OF

ENGLAND AND WALES;

EMBRACING RECENT CHANGES IN COUNTIES, DIOCESES, PARISHES, AND BOROUGHS; GENERAL STATISTICS; POSTAL ARRANGEMENTS; RAILWAY SYSTEMS, &C.,

AND FORMING

A COMPLETE DESCRIPTION OF THE COUNTRY

BY

JOHN MARIUS WILSON,

AUTHOR OF TOPOGRAPHICAL GAZETTEERS OF IRELAND AND SCOTLAND,
SCOTTISH [illegible] &C. &C.

VOL. I.

AARON END—CHARTLEY-HOLME.

A. FULLARTON & CO.
EDINBURGH, GLASGOW, LONDON, DUBLIN
1870

PREFACE.

THE IMPERIAL GAZETTEER OF ENGLAND AND WALES supersedes a previous Gazetteer, issued by the same publishers. That work was called the "Parliamentary Gazetteer of England and Wales," and was published in 1838 and following years. It embodied what was good in previous Gazetteers, added information from historians, antiquaries, and statists, engrossed the substance of many parliamentary documents on topographical, commercial, and social affairs, and aimed to be a complete and detailed description of all England and Wales. It was highly popular, it would have continued to be so but for immensely numerous changes, which rendered it in great degree obsolete, and, on account of these changes, as well as for sake of introducing important new features and topics, it is now superseded by the present work.

The Imperial Gazetteer professes to be as superior to the Parliamentary Gazetteer as it was superior to all previous Gazetteers, and aims to be much the best work of its class which has ever yet been produced. Its articles are about twice as numerous as those of the Parliamentary Gazetteer, they include names, subjects, and arrangements which do not occur in any other work, and they are framed with the best adaptations, which long experience in the preparation of Gazetteers could suggest, to all the purposes of an easy and perfect book of reference. They exhibit all sorts of inhabited places down to villages and hamlets, territorial divisions of the different kinds, political, registrational, and ecclesiastical, natural objects, such as mountains, headlands, caverns, streams, and waterfalls, industrial works, such as railways, canals, great bridges, and ancient roads, notable spots or objects, such as historical scenes, archæological sites, ancient camps, castles, and ruins. Every place is described in its position distances, and communications and also, when such exist, in its history, antiquities, property, administration, edifices, institutions, productions, traffic, taxes, and population.

Some features of the work are new, or not found in any other Gazetteer, and others, though not new, are larger, more distinct, or better drawn. The most recent changes in the limits, divisions, or constitution of counties boroughs, dioceses, and parishes are stated. The differences between the electoral counties and the registration ones are shown. Statistics of all kinds, in relation to counties, districts, boroughs, ports, dioceses, parishes chapelries, and other localities, are given. All post-offices, all money-order offices, all post-office savings' banks, and the nearest or proper post-office to any parish or chapelry which has not one of its own are indicated. All railways are described, all railway stations and all telegraph offices are noted, and the distance and direction of the nearest or most suitable station to every parish chapelry, or considerable township, are mentioned. New public buildings of every kind new public works new churches, new institutional erections, new schools, and even many new mansions new hotels, and new great warehouses, so far as could be known till the time of going to press, are described. Views of the social condition of the country, as to employments of the people, distribution of property, agriculture, manufactures, commerce, crime, pauperism, and other matters, as well from general information as from statistics, are interwoven. Objects or features interesting to tourists, to invalids, to sportsmen, to geologists to antiquaries, or to the curious—picturesque details even in spots little visited, spas, watering-places, trouting-waters, coursing-grounds, rock formations, bone caverns, land-slips, ancient and mediæval works, many things of a striking or peculiar kind, natural or artificial, are mentioned or described. And the account of every place, large or small, is so framed as to present all the information upon it at a glance

The technical treatment of the work also is on an improved plan Old modes of treatment are made more distinct, and some new ones are introduced The spellings of names are the most modern or approved,—generally after the revised form of the Commissioners of the Census, and in cases where two spellings still prevail, at different points of the alphabetical arrangement, both are inserted, with a reference from the one to the other Every concentric set of places, as of a village, a township, a parish, a sub-district, and a district, is treated under one name, in a continuous article, and in regular order from the centre to the circumference All places capable of being so spoken of are designated as situated on a river, on a railway, on a Roman road, under a height, or in some other marked relative position. The recent subdivision of England and Wales into registration districts, for fixing the locality of towns, parishes, and other included places, is everywhere followed, and that arrangement is found to possess great and numerous advantages The Census Commissioners of 1851 used it for all their statistics, retaining only so much reference to the old divisions as might form a nexus between the population tables of 1851 and those of the previous decades, and the Census Commissioners of 1861 discarded the old divisions altogether One use of following the district divisions, in the Imperial Gazetteer, has been to save much space for useful information, by avoiding prolix and multiform designations, another has been to exhibit the entire country in far more equal sections than on the plan of the old divisions, another has been to show places in their practical connexion with the principal administrations, and another has been to introduce statistics of poor rates births, marriages, and deaths at the date of the latest report before going to press, and statistics of places of worship and of schools according to the only Census of them which has been taken, the Census of 1851 The use of the new divisions, nevertheless, is still accompanied with sufficient notice of the old ones The poor law unions, in the vast majority of instances, are conterminate with the districts, or, when two or more are included in a district the fact is duly noticed and defined, so that these divisions are all constructively shown in the accounts of the districts. And as to the old divisions of hundreds, rapes, wapentakes and wards, these are still noticed in articles on themselves and in the articles on the counties.

The Imperial Gazetteer has had the benefit of long experience in the preparation of other Gazetteers, and it can scarcely have failed to derive considerable value from that circumstance alone Among other things brought thence to bear upon it were an acquaintance with authorities to be used and with the best modes of using them, an expertness in sifting and assorting materials according to their value, and a skill in putting facts together in fewest words and in clearest order,—in proportioning statements according to their degree of importance,—and in symmetrizing articles, making those of a class everywhere similar, and the earlier parts of the work neither broader nor narrower than the concluding ones These things, owing to the immense multitudinousness of its ingredients, affect a Gazetteer more strongly than almost any other compilation

The Imperial Gazetteer does not profess to be perfect. No Gazetteer ever was, no Gazetteer ever will be Mistakes and discrepancies in authorities and changes in places and structures, always occasion some errors But much care has been used to insure correctness, inquiries have been made to clear away doubts, and all articles which seemed in the least likely to want perfect freshness, including thousands of only a few lines each, have undergone revision by intelligent residents in the places which they describe, so that the amount of possible errors, throughout the work, may be presumed to have been reduced to a minimum

The only abbreviations used, such as r station for railway station, and the mere initial of a proper name when the name itself has immediately gone before, are all so obvious as not to require explanation. The statements of acreage are from the Census of 1861 The water-areas of places on coasts, estuaries, and tidal rivers, are generally foreshore The statements of real property are from the return of 1860, and those of rated property, from the return of 1859 The population of towns and parishes, when no year is specified, is always of 1861 The values of very many of the benefices are given as admitted or corrected by the incumbents themselves All the tracts designated parishes are parishes in the civil or political sense, and the great majority of them, or all not stated to include separate benefices, are also parishes ecclesiastical. All the tracts designated chapelries or parochial chapelries, and at the same time indicated to have been formed at a given date, or to have a defined population, are ecclesiastical parishes, and may be readily distinguished, by the fact of their definite population, from chapelries in the lower sense Most of them are simply sections of civil parishes, some are sections cut curiously through the core of townships, not a few comprise portions of several political parishes, and most were so obscurely defined at the Census of 1861 that "the exact limits of them were known to few persons in the locality except the incumbents," so that to have designated them parishes, or even new parishes, would have both involved much tedious language respecting their boundaries, and produced extreme confusion in the correlative statistics The Census calls them ecclesiastical districts, and exhibits them apart from parishes in supplemental tables, and it evidently required to adopt some such course in order to make its main statistics clear The Imperial Gazetteer also might have called them ecclesiastical districts, if that could have been thought a better name than chapelries, but, to prevent ambiguity, it has all been written on the rule of applying the term district only to a registration district The tracts called extra-parochial were, by a recent enactment, declared to be civil parishes for poor-law purposes, but as many of them have been found too small to be workable parochially, the Gazetteer designates them all as extra-parochial

A comprehensive article on all England and Wales, similar in structure to each of the articles on each of the counties, but more in detail, with a wider range of topics, exhibiting all England and Wales in one view, and serving as both centre and cincture to the entire work, is an important portion of the Gazetteer A thought was at first entertained to place it at the beginning, by way of Introduction, but mature consideration decides to place it at the end It will figure there, not as an Appendix, but as a Summary, and, while presenting information peculiar to itself, will throw reflected light on words, phrases, statements descriptions, or other matters in almost all the articles

The engraved illustrations given with the Gazetteer aim at combining novelty and utility with artistic excellence Besides plates of scenery and architecture, they comprise a series of interesting and beautifully-executed-and coloured maps and plans of estuaries, harbours, havens, cities, and towns—the Thames the Humber, the Severn, the Mersey—London Liverpool, Bristol, Manchester, Leeds Plymouth, Portsmouth, Hull, Whitby, and many others of lesser name—brought up to the present time, each and all illustrating the letterpress of the book, instructive to the stranger and a subject of pleasurable interest to the resident.

The Imperial Gazetteer is accompanied with a Sheet Atlas, or large map, of England and Wales This supplies a very great desideratum The county maps hitherto issued with Gazetteers are very unsatisfactory They commonly amount to about sixty,—one for each of most of the counties, and two or three for each of the larger ones, they are usually all of one size and shape, so as to give for their several territories a uniform extent of space, and they, therefore, are drawn on widely different scales. The larger counties, which are also the richest in local features, are shown on a scale unduly small, and the smaller ones, which are also the poorest in striking features, are engraved on a scale unduly large Devon, for example, which has an area of 1,657,180 acres, and abounds in features of local interest, is shown on the same space as Rutland, which has an area of only 95,805 acres, and possesses very little salient feature. The maps, as taken together, are no fair atlas, they do not exhibit the face of the country continuously, they convey, on a rough view, a vastly contorted notion of the porportions of its parts, and they fail, even with the aid of full observation of their several scales, to give a ready view of the connexions among the multitudes of places on opposite sides of county boundary-lines Their very margins are confusing, and their differences of execution, suited to their differences of scale, make wrong impressions

The Sheet Atlas of the Imperial Gazetteer would have been a great improvement had it done no more than merely avoid the faults of these county maps But it also possesses great positive advantages. It is a reduction from the Ordnance and other actual surveys, on a scale so large, and in such a manner, as to give a complete and correct picture of the country It is engraved on the uniform scale of 4 miles to an inch, it comprises 16 sheets, each having an engraved portion of 26 inches by 18, it measures, when put together, 8 feet 3 inches by 6 feet 6 inches, and it can either be retained in its sheet form or pieced up as one large wall-map It is executed in the best style, and has been produced by immense labour and at great cost It shows the lines of railway as corrected, and brought up to the time of publication, by the engineers of the respective companies It distinctly exhibits every hill, valley, stream, canal, railway, railway branch, railway station, road, cross-road, and important tourists' foot-path, every town, village, parish church, gentleman's seat, castle, important ruin, and site of battle, every object of historical, antiquarian, and tourist interest, and all lights, beacons, banks, shoals, and other objects of marine interest on or near the coast. It is divided by engraved lines into equal rectangular spaces, with reference-letters for indicating positions. And it is accompanied with an index of names and positions, printed to bind up with it if a book, or to be placed separately if mounted

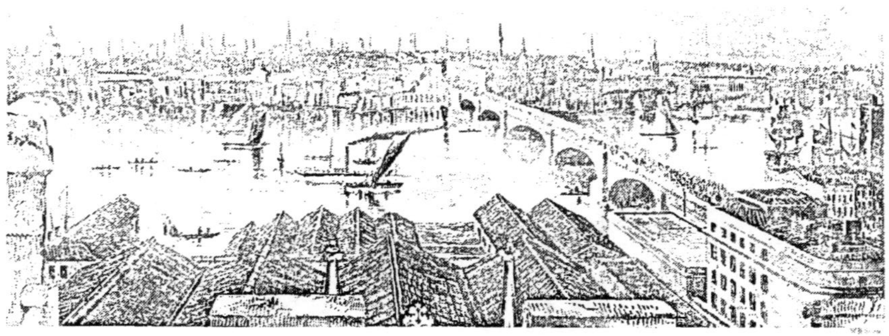

THE

IMPERIAL GAZETTEER

OF

ENGLAND AND WALES.

The sign * denotes that there is a habitable glebe house, † that there is a money order office, ‡ that there are a money order office and a savings bank.

AARON END, a mountain on the S side of the pass from Borrowdale over Sty Head toward Wastdale, Cumberland

ABBANDUNE See ABINGDON

ABBAS-COMBE See COMBE ABBAS

ABBAS COMPTON See COMPTON ABBAS

ABBENHALL See ABINGHALL.

ABBERBURY See ALBERBURY

ABBERFORD See ABERFORD

ABBERLEY, a parish in Martley district, Worcester, near the river Teme, 5 miles SW of Stourport r station. It has a post office under Stourport Acres, 2,636 Real property, £4,238. Pop, 692 Houses, 132 The property is much subdivided Abberley hills are about 800 feet high. The rocks display the caradoc formation, and include lime and coal An ancient camp occurs at Woodbury The poet William Walsh, the friend of Pope, was a native The living is a rectory in the diocese of Hereford Value, £249 * Patron, J Moilliet, Esq The church was rebuilt in 1852 There are a Wesleyan chapel and charities £15.

ABBERLEY, Kidderminster See HABBERLEY

ABBERTOFT a hamlet in Willoughby parish 2 miles SE of Alford, Lincoln. Pop., 23.

ABBERTON, a parish in Lexden district, Essex, on the river Roman, 5 miles south of Colchester r station It has a post office under Colchester Acres, 1,067 Real property, £1,574 Pop., 269 Houses, 59 The property is divided among a few The living is a rectory in the diocese of Rochester Value, £289 * Patron, the Lord Chancellor The church is plain but good, and there is a Wesleyan chapel

ABBERTON, a parish in Pershore district, Worcester, on the river Piddle, 3 miles SSW of Inkberrow and 4 NNE of Pershore r station It has a postal box under Pershore Acres, 1,001 Real property, £1,337 Pop, 82 Houses, 17 The property is all in one estate There are saline springs, similar to the waters of Cheltenham The living is a rectory in the diocese of Worcester Value, £161 Patron, W Laslett, Esq The church is good.

ABBERWICK, a township in Edlingham parish, Northumberland, on the river Alne, 3½ miles W of Alnwick Acres, 1 673 Pop, 137 Houses 26

ABBEY, an extra parochial tract in the district of Llanrwst, and county of Carnarvon, on the Conway river, 3 miles N of Llanrwst Pop 18 Houses, 3

ABBEY a sub district of Bath district, Somerset It comprises three parishes Pop, 11,086 Houses, 1,388 See BATH

ABBEY, a railway station in Cumberland, on the Carlisle and Silloth railway, at Abbey Holme, 17 miles WSW of Carlisle

ABBEY, Devon See HARTLAND

ABBEY, Hertford See ALBANS (ST)

ABBEY, Pembroke See DOGMEL (ST)

ABBEY CWM HIR, a parochial chapelry in Rhayader district, Radnor, 6 miles NNW of the Central Wales railway below Penybont, and 6½ ENE of Rhayader. Post-town, Penybont. Acres, 10,965 Pop 537 Houses, 96 The name signifies the Abbey of the Long Vale The surface lies along the Clywedog, a tributary of the Ithon, and is a charming, fertile bottom, environed and overhung by picturesque wooded hills A Cistertian abbey was founded here, in 1143, by Cadwathelan ap Madoc, and destroyed, in 1401, by Owen Glendower The property belonged, in the 17th century, to Sir Wm Fowler, concerning whom it was said,—

> "There is neither a park nor a deer
> To be seen in all Radnorshire,
> Nor a man with five hundred a year
> Save Fowler of Abbey Cwm Hir"

The abbey church was 255 feet long and 73 feet wide, but only a few fragments of it remain The mansion of F Philips, Esq partly built with the stones of the church in 1816, stands adjacent A Roman road goes up the vale past the abbey, toward the valley of the Marteg The living of Abbey Cwm Hir is a vicarage in the diocese of St. David's Value, £61 Patron, G H Philips Esq The church was rebuilt in 1867, and is in the Continental first pointed style

ABBEY DALE, a hamlet in Ecclesall Bierlow township, W R Yorkshire, 3 miles SW of Sheffield

ABBEY DEMENSES, a hamlet in the parish of Winchcombe, Gloucester See WINCHCOMBE.

ABBEYDORE, a village and a parish in the district and county of Hereford The village stands on the river Dore, 2 miles NW of Pontrilas r station, and 11 SW of Hereford, and has a post office under Hereford It is an old fashioned place, and offers facilities for anglers. The parish comprises 5,390 acres. Real property, £4,593. Pop., 501 Houses, 99 The property is divided among a few The living is a rectory in the diocese of Hereford Value, £680 * Patrons, the co heirs of the late duchess of Norfolk A Cistertian abbey was founded here, by Robert de Ewyas, in the time of King Stephen, and passed, at the dissolution, to the Scudamores The present church belonged to the abbey was recently repaired, and contains a fine old pulpit, some beautiful painted windows, and several ancient monuments Charities, £44

ABBEY FARM, an extra-parochial tract the site of the ancient abbey of Cockerham, 4½ miles SSW of Lancaster Pop, with Crook Farm, 42

ABBEY FORD See FORD ABBEY

ABBEY FOREGATE See SHREWSBURY

ABBEY GATE See LEICESTER.

ABBEY HOLME, or ABBEY TOWN, a township and a sub district in Wigton district, Cumberland The township is in the parish of Holme-Cultram, and lies on the river Waver, and on the Carlisle and Silloth railway, near the head of Morecambe bay, 6 miles WNW of Wigton. It has a station of the name of Abbey on the railway, and a post office‡ of the name of Abbey Town under Carlisle It was formerly a market town, and it still has a fair on 29 Oct A Cistertian abbey was founded here, in the 12th century, by Henry I, and rose to such consequence that its abbots were frequently summoned to sit in parliament, in the reigns of Edward I and II It was demolished by Robert Bruce, but afterwards splendidly rebuilt. It sustained much injury in the time of Henry VIII, but its church continued in good condition till 1600, but then the steeple fell, and destroyed great part of the chancel, and in 1604, most of the rest was ruined by an accidental fire Pop of the township, 982 Houses, 200 A bill was introduced in 1864 to make a railway from the Carlisle and Silloth at Abbey Holme to the Maryport and Carlisle, in the parish of Wigton, with a branch to Bolton, and branches therefrom to the Maryport and Carlisle, and near Priest croft —The sub district comprises the greater part of Holme Cultram, parts of two other parishes, and two entire parishes. Acres, with the rest of Holme Cultram, 71,720 Pop, 8,024 Houses 1 621

ABBEY HULTON, a lordship in Burslem parish, Stafford near Burslem r station. It contains the hamlets of Milton and Sneyd green, and has remains of a Cistertian abbey, founded in 1223 by Henry de Audley Pop, 726 Houses, 145

ABBEY LANDS, a township in Alnwick parish Northumberland, 2 miles NW of Alnwick It contains the hamlets of Broomhouse, Heckly, Heckly-Farm, Heckly Grange, and Whitehouse, and it contained anciently an abbey of canons Pop, 288 Houses, 52

ABBEY LANERCOST See LANERCOST

ABBEY MALMESBURY See MALMESBURY

ABBEY-MILTON See MILTON ABBAS

ABBEY STREET See CARLISLE

ABBEY-TOWN See ABBEY HOLME

ABBEY-WOOD, a hamlet in Erith parish, Kent, on the North Kent railway, 2¾ miles E of Woolwich It is named from the abbey of Lessness, about a mile distant, it has become a sort of metropolitan suburb, and it has a r station with telegraph, and a postal pillar box

ABBEY WOOD, Devon See DUNKESWELL

ABBORN See AUBURN

ABBOTS a tything in Portbury parish Somerset, 6½ miles WNW of Bristol It had a cell of the Augustinian priory of Bromere

ABBOTS ANN, a parish in Andover district, Hants, on the river Ann or Anton, adjacent to the Basingstoke and Salisbury railway, 2½ miles SW by W of Andover It has a post office under Andover Acres 3,351 Real property, £3,932 Pop, 640 Houses, 140 The property is all in one estate Red Rice House, an ancient mansion, is the place where George IV was married to Mrs. Fitzherbert The living is a rectory in the diocese of Winchester Value £645 * Patrons, the heirs of Sir J Burrough. The ancient church belonged to the abbey of Cornelies, in Normandy The present church is a deformed structure of last century There is an Independent chapel

ABBOTS ASTLEY See ASTLEY ABBOTS

ABBOTS BICKINGTON, a parish in Holsworthy district Devon, on the river Torridge, 2 miles SW of Umberleigh r station, and 7 NNE of Holsworthy Post town, Torrington Acres, 1,078 Real property, £584 Pop, 71 Houses, 13 A blue limestone, used for building is quarried The living is a vicarage in the diocese of Exeter Value, £93 Patrons, the trustees of Lord Rollo. The ancient church was a cell of the abbey of Hartland The present church is a small structure of chancel, nave two aisles, and low tower

ABBOTS BROMLEY, or BROMLEY ABBOTS, a small town, a parish and a sub district in the district of Uttoxeter, Stafford The town stands near the river Blythe, 6 miles NNE of Rugeley r station and 12 E of Stafford It has a post office‡ under Rugeley, and is a polling place It was formerly a market town, and still has fairs on the Tuesday before Midl, 22 May and 4 Sept It consists chiefly of a long street, containing some good houses and an ancient market cross The parish includes also the liberty of Bromley Hurst and the lordship of Bagots-Bromley Acres, 9,391 Real property, £4,409 Pop 1,538 Houses, 300 Blithfield, the seat of Lord Bagot, stands 2½ miles W of the town A Benedictine abbey was founded at Blithbury, on the Blythe, by Hugh Malveysin in the reign of Henry I or of Stephen, and passed, at the dissolution to the Chadwick family The living is a vicarage in the diocese of Lichfield Value, £235 Patron, the Marquis of Anglesey The church is an ancient structure in various styles, chiefly later English, but has been modernized There is an Independent chapel There are also a free school, a national school, and other charities with £193 a year Mrs. Cooper who saw her descendants to the sixth generation, lived at Abbots Bromley —The sub district comprises three parishes and part of a fourth Acres, 17,355 Pop., 2,976 Houses, 648

ABBOTSBURY, a village, a parish, and a sub district, in the district of Weymouth, Dorset The village stands in a vale, about a mile from the sea, 7½ miles W of the Weymouth railway, and 9 SW of Dorchester It has a post office‡ under Dorchester, and an inn It was formerly a market town, and has now a fair on 10 July Most of its inhabitants engage in fishing The parish contains also the hamlets of Rodden and Elworth; and exhibits picturesque features of both shore and surface. Acres, 5,816, of which 545 are water Real property, £5,631 Pop., 1,089 Houses, 213 The property is divided among a few The rocks belong to the shelly oolite The coast commands brilliant views, and is flanked by Chesil Bank, occasioning tumultuous tides. See CHESIL BANK St Catherine's Chapel, romantically situated on the crown of a hill between the village and the sea, is a very strong edifice of the 15th century, with large buttresses, a clerestory, and an octagonal tower and serves as a landmark to mariners A Benedictine abbey was founded at Abbotsbury, in 1044, by Orcus, steward of King Canute, and passed at the dissolution, to the Strangeways The gateway of its church, the walls of a dormitory and barn, and some fragments scattered over a large area, still remain A swannery, which belonged to the abbey, and is said to have contained about 8,000 swans, still exists, with about 1 000 swans, and is connected with a decoy for the extensive capture of wild fowl A castellated seat of the Earl of Ilchester, the present proprietor is adjacent An ancient fortification, 1½ mile to the west, occupies 20 acres, comprises very high ramparts, ditches, and redoubts, and commands a noble view Hardy's Monument, about 3 miles distant, commands a still nobler view, and the key for it may be had at Portisham The living is a vicarage in the diocese of Salisbury Value, £140 * Patron, the Earl of Ilchester The church adjoins the abbey ruins, and is an old embattled edifice with a curious weather worn sculpture over the west door A school has £20 a year from endowment, and other charities £19 —The sub district includes three parishes. Acres, 11,358 Pop, 2,034 Houses, 405

ABBOTS CARSWELL See ABBOTS KERSWELL

ABBOTS CHARLETON See CHARLETON ABBOTS

ABBOTS CLIFF See DOVER

ABBOTS COURT, an extra parochial tract in Winterborne Kingston parish, Dorset, 5½ miles SSW of Blandford

ABBOTSHAM, a parish in Bideford district Devon, between Taw river and Barnstaple bay, 1½ mile W of Bideford r station It has a post office under Bideford, and contains the hamlet of Shepperton Acres, 1,758 Real property, £2,267 Pop 365 Houses 67 The property is subdivided. Odun, Earl of Devon, in 878 vanquished and slew here the Danish invader Hubba, at Kenwith Castle The living is a vicarage in the diocese of Exeter Value, £139 * Patron, E U Vidal, Esq The church is a plain old structure with a square tower There are a small Baptist chapel and charities £11

ABBOTS HILL, a hamlet on the north border of Dorset, 5 miles SW of Yeovil.

ABBOTSIDE (HIGH and LOW), two townships in the parish of Aysgarth, N R Yorkshire The former lies 2 miles NNW of Hawes, and the two are separated from each other by Whitfield gill. Acres of High Abbotside 11,150 Pop 532 Houses, 1.1 Acres of Low Abbotside, 5 080 Pop 163 Houses, 37 High Abbotside contains the hamlets of Hardraw, Cotterdale, Fossdale Simonstone, Sedbusk, Shaw, Helbeck Lunds, Birkriggs, Camhouses and Litherskew, and Low Abbotside contains the hamlets of Grange, Bowbridge, Helme, and Shawcote Much of both townships is high moorland and lofty fell, intersected by ravines and deep narrow vales, all within the upper basin of the river Ure A remarkable waterfall, called Hardraw force, occurs in one of the ravines, and a picturesque waterfall, called Whitfield force, occurs in another See HARDRAW FORCE and URE (THE)

ABBOTS ISLE See ISLE ABBOTS

ABBOTS KENSINGTON See HOLLAND HOUSE.

ABBOTS KERSWELL, or ABBOTS CARSWELL, a parish in Newton Abbot district, Devon, on the South Devon railway 2 miles south of Newton Abbot Post town, Newton Abbot Acres, 1,461 Real property, £3,043 Pop. 437 Houses, 106 The property is much divided. The minerals comprise limestone, coal, potters clay, and alum. The living is a vicarage in the diocese of Exeter Value, £293 * Patron, the Lord Chancellor The ancient church was a cell of Montacute Abbey The present church is a neat small edifice of nave, chancel, and aisles, with a square tower There are two small dissenting chapels Baptist and Wesleyan

ABBOTS LANGLEY, a parish and a sub district in Watford district, Herts. The parish lies on the Grand Junction canal and the Northwestern railway, 1 mile SE of Kings Langley station, and has a post office under Watford. Acres, 5,213 Real property, £13,033 Pop, 401 Houses, 520 The property is subdivided A [illegible] n of Claudius was found at Langley House The parish gave birth to Nicholas de Breakspear, Pope Adrian IV, and was given to the abbots of St Albans "to find them in clothes" Here is the Booksellers Provident Retreat The living is a vicarage in the diocese of Rochester Value, £315 Patron, W Jones Lloyd, Esq The church is partly Norman, partly of later date, and contains an ancient font and some handsome monuments There are Independent and Wesleyan chapels, national schools, and extensive paper mills —The sub district is co extensive with the parish

ABBOTS LEIGH, a parish in Bedminster district, Somerset, on the left bank of the Avon, near Rownham ferry, 3½ miles WNW of Bristol It has a post office under Bristol Acres, 2 228 Real property, £3,822 Pop, 765 Houses, 63 Limestone is quarried Leigh Court the seat of Sir William Miles, Bart, is an elegant structure with Ionic porticoes, commanding a fine view across the Bristol channel, and contains a splendid collection of pictures An ancient manor house near the site of this mansion, belonging to the ancient family of Norton, and gave concealment to Charles II after the battle of Worcester The living is a vicarage in the diocese of Gloucester and Bristol Value, £77 * Patron the Bishop of Gloucester and Bristol The church was much burnt down about 1848, and afterwards partly [illegible] and partly rebuilt Charities £[illegible]

ABBOTS LENCH, a hamlet in the parish of Fladbury, Worcester Acres 870 Pop 60 Houses, 13

ABBOTSLEY, a parish in St Neots district Huntingdon, 3½ miles [illegible] of the Great Northern railway and [illegible] SE of St. Neots Post town, St Neots Acres, 2 110 Real property, £2,905 Pop, 180 Houses 91 The property is subdivided The living is a vicarage in the diocese of Ely Value £55 * Patron, Balliol College Oxford The church is good and there are a Wesleyan chapel, a national school, and charities £9

ABBOTS MORTON, a parish in the district of Alcester and county of Worcester, 6 miles N by E of Fladbury r station, and 7 WSW of Alcester It has a post office under Bromsgrove Acres, 1,420 Real property, £2,091 Pop. 245 Houses, 57 The property is all in one estate The living is a rectory in the diocese of Worcester Value £146 Patron, C J A Walker, Esq The church is good

ABBOTS NEWTON See NEWTON ABBOTS.

ABBOTS-NORTON See NORTON WITH LENCHWICK.

ABBOTS RIPTON See RIPTON ABBOTS

ABBOTS ROOTHING See ROOTHING ABBOTS

ABBOTS-STOKE See STOKE ABBAS

ABBOTSTON, a hamlet and a parish in Alresford district, Hants The hamlet lies 2¼ miles NW of Alresford, and 7 ESE of Micheldever r station The parish is a rectory, united with the vicarage of Itchin Stoke, in the diocese of Winchester It contains a ruined church, and part of an old mansion of the Paulets See ITCHIN-STOKE

ABBOTSTON, a tything in the parish of Whiteparish, Wilts, 2 miles S of Dean r station, and 8 SE of Salisbury It is a resort of sportsmen.

ABBOTSTON, Gloucester See ABSON

ABBOTSTREET See WIMBORNE MINSTER.

ABBOTSWORTHY, a tything in the parish of Kings worthy, 2 miles NNE of Winchester Hants

ABCOTT, a township in Clungunford parish, Salop, on the river Clun, 8½ miles WNW of Ludlow

ABDASTON See ADBASTON

ABDICK AND BULSTONE, a hundred in Somerset It contains the parish of Ashill and twenty five other parishes. Acres 38,575 Pop in 1851, 12,401, in 1861, 12,047 Houses 2 498

ABDON, a parish in Ludlow district, Salop, under the Clee hills, 7 miles E of Marsh Brook r station and 9 NNE of Ludlow Post town Burwarton under Bridgnorth Acres, 1,104 Real property £890 Pop., 170 Houses 33 The property is divided among a few The living is a rectory in the diocese of Hereford Value, £147 * Patron, the Earl of Pembroke The church is tolerable

ABENBURY FAWR, a township in the part of Wrexham parish within Denbigh Acres, 1,078 Pop, 167 Houses, 38

ABENBURY FECHAN, a township in the part of Wrexham parish within Flint Acres, 138 Pop 145 Houses, 32

ABENHALL See ABINGHALL

ABER, a local name of the ancient Britons designating any place of a marked character near the mouth of a stream, whether on the coast or inland It occurs seldom by itself but often and prominently as a prefix

ABER, a village and a parish in Bangor district, Carnarvon The village stands on the coast, at the mouth of the Gwyngregyn rivulet, 4½ miles E of Bangor It has a post office under Bangor, a station on the Chester and Holyhead railway, and a comfortable inn It is a charming place, and is much frequented by tourists The views all round, and in the neighbourhood over sea and land, are rich and varied, and some of them are panoramic and extensive The Lavan sands extend in front of it for 4 miles at low water and may be crossed on foot, with a guide to the ferry of Beaumaris. The glen of the Gwyngregyn narrow and romantic, strikes about 2 miles inland, flanked on one side by a well-wooded lofty hill,—on the other side by the stupendous rock of Maes y Gaer, and is blocked at the head by the dark, vast concave precipice of the hill Bera over which falls the famous cataract Rhaiadr Mawr The cataract is fringed with ash trees, and first breaks on the cliffs into three or four parts, then makes a sheer leap of more than 60 feet An artificial conical mound, near the village was the site of a palace of the Welsh princes, where Llewelyn the Great received the summons to surrender his rights to Edward I of England A field, not far off, called

Cae Gwilym Dhu, "Black William's Field," was the scene of the summary execution of the Norman baron, William de Braose, whom Llewelyn ap Iorwerth had taken prisoner, and whom he suspected of an intrigue with his princess. A well known Welsh distich, alluding to this event, records the following question and answer —

"'Lovely princess,' said Llewelyn,
'What will you give to see your Gwilym?'
'Wales and England, and Llewelyn,
I'd give them all to see my Gwilym.'"

The parish of Aber comprises 8,833 acres, of which 1,515 are water. Real property, £2,454. Pop., 582. Houses, 116. The property is divided among a few. The living is a rectory in the diocese of Bangor. Value, £340.* Patron, the Hon. Col. D. Pennant. The church is ancient, with a square tower, in moderate condition. There are chapels for Calvinistic Methodists and Wesleyans. There is also a free school, which was founded about 1719 by Dr. Jones, Dean of Bangor.

ABER, a village in Llandyfriog parish, Cardigan, on the river Teifi, 2 miles NE of Newcastle Emlyn.

ABERAERON. See ABERAYRON.

ABERAFON. See ABERAVON.

ABERAMAN, a village at the influx of the Aman to the Cynon, 2 miles SE of Aberdare, Glamorgan. It has a post-office† under Aberdare. The ironworks and the mansion of C. Bailey, Esq., are adjacent.

ABERANGEL, a railway station 3¼ miles S by W of Dinas Mowddwy, in Merioneth.

ABERARAD, a village in the parish of Kenarth, Carmarthen, a mile east of Newcastle Emlyn.

ABERARTH. See LLANDDEWI ABERARTH.

ABERAVON, a town and a parish at the mouth of the river Avon, in the district of Neath, Glamorgan. The town stands on the South Wales railway, in the western vicinity of Taibach, 5½ miles SSE of Neath, and 32½ WNW of Cardiff. It is a borough, municipal and parliamentary, and a sub port under the port of Swansea. It consists of an old part, a little inland, which is Aberavon proper, and a new part on the shore, which embraces the harbour, and is called Port Talbot. It has a post office‡ of its own name under Taibach, and a station of the name of Port Talbot on the railway. It was recently a small village, but has grown rapidly in connexion with neighbouring mines and the export of their produce. Its harbour was highly improved in 1838 by a new cut for the river, and gives floating accommodation with considerable depth. Numerous coasting vessels frequent it, and steamers come from Bristol. Fairs are held on the second Friday in May, and on 24 June, 1 July, 14 Aug., 7 Oct., and 1 Nov. The municipal borough lies wholly in Aberavon parish, and is governed by a portreeve and two aldermen. The parliamentary borough includes also part of Margam parish, and part of the hamlet of Upper Michaelstone, and is linked in the franchise with Swansea. Pop. in 1851, 6,557, in 1861, 7,754. Houses, 1,423. —The parish comprises 1,943 acres of land and 655 of water. Real property £5,073. Pop. in 1831, 573, in 1861, 2,916. Houses, 531. The property is much subdivided. The living is a vicarage, united to Baglan, in the diocese of Llandaff. Value, £134.* Patron, G. Llewellyn, Esq. The church is an edifice in the middle pointed style, consists of nave, chancel, and south aisle, with a tower, and was built in 1860, at a cost of £2,120. There are chapels for Independents, Baptists, Calvinistic Methodists, Primitive Methodists, Bible Christians, and Roman Catholics. Some remains exist on Aberavon Mynydd hill of the castle of Caradoc ab Iestyn, which was destroyed in 1150. Some interesting localities are in the neighbourhood. See TAIBACH, MARGAM, CWM AVON, and BAGLAN.

ABERAYRON, a small seaport town and a district in Cardigan. The town stands in the parishes of Henfynyw, and Llanddewi Aberarth, at the mouth of the Ayron river, 16 miles SSW of Aberystwith, and 13 miles NW of Lampeter r. station. It has two piers, enclosing a small harbour, and owns about 40 vessels. It was long a retired village, but has become a market town and an esteemed watering place. The views around it are delightful, and the climate is about the healthiest in South Wales. The town has a post office‡ under Carmarthen, a comfortable hotel, warm baths, a town hall, a new sno parochial church, and three dissenting chapels, Independent, Calvinistic Methodist, and Wesleyan. The church is served by a perpetual curate, who is appointed by the inhabitants, and has a salary of £50. The quarter sessions for the county are held at Aberayron in Jan., April, July, and Oct., and markets are held on Wednesday and Saturday, and a fair on 13 Dec. A circular camp, called Castell Cadwgan, and believed to have been formed in 1148 by Cadwgan ap Bleddyn, is on the shore. Mynachdy, the seat of the proprietor of the town, is in the neighbourhood, and is supposed to occupy the site of a monastery. Pop. of the town not separately returned.—The district of Aberayron comprehends the sub district of Llandisilio, containing the parishes of Dihewid, Llanarth, Llandisilio Gogo, Llanllwchaiarn, and Llanina, and the sub district of Llansaintffraid, containing the parishes of Llanfihangel-Ystrad, Cilcennin, Cilie Aeron, Llanerch Ayron, Henfynyw, Llanddewi Aberarth, Llanbadarn Tref Eglwys, and Llansaintffraid. Acres, 67,704, of which 556 are water. Poor rates in 1866, £5,109. Pop. in 1841, 12,875, in 1861, 13,540. Houses, 3,163. Marriages in 1863, 82, births, 405,—of which 47 were illegitimate, deaths, 239,—of which 51 were at ages under 5 years, and 13 at ages upwards of 85. Marriages in the ten years 1851–60, 880, births, 3,953, deaths, 2,643. The places of worship in 1851 were 16 of the Church of England, with 3,537 sittings, 11 of Independents, with 3,168 s., 11 of Calvinistic Methodists, with 3,260 s., 3 of Wesleyan Methodists, with 330 s., 2 of Baptists, with 360 s., and 4 of Unitarians, with 698 s. The schools in 1851 were 12 public day schools, with 930 scholars, 15 private day schools with 537 s., and 44 Sunday schools, with 5,121 s. The workhouse is in Llanddewi-Aberarth.

ABERBAIDAN. See LLANELLY.

ABERBARGOED. See BARGOED.

ABERBECHAN, a township in Llanllwchaiarn parish, Montgomery, at the influx of the Bechan to the Severn, in the NE neighbourhood of Newtown. Pop., 147. A House is the seat of Sir J. Clifton, Bart.

ABERBEEG, a station on the Western Valleys Monmouth railway, 15 miles NNW of Newport, Monmouth. Here is a post office under Newport, Monmouth.

ABERBRAN, a station on the Neath and Brecon railway, 4½ miles SW of Brecon.

ABERCARN, a town in Mynyddyslwyn parish, Monmouth, on the W. Valleys railway, 10½ miles NW of Newport. It has a post-office‡ under Newport, Monmouth, a r. station, chemical works, iron and tin plate works, and extensive collieries. A House is a seat of Lord Llanover.

ABERCASTLE, a village in Mathry parish, Pembroke, on the coast, 6½ miles NNE of St. David's. It has a small harbour, frequented by coasters. On the farm of Longhouse, above it, is a cromlech, comprising a massive capstone 16 feet long, four supporting stones 5½ feet high, and two other stones.

ABERCONWAY. See CONWAY.

ABERCRAVE, a locality 3 miles from Ystradyngläis, Brecon. It has a post office under Swansea, and was a seat of the Gwynnes.

ABERCWHILER, a township in Bodfary parish, Denbighshire, at the confluence of the Cwhiler and the Clwyd, 3½ miles NE of Denbigh. Acres 3,346. Pop., 430. Houses 99. Here is a Calvinistic Methodist chapel.

ABERDARE, a town, a parish, and a sub district, in the district of Merthyr Tydvil, Glamorgan. The town stands at the confluence of the Dare and the Cynon, 4 miles SW of Merthyr Tydvil, and 24 NNW of Cardiff. A railway and a canal connect it with Cardiff, and a junction branch, 1½ mile long, connects it with the railway from Merthyr Tydvil to Neath. The scenery around it is picturesque. Extensive collieries and iron works are adjacent, and these have raised the place, since about the year 1835, from the condition of a village to the condi tion of a large and flourishing town The town has a telegraph station, a head post office,‡ two hotels three banking-offices an elegant church called St Elvan's, another church in the French pointed style built in 1865, two other churches, several dissenting chapels, a public park formed in 186, markets on Wednesday and Saturday, and three annual fairs

The parish contains the hamlets of Cefnpennar Cwmdare Forchaman, and Llwydcoed, and is all within the parliamentary burgh of Merthyr Tydvil Acres, 16,310 Real property in Cefnpennar £32,867 —of which £23,096 are in mines and ironworks in Cwmdare £32,794, —of which £12 374 are in mines and ironworks, in Forchaman, £5,871,—of which £31 718 are in mines and ironworks, in Llwydcoed, £29,874,—of which £26 407 are in mines and ironworks Pop of the parish in 1841 6,471, in 1861 32,299 Houses, 5,834 The property is subdivided. Abernant House, the seat of one of the principal proprietors adjoins the town The living is a vicarage, united with the chapelries of St. Elvan Hirwain and St. Mary in the diocese of Llandaff Value, £305 * Patron, the Marquis of Bute The vicarage of St. Fagan and the p. curacy of Mountain Ash are separate Value of St. F, £300 * Patron, the Bishop of L The Welsh poet Owen was a native, and the dissenting theologian E Evans died here.—The sub district comprehends three parishes Pop, 37,487

ABERDARE JUNCTION, a railway station with telegraph in Glamorgan, 7¼ miles SSE of Aberdare

ABERDARON, a village, a parish, and a sub district, in the district of Pwllheli, Carnarvon The village stands in a vale overhung by lofty cliffs, at the head of a small bay of its own name, near the extremity of the peninsula of Lleyn, 4 miles N of Bardsey Island and 17 SW of Pwllheli r station. It is a small sequestered place, but has a post-office under Pwllheli, and a fair on 12 Aug The scenery around it is very grand, and attracts distant visitors The distinguished linguist, Richard Robert Jones, was a native The parish comprises 6,908 acres of land, and 175 of water Real property, £4,071 Pop 1 266 Houses 269 The property is not much divided. Bodwrdda a large, well constructed mansion, about 250 years old now a farm house, stands about a mile from the village. The fragment of an ancient edifice, called Capel Vair, stands at the end of the peninsula. The scenery here, and at other parts of the coast, is equal in sublimity to some of the most striking parts of the Scottish Hebrides, and a sheer descent of 600 feet to the ocean occurs at Parwyd The living is a vicarage in the diocese of Bangor, and includes the vicarage of Llanvaelrhys Value £ 20 Patron, the Bishop of Bangor The old church is an ancient structure of different styles, with a beautiful Norman door, and was formerly collegiate, and had the privilege of sanctuary, but was some years ago, abandoned The new church is a recent tasteless structure There are three dissenting chapels, and charities £12 The sub district comprehends eight parishes, a chapelry, and Bardsey Isle Acres 29,133 Pop, 3,800 Houses 830

ABERDINAS See DINAS, Pembroke

ABERDOVEY or ABERDYFI a seaport village and a chapelry in Towyn parish Merioneth The village stands on the Dovey estuary adjacent to the Llwyngwrill railway 10 miles N of Aberystwith, has a station on the railway, a post office‡ under Shrewsbury, a good hotel and a few respectable lodging houses, and is a watering place and a seat of petty sessions The Dovey here is about a mile wide, and is crossed by a ferry to the Borth sands, leading toward Aberystwith The chapelry includes the village and was constituted in 1844 Pop 1 186 Houses 267 The living is a vicarage in the diocese of Bangor Value, £90 Patrons, Trustees

ABERDULAIS, a village at the influx of the Dulais river to the Neath 2¾ miles NE of Neath Glamorgan It has a post office under Neath, and a station on the Neath and Merthyr Tydvil railway Extensive tin works and a small cascade are in the neighbourhood

ABERDYFI See ABERDOVEY

ABERDYLAIS See ABERDULAIS

ABEREDW, a parish with a r station, in Builth district Radnor, at the influx of the Edw to the Wye and on the Mid Wales railway, 4 miles SE of Builth. Post-town, Builth Acres, 4 300 Real property, £2,022 Pop., 281 Houses, 56 The property is much subdivided. Aberedw Court is the seat of the Minors of Treago Aberedw Castle, now reduced to mouldering walls, much hidden by foliage on the summit of a mound, was the hunting seat of Llewelyn ap-Griffith, the last native prince of Wales. The adjacent scenery up the glen of the Edw, is highly picturesque Prince Llewelyn was slain in the vicinity, and an excavation in the rock, about 6 feet square, still bears the name of Llewelyn's Cave The living is a rectory, united with Llanvareth, in the diocese of St David's Value, £355 Patron, the Bishop of St. David's The church is an old edifice, in good condition, on an eminence a short way above the castle T Jones, the painter, who died in 1803, was a native

ABERERCH a parish in Pwllheli district, Carnarvon on the river Erch and thence to the coast, 1½ mile ENE of Pwllheli r station It has a post office under Pwllheli Acres, 5,962, of which 358 are water Real property, £5 101 Pop, 1,632 Houses, 398 The property is not much divided The living is a vicarage united with the curacy of Penrhos, in the diocese of Bangor Value, £132. Patron the Lord Chancellor The church is partly early English There are chapels for Independents, Calvinistic Methodists, and Wesleyans Charities, £6

ABERFFRAW, a seaport village and a parish in the district and county of Anglesey The village stands at the mouth of the Ffraw rivulet, on a creek of Carnarvon bay, 2¾ miles WSW of Bodorgan r station, and 12 SE of Holyhead It has a post office under Bangor, and an inn. It was formerly a market town, and it still has fairs on 7 March, the Tuesday before Easter the Wednesday after Trinity, 15 Aug, and 11 Dec It is now a poor place, inhabited chiefly by fishermen and farm labourers, but it anciently for four centuries, till the death of Llewelyn ap Griffith, was a capital of the princes of Wales No remains of the palace exist, but a garden, at the S end of the village still bears the name of Gardd y Llys or "palace garden The eisteddfodds, or assemblies of the bards, were anciently held here, and a spirited commemorative one was held in 1849 The parish comprises 6,214 acres of land, and 138 of water, and it contains eight tythings Real property, £5,044 Pop, 1,238 Houses, 274 The property is not much divided A lake, called Llyn Coron, about 2 miles in circumference, lies a little east of the village, and is much frequented by anglers The living is a rectory in the diocese of Bangor Value, £583 * Patron, the Prince of Wales The old church contains a very interesting doorway of the 12th century, and is in good condition There are four dissenting chapels and charities £24

ABERFORD, a village, a township, a parish, and a sub district, in the district of Tadcaster, W R Yorkshire The village stands on the rivulet Cock 3 miles NNE of Garforth r station, and 6 SW of Tadcaster It has a post office‡ under South Milford, and is a seat of petty sessions and a polling place It consists of a long straggling street, on a gentle acclivity of limestone rock, and it had ruins of a castle said to have been built soon after the Conquest It was formerly a market town, and it still has fairs on the last Monday of April and May, the first Monday of Oct, the Monday after 18 Oct and the Monday after 2 Nov A famous pin manufacture once flourished in it but has disappeared Coal, limestone and a fine white building stone are worked in its neighbourhood The township includes the village Acres, 1,5?0 Real property, £2,921 Pop, 759 Houses, 147 The parish comprises the townships of Aberford, Sturton and Parlington Acres 4,120 Real property £7,?01, of which £2,596 are in mines Pop 1,009 Houses, 200 The property is divided among a few Huddleston Hall, a very ancient building, is 3 miles distant and Watling Street bisects the parish The living is a vicarage in the diocese of York Value, £305 * Patron, Oriel College, Oxford. The church is excellent There are a Methodist chapel, a Roman Catholic chapel, and charities £18 —The sub district comprehends two entire parishes and parts of three other parishes Acres, 23,419 Pop, 5,973 Houses, 1,256

ABERFORD, Sherburn, W R. Yorkshire See LOTHERTON CUM ABERFORD

ABERGARW, a village in Llangeinor parish, Glamorgan, 9 miles N of Bridgend.

ABERGAVENNY, a town, a parish, a sub-district, a district, and a hundred, in Monmouth The town stands at the confluence of the Gavenny with the Usk, on the road from Monmouth to Brecon, and on the railway from Newport to Hereford, a mile E of the Monmouth and Brecon canal, 13½ miles W of Monmouth, and 17½ N of Newport Its environs comprise a picturesque reach of the Usk's valley amid a near amphitheatre of mountains, with the Skyrrid Vawr, the Blorenge, the Sugar Loaf, and other summits, and are flecked with wood and studded with mansions Its site was occupied by the Roman Gobannium, and has yielded coins and bricks with the inscription "Leg II Aug," and other Roman relics The place, owing to its position on the verge of the hill-country, was long an important post in the Border warfare, and witnessed many a strife between the Normans and the Welsh. The town was described by Leland, in the time of Henry VIII, as, "a fair walled town, well inhabited," and one of its gates, called Tudor's gate, stood till only a few years ago, and was then needlessly destroyed. The present streets are chiefly three, leading out to Monmouth, Hereford, and Brecon, and they are, for the most part, narrow and irregular, and show a mixture of old and new buildings. A castle, on an eminence near the S end, was built by the Norman, Hamaline de Bohun, soon after the Conquest, and passed to successively the Braoses, the Cantilupes, the Hastingses, the Valences, the Herberts, the Greys, the Beauchamps, and the Nevilles It is now a fragmentary, shattered, uninteresting ruin, blended with a private house, which was built about 1805, on the site of the keep, but a public terrace walk goes round it and commands a delightful view The poet Churchyard, in 1587, sang of its "most goodly towers," and a more modern poet speaks of it as

> "The rent Norman tower that overhangs
> The lucid Usk."

Some remains of a Benedictine priory, of early date, stand on the SE side of the town, but now form part of a private residence The priory church, called St Mary's, was formerly a very fine cruciform structure, but has been excessively injured by modern alterations, yet attracts the antiquary and the artist by many curious monuments, especially Norman effigies. St John's the original parish church, was converted by Henry VIII into a free grammar school, and this has an endowed income of £265 and a fellowship and exhibitions at Jesus College, Oxford Trinity church was erected and endowed in 1839 by Miss Rachel Herbert The Roman Catholic chapel of Our Lady and St. Michael is an edifice in decorated style, with Bath stone dressings, erected in 1860 There are five dissenting chapels, Independent, Baptist and Wesleyan An old bridge of 15 arches takes the public road across the Usk, and an adjacent bridge on a higher level, takes across a rail road toward Tredegar The market house is a well arranged building erected about 1830 on the site of a previous structure The Cymreigyddion hall is a plain edifice, remodelled out of an old malt house, by the Cymreigyddion Society who made efforts for the revival of old national art, and the encouragement of native manufacture but became defunct in 1855, and it is now used by the Volunteers as a drill room, and called the Volunteers hall, and is used also for large public meetings. The town was formerly famous for fine Welsh flannel, for fashionable Welsh wigs, made of goats' hair and sometimes sold at 40 guineas each, and for the resort of invalids to drink goats' whey, but it now figures chiefly for coarser flannel, for boots and shoes, for the traffic of neighbouring coal and iron works, and especially for crowded markets The markets are held on Tuesday, and fairs are held on the third Tuesday in March, on 14 May, on 24 June, on the Tuesday before 20 July, on 25 Sept, and on 19 Nov The town has a head post office,‡ a telegraph station, two banking offices, and two hotels. It is a seat of petty sessions and a polling place, and it was anciently a corporate town, governed by a bailiff, a recorder, and 27 councillors, but it forfeited its charter in the time of William III Races are held in April on a one mile course Bishop Cantilupe, who died in 1267, and Baker, the Benedictine historian, were natives. The town gives the title of Earl to the family of Neville Pop in 1851, 4,797, in 1861, 4,621 Houses, 989

The parish includes the town, and contains the hamlets of Hardwicke and Lloyndu Acres, 4 229 Real property, £22,077 Pop, 6,086 Houses, 1,157 The property is much subdivided A large proportion of the surface is hill sheepwalk The living is a vicarage in the diocese of Llandaff Value, £510 Patron, Sir John Guest, Bart Trinity church is a separate benefice, a p. curacy, in the patronage of Miss Rachel Herbert.—The sub district comprises four entire parishes, and parts of three other parishes. Acres, 20,674. Pop, 8,669 Houses, 1,692.—The district consists of two poor law unions, Abergavenny and Bedwelty and is divided into the sub district of Llanarth, containing the parishes of Bettws Newydd, Bryngwyn, Llanarth, Llanvair Kilgidin, Llanfihangel nigh Usk, Llansaintfraed, and Llanthewy Rhytherch, the sub district of Llanfihangel, containing the parishes of Llanvapley, Llanthewy Skirrid, Llanvetherine, Llangattock Lingoed, Llanfihangel, Cwmyoy, and Oldcastle the sub district of Abergavenny, containing the parishes of Abergavenny, Llantilio Pertholey Llangattock nigh Usk, and Llanellen and parts of the parishes of Llanover, Llanwenarth, and Llanfoist, the sub-district of Blaenavon containing parts of the parishes of Llanover Llanwenarth, and Llanfoist, the sub-district of Aberystruth, co extensive with the parish of Aberystruth, and the sub districts of Tredegar and Bedwelty, containing the parish of Bedwelty Acres 58 178 Poor rates in 1866 £22,733 Pop. in 1851, 50,815, in 1861, 67,087 Houses, 12,461 Marriages in 1866 597, births, 2,765,—of which 140 were illegitimate, deaths, 1,691,—of which 653 were at ages under 5 years, and 40 at ages upwards of 85 Marriages in the ten years 1851-60, 5,699, births, 24,769, deaths, 15,909 The places of worship in 1851 were 34 of the Church of England, with 9,172 sittings 13 of Independents with 5,690 s, 30 of Baptists with 12,750 s, 13 of Calvinistic Methodists, with 5,111 s, 16 of Wesleyan Methodists, with 5 754 s, 11 of Primitive Methodists with 2 149 s 2 of Roman Catholics, with 510 s, 4 of Latter-day Saints with 100 s, and 1 undefined, with 200 s The schools in 1851 were 28 public day schools, with 3,102 scholars, 54 private day schools with 1,303 s, 94 Sunday schools, with 11,001 s, and evening schools for adults, with 170 s.—The hundred is mainly identical with the district, but extends beyond it in some parts, and does not extend so far in others and is cut into two divisions, Higher and Lower Acres, 47,583 and 28,357 Pop in 1851, 50 036 in 1861, 54,742 Houses, 10,483

ABERGELE, a village, a parish, and a sub district on the coast of the district of St. Asaph, Denbigh The village stands near the Chester and Holyhead railway, 7 miles WNW of St Asaph, and 34½ W of Chester It has a station, with telegraph on the railway, a head post office,‡ and two hotels, and it is a seat of petty sessions, a seaport, and a watering place It consists chiefly of one wide, irregular street, along the highway, about ½ a mile from the shore. A weekly market is held on Saturday, and fairs are held on 2 April, on the day before Holy Thursday, on 15 June, 20 Aug, 9 Oct and 6 Dec. The beach is excellent bathing ground, and the surrounding scenery of coast and mountain is magnificent Limestone is extensively shipped, lead, copper and manganese occur in the neighbourhood, and some fine studies for the geologist in varieties of rock, are near Castell Cawr, on a high rock about a mile inland from the church, is one of the most perfect Roman camps in Wales and Gorddyn Mawr, on Coppar Wylfa, or "the mount of the watch tower," a mile farther W, is a large strong British hill fort Gwrych Castle, the seat of L. H B Hesketh Esq under a high hill on the coast about a mile W of the village, is a modern castellated edifice, with a frontage of 480 yards a tower 93 feet high and 17 turrets, and the grounds around it command delightful views, but they are not open to the public Cave hill, in the vicinity of Gwrych, is a calcareous rock, pierced with several curious caverns and one of these, called Cefn Ogo has an entrance arch 30 feet high, mi es a brilliant display of stalactites and stalegmi es goes very far into the bowels of the hill, but cannot be safely explored beyond 40 yards, and was the place where Richard II lay concealed, when betrayed to Bolingbroke by Percy Brynffanigle, within Abergele, was the residence of Marchudd ab Cynon, Prince of North Wales and an old mansion, now demolished, was the home of some of the early life of the poet, Mrs Hemans The parish includes the townships of Abergele, Bodorryn, Botegwel, Brynffanigle, Dolganned, Towyn Isaf Garth Gogo, Gwrych, Hendre Gyda-Isaf, Hendre Gyda Uchaf, Nant, Sirioi and Twyn Isaf and Uchaf Acres, together with the parish of St George, 1,998 of land, and 2,055 of water Real property, £9,350 Pop, 3,308 Houses, 727 The property is not much divided The living is a vicarage in the diocese of St Asaph Value, £400 Patron, the Bishop of St Asaph The church is a neat good structure of the time of Henry VIII There are Independent, Baptist, Calvinistic Methodist, and Wesleyan chapels, and charities £13 —The sub district comprises five parishes Acres, 22 115 Pop, 6,548 Houses, 1,455

ABERGLASLYN, a pass in the southern vicinity of Bedgelert, 8 miles S of Snowdon, on the boundary between the counties of Carnarvon and Merioneth It is a gorge between cliffs about 700 feet high, which answer face to face, and look as if they had been split from each other by the vertical stroke of an earthquake, it forms, from end to end, a scene of terrific grandeur, and it is traversed by the eastern road from Carnarvon to Aberystwith and has barely breadth enough of bottom to allow the road to pass A rock in it is said to have been the favourite haunt of the poet Rhys Goch O'rvri, who flourished in the time of Owen Glendower The rivulet Glaslyn scours the pass and makes a grand cataract on leaving it at a one-arch bridge, called Pont Aberglaslyn, which stretches from rock to rock.

ABERGLASNEY a seat on the river Glasney near Llandilofawr, in Carmarthen It once belonged to the Dyers one of whom was the poet of ' Grongar Hill

ABERGORLECH, a village and a chapelry, in Llanybyther parish, Carmarthen, at the confluence of the Gorle with the Cothi, 7 miles WNW of Llangadock station and 7 NW of Llandeilofawr Post town, Llandeilo under Carmarthen The chapelry is a p curacy in the diocese of St Davids Value, £60 Patron, the Vicar of Llanbyther

ABERGWAIN See Fishguard

ABERGWESSIN, a sub district in the district of Builth Brecon It comprises three entire parishes, and parts of two other parishes Acres, 46,141 Pop, 2,897 Houses, 51-

ABERGWILLY, a village and a parish in the district and county of Carmarthen The village stands at the confluence of the Gwilly with the Towy, and on the Llandilo and Carmarthen railway, 1½ mile NE of Carmarthen It has a station on the railway and a post office under Carmarthen Fairs are held on 4 May 23 June 2 and 27 Oct The palace of the Bishop of St Davids, an edifice in the Tudor style, built in 1830, is adjacent Merlin's hill, an eminence on the side of a dell, nearly 1½ mile above the village is said to have been the birth place and the favourite haunt of the sorcerer Merlin, and a rocky cavity near its summit still bears the name of Merlin's Chair A battle was fought in the neighbourhood, in 1020, between Llewelyn ab Sytsylt and the adventurer Run.—The parish contains also the hamlets of Cricklas, Glantawy, Hengd, Veney, and Ystyngwilly Acres, 10,748. Real property, £9,078 Pop. 2,197 Houses, 451 The property is much subdivided There are slate quarries. The living is a vicarage in the diocese of St Davids Value, £172.* Patron, the Bishop of St Davids The ancient church was made collegiate in 1287, but was annexed in 1531 to the college at Brecon The present church is a handsome edifice, in the early English style, with a spire A sub parochial church stands at Llanfihangel Uwchgwilly, and is served by a perpetual curate, on a salary of £75, appointed by the Vicar There are Independent, Baptist, and Calvinistic Methodist chapels, and charities £14

ABERGWYNOLWYN, a village with a r station and an inn, in Merioneth, on the Talyllyn railway, opened in 1868, 6¾ miles NE of Towyn

ABERHAFESP, a parish in Newtown district, Montgomery, at the confluence of the Hafesp with the Severn, near the Central Wales railway 2½ miles WNW of Newtown Post town, Newtown Acres, 4,568 Real property £3,335 Pop., 486 Houses 94 The property is held by two proprietors Aberhafesp Hall and the parsonage command fine views of the Severn Fishing and quarrying are carried on Traces exist of a Roman road and there is a medicinal spring. The living is a rectory in the diocese of St Asaph Value, £356 * Patron, the Bishop of St Asaph The church is early English, and in very good condition There are chapels for Independents and Baptists

ABERHALE, a township in Tregynon parish, Montgomery 5½ miles N of Newtown

ABERHONDDU See Brecon

ABERKENFIG a village in Newcastle parish, Glamorgan, 3 miles NNW of Bridgend It has a post office‡ under Bridgend, and a railway station Pop, 257

ABERLLUNVEY, formerly a parish, but now a hamlet in Glasbury parish, Brecon, at the confluence of the Llunvey with the Wye, 4½ miles SW of Hay Acres 626 Real property, £2,575 Pop, 132 Houses, 23

ABERMARCHNANT, a township in the parish of Llanrhaadr yn Mochnant, Montgomery, 4½ miles NNW of Llanfyllin Pop., 27

ABERMARLAIS a place on the river Towy, in Carmarthen, 1½ mile NW of Llangadock It was the seat of the Griffiths, of the celebrated Sir Rhys ab Thomas, and of the Foleys

ABERMAW See Barmouth

ABERMENAI, the contraction at the SW end of the Menai strait, between Carnarvon and Anglesey Here is a ferry

ABERMULE, a village at the influx of the Mule to the Severn, 4½ miles NE of Newtown, Montgomery It has a station on the Oswestry and Newtown railway and a post office under Shrewsbury

ABERNANT, a village and a parish in the district and county of Carmarthen The village stands near the river Cywyn 2¾ miles N of the South Wales railway, and 5 WNW of Carmarthen, and is a seat of petty sessions. Post town, Carmarthen The parish comprises 6,321 acres Real property, £3 718 Pop, 798 Houses, 16 The property is subdivided The living is a vicarage, united to the vicarage of Conwil, in the diocese of St. Davids Value, £131 * Patron, the Duke of Leeds The church is good

ABERNANT, a station on the Vale of Neath railway 4 miles SW of Merthyr Tydvil Glamorgan. Extensive iron works and collieries are adjacent

ABERPERGWM a chapelry in the parish of Cadoxton Glamorgan at Glyn Neath r station Post town, Glyn Neath under Neath The scenery of vale and mountain with the vale of the Pergwm rivulet, a waterfall, and the fine grounds of Aberpergwm House, is very rich Coal is worked The living is a vicarage in the diocese of Llandaff Value, £119 Patron Lees Williams, Esq

ABERPORTH a village and a parish in the district and county of Cardigan The village stands on the coast, at the mouth of the Howni rivulet 7 miles NE of Car digan, and is partly in the parish of Blaenporth It has a post-office under Cardigan, and is a seaport, a fishing station, and a watering place The parish contains also the hamlets of Rectorial and Llanannerch Acres, 2,200 Real property, £1,209 Pop., 454 Houses, 108 The property is much subdivided Great portion of the sur face is bare hill, and one of the summits is within view of the coast of Ireland. Plas, belonging to the Morgan family, is an ancient cruciform mansion The living is a rectory in the diocese of St David's Value, £136 Patron, the Bishop of St David's The church is very good. There is a Calvinistic Methodist chapel

ABERPWL See BANGOR

ABERRHEIDOL. See ABERYSTWITH

ABERRHIW See BERRIEW

ABERSOCH, a village, with a harbour, on St Tud well's bay, Carnarvon 7 miles SW of Pwllheli It has a post office under Pwllheli

ABERSYCHAN, a village in Trevethin parish Mon mouth, at the influx of the Sychan to the Avon, 2 miles NNW of Pontypool It has a post office‡ under Ponty pool, and a r station on the Eastern Valleys Monmouth railway It is a straggling populous place, connected with the British Iron works, on the neighbouring hill-side Here is a sub parochial church, for a pop of 7,979, served by a vicar, with a salary of £300, appointed by the vicar of Trevethin

ABERTANAT, a township in Llanyblodwell parish, Salop, on the river Tanat, 4½ miles SW of Oswestry Pop, 102

ABERTAWEY See SWANSEA.

ABERTEIFI See CARDIGAN

ABERTHAW, a seaport village in Penmark parish, Glamorgan, at the mouth of the Ddaw or Thaw river, 5½ miles SSE of Cowbridge Hydraulic lime, got from lias pebbles on the beach adjacent to it, is shipped The ruins of Penmark and East Orchard castles are near

ABERTHIN, a hamlet in Llanblethian parish, Glamorgan, 1 mile NE of Cowbridge

ABERTILLERY, a village in Aberystruth parish, Monmouth, 5 miles N of Crumlin. It has a station on the Western Valleys railway, a post office‡ under New-port, Monmouth, and a sub parochial church

ABERWHEELER See ABERCHWHILER

ABERYSCIR, a parish in the district and county of Brecon, 2¼ miles W by N of Brecon r station Post town Brecon. Acres, 1,918 Real property, £1,224 Pop, 125 Houses, 26 The Yscir river falls here into the Usk, and has, on the right bank, the parish church, surrounded with yew,—on the left bank a rectangular camp and several ramparts, together with substructions of walls, supposed to have been a station of the Roman general Ostorius Scapula, preceded by the British town Bannium. The living is a rectory in the diocese of St David's Value, £186 Patron, the Rev W L. Jones. The church belonged anciently to Malvern priory, and is a poor structure

ABERYSTRUTH, a parish, which is also a sub district, in the district of Abergavenny, Monmouth, at the Blaina station of the Western Valleys railway, 9 miles WSW of Abergavenny Post town, Blaina under Tredegar Acres, 11,788 Real property, £63,055,—of which £38,673 are in mines and iron works Pop in 1811, 11,272, in 1861, 16,055 Houses, 2,865 The property is held in two estates The surface is chiefly upland, round the higher reaches of the Ebbw river Collieries and iron works, round Nantyglo, Beaufort, and other centres, employ a great proportion of the inhabitants, and have undergone great recent increase The living is a rectory in the diocese of Llandaff Value, £265 Patron, the Earl of Abergavenny The curacy of Abertillery is included, and the vicarage of Nantyglo and cur of Beau fort are separate benefices The parish church is good Aberystruth is sometimes called Blaen Gwent

ABERYSTWITH, a town, a chapelry, a sub district, and a district on the coast of Cardigan The town is in the parish of Llanbadarn Fawr, stands on both banks of the river Rheidol, and on the Welsh coast railway sys tem, 39 miles NE of Cardigan, and is a fashionable water ing place, a head seaport, and a borough. The part of it on the right bank of the Rheidol sometimes bears the name of Aberrheidol, and the part on the left bank is called Trefechan The Rheidol is crossed by a five-arched bridge, forms a sort of inner harbour, is joined there by the Ystwith, and then scours the outer harbour to the sea The town chiefly occupies a gentle eminence, de clining all round from the centre, and commands exten sive superb views of sea and coast and lofty mountains The streets are uneven and steep, but some are broad and well-edificed, and the Marine terrace forms a fine crescent, with about 60 elegant dwellings. Two heights, at the end of the terrace, are pleasantly laid out in public walks The remains of a castle, consisting of a gateway and fragments of towers and walls, crown the south western height, overlooking the sea. The original castle was built in the time of Henry I by Gilbert de Strong bow, and destroyed by Owen Gwynedd, and the present castle was built by Edward I, as a means of securing his conquest of Wales, and dismantled by the Parlia mentarians after the defeat of Charles I The Castle House, at the end of the terrace, below the castle, is an edifice of fantastic design, in mixed Gothic and Italian, built by Nash for the late Sir Uvedale Price, Bart An ancient church stood in front of the site of the Castle House, and was overwhelmed about the year 1650 by the sea. The present church stands near the castle ruins, and is a plain, quasi-cruciform edifice, built in 1830, at a cost of nearly £4,000 There are chapels for Inde pendents, Baptists, Calvinistic Methodists, Wesleyans, and Roman Catholics The court house, built in 1860, is a handsome edifice with a tetrastyle Ionic portico The assembly rooms, built in 1820, have Grecian features, and contain a ball room 45 feet by 20, card, billiard, and reading rooms Other public buildings are the grammar school, the market houses, the infirmary, the poor house, and the prison

The town was incorporated by Edward I, but has no charter It is governed by a mayor, 4 aldermen, and 12 councillors, it was designed, at the building of the court house, to be made a seat of quarter sessions and of assizes, and it joins with Cardigan, Lampeter, and Ad-bar in sending a member to parliament The borough boundaries include all Aberystwith chapelry and parts of Issavndre and Lower Vainor townships The port has jurisdiction northward to the Diswynnig river, and south-ward to Llan St Fraid. The vessels registered at it in 1867 were 86 small ones of aggregately 2,984 tons, and 296 large ones of aggregately 37,995 tons The vessels which entered from British colonies or foreign countries were 23, of aggregately 4,633 tons, and those which entered coastwise were 409 sailing vessels of 17,225 tons, and 71 steam vessels of 6,675 tons The amount of customs, in that year, was £87 The exports include lead ore and other minerals, timber, bark, and corn, and the imports include all kinds of goods from Liver-pool, Bristol and London. The harbour was much ob structed by a bar, but has been greatly improved by artificial cuttings of the river by a new pier 260 yards long and by other works. The town has a head post-office,‡ a r station with telegraph, two banking offices, three hotels, markets on Monday and Saturday, and fairs on the Monday before 5 Jan., Palm Monday, Whit Monday, and the Monday after 13 Nov About two thousand temporary residents, and several thousands of casual visitors frequent the town as a watering place in autumn. The bathing beaches are excellent, bathing-machines are plentiful, hot salt water baths are at hand, a chalybeate spring, of similar qualities to the water of Tunbridge, is on a neighbouring common, recreations in variety, are abundant and the walks and drives in the vicinity are charming Races are held on two days in September at Gogerddan, 3 miles distant. Cornelians, jaspers, agates, mochos, and other precious pebbles are often picked up by loungers on the beach Public coaches used to run to distant towns, east south, and north, railway trains have now superseded them, and steamers ply to Bristol and Liverpool Plas crug, a ruined castel lated edifice, in the environs, on the banks of the Rheidol is said to have been the residence of Owen Glendower The grave of the poet Taliesin, who flourished in the 6th century is 8 miles distant Pop of the town in 1851, 5,231 in 1861, 5,641 Houses, 1 089 A system of railway, called the Aberystwith and Welsh Coast ramifying northward and eastward from Aberystwith, to an aggregate length of 86 miles, was authorized in 1861, underwent extensions and alterations under acts of 1862-1867, became amalgamated with the Cambrian system, and connects, at Aberystwith, with a line southward to the South Wales system at Carmarthen

The chapelry comprises 559 acres of land and 175 of water Pop, 5 361 Houses 1,068 The living is a vicarage in the diocese of St David's Value, not reported Patron, the Bishop of St David's —The sub district comprises Llanychaiarn parish and part of Llanbadarn Fawr Acres, 15,440 Pop, 8,772 Houses, 1,720 The district comprehends also the sub district of Llanrhystyd, containing the parishes of Llanrhystyd, Llanddeinol, Llangrwyddon, Llanilar, and Rhostie, the sub-district of Geneur Glynn, containing the parish of Llancynfelin, and parts of the parishes of Llanbadarn Fawr and Llanbhangel Geneur-Glynn and the sub district of Rheidol, containing the parishes of Llanafan and Llanbhangel y Croyddin, and part of the parish of Llanbadarn-Fawr Acres, 132,592 Poor rates in 1866, £3,027 Pop. in 1841, 22 242, in 1861, 25,461 Houses, 5,083 Marriages in 1866, 244, births, 916,—of which 70 were illegitimate, deaths, 523,—of which 148 were at ages under 5 years, and 22 at ages upwards of 85 Marriages in the ten years 1851-60, 1 935, births, 7,458, deaths, 4,697 The places of worship in 1851 were 20 of the Church of England, with 5,951 sittings, 11 of Independents, with 1,996 s, 27 of Calvinistic Methodists, with 7 227 s, 10 of Wesleyan Methodists, with 2,519 s., 1 of Primitive Methodists, with 212 s., 1 of the Wesleyan Association with 238 s, and 9 of Baptists, with 2,095 s The schools in 1851 were 20 public day schools, with 1,409 scholars, 27 private day schools, with 732 s, and 67 Sunday schools, with 9,835 s

ABINGDON, a town, two parishes, a sub district, and a district in Berks The town comprises parts of the two parishes, and is a borough It stands on a rich flat plain at the influx of the Ock to the Thames, at the junction of the Wilts and Berks canal with the Thames, and at the terminus of a sub branch railway of 1¾ mile from the Oxford branch of the Great Western 6 miles by road S of Oxford and 60¼ by railway W by N of London It was called originally Scheovesham softened into Shovesham and afterwards Abandune, altered into Abingdon It was a place of note in the time of the Britons, and became a royal residence in the times of the Saxons Synods were held at it in 742 and 822, and the royal courts of Mercia and Wessex made it long a seat of state assemblies A manuscript in the Cottonian library, called "the old book of Abendon," describes it as "in ancient times a famous city, goodly to behold, and full of riches Some foundations of its royal palace can still be traced in a meadow on the E side of the bridge The town was visited by William the Conqueror, by Henry III and by Henry VIII It was garrisoned for Charles I, made the head quarters of his horse, and the temporary retreat of all his family, and became the scene of sharp struggles and great excesses before he was subdued A sharp practice of its garrison, of hanging all Irish prisoners without trial, gave rise to the proverb of "Abingdon law"

The town consists of several wide streets, diverging from a spacious market place The market house is a curious edifice, of ashlar and rough freestone, with a tower erected in 1678 The county prison is a substantial structure with capacity for 45 male and 16 female prisoners, built in 1812, at a cost of £23 000 The grammar school, founded in 1563 by J Roysse, was rebuilt outside the town in 1869 has an endowed income of £241 holds five scholarships at Pembroke College, Oxford, and numbers among its pupils Lord Chief Justice Holt Archbishop Newcome, Godwin and Mount, the antiquaries Holland the linguist, and Graves the author of the "Spiritual Quixote" Christ's hospital, founded in 1553 by Sir John Mason, is a curious cloistered edifice of brick and timber, with turret and dome, contains an oak hall with pictures and stained glass shows, at the E end of its cloister, a representation of a famous octagonal market cross, which was destroyed in 1644, and has an endowed income of £632 Other charities have £930 The bridge across the river is a picturesque structure with six pointed arches, erected in 1416, was regarded, at the time of its erection, as a grand boon to all the surrounding country, and is the subject of some quaint old verses preserved in Christ's Hospital Prince Albert's cross is an elegant erection of 1864, after designs by Gibbs It has a quadrangular base, with medallions, a central octagonal shaft, with rich entablature, side columns, with carved capitals supporting heraldic lions, and a surmounting pyramidal pedestal, crowned by a statue of the Prince

St Helen's church occupies the site of an ancient nunnery, and was about to be restored in July 1869 It has a nave, three aisles, and a south chapel, and forms altogether a spacious rectangle The north aisle has rich timber ceilings of the time of Henry VI, and the south aisle was built in 1539 A tower, in the early English style rises at the NE corner, and is surmounted by a lofty octagonal spire in the perpendicular style, which figures conspicuously for miles St Nicholas church was built about the year 1300, on the site of an earlier edifice, and it has a good Norman doorway and a tower A graceful gateway, in the perpendicular style, adjoining St Nicholas' church, and part of a refectory behind, now used as a stable, and containing a beautifully decorated window, are the chief remains of the Mitred Benedictine abbey of St Mary, which was one of the richest in England The original abbey was founded in Bagley-wood, in the neighbouring parish of Sunningwell, about the year 680, by Cissa, viceroy of Centurin, king of Wessex, but was totally destroyed, in the time of Alfred, by the Danes The subsequent edifice was founded at Abingdon by King Edred, and completed in the reign of King Edgar The nave was 180 feet long, the choir 65 feet long, the Lady Chapel, 36 feet long, the transept, 156 feet long, the western tower, 100 feet high The Independent chapel was built in 1863, and is in the Italian style The Roman Catholic chapel was built in 1866, at a cost of more than £5,000, and is in the second pointed style

The borough comprises 239 acres It received a charter of Queen Mary in 1557 It is governed by a mayor 4 aldermen, and 12 councillors, it holds a commission of the peace and a court of quarter sessions, it is the seat of summer assizes for Berks, and it sends a member to parliament. The average annual revenue is £750, the amount of taxation in 1860 was £3,759, the number of electors in 1868 was 329 Real property in 1860, £20 425. Pop in 1851, 5,954, in 1861, 5 680 Houses, 1 189 A large trade is carried on in clothing, and a little is carried on in matting hemp dressing, and sack and sail cloth making A weekly market is held on Monday a wool fair on the first Monday in July, a hiring fair, on the Monday before Old Michaelmas day, lamb fairs, on 5 Aug, 19 Sep, and 11 Dec, and other fairs on the first Monday in Lent, 6 May and 20 June Races are run annually, on a 1¼ mile course The town has a head post office‡ a telegraph office, two banking offices, two principal hotels, four dissenting chapels, and a variety of local institutions It gives the title of Earl to the family of Bertie, and it numbers among its natives or celebrities Archbishop St Edmund Archbishop Newcome, Sir John Mason, Sir T Smith Abbot the Speaker, Moore who wrote the "Gamester," and W Stevens the poet

The parish of St Helen comprises 3 184 acres, and includes the farms of Barton and Pumney, the hamlets of Northcourt and Cholswell, and the townships of Sandford and Shippon Rated property, £14 342 Pop, 5 958 Houses 1,214 The parish of St Nicholas comprises 177 acres. Rated property, £2,212 Pop, 742 Houses, 143 The living of St H is a vicarage, that of St N a rectory, in the dio of Oxford, and the two are conjoined. Value, £255 Patron, the Bishop of O The vicarages of Drayton, Sandford, and Snippon are separate benefices —The sub-district of Abingdon comprises five parishes and two extra parochial tracts Acres, 12,983 Pop., 8,672. Houses, 1,759 The district of Abingdon, though all in the registration county of Berks, is partly in the parliamentary county of *Oxford* It comprehends the sub district of Fyfield, containing the parishes of Kingston Bagpuize, Fyfield, Tubney, and Appleton, and parts of the parishes of West Hanney and Longworth, the sub district of Abingdon, containing the parishes of Marcham, St Helen, St Nicholas, Radley, and Sunningwell, and the *extra-parochial tracts of* Bagley wood and Chandlings-farm, the sub district of Cumnor, containing the parishes of Besselsleigh, Cumnor, Wootton, Wytham, North Hinksey, South Hinksey, and Binsey (the last in Oxfordshire), and the extra-parochial tract of Seacourt, the sub-district of Sutton Courtenay, *containing the parishes of Sutton* Courtenay, Milton, Drayton Steventon, and Culham (the last in Oxfordshire), and the sub district of Nuneham Courtenay, all in Oxfordshire, and containing the parishes of Sandford, Nuneham Courtenay, Baldon Marsh, Baldon Foot, Chiselhampton, Stadhampton, *Drayton*, and Clifton Hampden, and *parts of the parishes* of St Mary Oxford and Dorchester Acres, 56,445 Poor rates in 1866, £14,319 Pop in 1841, 18,780 in 1861, 20,861 Houses, 4,328 Marriages in 1866, 162, births, 652,—of which 48 were illegitimate deaths, 388, —of which 100 were at ages under 5 years, and 18 were at ages above 85 Marriages in the ten years 1851–60, 1,409, births, 6,940, deaths, 4,911 The places of worship in 1851 were 37 of the Church of England, with 9,073 sittings, 2 of Independents, with 740 s, 8 of Baptists with 2,730 s, 11 of Wesleyan Methodists, with 986 s, 2 of Primitive Methodists, with 312 s and 2 undefined, with 339 s The schools in 1851 were 27 public day schools, with 1,742 scholars, 33 private day schools with 768 s, 43 Sunday schools, with 2,707 s and 3 evening schools for adults with 133 s The work house is in Northcourt hamlet and was built at a cost of £8,500

ABINGER, a village and a parish in Dorking district Surrey The village is 2½ miles SE of Gomshall and Shere r station, and 4½ miles SW of Dorking, and has a post office under Dorking It was for many years the residence of Hoole, the translator of Ariosto, and it gives the title of Baron to the family of Scarlett. The parish is overhung on the SE by Leith hill, and drained westward by a tributary of the Wey Acres, 5,547 Real property, £4,265 Pop, 906 Houses, 177 The property is not much divided Abinger Hall is the seat of Lord Abinger, and was long the residence of the Countess of Donegal, Swift's "Glory of the Granard race." The living is a rectory in the diocese of Winchester Value, £453 * Patron, W J Evelyn, Esq The church is an ancient edifice, partly in the earliest Norman, partly in early English, was recently restored at a cost of about £1,500, and has some good coloured windows Charities, £9 This parish is a meet for the Surrey Union hounds

ABINGHALL or ABBENHALL, a parish in Westbury on Severn district, Gloucester, in *Dean forest* 1½ mile SSW of Longhope r station, and 5 N of Newnham Post town, Longhope under Newnham Acres, 751 Real property, £1,718 Pop, 228 Houses 43. The property is not much divided There is a mineral spring The living is a rectory in the diocese of Gloucester and Bristol *Value £112 * Patron, J F Sevier, Esq* The church is an old Norman edifice, in good condition, and contains some ancient tombs.

ABINGTON, a parish in the district and county of Northampton, near the river Nen and the Peterborough railway, 1½ mile NE of Northampton Post town, *Northampton* Acres, 1,112 Real *property*, £2,851 Pop, 164 Houses, 24 A spot here was the grave of Shakspeare's favourite grand daughter, and is marked by a mulberry tree planted by Garrick Abington Abbey is a lunatic asylum The living is a rectory in the diocese of Peterborough Value, £200 * Patron Lord Overstone The church is early English, and contains tombs of the Berhards Charities £20

ABINGTON, a village in Great Abington parish, Cambridge, near the C and Haverhill railway, 2½ miles NW of Linton It has a post office under Cambridge, and a r station, and was formerly a market town

ABINGTON (GREAT), a parish *in Linton district*, Cambridge It contains the village of Abington, and the seats of Abington House, Abington Hall, and Abington Park Acres, 1,500 Real property, £2,291 Pop, 330 Houses, 62 The living is a vicarage in the diocese of Ely Value, £120 Patron, T Mortlock, Esq The church is early English.

ABINGTON (LITTLE), a parish in Linton district, Cambridge, adjoining the N side of Great Abington Acres, 1,120 Real property, £1,680 Pop, 316 Houses, 66 The property is divided among a few The living is a vicarage in the diocese of Ely Value, £87 * Patron, T Mortlock, Esq The church belonged to Pentney Abbey, is in good condition, and contains tombs of the Daltons.

ABINGTON IN THE CLAY, or ABINGTON PIGOTTS, a parish in Royston district, Cambridge 5 miles NW of Royston, and 4 from Royston r station Post town, Royston Acres, 1,237 Real property, £2,206 Pop, 228 Houses, 41 The manor has been held by the family of Pigott since the Conquest The living is a rectory in the diocese of Ely Value, £310 * Patron, M G F Pigott Esq The church is good.

AB-KETTLEBY, a township and a parish in Melton Mowbray district, Leicester The township lies on an affluent of the river Wreak, at Broughton hill, 2¾ miles N by E of Asfordby r station, and 3 NW by N of Melton Mowbray, and has a post office under Melton Mowbray Pop, 224 Houses, 50 The parish contains also the township of Holwell Acres, 2 930 Rated property, £1 805 Pop 3 1 Houses, 52 The property is subdivided The living is a vicarage in the diocese of Peterborough Value, not reported Patron, Rev T Bingham The church belonged anciently to Laund priory, was recently restored, and has a tower and spire There are a Wesleyan chapel and charities £8

ABLINGTON, a tything in Bibury parish, Gloucester, on the river Coln, 5½ miles NW of Fairford Pop, 113 Houses, 21

ABLINGTON, a hamlet in Figheldean parish, Wilts, on the river Avon, 4½ miles N of Amesbury Pop, 137

ABNEY, a hamlet in Hope parish Derby on a tributary of the river Derwent, 4 miles NE of Tideswell

ABNEY PARK, a suburb of London 3½ miles N of St Paul's It has a post office under Stoke Newington, London N A mansion on its site was the seat of Sir Thomas Abney and the residence of Dr Watts, and a cemetery now here has a chapel in the centre, and contains a monument to Dr Watts

ABOVE DERWENT See ALLERDALE

ABOVE SAWTHE, a tract called a hamlet, containing Ergob, Cnwchroen Hall, and the town of Llangadock, in the parish of Llangadock Carmarthen Pop, 746 Houses, 169 See LLANGADOCK

ABRAHAM (HEIGHTS OF) See MATLOCK

ABRAM, a *chapelry in Wigan parish*, Lancashire on the Wigan and Newton railway and Wigan and Leigh canal 3½ miles SSE of Wigan Acres, 1,965. Real property, £8,925 —of which £4,125 are in mines. Pop, 911 Houses, 173 The property is much subdivided The living is a vicarage Value £120 Patron, the Rector of Wigan The church was built in 1813 There are an endowed school, and charities £30

ABRIDGE, a village in Lambourne parish, Essex, on the river Roding 5 miles S of Epping It has a post-office under Romford, and a fair on 2 June, and it forms a curacy with the rectory of Lambourne

ABSON ABSTON, or ALBOTSTON, a village and a parish in Chipping Sodbury district, Gloucester The village stands on a small tributary of the Avon, 3 miles SE of Mangotsfield r station, and 7 E by N of Bristol The parish contains also the villages of Bridgegate and Holbrook, and is sometimes called Abson cum Wick and sometimes Wick and Abson Post town, Wick under Bath Acres, 2 315. Real property, £5,541 Pop 833. Houses, 185 The manor belonged anciently to Glastonbury abbey and belongs now to Messrs Batterbury and Tolman. There are romantic rocky heights, a Roman camp, two Druidical stones, lead and tin ores, and two iron rolling mills The living is a p curacy, annexed to Pucklechurch in the diocese of Gloucester and Bristol There are a church for Abson, of early English date, a church for Wick, built in 1850, Independent and Wesleyan chapels and a national school

ABTHORPE a village, a parish, and a sub district in the district of Towcester, Northampton The village stands on the river Tove, 3 miles WSW of Towcester, and 8 SW by W of Blisworth r station and has a post office under Towcester The parish includes the hamlet of Foscote Acres, 1,919 Real property, £2,903 Pop., 511 Houses, 110 The property is divided among a few The living is a vicarage in the diocese of Peterborough Value, £215 * Patron alternately the Bishop of Lichfield and the Trustees of Leeson's charity The church is good. Charities, £191 —The sub district comprises seventeen entire parishes, and parts of two others. Acres, 22 323 Pop, 5,473 Houses, 1,237

ABURY See AVEBURY

ABY, a parish in Louth district Lincoln, 1 mile W of Claythorpe r station, and 3 NW of Alford. Post town, Alford Acres 1,440 Real property £2,018 Pop, 407 Houses, 87 The hamlet of Greenfield is included. The living is a vicarage, united to the rectory of Belleau, in the diocese of Lincoln There are a Wesleyan chapel, a national school and remains of a Cistertian nunnery founded about the year 1150

ACASTER-MALBIS a township and a parish in York district, W R. Yorkshire. The township lies on the river Ouse, 2 miles E of Copmanthorpe r station, and 5 S of York and has a post office under York The parish includes also part of the township of Naburn Acres, 1 750 Real property, £2,894 Pop, 359 Houses 61 The property is all in one estate, and it derived its name from the Malbisse family, who flourished here for several centuries after the Conquest The living is a vicarage in the diocese of York Value £56 Patron F Lawley, Esq The church is very good. Charities £35

ACASTER SELBY, a township chapelry in Stillingfleet parish, W R Yorkshire on the river Ouse, 3 miles E of Bolton Percy r station, and 8 S of York Post town, Tadcaster Acres, 1 523 Real property, £2,639 Pop 151 Houses, 26 The property belonged anciently to the abbey of Selby, and it still is undivided. A college for a provost and two or three fellows was founded on it by Robert Stillington The chapelry was constituted in 1850, and is a vicarage in the diocese of York Value, £40. Patron, Sir W M Milner, Bart The church is very good.

ACCONBURY See ACORNBURY

ACCOTT a hamlet in Swimbridge parish Devon, 5 miles E of Barnstaple

ACCRINGTON, a town, two townships, two chapelries, and a sub district in Whalley parish, Lancashire The town adjoins the E Lancashire railway, near the Leeds and Liverpool canal, 4 miles by road and 5½ by railway E of Blackburn It is large and thriving, has sprung up within the present century is a seat of petty sessions and county courts, publishes a weekly newspaper carries on industry in twenty cotton factories, three print works, extensive turkey red dye works several large chemical works, foundries, steel works and a brewery, is well supplied with water from reservoirs, and has a head post office ‡ a r station with telegraph, a banking office four hotels, a market house of 1868, public rooms of 18[illegible] in the Italian style at a cost of £5,000, a mechanics institution, a museum and pleasure gardens a church enlarged in 1826 a church of 1841 in the early English style at a cost of £8 000 a church of 1865 two new Wesleyan chapels of 1815 and 1866 nine other dissenting chapels a Roman Catholic chapel seven public schools, and two annual fairs Pop in 1851, 7,481 in 1861, 13,872 Houses, 2 579 —The townships are New A and Old A Acres, 2 450 and 740 Real property, £52,634, of which £8 400 are in mines Pop, 11,853 and 5,835.—The chapelries are St James and Christ church, and both are p curacies in the diocese of Manchester Value of each £300 * Patrons of St J, Hulme's Trustees, of C, Trustees —The sub district is conterminate with the two townships

ACHURCH See THORPE ACHURCH

ACKENTHWAITE, a hamlet in Heversham parish, Westmoreland, adjacent to Milnthorpe, and to the Lancaster and Carlisle railway

ACKHAMPSTEAD See ASHAMPSTEAD, Oxford

ACKLAM, a township and a parish in Malton district, E R Yorkshire The township is called Acklam with Barthorpe and lies 5 miles ESE of Kirkham r station, and 7 S of Malton Acres, 1,800 Pop. 366 Houses, 82. The parish is called East Acklam, and contains also the township of Leavening Post town, Kirby Underdale under York Acres, 2 970 Real property, £1,621 Pop, 774 Houses, 154 The surface is on the Wolds, and commands a very extensive view The property is much subdivided. The living is a rectory in the diocese of York Value, £108 * Patron, the Archbishop of York The church was rebuilt in 1868 There are chapels for Wesleyan and Primitive Methodists Some ancient entrenchments and other works, British or Roman, are on the hills

ACKLAM (WEST), a parish in the district of Stockton, and N R Yorkshire 2 miles S of Newport r station, and 4 ESE of Stockton Post town, Stainton under Stockton. Acres 1,470 Real property, £1,029 Pop, 103 Houses, 19 The property is divided among a few Acklam Hall is the seat of T Hustler, Esq The living is a vicarage in the diocese of York Value, £77 * Patron, T Hustler, Esq The church is good Charities, £5

ACKLETON, a township in Worfield parish, Salop, 5½ miles NE of Bridgnorth. It has a post-office under Bridgnorth

ACKLEY a township in Forden parish, Montgomeryshire 3½ miles N of Montgomery Pop, 84

ACKLINGTON, a township and a chapelry in Alnwick district, Northumberland The township is in Warkworth parish, lies on the Northeastern railway and the river Coquet, 11¾ miles north of Morpeth, and has a station on the railway, and a head post office ‡ Acres, 2 072 Pop 255 Houses, 52 —The chapelry comprises parts of Warkworth and Shilbottle parishes, was constituted in 1859, and is a vicarage in the diocese of Durham Pop., 635 Houses, 124 Value, not reported Patron the Duke of Northumberland The church is in the early English style, and was erected in 1861 after designs by Deason, at the Duke of Northumberland's expense

ACKLINGTON PARK, a township in Warkworth parish, Northumberland adjoining Acklington Acres, 766 Pop 163 Houses, 31

ACKTHORPE a hamlet in South Elkington parish, Lincolnshire, 2 miles W of Louth Pop 35

ACKTON See ACTON

ACKWORTH a parish in Hemsworth district, W R Yorkshire, 3½ miles S of Pontefract r station It contains Ackworth village and three hamlets, and has a post office ‡ under Pontefract Acres 2 270 Real property, £9,72[illegible] Pop 1,813 Houses 333 A Park, A House, and several good villas are chief residences Stone is largely quarried, and the kennels of the Badsworth hunt are here The living is a rectory in the diocese of York Value, £493 * Patron the Duchy of Lancaster The church was rebuilt in 1851 There are chapels for Quakers Wesleyans and Roman Catholics a large and famous Quakers school, a training school for masters, two endowed schools, two other public schools, and charities £144

ACLE a village and a parish in Blofield district, Norfolk The village stands near the river Bure, 4 miles N of Brundall r station, and 11 E of Norwich It has a post office ‡ under Norwich and was formerly a market town, and a fair is held at it on Midsummer day The parish lies chiefly around the village, but part of it is at some distance, in the Marshes Acres, 3,209 Real property, £8 417 Pop, 926 Houses, 197 The property is much subdivided The living is a rectory in the diocese of Norwich Value, £603 * Patron, Lord Calthorpe The church is old A Wesleyan chapel was built in 1867 There is a national school An Augustinian priory anciently stood at Vale Dam

ACLEA See OCKLEY

ACLETON See ACKLETON

ACOCK'S GREEN, a chapelry in Yardley parish, Worcester, on the Oxford and Birmingham railway, 4¼ miles SE of Birmingham. It was constituted in 1867, and it has a r station, a post-office‡ under Birmingham, a church of 1867 at a cost of £4,000, a recent handsome Independent chapel, and a Wesleyan chapel The living is a vicarage Statistics, not reported

ACOL, or WOOD, a ville in Thanet, Kent, 3 miles SW of Margate Acres, 1,176 Pop, 260

ACOMB, a township and a parish in York district, W R Yorkshire. The township lies 2 miles W of York, and has a post office under that city Acres, 1,440 Pop, 897 Houses, 195 The parish includes also most of the township of Knapton and part of the township of Drinkhouses, and is traversed by the Northeastern railway Acres, 2,273 Real property, £5,361 Pop, 1,034 Houses, 226 The property is much subdivided An eminence called Severs hill is traditionally said to have been the place where the body of the Emperor Severus was consumed to ashes The living is a vicarage in the diocese of York Value, £190 Patron, F Barlow, Esq The church is old, but good. There is a Wesleyan chapel Charities £12

ACOMB, a township in St. John Lee parish Northumberland, on the Tyne, 2 miles NNW of Hexham It has a post office under Hexham, and a Wesleyan chapel Acres, 2 745 Pop, 800 Houses, 128

ACOMB (EAST), a township in the parish of Bywell St Peter Northumberland, on the Tyne, 4 miles E of Corbridge Acres, 391 Pop, 62 Houses, 9

ACONBURY, or ACORNBURY, a village and a parish in the district and county of Hereford The village stands 2¾ miles WSW of Holme Lacey r station, and 4½ S of Hereford, and is an old fashioned place The parish comprises 1,591 acres, and its post town is Holme Lacey under Hereford Real property £1,132 Pop, 183 Houses, 37 The property is divided among a few Aconbury hill, to the S of the village, commands an extensive and very fine prospect, and shows distinct traces of a large Roman camp An Augustinian nunnery anciently stood in Aconbury forest. The living is a vicarage in the diocese of Hereford. Value £53 * Patron, the Rev S Thackwell The church is neat

ACREFAIR, a village, with a railway station, in Denbigh, 2 miles SSW of Ruabon.

ACRE (SOUTH) See SOUTH ACRE

ACRE (WEST) See WEST ACRE

ACRISE, a parish in the Elham district, Kent, 5 miles NNW of Folkestone r station Post town, Elham under Canterbury Acres, 1,034. Real property, £1,196 Pop, 173. Houses, 34 The property is divided among a few The living is a rectory in the diocese of Canterbury Value, £171 * Patron, W A. Mackinnon Esq The church has a Norman chancel arch, and is very good The East Kent hounds meet at Acrise and a fair is held on 16 Oct at Acrise Mill

ACTON, a name signifying "oak town," and designating a seat of population which anciently was occupied by oak trees

ACTON a township in Weaverham parish, Cheshire, 4½ miles WNW of Northwich It lies on the Northwestern railway and on the Weaver river, and has a station on the railway Acres. 1,139 Pop, 434 Houses, 100 A bridge on the Weaver here was built of stones from Vale Royal abbey Fairs are held at Acton Bridge on 14 April and 14 Oct

ACTON, a township and a parish in Nantwich district, Cheshire. The township lies on the Birmingham and Liverpool canal, near the Shropshire Union railway 1¼ mile WNW of Nantwich, and has a post-office under Nantwich Acres, 722 Pop, 297 Houses, 57 The parish comprises the townships of Acton, Cool Pilate, Austerson, Baddington, Edleston, Burland, Faddiley, Brindley, Henhull, Hurleston, Poole, Stoke, Cholmondestone, Aston juxta Mondrum, and Worleston Acres, 15,542 Real property, £2,978 Pop. 3,125 Houses 625 The manor belonged to the Saxon earl Morcar, and passed, through the Lovels, Ardens and Wilbrahams to the Tollemaches The parish church and Dorfold Hall were garrisoned, during the civil war, by successively the regal and the parliamentary forces The church is early English, and contains some ancient monuments Dorfold Hall was built in 1616, consists of dark brick, has large bay windows and massive chimneys, and contains some well preserved, rich, plaster ornaments. The living is a vicarage in the diocese of Chester Value, £627 * Patron, J Tollemache, Esq The p curacy of Burley Dam is a separate benefice Charities, £100

ACTON, a village a parish and a sub district in Brentford, Middlesex. The village stands 8½ miles W of St. Paul's, London, is linked to the metropolis by an almost continuous line of houses, bisected by the Junction railway, connecting the Northwestern railway with the Southwestern, and it has a station on the railway and a post-office‡ under London W The parish contains also the hamlets of East Acton and Steyne Acres, 2,286 Real property, £18,477 Pop, 3,151 Houses, 610 The property is subdivided Old Oak Common, traversed by the Great Western railway and by the North and Southwestern junction, was anciently a thick oak forest Acton Wells, on the common, were in much repute, about the middle of last century, for their medicinal waters Berrymead Priory was once the seat of the Savilles and the Evelyns Sir P Skippon, Richard Baxter, Sir Matthew Hale, Bishop Lloyd, Provost Rous Thicknesse, the traveller, and Ryres, the author of "Mercurius Rusticus," resided in Acton The living is a rectory in the diocese of London Value, £968 * Patron the Bishop of London The church is early English, and was restored in 1865 There are Independent and Wesleyan chapels, a literary institution, handsome national schools, Wesleyan schools, and well-endowed alms houses —The sub-district comprises four parishes Acres, 5,963 Pop 6 443 Houses, 1,041

ACTON, a township in Featherstone parish, W R Yorkshire, 3½ miles W of Pontefract It contains Acton Hall Acres, 934 Pop, 67 Houses, 17

ACTON, a parish in Sudbury district Suffolk, near the river Stour 2½ miles N by E of Sudbury r station It has a post office under Sudbury Acres, 2 811 Real property £4,159 Pop, 558 Houses, 122 The property belongs chiefly to two Acton Place contains some old paintings and other interesting objects. The living is a vicarage in the diocese of Ely Value, £255.* Patron Earl Howe The church contains five brasses, and is good

ACTON, a township in Wrexham parish, Denbigh, on the Shrewsbury and Chester railway, 1 mile NNE of Wrexham Acres, 852 Pop, 220 Houses, 42 Acton Park is the seat of Sir Robert H Cunliffe, Bart, and occupies the site of the house in which the notorious Judge Jeffreys was born

ACTON a hamlet in Langton Matravers parish Dorset, 3½ miles SE of Corfe Castle

ACTON, a township in North Lydbury parish, Salop, 2¼ miles SSW of Bishop's Castle Pop, 108

ACTON, a township in Swinnerton parish, Stafford 3½ miles SW of Newcastle under Lyne

ACTON AND OLD FELTON, a township in Felton parish, Northumberland, near the river Coquet, 3 miles ENE of Acklington r station, and 7½ S of Alnwick Acres 1,244 Pop., 93 Houses, 21

ACTON BEAUCHAMP, a parish in the district of Bromyard and county of Worcester, 5 miles SE of Bromyard, and 5½ SW by N of Colwall r station. It has a post office under Worcester Acres, 1,529 Real property £2 026 Pop., 205 Houses, 42 The property belonged anciently to the Beauchamps, but is now much subdivided. There are mineral springs. The living is a rectory in the diocese of Worcester Value, £320 * Patron, Rev R. Cowpland The church is very good

ACTON BRIDGE See Acton, Weaverham, Cheshire

ACTON-BURNELL, a township and a parish in Atcham district, Salop The township lies 4 miles ENE of Dorrington r station, and 8¼ SSE of Shrewsbury, and it has a post office under Shrewsbury, and is the meet of the Wheatland hounds Pop, 283 Houses, 56 The parish contains also the townships of Ruckley and Langley Acres, 3,141 Real property, £3,839 Pop, 361 Houses, 72 Acton Park is the seat of Sir C F Smythe, Bart, the only landowner A ruin on Acton hill, with very thick walls and curiously carved pointed windows, is part of a castle which was built in the 13th century, and belonged to the family of Burnell The lords of Edward I 's parliament of 1283, which passed "Statutum de mercatoribus," sat in a hall of the castle, while the commons sat in an adjacent barn The living is a rectory in the diocese of Lichfield, and includes the chapelry of Acton Pigott Value, £350 * Patron, Rev R Meyricke The church contains a canopied brass of a Burnell, and is good.

ACTON DELAMARE See Acton, Weaverham, Cheshire

ACTON GRANGE a township in Runcorn parish, Cheshire, on the Northwestern railway and the Bridgewater canal, 2½ miles SW of Warrington Acres, 1,004 Pop., 130 Houses 28

ACTON IRON See Iron Acton

ACTON PIGOTT a chapelry in Ruckley township Acton Burnell parish, Salop, 1 mile NE of Acton Burnell See Acton Burnell.

ACTON REYNOLD, a township in Shawbury parish, Salop, near the river Roden, 7 miles NNE of Shrewsbury Pop, 159

ACTON ROUND a parish in Bridgnorth district, Salop, near Wenlock Edge 5 miles W by S of Linley r station, and 6½ WNW of Bridgnorth Post town, Burton under Wellington, Salop Acres 2 126 Rated property, £1,400 Pop., 173 Houses 36 Sir F R E Acton, Bart, of Aldenham Hall, is the chief proprietor and Cardinal Acton belonged to his family The living is a vicarage in the diocese of Hereford Value, £85 Patron, Sir F R F Acton The church is ancient and cruciform, has a small tower, contains three fine monuments of the Acton family, and was recently restored

ACTON SCOTT, a parish in Church Stretton district, Salop, near the river Onny, under Wenlock Edge, 2 miles E of Marsh Brook r station, and 3 S of Church Stretton Post town Church Stretton Acres, 1,889 Real property, £2 012 Pop, 207 Houses, 41 The property is divided among a few The living is a rectory in the diocese of Hereford Value, £238 * Patron, F W Lendarvis, Esq The church is very good.

ACTON STONE a township in Rushbury parish, Salop, 3 miles E of Church Stretton

ACTON TRUSSELL AND BEDNALL, a township chapelry in Baswich parish Stafford, on the river Trent and the Stafford canal, near Cannock Chase, and near the Northwestern railway, 3 miles N of Penkridge It has a post office, of the name of Bednall, under Stafford Acres, 2,547 Real property, £4,782 Pop, 617 Houses, 123 The property is divided among four proprietors The living is a vicarage in the diocese of Lichfield Value, £231 Patrons, Hulme's Trustees The church is in disrepair

ACTON TURVILLE, a parish in Chipping Sodbury district Gloucester near the Fosse way and under the Cotswold hills 5½ miles E by S of Chipping Sodbury, and 7½ E of Yate r station Post town Chipping Sodbury Acres, 1 009 Real property £1 421 Pop 310 Houses 68 The manor belongs to the Duke of Beaufort The living is a vicarage annexed to the rectory of Tormarton, in the diocese of Gloucester and Bristol The church is early English, restored and enlarged There is a Baptist chapel and a free school of 1842

ADBASTON, a township and a parish in the district of Newport-Salop and county of Stafford The township lies near the Grand Junction canal, 4½ miles W by S of Eccleshall, and 6 SW of Standon Bridge r station, and has a post office under Newport Salop Real property, £2 329 Pop, 210 Houses 40 The parish contains also the townships of Flashbrook, Bishops Offlow, and Tunstall. Acres 4 560. Real property, £6 895 Pop 593 Houses, 116 The property is much subdivided The living is a vicarage in the diocese of Lichfield. Value £100 * Patron, the Dean of Lichfield The church is good Charities, £8 Adbaston gave the title of Viscount to Earl Whitworth

ADBEER, a hamlet in Trent parish, Somerset, 4 miles NE by N of Yeovil

ADBOLTON, a hamlet, formerly a parish on the river Trent, near Grantham canal, 1½ mile SE of Nottingham It is now included in Holme Pierrepoint parish Pop., 29

ADCOT, a township in Little Ness chapelry, Salop, near the river Perry, 6½ miles NW of Shrewsbury Pop 26

ADDERBURY a village, two townships, and a parish, in Banbury district Oxford The village stands near the Oxford canal and the river Cherwell, 1¾ mile NW of Aynhoe r station, and 3½ S of Banbury, and has a post office under Oxford Its church is cruciform, and chiefly perpendicular English, with a lofty decorated spire The chancel was built by William of Wykeham, and has his arms on the outer wall The ancient parsonage and the old tythe barn are adjacent. A Norman castle, and afterwards a palace of the Dukes of Buccleuch, stood at Adderbury, but are extinct An impostor, who pretended to be the Saviour, was crucified here in 1219, by order of an Episcopal synod Adderbury Lodge, in the neighbourhood, contains a portrait of Luke, the hero of "Hudibras Wilmot, the witty, profligate Earl of Rochester, took from Adderbury the title of Baron, and lived and died in the manor house near Adderbury Green, and Pope the poet afterwards made a visit there to the great Duke of Argyle, and wrote,—

"With no poetic ardour fired
I press the bed where Wilmot lay

The townships of Adderbury are called East and West Real property of East A, £7,019 Pop, 895 Houses 214 Real property of West A, £2,995 Pop, 346 Houses, 89 The parish includes also the hamlet of Milton and the chapelries of Barford St John, and Bodicott Acres, 6 380 Real property, £17 615 Pop, 2,140 Houses, 535 The property is subdivided The living is a vicarage in the diocese of Oxford Value £818 * Patron, New College, Oxford The curacies of Milton and Barford are included while the vicarage of Boddicott is a separate benefice There are three dissenting chapels, an endowed school, and charities £270

ADDERLEY, a township and a parish in Market Drayton district, Salop. The township lies on the Weaver river and the Nantwich and Market Drayton railway, 4 miles N of M Drayton and has a station on the railway, and a post office under Market Drayton The parish includes also the township of Shavington and part of the township of Spoonley Acres, 2,850 Real property, £5 616 Pop 428 Houses, 75 Adderley Hall is the seat of Richard Corbet Esq, and Shavington Hall is the seat of the Earl of Kilmorey The living is a rectory in the diocese of Lichfield Value, £665 * Patron, R Corbet, Esq The church is good Charities, £58

ADDERLEY GREEN, a hamlet in Caverswall parish Stafford, 1 mile E of Lane End It is a meet of the North Stafford hounds

ADDERLEY PARK, a station on the Birmingham fork of the Northwestern railway, between Stechford and Birmingham

ADDERMINTON See Admington

ADDERSTONE, a township in Bamborough parish Northumberland, 2 miles W of Lucker r station and 3 SSE of Belford Acres 2 603 Pop, 321 Houses, [illegible]

ADDINGTON See Adwalton

ADDINGHAM, a parish in Penrith district Cumber

land, on the river Eden, 6 miles E of Plumpton r station and 6½ NE of Penrith. It contains the townships of Hunsonby and Winskel, Little Salkeld, Glassonby, and Gamblesby Post town Kirkoswald under Penrith Acres, 9,520 Real property, £6,778 Pop, 754 Houses, 148 The property is much sub-divided The living is a vicarage in the diocese of Carlisle Value, £280 * Patron the Dean and Chapter of Carlisle The church is good, and there are chapels for Independents and Wesleyans Two schools have £85 and £80 from endowment, and other charities £69 Dr Paley was vicar from 1792 till 1795 The Roman Maiden way runs through the parish, and a remarkable Druidical monument, called Long Meg and her Daughters, with a splendid view from the Crossfell mountains to Helvellyn, occurs on an eminence about a mile ENE of the church The monument comprises seventy two large stones, most of them in a circle of 350 feet in diameter, and a predominant upright block 15 feet in girth and 18 feet high Wordsworth pronounces this "family of Druid stones unrivalled in singularity and dignity of appearance, and says,—

"A weight of awe not easy to be borne
Fell suddenly upon my spirit—cast
From the dread bosom of the unknown past,
When first I saw that family forlorn

ADDINGHAM, a township, a parish, and a sub-district, in Skipton district, W R Yorkshire The township adjoins the river Wharfe, 4 miles NNW of Kildwick and Crosshills r station, and 6 ESE of Skipton, and has a post office‡ under Leeds It formerly carried on much industry in cotton, worsted, and woollen factories, but began to suffer great reverses about 1835 Fairs are held on 22 March 16 April, and 3 Oct Acres, 4 293 Pop in 1831, 2,179, in 1861, 1,850 Houses, 420 The parish includes also part of the township of Beamsley Acres, 5,472 Real property, £7,478 Pop, 1,938 Houses, 440 The property is much sub divided The living is a rectory in the diocese of Ripon Value, £360 * Patron, Mrs M Cunliffe The church is Norman, was restored in 1858, and stands in a beautiful situation There are three dissenting chapels, a national school and charities £13.—The sub district comprises all Addingham parish, and parts of two other parishes Acres, 22,890 Pop., 3 157 Houses, 635

ADDINGTON, a parish in the district and county of Buckingham, on a tributary of the Ouse, 1¾ mile WNW of Winslow r station Post town, Winslow Acres, 1,320 Real property, £2,718 Pop, 111 Houses, 21 The property is divided among a few Addington House was formerly the seat of Admiral Poulett, late Lord Nugent. Gallows Gap was a place of feudal capital punishment by the ancient proprietors the Moulines The living is a rectory in the diocese of Oxford Value £300 * Patron, J G Hubbard, Esq The church is good.

ADDINGTON, a parish in Malling district Kent, 3¾ miles WSW of Snodland r station, and 7 WNW of Maidstone It has a post office under Maidstone Acres, 942. Real property, £1,662. Pop, 262 Houses, 46 The property is somewhat divided Two ancient stone circles occur in the grounds of Addington Park, and seem to have had connexion with other neighbouring Druidical monuments A nailbourne spring in the parish breaks out at intervals of seven or eight years, and sends off its waters to the Leyborne rivulet. The living is a rectory in the diocese of Canterbury Value, £253 * Patron, the Hon J W Stratford. The church was built about 1402, is in good condition, contains two brasses, and stands on a finely picturesque wooded eminence Charities, £20

ADDINGTON a village and a parish in Croydon district, Surrey The village stands on the verge of the county, 3 miles ESE of Croydon r station, and has a post-office under Croydon Tradition asserts it to have been anciently a place of some note The parish comprises 3,900 acres Real property, £4,148 Pop, 630 Houses, 122 The manor was given by William the Conqueror to his cook Tezelin, to be held on the tenure of presenting a mess of pottage to the king at his coronation, and it passed, with its curious tenure in 1807, to the Archbishop of Canterbury The mansion on it was built about 1780 by Alderman Trecothick, and improved in 1830 by Archbishop Howley The higher ground of the park, and the hills above them, command fine views About twenty five tumuli, or remains of tumuli, altered by having been opened, occur on a common above the village The living is a vicarage in the diocese of Canterbury Value, £206 Patron, the Archbishop of Canterbury The church is ancient, but was renovated in 1848, and it shows the late Norman style in the interior, and contains monuments and brasses There are a national school, and charities £6

ADDINGTON (GREAT), a parish in Thrapston district Northampton on the river Nen near Ringstead r station, 4½ miles SW of Thrapston Post town, Ringstead under Thrapston. Acres, 1,230 Real property, £1,919 Pop, 307 Houses, 67 The property is somewhat divided. The living is a rectory in the diocese of Peterborough. Value, £420 * Patron, Mrs Clay The church is ancient

ADDINGTON (LITTLE), a parish in Thrapston district, Northampton, immediately S of Great Addington, and also near Ringstead r station Post town, Ringstead under Thrapston Acres, 1,170 Real property £1,951 Pop, 337 Houses, 76 The manor belonged anciently to Sulby monastery The living is a vicarage in the diocese of Peterborough Value, £245.* Patron, John Boodle Esq The church is good, and there is a Wesleyan chapel

ADDISCOMBE, a locality 1¼ mile E of Croydon, with a post-office under that town, in Surrey An edifice here, within a pleasant small park, was built by Vanburgh, inhabited by the Herons, Lord Chancellor Talbot, Lord Liverpool and the Clarkes, purchased in 1812 by the East India Company, and made a military college for their cadets The estate was sold, in 1861, for £33,600 to the British Land Company

ADDLE, or ADILL, a township and a parish in Otley district, W R Yorkshire The township lies near Horsforth r station, and 6 miles NNW of Leeds, and it is joined to Eccup, forming Addle cum Eccup Acres, 4,576 Real property £6,160 Pop., 801 Houses, 145. The parish contains also the township of Arthington Post town, Horsforth under Leeds. Acres, 6,356 Real property, £9,900 Pop., 1,145 Houses, 209 The Leeds water works are within Addle township Remains of the Roman town Burgodunum and other antiquities, are on Rumbold's Moor, 1,808 feet high The living is a rectory in the diocese of Ripon Value, £623 * Patron, John Murray Esq The church is a very fine Norman edifice, of date prior to 1100 The vicarage of Arthington is separate Charities, £34

ADDLESTONE a village and a chapelry in Chertsey parish, Surrey The village stands 2 miles SSE of Chertsey, and has a station on the Chertsey branch of the South western railway, and a post office under Chertsey It contains the residence of Mrs S. C Hall, and is noted for a very large oak tree called the Crouch Oak, beneath which tradition asserts Wickliffe to have preached and Queen Elizabeth to have dined The chapelry was constituted in 1838, and is a vicarage in the diocese of Winchester Value £150 * Patron, the Bishop of Winchester Pop 2 896 Houses, 535

ADDLESTROP a parish in Stow on the Wold district, Gloucester on the river Evenlode, 3½ miles ENE of Stow on the Wold It has a station with Stow Road, on the West Midland railway Post town, Stow on the Wold, under Moreton in the Marsh Acres, 1,285 Real property, £1 913 Pop 184 Houses, 42 The manor belonged to the abbey of Evesham, passed at the dissolution to Sir Thomas Leigh, and is now the property of Lord Leigh. Addlestrop House, the seat of his lordship, is a large and interesting mansion, partly of considerable antiquity, amid beautiful grounds laid out by Adey Repton The living is a rectory annexed to the rectory of Broadwell, in the diocese of Gloucester and

Bristol The church was built in 1764, and is in good condition.

ADDLETHORPE, a parish in Spilsby district, Lincoln, on the coast 4½ miles NE of Burgh r station, and 7½ SE of Alford Post town, Ingoldmells under Boston Acres, 2,093 Real property, £4,653 Pop, 302 Houses, 53 The property is subdivided The living is a rectory in the diocese of Lincoln Value, £72 * Patron, the Lord Chancellor The church is rich perpendicular English, and has several oak stalls and a chancel wooden screen There are a Wesleyan chapel, and charities £18

ADEL See ADDLE

ADENEY See ADNEY

ADFORTON, a township with Stanway, Paytoe, and Grange, in the parish of Leintwardine, Hereford, 2 miles NW of Wigmore. Pop, 250 Houses, 57

ADGARLEY, a township in Urswick parish, Lancashire, 4 miles SSW of Ulverstone Pop, 4[illegible]

ADGETON, a hamlet in Brading parish, a mile SW of Brading Isle of Wight. It was a frequent scene of Legh Richmond's labours

ADHELM'S HEAD (ST) See ALBAN'S HEAD (ST)

ADISHAM, a parish in Bridge district, Kent on the Dover railway, 6 miles SE of Canterbury It has a station on the railway and its post town is Wingham under Sandwich Acres, 1,815 Real property, £3,004 Pop, 432 Houses, 84 The manor was given in 616 to Christ Church, Canterbury, and is now held by the Ecclesiastical Commissioners The living is a rectory in the diocese of Canterbury, and, till 1864, was united with the p curacy of Staple Value £750 * Patron, the Archbishop of Canterbury The church is cruciform, and early English, with a central tower Charities, £20

ADLESTROP See ADDLESTROP

ADLINGFLEET a township and a parish in Goole district, W R Yorkshire The township lies near the confluence of the Ouse and the Trent, 5½ miles E of Goole station, and has a post office under Howden Acres, 1,650 Real property, £2,542 Pop, 225 Houses, 53 The parish includes also the townships of Fockerby, Haldenby, and Eastoft Acres, 5,295 Real property, £7,303 Pop, 450 Houses, 107 The living is a vicarage in the diocese of York Value £330 * Patron, the Lord Chancellor The church is good The vicarage of Eastoft is separate There are a Wesleyan chapel, a national school and charities £69

ADLINGTON, a township in Prestbury parish Cheshire, on the river Bollin and the Northwestern railway 5 miles N of Macclesfield It has a station on the railway Valuable mines of coal and flagstone are in the neighbourhood. Acres 3,030 Real property, £7,553 Pop, [illegible] Houses, 187 Many of the inhabitants are silk weavers. Adlington Hall is an old seat, and was taken in 1645, by the Parliamentary forces, after a fourteen days' siege. There is a Wesleyan chapel

ADLINGTON a township and a chapelry in Standish parish Lancashire The township lies on the Bolton and Preston railway near the Leeds and Liverpool canal, 3½ miles SE of Chorley, and has a station on the railway, and a post office under Chorley Cotton manufacture is carried on, and coal mines were formerly worked, but are exhausted Acres, 1,062 Real property, £4,324 Pop, 1,[illegible] Houses, 30[illegible] The chapelry was constituted in 1542 and is more extensive than the township. Pop, 3,3[illegible] Houses, [illegible] The living is a vicarage in the diocese of Manchester Value £150 * Patron, the Rector of Standish The church was built in 1838, and is in the Norman style There are a Wesleyan chapel and a national school

ADMARSH See PERYSDALE

ADMASTON, a hamlet in Blithfield parish Stafford, 4 miles N of Rugeley It has a post office under Rugeley Pop [illegible]

ADMASTON a township in Wrockwardine parish, Salop 1½ mile NW of Wellington It has a station on the Shropshire Union railway, and a post office under Wellington Pop, 13[illegible]

ADMERGILL See [illegible]

ADMINGTON, or ADDERMINSTON, a hamlet in Quinton parish, Gloucester, 6 miles NE of Chipping-Campden

ADMISTON, or ATHELHAMPTON, a parish in Dorchester district, Dorset, on the river Piddle, 5 miles NW of Moreton r station, and 6 NE of Dorchester Post town, Piddletown under Dorchester Acres, 471 Real property, £1,026 Pop, 93 Houses, 13 This place is said to have been at one time the principal residence of the kings of Wessex The living is a rectory, united to the rectory of Burrelston, in the diocese of Salisbury Value, £200 Patron, G J Wood, Esq The church is perpendicular English, and has a tomb of Sir W Martin

ADMISTON, Berks See ALDERMASTON

ADNEY, a township in Edgmond parish, Salop, near the river Strine, 3½ miles WSW of Newport Salop Pop, 71

ADPAR, or ATTAR, a small ancient town in Llandyfriog parish, Cardigan It stands on the river Teifi, opposite Newcastle Emlyn, separated from that town only by the river, and is practically a suburb of it But politically it is a borough by prescription, and now includes Newcastle Emlyn within its borough limits, and it unites with Cardigan, Aberystwith, Lampeter, and Tregaron, in sending a member to parliament Pop of the old borough, 355, of the new borough, 1,473 Houses, 136 and 358 See NEWCASTLE EMLYN

ADRIAN'S WALL See ROMAN WALL (THE)

ADSTOCK, a parish in the district and county of Buckingham, on the Bucks railway, midway between Buckingham and Winslow Post town, Buckingham. Acres, 1,130 Real property, £2,102 Pop, 385 Houses 83 The property is not much divided The market for Buckingham and Winslow was held here during the plague of 1665 The living is a rectory in the diocese of Oxford Value, £444 * Patron Philip Hart, Esq The church is ancient but good, and there is a Wesleyan chapel

ADSTON a township in Wentnor parish, Salop 4½ miles W of Church Stretton Pop, 100

ADSTONE, a chapelry in Ashby Canons parish, Northampton, 5¾ miles SSW of Weedon r station, and 6¾ WNW of Towcester Post town, Blakesley, under Towcester Acres, 1,190 Real property, £2,28[illegible] Pop, 165 Houses, 36. The living is a p curacy in the diocese of Peterborough Value, £130 Patrons the Sons of Clergy Corporation There is a Wesleyan chapel

ADUR, or ALDER (THE), a river of Sussex It rises in St Leonard's forest, in the neighbourhood of Horsham and runs about 20 miles southward past Ashurst and Steyning to the English Channel at Shoreham It affords good trouting above Bolney, and is noted for its mullet further down It is navigable to Binesbridge

ADVENT, a parish in Camelford district, Cornwall, on Camel river, 2 miles S of Camelford, and 11 N of Bodmin Road r station, Post town Camelford Acres, 4,059 Real property £1 626 Pop., 203 Houses, 45 The property is much subdivided A copper mine is worked. The living is a rectory, annexed to Lanteglos, in the diocese of Exeter The church is bad An ancient weather worn granite cross, about 9 feet high, stands in a field a short way from the church

ADWALTON, or ADDERTON, a hamlet in Drighlington township, Birstal parish W R Yorkshire, 5½ miles SW of Leeds It has a joint station with Drighlington on the Gildersome branch of the Leeds Bradford and Halifax Junction railway It was formerly a market town, and it still has fairs on 26 Jan 6 Feb, 9 Mar, Easter Thursday, Whit Thursday, 5 Nov, and 23 Dec Adwalton Moor, in the neighbourhood, was the scene, in 1642 of the defeat of Fairfax by the Earl of Newcastle

ADWELL, a parish in Thame district, Oxford, near the Chiltern hills 2 miles SSE of Tetsworth, and 12 NE of Wallingford Road r station Post town Tetsworth. Acres, 439 Real property £798 Pop. 63 Houses 12 Adwell House is the chief residence Adwell Cop is an ancient entrenchment supposed to have been constructed by the Danes when they burnt Oxford in 1010 The living is a rectory in the diocese of Oxford Value £125 Patron H B Reynardson, Esq The church was rebuilt in 1865

ADWICK LE STREET, a township and a parish in Doncaster district, W R. Yorkshire The township lies on Ermine street and near the West Riding and Grimsby railway, 4 miles NW of Doncaster, and near a r station Acres, 1,614 Pop, 280 Houses 61 The parish includes also the township of Hampole Post town, Doncaster Acres, 3 034 Real property, £2,987 Pop, 440 Houses, 95 The manor belongs to C S A Thellusson, Esq The living is a rectory in the diocese of York Value, £450 * Patron, J Fullerton, Esq The church is good, and there are two Wesleyan chapels, an endowed school with £10 a year, and charities £19

ADWICK UPON DEARNE, a parish in Doncaster district, W R. Yorkshire, on the river Dearne, near Bolton upon Dearne r station, 6¾ miles NNE of Rotherham Post town, Bolton upon Dearne under Rotherham. Acres, 1 107 Real property, £1,473 Pop, 226 Houses, 44 The living is a vicarage, annexed to the vicarage of Wath, in the diocese of York The church is ancient

AEPON (THE) See AYRON (THE)

ÆSCENDUNE See ASHDOWN PARK

AFF PUDDLE, a parish in Wareham district, Dorset, on the river Piddle, 4 miles N of Moreton r station and 8 ENE of Dorchester It contains the hamlet of Pallington and the tything of Bryants Puddle. Post town, Piddletown under Dorchester Acres, 3,818 Real property, £2,923 Pop, 455 Houses, 97 The manor belonged anciently to Cerne abbey The property is divided. The living is a vicarage, annexed to the rectory of Turners Puddle, in the diocese of Salisbury The church is ancient but good. Charities, £5

AFON See AVON

AFTON, a village 2 miles S of Yarmouth, Isle of Wight Afton House adjoins it, on a pleasant slope toward the Yar Afton Down rises in the south eastern neighbourhood overhangs the English Channel, has an altitude of about 500 feet, and is crowned by tumuli.

AGAPEMONE See CHARLINCH

AGAR TOWN, a metropolitan suburb in St Pancras parish, Middlesex, 2½ miles NW of St Paul's A chapelry is here, and the living is a vicarage See LONDON

AGBRIGG, a village in Warmfield with Heath township, W R Yorkshire 2 miles E of Wakefield

AGBRIGG AND MORLEY, a wapentake of three divisions, Lower, Upper, and Morley, W R Yorkshire The Lower div comprises Warmfield parish, nine other parishes, and 4 parts, the Upper div, Almondbury parish, three others, and two parts, the Morley div, Bradford parish, three others, and two parts. Acres, 67 481, 83,910 and 129,532 Pop in 1851, 81,935, 139,275, and 219,107, in 1861, 475,985 Houses, 99 096

AGDEN, a township in Malpas parish Cheshire, 3 miles NW of Whitchurch Acres, 548 Real property, £699 Pop, 110 Houses, 21

AGDEN, a township in Bowden and Rostherne parishes, Cheshire, 3½ miles SW of Altrincham Acres, 520 Real property, £1,394 Pop, 93 Houses, 15

AGGLESTONE, a large isolated block of ferruginous sandstone about a mile NW of Studland village, in the parish of Studland, Dorset It crowns a hillock nearly a mile from the shore, measures 37 feet in length 19 feet in breadth, and 15 feet in height, and is regarded by some persons as merely a boulder,—by others as a Druidical monument. The common people allege it to have been thrown by the Devil, from the Isle of Wight, to demolish Corfe Castle, and call it the Devil's Nightcap.

AGGLETHORPE, a joint township with Coverham, in Coverham parish, W R Yorkshire See COVERHAM

AGLIONBY, a township in Warwick parish Cumberland, near the river Eden and the Carlisle and Newcastle railway 3½ miles E of Carlisle Pop, 119 Houses, 23

AGMONDESHAM See AMERSHAM

AGNES (ST) a town a parish, and a sub district, in the district of Truro Cornwall The town is a sea port, on a small bay of Bristol Channel 4 miles N of Chacewater r station and 9 NW by W of Truro It has a post office‡ under Scorrier, and is the centre of a rich mining district A weekly market is held on Thursday, and an annual fair on 1 May The harbour is small, and can be entered only near high water, and only by vessels of not more than 100 tons' burden Coal, lime, and slate are imported. Most of the inhabitants are connected with neighbouring mines —The parish comprises 8,234 acres of land, and 60 of water Real property, £10,321,—of which £2,514 are in mines Pop. 6,550 Houses, 1,395 The property is much subdivided Granite is the prevailing rock, and copper, tin, and iron are worked The scenery of coast and surface is picturesque St Agnes Beacon, 621 feet high, immediately NW of the town, shows remarkable deposits of sand and clays at heights of from 300 to 400 feet, and was a beacon station during the French war, and a chief station of the Trigonometrical survey Harmony Cot, 2 miles from the town, on the road to Perran Porth, was the birthplace of the painter Opie. The living is a vicarage in the diocese of Exeter Value, £280 * Patrons, the Dean and Chapter of Exeter The church was built in 1482, has been restored, and shows interesting features Chapels for Independents, Wesleyans, and Primitive Methodists, are in the parish Ruins of ancient chapels are at Mawla and St Agnes' Well —The sub-district comprises two parishes. Acres, 19,694 Pop, 9,509 Houses 1,998

AGNES (ST), one of the Scilly Islands, near the southern extremity of the group, separated on the NE from St Mary's by St Mary's Sound It consists of two parts, St Agnes proper and the Gugh, divided from each other by high water of spring tides The former measures about 1 mile by ½, the latter, about ⅔ of a mile by ¼ Much of the land is fertile and well cultivated St Agnes proper displays some interesting features, contains a church and is crowned by a lighthouse, 72 feet high, having a revolving light, with one minute flash The Gugh has a curious rock pillar 9 feet long and several stone covered barrows. Pop, 200

AGRICOLA'S WALL. See ROMAN WALL (THE)

AIGBURTH a chapelry in Childwall parish, Lancashire, 4½ miles E of Liverpool It has a post office‡ under Liverpool Pop, 1,994 Houses, 338 The living is a vicarage in the diocese of Chester Value, £400 Patrons Trustees The church was built in 1853. There are Wesleyan and Roman Catholic chapels.

AIGHTON, one of three hamlets forming a township in the parish of Mitton, Lancashire It lies near Hodder river, under Longridge fell, 3½ miles NNW of Whalley r station, and 5 WSW of Clitheroe It contains cotton factories, a workhouse, and the Roman Catholic college of Stonyhurst —The other hamlets of the township are Bailey and Chaighley Acres in the three, 5 750 Real property, £6,726 Pop, 1 500 Houses 244

AIKBAR or AKEBAR, a township in Finghall parish, N R Yorkshire near the Leyburn railway, 4 miles NW of Bedale Acres, 750 Pop, 37 Houses, 4

AIKE, a township in the parishes of Lockington and St John Beverley E R Yorkshire, near the river Hull 2 miles E of Lockington r station, and 6 N of Beverley Acres 630 Pop, 103 Houses, 19

AIKTON, a township and a parish in Wigton district Cumberland The township lies E of the Wampool river, 2¾ miles ESE of Kirkbride r station, and 4 NNE of Wigton Real property £2,088 Pop, 284 Houses, 58 The parish includes also the townships of Wampool, Wiggonby, Biglands and Gamblesby Post town, Wigton Acres 6,177 Real property, £7,299 Pop, 806 Houses, 154 The property is much subdivided The living is a rectory in the diocese of Carlisle Value, £346 * Patron the Earl of Lonsdale The church is small and old Charities, £176

AILBY, a hamlet in Rigsby parish, Lincoln 1 mile NW of Alford Pop, 53

AILESBURY See AYLESBURY

AILSWORTH, a hamlet in Castor parish, Northampton, near the river Nen, 5 miles W of Peterborough Pop, 306 Houses 77

AILSTON a village in Atherstone on Stour parish, Warwick 3 miles S of Stratford on Avon Pop, 47

AINDERBY, a station on the Bedale and Leyburn

branch of the Northeastern railway, adjacent to Ainderby Steeple, 3½ miles west of Northallerton, N R Yorkshire

AINDERBY MYERS WITH HOLTBY, a township in Hornby parish N R Yorkshire, 3½ miles NNW of Bedale Acres 917 Real property, £1,364 Pop, 97 Houses, 15

AINDERBY QUERNHOW a township in Pickhill parish, N R Yorkshire, near the Northeastern railway 7 miles NNE of Ripon Acres, 527 Real property, £1 058 Pop, 90 Houses, 23

AINDERBY STEEPLE a township and a parish in Northallerton district, N R Yorkshire The township lies on the river Swale adjacent to Ainderby r station, 3 miles W of Northallerton, and has a post-office under Northallerton Acres, 1,138 Real property, £2,755 Pop., 319 Houses, 75 The parish includes also the townships of Warlaby, Morton upon Swale, and Thrintoft. Acres 4 605. Real property, £9,205 Pop, 848 Houses, 191 The property is divided among a few The living is a vicarage in the diocese of Ripon Value, £280 Patron the Lord Chancellor The church is good. Charities, £8

AINSDALE, a hamlet in Formby chapelry, Lancashire 3½ miles S of Southport It has a station on the Liverpool and Southport railway

AINSTABLE, a parish in Penrith district Cumberland, between the Croglin and the Eden rivers, 7 miles E of Southwaite r station, and 11 N by E of Penrith It is divided into the High and Low quarters, and includes the village of Ruckcroft Post town Kirkoswald under Penrith Acres, 4,178 Real property, £3,957 Pop, 543 Houses, 113 The property is subdivided A Benedictine nunnery was founded here by William Rufus, and its site, on high ground, is now marked by a stone pillar Nunnery a mansion taking name from it, stands on lower adjacent ground, amid scenery which is highly picturesque, and has been sung by Wordsworth The living is a vicarage in the diocese of Carlisle Value, £225 Patrons the presentatives of Mrs Aglionby The church was built from the Plumpton Walls, contains a tomb of John de Denton, and is in tolerable condition Charities, £15 Dr John Leake, the founder of the Westminster lying in hospital, was a native

AINSTY, a wapentake, bounded by the rivers Ure Ouse and Wharfe, in Yorkshire It was originally a forest was annexed, by Henry VI, to the city of York, as the county of the city, was made in 1837 a wapentake of the west riding but, for parliamentary purposes, is in the north riding It contains the parish of Acomb, fifteen other parishes and parts of six others Acres 50 161 Pop in 1851, 9 599, in 1861, 9,806 Houses 2 032

AINSWORTH, or COCKEY a chapelry in Middleton parish Lancashire, at Bradley-Fold r station, 2½ miles E of Bolton Post town, Bolton Acres, 1,296 Real property £7 043,—of which £1,652 are in mines. Pop 1 773 Houses, 348 Cotton manufacture is carried on The living is a vicarage in the diocese of Manchester Value £135 Patron, the Rector of Middleton The church is good and there are two dissenting chapels, a national school and charities £12

AINTHORPE See ANTHORPE

AINTHORPE, a village in Danby parish, N R Yorkshire

AINTREE, a township in Sephton parish, Lancashire, on the Alt river and the Leeds canal, 6 miles NNE of Liverpool It has a post office under Liverpool, a station on the Lancashire and Yorkshire railway, and an Episcopalian chapel and it contains, with a grand stand built in 1830, a race course, 1½ mile round where the Liverpool races are run in February and July Acres 825 Pop 300 Houses 52

AIR (POINT OF) See AYRE

AIRA or AIRY (THE) a rivulet running 5 miles eastward to Ulleswater, on the boundary between Westmoreland and Cumberland It rushes along a wooded rocky ravine and makes a very romantic fall of 80 feet, called Aira Force A castellated shooting box called Lyulph's Tower, stands at its mouth on the site of an ancient tower of the same name The present structure was built by the late Duke of Norfolk and the ancient one perhaps took its name from L Ulph, the first baron of Greystoke A pathetic old legend respecting L'Ulph's Tower and Aira Force is embodied in Wordsworth's poem of the "Somnambulist"—

"List ye who pass by Lyulph s Tower
At eve,—how softly then
Doth Aira Force, that torrent hoarse
Speak from the woody glen

AIRE (THE) a river of Yorkshire It rises in wild moors near Malham in the north west quarter of the west riding, runs about a mile underground to Malham cove, then goes ESE, past Skipton and Bingley, to Leeds, then assumes a more easterly direction till below Snaith, then turns to the NE and goes to the Ouse, a little below Armin, 3 miles SW of Howden Its entire length is about 70 miles It is joined at Leeds by the Liverpool canal, which follows it thither from Gargrave, at Castleford, by the river Calder, and at Birkin by the Selby canal

AIREDALE, the valley of the Aire in Yorkshire Airedale college, for the education of young men to be Congregational ministers, is situated at Undercliffe, in the vicinity of Bradford

AIREY See AIRA.

AIRSHOLME, a hamlet in Linthorpe township, N R Yorkshire, near the river Tees, 3½ miles E of Stockton

AIRTON, a township in Kirkby in Malham dale parish, W R Yorkshire, on the river Aire near the Midland railway, 6 miles SE of Settle Acres, 2,790 Real property £2,693 Pop, 236 Houses, 42

AIRYHOLME See AIRSHOLME

AISBY, a village in Corringham parish, Lincoln, 4½ miles NE of Gainsborough Pop, 63

AISBY, a village in Heydor parish, Lincoln 5½ miles NW of Folkingham Pop, 190

AISENBY See ASENBY

AISHOLT, or ASHOLT, a parish in Bridgewater district, Somerset, 4½ miles E of Crowcombe Heathfield r station, and 7½ W by S of Bridgewater It has a post-office under Bridgewater Acres, 1 252 Real property, £2,643 Pop, 181 Houses, 41 The property is much subdivided The living is a rectory in the diocese of Bath and Wells Value, £280 Patron, Rev Josh West The church is good. Charities, £5

AISKEW, or ASKEW a township in Bedale parish N R Yorkshire, ½ mile ENE of Bedale. It contains Little Leeming hamlet Baptist and Roman Catholic chapels, and an endowed school Pop, 759 Houses 164

AISLABY, a township in Egglescliffe parish Durham on the Tees river near the Stockton and Darlington railway, 1½ mile W by N of Yarm Acres, 2,200 Real property, £2 804 Pop, 152 Houses, 28.

AISLABY, a township in Middleton parish N R Yorkshire, near the Whitby railway, 2 miles WNW of Pickering Acres, 1,110 Real property, £1,319 Pop, 180 Houses, 36

AISLABY, a chapelry in Whitby parish, N R Yorkshire, on the Esk river and the Whitby railway, at Sleights station 3 miles SW of Whitby Post town Sleights under Whitby Acres 1,008 Real property £1,568 Pop, 330 Houses, 70 A building limestone is quarried here, and was the material of Whitby abbey and of several great modern works The living is a p curacy in the diocese of York. Value, £87 Patron, J Boulby Esq Charities, £11

AISMUNDERBY WITH BONDGATE a township in Ripon parish, partly within Ripon borough, W R Yorkshire Acres, 1 055 Pop 620 Houses, 140

AISTHORPE, or EAST THORPE, a parish in the district and county of Lincoln, on the Wolds, near Ermine street, 4 miles NE of Saxelby r station, and 6½ NNW of Lincoln Post town, Saxelby under Lincoln Acres, 803 Real property, £1 211 Pop 100 Houses, 18 The property and that of West Thorpe are divided among four proprietors The living is a rectory, united to the vicarage of West Thorpe, in the diocese of Lincoln. Value, £289 Patron, J Milnes, Esq The church is tolerable

AIS WATER See HAYS WATER.

AITS or EYOTS (THE) picturesque islets in the Thames, in the neighbourhood of Henley and of Richmond They occur sometimes singly, sometimes in groups, and, being generally planted with osiers, are sometimes called the Osier Islands

AKA See ROCK, Northumberland

AKEBAR. See AIKBAR

AKELD, a township in Kirknewton parish, Northumberland, near the river Glen, 2 miles NW of Wooler Acres 2,208 Pop, 162 Houses, 33

AKELEY CUM-STOCKHOLT, a parish in the district and county of Buckingham, 3¼ miles N by E of Buckingham r station Post-town, Buckingham Acres, 1,080 Real property, £1 924 Pop 366 Houses, 81 The property is much subdivided The Living is a rectory in the diocese of Oxford Value, £255 Patron, New College, Oxford The church is good, and there is a Methodist chapel Charities, 7 allotment acres

AKEMAN STREET, a Roman road from Akemancester, now the city of Bath, north north eastward by Cirencester, through Wychwood forest, and by Alcester, to Watling Street It still exists from Tetbury to Cirencester, and can be traced at Blenheim.

AKENHAM, a parish in Bosmere district, Suffolk, near Gipping river, 2 miles E of Claydon r station, and 4 N by W of Ipswich Post town, Claydon under Ipswich Acres, 993 Real property, £1,630 Pop., 94 Houses, 22 The living is a rectory, annexed to Claydon, in the diocese of Norwich. The church is old but good

ALAN, or CAMEL (THE), a river of Cornwall It rises near Davidstow, runs southward, past Camelford, Michaelstow, and Helland, to Bodmin, then goes west north westward, past Wadebridge, to the Bristol Channel below Padstow Its entire length is about 27 miles, and its lowest reach is estuary, and forms Padstow harbour

ALANNA See ALCESTER, Warwick.

ALBANS (ST) a town three parishes, a sub district, and a district in Herts. The town stands near the southern extension of the Midland railway, and at the termini of branches of the Great Northern and the North western railways, 21 miles NNW of London Its site is the summit and the northern declivity of a hill, skirted by the rivulet Ver, a tributary of the Colne, near the vestiges of the ancient town of Verulam and the line of the Roman Watling street. Verulam or Verulamium, according to the Roman historians, was founded by the Britons at an earlier period than London According to Camden, it is the city or fortress of Cassibelan, or Cassivellaunus, which was forced by Cæsar Milton calls St. Albans "jugera Cassibelauni" In Nero's reign it ranked as a municipium, or free city, enjoying the privileges of Roman citizenship Boadicea, queen of the Iceni, surprised it in the reign of Claudius, and put the chief part of the inhabitants to the sword, but it soon recovered from this calamity In A.D 293, Alban, a citizen of Verulam, who had embraced the Christian faith, was beheaded on a hill in the neighbourhood In 429, Germanus, bishop of Auxerre, and Lupus, bishop of Troyes, held a synod here, to confute the Pelagian heresy Verulam fell not long after into the hands of the Saxons but was retaken by the Britons and again reverted to the Saxons While yet in ruins after these successive contests, Offa, king of Mercia, founded an abbey here in honour of St Alban, whose remains had just been discovered on the spot of his martyrdom Matthew Paris—who was himself a monk in the abbey of St Albans—says that Alsinus, the 6th abbot, about 950, built a church on each of the three principal roads leading from the monastery and that around these the present town of St Albans gradually arose Pope Adrian IV constituted the abbot of St. Albans first abbot in England in order and dignity, and Pope Honorius in 1218, exempted the abbot from the jurisdiction of the bishop of Lincoln, his diocesan A sanguinary battle was fought here in 1455 between Henry VI and the Duke of York, in which the Lancastrians were defeated Money is said by Camden to have been coined here in the time of the Romans On the introduction of printing into England, a press was put up in the abbey of St Albans, from which issued some of the earliest English specimens of the art. Giles, the physician, Sir John Mandeville, the traveller, Alexander Neckham, the poet, Sir John King, the lawyer, Chief Justice Pemberton, and Humphry, the nonconformist, were natives Bacon, the philosopher, resided at the neighbouring seat of Gorhambury, and had the titles of Baron Verulam and Viscount St. Albans Verulam now gives the title of Earl to the family of Grimston, and St. Albans gives that of Duke to the family of Beauclerk

Verulam long continued to present great attractions to antiquaries, but now possesses nothing of interest except vestiges and associations Parts of its walls and ditches still exist. Its streets also are still traceable in the green field, by the thin short grass that covers them, and by Roman bricks which can be dug from below Even substructions of its buildings, matted with weeds or shaded with shrubs and trees, still draw the attention of the curious visitor But coins, sculptures, and other valued relics, were all long ago carried off by thousands of investigators, and now the best things to be found are merely shingle, mortar, and layers of brick,—the last generally carbonized in the centre Such multitude and variety of curiosities were gathered here, in former times, by antiquaries and others, that Camden says, "Were I to relate what common report affirms respecting them, I should scarcely be believed" Philosophers and poets alike loved to saunter among the ruined fragments of the town, Sir Thomas More desired to live and die in its vicinity, and Spenser assumed the character of its presiding genius, to sing its grandeur and melancholy glory:—

"I was that city which the garland wore
Of Britain's pride, delivered unto me
By Roman victory which it wore of yore,
Though nought at all but ruins now I be,
And lie in my own ashes, as ye see
Verlame I was what boots it that I was,
Sith now I am but weeds and wasteful grass"

St. Albans consists principally of three streets. Many of the houses are ancient, but others, particularly on the new line of road to the S, are modern The town hall was rebuilt in 1830 The corn exchange was built in 1857, and is used also as a public hall The prison consists partly of the tower of the Abbey gateway, partly of a modern addition, and has capacity for 85 male and 15 female prisoners The free grammar school is in the Lady chapel formerly a part of the Abbey church, was chartered in 1553 by Edward VI and further endowed by Elizabeth and James I and has an endowed income of £137 The Marlborough buildings are alms houses for 36 decayed men and women, founded and endowed by Sarah, Duchess of Marlborough, and have an income of £797 There are other charities £626 four churches, six dissenting chapels, a literary and scientific institution, a blue coat school, four national schools, and a British school

The original abbey, founded by King Offa, became ruinous about the time of the Conquest The subsequent abbey was of vast extent and great magnificence, but most of it, except the church, has fallen The church, however, with enormous nave, pinnacled transept, graceful choir, lofty square tower, and grand, ornate, rich interior is an imposing object, inferior to no minster in the kingdom either as a feature in the landscape or for its own attractions It comprises a nave of thirteen bays with aisles, a choir with aisles, a transept without aisles a presbytery and ambulatory to the east, and a Lady chapel, of three bays, with vestibule The nave is 276 feet long 65 feet broad and 65 feet high, the choir is 175 feet long, the transept, 175½ feet, the entire edifice, 518½ feet Three noble towers in fine symmetry formerly rose above it, but only the central one without spire or pinnacles, now stands, and this is 32½ feet long 30¾ feet broad, and 144 feet high. The church was chiefly built in 1077-93 by Abbot Paul of Caen, but was extended and altered at subsequent periods by other abbots, and it exhibits specimens of every style from the Saxon through the Norman, to the English of the time of Edward IV This edifice, remarks Lady Morgan "though but a fragment of the once magnificent, mitred, parliamentary abbey, attests the grandeur of the whole, and the perfection of ecclesiastical architecture in England during the middle ages. There is still extant, in the interior, specimens of genuine Saxon architecture a part of the original building the rounded arch, the massy tower, and enormous pillar whose rude but noble simplicity is forcibly contrasted to the elaborated elegance of the Gothic style. Screens of the most minute tabernacle work, pointed arches, feathery shafts and a profusion of richly sculptured tracery, display all the characteristic beauty of that most picturesque and fanciful epoch of the art The high altar, the after part of the choir, the chapel of Abbot Lambridge, and that of St Alban, are the most remarkable There are also existing beneath the fretted roof of this beautiful abbey church monuments and tombs well-suited to revive remote associations with great events, and to awaken a poetic nationality in the most phlegmatic temperament Of these, the tomb of the Protector, Duke of Gloucester, familiarly called the good Duke Humphry stands on the southern side" The church has acquired dramatic interest, too, from the pen of Shakspeare, and it has been splendidly illustrated by the Society of Antiquaries The cloister connected with it was 150 feet square A part of the south wall of the chapter house, situated on the south side of the transept, is standing. The gate house, which formed the original grand entrance to the Abbey court and is now the chief part of the borough prison, stands parallel with the west end of the church, at the distance of about 150 feet

St Michael's church was founded about the middle of the 10th century, underwent careful restoration by ... in 1806, and contains the tomb of Bacon, with a beautiful sitting statue of him, erected by Sir T Meautys St Peter's church was rebuilt on the site of a Saxon one, the many of the slain in the two battles of St Albans had been buried, and it contains a tomb of Dr Cotton The ruins of a nunnery founded in 1140, stand at Sopwell in the south eastern vicinity of the town Lady Juliana Berners who wrote treatises on hunting, hawking and heraldry, was one of the superiors of this nunnery, and Henry VIII is said to have been married to Anne Boleyn in its chapel

The town was incorporated in 1554 by Edward VI It sent two members to parliament till 1852, and was then disfranchised It is governed by a mayor, four aldermen and twelve councillors It possesses a liberty or district, with peculiar jurisdiction The borough comprises 425 acres including all Abbey parish main parts of St Michael and St Peter parishes and small part of St Stephen parish and the liberty includes the rest of these parishes, and also the parishes of Abbots Langley, Aldenham Barnet Sandridge Redbourn, Codicote, Shephall, Brantfield Elstree, Sarratt Hexton, Norton, Ridge St Pauls Walden Northaw, Newnham, Rickmansworth, and Watford Quarter sessions are held in the same weeks as at Hertford, county courts and petty sessions also are held The town has a head post office, two banking offices and several good inns, it publishes two weekly newspapers, and it has a thriving general business A market is held on Saturday, and fairs on 25 March and 11 Oct Straw plaiting and silk throwing are carried on Real property £18 035 Pop., in 1851, 7,000, in 1861 7,675 Houses 1,503

The parishes of St Albans are in the diocese of Rochester Abbey or St Albans proper comprises 165 acres, St Michael 190 acres, and St Peter 5,715 acres, and the last includes the hamlets of Sleep and Tittenhanger, and part of the hamlet of Smallford St Albans proper is a rectory and includes, as a separate benefice, the p curacy of Christ Church Value of the rectory, £200.* Patron, the Bishop of Rochester Value of the curacy, £100 * Patron, Mrs Worley St Michael is a vicarage and includes, as a separate benefice the vicarage of Leverstock Green Value of the vicarage, £300,* of the curacy, £ 0 Patron of both, the Earl of Verulam St Peter also is a vicarage and includes, as a separate benefice, the vicarage of Colney Heath. Value of the vicarage, £308.* Patron, the Crown Value of the curacy, £330 * Patrons Trustees. Leverstock Green church was built in 1849

The sub district of St Albans comprises the parishes of Abbey, St Michael, St. Peter and St Stephen Acres, 14,240 Pop, 11,926 Houses, 2 320 The district comprehends also the sub district of Harpenden containing the parishes of Wheathampstead, Harpenden, Redbourn, and Sandridge Acres, 34,615 Poor rates in 1867, £7,333. Pop in 1841 17 048, in 1861, 18 926 Houses, 3,762 Marriages in 1866 150, births, 64?,—of which 57 were illegitimate, deaths, 361,—of which 123 were at ages under 5 years, and 12 were at ages above 85 Marriages in the ten years 1851-60, 1,136, births, 5,6?5 deaths, 3,593 The places of worship in 1851 were 12 of the Church of England, with 5,723 sittings, 4 of Independents, with 1,198 s, 2 of Baptists, with 9?0 s, 1 of Unitarians with 150 s, 6 of Wesleyan Methodists, with 1,458 s., 1 of Primitive Methodists, with 333 s 1 of Roman Catholics, with 50 s, 1 of Latter Day Saints, with 42 s, and 5 undefined, with 630 s The schools in 1851, were 17 public day schools, with 1,490 scholars, 36 private day schools, with 600 s, 22 Sunday schools, with 2,726 s., and 2 evening schools for adults, with 16 s

ALBANS (ST) See LONDON and WORCESTER

ALBANS COURT (ST) See NONINGTON

ALBANS HEAD (ST), a promontory in the parish of Worth Matravers, 4 miles S of Corfe Castle, Dorset Its skirt is pierced with the subterranean workings of Winspit quarry Its face exhibits, in section, three beds of the Portland oolite. Its summit has an altitude of 441 feet, is crowned by an ancient chapel, with Norman doorway, and commands a brilliant and extensive view It is sometimes called St Adhelm's or Aldhelm's Head

ALBANY BARRACKS See PARKHURST

ALBERBURY, or ABERFORD, a township and a sub district in the district of Atcham, Salop, and a parish, partly in the same district and county, and partly in the district and county of Montgomery The township lies on Watling street, near the Severn, 4 miles SW of Baschurch r station, and 9 W by N of Shrewsbury and has a post office under Shrewsbury Acres, with Wolleston chapelry, 6,471 Pop, exclusive of Wollaston, 632 Houses, 110 The township is called Alberbury Lower Quarter, and the chapelry is called Alberbury Upper Quarter Loton Hall, the seat of Sir Baldwin Leighton, Bart., is adjacent A priory for black monks was founded at Alberbury by Fitzwarren, in the time of Henry I and was given by Henry VI to All Souls' College Oxford The sub district of Alberbury comprises two parishes and part of a third Acres, 12,034 Pop., 2,235 Houses, 440 The parish of Alberbury comprises the two Alberbury Quarters in Salop, and the townships of Bansley, Middletown, and Uppington, and the chapelry of Cruggion in Montgomery Acres ?,??? Real property £? 429 Pop 1 918 Houses, 3?? The property is subdivided. The living is a vicarage in the diocese of Hereford Value £187 * Patron, All Souls College Oxford The church is ancient The vicarages of Wollaston and Cruggion are separate benefices Charities, £17 Glyn, a hamlet in this parish, was the birth place of old Parr

ALBERT BRIDGE, a grand tubular viaduct, on the line of the West Cornwall railway, over the estuary of the Hamoaze, between Devon and Cornwall It was designed by Brunel and opened, on 2 May 1859, by Prince Albert "The bridge is 2,240 feet long, by 30 feet broad, and rises 260 feet from the foundations to the summit so that line of battle ships can sail under it. It consists of 19 spans—double chains composed of ..

bars, 17 of them are wider than the arches of Westminster Bridge, and the two central spans cross the Tamar with a leap of 900 feet The latter rest upon the main central pillar, built into the solid rock, which was reached through 70 feet of sea and 20 feet of mud and gravel, by means of a coffer dam, on this are four octagonal columns, 10 feet in diameter and 100 feet high On this the great spans are laid, composed of two bows, the lower, with a curve of 28 feet, carries the roadway, the upper, a tube of wrought iron, is attached to the lower by supports Each span was floated out and lifted into its place by hydraulic presses. The main columns, on either side of the river, are built of solid masonry, 11 feet square, which rests on granite piers, measuring 29 feet by 17 feet They are 190 feet from the foundation to the summit. In the construction of this wonderful structure, 2,700 tons of wrought iron 1 300 of cast iron, 17,000 cubic yards of masonry, and 14,000 cubic yards of timber have been used It is 300 feet longer than the Britannia Bridge, and 60 feet higher than the Monument

ALBERT TOWN, a suburb of London, with post office‡ under Stoke Newington, London N

ALBION, the ancient Roman name of England, derived from *Albus* ' white, ' in allusion to the white cliffs first seen in the approach from the Continent

ALBION, a station on the Birmingham and Stafford railway, 6 miles WNW of Birmingham

ALBOROUGH See ALDBOROUGH

ALBOURNE, a parish in Cuckfield district, Sussex 3½ miles W of Hassocks Gate r station, and 6½ SW of Cuckfield It has a post office under Hurstperpoint Acres, 1,740 Real property £2 641 Pop. 341 Houses, 68 The property is somewhat divided Albourne Place is said to have been built by Archbishop Juxon, who attended Charles I on the scaffold, and was the residence of the eccentric Sir R Figge The living is a rectory in the diocese of Chichester Value, £225 * Patron John Goring, Esq The church is good Charities £11

ALBRIGHTLEE, a township in St Alkmond parish, Salop 3½ miles NE of Shrewsbury Pop, 45

ALBRIGHTON, a village, a parish, and a sub district, in the district of Shiffnal Salop The village adjoins the Shrewsbury and Birmingham railway, 5½ miles ESE of Shiffnal, and has a station on the railway, and a post office‡ under Wolverhampton It was formerly a market town, and it still has fairs on the second Monday in Jan, the first Monday in March 23 May and the third Monday in Oct The parish comprises 3 424 acres Real property, £8,393 Pop, 1,156 Houses, 249 The manor anciently belonged to Dore abbey The property is divided The living is a vicarage in the diocese of Lichfield Value, £651 Patrons, alternately the Haberdashers Company and Christ s Hospital The church is early English, with perpendicular transoms Charities, £65 The sub district comprises ten parishes and an extra parochial tract Acres, 22,511 Pop, 4,145 Houses 820

ALBRIGHTON, a chapelry in the parish of St Mary district of Atcham, Salop, near the Shrewsbury and Chester railway, 4 miles N of Shrewsbury It has a post office under Shrewsbury Acres, 750 Pop, 78 Houses 12. The living is a vicarage in the diocese of Lichfield Value, £52 * Patron, W Spurrier, Esq The church is very good

ALBURGH a parish in Depwade district, Norfolk on an affluent of the river Waveney near the Bungay railway, 3½ miles NNE of Harleston It has a post office under Harleston, and a fair on 21 June Acres, 1,512 Real property £3 699 Pop, 537 Houses, 130 The property is much subdivided The living is a rectory in the diocese of Norwich Value, £395 * Patron, St John s College, Cambridge The church has a large Norman porch There are a national school, and charities £240

ALBURY, a parish in Bishop Stortford district Herts, on the river Ash 4 miles W of Stanstead r station, and 4½ NW of Bishop Stortford It has a post-office under Ware and a fair is held in it at Patmore Heath, on 17 July Acres, 3,182 Real property, £5,275 Pop, 700 Houses, 147 The property shows pleasant scenery, and is much subdivided The living is a vicarage in the diocese of Rochester Value, £300 * Patron, the Treasurer of St Paul s The church contains a brass of Sir R Verney, and a tomb of De la Lee of Albury Hall Charities, £19

ALBURY, or ALDBURY, a parish in Thame district, Oxford near the river Thame, 3 miles NW of Tetsworth, and around Tiddington r station It includes Tiddington hamlet Post town, Tetsworth Acres, 1,110 Real property, £1,281 Pop, 183 Houses, 40 The property is divided among a few The living is a rectory in the diocese of Oxford. Value, £276 * Patron, the Earl of Abingdon The church is very good Charities, £10

ALBURY, ALDBURY, or ALDEBURY, a village a parish, and a sub district in the district of Guildford, Surrey The village stands on a tributary of the river Wey, under the north downs 1 mile N of Gomshall and Sheire r station, and 5 ESE of Guildford and has a post office under Guildford. The new parish church at it is an edifice of red brick in the Norman style, after the model of a church at Caen The author of "Proverbial Philosophy ' resided at the village The adjacent country abounds in charming walks and rides and a spot, called Newland's Corner, commands a most extensive view —The parish comprises 4,503 acres. Real property, £4,905 Pop, 1,041 Houses 199 Albury estate belongs to Earl Percy, belonged previously, from 1819, to H. Drummond, Esq, and belonged previously to the Finches and the Howards The grounds of its park possess interesting artificial features, some derived from Henry Howard afterwards Duke of Norfolk, others mentioned in the book of Domesday The mansion has been modernized from designs by Pugin The old parish church in Early Norman with a tower, adjoins the mansion The cathedral of the Catholic Apostolic church a cruciform edifice in the perpendicular style, built by Mr Drummond at a cost of £10,000, stands in the park The living of Albury is a rectory in the diocese of Winchester Value, £600 * Patron, the Duke of Northumberland Charities, £31 --The sub district comprises seven parishes. Acres, 19 760 Pop, 4,453. Houses 892

ALBURY HATCH See ALDBOROUGH HATCH

ALBY, or ALDBY, a parish in Aylsham district, Norfolk, near the river Bure, 4½ miles NNE of Aylsham, and 17 ENE of Elmham r station Post town Hanworth under Norwich Acres 811 Real property £1,974 Pop, 231 Houses, 58 The property is divided The living is a rectory in the diocese of Norwich Value, £140 * Patron, R Buckley, Esq The church is old but good.

ALCANNINGS See ALLCANNINGS

ALCESTER, the vestige of the Roman Alia Castra on Akeman Street 1½ mile SW of Bicester Oxford The place shows faint traces of a square enclosure divided by four ways.

ALCESTER, a liberty in the parish of St James Shaftesbury, within the parliamentary borough of Shaftesbury, but without the municipal borough, Dorset Pop, 342 Houses, 76

ALCESTER, a town a parish, a sub district and a district in Warwick The town stands at the confluence of the Alne and the Arrow, and on the Birmingham and Malvern railway, 9 miles NNE of Evesham The Roman station Alauna stood on its site, and the Roman road, Icknield street passed through and may still be traced in the vicinity Roman pavements, substructions, coins and urns have been found The place had great importance in the times of the Saxons and was a royal residence at the period of the Conquest A Benedictine abbey was founded in 1140, on an island about ½ a mile to the N, but fell into decay became a cell of Evesham abbey, and has long disappeared Alcester was made a borough by Henry I, and it continued to be of note in the 16th and 17th centuries, but it is now within the jurisdiction of the county magistrates It consists of one principal street, and some small diverging ones, and presents a clean and neat appearance The town hall was built in 1641, the corn exchange, in 1857 The parish church rebuilt in 1732, and retaining the previous tower, is a fine Gothic structure, and contains a well preserved altar tomb of Sir Fulke Greville and his lady, and a splendid monument of the Marquis of Hertford. There are three dissenting chapels, two public schools, eight alms houses, and other charities £270 The town has a post office‡ under Redditch, a r station a banking-office, a weekly market on Tuesday and fairs on the Tuesday before 29 Jan, on the Tuesday before 25 March, on the third Tuesday of April, May, and Sept, on the second Tuesday of July, on 17 Oct, and on the first Tuesday of Dec. The manufacture of needles and fish hooks is carried on Pop, not separately returned The railway past Alcester was partly projected in 1861, but not all opened till 1868

The parish of Alcester comprises 1,530 acres Real property, £8,920 Pop, 2,128 Houses, 491 The manor belongs to the Marquis of Hertford, whose seat, Ragley Park, is about 2 miles SW of the town The living is a rectory in the diocese of Worcester Value, £259 * Patron, the Marquis of Hertford —The sub district includes six entire parishes and part of another Acres, 15,419 Pop., 4 787 Houses, 1,066 The district, while all within the registration county of Warwick, is partly within the county proper of Worcester It comprehends the sub district of Studley, containing the parishes of Oldberrow, Morton Baggott, Spernall, Studley, and Ipsley, and part of the parish of Coughton, the sub-district of Alcester, containing the parishes of Great Alne, Aston Cantlow, Haselar, Kinwarton, Alcester, and Arrow, and part of the parish of Coughton, the sub district of Feckenham, containing the parishes of Feckenham, Inkberrow, Abbots Morton, and Weethley, and the sub district of Bidford, containing the parishes of Salford, Bidford Wixford, and Exhall Acres 52,430 Poor rates in 1866, £11,054 Pop in 1841, 16 838 in 1861, 16,878 Houses, 3,750. Marriages in 1866, 119, births, 548,—of which 45 were illegitimate, deaths 374, —of which 142 were at ages under 5 years, and 15 were at ages above 85 Marriages in the ten years 1851–60, 950, births, 5 439, deaths 3,553 The places of worship in 1851 were 23 of the Church of England, with 6,336 sittings, 1 of Independents, with 160 s, 9 of Baptists, with 1,768 s, 1 of Unitarians, with 500 s 8 of Wesleyan Methodists, with 1,232 s, 1 of Primitive Methodists, with 100 s and 3 of Roman Catholics with 1,180 s The schools in 1851 were 18 public day schools, with 1 150 scholars, 22 private day schools, with 353 s, 30 Sunday schools, with 2,334 s and 3 evening schools for adults, with 69 s The work house is in Oversley hamlet

ALCISTON a parish and a hundred in Sussex The parish lies in the district of Lewes, 1 mile S of Berwick r station, and 6½ SE of Lewes. Post town Selmeston under Lewes Acres 2,079 Real property, £1,596 Pop, 220 Houses 47 The manor belonged anciently to the Abbey of Battle The surface is hilly The living is a vicarage, united to Selmeston in the diocese of Chichester The church shows features of Norman and of early English, and is in tolerable condition.—The hundred of Alciston is in the rape of Pevensey, and comprises the parishes of Alciston Alfriston, and Lullington. Acres, 5,666 Pop in 1851, 859 Houses, 181

ALCOMBE, a hamlet in Dunster parish, Somerset, 1 mile NW of Dunster Pop 259

ALCONBURY, or ALKMUNDBURY, a parish in the district and county of Huntingdon, on Alconbury brook near Ermine street and the Eastern Counties railway, 5 miles NW of Huntingdon It has a post office under Huntingdon and a fair on 24 June Acres 3,700 Real property, £5,087 Pop, 909 Houses, 200 Alconbury Lodge is the chief residence Alconbury hill commands a fine view Alconbury brook rises on the confines of Northamptonshire, and runs about 3 miles south east ward to the Ouse at Huntingdon The living includes Alconbury Weston, and is a vicarage in the diocese of Ely Value, £162 * Patrons, the Dean and Chapter of Westminster The church is good, and there is a Wesleyan chapel

ALCONBURY WESTON, a parish in the district and county of Huntingdon contiguous, on the NW, to Alconbury Acres 1,540 Real property, £2,770 Pop, 566 Houses, 111 See ALCONBURY

ALCOTT END See AMPNEY CRUCIS

ALDATE (ST) See GLOUCESTER and BRISTOL

ALDBOROUGH, a parish in Erpingham district, Norfolk, on the river Bure, 4¾ miles N by W of Aylsham, and 7 NW of N Walsham r station It has a post-office under Norwich. Acres, 788. Real property, £2,051 Pop, 305 Houses, 79 The property is subdivided. The living is a rectory in the diocese of Norwich. Value, £173 * Patron, Lord Suffield The church was restored in 1849 There is a P Methodist chapel

ALDBOROUGH a decayed ancient town and a township in the district of Knaresborough, W R. Yorkshire, and a parish chiefly in the same district, but partly in Ripon district, N R The town stands on the river Ure and on Watling street near the Boroughbridge and Pilmoor railway, 1 mile E by N of Boroughbridge, and it has a post office under York It was the capital of the Brigantes the Isurium of the Romans, and the Ealdburg of the Saxons It became a borough in the time of Queen Mary, and it sent two members to parliament till disfranchised by the act of 1832 It anciently covered about 60 acres, within defensive walls about 12 feet thick, but it is now a mere village, irregularly built. Some vestiges of the walls remain, and many Roman coins, urns, utensils and other relics have been found A Roman citadel is supposed to have stood in its centre, a Roman bridge crossed the Ure contiguous to it, and Roman works of art, including sculptures, wall paintings, baths, and fine pavements, have left sufficient remains in it to show that it must have been a scene of luxury and power during a considerable period of the Roman occupation Many of the relics are preserved for the inspection of the curious The parish church adjoins the site of the supposed citadel, is an edifice of some antiquity, and probably was built with materials from the ancient town A statue of Mercury occurs in the outside of the vestry wall, and a gravestone, believed to be Saxon, is in the churchyard Aldborough Hall is at the east gate of the ancient town, and Aldborough Manor is at the west gate —The township includes the village, and comprises 1 890 acres Real property, £6,300 Pop, 522 Houses 115 —The parish includes also the townships of Boroughbridge, Rocliffe, Minskip, Ellenthorpe, and Lower Dunsforth, and parts of the townships of Humberton with Milby and Upper Dunsforth cum Branton Green Acres 9,323 Real property of Aldborough Boroughbridge Rocliffe Minskip, and Dunsforth townships £17,002 Pop of the parish 2,279 Houses, 519 The property is much subdivided The living is a vicarage in the diocese of Ripon Value, £380 * Patrons, the Dean and Chapter of York The vicarages of Boroughbridge, Rocliffe, and Dunsforth are separate benefices

ALDBOROUGH, or ALDEBURGH a seaport town, a parish, and a sub district in the district of Plomesgate, Suffolk The town stands at the terminus of a branch of the Eastern Union railway, 7 miles SE of Saxmundham, and 91¾ NE of London It occupies a pleasant site in Slaughden Valley, on the river Alde, between Aldborough bay and Aldborough mere, overlooked by a steep hill which commands a fine prospect The beach adjacent to it consists of fine firm sand, slopes gradually to the sea, and is well suited for bathing A shoal in the vicinity 2 miles long called Aldborough Knape causes strong breakers in easterly winds The sea has made great encroachments on the shore within the last two centuries. The town has become an esteemed watering-place and though containing many old houses, chiefly inhabited by fishermen, has also handsome new ones and villas for the accommodation of fashionable visitors. The parish church, on the summit of the hill, is perpendicular English, was recently restored has a tower with an octagonal turret contains six brasses and a Tudor pulpit, and presents a good landmark to mariners There are two dissenting chapels, a public library, and a national school The town hall is a half timbered edifice restored in 1853 The town was made a borough by Elizabeth, and it sent two members to parliament till disfranchised by the act of 1832 It has a post-office‡ under Saxmundham, and it formerly had a market and two fairs. Herring and lobster fishings are carried on, corn and wool are exported, and coal and timber are imported About 10 vessels of aggregately about 1,800 tons belong to the port Crabbe, the poet, was a native The title of Viscount Aldborough was borne by an ancestor of F J V Wentworth, Esq, the proprietor of the manor The parish comprises 1,782 acres of land and 50 of water Real property, £6,1?6 Pop, 1,721 Houses, 391 The living is a vicarage in the diocese of Norwich Value, £383 * Patron, F J V Wentworth, Esq Charities, £40 —The sub district includes eight parishes Acres, 12,946 Pop, 4,049 Houses, 925

ALDBOROUGH, N R and E. R Yorkshire See ALDBROUGH

ALDBOROUGH HATCH, a chapelry in Great Ilford parish Essex, 1½ mile NE of Ilford r station, and 8½ miles ENE of Bishopsgate It has a post office under Ilford, London E The famous Fairlop oak stood near it 36 feet in girth of bole, and 300 feet in circumference of head. Hainault forest, adjacent on the N, was part of the old great forests of the country The living is a vicarage in the diocese of London Value not reported Patron, the Crown A new church was built in 1863

ALDBOURNE a village and a parish in the district of Hungerford and county of Wilts The village stands 7 miles NW of Hungerford r station and 9 SE of Swindon, and has a post office under Hungerford It was formerly a market town, but it suffered great devastation by fire in 1760, and it has never recovered its old prosperity Aldbourne Chase, adjacent to it on the N, was a favourite hunting ground of king John, given by Henry VIII to the Duke of Somerset, and the scene of the defeat of the Parliamentarians under the Earl of Essex, by the Royal forces under Prince Rupert, but is now enclosed and cultivated The parish includes the tythings of Preston, Lower Upham, and Upper Upham Acres, 8,495 Real property, £10 301 Pop, 1,539 Houses, 343 The property is subdivided The living is a vicarage in the diocese of Salisbury Value, £367 * Patron, the Bishop of Salisbury The church is ancient has Norman features and a brass, and is good. Part of the parsonage is supposed to be a remnant of the ancient royal hunting seat Remains of an ancient British encampment occur near a farm house called Pierce's Lodge. There are a Wesleyan chapel, and charities £43

ALDBROUGH, a township and a sub district in the district of Richmond, N R. Yorkshire The township is in the parish of St John Stanwick on a tributary of the Tees 7 miles N by E of Richmond, and has a post office under Darlington. Acres, 1,636 Real property, £3,093 Pop, 420 Houses, 109 There is a Wesleyan chapel.—The sub district comprises two entire parishes and part of a third Acres 11,996 Pop, 1 706 Houses 390

ALDBROUGH, or ALDBURGH, a township, a parish, and a sub district in the district of Skirlaugh E R Yorkshire. The township lies on the coast, 8 miles NNE of Hedon r station, and 13½ E of Beverley, has a post office‡ under Hull and includes the hamlets of Bewick Carlton with Fosham, Etherdwick, and Tunstall A fair is held on 4 Sep Acres 4 911 Real property £6 020 Pop, 831 Houses 191 —The parish includes also the townships of East Newton and West Newton Acres, 6 319 Real property, £10,147 Pop, 1 095 Houses, 228 The property is much subdivided The living is a vicarage in the diocese of York Value, £476 Patron the Lord Chancellor The church is ancient and tolerable and has a curious Danish monumental stone The p curacy of Colden Parva is a separate benefice Towrie's charity, founded in 1663, has an income of £200 and includes almshouses and school There is a Wesleyan chapel —The sub district comprises two entire parishes and part of a third Acres, 10,603. Pop, 1 735 Houses 373

ALDBURGH See ALDBOROUGH and ALDBROUGH.

ALDBURY, a parish in Berkhampstead district Herts, under the Chiltern hills 1 mile E of Tring r station and 3½ NNE of Berkhampstead It has a post-office under Tring Acres, 2,071 Real property £2,962 Pop, 848 Houses, 179 The manor was possessed by the Verneys, the Andersons, and the Hydes, and now belongs to the Duke of Leeds The living is a rectory in the diocese of Rochester Value, £448 * Patron, Earl Brownlow The church is early English, with a square embattled tower, and contains some ancient tombs Charities, £20 and poors' cottages.

ALDBURY, Oxford and Surrey See ALDERLEY

ALDBY See ALBY

ALDCLIFFE, a township in Lancaster parish, on the estuary of the Lune, 1½ mile SSW of Lancaster Acres, 652 Pop 74 Houses, 13

ALDE (THE), a river of Suffolk It rises near Haxted, runs south eastward to the vicinity of Aldborough, and goes thence southward to the sea at Oxford haven Its entire length is about 30 miles, and its lower reaches, to the extent of 10 miles, are narrow, winding estuary, past the Lantern marshes

ALDEBURGH See ALDBOROUGH Suffolk

ALDEBY a parish and a sub district in the district of Loddon Norfolk The parish lies on Waveney river, 3 miles NE of Beccles, and it has a station on the Yarmouth branch of the Eastern Union railway, and a post office under Beccles Acres, 3,056 Real property £5,108 Pop, 557 Houses 118 The manor belonged anciently to the cathedral of Norwich, and was made the site of a Benedictine cell The property is divided The living is a vicarage in the diocese of Norwich Value, £120 * Patrons, the Dean and Chapter of Norwich The church is ancient and good and has a fine door The sub district comprises sixteen parishes. Acres, 24,373 Pop 4,954 Houses, 1 102

ALDENHAM, a parish in Watford district, Herts near the Colne river and the St Albans railway, 3 miles NE of Watford Post town Watford Acres 5,810 Real property £13 801 Pop, 1,760 Houses 35? The hamlet of Theobald Street is in it The property is divided The chief residences are Aldenham Abbey and Aldenham Lodge The living is a vicarage in the diocese of Rochester Value, £425 * Patrons, the Trustees of P Thellusson, Esq The church is early English of cemented flint stones, in very good condition Radlett chapelry, formed in 1865, is a separate vicarage Platt's almshouses and free grammar school have an income of £1,141, and were founded in 1599, and rebuilt in 1825 Other charities, £24

ALDENHAM HALL, the seat of Sir J E D Acton Bart 3½ miles WNW of Bridgenorth, Salop

ALDER (THE) See ADUR

ALDERBURY a village a parish, a sub-district, a hundred, and a district in Wilts The village stands on the river Avon, near the Salisbury branch of the Southwestern railway 3 miles SE of Salisbury, and has a post office under Salisbury —The parish includes also the chapelries of Pitton and Farley Acres 4,332 Real property of Alderbury Whaddon, and West Grimstead £4 270 of Pitton and Farley £2 921 Pop of the parish 1,334 Houses 288 The property is divided among a few Alderbury House, the seat of the Forts, in the vicinity of the village, was built of materials from the ancient belfry of Salisbury cathedral Ivy Church, some remains of which exist in a school house on an eminence, was an Augustinian priory founded by King Stephen The living of Alderbury is a vicarage in the diocese of Salisbury, and includes the curacies of Pitton and Farley Value £477 Patron the Bishop of Salisbury The church is excellent There are a Wesleyan chapel, and charities £16 —The sub district comprises five parishes part of another parish, and three extra parochial tracts Acres 24 751 Pop. 4,357 Houses 924 —The hundred comprises most of the parishes and tracts of the sub district, and includes so many others

as to be more extensive Acres, 32,790 Pop, 4,377 Houses, 1,019 —The district comprehends the sub district of Alderbury, containing the parishes of Alderbury, Winterslow, West Grimstead, Whiteparish, and Landford, part of the parish of West Dean, and the extra parochial tracts of Clarendon Park, Melchet Park and Earldoms, the sub-district of Downton, containing the parishes of Downton, Standlinch, Nunton with Bodenham, Odstock, Homington, Coombe Bisset, and Stratford St Anthony, and the sub district of Britford, containing the parishes of Britford, West Harnham, Laverstock, Stratford under the Castle, and Fisherton Anger, part of the parish of St Martin, the liberty of Salisbury Close, and the extra parochial Old Sarum Acres, 53 490 Poor rates in 1866, £11,080 Pop in 1841, 14 174, in 1861, 14,770 Houses, 2,977 Marriages in 1866 91, births, 472, - of which 26 were illegitimate, deaths 337,—of which 82 were at ages under 5 years, and 8 were at ages above 85 Marriages in the ten years 1851–60, 1,069, births, 4,550 deaths 3 305 The places of worship in 1851 were 23 of the Church of England, with 4,827 sittings, 1 of Independents, with 35 s 7 of Baptists, with 894 s, 12 of Wesleyan Methodists, with 1,346 s, and 2 of Primitive Methodists, with 822 s The schools in 1851 were 27 public day schools, with 1 633 scholars, 17 private day schools, with 325 s 36 Sunday schools, with 2 317 s and 5 evening schools for adults, with 86 s. The workhouse is in Britford

ALDERBURY, Surrey See ALBURY, Surrey

ALDERFORD, a parish in St Faith district, Norfolk, on the river Wensum 9 miles NNE of Thuxton r station, and 10 NW of Norwich. It has a post office under Norwich Acres, 492 Real property, £835 Pop, 2[illegible] Houses [illegible] The manor belonged anciently to Norwich cathedral The living is a rectory, united with the vicarage of Attlebridge, in the diocese of Norwich Value, 219 * Patrons, the Dean and Chapter of Norwich The church is old but good

ALDERHOLT a tything and a chapelry in Cranborne parish, Dorset The tything lies on the verge of the county 4½ miles E of Cranborne, and 5½ N of Ringwood r station, and has a post office under Salisbury Pop, 4[illegible] The chapelry includes the tything, but is larger and was constituted in 1849 Pop, 708 Houses, 145 The living is a vicarage in the diocese of Salisbury Value, £105 * Patron, the Vicar of Cranborne The church was built by the Marquis of Salisbury

ALDERLEY, a parish and a sub district in the district of Macclesfield Cheshire The parish lies on an affluent of the river Bollin, and on the Manchester and Birmingham railway 7 miles SSW of Stockport It has a station on the railway and a post office under Congleton and it includes the townships of Nether Alderley, Over Alderley and Great Warford Acres in Nether Alderley, 2,755 Real property, £8,708 Pop, 617 Houses, 1[illegible] Acres in Over Alderley 2,146 Real property, £3,388 Pop, 421 Houses 77 Acres in the parish, 6,175 Real property, £14 931. Pop, 1,418 Houses 257 The property is subdivided Alderley Edge has a height of 360 feet, commands an extensive view and yields excellent sandstone Alderley Park is the seat of Lord Stanley of Alderley, and has fine grounds Numerous neat residences have recently been built on Alderley Edge, and excursion trains run to it in summer from Manchester Copper ore is worked The living is a rectory in the diocese of Chester Value, £7[illegible] * Patron Lord Stanley of Alderley The church is good and there are a Baptist chapel and a Wesleyan —the latter a Gothic edifice of 1853 Charities £21 —The sub district includes also parts of three other parishes Acres 13 [illegible] Pop 4 52[illegible] Houses 798

ALDERLEY a village and a parish in Chipping Sodbury district, Gloucester The village stands on a hill of the Cotswolds above the confluence of two rivulets, 9 miles ESE of Charfield r station and 4 SE of Wickwar, and has a post office under Wotton under Edge The parish comprises 678 acres Real property £1 600 Pop 93. Houses 23 The property is not much divided The hill on which the village stands has yielded many curious fossils The parish was formerly the boundary of Kingswood forest The estate of Alderley was the birthplace of Sir Matthew Hale, and continues to be held by his descendants The living is a rectory in the diocese of Gloucester and Bristol Value, £200 * Patron R H B Hale, Esq The church is a handsome building, conspicuously situated on the hill, and contains the grave and monument of Sir Matthew Hale

ALDERMAN HAW, a village in Woodhouse chapelry, 2 miles W of Mount Sorrel, Leicester It had a cell of Bermondsey abbey Pop, 25

ALDERMASTON, or ADMISTON a village and a parish in Bradfield district, Berks —The village stands at the influx of the Emborne to the Kennet, 8 miles E of Newbury, and it has a station, 1½ mile distant on the Great Western railway, and a post office under Reading It was formerly a market town, and it still has fairs on 6 May, 7 July and 11 Oct The Earl of Essex occupied it in 1644 The parish comprises 3,669 acres Real property, £4,718 Pop, 587 Houses, 129 The property is not much divided Much of the surface is heathy The park of Aldermaston Court includes 1,000 acres, and is one of the wildest and most diversified in the south of England The mansion on it is a Tudor edifice, built in 1851, and contains many interesting relics of a remarkable structure which preceded it, the seat of the Forsters and the Congreves, and the old lodges, with spired tower and roof are still standing An ancient camp occurs near Aldermaston Soak The living is a vicarage in the diocese of Oxford Value and patron, not reported The church is an ancient edifice, with fine Norman doorway and interesting monuments

ALDERMINSTER, a parish in the district of Stratford on Avon and county of Worcester, on the river Stour and on the Stratford and Moreton railway, 5 miles SSE of Stratford It has a post office under Stratford Acres, 3,167 Real property, £3,777 Pop, 520 Houses 105 The property is not much divided. The living is a vicarage in the diocese of Worcester Value, £170 * Patron the Lord Chancellor The church is cruciform, with a low tower, and partly Norman

ALDERMOOR, an eminence, crowned by a windmill, and commanding a grand prospect, 1¼ mile SSW of Ryde, Isle of Wight

ALDERNEY one of the Channel Islands It lies 10 miles W of Cape La Hogue in France 15 NNE of Guernsey, and 57 S by E of Portland Bill the nearest part of the English coast Its length is 3½ miles, its breadth a little more than 1 mile its circumference, about 8 miles It was the Riduna of the Romans and is called Aurigny by the French It is surrounded by rocks islets, and conflicting currents so that the approach to it is often dangerous Small bays indent its coast, and that of Braye, on the NW affords good anchorage Communication is maintained twice a week, by a small steamer, with Guernsey The surface is variously high and low all destitute of trees but contains some fertile land in good cultivation The Alderney cow, a small straight backed animal, has a world-wide fame for its milking properties, but is supplied to the English market from Jersey and Guernsey, very rarely from Alderney, and is of much smaller size in Alderney than in Jersey, and smaller in Jersey than in Guernsey Many Roman coins and other Roman relics have been found in Alderney Celtic monuments formerly were numerous but only one, a dilapidated cromlech, now remains A castle of the Earl of Essex and a number of forts on the coast but are now represented by a modern fort and a barrack Vast works, comprising forts, a capacious harbour and a breakwater, recommended by the late Duke of Wellington are in the course of construction by Government to check the great French works at Cherbourg, and maintain command of the English Channel They were originally estimated to cost £600 000, but they actually cost £1,000,000 at a point in 1860 and were then computed to require about £300 000 more The town of St Anne stands within ½ a mile of the harbour nearly in the centre of the island and contains the dwellings of nearly all the inhabitants It has two main streets, a government house, a new court house, a parish church, and chapels for Presbyterians, Wesleyans, Primitive Methodists, and Roman Catholics. The parish church is an elegant cruciform edifice, in the semi Norman style, with central tower, built in 1850, at a cost of £8,000 The island is governed by a court of its own, subject to the court of Guernsey, it has a post office‡ under Guernsey, and it forms a parish in the diocese of Winchester The living is a p curacy of the value of £300,* in the patronage of the Governor of Guernsey Both English and French are spoken by the inhabitants, but English more than French. Pop. in 1841, 1,038, in 1861, 4,932 —The strait between the island and France is swept by a tidal current of 6 miles an hour, and bears the name of the Race of Alderney The French fleet escaped through it in 1692, after the battle of La Hogue, and Admiral Balchen was lost in it in 1774 Alderney gave the title of Baron to a son of George II —See CASKETS (THE)

ALDERSBROOKE, a locality in Epping forest, Essex, near the river Roding, 1 mile WNW of Ilford r station, and 6 miles NE of St. Paul's, London. It has a post-office under Ilford, London E Here is the City cemetery, and here was the seat of the antiquary Lethieullier

ALDERSEY, a township in Coddington parish, Cheshire, on an affluent of the river Dee, 4 miles SW of Tattenhall r station, and 8 SSE of Chester Acres, 784 Real property, £1,175 Pop., 119 Houses, 21 The proprietor's seat is Aldersey Hall

ALDERSHOLT See ALDERHOLT

ALDERSHOT, a town, a camp, and a parish in the district of Farnham and county of Hants The town stands near the Basingstoke canal, and near the Ash, the Tongham, the Farnham, and the Farnborough r stations, 3 miles NE by N of Farnham It has a post office‡ under Farnborough station a church, and three dissenting places of worship, and it publishes two weekly newspapers It suddenly rose from seclusion to importance by the formation of the neighbouring camp The church at it contains several monuments of the Tichbourne family who formerly resided in the parish.—The camp is situated close to the town, on Aldershot Heath, which consists of the Bagshot sand, and stretches away to the downs of Surrey, and it also has a post-office‡ under Farnborough station. It was formed in 1854, at a cost of upwards of £600,000 It is practically a wooden town covers an area of 7 square miles, and is divided by the Basingstoke canal into two parts, containing accommodation for respectively 12,000 and 8 000 men Two churches of wood, and another church of cast iron, are in it, for the use of the troops Quarters for the commanding officers are on a rising ground overlooking it from the SW, the Queen's Pavilion, built at a cost of £5,000, is beyond these quarters, and permanent barracks, erected in 1857 at great cost, with accommodation for about 7,000 men, and a large church, built in 1863, at a cost of £14,000, are near the Pavilion —The parish comprises 4,144 acres Real property, £12,073 Pop in 1841, 685, in 1861 16,720 of whom 11,720 were military in the camp. Houses, 763 The manor belonged anciently to Merton priory The living is a vicarage in the diocese of Winchester Value £164 * Patrons, F Eggar C Andrews, P Alden and H Tice, Esqs

ALDERTON, a parish in Winchcombe district, Gloucester 5 miles ESE of Ashchurch r station, and 9 NNE of Cheltenham It has a post office under Cheltenham, and contains the hamlet of Dixton Acres, 1,750 Real property, £2,067 Pop, 487 Houses, 109 The property is subdivided Here are remains of a Saxon camp The living is a rectory in the diocese of Gloucester and Bristol Value, £450 * Patron, the Rev C Covey The church is good Charities, £20

ALDERTON, a parish in Potterspury district, Northampton, near Watling street, the Tove river, and the Grand Junction canal, 3¼ miles W of Roade r station, and 3½ SE of Towcester Post town, Towcester Acres, 910 Real property £1,292 Pop, 131 Houses, 34 The property is divided among a few Lace making is carried on The living is a rectory, annexed to Grafton Regis, in the diocese of Peterborough The church is modern, and in the perpendicular English style Charities, £4 and five poors' cottages.

ALDERTON, a parish in Woodbridge district, Suffolk, on the coast, between the Deben river and Hollesley bay, 8 miles SSE of Woodbridge r station It has a post office under Woodbridge. Acres, 2 513 Real property, £4,390 Pop, 634 Houses, 137 The property is not much divided The living is a rectory in the diocese of Norwich Value, £720 * Patrons, T Archer, Esq, and the Bishop of Norwich The church is a modern brick edifice, and a previous church is in ruins, and serves as a landmark Charities, £23. Giles Fletcher, the poet, was rector of Alderton, and died here in 1623

ALDERTON, a parish in Malmesbury district, Wilts, near Akeman street, 9 miles NNW of Chippenham r station It has a post office under Chippenham Acres, 1,587 Real property, £2,404 Pop., 192 Houses, 44 The living is a vicarage in the diocese of Gloucester and Bristol Value, not reported Patron, Sir J Neeld, Bart Gore, the antiquary, who flourished in the 17th century, was a native of Alderton, and was buried in the church

ALDERTON, a township in Great Ness parish, Salop, near the river Severn, 8 miles WNW of Shrewsbury Pop, 54

ALDERTON, a township in Hadnall chapelry, Salop, 6 miles NNE of Shrewsbury Pop, 25

ALDERWASLEY, a township chapelry in Wirksworth parish, Derby, near the Derwent river, the Cromford canal, and the Whatstandwell Bridge r station, 2½ miles ESE of Wirksworth Post town, Wirksworth Real property, £4,356,—of which £1,000 are in iron works. Pop, 372 Houses, 70 The scenery is picturesque Alderwasley Hall is a beautiful seat Coal, iron, and lead are worked The living is a donative in the diocese of Lichfield Value, £120 * Patron, F Hurst, Esq

ALDFIELD, a township and a chapelry in Ripon parish, W R. Yorkshire The township lies on the rivulet Skell, 4 miles SW of Ripon r station Post town, Ripon Acres, 1,223 Real property, £1,375 Pop., 128 Houses, 27 A sulphuretted spring exists here, in a picturesque spot and, but for being so near Harrowgate, would probably be in high request The chapelry comprises the townships of Aldfield, Studley-Roger, and Studley Royal and bears the name of Aldfield with Studley Pop in 1851, 327 The living is a p curacy in the diocese of Ripon Value, £72 Patron, Countess Cowper

ALDFORD See ALFORD

ALDFORD, a village, a township, and a parish in Great Boughton district, Cheshire The village stands on an affluent of the Dee 2½ miles ESE of Saltney r station, and 6 miles S by E of Chester It has a post office under Chester, and it was formerly a market town A bridge here crosses an 'old ford' on the line of a Roman road into Wales, and that old ford gave the place its name Remains of a castle are in the neighbourhood, erected in the reign of Henry II, and garrisoned by Brereton in the civil war The township comprises 1,273 acres. Pop 438 Houses, 88 The parish includes also the townships of Edgerley Buerton, and Churton by-Aldford Acres 2,638 Real property, £4,572 Pop, 731 Houses 150 The manor with Eton Hall belongs to the Marquis of Westminster The living is a rectory in the diocese of Chester Value, £330 * Patron, the Marquis of Westminster The church was rebuilt in 1866, and is in the early English style There are a Wesleyan chapel and a free school

ALDGATE. See LONDON

ALDHAM, a parish in Lexden district, Essex, near Colne river 3 miles N of Marks Tey r station, and 3 ENE of Coggeshall Post town, Marks Tey under Colchester Acres 1 925 Real property £2 598 Pop, 406 Houses, 94 The manor belonged to the De Veres The property is subdivided The place is a meet for the East Essex hounds. The living is a rectory in the di cese of Rochester Value, £327 * Patron, the Bishop of Rochester The church is very good Charities, £32 Morant the historian was rector of Aldham

ALDHAM, a parish in Cosford district, Suffolk, near the river Bret, 2 miles N of Hadleigh r station Post town Hadleigh, under Ipswich Acres, 1,744 Real property, £1 360 Pop 267 Houses, 60 The property is divided among a few The living is a rectory in the diocese of Ely Value, £290. Patron, T B Lennard, Esq The church is very ancient, and has a Norman round tower A priory cell stood at Priory Farm Rowland Taylor was burned, in 1555, on Aldham Common

ALDHELM'S (ST). See ALBAN'S HEAD (ST)

ALDINGBOURN, a parish in Westhampnett district, Sussex 1 mile north of Woodgate r station, and 4 E of Chichester It contains the hamlets of Lidsey and Westergate Post town, Chichester Acres, 3,069 Real property, £6,678 Pop, 772 Houses, 162 Aldingbourn House was a seat of the Howards The living is a vicarage in the diocese of Chichester Value, £220 * Patron, the Bishop of Chichester The church is early English and has a black marble font

ALDINGHAM, a parish in Ulverstone district, Lancashire, on Morecambe bay, 4 miles E of Furness Abbey r station, and 5 S by W of Ulverstone It includes the divisions of Gleaston and Leece Post town, Bardsea under Ulverstone Acres, 4,694 Real property, £8,497 Pop 1,011 Houses, 186 The property is much subdivided Much land formerly in the parish has been carried off by the sea Gleaston Castle, now a ruin of three towers, with connecting walls, was a seat of the Flemings, and of the Duke of Suffolk, the father of Lady Jane Grey The living is a rectory in the diocese of Carlisle Value, £1,093 * Patron, the Crown The church is very good The p curacy of Dendron is a separate benefice Charities £15.

ALDINGTON, a village, a parish, and a sub-district in the district of East Ashford, Kent The village stands near the Grand Military canal, 1½ mile S of Smeeth r station and 6 SE of Ashford It has a post office under Hythe and is in the lib of Romney Marsh —The parish comprises 3 576 acres Real property £5,357 Pop, 678 Houses, 144 The property is not much divided. The Roman road from Lymne to Pevensey went through the parish Court of Street, on the line of that road, about a mile E of the village, was the scene of the imposture of Elizabeth Barton, the nun of Kent, who made so great a figure in the political party of Queen Catherine the living is a rectory in the diocese of Canterbury, and till 1 68 was united with Smeeth Value, £850 * Patron the Archbishop of Canterbury The church is early English, with a tower in late perpendicular, and formerly had a brass of 1475 Charities, £9 The celebrated Erasmus of Rotterdam, and Richard Moster, who suffered death for aiding the imposture of Elizabeth Barton, were rectors of Aldington —The sub-district comprises seven parishes Acres, 16,127 Pop, 2,487 Houses 509

ALDINGTON a hamlet in Badsey parish, Worcester, 2 miles E of Evesham Pop, 141 Houses, 35

ALDMONBURY See ALMONBURY

ALDON, a township in Stokesay parish Salop, near the river Onny, 6¼ miles NW of Ludlow Pop, 236

ALDON, a hamlet in Addington and Ryarsh parishes, Kent 6½ miles NW of Maidstone

ALDRETH, a hamlet in Haddenham parish, Cambridge

ALDRIDGE, a small town, a parish and a sub district in the district of Walsall, Stafford The town stands near the Worley canal 2¼ miles ESE of Pelsall r station, and 3½ NE of Walsall, and it has a post office under Walsall An extensive distillery is here, and fine potter's clay and coal are worked in the neighbourhood Pop, 1,179 Houses 231 —The parish includes also the town of Great Barr Acres, 7 752 Real property £6,041 Pop, 2,2 4 Houses, 451 The property is divided among a few A height called Barr Beacon is said to have been a place of Druidical sacrifices and a pool called Druid Mere, makes an occasional overflow, and has been popularly imagined to possess some supernatural quality Barr-Hall Park is the seat of Sir E D Scott, Bart The living is a rectory in the diocese of Lichfield. Value, £375 * Patron, the Rev J F Smith The church contains a monument of a Stapleton, and is good The vicarage of Great Barr is a separate benefice Jordan's schools have £118 from endowment, and other charities £64 —The sub district comprises two parishes and part of a third Pop, 7,026 Houses, 1,413

ALDRIDGE HILL, an extra parochial tract contiguous to Brockenhurst parish, Hants

ALDRINGHAM, a village and a parish in Blything district, Suffolk The village stands near the coast and near the Aldborough railway, 2¼ miles N of Aldborough It was formerly a market town, and it still has fairs on 11 Oct and 1 Dec The parish contains also the hamlet of Thorpe Post town, Aldborough under Saxmundham Acres, 1,783, of which 80 are water Real property, £1,913 Pop., 471 Houses, 111 The property is divided among a few The living is a vicarage in the diocese of Norwich, and includes the curacy of Thorpe Value, £59 Patron, the Rev E. Hollond The church is transition Norman, and has an octagonal font There is a Baptist chapel

ALDRINGTON, or ATHERINGTON, a parish in Steyning district, Sussex, on the coast, near the South Coast railway, 3 miles W of Brighton. Post town, Brighton Acres, 776. Pop, 7 Houses 2 A village here which antiquaries suppose to have been the Portus Adurni of the Romans which some also suppose to have been given by King Alfred to his younger son, and which came to bear the same name as the parish, was destroyed at no very late period, by encroachment of the sea. So much of the parish also was carried away that not an inhabitant was found in it at the Censuses of 1801-31 The ruins of the church, in early English architecture still exist The living is a rectory in the diocese of Chichester Value, £294 Patron, Magdalene College, Cambridge

ALDSTONE See ALSTON, Cumberland

ALDSWORTH, a parish in Northleach district, Gloucester near the river Leach, 10 miles NE of Cirencester r station It has a post office under Cheltenham Acres, 3,460 Real property £3,107 Pop, 430 Houses, 82 The property is divided among a few The living is a vicarage in the diocese of Gloucester and Bristol Value £66 Patron, Christ's Church, Oxford The church stands on a hill and commands an extensive view

ALDSWORTH, a tything in Westbourne parish, Sussex, near Stanstead Park, 6½ miles WNW of Chichester Pop, 118

ALDWARK, a township in Bradbourne parish, Derby near Mouldridge-hill and the Peak railway, 4½ miles NW of Wirksworth Acres, 935 Pop, 65 Houses 13

ALDWARK, a township in Alne parish N R York shire, on the river Ouse, 3½ miles W of Tollerton r station, and 12 NW of York Acres, 2 217 Real property, £2 012 Pop, 155 Houses 37

ALDWARK, a hamlet in Ecclesfield parish, W R. Yorkshire, on the river Don 2 miles NE of Rotherham Aldwark Hall, in the vicinity, was once a seat of the Fitzwilliam family

ALDWICK, a tything and a hundred on the coast of Sussex The tything is in Pagham parish, a mile SW of Bognor, and has a post office under Bognor The hundred is in the rape of Chichester, and comprises Bognor, and parts of five parishes. Acres, 13,516 Pop in 1851, 4,?77

ALDWINKLE ALL SAINTS, a parish in Thrapston district, Northampton, on the river Nen at Thorpe r station, 2½ miles NNE of Thrapston Post town, Thrapston Acres, together with Aldwinkle St Peter 2,450 Real property £4, 24 Pop of Aldwinkle All Saints 361 Houses 83 The property is divided The living is a rectory in the diocese of Peterborough Value £311 * Patron the Rev Dr Roberts The church shows beautiful features of decorated English, and has a handsome tower Thorpe's school has £16 from endowment, and other charities have £35 The father of the poet Dryden was rector of Aldwinkle-All Saints, and the poet was born in the parsonage

ALDWINKLE ST PETER, a parish in Thrapston district, Northampton, on the river Nen, a mile W of Thorpe r station, and 3 miles N by W of Thrapston Post town, Thrapston. Acres and property returned with Aldwinkle All Saints. Pop, 222 Houses, 46 The property is subdivided A curious cruciform building, called Liveden, stands here on the Nen, erected by the Tresham family, and richly decorated with sculpture The living is a rectory in the diocese of Peterborough Value, £230 Patron, Lord Lilford The church is good. Thomas Fuller, the historian, was a native

ALDWORTH, or ALLDER, a parish in Wantage district, Berks, in a high hilly tract, near Icknield street, 3 miles WSW of Goring r station, and 4 E by S of East Ilsley Post town, Ashampstead under Reading Acres, 1,960 Real property, £2,119 Pop, 275 Houses, 64 The manor belonged to the family of De la Beche, one of whom was tutor to the Black Prince, and a farm called Beach was the site of their baronial castle The living is a vicarage in the diocese of Oxford Value, £449 Patron St John's College, Cambridge The church contains nine remarkable monuments of the De la Beches, two of them altar tombs, and all so interesting that Queen Elizabeth made a journey on horseback to see them A yew tree, 27 feet in girth, is in the churchyard

ALED (THE), a stream of North Wales It rises at Llyn Aled, in the SW of Denbigh, and runs 10 miles northward, past Dyffryn Aled, to a confluence with the Elwy, 2 miles NE of Llanfair

ALEMOUTH See ALNMOUTH

ALEN (THE) See ALWEN (THE)

ALESHAM See AYLSHAM and HAILSHAM

ALESWORTH See AILESWORTH

ALETHORPE an extra-parochial tract, in Walsingham district, Norfolk, 2 miles ENE of Fakenham Acres, 239 Pop, 6 House, 1

ALEX'S TOR, a peak near Brown Willy, 5½ miles SE of Camelford, Cornwall

ALEXTON, a parish in Billesdon district, Leicester, on the river Eye, 3 miles W by N of Uppingham, and 6 NW of Medbourne Bridge r station. Post town, Uppingham. Acres 997, but only 76 arable Real property, £1,797 Pop 67 Houses, 15 The property is divided among a few Alexton Hall now a farm house, was till lately a seat of Lord Berners The living is a rectory in the diocese of Peterborough Value, £140 * Patron, Lord Berners The church was restored in 1863

ALFOLD, ALDFOLD, or AWFOLD, a parish in the district of Hambledon, and counties of Surrey and Sussex, on the Wey and Arundel canal, 6½ miles SE of Witley r station, and 8 SSE of Godalming It has a post office under Horsham Acres, 2,883 Real property, £1,970 Pop 535 Houses, 96 Much of the surface is woodland, and little yields any grain but oats. Several French refugees from the massacre on St. Bartholomew's day settled here, and erected a glass manufactory The living is a rectory in the diocese of Winchester Value, £205 * Patron, the Rev L W Elliott The church is Norman

ALFORD, a small town, a parish, and a sub district in the district of Spilsby, Lincoln The town stands on a rivulet, adjacent to the East Lincoln railway, 10½ miles SSE of Louth, and 23½ NNE of Boston, took its name from an old ford on the rivulet, gives the title of Viscount to Earl Brownlow comprises three main streets and a market place, is a seat of petty sessions, and a polling place, carries on brewing, tanning dyeing, rope making and other employments and has a r station with telegraph, a head post-office,‡ two banking offices, three chief inns, a police station a handsome recent corn exchange, a neat mechanics institute of 1854 with lecture hall and library an early English church, five dissenting chapels, a grammar-school with £354 a year from endowment, and with a fellowship and three scholarships at Cambridge, an endowed school for girls, a mixed national school, six alms houses, some other charities, a weekly market on Tuesday, and stock fairs on Whit-Tuesday and 8 Nov —The parish comprises 1,410 acres Real property, £7,893 Pop, 2,658 Houses, 502 The property is subdivided There are a mineral spring and barrows The living is a vicarage, united to the curacy of Rigsby, in the diocese of Lincoln Value, £163 Patron, the Bishop of Lincoln —The sub district comprises nineteen parishes. Acres, 32,570 Pop, 7,501 Houses, 1,633.

ALFORD a village and a parish in Wincanton district, Somerset The village stands on the river Brue, near Castleeary r station 8 miles SE of Glastonbury It has a post office under Bath A chalybeate spring in its neighbourhood was formerly much resorted to, but is now neglected The parish comprises 722 acres Real property, with Lovington and Wheathill, £3,793 Pop, 109 Houses, 21 The property is all in one estate The living is a rectory, united with the rectory of Hornblotton, in the diocese of Bath and Wells Value, £788 * Patron, the Rev J G Thring The church is early perpendicular of the time of Henry VI, with very fine features of structure and carving

ALFRED See ASHFORD Kent

ALFRED S CASTLE See ASHDOWN PARK

ALFRED S TOWER, a monumental edifice in Stourhead Park, on the confines of Wilts and Somerset, 5 miles NNE of Wincanton It stands on Kingsettle hill, 800 feet high, 3 miles WNW of Stourhead House, and commands an extensive view over the circumjacent counties It is a triangular structure of red brick, 150 feet high, with turrets at the corners, and surmounted by a colossal statue of Alfred the Great. It was built by the proprietor of the park, Henry Hoare, Esq, to commemorate the achievements of Alfred, and it bears an appropriate inscription Alfred, on issuing from his retreat in the Isle of Athelney, fixed his standard here against the Danish invaders. Hence the name Kingsettle given to the hill A huge mound, called Jack s Castle, occurs a mile S of the tower, and was long believed to have been formed for beacon fires, but is now known to have been sepulchral. See STOURTON

ALFRETON, a small town, a parish, and a sub district, in the district of Belper, Derby The town stands on the brow of a hill, about a mile from the new branch railway connecting the Erewash line with the main Midland, and 14 miles NNE of Derby It is said, but without good reason, to have got its name and origin from a residence of King Alfred Its form is irregular and straggling, and many of its houses are old The parish church is variously early, decorated, and later English and was restored and enlarged in 1869 The town has a railway station, a head post-office,‡ two banking offices, and two chief inns, and is a polling place Stocking manufacture is carried on, and potteries, stone quarries, collieries, and iron works are in the neighbourhood A weekly market is held on Friday, and fairs on 26 Jan, Easter Tuesday, Whit Tuesday, 31 July, 8 Oct, and 22 Nov —The parish contains also the villages of Greenhill Lane and Birchwood, the manor of Riddings with Ironville, and the hamlets of Summercotes and Swanwick Acres, 4,550 Real property, £27,414,—of which £7,472 are in mines, and £2,000 in iron works Pop, 11,549 Houses, 2 092 The property is divided among a few The manor of Alfreton belonged to successively the De Alfretons the Chaworths, the Babingtons, and the Zouches and now belongs to W P Morewood, Esq Roman relics have been found at Greenhill Lane The living is a vicarage in the diocese of Lichfield Value, £150 * Patron W P Morewood, Esq The p curacy of Swanwick, the vicarage of Ironville, and the vicarage of Riddings-with Summercotes, are separate benefices The ancient parish church belonged to Beauchief abbey There are chapels for Independents Baptists, Wesleyans, and Primitive Methodists An endowed school has £50 a year, and other charities £145 The sub district is co extensive with the parish

ALFRICK, a township chapelry in Suckley parish, Worcester, near the river Teme, 7½ miles W of Worces ter It has a post-office under Worcester Acres, 1,790 Pop, 474 Houses, 93 The living is a curacy annexed to the rectory of Suckley Charities, £14.

ALFRISTON, a village and a parish in Eastbourne district, Sussex. The village stands on the Cuckmere river, 2½ miles S of Berwick r station, and 8 SE of Lewes. Its name is a corruption of Alfred's Town, and points to ancient *entrenchments in the neighbourhood*, formed by King Alfred It has a post-office under Lewes, and it formerly had two fairs The Star Inn here, a building about 360 years old, contains some curious sculptures. The parish comprises 2,425 acres Real property, £2 617 Pop, 522 Houses, 113 The manor belonged anciently to Michelham priory The property is subdivided Two fine varieties of apples, one of them called the Alfriston apple, are grown Roman coins and Anglo Saxon sceattas have been found. The living is a vicarage in the diocese of Chichester Value, £135 Patron, the Lord Chancellor The church is chiefly decorated English, and has stone stalls and an ancient tomb There is an Independent chapel

ALGAPKIRK a parish in Boston district, Lincoln, on the *Peterborough* and *Boston railway, near Fosdyke* Wash 6½ miles S by W of Boston It has a station, with Sutterton, on the railway Post town, Sutterton under Spalding. Acres, 6,050 Real property, £10,828 Pop 772 Houses, 155 The property is subdivided. Much of the surface is fen Algarkirk House is the seat of the Rev B Beridge The living is a rectory, united with Fosdyke, in the diocese of Lincoln Value, £1 310 * Patron, the Rev B Beridge The church is cruciform, with a low central tower, shows successive characters from traces of Norman to later English, has a beautiful new reredos, and *contains sedilia* and an octagonal font. A pillar in the churchyard is said to mark the grave of Algar, Earl of Mercia, who fell in battle against the Danes at Threkingham, in 870 Hence the name Algarkirk Charities £24, and a share in Fosdyke hospital.

ALHAMPTON, a tything in Ditcheat parish, Somerset, near the river Brue, 3 miles NNW of Castlecary Pop 3?6

ALICANA. See ILKLEY

ALICE HOLT FOREST, a royal forest on the E border of Hants, near the Alton railway, between Binstead and Farnham It measures about 2 miles by 2 It was formerly stocked with fallow deer and kept thickly wooded, and it still contains many stately trees Much rude ancient pottery has been found in it, and is supposed to have been manufactured on the spot by the aboriginal Britons

ALKBOROUGH, or AUKBOROUGH, a parish in Glanford Brigg district, Lincoln, at the mouth of the river Trent, 5 miles S of Brough r station and 10½ W of Barton upon Humber It has a post office under Brigg, and contains the hamlet of Walcot Acres, 2,875 of which 305 are water Real property, £3 394 Pop, 437 Houses, 93 The property is divided between two A high ground with cliff, overhanging the Trent, commands a brilliant *view of the basins of the Trent*, the Ouse, and the Humber and forms a strong, natural, military post for overawing great part of the coast of England A Roman camp occurs here, of square outline 300 feet each side with vallum and ditch nearly entire, and now bears the name of Countess Close, from a tradition that it was inhabited by a Countess of Warwick Alkborough is thought to have been the Roman Aquis. The living is a vicarage, united with the vicarage of Whitton in the diocese of Lincoln Value, £209 Patrons, the Bishop of Lincoln and the Rev C Constable. The church is ancient. There are two Methodist chapels and a large alms house

ALKERTON, a tything in Eastington parish, Gloucester 4 miles W of Stroud Pop 1 003 Houses, 2?5 Here are a Baptist chapel and a Methodist chapel

ALKERTON or AWKERINGTON, a parish in Banbury district, Oxford on the verge of the county 6 miles W NW of Banbury r station Post town, Shennington under Banbury Acres, 650 Real property, £1,316 Pop, 194 Houses, 40 The property is not much divided. The living is a rectory in the diocese of Oxford Value, £153 Patron, the Rev R F Hughes. The church contains, in its external courses some curious figures of acolytes censing, and is in tolerable condition The learned but unfortunate mathematician, Thomas Lydiat, who lived in 1572-1646, was a native of the parish, and for some time its rector

> "If dreams yet flatter once again attend,
> Hear Lydiat's life, and Galileo's end

ALKHAM, a parish in Dover district, Kent 3 miles SW of Ewell r station, and 4 W of Dover Post town Ewell under Dover Acres, 3,200 Real property, £3,567 Pop, 520 Houses, 102 The property is much subdivided A nailbourne here breaks out occasionally with such "store of water as would carry a vessel of considerable burden" The living is a vicarage, united with the vicarage of Capel le-Ferne, in the diocese of Canterbury Value, £152 Patron, the Archbishop of Canterbury The church is partly Norman, partly early English, and in very good condition Reinden House, contiguous to Alkham, is extra parochial.

ALKINGTON, a tything in Berkeley parish, Gloucester, adjacent to the town of Berkeley Pop, 1,010 Houses 221

ALKINGTON, a township in Whitchurch parish, Salop, 1 mile SSW of the town of Whitchurch Pop, 135

ALKMERE See BETTON

ALKMONTON, a township and a chapelry in Longford parish, Derby The township lies 5 miles NNE of Sudbury r station, and 6 S by E of Ashborne Post town, Longford under Derby Pop, 82 Houses, 15 A chapel and an hospital were founded here in 1474, by Lord Mountjoy but are now extinct The present chapelry was constituted in 1849, and is more extensive than the township. Pop 164 Houses, 27 The living is a vicarage in the *diocese of Lichfield* Value, £50 * Patron, W Evans, Esq The church is very good

ALKMUNDBURY See ALCONBURY

ALKRINGTON, a township in Prestwich cum Oldham parish, Lancashire, 1 mile W of Middleton Junction r station, and 4½ N by E of Manchester Acres, 758 Real property £1,957 Pop, 443 Houses 77 The inhabitants are employed chiefly in the neighbouring cotton factories Alkrington Hall is the seat of the Lever family, and is noted for Sir Aston Lever's collecting a museum at it, which was sold in London

ALLALEIGH, a hamlet in Cornworthy parish, Devon 4½ miles SE of Totnes. Pop, 93

ALLAN BANK See GRASMERE

ALLAPTHORPE. See ALLERTHORPE

ALLATHORNE See ALLERTHORNE.

ALLCANNINGS, a tything and a parish in Devizes district, Wilts The tything lies on the Avon canal 2 miles S of Wans Dyke, 4 miles E by N of Devizes r station, and has a post office under Devizes Pop, 602 Houses, 138 The parish contains also the tythings of Allington, Etchilhampton, and Fallaway Acres, 5,483 Real property £8,647 Pop, 1,013 Houses 230 The manor house is a building of the 15th century, now used as a farm house The living is a rectory, and was formerly a prebend, in the diocese of Salisbury Value, £1,100 * Patron, Lord Ashburton The church was partly built in the 17th century Charities, £19

ALLDER. See ALDWORTH

ALLEN (THE), a stream of Cornwall which runs 6 miles southward to the Fal at Truro Also a stream of Dorset, which runs 9 miles southward to the Stour in the vicinity of Wimborne Minster Also a stream of Flint, which runs a short distance underground near Mold and falls into the Dee below Caergwrle Also a stream of Northumberland, which rises, in two head streams E and W on the confines of Durham and Cumberland, and runs 11 miles *northward to the South Tyne*, 3 miles above Haydon Bridge

ALLEN (ST), a parish in Truro district, Cornwall, on the Allen rivulet, 1½ miles N by W of Truro r station Post town, Truro Acres, 3,501 Real property

£2,735 Pop, 687 Houses 133 The property is divided among a few Many of the inhabitants are miners An old edifice, now a farm-house, was the seat of the Bevills An ancient camp, with triple ditch, occurs at Gwarnike The living is a rectory in the diocese of Exeter Value, £174 * Patron, the Bishop of Exeter The church is good

ALLENDALE, a small town, a parish, and a sub district in the district of Hexham, Northumberland The town stands on the Allen rivulet, and on the Allendale railway, 9 miles SW of Hexham It has a post office‡ under Carlisle, and is a polling place A weekly market is held on Friday, and fairs on the Friday after 12 May, and 29 Oct, and 22 Aug —The parish is cut into eight divisions (some of them called grieveships), Allendale town, Catton, Keenty, Broadside, High Forest, Low Forest, Park, and West Allen, and it contains the townships or villages of West Allendale, Catton, Keenty, Broadside with Forest, and Allenheads. Acres, 37,267 Real property, £64,716,—of which £27,373 are in mines Pop, 6,401 Houses, 1,155 Much of the surface is moorish, bleak, hilly and mountainous The property is much subdivided Lead mines are worked to the extent of about 2,500 tons of metal in the year, and there are several smelting houses, with very extensive flues. Coal also is worked, and some silver and rock crystal are found Allenheads, at the sources of the Allen, 7 miles S of the town of Allendale, is in the neighbourhood of the lead mines, and has a post office of its own name under Carlisle An ancient camp occurs at Old Town The living of Allendale is a rectory in the diocese of Durham. Value, £250 * Patron, W B Beaumont, Esq The church was built in 1807 The p curacies of St. Peter, Ninebanks, and West Allen are separate benefices Values, £120, £150,* and £100 Patron of all, W B Beaumont, Esq There are Wesleyan and Primitive Methodist chapels and a free grammar school The Allendale railway was authorized in 1865, joins the Newcastle and Carlisle near Hexham, was opened to Langley in 1867,—to Catton road in 1868, and was to be prolonged to Allenheads —The sub district of Allendale comprises Allendale parish and Haydon chapelry Acres, 50,955 Pop, 8 622 Houses, 1,589

ALLENFORD See LOYD FARM

ALLENHEADS See ALLENDALE

ALLENSMORE, a parish in the district and county of Hereford, near Tram Inn r station, 4 miles SW of Hereford It has a post office under Hereford. Acres, 2 007 Real property, £3,061 Pop, 612 Houses, 156. The property is not much divided The living is a rectory in the diocese of Hereford Value, not reported Patron, the Bishop of Hereford The church is in disrepair There are Wesleyan Methodist and Primitive Methodist chapels Charities, £15

ALLENTON, or ALWINTON, a township and a parish in Rothbury district, Northumberland The township lies on the Coquet river at the influx of the rivulet Allen or Alwin, 13 miles NNW of Scots Gap r station, and 19 WSW of Alnwick Acres, 1,550 Pop, 87 Houses, 18 There were formerly two annual fairs The parish contains also the townships of Farnham, Sharperton, Peals, Clennel, Burrowden, Biddlestone, Linbridge, Fairhaugh, Netherton North Side, and Netherton South Side. Post-town, Harbottle, under Morpeth Acres, 31 940 Real property, £16,869 Pop, 899 Houses, 167 The property, together with that of Holystone, is held chiefly by two proprietors Much of the surface is moor and hill, rising toward the Central Cheviots The living is a vicarage, united to the p curacy of Holystone, in the diocese of Durham Value, £160 * Patron, the Duke of Northumberland The church is early English and cruciform, and was restored in 1853 Charities, £25

ALLEN (WEST) See ALLENDALE

ALLER a hamlet in Hilton parish Dorset, on an affluent of the Trent 8½ miles WSW of Blandford Pop, 91

ALLER, a village and a parish in Langport district Somerset The village stands near the river Parret and the Durston and Yeovil railway, 2½ miles N of Langport, and has a post office under Taunton This is said to be the place where Guthrum and his Danes were baptized after their defeat by Alfred at Edington The parish includes also the tything of Cath Acres, 3,651 Real property £6,454 Pop 518 Houses, 115 The property is much subdivided The living is a rectory in the diocese of Bath and Wells Value, £623 * Patron Emmanuel College, Cambridge The church was restored in 1861 There are an Independent chapel, a national school, and charities £8 Dr Ralph Cudworth, the author of the "Intellectual System of the Universe," was a native, and his father was rector A detachment of Goring's army was defeated, in 1645, on Aller Moor

ALLERBY See OUGHTERSIDE

ALLERDALE, two wards in Cumberland The one is called Allerdale above Derwent, the other Allerdale below-Derwent The former contains Cockermouth and Ravenglass, and is bounded mainly by Bassenthwaite water, Derwent water, Lancashire, and the Irish sea while the latter contains Maryport and Allerby, and extends conterminously with the former from the Irish sea to the E Acres in A above D, 207,579 Pop in 1851, 48,168, in 1861, 65,046 Houses 12,988 Acres in A below D, 155,080 Pop in 1851, 21,730, in 1861 34,841 Houses, 7,208

ALLERFORD, a tything in Selworthy parish, Somerset, 4½ miles W of Minehead It has a post office under Taunton Pop, 181

ALLERSTON, a parish and a sub district in the district of Pickering, N R Yorkshire The parish lies near the river Derwent, 3½ miles ENE of Marishes Road r station, and 4 E by S of Pickering Post-town, Ebberston under York Acres, 10,012 Real property, £4,101 Pop, 413 Houses 82 The property is divided The living is a p curacy annexed to the vicarage of Ebberston, in the diocese of York The sub-district comprises four parishes Acres, 22,018 Pop, 2,526 Houses, 535

ALLERTHORPE, a township and a parish in Pocklington district E R Yorkshire The township lies near the Pocklington canal and the Market-Weighton railway, 2 miles SW of Pocklington Acres 1,565 Real property, £1,949 Pop, 147 Houses, 36 Part of the area is common The parish includes also the township of Waplington Post town, Pocklington under York Acres, 2,355 Real property, £2,125 Pop. 205 Houses, 43 The living is a p. curacy, annexed to the vicarage of Thornton, in the diocese of York Charities, £19 and two houses

ALLERTHORPE, W R Yorkshire See ALVERTHORPE

ALLERTHORPE N R Yorkshire See SWAINBY

ALLERTON, a township with a r station in Childwall parish, Lancashire, 4½ miles SE of Liverpool Acres, 1,531 Real property, £8 361 Pop 559 Houses, 94 Here are Allerton Hall Allerton Priory, the famous Allerton oak, and the ancient monument of Calder stone, supposed to be Druidical Allerton Hall was at one time the seat of Mr Roscoe, author of the "Life of Lorenzo de Medici

ALLERTON a township in Bradford parish, W R. Yorkshire, 3½ miles WNW of Bradford It has a post office under Bradford, and it includes the villages of Allerton Lanes, Fairweather, Green, Upper Green, Lee, Moor House Moor Pikeh, Harrop Edge, and Crosky-Hall Acres, 1,970 Real property, with Wilsden, £11,536,—of which £1,206 are in quarries, and £762 in mines Pop, 2 014 Houses, 433 Most of the inhabitants are employed in manufactories and collieries. A chapelry for Wilsden with Allerton was constituted in 1828 and there are three dissenting chapels

ALLERTON a railway station in W R. Yorkshire, on the Knaresborough railway, 1½ miles ENE of Knaresborough See ALLERTON MAULEVERER

ALLERTON BYWATER, a chapelry in Kippax parish W R Yorkshire, on the Aire navigation, 5 miles NNW of Pontefract. Acres, 870 Real property, £5,271,—of which £3,000 are in mines Pop, 704 The living is a vicarage The church was built in 1866

ALLERTON CHAPEL, a parish in Axbridge district, Somerset, 4 miles N of the Glastonbury railway, and 3 SSW of Axbridge. It has a post-office under Weston super Mare, and contains the hamlets of Arston and Stone Allerton. Acres, 1,160. Real property, with Churchill and Upper Weare, £13,268. Pop., 292. Houses, 59. The property is much subdivided. The living is a rectory in the diocese of Bath and Wells. Value, £223. Patrons, the Dean and Chapter of Wells. The church was restored in 1860.

ALLERTON CHAPEL, or CHAPEL ALLERTON, a chapelry in Leeds parish, W R Yorkshire, 2½ miles N of Leeds. It has a post-office‡ of the name of Chapel Allerton under Leeds, and it contains the hamlets of Moor-Allerton, Gledhow-wood and Allerton Gledhow. Acres, 2,747. Real property, £13,254. Pop., 3,083. Houses, 6?2. The property is much subdivided, and there are many handsome residences. The living is a vicarage in the diocese of Ripon. Value, £361.* Patron, the Vicar of Leeds. The church is in the Corinthian style. There are a Wesleyan chapel and public schools.

ALLERTON GLEDHEW. See preceding article.

ALLERTON MAULEVERER, a township and a parish in Knaresborough district, W R Yorkshire. The township includes Hopperton, and lies on an affluent of the Nidd, at the Allerton r. station, 4½ miles ENE of Knaresborough. Pop., 2?1. Houses, 52. The parish includes also the township of Clareton. Post town, Whixley under York. Acres, 2,800. Real property, £3,63?. Pop., 2?3. Houses, 55. The property is all in one estate. It belonged anciently to the family of Mauleverer, passed to Lord Galloway, and was sold, since 1?5, to successively the Duke of York, Colonel Thornton and Lord Stourton. The mansion on it, the seat of Lord Stourton, is a superb structure, and was called some time Thornville Royal, but now Allerton Mauleverer House. Clare hill, on the estate, is a remarkable eminence. The living is a vicarage in the diocese of Ripon. Value, £63. Patron, Lord Stourton. The church is tolerable. The Roman Catholics have a chapel, a school, and a cemetery. An alien Benedictine priory was founded here in the time of Henry II, and given by Henry VI to King's College, Cambridge.

ALLERTON (NORTH). See NORTHALLERTON.

ALLERTONSHIRE, a wapentake in N R Yorkshire. It contains Northallerton parish, seven other parishes, and parts of three others, and is bounded on the N by the river Tees. Acres, ?3,336. Pop. in 1851, 9,201; in 1861, 9,603. Houses, 2,057.

ALLESLEY, a parish in Meriden district, Warwick, near the Northwestern railway, 2 miles NW of Coventry. It has a post-office under Coventry. Acres, 4,225. Real property, £9,?73. Pop., 971. Houses, 207. The property is much subdivided. The manor belongs to E. A. Neale, Esq. The living is a rectory in the diocese of Worcester. Value, £749.* Patron, the Rev. W. T. Bree. The church was restored and enlarged in 1864. There are an educational establishment called Allesley Park College, an endowed school for boys, a subscription school for girls, and charities £60.

ALLESLEY GATE, a station on the Coventry and Nuneaton railway, 3½ miles N by E of Coventry.

ALLESTREE, a parish in Belper district, Derby, near Derwent river and the Midland railway, 2 miles N of Derby. Post town, Derby. Acres, 990. Real property, £?,6?? Pop., 529. Houses, 106. The property is divided among a few. The chief residences are Allestree Hall and Markeaton. The living is a vicarage in the diocese of Lichfield. Value, £?51.* Patron, not reported. The church is ancient; contains tombs of the Mundys, and is very good. There are a Wesleyan chapel and charities £?.

ALLERTON. See ALLERTON.

ALLHALLOWS, a parish in Wigton district, Cumberland, on the river Ellen, 2 miles SE of Brayton r. station and 7 SW of Wigton. Post town, Aspatria under Carlisle. Acres, 1,?? Real property, £2,19?. Pop., 2?. Houses, ?7. The property includes the manors of Harby, Ukmanby, and Whitthall. Coal, lime, and freestone are worked. The living is a vicarage in the diocese of Carlisle. Value, £90. Patron, the bishop of Carlisle. The church is good.

ALLHALLOWS, or HOO ALLHALLOWS, a parish in Hoo district, Kent, on the Thames, 8½ miles NE of Strood r. station. Post town, Hoo under Rochester. Acres, 5,165, of which 2,705 are water. Real property, £3,089. Pop., 230. Houses, 45. The property is divided among a few. The coast guard station of Yantlet Creek is on the shore. The living is a vicarage in the diocese of Rochester. Value, £247. Patrons, the Dean and Chapter of Rochester. The church is very good.

ALLHALLOWS, Berks. See WALLINGFORD.

ALLHALLOWS, Devon. See EXETER.

ALLHALLOWS, Middlesex. See LONDON.

ALLINGHAM. See THORNHAM.

ALLINGTON, a township in Gresford parish, Denbigh, 3½ miles N of Wrexham. Acres, 3,529. Pop., 5?3. Houses, 130.

ALLINGTON, a parish in Bridport district, Dorset, on the river Brit, and on the Roman road from Old Sarum to Silchester, adjacent to the Bridport railway, ½ a mile N of Bridport. Post town, Bridport. Acres, 5?4. Real property, £5,511. Pop., 1,915. Houses, 376. The property is subdivided. The living is a vicarage in the diocese of Salisbury. Value, £103.* Patron, the Rev. H. Fox. The church is good. There was formerly a lepers hospital founded in 1553. A fair is held on the first Wednesday in Aug.

ALLINGTON, a tything in South Stoneham parish, Hants, near the river Itchin and the Southwestern railway, 5½ miles NE of Southampton. Pop., 475. Houses, 107.

ALLINGTON, a parish in Malling district, Kent, on the river Medway and the Maidstone railway, 1½ mile NNW of Maidstone. Post town, Maidstone. Acres, 612. Real property, £1,495. Pop., 66. Houses, 10. The manor was granted, at the Conquest, to William de Warrene, passed to the family of Allington, to Sir Stephen de Penchester, to the Cobhams, the Brents, and the Wyatts; was the birthplace of Sir Thomas Wyatt the poet and of his son Sir Thomas, who headed the insurrection against Queen Mary; was given, at the confiscation of manors, to Sir John Astley; and passed, in 1720, to the Earl of Romney. A castle was built on it by Warrene, rebuilt by Penchester, extended by the Wyatts, and abandoned to ruin by Astley. Considerable part of the structure still stands, and presents interesting features. The exterior is a long parallelogram with projecting circular towers, and the interior is divided by a range of low building with archway into two distinct courts. A wide moat, fed from the Medway, nearly encircles the pile, and a farm house, of picturesque character, built out of fallen parts of the castle, stands adjacent. Gentle hills mostly covered with wood rise in the vicinity, and irregular mounds, which probably were ornamental features in the once noble park, lie between the castle and the river. Wyatt, the poet, describing his life here, says,—

> "This maketh me at home to hunt and hawk,
> And in foul weather at my book to sit;
> In frost and snow then with my bow to stalk;
> No man doth mark whereto I ride or go;
> In lusty leas at liberty I walk,
> And of these news, I feel nor weal nor woe."

The living is a rectory in the diocese of Canterbury. Value, £145.* Patron, the Earl of Romney. The church is decorated English in very good condition.

ALLINGTON, a tything in Allcannings parish, Wilts, near the Kennet and Avon canal, 4 miles ENE of Devizes. Real property, £1,433. Pop., 159. Houses, 34.

ALLINGTON, a tything in Chippenham parish, Wilts, 2½ miles NW of Chippenham. Real property, £1,743. Pop., 120.

ALLINGTON, a parish in Amesbury district, Wilts, on an affluent of the river Avon, and on the Roman road from Old Sarum to Silchester, 2½ miles NE of Porton r. station and 3¾ ESE of Amesbury. Post town, Salisbury.

Acres, 936 Real property, with Cholderton and Newton Toney, £4,637 Pop., 93 Houses, 20 The living is a rectory in the diocese of Salisbury Value, £270 Patron, the Earl of Craven The church is very good

ALLINGTON (EAST) a parish in Kingsbridge district Devon, 4¾ miles NW of Start bay and 8 SSW of Totnes r station Post town, Blackawton under Totnes Acres, 3,646 Real property, with Blackawton, £11,644 Pop., 521 Houses, 111 The property is divided among a few The parish is a meet for the Slapton harriers The living is a rectory in the diocese of Exeter Value, £510 * Patron, W B Fortescue, Esq The church has a screen, contains monuments of the Fortescue family, and is good

ALLINGTON (EAST and WEST), two parishes in the district of Newark and county of Lincoln, 2½ miles N of Sedgebrook r station, and 4 NW of Grantham They have a post office, of the name of Allington, under Grantham. Acres in both 2,070 Real property, £3,535 Pop of E A, 275 Houses, 64 Pop of W A, 135 Houses, 27 The property is not much divided. Allington House is an edifice in the Tudor style. The livings are in the diocese of Lincoln, and that of E A is a curacy annexed to the rectory of Sedgebrook, while that of W A is a rectory, of the value of £262, in the patronage of the Lord Chancellor The church is very good and there are charities £17

ALLINGTON, or ALVINGTON (EAST), a hamlet in Chivelstone parish, Devon, 5½ miles SE of Kingsbridge

ALLINGTON, or ALVINGTON (WEST), a parish and a sub district in the district of Kingsbridge, Devon The parish lies on the Marlborough creek, 1 mile SW of Kingsbridge, and 9½ S of Kingsbridge Road r station It has a post office, of the name of West Alvington under Kingsbridge, and it contains the hamlets of Woolstone, Easton, Sorley, and Bawcombe, and part of the hamlet of Marlborough. Acres [illegible] 110, of which 270 are water Real property, with Thurlestone and South Milton £13,111 Pop., 925 Houses, 199 The property is much subdivided. Allington manor belonged anciently to the Bastards Garston gardens were famous for producing, on wall trees, oranges and lemons of as fine a quality as any in Portugal The right to a weekly market was granted to West Allington in 1270, but went into disuse. The living is a vicarage united with the curacies of Malborough, South Huish, and South Milton in the diocese of Exeter Value, £888. Patrons, the Dean and Chapter of Salisbury The church has a screen, contains tombs of the Bastards, and is very good The vicarage of [illegible]combe is a separate benefice Charities, £9 —The sub district comprises six parishes. Acres, 15,901 Pop 4,835 Houses, 999

ALLITHWAITE, two townships and a chapelry in Cartmel parish, Lancashire. The townships are Lower and Upper, and lie near Cark r station Acres, 2,360 and 3,710 Real property, £5,142 and £3,123 Pop., 933 and 729 Houses, 190 and 162 The chapelry was formed in 1865 Pop., 480 The living is a p. curacy Value, £150 * Patron, the Bishop of Carlisle

ALLONBY, a seaport village, a chapelry, and a township, in Bromfield parish, Cumberland. The village stands on a wide open bay of its own name opposite R.gg light vessel, 2½ miles N of Bull Gill r station, and 6 NNE of Maryport It has a post office under Maryport and it carries on a fishing trade and is a summer resort for sea-bathing. It was the birthplace of the distinguished hydrographer, Huddart, who died in 1816 The chapelry includes the village Pop in 1851, 749 The living is a p curacy in the diocese of Carlisle Value, £94 * Patron, the Vicar of Bromfield. There are a Quaker's meeting house and a slightly endowed school —The township includes West Newton and bears the name of West Newton and Allonby Acres, 1,794 of which 573 are water Real property, £5,627,—of which £2,423 are in West Newton Pop., 1,002 Houses 2[illegible]2

ALLOSTOCK, a township in Great Budworth parish, Cheshire on an affluent of the river Weaver 5 miles S by W of Knutsford. Acres, [illegible] 92[illegible] Real property, £4 739 Pop., 536 Houses 100

ALLOW (THE), a stream of Durham, running 6 miles northward to the Tyne, in the vicinity of Swalwell Also a stream of Anglesey, running 9 miles south westward to Holyhead bay in the vicinity of Pen y gored

ALLOWENSHAY a hamlet in Kingston parish, Somerset, 2 miles NNW of Ilchester Pop., 219

ALL SAINTS See BRISTOL, CAMBRIDGE CANTERBURY, CHICHESTER, COLCHESTER, DERBY DORCHESTER, EVESHAM, HASTINGS, HEREFORD, HERTFORD, HUNTINGDON, KING'S LYNN, LEICESTER, LEWES, LONDON, MALDON, NEWCASTLE UPON-TYNE, NORTHAMPTON, NORWICH, NORWOOD, OXFORD, SOUTHAMPTON, STAMFORD, SUDBURY, WORCESTER, and YORK

ALLSCOT, a township in Worfield parish, Salop, near the Severn, 2 miles NNE of Bridgnorth

ALLSCOTT, a township in Wrockwardine parish, Salop, on the river Tern, 3¾ miles WNW of Wellington Pop., 94

ALLSOP LE DALE See ALSOP LE DALE

ALLSTONEFIELD, or ALLSTONFIELD, a village, a township, and a parish on the NE border of Staffordshire, contiguous to Derbyshire The village stands on the river Dove, 8 miles NNW of Ashborne r station, and has a post-office under Ashborne The township contains also the hamlet of Stanshope and a work house, and is in the district of Ashborne Acres, 2 700 Real property, £4,438 Pop., 601 Houses, 110 The parish contains also the townships of Heathylee, Quarnford Hollinsclough Longnor, Fairfieldhead, Warslow, and Elkstone in the district of Leek Acres, 21,560 Real property, £19,824 Pop., 4,117 Houses, 917 The property is divided among a few Coal lead ore, and copper are worked Isaac Walton indulged his angling propensities here, with his friend Cotton of Beresford Hall The living is a vicarage in the diocese of Lichfield Value £300 * Patron, Sir John Crewe Bart The church is a beautiful structure in early English style with a pinnacled tower The p curacies of Quarnford, Longnor, Warslow, and Elkstone are separate benefices Charities, £54

ALL STRETTON a township in Church Stretton parish, Salop, 1½ mile N of Church Stretton

ALLT, a township in Berriew parish, Montgomeryshire, 3 miles NW of Montgomery Pop., 17

ALLTGREIG, a hamlet in Llanguick parish, Glamorgan, 5½ miles NW of Neath Pop., 1 078

ALLTGYMBYD, a township in Llanarmon parish, Denbigh, 10 miles WNW of Wrexham Pop., 1[illegible]

ALLTMAWR, a parish in Builth district, Brecon on the river Wye 3½ miles SSE of Builth and 6½ SE of the Central Wales railway Post town Builth Acres 49[illegible] Real property, £272 Pop., 15 Houses, 6 The living is a vicarage in the diocese of St David's Value, £4[illegible] Patron the Vicar of Llanavan Fawr

ALLTON See IDRIDGEHAY

ALLTYGAF, a hamlet in Llangathen parish, Carmarthen, 3½ miles W of Llandeilofawr

ALLWESTON, a hamlet in Folke parish Dorset, 2 miles SE of Sherborne

ALLWINTON See ALWINTON

ALMELEY or ALMERLEY a parish in Weobly district Hereford, on Kington railway, 4½ miles SE of Kington It includes the township of Hopley's Green and Logaston Post town, Weobley Acres, 3,3[illegible] Real property £3 922 Pop., 637 Houses, 140 The property is much subdivided The living is a vicarage in the diocese of Hereford Value, £25[illegible] * Patron the Bishop of Worcester The church is ancient, had once a chantry, and was recently restored

ALMER, a parish in Blandford district Dorset on an affluent of the Stour, 3½ miles S by W of Spettisbury r station and 7 W by S of Wimborne Minster It contains the hamlet of Mapperton Post town, Shapwick under Blandford Acres, 1,161 Real property, £2 686 Pop., 155 Houses, 34 The manor belongs to T S Drax, Esq of Charborough, and much of the surface is included in Charborough Park. The living is a rectory in the diocese of Salisbury Value, £284 * Patron Miss Drax

ALMER-COMBE a tything in Sturminster Marshall parish Dorset, on the river Stour, 4 miles W of Wimborne Minster

ALMEPLFY See ALMELEY

ALMES CLIFF, a gritstone crag 5 miles SW of Harrogate W R Yorkshire It crowns a hill 716 feet high, and commands a brilliant, extensive, panoramic view Numerous hollows are on its summit whether formed naturally or artificially is doubtful, and a fissure, of great length, called the Fairy Parlour is on its west side Another crag, called Little Almes Cliff, 121 feet higher than this is about 3 miles to the NW

ALMHOLME, a hamlet in Bentley parish, W R Yorkshire, near the river Don, 3¼ miles NNE of Doncaster

ALMINGTON, a township in Drayton parish, Stafford, on the river Tern, 1 mile E of Market Drayton

ALMINGTON AND STONY DELPH, a township in Tamworth parish Warwick, on the river Anker, near the Coventry canal and the Midland Counties railway, 2 miles NE of Tamworth Pop., 419 Houses, 85 Almington Hall was formerly the seat of the Clintons, and is now the seat of the Repingtons

ALMODINGTON, a tything in the parishes of Earnley and Siddlesham, Sussex near Pagham harbour, 4¼ miles SSW of Chichester It was formerly a parish, and it contains the ruins of a church

ALMONDBURY, a town, a township, a sub district and a parish in the district of Huddersfield, W R Yorkshire The town stands near the Colne river and the Sheffield railway, 2 miles SE of Huddersfield. It has a post office under Huddersfield, and a fair on Easter-Monday It was anciently called Albanbury It is supposed by some antiquaries to have been the Campodunum of the Romans and it seems certainly to have been a seat of the Kings of Northumbria. An ancient castle crowned an eminence at it, strongly fortified by double walls and trenches, and interiorly disposed in outer and inner courts, and a few traces of this still exist, in an almost vitrified state, proving it to have been destroyed by fire The township includes also the hamlets of Coldmill, Fenny bridge, Castlehillside, Oaks, Newsome, and Thorpe Acres, 2,585 Real property, £22,943 Pop, 10,361 Houses, 2,225 —The sub district comprises the townships of Almondbury and Farnley Tyas Acres, 4,293 Pop, 11,063 Houses, 2,376 The parish, in addition to this sub district, comprises the sub districts of Lockwood, Meltham, and Honley, and part of the sub districts of Slaithwaite and Holmfirth Acres 28,092 Rated property, exclusive of the chapelries of Nether Thong, Armitage Bridge, and Helme, £177,443 Pop in 1841, 37,315, in 1861, 42,889 Houses, 8,884 The property in many parts is much subdivided. A large proportion of the inhabitants are employed in cotton and woollen factories The living is a vicarage in the diocese of Ripon Value, £571 * Patron, Sir J W Ramsden, Bart The church is in the perpendicular English style The chapelries of Honley Meltham Marsden, Linthwaite, Lockwood Crossland, Nether Thong Upper-Thong, Holme Bridge, Farnley Tyas, Meltham Mills, Milns Bridge, Armitage Bridge, Rash lift Wilshaw, and Helme, are all within the parish, and there are various chapels for Independents, Baptists, and Methodists A free grammar school was founded in the time of James I and has £73 a year from endowment, and other charities have £348

ALMONDINGTON See ALMODINGTON

ALMONDSBURY, a village, a parish, and a sub district in the district of Thornbury Gloucester The village stands near the rivulet Boyd, at the foot of a ridge of limestone rocks, 1¾ mile from the Bristol and South Wales railway, 8 miles N of Bristol, and has a post office under Bristol It is said to have derived its name from Alemond, King Egbert's father who was buried in the church, and from a fortification in the neighbourhood The heights above it and the grounds of Knole House adjacent on the SW, command a very noble and extensive view, embracing the estuary of the Severn and the hills of Monmouth and Wales —The parish includes the tythings of Almondsbury Lea, Over, Gaunts Eartheote, Lower Tockington, and Hempton and Patchway Acres, 6,927 Real property, £15,073 Pop, 1,864 Houses 394 The property is much subdivided. Some lands belonged anciently to the priory of St Augustine in Bristol The living is a vicarage in the diocese of Gloucester and Bristol Value, £915 Patron, the Bishop of Gloucester and Bristol The church is cruciform and early English, with tower and spire at the intersection There are a neat little chapel of ease at Cross Keys, two dissenting chapels, a national school, and charities £255 —The sub-district comprises six parishes. Acres, 23,087 Pop, 5,233 Houses, 1,084

ALMPTON See OMPTON

ALMSFORD, or ANSFORD, a parish in Wincanton district, Somerset, adjacent to Castlecary, the river Brue, and the East Somerset railway Post town Castlecary Acres, 844 Real property, returned with contiguous parishes. Rated property, £1,828 Pop, 306 Houses, 69 The property is much subdivided The living is a rectory in the diocese of Bath and Wells Value, £297 * Patron, J Woodford, Esq The church was restored in 1861, at a cost of about £1,000

ALMWYCH See AMLWCH

ALNE (THE), a river of Northumberland It rises a little west of Alnham, and runs about 16 miles eastward, past Whittingham, Hulme abbey, and Alnwick, to the sea at Alnmouth It is a fine fishing stream

ALNE (THE), a river of Warwick It rises near Beardmore, and runs 15 miles southward past Great Alne and Alcester, to the Avon at Salford Priors It is joined by the Arrow at Alcester

ALNE, a township and a parish in Easingwold district, N R Yorkshire The township lies on an affluent of the Ouse, and on the Northeastern railway, 11½ miles NW by N of York, and it has a station on the railway, and a post office under Easingwold Acres 2,240 Real property £2,428. Pop, 453. Houses, 99 The parish includes also the townships of Youlton, Aldwark, Tollerton, Flawith, and Tholthorpe Acres 9,947 Real property, £12,424 Pop 1,592 Houses 333 The property is much subdivided A chief residence is Alne House The living is a vicarage in the diocese of York and includes the curacy of Aldwark Value, £215 * Patron, Sir C Codrington The church is Norman and has a carved oaken pulpit a Norman font a piscina and a recumbent alabaster effigies. There are a Wesleyan chapel and charities £47

ALNE (GREAT), a parish in Alcester district, Warwick, on the river Alne, 5 miles W by S of Bearley r station, and 6½ NW of Stratford on Avon It has a post-office under Birmingham Acres, 1,753 Real property, £3,028 Pop, 347 Houses 89 The property is subdivided The living is a p curacy annexed to the rectory of Kinwarton, in the diocese of Worcester The church is good Charities, £28.

ALNE (LITTLE), a hamlet in Aston Cantlow parish, Warwick, on the river Alne, 2 miles NE of Great Alne Pop., 80

ALNESBOURNE PRIORY, a depopulated hamlet in Nacton parish Suffolk; near the river Orwell, 4½ miles SE of Ipswich A small Augustinian priory anciently stood here and was annexed, in the 13th century, to the monastery of Woodbridge

ALNEY (ISLE OF) an islet in the Severn, in the vicinity of Gloucester Edmund Ironsides and Canute fought a single combat here in 1016, and proving equal in the strife, concluded a peace, and agreed to divide the kingdom between them

ALNHAM, a township and a parish in Rothbury district, Northumberland The township lies near the source of Alne river under the southern offsets of the Cheviots, 13 miles W of Alnwick r station, and has a post office under Alnwick Acres, 9,535 Pop, 119 Houses, 22 The parish includes also the townships of Prendwick Unthank and Screnwood Acres, 12,859 Real property, £1,320 Pop 295 Houses 47 The property is divided among a few Much of the surface is moor and mountain A semicircular ancient camp,

300 feet in diameter, with encircling double rampart and deep trench, occurs on a hill about a mile W of the village The living is a vicarage in the diocese of Durham. Value, £200 * Patron, the Duke of Northumberland The church is cruciform and old The parsonage was built in the time of Edward III, and restored in 1814, and includes a peel tower

ALNMOUTH, or ALEMOUTH, a seaport village, and a township chapelry in Lesbury parish, Northumberland The village stands on a small bay at the mouth of the river Alne, 2 miles E of Bilton r station, and 5 ESE of Alnwick, has a post office under Alnwick, and is a sub port to Berwick Its harbour admits vessels of from 50 to 150 tons, and is used chiefly for coasting trade A chapel anciently stood adjacent on an eminence at the shore, and a burying ground connected with it was in use till about the year 1815, but has been washed away by the sea Horses' bones were once found here, and gave rise to a foolish belief that the neighbouring country was formerly peopled by giants —The chapelry includes the village, and was recently re constituted Acres, 579 Pop., 452 Houses 100 The living is a p cu racy in the diocese of Durham Value, £100 Patron, the Duke of Northumberland The church was built in 1860, and there is a Wesleyan chapel

ALNWICK, a town, a castle, two townships, a parish, a sub district, and a district, in Northumberland. The town stands on the river Alne, at the terminus of a branch railway of 3 miles from the Bilton Junction of the Northeastern, 34 miles by road, and 38½ by railway, N by W of Newcastle on Tyne Its name signifies "the town on Alne" The town probably dates from the time of the Romans, or, at least, grew up as a dependency of a strong baronial mansion, the original castle, in the time of the Saxons The barony belonged to William Tyson, who fell at the battle of Hastings, it was given by the Conqueror to Ivo de Vesco, the ancestor of the De Vescis, and it passed, in 1310, to the family of Percy, the ancestors of the Dukes of Northumberland Malcolm III of Scotland besieged the town in 1093, and was killed before its walls in 1098 David of Scotland captured it in 1135 William the Lion besieged it in 1174, but was surprised by Ralph de Glanville, and taken prisoner to London King John burnt it in 1215 Gualo, the Pope's legate, convoked a meeting of the Scottish bishops at it in 1220 Robert Bruce's nobles, Douglas and Randolph, besieged it without success in 1328 Additional fortifications of both the town and the castle were made in 1411 The Scots took the town and burnt it in 1448, in revenge for the burning of Dumfries The Earl of Warwick laid siege to the castle in 1463, after the battle of Hexham, and Sir George Douglas, with a considerable force, came to its relief, and enabled its garrison to retire unmolested

The town stands chiefly on a declivity on the south bank of the Alne It is well laid out, and has a spacious market place in the centre The streets are wide and well paved The houses are chiefly modern, mostly built of freestone, many of them of considerable elegance Four gates formerly pierced the town walls, and one of them, Bondgate, is still standing, and gives name to a street A handsome stone bridge of three arches, erected by the Duke of Northumberland, takes the highway over the Alne The town hall, on one side of the market-place, is a large edifice, surmounted by a square tower Another building, on another side, is a modern structure, disposed below in meat and fish market, and containing above an elegant assembly room and a spacious reading room The corn exchange was opened in 1862. The prison contains accommodation for 12 male and 6 female prisoners The parish church is a large edifice, of the 14th century, with richly groined chancel and carved stalls, and was restored by the fourth Duke of Northumberland, at a cost of £6,000 St Paul's church was built in 1846, at a cost of £20 000, is a handsome edifice, in the decorated English style, has a memorial window to the third Duke of Northumberland, produced at Munich in 1856, and contains an effigies of the Duke in Caen stone by Carew The English Presbyterians or Free Churchmen the United Presbyterians, the Independents, the Wesleyan Methodists, the New Connexion Methodists, the Unitarians, and the Roman Catholics have places of worship, and there are a mechanics institute a dispensary and infirmary, two endowed schools with £22 a year, and other charities with £37

Alnwick claims to be a borough by prescription, and is governed by four chamberlains and 24 common council men It is a seat of quarter sessions, and a polling place, and has a head post office,‡ a telegraph station, four hotels, and an office of the Alnwick and county bank. A weekly market is held on Saturday, and fairs are held on Palm Sunday Eve, 12 May the last Monday in July, the first Tuesday in Oct., 28 Oct, and the Saturday before 25 Dec Trade in corn and cattle is extensive, tanning and brewing are carried on, and brick works, limestone quarries, and building stone quarries are in the neighbourhood. Two monthly newspapers are published Earl Beverley, who became fifth Duke of Northumberland in 1865, is Baron Alnwick The friar Martin of Alnwick and the Bishop William of Alnwick were natives. Pop, 5,670 Houses, 837

Alnwick Abbey, beautifully situated on the north bank of the Alne, was the first house of the Premonstratensian canons in England It was founded in 1147 by Eustace Fitz John, and dedicated to the Virgin, and, at the dissolution of monasteries, it had about 13 canons, and was valued at £190 It became the seat of successively the Brandlings and the Doubledays, and then was sold to the Duke of Northumberland. A gateway tower of it still stands, and has armorial shields of the Percys, crosses, and a niche richly canopied with open Gothic work

Alnwick Castle, the seat of the Duke of Northumberland, situated on an eminence on the south side of the Alne, is a most imposing pile. It retains some vestiges of Saxon architecture, but probably none of the original castle, and, after having passed almost to ruin by the shocks of war and the wear of time, it was reconstructed and embellished, at a modern period, in the Gothic style, and has just been undergoing extensive renovations, partly in a very fine light tinted stone, after designs by the Commendatore Canina of Rome It consists mainly of freestone or moorstone, covers or encloses about five acres, is disposed in three courts, exhibits sixteen towers and turrets, and is altogether a most noble and magnificent specimen of a great baronial seat A notice of it in 1860 said,—"The new grand staircase forms the approach to the vestibule, in which the recesses will be filled with illustrations of the ballad of Chevy Chase The ceiling will be painted with a subject from English history Stettin damask hangings line the walls of the domestic apartments. The drawing room has a ceiling of carved wood, gilt and coloured The dining room, 60 feet by 24, stands on the site of the old banqueting hall The foundation stone of the Prudhoe tower was laid on 25 Nov 1854 It now rises 20 feet above the cluster of towers, breaks the hitherto long uniform sky line, and forms a fine bold feature in the landscape In the SW front is a deeply recessed triple-corbelled window The high roofed chapel, early English, has a stone vault and an apsidal west end and will be furnished with marbles and mosaics from Rome It contains a tomb to the Duchess Elizabeth, daughter of Algernon, Duke of Somerset In the state apartments are exquisite carvings by Bulletti, copies by Nucci, of slaves from Constantine's Arch and the Greek Canephora and colossal friezes by Mantovani, inlaid wood pure white marbles and carved walnut panels contribute to the magnificence of these rooms A vaulted kitchen has been built on the SE side, which rivals a mediæval structure of the sort The octagonal Donjon tower contains a square dungeon, 11 feet by 9¾" The grounds connected with the castle lie along both sides of the Alne, are upwards of 3 miles long exhibit great wealth and variety of both natural and artificial beauty, and contain the remains of Alnwick and Hulne abbeys, a picturesque cross on the spot where King Malcolm of Scotland fell, a monument on the spot where William the Lion was taken prisoner, and the tower of Brislee, 66 feet high, erected in 1782, and commanding a superb extensive view

The two townships of Alnwick are Alnwick and Alnwick South Side —The former comprises 4 604 acres, the latter, 4 760 and the latter includes the hamlets of Canledge Park Greenshell, Grimwells Park Hobberlaw, Pugley Shieldykes, and Snipe House Pop of A township 5,958 Houses, 876 Pop of A S S township, 203. Houses, 53 —The parish includes also the townships of Abbey Lands, Canongate, Denwick, and Hulme Park. Acres, 16,250 Real property, £31 183 Pop., 7,350 Houses, 1,110 The living is a vicarage in the diocese of Durham Value, £175 * Patron, the Duke of Northumberland. The chapelry of St Paul's was constituted in 1846, and is a perpet curacy, with salary of £200, in the patronage of the Duke of Northumberland.—The sub district differs only so far from the parish as to include a small additional township Acres, 16 184 Pop , 7 359 Houses, 1,112

The district of Alnwick comprehends the sub district of Warkworth, containing the parishes of Lesbury and Shilbottle and parts of the parishes of Warkworth and Felton, the sub district of Alnwick, containing the parish of Alnwick and a township of the parish of Eglingham and the sub district of Embleton, containing the parishes of Embleton, Howick, Long Houghton, and Edlingham, and parts of the parishes of Whittingham, Eglingham and Ellingham Acres, 98,935 Poor rates in 1866 £9 850 Pop in 1841, 18,799 in 1861, 21,053 Houses, 3,800 Marriages in 1866, 90, births, 595 — of which 60 were illegitimate deaths, 355,—of which 92 were at ages under 5 years, and 15 at ages above 85 Marriages in the ten years 1851-60, 907, births, 6,359 deaths 3,910 The places of worship in 1851 were 13 of the Church of England, with 4 375 sittings, 3 of the United Presbyterian Church with 1 248 s , 2 of the Presbyterian church in England with 1,158 s , 2 of Independents with 1,080 s , 1 of Unitarians, with 210 s 7 of Wesleyan Methodists, with 1 339 s , 2 of the New Connexion Methodists with 370 s , and 2 of Roman Catholics with 350 s The schools in 1851 were 33 public day schools, with 2,488 scholars 22 private day schools, with 590 s , 37 Sunday schools with 2,512 s , and 4 evening schools for adults, with 36 s

ALOESBRIDGE a hundred in the lathe of Shepway, Kent It adjoins Romney marsh the English channel, and Sussex, and contains Brookland, Fairfield, Snargate, and Stone parishes, and part of Ivychurch Acres, 7,923 Pop in 1851, 802 Houses, 168

ALPERTON, a hamlet in the parish of Harrow on the Hill, Middlesex near the river Brent, the Paddington canal and the Northwestern railway 8 miles WNW of St Paul's, London It has a post office under Ealing, London W Pop , 212

ALPHAGE (St) See CANTERBURY

ALPHAMSTONE a parish in Sudbury district, Essex, near the river Stour 2½ miles WNW of Bures r station and 5 S of Sudbury Post town Bures under Colchester Acres, 1,557 Real property £2 61 Pop , 317 Houses 72 The property is divided among a few The living is a rectory in the diocese of Rochester Value, £207 * Patron, the Lord Chancellor The church is tolerable Charities, £13

ALPHETON, a parish in Sudbury district, Suffolk, on an affluent of the river Stour, 7 miles N of Sudbury r station Post town Lavenham under Sudbury Acres, 1 292 Real property, £1 911 Pop 298 Houses, 69 The property is not much divided The parish is a meet for the Suffolk hounds The living is a rectory in the diocese of Ely Value, £275 Patron, the Rev W J Aislabie The church is tolerable

ALPHINGTON, a village, a parish, and a sub district in the district of St Thomas Devon The village stands near the South Devon railway and the river Exe, 1½ miles S of Exeter, and has a post office under Exeter, and fairs on the Wednesday after 20 June and after 29 Sept It was one of the head quarters of Fairfax's army, 1646 at the blockading of Exeter —The parish comprises 2,471 acres Real property, £8,598 Pop , 1,250 Houses, 270 The property is divided among a few The manor was acquired, in the reign of Richard II , by the family of the Earl of Devon , and the greater part of it continues still in their possession The living is a rectory in the diocese of Exeter Value £937 * Patron, the Rev F A Savile The church contains a Norman font with interlaced arches, scroll ornaments, and grotesque figures over the arches , has a red turretted tower in perpendicular English and, excepting the south wall is in good condition Charities £20, and some poors' cottages.—The sub district comprises seven entire parishes and parts of two others Acres. 17,470 Pop , 4,097 Houses, 844

ALPINGTON a parish in Loddon district, Norfolk , 4 miles E of Swainsthorpe r station, and 6 SE of Norwich Post town, Rockland under Norwich Acres, 630 Real property, £1,285 Pop , 208 Houses, 47 A chief residence is Alpington Hall The living is a rectory, annexed to Yelverton, in the diocese of Norwich

ALPRAHAM, a township in Bunbury parish, Cheshire, near the Chester canal, 2 miles N of Calverley r station, and 3½ ESE of Tarporley It has a post office under Tarporley Acres, 1,596. Real property, £2 691 Pop., 530. Houses, 99 There is a Wesleyan chapel

ALRESFORD a parish in Tendring district, Essex , 5 miles SE of Colchester It has a post office under Colchester, and a r station Acres, 1,583, of which 75 are water Real property, £2,195 Pop , 248 Houses 62 The property is divided among a few The living is a rectory in the diocese of Rochester Value, £378 * Patrons, Hulme's Trustees The church is good

ALRESFORD, or NEW ALRESFORD a small town, a parish, a sub district and a district in Hants The town stands along a hill contiguous to the Arle river, with a st on the Alton and Winchester railway 7 miles ENE of Winchester The tract around it was given by Kynewald second Christian king of Wessex, to the church of Winchester, and was thenceforth much controlled by the bishops The town seems to have been soon formed by them, and, falling into decay was restored in the time of King John, by Bishop Godfrey de Lucy A pond was then excavated adjacent to it along the course of the Itchen, 1½ mile in length and about 200 acres in area with the view of bringing up navigation hither from the sea , but failed eventually to serve the purpose and is now reduced to about 60 acres The embankment on the north side, to the extent of nearly 500 yards, is said to have been originally a Roman causeway The town was incorporated at an early period, and is said to have sent a member to parliament in the time of Edward I , and it had at one time a considerable cloth manufacture and many fulling mills , but it is now merely a marketing centre for country produce with right to some rents and tolls It was burned by the royalist troops in 1644, and again suffered severely from fire in 1689 and in 1736 It has a head post office,‡ two banks, a market house of 1866 a weekly market on Thursday, and fairs on Holy Thursday, the last Thursday in July, the first Thursday in Sept , 17 Oct , and the last Thursday in Nov Mrs. Mitford, the author of "Our Village, was a native Many silver coins of the reign of William I were found in 1833, in a leaden box, in a neighbouring field The Alton and Winchester railway, opened in 1865 passes close to the town, and gives ready access to London and Southampton The parish comprises 683 acres. Real property, £5 411 Pop 1,546 Houses, 274 The property is subdivided The living is a rectory in the diocese of Winchester Value, £240 * Patron the Bishop of Winchester The church was built in 1690 and has a square embattled tower There are an Independent chapel a free grammar school, with £149 a year and other charities with nearly £40

The sub district contains the parishes of New Alresford, Old Alresford, Ovington, Itchen Stoke, Bighton, Swarraton Northington Brown Candover, and Chilton Candover and the extra parochial tract of Godsfield Acres 16 019 Pop , 3 674 Houses 679 The district includes also the sub district of Ropley containing the parishes of Ropley, West Tisted, Bramdean, Hinton Ampner, Kilmiston, Beauworth, Cheriton, Titchborne, and Bishops-Sutton Acres, 39,761 Poor rates in 1866, £5,176 Pop in 1841, 7,094, in 1861, 7,182 Houses, 1,407 Marriages in 1866, 40, births, 221,—of which 11 were illegitimate, deaths, 118,—of which 39 were at ages under 5 years, and 8 at ages above 85 Marriages in the ten years 1851-60, 433, births, 2,107, deaths, 1,190 The places of worship in 1851 were 18 of the Church of England, with 3,973 sittings, 2 of Independents, with 290 s, 1 of Baptists, with 40 s, 2 of Primitive Methodists, with 130 s, and 1 of Roman Catholics, with 70 s The schools in 1851 were 16 public day schools, with 917 scholars 13 private day schools, with 243 s, 14 Sunday schools, with 780 s, and 1 evening school for adults with 22 s The workhouse is in Alresford

ALRESFORD (OLD), a parish in Alresford district, Hants, adjoining the W side of Alresford parish Post town, Alresford Acres, 3,618 Real property, £4,314 Pop, 526 Houses 99 The property is divided among a few Old Alresford House belongs to Lord Rodney, and was the residence of his ancestor, the Admiral The living is a rectory in the diocese of Winchester Value, £556 * Patron the Bishop of Winchester The church was built in 1753, but has an ancient tower

ALREWAS, a village and a parish in Lichfield district, Stafford The village stands on the Grand Trunk canal, near the South Stafford railway, the river Trent, the river Tame, and Ryknield street, 5 miles NE of Lichfield. It has a station on the railway ¾ of a mile distant, a post office under Lichfield ‡ and an inn Pop., 1 125 Houses 264 The parish includes also the townships of Orgreave and Fradley Acres, 4,329 Real property, £11 237 Pop, 1,633 Houses, 379 The property is divided among a few The manor was given to Lichfield cathedral in 822 The living is a vicarage in the diocese of Lichfield. Value, £328 Patron, the Bishop of Lichfield The church is good There are chapels for Wesleyan and Primitive Methodists Charities, £26

ALREWAS HAYS, an extra parochial tract in Lichfield district, Stafford, contiguous to Alrewas parish It was formerly a common, but has been reclaimed Acres, 1,689 Real property, £1,356 Pop, 48 Houses, 10

ALSAGER, a chapelry in Barthomley parish, Cheshire, near the river Wenlock, the Grand Trunk canal, and the North Stafford railway, 4½ miles SSE of Sandbach It has a station on the railway, about a mile distant, and its post town is Lawton, under Stoke on Trent Acres, 2,184 Real property, £4,202 Pop, 703 Houses, 139 Part of the land was a common recently enclosed The living is a p curacy in the diocese of Chester Value, £100 Patrons, the proprietors of the manor There is a Wesleyan chapel of 1809 Charities, £41

ALSCOTT See ALVERDISCOTT

ALSOP LE DALE AND EATON, a chapelry in Ashborne parish, Derby, near the river Dove, 6 miles N by W of Ashborne r station Post town, Parwich under Ashborne Acres, with Newton Grange hamlet, 2,264 Rated property, £1,568. Pop, 76 Houses, 12 The property is not much divided The living is a p curacy in the diocese of Lichfield. Value £49 Patrons, the Inhabitants and Freeholders The church is good

ALSTOE, a hundred in Rutland It adjoins the counties of Leicester and Lincoln, and contains twelve parishes. Acres, 27,202 Pop, 4,296 Houses 930

ALSTON, a township and a sub district, in the district of Preston, Lancashire The township is in the parish of Ribchester, and lies adjacent to Longridge railway, near Longridgefell, 2 miles N of the river Ribble 7 miles NE of Preston Acres, 1,989 Real property, £[illegible],268 Pop 1,098 Houses 213 A chief residence is Alston Lodge —The sub district comprises all the parish of Ribchester and part of the parish of Preston Acres, 11 773 Pop, 4 414 Houses, 850

ALSTON, a town, a parish, a sub district, and a district, in Cumberland The parish is also designated Alston Moor The town stands on the South Tyne river, a little W of Middlefell, not far from the boundaries with Northumberland, Durham, and Westmoreland, at the terminus of a branch railway of 13 miles from the Haltwhistle station of the Carlisle and Newcastle railway, 26 miles by road and 35 by railway, ESE of Carlisle Its site is a declivity, near the influx of the Nent to the South Tyne, amid a region of high, moorish uplands, and its appearance is relieved and beautified by the vales of the streams and by the neighbourhood of woods Its houses are irregular, but consist chiefly of stone The chief public buildings are a new town hall, the parish church, several dissenting chapels a grammar school, a workhouse, and a stone bridge The chief employments are connected with a woollen factory and an extensive mineral traffic A weekly market is held on Saturday, and fairs on the third Saturday of March, the last Thursday of May, 27 Sept and the first Thursday of Nov The town has a post-office‡ under Carlisle, a telegraph station a banking office, and two hotels, and it is a seat of petty sessions and a polling place

The parish includes also the chapelries of Garrigill and Nenthead Acres, 35,060 Real property, £12,573,—of which £4,243 are in mines Pop, 6,404 Houses, 1,282 Much of the property belonged to the Earls of Derwentwater, and, after the attainder and execution of the last earl, was given to Greenwich hospital The land is chiefly moor and mountain, either utterly sterile or grazed by sheep, but the rocks abound with rich ores, and the hills in some parts are pierced with spar caves Lead mines began to be worked in the time of Henry III, they became greatly extended about 1688, they increased to 119 in 1768, with an annual produce of about 167,544 cwt, and they then began to decrease, but still amounted to 102 in 1814, with an annual produce of about 91,968 cwt An aqueduct level, 5 miles in length, called Nent Force, was cut from the Nenthead mines to the town for carrying off the water The lead ore generally contains so much silver as to yield from 8 to 10 ounces per ton, and that of Yadmoss mine, opened in 1829, has yielded 96 ounces per ton Copper ore has been found in the same mines as the lead Some of the caves in the hills make both a beautiful and an opulent display of minerals, and one, called Tutman s Hole, has been explored to the extent of a mile from the entrance Traces of the Roman Maiden way are seen about a mile W of the town, and remains of Whitley castle, consisting of earthworks, substructions, and a moat, occur on Hall Hill The living is a vicarage in the diocese of Durham, and includes the curacy of Garrigill Value, £210 * Patron, Greenwich hospital The chapelry of Nenthead is a separate benefice The grammar school in the town has £40 a year from endowment, and other charities have £65

The sub district and the district of Alston are co extensive with the parish Poor-rates in 1866, £1,8[illegible]8 Marriages in 1866, 31, births, 214,—of which 28 were illegitimate, deaths, 114 —of which 34 were at ages under 5 years, and 2 at ages above 85 years Marriages in the ten years 1851-60, 336, births 2,294, deaths, 1 315 The places of worship in 1851 were 3 of the Church of England, with 1 090 sittings 2 of Independents, with 520 s, 1 of Quakers, with 200 s, 8 of Wesleyan Methodists, with 1,801 s, and 5 of Primitive Methodists, with 1,118 s The schools in 1851 were 10 public day schools, with 910 scholars, 5 private day schools, with 117 s, 13 Sunday schools, with 1,393 s, and 2 evening schools for adults with 39 s

ALSTONE, a chapelry in Overbury parish, Gloucester, 3½ miles ESE of Tewkesbury r station, and 4½ NW of Winchcomb Post town, Tewkesbury Acres, with Little Washbourne, 1,060 Rated property, £610 Pop, 90 Houses, 20 The property is divided among a few The living is a curacy, united to the vicarage of Overbury, in the diocese of Worcester The church is very dilapidated

ALSTONE, a hamlet in Gnosall parish, Staffordshire, 5½ miles SW of Stafford

ALSTONE, Cheltenham See CHELTENHAM

ALSTONFIELD See ALSTONEFIELD

ALT (THE), a small river of Lancashire It rises near Knowsley Park a little W of Prescot and runs about 12 miles north westward to the Irish sea, in the vicinity of Formby

ALT, ALT EDGE and ALT HILL, three hamlets in the Knott Lanes sub district of the parish of Ashton under Lyne, Lancashire

ALTARNUN See ALTERNON

ALTBACH, a township in Heathland parish, Hereford, 4½ miles NW of Ross

ALTCAR a parish in Ormskirk district, Lancashire on the river Alt 3 miles SE of Formby r station and 6 WSW of Ormskirk. It includes the hamlet of Little Altcar Post town, Formby under Liverpool Acres, 4 284 of which 205 are water Real property, £5,988 Pop, 540 Houses, 82. The property is divided among a few The surface includes some marsh. The living is a vicarage in the diocese of Chester Value, £150 * Patron, the Earl of Sefton. The church is very good Charities £7

ALT EDGE See ALT

ALTERNON, or ALTARNUN, a parish and a sub district in the district of Launceston, Cornwall The parish lies round the head streams of the rivers Inny and Lynher 8 miles WSW of Launceston, and 12 N of Doublebois r station It has a post office under Launceston Acres, 15,014 Real property, £6 272 Pop, 1,389 Houses, 279 The property is much subdivided. Much of the land is very poor or barren The minerals include granite, hornblende, and stream tin The living is a vicarage in the diocese of Exeter Value, £320 * Patrons, the Dean and Chapter of Exeter The church is a fine building and has the highest tower in Cornwall, except that of Probus St. Nunn, the mother of St David of Wales is said to have been buried here and Isbell the clerk in the time of Charles II, died at the age of 150 There are chapels for Wesleyan Methodists and Bible Christians Charities, £6 The sub district comprises 4 parishes Acres, 22,499 Pop, 2 406 Houses, 501

ALTHAM, a township chapelry in Whalley parish Lancashire, on the Henburn river, near the Leeds and Liverpool canal, 1 mile N of Huncoat r station, and 5 W of Burnley It includes the village of Sykeside, and its post town is Accrington Acres, 1,406 Real property, £2 580 Pop, 410 Houses, 75 The property is not much divided The living is a vicarage in the diocese of Manchester Value, £150 * Patron R T R Walton, Esq The church was almost entirely rebuilt in 1859

ALT HILL See ALT

ALTHORNE, a parish in Maldon district, Essex, near the river Crouch, 7 miles SE of Maldon r station It has a post office under Maldon Acres, 2,230 Real property, £2 607 Pop 386 Houses 79 The property is subdivided Much of the land lies lower than spring tide mark and is protected by embankments constructed by Dutchmen, whose descendants remain here The living is a vicarage united to the rectory of Creeksea in the diocese of Rochester The church is good A f[illegible] held on 5 June

ALTHORP an extra parochial tract in Brixworth district Northamptonshire contiguous to [illegible] parish, 6 miles NW of Northampton Pop 75 Houses 10 It gives the title of Viscount to Earl Spencer, and Althorp Park here is the Earl's seat "The domain of Althorp says Dibdin "has been possessed by the Spencer family upwards of three centuries, but the exact period of the erection of the house seems to be unknown There is however, no question of its having received its principal improvements during the time of the first Earl of Sunderland (1636–1643), who was the son of the second baron Spencer The lady of this earl (daughter of Robert Sidney second earl of Leicester and better known as the Sacharissa of Waller the poet) erected and covered in the great staircase, which had been formerly an interior courtyard, in the fashion of the times From this period to the present, both the house and park have continued to receive improvements The family of the Spencers became possessed of the park at Althorp about the year 1512 This originated in a license from the king to John Spencer, afterwards Sir John Spencer At that time the park is described as containing 300 acres of land, 100 acres of wood, and 40 acres of water in 'Oldthorpe' but this seems to have been only an extension of some property previously acquired there for it is certain that Althorp, so called, was purchased by this Sir John Spencer as early as the year 1508" The great attraction of Althorp House is its noble library, which Dibdin says is the finest collection of books perhaps in Europe. "It occupies a suite of rooms, four in number, and measuring in the whole about 170 feet in length. These are garnished from top to toe with the choicest copies of the choicest editions of the choicest authors in the choicest bindings." The collection of pictures also is very rich. The queen and son of James I, when on their journey from Scotland to London in 1603 rested some days at Althorp, and a mask, composed by Ben Jonson, was exhibited for their entertainment

ALTHORPE, a township and a parish in the district of Thorne and county of Lincoln The township lies on the river Trent, and on the Doncaster, Barnetby, and Grimsby railway, 4½ miles SE of Crowle, enjoys advantages of the Trent navigation, includes the hamlet of Derrythorpe, and has a post office under Bawtry, and a r station Real property, £3 098 Pop, 324 Houses, 88 The parish includes also the townships of Keadby and Amcotts Acres, 5,460 Rated property, £10 346 Pop, 1 316 Houses, 243 The property is much subdivided The living is a rectory in the diocese of Lincoln Value, £407 * Patron, the Crown The church is of the time of Edward IV There are two Methodist chapels and a national school

ALTHORPE, Norfolk. See ALETHORPE.

ALTOFTS, a township in Normanton parish W R Yorkshire, on the North Midland railway, at its transit over the Calder river and the Aire and Calder canal, about a mile from Normanton station 3½ miles NE of Wakefield It has a post office under Normanton Acres, 1,701 Pop, 1,210 Houses 224

ALTON a small town, a parish, a sub district, a district, and a division, in Hants The town stands on the Guildford, Farnham and Winchester line of the South-western railway 8¾ miles SW by S of Farnham, and has a railway station with telegraph It dates from the time of the Saxons, was the scene of a meeting in 1001 with the Danes, sent a member to parliament in the time of Edward I, and was taken, in 1643, by the parliamentarian force of Sir William Waller from the royalist force of Colonel Boles. It consists chiefly of one long steep street, and contains some handsome houses It is a seat of petty sessions and a polling place, and it has a head post office,‡ two banking offices, and a hotel It formerly had a considerable manufactory of bombazines, and it afterwards had manufactures of silk, druggets serges and other fabrics, and it now has extensive breweries of much note and a large paper mill A weekly market is held on Tuesday and fairs on the Saturday before 1 May, 11 July, and 29 Sept The market house was recently enlarged, and other aids to the market effected The parish church is a spacious edifice variously Saxon, Norman, and later English, with square embattled tower and spire, and contains some wall paintings of the 15th century There are chapels for Independents, Wesleyan Methodists, and Quakers. A popular adage makes the town noted for its Quakers and Pennard Bolton has embalmed them in his verse The Dominican friar, William de Alton, in the time of Edward II the biographical author John Pits, born in 1560, and the botanical writer William Curtis born in 1746, were natives Pop, 3,286 Houses, 616 The railway from Alton past Alresford, to Headbourne-Worthy near Winchester was formed under an act of 1860

The parish comprises 3,896 acres Real property £17,293 Pop 3,769 Houses 710 The property is much subdivided A chief residence is The Alton Grange

Hops are extensively grown The living is a vicarage in the diocese of Winchester, and, till 1863, had annexed to it the living of Holybourne Value, £496 * Patrons, the Dean and Chapter of Winchester There are a grammar school with £81 a year from endowment, other charities with £22, a mechanics' institute, and a lunatic asylum —The sub district contains the parishes of Alton Wield, Medsted, Bentworth, Lasham, Shalden, East Tisted, Chawton, Farringdon, and Newton Valence. Acres, 25,575 Pop, 7,197 Houses, 1,352 The district includes also the sub-district of Binsted, containing the parishes of Binsted Selborne, Hartley Mauditt, West Worldham, East Worldham, Holybourne, Frovle, and Bentley, and the extra parochial tract of Coldrey Acres, 53,057 Poor rates in 1866, £8,650 Pop in 1841, 11,299 in 1861. 12,063 Houses, 2,332 Marriages in 1866, 97, births, 389 —of which 29 were illegitimate, deaths, 210,—of which 78 were at ages under 5 years and 7 were at ages above 85 Marriages in the ten years 1851–60, 780, births, 3,824, deaths 2,129 The places of worship in 1851 were 18 of the Church of England, with 4,943 sittings, 4 of Independents with 880 s, 1 of Baptists, with 20 s, 1 of Quakers, with 185 s, 2 of Wesleyan Methodists, with 208 s., 1 of Primitive Methodists, with 86 s, and 2 of Bible Christians with 104 s The schools in 1851 were 17 public day schools, with 1,503 scholars, 13 private day schools, with 248 s. 22 Sunday schools, with 1,118 s and 1 evening school for adults, with 10 s.—The division of Alton is considerably identical with the district but more extensive, and it is subdivided into the towns of Alton and Alresford, and the hundreds of Alton, Bishops Sutton, and Selborne. Acres, 70,811 Pop, 14,048 Houses, 2,770 Alton hundred is divided into Lower Half, comprising 16,152 acres, and Upper Half, comprising 14,027 acres The work house and lunatic asylum are in Alton

ALTON, a constablewick in Rock parish, Worcester, near Wyre forest 4½ miles W of Bewdley

ALTON, or ALVETON, a township a parish, and a sub-district, in the district of Cheadle, Stafford. The township lies on the Churnet river, the Uttoxeter canal and the North Stafford railway, 7½ miles NNW of Uttoxeter It has a station on the railway, a post office under Stafford, and an inn Real property, £3,553 Pop., 1,173 Houses, 253 —The parish includes also the town ships of Farley, Denston, and Upper and Lower Cotton Acres, 7,379 Real property £10,325 Pop, 2,250 Houses 476 The manor belongs to the Earl of Shrewsbury Alton Towers, the seat of the Earl, is a splendid edifice, in a variety of styles, built in 1814, and contains a mag nificent hall, an armory, 120 feet long, a picture gallery, 150 feet long, with superb collection of pictures, a chapel with stained windows by Pugin, and a state drawing room with some ornaments of Queen Catherine The gardens connected with it are richly ornate, and contain a Choragic temple, a Chinese conservatory, an imitation Stonehenge, a pagoda 95 feet high, and a Gothic temple commanding an extensive view The ruins of a castle of the De Verdons, of the time of Henry II, stand on a rock by the Churnet 300 feet high St John's hospital founded by the Talbots, for a warden and fellows, with church and school, is near the castle An ancient camp, with double fosse, occurs at Bonebury The living is a vicarage in the diocese of Lichfield. Value, £151 * Pa tron the Earl of Shrewsbury -The church is modern Cotton and Denston are separate charges, and there are chapels for Independents Methodists and Roman Catholics and charities £25 —The sub district comprises three parishes. Acres, 9,487 Pop, 2,693 Houses, 561

ALTON BARNES, or ALTON BERNERS, a parish in Devizes district Wilts on the Kennet and Avon canal, near Wans Dyke, 7 miles E of Devizes r station. Post town, Pewsey under Marlborough Acres, 1 053. Real property, £1,520 Pop, 177 Houses, 37 The pro perty is divided among a few The living is a rectory in the diocese of Salisbury Value, £294 * Patron, New College Oxford. The church is good

ALTON PANCRAS, a parish and a liberty in Dorchester district, Dorset The parish lies on the Downs, 2½ miles NE of Cerne Abbas, and 7 E by S of Evershot r station Post town, Cerne under Dorchester Acres, 2,343 Real property, £2,612 Pop, 270 Houses 55 The property is subdivided The parish is a meet for the Blackmoor harriers The living is a vicarage in the dio cese of Salisbury Value £208 * Patrons, the Dean and Chapter of Salisbury The church is good. The liberty is co extensive with the parish

ALTON PRIORS, a chapelry in Overton parish, Wilts, on the Kennet and Avon canal, contiguous to Alton Barnes, 7 miles E of Devizes r station. It includes the tything of Stowell, and its post town is Pewsey under Marlborough Acres 2,630 Real property, £2,038. Pop, 207 Houses, 46 The manor belonged anciently to Winchester monastery The living is a curacy, an nexed to Overton vicarage, in the diocese of Salisbury The church has a curious brass of 1528.

ALTON TOWERS See ALTON Stafford

ALTRINCHAM, or ALTRINGHAM, a town, a township, two chapelries, a sub district, and a district, in Cheshire The town is in the parish of Bowdon, at an intersection of railways, adjacent to the Bridgewater canal, 8 miles SSW of Manchester, comprises good streets and some handsome villas, is a seat of petty sessions and county courts, and a polling place, publishes a weekly news paper, carries on iron founding, bone-grinding, timber sawing, much trade from neighbouring market gardens, and much transit traffic, and has a head post office,‡ three r stations, two chief inns, a town hall of 1849, a literary institution in the Tudor style enlarged in 1864, a plain church of 1799, a church in the decorated English style built in 1867, a Wesleyan chapel in the Byzantine style built in 1864, five other dissenting chapels, a Roman Catholic chapel, five public schools, a medical hospital, charities £97, a weekly market on Tuesday, and three annual fairs —The township comprises 657 acres. Real property, £24,087 Pop., 6,628 Houses, 1 240 —The chapelries are St George and St John The livings are p curacies Value of St G, £210 * Patron of St G, the Vicar of Bowdon, of St J, the Bishop of Chester

The sub district comprises part of the parish of Bowdon and all the parish of Ashton upon Mersey Acres, 17,796 Pop, 18,214 Houses 3 453 The district comprehends also the sub district of Wilmslow, containing the parishes of Mobberley, and Northen, and part of the parish of Wilmslow, the sub district of Lymm, containing the pa rishes of Lymm and Warburton, and parts of the parishes of Bowdon, Rosthern, and Great Budworth and the sub district of Knutsford containing the parish of Knuts ford, and parts of the parishes of Rostherne and Great Budworth Acres 73,605 Poor rates in 1866 £15,917 Pop in 1841, 31 019, in 1861, 40 517 Houses 7,782 Marriages in 1866, 230, births, 1,385 —of which 115 were illegitimate, deaths, 855 —of which 317 were at ages under 5 years, and 16 were at ages above 85 Mar riages in the ten years 1851–60, 2,012, births, 12,179 deaths, 7 387 The places of worship in 1851 were 20 of the Church of England, with 8,832 sittings, 12 of Inde pendents, with 2 495 s., 4 of Baptists with 615 s, 1 of Quakers, with 200 s 6 of Unitarians, with 684 s., 2 of Moravians, sittings not reported, 21 of Wesleyan Metho dists, with 3,672 s, 1 of New Connexion Methodists, with 500 s, 9 of Primitive Methodists, with 879 s, 1 of Wesleyan Association and 1 of Brethren sittings not reported 1 of Latter Day Saints, with 50 s., and 2 of Roman Catholics, with 130 s. The schools in 1851 were 42 public day schools, with 2,755 scholars, 64 private day schools, with 1 590 s, 63 Sunday schools, with 5,649 s, and 2 evening schools for adults, with 55 s The work house is in the township of Knutsford Inferior

ALUM BAY, a semicircular bay, about 7 furlongs wide on the N side of the western extremity of the Isle of Wight, near the Needles, and 2¾ miles WSW of Freshwater Gate Cliffs of snowy chalk overhang it on one side, cliffs of bright variegated colours streaked like a ribbon overhang it on the other, and these com bine with green turf above them, and with the fine bold headland of Headon Hill on the E to form a sc[illegible] of uncommon force and beauty "The chalk, says Sir H Englefield, "forms an unbroken face, everywhere nearly perpendicular, and in some parts formidably projecting, and the tenderest stains of ochreous yellow and greenish moist vegetation vary without breaking its sublime uniformity This vast wall extends more than a quarter of a mile and is probably nearly 400 feet in height Its termination is by a thin edge of bold broken outline, and the wedge like Needle Rocks, rising out of the blue waters, continue the cliff in idea, beyond its present boundary, and give an awful impression of the stormy ages which have gradually devoured its enormous mass The pearly hue of the chalk is beyond description by words, and probably out of the power of the pencil Deep rugged chasms divide the strata in many places, and not a vestige of vegetation appears in any part, all is wild ruin The tints of the other cliffs are so bright and so varied that they have not the appearance of anything natural Deep purplish red, dusky blue, bright ochreous yellow, grey nearly approaching to white, and absolute black succeed each other as sharply defined as the stripes in silk and after rain the sun, which from about noon till his setting, in summer, illuminates them more and more, gives a brilliancy to some of these nearly as resplendent as the high lights on real silk.' Copperous stones, lignite, alum, pipe clay, shells, and fossils are found on the shore, and a siliceous silvery looking sand long in high request for the glass and porcelain works of London Bristol, and Worcester, abounds at the sea base of Headon Hill Landslips sometimes occur of considerable extent, and one, not many years ago, fell with a depth of between 200 and 300 yards, and carried off to the sea the tools and works of the diggers at the sand pits A cavern called Mother Larges Kitchen, pierces the chalk cliffs at a part which can be reached by the shore. A strong fort, called Victoria Fort, mounting 52 guns, was recently constructed at Cary's Sconce where the cliffs decline. An excellent hotel, the Needles, is near the head of the bay

ALUM GREEN, an extra parochial tract in New Forest district, Hants, contiguous to Lyndhurst parish, 9 miles NNW of Lymington Pop 13

ALUM POT, a deep pond ¼ a mile SW of Selside and 3¼ miles NNE of Kendal, Westmoreland Its circumference is at least 150 feet, its depth, from the rim, at least 165 feet, and from the surface of the water, after a drought, 130 feet.

ALUN or ALLYN (THE) See ALLEN

ALVANLEY, a township chapelry in Frodsham parish, Cheshire, near Delamere forest, 1¾ mile S of Dunham r station and 3 SSW of Frodsham Post town, Frodsham under Preston Brook, Acres, 1,532 Real property, £2,171 Pop., 330 Houses, 55 The manor has belonged, for many generations, to the Arden family and gives them the title of Baron The living is a v carage in the diocese of Chester Value, £160 * Patrons the Hon Miss Arden and others The church was built in 1860, and a national school in 1861

ALVASTON a township in Nantwich parish, Cheshire, 1¼ mile N of Nantwich. It includes part of Beam Heath. Acres, 616 Real property, £1,350 Pop, 28 Houses, 6

ALVASTON a township chapelry in St Michael parish, Derby, on the Derwent river near the Midland railway, 3 miles SE of Derby It has a post office under Derby Acres, 870 Rated property £2,930 Pop, 583 Houses, 117 The property is much subdivided The living is a vicarage in the diocese of Lichfield Value, £116 Patrons the parishioners The church was rebuilt in 1856 There are Presbyterian and Wesleyan chapels and a church school

ALVECHURCH, a village and a parish in Bromsgrove district, Worcester The village stands adjacent to the Worcester and Birmingham canal and to the Redditch branch of the Bristol and Birmingham railway near Ikneild Street 5 miles NE of Bromsgrove, and it has a station on the railway, and a post office‡ under Bromsgrove It was formerly a borough and it had, from the time of Henry II till the time of Charles I, a palace of the Bishops of Worcester Fairs are held on 3 May and 11 Aug The parish is cut, for local purposes, into the sections of Yields of Town Green, Barn Green Ferrill with Hopwood and Lea End. Acres, 6,747 Real property, £12,518 Pop 1 713 Houses, 352 The property is much subdivided A chief residence is Bordesley Park, 1½ mile SE of the village A tunnel of the canal, nearly 3 miles long, begins at Hopwood The living is a rectory in the diocese of Worcester Value £1,200 * Patron, the Bishop of Worcester The church, excepting the tower, was recently rebuilt, at a cost of £3,200 There are a mission chapel, a Baptist chapel, an endowed school with £36 a year, and charities £33 Moore the nonconformist, and Hicks, the author of Thesaurus " were rectors

ALVECOTE PRIORY See SHUTTINGTON

ALVEDISTON See ALVESDISTON

ALVELEY, a township and a parish in Bridgnorth district, Salop The township lies on the river Severn, adjacent to the Severn Valley railway, near Highley r station, 8 miles NNW of Kidderminster, and has a post office under Bridgnorth. Pop, 882 Houses, 194 The parish includes also the township of Nordley Regis and the liberty of Romsley Acres, 6,788 Real property, £8,423 Pop, 1,018 Houses, 225 The property is much subdivided. Lead ore occurs The living is a vicarage in the diocese of Hereford Value, £103 Patron Mrs Wakeman The church had a chantry A school has £26 a year from endowment, and other charities £97

ALVERBANK, a group of Gothic villas on the shore, 2 miles SW of Gosport, Hants One of them, built by the late Right Hon John W Crocker, was, in 1857, the residence of Prince Alfred

ALVERDISCOTT, or ALSCOTT, a parish in Torrington district Devon, 4 miles SE of Instow r station and 5 E of Bideford Post-town, Newton Tracey under Barnstaple Acres, 2,273 Real property £1 870 Pop, 336 Houses, 64 The property is not much divided The living is a rectory in the diocese of Exeter Value £183 * Patrons, Rev E. Sturges, Rev W H Bond and H Gibson, Esq The church is old A small Methodist chapel stands at Stone Cross

ALVERSTOKE, a village, a parish, a liberty, a sub district, and a district in Hants The village stands adjacent to Stoke bay r station, opposite Spithead 1¾ mile SSW of Gosport, and has a post office under Gosport It is a pleasant place with charming environs.—The parish includes also the town of Gosport the villages of Forton, Hardway, and Elson, the watering place of Anglesey the villas of Alverbank, the Forton military prison, the royal marine barracks, the Haslar barracks, the royal naval hospital, Blockhouse fort, and Fort Monckton Acres 5 222 Real property, £48 097,—of which £18,363 are in Gosport Pop in 1841, 13,510 in 1861, 22,653 Houses, 3,436 The manor was given by the noble Saxon lady Alwara to the church of Winchester, and it still belongs to the Bishop of Winchester as superior Many excellent mansions, villas, and other residences, with gardens and terraces, adorn the surface and the shores, and a rich extensive prospect is enjoyed of the Solent and the Isle of Wight Stoke bay is now a noted roadstead, where all the steam war ships, when newly fitted with their engines, test their speed at the measured mile The living is a rectory in the diocese of Winchester, and includes the curacy of Anglesey Value £1 087 * Patron the Bishop of Winchester The vicarages of Trinity Gosport, St Matthew Gosport, St John Forton and St Thomas Elson are separate benefices The parochial church is Saxon built in 1130, repeatedly restored and now chiefly modern Christ church, in the decorated English style, was opened in June, 1865 Charities, £17 Dr Wilberforce the present bishop of Oxford was once rector here, and Dr French the present Archbishop of Dublin, was his curate

The liberty, the sub district and the district of Alverstoke, are co extensive with the parish The administration for the poor is still under the act of 43 Eliz Poor rates in 1867, £8,270 Marriages in 1866 2.., births, 757,—of which 23 were illegitimate, deaths, 474,—of which 134 were at ages under 5 years, and 6 were at ages above 85 years. Marriages in the ten years 1851–60, 2,099, births, 6,287, deaths, 5,110 The places of worship in 1851 were 7 of the Church of England, with 6,102 sittings, 3 of Independents, with 1,050 s, 2 of Baptists, with 320 s, 2 of Wesleyan Methodists, with 754 s, 1 of the Wesleyan Methodist Association, with 210 s., 1 of Latter Day Saints, with 85 s, 1 of Roman Catholics with 200 s, and 1 undefined, with 60 s The schools in 1851 were 9 public day-schools, with 1,076 scholars, 35 private day schools, with 794 s, and 13 Sunday schools, with 1,406 s

ALVERSTON, an ancient manor in Brading parish, Isle of Wight, on the Yar river, 2 miles SW of Brading Its Saxon proprietor, Tovi, was allowed to retain possession at the Conquest A free chapel was founded on it by the Strangways, but has gone to ruin

ALVERTHORPE, a village, a township a chapelry, and a sub district in Wakefield parish, W R Yorkshire The village stands near the Midland railway, 1½ mile NW of Wakefield, and has a post office under Wakefield The township bears the name of Alverthorpe with Thornes, lies partly within the borough boundaries of Wakefield, and contains the hamlets of Fanshaw, Kirkham Gate, and Silcoates, and part of the hamlet of Newton Acres, 3,153 Real property, £23,690 Pop, 6,645. Houses, 1,423 The property is much subdivided —The chapelry was constituted in 1830 Pop., 4,590 The living is a vicarage in the diocese of Ripon Value, £300 * Patron, the Vicar of Wakefield The church is large, modern, and handsome There are three Methodist chapels, the Northern Congregational grammar school, four national schools, and charities £50 —The sub-district is co extensive with the township.

ALVERTON, a hamlet in Kilvington parish, Notts, 7 miles S of Newark. Pop., 40 Houses, 7

ALVERTON, a hamlet in the western vicinity of Penzance, Cornwall.

ALVESCOTT, a parish in Witney district, Oxford, near the Cheltenham and Faringdon railway 3½ miles WNW of Bampton Post-town, Bampton, under Faringdon Acres, 2,690 Real property, £2,961 Pop 407 Houses, 85 The property is subdivided The living is a rectory in the diocese of Oxford Value, £371 Patron, Rev A Neate. The church is cruciform, in early English, with plain Norman tower There are a Baptist chapel, a free school, and charities £22

ALVESDISTON, or ALVEDISTON, a parish in Tisbury district, Wilts, on an affluent of the Avon, under White sheet hill, 4 miles SSE of Tisbury r station, and 3 E of Shaftesbury Post town, Broad Chalk under Salisbury Acres, 2 531 Real property, with Berwick St John and Tollard Royal, £7 280 Pop 267 Houses, 56 The property is not much divided The living is a vicarage in the diocese of Salisbury Value, £82 * Patron, the Vicar of Broad Chalk The church is good

ALVESTON, a parish in Thornbury district Gloucester, 1¾ mile S of Thornbury, 2½ E of the Bristol and Wales railway, and 6 WNW of Yate r station. It has a post office under Bristol, and contains the hamlets of Grovening and Urcat Acres, 2 518 Real property, £5,384 Pop, 841 Houses, 188 The property is much subdivided. Vestiges of Roman camps occur on Oldbury hill and Castle hill The living is a vicarage in the diocese of Gloucester and Bristol Value, £250 Patrons, the Dean and Chapter of Bristol The church is ancient There are two Methodist chapels, a national school, and charities £6

ALVESTON, a village and a parish in Stratford on Avon district Warwick The village stands near the Avon under Welcombe hills, amid charming environs, 2¼ miles ENE of Stratford on Avon r station, was pronounced by Dr Parry the Montpelier of England, and has a post office under Stratford on-Avon The parish contains also the pleasant village of Tiddington Acres, 4,800 Real property, £8,531 Pop., 811 Houses, 191 The property is much subdivided A chief residence is Alveston House The living is a vicarage in the diocese of Worcester Value £220 Patron, the Rector of Hampton Lucy The church contains some fine tombs of the Lucys, and is very good Charities, £46

ALVETON See ALTON, Stafford.

ALVINGHAM, a parish in Louth district, Lincoln, on the Louth canal, 3½ miles NE of Louth r station Post town, Louth Acres, 1,940 Real property, £2,802 Pop, 350 Houses, 74 The property is much subdivided A Gilbertine priory stood here, dedicated to the Virgin and St. Adelwold, and was given, at the dissolution, to the Clintons. The living is a vicarage, united with Cockerington, in the diocese of Lincoln Value, £170 * Patron, the Bishop of L The church is ancient There are three Methodist chapels

ALVINGTON, a parish in the district of Chepstow and county of Gloucester, on the estuary of the Severn, and the South Wales railway, near Wollaston r station, 2 miles SW of Lydney Post town, Lydney Acres, 2,553, of which 500 are water Real property, £2,709 Pop 369 Houses 79 The manor belongs to the family of Noel The living is a p curacy annexed to the rectory of Wollaston, in the diocese of Gloucester and Bristol. The ancient church was a cell to Llanthony abbey

ALVINGTON, a hamlet in Brimpton parish, Somerset, 2 miles W of Yeovil Pop 65

ALVINGTON, Devon See ALLINGTON

ALWALTON, a parish in the district of Peterborough and county of Huntingdon, on the river Nen 2 miles SW of Overton r station, and 5 WSW of Peterborough It has a post office under Peterborough, and contains the mansion of Alwalton Castle Acres, 1,010 Real property, £1 704 Pop, 342 Houses 68 The manor was given anciently to the monks of Peterborough, and transferred by Henry VIII to the Dean and Chapter of Peterborough The property is not much divided The living is a rectory in the diocese of Ely Value, £200 * Patron, the Hon G W Fitzwilliam The church is partly Norman, and was recently restored. There are a Wesleyan chapel and a British school

ALWARDBY See ALLERBY

ALWEN (THE), a stream of North Wales It issues from Llyn Alwen, a small lake 7½ miles FSE of Llanrwst, and runs 14 miles south eastward to the Dee, about 1¾ mile above Corwen.

ALWINGTON, a parish in Bideford district, Devon, on the river Yeo, 4 miles SW by W of Bideford r station It contains the hamlets of Fairy Cross, Ford, and Woodtown, and its post town is Bideford Acres 2,6?? Real property, £1,802 Pop 359 Houses, 74 The Coffin family have held the manor since the Conquest and have a handsome residence on it called Portledge The living is a rectory in the diocese of Exeter Value, £243 * Patron, J P P Coffin, Esq The church is a very ancient pile, with lofty pinnacled tower, and contains several monuments Remains of an ancient chapel occur at Yeo vale, and there is a small Wesleyan chapel at Ford Charities, £16

ALWINTON See ALLENTON

ALWOODLEY, a township in Harewood parish, W R Yorkshire, 4½ miles N of Leeds Acres, 1,511 Pop 110 Houses, 28

ALWYE (THE) See OLWY

AMAN (THE) See ABERAMAN

AMASTON, a township in Alberbury parish, Salop, 8 miles W of Shrewsbury

AMBER (THE), a streamlet of Derbyshire, about 4 miles long falling into the Derwent, 3½ miles N of Belper

AMBERGATE, a station on the Midland railway, near the mouth of the Amber rivulet, 10½ miles N of Derby Here are a post office under Derby, and extensive lime works A branch railway of 11½ miles, goes off hence north north westward to Rowley, and traverses one of the most grandly picturesque districts in the empire See NOTTINGHAM AND GRANTHAM RAILWAY

AMBERLEY, a township in Marden parish Hereford 4 miles ENE of Moreton r station Acres, 377 Pop. 30 Houses, 7

AMBERLEY, a hamlet in Minchinhampton parish,

and a chapelry in Minchinhampton and Rodborough parishes, Gloucester The hamlet stands near Nailsworth, 3 miles S of Stroud r station, and its post town is Nailsworth under Stroud The chapelry includes the hamlet, and was constituted in 1841 Pop, 1,438 Houses, 364 The living is a rectory in the diocese of Gloucester and Bristol. Value, £300 * Patron, D Ricardo Esq

AMBERLEY, a village in Worthing district, and a parish partly also in Thakeham district, Sussex. The village stands on the river Arun, and on the Arundel railway under the South Downs, 4½ miles N by E of Arundel, and has a station on the railway It is a quaint, old fashioned, picturesque place, and has a post office under Arundel A palace at it, now used as a farm house, was a residence of the Bishops of Chichester, originating soon after the Conquest, castellated in 1379, forming a parallelogram, with square towers at the corners, and round towers at the gateway, and seized and dismantled by Waller in 1643 The parish church is variously Norman and early English, and has a fine Norman chancel arch, and a very rich early English south door The Wild Brook marsh adjacent is flooded in winter, but yields profusion of turf and cranberries in summer, and the river Arun runs through it, and contains here choice salmon peel, which have long been noted as Amberley trout The parish includes also the hamlet of Rackham. Acres, 2,900 Real property, £4,575 Pop., 650 Houses, 135 The property is much subdivided The living is a vicarage, united with the vicarage of Houghton, in the diocese of Chichester Value, £166 * Patron, the Bishop of Chichester A school has an endowed income of £105, and other charities £12

AMBERSHAM (NORTH and SOUTH), two tythings in Midhurst district, Sussex, on the river Rother, 2½ miles ESE of Midhurst They belong to Steep parish, but lie detached from the rest of it, and, prior to 1844, they were in Hampshire Acres of N A, 1,112. Pop., 111 Houses, 19 Acres of S A, 1,506 Pop, 113. Houses, 28

AMBERWOOD, a small extra parochial tract in New Forest district, Hants, 6½ miles SW of Romsey

AMBLE, a township in Warkworth parish Northumberland, on the coast, and on the Coquet branch railway, 1½ mile SSE of Warkworth It contains a village of its own name, well built and chiefly modern, has a post office‡ under Acklington, Independent, Wesleyan, and Roman Catholic chapels, and extensive coal mines, and carries on commerce at Coquet harbour Acres, 1,112 Pop, 1,275 Houses, 264

AMBLECOAT, a hamlet and a chapelry in Old Swinford parish Stafford. The hamlet stands on the southern verge of the county, at the river Stour, and is suburban to Stourbridge being separated from it only by the river Acres 689 Real property, with Kingswinford, £273,463 —of which £66,786 are in mines, £123 936 in iron works, and £3,530 in canals Pop, 2 613 Houses, 531 The inhabitants are employed chiefly in potteries, glass works, collieries, and iron works —The chapelry was constituted in 1845 and originally included Woolaston but since 1860, has been co extensive with Amblecoat hamlet The living is a vicarage in the diocese of Worcester Value, £100 * Patron the Earl of Stamford The church stands on an eminence was opened in 1844 and is a pleasing structure of fire bricks

AMBLESIDE, a small town, a township, a chapelry, and a sub-district, in Westmoreland The town stands on a central spot of the Lake country, at the mouths of Stockgill glen and Rothay vale under Wansfell and Fairfield mountain, 1 mile above the head of Windermere Lake and 4½ NNW of Windermere r station It is a great resort of tourists for visiting the Lakes and it commands a very noble circle of views and drives It presents an irregular appearance, but has of late years, been much extended and improved and it contains three large hotels some comfortable lodging houses and many good shops It has a post office‡ under Windermere, a banking office, a library, a national school, and a free grammar school, and is a polling place, and a seat of petty sessions. Coaches run from it daily to Windermere, Grasmere, Keswick, and Cockermouth A market is held on Wednesday, and fairs on Whit Wednesday, and on 13 and 29 Oct An ancient cross stood in the market place A church, built in 1812, stands within the town, continues to be in use, and a new church built in 1851 in the mediæval style, with a memorial window to Wordsworth, and a disproportionately large steeple, stands in the vale to the west There are a chapel for Methodists, a town hall built in 1858, and a mechanics institute A bobbin mill, of picturesque appearance, is in the mouth of Stockgill glen The Roman station Dictis was in the neighbourhood, near the head of Windermere, and can still be faintly traced Many Roman coins and other Roman relics have been found there, and some of them are preserved at Oxford Ambleside dates from remote times, and was called first Amelsate, and afterwards Hamelside A peculiar ceremony, which originated in the time of Pope Gregory IV, and includes a procession of school children bearing flower-garlands to the church, is observed annually on the eve of the last Sunday in July Hence the lines of Wordsworth,—

"Forth by rustic music led,
The village children, while the sky is red
With evening light advance in long array
Through the still churchyard each with garland gay
That carried sceptre like, o'ertops the head
Of the proud wearer

The township of Ambleside is partly in the parish of Windermere, partly in that of Grasmere Acres, 3,244, —of which 454 are water Real property, £7,482 Pop, 1,603 Houses, 306 The property is much subdivided Many parts are adorned with fine residences, and with gardens lawns, or woods One part in the west contains a large slate quarry, and the mountains contain lead and copper ore The chapelry is co extensive with the township, and is a vicarage in the diocese of Carlisle Value, £93 Patron, General Le Fleming Charities £144 —The sub district comprises twelve townships in the parishes of Windermere, Grasmere, and Kendal Acres, together with Grayrigg sub district 110 616 Pop, exclusive of Grayrigg, 8,404 Houses 1 527

AMBLESTON, a parish in Haverfordwest district, Pembroke on an affluent of the river Cleddau 5 miles NNW of Clarbeston road r station, and 8 NNE of Haverfordwest Post town, Haverfordwest Acres 3,955 Real property, £2 980 Pop, 524 Houses, 118 The Roman station Ad Vigesimum on the Via Julia Maritima, occurs about a mile NE of the church and bears popularly the name of Castle Flemish The living is a vicarage in the diocese of St David's Value £193 Patron, the Lord Chancellor There is a Calvinistic Methodist chapel

AMBRESBURY See AMESBURY

AMBROSDEN, a village and a parish in Bicester district, Oxford. The village stands near the river Ray, adjacent to the Oxford and Bletchley railway, 2½ miles SE by S of Bicester Its name is supposed to have been derived from Ambrosius Aurelius, the British Merlin who encamped here during the siege of Alchester by the Saxons. Ambrosden Park, adjacent on the NW, was the seat of the late Sir G Page Turner Bart The parish includes also the hamlets of Blackthorn and Arncott Post town Bicester Acres 4,865 Real property, £4 218 Pop, 871 Houses, 210 The living is a vicarage in the diocese of Oxford Value, £228 * Patrons the trustees of the late Sir G P Turner The church is decorated early English Charities £40 Bishop Kennet the author of "Parochial Antiquities," was for some time vicar

AMBROTH See AMROTH

AMCOTTS, a township chapelry in Althorpe parish, Lincoln, on the river Trent, 5 miles E by N of Cowle Post town, Althorpe under Bawtry Pop. 374 Houses,

75. The living is a rectory in the diocese of Lincoln, and was formerly annexed to the rectory of Althorpe, but was recently made a separate benefice Value, £260 Patron, the Crown The church is new A former church, dedicated to St Thomas à Becket, fell down in 1849 There is a Wesleyan chapel

AMELSATE. See AMBLESIDE.

AMERDALE, an upland vale in the parish of Arncliffe, W R Yorkshire. The Skirfare rivulet runs along its bottom on a rocky bed, and, in dry seasons, alternately merges and reappears

AMERSHAM, a town, a parish, a sub district, and a district in Bucks The town was formerly called Agmondesham It stands in a pleasant valley near the Misbourne tributary of the river Colne, surrounded by wood crowned hills, 7½ miles ENE of Wycombe r station, and 8½ SSW of Berkhampstead. It consists chiefly of a long street crossed by a shorter one The town house was erected, in 1682, by Sir William Drake, and is a substantial brick edifice, with arched and pillared basement, used as a market place, and a surmounting clock lantern The parish church is a Gothic edifice of brick coated with stucco, has a fine east window, filled with ancient stained glass, and contains monuments of the Drakes, the Dents, and the Curwens. There are four dissenting chapels, a free grammar school, founded in 1620, with endowed income of £86, and three exhibitions at Oxford, endowed writing school, Sunday school, alms houses and other charities with aggregately £312, and a workhouse A weekly market is held on Tuesday, and fairs, on Whit Monday and 19 Sept. Manufactures of straw plait, black lace, silk crape, and wooden chairs are carried on The town has a head post office‡ and two hotels, and publishes a bi weekly newspaper It was a borough, from the time of Edward I, sending two members to parliament, but was disfranchised by the act of 1832 The Drakes represented it for upwards of two centuries, the poet Waller, in the reign of Charles I, and Algernon Sydney, in 1679 Several of its inhabitants were burnt at the stake, as martyrs, in the times of Henry I and of Mary, and John Knox preached in its church Pop, 3,019 Houses, 578

The parish includes also part of the hamlet of Coleshill Acres, 10,544 Real property, £6,677 Pop, 3,550 Houses, 698 The property is not much divided The manor belonged to the Nevilles, to Warwick the king maker, and to the Tothills, and passed to the Drakes Shardeloes, the manor house, stands about a mile NW of the town, and is a fine edifice designed by Adams The living is a rectory in the diocese of Oxford Value, £1,331 * Patron, T T Drake, Esq —The sub district is co extensive with the parish —The district comprehends also the sub district of Missenden, containing the parishes of Lee and Great Missenden, the sub district of Chesham, containing the parishes of Chesham, and Chesham Bois, the sub district of Chalfont, containing the parishes of Chenies, Chalfont St Giles, and Chalfont St Peter, and the sub district of Beaconsfield, containing the parishes of B and Penn, and the chapelry of Seer Green Acres, 49,540 Poor rates in 1866, £10,021 Pop in 1841, 18,212, in 1861, 18,240 Houses, 3,826 Marriages in 1866, 111, births, 617,—of which 42 were illegitimate, deaths, 351,—of which 148 were at ages under 5 years, and 11 at ages above 85 Marriages in the ten years 1851-60, 1,197, births, 6,167, deaths, 4,053 The places of worship in 1851 were 14 of the Church of England, with 6,109 sittings, 3 of Independents, with 1 150 s, 18 of Baptists, with 4,458 s, 2 of Quakers, with 430 s, 3 of Wesleyan Methodists, with 360 s, 5 of Primitive Methodists, with 630 s., and 1 of Wesleyan Methodist Reformers, with 143 s The schools in 1851 were 27 public day schools, with 1,783 scholars, 47 private day schools, with 802 s., 33 Sunday schools, with 3,307 s, and 2 evening schools for adults, with 60 s

AMERTON, a township in Stowe parish, Staffordshire 5½ miles NE of Stafford Pop, 120

AMESBURY, a small town, a parish, a sub district, a hundred, and a district, in Wilts The town stands in the valley of the Avon, 4 miles NW of Porton r station, and 7½ N of Salisbury It was formerly called Ambrosbury, Ambresbury, and Amblesberie, and it probably derived its name from the ancient British chief Ambrosius Aurelius. It dates from a high antiquity, and was the meeting place of a synod, in the time of King Edgar for settling disputes between the regular and the secular clergy A densely wooded hill in its western vicinity bears the name of Vespasian's camp, and is marked by military defences round an area of 39 acres, which are believed to have been first formed by the ancient Britons, and afterwards strengthened and held by the Romans Stonehenge and the Cursus are only 1½ mile beyond this hill, and several other ancient monuments are near A monastery for 300 monks was founded at the town either by the British Ambrosius or by a contemporary churchman, and this was succeeded, about the year 980, by a Benedictine nunnery founded by Queen Elfrida, on account of the murder of her son in law, Edward, at Corfe Castle The nunnery was converted by King Henry II into a cell to the great convent of Font Evrault in Anjou, became the retreat of several royal and noble ladies,—particularly Mary, daughter of Edward I, and Eleanor, queen of Henry III, and rose again to be an independent monastery, one of the richest non mitred abbeys in England A noble mansion now occupies the site of the abbey, and bears its name This was the seat of the Duke of Queensberry, built by Webb, from designs by Inigo Jones, and subsequently improved by the Earl of Burlington, it was also the retreat of the poet Gay, where he wrote the Beggar's Opera, and it passed, in 1824, to Sir Edmond Antrobus, Bart, and was afterwards in great measure rebuilt, and adorned with a Corinthian portico The parish church belonged originally to the abbey, was well restored in 1853, and contains rich features of the early pointed style The town has fallen greatly into decay, but still possesses interest for sake of the attractions around it, and it has a post office‡ under Salisbury, a hotel, a Methodist chapel, two free schools, and a workhouse The two schools have an endowed income of £115, and other charities have £42 A weekly market was formerly held on Friday, but has been discontinued, and fairs are held on 17 May 22 June, and 21 Dec The immediate environs, along the Avon, are wooded and charming while the country beyond is bleak and dreary, but celebrated for coursing Prime pipe clay is sometimes found in diggings, and famous loaches are caught in the streams

The parish contains also the hamlet of Little or West Amesbury Acres, 5,890 Real property, £7,490 Pop 1 138. Houses, 229 The property belongs chiefly to the estate of Amesbury Abbey The living is a vicarage in the diocese of Salisbury Value, £141 * Patrons, the Dean and Chapter of Windsor —The sub district comprises eight parishes. Acres, 27,363 Pop, 3,756 Houses, 783 —The hundred includes thirteen parishes, and parts of four other parishes Acres, 35,832 Pop, 5,242 Houses, 1 104 —The district comprehends the sub district of Amesbury, containing the parishes of Amesbury, Woodford, Durnford, Wilsford, Bulford, Durrington, Milston, and Figheldean, the sub district of Orcheston, containing the parishes of Orcheston-St. Mary, Orcheston St. George, Tilshead, Shrewton, Maddington, Rolstone, and Winterbourne Stoke and the sub district of Winterbourne, containing the parishes of Winterbourne Gunner, Winterbourne Dantsey, Winterbourne Earls, West Cholderton, Newton Toney, Allington, Boscombe, and Idmiston Acres, 62,420 Poor rates in 1866, £5,919 Pop in 1841, 7,705, in 1861, 8,127 Houses, 1,723 Marriages in 1866, 41, births 234,—of which 18 were illegitimate, deaths, 129,—of which 39 were at ages under 5 years, and 6 were at ages above 85 Marriages in the ten years 1851-60, 563, births, 2 536, deaths, 1 636 The places of worship in 1851 were 24 of the Church of England, with 4,195 sittings 2 of Independents with 350 s., 1 of Baptists, with 550 s., 5 of Wesleyan Methodists, with 802 s, and 2 of Primitive Methdists, with 130 s The schools in 1851 were 21 public day schools with 966 scholars, 9 private day schools, with 116 s and 24 Sunday schools, with 1 284 s.

AMICOMBE HILL, a mountain on the NW of Dartmoor, Devon, 6½ miles SSW of Okehampton It has an altitude of 2 000 feet and commands an extensive view.

AMINGTON See ALMINGTON

AMLWCH, a seaport town, a parish, and a sub district, in Anglesey The town stands on a small bay, 17 miles NW of Beaumaris, and is at the terminus of the Anglesey Central railway, opened in 1866 It was a fishing hamlet of only six houses in 1766, but it speedily acquired bulk and importance by the working of the mines in the Parys mountain It is itself dingy and disagreeable, but its neighbourhood contains very fine coast scenery, and commands some noble views. The harbour was cut out of slate rock, is protected by a breakwater, and has capacity for thirty vessels of 200 tons burden A fixed light is on the north pier, 26 feet high, visible at the distance of 8 miles, and a number of rocks or small islets, one of them serving as a sea mark, lie off the entrance A small steamer plies weekly to Liverpool and Holyhead The town has a post office‡ under Bangor, a banking office, two hotels, a parish church, four dissenting chapels, several good schools, and a scientific and literary institution The parish church is a large and handsome edifice, built by the Parys mine company, at a cost of £4,000 Many of the inhabitants are miners, and others are employed in alum and vitriol works and in shoemaking Fairs are held on 8 March, 4 May, 12 Aug, and 21 Oct Amlwch is a parliamentary borough under the Reform bill, united in the franchise with Beaumaris and Holyhead Pop, 3,207 Houses 825.

The Parys mountain is situated 2 miles S of the town Its aspect rising into vast rocks of aluminous shale and whitish quartz is very rugged and impressive, and its picturesque appearance has been greatly increased by the mining operations The Romans are believed to have obtained copper ore on it, and various vestiges of ancient workings have been observed, and some very ancient stone utensils found. Trials in quest of ore began to be made in 1761, and resulted in splendid discoveries on 2 March, 1768,—a day which has ever since been celebrated here by an annual festival Rich lodes were found at a depth of only 7 feet from the surface, and two great mines called the Parys mine and the Mona mine, were worked most productively, chiefly in the manner of quarries, till 1800 The Mona mine then became unprofitable, and the Parys fell greatly off, but in 1811, by means of sinking and improved management, they again became valuable. The ore is chiefly a sulphate of copper, and the bed of it in the Mona mine was 300 feet broad, and in some parts 72 feet thick A lead ore yielding from 60 to 1,000 pounds of lead and 57 ounces of silver per ton, occurs occasionally in a stratum of yellow saponaceous clay above the copper ore The produce of copper at the richest period of the workings, was worth £300 000 a year The deepest shaft sunk is about 200 fathoms The mines belong to the Marquis of Anglesey and the representatives of the late Lord Dinorben

The parish of Amlwch includes the borough of Amlwch the chapelry of Llanwenllwyfo, and most of the town and chapelry of Llanerchymedd Acres, 10 077 Real property, £7,590 Pop, 5 949 Houses, 1,430 The property is not much divided The living is a vicarage in the diocese of Bangor Value, £217 Patron, the bishop of B The vic of Llanerchymedd is separate —The sub district comprises two parishes Acres, 13,37, Pop, 7 777 Houses, 1,886

AMMAN, or AMMOND (THE) a streamlet of Carmarthen, rising in the Black Mountains and running 10 miles WSW to the Loughor in the vicinity of Bettws

AMMINGTON See ALVINGTON and EMMINGTON

AMMOND See AMMAN

AMNEY See AMPNEY

AMOLH, a village in Batheaston parish, Somerset, 2 miles NE of Bath

AMOTHERBY, a township in Appleton le Street parish, N R Yorkshire, on the Thirsk and Driffield railway, near the river Rye, under the Cleveland moors, 4½ miles WNW of Malton It has a station on the railway Acres, 1,250 Real property, £2,779 Pop, 256 Houses 54 A church was built in 1858

AMOUNDERNESS, a hundred in Lancashire It extends from the coast to Yorkshire, and contains Fleetwood Garstang, and parts of Lancaster and Ribchester Acres, 175 ,28 Pop in 1851, 43,702, in 1861, 47,716 Houses, 8 ,81

AMPFIELD a village and a chapelry in Hursley parish, Hants. The village stands 4 miles ENE of Romsey r station, and has a post office under Romsey The chapelry was constituted in 1841, and is a vicarage in the diocese of Winchester Value not reported.* Patron, the Vicar of Hursley The church is a neat Gothic structure, erected at the expense of Sir William Heathcote, Bart, and surrounded by a model burying ground Pop 531

AMPLEFORTH, a village three townships, and a parish in Helmsley district, N R Yorkshire The village lies near the Thirsk and Driffield railway, 4 miles SW of Helmsley, it comprises the townships of Ampleforth St Peter and Ampleforth Birdforth in the parish of Ampleforth, and the township of Ampleforth Oswaldkirk, in the parish of Oswaldkirk, and it has a station on the railway, and a post office under York Pop, 605 A Roman Catholic college was established at Ampleforth Lodge, in Ampleforth Oswaldkirk, in 1802, grew from a small commencement to great size and consequence received the addition of a church in 1856, and of new college buildings in 1861, is now a massive quadrangular pile in the pointed style of the 14th and 15th centuries, and numbers among its pupils many members of the English Romanist aristocracy Ampleforth and Oswaldkirk parishes are interlocked with each other through the village Acres of the two, 3 573 Real property, £6,516 Pop of Ampleforth alone, 450 House, 90 The property is much subdivided The living is a vicarage in the diocese of York Value, £261 Patron, the Archbishop of York The church is good, and there are two Methodist chapels Charities £29

AMPNEY CRUCIS, a parish in Cirencester district, Gloucester, on Ampney brook, near Ermine-street 3 miles E of Cirencester r station It contains the hamlet of Alcott End and its post town is Cirencester Acres, 2 660 Real property, £4 728 Pop, 618 Houses 132 The property is not much divided Ampney Park is the seat of Earl Ducie The living is a vicarage in the diocese of Gloucester and Bristol Value, £84. Patron Rev F T Brewster The church is an ancient structure, dedicated to the Holy Cross, and in good condition A free school, founded and endowed, in 1722, by Sir Robert Pleydell, has an endowed income of £80

AMPNEY DOWN or DOWN AMPNEY, a parish in Cirencester district Gloucester on Ampney brook, the Thames and Severn canal and Ermine street 3 miles NNE of Cricklade, and 6 ESE of Cirencester r station It has a post office under Cricklade Acres, 2,510 Real property, £3 713 Pop 429 Houses, 82 The property is undivided The manor belonged at Domesday to Ralph de Todeni, and passed to the Duchy of Lancaster to the Villierses to Speaker Hungerford, to the Dunches, to Secretary Craggs, to the Eliots and to the Bouveries A mansion built on it in the time of Henry VIII by Sir Anthony Hungerford, still stands, but has been much altered by modern additions The living is a vicarage in the diocese of Gloucester and Bristol Value, £116 Patron Christ Church college Oxford The church is early English built about the year 1260 by the knights templars, and was partly rebuilt about 1545, partly repaired in 1863

AMPNEY ST MARY, or ASHBROOK, a parish in Cirencester district, Gloucester on Ampney brook, 4 miles E of Cirencester r station Post town, Cirencester Acres, 1,170 Real property, £2,5?? Pop, 12? Houses, 28 The property is not much divided The living is a vicarage in the diocese of Gloucester and Bristol Value, £71 Patron, M H Beach, Esq The church is an ivy-clad, quaint looking, very ancient edifice, recently repaired

AMPNEY ST PETER, or EASINGTON, a parish in Cirencester district, Gloucester, contiguous to Ampney St Mary, 4½ miles E of Cirencester r station Post town, Cirencester Acres, 533 Real property, £1,291 Pop, 188 Houses 49 The property is divided among a few The living is a vicarage in the diocese of Gloucester and Bristol Value £60 Patron, the Bishop of Gloucester and Bristol The church is good

AMPORT, a parish in Andover district, Hants on the Basingstoke and Salisbury railway, near Grateley station, 5 miles WSW of Andover It includes the tythings of Sarson and East Cholderton and has a post office‡ under Andover Acres, 3,933 Real property, with Monxton, £6,988 Pop. of Amport, 705 Houses, 156 The manor belongs to the Marquis of Winchester, and has descended to him from the Norman house of De Port, the common ancestors of the Paulets and the St Johns Amport House, the seat of the Marquis, has just been rebuilt, in the Tudor style, after designs by Mr Burns and stands in a pleasant undulating park much marked with single trees The living is a vicarage, united till 1863 with Appleshaw, in the dio of Winchester Value, £590 * Patrons, the Dean and Chapter of Chichester The church is chiefly in the late decorated style, with a central tower There is a Primitive Methodist chapel. There are also an endowed school and endowed almshouses, with jointly £150 a year

AMPTHILL, a small town a park, a parish, a sub district, and a district, in Beds The town stands on a pleasant spot, overlooked by hills, 2½ miles SE of the Ampthill or Marston station of the Northwestern railway, and 7 S by W of Bedford It is neat and regular, and has a head post office ‡ a banking office, two chief inns, an old moot hall a new market house, a parish church three chapels for Independents, Wesleyan Methodists, and Quakers, a national school a workhouse, and two alms houses The parish church consists of nave, aisles, and chancel, is in the later English style, with a tower at the west end, and contains a mural monument to the memory of Governor Nicholl, who fell in the sea fight off Solebay in 1672 The town is a seat of petty sessions and a polling place Most of its inhabitants are agricultural, but some are employed in an extensive brewery, and many are employed in straw platting and bonnet sewing. A weekly market is held on Thursday, and fairs on 4 May and 30 Nov

Ampthill Park adjoins the town on the NW, and is united to Houghton Park on the NE It was the seat of the late Lord Holland, and is now occupied by Lord Wensleydale A castle was built on it in the time of Henry VI, by Sir John Cornwall afterwards Lord Fanhope, and was the residence of Catherine of Arragon, during the process instituted against her by Henry VIII A cross, in commemoration of this event, was erected in 1770 by the Earl of Ossory, then proprietor of the estate and bears an inscription from the pen of Horace Walpole The present mansion stands on lower ground than the site of the ancient castle, yet commands an extensive view of the vale of Bedford and is a magnificent edifice, built by Lord Ashburnham, and containing some valuable paintings and a museum The estate was constituted by Henry VIII a royal domain, under the name of the Honour of Ampthill The park is spacious, well diversified with picturesque scenes, and much studded with venerable oaks Houghton Park contains the pear tree under which Sir Philip Sidney is said to have written part of his "Arcadia" and remains of the house built by "Sidney's sister, Pembroke's mother" A beautiful grove of lime trees, called the Alameda was planted by Lord Holland for the recreation of the townspeople

The parish of Ampthill comprises 1,928 acres Real property, £8,651 Pop, 2,144 Houses 439 The living is a rectory in the diocese of Ely Value, £280 * Patron, the Lord Chancellor —The sub district comprises 9 parishes and part of another Acres, 19,115 Pop, 9,076 Houses 1,897 —The district comprehends the sub district of Cranfield, containing the parishes of Cranfield, Lidlington, and Marston Moretaine, the sub district of Shillington, containing the parishes of Shillington, Upper Gravenhurst, Lower Gravenhurst, Higham Gobion, Clophill, and part of Flitton, and the sub district of Ampthill, containing the parishes of Ampthill Houghton-Conquest, Hawnes, Maulden Pulloxhill, Westoning, Flitwick, Steppingley, Millbrook and part of Flitton Acres, 51 591 Poor rates in 1866, £10,261 Pop in 1861, 16,970 Houses, 3,519 Marriages in 1866, 159, births, 646,—of which 47 were illegitimate, deaths, 370,—of which 160 were at ages under 5 years, and 8 at ages above 85 years. Marriages in the ten years 1851–60, 1,293, births, 5,742, deaths, 3,565 The places of worship in 1851 were 20 of the Church of England, with 6,305 sittings, 1 of Independents, with 290 s; 6 of Baptists, with 1 052 s, 1 of Quakers, with 220 s. 13 of Wesleyan Methodists, with 2,360 s, 3 of Primitive Methodists, with 309 s., and 3 undefined, with 672 s The schools in 1851 were 18 public day schools with 1,209 scholars, 19 private day schools, with 423 s, 36 Sunday schools, with 3,607 s, and 3 evening schools for adults, with 91 s.

AMPTON a parish in Thingoe district, Suffolk, 5 miles N of Bury St. Edmunds r station It has a post office under Bury St Edmunds Acres, 716 Real property, £910 Pop., 131 Houses 23 Ampton Hall, the seat of H Rodwell Esq, is a large brick edifice, in a spacious park The living is a rectory in the diocese of Ely Value, £172 * Patron, Hun Rodwell, Esq The church is a plain brick building, with a stone tower, and has a brass Charities, Calthorpes school, almshouses, &c £440

AMPORTH, or AMROTH, a parish and a sub district in the district of Narberth Pembroke The parish lies on Carmarthen bay, 6 miles SE of Narberth, and 6½ S by W of Whitland r station, and has a post office under Tenby Acres, 2,578, of which 230 are water Real property, £2,754 Pop, 889 Houses, 195 The property is divided among a few Coal is worked, and fishing is carried on Amroth Castle, delightfully situated on the coast, was formerly a grand feudal residence, the seat of a follower of Arnulph de Montgomery, called Earo Wear, but passed to the family of Ackland, and is now a splendid modern mansion. The living is a vicarage in the diocese of St Davids Value, £75 Patron J L P Lewis, Esq The church is early English and has a curiously formed tower Charities, £20 —The sub district comprises eight parishes and part of another Acres, 24 608 Pop, 3,265 Houses, 659

AMSTEY See ANSTEY, Herts.

AMWELL. See CLERKENWELL.

AMWELL-END See WARE

AMWELL (GREAT), a village and a parish in Ware district, Herts The village stands near the sources of the New river and near the Eastern Counties railway, 1½ mile SE by S of Ware, and has a post office, of the name of Amwell, under Ware Its name is supposed to have been derived from Emma's Well a fountain which issues from a hill, and forms one of the sources of the New river The parish comprises 2,437 acres. Real property, £9,463 Pop, 1 600 Houses 314 The property is not much divided Amwell Place was the seat of the Quaker poet Scott, who described the picturesque beauty of the neighbourhood, and wrote the lines, "I hate the drum's discordant sound. Amwell Bury, near Parrot hill has yielded some ancient relics Haileybury college belonged to the East India Company and is now a first class school similar to Marlborough schools A monument stands on an islet in the New river, erected in 1800 by Mr Mylne the architect, to the memory of the ill requited Sir Hugh Myddleton who impoverished himself by the formation of that work to which London owes a large supply of water This artificial river is 36 miles long, has 43 sluices and 218 bridges, and was begun in 1608 and completed in 1613 Sir Hugh, notwithstanding aids from Parliament and from London, was so reduced by the work as to be driven to spend his subsequent life in penury and ob-

recently,—some accounts say in mean manual labour Isaac Walton was a frequent visitor at Amwell, and Hoole, the translator of Tasso, was a resident The living is a vicarage in the diocese of Rochester Value, £140 * Patrons, Trustees of late W M'Nab Esq The church stands on an eminence, and is an edifice of the 14th century The church yard contains the graves of Reed the editor of Shakspeare, and of the poet Warner, who wrote Albion's England The vicarage of Hoddesdon is a separate benefice

AMWELL (LITTLE), a chapelry in All Saints parish Hertford 1 mile W by S of Ware Acres, 491 Real property £3 010 Pop, 500 Houses, 96 The living is a vicarage Value, £90 * The church was built in 1863

ANCASTER, a village and a parish in Grantham district, Lincoln The village adjoins the Grantham and Boston railway, on the line of Ermine street 8 miles NE of Grantham It has a station on the railway, and a post-office under Grantham It gave the title of Duke, now extant, to the Berties of Uffington A Roman station, either Causennæ or Crocolana, occupied its site, and many Roman coins bricks and other relics have been found A spot in the neighbourhood was the scene of a victory, in 1643 over the Parliamentarians The parish contains also the hamlets of Sudbrooke and West Willoughby Acres, 2,800 Real property £4,241 Pop., 622 Houses, 139 The property is much subdivided The chief residences are Ancaster Hall, Sudbrooke Hall and West Willoughby Hall A tract which formerly was a common wild and barren, is now enclosed and tilled A fine oolitic building stone is extensively quarried, has been used for Belvoir Castle, Wollaton Hall and other great edifices, and is well exemplified in the parsonage which was built in 1842 The living is a vicarage in the diocese of Lincoln Value, £190 * Patron, the Rev Z S Warren The church is a mixture of Norman and early English There are two Methodist chapels, and charities £7

ANCHOLME (THE), a river of Lincoln It rises in the Wolds near Market Rasen, and runs about 22 miles, northward, past Brigg, to the Humber near Ferriby The Caistor canal joins it at Kelsey, and an artificial cut, called New Ancholme river, goes, in nearly a straight line, along its whole course It is navigable from the Humber to Brigg An old adage says,

"Ancholme eel and Witham pike,
In all England is none like"

ANCHOR CHURCH a rock on the river Trent, 6½ miles SSW of Derby It has an outline somewhat resembling that of a Gothic church, and was once the residence of an anchorite

ANCHOR HEAD, or WESTON HEAD, a headland in Bristol Channel between Sand bay and Uphill bay, adjacent to Weston super Mare, Somerset Worle mill on it is a sea-mark and Pilean rock and Weston ledge are in front

ANCHOR STONE, a rock in the river Dart, a little S of Dittisham Devon It rises steeply from a depth of fully ten fathoms, and is visible at low water It is said to have been frequented by Sir Walter Raleigh, from his adjacent seat of Greenway for the purpose of smoking A project was recently afoot for using it as a pier in constructing a railway viaduct over the Dart

ANCOATS See MANCHESTER

ANCROFT, a township and a parochial chapelry in Berwick district, Northumberland The township lies in a pleasant vale, 6 miles NW of Scremerston r station and 5 S of Berwick, and has a post office under Berwick The chapelry comprises also the townships of Cheswick, Haggerston, and Scremerston, lies along the coast, and is traversed by the North Eastern railway Acres, 10,2[illegible], of which 610 are water Real property, £15,055,—of which £2,011 are in mines quarries and fisheries Pop, 2,133 Houses, [illegible] The property is divided among a few The chief residences are Cheswick House and Haggerston Castle The living is a vicarage in the diocese of Durham Value, £131 * Patrons, the Dean and Chapter of Durham The church is a very old edifice with a square tower, belonged formerly to Holy Island, and is in good condition The vicarage of Scremerston is a separate benefice

ANDERBY, a village and a parish in Spilsby district, Lincoln The village stands within a mile of the coast, 3¾ miles ENE of Willoughby r station, and 5 E by S of Alford A rivulet goes past it to the sea, and forms a small harbour, and a canal, cut in 1828, at a cost of £37 000, connects it with Alford The parish comprises 1 080 acres of land, and 765 of water Post town, Huttoft under Alford Real property, £2 389 Pop, 276 Houses 62 The property is much subdivided The living is a rectory, united with Cumberworth, in the diocese of Lincoln Value, £548 * Patron, Magd College Cambridge The church is good, and there is a Wesleyan chapel

ANDERBY, YORKSHIRE See AINDERBY

ANDERIDA, an ancient strong Roman town, or great fortress, at the end of Ermine-street, on the coast of Sussex It was attacked and destroyed, in the latter part of the 5th century, by the Saxons Its site has been claimed by seven places in Sussex, and one in Kent, but is now fixed, by the best antiquaries, at Pevensey The tract around it was called Silva Anderida, signifying the "uninhabited forest," and continued to be known by the Saxons as Andreaswald

ANDERSFIELD a hundred in Somerset It contains the parishes of Broomfield, Creech St Michael, Enmore Goathurst, and Lyng, and parts of the parishes of Durleigh, Chilton Trinity, and North Petherton Acres, 13,701 Pop, 2,807 Houses, 575

ANDERSON, or ANDERSTONE WINTERBOURNE, a parish in Blandford district, Dorset on an affluent of the river Stour, 7 miles S of Blandford, and 7 WNW of Poole Junction r station Post town, Winterbourne Kingston under Blandford Acres, 570 Real property £1,149 Pop, 62 Houses, 12 The chief residence is Anderson House The living is a rectory in the diocese of Salisbury Value, £146 Patron, Sir B Tregonwell

ANDERTON, a township in Great Budworth parish Cheshire, on the Grand Trunk canal, 2 miles NW of Northwich Acres, 481 Real property, £4,13[illegible] Pop., 3[illegible]4 Houses [illegible]

ANDERTON a township in Standish parish, Lancashire, under Rivington Pike, near the Bolton railway and the Manchester and Leeds canal, 3½ miles SE of Chorley Acres 1,175 Real property, £2 211 Pop, 243 Houses 47

ANDERWYKE See ANKERWYKE

ANDOVER, a town, a parish a sub district a district a hundred and a division in Hants The town stands on the Anton river and on the Andover, Romsey and Southampton railway, ¾ mile S of that railway's junction with the London, Yeovil, and Exeter railway and 17½ miles N of Romsey, and has a station with telegraph on the former railway, and another station at the junction A canal, 22½ miles long, with a fall of 179 feet and 24 locks, formerly commenced at the town, and went down the line of the Anton river, past Stockbridge and Romsey, to Southampton water at Redbridge The Andover, Romsey, and Southampton railway was constructed principally by transmutation of that canal down to Redbridge, was connected there with the Weymouth and Southampton railway, and was opened in 1865 The vale of the Anton is for the most part beautifully wooded and presents a striking contrast to the bare downs which flank and overlook it Bury hill, about 1½ mile W of the town, commands a picturesque view of the vale together with an extensive prospect toward the borders of Berks and Wilts, and is crested with a large strong ancient camp, which probably was first formed by the aboriginal British, and afterward occupied by the Romans and the Saxons The town stands on the Roman road from Salisbury to Silchester and possibly occupies the site of a Roman station and it took its name from a ford of the Anton, called Andoven by the Romans and Andeafaran by the Saxons It probably is indicated by the letters A N D O on some Celtic gold coins in the British museum and it was a royal manor and the place of several witenagemots in the time of the Saxons Ethel red concluded a peace here, in 993, with the Norse king Olaf Tryggvason, and many a conflict must have taken place, at prior periods, among the neighbouring strong chalk hills.

The town is compactly built, and extends on either side about a third of a mile from the market place. The town hall, with corn market below, is a handsome stone edifice, with Grecian front, supported on arches, and was built in 1825, at a cost of £7,000 The parish church is a spacious structure, in the early English style, surmounted by a lofty tower, with crocketted pinnacles, and was built in 1849, at a cost of £30,000 furnished by the Rev Dr Goddard, head master of Winchester college, and afterwards vicar of Andover The previous church was an edifice of the time of William the Conqueror, subsequently altered, and in various styles, and a very rich late Norman doorway of it now forms one of the entrances to the church yard This church was long a cell to the abbey of St Florence in Anjou, and afterwards was given to the college of Winchester The other noticeable buildings are four dissenting chapels, a free grammar school, two other free schools, two sets of alms houses, a workhouse, and a borough jail Income of the charities, £183 The town has a large trade in agricultural produce, it shares much in the business of the great Weyhill fair, held in October, 3 miles to the NW, it carries on malting and the manufacture of silk shag, and it is much frequented, during the sporting season, by parties following the hounds over the extensive neighbouring downs. It has a head post-office,‡ a telegraph station, two banking offices, and two chief inns, and it publishes two weekly newspapers. Markets are held on Saturdays, and fairs on Mid Lent Friday and Saturday, 13 May, and 17 and 18 Nov The town was incorporated under King John, it sent two representatives to parliament in the times of Edward I and II and from the 27th year of Elizabeth till 1867, but, by the reform act of 1867, it was reduced to the right of sending only one It is governed by a mayor, four aldermen, and twelve councillors and is a seat of petty sessions and a polling place Its municipal limits are conterminate with the parish of Andover, and its parliamentary limits comprise the parishes of Andover, Knights-Enham, and Foxcott It gives the title of Viscount to the Earl of Suffolk and Berkshire Pop of the m borough, 5,221 of the p borough, 5,430 Houses, 1,053 and 1,102 Electors in 1868, 263 Direct taxes, £3,603

The parish contains also the hamlets of Charlton, Enham Kings Little London, Smannell or Swanhill, Wildhern, Woodhouse, and part of Hatherden. Acres, 7,670 Real property, £19,340 Pop, 5,221 Houses, 1,053 The living is a vicarage, conjoined with the curacy of Foxcott, in the diocese of Winchester Value, £400 Patron, Winchester college The p curacy of Smannell with Hatherden is a separate benefice —The sub-district comprises six parishes Acres, 12,706 Pop, 6,435 Houses, 1,323 —The district comprehends the sub district of Longparish, containing the parishes of Longparish, Bullington, Barton Stacey, Chilbolton, Wherwell, Goodworth Clatford, Upper Clatford, and Abbots-Ann, the sub district of Andover containing the parishes of Andover, Knights Enham, Foxcott, Penton Mewsey Appleshaw and Weyhill or Penton Grafton, the sub district of Ludgershall, containing the extra parochial tract of Park House, and the parishes of Monxton, Amport, Thruxton, Quarley, Grately, Shipton Bellinger, Kimpton, Fyfield, South Tidworth, North Tidworth, and Ludgershall —the two last electorally in Wilts; and the sub district of Hurstbourne Tarrant, containing the parishes of Hurstbourne Tarrant, Faccombe, Tangley, Vernhams Dean, Linkenholt and Chute, and the tract of Chute Forest Acres, 83,615 Poor rates in 1866, £11 937 Pop in 1851, 16,903, in 1861, 17,132 Houses, 3,627 Marriages in 1866, 94 births, 524,—of which 36 were illegitimate, deaths, 290—of which 86 were at ages under 5 years, and 15 at ages above 85 Marriages in the ten years 1851-60, 1,096 births, 4,993, deaths, 3,170 The places of worship in 1851 were 31 of the Church of England, with 6,394 sittings, 7 of Independents, with 1,201 s, 4 of Baptists, with 850 s, 10 of Wesleyan Methodists, with 1,110 s, 11 of Primitive Methodists, with 1,272 s, and 1 undefined, with 70 s The schools in 1851 were 36 public day schools, with 1,672 scholars, 27 private day schools, with 449 s, and 36 Sunday schools, with 2,019 s

The hundred consists of lower half and upper half The lower half contains Knights Enham, Foxcott, Upper Clatford, Monxton, Penton Mewsey, Weyhill and part of Abbots Ann Acres, 10,981 Pop in 1851, 2,272. Houses 476 The upper half contains Amport, Appleshaw, Fyfield, Grately, Kimpton, Quarley, Shipton Bellinger, Thruxton, and South Tidworth Acres, 19,372 Pop in 1851, 2,805 Houses, 586 —The division comprises the hundreds of Lower and Upper Andover, Barton Stacey, Upper-Pastrow, Upper Thorngate, and Lower and Upper Wherwell Acres, 81,507 Pop in 1851, 13,422, in 1861, 14 758 Houses, 3,197

ANDOVERSFORD, a village in Dowdeswell parish, Gloucester, on the river Isborne, under the Cotswolds, 5¾ miles ESE of Cheltenham It has a post office under Cheltenham

ANDREAS or KIRK ANDREAS, a village and a parish in the Isle of Man The village stands 5¼ miles NW of Ramsey, and has a post-office of the name of Kirk Andreas, under Douglas. Fairs are held on St. Andrew's and St John's days. Pop, 76 Pop. of the parish, 1,955 Houses 372. The land is very fertile Many barrows and a camp occur near Ballacurry The living is a rectory in the diocese of Sodor and Man Value, £750 * Patron, the Crown The church was rebuilt in 1802 on the site of a preceding one which was the oldest in the island, and it has an ancient marble font, which belonged to Philip I of France Two runic monuments are in the church yard St Jude's p. curacy is a separate benefice, of the value of £100,* in the patronage of the Archdeacon

ANDREDSWALD, a quondam great forest round the ancient Roman Anderida over much of Sussex and Kent, and westward to Privet in Hants It was 120 miles long, and 30 miles broad Sigebert, king of Wessex, was slain in it by a swine herd Fragments of it remain in Woolmer forest, Alice holt, and the forest of Bere

ANDREW (St), a parish in Cardiff district, Glamorgan, 3 miles S by W of St Fagans r station and 5 SW of Cardiff It contains the village of Dinas Powis with a post office under Cardiff Acres, 3,149 Real property, £3,518 Pop, 570 Houses, 114 Remains exist of Dinas Powis castle, built by Gestyn ap Gwrgan, and named after his wife Denis, daughter of the prince of Powis The living is a rectory in the diocese of Llandaff Value, £410 * Patron, the Bishop of Llandaff The church has monuments of the Howells

ANDREW (St), a parish in Guernsey, 2 miles WSW of St Peters Port. It contains a village of the same name, the manor house of St Helena, and the estate of Vaubellets. Pop, 1,049 Houses, 203 The living is a rectory in the diocese of Winchester Value £150 * Patron, the Governor The church is a handsome Gothic edifice, the finest in the island, with an embattled tower and a spire There is a small dissenting chapel embosomed in trees

ANDREW (St) See PLYMOUTH, CANTERBURY, HASTINGS, CHICHESTER LONDON, DROITWICH HERTFORD, NEWCASTLE ON TYNE, NORWICH PERSHORE, CAMBRIDGE WELLS, WORCESTER, and YORK

ANDREW (St), Ilketshall. See ILKETSHALL ST ANDREW

ANDREW (St) MINOR, a parish in Bridgend district, Glamorgan, 4¼ miles SSE of Bridgend r station. It is a sinecure rectory in the diocese of Llandaff, of the value of £5 and contains but one house, Clemenston, the seat of T Franklin, Esq Pop, 12

ANDWELL, an extra-parochial tract in Basingstoke district, Hants contiguous to Up Nately parish, 3 miles E of Basingstoke Acres, 143 Pop, 20 Houses, 4

ANERLEY, or ANNERLEY, a village on the Croydon

railway, a mile SSW of Sydenham Surrey It has a r station, a post-office‡ under Norwood, tea gardens, and an entrance to the Crystal Palace

ANGEL ROAD, a railway station with telegraph, at the junction of the Enfield railway with the Hertford, on *the NE border of Middlesex*

ANGLETOWN, a village in the higher section of Newcastle parish Glamorgan Pop, 48

ANGERSLEIGH, a parish in Taunton district, Somerset, on the verge of the county, under Black Down hills, 4 miles SSW of Taunton r station Post-town, Wellington, Somerset Acres, 403 Real property, £656 Pop 30 Houses 8 The property is not much divided The living is a rectory in the diocese of Bath and Wells Value, £111 Patron, the Rev H T Tucker The church has a painted window representing the arms and alliances of the ancient family of Lyte

ANGERTON (HIGH and LOW), two townships in Hartburn parish, Northumberland, on the Wansbeck river and railway, with a r station, 6½ miles W of Morpeth Acres, 2,272 Pop., 185 Houses, 25

ANGLE or NANGLE, a village and a parish in the district and county of Pembroke. The village stands in a nook or "angle" of the south side of Milford haven, 7 miles SW of Milford road r station, and 9 W of Pembroke, bears marks of having been a place of some importance in former ages, and has a post office under Pembroke The parish comprises 2 276 acres of land, and 2,305 of water Real property, £2,107 Pop, 512 Houses, 82 The property is divided among a few The chief residence is Angle Hall Limestone is quarried Angle bay affords good anchorage The living is a vicarage in the diocese of St David's Value, £80 Patron, the Bishop of St David's The church is good

ANGLE TARN, a mountain lakelet on the fell on the E side of Patterdale a short way N of Hartsop, Westmoreland It has an area of about five acres and a curious outline, contains two rocky islets, and abounds with good trout Its efflux descends rapidly westward to Patterdale water

ANGLE TARN a mountain lakelet in a hollow high up Bow fell, 10½ miles S of Keswick, Cumberland It contains fine trout and sends down a streamlet north eastward into Borrowdale

ANGLESEY, an insulated county of North Wales It is separated on the SE, by the Menai strait from Carnarvonshire, and is surrounded elsewhere by the Irish sea. It consists chiefly of the island of Anglesey, but includes also the island of Holyhead and the islets of Skerries, Priestholm, and Llanddyn, with some others. Its length, south-eastward, is 20 miles, its breadth, south westward, 16 miles, its circumference, 76 miles, its area, 193,453 acres Its outline has long sweeps which might occasion it to be pronounced triangular or pentagonal, but is indented by several considerable bays and a number of small ones The coast is extensively rocky, and presents some fine scenery, but in the S, is partly desolated with sand The general surface is uninteresting, not much diversified with hill and dale, and quite devoid of lofty mountains or deep glens, flat in the S and in the centre, and rising into only moderate hills in the N The climate is mild, but foggy The most extensive rocks are Cambrian the next most extensive lower Silurian, the next lower carboniferous limestone and shale, the next, granite and intrusive felspathic traps, the next, Permian conglomerate sandstone and red marl Some coal exists, but of most uncertain character,—sometimes in alluvial boulders of a ton or upwards, and is worked at present in only five pits Peat fuel is obtained in inexhaustible plenty, Gritstone, limestone coloured marble, lead ore, and copper ore, are worked and serpentine soapstone fullers earth potters clay, magnesia calamine, sulphur alum silver and zinc are found Much of the land is pastoral and unenclosed The arable soils are chiefly a sandy loam, a stiff reddish earth and a blackish vegetable mould, all pretty fertile and receiving improvement by means of shell sand from various parts of the shore Wood occurs along the banks of the Menai, but is elsewhere scarce The enclosures are not quickset hedges, but stone or turf walls, and they combine with the bleakness of the surface to render the general aspect tame and cold The farm buildings and the cottages are generally poor and mean Agriculture has undergone great improvement, yet is still in a backward condition Oats barley, rye, and potatoes, are the chief crops The black cattle are of the kind called runts, and are much esteemed for the flavour and tenderness of their flesh and about 5,000 are annually exported The native sheep are the largest breed in North Wales, and many are reared for exportation Not a few sheep also of the mountain districts are sent hither to fatten The chief streams are the Braint, the Cevin the Devon, the Allow, and the Dulas, but all are small Numerous kinds of fish some of them not common in other parts, are plentiful along the coast Shell fish also abound, and good oysters, in particular, are taken at Penmon Coarse woollen fabrics, for home use are manufactured The Chester and Holyhead railway goes through the southern part of the county, from the Britannia bridge to Holyhead, and the Anglesey Central, opened in 1866, goes from a junction at Gaerwen northward to Amlwch

The towns and chief villages are Beaumaris, Amlwch Llangefni, Holyhead, Llanerchymedd, Newborough, and Aberfraw The ports are Beaumaris Amlwch, Holyhead Cremlyn, Dulas, Red Wharf, and Maltraeth The political divisions were first, three cantrefs next, six hundreds, and now, one district and parts of two other districts. The ecclesiastical divisions are 74 cures, 42 parishes, and 6 deaneries, in the archdeaconry and diocese of Bangor The hundreds are Tyndaethwy, in the NE, Menai, in the SE Twrcelyn in the middle N, Maltraeth in the middle S, Talybolion, in the NW, and Llyfon, in the SW The district is Anglesey constituting the registration county of Anglesey and will be noticed below, and the parts of districts are four parishes in the district of Carnarvon and eleven in the district of Bangor, both in the registration county of Carnarvon The county is governed by a lord-lieutenant high sheriff, deputy lieutenants and about twenty six magistrates, and it is in the North Wales circuit and the Home military district The county jail is at Beaumaris The number of known thieves and depredators and of suspected persons at large, in 1861, was 13 at ages under 16 years and 100 at ages above 16 years and the number of crimes committed in that year was 34 and the number of criminals apprehended 15 One member is sent to parliament by the county at large, and another by the boroughs of Beaumaris, Holyhead Amlwch, and Llangefni Electors of the county, in 1868, 2,352, of the boroughs, 503 Real property in 1815, £92,589, in 1843 £165,523 —of which £ 231 was in mines and £63,495 was on rentals, in 1860 was assessed to the property and income tax £206 693, —of which £19,626 were in mines and £365 in quarries Pop. in 1801 33,806 in 1821, 45,063, in 1841, 50 891, in 1861, 54,609 Inhabited houses, 12,325 Uninhabited, 534. Building, 55

Anglesey was called by the ancient natives Ynys Mon, or Mon signifying "remote," and by the Romans Mona Its present name was given by the Saxons, is strictly Anglesel, or Anglesea Eye, and signifies "the Englishman's island Lambard says —"Some, as Polydore, will have Mona or Monia to be the Isle of Man, which others call Menavia or Eubonia, reputinge Monia to be that which at this day is called Anglisey, amongest whome is Leland Of whose opinion I am for two causes, thone for that it contineth the name of Mon to this day in the Brittishe or Welshe speche, as by the common proverb, expressinge the fruitfulness thereof may appeare *Terr mam Kymbry*, i e, Anglisey is the mother or nurse of Wales Thother for that Silvester Gyraldus in his booke called Itinerarium Walliæ sayethe, that Caernarvon is soe called because it is a citie standinge over against Mon This Gyraldus was a Welshman learned in the antiquities of his countrie and lived in Hen II tyme, and before Of the same mynd also is he that wrote 'Additamenta Prosperi Aquit This is generally believed to have been the chief seat of the Druids, and, so far as we know anything of the Druids, there is some probability in the supposition, especially considering the number of cromlechs, or altars, which have been found in the island In A D 61, Anglesey was invaded by the Romans under Suetonius Paulinus, who cut down the groves—"sævis superstitionibus sacra," and suppressed the order of Druids Their complete extirpation, however, was not effected till some years after by Julius Agricola At this period, says Lambard, it "was to be waded over on foote betwene that and the mayne land, wherby that seamethe the more likely, which Paulus Jovius writethe of it, saying, that it was somtyme part of the continent, and was by rage of sea (like to Scicile) rent therfroe, as by a bridge which dothe yet somtyme appeare, dothe seme manifest Traces of a natural isthmus are still visible at Portaethwy, where a line of rocks juts out nearly across the channel It is, perhaps, to this that Lambard alludes in the preceding extract. From that period Anglesey remained under the dominion of the Romans till they withdrew from Britain A sovereignty was established here in 450 by Caswallon Llawhir, a British prince, who was sent hither to expel invaders. Aberffraw was the royal residence, and Cadwallader the last king of the Britons, is said to have been a descendant of this family In the reign of William Rufus, Hugh, earl of Chester and Hugh, earl of Shrewsbury, are said to have assisted the inhabitants to repel an invasion of Griffith ap Conan prince of Wales, and about the same time the island was invaded by Magnus, king of Norway From this period it became a part of the kingdom of Wales and was even regarded as the seat of government, till the final extinction of Welsh independence by Edward I After the subjugation of the island by Edward I, he built a castle at Beaumaris to intimidate the inhabitants and fortified the town with a wall "Eve-sythens" says Lambard "they have lyved in better quie Anglesey was afterwards incorporated with England, and in the reign of Henry VIII was constituted a county The chief antiquities are eight or nine standing cromlechs, remains or memorials of about twenty other cromlechs traces of the royal residence at Aberffraw, the castle of Edward I at Beaumaris, a priory and cross at Penmon, a friary at Llanvaes, and a number of churches of the 14th and 15th centuries Anglesey gives the title of Marquis to the family of Paget

The district of Anglesey or the registration county, consists of the two poor law unions of Anglesey and Holyhead, and is divided into the sub-district of Llangefni, containing the parishes of Llangefni, Llangwyllog, Llangristiolus, Heneglwys, Cerrig Ceinwen, Trefdraeth, Aberffraw, and Llangadwaladr or Eglwysael and the parochial chapelry of Tregaian, the sub-district of Bryngwran, containing the parishes of Llanbeulan, Llanllygain with Gwyndu, and Llantrisaint, the parochial chapelries of Llangwyfan, Llanfaelog, Llechylched Ceirchiog Trewalchmai Bodwrog Llanllibio, Llechgwenfarwydd, and Rhodogeidio or Ceidio, the village of Llanerchymedd, and the extra parochial tract of Gwredog, the sub district of Llandyfrydog, containing the parishes of Llandyfrydog, Llanddyfnan, Llaneugrad, and Perrhos lligwy, and the parochial chapelries of Llanthangel Tre r Beirdd, Llanfair-Mathafarn Eithaf, Coedana, Pentraeth, Llanbedr Goch, and Llanallgo, the sub-district of Amlwch containing the parishes of Amlwch and Llaneilian, and the parochial chapelry of Llanwenllwyfo the sub-district of Llanddausaint containing the parishes of Llanddausaint Llanbadrig, Llanfechell, Llanrhyddlad Llanbabo, Llanfaethly, and Llanfachreth and the parochial chapelries of Rhosbeirio, Lodewryd, Llanrhwydrys, Llanfairynghornwy, Llanfflewyn, Llanfwrog and Llanfigael, and the sub district of Holyhead, containing the parishes of Holyhead Rhoscolyn, Poblern, and Llanfihangel yn Howyn, and the parochial chapelries of Llanynghenedl and Llanfair yn Fubwll Acres, 138 884 Poor rates in 1866, £21,843. Pop in 1841, 38 106, in 1861 35,157 Houses 8,364 Marriages in 1866, 216, births, 1,011 — of which 80 were illegitimate, deaths, 786, —of which 185 were at ages under 5 years, and 46 at ages above 85 Marriages in the ten years 1851-60, 2,537, births, 11 047, deaths, 7,663 The places of worship in 1851 were 53 of the Church of England, with 8 654 sittings, 25 of Independents, with 4,606 s., 15 of Baptists, with 2 718 s., 52 of Calvinistic Methodists, with 12,912 s, 14 of Wesleyan Methodists, with 2,506 s, and 1 undefined with 329 s. The schools were 31 public day schools, with 2 504 scholars, 16 private day schools, with 385 s, and 115 Sunday schools, with 11,662 s There is no workhouse, out-door relief being given in all cases

ANGLESEY, a charming watering place in Alverstoke parish, Hants, 2 miles SW of Gosport, opposite Spithead and the Isle of Wight It was founded in 1826, by the Marquis of Anglesey, it includes a terrace, a crescent, public gardens, marine villas, a hotel, reading rooms, baths, and a church, and it commands splendid views and has delightful environs The church is an edifice in the Tudor style, built in 1844, and united with the rectory of Alverstoke

ANGLEZARKE, a township in Bolton le Moors parish Lancashire, 3 miles E of Chorley Acres, 1,279 Real property, £946 Pop, 134 Houses, 28 Building stone is quarried, and lead ore, witherite, and carbonate of barytes are found

ANGLIA See EAST ANGLIA.

ANGMERING, a parish in Worthing district, Sussex, on the South Coast railway, 4 miles SE of Arundel It has a station on the railway, a post-office‡ under Arundel, and a fair on 3 July Acres, 3,150 Real property, £6,352 Pop, 953 Houses, 193 Angmering Park belongs to the Duke of Norfolk Ham House is the seat of W K Gratwicke Esq New Place, now inhabited by work people, was the seat of Sir Edward Palmer in the time of Henry VIII, and the birthplace of his three sons, who all were knighted The living is a rectory and a vicarage—rectory of East Angmering vicarage of West Angmering—in the diocese of Chichester Value, £238 * Patron, Sir G R Pechell, Bart East Angmering church has disappeared West Angmering church, excepting the tower and small part of the chancel, was rebuilt in 1852 There are an Independent chapel and a free school

ANGRAM, a township in Long Marston parish, W R Yorkshire, 4 miles NE of Tadcaster Acres, 518 Pop 59 Houses, 14

ANGRAM, a hamlet in Muker chapelry N R Yorkshire, on the river Swale, near Shunner fell, 2 miles NW of Muker

ANGRAM GRANGE, a township in Coxwold parish, N R Yorkshire 4½ miles N of Easingwold Acres, 438. Pop, 31 Houses, 5

ANICK AND ANICK GRANGE, two townships in St John Lee parish, Northumberland near the Tyne, 1½ mile NE of Hexham Acres, 451 and 2,220 Pop, 137 and 45 Houses 27 and 8

ANKER (THE), a stream of the NE of Warwickshire It rises near Bulkington, and runs about 17 miles north-westward past Nuneaton and Atherstone to the Tame at Tamworth Its course is mainly followed by the Coventry canal and the Trent Valley railway, and it crosses Watling street near Atherstone, and is crossed by the railway on a nineteen arched viaduct 260 yards long

ANKERWYKE or ANKERWYKE, an estate in Wyrardisbury parish Bucks, on the Thames, 2 miles WNW of Staines A Benedictine nunnery was founded here, in the time of Henry II, by Sir Gilbert Montfichet and was given by Edward I to Sir Thomas Smith, provost of Eton A mansion now occupies the site, and only the hall of the nunnery remains A famous old yew tree, 28 feet in girth, is in the grounds, and tradition says that Henry VIII had a meeting beneath it with Anne Boleyn

ANKTON, a hamlet in Felpham parish, Sussex, in the eastern vicinity of Bognor

ANLABY, a township in Kirk Ella and Hessle parishes E R Yorkshire, near Selby railway 4 miles W of Hull Acres, 2,020 Real property, £8,777 Pop.,

493 Houses, 103 Arlaby House has been the seat of successively the Antabus, the Legards, and the Vauses There is a Wesleyan chapel

ANMER, a parish in Docking district, Norfolk, near Peddar way, 4 miles E by S of Dersingham r station and 11 NE of King's Lynn Post town, Dersingham, under Lynn Acres, 1 4_0 Real property, £1 290 Pop, 142 Houses, 30 The manor belongs to H Coldham Esq whose seat is Anmer Park The living is a rectory in the diocese of Norwich. Value, £222 Patron, H Coldham Esq The church is small

ANN ABBOTS See ABBOTS ANN

ANN (ST) See LEWES, NOTTINGHAM, and KIRK ST ANN

ANNE (ST) See ALDERNEY and LONDON

ANNERLEY See ANERLEY

ANNERY a residence in the valley of the Torridge, 3 miles NW of Torrington, Devon It was long the seat of the Hankfords, and was the birthplace and death place of Chief Justice Sir William Hankford who committed Philip Henry, and is now the property of W Tardrew Esq

ANNE'S HILL (ST), a hill about a mile W of Chertsey, in Surrey It rises abruptly from the low ground of the Thames to a height of 240 feet, and looks, from some points of view, to be almost conical An ancient camp was on it, and gave it the name of Eldebury hill, but is now effaced A chapel, dedicated to St Anne was built on it in 1334, and a dwelling house is said to have been constructed out of the chapel by Lawrence Tomson, translator of the New Testament, but only a piled heap of the stones remains St Anne's House once the seat of Charles James Fox and of the late Lord Holland, is on the SE side of the hill, and Monk's Grove, the seat of Lady Mount... is on the NE side

ANNE'S HILL (ST), the highest summit of the Marlborough Downs, 6 miles ENE of Devizes, in Wilts It has an elevation of about 1,000 feet above the level of the sea The Wans Dyke goes along its summit and the camp of Rybury a primitive military work of the aboriginal inhabitants, is on a southerly projection A fair known throughout Wilts and the neighbouring counties, as Tan Hill fair is held on St Anne's Hill on 6 Aug

ANNE'S IN THE GROVE (ST) See BRIER'S

ANNESLEY a parish in Basford district, Notts on the border of Sherwood forest, 2½ miles NW of Linby r station, and 6½ SSW of Mansfield It contains the hamlets of Annesley, Woolhouse, and Wansley, and its post town is Linby under Nottingham Acres, inclusive of the extra parochial tract of Felley, 3,360 Real property £2 743 Pop, 288 Houses, 57 Annesley Park was the birthplace of Mary Chaworth, the object of the early attachment of Lord Byron, celebrated in the poem of The Dream, and is now the seat of J Chaworth Musters, Esq The manor belonged, for some time after the Conquest to the Annesleys, now of Bletchingdon, who built a castle in the park and a priory in Felley The living is a vicarage in the diocese of Lincoln Value, £91 Patron J Chaworth Musters, Esq The church is old but good, and contains monuments of the Annesleys There are two Wesleyan chapels, a free school, and charities £...

ANNESLEY, Stafford See ANSLOW

ANNESLEY, Surrey See ANNINGSLEY

ANNET one of the Scilly islands. It lies W of St Agnes separated by Smith's sound, was formerly much larger than now, and is uninhabited Annet Head at its north western extremity overlooks very whirling tides among obstructing rocks the "dogs" of Scilly

ANNELEY (THE) a stream of Pembroke It rises in the N... of the Precelly mountains, and runs 10 miles west north westward to Newport bay

ANNINGSLEY, or ANNESLEY an estate 3 miles SSW of Weybridge in Surrey It was purchased in 1771 by Thomas Day, the author of "Sandford and Merton," was the scene of his eccentric experiments, and passed by marriage of his grand niece to the Hon James Norton

ANN (LITTLE), a tything in Abbots-Ann parish, Hants

ANN'S (ST) See LEWES NOTTINGHAM, KIRK ST ANN, ALDERNEY and LONDON

ANN'S HEAD (ST), a headland at the W side of the entrance of Milford Haven Pembroke Two fixed lights are on it, 159 and 192 feet high, seen at the distances of 17 and 19 miles

ANN'S HILL (ST) See ANNE'S HILL (ST)

ANSFORD See ALMSFORD

ANSLEY, a parish in Atherstone district, Warwick, on the river Bourne, 5 miles W of Nuneaton r station It has a post office under Atherstone Acres 2,869 Real property, £5 023 Pop 655 Houses 160 The property is not much divided Ansley Hall belonged once to the Ludfords, and belongs now to the Astleys, and it stands in an extensive park which abounds with both natural and artificial beauties, and contains a hermitage and a Chinese temple The hermitage was formed out of an ancient oratory, and was the place where Wharton wrote his lines "Beneath this stony roof reclined" and the Chinese temple was constructed by Sir W Chambers and contains a monument of the Purefoy family, brought from Caldecote church The living is a vicarage in the diocese of Worcester Value, £116 * Patron, the Rev Theoph Sharp The church is partly Norman, has a fine square tower, and is in good condition There is an Independent chapel Charities £47

ANSLOW or ANNESLEY, a township chapelry in Rolleston parish, Stafford, near the Grand Trunk canal, 3½ miles NW of Burton on Trent Post town, Burton on Trent Real property, £2,929 Pop, 348 Houses, 71 The living is a vicarage in the diocese of Lichfield Value, not reported Patron, Sir O Mosley, Bart There is a Wesleyan chapel

ANSTEY, a parish in Royston district, Herts on Ermine street, near the river Quin, 3½ miles NE of Buntingford, and 6½ SSE of Royston r station Post town, Buntingford Acres, 2,170 Real property £3 194 Pop, 478 Houses 93. A castle stood here upon a high round hill said to have been erected, soon after the Conquest, by Eustace, Earl of Boulogne, but was demolished, in the time of Henry III, "because it had been a nest of rebels" The moat which surrounded it and some works which were added in the time of King John still remain The living is a rectory in the diocese of Rochester Value, £501 * Patron, Christ's College, Cambridge The church was built out of the materials of the castle and is cruciform and of mixed architecture, from Norman to debased There are a P Methodist chapel a national school, and charities £8

ANSTEY, a chapelry in Thurcaston parish Leicester, on a branch of the river Soar, near Swanning on railway 4 miles NW of Leicester It has a post office under Leicester Acres about 1,400 Real property, £3 144 Pop, 734 Houses, 174 The manor belonged to Ulverscroft abbey and went to the Greys of Groby The living is a rectory in the do of Peterborough Value, £150 The church was recently rebuilt but retains an ancient tower There are three dissenting chapels, a national school, and charities £11

ANSTEY, a parish in Foleshill district Warwick on the Oxford canal, near the river Sow 2 miles SW of Bulkington r station and 5 NE of Coventry It has a post office under Coventry Acres 930 Real property, £2 340 Pop 171 Houses 47 The property is divided among a few Some of the inhabitants are ribbon weavers The living is a vicarage in the diocese of Worcester Value, £162 Patron the Lord Chancellor The church is very good There is a charity school

ANSTY, a parish in Tisbury district, Wilts under Whitesheet hill, 2 miles S by E of Tisbury r station and 5 SSE of Hindon Post town, Tisbury under Salisbury Acres, 840 Real property with Swallowcliff £3 775 Pop, 298 Houses, 59 The property is divided among a few A preceptory of the Hospitallers was founded here in 1210 and a barn belonging to it still remains The living is a donative in the diocese of Salisbury

Value £22 Patron, Lord Arundell The church is the oldest in the diocese, has an ancient font, and is in tolerable condition Dr Richard Zouch, judge of the court of admiralty in the reign of Charles I, was a native

ANSTEY, a hamlet in Hilton parish, Dorset, 9 miles WSW of Blandford Pop, 200

ANSTEY (EAST), a parish in South Molton district, Devon, on the river Yeo, 1½ miles WSW of Dulverton, and 12 NNW of Tiverton r station Post town, Dulverton under Tiverton Acres, 3,245 Real property, £1,810 Pop, 227 Houses, 32 The surface is hilly, and the property is not much divided The living is a rectory in the diocese of Exeter Value, £180 * Patron, T S Jessopp, Esq The church is tolerable

ANSTEY PASTURES, an extra parochial tract in Barrow upon Soar district, Leicestershire, contiguous to the parishes of Anstey and Glenfield 3 miles NW of Leicester It was included within the duchy of Lancaster, and now belongs to the proprietor of Anstey Hall Pop, 34 Houses, 6

ANSTEY (WEST), a parish in South Molton district, Devon, on the river Yeo, contiguous to East Anstey Post town, Dulverton under Tiverton Acres, 3,008 Real property, £1,845 Pop, 299 Houses, 50 The surface is hilly, and the property is not much divided The living is a vicarage in the diocese of Exeter Value, £132 * Patrons, the Dean and Chapter of Exeter The church is pretty good Charities, £7

ANSTILBURY, or HANSTIEBURY, an ancient circular camp with a double trench, in the eastern vicinity of Coldharbour, 4½ miles S of Dorking, in Surrey It comprises 10 acres, and is nearly covered with trees and brushwood Flint arrowheads and many Saxon coins have been found in its neighbourhood

ANSTIS COVE, a romantic little dell on the coast of Devon, in the southern vicinity of Babbacombe bay 4½ miles S of Teignmouth. Its sides consist of limestone cliffs, variously rugged, buttressed, and smooth, and partly covered with ivy or shaded with wood and its northern promontory commands a magnificent view of the coast from Teignmouth to Portland. Adjacent to it, on the Babbacombe road, are the terraces and towers of the Bishop of Exeter's Italian villa of Bishopstowe, which was partly burnt in 1858

ANSTON, a township, a parish and a sub district, in the district of Worksop, and W R. Yorkshire The township lies on the Chesterfield canal, about 1 mile N of Kiveton Park r station, and 10 ESE of Sheffield, is divided into North and South Anston, and has a post office, of the name of South Anston, under Rotherham Pop 1,126 Houses, 237 —The parish is called Anston cum Membris, and includes also the township of Woodsetts Acres, 4,490 Real property, exclusive of Woodsetts, £4,820 Pop, 1,290 Houses, 279 The property is divided among a few Nail making and starch making are carried on The living is a vicarage in the diocese of York Value, £280 Patron, the Archbishop of York The church is good The sub district comprises seven parishes Acres, 16,550 Pop, 3,222 Houses 679

ANSWELL TOP a hill on the left side of the river Dart, 1½ mile NW of Ashburton, Devon It is skirted with a wood of firs, and it commands a fine view to the S.

ANT (THE), a stream of Norfolk It rises near Antingham, and runs about 12 miles south south eastward, past North Walsham and Irstead, to the Bure below Horning

ANTHOLIN (ST) See LONDON

ANTHONY IN EAST See ANTONY

ANTHONY IN-MENEAGE (ST), a parish in Helston district, Cornwall, on the S shore of the estuary of the Helford, 5½ miles S by W of Falmouth, and 12 SE of Redruth r station Post town Mawnan under Falmouth Acres, 1,510 of land, and 330 of water Real property, £1,786 Pop, 252 Houses, 40 Picturesque creeks branch here from the Helford, Dinas promontory projects at its mouth and commands fine views, and the Great and Little Dinas entrenchments, originally ancient British camps, command its entrance, and were held as military posts in the civil war of Charles I The living is a vicarage in the diocese of Exeter Value, £101 * Patron, the Lord Chancellor The church stands on the shore, at the base of Dinas promontory, is an old edifice, with a granite tower and a font, and was a cell to Tywardreath priory founded before the time of Richard I

ANTHONY IN ROSELAND (ST), a parish in Truro district Cornwall, on the English Channel and the E side of Falmouth harbour, 3 miles E of Falmouth, and 9½ S of Truro r station Post town, St. Mawes under Grampound Acres, 652 of land, and 435 of water Real property, £1,200 Pop 169 Houses, 28 St Anthony's Head projects into the sea at the mouth of Falmouth harbour, and is crowned by a lighthouse, showing a white flashing light 65 feet high visible at the distance of 12 miles The Old Wall rock, with 26 feet of water, lies off the headland A bed of shell, 30 feet above high water mark, occurs at Porth Place House, a seat of Sir S T Spry, adjoins the church, and occupies the site of an Augustinian priory, which was founded in 1124, by Werlewast, Bishop of Exeter, and was a cell to Plympton The living is a donative in the diocese of Exeter Value, not reported Patron, Sir S T Spry The church is a beautiful small structure in early English, with a Norman doorway, was recently restored by Sir S T Spry, and contains a monument, by Westmacott, to Admiral Sir Richard Spry

ANTHONY (ST JACOB) See ANTONY

ANTHONY'S (ST) a locality 1½ mile NW of Walker, with a post office under Newcastle on Tyne, Northumberland

ANTHONY'S HEAD (ST) See ANTHONY IN ROSELAND (ST)

ANTHONY'S HILL (ST) See [illegible]

ANTHORN, or ANTHORN, a township in Bowness parish, Cumberland, on Anthorn lake and the N side of the Wampool estuary, 8 miles NNW of Wigton Pop, 197 Houses, 38

ANTINGHAM, a parish in Erpingham district Norfolk, at the source of Ant river, 3 miles NNW of North Walsham r station, and 16 N of Norwich Post town North Walsham under Norwich Acres 1,609 Real property, £2,166 Pop., 227 Houses, 54 The property is not much divided There are ecclesiastically two parishes St Mary and St Margaret, and both are rectories in the diocese of Norwich. St Mary is united with the vicarage of Thorpe Market and the donative of Bradfield Value, £262 Patron, Lord Suffield The church is a structure of flint, in good condition, and has a brass of Calthorpe. St Margaret is annexed to the vicarage of North Walsham, and the church is in ruins Charities, two coombs of wheat

ANTON (THE), a river of Hants It rises among the chalk hills in the neighbourhood of Penton Mewsey, runs 7 miles south eastward, past Andover, to a junction with the Test in the vicinity of Wherwell, and goes thence 17 miles southward, past Stockbridge and Romsey, to the head of Southampton water See ANDOVER

ANTONY, a parish and a sub district, in the district of St Germans, Cornwall The parish is called also Anthony in East and St Jacob Anthony, lies on Lynher creek and the Hamoaze, 4 miles S of Saltash r station and 4 SE of St Germans, and has a post office, of the name of Antony, under Devonport Acres, 3,222 of land, and 1,260 of water Real property, £14,508 Pop 3,887 Houses, 562 The manor of East Antony belonged formerly to the Dawneys, and belongs now to the Carews. Antony House, on that manor, is a large square edifice of Pentuan stone, built in 1721 by Gibbs and contains an interesting collection of old pictures West Antony village, or St Jacob, is a pleasant place, and owing to its proximity to Devonport and Plymouth, is a favourite residence of officers connected with the dockyards and the navy at these towns Antony Passage, at East Antony, has a ferry to Trematon. Beggars Island below the passage, was named after Ranteyeld Moone Carew, commonly called King of the Beggars The living is a vicarage in the diocese of Exeter Value, £282 *

Patron W H P Carew The church was built in 1420, but has a tower of the previous century, and it contains monuments of Lady Marjory Arundel, Richard Carew, who wrote the 'Survey of Cornwall,' and Captain Graves, R N, who figured in the time of George II The curacy of Merrifield is united with the vicarage, and the p curacy of Torpoint is a separate incumbency There is a Wesleyan chapel The workhouse of St Germans is in this parish Charities, £12 The sub district of Antony comprises four parishes. Acres, 9,740 Pop, 7,578 Houses, 1,336

ANTROBUS, a township and a chapelry in Great Budworth parish, Cheshire The township lies 3 miles NE of Acton r station, and 4½ NW of Northwich Acres, 2,086 Real property, £4,233 Pop 514. Houses, 99 Pop of the chapelry, 673. Post-town, Northwich The living is a vicarage in the diocese of Chester Value, £80 Patron, the Vicar of Great Budworth The church was built in 1848, and improved in 1863 There are a Wesleyan chapel and a national school

ANWICK, a parish in Sleaford district, Lincoln, near the Sleaford canal, 4½ miles ENE of Sleaford r station Post town, Sleaford Acres, 1,820 Real property, £2,773 Pop, 277 Houses, 58 The property is divided among a few The living is a vicarage annexed to the rectory of Brauncewell, in the diocese of Lincoln. The church is good

APESTHORPE See APPLETHORPE

APETHORPE, a parish in Oundle district, Northampton, on an affluent of the river Nen, 3¾ miles W by S of Elton r station, and 5 SW of Wansford It has a post-office under Wansford, and it includes Moornay Lodge in Rockingham forest, which some account extra parochial Acres 2,630 Real property, £1,335 Pop, 245 Houses, 50 Apethorpe Hall is the seat of the Earl of Westmoreland, has a statue of James I, and was the place where that monarch first met his favourite Villiers The living is a vicarage, united in 1868 to Woodnewton, in the diocese of Peterborough Value, £300 Patron, the Bishop of P The church is good, and contains a splendid monument to Sir W Mildmay, Chancellor of the Exchequer in the time of Queen Elizabeth, and founder of Emmanuel college, Cambridge Charities, £66

APETON a hamlet in Gnosall parish, Staffordshire, 5½ miles SW of Stafford.

APLEY, a parish in Lincoln district, Lincoln, near Langworth river, 3½ miles SW of Wragby and 5 N of Barlney r station Post town, Wragby Acres 1,658 Real property, £1,670 Pop, 221 Houses, 45 The manor belonged to the Tyrwhittses, and descended to the Drakes and the old mansion on it is now a farm house The living is a vicarage in the diocese of Lincoln Value, £20. Patron, T T Drake, Esq There is no church, but there is a Wesleyan chapel

APLEY, a seat on the edge of a wooded sea cliff, ¾ of a mile E of Ryde in the Isle of Wight It was built, in the early part of last century, by the noted smuggler, David Boyce, and it occupies one of the most enchanting spots in the island

APLEY CASTLE an old baronial seat, 1 mile NW of Wellington, and 2¾ miles N of the Wrekin, Salop It was the head house of the Charltons in the time of Leland

APLEY PARK the seat of the Whitmore family, on the river Severn 3 miles N of Bridgnorth, Salop. The grounds are richly picturesque, in both natural and artificial feature, and a terrace, about a mile long commands a superb panoramic view to the Clents, the Malverns Clee Wenlock Edge, and the Wrekin

APPLEBY, a township in Bywell St Peter parish Northumberland near the Tyne, 7 miles ESE of Corbridge Acres, 429 Pop., 20 Houses 4

APPERLEY BRIDGE a village in the townships of Calverley with Farsley and Eccleshill, parish of Calverley, W R Yorkshire, on the river Aire the Leeds and Liverpool canal and the Leeds and Colne railway 7¾ miles WNW of Leeds It has a station on the railway, a post office under Leeds and a large school of the sons of Methodist ministers, and it commands a fine view

APPERLEY WITH WHITEFIELD, a hamlet in Deerhurst parish Gloucester, on the river Severn, 4 miles SW of Tewkesbury It has a post-office under Tewkesbury, and a chapel of ease Pop, 427

APPERSETT, a hamlet in Hawes chapelry, N R Yorkshire, in Wedale, under Cam fell, at the head of the river Ure, 4 miles SW of Hawes

APPERTON See ALPERTON

APPLEBY, a parish in Glanford Brigg district, Lincoln, near the Doncaster and Grimsby railway, 7 miles NNW of Brigg It includes Raventhorpe hamlet and has a post-office under Brigg, and a r station. Acres, 6,164 Real property, £6 192 Pop, 579 Houses, 101 The property is divided between two Appleby House is the seat of C Winn, Esq The living is a vicarage in the diocese of Lincoln Value, £150 Patron, C Winn, Esq The church is a neat structure, with a tower

APPLEBY, a village and a parish in Ashby de la Zouch district, on the confines of Leicester and Derby The village stands 1½ mile WSW of the Mease river and the Ashby-de la Zouch canal, and 6 miles SW by S of Ashby de la Zouch r station It has a post office‡ under Atherstone, and is a meet for the Atherstone hounds. It is sometimes called Appleby Magna or Great Appleby, while a hamlet a little S of it, in the same parish, is called Appleby Parva or Little Appleby The parish comprises 2,020 acres Real property, £7 067 Pop, 1,070 Houses, 248 The property is not much divided Appleby Hall is the seat of G Moore, Esq The living is a rectory in the diocese of Peterborough Value, £750 * Patron, G Moore, Esq The church is a handsome structure with a spire, and has some good painted glass There are three dissenting chapels and a free grammar-school,—the latter founded in 1697, by Sir John Moore, lord mayor of London Endowed income of the grammar-school, £326, other charities £9

APPLEBY, a small town, two townships, two parishes, and a sub district in the district of East Ward, Westmoreland The town stands on the river Eden, and on the Eden Valley railway 9½ miles ENE of Shap, and 13 SE of Penrith It consists of Appleby proper, in the parish of Appleby St Lawrence, on the left bank of the river and Old Appleby or Bongate, in the parish of Appleby St. Michael, on the right bank It dates from the time of the Romans, and was long a place of similar importance to York It gave name to a sheriffdom under Edward the Confessor stood prominent at the Conquest, underwent surprise and demolition by William the Lion, king of Scotland, re acquired speedily its former strength and became the seat of a Court of Exchequer, suffered demolition again by the Scots in 1388, recovered but partially from the blow, and was desolated in 1598 by the plague, made a heroic resistance, under the direction of Anne, Countess of Pembroke, to the Parliamentarian army in 1648, but was constrained to yield It is supposed to have had a length or breadth of at least 2 miles, and the name Burrals belonging to a township now 1¼ mile distant from it is believed to be a corruption of Borough walls. The town was made a borough by Henry II and it sent two members to parliament from the time of Edward I till disfranchized by the act of 1832 It is governed by a mayor, twelve aldermen, and sixteen burgesses, is a seat of petty sessions, quarter sessions, and assizes, and is the place of nomination for the county members, one of the polling places, and the head quarters of the county militia But its ancient glory is represented mainly by antiquities and historical associations, and has not been followed by modern prosperity

Appleby proper stands on a hill slope, with the castle at its head, and the church of St Lawrence at its foot comprises one main street and three intersecting small ones, and is irregularly built, but contains some good houses The castle occupies the site of the Roman station Aballaba was built by the Saxons, and rebuilt, in the time of Henry VI, by Lord Clifford, and contains a portrait of the Countess Anne of Pembroke, many other family portraits, some valuable manuscripts, and some interesting old armour The church of St. Lawrence is an edifice in late English, chiefly rebuilt by the Countess Anne of Pembroke and contains tombs of that lady, of her mother the Countess of Cumberland, and of other Cliffords The county hall, in the Main street, is a large, ancient structure. The market house, built in 1811, after a design by Smirke, is a handsome Gothic edifice Queen Elizabeth's grammar school contained some curious ancient inscriptions, recording the misfortunes of the town, found here and put up by one of the masters, the friend of Camden, but which have been removed, and it possesses an endowed income of £216, with five exhibitions at Queen's college, Oxford Countess Anne's hospital, founded and endowed by the Countess Anne of Pembroke is a quadrangular building for thirteen aged widows, and has an endowed income of £812 Other charities have £182 An ancient two-arched bridge spans the Eden, and connects the two sections of the town The county jail, in Bongate, is an irregular structure of 1771, with capacity for 35 male and 8 female prisoners The church of St Michael, about ¾ of a mile SE of the town, is a neat edifice, and has tombs of the Hiltons of Murton A monastery for white friars, founded in 1281 by Lord Vessey, stood in Bongate, and was given to an ancester of the Earl of Lonsdale The town has a railway station, a post office‡ under Penrith, and a banking office A weekly market is held on Saturday, and fairs on 17 Feb, Whitsunday Eve, Whit Monday, the second Wednesday in June, the first Wednesday in July, and 21 Aug Thomas de Vitripont of the 13th century, Thomas de Appleby, bishop of Carlisle, Roger de Appleby, bishop of Ossory, Dr Bambridge, archbishop of York and Dr Christopher Potter dean of Durham, were natives, and Bedell, bishop of Kilmore, Barlow, bishop of Lincoln, Addison, dean of Lichfield, and Dr Langhorne, the translator of Plutarch, were educated at the grammar school

The township of Appleby is identical with Appleby proper Acres, 48 Pop, 960 Houses, 178 The township of Old Appleby, or Bongate, includes the part of the town on the right side of the Eden, but also extends into the country Acres, 3,261 Real property, £4,438 Pop, 654 Houses, 128 The parish of Appleby St Lawrence comprises the townships of Appleby, Scattergate, Colby, Burrals, Hoffe and Low, and Drybeck Acres 5,350 Real property, £6,291 Pop., 1 660 Houses, 300. The living is a vicarage in the diocese of Carlisle Value, £306 * Patrons, the Dean and Chapter of Carlisle The parish of Appleby St. Michael comprises the townships of Bongate, Crackenthorpe, Murton, and Hilton Acres, 14,550 Real property, inclusive of Bampton, £10,226 Pop, 1,255 Houses, 242 This living also is a vicarage in the diocese of Carlisle Value, £175 * Patron the Bishop of Carlisle The p curacy of St John's, Murton, is a separate incumbency There are, in the two parishes, several dissenting chapels The sub district comprises these two parishes and four others Acres, 55,873 Pop., 5,527 Houses 1,092

APPLEDORE, a tything in Burlescombe parish, Devon, near the Great Western railway, the Western canal, and the Culm river, 7½ miles ENE of Tiverton. Pop, 195

APPLEDORE, a seaport village and a chapelry in Northam parish, Devon The village stands on the bay at the mouths of the rivers Torridge and Taw, 3 miles N of Bideford r station, and has a head post office,‡ designated Appledore, North Devon It has pleasant environs, a fine bathing beach, and good accommodation for strangers, so that it has become an esteemed watering place It is a sub port to Bideford, and a number of its inhabitants are engaged in the coasting trade and in dock yards Hubba, the Dane landed here in the time of King Alfred, but was taken in the neighbourhood, and put to death The chapelry includes the village, and was constituted in 184- Pop 2 210 Houses, 513 The living is a vicarage in the diocese of Exeter Value £150 Patron, the Vicar of Northam The church is a neat edifice, and there are chapels for Independents Baptists and Wesleyans.

APPLEDORE, a village and a parish in Tenterden district, Kent. The village stands on the Military canal, on a branch of the river Rother, on the W border of Romney marsh 1¼ mile W of a station of its own name on the Ashford and Hastings railway and 6 ESE of Tenterden It has a post office‡ under Staplehurst, and it formerly had a weekly market and still has a fair on the 4th Monday in June It once was a seaport, on the quondam estuary of the Rother, and it was assailed by the Danes in the time of King Alfred, and by the French in 1380 The parish comprises 3,001 acres Real property, £6,184 Pop 640 Houses, 132 The property is divided among a few Much of the land is rich meadowy pasture The living is a vicarage in the diocese of Canterbury and includes the curacy of Ebony Value, £200 * Patron, the Archbishop of Canterbury The church has a singular projection from the N side of the nave, and is a strange mixture of Norman, early English, and decorated, but has been greatly altered, and is in good condition

APPLEDRAM, a parish in Westhampnett district, Sussex, on the E side of Chichester harbour, adjacent to the Arundel and Portsmouth canal and the South Coast railway, 2 miles SW of Chichester Post town, Chichester Acres, 1,197, of which 290 are water Real property, £1,763 Pop., 129. Houses, 29 The property is divided among four Appledram House is an old Tudor edifice A farm house near the church is said to have been part of a castle which William Rennan was stopped in building in the time of Edward II, and the rest of the materials for which he used in erecting the tower that bears his name at Chichester The living is a vicarage in the diocese of Chichester Value, £64 Patrons, the Dean and Chapter of Chichester The church is early English, and had a chantry

APPLEDURWELL See APPULDURCOMBE.

APPLEFORD, a chapelry in Sutton Courtney parish, Berks, on the river Thames and the Oxford branch railway, 1 mile S of Culham r station, and 3½ SE of Abingdon Post town, Abingdon Acres, 760 Real property, £1,768 Pop, 288 Houses, 61 The property is divided among a few The living is a p curacy annexed to the vicarage of Sutton Courtney, in the diocese of Oxford The church is good, and there is a free school

APPLEGARTH FOREST, a hamlet in Bowes township and parish, 12 miles N of Muker, N R Yorkshire

APPLESHAM a locality near the river Adur and the South Coast railway, 1 mile NW of Shoreham, Sussex It is a resort of sportsmen

APPLESHAW, a village and a parish in Andover district, Hants The village stands under the Downs, 5 miles WNW of Andover r station, and it has a post office under Andover, and fairs on 23 May, on the Friday and Saturday before Weyhill, and on 4 and 5 Nov The parish contains also the hamlet of Filly Down, and parts of the hamlets of Appleshaw Bottom and Dancey Acres, 697 Real property, £1,305 Pop., 284 Houses, 62 The property is divided among a few Appleshaw House is the seat of the family of Duke The living is a vicarage in the diocese of Winchester, and till 1865 was annexed to Amport The church is good

APPLESHAW BOTTOM, a hamlet in the parishes of Appleshaw and Weyhill with Penton, Hants Pop. 4-

APPLETHORPE, APESTHORPE, or HAPBLESTHORPE a parish in East Retford district, Notts, on the verge of the county, 1 mile E of Leverton r station, and 5¼ E of East Retford It contains the hamlet of Coates, and its post town is Sturton under Retford. Acres, 1,020 Real property, £1,309 Pop 142 Houses, 26 The living is a p curacy in the diocese of Lincoln Value, £81 Patron, the Bishop of L. There is no church, but there are a Wesleyan chapel, and charities £62.

APPLETHWAITE a township and a chapelry in Windermere parish, Westmoreland. The township contains Windermere village and r station includes part of Windermere lake, and extends southward from the mouth c Troutbeck vale to about a mile from Bowness Post town, Windermere Acres, 5,320 of land, and 911 of water Pop, 1,295 Houses, 187 An upland tract on the NE side, between Troutbeck and Kentmere is Applethwaite Common The chapelry is less extensive than the township and was constituted in 1856 Pop., 1,235 Houses, 179 The living is a vicarage in the diocese of Carlisle Value, £120 Patron, the Bishop of Carlisle See WINDERMERE.

APPLETHWAITE, a village on the ascent of Skiddaw, 2 miles N of Keswick, Cumberland It commands a brilliant view of Derwentwater and the encincturing mountains. A small property adjacent to it was given by Sir George Beaumont to the poet Wordsworth

APPLETON a village and a parish in Abingdon district Berks. The village stands near the Thames 5 miles NW of Abingdon r station, and has a post office under Abingdon. The parish includes also the township of Eaton Acres, 1,991 Real property, £2,820 Pop, 54 Houses, 121 The Fettiplaces had an old seat here, which is now reduced to a fragment The living is a rectory in the diocese of Oxford. Value, £307 * Patron, Magdalene College, Oxford. The church has tombs of the Fettiplaces, and a brass of a skeleton A school has £13 from endowment, and other charities £35 Edmund Dickenson, the famous chemist and physician, born in 1624, was a native

APPLETON a village in Widnes township, Prescot parish, Lancashire, near St Helen s railway, the Sankey canal, and the river Mersey 6½ miles NNW of Warrington It has a station on the railway, a post office under Warrington, a Wesleyan chapel, and a Roman Catholic chapel

APPLETON a hamlet in Flitcham parish, Norfolk, 3 miles NE of Castle Rising It is regarded ecclesiastically as a parish a vicarage, in the diocese of Norwich Value, £ Patron, Edmund Kent, Esq The church is in ruins

APPLETON or HULL and APPLETON, a township in Great Budworth parish Cheshire, near the Bridgewater canal, 3 miles SE of Warrington Acres, 3,324 Real property, £9,571 Pop, 1 828 Houses, 376 Here are Appleton Lodge, and Independent, Baptist, and Wesleyan chapels

APPLETON (EAST and WEST), a township in Catterick parish, N R. Yorkshire, 5½ miles SE of Richmond Acres, 1,533 Real property, £2,812 Pop 115 Houses 19

APPLETON LE MOORS, a chapelry in Lastingham parish, N R. Yorkshire 5 miles NW of Pickering Acres, 2,070 Real property, £2,023 Pop., 265 Houses, 53 The living is a vicarage Value, £301 The church was rebuilt in 1868 There is a Wesleyan chapel

APPLETON LE STREET a township and a parish in Malton district, N R Yorkshire The township lies on the Roman road to Aldborough, near the river Rye, 3½ miles WNW of New Malton r station Acres, 1,140 Real property, £1 815 Pop, 185 Houses, 35 The parish contains also the townships of Swinton, Broughton Amotherby, and Hildenley Post town, New Malton Acres 4 715 Real property, £8 117 Pop 937 Houses, 213 The property is subdivided The living is a vicarage in the diocese of York Value, £515 * Patron, the Rev J J Peach The church has an early Norman tower, contains two recumbent effigies, and was recently restored in a manner incongruous with its age and style Charities, £26

APPLETON NUN, a seat in Bolton Percy parish, W R Yorkshire, at the confluence of the Wharfe and the Ouse, 5½ miles SE of Tadcaster It was the site of a Cistertian nunnery, founded by Adeliza de St Quintin in the reign of Stephen, and it is now the property of Sir W M E Milner, Bart

APPLETON ROEBUCK a township and a sub-district in the district of Tadcaster W R Yorkshire The township is in the parish of Bolton Percy, near Appleton Nun, 1½ mile SE of Bolton Percy r station, and has a post office under Tadcaster, a church built in 1868, and a Wesleyan chapel Acres, 2,780 Pop, 622 Houses 141 —The sub district comprises the townships of Bolton Percy parish and another township Acres, 8,671 Pop, 1,272 Houses, 263

APPLETON WISKE or APPLETON UPON WISKE a chapelry and a sub district, in the district of Northallerton, N R Yorkshire The chapelry lies on the river Wiske, 3 miles NW of Welbury r station, and 7½ NNE of Northallerton, and it has a post office under Northallerton Acres, 1,827 Real property, £2,300 Pop., 466 Houses, 119 The property is much subdivided The living is a p curacy in the diocese of York, annexed to the rectory of Great Smeaton in the diocese of Ripon The church is very bad —The sub district comprises six parishes, and parts of three other parishes Acres, 26,590 Pop, 2,952 Houses, 620

APPLETREE, a hamlet in Aston le Walls parish, Northampton 7 miles NNE of Banbury Pop 88 Houses, 15

APPLETREE, a hundred in Derbyshire It is bounded on the W by Staffordshire, and it contains Belper, part of Ashborne, twenty nine parishes, and parts of five other parishes. Acres, 97,273 Pop in 1851, 35,348, in 1861, 34,702 Houses, 7,242

APPLETREEWICK, a village and a township in Burnsall parish, W R. Yorkshire The village stands on the river Wharfe near Bardon fell, 8½ miles NE by E of Skipton, and has a fair on 25th Oct Lord Mayor Craven was a native The township includes also Skireholme hamlet, and part of Greenhowhill village Acres, 7,740 Real property, £3,313 Pop, 354 Houses, 70

APPLEY BRIDGE, a railway station in Lancashire, on the Wigan and Southport railway, between Gathurst and Newburgh

APPREY See ALPEY

APPS COURT, a seat near the Thames, 4½ miles WSW of Kingston, in Surrey It belonged anciently to the Halls, belongs now to the Sharps and was the residence of "Conversation" Sharp, the author of "Letters.

APPULDURCOMBE, or APPLEDURWELL, a manor in Godshill parish, 2½ miles NW of Ventnor, Isle of Wight It was given by Isabella de Fortibus, in the time of Henry III, to the Benedictine abbey of Montebourg in Normandy, suffered seizure, in the time of Henry V, in reprisal of the hostilities of France, was granted by Henry VI to the Minoresses without Aldgate in London, went from them by lease to the Frys and from the latter by marriage to the Leighs and the Worsleys, passed, at the death of Sir Richard, the last of the Worsleys, to the noble family of Yarborough, and was sold by the present Earl to Winn Williams Esq A priory stood on it while it belonged to the Benedictines, and was afterwards converted into a manor house, and one of the Worsleys entertained here Henry VIII and his minister Cromwell The present mansion was founded in 1710 by Sir Robert Worsley, and completed by Sir Richard, the historian of the island, and is a square Corinthian edifice of Portland stone, with low projecting wings A very rich collection of pictures, statues and antiquities was made in it by Sir Richard and described in his magnificent and very costly work, the "Museum Worsleianum," but has been removed to the other seats of the Earl of Yarborough. The park is extensive, picturesque, and highly diversified, and commands noble views A granite obelisk, erected in 1774 in memory of Sir Robert Worsley, crowns the highest point at an elevation of 635 feet above the level of the sea, and was originally 70 feet high, but lost several feet of the top by a stroke of lightning in 1831

APSLEY WITH FORDHALL a hamlet in Ullenhall chapelry, 5½ miles NW of Henley in Arden, Warwick. Pop 126

APTHORPE See APETHORPE

AQUALATE MERE a lake on the W border of Staffordshire, 2 miles ENE of Newport, Salop It is nearly ½ a mile broad, and upwards of a mile long, possesses considerable beauty, abounds in several fish, of large size, and is the resort of various aquatic wild fowls Aqualate Hall, the seat of the baronet family of Boughey, is adjacent.

AQUIS See ALKBOROUGH

ARBORFIELD, a parish in Wokingham district, Berks, on the river Loddon, 4 miles W of Wokingham r station. Arborfield Cross, 1½ mile SE of the village, has a post-office under Reading Acres in the parish, 1,466 Real property, £3,975 Pop., 286 Houses, 65 The property is divided among a few The manor formerly belonged to the Bullocks, one of whom was "Hugh of the Brazen Band," and the old manor house, called in "Our Village, the "Old House at Aberleigh, was the deathplace, in 1730, of Edward Standen, Esq, the person alluded to in the ballad of "Molly Mogg of the Rose" The living is a rectory in the diocese of Oxford Value, £345 * Patron, Lord Braybrooke The church was built in 1663, and is in the middle pointed style

ARBOR LOW HILL, an eminence in the vicinity of Youlgreave, Derby Its summit is crowned by a Druidical circle of 150 feet in diameter, with 30 stones, and commands a fine view

ARBORY See KIRK-ARBORY

ARBURY, a hamlet in Winwick parish, Lancashire, on the Roman road, near the Liverpool railway, 3 miles N of Warrington See HOUGHTON

ARBURY, a Roman camp on Icknield street, 5½ miles NNE of Baldock, Herts

ARBURY, or HARBOROUGH, a Roman camp near Gogmagog hills 2 miles N of Cambridge

ARBURY BANKS, a Roman camp on Watling street, 1 mile W of Chipping Warden, Northampton

ARBURY HALL, the seat of the Newdegate family, in Chilvers Coton parish, 3 miles SW of Nuneaton, Warwick An Augustinian priory was built on its site in the time of Henry II, given, in 1538, to Charles Brandon, Duke of Suffolk, purchased, in the reign of Elizabeth, by Sir Edmund Anderson, and transferred, soon afterwards, in exchange for other property, to John Newdegate, Esq The priory was demolished, and a quadrangular mansion erected in its place, by Sir Edmund Anderson, and the mansion was transmuted into an elegant Gothic pile, of four fronts in different styles, by Sir Roger Newdegate who founded the Newdegate prize poem, and died in 1806 The interior is splendid, and possesses, among other attractions, a very curious and interesting picture of the time of Henry VI, brought hither from Astley Castle The park is extensive and richly ornate, and has been called the "Strawberry Hill of Warwickshire.

ARCHCLIFF See DOVER

ARCHDEACON NEWTON a township in Darlington parish, Durham, 3 miles NW of Darlington Acres, 1,040 Pop, 61 Houses 11

ARCHENFIELD See IRCHINGFIELD

ARCLEDON, a hamlet in Plumbland parish, Cumberland, 5 miles ENE of Maryport. Coal mines are in the neighbourhood

ARCLID, a township in Sandbach parish, Cheshire, 2 miles E by N of Sandbach It contains the Congleton workhouse Acres, 538 Pop, 265 Houses, 25

ARD, a prefix of Celtic names, signifying "high, and commonly applied to a high point or head

ARDDA, a hamlet in Dolgarrog township, Carnarvon, 4½ miles NW of Llanrwst.

ARDDLEEN, a railway station on the eastern verge of Montgomery, on the Oswestry and Newtown railway, 6½ miles NNE of Welshpool

ARDDYNWENT, a township in Mold parish, Flint, in the vicinity of the town of Mold. Pop, 463. Houses 105

ARDELEY, or YARDLEY a parish in Royston district, Herts, on the river Beane, 4 miles W of Westmill r station, and 4½ SW by W of Buntingford Post town, Buntingford Acres 2,405 Real property, £3,815 Pop, 574 Houses, 126 The manor was given by Athelstane to the Dean and Chapter of St Paul's Ardeley Bury belonged once to the Cornwalls, then to the Chaunceys and passed to the Murrays The living is a vicarage in the diocese of Rochester Value, £224 * Patrons, the Dean and Chapter of St Paul's The church was repaired in 1850 and has a brass of a priest Charities, £20

ARDEN, a part of Temple Grafton parish midway between Stratford on Avon and Alcester, in Warwick, or, more extensively, a tract about 17 miles long and 12 miles broad, extending northward from the Avon to the vicinity of Birmingham This was anciently a forest, and originally but part of a still greater forest, between the Severn and the Trent, held by the British Cornavii It was probably the type of Shakespeare's "Forest of Arden," and it gave the title of Baron to Earl Egmont. The name signifies "the high wood and much of the tract designated by it is now called the Woodland

ARDEN WITH ARDENSIDE, a township in Hawnby parish, N R Yorkshire, 7½ miles NW of Helmsley Acres, 4,613 Pop 129 Houses, 25. The surface is chiefly part of Humbleton moor A Benedictine nunnery was founded here in 1150 but has disappeared

ARDINGLY, a parish in Cuckfield district, Sussex near the Brighton railway, 2 miles SE of Balcombe r station, and 3 NE of Cuckfield It includes the hamlet of Hapsted, and its post town is Cuckfield Acres, 3,817 Real property, £3,564 Pop., 626 Houses, 114 Wakehurst Place, a short distance NE of the church, was formerly the seat of the Wakehursts and the Culpeppers and is now the seat of Sir Alex Cockburn The mansion was built in 1590, by one of the Culpeppers, and is a picturesque structure stained with lichens The living is a rectory in the diocese of Chichester Value, £498 * Patron, J F W Peyton Esq The church is ancient. There are an Independent chapel, a national school, and a great lower middle school, called Ardingly college The buildings of the college were completed in 1869, are in the first pointed style and comprise two quadrangles, with accommodation for 1,000 resident boy-pupils

ARDINGTON, a parish in Wantage district Berks on an affluent of the Thames, near the Wilts and Berks canal and the Great Western railway 2 miles E of Wantage, and 4 SW of Steventon r station Post town, Wantage Acres, 1,775 Real property, £3,518 Pop 354 Houses, 78 Ardington House was the residence of Clarke the antiquary, and the seat of Robert Vernon, Esq, who collected here the "Vernon Gallery of pictures, which he left to the nation, and died in 1849 The living is a vicarage in the diocese of Oxford Value not reported * Patron, Christ's Church, Oxford The church is good, and has a tomb of R Vernon

ARDLEIGH, a parish and a sub district in the district of Tendring, Essex The parish lies on the Eastern Union railway, 1½ NE of Colchester, and it has a station on the railway, and a post office under Colchester Acres, 4,905. Real property, £9 445 Pop, 1 532 Houses, 360 The property is divided among a few The living is a vicarage in the diocese of Rochester Value £380 * Patron, the Lord Chancellor The church is good, and there is a Wesleyan chapel.—The sub district comprises six parishes Acres, 18,037 Pop, 4,964 Houses, 1,136

ARDLEY, a parish in Bicester district, Oxford on the boundary ditch between Mercia and Wessex, 3½ miles ENE of Heyford r station and 4½ NW of Bicester Post town, Fritwell under Bicester Acres, 1,469 Real property, £1 728 Pop, 169 Houses, 36 The property is divided among a few Foundations exist of a Norman castle, built in the reign of Stephen, on the site of Offa's camp The living is a rectory in the diocese of Oxford Value £307 * Patron, the Duke of Marlborough The church is good

ARDSLEY, a township and a chapelry in Darfield parish, W R Yorkshire. The township lies on the Barnsley branch railway and on the Dearne and Dove canal 2½ miles ESE of Barnsley and it has a station on the railway and a post-office under Barnsley Acres, 1 212 Real property, £12 033,—of which £7,109 are in mines and quarries. Pop 1 772 Houses, 363 The chief residences are Ardsley Hall and Ardsley Park. The fanatical and ill used Quaker, James Nayler, who died in 1660, was a native The chapelry is less extensive than the township, and was constituted in 1844 Pop, 1,712 Houses 363 The living is a vicarage in the diocese of York Value, £120 * Patron the Vicar of Darfield. The church is in the Norman style and was built in 1841 There is a Wesleyan chapel

ARDSLEY, a railway station and a sub district in the district of Wakefield, W R Yorkshire The railway station is on the Leeds and Wakefield railway, 3 miles from Leeds, and 5 from Wakefield. The sub district comprises the parishes of Ardsley, East and West, and the township of Thorpe Acres, 4,414 Pop, 2,786 Houses, 537

ARDSLEY (EAST), a parish in Wakefield district, W R Yorkshire, on the Leeds and Wakefield railway, 1½ mile from Ardsley station, and 3¼ NW of Wakefield It has a post-office under Wakefield. Acres, 1,630 Real property, £3 963 Pop, 1,069 Houses, 219 The property is not much divided Coal abounds, and there is a large woollen factory The living is a vicarage in the diocese of Ripon Value £369 * Patron, the Earl of Cardigan The church is good, and there are a U Free Methodist chapel and charities £14

ARDSLEY (WEST) or WOODKIRK a parish in Wakefield district, W R Yorkshire, on the Leeds and Wakefield railway, at Ardsley station, 5 miles NW of Wakefield It includes six hamlets and has a post office o the name of West Ardsley, under Wakefield Acres 2 2[illegible] Real property, £5,139 Pop, 1,646 Houses, 335 Coal is worked, and bricks are made. The living is a vicarage in the diocese of Ripon Value, £265 * Patron, the Earl of Cardigan The church was rebuilt in 1831 There are two Methodist chapels a partially endowed school, and charities £10

ARDUDWY a hundred in the NW of Merioneth It contains Harlech, sixteen parishes, and part of another, and is cut into two parts, Is Artro and Uwch Artro Acres of A Is Artro, 59 415 Pop in 1851, 10,629, in 1861, 13,324 Houses, 775 Acres of A Uwch Artro 36 540 Pop in 1851 3,559, in 1861, 11 750 Houses, 2 4_5

ARDWICK, a township, three chapelries, and a sub district in Manchester parish, Lancashire The township is suburban to Manchester city, on the SE, and lies within the borough boundaries Acres, 470 Real property £57,895 Pop, 21,757 Houses, 4,414 The Manchester and Sheffield railway has a station here ¾ of a mile from the terminus, joins here the Manchester and Birmingham railway near Chancery lane, and is carried here on a succession of immense viaducts —The chapelries are Ardwick St Thomas Ardwick St Silas and Ardwick St Matthew, and were constituted in respectively 1833, 1844, and 1868 Pop of A St T, 10 147 Houses 2 029 Pop of A St S, 10,375 Houses, 2,1 3 The livings are rectories in the diocese of Manchester Value of St E and St S, each £300, of St M, not reported Patrons of St T, the Dean and Chapter of Manchester of St S and St. M, Trustees —The sub district includes also four other townships, and is in Chorlton district Acres, 4,031 Pop, 47,752 Houses, 9 322

ARELEY (KINGS), a parish in Martley district, Worcester, on the river Severn ½ a mile SW of Stourport r station It contains the hamlet of Dunley, and its post town is Stourport Acres 1 149 Real property £3 659 Pop 564 Houses, 138 The property is not subdivided An eminence on which the church is situated commands an extensive prospect Areley House and Areley Hall are chief residences The living is a rectory in the diocese of Worcester Value £346 * Patron the Rev H J Hastings The church is early English, with a Norman doorway A rude sepulchral monument inscribed with a quaint rhyming distich said to be to the memory of Sir Henry Coningsby of Hertfordshire is in the churchyard Layamon author of an ancient British history, was a native Charities, £19

ARELEY (UPPER) See ARLEY (UPPER)

ARGAM or ERGHAM, a parish in Bridlington district E R Yorkshire on the Wolds, 2½ miles WSW of Speeton r station, and 5 NW of Bridlington Post town Grindale under Hull Acres, 510 Real property, £798 Pop 27 Houses [illegible] The living is a sinecure rectory Value, £21 Patron, C Grimston Esq

ARGOED, a railway station in the W of Monmouth, between Blackwood and Tredegar

ARGOED, a township in Mold parish, Flint, 1½ mile from the town of Mold Pop, 874 Houses, 179

ARGOED AND YSTRAD a township in Caron ys Clawdd parish, Cardigan It contains the town of Tregaron Pop, 832 Houses, 213

ARK (THE), a stream of N R Yorkshire. It rises on Stonedale Moor, adjacent to the boundary with Westmoreland and runs 11 miles south eastward, through Arkengarth Dale, to the Swale below Reeth

ARKENDALE, a township chapelry in the parishes of Knaresborough and Farnham, W R Yorkshire, 2¾ miles N of Goldsborough r station, and 3¼ NE of Knaresborough It has a post office under Knaresborough Acres 1,620 Real property, £4,235 Pop, 242 Houses 47 The property is much subdivided The living is a p curacy in the diocese of Ripon Value, £80 * Patron the Vicar of Knaresborough The church is modern and good, and there is a Wesleyan chapel.

ARKENGARTH DALE, a parish in Reeth district, N R Yorkshire, on the river Ark, 2 miles NW of Reeth, and 10 W of Richmond r station It includes the hamlets of Arkle Booze, Langthwaite, Eskeleth, Seal Houses, Whaw, and Dale Head, and its post town is Reeth, under Richmond Acres, 14,235 Real property, £7 320,—of which £2,647 are in lead mines Pop, 1 147 Houses, 249 The lead mines belong to Sir J Lowther, Bart, and the other property is much subdivided The mines were worked so early as the time of King John, and are still so valuable as to have been estimated, a few years ago, at an annual produce of 2,000 tons Barytes and witherite ores are found Much of the land is moor The living is a vicarage in the diocese of Ripon Value, £123 Patron Sir J Lowther, Bart The church is good, and there are a Methodist chapel, and charities £37

ARKESDEN, a parish in Saffron Walden district, Essex, on an affluent of the river Stort 2½ miles W of Newport r station, and 5 SW of Saffron Walden Post town, Newport under Bishop Stortford Acres 2,320 Real property, £3,207 Pop, 506 Houses, 111 The property is not much divided The living is a vicarage in the diocese of Rochester Value, £181 * Patron, the Rev W B Wolfe The church is very good, and contains a brass of a knight

ARKHOLME, a township chapelry and a sub district in Lancaster district Lancashire The township is in Melling parish, lies on the river Lune and on the Furness and Midland railway, 3 miles NNE of Hornby, and has a post office under Lancaster, and a r station Acres, 3,022 Real property, £3,424 Pop, 331 Houses, 59 The living is a vicarage in the diocese of Manchester Value, £80 * Patron the Vicar of Melling Charities, £14 —The sub district comprises this township, the parish of Whittington and part of another parish Acres, 9,278 Pop, 910 Houses, 173

ARKLE See ARKENGARTH DALE

ARKLEBY a sub station on the Carlisle and Maryport railway 1½ mile SW of Aspatria, Cumberland

ARKLESIDE, a hamlet in Carlton Highdale township Coverham parish N R Yorkshire, 6¼ miles SW of Middleham

ARKLEY, a chapelry in East Barnet parish Herts a p curacy in the diocese of Rochester Statistics returned with the parish

ARKSEY or BENTLEY WITH ARKSEY, a parish in Doncaster district, W R Yorkshire on the Great Northern railway and the river Don 2 miles N of Doncaster It has a station on the railway it includes the hamlets of Almholme, Bodles, Doncaster Bridgend Scawthorpe Shaftholme and Stockbridge, and it has a post office, of the name of Bentley, under Doncaster Acres, 5,221 Rated property, £8 859 Pop 1,099 Houses 200 The living is a vicarage in the diocese of York Value £113 Patron Sir W B C Cooke Bart The church is ancient There are two Methodist chapels a free school 12 alms houses, and other charities £160.

ARLE, a tything in the parish and within the borough of Cheltenham, Gloucester

ARLE (THE), a head stream of the Itchen river in Hants

ARLECDON, a parish in Whitehaven district, Cumberland, 4¾ miles E by N of Parton r station, and 5½ ENE of Whitehaven It includes the townships of Frizington and Whillymore, and its post town is Whitehaven Acres, 5 700 Real property, £18,793, —of which £15,407 are in mines Pop, 1,550 Houses, 254 The property is much subdivided Coal, lime, and ironstone are worked, and there is a good chalybeate spring The living is a vicarage in the diocese of Carlisle Value, £100 Patron, the Bishop of Carlisle The church was built in 1829 There is a Wesleyan chapel

ARLEEN, a locality on the NW border of Montgomeryshire, 2½ miles S of Llanymynech, with a post office under Oswestry

ARLESCOTE, a hamlet in Warmington parish, Warwick, near Nadbury camp, 4¼ miles ESE of Kington Pop, 43. Arlescote manor, around the hamlet, was given at the Conquest to the Earl of Mellent, was, in great part, transferred by him to the monks of Preaux, and passed, at the dissolution, to the family of Andrews

ARLESEY, ARLSEY, or ARSLEY, a village and a parish in Biggleswade district, Beds The village stands on the river Hiz a little E of the Great Northern railway, 4 miles ESE of Shefford, and it has a station on the railway, and a post office under Baldock, and was formerly a market town The parish comprises 2,370 acres Real property, £5,357 Pop, 1,401 Houses, 270 The property is divided among a few An ancient castle stood at Etonbury, near the road to Baldock, and appears, from an entrenchment which still remains, to have been a place of considerable strength The living is a vicarage, united with Astwick rectory, in the diocese of Ely Value, £420 * Patron, James Curtis, Esq The church is a plain edifice, was recently fitted with new benches, and contains some ancient monuments There are a Wesleyan chapel, a national school, and extensive brick-works

ARLESTON, a hamlet in Wellington parish, Salop, 1 mile SE of Wellington Pop, 181

ARLESTON AND SINFIN, a liberty in Barrow upon Trent parish, Derbyshire, 3¼ miles SE of Derby Pop, 54 Houses, 10

ARLEY, a parish in Nuneaton district, Warwick, on the Birmingham and Leicester railway, with a r station 6 miles W by S of Nuneaton It includes a place called Sloley Hill, and its post town is Fillongley under Coventry Acres, 1,929 Real property, £3,366 Pop, 230 Houses, 56 The property is much subdivided. The living is a rectory in the diocese of Worcester Value, £351 * Patron, the Rev Roger R Vaughton The church is good, and there are charities £36

ARLEY, a locality in Great Budworth parish, Cheshire, 4½ miles NNE of Northwich, with a post office under that town Arley Hall, with an extensive park, is adjacent, and Arley Mere is in the park

ARLEY, a railway station adjacent to the meeting point of Stafford, Worcester, and Salop, on the Severn Valley railway, at Upper Arley, 4½ miles NNW of Bewdley

ARLEY (KING'S) See ARELEY (KING'S).

ARLEY (UPPER), a parish in the district of Kidderminster, and county of Stafford, in the southwestern projection of the county, on the river Severn, and on the Severn Valley railway, at Arley r station, 4½ miles NNW of Bewdley It has a post-office under Bewdley Acres, 3,912 Real property, £9,031 Pop., 886 Houses, 158 Arley Hall here is the seat of Viscount Valentia, and there is an ancient camp in the woods of its park The living is a vicarage in the diocese of Lichfield Value, £255 Patron, Viscount Valentia * The church is conspicuously situated, and has a fine prospect Charities £35

ARLINGHAM, a parish in Wheatenhurst district, Gloucester, on the left side of the Severn, within a fold of that river, nearly opposite Newnham r station, and 9 miles WNW of Stonehouse It has a post office under Stonehouse Acres, 3,225,—of which 835 are water Real property, £5,333. Pop, 693 Houses, 163 The property is divided among a few Much of the land is marshy Some spots command a fine view of the Severn and its screens A chief residence is Arlingham Court The living is a vicarage in the diocese of Gloucester and Bristol Value, £193 * Patron, John Sayer, Esq The church is good, and there are a Wesleyan chapel, and charities £80

ARLINGTON, a parish in Barnstaple district, Devon, near East Down 6 miles NNE of Barnstaple r station It has a post-office under Barnstaple Acres, 2,535 Real property, £2,622 Pop, 219 Houses, 37 The manor belongs to the Chichester family,—came into their possession in the time of Henry VII, and Arlington Court, the family seat is a very handsome edifice The living is a rectory in the diocese of Exeter Value, £272 * Patron, Sir A P B Chichester, Bart. The church, with the exception of the tower was rebuilt a few years ago, is in the Gothic style and contains many memorials of the Chichesters Charities, £4

ARLINGTON, a tything in Bibury parish, Gloucester, 4 miles NNW of Fairford Here is a Baptist chapel Pop., 415 Houses, 90

ARLINGTON, a parish in Hailsham district, Sussex, on the river Cuckmere, 1 mile NE of Berwick r station, and 4 SW by W of Hailsham It has a post office under Hurst Green Acres, 5,185 Real property, £5 631 Pop., 623 Houses, 123. The Roman Anderida Sylva occupied all the surface and the Roman camp of Burlow Castle is in the neighbourhood The living is a vicarage in the diocese of Chichester Value, £156 * Patron, the Bishop of London The Dicker p. curacy is a separate benefice

ARLSEY See ARLESEY

ARMATHWAITE, a village, a castle and a chapelry in Hesket in the Forest parish, Cumberland The village stands on the river Eden 4 miles E of Southwaite r station, and 10 N of Penrith It has a post office under Carlisle, and it was the site of a small Benedictine nunnery, built and endowed by King William Rufus The castle stands adjacent is a plain, modernized, ancient tower, was the seat of the satirical poet Skelton, noted for his attack on Wolsey, "Why come ye not to Court," and is now the property of the Earl of Lonsdale The surrounding scenery on the Eden is picturesque and includes a long wooded walk, a grand projecting crag, a cataract in the stream and a lake like expanse above, with the massive background of the Cooms and the Baron Wood The chapelry is a p curacy in the diocese of Carlisle Value, £90 Patron, the Earl of Lonsdale The church is plain but picturesque

ARMATHWAITE HALL, the seat of Sir Henry Vane, Bart, at the foot of Bassenthwaite water, 5½ miles ENE of Cockermouth, Cumberland The grounds are very beautiful, and a spot adjacent to them, on the road to Hesket-Newmarket, commands one of the richest views of Bassenthwaite water and its screens

ARMBOTH FELLS, a range of steep high hill, overhanging the W side of Thirlmere, and confronting Helvellyn, 5 miles SSE of Keswick, Cumberland The summit commands a magnificent view

ARMIN, a chapelry in Snaith parish, W R Yorkshire, at the confluence of the Aire and the Ouse, 1½ mile NW of Goole r station It has a post office under Howden Acres 3,660 Real property, £5,750 Pop, 557 Houses, 117 The living is a p curacy in the diocese of York Value, £74 * Patrons C Heber Percy, Esq, and G J Yarburgh, Esq The church had a chantry

ARMINGFORD, a hundred in Cambridge It is bounded by Herts on the S, by Beds on the W, and it contains thirteen parishes and part of another Acres, 29 307 Pop in 1851, 9,711 in 1861, 9,250 Houses, 1,902

ARMINGHALL, a parish in Henstead district Norfolk, near a branch of the river Yare, 3 miles SSE of

Swainsthorpe r station, and 3½ S by E of Norwich Post town, Norwich Acres, 650 Real property, £1,444 Pop, 75 Houses 21 The property is not much divided The living is a vicarage in the diocese of Norwich Value, £80 Patrons, the Dean and Chapter of Norwich The church is very good, and belonged anciently to Norwich priory Charities £6

ARMITAGE a parish in Lichfield district, Stafford, on the Northwestern railway and the Grand Trunk canal, 3½ miles NW of Lichfield It has a station on the railway, and a post office under Rugeley, and it includes the hamlet of Handsacre and part of the village of Brereton Acres, 1,921 Rated property, £4,943 Pop, 937 Houses, 206 The property is divided among a few Armitage Park is a fine mansion The Grand Trunk canal in its course within the parish, passes through a large tunnel The living is a vicarage in the diocese of Lichfield Value, £300 Patron, the Bishop of Lichfield The church stands on a rocky eminence has a Norman doorway, and an interior hand some arch, and is a picturesque object. A church stood formerly at Handsacre, but is now a ruin There are chapels for Independents and Wesleyans Charities, £9

ARMITAGE BRIDGE, a chapelry in Almondbury parish, near Huddersfield, W R Yorkshire It was constituted in 1848. Pop, 2,455 Houses, 561 The living is a vicarage in the diocese of Ripon Value, £196 * Patrons, the Vicar of Almondbury and J Brooke, Esq

ARMLEY, a township-chapelry in Leeds parish, W R Yorkshire, on the Leeds and Bradford railway, the Leeds and Liverpool canal, and the river Aire, 1¾ mile W of Leeds It has a station on the railway, and a post office under Leeds. Acres, 907 Real property £16,744 Pop 6,734 Houses, 1,491 A number of factories, in various departments of the woollen trade, are on the banks of the river Armley Park, the seat of the Gott family, and Leeds borough gaol, are near the railway station A Danish camp, called Giants Hill, was an object of much antiquarian interest, but was cut through at the forming of the canal, and has been nearly effaced The living is a p curacy in the diocese of Ripon Value, £204 * Patron, the Vicar of Leeds The church is a plain edifice, and there are four dissenting chapels

ARMSCOTT a hamlet in Tredington parish, Worcester near the river Stour, 2 miles NNW of Shipston on Stour Pop 139

ARMSTON, a hamlet in Polebrook parish, Northampton near the Peterborough railway and the river Nen 3½ miles SE of Oundle Pop., 26

ARMTHORPE, a parish in Doncaster district, W R Yorkshire, 3 miles NE of Doncaster r station Post town, Doncaster Acres, 2,810 Real property £3,485 Pop, 424 Houses, 83 The living is a rectory in the diocese of York Value £368 * Patron, J W Childers Esq The church is old but good There are a P Methodist chapel a national school, and charities £49

ARNCLIFFE, a township and a sub-district in the district of Settle, and a parish chiefly in that district but partly also in the district of Skipton, W R Yorkshire The township lies on the river Wharfe 10 miles NE of Settle r station and has a post office under Skipton Acres, 5,750 Real property, £1,884 Pop., 174 Houses, 36 The sub district comprises also the townships of Hawkeswick, Litton, and Halton Gill Acres, 20,797 Pop, 405 Houses, 87 The parish includes also the township of Buckden Acres, 34,021 Real property, £12,009 Pop, 740 Houses, 159 The property is considerably divided Much of the land is hilly and moorish, but many spots near the streams, are low and pleasant Manufacturing industry, in textile fabrics, employed many of the inhabitants, but has much declined The living is a vicarage in the diocese of Ripon Value £36 * Patron, University College Oxford The church is old and has been carefully restored The p curacies of Halton Gill and Hubberholme are separate incumbencies A school has £28 from endowment, and other charities £34

ARNCLIFFE INGLEBY See Ingleby Arncliffe

ARNCOTT, a hamlet in Ambrosden parish, Oxford, on the river Ray 3½ miles SE of Bicester Acres, 2,010 Real property, £1,018 Pop, 334 Houses, 87 Arncott Wood commands a fine view

ARNE, a parish in Wareham district, Dorset, on the W side of Poole harbour, 4 miles E of Wareham r station Post town, Wareham Acres, 4,190, of which 1,580 are water Real property, with Parlsmead and Haymoor, £521 Pop 139 Houses, 30 The living is a p curacy, annexed to the rectory of Wareham, in the diocese of Salisbury

ARNESBY, a parish in Lutterworth district, Leicester, 3½ miles SE of Countesthorpe r station, and 8 S by E of Leicester Post town, Shearsby under Rugby Acres, 1,510 Real property, £3,034 Pop., 573 Houses, 121 The living is a vicarage in the diocese of Peterborough Value, £119 Patron, the Rev W Pilling A Baptist church has existed here since 1702 Robert Hall was a native Charities, 57

ARNOLD, a hamlet in Swine and Long Riston parishes E R Yorkshire, 7 miles E of Beverley Pop, 192

ARNOLD, a village, a parish, and a sub district, in the district of Basford, Notts The village stands near Sherwood forest, 2½ miles ENE of Bulwell r station, and 5½ N by E of Nottingham It has a post office‡ under Nottingham Its inhabitants are employed chiefly in lace and stocking making The parish includes also part of Daybrook hamlet and the seats of Arnold Grove and Sherwood Lodge Acres, 4,670 Real property, £12,059 Pop, 4,642 Houses, 971 The property is much sub divided The living is a vicarage in the diocese of Lincoln Value, £310 * Patron, the Duke of Devonshire The church is later English, and has a tower There are chapels for Sc. Presbyterians, Baptists, Wesleyans and P Methodists A school has £23 from endowment and other charities £10 P Bonington the painter, born in 1801, was a native —The sub district comprises six parishes and an extra parochial liberty Acres, 18,520 Pop, 8,378 Houses, 1,779

ARNSIDE, a village in Beetham parish Westmoreland, on the coast, near the Lancaster and Ulverstone railway, at the influx of the river Kent to Morecambe bay, 4½ miles W of Burton in Kendal It has a station on the railway, a post office under Milnthorpe, and a church built in 1866 and is a sub port to Lancaster Arnside Knot is an adjacent eminence, commanding an extensive prospect and Arnside Tower, on that eminence, is the ruined ancient residence of the Stanleys

ARNWOOD, a tything in Hordle parish Hants, 2 miles NW of Lymington Pop, 543

ARRAM, a hamlet in Leckonfield parish E R Yorkshire, on the river Hull, 3 miles N of Beverley It has a station on the Hull and Scarborough railway Pop, 117

ARRAM a hamlet in Atwick parish, E R Yorkshire, 3 miles NW of Hornsey Pop., 25

ARRAN FOWDDY, ARRAN GESSEL, and ARRAN PENLLYN, three chief summits of the Berwyn mountains, on the mutual boundary of Montgomery and Merioneth They have altitudes of respectively 2,955, 2,221, and 2,004 feet above the level of the sea The headstreams of the Dee rise on their NW side See BWLCH Y GROES

ARRAS See MARKET WEIGHTON

ARRATHORNE See ARRATHORNE.

ARRENIG, a mountain, 2,809 feet high, 7 miles W of Bala, Merioneth

ARRETON, or ATHERTON a village and a parish in the Isle of Wight The village stands 2¾ miles SE of Newport, consists of a long straggling street, leading down to the river Medina, and has a post office under Newport. The parish contains also the hamlet of Budlesford Acres, 8,833 Real property, £12,527 Pop, 1,980 Houses 385 Arreton Down adjacent to the NW end of the village forms part of the range of chalk hills, extending from Culver Cliff to the Needles, commands an extensive and very brilliant view and is crowned by two barrows The living is a vicarage in the diocese of Winchester Value £220 * Patron J Fleming Esq The church stands in a vale at the foot of the Down, at the head of the village is an ancient struc ture, in mixed Norman and early English, with a low tower of perpendicular date and contains some fine monuments of the family of Holmes, and a curious brass of a knight of 1430 It was one of the six churches given by Fitz Osborne soon after the Conquest to the abbey of Lire in Normandy A school has £37 from endowment and other charities £27 Elizabeth Wallbridge the "Dairyman's Daughter of the Rev Leigh Richmond's well known narrative, was a native Her father's cottage is on the right of the road to Sandown, and her grave is in the churchyard, marked by a head stone, with an epitaph from the pen of her biographer, beginning,—

"Stranger! if e'er by chance or feeling led,
Upon this hallowed turf thy footsteps tread,
Turn from the contemplation of the sod
And think on her whose spirit rests with God.'

ARRINGTON, a village and a parish in Caxton district, Cambridge The village stands on Ermine street, near the bridge on the Cam 3½ miles WNW of Shepreth r station, and 7 N of Royston, and was anciently called Erminton It has a post office under Royston, and is a seat of petty sessions. Sixteen human skeletons were found near it in 1721, within 2 feet of the surface, supposed to have been the remains of soldiers killed in a skirmish, in the time of Charles I, for the possession of [illegible] over the Cam The parish comprises 1,388 acres Real property £1,201 Pop, 302 Houses, 59 The property is divided among a few The living is a vicarage in the diocese of Ely Value £69 Patron, Trinity College, Cambridge The church is ancient, and has a double piscina

ARROW, a township in Woodchurch parish, Cheshire, 3 miles SW of Birkenhead Acres, 732 Pop, 109 Houses, 19

ARROW, a township and a parish in Alcester district Warwick The township lies on the Alne or Arrow river, 1 mile SW of Alcester r station and 8 W of Stratford on Avon, and its post town is Alcester, under Redditch Real property, £4,137 Pop, 295 Houses, 69 The parish includes also the township of Oversley Acres, 4,220 Real property £6,811 Pop, 590 Houses, 111 The chief feature is the Marquis of Hertford's magnificent seat of Ragley Park. The living is a rectory in the diocese of Worcester Value, £248 * Patron, the Marquis of Hertford The church is ancient Charities £5 See RAGLEY PARK

ARROW (THE), a river of Worcester and Warwick It rises in the Lickey, near Alvechurch and runs 11 miles southward to a confluence with the Alne at Alcester

ARROW (THE), a river of Radnor and Hereford. It rises 2½ miles N of Glascwm, and runs about 25 miles eastward, past Kington and Pembridge, to the Lug below Leominster

ARSCOTT, a township in Pontesbury parish, Salop, 6½ miles SW of Shrewsbury Pop, 127

ARSLEY See APLESEY

ARTH (THE), a stream of Cardigan It rises at the S end of the Mynydd Bach mountains, and runs 8 miles westward to the Irish sea at Aberarth

ARTHINGTON, a chapelry in Adel parish, W R Yorkshire, on the river Wharfe and on the Leeds and Stockton railway, 4 miles E of Otley It has a station on the railway, 9½ miles from Leeds Acres, 1,780 Real property, £3,710 Pop. 341 Houses 63 A Cluniac nunnery was founded here, in the 12th century by Peter de Ardington The living is a vicarage in the diocese of Ripon Value, £110 * Patron, W Sheepshanks, Esq The church was built in 1864

ARTHINGWORTH, a parish in the district of Market Harborough and county of Northampton, on an affluent of the river Nen, 1½ mile NW of Kelmarsh r station, and 5 S by E of Market Harborough. Post town, Kelmarsh under Northampton Acres 2,030 Real property, £3,056 Pop, 275 Houses, 53 The property is divided among a few Arthingworth Hall is the seat of the family of Rokeby The parish is a meet for the Pytchley hounds The living is a rectory in the diocese of Peterborough. Value, £323 Patron, the Rev H R. Rokeby Charities, £39

ARTHUR (GREAT and LITTLE), two islets of the Scilly Islands They lie near St Martin's, and are of small extent

ARTHURET, a parish in Longtown district Cumberland on the river Esk and the Border Counties railway, 8 miles N of Carlisle It contains Longtown, with r station and post-office, the latter under Carlisle, and contains also the townships of Netherby, Brecouhill, and Lyneside Acres, 17,390 Real property, £9,617 Pop, 3,714 Houses, 615 The property is divided among a few Much of the surface is the low flat land of Solway moss, stretching toward the head of the Solway frith, and this, in 1543, was the scene of a famous battle in which the Scots under Oliver Sinclair were defeated by the English under Sir Thomas Wharton Netherby Hall is the seat of Sir F U Graham Bart., and contains a large collection of Roman coins, tablets, altars baths, and other relics found in the vicinity The living is a rectory in the diocese of Carlisle. Value, £847 * Patron, Sir F U Graham, Bart. The church was renovated in 1869 There is an endowed school with £40 a year Archy Armstrong, court jester to James I and Charles I, was a native, and was buried in the church yard.

ARTHUR'S CHAIR or CADER ARTHUR, two grand mountain peaks, 5 miles S of Brecon They rise to the height of 2,862 feet, are among the loftiest summits in South Wales, command a very extensive view, have a striking appearance, and are sometimes called the Brecknock Beacons.

ARTHUR'S GRAVE See GLASTONBURY

ARTHUR'S PALACE. See CADBURY (SOUTH)

ARTHUR'S ROUND TABLE, an ancient circular plot of ground on the left side of the river Lowther, 1½ mile S of Penrith, Westmoreland It measures 87 feet in diameter, is encompassed by a broad ditch and a high mound and is supposed to have been used in the time of Richard III and later, for tournaments Sir Walter Scott calls it

"Red Penrith's Table Round
For feats of chivalry renowned.'

ARTHUR'S ROUND TABLE, a series of ancient artificial cavities in rock in Llansannan parish Denbighshire, 6½ miles W of Denbigh. They are twenty four in number, and large enough for men to sit in

ARTHUR'S STONE, a cromlech on the N slope of Cefn Bryn, 9 miles W of Swansea, Glamorgan It comprises a mass of millstone grit, 14 feet long 7 feet 2 inches deep, and about 20 tons in estimated weight, resting apparently on nine upright supporters, but really upon only four, and all somewhat sunk in a hollow crowded with rough stones It ranks in the same class of great antiquities as Stonehenge See CEFN BRYN

ARTHUR'S STONE, a cromlech in Moccas parish, Hereford, on an eminence adjacent to the river Wye 6½ miles SSW of Weobly It consists of one chief stone and eleven supporters, and commands a fine view

ARTINGTON, or LARTINGTON a tything in St. Nicholas Guildford parish Surrey on the river Wey, 1¾ mile SSW of Guildford Acres, [illegible] 500 Pop 914 Houses 170

ARTILLBURY, a township in Worfield parish, Salop, near Bridgnorth

ARUN (THE), a river of Sussex It rises in St Leonard's forest, runs westward, past Horsham, to the vicinity of Loxwood, receives, by the way, a head-stream from Surrey turns to the S, goes to Stopham, and receives there the Rother, and proceeds southward past Arundel to the English channel at Little Hampton. Its length of course is about 33 miles It abounds with mullets which are much famed under the name of Arundel mullets, and it also contains trout of superior quality but in no great quantity It is navigable for some distance from the sea, and it opens the way for inland navigation through the Arundel and Portsmouth canal with Chichester —through the river Rother, with Petworth and Midhurst—and through the Arun and Wey canal, with Guildford and the Thames Causes of the ancient Bri tish appear to have plied on it and two formed of open trunks, were found in 1834 and 1857 at North Stoke and South Stoke one of them six feet below the surface of the soil, at 150 yards from the present edge of the river, and now preserved in the British Museum The Arun has been sung by Collins and by Charlotte Smith, and the former, alluding to a brother poet, says,—

> "Wild Arun too has heard thy strains,
> And Echo, midst thy native plains,
> Been soothed by Pity's lute
> There first the wren thy myrtles shed
> On gentlest Otway's infant head,
> To him thy cell was shown."

ARUN AND WEY CANAL, a canal connecting the rivers Arun and Wey It leaves the Arun below Stopham, goes northward past Loxwood and Bramley, and joins the Wey 2 miles S of Guildford It is 18 miles long, and has 23 locks

ARUNDEL, a railway station, a town, a castle, a parish, a hundred, a sub district, and a rape in Sussex The railway station is on the Horsham and Arundel railway 2 miles NNE of Ford junction, and 8¼ S by W of Pulborough, superseded a previous station, 2 miles S, on the Brighton and South Coast railway, and has a telegraph The town stands on the right bank of the Arun on the irregular ascent of a considerable hill, ¼ a mile W of the station It takes its name from the vale of Arun Arun dale, a word probably of ancient British origin, and it is supposed to have been influenced by the Roman station Ad Decimum at Bignor, and by the Roman Portus Adurni which may have been within the mouth of the river, but it is first mentioned in the will of King Alfred, who bequeathed it to his nephew Adhelm It consists of one street going steeply up from the Arun to the castle, and two others going off from this at right angles. It is a small place of little intrinsic interest, but it has always derived much consequence in many ways, from the castle Its houses, in general, are well built A neat bridge of three arches spans the river The town hall was erected by Bernard, Duke of Norfolk, at a cost of £9,000 The parish church is a cruciform edifice, of flint and stone 190 feet long with a low central tower surmounted by a short leaden spire It occupies the site of a Benedictine priory, founded soon after the Conquest, by Roger de Montgomery, and it was built in 1380, and made then collegiate for a master and twelve canons, under the name of the college of the Holy Trinity It is entirely perpendicular English, it has a college chapel E of the chancel, and a Lady chapel N of the former, and it contains six grand monuments of Earls of Arundel and several brasses A Maison Dieu a quadrangular edifice, with chapel and refectory, was built at the foot of the town, about the same time as the church, but only some fragments of it now exist There are two dissenting chapels a Roman Catholic chapel, a work house, and a considerable inn The town ranks as a head sea port, and vessels drawing 13 feet water come up to it but the real head port, and now the place of the custom house is Little Hampton, 3½ miles distant, at the mouth of the river The vessels belonging to the port, at the beginning of the year 1868, were 34 small sailing vessels, of aggregately 997 tons, and 42 larger sailing vessels, of aggregately 6 845 tons The sailing vessels that entered in 1867 were 432 of 40,590 tons, in the coasting trade, 4 of 246 tons from British colonies, and 86 of 3,983 tons, from foreign countries Chief imports are coal and fruit and chief exports, corn, timber, and oak bark The amount of customs in 1867 was £660 The town has a head post office ‡ a telegraph station and two banking offices, and it publishes a weekly newspaper A fortnightly market is held on Monday and fairs on 14 May, 21 Aug 25 Sept and 17 Dec. Arundel is a borough by prescription and it sent two members to parliament from the time of Edward I till 1832, but it was half disfranchised by the reform act of 1832, and wholly disfranchised by the act of 1868 for increasing the representation of Scotland The town is governed by a mayor four aldermen, and twelve councillors, and it is a seat of petty sessions, and a county polling place Real property £11,055 Assessed taxes, £1,879 Pop., 2,498 Houses 528

Arundel Castle is the chief seat of the Duke of Norfolk It stands adjacent to the church, at the head of the town, on the verge of a plateau which stoops precipitously, on two sides, at least 90 feet, to the low bank of the Arun Its position is a strong one, in a military view, and was well fitted, in the old times, to maintain high command over the surrounding country The original pile is said to have been built, in the Saxon times, by Bevis, a hero of romance, the next pile, possessing much military strength, was built, soon after the Conquest, by Roger de Montgomery who was related by blood to the Conqueror, and led the centre division of the victorious army at the battle of Hastings, and the greater part of the present pile, 250 feet long and 250 feet broad, was built, in 1791 and succeeding years, by Charles eleventh Duke of Norfolk The castle was visited, in 1097, by William Rufus, it was besieged in 1102 by Henry I and taken then from Robert de Belesme, Robert de Montgomery's heir, who had rebelled against the Crown, it was inhabited by Henry I's widow, Queen Alice or Adeliza, and gave hospitable shelter, under her, in 1139, to the Empress Maud, it passed from Queen Alice by marriages, to successively the De Albinis, the Fitzalans, and the Howards, it was declared by act of parliament in the second year of Henry VI to confer the title of Earl of Arundel without creation, and it was besieged and captured in 1643 by the Parliamentarian forces under Sir W Waller, recaptured by the Royalists, and again captured, in 1644 by Waller The structure, in its present state, covers an area of five acres The entrance gate way is magnificent, in the Norman style, machicolated, and flanked by two imposing towers, was commenced in 1861 and leads into a quadrangle, with extensive remains of the ancient castle on the one side and the grand Gothic pile of the modern mansion on the other A towered gateway, a raised causeway, a steep flight of steps, and a spacious court yard with four flanking towers lead up to the keep The towers have four stages, with dungeons below, and one of them called the Bevis tower is so clad with ivy as to look like a tall green pyramid The keep is proximately circular stands on an artificial steep mound, raised above a fosse measures from 8 to 10 feet in thickness of wall and variously 59 feet and 67 feet in diameter, and appears to be of late Norman architecture, with Caen stone facings, but is almost all mantled with ornamental foliage and rich ivy The modern mansion displays mixtures of Gothic in Whitby freestone, and is far from being congruous, but has a grandly imposing effect in its general mass The library is 120 feet by 24, with eight tall walls, the dining room, 45 feet by 24, with a window 20 feet by 10 the drawing room, 54 feet by 28, the long gallery, 195 feet by 12 with groined ceiling the baron's hall, 115 feet by 35 with a window of stained glass, representing the signing of Magna Charta, and eight other windows containing figures of the barons connected with the signing The castle contains a splendid collection of family portraits and other pictures The park is 7 miles in circuit, contains many hundreds of deer, and affords rich scenes and beautiful prospects

The parish of Arundel is also the hundred, is co extensive with the limits of the borough Its area is 1,968 acres, and most of this is within the ducal park The living is a vicarage in the diocese of Chichester Value, £222 * Patron, the Earl of Albemarle The sub district comprises also six other parishes and parts of two more and is in the district of Worthing Acres, 14,090 Pop 3,797 Houses, 751 The rape extends northward from the English channel to Surrey, is bounded on one side by the river Arun and contains the hundreds of Avisford, Bury Poling Rotherbridge, and West Easwrith Acres, 129 52* Pop in 1851, 30,700 in 1861, 29 975 Houses, 5,936

ARUNDEL AND PORTSMOUTH CANAL, a canal was cut from the river Arun to Chichester harbour with a branch to Chichester, and another, through Langston harbour, to Portsea. It was opened in June 1823, and cost £160,000. The main line leaves the Arun, at the tideway, 2 miles from the sea, passes Barnham, Merston and Donnington, is 12 miles long, and has a fall of 21 feet, with four locks. The branch to Chichester is 1¼ mile long. The branch to Portsea is 2¾ miles long, but has been partly filled up for the railway, and is now disused.

ARUNDEL SAMPFORD. See SAMPFORD ARUNDEL.

ARVANS (St), a parish in Chepstow district, Monmouth, near the river Wye, 2 miles NNW of Chepstow r station. It contains the hamlet of Portcasseg and the tract of Kingsmark, sometimes deemed extra parochial, and it has a post office under Chepstow. Acres, 2,309. Real property, £3,703. Pop, 379. Houses, 83. The property is subdivided. The living is a vicarage in the diocese of Llandaff. Value, £53. Patron, the Duke of Beaufort. The church is an ancient structure, with an octagonal tower, and is in good condition. There are remains of two ancient chapels.

ARWERTON. See ERWARTON.

ARYHOLME or ARYHOLME AND HOWTHORPE, a township in Hovingham parish, N R Yorkshire, 7½ miles WNW of New Malton. Acres, 690. Pop., 35. Houses, 4.

ASAPH (St), a city in Flint, a parish, a sub-district, and a district in Flint and Denbigh, and a diocese in Flint, Denbigh, Merioneth, Montgomery, Carnarvon, Salop, and Cheshire. The city stands in the parish, on an eminence between the rivers Elwy and Clwyd, adjacent to the Vale of Clwyd railway, 5¼ miles N by W of Denbigh, and 5¾ SSE of Rhyl. It was formerly called Llanelwy, from its position on the Elwy; it takes the name of St Asaph from the second bishop of its see, and the eminence on which it stands is called Bryn Paulin from having been encamped on by the Roman general Paulinus, on his way to Mona. It has a station on the railway, and a post office‡ under Rhyl, and it is a market town, a borough, and a place of petty sessions, but it ranks as a city solely on account of its being the seat of a bishopric, and is practically a village, consisting of little more than a single street. A fine arched bridge spans the Elwy, and another good bridge spans the Clwyd. The episcopal palace stands a little W of the cathedral, overlooking the Elwy, and is a large modern edifice, built by Bishop Carey. The deanery stands about ¼ of a mile distant, and is also a recent structure, erected by Dean Luxmore. The parish church stands at the foot of the eminence, and is a mean small edifice, of the time of Henry VIII, without a tower. The churchyard contains several ancient tombs, and a new cemetery was opened in 1849. The cathedral stands on the summit of the eminence, is a cruciform structure, with central, low, square, embattled tower, was built chiefly in 1490, and partly in 1783, has a very plain and simple exterior, is mostly in decorated English, but partly in modern perpendicular, measures 179 feet from E to W, and contains monuments of Bishops Owen, Griffith, Barrow, and Luxmore, Dean Shipley, and Mrs. Hemans. A fine view of the vale of Clwyd and of a long reach of sea coast is obtained from the summit of the tower, and has been sung by Robert Montgomery. There are four dissenting chapels, a free grammar-school, an alms house, a workhouse, and four chief inns. The grammar school has £57 a year from endowment, the alms house £31, and other charities £58. A market is held on Saturday, and fairs, on 2 March, Easter Tuesday, 15 July, 19 Aug, 16 Oct, 2 Nov, and 15 Dec. The borough unites with Flint and six other towns in sending a member to parliament. Pop, 2,063. Houses, 458. The town gives the title of Viscount to Earl Ashburnham. The environs include Bronwylfa and Phyllon, which were abodes of Mrs Hemans, and contain other objects of interest.

The parish contains the townships of Bodeigan, Bodllewyddan, Brynpolyn, Cilowen, Cyrchynen, Faenol, Gwerngliefryd, Gwernigron, Pengwern, Rhyllon, and Talar in Flint, and the townships Meriadog and Wigfair or Wickwer in Denbigh. Acres, 10,825. Rated property, £24,577. Pop, 3,592. Houses, 759. The property is much subdivided. The living is a vicarage of four parts, two of which are Bodllewyddan and Cefn chapelries. Value of each, £179. Patron, the Bishop.—The sub-district comprises also five other parishes and part of another, all in Flint. Acres, 33,589. Pop., 11,922. Houses, 2,587.—The district comprehends the sub district of Denbigh, containing the parishes of Denbigh, Llannefydd, Henllan, and Llansannan, all in Denbigh; the sub district of Abergele, containing the parishes of Abergele, St. George, Llanddulas, Llanfair talhaiarn, and Bettws yn Rhôs or Bettws Abergele, all in Denbigh, and the sub district of St. Asaph, containing the parishes of St Asaph, Rhuddlan, Meliden, Dyserth, Cwm, and Dymeirchion or Trewerchion, and part of the parish of Bodfary. Acres, 92,931. Poor rates, £13,396. Pop in 1841, 23,547, in 1861, 27,518. Houses, 5,963. Marriages, 186, births, 785,—of which 68 were illegitimate, deaths, 547,—of which 130 were at ages under 5 years, and 30 were at ages above 85. Marriages in the ten years 1851–60, 1,731, births, 7,379, deaths, 5,559. The places of worship in 1851 were 19 of the Church of England, with 7,704 sittings, 13 of Independents, with 2,807 s, 10 of Baptists, with 1,466 s, 25 of Calvinistic Methodists, with 5,776 s, 15 of Wesleyan Methodists, with 3,535 s, 2 of Latter Day Saints, with 300 s, and 1 of Roman Catholics, with 40 s. The schools in 1851 were 26 public day schools, with 1,862 scholars, 24 private day schools, with 673 s, 76 Sunday schools, with 8,208 s, and 2 evening schools for adults, with 27 s.

The diocese comprehends all Flint, all Denbigh, about half of Merioneth, the greater part of Montgomery, three parishes of Carnarvon, ten of Salop, and part of one of Cheshire. Acres, 1,067,583. Pop, 240,337. Houses, 52,242. An arrangement was made, in the recent revisal of dioceses, to unite it to Bangor, but this has not taken effect. The see was founded in 543 by Kentigern or St Mungo, the founder of the see of Glasgow, who was driven by persecution from the north, and found refuge here under the protection of Cadwallon, and it was held by Asaph or Hassaph, a bishop of good family and of great piety, who died and was buried here in 590. The most notable of the bishops, after Asaph, were Geoffrey of Monmouth, the Welsh Herodotus, Anian, the black friar of Schonau, John de Trevor, the Crusader, who pronounced the deposition of Richard II, Edmund de Birkenhead, and Goldwell, who sat in the council of Trent, Pocock the Wickliffite, Morgan and Davis, translators of the Bible, Owen who introduced sermons in Welsh, Griffith, the author of the "Form of Adult Baptism," Isaac Barrow who educated his nephew of his own name, the distinguished mathematician, Beveridge the author of "Thesaurus Theologicus" and "Private Thoughts," Tanner, the historian of monasteries, and Samuel Horsley, the eminent oriental scholar and biblical critic. The cathedral establishment includes the bishop, the dean and chancellor, four canons, nine honorary canons, two archdeacons, four minor canons, and four bishop's chaplains. The income of the bishop is £4,200, of the dean £700, of the chancellor, £150, of each of the canons, two of whom are the archdeacons, £350. The diocese is in the prov of Canterbury, and is divided into the archdeaconries of St. Asaph and Montgomery, the former comprising nine deaneries,—the latter three. Many of the livings have recently been raised in status and are named as they now stand in the separate articles on them in our work, but all will be named here as they stood in 1861.

The deanery of Mold includes the rectories of Hawarden, Llandegla and Llanferres, the vicarages of Hope, Llanarmon yn Ial, and Mold, the p curacies of Estre, Gwernafield, Llanfynydd, Nerquis, Pontblyddyn, and Treuddyn, and the donative of Llyn Eglwys. The deanery of Wrexham includes the rectories of Bangor Monachorum, Erbistock, Marchwiail, and Worthenbury, the vicarages of Wrexham, Gresford, Hanmer, and Ruabon, and the p curacies of Berse, Brymbo, Gwersyllt, Holt,

Isycoed, Minera, New Fens, Rhos Llanerchrugog Phos y Medre Forest, and Threapwood The deanery of Llangollen includes the rectory of Llanarmon Dyffryn-Ceiriog the vicarages of Chirk Llangollen, Llanrhaiadr Mochnant, Llansilin and Llansblodwel, and the p curacies of Llanarmon Mynydd Mawr, Llangadwaladr, Llangollen Pontfadog Trevor Llansantffraid Glyn Ceiriog, Llantysilio and Rhyd y Croesau The deanery of Oswestry includes the rectories of Knockin, Llanymynech Selattyn, and Whittington the vicarages of Kinnerley, Oswestry, and St Martin's, and the p curacies of Hengoed, Melverley, Morton, Trinity Oswestry, and Trefonen The deanery of Denbigh includes the rectories of Denbigh, Llanddulas, Llanelian, Llangernyw, Llysfaen and St. George, the vicarages of Abergele Bettws, Henllan Llansannan, Llannfydd, and Nantglyn and the p curacies of St David's Denbigh, Bylchau, Llanfair Talhaiarn, and Trefnant The deanery of Llanrwst includes the rectories of Llanrwst, Cerrig-y-Druidion Gwytherin, Llanddoget, Llanfihangel Glyn y Myfyr and Llansaintffraid Glan Conway, the vicarages of Eglwysfach, Llandrillo yn Rhos, and Llangwm, and the p curacies of St Mary-Llanrwst, Capel Garmon, Colwyn Foelas, Llangwstennin, Llanrhôs and Yspytty Ifan The deanery of St Asaph includes the rectories of Bodfary, Caerwys, and Gwaenysgor, the vicarages of St Asaph, Cwm, Dymeirchion Llanasa, and Rhuddlan, and the p cur of Cefn, Bodllewyddan, Diserth, Meliden Newmarket, and Rhyl The deanery of Holywell includes the rectories of Halkin Nannerch, and Ysceifiog, the vicarages of Holywell, Cilcain, Northop, and Whitford, and the p curacies of Bagillt, Brynford, Flint, Rhes y Cae Mostyn, and Connah's Quay The deanery of Dyffryn Clwyd or Ruthin includes the rectories of Clocaenog Derwen, Efenechdyd, Llanbedr Dyffryn-Clwyd Llandyrnog, Llanelidan, Llanfwrog, Llangwyfan Llangynhafal, Llanychan, and Ruthin Wardship-with-Llanrhydd the vicarages of Llanfair Dyffryn Clwyd, Llanrhaiadr-Kinmerch and Llanynys, and the p curacies of Pron and Gyffylliog

The deanery of Welshpool includes the rectories of Castle Caereinion, Llandrinio, Llandysilio, and Llangyniew the vicarages of Guilsfield Llanfair Caereinion Llansaintffraid yn Mechan, Meifod, and Welshpool, and the p curacies of Buttington Pont Dolanog, Pont Robert and Penrhôs The deanery of Llanfyllin includes the rectories of Garthbeibio, Hirnant Llanerfyl, Llanfechan, Llanfihangel, Llanfyllin, Llangadfan, and Llangynog, the vicarage of Pennant and the p curacies of Llan [illegible], Llw[illegible]rth, and Penybont The deanery of Penllyn and Edeirnion includes the rectories of Bettws Gwerfyl Goch Llanderfel Llangar, Llangower, Llansantffraid and Llanycil, the vicarages of Corwen, Gwyddelwern, Llandrillo, and Llanfawr, and the p curacies of Frongoch Llanwchllyn, Llawr y Bettws and Trinity

ASBY, formerly ASHBY or ASHEBY, a parish in East Ward district Westmoreland, on an affluent of the river Eden adjacent to the Eden Valley railway, near Warcop r station, and 4 miles S by E of Appleby It comprises the townships of Great Asby, Little Asby, Asby Coatsforth, and Asby Winderwath, and the tract of Grange Hall sometimes deemed extra parochial, and its post town is Warcop under Penrith Acres, 8,??5 Real property, £3 507 Pop 440 Houses, 89 The property is subdivided Great Asby belonged to Roger Clifford Little Asby had formerly a chapel with a chantry, and belonged to the Honeywoods Asby Coatsforth belonged to the Cotsforths and the Musgraves Asby Winderwath belonged to the Vanes Asby Overgrange belonged to Lyland abbey, and Gaythorne to St Leonards, York Asby Hall is the seat of the Fish family Great part of the parish is mountainous Three of the chief summits, Gathorneclingow, Oxenbush, and Castlefolds, have altitudes of respectively 1 53 , 1,620 and 1 700 feet Asby Scar is a ridge of rock extending about 2 miles from N to S, and 4 miles from E to W A cavern called Pate Hole, about a ¼ of a mile S of the hamlet of Great Asby, runs 430 yards in one direction, and 230 yards in another, and has, at the end of its first gallery, a pool 20 yards long and a lofty dome Some striking scenery occurs among the mountains Freestone, limestone, and copper ore, are worked Several tumuli, various in form, exist at Sayle Bottom , and two, which were found to contain human remains, are at Gaythorne Hall. The living is a rectory in the diocese of Carlisle, Value, £205 Patroness Miss Hill The church was rebuilt in 1866 at a cost of £2 000, and is in the decorated English style There are an endowed school, with £41 a year, an alms house, with £ 8, and other charities, with £20

ASCOT, a chapelry and a race course in Winkfield parish, Berks The chapelry adjoins the Staines and Reading railway, 6 miles W by S of Staines, was constituted in 1866, and has a post office under Staines, and a r station Pop , 900 Ascot Place is the seat of C C Ferard, Esq The living is a rectory in the diocese of Oxford Value, £100 Patron, the Bishop of Oxford There is a national school —The race course is adjacent to the SW extremity of the Great Park of Windsor, has a rich sward a grand stand with noble view, and the most complete range of racing chateaux in the empire, is circular, and only 66 yards short of 2 miles, and goes half the way on the descent the other half chiefly up hill The races were instituted by the Duke of Cumberland, uncle of George III , they take place early in June , and they are generally attended by the Royal Family in state, and by the élite of the court, the nobility, and the fashion A cup was given to them by the Emperor Nicholas of Russia after his visit to England, and discontinued at the Crimean war , and another has been given, in its stead, by the Emperor Napoleon of France

ASCOTE, a hamlet in Pattishall parish, Northampton, near Watling street, 3 miles N of Towcester

ASCOTE (CHAPEL), an extra parochial tract in Southam district, Warwick , contiguous to Bishops Itchington parish, 3 miles S of Southam.

ASCOTT, a hamlet in Whichford parish, Warwick , on the Wolds, 5½ miles SE of Shipston on Stour Pop., 158.

ASCOTT, a hamlet in Wing parish, Bucks , 3½ miles NW of Ivinghoe Pop , 98 Ascott Hall, the seat of the Stanhope family is adjacent

ASCOTT, a hamlet in Great Milton parish Oxford , near the Thame, 6 miles N of Wallingford Pop , 29 Houses, 6

ASCOTT, a station on the West Midland railway, 4 miles SE of Chipping Norton junction, and 17½ NW by W of Oxford

ASCOTT UNDER WYCHWOOD, a parish in Chipping Norton district, Oxford , on the river Evenlode and on the West Midland railway, at Ascott station, 3½ miles W of Charlbury It contains High Lodge in Wychwood forest , and has a post office under Enstone Acres, 1,793 Real property, £2,960 Pop , 453 Houses, 90 The property is divided among a few Ascott Earl is a chief residence The living is a vicarage in the diocese of Oxford Value, £80 Patron, the Bishop of Oxford The church is good, except the chancel There are chapels for Baptists and Wesleyans, and charities £45

ASENBY, ASENDBY, or AZENBY, a township in Topcliffe parish, N R Yorkshire , on the river Swale, 5½ miles SW of Thirsk Acres, 1 130 Real property, £2,146 Pop 202 Houses, 45

ASFORDBY See ASHFORDBY

ASGARBY, a parish in Sleaford district, Lincoln adjacent to the Boston and Grantham railway 3 miles E of Sleaford It includes the hamlet of Boughton , and its post town is Sleaford Acres, 838 Real property £1,424 Pop 83 Houses 14 The living is a rectory, annexed to the rectory of Kirkby la Thorpe, in the diocese of Lincoln The church is later English, and has a crocketted spire

[illegible], a parish in Horncastle district, Lincoln , on the Wolds, 4 miles ESE of Horncastle r station Post town, Hagworthingham under Spilsby Acres, 818 Real property £1,361 Pop 80 Houses, 17 The property is divided among a few Eight acres are an allotment in the West Fen The living is a [illegible] in the diocese of Lincoln Value, £50 * Patron, the Bishop of Lincoln The church is good.

ASH (THE), a stream of Herts It rises near Little Hadham, and runs about 8 miles south westward to the sea a little below Ware

ASH, a hamlet in Sutton on the Hill parish, Derbyshire, 8 miles W by S of Derby Acres, 691 Pop, 46 Houses, 7

ASH, a hamlet in Parkham parish, Devon, 6½ miles W of Torrington

ASH, a hamlet in South Tawton parish, Devon, 4¼ miles ESE of Okehampton Ash House in the vicinity, now a ruin, was a seat of the Drakes, and the birthplace, in 1650, of the mother of the Duke of Marlborough

ASH, a hamlet and a chapelry in Martock parish Somerset The hamlet stands near the Durston and Yeovil railway, 3 miles SW of Ilchester Pop., 322 The chapelry includes the hamlet, and was constituted in 1845 Post town, Martock under Ilminster Pop, 530 The living is a vicarage in the diocese of Bath and Wells Value £62 Patron, the Vicar of Martock.

ASH a tything in Crewkerne parish, near the town of Crewkerne, Somerset

ASH, a village in Farnborough district, and a parish in Farnborough and Farnham districts, Surrey The village stands near the Southwestern railway the Basingstoke canal, and the Blackwater river, 2 miles NW of Hog's Back and 4 NE of Farnham, and it has a station on the railway, and a post office under Farnborough station. The parish includes also the tything of Normandy, and the hamlet chapelry of Frimley Acres, 12,273 Rated property, £15,443 Pop, 4,164 Houses, 753 The property is much subdivided The southern tracts are hilly, and partly common Ash Lodge is a chief residence The living is a rectory in the diocese of Winchester Value, £473 * Patron, Winchester college. The church has a plain Norman doorway, and is good. The rectory of Frimley and the p. curacy of York Town are separate charges Charities, £16

ASH a chapelry in Whitchurch parish, Salop, 2¼ miles SE of Whitchurch r station It includes the townships of Ash Magna and Ash Parva, contains the residences of Ash House and Ash Grove, and has a post office under Whitchurch Pop, 545 Houses, 110 The living is a vicarage in the diocese of Lichfield Value, £145 * Patron the Rector of Whitchurch

ASH, Hants, Dorset, and East Devon See ASHE

ASH, Durham See ESH

ASH, North-East Kent See ASH NEXT SANDWICH

ASH, or ASH NEXT RIDLEY, a parish in Dartford district, Kent, 6 miles S of Northfleet r station, and 7 SSE of Dartford It includes the hamlets of Hodsol Street and West York and part of Culverstone Green and it has a post office under Sevenoaks Acres, 3,023 Real property, £4,761 Pop, 537 Houses, 132 The property is much subdivided The living is a rectory in the diocese of Rochester Value, £545 * Patron, W Lambarde, Esq The church is good, and there are a Baptist chapel and a national school

ASH ABBEY See CAMPSEY ASH

ASHAMPSTEAD, a parish in Bradfield district Berks 6 miles W of Pangbourne r station, and 10½ W by N of Reading It has a post office under Reading Acres 2,057 Real property, £2,316 Pop, 385 Houses, 87 Part of the land is common The living is a vicarage in the diocese of Oxford Value, £80 * Patrons, Rev W Sykes and Simeon's Trustees. There are two dissenting chapels a free school and charities £12

ASHAMPSTEAD, or ASHHAMPSTEAD, a chapelry in the parish of Lewknor and counties of Oxford and Buckingham 3¼ miles NW of Great Marlow, and 3¾ WSW of Wycombe station The part of it known as Sturridge and Cadmore End is in Oxford and the part known as the Moor and Finnemoor is in Berks Post town, Lewknor under Tetsworth Pop, 355 The living bears the name also of Cadmore End and is a vicarage in the diocese of Oxford Value, £150 * Patrons the Bishop of Oxford two turns, and All Souls College one turn

ASHAPCH, a village 3½ miles NE of Ludlow, Salop

ASHBADWELL See BADWELL ASH

ASHBEACON HILL, a hill 655 feet high, near Milborne Port, Somerset.

ASH BOCKING, or ASHBOCKING a parish in Bosmere district, Suffolk, 5 miles NE of Claydon r station, and 8 N of Ipswich Post town, Coddenham under Needham Market Acres, 1,408. Real property, £2,588 Pop., 324 Houses, 70 The property is not much divided The living is a vicarage in the diocese of Norwich Value, £333 * Patron, the Lord Chancellor The church has a brass of a Bocking of 1585, and is very good Charities £25

ASHBORNE, or ASHBOURNE, a small town, a township, a parish, a sub district, and a district in Derby The town stands on the river Henmore, 1¼ mile above its influx to the Dove, at the terminus of a branch of the North Stafford railway, 7½ miles NE of the junction with the main line at Rocester station, and 13½, by road, NW of Derby It was formerly called Ashburn, and anciently Esseburn It belonged to the Crown at the time of the Conquest, passed to the duchy of Lancaster, was taken by the Parliamentarian forces in 1644, retaken by the Royal forces, and visited by Charles I, in 1645, and occupied as head quarters by the Scottish army of Prince Charles Edward, on their march to Derby in 1745 Its situation is pleasant, and its vicinity rich in romantic scenery, so as to occasion it to attract many visitors Its houses, in general, are of red brick, roofed with slate, and its streets are tolerably neat It has a head post office,‡ a telegraph office, a banking-office, three chief inns a town hall, news rooms, a small jail, a grammar school, a national school, a parish church, a Calvinist chapel restored in 1869, three other dissenting chapels, a R. Catholic chapel, a workhouse of 1864, several alms houses, and large general charities, and is a seat of petty sessions and county courts and a polling place The grammar school was founded in 1585, has estates yielding £211 a year and is a substantial stone building The house once inhabited by Dr John Taylor, and visited by his intimate friend the great Dr Johnson stands opposite the grammar school The parish church is a spacious, cruciform, early English edifice of 1241, is surmounted by a central square tower, with lofty, ornamented, octagonal spire was renovated in 1845, at a cost of nearly £5,000, mostly raised by subscription and contains brasses and tombs of the Cockaynes the Bradburns and the Boothbys. The finest of the monuments is a statuary one, in white marble, from the chisel of Banks to the memory of Penelope, the only child of Sir Brooke Boothby, who died in 1791 in her sixth year and this is supposed to have suggested to Chantrey his beautiful group of the two children in Lichfield cathedral The town is in high repute as a mart for cattle cheese, and other agricultural produce, and it has a weekly market on Saturday,—general fairs on the first Tuesday in Jan, 13 Feb., 3 April, the last Thursday in April, 21 May, 5 July, 16 Aug, 20 Oct and 29 Nov or on the preceding day if the 29th be a Sunday,—fairs for cheese on the second Tuesday in March and the third Tuesday in Sept.,—and fairs for horned cattle, sheep, and horses on the days preceding each Malt making, lace making, and cotton manufacture are carried on Pop 3,501 Houses, 760

The township lies wholly in the town Real property, £6,605 Pop 2,120 Houses, 472 —The parish includes also the liberty of Offcote and Underwood, the townships of Sturston Yeldersley, Hulland, Hulland Ward Hulland Ward Intakes, and Clifton and Compton the hamlet of Newton Grange, and the chapelry of Alsop le Dale and Eaton Acres, 7,032 Rated property, exclusive of Hulland chapelry, £29,412. Pop of the whole, 5,078 Houses, 1,098 The property is much subdivided Ashborne Hall was long the seat of the Boothbys, was the quarters of Prince Charles Edward on his march to Derby, and is now the residence of Captain Holland R N Ashborne Green Hall belongs to the De Burghs, and is a meeting place of sportsmen Ashborne Grove belongs to the Dales Mayfield Cottage, in the neighbourhood, was, for a considerable time, the residence of the poet Moore, and the place where he wrote great part of his "Lalla Rookh" The Henmore and the Dove in their connexion with the parish, afford prime angling for trout and grayling, and were noted for it by Warton and Cotton Thorp Cloud Hill, 3 miles from the town, and 300 feet high, commands a fine view of the craggy flanks of the Dove The living is a vicarage, united with the rectory of Mappleton, in the diocese of Lichfield Value, £420 * Patron the Bishop of Lichfield The chapelries of Clifton, Hulland, and Alsop le Dale are separate charges. Sir Aston Cockaine, the Elizabethan poet, and Sir Brooke Boothby the author of "Tables and Satires" and of other works, were natives

The sub district comprises the parishes of Edlaston with Wyaston, Osmaston Bradley, and Kniveton, and parts of the parishes of Ashborne and Bradbourne Acres, 11 442 Pop, 4,876 Houses, 1,041 The district consists of Ashborne poor law union and part of Allstonefield Gilbert's incorporation, and comprehends, in addition to Ashborne sub district, the sub-district of Brailsford, containing the parishes of Brailsford, Longford, and Shirley and parts of the parishes of Ashborne, Mugginton, and Wirksworth,—the sub-district of Hartington, containing the parish of Parwich, and parts of the parishes of Ashborne, Hartington, and Bradbourne,—the sub district of Brassington, containing the parishes of Carsington, Hognaston, and Bonsall the extra parochial tract of Griff Grange, and parts of the parishes of Bradbourne, Kirk Ireton and Wirksworth —the sub district of Mayfield, containing the parishes of Snelston and Ellastone, the latter electorally in Stafford, and parts of the parishes of Ashborne and Mayfield, the latter electorally in Stafford,—and the sub district of Calton, containing the parishes of Tissington, Fenny Bentley, Thorpe, Mappleton, Okeover Blore, Ilam, and Waterfall, the four last electorally in Stafford, the extra parochial tract of Musden Grange, electorally in Stafford, and parts of the parishes of Bradbourne, Mayfield, and Allstonefield, the two last in Stafford Acres, 100,937 Poor rates in 1866, £8,029 Pop. in 1841, 21,358, in 1861, 20,648. Houses, 4,384 Marriages in 1866, 163, births, 620,—of which 51 were illegitimate, deaths, 397,—of which 114 were at ages under 5 years, and 12 at ages above 85 Marriages in the ten years 1851-60, 1,390, births, 6,252 deaths, 4,064 The places of worship in 1851 were 41 of the Church of England with 9 921 sittings, 4 of Independents, with 440 s 1 of Lady Huntingdon's Connection with 340 s, 1 of Baptists, with 300 s, 21 of Wesleyan Methodists, with 2,541 s. 24 of Primitive Methodists, with 2,301 s, 3 of Wesleyan Reformers, with 290 s, and one undefined, with 90 s The schools in 1851 were 60 public day schools, with 2,193 scholars, 40 private day schools, with 930 s, 57 Sunday schools, with 3,112 s, and 4 evening schools for adults, with 70 s

ASHBRITTLE, a parish in Wellington district, Somerset, on the verge of the county, and on the river Tone near the Western canal 3½ miles from the Bristol and Exeter railway 6 miles W by S of Wellington It includes the tything of Greenham, and its post town is Wellington, Somerset Acres, 2 489 Real property, £2,715 Pop 525 Houses, 100 The property is subdivided The living is a rectory in the diocese of Bath and Wells Value £150 * Patron J Quicke, Esq The church is mainly old, partly new There are a chapel of ease built in 1860, and a national school

ASHBROOK See Ampney St Mary

ASHBURN See Ashborne

ASHBURN (The), a stream of Sussex It rises near Kent's Hill, and runs about 8 miles southward to the Channel at Pevensey Its mouth up to Pevensey bridge, till about 1700, was a harbour for small vessels but has been rendered unnavigable by accumulation of sand and shingle

ASHBURNHAM, a parish in Battle district Sussex, 5 miles W of Battle r station It has a post office under Battle, and it gives the titles of Baron and Earl to the family of Ashburnham descendants of Bertram de Ashburnham, who was ... of Kent and Sussex at the landing of William the Conqueror Acres, 3 648 Real property £3 577 Pop., 844 Houses 154 Ashburnham Place, the seat of the Earl of Ashburnham, is a red brick mansion, mostly modern, and contains a rich collection of books and manuscripts, several rare pictures some fine old plate and ancient armour, and the shirt worn by Charles I on the scaffold, his watch, his white silk drawers, and the sheet thrown over his body after the execution These relics were given on the scaffold to the king's attendant John Ashburnham, and bequeathed by one of his descendants to the parish for ever, and were formerly preserved in the church A public path through the church yard commands grand views of the coast to Beachy head An iron furnace, in the north was noted for producing the best iron in England, and continued to be worked after every other iron furnace in Sussex was extinct, and the site of it may still be traced The living is a vicarage, united with the rectory of Penhurst, in the diocese of Chichester Value, £307 * Patron, the Earl of Ashburnham The church was rebuilt by the John Ashburnham who attended Charles I, and contains monuments of himself and of other members of the family Charities, £5

ASHBURTON a town, a parish, and a sub district in the district of Newton Abbot, Devon The town stands on the Yeo, about 1½ mile from the Dart, near the grandest part of Dartmoor, 7 miles NNW of Totnes and a railway to it, from the South Devon, was in advanced progress in 1869 It was anciently called Asperton and Aisbertone It belonged to the Crown at Domesday, was given to the see of Exeter before 1310 became a stannary town in 1328, on account of tin and copper mines in its neighbourhood, belonged to the Crown again in the time of Charles I, was taken by Fairfax in 1346 and went, after various changes, into the possession of Lord Clinton It consists principally of two long streets, and has a neat appearance The market house has a lofty basement for market purposes, and an upper story with public rooms, and is a fine edifice, in the Italian style, built in 1850, at a cost of upwards of £3,000 The parish church is a spacious cruciform structure, of perpendicular date, with modern alterations, surmounted by a central tower, 90 feet high was formerly collegiate, and contains some fine monuments There are four dissenting chapels, a grammar school, with £80 of endowed income and two exhibitions and two scholarships at Exeter college, Oxford, other charities with £322, a post office‡ under Newton Abbot, and three chief inns A weekly market is held on Saturday, and fairs on the first Thursday in March and June, 10 Aug, and 11 Nov The manufacture of serge and blanketting is carried on A great business formerly arose from the thoroughfare between London and Plymouth, but has died away since the opening of the South Devon railway The town is a borough by prescription, sent two members to parliament in the times of Edward I and Henry IV, and from 1640 till 1832 and was half disfranchised by the act of 1832, and entirely disfranchised in 1868 It is governed by a portreeve, a bailiff, and constables Acres, 6 936 Real property £13 670 Electors in 1868, 350 Pop, 3,062 Houses, 574 John Dunning solicitor general in 1767, Dr Ireland dean of Westminster, and William Gifford, the well known editor of the Quarterly Review, born in 1756, were natives A peerage, with the title of Baron Ashburton, was given to Dunning in 1782, and, becoming extinct in 1823, was revived in favour of Alexander Baring in 1835 —The parish as already noted, is co extensive with the borough The living is a vicarage in ... with the vicarage of Buckland in the Moor in the diocese of Exeter Value, £639 * Patrons, the Dean and Chapter of Exeter —The sub district includes six parishes and a chapelry Acres 21,590 Pop 6,362 Houses, 1,245

ASHBURY, a village and a parish in Farringdon district, Berks The village stands near the Ridge way or Icknield street, at the W end of Whitehorse vale 3 miles SSE of Shrivenham r station, and 7½ S of Farringdon, and it has a post office under Shrivenham The parish includes also the tythings of Idstone and Odstone, and the hamlet of Kingstone Winslow Acres, 5,520 Real property, £6,829 Pop., 712 Houses, 153 The property is divided among a few The living is a vicarage in the diocese of Oxford Value, £375 * Patron, Magdalen college, Oxford The church is partly Norman, partly decorated English There are a P Methodist chapel, a national school, and charities £14

ASHBURY, anciently Essebury, a parish in Okehampton district, Devon, on an affluent of the river Torridge, 5 miles SSW of Hatherleigh, and 11 WSW of Morchard Road r station Post town North Lew under Exbourne, North Devon Acres, 1,700 Real property, £748 Pop., 80 Houses 9 The manor, with most of the property, belongs to the owner of Ashbury House, a large old residence in a well wooded park. The living is a rectory in the diocese of Exeter Value, £96 * Patron, the Lord Chancellor The church is a small old edifice, with nave, chancel, and tower

ASHBURY'S, a station on the Manchester and Sheffield railway, 1½ mile ESE of Manchester It serves for Bellevue

ASHBY, a township in Bottesford parish, Lincoln, 7 miles WNW of Brigg It has a post office under Brigg. Real property, £2 611 Pop, 503. Houses, 111

ASHBY, a hamlet in Litton Cheney parish, Dorset, 9 miles W of Dorchester

ASHBY, a parish in Loddon district, Norfolk, 3 miles SW of Buckenham r station, and 7 SE of Norwich Post town, Rockland under Norwich Acres, 487 Real property, £1,360 Pop, 237 Houses, 58 The living is a rectory, annexed to the rectory of Carleton, in the diocese of Norwich.

ASHBY, a parish in Flegg district, Norfolk, near the river Bure, 8 miles NE of Brundall r station, and 12 ENE of Norwich Post town, Ludham under Norwich Acres, with Oby and Thurne, 1,408 Real property, with Oby, £3,085 Pop of Ashby, 16 Houses, 3. Ashby, Oby, and Thurne are three rectories forming one benefice in the diocese of Norwich Value, £690 * Patron, the Bishop of Norwich

ASHBY a parish in Mutford district, Suffolk, near the river Waveney 2½ miles N of Somerleyton r station, and 5½ NW of Lowestoft Post town, Somerleyton under Lowestoft. Acres, 1,109 Real property, £1,137 Pop, 70 Houses, 11 The living is a rectory in the diocese of Norwich Value, £214 Patron, Sir S M Peto, Bart. The church is mainly early English, and has a decorated east window, a square Norman font, and a circular west tower, with octagonal upper story

ASHBY, Westmoreland See ASBY

ASHBY BY PARTNEY, or ASHBY-EAST, a parish in Spilsby district, Lincoln, on the river Steeping, 2 miles E of Spilsby, and 3½ W of Burgh r station. Post town, Spilsby Acres, 1,210 Real property, £1,640 Pop, 148 Houses, 33 The living is a rectory in the diocese of Lincoln Value, £157 * Patron, the Rev L Fowler The church is plain There is a Wesleyan chapel

ASHBY (CANONS), a parish in Daventry and Towcester districts, Northampton, on the river Cherwell, 8 miles SW of Weedon r station, and 9 S of Daventry It includes the hamlet of Adstone, and its post town is Eydon under Daventry Acres, 2,600 Real property, £3,109 Pop, 220 Houses, 46 A priory of black canons was founded here, in the time of Henry II, by Stephen de Leye, and given, at the dissolution, to Sir Francis Bryan Canons Ashby House is the seat of Sir H E L Dryden, Bart, and contains a very large apartment floored with oak from one tree The living is a donative in the diocese of Peterborough Value, not reported Patron, Sir H E L Dryden The church is good, and has tombs of the Drydens. The p curacy of Adstone is a separate charge

ASHBY (CASTLE), a parish in Hardingstone district, Northampton, near the Nen river and the Peterborough railway, 7 miles E of Northampton It has a station on the railway at White Mill, and includes the hamlet of Chadstone, and its post town is Grendon under Northampton. Acres, 1,926 Real property, £3,088. Pop, 183 Houses, 38 Castle Ashby House the seat of the Marquis of Northampton, stands within the parish, at the north end of a wide avenue of upwards of 3 miles through Yardley Chace, and is a large quadrangular edifice, with two lofty octangular towers, built in 1625-35 and contains a good picture gallery, with valuable portraits and very old oil paintings. The living is a rectory in the diocese of Peterborough Value, £238 * Patron the Marquis of Northampton The church stands in the park, has a Norman porch, and contains an altar tomb, with effigies of a crusader

ASHBY (COLD), a parish in Brixworth district, Northampton, 3½ miles S of Welford, and 5 SE of Stanford-Hall r station Post town, Welford under Rugby Acres, 1,910 Real property, £4,090 Pop, 446 Houses, 104 The property is subdivided The place is a meet for the Pytchley hounds. The living is a vicarage in the diocese of Peterborough Value, £230 Patron, the Rev W Mousley The church is tolerable, and contains tombs of the Langhams A school has £23 from endowment, and other charities £20 Richard Knolles, born in 1543, the author of a History of the Turks, was a native

ASHBY CUM FENBY See ASHBY WITH FENBY

ASHBY DE LA LAUND, a parish in Sleaford district, Lincoln, 4½ miles N of Sleaford r station Post town, Digby under Sleaford Acres, 2,880 Real property, £2,938 Pop, 176 Houses, 28 The property is not much divided Ashby Laund House is an old mansion, the seat of J W King, Esq The living is a vicarage in the diocese of Lincoln Value, £299 Patron, J W King, Esq The church is good Charities, £9

ASHBY DE LA ZOUCH, a town, a parish, a sub district, and a district, in Leicester The town stands in a pleasant situation, on the NW border of the county, on the rivulet Gilwiskaw, near the Midland railway and the Ashby de la Zouch canal, 18 miles by road and 20¾ by railway NW by W of Leicester It was anciently called Esseby, and it took the afterpart of its present name from the ancient Norman-French family of La Zouch It belonged to that family from the time of Henry III till 1401, it passed then to the Crown, and it was given to the family of Hastings, the ancestors of the present Marquis The castle of the La Zouches stood on a rising ground at the S end of the town, and a stronger one was built on its site, out of its materials, in 1480, by Sir William Hastings This gentleman was master of the mint, and introduced a new gold coinage, and he was created Baron Hastings by Edward IV, and beheaded in the Tower by Richard III Mary, Queen of Scots was for some time confined in the castle, James I s queen and son Henry were entertained in it, on their journey to London in 1603, James I himself visited it in 1617, and Charles I dined at it a few days before the storming of Leicester Colonel Henry Hastings, son of the Earl of Huntingdon, and afterwards created Baron Loughborough, garrisoned it for Charles was besieged in it by Fairfax, and surrendered it to Colonel Needham The parliament thought it more likely, if left entire, to be serviceable to the Royalists than to themselves, and they ordered it to be dismantled in 1648 Only portions of the hall, the chapel, and the kitchen are now standing, but they form an extensive and picturesque mass of ruin, perhaps the finest in the country, and they show Tudor features of architecture which indicate that some parts were of later erection than the original pile The scene of the grand tournament described in "Ivanhoe is about a mile to the W, near the village of Snibston, and some Roman coins have been found in the vicinity

The town consists chiefly of one principal street, with two smaller ones running in a parallel direction, and contains some well built houses The town hall was built in 1857, and is a noble edifice St Helen s church is fine decorated English, includes two chapels, separated by four lofty arches, springing from fluted pillars and contains tombs of the Earls of Huntingdon, and of the good Countess Selina, who figures largely in religious history, and spent £100,000 in works of benevolence Trinity church, at the west end of the town, is a handsome structure, in the early English style, with about 900 sittings, built in 1838, at a cost of £4,000 There are chapels for Independents, Baptists, Wesleyan Methodists, and Primitive Methodists, and the first was rebuilt in 1825, at a cost of nearly £2,000 The grammar-school is a large edifice, was founded, in 1567, by Henry, Earl of Huntingdon has endowments yielding £840 a year, holds ten exhibitions of £10 a year each, in Emanuel college, Cambridge, and had for its first master Joseph Hall, afterwards Bishop of Exeter, and author of well-known Christian writings Two other public schools have £50 and £36 from endowment, and other charities £150 Ivanhoe baths, constructed in 1826, have a fine Doric edifice 200 feet long, are supplied, by pipes, from springs 3 miles distant with mineral water containing bromine, and are noted for medicinal effect in scrofula and kindred diseases. The town is a summer resort of invalids and visitors, and has two good hotels, good lodging houses, a theatre, a railway station, a head post office, and a banking office A weekly market is held on Saturday, and fairs on the Monday before Shrove Tuesday, Easter Tuesday, Whit Tuesday, 14 Sept, and 8 Nov Trade is carried on in malting, stocking making, hat making and in the traffic of neighbouring brick fields, smelting works, and collieries A coal field lies around, of irregular outline, about 10 miles by 8, estimated to comprise 40,000 acres of workable area of coal, having nine seams, with an aggregate thickness of 33 feet, and includes pits at Swadlincote, Moira, Donisthorpe, and Oakthorpe, belonging to the Marquis of Hastings, and pits at Snibston, Whitwick, Church Gresley, Measham, Staunton Harrold, and elsewhere, belonging to other proprietors The town is governed by officers annually appointed at the court leet of the lord of the manor, and is a seat of petty sessions and a polling place Pop., 3,772 Houses, 830 Bishop Joseph Hall and Dr John Bainbridge were natives

The parish includes also part of Blackfordby chapelry Acres, 8,097 Real property, £39,884, of which £12,230 are in mines, and £1,130 are in railways Pop, 6,958 Houses, 1,347 The living is a vicarage in the diocese of Peterborough Value, £417 * Patron, the Marquis of Hastings. Trinity church is a separate charge, with income of £180,* in the patronage of the Vicar —The sub-district includes the parishes of Osgathorpe and Calke, the latter electorally in Derby, and parts of the parishes of Ashby-de la Zouch and Breedon on the Hill. Acres, 12,480 Pop, 8,290 Houses, 1,640 The district comprehends also the sub district of Hartshorn, containing the parishes of Willesley, Smisby, Hartshorn, and Ticknall, the extra parochial tract of Londary or Burton Road, and parts of the parishes of Ashby de la Zouch Seal, Stretton en le Field, Church Gresley, and Measham, all, except the parts of Ashby de la Zouch and Seal, electorally in Derby, the sub district of Measham, containing the parishes of Heather, Swepstone, and Snarestone, and parts of the parishes of Nailstone, Measham, and Appleby, the three last electorally in Derby, and the sub-district of Whitwick, containing the parishes of Whitwick Cole Orton, Packington, and Ravenstone parts of the two latter electorally in Derby, and part of the parish of Ibstock. Acres, 50,242 Poor rates in 1866, £11,636 Pop in 1861, 28,480 Houses, 5,931 Marriages in 1866, 239 births, 1,188,—of which 96 were illegitimate, deaths, 599,—of which 251 were at ages under 5 years, and 11 were at ages above 85 Marriages in the ten years 1851 60, 2,007, births, 9,902, deaths, 5,665 The places of worship in 1851 were 38 of the Church of England, with 10,081 sittings, 2 of Independents, with 655 s., 13 of Baptists, with 2,934 s, 27 of Wesleyan Methodists, with 4,155 s, 7 of Primitive Methodists, with 1 040 s, 3 of Wesleyan Reformers, with 160 s, and 2 of Roman Catholics, with 280 s The schools in 1851 were 49 public day schools, with 3,283 scholars, 48 private day schools, with 888 s, 60 Sunday schools, with 4,191 s, and 1 evening school for adults, with 29 s

ASHBY DE LA ZOUCH CANAL a canal from the neighbourhood of Moira, 3½ miles W of Ashby de la Zouch, to the Coventry canal, 2 miles S of Nuneaton It was opened in 1805 is 20½ miles long, all on a level, and goes in a S by easterly direction, past Market Bosworth and near Hinckley, but is very winding Tram railways connect its N end with Ashby de la Zouch, Ticknall, and Church Gresley

ASHBY (EAST) See ASHBY DE PARTNEY

ASHBY FOLVILLE, a township and a parish in Melton Mowbray district, Leicester The township lies on an affluent of the river Wreak, 5 miles ESE of Rearsby r station, and 6 SW of Melton Mowbray Acres, 1,993 Real property, £3,460 Pop, 160 Houses, 43 The parish includes also the chapelry of Barsby, and its post town is Gaddesby under Melton Mowbray Acres, 3 013 Real property, £5 679 Pop, 450 Houses, 106 The property is divided among a few The living is a vicarage in the diocese of Peterborough Value, £190 Patron, the Rev W Acworth The church is decorated English of the 14th century, has fine square headed windows, and needs repair Almshouses and other charities were founded by Lord Carrington, and have an income of £139 The Franciscan friar, William Folville who figured in the controversy "De pueris in ducendis," was a native

ASHBY (GREAT) See ASHBY-MAGNA

ASHBY (LITTLE) See ASHBY PARVA

ASHBY-MAGNA, a parish in Lutterworth district, Leicester, 2 miles ESE of Broughton Astley r station, and 4 N by E of Lutterworth. Post town, Leire under Lutterworth Acres, 1,720 Real property, £2,881 Pop, 315 Houses, 65 The property is divided among a few The living is a vicarage in the diocese of Peterborough. Value, £200 * Patron, the Earl of Aylesford The church was restored in 1861

ASHBY MEARS, or MEARS ASHBY, a parish in Wellingborough district, Northampton, 3 miles N by W of Castle Ashby r station, and 3½ WSW of Wellingborough Post town, Wilby, under Northampton Acres, 1 800 Real property, £3,220 Pop, 525 Houses, 117 A M Hall is the seat of H M Stockdale, Esq The living is a vicarage in the diocese of Peterborough. Value, £235 Patrons, Trustees The church was restored in 1858 There are two dissenting chapels and an endowed school

ASHBY PARVA, or LITTLE ASHBY, a parish in Lutterworth district, Leicester, 1½ mile NE of Ullesthorpe r station, and 3½ NNW of Lutterworth It has a post office, of the name of Ashby Parva, under Lutterworth. Acres, 1,357 Real property, £2,742 Pop, 169 Houses, 46 The property is divided among a few The living is a rectory in the diocese of Peterborough Value, £205 * Patron, the Lord Chancellor Charities, £187 of which £150 belong to an almshouse and a school

ASHBY PUERORUM, a parish in Horncastle district Lincoln, on the Wolds 4½ miles ENE of Horncastle r station It includes the hamlet of Stainsby and the tract of Holbeck, which is in some respects extra parochial, and its post town is Hagworthingham under Spilsby Acres, 1,620 Real property £2,229 Pop 149 Houses, 30 The property is divided among a few An estate was bequeathed to the Lincoln chorister boys, and this is alluded to in the distinctive name Puerorum A Roman sarcophagus or stone chest, containing a strong, well made, glass urn was found, in 1831, near the church The living is a vicarage in the diocese of Lincoln Value, £118 Patrons, the Dean and Chapter of Lincoln The church is a small antique structure, with a massive tower and is in very good condition

ASHBY ST LEDGERS, a parish in Daventry district, Northampton, near Watling street and the Oxford and Grand Junction canals, 2 miles W of Crick station, and 4 N of Daventry It has a post office under Rugby Acres, 2 050 Real property, £3 605 Pop, 300 Houses 63 The distinctive name St Ledgers is taken from the patron saint of the church Ashby Manor house a substantial old mansion belonged to the Catesbys, passed to the Ivesons, and is now the property of W Senhouse, Esq, and a small room in one of its offices was the place where Robert Catesby and his fellow conspirators concocted the gunpowder plot Ashby Lodge is another chief residence The parish is a meet of the Pytchley hounds The endowed charities in it amount to £44 The living is a vicarage in the diocese of Peterborough Value, £130 * Patron, W Senhouse, Esq The church is an edifice of nave and aisles, with tower and spire, has screen, rood loft, and three piscinas, and contains an altar tomb of William Catesby and his wife, of date 1493 This Catesby was the favourite of Richard III, fought for him at the battle of Bosworth, and was captured there and beheaded at Leicester, and he is "the cat" of the triumvirate—while Richard Ratcliffe is "the rat," Lord Lovel "the dog," and Richard III "the hog" in allusion to his crest of the boar—named in the satirical distich

"The rat and the cat, and Lovel the dog,
Do govern all England under the hog"

ASHBY (WEST), a parish in Horncastle district, Lincoln, 2 miles N by E of Horncastle r station It contains the hamlets of Farthorpe and Middlethorpe, and its post town is Horncastle Acres, 1,590. Real property, £4,853. Pop, 526 Houses, 118. Ashby-Thorpe House is a chief residence The living is a vicarage in the diocese of Lincoln Value £54 Patron, the Bishop of Carlisle The church is later English There are two Methodist chapels and some charities.

ASHBY WITH FENBY, a parish in Caistor district, Lincoln, on the Wolds 3 miles SW of Holton le Clay r station, and 6¼ S by W of Great Grimsby Post-town Holton le Clay under Grimsby Acres, 1,675 Real property, £2,640 Pop, 274. Houses 60 The property is subdivided. The living is a rectory in the diocese of Lincoln Value, £310 * Patron, the Lord Chancellor The church is ancient There are a Wesleyan chapel, and alms houses with £30 a year

ASH CAMPSEY See CAMPSEY ASH

ASHCHURCH, a parish in Tewkesbury district, Gloucester, on the Bristol and Birmingham railway, at the junction of the Tewkesbury branch 2 miles E of Tewkesbury It has a station on the railway, it includes the tythings of Pamington, Fiddington and Natton, Aston on Carron, and Northway and Newton, and its post-town is Tewkesbury Acres, 4,201 Real property, £11,801 Pop, 771 Houses, 152 The property is much subdivided There is a mineral spring of similar quality to the waters of Cheltenham The living is a rectory in the diocese of Gloucester and Bristol Value £270 * Patron, Rev C. N Williams The church is later English, with a Norman porch and a pinnacled tower There are a Wesleyan chapel, a national school, and charities £26 The junction of the Tewkesbury branch railway is at Ashchurch, and a railway from A to Evesham was formed under an act of 1862

ASHCOMBE, a parish in St. Thomas district Devon, 3 miles E of Chudleigh, and 4½ NW of Dawlish r station It has a post office under Dawlish Acres, 1,932 Real property, £1,957 Pop, 212 Houses, 41 The property is all in one estate, and about 500 acres are waste or wood The living is a rectory in the diocese of Exeter Value, £222 Patron, the Lord Chancellor The church is a small edifice, repaired and partly rebuilt in 1825, and has a square tower and a stained glass east window

ASHCOMBE, a hamlet in Weston super Mare parish, Somerset, near the Bristol channel and the Great Western railway, 8½ miles NW of Axbridge.

ASHCOMBE, an estate in Cranborne Chase, Wilts, 5 miles SE of Shaftesbury It belonged formerly to Lord Arundell, and belongs now to Mr Grove It comprises a romantic circular hollow, engirt with an amphitheatre of wooded hills, accessible only by a declivitous road, and has, in the centre, an isolated knoll, crowned by remains of an old mansion

ASHCOTT, a parish in Bridgewater district Somerset, near the Glastonbury railway, 5 miles WSW of Glastonbury It has a station on the railway, and a post-office under Bath, and includes the hamlet of Pedwell Acres, 2,272 Real property, £4,323. Pop, 817 Houses, 183 The manor belonged to Glastonbury abbey The living is a vicarage, annexed to Shapwick, in the diocese of Bath and Wells The church was restored in 1860 There are a Wesleyan chapel, and charities £70

ASHDON, a village in Saffron Walden district, Essex, and a parish chiefly in that district and county but partly also in Linton district, Cambridge The village stands on an affluent of the river Cam, 3½ miles NE of Saffron Walden, and 5½ ENE of Audley End r station, and has a post office under Cambridge Pop, 1,011 Houses, 220 The parish includes also the hamlet of Bartlow End Acres, 4,969 Real property, £6,969 Pop, 1,235 Houses, 270 The property is divided among a few The manor belongs to Viscount Maynard A place with a fine prospect and four barrows—the latter supposed to be sepulchral monuments of Danish chiefs—contends with Ashingdon in Rochford district the repute of being the battlefield of Canute's victory of Assandune, in 1016, over Edmund Ironside The living is a rectory in the diocese of Rochester Value, £909 * Patron Caius College, Cambridge The church is good, and there are a Baptist chapel and charities £21

ASHDOWN FOREST, an ancient forest, now a heath land, midway between East Grinstead and Uckfield, Sussex It lies within the manor of Maresfield, extending into five parishes, and comprises 13,991 acres It once was fenced, covered with wood, and stocked with deer, but was laid open during the civil war in the time of Charles I and allowed to be desolated Most of its timber was consumed as fuel in the iron furnaces which formerly abounded in the neighbourhood, and only a few trees, scattered and on the lower grounds, now remain The general surface is bare and wild, cut with ravines and glens, or rising into heights which command extensive views The manor, with the forest, belonged to the honour of Pevensey, was given among other lands, in lieu of Richmond castle, to John of Gaunt, and took then the name of Lancaster Great Park, passed, at the Restoration, to the Earl of Bristol, and is now divided among various proprietors

ASHDOWN PARK, the seat of the Earl of Craven, in Berks, on a high desolate spot, among bleak downs, near Ridge way or Icknield street, 3 miles SSW of White Horse vale, and 3¾ NW of Lambourn. The house was built by Webb, the nephew of Inigo Jones, is in the same style as Coleshill and contains interesting family portraits Stones called the Grey Wethers looking like a flock of sheep, remains of a stratum of Bagshot sand similar in nature to the stones of Stonehenge and Avebury, lie on the turf around the house, and a small circular camp, known as Alfred's Castle, lies to the E. Some neighbouring spot on the downs contests with Aston, Ashendon, Ashampstead, and Ilsley, the celebrity of having been the scene of the famous battle, in 871, between Alfred and the Danes, and is now thought by most antiquaries to have the best of the claim, so that, most probably, Ashdown was the Æscendune of the Saxons.

ASHE, a tything in Stourpaine parish, Dorset, on the river Stour, 3¾ miles NNW of Blandford Pop, 64

ASHE or ASH a tything in Netherbury parish, Dorset 1 mile SW of Beaminster It is a curacy annexed to Netherbury

ASHE or ASH, a hamlet in Musbury parish, Devon, 2¼ miles SW of Axminster An old mansion here, now a farm house, was the birthplace, in 1650, of John Churchill, the famous Duke of Marlborough

ASHE, or ASH, a parish in Whitchurch district, Hants, near the Southwestern railway in the vicinity of Overton station, 5 miles ENE of Whitchurch Post-town, Overton under Micheldever station Acres, 2,107 Real property, £1,759 Pop, 145 Houses, 25. Part of the surface is warren Ashe Park and Oakley Hall are chief residences The parish is a resort of sportsmen The living is a rectory in the diocese of Winchester Value, £410 * Patron W H Beach, Esq

ASHEBY See ASBY

ASHELDHAM a parish in Maldon district, Essex, near the coast, 10 miles ESE of Maldon r station Post town, Tillingham under Maldon Acres, 2 398 of which 700 are water Real property, £1,950 Pop, 212 Houses, 35 The surface is low, and partly marshy The living is a vicarage in the diocese of Rochester Value, £339 * Patron, the Bishop of Rochester

ASHELWORTH, or ASHLEWORTH, a parish in the district and county of Gloucester, at a ferry on the river Severn 5 miles N of Gloucester r station It has a post office under Gloucester Acres, 1,710 Real property, £3,710 Pop., 517 Houses, 136 The property is subdivided Ashelworth House is an old seat of the Haywards The living is a rectory in the diocese of Gloucester and Bristol Value, £280 Patron, the Bishop of Gloucester and Bristol The church is early English, and has a tower and spire There are a national school a police station and some charities

ASHEN, a parish in the district of Risbridge and county of Essex, on the verge of the county, at the river Stour, 2½ miles SW of Clare, and 3½ NNW of Yeldham r station Post town, Bumpstead Steeple under Halstead Acres, 1,498 Real property, £2,528 Pop, 341 Houses, 71 The property is subdivided An Augustinian priory was founded here in the time of Edward II The living is a rectory in the diocese of Rochester Value £300 * Patron, the Duchy of Lancaster The church was repaired in 1859

ASHENDON, a parish and a hundred in Bucks. The parish is in Aylesbury district, near the Julian way, 7½ miles W of Aylesbury r station, and includes the hamlet of Pollicot Post town, Brill under Tetsworth Acres 1,790 Real property, £3,498 Pop, 325 Houses 64 The property is divided among a few The manor of Ashendon has been held for centuries by the Grenvilles The manor of Little Pollicot was given about the year 1179 by John Bucktot, a priest, to one of the colleges of Oxford Ashendon figures repeatedly in the wars of the heptarchy, and claims against Ashdown to have been the scene of Alfred's victory in 871 The living is a vicarage, united with the vicarage of Dorton, in the diocese of Oxford Value, £106 Patron Christ Church College, Oxford The church contains the tomb of a crusader, and is good —The hundred is bounded on the SW and the W by Oxfordshire and contains twenty seven parishes and parts of four others Acres, 63,953 Pop in 1851, 13,360, in 1861, 13,389 Houses, 2,906

ASHERIDGE, a hamlet in Chesham parish, Amersham district, Bucks, 2 miles NW of Chesham Pop, 129

ASHRIDGE, Berkhampstead district See ASHRIDGE

ASHEY, an extensive ancient manor in the Isle of Wight, extending from the coast around Ryde southward to the hills which overhang the Main river It belonged to the abbess of Wherwell, near Andover, was alienated, in 1535 to Giles Worsley, and the northern part of it on which Ryde stands, was sold to Anthony Dillington, and passed afterwards to the family of Player Ashey Common, 2 miles S of Ryde, is now enclosed Ashey Farm a little further S, was the site of a cell of the nunnery of Wherwell Ashey Down, still further S, rises 424 feet above the level of the sea, and commands splendid views from Southampton to Chichester Ashey Sea mark on the summit of the down is a triangular pyramid, erected in 1735 by the Trinity Board, and guides the navigation into St Helen's Road at Spithead The Ryde water works, constructed in 1855, are at the foot of the down

ASHFIELD, or ASHFIELD WITH THORPE a parish in Bosmere district, Suffolk, 2 miles ESE of Debenham, and 9 NE of Needham r station Post town, Debenham under Stonham Acres, 1,505 Real property, £2,474 Pop, 300 Houses, 67 The living is a vicarage in the diocese of Ely Value, £53 Patron Lord Henniker The church is a brick structure of 1853

ASHFIELD (GREAT), a parish in Stow district, Suffolk 2½ miles N of Elmswell r station and 7½ NW of Stowmarket It has a post office of the name of Ashfield under Bury St Edmunds Acres 1,516 Real property, £2,709 Pop 408 Houses, 78 Ashfield Lodge is now the seat of Sir Henry C Blake, Bart, and was the birthplace of Lord Chancellor Thurlow, and of his brother, the Bishop of Durham The living is a vicarage in the diocese of Ely Value, £54 Patron, Lord Thurlow The church is a small brick edifice, with a tower Charities £104

ASHFIELD WITH RUTHALL, a township in Ditton Priors parish, Salop, 7½ miles SSW of Much Wenlock Pop., 55

ASHFIELD WITH THORPE See ASHFIELD.

ASHFORD, a village, a township and a chapelry in Bakewell parish, Derby The village stands on the river Wye, adjacent to the Buxton railway, in a charming situation surrounded by high hills near Monsal dale, 1 mile WNW of Hassop r station and 2 NW of Bakewell. It has a post office under Bakewell, and it carries on stocking making, spinning and a trade in marble Mills for the cutting and polishing of marble were erected in its vicinity in 1748, and are the oldest establishments of their kind in England Marbles of many tints, but chiefly black and grey, are found adjacent about 40 feet beneath the surface, in nine beds from 3 to 9 inches thick, and are manufactured at the mills into a great variety of ornamental articles. Ashford Hall, in the neighbourhood, is the seat of the Cavendish family, and the manor belongs to the Duke of Devonshire A spot near the church was the site of the mansion of Edward Plantagenet, of Woodstock, Earl of Kent, now traceable only by the moat —The township and the chapelry are co extensive Real property, £5,195 Pop, 829 Houses, 172 The living is a p curacy in the diocese of Lichfield Value £102 * Patron, the Vicar of Bakewell The church is ancient There are chapels for Methodists and Unitarians, free schools for boys and girls, and charities £20

ASHFORD, a parish in Barnstaple district, Devon, on the north side of the estuary of the Taw, 2½ miles NW of Barnstaple r station Post town Barnstaple Acres 359 Real property, £706 Pop, 157 Houses, 31 The property is much subdivided The living is a rectory in the diocese of Exeter Value, £110 Patron, the Lord Chancellor The church was built in 1854 and is a neat small edifice, with low square tower and a spire

ASHFORD a village and a parish in Staines district, Middlesex The village stands amid a rich, cultivated tract, near the London, Richmond, and Reading railway, 2 miles E of Staines, and has a station on the railway, and a post office under Staines The parish includes the western part of Old Hounslow Heath, once the retreat of highwaymen and the terror of travellers Acres, 1,378 Real property, £3,586 Pop, 781 Houses, 130 Ashford Common was formerly a field for military reviews but has now been long enclosed and cultivated Ashford Lodge, Manor House and Clock House are handsome seats The living is a vicarage in the diocese of London Value, £136 Patron, the Lord Chancellor The church was rebuilt in 1859 A Welsh charity school, an edifice in the Tudor style, for 200 children was founded in 1857

ASHFORD, a town a parish, a subdistrict, and two districts, East and West, in Kent The town stands on the Esshe or Esshet river, the western branch of the Stour and on the South eastern railway at the intersection of the line from Reigate to Folkestone with the line from Hastings to Ramsgate, 67 miles SE by E of London It was anciently called Esshetford, from its situation on the river, and it belonged to Hugo de Montfort, and passed to successively the Asshetfords, the Criols, the Leybornes, the Archers, the Smyths, and the Tootes The original town is situated on an eminence, on the N bank of the river, and has a High street, of considerable width, about ½ a mile long A new town, called Alfred or Newtown Ashford, was built by the railway company, adjacent to the station, and includes extensive workshops, constructed at a cost of upwards of £100,000, and about 200 dwellings and a school, used as a church The parish church, in the old town, is a spacious structure, in fine perpendicular English, built or restored by Sir John Fogge in the time of Edward IV, comprises nave, transept, and three chancels, with a lofty tower resembling the Bell Harry tower of Canterbury cathedral, and contains a figured font, the tomb of Sir John Fogge, a brass of the Countess of Athole of 1375, and some fine monuments of the Smyths of Westenhanger, one of whom was the Sacharissa of Waller. An ecclesiastical college was founded by Sir John Fogge as a pendant to the church but was dissolved in the time of Henry VII. A new church, in the second pointed style, was built in the new town in 1867. Charities exist to the amount of £309, and include two public schools. There are chapels for five dissenting bodies and Roman Catholics, a police station, built in 1864, a mechanics' institution, assembly rooms and reading room, a four arched bridge, a market house, a corn exchange erected in 1861, a head post office,‡ in High street, and a receiving office,‡ 1¼ mile distant, in the new town. There is also a neat cemetery, with two chapels. A great stock market is held on the first and third Tuesdays of every month, and fairs on 17 May, 9 Sept., and 12 13, and 24 Oct. There are two banking offices and two chief inns. Fine linen is manufactured, and a weekly newspaper is published. The town is one of the polling places for the county, and is under the jurisdiction of the county magistrates. Pop., 5,522. Houses, 1,049. Wallis, the mathematician, Glover, the antiquary, and Milles the herald were natives. The "headstrong Kentish man" of Shakespeare also, is "John Cade of Ashford." The Osborne family, Dukes of Leeds, are said to have originated here, and the Keppels, Earls of Albemarle, take from the place the title of Baron.

The parish of Ashford comprises 2,786 acres. Real property, £27,729. Pop., 6,950. Houses, 1,311. The living is a vicarage in the diocese of Canterbury. Value, £460.* Patrons, the Dean and Chapter of Rochester.—The sub-district of Ashford includes six parishes. Acres, 19,360. Pop., 9,826. Houses, 1,884.—The district of East Ashford comprehends the sub district of Aldington, containing the parishes of Aldington, Warehorne, Orlestone, Ruckinge, Bilsington, Bonnington and Hurst, the sub district of Brabourne containing the parishes of Brabourne, Mersham, Sevington, Willesborough, Hinxhill, Smeeth and Pircholt, and the sub district of Wye, containing the parishes of Wye, Hastingleigh, Brook, Kennington, Crundale, Boughton-Aluph, Eastwell, Challock, Moldash, Chilham, and Godmersham. Acres, 54,498. Poor rates, £8,292. Pop in 1841, 11,530, in 1861, 12,286. Houses, 2,444. Marriages, 80, births, 396,—of which 13 were illegitimate, deaths, 233,—of which 61 were at ages under 5 years, and 10 at ages above 85. Marriages in the ten years 1851-60, 892, births, 4,141, deaths, 2,234. The places of worship in 1851 were 21 of the Church of England, with 3,911 sittings, 1 of Baptists, with 203 s., 7 of Wesleyan Methodists, with 739 s., and 1 of Bible Christians, with 100 s. The schools in 1851 were 17 public day schools, with 1,169 scholars, 14 private day schools, with 329 s., and 19 Sunday schools, with 1,313 s. The workhouse is in Willesborough.—The district of West Ashford comprehends the sub district of Ashford, containing the parishes of Ashford, Hothfield, Bethersden, Great Chart, Kingsnorth, and Shadoxhurst, and the sub district of Calehill, containing the parishes of Westwell, Smarden, Egerton, Little Chart, Charing, and Pluckley and Pevington. Acres, 41,901. Poor rates, £7,318. Pop in 1841, 11,329, in 1861, 15,137. Houses, 2,891. Marriages, 195, births, 533,—of which 35 were illegitimate, deaths, 315,—of which 116 were at ages under 5 years, and 13 at ages above 85. Marriages in the ten years 1851-60, 1,085, births, 5,281, deaths, 2,820. The places of worship in 1851 were 13 of the Church of England, with 7,146 sittings, 1 of Lady Huntingdon's Connexion, with 370 s., 5 of Baptists, with 1,395 s., 1 of Quakers, with 150 s., 6 of Wesleyan Methodists, with 966 s., 1 of Bible Christians, with 115 s., 1 undefined, with 80 s., and 1 of Roman Catholics, with 30 attendants. The schools in 1851 were 14 public day schools, with 1,552 scholars, 19 private day schools, with 375 s., 21 Sunday schools, with 1,422 s., and 2 evening schools for adults, with 20 s. The workhouse is in Westwell.

ASHFORD BOWDLER, a parish in Ludlow district, Salop, on the river Teme, adjacent to Woofferton r. station, 2½ miles S of Ludlow. Post town, Ludlow. Acres, 575. Real property, £1,144. Pop., 106. Houses, 18. The property is not much divided. Ashford Bowdler Court and Ashford Bowdler Hall are chief residences. The living is a vicarage in the diocese of Hereford. Value, £55. Patron, C. Walker, Esq. The church is an old edifice, figuring picturesquely in a neat small village.

ASHFORDBY, or ASFORDBY, a parish in Melton Mowbray district, Leicester, on the Midland railway and the river Wreak, 3 miles W of Melton Mowbray. It has a station on the railway, and a post office under Melton Mowbray. Acres, 1,210. Real property, £3,902. Pop., 485. Houses, 125. The property is much subdivided. Stocking making is carried on. The living is a rectory in the diocese of Peterborough. Value, £455. Patron, the Rev. Frederick G. Burnaby. The church was recently repaired, and has a tower and spire. There are chapels for Wesleyan and Primitive Methodists, and charities £8.

ASHFORD CARBONELL, a parish in Ludlow district, Salop, on the river Teme, near Woofferton r. station, 3 miles S by E of Ludlow. It has a post-office under Ludlow. Acres, 1,478. Real property, £2,657. Pop., 282. Houses, 59. The property is divided among a few. The living is a rectory, annexed to the rectory of Little Hereford, in the diocese of Hereford. The church is good.

ASHFORD HILL, a locality on the north border of Hants, 3 miles from Kingsclere, with a post office under Reading.

ASHFURLONG, a village in Sutton Coldfield parish, Warwick, 2 miles NE of Sutton Coldfield.

ASHGILL, a hamlet in Coverham parish, N. R. Yorkshire, 2 miles SW of Middleham.

ASH HOLE, a cavern at Berry Head, on the south side of Tor bay, Devon. The bones of hyenas and of other animals, now known only in hot climates, have been found in it.

ASHILL, a parish in Swaffham district, Norfolk, near the river Stoke, 5 miles S of Dunham r. station, and 6 SE of Swaffham. It has a post-office under Thetford. Acres, 2,990. Real property, £5,260. Pop., 696. Houses, 151. The property is divided among a few. The manor was held by the Hastingses, on the tenure of serving the king's linen at the coronation. Part of the land is common, and some points command a fine view. The living is a rectory in the diocese of Norwich. Value, £850.* Patron, the Rev. B. Edwards. The church is later English, has a flint tower, and is good. Charities, £36 and 30 acres of allotment.

ASHILL, a village and a parish in Chard district, Somerset. The village stands near Chard canal, and near the Chard and Taunton railway, 4 miles NW of Ilminster, and 8 SSE of Taunton. It has a post-office under Ilminster, and fairs on Easter Wednesday, and on 12 Sept. or the following Wednesday. The parish comprises 1,790 acres. Real property, £3,324. Pop., 415. Houses, 92. The property is much subdivided. A spring which ebbs and flows is near the village. The living is a rectory in the diocese of Bath and Wells. Value, £300.* Patron, the Bishop of Bath and Wells. The church is ancient, and was recently restored.

ASHINGDON, a parish in Rochford district, Essex, near the river Crouch, 2½ miles N of Rochford, and 6 NNE of Leigh r. station. Post town, Rochford, under Ingatestone. Acres, 1,165. Real property, £1,878. Pop., 99. Houses, 17. The property is divided among a few. Ashingdon disputes with Ashdon being the ancient Assandune, the scene of Canute's victory over Edmund Ironside in 1016. An ancient camp was formerly at Canewdon, a great group of barrows, supposed to be the graves of the Danes, is in the neighbouring parish of Woodham Mortimer, and a church built by Canute, in commemoration of his victory, is said to have stood in the neighbouring village of Hockley. The living is a rectory in the diocese of Rochester Value, £254 Patron the Rev S Nottidge The church is ancient, and has a fine view

ASHINGDON, N W Essex See ASHDON

ASHINGTON, a parish in Yeovil district, Somerset, on the river Yeo and on the Durston and Yeovil railway, 3½ miles N of Yeovil. Post town, Ilchester under Taunton. Acres 5 4 Real property, with Draycott £1,957 Pop, 5 Houses, 10 The property is divided among a few The living is a rectory in the diocese of Bath and Wells Value, £162 * Patron, not reported The church is good

ASHINGTON a parish in Thakeham district, Sussex, 4 miles NW of Steyning and 5 ESE of Pulborough r station It has a post office under Hurstpierpoint, contains the hamlet of Banckton, and has fairs on 29 June and 21 July Acres, 1,273 Real property, £1,509 Pop 234 Houses, 52 The property is subdivided The parish is noted for coursing The living is a rectory united with the curacy of Banckton, in the diocese of Chichester Value, £288 * Patron, the Duke of Norfolk. The church is good

ASHINGTON AND SHEEPWASH, a township in Bothal parish, Northumberland on the river Wansbeck, 3½ miles E of Morpeth. Acres, 688 Pop, 76 Houses, 13

ASHLEWORTH See ASHELWORTH

ASHLEY, a township in Bowdon parish, Cheshire on the Knutsford and Altrincham railway near the river Bollin, 2½ miles S of Altrincham It has a station on the railway, and a post office under Manchester Acres 2,173 Real property, £3 900 Pop, 375 Houses, 59 Ashley Hall was a place of councils against the cause of the rebellion in 1715 A school church was built in 18 4 and a Wesleyan chapel in 1839

ASHLEY a tything in Milton parish, Hants near the Channel 4½ miles WSW of Lymington Real property £3,475 Pop 552

ASHLEY a hamlet in Box parish, Wilts, adjacent to the Great Western railway, 4½ miles WSW of Corsham

ASHLEY, a parish in Stockbridge district, Hants, 2 miles F of the Andover railway, and 7 W of Winchester Post town, Stockbridge under Winchester Acres, 1,857 Real property, £1 511 Pop, 104 Houses, 24 The property is subdivided There are vestiges of Roman camps and a Danish entrenchment. The living is a rectory in the diocese of Winchester Value, £329 * Patron the Rev James Hannay The church is Norman, has a very small chancel arch, and was restored in 18 5

ASHLEY a parish in the district of Market Harborough and county of Northampton, on the verge of the county at the river Welland in the vicinity of Medbourne Bridge r station, 7 miles ENE of Market Harborough Post town, Market Harborough under Rugby Acres 1,1 Real property, £2,620 Pop, 3 8 Houses, 82 The property is divided among a few The living is a rectory in the diocese of Peterborough Value, £32 * Patron the Rev R F Pulteney The church is good and there are a Baptist chapel, and charities £24

ASHLEY, a parish in the district of Market Drayton and county of Stafford 4 miles SW of Whitmore r station, and 5 ENE of Market Drayton It contains the village of Ashley Heath, and part of the hamlet of Hook Gate, and has a post office under Market Drayton Acres, 2,869 Real property, £5,303 Pop, 870 Houses, 1 5 The property is much subdivided There is a Roman camp on a site 803 feet high The living is a rectory in the diocese of Lichfield Value £316 * Patron, Mrs Kinnersley two turns, and H C Meynell Ingram, Esq, one turn The church is very good, has a font given by a soldier of the Black Prince and was enlarged by a chapel which contains handsome monuments of the Kinnersleys There are chapels for Independents and Roman Catholics, and charities £22

ASHLEY a parish in the district of Tetbury and county of W s, near Akeman street 3 miles NE of Tetbury, and SSW of T tbury road r station Post town Tetbury Acres 91 Real property, with Newn ton, £4,581 Pop, 90 Houses, 17 The property is all in one estate, belonged formerly to the Georges and the Hungerfords, and belongs now to the Estcourts There is a large mansion, and there was formerly a market. The living is a rectory in the diocese of Gloucester and Bristol Value £220 * Patron, the Duchy of Lancaster The church is ancient, with some arches round, others pointed and a square embattled tower, contains a large rude font, and tomb of the Georges, and was repaired in 1858

ASHLEY Gloucester See CLIFTON

ASHLEY COMBE, a summer residence of the Earl of Lovelace, 2 miles W of Porlock, Somerset It stands on the coast, on a high narrow terrace looking out on Porlock bay and Wales A glen adjacent to it leads up to a grand amphitheatre, streaked by five brooks on the side of a moorland height

ASHLEY CUM SILVERLEY, a parish in Newmarket district, Cambridge, on the verge of the county, at Ashley Gap, 4 miles ESE of Newmarket r station It has a post office, of the name of Ashley, under Newmarket Acres, 2,143 Real property, £3 2 3 Pop, 509 Houses, 109 The property is divided among a few The living is a rectory and a vicarage—Ashley rectory, Silverley vicarage—in the diocese of Ely Value, £150 * Patron, the Hon W R J North The church was built in 1845

ASHLEY (GREAT and LITTLE), two villages on the W border of Wilts, near the river Avon 1¾ and 2¼ miles NW of Bradford

ASHLEY GREEN, a hamlet in Chesham parish, Bucks, 2¼ miles NNE of Chesham Pop, 536

ASHLEY HAY, a township in Wirksworth parish Derby, 1 mile SE of Wirksworth Pop, 232 Houses, 49

ASHLEY HEATH See ASHLEY, Stafford

ASHLEY HILL, a station on the Bristol and South Wales Union railway, 3 miles N of Bristol

ASHLEY LODGE, an extra parochial tract in the New Forest, Hants, 3 miles ENE of Fordingbridge

ASHLEY (NORTH), a tything in Ringwood parish, Hants, contiguous to Ringwood. Pop, 237

ASHLEY PARK, the seat of Sir Henry Fletcher, Bart, on the N border of Surrey, on the Thames, 4½ miles E by S of Chertsey The mansion is an edifice of red brick, with Tudor features, but has been much modernized, and contains a gallery 100 feet long Some very large Scotch pines are in the park

ASHLEY WALK a portion of the New Forest, Hants partly extra parochial, and partly in the parishes of Breamore and Ellingham Acres, 5,245

ASHLING (EAST and WEST), two tythings in Funtington parish, Sussex, near the South Coast railway 4 miles NW of Chichester Pop 310 and 455 West Ashling has a post office under Chichester

ASH MAGNA and ASH PARVA See ASH Salop

ASHMANHAUGH a parish in Tunstead district, Norfolk, 9 miles NNE of Norwich r station Post town, Coltishall under Norwich Acres, 66 Real property, £1,172 Pop, 136 Houses, 32 The property is divided between two. The living is a vicarage in the diocese of Norwich Value, £12 Patron Sir J H Preston, Bart The church is good Charities, £12

ASHMANSWORTH, a parish in Kingsclere district Hants, 6½ miles NNW of Whitchurch r station, and 8½ SSW of Newbury Post town, East Woodhay under Newbury Acres, 1,898 Real property, £1,103 Pop 201 Houses, 44 The living is a p curacy, annexed to the rectory of East Woodhay, in the diocese of Winchester The church is early English

ASHMORE, a parish in Shaftesbury district, Dorset contiguous to Wilts 5 miles SE of Shaftesbury, and 7½ N of Blandford r station Post town, Shaftesbury under Salisbury Acres 2 33 Real property with Farnham £3, 20 Pop, 2 1 Houses, 61 The property is divided among a few The living is a rectory in the diocese of Salisbury Value £410 * Patron, the Rev C Chisholm The church is good, and there is a Wesleyan chapel

ASHNESS, a locality on the E side of Derwent water,

8 miles S of Keswick, Cumberland. It commands a good bird's eye view of the lake

ASH NEXT RIDLEY See Ash, Kent

ASH NEXT SANDWICH, a village and a parish in Eastry district, Kent. The village stands on a rising ground, by the side of Wingham brook, a tributary of the Stour, 3 miles W of Sandwich r station, and has a post office,‡ of the name of Ash, under Sandwich The parish comprises 6,871 acres. Real property, £20,467 Pop, 2,039 Houses, 439 Richborough Castle, the Roman Rutupiæ, is on the E border, about a mile N of Sandwich See RICHBOROUGH One of the earliest settlements of the Saxons was in the parish and many relics of the earliest Saxon times have been found Hops are grown, and pale ale is extensively brewed There are two livings, St Nicholas and Trinity, and both are vicarages in the diocese of Canterbury Value, £293* and £50 Patron, the Archbishop of Canterbury St. N church is cruciform, early English, and very fine, is surmounted by a spired central tower, which serves as a landmark has undergone some good recent restorations, and contains two altar tombs and some brasses The church of Trinity stands at Westmarsh, 2 miles distant, and there is a neat Independent chapel A school has £90 from endowment, and other charities have £17

ASHOLME, a hamlet in Lambley parish, Northumberland, near the South Tyne, the Alston railway, and the Maiden way, 5 miles S of Haltwhistle

ASHOLT See AISHOLT

ASHOP (THE), a stream of Derbyshire It rises at Ashop Head, on the N side of the Peak, and runs about 8 miles east south-eastward to the Derwent at Ashton inn

ASHORNE, a hamlet in Newbold Pacey parish, Warwick, on an affluent of the river Avon, 4½ miles S by E of Warwick

ASHOVER, a village, a township, a parish and a sub district in Derby The village stands in a deep narrow valley, near the rivers Amber and Milntown, 3 miles WNW of Stretton r station, and 7 SSW of Chesterfield It is a place of great antiquity, had a church at Domesday, and was once a market town Fairs are still held at it on 25 April and 15 Oct., and it has a post office under Chesterfield Lace making is carried on Tambour working and stocking weaving also were once prominent, but the former has ceased, and the latter is declining —The township includes the village, and is in the district of Chesterfield Acres, 9,180 Real property, £9,732 Pop 2,351 Houses, 542.—The parish includes also the chapelry of Dethwick Lea, in the district of Belper Acres, 11,290 Real property, £13,206 Pop, 3,286 Houses, 748 The property is much subdivided Limestone is quarried, and lead ore was formerly mined Overton Hall was the seat of Sir Joseph Banks, the president of the Royal Society Dethwick was the seat of the Babingtons, one of whom was executed for treason against Queen Elizabeth Lea Hurst, a fine Gothic mansion, is the seat of the Nightingales Robin Hood's Mark, a rocking stone about 26 feet in circuit, is on a slope of Ashover Common and the Turning stone, a remarkably shaped block 9 feet high, supposed to have been an object of Druidical veneration, is about 200 yards further off The living is a rectory in the diocese of Lichfield Value, £510* Patron the Rev J Nodder The church was built in 1419, and recently repaired, is surmounted by an embattled tower, and a handsome spire, has a grand window of stained glass, set up in 1845, and contains tombs of the Babingtons and two brasses. An endowed school, at High Ashover, has £28, and other charities £12 The p curacy of Dethwick Lea is a separate benefice There are Wesleyan and Primitive Methodist chapels —The sub district of Ashover is in Chesterfield district, and contains two parishes, and parts of three others. Acres, 21,234 Pop, 10,757 Houses 2 106

ASHOW, a parish in the district and county of Warwick, on the river Avon adjacent to Stoneleigh, near the Northwestern railway, 2½ miles ESE of Kenilworth It has a post office† under Kenilworth Acres 1 012 Real property, £1,527 Pop, 149 Houses, 40 The property is not much divided. The manor was given, in the time of Edward IV, to the abbey of Stoneleigh The living is a rectory in the diocese of Worcester Value £295* Patron, Lord Leigh The church is ancient. Charities, £45

ASHPERTON, a parish in Ledbury district Hereford, on the Worcester and Hereford railway, near the river Frome, 5 miles NW of Ledbury It has a station on the railway, and its post town is Ledbury Acres, 1,741 Real property £3,190 Pop, 534 Houses, 105 The property is divided among a few The living is a p curacy annexed to the vicarage of Stretton Grandison, in the diocese of Hereford. The church is good

ASHPRINGTON, a parish in Totnes district, Devon, at the influx of the Harborne river to the Dart, 2¾ miles SSE of Totnes r station Post town, Totnes Acres, 2,790 Real property with Cornworthy, £7,768 Pop, 537 Houses, 121 The property is not much divided Sharpham House, the seat of the Durant family, is an elegant edifice, and commands an extensive view along the Dart The living is a rectory in the diocese of Exeter Value, £537* Patron, the Rev G T Carwithen The church is a neat old edifice, of nave, chancel, and aisles, with square tower A dilapidated old chapel stands at Painsford

ASH PRIORS a parish in Taunton district, Somerset, near Bishops Lydeard r station, and 6 miles NW of Taunton Post town, Bishops-Lydeard under Taunton Acres, 635. Real property, £1,057 Pop, 207 Houses 45 The property is divided among a few The living is a vicarage in the diocese of Bath and Wells Value, £70 Patron, Sir T B Lethbridge, Bart The church is good

ASHREIGNEY, or RINGS ASH, a parish in Torrington district, Devon 4 miles WNW of Eggesford r station, and 4 WSW of Chumleigh Post town Chumleigh Acres, 5 663 Real property, £3,718. Pop, 842 Houses, 169 The property is subdivided The parish was a rendezvous of Fairfax in 1646, prior to his attack on Torrington The living is a rectory in the diocese of Exeter Value, £335* Patron, the Rev J T Johnson The church is an ancient structure, of nave, chancel, and south aisle, with low square tower Charities £10

ASHRIDGE PARK, the seat of Earl Brownlow, on the mutual border of Bucks and Herts, adjacent to the Northwestern railway, 3½ miles N of Berkhampstead A monastery of the order of Bonhommes was founded here in 1283, by Edmund Plantagenet, Earl of Cornwall, and put into high celebrity by means of an alleged portion of the blood of Christ which he brought to it from Germany Edward I kept Christmas and held a parliament in the monastery in 1290 The Princess Elizabeth, afterwards Queen Elizabeth, received a grant of the place, and resided in it and she was taken prisoner hence to London on the charge of being a party to Wyatt's conspiracy The church was destroyed in Elizabeth's time, the great hall and the cloisters stood till 1800, and only the crypt of the monastery now remains A new mansion was built in 1808-14, after designs by Wyatt, and "is a varied and irregular line of towers and battlements arched doorways, mullioned windows, corbels and machicolations, with a turreted centre, fine Gothic porch, and beautifully proportioned spire, surmounting the chapel, and it contains fine statues, ancient brasses, choice paintings and other objects of interest. The property was given by Elizabeth to her Lord Keeper of the Great Seal Baron Ellesmere, and passed through the Earls and Dukes of Bridgewater, to Earl Brownlow The pretended blood of Christ in the ancient monastery was publicly exposed, in 1538, at Paul's Cross, by the Bishop of Rochester and shown to be clarified and coloured honey An old poet says

"The Bonehommes at Asheridge beside Barcanstede,
Where the sange royal is, Christ's blode so rede
A plesaunter place than Asheridge is, harde were to finde,
As Skelton rehearseth with words few and playne"

ASHTEAD, a parish in Epsom district, Surrey, on the Croydon and Leatherhead railway, 2½ miles SW of Epsom It has a station on the railway and a post office under Epsom Acres, 2 522 Real property, £3,519 Pop., 729 Houses, 124 The property is divided among a few Ashtead House, the sea of the Howard family, is a splendid mansion, and contains some good pictures The park has some venerable old oaks and elms, and a long avenue of limes, and is well stocked with deer Ashtead Common, above the park commands picturesque views, and contains, among wood an ancient entrench ment The Roman Stone street passed through the pa rish, and has left relics in the materials of the church There is a mineral spring similar to that of Epsom The living is a rectory in the diocese of Winchester Value £499 * Patrons, the Heirs of the late Hon Col Howard The church is an ancient structure, with a tower, and embodies Roman bricks and tiles in its walls, but has undergone numerous alterations Sir Robert Howard used to entertain Charles II in a mansion which occu pied the site of the present Ashtead House An alms house for six poor widows has £32 from endowment, and other charities £16

ASHTED, a chapelry in Aston parish Warwick It includes the north eastern part of Birmingham, and has a post-office‡ of Ashted Row, in the street of that name, 1½ mile distant from the Birmingham head office Pop. in 1851, 11,198, in 1861, 13,392 Houses, 2 601 The living is a vicarage in the diocese of Worcester Value £143 Patrons, three Trustees The church is a plain edifice, built for a private residence by the physician, Dr Ash, converted into a chapel in 1789, purchased for the Church of England in 1791, and now used as well for the troops at the horse barracks as for the parishioners

ASHTON a township and a chapelry in Tarvin parish, Cheshire. The township lies near Delamere forest 3½ miles SE of Dunham Hill r station, and 7 NE of Ches ter It has a post office under Chester Acres 1,303. Real property, £2 732 Pop, 411 Houses, 81 —The chapelry is called Ashton Hayes, and was constituted in 1849 Pop, 626 Houses, 114 The living is a vicar age in the diocese of Chester Value, £160 * Patron, W Atkinson, Esq The church is in the later English style There are two Methodist chapels

ASHTON, a parish in St Thomas district, Devon adjoining the river Teign, 4 miles N of Chudleigh and 6½ WSW of Exminster r station Post town Chudleigh under Newton Abbot Acres 1 709 Real property £1,985. Pop, 3?7 Houses, 66 Viscount Exmouth is lord of the manor, and owns most of the land. The Chudleighs were proprietors for several hundred years, and their mansion, some remains of which still exist was garrisoned for King Charles I, and taken by the Parliamentarians. Manganese ore is mined The living is a rectory in the diocese of Exeter Value £230 Patron, the Rev George Ware The church is a small ancient edifice, with square turreted tower Charities £6

ASHTON, a township, conjoint with Eye and More ton, in Eye parish Hereford, near the Leominster ca nal, 4 miles NNE of Leominster

ASHTON, a tything in Bishops Waltham parish, Hants, 1 mile NW of Bishops Waltham Pop., 310

ASHTON a parish in Potterspury district Northamp ton, on the Northwestern railway and the Grand Junc tion canal near Salcey forest and the Blisworth tunnel, 1½ mile SSE of Roade r station, and 7 S of Northamp ton Post town Roade under Northampton Acres, 1 290 Real property, £1,787 Pop, 371 Houses 84 The property is divided among a few The inhabitants have a right of common in Salcey forest The living is a rectory in the dio of Peterborough Value, £275 Pa tron, the Lord Chancellor The church is good, and there are Baptist and Methodist chapels, and charities £20

ASHTON, a hamlet in Oundle parish Northampton, near the Peterborough railway and the Nen river 1 mile E of Oundle Real property, £1,?81 Pop 177 Houses 39

ASHTON a hamlet in Ufford parish, Northampton 2½ miles W of Helpston r station and 5 E by S of Stamford Acres, 9?0 Real property £1 0?? Pop 115 Houses 21 Ashton Wold is a resort of sportsmen

ASHTON, Lancashire See ASHTON IN MACKER FIELD, ASHTON ON RIBBLE, ASHTON UNDER-LYNE, and ASHTON WITH STODDAY

ASHTON BLANK. See ASTON BLANK

ASHTON (COLD), a parish in Chipping Sodbury dis trict, Gloucester on the verge of the county, under the Cotswolds, 5¾ miles N of Bath r station It includes the village of Pensylvania, and its post town is Marsh field under Chippenham Acres, 2,300 Real property, £4,284 Pop, ?13 Houses, 99 The property is sub divided The living is a rectory in the diocese of Glou cester and Bristol Value, £492 Patron, the Rev I Sayres The church has a stone pulpit, and is very good Charities, £10 Bishop Latimer was for some time rector

ASHTON COURT, the seat of Sir John H G Smyth Bart, in Long Ashton parish, Somerset, on the SE slope of Ashton Down, 2 miles SW of Bristol. The mansion belonged originally to the Lyons family, is an old edifice with a front 143 feet long by Inigo Jones, and contains a portrait gallery 90 feet by 20

ASHTON GIFFORD, a township in Codford St Peter parish Wilts, on the river Wiley, 2½ miles SE of Hey tesbury Pop, 141

ASHTON GREEN, a hamlet in Prescot parish, Lan cashire, 2½ miles E of St Helen's

ASHTON HALL, a seat in the township of Ashton with Stodday, Lancashire, between the Preston and Lan caster railway and the estuary of the Lune, 2½ miles S of Lancaster It belonged to the Lawrences, passed by marriage to the Dukes of Hamilton, and is now the residence of Le Gendre N Starkie, Esq The mansion is a large edifice with square embattled towers The park is finely wooded, and commands charming views over Morecambe bay

ASHTON HAYES See ASHTON Cheshire

ASHTON IN MACKERFIELD or ASHTON LE WIL LOWS a village and a township in Wigan district, and a parish partly also in Warrington district, Lancashire The village stands 2½ miles NW of Newton, and 3 WNW of Golborne r station, and has a post office ‡ of the name of Ashton in Mackerfield, under Warrington The town ship has long been noted for the manufacture of hinges, locks, files, and nails, and is maintained also by cotton factories and coal mines Acres, 5,5?7 Real property, £23,364,—of which £13,06? are in mines Pop in 1851, 5,679, in 1861, 6,?66 Houses, 1,176 —The parish in cludes also the township of Haydock and comprises 7,919 acres Real property, £42,630, —of which £20,893 are in mines Pop in 1851, 7,673, in 1861, 10,181 Houses 1 777 There are two livings, or ecclesiastically two parishes, Holy Trinity and St Thomas the former a rectory, the latter a vicarage, in the diocese of Chester Value of H T, £550,* of St T, £24? * Patron of H T, the Earl of Derby of St T, the Rector H T church is near the hamlets of Downhall Green and North Ashton, where is a post office under Wigan and St. T church is in the village of Ashton There is also a vicar age of St James Haydock There are likewise a hand some Independent chapel built in 1867, three other dis senting chapels, a Roman Catholic chapel an endowed school with £33 and charities £97

ASHTON INN See ASHOP (THE)

ASHTON KEYNES, a parish in Cricklade district Wilts, on an affluent of the Thames 2½ miles NNE of Minety r station and 4 W of Cricklade It includes the chapelry of Leigh, and has a post office under Crick lade. Acres, 3 820 Real property, £5,056 Pop 1,070 Houses 2?2 The property is much subdivided Ashton Keynes House is a chief residence The living is a vicarage in the diocese of Gloucester and Bristol Value, £32? * Patron J Swinford, Esq The church is good and there are two dissenting chapels, and chari ties £119

ASHTON LE WILLOWS See ASHTON IN MACKER FIELD

ASHTON (LONG), a parish and a sub-district in Bed minster district, Somerset The parish lies on the Bris tol and Exeter railway, near Wans Dyke and Dund y

Beacon, 3 miles SW of Bristol It contains Bedminster workhouse, and Bower Ashton, Kingscott Providence, Yanley, and Rownham hamlets, and has a post office under Bristol Acres, 4 237 Real property, £10,535 Pop., 2,000 Houses, 297 The centre is a fertile wooded vale, partly disposed in market gardens and orchards, for sending vegetables and fruit to Bristol The N rises into a range of bleak but picturesque hills, which command a grand view of the surrounding country The S goes up to Barrow Common, which is sometimes deemed extra parochial, and has remains of Roman camps at Stokeleigh and Burwalls The chief residence is ASHTON COURT which see Many Roman coins have been found The living is a vicarage in the diocese of Bath and Wells Value, £450 * Patrons, Sir J Smyth, Bart, and W G Langton, Esq The church dates from 1390, has a carved Gothic screen, dividing the chancel from the nave and aisles, contains figured stained windows and some handsome monuments, and is surmounted by a tower, with the arms of the Lyons family in stone There are an Independent chapel, an endowed school with £14, and other charities with £112. Collinson, the county historian, was vicar —The sub district comprises seven parishes Acres, 19,349 Pop., 5,861 Houses, 1,073

ASHTON ON MERSEY, a township and a parish in Altrincham district, Cheshire The township lies on the river Mersey, near the junction with it of the Bridgewater canal, 1½ mile NW of Sale r station, and 5¼ WSW of Manchester, it is not wholly within the parish of Ashton on Mersey, but extends into the parish of Bowden, and it has a post office under Manchester Acres, 1,61? Real property, £9,522 Pop, 1 47? Houses, 29? — The parish includes also the township of Sale Acres, 3,592 Real property, £28,806 Pop 4 307 Houses, 895 The living is a rectory in the diocese of Chester Value, £608 * Patron, the Rev C B Sowerby The vicarage of Sale is a separate benefice There are places of worship for Quakers, Wesleyans, and Primitive Methodists Charities, £7

ASHTON ON RIBBLE, a chapelry in Preston parish, Lancashire, on the river Ribble, adjacent to the Wyre and Preston railway, 2 miles W of Preston. It consists of the townships of Lea, Ashton, Ingol, and Cottam Post town, Preston Acres, 3,522, of which 175 are water Real property, £9,883 Pop, ?11 Houses, 176 The living is a p curacy in the diocese of Manchester Value, £106 * The church was built in 1836 There are a Roman Catholic chapel and a free school

ASHTON (STEEPLE), a village and a tything in Westbury district and a parish in Westbury and Melksham districts, Wilts. The village stands 2½ miles S of the Kennet and Avon canal and 3¼ E of the Great Western railway at Trowbridge It takes its distinctive name from a tall steeple which was destroyed by lightning in 1670 It formerly was a market town, and still has a fair on 19 Sept, and it is a seat of petty sessions, and has a post office under Trowbridge.—The tything comprises 2,808 acres. Real property, £5,846 Pop., 776 Houses, 177 —The parish includes also the tythings of Great Hinton, West Ashton, and Littleton, and the chapelry of Semington Acres, 6,789 Real property, £14,474 Pop, 1 767 Houses, 359 A considerable extent of the land was formerly common and recently enclosed. Rood Ashton House, the seat of the Long family, is about a mile SW of the village Very numerous fossils have been found and an ancient pavement, thought to have been Roman, but of different character from other Roman pavements, has been dug up The living is a vicarage united with the curacy of Semington, in the diocese of Salisbury Value, £852 Patron, the Master of Magdalene college, Cambridge The church is large and later English, with a four-spired tower, and was built, toward the end of the 15th century, chiefly by Robert Long, a clothier The vicarage of West Ashton is a separate charge

ASHTON TOWN See ASHTON UNDER LYNE

ASHTON UNDER HILL, a parish in the district of Evesham, and county of Gloucester, on the Ashchurch and Evesham railway with a r station, 5 miles SW of Evesham Post town, Beckford, under Tewkesbury Acres, 1,300 Real property, £2,475 Pop, 411 Houses 93 The living is a p curacy, annexed to the vicarage of Beckford, in the diocese of Gloucester and Bristol

ASHTON UNDER LYNE, a town, a parish, and a district, on the SE border of Lancashire The town stands on the river Tame at a convergence of canals and railways, 6¼ miles E by N of Manchester Its site is a rising ground, from ?0 to 40 feet high, on the N bank of the river, its environs are a low flat tract reclaimed from the condition of a marsh, overlying rich strata of coal and sandstone, and studded with factories, villages, and mining shafts, and many parts of both site and environs, previous to the introduction of the cotton trade in 176?, were bare, wet, and almost worthless. The Assheton family, now represented by the Earl of Stamford, were lords of the manor, shared their name with it, and maintained their power over it by means of dungeon and gallows and a commemoration of their rule is kept up, on Easter Monday, by what is called "riding the black lad" the parading of a figure in black armour through the streets The distinctive name "Under Lyne" probably refers to the vicinity of the remarkable line of hills called the "Back Bone of England."

The town comprises about 16 miles of street, is well supplied with water, and has undergone great and costly improvements Some of the oldest houses are at Boston and Charleston, which were built during the American war The old streets are narrow and dingy while the more modern ones are wide and regular, and contain many good houses The town hall was built in 1840, at a cost of more than £7,500, is in the Corinthian style, and contains police offices, rooms for petty sessions and county courts, and a public hall 83 feet by 40 St Michael's church is a spacious structure in later English built in the reign of Henry V, thoroughly restored in 1844, surmounted by a tower of more recent date, with a fine peal of bells, and contains tombs of the Asshetons. St Peter's church at the west end of the town, is a beautiful edifice, with pinnacled square tower and was built in 1821, at a cost of £12 689 Christ church, in Oldham road, is a cruciform building of 1847 One Independent chapel was built in 1804, at a cost of £3,200 another in 1852, at a cost of £5,500 One of two Wesleyan chapels was built in 1831 at a cost of £3,300 One of three New Connexion Methodist chapels was enlarged in 1833 Two Baptist chapels, a Primitive Methodist, an Independent Methodist a Swedenborgian, and two Roman Catholic are neat edifices The Jewish synagogue was built in 1825, at a cost of £9,500 but is now vacant The mechanics institute was built about 1840 at a cost of more than £4 000 A suite of school houses was built in 1863, at a cost of £3,500 There are six national schools, and three British The workhouse was built in 1850, at a cost of £12 000, the infirmary in 18?8 at a cost of £9,600

Ashton has upwards of 93 cotton factories, carries on the cotton trade in all its branches, does business in bleaching dyeing calico printing hat making and silk weaving, and derives importance from upwards of 70 factories and 80 coal pits throughout its neighbourhood Railway communication goes from it E, W, N and S to all principal towns and 3 canals lead respectively to Huddersfield and the German ocean to the Peak forest of Derbyshire, and to Manchester, Stockport and Oldham The town has a telegraph station, a head post office ‡ three banking offices and five chief inns and publishes two weekly newspapers Markets are held on Wednesday and Saturday and fairs on 23 March, 29 April 25 July 5 Aug 21 Nov and 3 Dec The privileges of a borough were enjoyed anciently, but went into disuse, and were lost The act of 1832 gave the right to send a member to parliament, and a charter of 1847 created a municipal governing body consisting of a mayor eight aldermen and twenty four councillors. The parliamentary borough is conterminate with the parochial division called Ashton Town Pop in 1811,

22,678, in 1861, 33,917 Houses, 6,460 The municipal borough includes also part of the parochial division called Audenshaw Pop in 1851 30 676 in 1861 34 886 Houses 6,647 Electors in 1868, 907 Direct taxes £14,798 Real property, £113,703 Police force, 21 Cost of police establishment, £1,126 Known depredators 70 Prisoners are committed to the county gaol at Lancaster or the house of correction at Salford

The parish consists of the four divisions of Ashton Town Audenshaw, Knott Lanes, and Hartshead, and includes the hamlets of Lees, Crossbank, Alt, Altedge, Althill, Taunton Knott Lanes, Wood Park, Hazlehurst, Heyrod, Smallshaw and Hartshead, the villages of Hooleyhill, Walkmill, Audenshaw Littlemoss, Woodhouses, North Street, Hurst, Hurstbrooks, Mossley, and Mossley Brow, and part of the town of Stalybridge Acres 9,300 Real property, £233,117 Pop in 1841, 46,304, in 1861, 66,801 Houses, 12,962 The Earl of Stamford has about 2,030 tenants within the manor and draws from it an income of upwards of £30,000 Ashton Hall a very ancient building long the residence of the Assheton family is occupied by his head steward The living is a rectory in the diocese of Manchester Value, £900 * Patron, the Earl of Stamford. St. Peter's is a separate p curacy Christ church a separate vicarage, each with an income of £300, the former in the patronage of the Rector, the latter in the patronage of alternately the Crown and the Bishop Audenshaw, Bardsley, Hurst, Leesfield, Lees, Mossley, Stalybridge Old and New, and Hurstbrook, also are separate charges

The district of Ashton under Lyne comprehends the sub district of Ashton Town, identical with the parochial division of Ashton Town, the sub district of Audenshaw, containing the parochial division of Audenshaw and the Manchester township of Droylsden, the sub district of Knott Lanes, identical with the parochial division of Knott Lanes, the sub district of Hartshead, identical with the parochial division of Hartshead, the sub district of Denton containing the Manchester townships of Denton and Haughton, the sub district of Dukinfield, containing the Stockport township of Dukinfield, electorally in Cheshire the sub district of Newton containing the Mottram townships of Newton and Godley, electorally in Cheshire, the sub district of Mottram, containing the townships of Mottram, Hattersley, Hollingworth, and Tintwistle, electorally in Cheshire, and the sub-district of Stayley containing the hamlet of Micklehurst, and the townships of Stayley and Matley, in Cheshire Acres 38,657 Poor rates in 1866, £30,767 Pop in 1841, 101,605, in 1861, 134,753 Houses, 26,500 Marriages in 1866, 1,320, births, 4,644,—of which 282 were illegitimate, deaths, 3,398,—of which 1,438 were at ages under 5 years, and 28 at ages above 85 Marriages in the ten years 1851-60 11,114, births 46,646 deaths 33,8?2 The places of worship in 1851 were 25 of the Church of England, with 20,844 sittings, 11 of Independents, with 5 197 s., 3 of Baptists with 1,830 s, 1 of Unitarians, with 710 s 2 of Moravians, with 846 s, 8 of Wesleyan Methodists, with 1,862 s, 13 of New Connexion Methodists, with 5 617 s 10 of Primitive Methodists, with 2,37? s 3 of the Wesleyan Association, with 433 s 1 of the New Church with 250 s, 5 of Brethren with 1 076 s, 2 of Latter Day Saints, with 170 s 2 of Roman Catholics, with 1 400 s and 3 undefined with 1 296 s The schools in 1851 were 38 public day schools, with 5,736 scholars, 108 private day schools with 5 2?3 s, 93 Sunday schools with 24,606 s, and 48 evening schools for adults, with 858 s

ASHTON UNDER LYNE CANALS two canals connecting Ashton under Lyne with the Huddersfield canal and Manchester, and sending off branches to Stockport and Oldham They were formed in 1793-1807 they are respectively 6¼ and 8 miles long, and the one has a fall of 162¼ feet, with 18 locks,—the other a fall of 83 feet with 8 locks

ASHTON UPON MERSEY See ASHTON ON MERSEY

ASHTON (WEST) a tything and a chapelry in Steeple Ashton parish Wilts. The tything lies near the Great Western railway, 2½ miles SE of Trowbridge Post-town Trowbridge Acres, 2,010 Pop, 314 Houses, 67 The chapelry is conterminate with the tything, and is a p curacy in the diocese of Salisbury Value, £200 * Patron, W Long, Esq, of Rood Ashton The church is a neat modern edifice, and has a stone pulpit and a good organ

ASHTON WITH STODDAY a township in Lancaster parish, Lancashire, on the Preston canal, between the Lancaster and Preston railway, and the estuary of the Lune, 3 miles S of Lancaster Acres, 1,439 Real property, £2 387 Pop, 134 Houses, 41 See ASHTON HALL.

ASHTON WOLD See ASHTON, Ufford, Northampton

ASHURST, a parish in Tunbridge district, Kent, on the verge of the county at the river Medway, 5 miles W of Tunbridge Wells r station Post town, Langton Green under Tunbridge Wells Acres, 891 Real property £1,956 Pop, 2?7 Houses 45 The property is divided among a few Ashurst Park the seat of G Field, Esq, is in the east The living is a rectory in the diocese of Canterbury Value, £207 * Patron, Countess Delawarr The church is tolerable

ASHURST, a parish in Steyning district, Sussex on the river Adur, 3½ miles N of Steyning, and 2 SSW of Partridge Green r station It has a post office under Hurstperpoint Acres, 2 355 Real property £2,701 Pop 274 Houses, 58 The property is subdivided The living is a rectory in the diocese of Chichester Value, £263 * Patron, Magdalene College, Oxford The church is small but good A fair is held on 16 Oct

ASHURST, a hamlet in East Grinstead parish Sussex

ASHURST BEACON, a sea mark on a hill, 4 miles WNW of Wigan, Lancashire. It guides the navigation up to Liverpool, and commands a magnificent view over the Irish sea with the Isle of Man, and from the mountains of the Lake district to the mountains of Wales

ASHWATER a village and a parish in Holsworthy district, Devon The village stands 7 miles SSE of Holsworthy, and 21 SSW of Bideford r station It has a post office under Launceston and fairs on the first Tuesday in May, and on the Monday after 1 Aug The parish includes also the hamlet of Quoditch Acres, 8,587 Real property, £3,887 Pop, 803 Houses, 161 The property is subdivided Good building stone is quarried The living is a rectory in the diocese of Exeter Value, £700 * Patron, W W Melhuish, Esq The church is an old structure, with lofty pinnacled tower, and contains several monuments and a very fine ancient font. There are two chapels of Bible Christians

ASH WEEK, a tything in Bishops-Lydeard parish, near Ash Priors, Somerset

ASHWELL, a village and a parish in Royston district Herts The village stands at the source of the river Rhee, an affluent of the Cam, 2 miles N of a station of its own name on the Hitchen and Cambridge railway and 4½ NNE of Baldock It is thought to have been of Roman origin, it bore anciently the name of Escewell, and it was a seat of the Saxon kings, a borough, and a market town It now consists of several scattered streets, and has a post office‡ under Baldock The parish comprises 3,852 acres. Real property, £7 ?09 Pop, 1 507 Houses 293 The manor was given, before the time of Edward the Confessor, to Westminster abbey, and passed at the dissolution, to the see of London The Roman road Icknield street passes ½ a mile S of the village, and the Roman camp of Arbury occurs there, covers an area of 12 acres and has yielded Roman coins, and other Roman relics. A small dell adjacent to the village leads up to a steep rocky bank, from the foot of which a number of springs gush out to form the river Rhee Building stone is quarried The living is a rectory in the diocese of Rochester Value £513 * Patron the Bishop of Rochester The church is ancient and good, consists of nave aisles and chancel, has a tower at the W end surmounted by a spire 175 feet high, and contains several old slabs formerly inlaid with brasses There are Independent, Baptist, Wesleyan, and Quaker chapels an endowed school with £17 a year, and other charities with £55 Cudworth was vicar till his death in 1688

ASHWELL, a parish in Oakham district, Rutland, on the Midland railway and an affluent of the river Wreak, near the Melton Mowbray canal, 3½ miles N of Oakham It has a station on the railway, and its post town is Oakham Acres, 1,799 Real property, £3,051 Pop, 206 Houses, 48 The manor was known, in the Saxon times, as Exwell, belonged to Earl Harold, and passed, in the time of Edward III, to the Touchets and afterwards to others The living is a rectory in the diocese of Peterborough Value, £401 * Patron, Viscount Downe The church is a handsome edifice, with a tower, and contains three interesting altar tombs

ASHWELL THORPE, a parish in Depwade district, Norfolk, on an affluent of the river Yare, 3 miles SE of Wymondham r station Post town, Wymondham Acres, 979 Real property, £2,191 Pop, 409 Houses, 88 The manor belonged anciently to the family of Thorpe, passed to that of Bourchier, and was held, in the time of Henry VII, by Sir John Bourchier, the translator of Froissart, and ancestor of the present Lord Berners The living is a rectory, united with the rectory of Wreningham, in the diocese of Norwich Value, £648 * Patron, Lord Berners The church contains some old monuments Charities, 1½ acre of fuel allotment

ASHWICK, a parish in Shepton Mallet district, Somerset, on the Fosse way, near Masbury camp, 3¾ miles NNE of Shepton Mallet r station. It includes part of the hamlet of Oakhill, which has a post office under Bath Acres, 1,525 Real property, £4,179 Pop, 778 Houses, 201 The property is divided among ten Ashwick Grove is the seat of the Stracheys Coal is worked The living is a vicarage in the diocese of Bath and Wells Value, £113 Patron, the Vicar of Kilmersdon The church is good, and there are three dissenting chapels, and charities £13

ASHWICKEN, or ASHWYKEN, a parish in Freebridge Lynn district, Norfolk, 1½ mile NW of East Winch r station, and 5½ E by S of Kings Lynn Post town, East Winch under Lynn Acres, 1,252 Real property, £1,143 Pop, 108 Houses, 23 The property is divided among a few The living is a rectory, united with the rectory of Leziate, in the diocese of Norwich Value £520 * Patron, the Rev J Freeman The church is very good

ASHWOOD, a hamlet in King's Swinford parish, Stafford, near the river Stour, 4½ miles NNW of Stourbridge Remains of a Roman camp, called Wolverhampton churchyard, are on an adjacent heath

ASHWORTH, a township chapelry in Middleton parish, Lancashire, on an affluent of the river Roch, 3 miles NE by E of Bury r station Post town, Rochdale Acres, 1,022 Real property, £2,143 Pop, 233 Houses, 45 The property is all held by one proprietor The living is a vicarage in the diocese of Manchester Value, £119 Patron, Lord Egerton The church is good

ASHWYKEN See ASHWICKEN

ASKE, a township in Easby parish, N R Yorkshire, 2½ miles N of Richmond Acres, 1,670 Real property, £1,537 Pop 140 Houses, 20 Aske Hall is the seat of the Earl of Zetland, belonged formerly to the Darcys, and commands a fine prospect up and down the Swale

ASKERN, a village, a township, and a chapelry in Campsall parish, W R Yorkshire The village stands on a rocky eminence, bordering on a plain, adjacent to the Lancashire and Yorkshire railway 6¼ miles N of Doncaster, and has a station on the railway, and a post office under Doncaster It was, not long ago, a paltry hamlet, but is now a pretty place, with hotels and lodging houses, much frequented by invalids and others, seeking benefit from medicinal waters and salubrious air A sulphureous spa is here, by the side of a small plain sheet of water, called Askern Pool, and possesses celebrity for the cure of rheumatism and scorbutic diseases The British prince Ambrosius is said to have defeated and killed the Saxon leader Hengist on the neighbouring plain —The township comprises 800 acres Pop, 379 Houses, 81 The chapelry is conterminate with the township, and is a vicarage in the diocese of York with income of £64,* in the patronage of the Archbishop There are a Wesleyan chapel, and a national school

ASKERSWELL, a parish in Bridport district, Dorset, on an affluent of the river Brid, 5 miles E of Bridport r station It has a post office under Bridport. Acres 1 161 Real property with Loders Up Loders, and Mattravers, £7,127 Pop, 223 Houses, 48 The surface is a pleasant valley surrounded by hills The living is a rectory in the diocese of Salisbury Value, £160 * Patron, Mrs H T Bower The church was built in 1858, but has a tower which belonged to a previous edifice Charities, £6

ASKERTON, a township in Lanercost parish, Cumberland, on an affluent of the river Irthing, 6 miles NNE of Brampton Real property, £3 911 Pop, 380 Houses, 68 Berethen Castle here was built by the Dacres, who derived their name from the exploits of one of their ancestors at the siege of Acre under Richard Cœur de Lion, and was, at one time, garrisoned for the Crown against the Scots

ASKETT a hamlet in Monks Risborough parish, Bucks, 1 mile NNE of Princes Risborough

ASKEW See AISKEW

ASKHAM a parish in East Retford district, Notts 3 miles WNW of Tuxford r station and 4½ SE of East Retford It includes the hamlet of Rockley, and its post town is Tuxford under Newark Acres, 1,302 Real property, £2,337 Pop, 287 Houses, 69 The living is a vicarage in the diocese of Lincoln Value, £243 Patrons, the Dean and Chapter of York Charities, £22

ASKHAM, a township and a parish in West Ward district, Westmoreland The township lies pleasantly on the Lowther river, opposite Lowther Castle, 2½ miles SW of Clifton r station, and 5 S of Penrith, and it has a post-office under Penrith Real property, £1,822 Pop, 323. Houses, 67 The parish includes also the township of Helton Acres, 4,327 Real property, £3,469 Pop, 503. Houses 105 Askham manor belongs to the Earl of Lonsdale and there is another manor Askham Hall, on Askham manor, is a gloomy edifice of 1574 with embattled roof Limestone is quarried The living is a vicarage in the diocese of Carlisle Value, £180 * Patron, the Earl of Lonsdale. The church is good, and there are charities £21

ASKHAM BRYAN, or EAST ASKHAM, a parish in the district and county of York, 2 miles NNW of Copmanthorpe r station, and 3½ SW of York Post town, York. Acres, 1,920 Real property, £4 124 Pop, 362 Houses, 68 The property is divided among a few The living is a vicarage in the diocese of York Value, £120 * Patron, W Morris, Esq The church is old but good A school has £10 from endowment and other charities £24

ASKHAM RICHARD, or WEST ASKHAM, a parish in the district and county of York, contiguous to Askham-Bryan 3 miles NW of Copmanthorpe r station and 4½ SW of York Post town York. Acres, 960 Real property, £1,649 Pop 235 Houses, 52 The property is divided among a few The living is a vicarage in the diocese of York Value, £200 Patron, John Wood, Esq The church is good, and there are charities £17

ASKRIGG, a small town a township, a chapelry, a sub district and a district, N R Yorkshire The town stands on the left side of the river Ure, 6 miles E of Hawes, and 10½ W of Leyburn r station, and has a post office under Bedale It is a very ancient place, and was once much more prosperous than now It resembles a mere village but has a weekly market on Thursday, and fairs on 11 May, the first Thursday of June, 11 July, and 28 Oct. A moorish, upland country lies around it, and embosoms some striking scenery, with the fine waterfalls of Millgill, Whitfieldgill, and Hardraw forces —The township includes also the hamlets of Newbigging, Nappa, and Wraxhall Acres, 4,741 Real property £4,357 Pop, 698 Houses, 157 The property is much subdivided. Lead ore occurs, and has been worked, but not very productively Roman remains exist at Newbigging, Nappa, and Woodhall.—The chapelry includes the township, but is more extensive The living is a p curacy in the diocese of Ripon. Value, £100 Patron, the Vicar of Aysgarth The church is an ancient and interesting edifice, in good condition There are Independent, Wesleyan, and Quaker chapels, an endowed school with £65 a year, and six alms houses for widows with £60 —The sub district comprises nine townships Acres 44 206 Pop, 3 207 Houses, 701 —The district is conterminate with Aysgarth parish, is not under the poor law amendment act, and is divided into the sub districts of Askrigg and Hawes,—the former containing the townships of Askrigg Aysgarth, Bainbridge, Carperby cum Thoresby, Burton cum Walden, Newbiggen, Thoralby, Bishopdale, and Thornton Rust,—the latter containing the townships of Hawes, High Abbotside, and Low Abbotside. Acres 77,308 Poor rates in 1866, £2,429 Pop in 1861, 5,649 Houses, 1,227 Marriages in 1866, 35, births 171, —of which 9 were illegitimate, deaths, 120,—of which 45 were at ages under 5 years and 14 at ages above 85 Marriages in the ten years 1851–60, 426, births, 1,879, deaths, 1,123 The places of worship in 1851 were 6 of the Church of England, with 2,474 sittings, 9 of Independents, with 460 s, 1 of Baptists, with 7 attendants, 2 of Quakers with 450 sittings 8 of Wesleyan Methodists, with 1,375 s, 3 of Primitive Methodists, with 372 s, and 4 undefined with 380 s The schools were 9 public day schools, with 438 scholars 19 private day schools, with 272 s, and 20 Sunday schools, with 932 s The workhouse is in Bainbridge township

ASKWITH, a township in Weston parish, W R Yorkshire, near the river Wharfe, 3 miles NW of Otley It includes the hamlets of Upper and Lower Snowden Acres, 3,180 Real property, £3,329 Pop, 338 Houses, 76

ASLACKBY, a parish and a sub district in the district of Bourn Lincoln The parish lies 2 miles S of Folkingham, and 7 N by W of Bourn r station, includes the hamlets of Graby and Millthorpe, and has a fen allotment Post town, Folkingham Acres, 3 934 Real property, £5,944 Pop, 534 Houses, 100 A commandery of the Knights Templars was founded here, in the time of Richard I, by John le Mareschal, belonged afterwards to the Knights Hospitallers, and passed at the dissolution, to Edward, Lord Clinton A farm house, called the Temple, now stands on the site of its church, and includes remains of a square embattled tower A castle also was founded here before 1082, and can still be traced in fosse and mounds The living is a vicarage in the diocese of Lincoln Value, £453 * Patron, R F Barstow, Esq The church is a handsome edifice, with an embattled tower —The sub district comprises ten parishes. Acres, 23,635 Pop, 4,730 Houses, 982

ASLACOE (East and West), two wapentakes in the parts of Lindsey Lincoln They lie toward the NW of the county, include Blyborough parish and twenty other parishes, and are traversed by Ermine street. Acres, 23,011 and 21,104 Pop 5 925 Houses, 1,211

ASLACTON, a parish in Depwade district, Norfolk, on an affluent of the river Yare, 1½ mile W of Forncett r station, and 6 ENE of New Buckenham Post town, Forncett under Long Stratton Acres 1,194 Real property, £2,300 Pop 356 Houses, 76 The property is much subdivided The manor belonged to the Le Neves, and was the native place of Sir William le Neve, the herald and antiquary in the time of Charles I The living is a p curacy in the diocese of Norwich Value, £59 Patron, the Rev F G Curtler The church is good and there are a Wesleyan chapel and 18 acres of fuel allotment

ASLACTON, or ASLOCKTON a township in Whatton, Notts on the river Smite adjacent to the Nottingham and Grantham railway 3½ miles E of Bingham It has a station on the railway, and its post town is Whatton under Nottingham Real property £2 103 Pop 410 Houses, 96 Chief residences are Aslacton Abbey and Aslacton House A chapel here was a peculiar of the collegiate church of Southwell, but is now a ruin Archbishop Cranmer was a native

I

ASPALL, a parish in Hartismere district, Suffolk, 1½ mile NNW of Debenham, and 11 miles NE of Needham r station Post town, Debenham under Stonham Acres, 834 Real property, £1,397 Pop, 156 Houses 27 The property is divided among a few The living is a vicarage in the diocese of Norwich Value, £140 Patron, Mrs. Chevallier The church is good

ASPALL STONEHAM See STONEHAM ASPALL.

ASPARAGUS ISLAND See KINANCE COVE

ASPATRIA, a small town and a township in the district of Wigton, and a parish in the districts of Wigton and Cockermouth, Cumberland The town stands on the right side of the river Ellen, adjacent to the Carlisle and Maryport railway, 7¾ miles NE of Maryport It has a station on the railway, a post-office‡ under Carlisle, and a weekly market on Thursday, and is a polling place Its site is the side of a hill and its appearance that of a long straggling village. Its name is a corruption of Aspatrick or Cospatrick, and was derived from one of the Cospatricks, Earls of Dunbar —The township bears the name of Aspatria and Brayton Acres, 4,611 Real property, £13,551 —of which £7 598 are in mines Pop, 1 210 Houses, 254 The parish includes also the townships of Hayton and Mealo, and Oughterside and Allerby Acres, 9,048, of which 438 are water Real property, £25,368 —of which £12,570 are in mines Pop, 2 305 Houses, 475 The property is much subdivided The surface is hilly Coal and red sandstone are worked A human skeleton, 7 feet long, supposed to have been that of some great chief, buried about the 2d century, together with a broad sword 5 feet long, and some fine ornaments of a warrior, was found, in 1790, beneath a barrow on Beacon hill, an eminence about 200 yards N of the town The living is a vicarage in the diocese of Carlisle Value, £240 * Patron, the Bishop of Carlisle The church was rebuilt in 1848. Hayton was made a separate charge in 1867, and is a rectory There are an Independent chapel, and charities £10

ASPEDEN, a parish in Royston district Herts on the river Rib, 8 miles SE of Baldock r station It includes part of the post town of Buntingford Acres, 1,351 Real property, £3,539 Pop, 577 Houses 114 The property is divided among a few The manor belonged to the Cliffords the Freemans, and the Jocelyns, and passed to Earl Hardwicke and the Polderos Aspeden Hall and its park are a prominent feature The living is a rectory in the diocese of Rochester Value, £357 * Patron, the Countess of Mexborough The church contains a curious monument to Sir Robert Clifford, master of the ordnance to Henry VIII, and other tombs and brasses, and is in good condition An endowed school has £17 a year, and other charities £37

ASPERTON See ASHBURTON

ASPLEY, a township in Eccleshall parish Stafford near the Northwestern railway, 3½ miles NNW of Eccleshall Acres 540 Pop 30 Houses 3

ASPLEY GUISE, a parish in Woburn district Beds, 1½ mile WNW of Ridgemount r station and 2 N of Woburn It has a post office under Woburn, and formerly had a market Acres, 1,930 Real property, £4,815 Pop, 1 437 Houses, 324 The property is subdivided The manor belonged anciently to the Guises Aspley House and Aspley Guise House are chief residences Aspley Heath and Aspley Wood give fine views. Fuller's earth occurs The living is a rectory in the diocese of Ely Value, £325 * Patron the Duke of Bedford The church is elegant and a new church and three dissenting chapels are at Woburn Sands

ASPS, a village in Bishops Tachbrook parish, Warwickshire, 1½ mile SE of Warwick Pop, 32

ASPULL a township and a sub district in Wigan district Lancashire The township is in Wigan parish, 3 miles NE of Wigan, and has a post office, of the name of Aspull-Moor under Wigan Acres 1,879 Real property, £27,151 of which £19,863 are in mines Pop 4,290 Houses, 753 The inhabitants are employed chiefly in collieries and cotton mills There are a school church, Independent Wesleyan, and Roman Catholic

K

chapels and four public schools —The sub district comprises three townships Pop, 8,372 Houses, 1,534

ASSANDUNE See ASHDON and ASHINGDON

ASSELBY a township in Howden parish, E. R. Yorkshire, near the Hull railway and the river Ouse, 2 miles W of Howden Acres, 1,117 Real property, £2,331 Pop 276 Houses, 58.

ASSENDON, a liberty in Pirton parish, Oxford, 4 miles NW of Henley-on-Thames It has a post office under Henley A land spring here breaks out after a run of wet weather, and is so copious as to inundate neighbouring low tracts

ASSERBY See BILSBY

ASSINGTON, a parish in Sudbury district, Suffolk, on an affluent of the river Stour, 3½ miles NE of Bures r station, and 5 SE of Sudbury It has a post office under Sudbury Acres, 2,986. Real property, £5,020 Pop, 747 Houses, 162 The manor belonged formerly to the Corbets and belongs now to J Gurdon, Esq, whose seat is Assington Hall The living is a vicarage in the diocese of Ely Value, £390 * Patron, J Gurdon, Esq The church was recently restored at a cost of £3,000 There are a national school, and charities £7

ASTBURY, a village and a parish in Congleton district Cheshire The village stands on an affluent of the river Dane, adjacent to the North Staffordshire railway, near the Macclesfield canal, 1¼ mile SW of Congleton, and has a post-office under Congleton, and fairs on 30 April and 30 Oct The parish includes the townships of Davenport, Somerford Booths, Hulme Walfield, Radnor, Buglawton, Congleton, Newbold Astbury, Moreton-cum Alcumlow, Smallwood, and Odd Rode Acres, 19,602 Real property, £66,903. Pop. in 1841, 14,619, in 1861, 19,351 Houses, 4,009 There are six chief proprietors Coal, limestone, and building stone are worked Very many of the inhabitants are employed in silk factories, and some in cotton mills The living is a rectory, united with the curacy of Hulme Walfield in the diocese of Chester Value £2,040 * Patron, Lord Crewe The church is early English, with a good spire, and contains chancel stalls, a rood loft, some fine screen work, stained windows, and carved oaken ceilings Two very ancient monuments, with insignia of knighthood, are in the churchyard. The chapelries of Buglawton, Congleton, Congleton St James', Congleton St. Stephen's, Eaton, Mossley, Odd Rode, and Smallwood, and the donative of Somerford, are separate charges Charities, exclusive of Congleton, £63 See CONGLETON

ASTERBY, a parish in Horncastle district, Lincoln, on the Wolds near the river Bain, 6 miles N by E of Horncastle r station Post town, Scamblesby under Horncastle Acres, 620 Real property, £1,838 Pop, 304 Houses, 68 The property is not much divided Asterby Hall is the seat of T Southwell, Esq The living is a rectory in the diocese of Lincoln Value, £210 * Patron, W H Trafford, Esq The church is ancient There are a Baptist chapel, and charities £13

ASTERLEY, a township in Pontesbury parish, Salop, near the river Rhea, 9 miles SW of Shrewsbury Pop, 305

ASTERLEY FARM AND HOUSE, an extra parochial tract in Woodstock district, Oxford, contiguous to Kiddington parish, 4½ miles NW of Woodstock It was anciently a parish, and had a church at Chapelbroke, but was annexed to Kiddington in 1466.

ASTERTON, a township in Norbury parish, Salop, on Long Mynd hills, 4½ miles SW of Church Stretton Pop 164

ASTHALL a village and a parish in Witney district, Oxford The village stands on the Windrush river, and on Akeman street at the SW end of Wychwood forest, 2¾ miles ESE of Burford, and 5 S of Ascott r station It was known to the Saxons as Esthale and belonged to Roger d'Ivri The parish includes also the hamlet of Asthall Leigh Post town, Burford under Faringdon Acres, 1,180 Real property, £2 350 Pop, 424 Houses, 89 The manor belonged to the Lumleys the Joanses and the Fettiplaces and the manor house is now a farm house. A large barrow believed to be the sepulchre of some person of note, is on Akeman street The living is a vicarage in the diocese of Oxford Value, £100 Patron, Eton College The church is ancient, and a new one, at Asthall Leigh, was recently built There are two small free schools, and charities £25

ASTHORPE, a hamlet in Willoughby parish, Lincoln, 4½ miles SSE of Alford

ASTHORPE, Herts See MARSTON (LONG)

ASTLEY, a chapelry in the parish of St Mary Shrewsbury, Salop, 2¾ miles ENE of Hadnall r station, and 6½ miles NE of Shrewsbury Post town, Shawbury under Shrewsbury Acres, 1,168 Rated property, £1,670 Pop, 209 Houses, 54 The property is divided among a few The living is a vicarage in the diocese of Lichfield Value, £56 Patrons, Trustees The church is good

ASTLEY, a parish in Nuneaton district, Warwick, on the Sow brook, 3½ miles W by S of Chilvers Coton r station, and 4½ SW by W of Nuneaton It contains a place called Soley End, and has a post office under Nuneaton Acres, 2,350 Real property, £3,820 Pop, 332 Houses, 70 The manor belonged to the family of Astley, one of whom fell on the field of Evesham fighting against Henry III, two taken prisoners on the field of Bannockburn, and one distinguished highly for military services in the time of Henry VIII, it passed by marriage to the Greys of Ruthin, of whom were the Duke of Suffolk and his daughter, Lady Jane Grey, who suffered on the block for their claim to the crown, and it now belongs to C N Newdegate, Esq, of the neighbouring grand seat of Arbury Hall. Astley Castle, the ancient residence of the Greys, rebuilt in the time of Queen Mary, was allowed to fall into neglect, and used as a farm house, but is now a renovated and elegant residence, and contains some old armour, and a portrait of the last Duke of Suffolk. The old parts of it are picturesquely clothed with ivy, and a moat around it has remains of massive masonry along the inner edge, and is overshadowed with fine trees The living is a vicarage in the diocese of Worcester Value £60 Patron, C N Newdegate, Esq The church is part of an edifice built, in the time of Edward III by Sir Thomas de Astley for a dean, two canons, or prebendaries, and three vicars, and adorned with a tall spire, which served as a landmark in the broad surrounding woodlands, and was popularly called "the Lanthorn of Arden," but even what remains of the structure has been much injured by neglect and maltreatment There is a free school

ASTLEY a parish in Martley district, Worcester, on the river Severn, 3 miles SW by S of Stourport r station Post town Stourport Acres, 2,998 Real property, £6,862 Pop., 864 Houses, 198 A Benedictine priory, subordinate to the abbey of St Taurinus in France, was founded here, in the time of William the Conqueror, by Ralph de Todeni, suffered frequent seizure by the Crown during the wars with France, passed, in the time of Richard II, to John Beauchamp, and in that of Edward IV to the college of Westbury, and was given by Henry VII to Sir Ralph Sadleir, the compiler of the state papers. A hermitage was cut out of the solid rock at Astley Cliff, near Redstone ferry, was a place of great resort for devotees in the Roman times, and is now an alehouse. The living is a rectory in the diocese of Worcester Value, £620 * Patrons, the Trustees of the Rev D J J Cookes The church stands on an eminence, is Norman, and has a font and some monuments. An endowed school has £20 and other charities £6

ASTLEY, a hamlet in the parishes of Swillington and Kippax, W R Yorkshire, 6½ miles SE of Leeds

ASTLEY or EAST LEIGH, a township chapelry in Leigh parish, Lancashire, near the Bridgewater canal and the Manchester and Liverpool railway 5½ miles W of Manchester It has a station on the railway, and a post office under Manchester Acres, 2 625 Real property, £11 967,—of which £5,000 are in mines Pop 2,109 Houses 437 There are collieries and a large cotton mill The living is a vicarage in the diocese of Manchester Value £250 * Patron, the Vicar of Leigh The church is modern, and has been thrice enlarged

There are a Wesleyan chapel a free grammar school, a national school and some small charities.

ASTLEY-ABBOTS, a parish in Bridgnorth district Salop on the river Severn, and on the Severn Valley railway, 1½ mile S of Linley r station, and 2½ N of Bridgnorth. Post town, Bridgnorth Acres, 3,228 Real property, £4,716 Pop, 608 Houses, 137 The property is divided among a few Astley-Abbots House is the seat of T Whitmore, Esq The living is a rectory in the diocese of Hereford. Value, not reported Patron, W A Warwick, Esq The church is Saxon, in tolerable condition, and has some ancient monuments Charities £11

ASTLEY BRIDGE, a village and a chapelry in Bolton le Moors parish Lancashire The village is partly in the township of Sharples, stands near the Bolton and Blackburn railway, 3 miles N of Bolton, and has a post office† under Bolton The chapelry was constituted in 1844 Rated property, £9,729 Pop, 3,210 Houses, 670 The property is subdivided The living is a vicarage in the diocese of Manchester Value, £150 Patrons, the Crown and the Bishop alternately The church was built in 1848 There are Baptist and Wesleyan chapels, and national and British schools.

ASTON, a township in Hope parish, Derby, 2 miles ENE of Castleton Acres, 714 Pop., 103

ASTON, a township in Aston upon Trent parish Derbyshire, on the Grand Trunk canal and the river Trent, 6 miles SE by S of Derby The right of a market and fair was obtained in 1256, but has long been in disuse Some of the inhabitants are employed in potteries The place is a meet for the Donnington hounds

ASTON, a township in Hawarden parish, Flint, adjacent to Queen's Ferry r station, near the river Dee, 1½ mile N by W of Hawarden Acres, 613 Real property, £3,918,—of which £2,600 are in railways Pop, 333 Houses, 64 Most of the inhabitants are employed in an extensive iron foundry The manor, with an ancient castle, was held by the Whitleys from the time of Edward III, and now belongs to the Dundas family, whose seat is Aston Hall

ASTON, a parish in the district and county of Hertford, on the river Beane, 3 miles SE of Stevenage, and 4 SE by S of Stevenage r station Post town, Stevenage Acres, 2,052 Real property, £3,697 Pop, 639 Houses, 122 The manor belonged to the Saxon kings, was given, by the queen of Henry I, to Reading abbey, and passed, at the dissolution, to the Botelers of Walton. The manor house, at Aston Place, is a building of older date than the time of Henry VIII Six large barrows, supposed to be Danish, occur contiguous to the public road. The living is a rectory in the diocese of Rochester Value, £380 * Patron, the Rev G A. Oddie

ASTON, a township in Lydham parish, Montgomery, 7 miles W by S of Church Stretton Acres, 1,125 Pop, 62 Houses, 10

ASTON, a township in Wem parish, Salop, on the river Roden, 1 mile E of Wem Pop, 212

ASTON a township in Mucklestone parish Stafford, 3 miles W of Whitmore r station, and 6½ NE of Market Drayton Acres 910 Pop, 237 Houses, 47

ASTON, a hamlet in Avening parish, Gloucester, 2 miles 1 SE of Minchinhampton

ASTON, a township in Kingsland parish, Hereford, on the river Lug 3½ miles W NW of Leominster Pop 109

ASTON, a township in Claverley parish, Salop, 6½ miles E of Bridgnorth Pop 126

ASTON, a township in Hopesay parish, Salop, on the river Clun, 6½ miles SE of Bishop's Castle Pop, 202 It has a head post office‡ of the name of Aston on Clun

ASTON, a township in Munslow parish Salop near the river Corve, under Wenlock Edge, 7½ miles N of Ludlow Pop, 16?

ASTON a chapelry in Oswestry parish, Salop on the Llanymynech canal and the Shrewsbury and Oswestry railway 3½ miles SE of Oswestry Post town, Oswestry The living is a p curacy in the diocese of St Asaph Value not reported Patron Mrs Lloyd of Aston Hall

ASTON, a township in Wellington parish, Salop, near Watling street, under the Wrekin, 2 miles SW of Wellington Pop, 84

ASTON, a chapelry in Stone parish, Stafford, on the river Trent, the Grand Trunk canal, and the North western railway, 2 miles SE of Stone It includes the hamlet of Little Aston, and has a post office under Stafford. Real property, with Burston, Stoke, and Little Aston, £6,183 Pop., 625 Houses, 149 The manor belonged anciently to the Astons, and passed to the Heveninghams and the Simeons. The living is a p curacy, united with the curacy of Burston in the diocese of Lichfield Value, £105 Patron, the Hon E S Jervis. The church is a neat edifice in the English style, with a tower There is a Roman Catholic church.

ASTON, a hamlet in Ivinghoe parish, Bucks, 1 mile NE by N of Ivinghoe Acres, 1 180 Real property, £1,607 Pop., 446 There is a Wesleyan chapel

ASTON, a parish and a district in Warwick The parish partly lies within Birmingham on the E, partly spreads adjacent It is traversed by Icknield street, the river Tame, the Fazeley canal and the Northwestern, the Tamworth, the Oxford, and the Bristol railways. It contains the sub post offices of Aston street, Ashted row, Aston Park, and Deritend each about 1½ mile distant from Birmingham head office It comprises the hamlets of Deritend, Bordesley, and Duddeston cum Nechells, the manor of Aston, and the hamlets of Witton Erdington, Little Bromwich, Saltley and Washwood Castle Bromwich, and Water Orton. The hamlets of Deritend and Bordesley form one of the borough wards of Birmingham, the hamlet of Duddeston cum Nechells forms another ward, and the manor and the other hamlets are suburban or rural Acres within the borough, 2,026, without the borough 11,251 Real property of Aston manor, £53,188, of the suburban or rural hamlets, £43,452, of the entire parish, £271,514 Pop in 1831, 19,189, in 1841, 45,718, in 1861, 94,995 Houses, 19,256 The manor belonged to the Saxon Earls of Mercia, was given, at the Conquest, to William Fitz Ansculf, and passed to the Pagenels, the Erdingtons, and the Holts The manor house, Aston Hall, stands on a rising ground, at the end of a fine avenue, in the north eastern outskirts of the town, is a noble edifice in the Tudor style built in the time of James I by Sir Thomas Holt, gave entertainment to Charles I prior to the battle of Edge Hill and suffered a cannonade afterwards from the parliamentarian forces, and was for some years, the residence of the late James Watt son of the famous engineer Most of a beautiful park which surrounded it has been aligned for streets and let on building leases, and a tract of about 43 acres immediately around the hall was sold, in 1857, to a public company, for £35,000, with the view of being made free to the inhabitants of Birmingham The hall itself was included in the sale, and designed to be used for a permanent exhibition of manufactures and works of art, and was inaugurated, in 1858, by Queen Victoria The parish church stands 300 yards E of the hall, is an interesting edifice in varieties of English from Edward II to Henry VII with fine tower and spire, suffered great change and mutilation in 1790, and contains four altar tombs, some fine antique stone seats a carved church yard cross of early English date, and beautiful windows of stained glass The living is a vicarage in the diocese of Worcester Value £1,600 * Patron, Trustees The chapelries of Ward end, Ashted, Castle Bromwich, Bordesley, (two are here,) Aston Brook Deritend, Erdington, Duddeston, Nechells, Lozells Saltley, Water Orton St Lawrence, and Sparkbrook are separate charges There are chapels for Independents Baptists, Wesleyans and others public schools an alms house with £— a year and other charities £33.

The district of Aston comprehends the sub district of Deritend, containing the hamlets of Deritend and Bordesley, the sub district of Duddeston, conterminate with the hamlet of Duddeston cum Nechells, the sub district of Erdington, containing the other parts of Aston parish, and the sub district of Sutton Coldfield containing the parishes of Sutton Coldfield, Curdworth, and Wishaw

Poor rates in 1866, £9,823 Pop in 1841, 50,977, in 1861, 100,522. Houses, 20,415 Marriages in 1866, 951, births, 5,224, —of which 183 were illegitimate, deaths, 2,493—of which 1,326 were at ages under 5 years, and 32 at ages above 85 Marriages in the ten years 1851-60, 7,635, births, 32,988, deaths 17,585 The places of worship in 1851 were 17 of the Church of England, with 11 520 sittings, 7 of Independents, with 1,765 s, 3 of Baptists, with 1,817 s, 11 of Wesleyan Methodists, with 2,901 s, 1 of Primitive Methodists, with 90 s, 1 of Wesleyan Reformers, with 150 s, 1 of the Catholic and Apostolic church, with 300 s, 5 of Roman Catholics, with 1,070 s, and 1 undefined, sittings not reported The schools were 28 public day schools, with 3,300 scholars, 118 private day schools, with 2,553 s, 31 Sunday schools, with 5,483 s., and 1 evening school for adults, with 25 s The workhouse is in Erdington

ASTON, Oxford See COATE and ASTON

ASTON, Yorkshire. See ASTON-WITH AUGHTON

ASTON, N Cheshire See ASTON BY SUTTON

ASTON, S Cheshire. See ASTON JUXTA MONDRUM

ASTON, or PIPE ASTON, a parish in the district of Ludlow and county of Hereford, near the river Teme, 3½ miles WSW of Woofferton r station, and 4 SW of Ludlow Post town, Ludlow Acres, 920 Real property, with Burrington and Downton, £3,750 Pop., 31 Houses, 9 The living is a rectory in the diocese of Hereford. Value, £84 Patron, A R B Knight Esq

ASTON-ABBOTS, a parish in Aylesbury district, Bucks, among the Chiltern hills, 5 miles E of the Buckinghamshire railway, and 5 NNE of Aylesbury r station. Post town, Wingrave under Aylesbury Acres, 2 180 Real property, £4,342 Pop., 311 Houses, 69 The property is divided among a few The parish is a meet of the Rothschild hounds. The living is a vicarage in the diocese of Oxford. Value, £143 * Patron, Lord Overstone The church is good, and there are two dissenting chapels and a national school

ASTON AIR. See ASTON EYRE

ASTON BAMPTON See BAMPTON, Oxford

ASTON-BLANK, or ASHTON BLANK, a parish in Northleach district, Gloucester, under the Cotswolds, near the Fosse way and the Windrush river, 4 miles NNE of Northleach, and 8 SW by W of Addlestrop r station It has a post office under Cheltenham Acres, 2 200 Real property, £2,381 Pop 325 Houses, 68. The property is not much divided The living is a vicarage in the diocese of Gloucester and Bristol Value, £186 * Patron, the Lord Chancellor The church is good, and there are charities £39

ASTON BOTTERELL, a parish in Cleobury Mortimer district, Salop, under the Clee hills, 6½ miles NNW of Cleobury Mortimer, and 9¼ NE of Ludlow r station It contains the hamlet of Bold, and its post town is Burwarton, under Bridgnorth Acres, 2,238 Real property, £3,978 Pop, 171 Houses, 35 The manor belonged anciently to the Bottercells The living is a rectory in the diocese of Hereford. Value £367 * Patron, the Duke of Cleveland The church is good

ASTON BROOK, a new chapelry in Aston parish, suburban to Birmingham. Pop, 6,360 The church was built in 1864 and is in mixed Gothic, French and English

ASTON BY BUDWORTH, a township in Great Budworth parish, Cheshire, 3½ miles N of Northwich Acres, 2,859 Real property, £4,958 Pop, 459 Houses 77

ASTON BY-SUTTON, or ASTON SUTTON, a township chapelry in Runcorn parish, Cheshire, on the Northwestern railway and the Weaver river, near Preston Brook r station, and 3 miles E by N of Frodsham. It includes a place called Middleton Grange sometimes deemed extra parochial, and its post town is Preston Brook. Acres, 1,012 Real property, £3,021 Pop, 207 Houses, 38 Aston Hall here is the seat of Sir Arthur Aston, Bart. The living is a vicarage in the diocese of Chester Value, £88 Patron Sir A Aston, Bart. The original church was at Middleton, and the present one contains an old lectern

ASTON CANTLOW, or ASTON CANTELUPE, a parish in Alcester district, Warwick, on the river Alne near the Birmingham and Stratford canal, 2½ miles W by S of Bearley r station, and 5½ NW of Stratford on Avon It includes the divisions of Newnham, Shelfield, Little Alne, and Pathlow, and part of the hamlet of Wilncott, and its post town is Henley in Arden, under Birmingham Acres, 4,300 Real property, £7,611,—of which £1,563 are in quarries. Pop., 1,055 Houses, 230 The manor belonged anciently to the Cantelupes. The right to a market was obtained by one of the Cantelupes in the time of Henry III, but has gone into disuse The living is a vicarage, united with the p. curacy of Wilmcote, in the diocese of Worcester Value, £93 * Patron, the Rev E B K. Fortescue The church has an embattled tower

ASTON-CHETWYND See CHETWYND ASTON

ASTON CHURCH See CHURCH ASTON

ASTON CLINTON, a township, a parish, and a sub district in the district of Aylesbury, Bucks The township lies near Icknield street and the Wendover and Aylesbury canals, 3½ miles ESE of Aylesbury r station It has a post office under Tring, and is a meet of the Rothschild hounds Acres, 2,670 Real property, £4,532 Pop, 1,108 Houses, 232.—The parish includes also the hamlet of St Leonard Acres, 3,640 Real property, £5,509 Pop., 1,297 Houses, 267 The property is divided among a few Aston Clinton House was the seat of Viscount Lake, who died in 1808 The living is a rectory in the diocese of Oxford. Value, £506 * Patron, Jesus College, Oxford. The church is good, and there are a Baptist chapel, and charities £192 The p. curacy of St Leonard is a separate charge.—The sub district comprises ten parishes. Acres, 17,752 Pop, 5,246 Houses, 1,073.

ASTON (COAL or COLD) See COAL ASTON

ASTON-CROSS See ASTON ON CARRON

ASTON (EAST and WEST), two tythings in the parish of Longparish, Hants, on the river Anton, 3 miles SW of Whitchurch

ASTON EPISCOPI See WHITE LADY ASTON

ASTON EYRE, a township in Morvill parish, Salop, 4 miles W by N of Bridgnorth, Acres, 1,330 Pop, 85 Houses, 12 It forms a curacy annexed to the vicarage of Morvill

ASTON FLAMVILLE, a township and a parish in Hinckley district, Leicester The township lies near the river Soar, the Fosse way, and Watling street, 3½ miles ESE of Hinckley r station and 9 NW of Lutterworth Real property, £1,870 Pop, 81 Houses, 15 The parish includes also the chapelry of Burbage and the hamlet of Sketchley Post town, Hinckley Acres, 4,670 Real property, £9,601 Pop., 1,946 Houses, 431 The living is a rectory, united with the curacy of Burbage, in the diocese of Peterborough Value, £878 * Patron, Countess Cowper The church is ancient, and was partly restored in 1855 Charities, £22

ASTON GRANGE, a township in Runcorn parish, Cheshire, near the Northwestern railway and the river Weaver, 3 miles E of Frodsham Acres, 437 Real property, £837 Pop, 42 Houses 6

ASTON HALL See ASTON, Flint, and ASTON, Warwick

ASTON INGHAM, a parish in the district of Newent and county of Hereford, on the verge of the county, 2½ miles N by E of Mitcheldean Road r station, and 5¾ E of Ross Post town, Linton under Ross Acres, 2,378 Real property, £3,698 Pop, 568 Houses 123 The living is a rectory in the diocese of Hereford Value, £350 * Patron, the Rev H. T Whatley The church is old Charities £10

ASTON IVINGHOE See ASTON, Bucks.

ASTON-JUXTA MONDRUM, a township in Acton parish, Cheshire, near the Chester and Crewe railway, 4 miles N of Nantwich. It has a post office of the name of Aston under Nantwich Acres, 1,255 Real property, £1,797 Pop, 146 Houses, 29

ASTON LE WALLS, a parish in the district of Banbury and county of Northampton, on the verge of the county, on the Roman road to Dorchester, near the Ox ford canal 4½ miles NE of Cropredy r station, and 8 NNE of Banbury It includes the hamlet of Appletree, and its post town is Chipping Warden under Banbury Acres, 1,270 Real property, £3,436 Pop, 221 Houses, 42. The property is divided among a few The living is a rectory in the diocese of Peterborough Value, £535 * Patron, St John s College, Oxford. The church is of the 13th century The Roman Catholics have a chapel and a school.

ASTON (LITTLE), a hamlet in Shenstone parish, Stafford, 5½ miles ENE of Walsall Pop, 115 Also a hamlet in Aston chapelry, Stone parish, Stafford

ASTON MAGNA, a chapelry in Blockley parish, Worcester, near the Fosse way, adjacent to the West Midland railway, near Blockley station, 3 miles NW by N of Moreton in the Marsh Post town, Blockley under Moreton in the Marsh Real property, £1,851 Pop, about 300 The property is not much divided. The living is a vicarage in the diocese of Worcester Value, £246 * Patron, Lord Redesdale. The church is very good

ASTON (MIDDLE), a township in Steeple Aston parish, Oxford, near the Cherwell river and the Oxford canal, 1¾ mile N by W of Heyford r station, and 3 miles S of Deddington Real property, £1,368 Pop, 86 Houses, 21

ASTON MOLLINS, a hamlet in Dinton parish, Bucks, 3½ miles SW of Aylesbury

ASTON (NORTH), a parish in Woodstock district, Oxford, on the river Cherwell, adjacent to the Oxford canal, 1 mile W of Somerton r station, and 2 SSE of Deddington Post town, Deddington under Oxford Acres, 1,272 Real property, £3,129 Pop, 296 Houses, 68 Aston Park is a chief residence The parish is a resort of sportsmen The living is a vicarage in the diocese of Oxford. Value £199 Patron, J Wills, Esq The church was rebuilt in 1865

ASTON ON CARRON, or ASTON CROSS, a tything in Ashchurch parish, Gloucester, near the Birmingham and Gloucester railway, 3 miles ENE of Tewkesbury. It has a post office, of the name of Aston Cross, under Tewkesbury Real property, £1,414 Pop, 298

ASTON ON-CLUN See ASTON, Hopesay, Salop

ASTON ON TRENT See ASTON UPON TRENT

ASTON PARK See ASTON, Warwick, and ASTON (NORTH)

ASTON PIGOTT, a township in Worthin parish, Salop, near the river Rhea, 2 miles NE of Worthin. Pop., 78

ASTON ROGERS, a township in Worthin parish, Salop, near the river Rhea, ½ a mile NE of Aston Pigott. Pop, 174

ASTON ROWANT, a parish in Thame district, Oxford, under the Chiltern hills, near Icknield street, 3½ miles SE of Tetsworth and 4 miles SSE of Thame r station It includes the liberties of Chalford and Kingston Blount,—the latter containing the hamlet of Kingston Stirt, and its post town is Tetsworth Acres 2,980 Real property, £4,357 Pop 884 Houses, 182 Aston House is the seat of Thomas Taylor, Esq Marcasite or crow iron occurs in the hills Roman remains have been found in Kingston field, a short distance from Icknield street The living is a vicarage in the diocese of Oxford Value, £190 * Patron, the Bishop of Oxford. The church is early English, was repaired in 1850, and contains an elegant ancient font There are an Independent chapel, an endowed school with £41 a year, and charities £80

ASTON ST LEONARD See LEONARD (ST), Bucks.

ASTON SANDFORD, a parish in Aylesbury district, Bucks, on a branch of the river Thame, 6 miles SW of Aylesbury r station Post town Dinton under Aylesbury Acres, 669 Real property £385 Pop, 59 Houses 14 The property is not much divided The living is a rectory in the diocese of Oxford Value, £135 * Patrons Trustees The church is later English and small, with a gable roofed porch Scott the commentator was rector from 1803 till his death in 1821

ASTON SOMERVILLE, a parish in the district of Evesham and county of Gloucester, on the river Isborne, 4 miles S by E of Evesham r station. Post town, Broadway Acres, 993 Real property, £1,475 Pop, 105 Houses, 21 The manor has been held, for upwards of six centuries, by the family of Somerville, of whom were William Somerville the poet, author of "The Chase, and Lord Somerville, the distinguished agriculturist, who died in 1819 A salt spring occurs, and interesting fossils have been found The living is a rectory in the diocese of Gloucester and Bristol Value, £272 * Patron, Lord Somerville The church is very good.

ASTON STEEPLE, a township and a parish in Woodstock district, Oxford The township lies on the river Cherwell, the Oxford canal, and the Oxford and Rugby railway, adjacent to Heyford r station, 6½ miles NNE of Woodstock, and has a post office under Oxford Real property, £2,846 Pop., 650 Houses, 150 The parish includes also the township of Middle Aston Acres, 1,870 Real property £4,214 Pop, 736 Houses, 171 The property is subdivided The manor belonged anciently to the Molines, and passed to the Hungerfords. A tesselated pavement was ploughed up in the 17th century The living is a rectory in the diocese of Oxford Value, £582 Patron, Brasenose college, Oxford The church is ancient, but very good There are a Wesleyan chapel and a national school. Dr Samuel Radcliffe, principal of Brasenose college, was for some time rector, and founded a free school and alms houses

ASTON SUB EDGE, a parish in the district of Evesham and county of Gloucester, on the West Midland railway, under Bredon hill, 2 miles SSW of Honeybourne r station and 6 FSE of Evesham Post town Campden, under Moreton in the Marsh Acres, 755 Real property, £1,503 Pop, 128 Houses, 27 The property is divided among a few The living is a rectory in the diocese of Gloucester and Bristol Value, £204 * Patron, Earl Harrowby The church is tolerable.

ASTON SUTTON See ASTON BY SUTTON

ASTON TIPPOLD, a parish in Wallingford district, Berks, 2½ miles NW by N of Wallingford Road r station, and 4 SW of Wallingford It has a post office under Wallingford Acres, 1,674 Real property, £2 501 Pop, 395 Houses, 82 The property is divided among a few The living is a rectory in the diocese of Oxford Value, £233 * Patron, Magdalene college, Oxford The church is good There are an Independent chapel, and charities £14

ASTON UNDER EDGE See ASTON SUB EDGE

ASTON UPON CARRON See ASTON ON CARRON

ASTON UPON TRENT, a parish in Shardlow district Derbyshire, on the verge of the county, Grand Trunk canal, and the river Trent, 3¾ miles S of Spondon r station, and 6 SE by S of Derby It contains the townships of Aston and Shardlow with Far Wilne, and its post town is Shardlow under Derby Acres, 3,290 Real property, £4,933. Pop, 551 Houses 135 The property is divided among a few Aston Hall is the seat of the Holdens, and Aston Lodge of the Rev J Miller The living is a rectory in the diocese of Lichfield Value, £1,000 * Patron, E A Holden, Esq The church is good Shardlow is a separate charge, and contains the district workhouse There are a Wesleyan chapel, a national school and charities £22 See ASTON

ASTON UPTHORPE, a chapelry in Blewberry parish, Berks 3½ miles NW of Wallingford r station, and 4 SW of Wallingford Post town, Blewberry under Wallingford Acres 1,320 Real property, £1 210 Pop, 169 Houses, 30 The property is divided among a few Kenowwalch of Wessex was overthrown here, in 650, by Wulfhere of Mercia The living is a vicarage, united with the vicarage of Upton, in the diocese of Oxford Value, not reported Patron, the Bishop of Oxford The church is ancient

ASTON (WEST) See ASTON (EAST and WEST)

ASTON WHEATON, See WHEATON ASTON

ASTON WHITE LADY See WHITE LADY ASTON

ASTON WITH AUGHTON, a township and a parish in Rotherham district, W R Yorkshire The township lies near the river Rother, 2 miles SSW of Beighton r station, and 5 E of Rotherham, and has a post office, of the name of Aston, under Rotherham. Real property, £7,105,—of which £2 002 are in mines Pop., 995 Houses, 195 The parish includes also part of the township of Ulley Acres, 2 915 Real property, with the rest of Ulley, £8,569 Pop, 1,032 Houses, 233 The property is sub divided The manor belonged formerly to the D'Arcys, and belongs now to the Duke of Leeds A Hall is the seat of T Tillotson, Esq The living is a rectory in the diocese of York Value, £760 * Patron, the Duke of Leeds. The church is ancient, and contains a monument to Lord D'Arcy and his three wives, a splendid screen, and a Norman font There are Methodist chapels, national schools, and charities £37 The Rev William Mason, the editor of Gray's poems and the author of "Isis" and other poems of his own, was rector

ASTRAD, a township in Llandyrnog parish, Denbighshire, 1¼ mile SE of Denbigh Pop, 49

ASTROP, a hamlet in Kings Sutton and Newbottle parishes, Northampton, near the river Cherwell, 6 miles W of Brackley Pop, 224 A mineral spring here, called St Rumbald's well, was formerly much frequented for cutaneous diseases Astrop Hall is the seat of E Cunliffe, Esq

ASTWELL, a hamlet in Wappenham parish, Northampton, on an affluent of the river Tove, 6 miles NNE of Brackley Real property, with Falcutt, £2,465 Pop, 83. Houses, 12 The property belonged formerly to the Billing, the Lovett, and the Ferrers families, and belongs now to the Duke of Buckingham The old seat of the Earl of Ferrers still stands, and is now used as a farm house The hamlet is a resort of sportsmen

ASTWICK, a parish in Biggleswade district, Beds, on the river Ivel, 2½ miles ENE of Arlesey r station, and 4 N by W of Baldock Post town, Arlesey under Baldock. Acres, 570 Real property, £1,117 Pop, 64 Houses, 14 The property is not much divided. The living is a rectory annexed to the vicarage of Arlesey, in the diocese of Ely The church is good

ASTWICK, a decayed hamlet in Evenly parish, Northampton, 3 miles SSW of Brackley It was formerly a large town, and it retains traces of a capital manor house Several Roman coins have been found in Astwick field

ASTWICK, Yorkshire See AUSTWICK.

ASTWOOD, a parish in Newport Pagnell district, Bucks, on the verge of the county, 5½ miles ENE of Newport Pagnell, and 7 N of Ridgmount r station Post town, Newport Pagnell. Acres, 1,259 Real property, £1,880 Pop, 247 Houses, 65 The property is divided among a few The living is a vicarage in the diocese of Oxford Value, £230 * Patron, the Lord Chancellor The church is good.

ASTWOOD BANK, a village in Feckenham parish, Worcestershire, near Studley r station, 3½ miles S of Redditch. It has a post office ‡ under Redditch, needle factories, and Baptist and Wesleyan chapels

ASWARBY, a parish and a sub district in the district of Sleaford, Lincoln The parish lies in the Fens, 5 miles S of Sleaford r station Post town, Osbournby under Folkingham Acres, 1,348 Real property, £2,213 Pop., 128 Houses, 18. The manor belonged formerly to the Harveys, and belongs now to Sir T Whichcote, Bart, whose seat is Aswarby House. The living is a rectory in the diocese of Lincoln Value, £285 * Patron, Sir T Whichcote The church is a good edifice of lofty nave, aisle, and chancel, with fine tower and spire Charities, £5 Bass, the discoverer of Bass's Straits, was a native —The sub district comprises ten parishes Acres, 17,740 Pop, 3,059 Houses, 621

ASWARDBY, a parish in Spilsby district, Lincoln, on the river Steeping, 4 miles NW of Spilsby, and 6 SW of Alford r station Post town, Hagworthingham under Spilsby Acres 741 Real property, £1,755 Pop, 68 Houses, 15 The property is all in one estate The living is a rectory in the diocese of Lincoln Value, £266 Patron, R. Brackenbury, Esq The church is good

ASWARDHURN, a wapentake in the parts of Kesteven, Lincoln It includes the parish of Asgarby and nineteen other parishes Acres, 47,660. Pop in 1851 8,070, in 1861, 7,635 Houses, 1,608

ATCHAM, a township, a parish, a sub district, and a district in Salop The township lies at the influx of the Tern to the Severn, 2 miles SSW of Upton-Magna r station, 4 SE of Shrewsbury, and 6¼ W by N of the Wrekin It also bears the name of Attingham, and has an inn The parish includes also the townships of Berwick, Chilton, Cronkhill, Emstrey, and Uckington, and has a post-office under Shrewsbury Acres, 3,762 Real property, £4,851 Pop, 406 Houses, 92 The property is divided among a few Attingham Hall is the seat of Lord Berwick, and contains a fine gallery of paintings, chiefly by the early Italian masters, also a fine collection of Etruscan vases and other antiquities from Herculaneum The living is a vicarage in the diocese of Lichfield Value, £330 Patron, R. Burton, Esq The church has a good Norman doorway, an old porch, a reading desk with carved panels, and an ivy covered square tower, but is in very bad condition Charities, £84 Ordericus Vitalis, the historian, born in 1074, was a native.—The sub district comprises the parishes of Atcham, Uppington, Leighton, Eaton Constantine, and Wroxeter Acres, 12,316 Pop., 1,699 Houses, 347 —The district comprehends also the sub-district of Battlefield, containing the parishes of Battlefield, Preston Gubbals, Uffington, Upton-Magna, and Withington, the extra parochial tract of Haughmond Demesne, and part of the parish of St Mary Shrewsbury the sub district of Montford, containing the parishes of Montford, Melverley, Shrawardine, and Fitz, the sub-district of Alberbury, containing the parishes of Cardeston and Ford, and part of the parish of Alberbury, portions of which are electorally in Montgomery, the sub district of Westbury, conterminate with the parish of Westbury, the sub-district of Pontesbury, containing the parishes of Pontesbury, Habberley, and Great Hanwood, and the sub district of Condover, containing the parishes of Condover, Harley, Shineton, Cound Kenley, Hughley, Church Preen, Acton-Burnell, Frodesley, Pitchford, Berrington, Sutton, Stapleton, and Church-Pulverbatch Poor rates in 1866, £8,072 Pop in 1841, 18,842, in 1861, 19,455 Houses, 3,848 Marriages in 1866, 105, births, 538,—of which 36 were illegitimate, deaths, 344,—of which 75 were at ages under 5 years, and 27 at ages above 85 Marriages in the ten years 1851-60 974, births, 5,352, deaths, 3,499 The places of worship in 1851 were 43 of the Church of England, with 9,027 sittings, 9 of Independents, with 1,299 s, 4 of Baptists, with 433 s, 5 of Wesleyan Methodists, with 290 s, 1 of New Connexion Methodists, with 96 s, 16 of Primitive Methodists, with 1,219 s, 1 of Calvinistic Methodists, with 125 s, 1 of Latter Day Saints, with 40 s, and 1 of Roman Catholics, with 170 s The schools were 29 public day schools, with 1,703 scholars, 24 private day schools, with 383 s, and 32 Sunday schools, with 1,391 s The workhouse is in Berrington

ATCH LENCH, a hamlet in Church Lench parish, Worcester, 5 miles N of Evesham Pop., 77

ATFORD See ATWORTH

ATHAN (ST), a parish in Bridgend district, Glamorgan, on the coast, 5 miles S by E of Cowbridge, and 8 SW of St Fagans r station It has a post office under Cowbridge Acres, 1,771, of which 285 are water Real property, £2,574 Pop, 357 Houses 79 The property is divided among a few Breaksea Point is on the coast, and commands a fine view Remains of Roger Berkrols castle, built in 1091, are at East Orchard, and remains of two other castles, of later date, are at West Orchard and Castleton The living is a rectory in the diocese of Llandaff Value, £369 * Patron, W C Rayer, Esq The church is good, and contains two interesting Gothic monuments of the Berkrols family There is a Wesleyan chapel

ATHELHAMPTON See ADMISTON

ATHELLINGTON, or ALLINGTON, a parish in Hoxne district, Suffolk, 5 miles SE by E of Eye and 8 NW of Framlingham r station Post town, Horham under Wickham Market Acres, 437 Real property, £926.

Pop., 115 Houses, 24 The property is not much divided. The living is a rectory in the diocese of Norwich. Value, £155 * Patron, the Lord Chancellor The church is good.

ATHELNEY, a railway station and quondam island in Lyng parish, Somerset The station is on the Durston and Yeovil branch of the Bristol and Exeter railway, 4½ miles WNW of Langport The quondam island is a rising-ground, or small hill, of about 100 acres, surrounded by marshes, at the confluence of the rivers Tone and Parret. King Alfred took refuge here, in 879 after his defeat by the Danes, made frequent incursions hence against them till he became able to take the field for their complete overthrow, and founded here, in 888, a Benedictine abbey, in expression of gratitude for his victories The abbot did not sit in parliament yet enjoyed great privileges, and was regarded as a spiritual lord The edifice is extinct, but recent traces of it show it to have been large A stone pillar, with an appropriate inscription was erected on the spot, in 1801 by John Slade Esq, the then proprietor An amulet of enamel and gold, inscribed with words signifying "Alfred caused me to be made," was found on Athelney in the 17th century, and is now in the Ashmolean museum

ATHELSTAN ABBEY See EGGLESTON ABBEY

ATHERFIELD a tything in Shorwell parish Isle of Wight, on the S coast, 6½ miles SSW of Newport Atherfield rocks here are subject to landslips, and then, after being washed by the waves, show very strikingly the juxtaposition of the lowermost of the greensand deposits with the uppermost of the Wealden

ATHERINGTON, a village and a parish in Barnstaple district, Devon The village stands on a hill adjacent to the river Taw, in the vicinity of Umberleigh r station 7 miles SSE of Barnstaple, and has a post office under Barnstaple The parish comprises 3,326 acres. Real property, £3,270 Pop, 598 Houses, 120 The property is divided among a few The manor belongs to the Bassetts. A palace of King Athelstan is said to have stood at Umberleigh, and an ancient chapel was there, which also is said to have been built by him The living is a rectory in the diocese of Exeter Value, £403 * Patron, the Rev J Arthur The church is an ancient edifice, of nave, chancel, and north aisle, in bad condition, was a cell to Caen abbey, and contains a very handsome carved screen, and two recumbent effigies of the 15th century, brought to it in 1800 from the chapel at Umberleigh There are a Baptist chapel in the village, and a Wesleyan chapel at Langridge

ATHERINGTON Sussex. See ALDRINGTON

ATHERSTONE, a hamlet in White Lackington parish, Somerset, 1 mile NE of Ilminster

ATHERSTONE, a market town a township, a chapelry, a sub district, a district, and a division, in Warwick The town stands on Watling street and the Trent Valley railway, adjacent to the Anker river and the Coventry canal at the northern extremity of the forest of Arden, 8 miles SE of Tamworth It was anciently called Adrestone and Edrestone It was given at the Conquest to the monks of Bec in Normandy who obtained for it the right of a market and an annual fair An Augustinian friary was founded at it, in 1376, by Ralph Basset of Drayton, and given, at the dissolution, to the Cartwrights The Earl of Richmond and other disaffected nobles of Richard III concerted in it, in 1485, the measures which led next day to their victory on Bosworth field The place where they held their conference is said to have been the Three Tuns Inn, which still exists and the place on which their troops encamped was a meadow N of the church The field of Bosworth lies 8 miles to the NE within Leicester The town of Atherstone consists chiefly of one principal street, well-built, and nearly a mile long The market house stands on pillars, and has a spacious assembly room above The corn exchange is large and recent. The church was mainly re edificed in 1850, and is in the decorated English style The grammar-school was founded, in 1573, by Sir William Devereux and two other persons has a free income of £350, and was recently removed to new buildings There are chapels for Independents, Methodists Unitarians, and Roman Catholics, a Benedictine nunnery, an endowed school with £42 a year, other charities £293, a library and news room, a dispensary, and a work house The town is a seat of petty sessions, and a polling place, and has a station on the railway, a head post office,‡ a banking office, and two chief inns. A weekly market is held on Tuesday, and fairs, in Feb, April, June, Aug, Oct, and Dec. The manufacture of ribbons, hats, and shalloons is carried on, and a considerable traffic from neighbouring quarries and coal mines exists. Drayton, who wrote the "Polyolbion," and Dr Grew, the botanist, were natives Pop, 3,857 Houses, 860

The township includes the town, and is in the parish of Mancetter Real property, £11,854 Pop., 3,877 Houses, 864 Atherstone Hall is the seat of C A Bracebridge, Esq and stands on a pleasant bank, commanding an extensive view The park contains some very grand old oaks A very hard quartzose sandstone is largely quarried, and sent to distant parts, for road making Manganese has been extensively brought from the contiguous hamlet of Hartshill, and coal from the neighbouring moor of Baddesley —The chapelry is conterminate with the township. The living is a vicarage in the diocese of Worcester Value, £150 * Patron, Church Pat Society —The sub district and the district are co-extensive and comprehend the parishes of Mancetter Ansley, Baxterley, Baddesley Ensor Polesworth, Grendon, Merevale, Sheepy Magna, Sheepy Parva, Witherley, and Fenny Drayton, the extra parochial tract of the Mythe, and part of the parish of Shustoke, and four of these parishes, part of another, and the extra parochial tract are electorally in Leicester Acres in the district, 27,883 Poor rates in 1866, £4,980 Pop in 1861, 12 118 Houses, 2,605 Marriages in 1866 89 births 426,—of which 23 were illegitimate deaths 244,—of which 64 were at ages under 5 years, and 7 at ages above 85 years. Marriages in the ten years 1851-60, 760, births, 3,949, deaths, 2,336 The places of worship in 1851 were 15 of the Church of England, with 5 220 sittings 7 of Independents, with 1,976 s, 2 of Baptists, with 350 s, 6 of Wesleyan Methodists, with 770 s, 2 of Primitive Methodists, with 170 s, 1 of the Independent Methodist Society, with 176 s, and 1 of Roman Catholics with 140 s The schools were 16 public day schools with 1,047 scholars, 30 private day schools, with 564 s, 24 Sunday schools with 2,124 s, and 3 evening schools for adults, with 43 s —The division is in Hemlingford hundred, and excludes the parts of the district which are electorally in Leicester but includes ten other parishes which are electorally in Warwick Acres, 55,495 Pop in 1851 26,144 Houses 5,722

ATHERSTONE ON STOUR, a parish in Stratford on Avon district, Warwick, on the Moreton and Stratford railway and the river Stour, 3 miles S by E of Stratford on Avon It contains the village of Ailstow, and its post town is Stratford-on-Avon Acres 1,060 Rated property, £1 412 Pop, 90 Houses, 21 The property is undivided The manor belonged in the time of Edward III to John de Langley, and passed to successively the Mortons, the Hawkses, and the Ladkotes The living is a rectory in the diocese of Worcester Value, £238 * Patrons Representatives of late Rev Dr Cox The church is good Dr Thomas, the continuator of Dugdale's "Antiquities," was a native

ATHERTON a town, a township, a chapelry, and a sub district in the parish and district of Leigh, Lancashire The town stands about a mile E of the Bolton and Kenyon railway, 2 miles NNE of Leigh, and 13 WNW of Manchester It bears also the name of Chowbent and it has a station of the name of Atherton on the railway, and a post office‡ of the name of Chowbent under Manchester The inhabitants are employed variously in cotton factories iron works, nail factories, and collieries Pop, 2 692 Houses 633 The township includes also part of the town of Leigh, and is partly rural Acres, 2,323 Real property £2? 683, of which £8,920 are in mines. Pop, 5,907 Houses, 1,222

Atherton Hall stands near the site of a quondam seat of the Athertons, and is the property of Lord Lilford.—The chapelry is a p curacy in the diocese of Manchester Value, £100 Patron, Lord Lilford. The church was rebuilt in 1810 There are Baptist and Unitarian chapels, and a national school.—The sub district includes Tyldesley-cum Shakerley Pop, 11,936

ATHERTON, Isle of Wight See ARRETON

ATLOW, a chapelry in Bradbourne parish, Derby, on a branch of the river Dove, 4½ miles NE by E of Ashborne r station Post town, Ashborne Acres, 1,530 Real property, £1 926 Pop, 129 Houses, 26 The property is not much divided The Living is a rectory in the diocese of Lichfield. Value, £118. Patron, C H Okeover, Esq The church is tolerable

ATPAR. See ADPAR.

ATRE (THE) See ATTERY

ATTENBOROUGH, a village and a parish in the district of Shardlow and county of Nottingham The village stands at the confluence of the Erwash and the Trent, adjacent to the Nottingham railway, 1¼ mile NE of Long Eaton junction, and 5 SW of Nottingham The parish comprehends the township of Toton and the hamlet of Chilwell, the latter of which has a post office under Nottingham Acres, 2,343 Real property, £8,507 Pop, 1,110 Houses, 240. The property is much subdivided The living is a vicarage, united with the curacy of Bramcote, in the diocese of Lincoln Value, £250 * Patron, G S Foljambe, Esq The church is large and good. Charities, £19 Henry Ireton, the son in law of Oliver Cromwell, was a native

ATTERBY, a township in Bishop Norton parish, Lincoln, near Ermine street, 9 miles NW by W of Market Raisen. Acres, 1,190 Real property, £1,354 Pop, 95 Houses, 22

ATTERCLIFFE, a chapelry, a township, and a sub district in the parish and district of Sheffield, W R. Yorkshire The chapelry lies on the Rotherham railway, the Tinsey canal, and the river Don, 1¼ mile NE by E of Sheffield, and within that town s borough boundaries, and was constituted in 1847 Rated property, £7,306 Pop., 5,061 Houses, 1,059 The living is a vicarage in the diocese of York Value, £130 * Patron, the Vicar of Sheffield. The church was built in 1826, at a cost of £12,800, and is in the later Gothic style There are four dissenting chapels, a Roman Catholic chapel built in 1868 at a cost of £4,700 a news room, two public schools, and charities £36 —The township is conjoined with Darnall, and has a post office,‡ of the name of Attercliffe, under Sheffield Acres, 1,270 Real property, £15,412 Pop, 7,464 Houses, 1,554 The inhabitants are chiefly cutlers, mechanics, and colliers Cast-steel was first made here, and cannel coal is mined Attercliffe Hall is the seat of J Milner, Esq An abrupt precipice overhangs the Don, and probably gave name to the township. Archbishop Secker was educated at Attercliffe dissenting academy —The sub district is conterminate with the township.

ATTERLEY, a township in Much Wenlock parish, Salop 2 miles SE of Much Wenlock Pop., 52

ATTERTON, a hamlet in Witherley parish, Leicester, 3 miles E by N of Atherstone Real property, £1,184 Pop., 78 Houses, 17

ATTERY, or ATRE (THE), a stream of Cornwall It rises on Wilsey down, near Trenegloss and runs about 14 miles east-south eastward to the river Tamar, in the vicinity of Launceston

ATTINGHAM See ATCHAM

ATTINGTON, an extra-parochial tract in Thame district, Oxford, 3 miles S of Thame. Acres, 435 Pop, 15 Houses 3

ATTLEBOROUGH, a chapelry in Nuneaton parish, Warwick on the Trent Valley railway and the river Anker, near the Coventry canal, 1 mile S of Nuneaton It was constituted in 1843 It has a post office under Nuneaton Real property, £4,539 Pop, 1,393 Houses, 322 The property is subdivided The living is a vicarage in the diocese of Worcester Value, £170 * Patron the Vicar of Nuneaton The church was built in 1841, and is in the early English style There are a Baptist chapel and a national school.

ATTLEBOROUGH, or ATTLEBURGH, a small town, a parish and a sub district, in the district of Weyland, Norfolk. The town stands adjacent to the Norfolk and Eastern Union railway, 16 miles SW of Norwich. It was the capital of East Anglia, and had strength enough to check the incursions of the Danes, and it retained fortifications of some note till the time of Henry II It is now decayed and small, yet serves still as a county centre It has a station with telegraph on the railway, a head post office,‡ a banking office, and a chief inn A corn market hall was built in 1863, at a cost of £1,000 A weekly market is held on Thursday, and there are three annual fairs A college, for a custos and four fellows, was founded, in the time of Richard II, by Sir Robert de Mortimer, and given, in the time of Henry VIII, to Robert, Earl of Sussex The church of the college still stands is a spacious cruciform edifice in Norman and early English, with square tower rising from the centre, and contains monuments to distinguished members of the families of Mortimer, Ratcliffe, and Blickley —The parish comprises 5 260 acres Real property, £12,682 Pop, 2,221 Houses, 494 The property is much subdivided. A Hall, Hill House, and the Point are chief residences The first turnpike road in England was made in this parish The living is a rectory in the diocese of Norwich. Value, £1,226 * Patron, Sir W B Smyth There are three dissenting chapels Charities, £76 and 57 acres of poors allotment —The sub district includes eleven parishes. Acres, 22,885 Pop, 5,506 Houses, 1,223.

ATTLEBRIDGE, a parish in St Faith district, Norfolk, on the river Wensum, 9 miles NW of Norwich r station It has a post-office under Norwich Acres, 1,267 Real property, £1,374 Pop., 93 Houses, 19 The living is a vicarage annexed to the rectory of Alderford in the diocese of Norwich

ATTLEBURGH See ATTLEBOROUGH, Norfolk

ATWICK, a hamlet and a parish in Skirlaugh district E R Yorkshire The hamlet stands on the coast, 2 miles N of Hornsea r station, and 13 NE of Beverley, and has a post office under Hull The parish includes also the hamlets of Arram and Skirlington Acres, 2 350, of which 165 are water Real property, £3,186. Pop, 319 Houses, 69 The property is much subdivided The land is undergoing encroachment by sea. The living is a vicarage in the diocese of York. Value, £149 * Patron, the Lord Chancellor The church is good There is a Wesleyan chapel Fenwick s charity, for educating and apprenticing boys, has an income of £46, and other charities £13.

ATWORTH, or ATFORD, a chapelry in Bradford parish Wilts, near the Roman road, 3 miles WNW of Melksham r station Post town, Melksham Acres, 1 170 Real property, with South Wraxall, £5,337 Pop, 949 Houses, 225. The property is not much divided. The living is a vicarage with South Wraxall, in the diocese of Salisbury Value, £255 Patrons, the Dean and Chapter of Bristol. The church was built in 1828 There are an Independent chapel, and charities £17

AUBIN (ST), a small town in St. Brelade parish, Jersey, on the west side of a bay of its own name, 3¾ miles W of St. Helier The bay is semicircular, has a picturesque appearance, fills all the space eastward to St. Helier, and is defended on the west side by St. Aubin Castle, on the SE by Elizabeth Castle It forms a good roadstead, but has several shoals St Aubin Castle is a tower mounted with 14 guns, and has done service in the defence of the island The town is the second in Jersey, and has a post office under St Helier a weekly market on Monday, a pier, inns, a chapel of ease, and an alms house. The chapel is served by a curate, with a salary of £60, appointed by proprietors Several handsome villas are in the neighbourhood Pop, about 800

AUBOURN, a township and a parish in the district and county of Lincoln The township lies on the river

Witham, near the Fosse road and the Nottingham and Lincoln railway, 3½ miles SE of Thorpe r station, and 6½ SW by S of Lincoln, and includes the hamlet of Marlborough Acres, 1,843 Real property, £2,474. Pop, 308. Houses, 61 The parish includes also part of the township of Haddington Post town, Waddington under Lincoln Acres, 2,109 Real property, with the rest of Haddington, £3,636 Pop, 376 Houses, 73 The property is divided among a few The living is a vicarage in the diocese of Lincoln Value, £209 Patron, the Rev H Neville. The church is Norman There are a Wesleyan chapel, and charities £19

AUBREY ARMS See COWBRIDGE

AUBURN, or AWBURN, a township chapelry in Fraisthorpe parish, E. R. Yorkshire, on the coast, 2 miles SE of Carnaby r station and 3½ miles S by W of Bridlington Post town, Bridlington under Hull Pop, 16 Houses, 2 Much of the land has been washed away by the sea. The living is a p. curacy, annexed to Fraisthorpe, in the diocese of York

AUCKLAND, a district in Durham It comprehends the sub district of Bishop Auckland, containing the parish of Whitworth, the parochial chapelry of Escomb, and parts of the parishes of St Andrew Auckland, Merrington, and Brancepeth, and the sub-district of Hamsterley, containing the parochial chapelry of Witton le Wear, and parts of the parishes of St Andrew Auckland, Brancepeth, and Gainford Poor rates in 1866, £16,479 Pop in 1841, 21,988, in 1861, 50,491 Houses, 9,653 Marriages in 1866, 542, births 2,809,—of which 146 were illegitimate, deaths, 1,306,—of which 727 were at ages under 5 years, and 15 at ages above 85 years. Marriages in the ten years 1851-60, 3,792, births, 17,932, deaths, 9,447 The places of worship in 1851 were 16 of the Church of England, with 4,734 sittings, 1 of Independents, with 200 s., 2 of Baptists, with 400 s., 2 of Quakers, with 350 s, 18 of Wesleyan Methodists, with 2,852 s, 19 of Primitive Methodists, with 2,823 s, 2 of the Wesleyan Methodist Association, with 420 s, and 1 of Roman Catholics, with 240 s The schools were 34 public day schools, with 2,536 scholars, 33 private day schools, with 1,189 s., 43 Sunday schools, with 3,122 s, and 2 evening schools for adults, with 30 s The workhouse is in Bishop Auckland

AUCKLAND (BISHOP) See BISHOP AUCKLAND

AUCKLAND (ST ANDREW), a township and a parish in Auckland district, Durham The township lies on the Bishop Auckland and Weardale railway, and at the confluence of the Gaunless and the Wear rivers, 1 mile SE of Bishop Auckland. Acres, 1,186 Real property, £12 242 —of which £9,373 are in mines Pop, 1,401 Houses, 283 The parish includes also the town of Bishop Auckland, and the townships of Bishop Auckland, St Helen Auckland, Middlestone, Westerton, Old Park, Binchester, Newfield, Byers Green, Hunwick and Helmington, Newton Cap, Pollards Lands Coundon, Coundon Grange, Windlestone, Eldon, Middridge Grange East Thickley, Shildon, Middridge, West Auckland, Barony, Lynesack and Softley, Hamsterley, North Bedburn, and South Bedburn, and its post town is Bishop Auckland under Darlington Acres, 45,868 Real property, £134,725 Pop in 1841, 19,100, in 1861 32,111 Houses 6,301 The property, in most parts, is subdivided, in many parts, much subdivided Coal and limestone are extensively worked The living, with St Ann, is a vicarage in the diocese of Durham Value, £557 * Patron, the Bishop of Durham The church is a cruciform structure, with a tower at the west end, was made collegiate by Bishop Beck, in 1292, for a dean and nine prebendaries, contains brasses and the effigies of a crusader, and needs repair The chapelries of St Helen Auckland, Byers Green Etherley, Hamsterley Shildon Witton le Wear Coundon, Escomb, Fir Tree, Hunwick, Lynesack, Evenwood and New Shildon, are separate charges. Three endowed schools have an income of £485, and other charities have £30.

AUCKLAND (ST HELEN), a township chapelry in the parish of St Andrew Auckland, Durham, on the river Gaunless and on the Haggerleases branch railway, 2½ miles SW of Bishop Auckland It has a station on the railway, and its post-town is West Auckland under Darlington Acres 1,480 Real property, £7 570,—of which £5,102 are in mines. Pop., 842 Houses, 167 The property is subdivided The living is a p curacy in the diocese of Durham Value, £220 Patron, the Bishop of Durham The church is tolerable

AUCKLAND (WEST), a township in St. Andrew-Auckland parish, Durham, on the river Gaunless and on the Haggerleases branch railway, 3 miles SW of Bishop Auckland It has a post office‡ under Darlington Acres, 3,720 Real property, £7,019,—of which £2,300 are in mines. Pop, 2,581 Houses, 535 Here are chapels for Wesleyan and Primitive Methodists, a large brewery, and a lunatic asylum

AUCKLEY, or AWKLEY a township in the parish of Finningley and partly in Notts, partly in W R Yorkshire, 3 miles E by N of Rossington r station, and 5 ESE of Doncaster Acres, 1,970 Pop, 309 Houses, 69

AUDELEY END See AUDLEY END

AUDENSHAW, a village, a chapelry, a parochial division, and a sub district, in the district of Ashton under Lyne, Lancashire The village stands adjacent to the Ashton canal and the Manchester and Sheffield railway, 3 miles SW of Ashton, and has a post office under Manchester —The chapelry was constituted in 1844 Rated property, £9,000 Pop, 5,185 Houses, 1,037 The living is a p curacy in the diocese of Manchester Value £150 * Patron, altern the Crown and the Bishop The church is in the early English style There are Methodist chapels and good schools —The division includes the villages of Hooley hill, Waterhill, Littlemoss, Woodhouses, and North Street, and part of the borough of Ashton under Lyne Real property £20,814 Pop., 6,327 Houses, 1,277 Many of the inhabitants are employed in hat making, cotton spinning, calico printing, and silk weaving The large reservoirs of the Manchester and Salford water works are in the SW High Ash is an old hall of the Stopfords, where coats of arms and portraits of the kings of England were once preserved, and Shepley Hall is a modern seat, well known for its collection of pictures —The sub district includes also a township of Manchester parish Acres, 1,611 Pop, 15,125 Houses, 2,995

AUDLEBY, a hamlet in Caistor parish, Lincoln, on the Wolds, 1 mile N of Caistor It is a resort of sportsmen Pop, 23

AUDLEM, a township in Nantwich district Cheshire, and a parish chiefly in that district, and wholly in that county, but partly also in the district of Market Drayton. The township lies on the Nantwich and M Drayton railway, 6 miles S of Nantwich, and has a st. on the railway a post office‡ under Nantwich, and fairs on 24, 25, 26 July and 28 Nov Acres, 2,358 Real property, £7 156 Pop, 1,510 Houses, 344 The parish includes also the townships of Buerton, Hankelow, and Tittenley Acres, 10,525 Real property, £14,092 Pop., 2,287 Houses, 505 The property is divided among a few The living is a vicarage in the diocese of Chester Value not reported Patron, Lord Combermere The church is good There are five dissenting chapels an endowed school with £40 a year, and charities £292

AUDLEY, a township a parish and a sub district in the district of Newcastle under Lyne, Stafford. The township lies 3 miles W of Harecastle tunnel on the Grand Trunk canal, 3 S of Alsager r station, and 5½ NW by N of Newcastle under Lyne It has a post office‡ under Newcastle under Lyne, and it gives the title of Baron to the family of Touchet Real property, £4,189 Pop, 1 556 Houses 317 The parish includes also the liberty of Halmer End and the townships of Talk o' th Hill, Eardley End Knowl End, Bignall End and Park End Acres, 8 530 Real property, £30,383,—of which £11,431 are in mines Pop. 6,494 Houses 1,330 The property is much subdivided Heleigh Castle, now a ruin, was the seat of the Audleys Coal and ironstone are worked The living is a vicarage in the diocese of Lichfield Value, £520 * Patron the Rev E Gilbert The church was restored in 1846 and

1856, and has some fine features The vicarage of Talk-o th Hill is a separate charge There are Methodist chapels Vernon's grammar school has an endowed income of £115, and other charities have £35.—The sub-district comprises two parishes and part of a third Acres, 11,171 Pop, 7,625 Houses, 1,566.

AUDLEY END, a railway station and a noble park near Saffron Walden, Essex The station is on the Eastern Counties railway, 1½ mile W by S of Saffron Walden, and at the junction of the branch railway thither The park lies between the station and the town, on the river Granta, and is the seat of Lord Braybrooke. A bridge is in it by Adams, and a camp, on Ermine street The mansion is part of a splendid Tudor pile, built in 1603-16 It occupies the site of a Benedictine priory of 1136, and was erected by Howard, Earl of Suffolk, afterwards Lord High Treasurer of England, and named after his uncle, Audley It was offered by the Earl to James I, who declined to have it on account of its being too costly, was sold by a succeeding Earl to Charles II, who failed to pay the purchase money, and renounced possession, and was found by its owners to be so intolerably expensive, in the maintaining of a due establishment for it, that a large portion of it had to be taken down What remains of it is magnificent, and it contains some valuable paintings and a fine museum

AUGHTON, a parish and a sub district in the district of Ormskirk, Lancashire The parish lies on a branch of the river Alt, and on the Liverpool and Preston railway, at Town-Green station, near the Liverpool and Leeds canal, 2½ miles SSW of Ormskirk. It has a post office under Ormskirk Acres, 4,462. Real property, £13,804 Pop, 1,870 Houses, 360 The property is much subdivided. Aughton Hall is a chief residence The living is a rectory in the diocese of Chester Value, £830 * Patron, J P Tempest, Esq The church was rebuilt in 1867, at a cost of £6,000 There is a Roman Catholic chapel —The sub district includes also two chapelries Acres, 8,530 Pop., 3,862 Houses, 708

AUGHTON, a chapelry in Halton parish, Lancashire, on the river Lune, 2 miles N of Caton r station, and 7 NE of Lancaster Post town, Caton, under Lancaster Acres, 1,900 Pop, 132. The living is a p. curacy in the diocese of Manchester Value, £140 * Patron, the Rector of Halton The church was rebuilt in 1864

AUGHTON, a township in Howden district, and a parish in Howden and Pocklington districts, E R. Yorkshire The township lies on the river Derwent, 1¾ mile NNW of Bubwith r station, and 7 NE of Selby Acres, 1,790 Real property, £2,216 Pop, 202 Houses, 38 The parish includes also the townships of Laytham and East Cottingwith, and its post-town is Bubwith, under Howden Acres, 4,295 Real property, £5,711 Pop, 633. Houses, 134. The property is divided among a few Traces exist of a castle which was the seat of successively the family of Hai and the family of Aske. Here lived Sir Robert Aske, who was executed as a leader of the insurrection called "the pilgrimage of grace," occasioned by the suppression of the monasteries in the reign of Henry VIII, and here lived also the Aske who was one of the judges of Charles I The living is a vicarage, united with the p curacy of Cottingwith, in the diocese of York Value £90 * Patron, A J Fletcher, Esq The church is fair, and there are charities £48

AUGHTON, a tything in Collingbourne Kingston parish, Wilts, 4½ miles NW of Ludgershall.

AUGHTON, W R. Yorkshire See ASTON WITH AUGHTON

AUGUSTINE FRIARS. See LEICESTER.

AUGUSTINE (ST), a lathe in Kent It forms the eastern part of the county, measures 19 miles by 20, and contains the hundreds of Beaksbourne, Bewsborough, Bleangate, Bridge and Petham, Cornilo, Downhamford, Eastry Kinghamford, Preston, Ringslow, Seasalter, Westgate, Whitstable, and Wingham Acres, 172,494 Pop in 1851 78,146, in 1861, 66,143 Houses, 12,908.

AUGUSTINE (ST) See BRISTOL, CANTERBURY, LONDON, and NORWICH

AUKBOROUGH See ALKBOROUGH

AULKLEY See AUCKLEY

AULT HUCKNALL, or HAULT HUCKNALL, a parish in the district of Mansfield and county of Derby, on the verge of the county, adjacent to Hardwick Park, 5 miles ENE of Clay-cross r station, and 6½ SE of Chesterfield It contains the hamlets of Rowthorne and Stainsby, and its post town is Heath under Chesterfield Acres, 3,730 Rated property, £3 191 Pop., 686 Houses, 134 The property is not much divided The living is a vicarage in the diocese of Lichfield Value, £168 * Patron, the Duke of Devonshire. The church is good, and contains monuments to the first Countess of Devonshire and to the philosopher Hobbes See HARDWICK HALL

AUNBY See HOLYWELL WITH AUNBY

AUNSBY, a parish in Sleaford district, Lincoln, 5¼ miles ESE of Honington r station, and 5¼ SSW of Sleaford Post town, Osbournby under Folkingham Acres, 1,183. Real property, £1,786 Pop, 140 Houses, 27 The living is a rectory in the diocese of Lincoln Value, £291 Patron, J A. Houblon, Esq The church is early English, and has a figured font.

AURIGNY See ALDERNEY

AUST, or AUST CLIVE, a village and a chapelry in Henbury parish, Gloucester The village stands on the E shore of the Severn, 2 miles distant from the South Wales and the Bristol and Wales railways, 3½ W by S of Thornbury, and has a post office, of the name of Old Passage, under Bristol A ferry is here on the Severn, 2 miles over, to Chepstow, and bears the name of the Old passage, to distinguish it from the New passage, which is 2 miles lower down the river This was the ancient Trajectus, where the Roman legions used to be ferried over, and was also the place where Edward I passed over to hold a conference with Llewelyn. The chapelry is a tything Acres, 1,200 Real property, £2,398 Pop, 187 Houses, 39 The property is not much divided. Much of the surface is marshy Clays, alabaster, strontian, and some interesting fossils are found. The living is a p curacy, annexed to the vicarage of Henbury, in the diocese of Gloucester and Bristol. The church is externally good.

AUSTELL (ST), a market town, a parish, a sub district, and a district in Cornwall The town stands adjacent to the Cornwall railway, 1¾ mile NW of a bay of its own name and 39¼ W by S of Plymouth Its site is the side of a hill, which descends to a narrow vale watered by a rivulet The original town, or rather village, stood a short distance to the E, and is still represented by a few cottages The present town dates from about the time of Henry VIII, was taken by Charles I, in 1644, from the parliamentarian forces, and has risen to importance in connexion with neighbouring tin mines, and as a centre of great mineral traffic It has narrow streets, and a somewhat gloomy aspect, yet shows interesting features, and is skirted with pleasant villas. The market house and the town hall are large granite buildings. The Devon and Cornwall bank is a tasteful edifice of granite and marble The parish church is a spacious ancient structure, of nave, chancel, and aisles, with a remarkably fine tower, and many curious sculptures, the chancel early English, the nave and the tower perpendicular A communion cup used in the church is very ancient, was found by tinners, in 1774, about 17 feet below the surface of the ground, in the neighbourhood of the town, and contained several costly personal ornaments of silver and gold and a large collection of curious Saxon coins The town has a station on the railway, a head post office,‡ four banking offices, three chief inns, seven dissenting chapels, an alms house, a work house, and several blowing houses, not now worked for grain tin, and it is a seat of petty sessions, and a polling-place. A weekly market is held on Friday, and fairs, on the Thursday before Easter, Whit Thursday, the Friday after 23 July, 16 Oct, and 30 Nov A small manufactory of serges is carried on, a fishery for pilchards, in St. Austell bay, is extensive, and the mineral traffic embraces a large tract of surrounding country, and includes tin, copper, nickel, porcelain clay, china stone, porphyry granite, and Pentuan stone The principal mines are Polgooth, Carclaze, Crinnis, Pembroke Lanescot, and Pentuan Harbours exist at Pentuan and Charlestown, and railways go down to them from the town The name St Austell is of uncertain origin, but most probably is a corruption of St Auxilius Pop., 3,825 Houses, 777

The parish comprises 12,125 acres Real property, £37,325, of which £14 010 are in mines, and £2,157 in quarries Pop in 1841, 10,320, in 1861, 11,893 Houses, 2,309 The property is subdivided St Austell bay is 4 miles wide and 5 miles long, and forks in the N into the bay of St Blazey Hensbarrow hill about 2½ miles N of the town, is one of the loftiest heights in Cornwall The general surface of the parish, together with that of adjacent tracts, is bleak and desolate, and acquires increase to its ruefulness from the appearance of the mines and miners. The quarries in Pentuan vale supply a famous building stone, which has been used in the construction of many churches and mansions. One of the best tin stream works, not far from the quarries has thrown out fossil bones of men, of a whale, of enormous oxen, and of extinct species of animals An ancient holy well, with remains of a small chapel or baptistry, occurs in a pretty spot, beside a cataract, at Menacuddle hill, on the grounds of Mr Martin Penrice, 1½ mile S of the town, on the road to Pentuan is the seat of Sir C B G Sawle, Bart Polruddon and Treverbyn were ancient residences. The living is a vicarage in the diocese of Exeter Value, £537 * Patron, the Crown The vicarages of Charlestown and Treverbyn are separate charges

The sub district contains the parishes of St Austell, St Dennis, and Roche Acres, 21,665 Pop, 14,768 Houses, 2,946 —The district comprehends also the sub district of Fowey, containing the parishes of Fowey, Tywardreath, St. Sampson, and St Blazey, the sub district of Mevagissey, containing the parishes of Mevagissey, Gorran, St Ewe, and St. Michael Carhayes, and the sub district of Grampound, containing the parishes of Creed, St. Mewan, and St Stephen in Brannel, and part of the parish of Probus. Acres, 57,446 Poor rates, £10,449 Pop in 1841, 31,408, in 1861, 33,797 Houses, 6,829 Marriages, 286, births, 1,200,—of which 47 were illegitimate, deaths, 675,—of which 292 were at ages under 5 years, and 21 at ages above 85 years. Marriages in the ten years 1851-60, 2 804 births, 12,239, deaths, 6,577 The places of worship in 1851 were 18 of the Church of England, with 7,701 sittings, 5 of Independents, with 1,502 s, 1 of Baptists, with 350 s, 1 of Quakers, with 325 s, 31 of Wesleyan Methodists, with 7,020 s, 6 of Primitive Methodists, with 1,001 s, 2 of the Wesleyan Association, with 440 s, 27 of Bible Christians, with 4 052 s, 2 of Brethren, with 161 s., and 2 undefined, with 400 s The schools were 18 public day schools, with 1,166 scholars, 89 private day schools, with 2 070 scholars, 56 Sunday schools, with 5,651 s, and 2 evening schools for adults, with 24 s

AUSTERFIELD, a township chapelry in Blyth parish, W R. Yorkshire, adjacent to Notts, and to the Retford and Doncaster railway, 1½ mile NNE of Bawtry Post town, Bawtry Acres, 2,776 Real property, £3 477 Pop., 359 Houses 89 A Roman camp occurs here on the line of North Watling street, and a great battle is supposed to have been fought adjacent between the Britons and the Romans under Ostorius The living is a curacy, joined with Bawtry, in the diocese of Lincoln The church is Norman

AUSTERSON, a township in Acton parish, Cheshire, on the river Weaver, 2 miles S of Nantwich Acres, 890 Real property, £1,150 Pop, 57 Houses, 6

AUSTHORPE, a township in Whitkirk parish, W R Yorkshire, on the Selby railway 4 miles E of Leeds It includes the hamlets of Barrowby and Great and Little Manston Acres 600 Real property, £1 966 Pop., 231 Houses, 44 Smeaton, the civil engineer, born in 1724, was a native, and his monument, with a representation on it of his greatest work, the Eddystone light house, is in Whitkirk church.

AUSTHWAITE See BIRKER AND AUSTHWAITE

AUSTIN See HULL

AUSTINDYKE, a hamlet in Moulton parish, Lincoln 6½ miles NE of Crowland

AUSTLE (ST) See AUSTELL (ST).

AUSTONLEY, a township in Almondbury parish, W R. Yorkshire, on the river Colne, 2 miles SW of Holmfirth r station, and 6½ SSW of Huddersfield Acres, 1,760 Real property, £5,698 Pop, 1,901 Houses, 363. Many of the inhabitants are employed in manufactories See HOLME BRIDGE.

AUSTREY a parish in the district of Tamworth, and county of Warwick 4 miles NE of Polesworth r station, and 6½ E by N of Tamworth It has a post office under Atherstone Acres, 2,097 Real property, £4,735 Pop, 557 Houses, 126. The property is much subdivided The living is a vicarage in the diocese of Worcester Value, £162 * Patron, the Lord Chancellor The church presents some curious specimens of stained glass in the windows, and is very good There is a Baptist chapel Monk's school has an endowed income of £20, and other charities have £27

AUSTWICK, a township chapelry in Clapham parish, W R Yorkshire, near Ingleborough hill, 2 miles NE of Clapham r station, and 4½ NW of Settle Post town, Clapham, under Lancaster Acres 5,400. Real property, £5,224 Pop 561 Houses, 128 Austwick Hall is the seat of J R. Clapham, Esq The living is a p curacy, annexed to the vicarage of Clapham, in the diocese of Ripon The church is modern There are a Wesleyan chapel, a national school, and charities £27

AUTHORPE, a parish in Louth district, Lincoln, on the Wolds, and on the East Lincoln railway, 4½ miles NW of Alford It has a station on the railway, and its post-town is Withern under Alford. Acres, 921 Real property, £1,024 Pop, 134 Houses, 26 The property is divided among a few The living is a rectory in the diocese of Lincoln. Value, £166 Patron, R Vyner Esq The church is very good, and there are charities £6

AVEBURY, or ABURY, a village and a parish in Marlborough district, Wilts The village adjoins a head stream of the Kennet river 1½ mile N of Silbury hill, 4 miles N of Wansdyke, 6½ W of Marlborough r station, and 8 SSE of Wootton Bassett, and has a post office under Chippenham Its site is a flat area of 28 acres, once occupied by a vast Druidical temple Dr Stukeley, who examined the temple in 1720, supposed it to have originally consisted of 650 stones, and to have included the whole site of the present village It is surrounded by a broad ditch, outside of which is a lofty vallum, intended, it is supposed, to enable spectators to observe the ceremonies over the whole extent of the area. Within the ditch was a circle, 1,400 feet in diameter, formed of 100 upright stones, from 15 to 17 feet in height, and about 40 in circumference, placed at a distance of 27 yards from one another Within this were two circles each consisting of two double concentric rows, composed of the same number of stones, and arranged in a similar manner The grand circle had two entrances, consisting *of double rows of 100 upright stones each* placed at equal distances, and extending a mile in length, the one terminating in a double concentric circle of smaller diameter, and the other having a stone larger than the rest at the extremity Of this vast structure few traces now remain, the stones having been broken down and used in the construction of the houses of the village, and in repairing the roads Many barrows and tumuli, together with Druidical stones, are in the neighbourhood, and a most remarkable one is that called SILBURY HILL which see —The parish includes the tythings of Beckhampton and East and West Kennet Acres, 4 511 Real property, £6,717 Pop, 725 Houses, 153 The manor was given, in the time of Henry I, to the abbey of Boscherville in Normandy, passed first to Winchester college, Oxford, next to the collegiate church of Fotheringhay in Northamptonshire, and went, at the dissolution, to Sir William Sharington Avebury house is the manor house The living is a vicarage, united till 1965 to the vic of Winterbourne Monkton, in the diocese of

Salisbury Value, £250 * Patron, the Lord Chancellor The church is an ancient structure of stone and flint, with some Norman features, but much altered by modern repairs, and has a curious Norman font Charities £10

AVECOTE See SHUTTINGTON

AVELAND, a wapentake in the parts of Kesteven, Lincoln It contains the parish of Aslackby and twenty two other parishes Acres 47,012 Pop. in 1851, 10,782, in 1861, 11,868 Houses, 2,431

AVELEY, a village and a parish in Orsett district, Essex. The village stands adjacent to the Purfleet station of the Tilbury railway, near the Thames, 7 miles SE of Romford It has a post office under Romford, and a fair on Easter Monday, and was formerly a market town. The parish comprises 2,934 acres of land, and 105 of water Real property, £5,944. Pop, 930 Houses, 195 The property is not much divided. The living is a vicarage in the diocese of Rochester Value, £266 * Patron, the Bishop. The church is very old There are an Independent chapel and a national school

AVEN See AVON

AVENBURY, a parish in Bromyard district, Hereford, on the river Frome, 1½ mile SSE of Bromyard, and 7½ E of Dinmore r station It includes a detached tract, situated near Bridenbury and its post town is Bromyard under Worcester Acres, 3,233 Real property, £4,155 Pop, 371 Houses 74 The property is divided among a few Limestone occurs The living is a vicarage in the diocese of Hereford. Value, £105 * Patron, John Freeman, Esq The church is good There was anciently a small priory

AVENING a parish in Stroud district, Gloucester, 3½ miles S of Brimscombe r station, and 6 SSE of Stroud It lies within the parliamentary borough of Stroud, has a post office under that town, and includes the hamlets of Aston, Forest Green, Freeholds, West End, Bell Street, and Windsors Edge, and part of the chapelry of Nailsworth Acres, 4,425 Real property, £5,443 Pop, 2,070 Houses, 479 The manor belonged anciently to the nunnery of Caen in Normandy, and passed to the Shepheards A large tumulus, known as the Longstone, and supposed to be the sepulchre of a Danish chief, occurs in a field near Gatcombe Park, and there are several barrows in which human skeletons have been found A small manufacture of woollen cloth is carried on The living is a rectory in the diocese of Gloucester and Bristol Value, £769 * Patron, the Hon L H Harman The church is thought to have been erected by an abbess of Caen The p curacies of Nailsworth and Inchbrook are separate charges There are three dissenting chapels, a school with £22 a year from endowment, and other charities £9

AVENIS, a tything in Bisley parish, Gloucester, 4½ miles E of Stroud

AVENUE (THE), a railway station in Northumberland, on the Morpeth and Tynemouth railway, between Hartley junction and Whitley It serves for Seaton Sluice and Delaval Hall

AVERHAM a township and a parish in Southwell district, Notts The township lies at the confluence of the Greet river with the Trent adjacent to the Great Northern railway 2 miles W by N of Newark. Real property, £4,049 Pop., 175 Houses, 36 The parish includes also the township of Staythorpe, and its post town is Newark Acres, 2,646 Real property, £5,299 Pop, 237 Houses, 48 The property is divided among a few The manor belonged to Sir William Sutton, who is commemorated by a curious monument in the church Averham Hall is the parsonage. The living is a rectory, united with the rectory of Kelham, in the diocese of Lincoln Value, £1,135 * Patron, J H M Sutton, Esq The church is good. The monument to Sir William Sutton records that he had sixteen children, one half of whom

> "Ushered to heaven their father, and the other
> Remained behind him to attend their mother

AVETON GIFFORD a village and a parish in Kingsbridge district Devon The village stands on the river Avon, 3½ miles NW of Kingsbridge, and 7½ S of Kingsbridge Road r station It has a post office under Ivybridge, and was anciently a market town The parish comprises 3,052 acres of land, and 130 of water Real property, £5,909 Pop, 839 Houses, 178. The property is much divided The manor belonged formerly to the family of Gifford The living is a rectory in the diocese of Exeter Value, £667 Patron, the Rev W P Pitman The church is early English and cruciform, with central tower, one of the finest old churches in South Devon, but is in indifferent condition There are chapels for Baptists, Methodists, and Bible Christians, good national schools, and charities £7

AVILLE, a hamlet in Dunster parish, Somerset Pop, 17

AVINGHAM See OVINGHAM

AVINGTON, a parish in Hungerford district, Berks, on the Kennet river, the Kennet and Avon canal, and the Newbury branch of the Great Western railway, 2½ miles E of Hungerford. Post town, Hungerford Acres, 1,143 Real property, £1 285 Pop, 104 Houses, 18. The property is not much divided. The living is a rectory in the diocese of Oxford Value, £300 * Patron Sir R Burdett, Bart The church is an interesting specimen of Norman architecture with two early English windows, and a small early English spire bell turret The chancel is separated from the nave by an arch, richly ornamented with zigzag moulding and a great variety of grotesque heads, which has so settled as to look almost like two arches and springs from enriching piers leaning outwards The font also is Norman, of a circular form, and adorned with rudely sculptured figures. The church was repaired in 1849 The parsonage stands adjacent and is picturesque

AVINGTON, a parish in Winchester district, Hants, on the river Itching, 3 miles E of the Southwestern railway, and 5 NE of Winchester Post town, Itchen Abbots under Winchester Acres, 1,794 Real property, £1,833 Pop, 162 Houses, 33. The manor belonged anciently to the Crown, was given, in 961, by King Edgar, to the monastery of St Swithin at Winchester passed, at the dissolution, to the Clerks of Mitcheldever, and went, in the reign of Elizabeth, to the family of Bruges or Brydges, who afterwards became Dukes of Chandos and Buckingham. The infamous Countess of Shrewsbury who married into this family, was often visited here by Charles II The present house is a modern brick structure, on the site of the ancient mansion The park lies in a sequestered valley, nearly surrounded with high downs, is well wooded and measures about 3 miles in circuit The living is a rectory in the diocese of Winchester Value, £205 * Patron, the Bishop of Winchester The church stands in the park, and is modern Charities, £20

AVISFORD, a hundred in the rape of Arundel, Sussex It contains the parish of Barnham, and eleven other parishes. Acres, 16,258 Pop in 1851, 3,120 Houses, 563 Avisford House, the seat of the Houston family, is 4½ miles W of Arundel

AVON, an ancient British word, signifying "stream or "river," and specially applied to a stream of easy and gentle course It is used both as a complete name and as a prefix, and it occurs in the hydrographical nomenclature of all the divisions of the United Kingdom The closest form of spelling it perhaps would be Abhuin, but the various forms of Avon, Aven, Afon, Alen, Awin, Owen, Awn, Aun, and Aan, are used

AVON (THE), a river of Monmouth. It rises 1½ mile E of Nantyglo, and runs about 16 miles south southeastward, past Pontypool, to the Usk at Caerleon Most of its valley is traversed by one of the Monmouth railways, and part, by the Brecon and Monmouth canal It is sometimes called the Avon Llwyd, and sometimes the Torryden

AVON (THE), a river of Glamorgan It rises near the sources of the Taff, 3 miles SE of Aberpergwm, and runs about 15 miles south westward to the British channel at Aberavon

AVON (THE), a river of Devon It rises in Dartmoor forest, 6 miles WSW of Ashburton, and runs, in a gen easterly curve, with prevailing direction to the S, about 20 miles, past Diptford and Aveton Gifford to the English channel at Bigbury bay

AVON (THE), or EAST AVON, a river of Wilts and Hants It rises 2¾ miles E of Devizes, runs about 6½ miles south-eastward, to Upavon, and goes thence about 41½ miles southward, past Amesbury, Salisbury, and Fordingbridge, to the English channel at Christchurch It is navigable to Salisbury Its chief affluent is the Stour Its waters abound with small delicate loach.

AVON (THE), or LOWER AVON, a river of Gloucester, Wilts, and Somerset. It rises near the sources of the Thames, in the vicinity of Tetbury, on the SE border of Gloucester, goes southward into Wilts, past Malmesbury, Chippenham, and Melksham, to within 1¾ mile of Trowbridge, strikes westward there 4 miles, past Bradford, to the boundary with Somerset, goes northward 4½ miles along or near that boundary, and proceeds then westward and west north westward, past Bath to Keynsham, and along the boundary with Gloucester, past Bristol, to the Bristol channel at King's Road. Its length of course is about 80 miles, and its bed is chiefly a deep channel, in many places through very rich and picturesque valleys. It is navigable to Bath, and is connected thence eastward, past Bradford, Semington, Devizes, Tottenham Park, Hungerford, and Newbury, to Midgham, by the Kennet and Avon canal, with the Thames A lighthouse at its mouth, in the Bristol channel, was constructed in 1840, is 70 feet high, and shows a fixed light visible at the distance of 13 miles.

AVON (THE), or MIDDLE AVON, a river of Gloucester It rises on the Cotswolds, SE of Alderley, and runs about 15 miles north westward, past Wootton under Edge, to the estuary of the Severn in the vicinity of Berkeley

AVON (THE), or UPPER AVON, a river of Northampton, Leicester, Warwick, Worcester, and Gloucester It rises at Avon Well, near Naseby in Northampton, runs 8 miles west south westward, along the boundary with Leicester, goes south westward, nearly through the centre of Warwickshire, past Rugby, Warwick, and Stratford on-Avon, and proceeds in the same direction, on the boundary with Gloucester, across the S of Worcester, and into the NW corner of Gloucester, past Evesham and Pershore, to a confluence with the Severn at Tewkesbury Its length of course is about 96 miles Its channel, in many parts, as at Warwick and Stratford, is picturesque, and in other parts, through long reaches, lies along rich low country Its chief tributaries are the Alne, the Leame, the Stour, the Sow, and the Swift It is navigable for barges to Stratford, and is connected thence, by a branch canal, with the Worcester and Birmingham canal

AVON, an extra parochial tract in Chippenham district, Wilts, on the river Avon, adjacent to the Great Western railway, 3¼ miles NE of Chippenham Acres, 156 Pop, 20 Houses, 3

AVON, a tything in Sopley parish, Hants, on the river Avon, 4½ miles N by W of Christchurch Pop, 207

AVON a hamlet in the parish of Stratford under the Castle Wilts 2 miles NW of Salisbury Pop, 23.

AVON, a tything in Christian Malford parish, Wilts, 3¼ miles NE of Chippenham Pop, 76

AVON DASSET a parish in the district of Banbury and county of Warwick, 2 miles SW of Fenny Compton r station, and 6½ NNW of Banbury It has a post office under Banbury Acres, 1,530 Real property, £3,038. Pop, 280 Houses, 57 The living is a rectory in the dio of Worcester Value, £366 * Patron the Rev R G Jeston The church was rebuilt in 1869

AVONMOUTH, a new sea port in the SW of Gloucester, at the mouth of the river Avon and at the terminus of the Bristol Port and Pier railway, 5¼ miles NW by W of Clifton The railway and the pier were opened in 1865, and a dock 1,400 feet long and 85 wide, was being constructed in 1869 The port is to accommodate such large vessels as cannot readily go up the Avon to Bristol

AVONMOUTH, a hamlet in Thurlestone parish, Devon on the river Avon 4½ miles W of Kingsbridge

AVON (NETHER) See NETHER AVON

AVON WEN, a railway station in the Lleyn peninsula, Carnarvon 4 miles NE by E of Pwllheli

AWBRIDGE, a hamlet in Mitchelmersh parish, Hants, 2½ miles NW of Romsey It has a post office under Romsey Pop, 345

AWBURN See AUBURN

AWFOLD See ALFOLD

AWKERINGTON See ALKERTON

AWKLEY See AUCKLEY

AWLISCOMBE a village and a parish in Honiton district, Devon The village stands near the river Otter and near the Yeovil and Exeter railway, 2 miles WNW of Honiton It has a post-office under Honiton, and was formerly a market town The parish comprises 2,569 acres Real property, £4,022 Pop, 579 Houses, 125 The property is much subdivided. The manor was given, in 1491, by Thomas Calwoodley, to the corporation of Exeter, but comprised then only 203½ acres The living is a vicarage in the diocese of Exeter Value, £213 * Patron, the Duke of Bedford. The church is a neat Gothic edifice, mostly rebuilt in 1846, consists of nave, chancel, and aisles, and has a beautiful carved stone screen, and a tower There are a Unitarian chapel, and charities £10 Thomas Charde, the last abbot of Ford, was a native

AWNBY See HOLYWELL WITH AWNBY

AWRE, a tything and a parish in the district of Westbury on Severn, Gloucester The tything lies on the river Severn, and on the South Wales railway, 2 miles SE of Newnham, and has a post office under Newnham, and a r station The parish includes also Bledisloe, Hagloe, Etloe, and Blakeney Acres, 6,115, of which 2,035 are water Real property, £10,888 Pop, 1,526 Houses, 287 The property is much subdivided Part of the land has been washed away by the Severn Iron pyrites occur The weaving of cloth is carried on The living is a vicarage in the diocese of Gloucester and Bristol Value £530 * The church is in good repair The vicarage of Blakeney is a separate charge Sternhold, one of the translators of the English metrical version of the Psalms, was a native

AWSWORTH, a chapelry in Nuthall parish, Notts, 3½ miles W of Bulwell r station, and 6 NW of Nottingham Post town, Bulwell under Nottingham Rated property, £900 Pop, 294 The property is subdivided Most of the inhabitants are colliers or stocking weavers The living is a p curacy in the diocese of Lincoln Value, £101 * Patron, the rector of Nuthall The church is modern There is a P Methodist chapel

AXBRIDGE a small town, a parish, a sub district, and a district, in Somerset The town stands near the river Axe, and near the Cheder valley and Yatton railway, at the NW end of the Mendips, 10 miles NW of Wells, and has a railway station It is an ancient place and Roman roads went from it to Portishead and Ilchester It consists chiefly of a tolerably neat street, running in a winding manner from east to west and is practically no more than a village The guild hall and market house stands at the east end and is a modern edifice, rebuilt at a cost of about £1,800 The parish church stands on an eminence near the market house, is a large, cruciform, early English structure, with a handsome tower, and contains old monuments to the family of Prowse The town has a post office‡ under Weston super Mare, two banking offices, and a chief inn, and is a polling place, and a seat of petty sessions Markets are held on Saturdays, and fairs, on 3 Feb, 25 March, and 2d Tues. of Oct Axbridge was formerly a borough by prescription and sent members to parliament during the reigns of the first three Edwards, but was afterwards excused on the ground of poverty, and it still is governed under charter from Queen Elizabeth, by a mayor a bailiff, and ten aldermen A tract adjacent to it was so improved by drainage of the Axe, about the year 1800, at a cost of £70,000, that land which previously was worth only about 2s 6d. yearly per acre, is now rented at £5 and £6 —The parish comprises 540 acres Real property, £2,625 Pop, 799 Houses 173 The living is a rectory in the diocese of Bath and

Wells Value, £158.* Patron, the Bishop of Bath and Wells. There are chapels for Wesleyans and Plymouth Brethren, and charities £101

The sub district contains the parishes of Axbridge, Christon, Loxton, Compton Bishop, Winscombe, Rowberrow, Shipham, Cheddar, and Nyland Acres, 18,297 Pop, 5,856 Houses, 1 234 —The district comprehends also the sub district of Wedmore, containing the parishes of Wedmore, Mark, Chapel Allerton, Weare, Badgworth, and Biddisham, the sub district of Burnham, containing the parishes of Burnham, East Brent, South Brent, Berrow, Brean, Lympsham, and Bleadon, the sub district of Banwell, containing the parishes of Banwell, Worle, Uphill, Hutton, Locking, Weston super-Mare, Kewstoke, and Wick St. Lawrence, and the sub district of Blagdon, containing the parishes of Blagdon, Burrington, Churchill, Puxton, Congresbury, Wrington, and Butcombe, and the ville of Charterhouse on-Mendip Poor rates in 1866, £21,819 Pop in 1841, 32,204, in 1861, 36,106 Houses, 7,053 Marriages in 1866, 254, births, 1,071,—of which 45 were illegitimate, deaths 792,—of which 291 were at ages under 5 years, and 29 at ages above 85 years Marriages in the ten years 1851-60, 1,903, births, 9,637, deaths, 6,029 The places of worship in 1851 were 41 of the Church of England, with 13,148 sittings, 3 of Independents, with 730 s, 13 of Baptists, with 2,729 s, 2 of Quakers, with 600 s, 24 of Wesleyan Methodists, with 3,856 s, 2 of the Wesleyan Association, with 538 s., 7 of Bible Christians, with 820 s, and 1 undefined, with 30 attendants The schools were 36 public day schools, with 2,271 scholars, 67 private day schools, with 1,036 s, 54 Sunday schools, with 3,444 s, and 1 evening school for adults, with 12 s. The workhouse is in Compton Bishop

AXE (THE), a river of Somerset It rises on the Mendip hills, 2 miles NW of Wells, and runs about 20 miles north westward, past Axbridge, to the Bristol channel at Uphill bay It is a good trouting stream

AXE (THE), a river of Dorset and Devon It rises near Cheddington, in Dorset, runs south westward to Ford, where it enters Devon, and goes thence south south-westward, past Axminster, to the English channel at Axmouth. Its length of course is about 21 miles It is navigable for about 4 miles from its mouth

AXE EDGE HILL, a hill on the meeting point of Derby, Stafford, and Cheshire, at the sources of the rivers Dove, Wye, and Dane, 4 miles SW of Buxton It has a savage outline, rises to the height of 1,756 feet, and commands a view from Lincoln cathedral to Snowdon

AXEL. See AXHOLME

AXFORD, a tything in Ramsbury parish, Wilts, on the river Kennet, 3 miles ENE of Marlborough Pop, 362 Houses, 74

AXHOLME (ISLE OF), an insulated tract, between the rivers Trent, Idle, and Don, in the extreme NW of Lincolnshire It comprises the parishes of Althorpe, Belton, Crowle, Epworth, Haxey, Luddington, and Owston Its length, north north eastward, is 17 miles, and its mean breadth is about 4½ miles. The surface is low, flat, and naturally marshy A forest seems anciently to have covered it, and remains of trees are found a few feet below the surface The body of a woman, supposed to have lain from the time of Edward I, was found in a state of entire preservation in 17‑7, in a morass near Amcotts A castle of the Mowbrays, razed in 1174 stood at Haxey, then called Axel, and thence arose the name of Axelholm, now altered into Axholme

AXIUM See I[illegible]

AXMINSTER, a town, a sub-district a hundred, and a district, in Devon, and a parish partly also in Dorset The town stands on a rising ground, adjacent to the river Axe, above the influx of the Yarty, and contiguous to the Yeovil and Exeter railway 2½ miles E by N of Exeter It has a station on the railway, which serves also for Lyme Regis It dates from a period prior to the Roman invasion, it was called by the Anglo Saxons Brunenburgh, and gave that name to the battle field of Athelstan's famous victory, in 937, over the Danes, the Scotch, and the Irish, and it took the name of Axminster from a great church or minster, for seven priests, said to have been founded at it by Athelstan, in commemoration of his victory A party of the Royal troops were stationed in it in 1644, and fought an action, in its neighbourhood, with the Parliamentarians The Prince of Orange abode some days in it in 1689, on his way to London Its streets are irregularly formed, but spacious. A central place in it, called Trinity square was laid out after a great fire in 1834 The parish church is a large edifice of nave, aisles, and chancel, with massive central tower, consists variously of ancient parts and modern renovations, and perhaps includes some portion of Athelstan's minster, possesses a fine Norman doorway, and displays elsewhere the three styles of pointed architecture,—early English, decorated, and perpendicular, and contains two monumental effigies, a number of armorial shields, and a painting of the twelve apostles A new cemetery is about ½ mile distant on the Chard road There are chapels for Independents, Wesleyans and Roman Catholics, likewise a national school, and a free education charity The work house was erected in 1836, at a cost of £7,000, and afterwards enlarged at a further cost of £2,500. The town has a head post office,‡ two banking offices, and three chief inns, and is a seat of petty sessions, and of county courts Markets are held on Thursdays and Saturdays, and fairs, on the Tuesday after 25 April, the Tuesday after 24 June, and the Wednesday after 10 Oct A manufacture of famous carpets, rivalling those from Turkey, was begun in 1755, but came to an end in 1836, and silk throwing then was tried The environs of the town are pleasant, the views in the vicinity, extensive and beautiful and all the approaches, good and wide A tunnel on the road from Charmouth, opened in 1832 pierces one of the steepest hills between London and Exeter, and is about 70 yards long and of sufficient capacity to permit two of the largest stage waggons to pass each other A bill was introduced in 1860 for an Axminster, Seaton and Beer Junction railway, with bridge over the Axe

The parish includes the tythings of Abbey, Shapwick, Smallridge Trill, Uphay, West Water, Weycroft, and Wyke or Week, in Devon and the tything of Beerhall in Dorset Acres, 7,697 Real property, £16,208 Pop, 2,918 Houses, 547 The manor belonged to the Crown till after the Norman conquest was given by King John to Lord Brewer, passed to Lord Reginald de Mohun, who gave it to the abbey of Newenham, went, at the dissolution, to the Duke of Norfolk and was sold in the time of James I, to Lord Petre The rest of the landed property is subdivided. The living is a vicarage, united with the curacies of Kilmington and Membury, in the diocese of Exeter Value, £975 * Patrons, the Reps of Dean Conybeare Dr Buckland, the famous geologist, was a native —The sub district comprises 5 parishes. Acres, 19,219 Pop 5,537 Houses, 1,098 —The hundred contains thirteen parishes, and an extra parochial tract Acres, 43 699 Pop, 10,823 Houses, 2 273 — The district comprehends the sub district of Axminster, containing the parishes of Axminster, Kilmington, Combpyne Thorncombe, and Hawkchurch, the two last electorally in Dorset the sub-district of Lyme, containing the parishes of Uplyme, Charmouth, and Lyme Regis, the two last electorally in Dorset, the sub district of Chardstock, containing the parishes of Membury, Stockland, Dalwood, and Chardstock, the last electorally in Dorset and the sub district of Colyton, containing the parishes of Colyton, Shute Musbury Axmouth, and Seaton, and the extra parochial tract of Roosdown Acres, 61 738 Poor rates in 1866, £12,875 Pop in 1861, 19,758 Houses, 3 997 Marriages in 1866, 128, births, 605,—of which 31 were illegitimate, deaths, 427,—of which 119 were at ages under 5 years, and 17 at ages above 85 years Marriages in the ten years 1851-60, 1,370, births, 5,729, deaths, 3,921 The places of worship in 1851 were 20 of the Church of England, with 8,630 sittings, 8 of Independents, with 2,255 s 4 of Baptists with 900 s, 1 of Unitarians with 105 s, 7 of Wesleyan

Methodists, with 1,061 s, 3 of Bible Christians, with 170 s, and 2 of Roman Catholics, with 96 s The schools were 23 public day schools, with 1,397 scholars, 43 private day schools, with 884 s, 32 Sunday schools, with 2,551 s, and 2 evening schools for adults, with 21 s.

AXMOUTH, a village and a parish in Axminster district, Devon The village stands at the mouth of the river Axe, under Hawksdown hill, 6 miles SSW of Axminster It has a post office under Axminster, and is a coast guard station, and a station of the survey commenced in 1837 to detect the differences of level between the English and the British channels. A harbour here gave refuge, in ancient times, to vessels under stress of weather, was much improved in the early part of the 17th century, and now has piers for the moorage and discharge of vessels of 150 tons burden A range of cliffs extending hence east-north eastward to Lyme Regis has been remarkably subject to land slips, and commands magnificent views of nearly the whole coast of Devon and Dorset A great land slip occurred on the 25th of December 1839, destroying two cottages and 45 acres of fine arable land, and forming a chasm 300 feet or more broad, 150 feet deep, and ¾ of a mile long, and another, of much smaller extent, occurred on the 3d of February 1840 The parish comprises 4,533 acres of land, and 190 of water Real property, £5,631 Pop, 662. Houses, 126 The manor was given by Rivers, Earl of Devon, to the abbey of St Mary, Mountbarrow, in Normandy, passed, at the suppression of alien monasteries, to the abbey of Sion, went, at the final dissolution of monasteries, to Catherine, queen of Henry VIII, was granted, in 1552, to Walter Erle, Esq, passed from him to Sir W Yonge, was purchased in 1691, by R Hallett, Esq, and belongs now to that gentleman's descendant, W T Hallett, Esq, whose residence is a fine mansion, called Stedcombe House The living is a vicarage in the diocese of Exeter Value, £230 * Patron, W T Hallett, Esq The church consists of nave, chancel, and south porch, is early English and perpendicular, but has an Anglo Norman doorway and some wildly grotesque gurgoils, and contains monuments of the Erles and the Halletts.

AXTON, a township in Llanasa parish, Flint, 6½ miles ENE of Rhyddlan

AXTON, a hundred in the lathe of Sutton at Hone, Kent It contains the parish of Ash and sixteen other parishes. Acres, 34,139 Pop in 1851, 9,869 Houses, 1,852

AXWELL PARK, the seat of Sir W A Clavering, Bart on the north border of Durham, on the rivulet Derwent, a little above its influx to the Tyne, 3 miles S of Blaydon

AYCLIFFE, a village, a township, and a sub district in the district of Darlington, and a parish in the districts of Darlington and Stockton, Durham The village stands adjacent to the river Skerne, ¼ of a mile W of the York and Berwick railway, 5½ miles N of Darlington It has a station on the railway, and a post-office under Darlington It is an ancient place, belonged to the see of Lindisfarne, and was the meeting place of synods in 782 and 789 —The township bears the name of Great Aycliffe, and comprises 2,104 acres Real property, £8,131 Pop, 840 Houses, 185 Extensive lime quarries are worked —The sub district includes another township of the same parish, parts of two other parishes, and two entire parishes Acres, 27,745 Pop, 4,935 Houses, 1,043 —The parish includes the townships of Great Aycliffe and Brafferton, in the district of Darlington, and the townships of Preston le Skerne and Woodham, in the district of Stockton Acres, 10,858 Real property, £10,234 Pop, 1,458 Houses, 290 The property is divided among a few The living is a vicarage in the diocese of Durham Value £350 * Patrons, the Dean and Chapter of Durham The church is mixedly Norman and pointed, consists of nave, chancel, aisles, and porch, with a western tower 85 feet high, and is in good condition There are remains of two Saxon crosses in the churchyard There are chapels for Wesleyan and Primitive Methodists and charities £8

AYCLIFFE (SCHOOL), a township in Heighington parish, Durham, near the Clarence railway, 2 miles WNW of Aycliffe. Acres, 524 Pop, 25 Houses, 4

AYDON, a township in Corbridge parish, Northumberland, 2 miles NE of Corbridge, midway thence to the Roman wall Acres, 750 Pop, 78 Houses, 15 Lead ore and coal occur, and Roman remains have been found

AYDON CASTLE, a township in Corbridge parish, Northumberland, 1½ mile N of Corbridge Acres 393 Pop, 39 Houses, 5 A fortified house of the Aydon family was built here, in the time of Edward I, on the side of a ravine, and still stands well in a state of ruin It has the form of the letter H with a tower at the end of each of the four wings. The walls are very thick and one of the towers is upwards of 60 feet high

AYES WATER. See HAYS WATER.

AYLBURTON, a tything in Lydney parish, Gloucester, about a mile W of Lydney It has a post office under Lydney Pop, 604 Houses, 106 It forms a curacy, annexed to the vicarage of Lydney, and its church was rebuilt in 1857

AYLESBEAR, a village and a parish in St Thomas district, Devon The village stands on the eastern declivity of the bold range of hills, between the basins of the Otter and the Exe 3½ miles S by W of Whimple r station, and 8 E of Exeter It has a post office under Exeter, is a very straggling place and was anciently the inheritance of the Earls of Devon, and then bore the name of Earlesbear The parish includes also the tything of Newton Poppleford Acres, 2,948 Real property, £3,530 Pop, 1,079 Houses, 227 The property is divided among a few The living is a vicarage, in the diocese of Exeter Value, £210 Patron the Rev W H Carwithen. The church is an ancient edifice, of nave, chancel, north aisle, and western tower and contains a memorial window to Cecilia Yates and mural tablets to the Markers, the Stokes, and others The vicarage of Newton Poppleford is a separate benefice There is an Independent chapel

AYLESBURY, or AILESBURY, a town, a parish, a sub district, a hundred, and a district, in Bucks The town stands on a rising ground and on a small affluent of the river Tame, in the rich vale of Aylesbury, at railway termini, 16 miles SSE of Buckingham, and 38 by road, or 43½ by railway, NW of London One railway goes from it into junction with the Northwestern, another goes into junction with the Great Western, and another, 12½ miles long, the Aylesbury and Buckingham, authorised in Aug 1860, and opened in 1868, goes north north westward to the Buckinghamshire at Claydon A canal also, 6 miles long, rising 95 feet, with 16 locks goes eastward to the Grand Junction canal at Marsworth Aylesbury was a strongly fortified seat of the ancient Britons, and was maintained by them in independence till captured in 571, by Cuthwolf, brother of Ceawlin, king of the West Saxons, and it was then called Æglesberg or Elisberie It became a royal manor at the Conquest, was soon given to one of the followers of the court, belonged for ages to the Pickingtons, passed, in the time of Henry VIII, to Sir John Baldwin, chief justice of the common pleas, and was an important post of the parliamentarian forces in 1644 and 1645

The town is irregularly built, and consists of a spacious central, rectangular market place and diverging streets and thoroughfares The corn exchange and market house were built in 1865, at a cost of £10,000, and are in the Tudor style The county hall is a large handsome edifice of red brick The county gaol was built in 1847, contains 220 cells for male prisoners, 17 cells for female prisoners, and very ample accommodation for debtors and stands within an enclosure of 5 acres, entered by an arched way The work house was built in 1844, and is an edifice of red brick, in Tudor architecture The parish church is a cruciform structure, of successive ages from early English to the latest perpendicular, is surmounted at the centre by successively a low embattled tower a square turret, a short spire, and a cross 9 feet high, was restored by Scott in 1849 contains beautiful stained windows, and two canopied de corated tombs, and is so situated as to command a fine view, and be seen for many miles round. The church yard is extensive, and is laid out in walks, and planted with trees. The prebendal house, adjoining the church yard, occupies the site of an ancient monastery, was formerly the residence of the prebendaries of Aylesbury, and became the private property of the vicar, Archdeacon Bickersteth. The new county infirmary was erected in 1862, and has accommodation for 54 patients. There are chapels for Independents, Baptists, Methodists, and Quakers. A grammar school has an endowed income of £639, and other charities have £1,056.

The town has a head post office,‡ three banking offices, and four chief inns, and publishes three newspapers, two of them weekly, the other twice a week. Markets are held on Saturdays, and fairs on the Friday after 18 Jan., Palm Saturday, 8 May, 14 June, 25 Sept., and 12 Oct. Public conveyances run daily to Princes Risborough and to Thame. Lace making once flourished, but has greatly declined; straw plait making is prosperous; there is a silk factory, and about £22,000 worth of ducks are annually sent to London. Aylesbury is the seat of the assizes for the county, the principal place of the county elections, and the seat of the county quarter sessions. It was a borough, governed by a corporation under a charter of Mary dated 1554; but, from neglect and disuse of its privileges, it forfeited the charter in the time of Elizabeth. It sends two members to parliament, but, in 1804, in consequence of excessive corruption by bribery, the franchise was extended to the whole hundred of Aylesbury. The number of electors in 1868 was 1,329; and the amount of direct taxation in 1859 was £13,845. The town gives the titles of Earl and Marquis to the family of Bruce. The vale of Aylesbury is a fertile tract, described by Drayton as "lusty, firm and fat," affording pasturage to an extraordinary number of sheep, interesting to geologists for abundance of ammonites and other fossils, and bounded along the S and the N by chalk hills. Pop. of the town, returned with the parish, of the borough, the same as that of the hundred.

The parish includes the hamlet of Walton. Acres, 8,200. Real property, £19,694. Pop., 6,168. Houses, 1,313. The living is a vicarage in the diocese of Oxford. Value, £300.* Patron, the Bishop of Oxford. The vicarage of Walton is a separate charge.—The sub district contains five parishes. Acres, 11,239. Pop., 8,272. Houses, 1,715.—The hundred, which is also the borough, comprises the parishes of Aylesbury, Aston Clinton, Bierton with Broughton, Buckland, Cuddington, Haddenham, Halton, Hartwell, Hulcott, Stone, and Weston-Turville, and part of the parish of Dinton, in the district of Aylesbury; the parishes of Lee and Great Missenden, in the district of Amersham; and the parishes of Bledlow with Ridge, Ellesborough, Great Hampden, Little Hampden, Horsendon, Great Kimble, Little Kimble, Little Missenden, Monks Risborough, Princes Risborough, Stoke Mandeville, and Wendover, and part of the parish of Hitchenden, in the district of Wycombe. Acres, 71,069. Pop. in 1851, 26,794; in 1861, 27,090. Houses, 5,718.

The district of Aylesbury comprehends the sub district of Aylesbury, containing the parishes of Aylesbury, Hartwell, Stone, Aston Sandford, and Dinton; the sub district of Haddenham, containing the parishes of Haddenham, Cuddington, Chearsley, Nether Winchendon, Ashendon, Wotton Underwood, Grendon Underwood, Ludgershall, Upper Winchendon, and part of Waddesdon; the sub district of Aston Clinton, containing the parishes of Aston Clinton, Weston Turville, Halton, Hawridge, Cholesbury, Drayton Beauchamp, Buckland, Hulcott, Bierton with Broughton, and Wingrave with Rowsham; and the sub district of Waddesdon, containing the parishes of Aston Abbotts, Cublington, Creslow, Whitchurch, Hardwicke, Quarrendon, Fleet Marston, Quainton, Pitchcott, Oving, and part of Waddesdon. Acres, 73,364. Poor-rates in 1866, £15,993. Pop. in 1861, 23,600. Houses, 5,063. Marriages in 1866, 160; births, 802,—of which 65 were illegitimate; deaths, 490,—of which 147 were at ages under 5 years, and 16 were at ages above 83 years. Marriages in the ten years 1851-60, 1,601; births, 7,781; deaths, 5,026. The places of worship in 1851 were 35 of the Church of England, with 9,879 sittings; 2 of Independents, with 590 s.; 13 of Baptists, with 2,695 s.; 1 of Quakers, with 182 s.; 13 of Wesleyan Methodists, with 2,669 s.; 6 of Primitive Methodists, with 809 s.; 1 of Roman Catholics, with 120 s.; and 4 undefined, with 1,033 s. The schools were 22 public day schools, with 1,787 scholars; 19 private day schools, with 337 s.; 55 Sunday schools, with 4,096 s.; and 4 evening schools for adults, with 41 s.

AYLESBY, a parish in Caistor district, Lincoln; on the Wolds, 2¼ miles WSW of Great Coates r. station, and 4 W of Great Grimsby. Post town, Laceby, under Grimsby. Acres, 2,110. Real property, £2,851. Pop., 130. Houses, 26. The living is a p. curacy in the diocese of Lincoln. Value, £73. Patron, T. T. Drake, Esq.

AYLESFORD, a small town, a parish, a sub district, a district, and a lathe, in Kent. The town, the parish, and the sub district, are in the district of Malling. The town stands at the foot of a hill, on the right bank of the Medway, adjacent to the North Kent railway, 3 miles NNW of Maidstone; and it has a station on the railway, and a post office‡ under Maidstone. It dates from the times of the Saxons, and was then called Eaglesford. A battle was fought at it, in 455, between the British king Vortimer and the Saxon chiefs Hengist and Horsa, and terminated in favour of the Britons. The alleged grave of Horsa is shown in a heap of flint-stones, at Horsted, 2 miles to the N.; but is claimed also at Horsham and Horsted in Sussex. Victorious battles against the Danes also were fought in the vicinity, in 893 by Alfred, and in 1016 by Edmund Ironside. The town consists of one long street. Remains of a Norman keep, about 10 feet high, are in it; and a six arched bridge, of considerable antiquity, is adjacent on the river. A Carmelite priory was founded at it, in 1240, by Richard Lord Grey of Codnor; passed, at the dissolution, to Sir Thomas Wyatt of Allington; went, in the time of Elizabeth, to John Sedley of Southfleet; was sold, in the time of Charles I., to Sir Peter Rycaut; and came eventually to Heneage Finch, who was created Earl of Aylesford in 1714, and whose representatives still possess it. The existing edifice retains much of the ancient buildings, but includes additions and alterations, from the 17th century downward, by its successive occupants. The parish church crowns an abrupt rising ground at the end of the town, is principally Norman, with a square tower at the west end, and contains a brass of 1426, monuments of the Colepeppers, the Sedleys, and the Rycauts, and a costly one to Sir John Banks, who died in 1699. There are a neat Wesleyan chapel, a literary institution, national schools, an alms-house hospital with £135 a-year, restored in 1841, and other charities £43. An extensive stone ware pottery and a large paper mill are on the river a short way to the E. A remarkable Druidical monument, called KIT'S COTTY HOUSE (which see) is on the hill side, above the town. Cosenton, the seat of a family of its own name, from the time of King John till that of Henry VIII., but now a farm house, is on the same hill side. Sir Charles Sedley, the poet, and Sir Paul Rycaut, the oriental traveller, were natives of Aylesford.

The parish comprises 4,391 acres. Real property, £10,104. Pop., 2,057. Houses, 327. The property is subdivided. The living is a vicarage in the diocese of Rochester. Value, £531.* Patrons, the Dean and Chapter of Rochester.—The sub district contains ten parishes. Acres, 19,208. Pop., 8,036. Houses, 1,437.—The district of Aylesford lies N of Malling district, and bears the name of North Aylesford. It consists of the sub district of Northfleet, containing the parishes of Northfleet, Ifield, Nursted, Meopham, Luddesdown, Cobham, Denton, Chalk, and Shorne and Merston; and the sub district of Strood, containing the parishes of Strood, Higham, Cliffe at Hoo, Frindsbury, Cuxtone, and Halling. Acres, 41,732. Poor rates, £11,138. Pop. in 1851, 14,676; in 1861, 19,121. Houses, 3,579. Mar riages, 206, births 643,—of which 27 were illegitimate, deaths, 327,—of which 131 were at ages under 5 years, and 6 at ages above 85 years. Marriages in the ten years 1851-60, 1,868, births, 6,390, deaths, 3,648 The places of worship in 1851 were 14 of the Church of England, with 4,484 sittings, 3 of Independents, with 744 s, 3 of Baptists, with 571 s, 3 of Wesleyan Methodists, with 514 s 2 of Primitive Methodists, with 220 s., and 1 of the Wesleyan Methodist Association, with 55 s The schools were 12 public day schools, with 1,277 scholars, 37 private day schools, with 857 s., and 24 Sunday schools, with 1,933 s The workhouse is in Strood —The lathe of Aylesford extends from the Thames to Sussex, is from 7½ to 23 miles bread, and contains the hundreds of Brenchley and Horsemonden, Chatham and Gillingham, Eyhorne, Hadlow, Hoo, Larkfield, Littlefield, Maidstone, Shamwell, Toltingtrough, Lowey Tunbridge, Twyford, Washlingstone, West Malling, and Wrotham Acres, 261,743 Pop in 1851, 121,109, in 1861, 138,752 Houses, 24,897

AYLESHAM See HAILSHAM

AYLESTONE, a village and a parish in Elaby district, Leicester The village stands at the junction of the Union canal with the river Soar, near the Fosse way 1½ mile WNW of Wigston r station, and 2½ S by W of Leicester Pop, 392 Houses, 90 The parish includes also the township of Glen Parva and the chapelry of Lubbesthorpe, and its post town is Leicester Acres, 3,850 Real property, £5,444 Pop, 575 Houses, 132 The property is not much divided Aylestone Hall was formerly the seat of the Rutland family, and is an ancient mansion recently restored The living is a rectory in the diocese of Peterborough Value, £845 * Patron, the Duke of Rutland The church is a substantial structure, with tower and lofty spire A neat national school, in the Gothic style, was recently built

AYLMERTON, a parish in Erpingham district, Norfolk near the coast, 3 miles WSW of Cromer, and 18 E of Walsingham r station Post town, Cromer under Norwich Acres, 1,679 Real property, £1,484 Pop., 250 Houses, 66 The property is divided among a few Beacon Hill commands a fine prospect The living is a rectory, united with the rectory of Runton, in the diocese of Norwich Value, £500 Patron, John Ketton, Esq The church is later English, and was restored in 1865

AYLSHAM, a small town, a parish, and a district, in Norfolk. The town stands on the river Bure amid one of the most pleasant tracts in the county, 12 miles N by W of Norwich r station It has a post office† under Norwich, a good inn, a police station, and a corn exchange, is a seat of petty sessions and county courts, had a county bridewell, now converted into dwelling houses, and conducts some commerce by barges on the Bure. A manufacture of linen, known as Aylsham web was carried on in the times of Edward II and Edward III, and a manufacture of woollen fabrics sprung up at a later period, but both have disappeared The chief employments now are in the corn trade, the timber trade, and country business A weekly market is held on Tuesday, and fairs, on 23 March and the last Tuesday of Sept The parish church is decorated English, said to have been built by John of Gaunt consists of nave, chancel and transepts, with a square tower, and spire, and contains an ancient rood screen a carved font, and numerous brasses The churchyard contains the grave of Humphrey Repton, the landscape gardener, who died in 1818 There are chapels for Baptists, Wesleyans, and Primitive Methodists, a free school, and charities £25 The interesting seat of Blickling Hall is in the vicinity, within the contiguous parish of Blickling. Pop of the town, 2 388 Houses, 524

The parish comprises 4,308 acres Real property, £15 153 Pop, 2,623 Houses, 572 The property is much subdivided The living is a vicarage in the diocese of Norwich Value, £125.* Patrons, the Dean and Chapter of Canterbury —The district comprehends the sub district of Buxton, containing the parishes of Aylsham, Buxton, Ingworth, Erpingham, Thwaite, Alby Colby, Banningham, Tuttington, Skeyton, Swanton Abbot, Scottow, Coltishall, Belaugh, Hautbois Magna, Hautbois Parva, Lammas, Oxnead, Burgh, Brampton, Marsham, Hevingham, and Stratton Strawless, and the sub district of Reynsford, containing the parishes of Thurning, Hindolveston, Wood Norton, Foulsham, Themelthorpe, Guestwick, Wood Dalling, Hackford-by Reepham, Whitwell, Reepham, Kerdiston, Sall, Cawston, Heydon, Corpusty, Saxthorpe, Irmingland, Oulton, Itteringham, Mannington, Barningham Parva, Wickmere, Wolterton Calthorpe, and Blickling Acres, 68,123. Poor rates in 1866, £9,887 Pop in 1861, 19,052 Houses, 4,297 Marriages in 1866, 112 births, 563,—of which 69 were illegitimate, deaths, 327,—of which 121 were at ages under 5 years, and 26 were at ages above 85 years. Marriages in the ten years 1851-60, 1,342 births, 6,256 deaths, 4 113 The places of worship in 1851 were 42 of the Church of England, with 8,803 sittings, 4 of Independents, with 938 s, 5 of Baptists, with 1,260 s, 1 of Quakers, with 180 s, 14 of Wesleyan Methodists with 2 430 s, 16 of Primitive Methodists, with 1,609 s, and 10 of Wesleyan Reformers, with 1,168 s The schools were 24 public day schools, with 1,411 scholars, 41 private day schools, with 1,001 s, 51 Sunday schools, with 2 192 s, and 3 evening schools for adults, with 53 s The work house is in Aylsham

AYLTON, a parish in Ledbury district, Hereford, 1¾ mile SE of Ashperton r station and 3½ W of Ledbury Post town, Ledbury Acres, 825 Real property, £1,174 Pop, 89 Houses, 21 The property is subdivided The living is a rectory in the diocese of Hereford. Value, £149 * Patron, the Earl of Oxford The church needs repair

AYLWORTH, a hamlet in Naunton parish, Gloucester, near the Cotswolds, 6½ miles SW of Stow

AYMESTREY, a township and a parish in Leominster district, Hereford The township lies on the river Lug, 3½ miles NNW of Kingsland r station, and 7 NW of Leominster The village in it is pleasant, the neighbouring banks of the Lug are singularly rich and beautiful, and a circumjacent limestone formation is famous for fossils picked up either in quarries or on the public road Real property, £1 893 The parish includes also the townships of Leinthall Earls, Nether Lye, Over Lye, Yatton, Shirley, and Covenhope or Conhope, and its post-town is Kingsland, Herefordshire Acres, 6,349 Real property, with Elton and Leinthall Starkes, £8,324 Pop, 855 Houses, 178 The property is much subdivided Traces of Roman and British camps are near the village The living is a vicarage in the diocese of Hereford Value, £249 * Patron, the Lord Chancellor The church is good The p curacy of Leinthall Earls is a separate charge Two endowed schools, an almshouse, and other charities have aggregately an income of £50

AYNHO, a village and a parish in Brackley district, Northampton The village stands on the Roman Portway, near the Oxford and Birmingham railway the Oxford canal, and the river Cherwell, 6 miles SE by S of Banbury, and it has a station on the railway, and a post-office under Banbury It was once a market town, and it had anciently an hospital for the accommodation of travellers, founded by the Fitz Richards in the time of Henry II, and eventually given to Magdalene college, Oxford A spring, called the Town well, runs from it to the Cherwell, and traces exist at its E end of the Roman Portway The parish comprises 2,330 acres Real property, £4,724 Pop, 505 Houses, 131 The property is not much divided Aynho Park, adjacent to the village, the seat of W C Cartwright, Esq is a prominent feature, and contains a good collection of pictures. The living is a rectory in the diocese of Peterborough Value, £500 * Patron, W C Cartwright, Esq The church was restored in 1861 There are an endowed school with £20 a year, a national school and charities £170 Robert Wild, a poet and satirist was rector in the time of the Commonwealth, and ejected from it in 1662 Shakerley Marmion the dramatist, and Sir Ralph Winwood, the statesman, were natives

AYOTT ST LAWRENCE, or AYOTT MAGNA a parish in Hatfield district, Herts, near the river Marin, 2¾ miles WNW of Welwyn r station Post town, Welwyn Acres, 747 Real property, £1,568 Pop., 122 Houses, 23 The property is not much divided. The manor belonged anciently to King Harold, and belongs now to the Lydes of Ayott Park The living is a rectory in the diocese of Rochester Value, £180 * Patron, Lionel Lyde, Esq The church was rebuilt, in 1778, at the expense of Sir Lionel Lyde, in the Grecian style, after a design by Revett The previous church still stands as a ruin, and contains some curious monuments.

AYOTT-ST PETER, or AYOTT PARVA, a parish in Hatfield district Herts, 2 miles SW of Welwyn r station It has a post office under Welwyn Acres, 1,100 Real property, £1,558 Pop, 234 Houses, 53 The property is not much divided The living is a rectory in the diocese of Rochester Value £250 * Patron, Rev E Prodgers The church was rebuilt in 1863

AYRE (POINT OF), the northern extremity of the Isle of Man A lighthouse stands on it, erected in 1818, with lanthern 106 feet above high water, showing a revolving two-minute light, alternately bright and red, visible at the distance of 15 miles The Whitestone and Strana-kiley sands are adjacent

AYRE (POINT OF), a headland at the W side of the mouth of the estuary of the Dee, in Flint A lighthouse adjoins it, erected on piles in 1844, with lanthern 42 feet high, showing a fixed bright and red light, visible at the distance of 9 miles.

AYRON, or AERON (THE), a river of Cardigan It rises on the Ayron hills, near the middle of the county, 6 miles NW of Tregaron, and makes a circuitous course, of about 17 miles southward, south westward, and north westward to Cardigan bay at Aberayron

AYSFORD See ALMSFORD

AYSGARTH, a township and a parish in Askrigg district, N R. Yorkshire The township lies on the river Ure, at the junction of Wensley dale and Bishopdale, 4 miles ESE of Askrigg, and 7¼ WSW of Leyburn r station It has a post office under Bedale Acres, 1,174 Real property, £1,513 Pop, 283 Houses, 64 A remarkably fine fall of the Ure, called Aysgarth force, is adjacent The river flows in a narrow channel over a rugged bed of limestone, between picturesquely wooded banks, and makes a series of cascades which are variously grand or beautiful according to the fluctuations of its volume. "In floods it is a great, a mighty river, bursting with a prodigious effect through magnificent rocks, but in droughts, only a few gentle rills, the tears of the Naiads, run over the ledges of limestone " The parish church, an ancient structure, restored in 1536, by the last abbot of Jervaux, and containing a splendid carved wooden screen which belonged to Jervaux abbey, occupies a fine picturesque site above the rapids A bridge of a single arch, 71 feet in span, stands immediately above the falls, and commands a fine view of the church and the river Another waterfall, called Foss Gill, occurs in Bishopdale The parish is identical, in extent and statistics with the district. See ASKRIGG Real property, £48,154 The property is much subdivided The living is a vicarage in the diocese of Ripon Value, £137 Patron, Trinity college, Cambridge The p curacies of Askrigg, Hawes, Stalling Busk, and Hardrow with Lunds, are separate charges An endowed school has £65, and other charities £107

AYSLEBEY See AISLABY, Yorkshire

AYSTON a parish in Uppingham district Rutland, 1 mile NNW of Uppingham, and 3 miles SSW of Manton r station. Post town, Uppingham Acres, 897 Real property, £1,745 Pop, 97 Houses, 21 Ayston House is the seat of G Fludyer, Esq The living is a rectory in the diocese of Peterborough Value, £183 * Patron, G Fludyer, Esq The church is good

AYTHORP ROOTHING See ROOTHING AYTHORP

AYTON, two townships and a parish in Stokesley district, N R Yorkshire The townships are distinguished from each other as Great and Little Great Ayton lies on the river Leven, and on the Guisbrough railway, 3 miles NE of Stokesley, includes the hamlet of Langbaurgh, and has a post office under Northallerton, and a r station Acres, 3,146 Real property, £5,778 Pop, 1,450 Houses, 320 Little Ayton lies contiguous on the E, also on the river Leven, and includes the hamlet of Tunstall Acres, 1,331 Real property, £1,100 Pop, 78 Houses, 14 The parish contains likewise the township of Nunthorpe. Acres, 5,990 Real property £8,727 Pop, 1,688 Houses, 361 The property is subdivided Freestone is quarried, and appearances of iron ore exist. An agricultural school and model farm were established at Ayton House by T Richardson Some of the inhabitants are employed in linen factories. The living is a vicarage in the diocese of York Value, £82 Patron, the Rev G Marwood The church is tolerable The p curacy of Nunthorpe is a separate charge There are chapels for Independents, Methodists, and Quakers A charity school, with £10 a year, was founded, under Rose Topping hill, in 1704, by Michael Postgate, and here the celebrated navigator Captain Cook, received part of his education Other charities have £17

AYTON (EAST) a township in Seamer parish N R Yorkshire, near the river Derwent, 1¼ mile W of Seamer r station, and 4 SW of Scarborough It has a post-office under York Acres, 2,610 Real property, £2,772 Pop, 406 Houses, 78 Ironstone occurs and is worked There are a chapel of ease and a Primitive Methodist chapel The insurrection of 1548 began here

AYTON (GREAT and LITTLE) See AYTON

AYTON (WEST), a township in Hutton Bushell parish, N R Yorkshire, on a tributary of the Derwent river, 3½ miles W of Seamer r station, and 5 WSW of Scarborough Acres 2,160 Real property, £2 704 Pop., 385 Houses, 78 Remains exist of an ancient castle which belonged to the Evers or Eures and the Cliffords

AYTROP ROOTHING See ROOTHING AYTHORP

AZERBY See ASENBY

AZERLEY, or COZENLEY, a township in Kirkby Malzeard parish, W R Yorkshire, on a head stream of the river Ure, 4¼ miles NW of Ripon It includes the hamlets of Galphay and Mickley Acres, 3 919 Real property, £3,901 Pop, 606 Houses, 147

B

BABBICOMBE, a chapelry in St Marychurch parish, Devon, on the coast, 1¼ mile NE of Torquay It has a post office under Torquay, and an inn. It was recently a sequestered place, but has now a well built and rapidly increasing village The scenery is very fine The living is a vicarage The church is a splendid edifice, built in 1863

BABCARY, a parish in Langport district, Somerset near the river Parret, 3¾ miles ENE of Ilchester r station It includes the hamlets of Higher Farrington,

Lower Farrington, and Stort, and its post town is Charlton Mackerel under Taunton Acres, 2,393 Real property, £3,923 Pop, 426 Houses, 94 The property is much divided The living is a rectory in the diocese of Bath and Wells Value, £450 * Patron, Mrs Burke The church is good, and there is a Wesleyan chapel

BABERGH, a hundred in the SW of Suffolk. It adjoins Essex, includes Sudbury, and contains thirty parishes and parts of two others Acres, 73,425 Pop. in 1851, 24 401, in 1861, 24,198 Houses, 5,430

BABINGLEY, or BABUTCHLEY, a parish in Freebridge Lynn district, Norfolk, on a rivulet of its own name, near Lynn Deeps, 1½ mile S of Wolferton r station Post town, Castle Rising under Lynn Acres, 849 Real property £924 Pop, 67 Houses, 12 The first Christian church in East Anglia was erected here, and several hills in the neighbourhood are called Christian Hills The living is a rectory, annexed to the rectory of Sandringham, in the diocese of Norwich The church has a nave and a tower, but its chancel is ruined

BABINGTON, a parish in Frome district, Somerset, 5 miles WNW of Frome r station Post town, Mells under Frome Acres 607 Real property, £1,448 Pop, 129 Houses, 25 The property is divided among a few Babington House is the seat of W F Knatchbull The living is a rectory in the diocese of Bath and Wells. Value, £170 Patron, the Rev T R Jolliffe The church is good, and there are an endowed school with £15, and other charities with £10

BABLOCK HYTHE, a ferry on the river Isis, 4 miles by road, and 7½ by river, WSW of Oxford Arnold sings it as "crossing the stripling Thames at Bablock Hythe"

BABRAHAM, anciently BADBURHAM, a village and a parish in Linton district, Cambridge The village stands on an affluent of the river Cam, near the Gogmagog hills 2½ miles ENE of Whittlesford r station, and 6½ SE of Cambridge. It has a post office under Cambridge, and was formerly a market town The parish comprises 2,350 acres Real property, £2,700 Pop, 304 Houses, 67 The manor belonged to Algar, Earl of Mercia, passed, about the year 1576, into the possession of Sir Horatio Palavicini a Genoese, and now belongs to H J Adeane, Esq Sir H Palavicini collected the pope's taxes in England during the reign of Mary, converted them to his own use, and became Protestant, on the accession of Elizabeth, became a favourite of that queen, one of her negotiators in Germany, and a commander of one of her ships against the Spanish armada, and died at his seat in Babraham, and his widow was married to Sir Oliver Cromwell, the uncle of the Protector A curious epitaph on him is given in "Lord Orford's Anecdotes of Painting" The living is a vicarage in the diocese of Ely Value, £106 Patron, H J Adeane, Esq An almshouse and a free school, with income of £134, were founded in 1723 by Lebinus Bush and Judith Bennet, and a monument to her is in the church

BALTHORPE See MENTHORPE WITH BOWTHORPE

BABURGH See BAWBURGH

BABURGHLEY See BABINGLEY

BABWORTH, a village and a parish in East Retford district, Notts The village stands near the Chesterfield canal and the Great Northern railway, 1½ mile W of East Retford, and has a post office under Retford The parish includes also the hamlets of Great and Little Morton and Morton Grange, and part of the hamlet of Ranby Acres, 6,165 Real property, £7 205 Pop, 701 Houses, 133 The property is divided among a few Babworth Hall is the seat of the Simpson family, and stands in very fine grounds, which were laid out by Repton The living is a rectory in the diocese of Lincoln Value, £828 * Patron, the Hon B J Simpson The church is a neat Gothic structure with a small steeple, and was repaired in 1859 A charity school has £8

BACHALON, a hamlet in Higher Kinnerton township, Flint 3½ miles NE of Caergwrle

BACHALTON HILL, an eminence on the mutual border of Dorset and Somerset, about a mile E of Yeovil It commands a fine view

BACHE, a township in St. Oswald parish, Cheshire 1½ mile N of Chester Acres, 94 Real property, £514 Pop, 34 Houses, 4. Bache Hall is the seat of the Hughes family

BACHE, a township in the Llangollen Trian division of Llangollen parish, Denbigh Real property, £2,066 Pop., 507

BACHE AND NORTON, a township in Culmington parish, Salop, 6½ miles SE of Church Stretton Pop, 38

BACHELDRE, a township in Church Stoke parish, Montgomeryshire, 1½ mile SE of Montgomery It belongs to Earl Powis Pop, 137

BACHIE, a township in Llanfyllin parish, Montgomery Pop., 356.

BACH MILL, a hamlet in Munslow parish, Salop

BACHPHYD See BOUGHROOD

BACHWELL See BACKWELL

BACHWY, or MACHWY (THE), a stream of Radnorshire It rises a little north of Llanbedr, fetches a compass round by the east, and goes west south westward, past Pains' Castle and Llanbedr, through some fine scenery, to the Wye, near Erward, 7 miles below Builth Its length of course is about 10 miles

BACHYGRAIG, a township in Dymeirchion parish near St Asaph, Flint Pop., 53 Here is an old seat which belonged to Sir R Clough, and passed to Dr Johnson's friend Mrs Thrale.

BACHYMBYD, a township in Llanynys parish, Denbigh, 3 miles NNW of Ruthin Here is a seat of Lord Bagot, formerly a seat of the Salusburys, and on the grounds is a grove of unusually large chestnut trees

BACH YNYS, MACHYNIS, or MYNACH YNYS, an islet on the SE border of Carmarthen, in the mouth of the river Loughor, 3½ miles E of Llanelly A monastery was founded on it, in 518, by St Piro, and it became a seat of the Stepneys

BACK, a hamlet in the parish of St Clement, within the borough of Ipswich, Suffolk, 1 mile SE of Ipswich Pop, 272

BACKBARROW, a locality on the SW border of Westmoreland, adjacent to the Lancaster and Carlisle railway, 8½ miles SSW of Kendal It has a post office under Newton in Cartmel

BACKFORD, a township and a parish in Great Boughton district, Cheshire The township lies on the Ellesmere canal, 1 mile NE of Mollington r station, and 3½ N of Chester Acres, 749 Real property £1,271 Pop, 150 Houses, 29. The parish includes also the townships of Lea, Caughall, Chorlton by Backford, and Mollington Tarrant or Great Mollington, and its post town is Chester Acres, 3,109 Real property, £4,052 Pop, 525 Houses 83 The property is divided among a few Backford Hall is the seat of the Gleggs The living is a vicarage in the diocese of Chester Value £230 * Patron, the Bishop of Chester The church has monuments of the Birkenheads and the Morgalls. Charities, £26

BACKWELL or BACHWELL a parish in Bedminster district, Somerset, 1 mile SE of Nailsea r station, and 7 WSW of Bristol It includes the hamlets of Church Town, Downside, Farley, Mooreside, and West Town, and its post town is Nailsea. Acres, 2,902 Real property, £6,223 Pop, 926 Houses, 183 The property is subdivided Coal is extensively mined, and building stone is quarried The living is a vicarage, and a sinecure rectory in the diocese of Bath and Wells Value of the vicarage, £111, of the rectory £253 * Patron of the vicarage Mrs Uniacke, of the rectory, the Marquis of Bath The church is good and has a very fine tower and there are a Wesleyan chapel, a national school, and charities £45

BACKWORTH, or BLACKWORTH, a township in Earsdon parish Northumberland, on the Morpeth and Tynemouth railway, 4½ miles NW of North Shields It has a station on the railway, which serves also for Holywell and Earsdon Acres, 1,360 Pop, 954 Houses, 189 The manor belonged anciently to the priory of

Tynemouth, and belongs now to the Duke of Northumberland A coal mine here produces the Northumberland Wallsend or Earsdon Main coal

BACON HOLE, a cave on the coast of Glamorgan, at the E side of the mouth of Oxwich bay, 8 miles SW by W of Swansea. Its floor is about 20 feet above the level of the sea, and its interior has been much altered by blasting Fossil remains of great interest, and in successive layers, have been found in it,—first, bones of the ox, the red deer, the roebuck, and the fox, in alluvial earth, next, bones of the ox, the deer, and the bear, next, bones of the ox, the deer, the bear, the wolf, the hyena, the rhinoceros, and the mammoth, next, bones of the polecat, the badger, and the mammoth, all the successive layers separated from one another by deposits of stalagmite The mammoth bones are remarkably large, and may be seen in Swansea museum

BACONSTHORPE, or BEACONSTHORPE, a parish in Erpingham district, Norfolk, 4 miles SE by E of Holt, and 15 E by N of Fakenham r station It has a post office under Thetford Acres, 1,360 Real property, £1 968 Pop, 328 Houses, 67 The property is divided among a few The old hall, built in 1495, retains a central tower, but is otherwise a ruin The living is a rectory in the diocese of Norwich Value not reported * Patron, J T Mott, Esq The church is later English There are a Wesleyan chapel, a national school, and charities £5

BACOP, or BACUP, a town and three chapelries in Whalley and Rochdale parishes, Lancashire The town stands on the river Irwell, at the terminus of a branch of the Lancashire and Yorkshire railway, 7 miles NNW of Rochdale, is a seat of petty sessions and county courts, and carries on industry in cotton factories, woollen print works, Turkey red dye works, iron foundries, corn mills, and coal mining, has been much improved, by a local board, since 1864, and has a post office‡ under Manchester, a r station with telegraph, a banking office, a police station, water works, a market hall of 1867 built at a cost of £6,000, a plain church of 1788, two churches of 1854 and 1865 in the early English style, two recent handsome Wesleyan chapels, seven other dissenting chapels, a Roman Catholic chapel, a mechanics institution, with public hall and reading rooms, several public schools, a weekly market on Saturday, and two annual pleasure fairs. Pop in 1851, 6,981, in 1861, 10,935 Houses, 2,085 The chapelries are St. John, Christchurch, and St Saviour Pop, 6,981, 5,730, and 2,350 The livings of St J and C are vicarages, and that of St S is a p. curacy, in the dio of Manchester Value of St J and C, each £300, of St S, £159* Patrons of St J, Hulme's Trustees, of C, Five Trustees of St S., J M Holt, Esq

BACTON, a parish in the district and county of Hereford, near the Dore river, 4 miles NW of Pontrilas r station, and 11 SW of Hereford Post town Abbeydore under Hereford. Acres, 1 155 Real property, £1,172 Pop, 154 Houses, 28 The property is divided among a few The living is a rectory in the diocese of Hereford Value, £129 Patron, F Hamp, Esq The church is good, and there are charities £30

BACTON, a parish in Tunstead district, Norfolk on the coast, 4½ miles NE of North Walsham r station, and 19 NNE of Norwich It includes the hamlets of Bacton Green, Bromholm, and Keswick, and has a post-office under Norwich Acres, 1,770, of which 170 are water Real property, £3 058 Pop, 490 Houses, 129 The property is subdivided Considerable encroachments have recently been made by the sea A church formerly stood at Keswick, but has been completely washed away Ruins of a Cluniac priory founded in 1113 by Baxton de Glanville, stand at Bromholm The living is a vicarage in the diocese of Norwich Value £263* Patron, Lord of Kimberley The church is an ancient structure, with a square tower, has a good font and is in good condition. There are a Baptist chapel, a national school, and a coast guard station

BACTON, a parish in Hartismere district, Suffolk, on the East Union railway, near Finningham station, 6 miles N of Stowmarket It has a post office under Stowmarket Acres, 2,204 Real property, £4,642 Pop, 733 Houses, 161 The property is subdivided. The living is a rectory in the diocese of Norwich Value, £700* Patron, the Rev A B Hemsworth The church is good, and there are charities £86

BACUP See BACOP

BADBURHAM See BABRAHAM

BADBURY a tything in Chisledon parish, Wilts, 3½ miles SE of Swindon Pop, 395 An ancient camp here, called Badbury or Siddington Castle, is supposed to be the Mons Bodonicus of the Romans and the Baddiebrigg of the Saxons, and was the scene, in 520, of King Arthur's defeat of Cerdic

BADBURY, a tything and a hundred in Dorset. The tything is in Wimborne Minster parish, 4½ miles NW of Wimborne An ancient camp here, called Badbury Rings, crowns a naked hill commands an extensive panoramic view, is planted with firs, consists of three concentric ramparts, each with an outer ditch, the outermost a mile in circumference, occurs on the line of a Roman road to Old Sarum, seems to have been originally British, but to have been afterwards occupied by both the Romans and the Saxons, and was held by Edward the Elder after the death of Alfred the Great —The hundred lies in Wimborne division, and includes eight parishes Acres, 26,880 Pop in 1851, 6,941 Houses, 1,414

BADBURY HILL, a hill crowned by a Danish camp, in Berks, 2 miles SW of Farringdon

BADBURY RINGS See BADBURY, Dorset.

BADBY, a village and a parish in Daventry district, Northampton The village stands on the ascent of a hill, amid a sandy heath called Badby Down, near the source of the river Nen, 2½ miles SSW of Daventry, and 4¾ W of Weedon r station It has a post office under Daventry The parish comprises 2,370 acres Real property £4 455 Pop, 618 Houses 161 The property is much subdivided The manor belongs to Sir C. Knightly Hard blue rag stone is quarried An ancient camp, ten acres in area, with wide deep fosse and very steep ramparts, occurs on Arbury hill, and is supposed to be Roman The living is a vicarage, united with the curacy of Newnham, in the diocese of Peterborough Value, £306* Patron, Christchurch, Oxford The church is a fine old structure There are a free school for girls, a national school and charities £10

BADDESLEY CLINTON, a parish in Solihull district, Warwick, on the Warwick and Birmingham canal and the Warwick and Birmingham railway, at Kingswood station, 8½ miles NW of Warwick. Post town, Knowington under Warwick Acres, 1,329 Real property, £1 787 Pop, 143 Houses, 25 The manor belongs to M E Ferrers, Esq of Baddesley Hall The living is a rectory in the diocese of Worcester Value, £27 Patron, M E Ferrers, Esq The church is ancient There are a Roman Catholic chapel and a nunnery

BADDESLEY-ENSOR a parish in Atherstone district, Warwick, 3 miles NW of Atherstone r station It has a post office under Atherstone Acres 1,100 Real property, £2,278 Pop, 872 Houses, 171 The property is divided among a few The living is a vicarage in the diocese of Worcester Value, £106* Patrons, the Inhabitants. The church is good There are chapels for Independents and Wesleyans

BADDESLEY (NORTH), a parish in Winchester district, Hants on the Gosport and Salisbury railway, near Chandler's Ford station, 3½ miles E by S of Romsey Post town Romsey Acres, 2 570 Real property, £1,419 Pop, 253 Houses 53 The property is divided among a few Baddesley Hall is a chief residence The parish is a meet for the Hursley hounds The living is a vicarage in the diocese of Winchester Value, £112 Patron, T Chamberlayne, Esq The church is good

BADDESLEY (SOUTH) a tything chapelry in Boldre parish, Hants, 2 miles ENE of Lymington, and 6 SSE of Brockenhurst r station Post town, Lymington Real property, £2,835 Pop, 561 Houses, 116 A famous tree, a young elm known as "the groaning tree" ex listed here toward the middle of last century, emitting a singular noise from its roots similar to the groans of a person in extreme agony, and drawing many persons from a distance to visit it The sound continued for about a year and a half, not regularly but fitfully, and could not be explained by any naturalist, and at length stopped by the tree first being bored, then rooted up, but could not even then be explained A preceptory of Knights Templars, afterwards of Knights Hospitallers, stood at South Baddesley, and the chapel was taken down so late as 1818 The living is a p curacy in the diocese of Winchester Value, £100 Patron, P W Freeman, Esq

BADDIEBRIGG See BADBURY, Wilts

BADDILEY, a parish in Nantwich district, Cheshire, on the Ellesmere canal and the Shropshire Union railway, 3 miles SW by W of Nantwich r station. Post town, Nantwich. Acres, 1,962 Real property, £3,258 Pop., 272 Houses, 49 The property is not much divided The manor formerly belonged to the Mainwaring family, and their seat, Baddiley Hall, a very ancient structure of timber and plaster, was first converted into a farmhouse and then recently pulled down The living is a rectory in the diocese of Chester Value £219 * Patron, J Tollemache, Esq The church dates from times when public buildings were generally constructed of timber, consisted entirely of oak till 1811, but was then encased with brick is still in pretty good condition, and contains two fine marble monuments of the Mainwarings Charities, £48

BADDINGHAM See BADINGHAM

BADDINGTON, a township in Acton parish Cheshire, on the Grand Junction canal, 2 miles SSW of Nantwich. Acres 1,401 Real property, £1,715 Pop, 135 Houses, 20

BADDOW (GREAT), a village a parish, and a sub district, in the district of Chelmsford Essex The village stands near the river Chelmer, 2 miles ESE of Chelmsford r station, has a post-office under Chelmsford, and is a pleasant place, with a considerable number of genteel residents. The parish comprises 3,821 acres Real property, £11,061 Pop, 2 061 Houses 473. The property is much subdivided The manor belonged to Algar, Earl of Mercia, was given by William the Conqueror to the abbey of Caen in Normandy, passed, in the time of Henry I, to the Earl of Gloucester, and went through a series of proprietors, to the family of Houblon The living is a vicarage in the diocese of Rochester Value, £402 * Patron, Mrs Bullen The church formerly had two chantries, and is very good. Parker's school has an endowed income of £169, and other charities have £86 Richard de Badew, the founder of Clare Hall, Cambridge, was a native The sub district contains four parishes Acres, 14,685 Pop, 6 857 Houses, 1,490

BADDOW (LITTLE), a village and a parish in Chelmsford district, Essex The village stands on a tributary of the Chelmer river, 2 miles S of the Eastern Counties railway and 4 miles E by N of Chelmsford, and has a post office under Chelmsford The parish includes also the hamlet of Middlemead Acres, 2,779 Real property, £3,246 Pop, 605 Houses, 131 The property is subdivided The living is a rectory in the diocese of Rochester Value, £490 * Patron, Lord Rayleigh The church is good, and contains a costly and splendid monument to the memory of Sir Henry Mildmay, Bart, who died in 1639 There is an Independent chapel Free schools here and at Loreham founded in 1817 by Edward Butler, Esq, have an income of £200

BADECANWYLLA See BAKEWELL

BADGENDON See BADGINGTON

BADGER, or BAGSORE, a parish in Shiffnall district, Salop on the eastern verge of the county, 4½ miles SW of Albrighton r station, and 6 S by E of Shiffnall Post town, Beckbury under Shiffnall Acres, 920 Real property £1 801 Pop 178 Houses 37 The property is divided between two Badger Hall is the seat of R H Cheney, Esq, and Badger Dingle in the grounds connected with it, is a picturesque dell of red rock wood, and water, liberally open to the public and much visited The living is a rectory in the diocese of Hereford. Value, £230 Patron, R. H Cheney, Esq The church is good

BADGEWORTH, a village and a parish in Cheltenham district, Gloucester The village stands on a small stream, 2 miles S of the Gloucester and Birmingham railway, and 4 SW of Cheltenham The parish includes also the hamlets of Lentham, Little Shurdington, and Little Witcombe, and its post town is Shurdington under Cheltenham Acres, 3 927 Real property, £7,202. Pop., 1,048 Houses, 227 The manor belongs to J E Viner, Esq, of Badgeworth House There is a mineral spring The living is a vicarage, united with the curacy of Great Shurdington, in the diocese of Gloucester and Bristol Value, £295 * Patron, J E. Viner, Esq The church is later English, consists of nave, north aisle, and chancel, with tower at the west end of the nave, and is in good condition. Cox's charities for the poor yield £100 a year, and other charities £10

BADGEWORTH, Somerset. See BADGWORTH

BADGINGTON, or BADGENDON, a parish in Cirencester district, Gloucester, on the river Churn and near Ermine street, 4 miles N by W of Cirencester r station Post town, North Cerney under Cirencester Acres, 1 106 Real property, £1,604 Pop, 175 Houses, 40 The property is divided among a few Remains exist of two entrenchments which are supposed to have been thrown up in 556, on occasion of a battle between the Britons and the West Saxons The living is a rectory in the diocese of Gloucester and Bristol. Value, £191 Patron, Jesus' College, Oxford The church is good

BADGWORTH, a parish in Axbridge district, Somerset, 3 miles SW of Axbridge, and 10 SE of Weston super Mare Junction r station. Post town, Axbridge near Weston-super Mare. Acres, 1,815 Real property £2,563 Pop, 279 Houses, 63 The property is subdivided The living is a rectory in the diocese of Bath and Wells Value, £482 Patron, Sir C Mordaunt The church is good

BADINGHAM, a parish in Hoxne district, Suffolk, 3½ miles N by E of Framlingham r station It has a post office under Saxmundham Acres, 3,172 Real property, £5,814 Pop, 749 Houses, 166 The property is subdivided Badingham Hall and Badingham Green are chief residences. The living is a rectory in the diocese of Norwich Value, £582 * Patron, Rev R G Gorton The church is good and there are a Wesleyan chapel, a free school, and charities £24

BADINGTON See BAINTON, Northampton

BADLAND See KINNERTON, SALFORD, and BADLAND

BADLESMERE, a parish in Faversham district, Kent, 4½ miles S of Faversham r station It has a post office under Faversham Acres, 778 Real property, £1,060 Pop, 133 Houses, 23 The property is not much divided The manor belonged, in the times of Edward I and Edward II, to the potent family of De Badlesmere, was forfeited by the attainder and execution of John Earl of Oxford and Baron Badlesmere, and passed into the possession of the family of Sondes, now represented by Lord Sondes A house of regular canons was founded in the 13th year of Edward II by Bartholomew de Badlesmere The living is a rectory, united to the rectory of Leaveland, in the diocese of Canterbury Value, £323 * Patron, Lord Sondes The church is a small, plain, Saxon structure in very good condition A fair is held on 17 Nov

BADLEY, a parish in Bosmere district, Suffolk, near the river Gipping 2 miles WNW of Needham Market r station. Post town Needham Market Acres 1,050 Real property £1,430 Pop, 70 Houses, 15 The property is all in one estate The living is a vicarage in the diocese of Norwich Value £40 Patron, the Earl of Ashburnham The church is good

BADLINGHAM, a hamlet in Chippenham parish, Cambridge, 5½ miles NE of Newmarket

BADMINSTONE a hamlet in Fawley parish, Hants 5½ miles SW of Fareham

BADMINTON, or GREAT BADMINTON, a village, a

parish, and a ducal park in Chipping Sodbury district, Gloucester The village stands under the Cotswolds, on the SE verge of the county, 5 miles E by N of Chipping Sodbury, and 7 E of Yate r station It has a post office‡ under Chippenham, a reading room of 1862, a free school for girls, and six alms houses —The parish comprises 1,735 acres Real property, £2,990 Pop, 524 Houses, 107 The property belongs all to the Duke of Beaufort, and most of it is included in his park The living is a vicarage in the diocese of Gloucester and Bristol Value, not reported. Patron, the Duke of Beaufort The ancient church belonged to the abbey of Pershore; and the present one was built by the late Duke of Beaufort in 1785, stands within the park, lifts a pinnacle tower into view over the mansion, is a remarkably elegant structure, and contains many monuments of the Beaufort family, and the remains of Field Marshal Lord Raglan A free school and an alms house have an income of £94, left in 1705 by the then Duchess-Dowager of Beaufort The park is about 3 miles long, nearly 2 miles wide, and upwards of 9 miles in circuit, and contains some very fine woods and beautiful drives The mansion in it was erected in 1682, by the first Duke of Beaufort, and succeeded Raglan castle, in Monmouthshire, as the principal seat of his family The edifice is very extensive, consists of centre and wings is in the Palladian style, with rusticated basement and two surmounting cupolas, and contains many family portraits, downward from John of Gaunt, some rare and curious pictures by the Italian masters, and the remarkable satirical piece by Salvator Rosa, which occasioned that artist's expulsion from Rome

BADMINTON (LITTLE), a tything in Hawkesbury parish, Gloucester, 1 mile N of Great Badminton. Real property, £1,478. Pop, 113 Houses, 24

BADSEY, a village and a parish in Evesham district, Worcester The village stands on a tributary of the river Avon, adjacent to the Great Western railway, 2 miles ESE of Evesham The parish includes also the hamlet of Aldington Post town, Evesham Acres, 1,770 Real property, £4,268 Pop., 546 Houses, 119 There are mineral springs, and a silk mill. The living is a vicarage in the diocese of Worcester Value, £150 * Patron, Christchurch, Oxford The church is ancient There are a national school, and charities £18

BADSHOT AND RUNFOLD, a tything in Farnham parish, Surrey, 2 miles NE of Farnham It contains the work house of Farnham district, and is prominent in hop culture. Real property, £8,057 Pop, 1,733. Houses, 308

BADSWORTH, a township and a parish in Hemsworth district, W R. Yorkshire. The township lies 5 miles S of Pontefract r station, and has a post-office under Pontefract Acres, 1,529 Real property, £2,073 Pop, 219 Houses, 44 The parish includes also the townships of Upton and Thorpe Audlin Acres, 3,815 Real property, £5,915 Pop, 744 Houses, 158 The property is divided among a few Badsworth Hall is a chief residence The living is a rectory in the diocese of York Value, £596 * Patron, the Earl of Derby, The church is later English There are three Methodist chapels a national school, and charities £47

BADWELL ASH, or LITTLE ASHFIELD, a parish in Stow district, Suffolk, 3½ miles N by E of Elmswell r station, and 8 NNW of Stowmarket It has a post office, of the name of Badwell Ash, under Bury St. Edmunds Acres 1,860 Real property, £3,263 Pop, 527 Houses, 112 The property is subdivided. The living is a vicarage in the diocese of Ely Value, £69 Patron, Miss Clough The church is good, and there are a national school of 1861, and charities £18.

BAFBBANBUPGH See BAMBROUGH

BAGBERF, a tything in the parish of Sturminster-Newton Castle, Dorset, 1 mile N of Sturminster Pop, 402

BAGBOROUGH (EAST), a tything in Bishops Lydeard parish, Somerset, 7 miles WNW of Taunton

BAGBOROUGH (WEST) a parish in Taunton district, Somerset, in a pleasant hilly tract, on the Taunton and Watchet railway, between Bishops Lydeard and Crowcombe Heathfield stations, 8 miles NW of Taunton. It has a post office, of the name of Bagborough, under Taunton, and a fair on 23 May Acres, 1,972 Real property, £3,017 Pop, 495 Houses, 97 The property is divided among a few Bagborough House is the seat of the Popham family The living is a rectory in the diocese of Bath and Wells Value, £550 * Patron, Adam Clarke, Esq The church is good

BAGBURY, a hamlet in Evercreech parish, Somerset, 1 mile S of Shepton Mallet. Pop, 23

BAGBY WITH ISLEBECK, a chapelry in Kirby Knowle parish, N. R. Yorkshire, on an affluent of the river Codbeck, 2½ miles SE of Thirsk r station Post town, Thirsk. Acres, 1,795 Real property, £3,102 Pop, 302 Houses, 62 The living is a p curacy, annexed to the rectory of Kirby Knowle, in the diocese of York

BAGDEN (LOWER and UPPER), two hamlets in the township of Denby and parish of Penistone, W R. Yorkshire, 5½ miles NW of Barnesley

BAGDON HILL, a hill with a Roman camp, 3½ miles N of Devizes, Wilts.

BAG ENDERBY See ENDERBY BAG

BAGENDON See BADGINGTON

BAGGEARN HUISH, a hamlet in Nettlecombe parish, Somerset, 4½ miles S of Watchet

BAGGRAVE, a liberty in Hungerton parish, Leicestershire, 7½ miles ENE of Leicester Pop, 26 Baggrave Hall is the seat of the Burnabys

BAGGROW, a station on the Bolton branch railway, Cumberland 2 miles NNE of Aspatria

BAGGY POINT, a small headland at the S side of Morte bay, Devon, 5 miles NNW of the mouth of the river Taw A dangerous reef, called Baggy Leap, lies about ½ a mile off it.

BAGILLT, a village, a township, and a chapelry in Holywell parish, Flint The village stands on the S side of the estuary of the Dee, contiguous to the Chester and Holyhead railway 2 miles NW of Flint, and 2½ SE of Holywell It has a station on the railway, and a post office‡ under Holywell and is a sub port to Chester The tract around it is rich in minerals and yields a great out put of coals, and the village itself is the seat or centre of extensive lead, iron, and alkali works So large a quantity of lead ore as 100,000 tons, accompanied by 42,000 ounces of silver, has been annually smelted One of the adjacent hills bears the name of Bryn Dychwelwch signifying "the hill of retreat," and was the place at which Owen Gwynedd sounded his retreat from the pursuit by Henry II Bagillt Hall, in the vicinity is an old seat of the Griffiths —The township bears the name of Bagillt Fawr, and includes the hamlets of Bagillt Bach and Bagillt Fechan Real property, £7,040, of which £927 are in mines —The chapelry was constituted in 1844 Pop., 2 935 Houses, 657 The living is a p curacy in the diocese of St Asaph Value, £155.* Patron, the Vicar of Holywell. The church is in the early English style, and was opened in 1839 There are chapels for Independents, Baptists, Wesleyans, and Welsh Methodists

BAGINTON a parish in the district and county of Warwick, on the river Sow, 1¾ mile E of the North-western railway, and 3 S by E of Coventry Post town, Coventry Acres 1 667 Real property, £2,077 Pop, 213 Houses, 49 The property is all in one estate Baginton Hall, the seat of the proprietor, was built by W Bromley, Speaker of the House of Commons in the time of Queen Anne, and is now held by his descendant Slight traces exist of a castle of Sir William Bagot, a strong partizan of Richard II, where the Duke of Hereford, afterwards Henry IV, spent the night prior to his duel with the Duke of Norfolk, in the presence of Richard II, on Gosford Green, as described by Shakspeare The living is a rectory in the diocese of Worcester Value, £350 * Patron, the Rev W Bromley The church is good, has a fine bell turret, and contains a brass of Sir W Bagot and his lady A school has an endowed income of £228 and other charities £23

BAGLAN, a parish in Neath district, Glamorgan, on the E side of the mouth of Neath river, and on the South Wales railway, 1¼ mile S by W of Briton Ferry r station, and 3¼ S of Neath. It comprises the hamlets of Lower Baglan and Upper Baglan, and its post town is Briton Ferry, under Neath Acres 6,479, of which 1,240 are water Real property, £3,471, of which £550 are in mines. Pop of Lower Baglan 456 Houses, 92 Pop of Higher Baglan, 259 Houses, 28. The scenery possesses much beauty and some romance, and the higher grounds command very brilliant views. Earl Jersey's park spreads away, in extensive woods, over several bold hills, and Baglan House, the mansion in it, though without attraction as a building, possesses interest as once the resort of Mason, who wrote here his elegy —

"Coventry is dead! attend the strain,
Daughters of Albion"

Coal and fire-clay are worked. The living is a vicarage, annexed to the vicarage of Aberavon, in the diocese of Llandaff. The church is very picturesquely situated, and there is a Calvinistic Methodist chapel

BAGLEY, a hamlet in Calverley with-Farsley township, Calverley parish, W R Yorkshire, 4½ miles NE of Bradford

BAGLEY-WOOD, an extra parochial tract in Abingdon district, Berks, 3 miles S of Oxford. Acres, 390 Pop, 8 Houses, 3 A spot here, on Chilswell farm, was the site of the original Abingdon abbey, and another spot, on the top of a hill, commands a splendid view of Oxford

BAGNALL a hamlet in Basford parish, Notts, 2 miles SSW of Nottingham

BAGNALL, a township chapelry in Bucknall parish, Stafford, near the Churnet river and the Uttoxeter canal, 2 miles S of Endon r station Post town, Leek, under Stoke on Trent. Real property, £2,345 Pop, 424 Houses, 75 The living is a p. curacy, annexed to the rectory of Bucknall, in the diocese of Lichfield.

BAGNALL END See BIGNALL END

BAGNIGGE WELLS, a locality in St. Pancras parish, London, 1¼ mile NW of St Paul's Cathedral It is named from two mineral springs, which were once in repute, near Nell Gwynne's house.

BAGNOR, a tything in Speen parish, Berks, on the river Kennet 2 miles NNW of Newbury Pop, 165

BAGOTS BROMLEY See ABBOTS BROMLEY

BAGSHOT, a hamlet in Shalbourn parish, Berks, on the verge of the county 2 miles SSW of Hungerford Pop, 194

BAGSHOT, a village and a chapelry in Windlesham parish, Surrey, and an extensive heath in Surrey and Berks. The village stands on the Great Western road 5½ miles NNE of Farnborough r station, and 10 SW of Staines. It has a post office‡ under Farnborough station, and an inn, and a fair is held at it on 15 July It was a place of hotels, posting horses, and much thoroughfare prior to the railway period, and it bore the name of Holy Hall in the times of the Stuart kings. Bagshot Park, to the N of it, was a hunting seat of these kings, and a residence of George IV when Prince of Wales, and passed afterwards to the Duke of Gloucester An American garden here and a neighbouring large nursery are remarkable for very fine azaleas and rhododendrons —The chapelry includes fully one half of Windlesham parish The rated property amounts to £2,250, and is much subdivided The living is a p curacy annexed to the rectory of Windlesham The church was built by the Duke of Gloucester about 1816 There is a Baptist chapel —The heath contains 31,500 acres, and is a sandy flat diversified with long dusky ridges, at an elevation of 463 feet above sea level It was once an enclosed royal hunting ground, but was disparked during the civil war in the time of Charles I, and it afterwards lay long waste, and was the scene of many highway robberies. Much of it has been again enclosed, and subjected to the plough, and produces tolerable corn crops, and the rest is notable for depasturing small sheep, with very excellent mutton The geognostic nature of it is so peculiar as to give the name of Bagshot sand to the uppermost deposit of the so-called London basin

BAGSORE See BADGER.

BAGTHORPE, a parish in Docking district, Norfolk, 7½ miles N by W of Rougham, and 9 WNW of Fakenham r station Post town, Bircham under Rougham. Acres, 750 Real property, £830 Pop, 69 Houses, 14 The property is divided among a few Bagthorpe Hall is a chief residence The living is a rectory in the diocese of Norwich Value, £125 Patron, the Rev S R. Cattley The church is good

BAGTHORPE, a hamlet in Selston parish, Notts, on the western verge of the county, 11 miles NNW of Nottingham Pop, 536

BAGTHORPE, a hamlet in Basford parish, Notts, near the Mansfield railway, 2 miles NNW of Nottingham

BAGTOR, a seat of Lord Cranstoun, 3½ miles N of Ashburton, in Devon It was the birthplace, in 1586, of Ford, the dramatist.

BAGULEY, a chapelry, with a r station, in Bowdon parish, Cheshire, 3½ miles ENE of Altrincham Acres, 1,769 Real property, £5,028 Pop, 611 Houses, 118 Market gardening is largely carried on The chapelry was constituted in 1868 Living, a p curacy

BAGWORTH a chapelry in Thornton parish, Leicester, on the Leicester and Burton railway, 5½ miles NE of Market Bosworth It has a station on the railway, and a post office under Leicester Real property £2,912 Pop, 534 Houses, 102 A chief feature is Bagworth Park The living is annexed to Thornton.

BAHAITHLON, a township in Kerry parish, Montgomery, 3½ miles E of Newtown. Pop, 108

BAHAMA BANK, a shifting sand across Ramsey bay, in the Isle of Man It extends from NW to SE, and is 10 miles long and 1 mile broad A light vessel is moored at its SE end, in 9 fathoms, and shows two fixed lights, 20 and 33 feet high, visible at the distance of 10 miles

BAHANTUNE See BAMPTON

BAILDON, a village, a township, and a chapelry, in Otley parish, W R Yorkshire. The village stands near the river Aire and the Leeds and Liverpool canal, 2 miles NNE of Shipley r station, and 5 N of Bradford. It has a post office under Leeds, and fairs on 2 March and 4 Nov Its inhabitants are employed chiefly in woollen and worsted manufactures.—The township comprises 1,722 acres. Real property, £9,123 Pop, 3 895 Houses 834 Baildon Hill in the W, is 922 feet high, and has ancient entrenchments and tumuli —The chapelry is conterminate with the township. The living is a p curacy in the diocese of Ripon Value, £148* Patrons, Trustees. There are three dissenting chapels and a national school

BAILEY, a hamlet in Mitton parish, Lancashire, contiguous to Aighton, 5 miles N of Blackburn Pop 209 Houses, 43

BAILEY or BAILIE a township in Bewcastle parish, Cumberland, on a small tributary of the Esk 9 miles NE of Longtown. Real property, £3,526 Pop, 393 Houses, 65

BAILEY GATE a railway station in Dorset, on the D and Somerset railway, 2¾ miles NW of Wimborne

BAILEY (NORTH and SOUTH) See DURHAM

BAIN (THE), a stream of Aysgarth parish, N R. Yorkshire It rises in Raydale side, among high mountains, and runs 8 miles northward to the river Ure at Bainbridge. It expands into Simmer water 3 miles above Bainbridge, and makes two fine waterfalls. Simmer water is a lakelet of about 105 acres, a resort of water fowl, and abounding with fish, and borrows picturesqueness from surrounding scenery

BAINBRIDGE a village and a township in Aysgarth parish N R. Yorkshire The village stands on the river Ure 1½ mile SW of Askrigg, and has a post office under Bedale Here are a three arched bridge two dissenting chapels a free grammar school, and the Askrigg workhouse Here also was the Roman station Bracchium Traces of the rampart of the Roman camp, enclosing an area of about 5 acres, may be seen on the Borough Hill in the vicinity, some substructions of buildings occur at the foot of the same hill and a statue of the Emperor Commodus was found in the neighbourhood —The township includes also the hamlets of Counterside Marside, Cart End, Stalling Bush, High and Low Plean, and Cubeck and Morton Acres, 14,983 Real property, £8,185 Pop, 807 Houses, 160

BAINTON, a township, a parish, and a sub district, in the district of Driffield, E R Yorkshire The township lies on the Wolds, 4½ miles W by S of Hutton-Cranswick r station, and 6 SW of Great Driffield It has a post office under Driffield, and is a seat of petty sessions Acres, 2,320 Real property, £4,411 Pop, 399 Houses, 78 The parish includes also the township of Neswick Acres, 3,280 Real property, £6,086 Pop, 465 Houses, 90 The property is divided among a few The living is a rectory in the diocese of York Value, £757 * Patron, St John's college, Oxford. The church is ancient but very good.—The sub district comprises seven parishes and part of another Acres 31,014 Pop, 4 009 Houses, 759

BAINTON, or BADINGTON, a parish in the district of Stamford and county of Northampton, near the river Welland, 2 miles ESE of Uffington r station, and 4½ E by S of Stamford. Post town, Uffington under Stamford. Acres, 760 Real property, £1,730 Pop., 217 Houses, 42. The living is a p curacy, annexed to the rectory of Ufford, in the diocese of Peterborough The church is early English Charities, £51

BAINTON, or BEANTON, a hamlet in Stoke Lyne parish Oxford 3 miles N of Bicester Pop., 34

BAINTON BEACON, a division of Harthill wapentake E R Yorkshire It contains Bainton, Driffield, and twelve other parishes, and it takes its name from a warning signal formerly used in times of danger in Bainton. Acres, 55,635 Pop in 1851, 11,045 Houses, 2,219

BAKE, a property of Sir Joseph Copley, Bart, 4½ miles WSW of St Germains, in Cornwall It formerly was the seat of the Moyles, one of whom was Speaker in the time of Henry VIII

BAKEWELL, a small town, a parish, a sub district, and a district in Derbyshire The town stands at the foot of a hill, on the river Wye, adjacent to the Buxton railway, 11 miles W by S of Chesterfield Its name is a corruption of Bath well, originally Bath quelle, and was derived from a mineral well, used for the supply of baths, and supposed to have been in repute prior to the year 924 The manor of it was known to the Saxons under the name of Badecanwylla, probably had a Roman station, and certainly had a castle of Edward the Elder, on Castle hill, on the road to Chatsworth, was given at the Conquest to the family of Peveril, passed to successively the Gernons and the Vernons, and belongs now to the Duke of Rutland The town is clean and pleasant, exults in picturesque environs, and is much visited by strangers, both for its own sake, and for sake of the splendid neighbouring scenery It is a seat of petty sessions, and a polling place, and it has a railway station, a head post office,‡ a banking office, a parish church, two dissenting chapels, an endowed grammar school, an hospital and other charities with £382, a work house, a six arched bridge, a public library and reading room, a museum, public baths, and seven good inns The parish church stands on an eminence, is a spacious cruciform structure, in Saxon, Norman, and early English; has new transepts, and a new octagonal tower and spire, erected in 1841, and contains an ancient font and interesting tombs of the Vernons, the Foljambes, the Manners, and others. A very ancient cross, 8 feet high, decorated with rude sculpture, but much mutilated, is in the churchyard The public baths have been rebuilt by the Duke of Rutland, contain good accommodation, and include a large swimming bath, and separate shower and warm baths The water from the mineral spring is chalybeate and slightly tepid, and that for the warm baths may be had of any temperature by artificial heating A pleasant promenade is attached, called the Bath Garden, well laid out in walks and grottoes The public museum contains a great variety of British Roman and Saxon relics, obtained from places in the neighbourhood, and a private museum, connected with a shop, exhibits splendid specimens of spar ornament and inlaid marble A number of the inhabitants are employed in the working of marble and chert, and others are employed in a cotton mill A weekly market is held on Monday, and fairs, on Easter Monday Whit Monday, 26 Aug, the Monday after 10 Oct, and the Monday after 22 Nov —The township of Bakewell includes the town, together with a circumjacent tract. Real property, £10,474 Pop, 2,704 Houses, 485

The parish includes also the townships of Froggatt, Curbar, Calver Rowland, Hassop, Great Longstone and Holme, Little Longstone, Ashford, Sheldon, Taddington and Priestcliff, Brushfield, Chelmorton, Monyash, Over and Nether Haddon, Hartle or Harthill, Great Rowsley Beeley, Baslow with Bubnell, Blackwell, and part of Wardlow, all in the district of Bakewell, and the township of Buxton, in the district of Chapel en le Frith Acres, 43,020 Real property, with the rest of Wardlow, £62,699 Pop in 1841, 10,363, in 1861, 11,254 Houses, 2,164 Two objects of grand interest are the ducal seats of CHATSWORTH and HADDON HALL which see. Mines of coal, lead, and zinc, and quarries of stone and marble are worked Rocking stones and a Druidical circle occur on Stanton manor The living is a vicarage in the diocese of Lichfield Value, £460 * Patrons, the Dean and Chapter of Lichfield The chapelries of Ashford, Baslow, Beeley, Buxton, Chelmorton, Great Longstone, King's Sterndale, Monyash, Rowsley, Sheldon, and Taddington, are separate charges

The sub-district includes the greater part of Bakewell parish, parts of Youlgreave and Hartington parishes, and all Edensor Acres, 56,916 Pop., 12,547 Houses, 2 490 The district comprehends also the sub district of Tideswell, containing the parishes of Eyam and Hope, and parts of the parishes of Bakewell, Tideswell, and Hathersage, and the sub district of Matlock, containing the parishes of Matlock and Darley, and parts of the parishes of Youlgreave, Crich, Wirksworth, and Bradbourne Acres, 107 105 Poor rates in 1866, £8,519 Pop in 1861, 31,378 Houses, 6,448. Marriages in 1866, 170, births, 949,—of which 67 were illegitimate, deaths, 650, of which 191 were at ages under 5 years, and 17 at ages above 85 years Marriages in the ten years 1851-60, 1,909, births, 9,323, deaths, 6,157 The places of worship in 1851 were 33 of the Church of England, with 10,546 sittings, 8 of Independents, with 1,553 s, 2 of Baptists, with 100 s, 1 of Quakers, with 90 s, 5 of Unitarians with 290 s, 34 of Wesleyan Methodists, with 4,955 s., 20 of Primitive Methodists, with 2,589 s 7 of Wesleyan Reformers, with 586 s, 3 of Roman Catholics, with 200 s, and 1 undefined, with 70 attendants The schools were 37 public day schools with 2,298 scholars, 62 private day schools, with 1,371 s, 80 Sunday schools, with 6,141 s., and 4 evening schools for adults with 83 s

BAL, a prefix in many topographical names of Celtic origin It is commonly taken to mean a town, but it originally bore that meaning only in reference to the central seat of population on a single estate,—the town or homestead of a landlord. It does not occur often in England and Wales but is plentiful in Scotland, and exceedingly so, in the kindred form of Bally, in Ireland.

BALA a small town, a sub district, and a district, in Merioneth The town is in Llanycil parish, stands at the foot of Bala lake, and on the Ruabon and Dolgelly railway, 14 miles SW by W of Corwen, and has a railway station with telegraph An artificial mount called Tomen y Bala, probably of Roman origin, adjoins it, and two anciently fortified hills, called Caer Gai and Castell Corndochan, the former believed to have been occupied by the Romans, are in the neighbourhood. The town consists chiefly of one wide street, with a few handsome houses. It has a post-office‡ under Corwen, a church of 1867, two dissenting chapels, a free grammar school, a fine Calvinistic Methodist college of 1866, an

Independent college, a townhall, a market house, a banking-office, and two good inns. A manufacture of woollen hose and gloves was at one time flourishing but has very greatly declined. A weekly market is held on Saturday, and fairs, on 14 May, 10 July, 27 Sept., 24 Oct., and 8 Nov. Bills were introduced in 1861 for railways to Corwen and Dolgelly. The town is a borough by prescription, governed by two bailiffs and a common council, and is a polling place for the county, a seat of petty sessions, the seat of quarter sessions in January and July, and the seat of the Lent assizes. Real property, £3,821. Pop. in 1851, 1,341. The Rev. Thomas Charles, one of the founders of the British and Foreign Bible Society, lived here till his death in 1813.

The sub-district and the district are identical with each other, and contain only the parishes of Llanycil, Llanuwchllyn, Llangower, Llandderfel, and Llanfawr or Llanfor. Acres, 58,292. Poor rates in 1866, £3,565. Pop. in 1861, 6,332. Houses, 1,373. Marriages in 1866, 50; births, 188,—of which 26 were illegitimate; deaths, 121,—of which 24 were at ages under 5 years, and 11 at ages above 85 years. Marriages in the ten years 1851-60, 447; births, 1,704; deaths, 1,178. The places of worship in 1851 were 7 of the Church of England, with 1,080 sittings; 10 of Independents, with 1,351 s.; 1 of Baptists, with 132 s.; 18 of Calvinistic Methodists, with 2,647 s.; and 1 of Wesleyan Methodists, with 178 s. The schools were 10 public day schools, with 433 scholars; 1 private day school, with 25 s.; 39 Sunday schools, with 3,079 s.; and 1 evening school for adults, with 20 s.

BALA LAKE, LLYN TEGID, or PEMBLE MERE, a lake in Merioneth. It extends north-eastward to Bala, is 4 miles long, 1 mile broad, and more than 100 feet deep, receives the river Dwyfrdwy at its head, and discharges the Dee from its foot. Its shores are gravelly, its borders are wooded, easy slopes, its flanks, hills of no great beauty, overlooked by interesting mountains. Its waters abound with pike, and contain perch, roach, eels, char, and gwiniad. The fishery belonged anciently to Basingwerk abbey, and is now the property of Sir W. W. Wynn, who has a fishing lodge at the head, called Glan-y-Llynn.

BALA SALLA. See BALLA SALLA.

BALASLEY. See BATSELEY.

BALBY WITH HEXTHORPE, a township-chapelry in Doncaster parish, W. R. Yorkshire, on the river Don, 2 miles SW of Doncaster r. station. It has a post office under Doncaster. Acres, 1,567. Real property, £4,844. Pop., 1,058. Houses, 241. Tanning, brickmaking, and sand digging are largely carried on. The living is a vicarage in the diocese of York. Value, £150. Patron, the Rev. J. J. Banks. The church was built in 1847. There are a Wesleyan chapel of 1868, a P. Methodist chapel, and a national school. The Quakers, under George Fox, held their first meetings here.

BALCOMBE, a village and a parish in Cuckfield district, Sussex. The village stands on a pleasant spot, adjacent to the London and Brighton railway, 4 miles N of Cuckfield; and it has a station on the railway, a post office under Cuckfield, a small inn, and a fair on 13 April. The parish comprises 4,786 acres, of which 1,180 are in Highbeach warren. Real property, £3,652. Pop., 880. Houses, 170. The property is divided among a few. Balcombe Place and Wakehurst Place are elegant mansions. A tunnel of the railway, 1,139½ yards long, goes through a hill within the parish; and the Ouse viaduct, 100 feet high and upwards of ⅓ of a mile long, with 37 arches of 30 feet each in span, is about 1½ mile from the station. The parish is a meet for the Horsham hounds. The living is a rectory in the diocese of Chichester. Value, £515.* Patron, the Rev. G. C. Bethune. The church is early English in part, and very good.

BALDERSBY, a township and a chapelry in Topcliffe parish, N. R. Yorkshire. The township lies on the river Swale and on the Leeds and Thirsk railway, 5 miles NE of Ripon. It has a station on the railway, of the name of Baldersby Gate; and its post town is Topcliffe, under Thirsk. Acres, 1,752. Real property, £3,360. Pop., 333. Houses, 67. The chapelry is more extensive than the township. Pop. in 1871, 687. The property belongs to two. The living is a p. curacy in the diocese of York. Value, £120.* Patron, Viscount Downe. The church is new.

BALDERSTON, a township-chapelry in Blackburn parish, Lancashire, near the river Ribble, 5 miles NW of Blackburn r. station. Post town, Mellor Brook, under Blackburn. Acres, 1,710. Real property, £2,593. Pop., 532. Houses, 105. The property is much subdivided. The living is a p. curacy in the diocese of Manchester. Value, £160.* Patron, the Vicar of Blackburn. The church is very good. Charities, £11.

BALDERSTONE ST. MARY. See ROCHDALE.

BALDERTON, a parish in Newark district, Notts, on the Great Northern railway, 2 miles SE of Newark. It has a post office under Newark. Acres, 4,050. Real property, £8,017. Pop., 987. Houses, 231. The property is much subdivided. The living is a vicarage in the diocese of Lincoln. The church is later English, but has a fine Norman porch. There are a Methodist chapel, a national school, and charities £50.

BALDHU, a chapelry in Kea and Kenwyn parishes, Cornwall, in the northern vicinity of Truro r. station. Post-town, Truro. Rated property, £2,000. Pop., 2,070. Houses, 427. The property is not much divided. The living is a vicarage in the diocese of Exeter. Value, £200.* Patron, Viscount Falmouth. The church is very good. The chapelry was constituted in 1846.

BALDOCK, a small town, a parish, and a sub-district, in the district of Hitchin, Herts. The town stands in a valley between two hills, on Icknield-street, adjacent to the Hitchin and Cambridge railway, near the source of the river Rhee, 5 miles NE of Hitchin. It has a station on the railway, a head post office,‡ a parish church, four dissenting chapels, almshouses, a banking office, and two good inns; and is a seat of petty sessions. Its name was anciently written Baudoc, and is supposed by some to have been taken from Baalbec in Syria, and applied by the Knights Templars. These military monks got a grant of the place in the reign of Stephen, from Gilbert, Earl of Pembroke; and they built upon it a church, and obtained for it the rights of a market town. The present parish church includes some portions of the Templars' church, is a spacious edifice, in later English, with a large chancel and an ancient tower, was recently renovated, and contains some monuments of the Templars, a finely carved oak screen, a very curious font, and part of the ancient rood loft. The principal street of the town is wide, and has many respectable houses. Much business is done in the corn and malting trades; and a great quantity of straw-plait is made here and in the neighbourhood. A weekly market is held on Friday; and fairs, on 7 March, the last Thursday in May, 5 Aug., 2 Oct., and 11 Dec.—The parish comprises 200 acres. Real property, £6,312. Pop., 1,974. Houses, 408. The living is a rectory in the diocese of Rochester. Value, £200.* Patron, Bishop of Rochester. Charities, £270.—The sub-district contains sixteen parishes. Acres, 28,000. Pop., 8,738. Houses, 1,811.

BALDON MARSH, a parish in the district of Abingdon and county of Oxford, on the Roman road from Alcester to Wallingford, 3½ miles E by N of Culham r. station, and 6 SE of Oxford. Post town, Nuneham Courtney, under Oxford. Acres, 570. Real property, £1,370. Pop., 342. Houses, 69. Baldon House belonged formerly to the Pollards, and passed to the baronet family of Willoughby. The living is a rectory in the diocese of Oxford. Value, £93.* Sir H. P. Willoughby, Bart. The church is later English. There are a free school and charities £9.

BALDON TOOT, a parish in the district of Abingdon and county of Oxford, 4 miles NE of Culham r. station, and 5 SE of Oxford. Post town, Nuneham Courtney, under Oxford. Acres, 2,010. Real property, £1,708. Pop., 260. Houses, 59. The living is a vicarage in the diocese of Oxford. Value, not reported. Patron, the Bishop of Oxford. The church is ancient.

BALDONFEE See BAULDONFEE

BALDSLOW, a hundred in the rape of Hastings, Sussex. It contains the parishes of Crowhurst and Hollington, and parts of four others Acres, 12,320 Pop in 1851, 3,957 Houses, 669

BALDUNTON, a township in Middle parish, Salop, 9 miles NNW of Shrewsbury Pop, 26

BALDWIN, a chapelry in Kirk Braddan parish, 1 mile W of Douglas, Isle of Man Post town, Douglas. Pop, returned with the parish The living is a p curacy in the diocese of Sodor and Man Value, £70 Patron, the Vicar of Kirk Braddan

BALDWINHOLME, a township in Orton parish, Cumberland, 5½ miles SW of Carlisle Real property, £2,371 Pop., 234 Houses, 46

BALE, or BATHLEY, a parish in Walsingham district, Norfolk, 4½ miles E by N of Walsingham r station Post town, Holt under Thetford Acres, 1,041 Real property, £1,850 Pop, 227 Houses, 50 The property is not much divided The living is a rectory, annexed to the rectory of Gunthorpe, in the diocese of Norwich The church was restored in 1864 Charities, £15

BALHAM, a hamlet and a chapelry in Streatham parish, Surrey The hamlet adjoins the West London and Crystal Palace railway, 4 miles WNW of the Crystal Palace, and has a station on the railway, and a post office‡ under Clapham, London S A bill was introduced in 1861 for a railway to connect the West London and Crystal Palace railway at or near Balham with the Windsor line of the Southwestern at Putney The chapelry bears the name of Balham Hill Pop, 1,786 The living is a vicarage in the diocese of Winchester Value, not reported Patron, the Rector of Streatham

BALK, a township in Kirby Knowle parish, N R Yorkshire, 4½ miles NE of Thirsk Acres, 780 Real property, £934 Pop, 86 Houses, 16

BALKHOLME, a township in Howden parish, E R Yorkshire, adjacent to the Hull and Selby railway, 2 miles E by S of Howden Acres, 1,199 Real property, £1,525 Pop, 184 Houses, 36

BALKING, or BAULKING, anciently BETHELKING, a hamlet and a chapelry in Uffington parish, Berks The hamlet stands near the Great Western railway, and the Berks and Wilts canal, 3 miles W by N of Faringdon Road r station, and 4 SSE of Faringdon It was formerly a market town, and its post town is Uffington under Faringdon The chapelry contains 1,443 acres. Real property £2,184 Pop, 181 Houses, 41 The property is not much divided The living is a vicarage united to Woolstone, in the diocese of Oxford. Value, £78 Patron, C Eyre, Esq The church is good

BALLASALLA, a village in Kirk Malew parish, Isle of Man, on the Silver burn, and on the road to Douglas, 2¼ miles NNE of Castletown It has a post-office under Douglas, and remains of a Cistercian abbey founded in 1098 by Mac Manus, King of Man, enlarged and richly endowed by his successors, and given in 1134 to Furness abbey Pop, 516 Ballasalla House, in the vicinity, is the seat of the Drinkwater family

BALLAUGH, or KIRK-BALLAUGH, a village and a parish in the Isle of Man The village stands on the W coast, 7 miles W of Ramsey, is watered by a small stream descending from Snawfell, straggles upward from the shore over a space of nearly 2 miles, and has a post office,‡ of the name of Ballaugh, under Douglas. The parish includes Ballamoor, and has marl-pits and several warrens Bones and horns of the great Irish elk have been found in the marl pits, and a skeleton of one was sent hence to the Hunterian museum at the university of Glasgow Pop, 1,228 Houses, 266 The living is a rectory in the diocese of Sodor and Man Value, £325 * Patron, the Crown The old church stands on the shore, and was recently well restored, and a beautifully carved Runic cross is in the churchyard A new church, built in the early part of the present century, stands fully a mile up the streamlet

BALLIDON, a chapelry in Bradbourne parish, Derby, near the North Stafford railway, 6 miles W by N of Wirksworth. Post town, Brassington under Wirksworth Real property, £2,488 Pop, 110 Houses, 1? The property is divided among a few The living is a p curacy, annexed to the vicarage of Bradbourne, in the diocese of Lichfield The church is good

BALLINGDON CUM BRUNDON, a parish in the district of Sudbury, and county of Essex, on the northern verge of the county, ½ a mile SW of Sudbury r station Post town, Sudbury Acres, 366 Real property, £4,392 Pop 861 Houses, 190 There are two manors, Ballingdon above-Bridge and Ballingdon below Bridge The whole tract was long a parish under the name of Brundon, and seems to have been part of the manor of Brundon, which in the earliest times belonged to the family of Limesi, but now is sometimes regarded as a portion of the parish of Sudbury The living is a vicarage, annexed to the vicarage of Sudbury, in the diocese of Ely There is no church

BALLINGHAM, a parish in Ross district, Hereford, on the river Wye, and on the Hereford and Gloucester railway, near Fawley station, 5½ miles NNW of Ross. Post town, Holme Lacey under Hereford Acres, 991 Real property, £1 802 Pop, 163. Houses, 40 The property is divided among a few The living is a vicarage in the diocese of Hereford Value, £165 Patron, Sir E F S Stanhope, Bart The church is good

BALL'S POND, a suburban tract in Islington parish, London, on the North London railway, near the New river, 2½ miles N of St Paul s The cattle market of 15 acres, projected by Perkins, is here B Pond is a chapelry, constituted in 1830, a vicarage in the diocese of London, of the value of £420 in the patronage of Trustees The church is in the pointed style, and was designed by Barry A chapel in Gloucester road is under the vicar, and two churches in Essex road and Mildmay-park are served by other vicars, each with income of £400, and both appointed by the vicar of B Pond

BALNE, a township in Snaith parish, W R Yorkshire, 3 miles S of Whitley Bridge r station, and 4½ SW of Snaith Acres, 2,870 Real property, £3,111 Pop, 367 Houses, 73 A recent church is here

BALSALL, BALSHALL, or TEMPLE BALSALL, a chapelry in the parish of Hampton in Arden, Warwick, 3 miles E of Knowle r station, and 9 W by S of Coventry Post town, Knowle under Birmingham Real property, £8,864 Pop, 1,140 Houses, 291 The manor was given, in the reign of Stephen, to the knights Templars, belonged afterwards to the Knights Hospitallers, passed, in the time of Edward VI, to the Earls of Warwick and Leicester, and afterwards to Lady Katherine Leveson, and was bequeathed by that lady for the erection and endowment of an hospital for poor women and boys A hall was built by the Templars as a commandery or preceptory, and remains of it still exist. The hospital of Lady Leveson was enlarged under an act of Queen Anne, is now an extensive and substantial suite of buildings, in the form of a square, on the border of a large green, and has an income of £1,421 The living is a vicarage in the diocese of Worcester Value, £50 * Patron, the Governor of Balsall Hospital The church was built by the Templars, about the middle of the 12th century, is 104 feet long, 39 feet wide, and 57 feet high, and has lofty, pointed, finely traceried windows, timber roof, and stone stalls Other charities than the hospital £26

BALSALL HEATH, a chapelry in Kings Norton parish, Worcester, on the Birmingham and Gloucester railway, 2¼ miles S of Birmingham It was constituted in 1853, and it has a post office under Birmingham Pop., 7,651 Houses, 1,616 The living is a vicarage in the diocese of Worcester Value £300 * Patron, the Vicar of King's Norton The church is ancient.

BALSCOTT a chapelry in Wroxton parish Oxford, on the verge of the county, 4½ miles WNW of Banbury r station Post town, Wroxton under Banbury Acres, 550 Pop, 211 Houses, 47 The name is a corruption of Beletscot, and was derived from Michael Belet, who founded Wroxton priory The living is a p curacy, annexed to the vicarage of Wroxton in the diocese of Oxford. The church is decorated English

BALSDEAN, a hamlet 4 miles NE of Brighton, Sussex. A building here, called the Chapel, now used as a stable, is ancient and seemingly decorated English

BALSHALL See BALSALL

BALSHAM, a village a parish, and a sub district, in the district of Linton, Cambridge The village stands near Worsted Street, 3½ miles S of Six Mile Bottom r station, and 4 NE by N of Linton, and has a post office under Cambridge The parish comprises 4,402 acres, and includes part of the Gogmagog hills. Real property, £5,854 Pop, 1,162 Houses, 266 The property is much subdivided The living is a rectory in the diocese of Ely Value, £1,101 * Patrons, the Governors of the Charterhouse London The church is handsome and has a tower There are an Independent chapel, and charities £49 Hugh de Bottesham, founder of Peterhouse College, Cambridge was a native. See GOGMAGOG HILLS —The sub district contains six parishes Acres, 17,772 Pop, 3,925 Houses, 866

BALSTON See BAYSTON

BALTERLEY, a township in Barthomley parish, Stafford, 6½ miles NW of Newcastle under Lyne Acres, 1,206 Real property, £2,218 Pop, 281 Houses, 52

BALTONSBOROUGH, a parish in Wells district, Somerset, on the river Brue, 4 miles SW of Glastonbury r station It includes the hamlet of Southwood, and has a post office under Glastonbury Acres, 2,472 Real property, £6,934 Pop, 763 Houses, 166 The living is a p curacy annexed to Butleigh, in the dio of Bath and Wells The church is later English There are Wesleyan and Moravian chapels, and two public schools

BALVAST, or POOLVASH BAY, a bay at the SW end of the Isle of Man It opens between Scarlet point and Spanish head, and is 4½ miles wide at the entrance, and 2¼ miles long

BAMBER BRIDGE, a village and a chapelry in Blackburn parish, Lancashire The village stands adjacent to the East Lancashire railway, 3 miles SE by S of Preston, and has a post office under Preston, and a r station The chapelry was constituted in 1832 Rated property, £6,231 Pop, 2,182 Houses, 408 There are two large cotton factories The living is a p curacy in the diocese of Manchester Value, £150 * Patron, the Vicar of Blackburn The church was built in 1836 There are a Wesleyan chapel and a national school.

BAMBROUGH, or BAMBOROUGH a village a township, a parish, and a ward in Northumberland The village stands on the coast, 2 miles NE of Lucker r station, and 5 E by N of Belford, and has a post office under Belford It was a seat of the kings of Northumbria, bore originally the name of Baebbanburg or Bebbanburg, signifying Queen Bebba's town, was afterwards a market town and a royal burgh, sending two members to parliament, gave name to an extensive district around it, called Bambroughshire, and had churches of St Oswald and St Aidan, a cell of Augustinian canons, a house of Blackfriars, a college and an hospital It now possesses none of its ancient characters, but has become a retired, pleasant, favourite summer resort for sea bathing —The township includes also a place called Fowberry Acres, 1 242 Pop, 403. Houses, 84 —The parish contains likewise the townships of Bambrough Castle, Budle, Glororum, Burton, Hoppen Elford, Shoreston or Shoston, North Sunderland Beadnell, Tughall, Swinhoe, Fleetham, Newham, Lucker, Adderstone, Bradford, Spindlestone, Outchester Monson or Mowson, Warenton, Warenford, Ratchwood, and Newstead, and is in the district of Belford Acres, 26 234, of which 1 131 are water Real property, £25,320 Pop, 4 105 Houses, 814 The surface exhibits diversity of texture, and is rich in at once geognostic, antiquarian, and modern interest The living is a vicarage in the diocese of Durham Value, £300 * Patrons the Trustees of Bishop Lord Crewe The church is early English and cruciform, with a western tower, and has an unusually long chancel, with good modern small work, three sedilia, an ambrey, and the effigies of a knight The chapelries of Beadnell, Lucker, and North Sunderland are separate charges —The ward is about 17 miles long, and about 8 miles broad, contains seven parishes, and consists of two divisions, North and South Acres of North B, 33,421, of South B, 35,842 Pop of both, 11,244 Houses, 2,222

BAMBROUGH CASTLE, a township in Bambrough parish, Northumberland on the coast, contiguous to Bambrough township, 5 miles E of Belford Acres, 1 724, of which 1,13_ are water Pop, 38 Houses, 5 A famous castle was founded here, about the year 554, by Ida, first king of Northumbria, consort of Queen Bebba, and gave rise to the adjacent town The site of it is a rugged, triangular, basaltic rock, projecting into the sea, rising 150 feet above the watermark, and accessible only from the SE side The original pile was formed chiefly of wood, yet made a great figure throughout the troubled times of the Northumbrian kings A stronger structure, with Norman tower and Norman keep, was built principally about 1070, and this acted a part in most of the contests which shook the country, down to the reign of Edward IV, but sustained very severe injury in a siege after the battle of Hexham It passed, along with the manor, by grant of the Crown in the time of James I to the family of Forster, underwent forfeiture in 1715 on account of its owner, Thomas Forster, having joined the Pretender, and was purchased by that gentleman's maternal uncle, Lord Crewe, Bishop of Durham, and bequeathed by him, under trustees, for charitable uses The structure, as it now stands, includes a space of eight acres, and contains stores, schools, and a public library for the benefit of the surrounding population, together with numerous, constant, effective appliances for the rescue and relief of shipwrecked mariners The Farn islands, with accompanying rocks and shoals, so dangerous to navigation, are in the offing, and the appliances at Bambrough Castle are held in continual readiness, under resident managers and continual patrols, to afford succour to the endangered or the shipwrecked The great tower commands an extensive view, and one of the apartments has some interesting portraits and four large ancient pieces of tapestry Grace Darling who acted so very heroically at the wreck of the Forfarshire steamer, lies interred in the neighbouring churchyard

BAMBURGH See BAMBROUGH

BAMFORD, a township chapelry in Hathersage parish, Derby on a head stream of the river Derwent, in the Peak, 4½ miles ENE of Castleton, and 9 N of Bakewell r station Post town, Hathersage under Sheffield Acres, 1 455 Real property, £1,456. Pop, 377 Houses, 73. The living is a rectory in the diocese of Lichfield Value, £100 * Patron, W C Moore, Esq The church was built in 1859, after designs by Mr Butterfield, is in the decorated English style, consists of nave, north aisle, and chancel, with tower and spire 108 feet high, and has floor of encaustic tiles There are a Methodist chapel and a national school

BAMFORD, a village in the township of Birtle cum Bamford parish of Middleton, Lancashire, 3 miles W of Rochdale It has a post office under Rochdale and an Independent chapel, and its inhabitants are employed chiefly in cotton factories Bamford Hall, the fine old seat of J Fenton, Esq, is adjacent

BAMPFYLD WESTON See WESTON BAMPFYLD

BAMPTON a small town a parish, a sub district, and a hundred, in Devon The town stands in a vale on the rivulet Batherne, about a mile above its influx to the Exe, 7 miles N of Tiverton r station It was anciently called Bahantune, Baunton, Bathampton, and Bathrumpton, and it disputes with Bampton in Oxfordshire being the Beamdune of the Saxon chroniclers, where in 614 the Britons were defeated with great slaughter by Cynegilsus, king of the West Saxons It is supposed by some to occupy the site of a Roman station, and it had a castle erected in 1336 by a member of the Cogan family, on a knoll at the east end of Castle street, now called the Mount, and crowned with firs. The town consists of stone houses, irregularly scattered over a space of about ½ a mile, and has picturesque environs It was formerly a borough, and sent two members to parliament it was governed by a portreeve and other officers and it is now a seat of petty sessions

It has a post-office under Tiverton, and two good inns, and it formerly had a manufacture of serges and pottery A weekly market is held on Saturday, fairs, on Whit Tuesday and the last Thursday in Oct, and great markets for cattle, sheep, and Exmoor ponies, on the last Wednesday in Nov and the Wednesday before Lady day John de Bampton, a Carmelite friar, who first read lectures on "Aristotle" at Cambridge, and died in 1391, was a native

The parish includes also the hamlets of Petton and Shillingford Acres, 7,785 Real property, £9,144 Pop, 1,971 Houses, 397 Limestone is worked, in about 15 quarries, for supplying the country as far as to South Molton There is a chalybeate spring of some celebrity The living is a vicarage in the diocese of Exeter Value, £130 * Patron, Rev F Rendell The church is decorated and perpendicular English, consists of nave, aisles, transept, and chancel, with western tower, and contains a fine carved oak screen, and monuments of the Bourchiers. A small chapel of ease is at Petton, and a small Baptist chapel in the town Charities, £9 —The sub-district contains four other parishes, and is in the district of Tiverton. Acres, 17,718 Pop, 3,296 Houses, 631 —The hundred contains seven parishes, and is noted principally for its quarries of limestone, and its fine breed of sheep Acres, 28,7?7 Pop, 6 628 Houses, 1,360

BAMPTON, an ancient village or township a parish, a sub district, and a hundred in Oxford The village stands on a small tributary of the Thames, 5½ miles SSW of Witney r station, and 6 NNE of Faringdon It was formerly called Bampton in the Bush and is sometimes designated, in union with the hamlet of Weald, as Bampton-with Weald It was a place of some importance in the times of the Saxons, and it rose to still more importance, as a market-town, after the Conquest It has a post office‡ under Faringdon, a town hall, a parish church a Baptist chapel, a weekly market on Wednesday, and a large horse fair on 26 and 27 Aug The church at it is a handsome cruciform edifice, with a tall spire, and possesses considerable portions of Norman architecture, yet includes features of almost every period from the Conquest till the time of George III, and was partially restored in 1869 A castle of Aylmer de Valence, Earl of Pembroke, stood near the church, and was described, in the time of the Commonwealth, as "a quadrangular building, moated round, with towers at each corner and a gatehouse of tower like character on the south and east sides and picturesque remains of it still exist as two farm houses, called Ham Court and Castle Farm Real property of the township £8,872, Pop. 1,713 Houses, 393

The parish includes also the chapelry of Shifford, and the hamlets of Weald, Brighthampton, Ler, Chimney, Coate, and Aston Acres, 8,750 Real property £17,492 Pop, 2,863 Houses, 601 The property is much subdivided The living is a three fold vicarage,—Bampton, Bampton-Aston, or Aston Bampton, and Bampton Lew, of the value of respectively £550,* £550,* and £300,* all in the diocese of Oxford, and in the patronage of the Dean and Chapter of Exeter Endowed schools have £78, and other charities £271 Phillips the author of "Cyder" and the "Splendid Shilling," was a native —The sub district contains six other parishes, and is in the district of Witney Acres, 20,300 Pop, 5,629 Houses, 1,269 —The hundred includes seventeen parishes and parts of two others, is bounded by Berks on the south and by Gloucester on the west, and measures about 13 miles by 11¼ Acres, 48 188 Pop in 1851, 16,539, in 1861, 16 123 Houses, 3 554

BAMPTON, a village and a parish in West Ward district, Westmoreland The village stands on the river Lowther, 2 miles NNE of Hawes water, 4 NW of Shap r station and 9 S of Penrith, and it has a post office under Penrith The parish extends upward to Haweswater, and includes part of Mardale chapelry Acres, 10,390 Real property, £3,672 Pop, 511 Houses, 111 The property is much subdivided A lead mine, belonging to the Earl of Lonsdale has been discovered A spot not far from the village was the scene of a skirmish in the rebellion of 1745 The living is a vicarage in the diocese of Carlisle Value, £101 * Patron, the Earl of Lonsdale The church is good A grammar school, founded in 1627, has an endowed income of £83, and other charities have £95 Dr Mill, the biblical critic, Bishop Gibson, the editor of "Camden," and Judge Wilson, were educated at the grammar school, and Bishop Law, the friend of Paley, and Dr Gibson, the author of a system of anatomy, were natives

BAMPTON GRANGE a hamlet in Bampton parish, Westmoreland, 1 mile SE of Bampton village

BAMPTON KIRK, a township and a parish in Wigton district, Cumberland The township lies 4½ miles NNW of Dalston r station, and 6½ W of Carlisle, and has a post office, of the name of Kirk Bampton, under Carlisle Acres, 1,260 Real property, £1,506 Pop, 205 Houses, 37 The parish contains also the townships of Little Bampton and Oughterby Acres, 3,502 Real property, £2,817 Pop, 497 Houses, 99 The property is much subdivided The living is a rectory in the diocese of Carlisle Value, £100 * Patrons, the Earl of Lonsdale and Sir W Brisco The church is bad

BAMPTON (LITTLE), a township in Bampton Kirk parish, Cumberland, 2 miles W of Bampton Kirk township Acres, 1,337 Real property, £1,366 Pop, 172 Houses 37

BANBURY, a town a parish, a sub district, a district, and a hundred in Oxfordshire The town stands on the Cherwell river, the Oxford canal and the Oxford and Birmingham railway, 22½ miles N by W of Oxford Its name, in the Saxon times, was Banesbyrig; and its site is supposed to have been a Roman station Roman coins and a Roman altar have been found at it, and a kind of amphitheatre, still existing, is thought to be Roman. A castle was built here, about the year 1125 by Alexander, Bishop of Lincoln, and continued to be an episcopal residence till the reign of Edward VI, but only a fragment of one of the walls remains During the wars between the houses of York and Lancaster, the forces of the Yorkists held possession of the town, and a memorable action, known as the battle of Banbury, was fought in 1469, about 3 miles distant, on Danesmoor near Edgecott In the wars of the time of Charles I the castle was garrisoned for the Parliamentarians, and aided by the townspeople, who were almost all Puritans but it was captured by the Royalists after the battle of Edgehill, and held by them during thirteen weeks, till relieved by the Duke of Newcastle, and afterwards it sustained a siege of ten weeks by Colonel Whalley, and surrendered on honourable terms

The town presents a cheerful appearance, and has undergone much recent improvement, but does not possess any claim to elegance The town hall, built in 1854, is a handsome edifice, in the prevailing style of the 15th century, with an apartment 60 feet by 34, and a conspicuous tower The parish church is a large costly structure, raised under an act of parliament of 1790, has a tower over the western entrance 133 feet high, and contains two monuments of the Pigott family The new cemetery contains two neat chapels in the early English style The Roman Catholic chapel, built in 1838 and a Wesleyan chapel, built in 1864, are fine structures. There are churches in Neithrop and South B, nine dissenting chapels, a school of science built in 1861 a mechanics' institution, a blue coat school with £70 a year, alms houses and other charities with £193, a workhouse in Neithrop, a jail, two corn exchanges, a theatre and a nunnery A free grammar school was once so famous that the statutes of it were taken as models for schools in London and Manchester, but is now extinct. A college, dedicated to St Mary, stood on the Oxford road and a fragment of it still exists A lepers' hospital stood on the east side of the town, at what is now called Spital farm A spire cross, with a fountain, was recently erected on or near the site of an ancient market cross of great note, and described by Leland The town has a head post office,‡ a station on the railway, three wharves on the canal, four banking offices, and four chief inns, and publishes two weekly newspapers. It has a large corn trade, is famous for cakes, and carries on malting, brewing, wool stapling, agricultural implement making, and the manufacture of plushes and other webbing. A weekly market is held on Thursday, and fairs on the Thursday after Old Twelfth day, on the third Thursday of Feb., March, and April, on Holy Thursday, on the third Thursday of June, July, Aug., and Sept., on the first and the third Thursdays after Old Michaelmas, on the third Thursday in Nov., and on the second Thursday before Christmas. The town was made a borough in the time of Queen Mary, is governed by a mayor, four aldermen, and twelve councillors, is a seat of petty sessions, and a court of record, and sends one member to parliament. The municipal borough consists of the parish, exclusive of Neithrop township, while the parliamentary borough includes all the parish, and also the hamlets of Grimsbury and Nethercote. Pop. of the m. borough, 4,059. Houses, 791. Pop. of the p. borough, 10,216. Houses, 2,068. Direct taxation, £8,117. Real property, £20,049. Electors in 1868, 763.—Banbury formerly gave the title of Earl to the family of Knollys. Whately, the Puritan author of the "Bride Bush," born in 1583, was a native. The seats of Neithrop House, Broughton Castle, Wroxton Abbey, and Wykham Park are in the neighbourhood. A sulphurous spring adjoins the Ram inn, a chalybeate spring is at a short distance from the town, and the pyrites aureus, or golden firestone, is frequently found in digging wells.

The parish includes the town, the Neithrop suburb, and a tract of circumjacent country. Acres, 3,150. Rated property, £23,750. Pop., 9,140. Houses, 1,833. The living is a vicarage, united with the p. curacy of Neithrop, in the diocese of Oxford. Value, not reported.* Patron, the Bishop of Oxford. South Banbury, or Christ Church, is a separate charge, a vicarage, of the value of £180,* also in the patronage of the Bishop of Oxford.—The sub-district contains five other parishes, and part of a sixth. Acres, 14,925. Pop., 18,293. Houses, 2,797.—The hundred consists of two portions, on the northern border of the county, separated 3¼ miles from each other by the hundred of Bloxham. Acres, 21,186. Pop., 10,393. Houses, 2,265.—The district comprehends the sub-district of Banbury, containing the parishes of Banbury, Warkworth, Middleton Cheney, Chalcombe, Edgcott, and Chipping Warden, and the chapelry of Wardington,—all excepting Banbury and Wardington, electorally in Northamptonshire; the sub district of Bloxham, containing the parishes of Bloxham, Hook Norton, Wigginton, South Newington, Barford St. Michael, and Adderbury; the sub district of Swalcliffe, containing the parishes of Swalcliffe, Broughton, Tadmarton, Alkerton, Shenington, Hornton, Horley, Wroxton, Drayton, Padway, and Patley,—the two last electorally in Warwickshire; and the sub district of Cropredy, containing the lordship of Prescot, the extra parochial tract of Clattercote, the parish of Hanwell, and great part of the parish of Cropredy, electorally in Oxfordshire,—the parishes of Upper Boddington, Lower Boddington, and Aston le-Walls, electorally in Northamptonshire,—and the parishes of Shotswell, Warmington, Avon Dassett, and Farnborough, and small part of the parish of Cropredy, electorally in Warwickshire. Acres, 75,321. Poor rates in 1866, £23,172. Pop. in 1861, 30,171. Houses, 6,742. Marriages in 1866, 250; births, 1,051,—of which 62 were illegitimate; deaths, 593,—of which 192 were at ages under 5 years, and 16 at ages above 85 years. Marriages in the ten years 1851-60, 2,257; births, 10,051; deaths, 6,391. The places of worship in 1851 were 42 of the Church of England, with 12,042 sittings; 7 of Independents, with 1,200 s.; 9 of Baptists, with 2,030 s.; 5 of Quakers, with 832 s.; 1 of Unitarians, with 325 s.; 23 of Wesleyan Methodists, with 3,585 s.; 14 of Primitive Methodists, with 1,602 s.; 1 of Latter Day Saints, with 20 s.; 2 of Roman Catholics, with 500 s.; and 1 undefined, with 90 s. The schools were 35 public day schools, with 2,751 scholars; 61 private day schools, with 1,062 s.; 61 Sunday schools, with 3,608 s.; and 2 evening schools for adults, with 98 scholars.

BANBURY LANE, a hamlet in Gayton parish, Northampton; 4¾ miles N of Towcester. Pop., 45.

BANCHOPIUM. See BANGOR IS-Y-COED.

BANF (THE), a river of Lincoln. It rises in the Wolds, near Kelstern, and runs 20 miles southward, past Horncastle, to the Witham, about a mile below Tattershall. The lower part of it is navigable, and has been improved.

BANE END. See BONE-END.

BANESBYRIG. See BANBURY.

BANGLEY, a liberty in Tamworth parish, Stafford; 3 miles SW of Tamworth. Pop., 12. Houses, 3.

BANGOR, a city, a parish, a sub district, and a district, in Carnarvon; and a diocese in Carnarvon, Anglesey, Merioneth, and Montgomery. The city stands adjacent to the Chester and Holyhead railway, on the rivulet Cegid, in a narrow fertile vale, near the Menai strait at its opening to the Lavan sands, 2¼ miles NE of the Britannia Bridge, 8¾ NNE of Carnarvon, and 59¾ W of Chester. Rocks and heights overlook it, and command magnificent views, over coast and mountain, away to Great Ormes Head and Snowdon. The environs include Beaumaris bay, the Menai and Britannia bridges, Penrhyn Castle and quarries, delightful promenades, and many picturesque attractions. The name is a corruption of Ban Chor, signifying "the high or white choir;" and, in contradistinction to Bangor-is-y Coed or Bangor-Monachorum, was formerly written Bangor Fawr, signifying Bangor the Great. A grit stone, 16 inches long, bearing an inscription in honour of Antoninus Pius, was found in 1806 at Ty Côch, about 2 miles distant, and has suggested the probability that the Romans had some settlement in the neighbourhood. The scattered remains of a British camp exist on the top of a hill on the N side of the city; and slight traces of a strong castle, erected in the reign of William Rufus, by Hugh, Earl of Chester, occur on the summit of a steep rock, opposite Friars School. A college was founded, in 525, on the site of the cathedral by St Deiniol or Daniel; and this, most probably, gave rise to the city. The place seems never to have acquired more than the bulk of a village before the early years of the present century, and then it had only 93 houses; but now, in consequence of the thoroughfare to Holyhead, the forming of the Menai bridges, the opening of the railway, and the rush of strangers to enjoy sea-bathing and the scenery of Wales, it has become a considerable and very thriving town, with crowded influx of tourists and temporary residents.

The town consists chiefly of one narrow street, nearly a mile long, in a waving line, between two ridges of rock; and has, within these few years, been greatly improved, and for the most part rebuilt. Extensions of it are in progress; and a kind of suburb, designed to comprise terraces, crescents, and fine isolated villas, has been commenced on ground belonging to the Railway company, midway between the Menai and the Britannia bridges. The chief public buildings in the city, or connected with it, are the cathedral, the episcopal palace, the deanery house, four dissenting chapels, a Roman Catholic chapel, Glynn's free school, the work house for the district, the infirmary for Carnarvon and Anglesey, the market house, the assembly rooms, a temperance hall, the railway station, two banking offices, two great hotels, and several respectable inns. The cathedral is small, and wants effect from the lowness of its site; yet contains some good architectural details. The original pile was destroyed in 1071 by the Anglo Normans; destroyed again in 1211; dilapidated about 1247, in the wars between Henry III. and the Welsh; burnt down in 1402, during the troubles which followed the revolt of Owen Glendower; and remained, for more than 90 years, in a state of ruin. The present pile is cruciform, with central massive tower 60 feet high; the nave and choir 233 feet long; the nave and side aisles, 60 feet broad; the transept, 96 feet long. The choir is perpendicular English, and was built in 1496; but its east window was put up, in the course of a general repair of the edifice, about 1826. The nave, the transept, and the tower were built from 1509 till 1532, and the windows of the nave retain some remnants of the previous pile in decorated tracery The choir is used for the cathedral service, the north aisle of it for the chapter house, and the nave for the parish church The only monuments of interest are the tomb of Gruffydd ap Cynan, Prince of North Wales, and a recumbent stone effigies of his celebrated successor, Owen Gwynedd The episcopal palace stands on a low secluded spot, a little N of the cathedral, and is an edifice of the early part of the 16th century, much altered, plain, and commodious The deanery house adjoins the cemetery, and is a good building Glynn's free school was founded in 1557, by Dr Jeffrey Glynn brother of Bishop Glynn, and has an income of £551 Jones museum contains a large collection of rare and curious articles The railway crosses the Cegid rivulet on a viaduct 200 yards long, approaches the station through a rock cut tunnel, 1,000 yards long, and immediately afterwards enters another tunnel The town has a station, telegraph station, and a head post-office,‡ and publishes a weekly newspaper Its chief trade consists in the export of slates, raised in quarries 6 miles distant, and brought on a railway to Port Penrhyn, at the mouth of the Cegid, and from another quarry to a newly formed shipping place at Garth Port Penrhyn has a quay upwards of 300 yards long, and is accessible at all states of the tide, by vessels of from 200 to 300 tons, and adjacent to it is a good building, with hot and cold sea-water baths A manufacture of slates is carried on into billiard tables, chimney piers, and many other objects Steam vessels ply to Liverpool, calling at Beaumaris and Llandudno Markets are held on Fridays, and fairs are held on the second Friday of February, March, and April, the first Friday of May, the third Friday of June, the fourth Friday of Aug, the third Friday of Sept and Oct, and the first Thursday of Dec The town is a seat of petty sessions and a coast guard station, and it unites with the Carnarvon boroughs in sending a member to parliament Pop in 1831, 4,751, in 1861, 6,738 Houses, 1,331

The parish includes also the village of Tynlon, and the places called Aberpwl, Garth, and Hirael Acres, 7,543, of which 740 are water Real property, £25,015 Pop, 10,662 Houses, 2,090 The living is a vicarage, in the diocese of Bangor, and includes the curacy of Pentir Value, £833 * Patron, the Bishop of Bangor A new cemetery is about a mile from the town, and two churches, for two new chapelries, were built in 1863-5 —The sub-district contains also the parish of Llandegai Acres, 23,643 Pop, 14,013 Houses 2 779 —The district comprehends likewise the sub district of Llanllechid, containing the parishes of Llanllechid, Aber, and Llanfair Fechan, and the sub district of Beaumaris, all electorally in Anglesey, and containing the parishes of Beaumaris, Llanfihangel Esceifiog Penmynydd, Llansadwrn, Llaniestyn, Llanfihangel Tyn Sylwy, Penmon, Llanfaes, Llandegfan, and Llanfair Pwllgwyngyll, and the parochial chapelries of Llanedwen Llanddaniel Fab, Llanfinnan, Llangoed, and Llandisilio Acres, 92,478 Poor rates in 1866, £18,948 Pop in 1861, 36,309 Houses, 7,673 Marriages in 1866, 285, births, 1,078, —of which 60 were illegitimate, deaths, 1,005, of which 271 were at ages under 5 years, and 41 at ages above 85 years. Marriages in the ten years 1851-60, 2,619, births, 10,772 deaths, 7,096 The places of worship in 1851 were 24 of the Church of England, with 7,085 sittings, 16 of Independents, with 4,018 s, 8 of Baptists, with 945 s, 15 of Wesleyan Methodists, with 3,907 s, 24 of Calvinistic Methodists with 9,593 s, 1 of Roman Catholics, with 200 s, and 1 of Latter Day Saints, with 30 attendants The schools were 23 public day schools, with 2,755 scholars, 21 private day schools, with 735 s, 76 Sunday schools, with 10,143 s, and 1 evening school for adults, with 5 s

The diocese comprehends all Anglesey, most of Carnarvon, about half of Merioneth, and part of Montgomery Acres 935,946 Pop 195,390 Houses, 41,970 The see was founded in 550 The first bishop was St Deiniol, the founder of the precurrent college The bishop, in the time of Edward I, was Anian, who baptized the young prince Edward and wrote a folio volume, which is preserved in the cathedral library A bishop in the time of George I was Hoadley, who preached a sermon which gave rise to a long and famous dispute, known as the Bangorian controversy Two other distinguished bishops were Sherlock and Herring The cathedral establishment consists of bishop, dean, chancellor, two archdeacons, three canons residentiary a prebendary, five honorary canons, and two minor canons The income of the bishop is £4,200, of the dean, £700, of each of the canons residentiary, £350, of the prebendary, £318 The archdeaconries are Bangor and Merioneth, and the former comprises nine deaneries, the latter five Some of the livings have recently been raised in status, and are named as they now rank in the separate articles on them in our work, but all will be named here as they ranked in 1861

The deanery of Arvon contains the rectories of Llanaelhaiarn, Llanberis, Llanddeiniolen, Llandwrog, Llanllyfni and Llanrug, the vicarages of Bangor, Llanbeblig, and Llanwnda, and the p curacies of Bettws Garmon, Carnarvon St Mary s, Llanddeiniolen, and Llanfairisgaer The deanery of Arllechwedd contains the rectories of Aber Llanfairfechan, Llangelynin Llanllechid, and Trefriw, the vicarages of Conway, Dwygyfylchi, and Llanbedr and the p curacies of Bettws y Coed, Capel Curig, Dolwyddelan, Glanogwen, Gyffin, Llandegai, Llandegai-St Ann's, Llandudno, and Penmachno The deanery of Caedewen contains the rectories of Aberhafesp, Llandyssil, Llanmerewig, Llanwyddelan, Manafon, and Newtown, the vicarages of Berriew, Bettws, Kerry, and Llanllwchaiarn, and the p. curacies of Llanllugan, Mochtre, and Tregynon The deanery of Llifon contains the rectories of Llanbeulan, and Llantrisaint, and the p. curacies of Bodedern, Llanddrygarn, and Talyllyn The deanery of Menai contains the rectories of Llangeinwen and Newborough, the vicarage of Llanidan, and the p. curacy of Llanfihangel Ysceifiog The deanery of Malltraeth contains the rectories of Aberffraw, Heneglwys, Llangadwaladr, Llangefni, Llangristiolus, and Trefdraeth, and the p curacy of Llangwyllog The deanery of Tyndaethwy contains the rectories of Llandegfan, Llanddyfnan, Llansadwrn, and Llanfairpwllgwyngyll, and the p curacies of Llanfaes, Llangoed, Llanddona, Pentraeth, and Penmynydd The deanery of Talybolion contains the rectories of Llanfachrath, Llanfaethle, Llanfechell, Llanrhuddlad, Rhoscolyn, and Llanddeusant, the vicarage of Llanbadrig and the p curacy of Holyhead The deanery of Twrcelyn contains the rectories of Llandyfrydog Llaneilian, and Llanengrad, and the p curacies of Amlwch, Bodewryd, Penrhoslligwy, and Llanerchymedd

The deanery of Eivionydd contains the rectories of Criccieth Llanfihangel y-Pennant, Llangybi, Llanystumdwy, and Penmorfa, and the p curacy of Beddgelert. The deanery of Ardwdwy and Estimaner contains the rectories of Dolgelly Festiniog Llanaber, Llanddwywe, Llanenddwyn, Llanfair near Harlech, Llanfrothen, and Trawsfynydd the vicarage of Towyn, and the p. curacies of Brynycoedifor, Llanegryn Llanelltyd, Llanfachreth, Llanfihangel y-Pennant, Llanfihangel y Traethau, Pennal, Tallylyn, and Aberdovey The deanery of Arwystli contains the rectory of Penystowed the vicarages of Llandinam, Llandloes, Llangurig, Llanwnog, Llanidloes, and Trefeglwys, and the p curacy of Carno The deanery of Cyfeiliog contains the rectories of Cemmaes, Llanwrin, Llan Mowddwy Mallwyd, Machynlleth, and Penegoes, and the vicarages of Darowen and Llanbrynmair The deanery of Lleyn contains the rectory of Bodfean Edern, Llanbedrog Llaniengan, Llaniestyn, Meyllteyrn, and Rhiw, the vicarages of Aberdaron and Llannor and the p curacies of Aberdaron, Pwllheli, Ceidio Llangwnadl, Nefyn, and Tudweiliog

BANGOR, a parish in Newcastle in Emlyn district, Cardigan, on the river Teifi, 5 miles E of Newcastle Emlyn r station Post town, Newcastle Emlyn, under Carmarthen Acres 1 392 Real property, £978 Pop, 204 Houses, 41 The property is divided among a few The manor belonged to the Pastogs. The living is a rectory united with Heollan in the diocese of St David's Value, £163 Patron, the Bishop of St. David's The church is good

BANGOR, or CAPEL BANGOR, a chapelry in Llanbadarn Fawr parish, Cardigan, on the river Rheidol, 5 miles E of Aberystwith Post town, Aberystwith Pop., 1,919 Houses, 354 The property is much subdivided. The living is a vicarage in the diocese of St David's Value £148 Patron, the Vicar of Llanbadarn Fawr The church is good.

BANGOR IS-Y COED, or BANGOR MONACHORUM, a township in the district of Wrexham and county of Flint, and a parish partly also in the county of Denbigh The township lies on the river Dee, in an open fertile country, 5½ miles SE of Wrexham railway station It has a post office,‡ of the name of Bangor Is y Coed, under Wrexham, and a bridge of five arches on the Dee It was the Roman Banchorium or Bovium, and the Saxon Bancornaburg, and it anciently had a large monastery, said to have been founded previous to the year 180, by Lucius, son of Coel, the first Christian king of Britain The monks increased in number to 2,100, and so many as 1,200 of them were massacred in 593 by king Ethelfrith of Northumbria. Gildas Ninnius, who lived in the 7th century, and wrote a history of England which is still extant, was one of the abbots The ruins of many churches and of other extensive buildings are described by William of Malmesbury as existing soon after the Conquest, but these, and all other traces of the ancient monastery long ago disappeared Real property of the township, £4,884 Pop, 585 Houses, 138 The parish includes also the townships of Eyton, Royton, Pickhill, and Sesswick Acres, 5 795. Real property, £11,400 Pop, 1,240 Houses 261 The property is divided among a few The living is a rectory in the diocese of St Asaph, and till 1868 was united with Overton Value, £700 * Patron, the Marquis of Westminster The church contains a curious, octagonal ancient font and is good A school has £39 from endowment, and other charities £37

BANGROVE See BECKFORD

BANHAGLOG, a chapelry in Llandinam parish, Montgomery, near Llandinam r station, and 4½ miles NE of Llanidloes. Post town, Llandinam under Shrewsbury The living is a p curacy in the diocese of Bangor Value, not reported Patron, the Bishop

BANHAM, a parish and a sub district, in the district of Guiltcross, Norfolk The parish lies 2½ miles SW of New Buckenham, and 4 E of Eccles Road r station, and has a post office under Attleborough Acres, 3,963. Real property, £8,131 Pop, 1,163 Houses, 253 The property is much subdivided The living is a rectory in the diocese of Norwich. Value £1,000 * Patron the Lord Chancellor The church is good, and there are two Methodist chapels, a national school, and charities, £136.—The sub district contains eight parishes Acres, 18,631 Pop., 5,516 Houses, 1 243

BANKEN, a township in Llandyrnog parish, Denbighshire, 4½ miles E of Denbigh Pop, 96

BANKFOOT, a chapelry in Bradford parish, W R Yorkshire It was constituted in 1850 Post town Bradford Rated property, £1,213 Pop 2 641 Houses, 600 The living is a p. curacy in the diocese of Ripon Value £120 * Patron, Rt H n G Hardy

BANKHEAD, a township in Rothbury parish, Northumberland, included in Cartington township, 2 miles N of Rothbury Pop, 16

BANKLAND, a hamlet in North Petherton parish, Somerset, 6½ miles NE of Taunton

BANK NEWTON, a township in Gargrave parish W R Yorkshire, on the Leeds and Liverpool canal, 6 miles W by N of Skipton Acres 2 326 Real property, £2 930 Pop 106 Houses, 19

BANKS, a constablewick in Lanercost parish Cumberland 2 miles N of Brampton

BANKS a chapelry in North Meols parish Lancashire 3 miles NE of Southport It was constituted in 1867 The living is a vicarage

BANKS (FEE), a hamlet in Longborough parish, Gloucester, 2 miles NW of Stow on the Wolds

BANK TOP, a village in Sharples township, Bolton-le Moors parish, Lancashire, 4½ miles NNW of Bolton

BANNAGOR CRAGS, picturesque crags, "scathed verdureless and shivered," amid a grand landscape, on the river Wye, 3 miles N by W of Chepstow, Monmouth

BANNAN BRECHEINOG, or BRECKNOCK BEACONS, two summits of the Black Mountains, 2,862 feet high, 5½ miles SSW of Brecon, South Wales

BANNAN SIR GAER, or CARMARTHEN BEACONS, two summits of the Black Mountains, about 2,600 feet high, the one within Brecknockshire, the other within Carmarthenshire, 8½ miles SSE of Llandovery, and 12½ W by N of the Bannan Brecheinog, South Wales.

BANNEL, a township in Hawarden parish, Flint, near the Mold railway 4½ miles E of Mold Acres, 376 Real property, £463 Pop, 124 Houses, 28

BANNER CROSS, a hamlet in Ecclesall Bierlow township, Sheffield parish, W R Yorkshire, 3 miles SW of Sheffield. A mansion here, built by General Murray, is in the later English style

BANNERDOWN, a tract containing the meeting point of Wilts Gloucester, and Somerset The point is 1¼ mile NW of the Box tunnel of the Great Western railway, and 4¾ miles W of Corsham It was marked, for upwards of a century, by three small stones, but is marked now by a cromlech, set up in 1858

BANNINGHAM, a parish in Aylsham district, Norfolk, on a tributary of the river Bure, 2½ miles NE of Aylsham, and 14 N of Norwich r station Post town, Aylsham under Norwich Acres, 920 Real property, £2,209 Pop, 302 Houses, 67 The property is divided among a few The living is a rectory in the diocese of Norwich Value, £446 * Patrons, J S Dawber, Esq and Rev W Leeper The church is old but good There are a national school, and charities £5

BANNIUM See ABERYSCIR

BANSTEAD, a village and a parish in Epsom district, Surrey The village stands under the SW side of Banstead Downs, 4 miles E of Epsom, and has a post office under Epsom, a r station, and a police station The parish comprises 5,518 acres Real property £7,214 Pop, 1 461 Houses, 277 The property is subdivided Banstead Park is a seat belonging to Mr Yong, and Burgh House, in the neighbourhood, is the seat of the Earl of Egmont Banstead downs rise to the height of 576 feet, command extensive views, and are famous for coursing, for hunting, and for fine sheep pasturage Here, said Pope

> "To Hounslow Heath I point and Banstead Down,
> Thence comes your mutton, and these chicks my own"

The living is a vicarage in the diocese of Winchester Value, £300 * Patron, the Earl of Egmont The church is chiefly perpendicular English, has a good tower, surmounted by a tall spire, stands on high ground, and serves well for miles round, as a landmark Charities, £39 The Banstead and Epsom Downs railway, from the Sutton station of the Croydon and Epsom, was authorised in 1862 and opened in 1865

BANTHAM a hamlet in Thurlestone parish, Devon, on the river Avon, ½ a mile above its mouth, and 4½ miles W of Kingsbridge A ferry is here across the river and a roadstead adjacent gives shelter to small craft

BANWELL, a village, a parish and a sub district, in the district of Axbridge, Somerset The village stands under Banwell Hill, at the NW extremity of the Mendip range 3 miles SE of the Bristol and Exeter railway and 4 NNW of Axbridge It has a station on the railway, a post office‡ under Weston super Mare, and two inns and was formerly a seat of petty sessions A fair is held at it on 18 January or on the following Monday A monastery was founded here by some early Saxon king, had for one of its abbots Asserius or Asser, the biographer of King Alfred, was destroyed by the Danes and afterwards restored, but seems to have given place to an Episcopal palace, and ceased to be monastic long before the dissolution of monasteries. A mineral well in the vicinity expands into a lakelet, drives two mills, and sends off a rivulet to the Bristol Channel near Wood spring priory The parish contains also the hamlets of Knightcot, East and West Rolston, Towerhead, Westwick and Waywick, Woolfords hill, and Yarborough Acres, 4,829 Real property, £15,880 Pop, 1,853 Houses, 362 The property is much subdivided Banwell hill belongs chiefly to Captain Law, grandson of the late Bishop of Bath and Wells, and has an obelisk, erected by that prelate. The manor has belonged, since the time of Edward the Confessor to the Bishops of Bath and Wells. A palace was built on it by Bishop Beckington, but went into neglect, and now is represented only by a large farm house and offices, called Banwell Court, and by a cottage ornee Two remarkable caverns, discovered in 1824, and now so famous as to draw many visitors, occur on the skirts of Banwell Hill, the one, called the Stalactite cavern, presenting many beautiful specimens of translucent stalactites, the other, called the Bone cavern, found to have contained many bones of bears, buffalos, deer, wolves, foxes, and other animals, mingled with diluvium Bowles depicts a geological crisis, at which he fancies the bones to have been deposited, in his poem of "Banwell Hill or Days Departed" The living is a vicarage in the diocese of Bath and Wells Value, £702 * Patrons, the Dean and Chapter of Bristol. The church is later English, and has a richly-carved screen a finely sculptured stone pulpit, a circular font, and three brasses There are a Wesleyan chapel and charities £17 —The sub district comprises eight parishes Acres, 19,906 Pop, 12,649 Houses, 2,043

BAPCHILD, a village and a parish in Milton district, Kent The village stands near the Chatham railway, 1 mile ESE of Sittingbourne, and has a post office under Sittingbourne It probably was the Saxon Bachancild, where Wihtred, king of Kent, in 694 held his great council for the repairing of churches The parish comprises 1,058 acres Real property, £3,160 Pop. 389 Houses, 85 The property is divided among a few The manor belonged to the Crown in the time of King John, and was then given to Chichester cathedral Bapchild Court, adjoining the village, is the seat of W Gascoigne, Esq A small oratory stood by the wayside, as a resting place for pilgrims in route to Canterbury, but has disappeared The living is a vicarage in the diocese of Canterbury Value, £192 Patrons, the Dean and Chapter of Chichester The church consists of nave, north aisle, two chancels, and a square tower, is principally Norman, but contains many parts in various dates of English, and is in very good condition

BAPTON, a hamlet in the parish of Fisherton de la Mare, Wilts, 5½ miles SE of Heytesbury Pop, 143

BARBARY See BARBURY

BARBER AND COCKLE SHOALS, two shoals off Caistor, north of Yarmouth harbour, Norfolk They separate Hemesby Gat from Cockle Gat, and are both well buoyed

BARBER NOOK, a hamlet in Ecclesall Bierlow township, Sheffield parish, W R Yorkshire, 4¼ miles SW of Sheffield

BARBON, a chapelry in Kirkby Lonsdale parish, Westmoreland, on the river Lune and the Ingleton railway, under Casterton fell, 3 miles NNE of Kirkby Lonsdale It has a station on the railway, and includes the hamlet of Beckfoot. Its post town is Kirkby Lonsdale, under Burton in Kendal Acres, 4,204 Real property, £2,568 Pop, 364 Houses, 60 The property is divided among a few The living is a p curacy in the diocese of Carlisle. Value, £80 Patron, the Vicar of K L.

BARBOURNE, a chapelry in Claines parish in the N vicinity of Worcester city Pop, about 1,400 Living a p curacy The church is a handsome edifice of 1864

BARBRIDGE, a hamlet in Cheshire, 3½ miles NW of Nantwich It has a post office under Nantwich

BARBURY, a hill at the northern extremity of Marlborough downs, 5 miles S of Swindon, Wilts It is a culminating height of the county, amid wild lonely downs, and commands an extensive view A long and obstinate battle was fought on it, in 556 between the Saxons under Cynric and the Britons which led to the annexation of Wilts to Essex A well preserved British camp is on it, called Barbury Castle, about 2,000 feet in diameter, with double ditch and rampart

BARBY, a village and a parish in the district of Rugby and county of Northampton The village stands near the Oxford canal, 1½ mile from the Kilsby tunnel of the Northwestern railway, 4 miles NW of Crick r station, and 4½ SE of Rugby, and has a post office under Rugby The parish is called also Barby with Onley Acres, 2,535 Real property, £6,960 Pop., 645 Houses, 156 The property is much subdivided The living is a rectory in the diocese of Peterborough Value, £1,150 * Patron, John Jackson, Esq The church is good Charities and town lands, £121

BARCHESTON a village and a parish in Shipston on Stour district, Warwick. The village stands on the verge of the county, at the river Stour, 1 mile SE of Shipston on-Stour and 7½ NE of Blockley r station, and was a place of some consequence at the Conquest. The parish includes also the hamlet of Willington, and its post town is Shipston on Stour Acres, 1,475 Real property, £2,609 Pop, 190 Houses, 41 The property is divided among a few The manor was purchased, in the reign of Henry VII, by William Willington, and passed to the family of Sheldon The living is a rectory in the diocese of Worcester Value, £240 * Patron, the Rev G D Wheeler The church was restored in 1869

BARCLAY See BARKELEY

BARCOMBE, a parish and a hundred in Lewes district, Sussex. The parish lies on the Uckfield railway and the Ouse river, 4 miles N by E of Lewes, and it has a station on the railway, and a post-office under Lewes Acres, 4 983 Real property, £7 286 Pop, 1,090 Houses, 203 The property is divided among a few Sutton Hurst and Barcombe Place are chief residences The living is a rectory in the diocese of Chichester Value, £719 * Patron, the Lord Chancellor The church is tolerable, and an endowed school has £63 —The hundred is in the rape of Lewes, and includes the parishes of Barcombe, Hamsey, and Newick Acres, 9,710 Pop, 2,570. Houses, 485

BARDEN, a township in Hawkswell parish, N R. Yorkshire, 3½ miles NE of Leyburn It includes the hamlet of Barden Dykes Acres, 1,330 Real property, £1,292. Pop., 76 Houses, 17

BARDEN, a township in Skipton parish, W R. Yorkshire in Wharfdale 7 miles ENE of Skipton It includes the hamlet of Drebley, and has a post office under Skipton Acres, 6,115 Real property, £1 332 Pop, 371 Houses, 63 Most of the surface is moor and fell, and anciently was a forest. Barden Tower, built by Henry Clifford, "the Shepherd Lord," after his restoration to his property and titles, a plain structure in the Tudor style, was in good repair so late as 1774, and is now a picturesque ruin A chapel of the same age, attached to an adjacent farm house, is still in use The Shepherd Lord, as says the poet Wordsworth,

> "——— did not in wars delight,
> *This* Clifford wished for worthier might,
> Nor in broad pomp, or courtly state,
> Him his own thoughts did elevate,—
> Most happy in the shy recess
> Of Barden's lowly quietness."

BARDFIELD (GREAT), a village and a parish in Dunmow district, Essex The village stands on Blackwater river, 9 miles NW of Braintree r station. It has a post-office‡ under Braintree, a new town hall a police station and a fair on 22 Jan, and is a seat of petty sessions The parish comprises 3,689 acres Real property £6,715 Pop, 1,065 Houses, 259 The property is subdivided The living is a vicarage in the diocese of Rochester Value, £262 * Patron, Representatives of late Rev B E. Lampet. The church is old. There are three dissenting chapels, two public schools, and charities £72

BARDFIELD (LITTLE), a parish in Dunmow district, Essex on Blackwater river, 11 miles NW of Braintree r station It has a post office under Braintree Acres, 1 710 Real property, £3,082 Pop, 420 Houses, 90 The property is much subdivided The living is a rectory in the diocese of Rochester Value, £590 * Patron, the Rev M Barnard The church is good Alms houses and other charities have £80

BARDFIELD SALING, or LITTLE SALING, a parish in Dunmow district, Essex, 5 miles NW by W of Braintree r station Post town, Saling, under Braintree Acres, 1,111 Real property, £1,757 Pop, 356 Houses, 84 The property is divided among a few The living is a donative in the diocese of Rochester Value, £75 Patron, W Sandle, Esq The church is good Charities, £7

BARDLEY, a township in Stottesden parish, Salop, 3¼ miles N of Cleobury Mortimer Pop, 178

BARDNEY, a village and a parish in the district and county of Lincoln The village stands on the river Witham, adjacent to the Lincoln and Boston railway, 5¼ miles E by S of Lincoln, and has a station on the railway and a post-office‡ under Wragby It dates from ancient times, and was called by the Saxons Bardanig or Bealthanig The parish includes also the hamlet of Southrow Acres, 5 490 Real property £8,653 Pop, 1,425 Houses, 298 An abbey was founded, about ½ a mile west of the village, in 697, by Ethelred, king of Mercia, who himself afterwards became abbot of it till his death It is said to have had 300 monks, but was destroyed, in 870, by the Danes, lay in ruins upwards of 200 years was re edified, in the time of William the Conqueror for Benedictine monks, by Gilbert de Gaunt, Earl of Lincoln, and passed, at the dissolution, to Sir Robert Tirwhit The later abbots were styled Lords of Lindsey, and were peers in parliament Not a vestige of the edifice now exists A large barrow occurs in the neighbourhood, said to have been the grave of King Ethelred, and is surmounted by a modern cross, erected to his memory The parish is a meet for the Burton Hounds The living is a vicarage in the diocese of Lincoln Value, £300 * Patron, the Bishop of Lincoln The church consists of nave, aisle, chancel, and tower There are three Wesleyan chapels A free school has £1 6 and other charities £70

BARDON, a hamlet in St. Decumans parish, Somerset, 2 miles SW of Watchet.

BARDON, an extra parochial tract in Loughborough district Leicester, on the Leicester and Burton railway, 10 miles by road and 14½ by railway, NW of Leicester It has a station on the railway, and contains the Birch Tree hotel, Bardon Park mansion, and an Independent chapel Acres, 1,710 Pop, 63 Houses, 13 Bardon Hill here is a peak of the Charnwood Forest range, has an altitude of 853 feet, and commands a panoramic view, said to include about one-fourth of England. Drayton sings of the dryads,

> On Sharpley that were seen and Cadman s ancient rocks,
> Against the rising sun to braid their silver locks,
> And with the harmless elves on heathy Bardon s height,
> By Cynthia s golden beams to play there night by night."

BARDON-MILL, a railway station in Northumberland, on the Newcastle and Carlisle railway, adjacent to the South Tyne river, 4 miles W of Haydon Bridge Here is a post office under Carlisle

BARDOP (THE), a rivulet of Northumberland, falling into the Reed at Rochester, 5½ miles NW of Otterburn

BARDSEA, a township chapelry in Urswick parish Lancashire, on Morecambe bay 3 miles S by E of Ulverstone r station It has a post office under Ulverstone Real property, £1,846 Pop, 272 Houses, 62 An hospital of the Knights of St John once stood here A project was at one time afoot to cut a ship canal hence to the foot of Windermere The chapelry was constituted in 1854 The living is a vicarage in the diocese of Carlisle Value, £100 Patron, the Rev F Lee The church is modern Gothic There is an endowed school

BARDSEY, a township in Tadcaster district, and a parish partly also in Otley d strict, W R Yorkshire The township is united to Rigton, under the name of Bardsey cum Rigton, lies 5 miles SW by S of Wetherby r station, and has a post office, of the name of Rigton, under Otley Acres 2,745 Real property, £2,920. Pop, 295 Houses, 65 The parish includes also the township of Wothersome, and part of that of Wike. Acres, 3,437 Real property, with the rest of Wike, £4,524 Pop, 318 Houses, 69 The property is divided among a few Bardsey Grange was probably the birthplace of Congreve, the poet and dramatist, and was the occasional residence and the deathplace of Francis Thorp, the notorious Baron of the Exchequer Castle Hill, a little north of the village, was the site of a Roman fort The living is a vicarage in the diocese of Ripon Value, £300 * Patron, G L. Fox, Esq The church is good early Norman A school has £20 from endowment, and other charities £5

BARDSEY ISLE, an extra parochial island in Pwllheli district, Carnarvon It lies at the NW extremity of Cardigan bay, 2¾ miles S by W of Braich y Pwll headland, and 15 SW of Pwllheli. The sound between it and Braich y Pwll has from 15 to 25 fathoms water, but is swept by so strong a current in spring tides as to be called Bardsey race The island is nearly 2 miles long, measures ¾ of a mile at the north end, contracts into a narrow headland on the south, and comprises 430 acres Pop, 81 Houses, 14 It belongs to Lord Newborough, and yields a rental of £122 Part of it, on the north east, is a high rugged hill, with precipitous sea face, but the rest is chiefly low fertile plain A lighthouse, built in 1821, and 108 feet high, stands on the southern headland, and shows a fixed light, visible at the distance of 5 miles. The islanders are employed variously in farming and fishing, and conduct a brisk coast trade in lobsters, oysters, and white fish, with Liverpool A small well-sheltered harbour, on the south east side, admits vessels of from 30 to 40 tons The island is called Ynys Enlli by the Welsh, signifying "the island of the current," in allusion to the tidal stream in the sound, but was called Bards-Y, or Bards Island, by the Saxons, whence its present name Bardsey, and Insula Sanctorum, or the island of the saints, by the monks, in allusion to its early ecclesiastical history A monastery was founded on it, prior to 516, by Cadfan, and became the retreat and the deathplace of Dubritius, archbishop of Caerleon, who died in 612, and also the asylum of numerous refugees from the massacre of the monks at Bangor Is y Coed The bards allege that 20,000 saints were buried here, and Fuller, in his "Worthies," remarks that "it would be more facile to find graves in Bardsey for so many saints, than saints for so many graves The monastery was reconstituted an abbey for canons in the 13th century, but is now represented by only a fragment of its church tower

BARDSLEY, a chapelry in Ashton under Lyne parish, Lancashire, 2 miles N by W of Ashton Pop 2 721 Houses, 529 The inhabitants are employed chiefly in cotton factories, iron works, and coal mines The living is a p curacy in the diocese of Manchester Value £221 * Patrons, Hulme s Trustees The church was built in 1844, and schools in 1846, at costs of £2,500 and £2,100

BARDWELL a village and a parish in Thingoe district, Suffolk The village stands on a tributary of the Little Ouse river, 6 miles N by W of Thurston r station, and 8 NE of Bury St Edmunds, and has a post office under Bury St Edmunds The parish comprises 3 144 acres Real property, £4,971 Pop, 852 Houses, 198 The property is much subdivided Some barrows occur on Bowbeck Heath The living is a rectory in the diocese of Ely Value, £597 * Patron, St John's college, Oxford The church has a tower, stained glass windows, and some good monuments, and was thoroughly renovated in 1853 There are two dissenting chapels, an endowed school, and charities £103

BARE, a hamlet in Lancaster parish, with a st on the Morecambe railway, 3 miles NW of Lancaster Pop., 120

BAREHAM See LINTON, Cambridge

BARF, a bold, rugged hill, on the upper part of the west flank of Bassenthwaite water, Cumberland

BARF-END, a hamlet in Melbecks township, Grinton parish near Reeth, N R Yorkshire

BARFIELD, a village in Whitbeck parish, Cumberland, near the coast, 6½ miles SSE of Ravenglass

BARFORD, a hamlet in Kingston Lacy manor, Dorset, 3 miles W of Wimborne

BARFORD, a sub district and a hundred in Beds The sub district is in the district of Bedford, and contains the parish of Great Barford and four other parishes Acres, 12,340 Pop, 3,100 Houses, 655 —The hundred includes the sub district and three other parishes, extends north eastward from Bedford to Hunts, and is 11½ miles long and 4½ broad Acres, 24,770 Pop, 6,938 Houses, 1,460

BARFORD, a parish in Forehoe district, Norfolk, on the river Yare, 5 miles NNW of Wymondham r station, and 9 W of Norwich Post town, Barnham-Broom under Wymondham Acres, 1,052 Real property, £2,506 Pop, 419 Houses 94 The property is sub divided The living is a rectory in the diocese of Norwich. Value, £288 Patron, Skinner Turner, Esq The church is good, and there are two Methodist chapels

BARFORD an extra parochial tract in Kettering district, Northampton, 2 miles ENE of Rothwell. Pop., 7

BARFORD, a village and a parish in the district and county of Warwick The village stands on the river Avon, amid pleasant environs, 3 miles S by W of Warwick r station, contains some fine houses, and has a post office under Warwick The parish comprises 1,540 acres Real property, £5,668 Pop, 751 Houses, 190 The property is much subdivided Barford House is the seat of Capt W Ryton, and commands a charming view The living is a rectory in the diocese of Worcester Value, £369 * Patron, John Mills, Esq The church was rebuilt in 1844, but includes the square tower of a previous edifice, and contains several monuments of the Mills family A school has an endowed income of £48, and other charities £12

BARFORD (GREAT), a parish in the district and county of Bedford, on the river Ouse, 3 miles NNW of Sandy r station, and 6 1 by N of Bedford It has a post-office under St Neots Acres, 2 830. Real property, £4,679 Pop, 907 Houses, 198 The property is subdivided The river Ouse here is crossed by a bridge of about the beginning of the 15th century, and is navigable. The living is a vicarage, annexed to Roxton, in the dio of Ely The church is later English There are a Wesleyan chapel, a national school, and charities £20

BARFORD (GREAT), Oxford See BARFORD ST MICHAEL

BARFORD (LITTLE), a parish in the district of St. Neot's and county of Bedford, on the river Ouse, and on the Great Northern railway, at the verge of the county, 3 miles S of St. Neots Post town, St Neots Acres, 1,138 Real property, £1,251 Pop, 91 Houses, 26 The property is all in one estate The living is a rectory in the diocese of Ely Value, £251 * Patron, W Allington Esq The church is old but good Charities, £7

BARFORD (LITTLE), Oxford See BARFORD (ST JOHN)

BARFORD (ST JOHN), a chapelry in Adderbury parish Oxford, on a tributary of the river Cherwell 2½ miles WNW of Deddington, and 4 W by N of Aynho r station Post town Deddington, under Oxford Acres, 480 Real property, £1,532 Pop, 107 Houses, 26 The living is a p curacy annexed to the vicarage of Adderbury, in the diocese of Oxford The church is ancient, and has a Norman door

BARFORD (ST MARTIN), a parish in Wilton district, Wilts, on a tributary of the river Avon, 3 miles W of Wilton r station, and 5½ W by N of Salisbury It has a post office under Salisbury Acres inclusive of the extra parochial tract of Grovely Wood 2,236 Real property, together with Baverstock £3,984 Pop, 519 Houses, 116 The property is divided among a few The living is a rectory in the diocese of Salisbury Value, £577 * Patron, All Souls' College Oxford The church is good, and there is an Independent chapel

BARFORD (ST MICHAEL), a parish in Banbury district, Oxford, on the river Swere, 2½ miles W by N of Deddington, and 4 W of Aynho r station Post town, Deddington, under Oxford Acres, 1,180 Real property, £2,234 Pop., 332 Houses, 85 The property is divided among a few The living is a vicarage in the diocese of Oxford Value, £67 * Patron, John Hall, Esq The church is early English, with fine Norman door There are two Methodist chapels, and charities £25

BARFORTH, a township in Forcett parish, N R Yorkshire, on the river Tees, 6 miles W by S of Darlington It had a Roman station, and was formerly called Old Richmond Acres, 1,750 Real property, £2,403 Pop, 167 Houses, 25

BARFRESTON, or BARSTON, a parish in Eastry district, Kent, on the Dover and Canterbury railway, near Shepherd's Well station, and 6½ miles NW of Dover Post town, Goodnestone, under Sandwich Acres 500 Real property, £641 Pop, 144 Houses, 26 The property is not much divided The manor belonged early to the see of Canterbury, and passed, in 1081, to Hugh de Port, constable of Dover The living is a rectory in the diocese of Canterbury Value, £182 * Patron, St John's College, Oxford The church consists of nave and chancel, separated by a circular arch, is one of the most remarkable structures of its class in England, exhibits rich exterior decorations, in corbels, wreaths, and other sculptures and was well restored in 1840

BARGOED, a station on the Rhymney railway, on the mutual border of Monmouth and Wales, 18½ miles N of Cardiff The Bargoed Rhymney valley here joins that of the Rhymney river, and is crossed by the railway on a handsome viaduct

BARHAM, a parish in the district and county of Huntingdon, on a tributary of the river Ouse, 7 miles WNW of Huntingdon r station. Post town, Spaldwick, under St. Neots Acres, 700 Real property, £703 Pop, 115 Houses, 28 The living is a vicarage in the diocese of Ely Value, £58 Patron, the Bishop of Ely Charities, £8

BARHAM a village, a parish, downs, and a sub district, in the district of Bridge, Kent. The village stands in a valley, under the downs about 3½ miles SW of Adisham station on the London, Chatham and Dover railway, and 6 SE of Canterbury, and has a post office‡ under Canterbury The parish comprises 4,600 acres Real property, £6,058 Pop, 1,390 Houses, 232 The subsoil is chiefly chalk The manor belonged early to the see of Canterbury and was held by Reginald Fitzurse, one of Thomas à Becket's murderers, and afterwards by Fitzurse's descendants till the time of James I The principal residences are Broome Park the seat of Sir Henry Chudleigh Oxenden, Bart, and Barham Court, belonging to George C Dering, Esq The living is a rectory in the diocese of Canterbury Value, £800 * Patron, the Archbishop of Canterbury The church is early decorated English, and has a lofty spire and some neat monuments Digges, the mathematician, had connexion with the parish, and Admiral Sir T Thomson was a native The downs extend from SE to NW along the line of Watling street, and are about 3 miles long Numerous barrows are on them, of times from early British to later Saxon showing them to have been scenes of many ancient public events King John with his army of 60,000 men, encamped on them, in 1213, prior to the resigning of his crown. Simon de Montfort assembled his troops on them, in the time of Henry III, to oppose the landing of Queen Eleanor Queen Henrietta Maria, after her landing at Dover in 1625 was met on them by the flower of the English nobility Several regiments lay posted on them, in the time of Napoleon Buonaparte, to oppose his threatened invasion from Boulogne Traces of the camp of these regiments, and also a small square ancient camp, still exist. The Canterbury races, now of little note, are held on the downs, and the election of members for East Kent takes place on them. The sub district comprises thirteen parishes Acres, 22,871 Pop, 6,296 Houses, 1,257

BARHAM, a parish in Bosmere district, Suffolk, on the river Gipping, 1½ mile NE of Claydon r station, and 5 N of Ipswich. Post town, Claydon, under Ipswich Acres, 1,506 Real property, £3,281 Pop, 568 Houses, 90 The property is divided among a few The living is a rectory in the diocese of Norwich Value £342 * Patron F W. Schreiber, Esq The church is good. The work house for Bosmere district is here

BARHAM COURT a manor on the river Medway, near East Farleigh r station, 4½ miles SW of Maidstone, Kent. It belonged to Reginald Fitzurse, the proprietor of Barham manor in Bridge district in the time of A' Becket, continued with his descendants, the De Berhams, till the time of James I, passed to successively the Botlers, the Bouveries, and Sir Charles Middleton, who was created Lord Barham, descended to Lord Barham's grandson, the present Earl of Gainsborough, and is now the property and seat of the Right Hon. T Pemberton Leigh. The mansion on it is modern.

BARHOLM, a parish in Stamford district, Lincoln, on the Glen river near the Great Northern railway 2¾ miles SSE of Corby r station, and 3½ W NW of Market Deeping Post town, Market Deeping Acres, 1,230 Real property, £1,876 Pop, 192 Houses, 42 The property is not much divided. The living is a vicarage, united with the vicarage of Stowe, in the diocese of Lincoln. Value, £147 Patrons, the Trustees of Oakham and Uppingham schools. The church is good

BARIPPER a locality 1 mile from Camborne, Cornwall, with a post office under that town

BARKBY, a township and a parish in Barrow upon-Soar district, Leicester The township lies on an affluent of the river Wreak, 1½ mile S by E of Syston r station, and 4½ NE of Leicester, and it includes the hamlet of Hambleton. Real property, £3,739 Pop., 504 Houses, 117 The parish contains also the township of North Thurmaston and the hamlet of Barkby-Thorpe, and its post town is Syston, under Leicester Acres, 2 290 Real property, exclusive of Thurmaston, £4,739 Pop, 791 Houses, 193 Barkby Hall is the seat of W Pochin, Esq The living is a vicarage in the diocese of Peterborough. Value, £250 * Patron, W Pochin, Esq The church is good, and there are two Methodist chapels and a national school

BARKBY-THORPE. See preceding article

BARKELEY, a hundred in the lathe of Scray, Kent Acres, 7,208. Pop., 1,457 Houses, 278

BARKESTONE, a parish in the district of Bingham and county of Leicester, in the vale of Belvoir, and on the Nottingham and Grantham railway, 1¾ mile W of Bottesford station, and 17 E of Nottingham It has a post office under Nottingham Acres, 2,870 Real property, £2 950 Pop, 411 Houses, 83 The property is divided among a few The living is a vicarage in the diocese of Peterborough Value, £114 * Patron, the Duke of Rutland The church is excellent A school has £25 from endowment, and other charities £40

BARKHAM, a parish in Wokingham district, Berks, on a small affluent of the Thames, 2½ miles SW of Wokingham r station Post town, Wokingham. Acres 1,355 Real property, £1,846 Pop, 280 Houses, 55 The property is not much divided The living is a rectory in the diocese of Oxford Value, £300 Patron, Rev A Roberts The church was rebuilt in 1862

BARKING, a village and a parish in Bosmere district, Suffolk The village stands 1¾ mile SW of Needham Market, on the road to Hadleigh Pop, 409 Houses 93 The parish contains also the hamlet of Darmsden and the town of Needham Market, the latter of which has a railway station and a head post office Acres, 3,164 Real property, £8,276 Pop., 1,850 Houses, 417 The property is divided among a few The living is a rectory, united with the curacy of Darmsden, in the diocese of Norwich Value, £540 * Patron the Earl of Ashburnham. The p curacy of Needham Market is a separate charge A school has an endowed income of £55, and other charities £77

BARKING, or BERKING, a town a sub district, and a parish, in the district of Romford, Essex The town stands on a rich flat tract, on the river Roding and on the Southend railway, 2 miles N of the Thames, and 7 E of Bishopsgate, London. Its name is a corruption of Burg ing, signifying the "fortification in the meadow," and seems to allude to an ancient entrenchment, enclosing upwards of 48 acres and still traceable The town rose to importance in 670, by the founding at it of an extensive abbey for Benedictine nuns, and it was the residence of William the Conqueror during the erection of the tower of London, and the place where the Earls of Mercia and Northumberland, and many other nobles, swore fealty to him on the restoration of their estates. The abbey was founded by Erkenwald, Bishop of London destroyed, in 870, by the Danes, rebuilt by King Edgar, governed, after his death, by his queen, and at other times by a long series of royal or noble ladies, served, throughout all its duration, as a prime seminary of the gentry of England, and passed, at the dissolution, to Edward, Lord Clinton Nothing now remains of it except a gateway at the entrance to the present church yard, a square embattled structure, with an octagonal turret at one corner, whose upper part is a room, formerly called the Chapel of the Holy Rood, having large windows in perpendicular English The parish church stands near the site of the abbey church, and possesses two Norman pillars in the N aisle, some lancet lights in the chancel, a curious niche at the NW of the nave, and some brasses and sculptured mural monuments, but is chiefly a structure of late and poor style, very tastelessly restored The market house or town hall is a timbered edifice of the time of Queen Elizabeth The town has a station on the railway, a post office under London E, two hotels, three dissenting chapels, a Roman Catholic chapel, an endowed school with £20 a year, alms houses with £185, and other charities with £125 A weekly market is held on Saturday, and an annual fair on 22 Oct The inhabitants are chiefly market gardeners, graziers, fishermen, or seamen, and the last are employed largely in bringing coal and timber to London The creek of the Roding bears the name of Barking creek, has a convenient wharf and a magazine, and is a coast guard station Pop of the town in 1841, 3,751, in 1861, 5,076 Houses, 1,059

The sub district includes also Ripple ward Pop, 5,591 Houses, 1,162 The parish includes likewise Chadwell and Great Ilford wards Acres, 12,741, of which 225 are water Real property, £54 5'0 Pop, 10,996 Houses, 2,246 Most of the tract between the railway and the Thames is a fertile meadowy flat, called Barking level, disposed in grazing ground for black cattle, and protected from high tides in the Thames by an immense embankment This work, as originally constructed, gave way in 1707, with the effect of about 5,000 acres being inundated, but it was repaired and strengthened at a cost of about £40,000 The contiguous reach of the Thames bears the name of Barking reach, is 1½ mile long, and has, in the middle, a dangerous shoal of 5 furlongs, called Barking shelf, on which the Grampus of 54 guns was wrecked in 1799 The great outfall of the new drainage of London is at Barking creek. This work comprises three gigantic parallel sewers, is 5½ miles long, crosses streams, roads, and railways, by means of bridges and tunnels, possesses more stupendous features than those of most railways, was undertaken at an estimate of £625,000, and employed, in 1861, ten steam engines and locomotives and about 1,500 workmen Eastbury House, about a mile ESE of the town, is an old brick building, said by some to have been the residence of Lord Monteagle, and alleged by tradition to have been the place where the Gunpowder plot was concocted The living is a vicarage in the diocese of London Value, £757 * Patron All Souls college, Oxford

BARKING ROAD, a chapelry, with a r station in West Ham parish, Essex, 1¾ mile S by E of Stratford It was constituted in 1867 Pop, about 5 050 Living, a p curacy Value £200 Patron, the Bishop of Rochester

BARKING SIDE, a chapelry in Great Ilford parish, Essex. It was constituted in 1841, and has a post-office under Ilford, London E. Pop., 1,712. Houses, 334. The living is a vicarage in the diocese of London. Value, £110. Patron, the Vicar of Great Ilford.

BARKISLAND, a township chapelry in Halifax parish, W. R. Yorkshire, 2¼ miles WSW of Elland r. station, and 5 SSW of Halifax. It includes part of the village of Riponden, and has a post office under Halifax. Acres, 2,420. Real property, £6,219. Pop., 2,003. Houses, 426. The property is much subdivided. The inhabitants are employed chiefly in woollen and worsted factories. There is a Druidical circle, called the Wolf Fold. The living is a p. curacy in the diocese of Ripon. Value, £91.* Patron, the Vicar of Halifax. The church is good. A school has an endowed income of £32, and other charities £51.

BARKSDON GREEN, a village in Herts, 2 miles SW of Buntingford.

BARKSTON, Leicester. See BARKESTONE.

BARKSTONE, a parish in the district of Newark and county of Lincoln, near the Great Northern railway, 4 miles NNE of Grantham. It has a post office under Grantham, and a r. station. Acres, 2,083. Real property, £3,539. Pop., 540. Houses, 114. The property is divided among a few. The living is a rectory in the diocese of Lincoln. Value, £600.* Patron, the Bishop of Lincoln. The church is handsome. An endowed school has £17, and other charities £69.

BARKSTONE, a township in Sherburn parish, W. R. Yorkshire, 1 mile W of Church Fenton r. station, and 4 S of Tadcaster. Acres, 1,260. Real property, £1,932. Pop., 319. Houses, 71.

BARKSTONE ASH, a wapentake in W. R. Yorkshire, bounded on the S by the river Aire, on the E by the river Ouse, on the N by the river Wharfe. It contains 4 market towns, 18 parishes, and 48 townships, and is cut into two divisions, Lower and Upper. Acres, of L. D., 43,852. Pop. in 1851, 13,514. Acres of U. D., 40,941. Pop. in 1851, 13,688. Pop. of both in 1861, 27,366. Houses, 6,049.

BARKWAY, a small town and a parish in Royston district, Herts. The town stands on a rising ground, near the sources of the Quin river, 4¼ miles SSE of Royston r. station. It has a post-office‡ under Royston, was formerly a market town, has still a fair on 20 July, and, prior to the railway times, was a great thoroughfare on the northern road from London. It consists principally of one street, and most of its houses are modern. Pop., 940. Houses, 195. The parish includes also the hamlets of Newsells and Nuthampstead. Acres, 5,060. Real property, £7,057. Pop., 1,221. Houses, 251. The property is divided among a few. The manor belonged to the Chesters and the Jenningses. The living is a vicarage, annexed to the rectory of Reed, in the diocese of Rochester. The church is an ancient structure, and was recently restored, and the tower rebuilt. There are an Independent chapel, a reading room, a national school, and charities £63.

BARKWITH (EAST), a parish in Horncastle district, Lincoln, 3¼ miles NE of Wragby, and 5¼ E by S of Wickenby r. station. Post town, Wragby. Acres, 990. Real property, £1,776. Pop., 387. Houses, 74. The property is divided among a few. The manor belongs to G. F. Heneage, Esq. Living, a rectory in the dio. of Lincoln. Value, £230.* Patrons, Dean and Chap. of Lincoln. The church is good, and there is a Wesleyan chapel.

BARKWITH (WEST), a parish in Horncastle district, Lincoln, 2¼ miles NE of Wragby, and 5 ESE of Wickenby r. station. Post town, Wragby. Acres, 500. Real property, £996. Pop., 150. Houses, 25. The property is divided among a few. The living is a rectory in the diocese of Lincoln. Value, £144.* Patrons, Trustees. The church is good.

BARLAND. See EVENJOBB.

BARLASTON, a parish in Stone district, Stafford, on the Grand Trunk canal and the North Stafford railway, 3½ miles NNW of Stone. It has a station on the railway, and a post office under Stone. Acres, 2,157. Real property, £5,078. Pop., 637. Houses, 121. The property is divided among a few. Barlaston Hall was formerly a seat of the Bagnalls, and is now the seat of a branch of the Adderleys. The living is a vicarage in the diocese of Lichfield. Value, £150. Patron, the Duke of Sutherland. The church is modern, but has an ancient tower. Charities, £24.

BARLAVINGTON, or BARLTON, a parish in Chichester district, Sussex, near the river Arun, 4½ miles S of Petworth r. station. Post-town, Petworth. Acres, 1,175. Real property, £1,136. Pop., 136. Houses, 23. The living is a rectory in the diocese of Chichester. Value, £68. Patron, T. Biddulph, Esq.

BARLBOROUGH, a parish in the district of Worksop and county of Derby, near the Chesterfield canal, 2 miles E of Eckington r. station, and 8 NE of Chesterfield. It has a post office under Chesterfield. Acres, 3,220. Real property, £7,029, of which £1,738 are in mines. Pop., 1,170. Houses, 231. The property is divided among a few. Barlborough Hall, an edifice in the Tudor style, is the seat of W. H. de Rodes, Esq. Coal and iron stone are worked. The living is a rectory in the diocese of Lichfield. Value, £770.* Patron, W. H. de Rodes, Esq. The church was repaired in 1859. An almshouse, founded in 1752, has £69, and other charities £13.

BARLBY, a chapelry in Hemingbrough parish, E. R. Yorkshire, on the river Ouse, 1 mile N of the Leeds and Hull railway, and 1¾ NE of Selby. It includes Barlby Bank hamlet, and its post town is Selby. Acres, 1,411. Real property, £2,825. Pop., 471. Houses, 95. The property is much subdivided. The living is a p. curacy in the diocese of York. Value, £65. Patron, the Vicar of Hemingbrough. The church is good. Charities, £7.

BARLE, or BARLEY (THE), a river of the western border of Somerset. It rises in Exmoor forest, and runs about 16 miles south eastward, past Simons Bath, Withypoole, Hawkridge, and Dulverton, to a confluence with the Exe, 2½ miles below Dulverton.

BARLESTONE, or BARLSTON, a chapelry in Market-Bosworth parish, Leicester, 2¼ miles NE of Market Bosworth, and 3 SW of Bagworth r. station. Post town, Market Bosworth, under Hinckley. Acres, 810. Real property, £2,910. Pop., 544. Houses, 140. The property is much subdivided. Many of the inhabitants are employed in the manufactory of hosiery. The living is annexed to Market Bosworth. The church is plain. There are two dissenting chapels and a free school.

BARLEY (THE). See BARLE.

BARLEY, a parish in Royston district, Herts, on the NE verge of the county, 3 miles SE of Royston r. station. It has a post office under Royston. Acres, 2,645. Real property, £4,222. Pop., 809. Houses, 171. The property is divided among a few. The living is a rectory in the diocese of Rochester. Value, £501.* Patron, the Crown. The church is ancient. There are a recent Calvinist chapel, and charities £36.

BARLEY, Yorkshire. See BARLOW.

BARLEY BOOTHS. See BARLEY-WITH-WHITLEY BOOTH.

BARLEY-HALL, a hamlet in Wentworth township, Wath upon Dearne parish, W. R. Yorkshire, near Wentworth Park, 5½ miles NW of Rotherham.

BARLEYTHORPE, a manor in Oakham parish, Rutland, 1 mile NW of Oakham. It was given to Westminster abbey by Edward the Confessor, and it belongs still to the dean and chapter of Westminster. Real property, £3,830. Pop., 168. Houses, 31.

BARLEY-WITH-WHITLEY BOOTH, a township in Whalley parish, Lancashire, 4½ miles W of Colne. Acres, 2,870. Real property, £2,233. Pop., 495. There are two cotton mills and a Wesleyan chapel.

BARLEY WOOD, a house in Wrington parish, Somerset, near the Mendip hills, 6 miles NE of Axbridge. It was built in 1800 by Hannah More, was for several years her residence, and contains a bust of Locke, the philosopher, given by Mrs. Montagu. Hannah More's grave is in Wrington churchyard, and a tablet to her memory is in the church.

BARLICHWAY, a hundred in Warwickshire, bounded on the W by Worcester, on the S by Gloucester and on the central E by the river Avon It contains 36 parishes or chapelries and is cut into the four divisions of Alcester, Henley, Snitterfield and Stratford Acres, 110,679 Pop in 1851, 28,448, in 1861, 25,604 Houses, 5,623

BARLINCH See BROMPTON REGIS

BARLING, a parish in Rochford district, Essex, on a creek of the Broomhill river, 4½ miles ESE of Rochford, and 5 NE of Southend r station. It has a post-office under Chelmsford Acres, 1,258 Real property, £2,801 Pop 354 Houses, 77 The property is subdivided. The manor was given by Edward the Confessor to St. Paul's Cathedral The living is a vicarage in the diocese of Rochester Value, £230. Patrons, the Dean and Chapter of St Paul's The church is a neat structure with chancel and tower

BARLINGS a parish in the district and county of Lincoln, 2½ miles SE of Reepham r station, and 7 ENE of Lincoln It includes the hamlet of Langworth, and its post town is Nettleham under Lincoln Acres 2,630 Real property, £3,117 Pop, 475 Houses, 96 The property is subdivided A Premonstratensian abbey was founded, in 1154, at Barling Grange, and afterwards refounded at Oxeney, and was given, at the dissolution, to Charles, Duke of Suffolk. The last abbot of it, Dr Mackerel, was executed at Tyburn, in 1537, for heading the Lincoln insurrection against the Crown Only a few mutilated pillars of the edifice now remain The living is a vicarage in the diocese of Lincoln Value £55 Patrons, T T Drake and C Turner, Esqs The church is tolerable

BARLOW, a township in Hopesay parish, Salop, 5½ miles SE of Bishops Castle

BARLOW, or BARLEY, a township chapelry in Brayton parish W R. Yorkshire, on the river Ouse, 3 miles SE of Selby r station Post town, Selby Acres, 2,278 Real property, £3,433 Pop, 239 Houses, 46 The living is a donative in the diocese of York Value, £90 Patron, G H Thompson, Esq

BARLOW (GREAT), a chapelry in Staveley parish Derby, on a small stream 4½ miles NW of Chesterfield r station. It has a post office, of the name of Barlow, under Chesterfield Acres, 3,760 Real property, £2,966 Pop, 682 Houses, 137 The property is divided among a few Barlow Grange is a chief residence The living is a p curacy in the diocese of Lichfield Value, £95 * Patron, the Rector of Staveley The church is good Charities, £8

BARLOW (LITTLE), a township in Dronfield parish, Derby 3½ miles NW of Chesterfield Pop 54

BARLOW MOOR, a chapelry in Manchester parish, Lancashire Pop, 1,018 Living, a rectory Value, £230

BARLTON See BARLAVINGTON

BARMBROUGH, BARMBOROUGH BARNBROUGH, or BARNBOROUGH, a village, a parish, and a sub district, in the district of Doncaster, W R Yorkshire The village stands 3½ miles NNW of Conisborough r station, and 6 W of Doncaster, and has a post office, of the name of Barmborough under Doncaster —The parish includes also the hamlet of Harlington Acres, 1,947 Real property, £3,435 Pop, 462 Houses, 111 The property is much subdivided Barmborough Hall is the seat of the Griffiths family, and contains two portraits of Sir Thomas More's family by Holbein The living is a rectory in the diocese of York Value £555 * Patron, Southwell Collegiate Church The church is later English, in tolerable condition and has interesting monuments of the Cresacres, formerly lords of the manor One of the monuments is a rude representation of a contest about the middle of the 15th century, between Percival Cresacre and a wild cat, said to have been begun in an adjacent wood and to have terminated fatally to both combatants in the porch of the church, and another is a rich altar tomb of the same gentleman There are a Wesleyan chapel, a national school and charities £31 —The sub district contains eleven parishes and two tracts Acres, 23,953 Pop, 5,860 Houses, 1,251

BARMBY ON THE-MARSH, a township chapelry in Howden parish, E R Yorkshire, at the confluence of the Derwent and the Ouse, 2 miles SSW of Wressel r station, and 4½ W of Howden Post town Hemingborough under Howden Acres, 1,711 Real property, £3,812 Pop, 456 Houses, 103 Some of the inhabitants are sacking makers There are two mineral springs, chalybeate and sulphurous The living is a p curacy in the diocese of York Value, £30 Patron, the Vicar of Howden There are a Wesleyan chapel, and charities £106

BARMBY ON THE MOOR, or BARMBY-MOOR, a parish in Pocklington district, E R Yorkshire, near the Market-Weighton railway, 1½ mile W of Pocklington It has a post office, of the name of Barmby Moor, under York. Acres, 2,290 Real property, £3,038 Pop, 537 Houses, 110 The property is subdivided The living is a vicarage in the diocese of York Value £263 * Patron, the Archbishop of York The church consists of nave and chancel, has a fine octagonal spire, and was repaired in 1828 There are chapels for Wesleyan and Primitive Methodists, and charities £53

BARMBY-UPON DON See BARNBY UPON DON

BARMER, a parish in Docking district, Norfolk, 3 miles SSE of Stanhoe r station, and 6 S by W of Burnham Westgate Post town, Syderstone, under Fakenham Acres, 890 Real property, £1,183 Pop, 62 Houses, 9 The living is a vicarage in the diocese of Norwich Value, £5 Patron, T Kearslake, Esq The church is now used only as a burial-place

BARMING, or BARMING (EAST), a parish in Maidstone district, Kent, on the river Medway, 1 mile NW of East Farleigh r station, and 2½ WSW of Maidstone It has a post office, of the name of Barming, under Maidstone Acres 749 Real property, £3,170 Pop 589 Houses, 117 The property is divided among a few Hops and fruits are richly cultivated, and Kentish rag is quarried Roman remains have been found near the church The living is a rectory in the diocese of Canterbury Value, £598 * Patron, the Lord Chancellor The church is a neat edifice, with a cemetery embosomed in fine elms. Mark Noble, the antiquary was rector, and Christopher Smart, the poet, was a resident.

BARMING (WEST) a parish in Maidstone district Kent, contiguous to East Barming, 3 miles WSW of Maidstone Post town, Barming, under Maidstone Acres, 331 Pop, 24 Houses, 5 The living is a rectory, annexed to the rectory of Nettlestead, in the diocese of Canterbury

BARMOOR, a township in Lowick parish, Northumberland 1 mile W of Lowick and 8 N of Wooler Barmoor Castle here, the seat of the Sitwells, is an elegant edifice of 1802, on the site of an ancient seat of the Muschamps Barmoor wood was the head quarters of the English general on the eve of the battle of Flodden

BARMOUTH, a small seaport town and a sub district in the district of Dolgelly, Merioneth The town is in the parish of Llanaber, and stands on the N side of the mouth of the river Maw, and on a branch of the Welsh Coast railway, 10 miles W by S of Dolgelly It is called by the natives Abermaw, or, abbreviatedly Barmaw, whence, by corruption, the English name Barmouth It consists partly of a street along the strand, but chiefly of successive tiers of houses on the steep slope of a lofty rock, accessible from below by steps It has a head post office,‡ a r station, two good inns, a public library, a chapel of ease, and three dissenting chapels. It is much frequented as a watering place, and it possesses excellent bathing facilities enjoys splendid views, and offers ready access to charming excursions and recreations A ferry plies across the Maw and ample railway communication exists northward, northeastward, and southward, by the Aberystwith and Welsh Coast, the Cambrian, and the Carnarvonshire systems, together with their branches and connexions Markets are held on Tuesday and Friday and fairs on 10 May, 19 Sept, 7 Oct, and 8 Nov Business is done in woollen manu facture ship building, and coasting The harbour is small, but has a pier and upwards of 100 small sloops, and is a sub port to Carnarvon An island, called Ynys y Brawd, divides the entrance of the Maw into two channels, and the large shoal, called Sarn Badrig, lies about 10 miles off Wilberforce used to spend his autumns at Barmouth when labouring against the slave trade and a tower anciently stood here which was a retreat of the Earl of Richmond, afterwards Henry VII, when planning his expedition against Richard III Pop of the town, about 950 —The sub district comprises six parishes Acres, 72,147 Pop, 7,643 Houses, 1,773

BARMPTON, a township in Haughton le Skerne parish, Durham, 3 miles NNE of Darlington Real property, £2,307 Acres, 1,520. Pop, 127 Houses, 24

BARMSTON, a township in Washington parish, Durham, on the river Wear, 5 miles W of Sunderland Acres, 893 Real property, £1,879 Pop, 475 Houses, 89

BARMSTON, a parish in Bridlington district, E R Yorkshire, on the coast, 4 miles SE of Burton Agnes r station, and 6 S by W of Bridlington Post town, Lissett under Hull Acres, 2,336, of which 156 are water Real property, £3,857 Pop, 206 Houses, 36 The manor belongs to Sir H. Boynton, Bart., and the ancient mansion on it is now a farm house The living is a rectory in the diocese of York Value, £1,065.* Patron Sir H Boynton, Bart The church is perpendicular English, has a Norman porch door, had once a chantry, and contains a circular font with cable moulding and a curious monument to Sir Martin de la Mare Charities, £22

BARNABY ON THE MOOR. See BARNBY MOOR.

BARNACK a village, a parish, and a sub district in the district of Stamford, the village and the parish in Northampton, the sub district variously in Northampton, Lincoln, Huntingdon, and Rutland The village stands 1½ mile SSE of Uffington r station, and 3½ ESE of Stamford, and has a post office under Stamford. Pop, 569 Houses 137 The parish includes also the hamlets of Pilsgate and Southorpe Acres, 4 440 Real property, £8,699 Pop, 947 Houses, 202 The property is divided among a few Building stone is extensively quarried, and was furnished hence for Peterborough and Ely cathedrals, and for several other churches. The living is a rectory in the diocese of Peterborough Value, £1,025* Patron, the Bishop of Peterborough. The church is partly early Norman, and in very good condition There are a Wesleyan chapel, a national school, and a poors' estate yielding annually £73 —The sub district contains sixteen parishes Acres, 28,722 Pop., 5,692 Houses, 1,148

BARNACLE, a hamlet in Bulkington parish, Warwick, near the Trent Valley railway, 4 miles SSE of Nuneaton

BARNACRE WITH BONDS, a township in Garstang parish, Lancashire, 2 miles NE of Garstang Acres, 4,316 Real property, £5,809 Pop, 907 Houses, 162

BARNARD CASTLE, a town, a township, a chapelry, and a sub district, in the district of Teesdale, Durham The town, the township, and the chapelry are in the parish of Gainford The town stands on the left bank of the river Tees on the line of railway from Darlington to Lancashire, 15½ miles W of Darlington Its site is the side of an eminence rising abruptly from the bank of the river Its principal street is spacious, and nearly a mile long, and is intersected by smaller streets The environs are remarkably pleasant, and present romantic scenery, especially along the Tees A narrow bridge of two pointed arches, built in 1596, spans the river The market house is an octagonal freestone building open at the sides The church is ancient and cruciform There are four dissenting chapels, a Roman Catholic chapel, a mechanics' institution, national schools, a dispensary, a workhouse, an hospital for aged persons and some minor charities. The hospital was founded in 1229 by John Baliol of Scotland, and is endowed with 180 acres of land Remains of an ancient castle, comprising entrance gateway and two towers, stand on the brink of a steep rock, about 80 feet above the Tees and command a charming prospect The castle was founded by Barnard Baliol, son of Guy, who accompanied William the Conqueror to England, and grandfather of John Baliol, king of Scotland, and it took its name of Barnard from him, and gave its name of Barnard Castle to the town It ruled an extensive domain in Teesdale and Marwood, granted by William Rufus, but was transferred, along with that domain, by Edward I to Guy Beauchamp, Earl of Warwick It remained for five generations with the Beauchamps, then went to the Crown, was inhabited and embellished by Richard III, and eventually passed by sale to an ancestor of the Duke of Cleveland The area which it occupied was about 6¾ acres, but this is now partly sheep pasture, and partly disposed in orchards The castle figures in Sir Walter Scott's poem of "Rokeby," and it gives the titles of Baron and Viscount to the Duke of Cleveland. The town has a head post office ‡ a r station with telegraph, three banks, and two chief inns, and is a seat of petty sessions, a polling place, and the head quarters of the county militia A weekly market is held on Wednesday, a fortnightly one, for cattle, sheep and horses, on every alternate Wednesday, and fairs, on Easter Monday, Whit Wednesday, and Magdalene day Manufactures of carpets, plaids, cloth, and shoe thread are carried on John Baliol and Hutchinson, the historian of the county, were natives Pop, 4,178 Houses, 757 —The township comprises 4,007 acres Real property, £13,337,—of which £1,352 are in mines Pop., 4,477 Houses, 810 —The chapelry includes three other townships, and it is a vicarage in the diocese of Durham Value, £400* Patron, Trinity College, Cambridge —The sub district contains five parishes and parts of five others Acres, 58,607 Pop., 8,555 Houses, 1,629

BARNARDISTON, corruptedly BERNISTON, a parish in Risbridge district, Suffolk, 3¾ miles NW of Clare r station, and 12 SSE of Newmarket Post town, Clare, under Sudbury Acres, 1,100 Real property, £1,489 Pop., 280 Houses, 51 The property is much subdivided. The living is a rectory in the diocese of Ely Value, £191 Patron, the Rev Val Ellis. The church is good, and there is a Primitive Methodist chapel

BARNARD SAND, a shoal 3 miles long extending parallel to the coast, off Lowestoft roads Norfolk Its breadth is about two furlongs, and its highest part has only two feet water

BARNARD'S GREEN, a village 1 mile ESE of Great Malvern, Worcester It has a post office under Great Malvern and is a curacy to that place

BARNARD'S INN See LONDON

BARNBOW, a hamlet in the township and parish of Barwick in Elmet, W R Yorkshire, 5½ miles E of Leeds.

BARNBROUGH See BARMBROUGH

BARNBY, a parish in Mutford district, Suffolk, near the river Waveney, and near Carlton Colville r station, 5 miles E by S of Beccles. Post town Mutford Bridge under Lowestoft Acres, 1,099 Real property, £1,418 Pop, 270 Houses, 59 The property is much subdivided The living is a rectory annexed to the vicarage of Mutford, in the diocese of Norwich The church is old but good Charities £9

BARNBY, or EAST BARNBY, a township in Lythe parish, N R Yorkshire on the coast, 4½ miles WNW of Whitby Acres, 1,435, of which 35 are water Real property, £2,133 Pop., 247 Houses, 50

BARNBY BASIN AND BARNBY FURNACE, two hamlets in Cawthorne parish, W R Yorkshire, 4½ miles WNW of Barnsley

BARNBY DUN See BARNBY UPON DON

BARNBY IN THE WILLOWS, a parish in Newark district Notts, on the river Fosdick, 2½ miles N by E of Claypole r station and 4½ E by S of Newark. Post town, Claypole, under Newark. Acres, 1,701 Real property, £2,736 Pop 302 Houses, 64 The property is divided among a few The living is a vicarage in the diocese of Lincoln Value £184 Patron, Southwell Collegiate Church The church is good, and there is a Wesleyan chapel

BARNBY LE WOLD See BARNETBY LE WOLD.

BARNBY MOOR, anciently BARNABY ON THE MOOR, a township in Blyth parish, Notts, 3½ miles NW of East Retford It includes Bilby and has a post office, of the name of Barnby Moor, under Retford Real property, £3 602 Pop, 245 Houses 49

BARNBY UPON DON, or BARNBY DUN, a township and a parish in Doncaster district, W R Yorkshire The township lies on the river Don and on the Doncaster and Thorne railway, 5 miles NE by N of Doncaster, and it has a station, of the name of Barnby Dun on the railway Acres 2,230 Real property, £4 259 Pop, 537 Houses, 118 The parish includes also the township of Thorpe in Balne and its post town is Doncaster Acres, 3 737 Real property, £5,698 Pop, 644 Houses, 141 The living is a vicarage in the dio of York Value, £115 Patron, J H Newsome, Esq The church was recently restored. There are two Methodist chapels an endowed school, and charities £59

BARNES, a parish in Richmond district, Surrey, on the Richmond railway and the river Thames, 7 miles WSW of Waterloo Bridge station, London. It has a station on the railway, and it contains the village of Barnes and the hamlet of Barnes Elms or Barn Elms both of which have post-offices under Mortlake, London, S W Acres, 1,051, of which 115 are water Real property, £18,738 Pop., 2,359 Houses, 414 The manor was given by King Athelstane to the canons of St Paul's London, and was then and afterwards called Berne A tract in the N, 1½ mile long is engirt by a semicircular sweep of the Thames Barnes common, contiguous to this on the S, comprises about 500 acres, and lies lower than the level of the Thames' spring tide Barnes terrace is a pleasant range of houses, chiefly let to summer sojourners. Barn-Elms House was the residence of Sir Francis Walsingham, visited by Queen Elizabeth, afterwards the residence of Heydegger, George II 's master of the revels, visited by the king, afterwards the property of Sir R. C Hoare, the antiquary, and now chiefly a modern mansion, belonging to the family of Chapman A house in the vicinity, the ' queen s dairy," was the residence of the celebrated bookseller Jacob Tonson, and the meeting place of the kitcat club, adorned with portraits of the members, painted by Sir Godfrey Kneller This house has gone to ruin, but the portraits have been preserved, and are now at Bayfordbury near Hertford Cowley, the poet, Fielding, the novelist, and Handel, the composer, were residents of Barnes, Bishop Wilson was for some time rector, and Sir William Blizard, the surgeon, was a native The duel between the Duke of Buckingham and the Earl of Shrewsbury, in January 1667-8, was fought near Barn Elms, and the assassination of the count and the countess D Antraigues, in 1812, was done in the parish A suspension bridge, 750 feet long, takes a thoroughfare hence across the Thames to Hammersmith, and a three arched iron bridge, each arch 100 feet in span, takes across a loop line of railway from the Barnes station toward the Windsor railway near Hounslow The living is a rectory in the diocese of London Value, £375 * Patrons, the Dean and Chapter of St Paul's The church was built in 1189, and looks to be mainly early English, but has been rendered uninteresting by numerous alterations A recess, with rose bushes on its S exterior, marks the grave of Edward Rose, a citizen of London, who died in 1653, leaving a bequest of £20 to the poor of the parish, on condition that his monumental tablet should be kept in repair, and have rose bushes trained around it A small chapel of recent erection stands at Castlenau, built and endowed by Major Boileau and is served by a curate with salary of £100 Charities, £43

BARNES CHINE, a small wild ravine on the SW coast of the Isle of Wight, 1½ mile SE of Brixton The cliffs which flank it rise to a considerable height, and a dangerous reef, known as the Shipledge, is near its mouth

BARNESLEY a hamlet in Kingston Lacy manor, Dorset, 2 miles N of Wimborne Minster

BARNESLEY, Yorkshire See BARNSLEY

BARNET, a town a parish, a sub district, and a district, in Herts and Middlesex. The town is called also Chipping Barnet and High Barnet It is partly in the parish of Barnet, Herts, and partly in the parish of South Mimms, Middlesex, and it stands on the top of an eminence on the great north road, 1½ mile WNW of a station of its own name on the Great Northern railway, 9¼ miles N by W of King s Cross, London It consists principally of one street upwards of a mile long. St John s church is an edifice of 1400, erected by John Moot, abbot of St Albans, has a square embattled tower, and contains monuments of the Ravenscrofts and others Christ church, on Barnet common, is a recent erection There are a chapel for Independents, a grammar school, founded by Queen Elizabeth in 1573, two sets of alms houses, founded in the time of Charles II and in 1729, charities altogether to the yearly value of £870, and a workhouse built at a cost of £3,757 The town has a head post-office, a telegraph office at the railway station, and two chief inns, and publishes a weekly newspaper A weekly market on Monday used to be largely attended but has become nearly extinct Fairs are held on 8 9, and 10 April, and on 4, 5, and 6 Sept, and races are run, on Barnet Heath, after the fairs Much business arose, in the ante railway times, from the daily transit of nearly 150 public coaches, but this has perished Several fine seats are in the vicinity, and the place has become a resort for summer residence by the merchants of London A mineral spring on Barnet Common was discovered in 1652 At the twelfth milestone from London, N of the town, stands a stone column, commemorative of the battle of Barnet Field, fought there in 1471, between the army of the House of York, headed by Edward IV, and that of the House of Lancaster, headed by the Earl of Warwick.

The parish of Barnet bears also the name of Chipping Barnet and lies wholly in Herts Acres, together with the parish of East Barnet, 3,185 Real property, £10,829 Pop, 2,989 Houses, 475 The manor belonged to the abbots of St Albans The living is a rectory, with Arkley chapelry, in the diocese of Rochester Value, £435 Patron, the Crown Christ church is a separate p curacy —The sub-district comprises the parish of Hadley in Middlesex, and the parishes of Barnet, East Barnet and Totteridge in Herts. Acres, 7,312 Pop, 5,466 Houses, 929 The district comprehends also the sub district of South Mimms, containing the parish of South Mimms, in Middlesex, and the parishes of Ridge tree, Shenley, and Ridge, in Herts, and the sub district of Finchley, containing the parishes of Finchley and Friern Barnet, in Middlesex Poor rates in 1866, £10,392 Pop in 1841, 13,759, in 1861, 19,128 Houses, 3,216 Marriages in 1866 108, births 592,—of which 14 were illegitimate, deaths, 570,—of which 127 were at ages under 5 years, and 6 at ages above 85 years Marriages in the ten years 1851-60, 596, births, 4,125 deaths, 4 179 The places of worship in 1851 were 16 of the Church of England, with 5,552 sittings, 5 of Independents, with 1,478 s, 1 of Baptists, with 200 s, 4 of Wesleyan Methodists, with 520 s, and 1 of Roman Catholics, with 40 s The schools were 31 public day schools, with 2,107 scholars, 32 private day schools, with 644 s., 15 Sunday schools, with 1,292 s, and 3 evening schools for adults with 70 s

BARNET (EAST), a parish in Barnet district, Herts, on the Great Northern railway, near Barnet station 1¼ mile ESE of Barnet Post town Barnet Acres, with Barnet, 3,185 Real property £7,090 Pop, 851 Houses 167 The property is divided among a few The living is a rectory in the diocese of Rochester, and till 1866 was united with Barnet Value, £695 * Patron, the Crown The church is an ancient structure in good condition, and belonged to the abbey of St Albans. There are a national school, and charities £5

BARNETBY LE WOLD, a parish in Glanford Brigg district, Lincoln, on the Manchester and Lincolnshire railway, 3¾ miles NE of Brigg It has a station, of the name of Barnetby on the railway and a post-office, of the same name, under Ulceby Acres, 1,630 Real property, £4,334 Pop, 828 Houses, 186 The living is a vicarage in the diocese of Lincoln Value, £400 * Patron, the Bishop of Lincoln The church is early English. There are three dissenting chapels

BARNET FRYERN, a parish in Barnet district, Middlesex, on the northern verge of the county, 1½ mile W by N of Southgate and Colney-Hatch r station and 3 miles SSE of Barnet It contains the hamlet of Colney Hatch and part of the village of Whetstone, both of which have post offices under London N Acres, 1,292 Real property, £6 552 Pop 3,344 Houses, 241 The property is subdivided The living is a rectory in the diocese of London Value, £255 * Patrons, the Dean and Chapter of St Paul's The church was restored in 1858 There are national schools, seven alms houses, and some other charities Walker, the author of "the Pronouncing Dictionary," was a native and Judge Popham a resident See COLNEY HATCH

BARNEWELL See BARNWELL

BARNEY, a parish in Walsingham district, Norfolk, 5 miles ENE of Fakenham r station. It has a post office under Thetford. Acres, 1,389 Real property, £2,105 Pop, 283 Houses, 73 The property is divided among a few The living is a vicarage in the diocese of Norwich Value, £129 * Patron, Lord Hastings The church is an old building, with a tower There are chapels for Baptists and Wesleyans.

BARNFIELD (EAST), a hundred in the lathe of Scray, conterminate with the parish of Hawkhurst, Kent. See HAWKHURST

BARN GREEN, a hamlet in Yardley parish, Worcester, near the Birmingham and Bristol railway, 4 miles NE of Bromsgrove It has a station on the railway See ALVECHURCH

BARN GREEN, a hamlet in Hambledon parish, Hants, 6½ miles SE of Bishops Waltham.

BARNHAM, a parish in the district of Thetford and county of Suffolk, on the Little Ouse river, 3 miles S of Thetford r station Post town, Thetford. Acres, 5,184. Real property, £2,455 Pop., 475 Houses, 87 Some tumuli in the N are supposed to mark the scene of a conflict, in 870, between King Edward the Elder and the Danes. An ivy clad square tower belonged to the church of the extinct or incorporated parish of Barnham St-Martin The living is a rectory, annexed to the rectory of Euston, in the diocese of Ely The church was restored and enlarged in 1864 There is a free school

BARNHAM, a parish in Westhampnett district, Sussex, on the South Coast railway, with a station at the junction of the Bognor branch, 1½ mile W of Yapton, and 4½ SW of Arundel Post town, Yapton under Arundel. Acres 730 Real property, £1,332 Pop, 125 Houses 27 The property is subdivided The living is a vicarage in the diocese of Chichester Value, £67 Patron, the Bishop of Chichester The church is very good.

BARNHAM-BROOM, a parish in Forehoe district, Norfolk, on the river Yare, 3 miles E of Hardingham r station and 5 NNW of Wymondham It has a post office under Wymondham. Acres, 1,776 Real property, £3,748 Pop, 481 Houses, 110 The property is not much divided The manor belongs to the Earl of Kimberley The living is a rectory united with the rectory of Bixton and the vicarage of Kimberley, in the diocese of Norwich Value, £604 * Patron, Earl of Kimberley The church is a neat structure, with an embattled tower, and has a fine screen

BARNHILL, a hamlet in Malpas parish, Cheshire, 10 miles SE of Chester It is a seat of petty sessions

BARNINGHAM, a parish in the district of Thetford and county of Suffolk, 2¾ miles S of the Little Ouse river, and 9 SE of Thetford r station It has a post office under Bury St Edmunds Acres, 1,580 Real property, £2,982 Pop 489 Houses, 109 Barningham Park is the seat of R Hunt, Esq The living is a rectory, united with the rectory of Coney Weston in the diocese of Ely Value, £770 * Patron, R Hunt, Esq The church is a brick building, with a stone tower, and has a brass of 1409 There are a Wesleyan Methodist chapel, and charities £55

BARNINGHAM, a township in the district of Teesdale, and a parish partly also in the district of Richmond N R Yorkshire The township lies on a tributary of the Tees, near Arkengarth forest, 5½ miles SE of Barnard Castle r station, and has a post office under Darlington Acres, 3,454 Real property, £3,350 Pop, 307 Houses, 78. The parish includes also the townships of Scargill and Hope, and part of the township of Newsham Acres, 10,771 Real property with the rest of Newsham, £8,998 Pop, 526 Houses, 129 Much of the surface is upland moor Barningham Park is the seat of the Milbanks The living is a rectory in the diocese of Ripon Value, £553 * Patron the Lord Chancellor There are a Wesleyan chapel, and charities £20

BARNINGHAM (GREAT) See BARNINGHAM TOWN

BARNINGHAM (LITTLE), or BARNINGHAM PARVA a parish in Aylsham district, Norfolk, 5½ miles NNW of Aylsham, and 13 E by N of Ryburgh r station Post town, Itteringham, under Norwich Acres, 1,224 Real property, £1,373 Pop, 273. Houses, 54 The property is divided among a few A market and a fair were formerly held here, under charter of Edward I to Walter de Berningham, lord of the manor The living is a rectory in the diocese of Norwich. Value, £180 Patrons, G D Graver, T I Graver, and G B. Knight, Esqrs. The church is old but good

BARNINGHAM MAGNA See BARNINGHAM TOWN

BARNINGHAM NORWOOD, a parish in Erpingham district, Norfolk, 4½ miles ESE of Holt, and 16 ENE of Ryburgh r station Post town, Holt, under Thetford Acres, 834 Real property, £1,065 Pop, 30 Houses, 8 The property is divided among a few The living is a rectory in the diocese of Norwich Value, £156 Patron, Trustees of late W H Wyndham, Esq The church has an ancient brass, and is tolerable

BARNINGHAM PARVA. See BARNINGHAM (LITTLE)

BARNINGHAM TOWN or B WINTER, or B MAGNA, or B GREAT, a parish in Erpingham district, Norfolk, 5 miles SE of Holt, and 15 ENE of Ryburgh r station Post town, Holt, under Thetford. Acres, 833 Real property, £1,036 Pop., 125 Houses, 23. The property is divided among a few Barningham Hall, a fine Tudor mansion, is the seat of J T Mott, Esq A market and a fair were formerly held in the parish, under grant of Edward II to Roger le Curzam The living is a rectory in the diocese of Norwich. Value, £135 * Patron, J T Mott, Esq The church is partly a ruin.

BARNOLDBY LE-BECK a parish in Caistor district, Lincoln, 3 miles W of Waltham r station, and 5 SW by S of Great Grimsby Post town, Waltham, under Grimsby Acres, 1,460 Real property, £1,731 Pop, 242 Houses 60 The living is a rectory in the diocese of Lincoln Value, £235 Patron, Southwell Church The church is good, and there are two Methodist chapels

BARNOLDSWICK, a township, a parish, and a sub district, in the district of Skipton, W R Yorkshire The township lies adjacent to the Leeds and Liverpool canal, 5 miles N of Colne, and has a post-office‡ under Colne A railway from it 2 miles long, to the Leeds and Bradford, was authorised in 1867 Acres, 2,020 Pop., 2,810 Houses, 550 The parish is also called Gill Kirk, from the situation of its church on the verge of a deep glen, and includes likewise the townships of Salterforth, Coates, and Brogden with-Admergill. Acres, 6,040 Real property, £12,515 Pop., 3,478 Houses, 687 The property is much subdivided Much of the surface is hilly and high. An abbey was founded here in 1147, but in consequence of local disputes, was removed to Kirkstall The living is a vicarage in the diocese of Ripon Value, £162 * Patron L Hodson, Esq The church is Norman There are four dissenting chapels and a national school.—The sub-district comprises four parishes Acres, 17,463. Pop, 5,986 Houses, 1,191

BARNSCAR, a ruined town on Birkby Fell, 3½ miles E of Ravenglass, Cumberland Traces of streets and houses occur throughout an area of about 300 yards by 100, and some silver coins have been found. But the history of the place has perplexed antiquaries.

BARNSDALE, a hamlet in the township and parish of Campsall, W R Yorkshire, 6½ miles N of Doncaster Barnsdale forest adjacent was the haunt of Robin Hood, and is noted in old song as the scene of his curious adventure with the Bishop of Hereford.

' Then Robin he took the bishop by the hand,
And led him to merry Barnsdale,
He made him to stay and sup with him that night,
And to drink wine, beer, and ale

BARNSHAW See GOOSTREY CUM BARNSHAW

BARNSIDE, a hamlet in Hepworth township, Kirkburton parish, W R Yorkshire, 6½ miles S of Huddersfield.

BARNSLEY, a township in Worfield parish, Salop, 2 miles E of Bridgnorth

BARNSLEY, a parish in Cirencester district, Gloucester, near the river Colne, 4 miles NE of Cirencester r station It has a post-office under Cirencester Acres, 2 090 Real property £1,852. Pop, 327 Houses, 64 The chief property belongs to Sir W Musgrave, Bart The manor belonged formerly to the Perrots and the Bourchiers, and the old mansion of the latter still stands Barnsley Park, the seat of the present proprietor, is extensive, and the mansion is in the Italian style, and contains some frescoes and antiques Freestone is quarried. The living is a rectory in the diocese of Gloucester and Bristol. Value, £320 * Patron, Sir W Musgrave, Bart The church is transition Norman, and was recently restored Charities, £15

BARNSLEY, a town, a township, three chapelries, a sub district and a district in W R. Yorkshire The town stands in a fertile tract, on the river Dearne, at a focus of railways and canals, 10 miles by road, and 11¼ by railway, south of Wakefield Railways go from it north westward, south westward, and south eastward, and canals connect it northward with Wakefield, and eastward with the Don It figures in Domesday as a manorial seat, under the name of Bernesley, and was known afterwards as Bleak Barnesley or Black Barnsley, but is now a busy and flourishing scene of manufacturing industry It consists chiefly of narrow streets, and is straggling and plain, yet has two large market places and some handsome houses, and is built principally of stone from quarries in the neighbourhood, and it is governed by a local board of health Its chief objects are waterworks, enlarged in 1868, a handsome court house, built in 1861, at a cost of about £4,000, a large corn exchange, in the Grecian style, a public park presented to the town by Joseph Locke, Esq, and containing a statue of him by Marochetti, erected in 1866, a church, rebuilt in 1821, two handsome churches, built in 1822 and 1858, the former at a cost of £3,918, a beautiful Independent chapel built in 1851, at a cost of £5,000, a fine and very spacious Wesleyan chapel eight other dissenting chapels, a Roman Catholic chapel, an ultra mural cemetery with two mortuary chapels formed at a cost of £7,000, a mechanics institution, a Franklin institution, an endowed grammar-school, a workhouse, and charities £806 a year

The town has a head post-office,‡ a telegraph station two banking offices, and three chief inns, and it is a seat of petty sessions and county courts, and publishes four weekly newspapers. A weekly market is held on Wednesday, and fairs on the Wednesday before 28 Feb, 13 May and 11 Oct Wire drawing was carried on from at least the time of James I, and had long the reputation of producing the best wire in the kingdom, but has now very greatly declined. The manufacture of linen cloth, damasks, diapers, ducks, checks, ticks, and similar fabrics, took the place of the wire drawing, and is very prosperous The yarn is partly spun in large mills on the spot, and partly brought from the mills of Leeds and is woven principally by the weavers in their own houses About 1,000 power looms and about 3,500 hand looms are employed Bleaching dyeing wool working, glass making, and iron working also are carried on Extensive coal mines likewise are in the neighbourhood In explosion, with loss of 72 lives, took place, in 1847, at the Oaks colliery, and another, with similar loss, took place, in December 1862, at Worsbrough. The pop in 1801 was little above 3,000, in 1861, was upwards of 17,000, in 1865, nearly 20,000

The township includes also the hamlets of Old Barnsley, Measborough, Kinston place, and Old Mill, and is in the parish of Silkstone Acres, 4 000 Real property, £69,154, of which £14,490 are in mines Pop, 17,890 Houses, 3,565 —The chapelries are St. Mary, of old date, St George, constituted in 1831, and St. John, in 1844 The three jointly comprise the township The livings are St. M a rectory, St G and St. J vicarages, in the dio of Ripon Value of St. M., £400,* of St G, £300,* of St J, £300 Patron of St M and St G, the Bishop of Ripon, of St J, alternately the Crown and the Bishop.—The sub district comprises parts of the parishes of Silkstone, Darton, Roystone, and Darfield Acres, 10,628 Pop., 25,468 Houses, 5,125. The district comprehends also the sub district of Darton, containing parts of the parishes of Darton and Roystone, the sub district of Darfield, containing parts of the parishes of Darfield and Wath-upon Dearne, and the sub-district of Worsbrough, containing parts of the parishes of Darfield and Silkstone Acres, 35,376 Poor rates in 1866, £19,024 Pop in 1861, 45,797 Houses, 9 094 Marriages in 1866, 448, births, 2,143,—of which 138 were illegitimate, deaths, 1,298,—of which 710 were at ages under 5 years, and 10 at ages above 85 years Marriages in the ten years 1851-60, 3,121, births, 16,907, deaths, 9,713 The places of worship in 1851 were 17 of the Church of England, with 9,014 sittings, 2 of Independents, with 377 s., 1 of Baptists, with 390 s, 2 of Quakers, with 300 s, 19 of Wesleyan Methodists, with 2,993 s, 6 of New Connection Methodists, with 1,408 s, 7 of Primitive Methodists, with 1,539 s, 4 of the Wesleyan Association, with 870 s, 5 of Wesleyan Reformers, with 180 s, and 1 of Roman Catholics, with 500 s The schools were 27 public day schools, with 2,875 scholars, 44 private day schools, with 1,217 s, 54 Sunday schools, with 6,100 s, and 5 evening schools for adults, with 154 s

BARNSLEY CANAL, a canal, 15 miles long, in W R Yorkshire It goes from Corthorn in the vicinity of Barnsley, to the river Calder near Wakefield, joins the Dove and Dearne canal, crosses the Dearne by an aqueduct of 5 arches, passes Roystone and Sandall, both in the vicinity of the North Midland railway, and makes an aggregate descent of 158 feet, with 21 locks. It was opened in 1799

BARNSLEY OLD, a hamlet in Barnsley township, W R Yorkshire 1 mile NW of Barnsley

BARNSTAPLE, a town, a bay, a parish, a sub district, and a district, in Devon The town is a seaport, a borough, and the capital of North Devon It stands on the right bank of the river Taw, about 6 miles from its mouth, at an elbow of the North Devon railway, 9 miles NE of Bideford, and 39½ NW of Exeter Its site is a pleasant valley, bounded by a semicircular range of hills, to which the river forms a chord, and its environs abound in charming spots, and command brilliant views over land and sea Two of the best views are from the road to Bideford, and from Codden hill, 628 feet high The town was known to the ancient Britons as Tunge Abertawe,—to the Saxons as Berdenestaple, and it is now popularly called Barum It formed part of a domain of the Saxon kings, was for some time a residence of Athelstane, and received from him various liberties and rights An ancient castle stood at it, built by Athelstane, and strengthened after the Conquest, but is now represented only by a mound The town fitted out three ships, in 1588 for the fleet raised to repel the Spanish Armada, and it took part with the Parliamentarians in the time of Charles I, and underwent some sharp events in the wars which followed Three monastic edifices were erected at it, a Cluniac monastery, an Augustinian friary, and an hospital to the Holy Trinity, but are all extinct

The town is well aligned, and one of the most agreeable in the county A bridge of 16 arches, supposed to have been built in the 13th century, spans the river and was widened in 1834 Queen Anne's Walk, on the quay, west of the bridge, is a colonnade, upwards of 60 feet long, erected in the time of Queen Anne, adorned with a statue of that monarch, used originally as an exchange, and reconstructed by the corporation in 1798. The North Walk, further west, is a promenade, by the side of the river, planted with trees The market place in High street was enlarged, and a new and elegant town hall erected, in 1855, at a cost of upwards of £8,000 The corn market is at the upper end, and a music hall is over it. The theatre, in Boutport-street, built in 1834, is small but very neat. The North Devon infirmary, at the foot of Litchdon street, is a fine massive edifice The borough jail is a substantial structure, with capacity for 10 male and 9 female prisoners There are also a custom house, a dispensary, a work house, five suites of almshouses, a free grammar school, a blue coat school, a variety of day schools and benefactions, and a literary and scientific institution The parish church, nearly in the centre of the town, is a spacious ancient structure bearing many evidences of the hand of time, and has a curious timber spire, covered with lead, warped by the sun, and leaning to the south Holy Trinity church, at the south end of the town, has a tower 133 feet high, and was built in 1843 St Mary Magdalene church is a plain structure, erected in 1846 The Independent chapel is a very fine building The Wesleyan chapel was rebuilt in 1869, and is in the decorated English style The Roman Catholic chapel is a recent erection in very chaste style There are three Baptist chapels, and a chapel for Bible Christians

The town has a head post office ‡ a railway station, three banking-offices, and two chief inns, and it is the head quarters of the North Devon militia, and publishes three weekly newspapers. A weekly market is held on Friday, and a fair on the Wednesday after 19 Sept The manufacture of woollens was formerly extensive, and is still carried on Manufactures of bobbin net, paper, pottery, leather, and malt also exist, and ship building is prominent The chief commerce is in exports of grain, wool, oak bark, leather, and earthenware, and in imports of coal, fruit, wine, and foreign timber The vessels belonging to the port and its sub ports, at the beginning of 1868, were 62 small ones of aggregately 2,058 tons, and 31 large ones of aggregately 2,866 tons, and those which entered, in 1867, were 11 of aggregately 2,457 tons from the colonies and foreign countries, and 1,484 of aggregately 74,923 tons coastwise, and 236 of the latter were steamers The customs, in 1867, were £7,447 The town was made a borough by Edward I, sends two members to parliament, is governed by a mayor, six aldermen and eighteen councillors, and is a seat of petty sessions and a polling place Its limits as a borough, both parliamentary and municipal, include all the parish of Barnstaple and parts of the parishes of Pilton and Bishops Tawton Electors in 1868, 763 Direct taxation, £4,959 Real property, £29,490 Pop in 1851, 11 371, in 1861, 10,743 Houses, 2,188 Bishops Jewel and Gay were educated at the grammar school, and Dr Parsons, the author of "Japhet," was a native

The bay expands north and south at the mouth of the Taw, has there a dangerous bar, measures 15 miles across the entrance, from Morte point to Hartland point, lies much exposed to westerly winds, and includes, on the south side Clovelly roadstead, with from 4 to 8 fathoms water The navigation up from it to Barnstaple is through a narrow channel, with never more than 12 feet water —The parish, though not containing all the borough, extends beyond the town. Acres, 1,102 Rated property, £18,826 Pop, 8,127 Houses, 1,624 The living is a vicarage in the diocese of Exeter Value, £245 * Patron, Lord Wharncliffe Holy Trinity is a p. curacy, St. Mary Magdalene a vicarage, the former of the value of £120, in the patronage of the Bishop of Exeter, the latter of the value of £150, in the patronage of alternately the Crown and the Bishop of Exeter —The sub district comprises the parishes of Barnstaple, Swimbridge, Landkey, and Goodleigh Acres, 12,711 Pop, 10,652 Houses 2,167 The district comprehends also the sub district of Paracombe, containing the parishes of Paracombe, Highbray, Challacombe, Brendon, Countisbury, Lynton, Martinhoe, and Trentishoe, and part of the extra parochial tract of Exmoor Forest, the sub district of Combmartin, containing the parishes of Combmartin, Kentisbury, Arlington Loxhore, Bratton Fleming, Stoke Rivers, and Sherwill, the sub-district of Ilfracombe, containing the parishes of Ilfracombe Bittadon, Berryn-arbor, East Down, and West Down, the sub district of Braunton, containing the parishes of Braunton, Morthoe, Georgeham, Heanton Punchardon, Marwood Ashford and Pilton, and the sub district of Bishops-Tawton, containing the parishes of Bishops Tawton, Fremington, Instow, Westleigh, Newton Tracey, Horwood, Tawstock, and Atherington Acres, 149,729 Poor rates in 1866, £18,117 Pop in 1861, 36,293 Houses, 7,550 Marriages in 1866, 245, births, 1,128, —of which 88 were illegitimate, deaths, 689,—of which 182 were at ages under 5 years, and 39 at ages above 85 years. Marriages in the ten years 1851-60, 2,621, births, 10,413, deaths, 6,568 The places of worship in 1851 were 40 of the Church of England, with 11 568 sittings, 13 of Independents, with 2,761 s., 15 of Baptists, with 2,334 s, 1 of Quakers, with 45 s, 14 of Wesleyan Methodists with 2,753 s, 10 of Bible Christians, with 1,554 s, 3 of Brethren, with 180 s, 4 undefined, with 1,120 s, and 1 of Latter Day Saints, s. not reported. The schools in 1851 were 44 public day schools, with 2,620 scholars, 82 private day schools, with 1,692 s, and 64 Sunday schools, with 4,489 s

BARNSTON, a township in Woodchurch parish, Cheshire 4 miles N of Great Neston. It has a post office under Birkenhead. There is a tunnel of the Grand Trunk canal here, 550 yards long. Acres, 1,068 Real property, £1,325 Pop, 252 Houses, 52

BARNSTON, or BARNSTON, a parish in Dunmow district, Essex, on the river Chelmer, 2 miles SE of Dunmow r station, and 7½ WSW of Braintree It has a post office under Chelmsford. Acres, 1,442. Real property, £2,415 Pop, 192 Houses, 40 The property is divided among a few Barnston Hall is a chief residence The living is a rectory in the diocese of Rochester Value, £335 * Patron, the Rev W Toke The church is Norman

BARNSTONE, a chapelry in Langar parish, Notts, 3½ miles S of Elton r station, and 5 SE of Bingham Post town, Elton, under Nottingham. Pop, 169 The living is a p curacy, annexed to the rectory of Langar, in the diocese of Lincoln

BARNT GREEN See BARNT GREEN, Worcester

BARNTON, a township and a chapelry in Great Budworth parish, Cheshire The township lies near the Northwestern railway, 2 miles NW of Northwich, and has a post office under that town Acres, 751 Real property, £3,052 Pop., 1,219 Houses, 264 The chapelry is more extensive than the township and was constituted in 1843 Pop, 1,431 Houses, 310 The living is a vicarage in the diocese of Chester Value, £120 * Patron, the Bishop The church is good, and there are three Methodist chapels

BARNWELL See BARNWELL ST ANDREW

BARNWELL, or ST ANDREW-THE LESS See CAMBRIDGE

BARNWELL-ALL SAINTS, a parish in Oundle district, Northampton on the Peterborough railway, ¾ a mile S of Barnwell station, and 3 miles SSE of Oundle Post town, Barnwell St Andrew, under Oundle Acres, 1,680 Real property, £1,938 Pop, 115 Houses, 29 The living is a rectory, annexed to the rectory of Barnwell St Andrew, in the diocese of Peterborough

BARNWELL ST - ANDREW, a village and a parish in Oundle district, Northampton The village stands adjacent to the Peterborough railway, 2½ miles SSE of Oundle, and has a station, of the name of Barnwell, on the railway, and a post office, of the name of Barnwell St. Andrew, under Oundle Its name is alleged to be a corruption of "Barn's well," and is said to have arisen from an old superstitious belief, that some wells in the neighbourhood had a miraculous efficacy to cure the diseases of children. The parish comprises 1,740 acres Real property, £2,339 Pop 240 Houses, 50 The property is divided among a few A castle was erected here in 1152, by Reginald le Moine, and passed to the family of Montague, and the ruin of it, comprising a quadrangular court, with massive circular towers at the corners, and a grand gateway on the south side, is an interesting specimen of early Norman castellated architecture The living is a rectory, united with the rectory of Barnwell All Saints, in the diocese of Peterborough. Value £303 Patron, the Duke of Buccleuch The church is early English, and has a tower and spire An hospital for the poor, founded in the time of James I, has an income of £316, and other charities have £193

BARNWOOD, a parish in the district and county of Gloucester on the Fosse way and Cheltenham railway, 2 miles ESE of Gloucester Post town, Gloucester Acres, 1 471 Real property, £5,133 Pop, 507 Houses, 110 The property is much subdivided Barnwood Court and Barnwood House are chief residences The living is a vicarage in the diocese of Gloucester and Bristol Value, £195 Patrons, the Dean and Chapter of Gloucester The church is tolerable

BAROG a township in Llanfairtalhaiarn parish, Denbighshire, 9 miles WNW of Denbigh Pop, 197

BARON-HILL, the seat of Sir Richard Bulkeley, Bart, in Anglesey, on the coast, 1½ mile N of Beaumaris The mansion comprises part of a structure of 1618 by Sir Richard Bulkeley, but consists chiefly of a fine edifice, built by the last Lord Bulkeley, after designs by Mr S Wyatt The grounds are beautiful, and are liberally open to the public, and they contain, a short distance from the house, under a monumental recess, the stone coffin of Joan, daughter of King John of England, and wife of Llewelyn ap-Jorwerth, prince of North Wales, originally placed in the neighbouring priory of Llanvaes, and brought hither in 1808 by Lord Bulkeley

BARON S PARK. See BARRON S PARK

BARONY, a township in St Andrew Auckland parish, Durham, on the river Gaunless, and on the Northern Counties Union railway, at Evenwood station, 7 miles SW of Bishop Auckland. It includes the hamlet of Evenwood, contains extensive coal mines, and belongs to the Bishop of Durham. Acres, 5 336 Real property, £10,247,—of which £4,820 are in mines. Pop, 2,674 Houses, 515

BARRAS a railway station in Westmoreland, on the South Durham and Lancashire Union railway, between Bowes and Kirkby-Stephen

BARR (GREAT) a village, a township, and a chapelry in Aldridge parish, Stafford The village stands 2½ miles SE of Walsall r station, has a post office under Birmingham, and is a seat of petty sessions The township comprises 4 060 acres Real property, £8,405, Pop, 1,075 Houses, 220 Barr Hall is the seat of Sir E D Scott, Bart, and stands amid charming grounds, in a beautiful valley An urn near the flower-garden, is monumental of Miss Mary Dolman, the cousin of Shenstone Barr Beacon, 653 feet high, is said to have been the seat of the Archdruid, and was used by the Saxons and the Danes as a place of alarm fires.—The chapelry is conterminate with the township, and is a vicarage in the dio of Lichfield Value £405 Patron, Sir E D Scott, Bart The church stands at the village, and is a handsome recent structure with an eastern painted window by Egginton A school has an endowed income of £67, and other charities have £35

BARR (PERRY) See PERRY BARR

BARRASFORD, a township in Chollerton parish, Northumberland, on the North Tyne river and on the Border Counties railway, 7½ miles NNW of Hexham It has a station on the railway, and a post office under Hexham The right of a weekly market for it was obtained by Robert de Umfraville from Edward I, but has long been in abeyance. Acres, 1,394 Pop, 215 Houses 47

BARRAWAY, or BARWAY, a hamlet in Soham parish, Cambridge, near the river Ouse, 3½ miles S by E of Ely Pop, 71 It is a chapelry to the vicarage of Soham.

BARRICANE, a creek on the N coast of Devon, between Morte point and Woolacombe sands, 4½ miles SW of Ilfracombe It is notable for great profusion and variety of ocean flowers, sea weeds, and shells

BARRINGTON, a parish in the district of Royston and county of Cambridge, on the river Cam, 6 miles W by S of Shelford r station, and 7 SSW of Cambridge. It has a post office under Royston Acres, 2,129 Real property, £3,792 Pop, 563 Houses, 111 The property is much subdivided. The living is a vicarage in the diocese of Ely Value, £107 * Patron, Trinity College, Cambridge The church is old but good, and there are a neat Independent chapel, and charities £43

BARRINGTON, a parish in Langport district, Somerset 3½ miles NE of Ilminster, and 5 SW of Langport r station It includes the hamlet of Barrington Hill, and part of the hamlet of Westport, and its post town is Ilminster Acres, 1,6?6 Real property, £3,857 Pop, 501 Houses, 104 The property is much subdivided Barrington Court was a seat of the Phelipses and the Strodes, visited in the time of the latter by the Duke of Monmouth The living is a vicarage in the dio of Bath and Wells Value, £84 Patrons, the Dean and Chapter of Bristol The church is ancient. There are a Wesleyan chapel and an endowed school

BARRINGTON (GREAT), a parish in the district of Stow on the Wold Gloucester, on the verge of the county, 3½ miles NW of Burford, and 7 SW of Shipton r station It has a post office, of the name of Barrington, under Faringdon Acres, 2,983 Real property, £3,517 Pop, 496 Houses, 107 The property is divided among a few The manor belonged, prior to the Conquest, to Earl Harold, and belongs now to Lord Dynevor The present mansion on it is an elegant modern edifice, within a park about 3 miles in circuit, and a previous mansion was built in 1734 by Lord Chancellor Talbot, and soon afterwards destroyed by fire Quarries of excellent freestone are worked, and supplied the material for Blenheim House and for the restoration of Westminster Abbey The living is a vicarage in the diocese of Gloucester and Bristol Value £221 Patron, Lord Dynevor The church is a handsome building, with pinnacled tower, was erected in the time of Henry VII, and has monuments of Captain Edward Bray and Lord Chancellor Talbot. Charities, £17

BARRINGTON HILL. See BARRINGTON, Somerset

BARRINGTON (LITTLE) a parish in Northleach district, Gloucester, 2¾ miles WNW of Burford, and 7 SW of Shipton r station Post town, Barrington, under Faringdon Acres, 925 Real property, £1,600 Pop., 151 Houses, 33. The property is divided among a few The living is a vicarage in the diocese of Gloucester and Bristol Value, £100 * Patron, the Lord Chancellor The church is very good, and there are charities £66

BARRON S PARK, a hamlet in Desford parish, Leicester, 6½ miles E of Market Bosworth Pop, 18

BARROW (THE), a stream of Westmoreland, falling into the Burbeck, near Howsehouse.

BARROW (THE), a rivulet of Cumberland, falling into Derwent water, 2¾ miles S of Keswick A cascade of two falls occurs on it, altogether 122 feet, and is approached through the beautiful grounds of Barrow House, the seat of S Z Langton, Esq

BARROW, a parish in Great Boughton district, Cheshire, on a stream which goes northward to the Mersey, 3½ miles S of Dunham r station and 5 ENE of Chester It includes the townships of Great Barrow and Little Barrow, and has fairs on 22 June and 22 Dec, and its post town is Tarvin, under Chester Acres 2 916 Real property, £4,951 Pop, 623 Houses, 118 The property is divided among a few The living is a rectory in the diocese of Chester Value, £263 * Patron, Lord H Cholmondeley The church is early English There are a Wesleyan chapel, a national school built in 1865, and charities £9

BARROW, a township in Boddington parish, Glou

cester 4 miles NW of Cheltenham A hill here commands an extensive view, including 36 churches

BARROW, a township in Holystone parish, Northumberland, 10 miles W N W of Rothbury Pop, 14

BARROW, a parish in Madely district, Salop, on the Much-Wenlock railway, 3 miles E of Much Wenlock. Post town, Much Wenlock, under Wellington Acres, 3 013. Real property, £3,780 Pop, 365 Houses, 65 The property is all in one estate The living is a p curacy, annexed to Willey, in the diocese of Hereford The church was restored in 1850 There is an endowed school, with £34 a year

BARROW, a parish, with a village, in Thingoe district, Suffolk, 1½ mile S of Higham r station, and 6 W of Bury St Edmunds It has a post office under Bury St. Edmunds, and a fair on 1 May Acres, 2,665 Real property, £4,698. Pop, 1,030 Houses, 216 The property is much subdivided The living is a rectory in the diocese of Ely Value, £690 * Patron, St John s College, Cambridge The church was restored in 1852 There is an Independent chapel A school has an endowed income of £20, and other charities £60 Francis, the translator of Horace, was rector

BARROW, a hamlet in Wath upon Dearne parish, W R Yorkshire, 3½ miles N of Rotherham

BARROW, Leicester See BARROW-UPON SOAR.

BARROW, or PERK a hamlet in Cottesmore parish, Rutland 5½ miles NNE of Oakham

BARROW, or BARROW IN-FURNESS, a seaport town and two chapelries in Dalton in Furness parish, Lancashire The town stands at the terminus of a branch of the Furness railway, opposite Walney Island, 8 miles SW of Ulverston, was only a village, with a pop. of 325, so late as 1847, rose to a pop of about 2,000 in 1847, and to a pop of more than 12,000 in 1868, owed its rise mainly to rapid development of mineral wealth in its vicinity, began, in 1867, to acquire a grand artificial harbour, with docks and wharves, estimated to cost about £300,000, imports large quantities of timber and coal, has a long range of blast furnaces, extensive foundries, and steel works, large timber yards, ship building yards, and saw mills, draws from neighbouring mines about 400,000 tons of iron ore a year, produces about 4,000 tons of pig iron weekly, converts about one fifth of that quantity into steel by the Bessemer process, exports, in addition to its iron produce, about 3,000 tons of copper ore and about 20,000 tons of slate a year, is built on a regular plan, chiefly with streets crossing at right angles, and has a head post office,‡ a fine new r station with telegraph, a spacious town hall and market house built in 1865, an assembly room, a temperance hall, a subscription news room and library, a mechanics institute, a police office, a custom house, a church in the geometric style built in 1859 another church built in 1867, an Independent chapel in the early English style, a Wesleyan chapel of 1863, a Welsh chapel of 1864, a Roman Catholic chapel of 1866, and a national school —The chapelries are St George and St James, and were constituted, the former in 1863 the latter in 1867 The livings are p curacies in the diocese of Carlisle Value of St G, £149 * of St. J, £150 Patron of St G, the Duke of Devonshire, of St J, Trustees

BARROWBY, a parish, with three hamlets in Grantham district, Lincoln, on the Grantham and Nottingham railway 1½ mile W of Grantham It has a post office under Grantham Acres 4,462 Real property, £7,969 Pop., 862 Houses, 187 The property is divided among a few The living is a rectory in the diocese of Lincoln Value, £1,200 * Patron, the Duke of Devonshire The church is good

BARROWBY, W R Yorkshire See AUSTHORPE, and BARWICK IN ELMET

BARROWBY, N R Yorkshire See BORROWBY

BARROW COMMON See ASHTON (LONG)

BARROWDEN, a parish and a sub district in the district of Uppingham, Rutland The parish lies on the river Welland, 3 miles NE of Seaton r station and 6 E of Uppingham Post town, Morcott, under Uppingham Acres, 2,073 Real property, £2,806 Pop, 653 Houses, 147 The property is divided among a few The living is a rectory in the diocese of Peterborough. Value, £483 * Patron, the Marquis of Exeter The church is good. There are a Baptist chapel, and charities £47 —The sub d contains ten parishes Pop, 3,887

BARROW (EAST and WEST), a shoal, partly dry at low water, about 12 miles E of Foulness, Essex It extends from NE to SW, is 15 miles long, and from 1 to 3 miles broad, and has from 1 to 4 fathoms water A floating light is near the inner end. A navigable channel, called Barrow Deeps, with from 5 to 10 fathoms water, is on the one side, and another, called the Swin Deeps, more used by ships, is on the other

BARROWFORD, a township and a chapelry in Whalley parish, Lancashire The township lies on the East Lancashire railway, 2 miles W of Colne, and has a post office under Burnley Acres, 1,540 Real property, £7,754 Pop, 2,880 Houses, 612. The property is much subdivided Many of the inhabitants are employed in cotton manufactories.—The chapelry was constituted in 1843, and bears the name of Barrowford Colne, or Colne Barrowford Pop, 2,796 Houses, 591 The living is a p curacy in the diocese of Manchester Value, £150 * Patrons, Hulme s Trustees The church is recent and there are four dissenting chapels

BARROW (GREAT) See BARROW, Cheshire

BARROW GREEN See OXSTEAD.

BARROW GURNEY, a parish in Bedminster district, Somerset, 1½ mile SSE of Burton r station, and 5 W SW of Bristol Post-town, Long Ashton, under Bristol Acres, 2 026 Real property, £3,360 Pop, 321 House, 61 The property is divided among four Barrow Court near Barrow Hill is a fine Tudor mansion, the seat of J H Blagrave, Esq, and occupies the site of a Benedictine nunnery founded by the Fitzhardinges The living is a donative in the diocese of Bath and Wells Value, £66 * Patron, J H Blagrave, Esq

BARROW HAVEN See BARROW UPON-HUMBER

BARROW-HILL, an eminence adjacent to Englishcombe village, Somerset, 3 miles SW of Bath It surmounts an elevated ridge, is about 100 feet high, figures conspicuously in the view from Bath, and, if artificial, is one of the largest barrows in England.

BARROW-HILL, a quondam Roman station on Watling street, near Daventry, Northamptonshire

BARROW-HILL, an eminence on Akeman street, in Wychwood forest, Oxford, 5½ NE of Burford

BARROW-IN FURNESS See BARROW, Lancashire

BARROW (LITTLE) See BARROW, Cheshire

BARROW-MINCHIN, a hamlet in Barrow Gurney parish Somerset

BARROW (NORTH), a parish in Wincanton district, Somerset, adjacent to the Wilts and Somerset railway, 3 miles SW of Castle-Cary Post town, Castle Cary, under Bath Acres, 751 Real property, with South Barrow, £2,481 Pop, 111 Houses, 24 The living is a rectory in the diocese of Bath and Wells Value, £148 * Patron Lord Portman The church is good.

BARROW (SOUTH) a parish in Wincanton district, Somerset, adjacent to the Wilts and Somerset railway, 4 miles SW of Castle Cary Post town, Castle Cary, under Bath Acres, 752. Real property, with North Barrow, £2,481 Pop, 140 Houses, 29 The living is a vicarage in the diocese of Bath and Wells Value, £80 Patron, Mrs. Toogood The church is good

BARROW-UPON HUMBER, a village and a parish in Glanford Brigg district, Lincoln The village stands 2½ miles E of Barton, and has a post office‡ under Ulceby The parish includes also New Holland, lies on the Humber, nearly opposite Hull, has a ferry there, at Barrow Haven, to Hull, and is traversed, along the coast by the Barton branch railway, with a regular station at New Holland and a road side one at Barrow Haven Acres, 5,990, of which 1,370 are water Real property, £10,107 Pop 2,443 Houses, 543 The property is much subdivided An ancient monastery, founded by Wulpher, king of Mercia, stood at a place called Al Barwe An extensive entrenchment called the Castle and supposed to have been an ancient British camp, exists about a mile

NW of the village The living is a vicarage in the diocese of Lincoln Value, £260 Patron, the Lord Chancellor The church is very good An endowment for an afternoon preacher yields £160 a year, and charities yield £41 There are chapels for Independents, Wesleyans, and Primitive Methodists

BARROW UPON SOAR, a village, a township a parish, a sub district, and a district, in Leicester The village stands on the river Soar, and on the Midland railway, 3 miles SE of Loughborough, and it has a station, of the name of Barrow, on the railway, and a post office, of the same name, under Loughborough It is inhabited principally by gentry, farmers, labourers, and quarrymen, together with workers in lace and hosiery, and it has long been noted for a hard blue limestone which contains interesting fossils, and makes an esteemed cement under water —The township includes the village, and comprises 2,510 acres. Pop, 1,800 Houses, 404 —The parish includes also the townships of Mountsorrel North End and Quorndon, the liberty of Beaumanor, the chapelry of Woodhouse, and the hamlets of Woodhouse Eaves and Maplewell Acres, 9,160 Real property £8,182. Pop., 5,621 Houses, 1,281 The manor was known to the Saxons as Barwe, and belonged to Hugh Lupus. The property is now much subdivided The living is a vicarage in the diocese of Peterborough. Value, £326 * Patron, St John's College, Cambridge The church is partly old,—was partly rebuilt in 1862 The vicarages of Mountsorrel North End, Quorndon and Woodhouse are separate charges There are chapels for Baptists, Wesleyans, Primitive Methodists, and Roman Catholics Perkins' grammar school has an endowed income of £110, Babington's alms houses, £475, Beveridge's benefactions, for certain religious ends, £224, and other charities £170 Bishop Beveridge, who died in 1708 was a native

The sub district comprises Barrow upon Soar township, and the parishes of Walton on the Wolds, Seagrave Thrussington, Ratcliffe-on the-Wreak, Cossington, and Sileby Acres, 13,521 Pop, 5,144 Houses, 1,169 The district comprehends also the sub district of Quorndon, containing the parish of Swithland, the extra parochial tract of Ulverscroft, and parts of the parishes of Rothley and Barrow upon Soar, the sub district of Rothley containing the parishes of Wanlip, Thurcaston, and Newton Linford, the extra-parochial tracts of Rothley Temple, Broadgate, Anstey Pastures, Beaumont Leys, Sherman's Grounds, Gilroes and Leicester Abbey, and parts of the parishes of Rothley and Belgrave and the sub district of Syston, containing the parishes of Syston, Pearsby, Queeniborough, South Croxton, Beeby, and Barkby, and part of the parish of Belgrave Acres, 47,868 Poor rates in 1866, £11,830 Pop. in 1861, 19,778 Houses, 4,460 Marriages in 1866, 127, births, 712,—of which 49 were illegitimate, deaths, 398,—of which 150 were at ages under 5 years, and 13 at ages above 85 years. Marriages in the ten years 1851–60, 1,428, births 6,494, deaths, 4,316 The places of worship in 1851 were 27 of the Church of England, with 7,964 sittings 14 of Baptists, with 2,209 s 17 of Wesleyan Methodists, with 2,551 s, 14 of Primitive Methodists, with 2 121 s, 3 of the Wesleyan Association, with 405 s, 2 of Latter Day Saints with 120 s, and 2 of Roman Catholics, with 204 s. The schools were 28 public day schools with 1 774 scholars, 44 private day schools, with 927 s, 58 Sunday schools, with 3 933 s, and 4 evening schools for adults, with 131 s The workhouse is in Rothley township, and was built at a cost of £6 400

BARROW UPON TRENT, a township and a parish in Derbyshire The township is in Shardlow district, and lies on the river Trent, adjacent to the Grand Trunk canal, 3½ miles E by N of Willington r station, and 6 S of Derby Real property, £2,345 Pop, 260 Houses 61 The parish is partly also in Burton upon Trent district, and includes likewise the liberty of Arleston and Sinfin and the township of Twyford and Stenson Post town Chellaston, under Derby Acres, 5,840 Real property, £6,303 Pop, 526 Houses, 111 The property is much subdivided The living is a vicarage united with the p curacy of Twyford, in the diocese of Lichfield. Value, £105 Patron, A Moore, Esq The church is old but good, and there are Independent and Wesleyan chapels and charities £30

BARRULE (NORTH and SOUTH), two eminences at the ends of the mountain ridge across the centre of the Isle of Man The former is 2 miles SSW of Ramsey, and 1 840 feet high, and the latter is 5 miles SSE of Peel, and 1,545 feet high

BARRY, a village, an island, and a parish in Cardiff district, Glamorgan The village stands on the coast opposite the island, 9 miles SE of Cowbridge, is a subport to Cardiff, and has acquired importance by a harbour act of 1866, and by acts of 1865–6 for railways to the South Wales line at Peterston, to Sully, and to Penarth —The island comprises about 300 acres, and is separated from the mainland only by a narrow channel, passable for carriages at low water —The parish contains 570 acres of land and 267 of water, and its post town is Barry under Cardiff Real property, £631 Pop, 87 Houses, 13 The property is divided among a few There are ruins of an ancient castle and an ancient chapel The living is a rectory, annexed to the rectory of Porthkerry, in the diocese of Llandaff. The church is good

BARSBY a chapelry in Ashby Folville parish, Leicestershire, 6 miles E of Syston r station, and 10 NE of Leicester Post town, Gaddesby under Melton Mowbray Acres, 1 030 Real property, £2,219 Pop., 29[illegible] Houses, 63 There is a Wesleyan chapel

BARSHAM, a parish in Wangford district Suffolk near the river Waveney, 2 miles W by S of Beccles r station. Post town, Beccles Acres, 1,871 Real property, £2 976 Pop, 239 Houses, 49 The property is much subdivided The living is a rectory in the diocese of Norwich Value, £531 * Patron, Mrs. Anna M Suckling The church has a remarkable east front of 1617–37, and a round west tower, and contains a round decorated font, a brass of 1380, and a brick altar tomb of 1599 Echard, the ecclesiastical historian and early gazetteer writer, who died in 1730, and Catherine, the mother of Lord Nelson, were natives

BARSHAM (EAST), a parish in Walsingham district, Norfolk, adjacent to the Norfolk railway, 2½ miles N of Fakenham Post town, Fakenham Acres, 1,167 Real property, £1 932 Pop., 221 Houses, 44 The property is divided among a few The living is a vicarage, united with the rectory of Little Snoring, in the diocese of Norwich. Value, £645 * Patron, Lord Hastings The church is old but good Henry VIII walked barefooted from East Barsham to Walsingham, in 1510, to make a votive offering of a necklace

BARSHAM (NORTH), a parish in Walsingham district, Norfolk, adjacent to the Norfolk railway 2 miles SW of New Walsingham Post town, New Walsingham under Fakenham Acres, 1,015 Real property, £1,600, Pop 57 Houses, 14 The property is divided among a few The living is a rectory in the diocese of Norwich Value, £244 * Patron, the Earl of Orford The church is good

BARSHAM (WEST), a parish in Walsingham district, Norfolk, adjacent to the Norfolk railway, 3 miles NNW of Fakenham Post town Fakenham Acres, 1,571 Real property, £1 925 Pop, 92 Houses, 17 The property is divided among a few The living is a vicarage in the diocese of Norwich. Value, £155. Patron, General Balders The church is good

BARSTABLE, a hundred in Essex It touches the Thames, 12 miles above and below Gravesend, extends from 7½ to 15 miles inland, and includes 33 parishes Acres, 77,400 Pop in 1851, 15,216, in 1861, 15,230 Houses 3 038

BARSTON, a parish in Solihull district, Warwick, 1¾ mile ENE of Knowle r station, and 9 W of Coventry Post town, Knowle under Birmingham Acres, 1,966 Real property £4,507 Pop, 336 Houses, 79 The property is much subdivided Barston Park is a chief residence The living is a vicarage, annexed to the rectory of Berkeswell, in the diocese of Worcester The church is excellent Charities, £8

BARSTON, Kent. See BARFRESTON

BARTESTREE, a chapelry in Dormington parish, Herefordshire, on the Worcester and Hereford railway, near the Wothington station, the Roman road, and the river Wye, 4 miles E of Hereford It has a post office under Hereford. Acres, 250 Rated property, £533 Pop., 61 Houses 13 The property is divided among a few The living is a p curacy, annexed to the vicarage of Dormington, in the diocese of Hereford The church is good

BARTHERTON See BATHERTON

BARTHOLOMEW (St), a tract contiguous to Sudbury, Suffolk, held by some to be extra-parochial, by others to be within Sudbury borough

BARTHOLOMEW (St), Sussex. See CHICHESTER

BARTHOLOMEW (St), Middlesex See LONDON

BARTHOLOMEW HOSPITAL, (St), an extra parochial tract in Eastry district, Kent, adjacent to the south side of Sandwich Acres, 6 Pop., 51 Houses, 16 An hospital was founded here, about 1190 by Thomas Crompthorn, and re endowed in 1244 by Sir Henry de Sandwich, and still exists, as an almshouse, with income of £766

BARTHOLOMEW HYDE (St) See WINCHESTER.

BARTHOMLEY, a township in Nantwich district, Cheshire, and a parish in Nantwich and Congleton districts, Cheshire, and in Newcastle under Lyne district Stafford The township lies adjacent to the North Stafford railway, 1 mile S by W of Radway Green station, and 5 SE of Crewe, and has a post-office under Crewe Acres, 1,982 Real property £3,164 Pop, 416 Houses, 78 The parish includes also the townships of Crewe, Haslington, and Alsager in Cheshire and the township of Batterley in Staffordshire Acres, 11,035 Real property, £19,825 Pop, 3,002 Houses, 572 The property is not much divided Barthomley Hall, on Alsager Heath, is a chief residence The living is a rectory in the diocese of Chester Value, £824 * Patrons, the Trustees of the late Lord Crewe The church is an ancient edifice, with Norman porch and richly carved roof, the latter put up in 1589, and it was the scene of a tragical onslaught, in 1643, by a troop of Lord Byron A school has an endowed income of £10, and other charities £41 The chapelries of Alsager, Crewe Green, and Haslington, are separate benefices.

BARTHORPE. See ACKLAM

BARTINGTON, a township in Great Budworth parish, Cheshire, 4 miles NW of Northwich Acres, 306 Real property, £756 Pop., 63 Houses 15

BARTINNEY, a hill in the vicinity of Lands End, Cornwall. It has an altitude of 689 feet, and commands a fine view Its name signifies "the hill of fires

BARTLEY, two tythings in Eling parish, Hants, near the Southampton and Dorchester railway, 7½ miles W of Southampton The one bears the name of Bartley Regis, the other is united with Bistern, under the name of Bistern and Bartley, and they have a post office of the name of Bartley, under Southampton Bartley House is the seat of Lord Vivian, and Bartley Lodge, the seat of the Blaquieres

BARTLEY, or BARTLEY GREEN, a subdivision of Northfield parish, Worcester, near the Birmingham and Worcester railway, 6 miles SSW of Birmingham It has a post office of the name of Bartley Green under Birmingham and it forms a curacy with Northfield

BARTLOW or GREAT BARTLOW, a parish, with a r station, in Linton district, Cambridgeshire, on the Cambridge and Haverhill railway, 2½ miles SE of Linton Post town, Linton, under Cambridge Acres, 370 Real property, £677 Pop, 120 Houses, 23 The property is divided among a few Bartlow House and Bartlow Cottage are chief residences. Four barrows, popularly called Bartlow Hills, command an extensive view, and are generally, but erroneously, regarded as graves of the slain in the battle of 1016 between Edmund Ironside and Canute The living is a rectory in the diocese of Ely Value, £250 * Patron, R Watkins, Esq The church has a round Saxon tower, and is very good

BARTLOW END STEVENTON END, or LITTLE BARTLOW, a hamlet in Ashdon parish, Essex contiguous to Great Bartlow, 3 miles SE of Linton. Pop, 216

BARTON, a chapelry in Whippingham parish, Isle of Wight, 2 miles NE of Newport Pop, 1,314 The living is a vicarage Value £190 * See OSBORNE HOUSE.

BARTON, a parish in Chesterton district, Cambridgeshire, on a tributary of the Cam river, and on the Hitchin and Cambridge railway 3 miles SW of Cambridge It has a post office under Cambridge Acres, 1,812 Real property £3,303. Pop, 324 Houses, 70 The property is divided among a few The living is a vicarage in the diocese of Ely Value £156 Patron, the Bishop of Peterborough The church has a brass of 1593, and is good The rectorial tithes were given to Merton priory

BARTON, a township in Farndon parish, Cheshire, 8½ miles S by E of Chester Acres, 511 Real property, £964 Pop., 131 Houses, 28 Here is a Calvinistic Methodist chapel.

BARTON, a township in Preston parish, and a chapelry in Preston, Kirkham, Lancaster, and Garstang parishes, Lancashire The township has a station on the Northwestern railway, 5½ miles N of Preston Acres, 2,536. Real property, £3,782 Pop., 343 Houses, 67 Barton Hall and Barton Lodge are within the limits — The chapelry was constituted in 1850, and its post town is Preston Pop, 856 The living is a vicarage in the diocese of Manchester Value, £120 * Patron, R Jacson, Esq, and G Marton, Esq

BARTON, a sub district in the district of Glanford Brigg, Lincoln, containing Barton St. Peter, Barton St. Mary, and eleven other parishes. Acres, 57,077 Pop, 12,599 Houses, 2,799

BARTON, a parish in West Ward district, Westmoreland, on the river Eamont 3½ miles W by S of Clifton r station, and 4 SW of Penrith It extends along Ulles water to its head at Patterdale, includes the townships of High Barton Low Winder, Stockbridge and Tirril, Yanwath and Eamont Bridge and the chapelries of Martindale and Patterdale with Hartsop, and contains the post offices of Pooley Bridge and Patterdale under Penrith Acres, 35,312, of which 1,622 are water Real property £19,825 Pop, 1 808. Houses, 345 The property throughout the townships is not much divided, and the greater part of it belonged to the Lancasters, and has descended from them to the Earl of Lonsdale, while that of the two chapelries is subdivided The scenery includes many of the most admired features of the Lake country, and will be noticed in our article on Ulles water, and in other articles. Various minerals are found in the hills, particularly a variety of spars and petrifactions, on Barton fell The living is a vicarage in the diocese of Carlisle Value, £170 * Patron, the Earl of Lonsdale The church is a low large building, with a heavy tower between the nave and the chancel, was recently repaired and improved, and contains the tomb of one of the Lancasters, and monumental memorials of several other families The chapelries of Martindale and Patterdale are separate benefices A grammar school has an endowed income of £91, and other charities £23 Dr Langbaine, the historian and antiquary, who died in 1657, was a native

BARTON, a township and a parish in Darlington district and N R Yorkshire The township lies on a tributary of the river Tees, 4½ miles W of Croft r station, and 5 SW of Darlington, and has a post office under Darlington Acres, 2,177 Real property, £4,546 Pop 507 Houses, 117 The parish includes also the township of Newton Morrel and part of the township of Stapleton Acres 2,790 Real property, with the rest of Stapleton, £7,012. Pop., 584 Houses, 132 Limestone occurs The parish is a meet for the Raby hounds. The living is a double vicarage of Barton St Cuthbert and Barton St Mary in the diocese of Ripon Value, £110 * Patrons, the vicar of Stanwick and the vicar of Gilling

BARTON, a hamlet in Piddletown parish, Dorset, 5½ miles NE of Dorchester

BARTON, a hamlet in Guyting Temple parish, Gloucester 4½ miles E of Winchcomb

BARTON, a tything in Cirencester parish and borough, Gloucester

BARTON, a hamlet in Bidford parish, Warwick, 6½ miles SW of Stratford Pop, 147

BARTON, South Lancashire See BARTON UPON-IRWELL.

BARTON, Notts See BARTON IN FABIS

BARTON, Suffolk See BARTON (GREAT)

BARTON, N R. Yorkshire See BARDEN

BARTON, BRADNOR, AND RUSHOCK, a township in Kington parish, Hereford, 1 mile N of Kington Pop, 426 A Benedictine monastery anciently stood in the neighbourhood.

BARTON AND EASTLEY, a tything in South Stoneham parish, Hants, on the Southwestern railway, 5½ miles NNE of Southampton Pop, 57

BARTON AND WALTON, a station on the Derby and Birmingham railway, adjacent to the river Trent 1 mile E of Barton under Needwood, and 15 SW of Derby

BARTON BENDISH, a village and a parish in Downham district, Norfolk. The village stands 5½ miles SSW of Narborough r station, and 7½ ENE of Downham, and has a post office under Brandon It took its distinctive name from a dyke, called Bendish, which the Saxons erected to mark the boundary of the hundred The parish includes also the hamlet of Eastmore Acres, 4,390 Real property, £4,849 Pop, 484 Houses, 94 The property is divided among a few Barton Bendish Hall is the seat of Sir H Berney, Bart The living consists of the rectory of St Mary with All Saints, and the rectory of St. Andrew, and is in the diocese of Norwich Value £569 * Patrons, Sir H Berney, Bart and the Lord Chancellor The church of St Mary with All Saints is good, and that of St Andrew has a fine screen, with hagiological figures, and was repaired in 1859 There are a Wesleyan chapel, and charities £36

BARTON BLOUNT, a parish in the district of Burton-upon Trent and county of Derby, on a tributary of the river Dove, 4 miles NNE of Tutbury r station, and 10 W of Derby Post town, Church Broughton, under Derby Acres, 1,150 Real property, £2,301 Pop, 73 Houses, 7 The property is not much divided Barton Hall is the seat of F Bradshaw, Esq The parish is a resort of sportsmen The living is a rectory in the diocese of Lichfield Value, £60 Patron, F Bradshaw, Esq The church is excellent

BARTON EARLS, a parish and a sub district in Wellingborough district, Northampton The parish lies on the river Nen, adjacent to the Peterborough railway, 1½ mile NE of Castle Ashby r station, and 3½ SSW of Wellingborough and has a post office‡ under Northampton Acres, 1 750 Real property, £6,251 Pop, 1,557 Houses, 315 The property is much subdivided The living is a vicarage in the diocese of Peterborough Value £105 * Patron, E Thornton Esq The church stands on the substructions of an ancient fort, is partly Saxon or nearly Norman, but exhibits other styles has a curious tower, striped with stone work, and faced by long and short quoins. There are Baptist and Wesleyan chapels national and British schools, alms houses, and other charities £30 —The sub district comprises nine parishes Acres, 19,234 Pop, 6,239 Houses, 1,329

BARTON (EAST). See BARTON (GREAT)

BARTON END, a hamlet in Horsley parish, Gloucester, 3 miles WSW of Minchinhampton

BARTON FARM, a tract in Abingdon St Helen parish ½ a mile E of Abingdon Pop, 8 Barton Court and Barton Lodge are adjacent

BARTON (GREAT), a parish in Thingoe district, Suffolk near the Bury St Edmunds railway, 2½ miles NE of Bury St. Edmunds It contains the villages of Great Barton and East Barton, and has a post office of the name of Barton under Bury St Edmunds Acres, 4 030 Real property £4,794 Pop, 819 Houses, 200 Barton Hall is the seat of Sir H E Bunbury, Bart The living is a vicarage in the diocese of Ely Value, not reported * Patron, Sir C J T Bunbury, Bart. The church contains several old monuments, and is good. There are a free school, and four alms houses

BARTON HARTSHORN, a parish in the district and county of Buckingham, on the verge of the county, 2½ miles S of the Buckinghamshire railway, and 4 WSW of Buckingham Post town, Buckingham Acres, 870 Real property, £1,341 Pop, 126 Houses, 27 The property is divided among a few The living is a vicarage, united with the vicarage of Chetwode, in the diocese of Oxford Value, £102 * Patron, Mrs. Bracebridge The church is good

BARTON (HIGH), a township in Barton parish, Westmoreland, on the river Eamont, 4 miles SW of Penrith. It extends beyond the source of the Eamont in Ulleswater, and includes the hamlet of Pooley, and it once had the right of a weekly market Acres, 5,653, of which 278 are water Real property, £3,134 Pop 303 Houses, 60

BARTON HILL, a station on the York and Scarborough railway, adjacent to the river Derwent, at the boundary between the E and N ridings of Yorkshire, 12 miles NE of York

BARTON IN FABIS, a parish in Basford district, Notts, on the river Trent, 2½ miles E of Long Eaton r station, and 5½ SW of Nottingham It has a post office of the name of Barton under Nottingham Acres 1,620 Real property, £2,682. Pop., 295 Houses, 73 The property is all in one estate A British camp occurs, and coins have been found on Barton moor The living is a rectory in the diocese of Lincoln Value, £360 * Patron, the Archbishop of York The church is good.

BARTON IN THE BEANS, a township in Market-Bosworth district, Leicester; chiefly in Nailstone parish, but partly also in Market Bosworth and Shackerstone parishes, 2 miles N of Market Bosworth. Acres, 820 Real property £1,712 Pop, 159 Houses, 39

BARTON IN THE CLAY, a parish in Luton district, Beds, on the verge of the county, 7 miles N of Luton r station It has a post office under Ampthill Acres, 2,270 Real property, £3,400 Pop, 956. Houses, 210 The property is divided among a few The living is a rectory in the diocese of Ely Value, £400 * Patron, the Crown The church is ancient and good There are Baptist and Wesleyan chapels, an endowed school with £50, and other charities with £33

BARTON LE STREET, a township and a parish in Malton district, N R Yorkshire The township lies on the Thirsk and Driffield railway, and on the line of a Roman road under the Cleveland Moors, 6 miles WNW of Malton, and it has a station on the railway and a post office under Malton Acres, 1,644 Real property, £1,419 Pop, 184 Houses, 37 The parish includes also the townships of Butterwick and Coneysthorpe Acres, 3 476 Real property, £3 395 Pop, 454 Houses, 93 The property is divided among a few The living is a rectory, united with the curacy of Butterwick, in the diocese of York Value, £450 * Patron, H C Meynell Ingram, Esq The church has two elaborately sculptured Norman doorways, and is good There is a Wesleyan chapel

BARTON LE WILLOWS, a township in Crambe parish N R Yorkshire, on the river Derwent and on the York and Scarborough railway, adjacent to Barton Hill station 10 miles SW of Malton It has a post office under York Acres, 950 Pop., 225 Houses, 43

BARTON (MIDDLE), a township in Barton Steeple parish, Oxford

BARTON-MILLS, or LITTLE BARTON, a parish in Mildenhall district, Suffolk adjacent to the river Lark, 1 mile SSE of Mildenhall, and 5 N of Kennet r station. Post town, Mildenhall, under Soham Acres, 2,050 Real property £3,547 Pop, [illegible]31 Houses, 131 The property is subdivided Barton Place is the principal residence The living is a rectory in the diocese of Ely Value £550 * Patron, the Lord Chancellor The church is old, was restored in 1840 and contains an ancient font and a carved oak pulpit There are a Baptist chapel, and charities £14

BARTON MOSS, a station on the Liverpool and Manchester railway, on the border of Chat Moss, 7¾ miles W of Manchester

BARTON ON THE HEATH, a parish in the district of Chipping Norton and county of Warwick, on the verge of the county, near the Four-shire stone, 3½ miles E of Moreton r station, and 6 S of Shipton-on Stour It has a post office under Moreton in the Marsh. Acres, 1,540 Real property, £2 408 Pop, 184 Houses 36 The property is divided among a few The manor belonged, from the time of Henry III, to the Marshalls, and passed, in the time of Elizabeth, to the Overburys The living is a rectory in the diocese of Worcester Value, £364.* Patron, Trinity College, Oxford The church is old and plain, but good. Dover, the lawyer, who instituted the Cotswold games, so famous in the times of James I and II, was a resident

BARTON REGIS, a hundred in Gloucester It adjoins Bristol includes Clifton and other parishes, and measures 6 miles by 4 Acres, 6,976 Pop, 19,853 Houses, 3,838

BARTON ST CUTHBERT See BARTON, N R. Yorkshire

BARTON ST DAVID, a parish in Langport district, Somerset, on the river Brue, 4 miles NE of Somerton, and 6 SE of Glastonbury r station Post town, Somerton, under Taunton Acres, 945 Real property, £2,002 Pop., 404 Houses, 88 The living is a vicarage in the diocese of Bath and Wells Value, £60 * Patron, the Rev Mr Garrett The church was restored in 1858 There is an Independent chapel

BARTON ST-LAWRENCE See BARTON, Lancashire

BARTON ST-MARY, a hamlet in the parish of St Mary de Lode, in the suburbs of Gloucester city, and within the boundaries of Gloucester borough Acres, with Tuffley hamlet, 1 470 Pop, 4,335 Houses, 828

BARTON ST MARY, Lincoln See BARTON UPON HUMBER

BARTON ST MARY, Yorkshire. See BARTON, N R Yorkshire

BARTON-ST-MICHAEL, a hamlet in St. Michael parish, in the suburbs of the city of Gloucester It has a post office under Gloucester Acres, 500 Pop, 2,315 Houses, 423

BARTON ST PETER See BARTON UPON HUMBER

BARTON SEAGRAVE, a parish in Kettering district, Northampton, on the Leicester and Bedford railway, 2 miles SE of Kettering. It has a post office under Kettering Acres, 1,782 Real property, £3,656 Pop, 199 Houses, 40 The property is divided among a few The manor belonged anciently to the Seagraves, who had a castle on it in the time of Edward II, and one of whom was marshal of England in the time of Edward IV The principal landowner now is Viscountess Hood The living is a rectory in the diocese of Peterborough Value, £492 * Patron, the Duke of Buccleuch The church is ancient but good, has a tower, and contains monuments of the Bridges Bishop Henchman born in 1592, and the two Bridges, father and son the former of whom was the first grower of sainfoin in these parts, while the latter made extensive collections for a history of the county and died in 1724, were natives

BARTON SESWELLS, a township in Barton Steeple parish Oxford

BARTON STACEY, a tything, a parish, and a hundred in Hants The tything lies on a headstream of the Anton river, and on the line of the Roman road to Winchester, 4¼ miles E of the Andover railway, and 5¼ SE of Andover, and has a post-office under Winchester and a fair on 31 July The parish includes also the townships of Bransbury, Drayton, and Newton Stacey Acres 4 943 Real property, £5 925 Pop, 516 Houses 108 The property is divided among a few A strong ancient entrenchment occurs at Bransbury The living is a vicarage in the diocese of Winchester Value, £266 * Patrons, the Dean and Chapter of Winchester The church is early English and cruciform, and has a fine perpendicular tower There are a Wesleyan chapel, and charities £44 The hundred is conterminate with the parish

BARTON STEEPLE, a township and a parish in Woodstock district, Oxford The township lies on a tributary of the Cherwell river, 2¼ miles W of Heyford r station, and 4½ SSW of Deddington The parish includes also the townships of Middle Barton and Seswells Barton, and its post town is Lower Heyford, under Oxford Acres, 2,710 Real property, £3 981 Pop, 859 Houses, 204 The property is divided among a few The manor belonged for centuries to the Dormers, passed in 1750 to Sir Clement Cottrell, and belongs now to H Hall, Esq, and the mansion on it is a picturesque structure of 1521, enlarged tastefully by the present proprietor The living is a vicarage in the diocese of Oxford Value, £123 * Patrons, the Duke of Marlborough and H Hall, Esq The church is an ancient edifice, recently restored There are Wesleyan and Primitive Methodist chapels

BARTON TURF, a parish in Tunstead district, Norfolk, 6½ miles SE by S of North Walsham r station, and 11 NE of Norwich Post town, Smallburgh, under Norwich Acres, 1,599 Real property, £2,643. Pop, 379 Houses 88 The living is a vicarage, united to the rectory of Irstead in the diocese of Norwich Value, £360 * Patron, the Bishop of Norwich The church is good, and has a lofty tower

BARTON UNDER NEEDWOOD, a village and a chapelry in Burton upon Trent district, Stafford The village stands near Icknield street, the Grand Trunk canal, the river Trent, and the Birmingham and Derby railway, 1 mile W of Barton and Walton station, and 5½ SW of Burton upon Trent It has a post office‡ under Burton upon Trent, is in the honour of Tutbury, and a seat of courts, and has fairs on 3 May and 28 Nov Several fine villas are in the neighbourhood The chapelry includes the village, and is in the parish of Tatenhill Acres, 3,520 Real property £12 054 Pop, 1,589 Houses, 339 The property is much subdivided The living is a p curacy in the diocese of Lichfield. Value, £135 * Patron, the Dean of Lichfield The church is later English, and was built, in the time of Henry VIII, by Dr John Taylor, a native of the village There are chapels for Wesleyan and Primitive Methodists Two endowed schools have £60, and other charities £39

BARTON UPON HUMBER, a town and two parishes in Glanford Brigg district Lincoln The town stands on a rising ground, about ¾ of a mile from the Humber, at the terminus of a branch of the Lincolnshire railway, 5 miles westward from New Holland, and 6 WSW of Hull It occupies the site of a Roman station and was a place of considerable commerce in the time of the Conqueror, but suffered much when Edward I made Hull a free borough It consists principally of spacious but irregularly built streets, and contains some good modern houses St Peter's church is a large edifice, of nave, aisles and chancel, chiefly in decorated English, with a tower partly Saxon, partly early Norman, and was renovated in 1859 at a cost of about £1,400 St. Mary's church is a structure of probably the 14th century There are three dissenting chapels, a Roman Catholic chapel, a national school charities £250, a newspaper, a head post office,‡ a banking office, and two chief inns A weekly market is held on Monday, and a fair on Trinity Thursday A good trade exists in corn and flour, manufactures are carried on in ropes, sacking, bricks, tiles, pottery and malt, and quarrying is done in chalk and oolite The town is a coast guard station, a seat of petty sessions, and a polling place The two parishes are St Peter and St Mary They are regarded politically as conterminate with the town, yet comprise 6 710 acres of land and 1,430 of water Real property, £16 799 Pop of St Peter, 1,672 Houses 384 Pop of St Mary, 2,185 Houses, 504 The property in both is much subdivided The manor belonged at one time to Lord Beaumont, and afterwards to the Crown R mains of ramparts and other works, raised for defence in the Saxon times, occur at Castle Dykes The livings are jointly a vicarage in the diocese of Lincoln Value, £250 * Patron, G C. Uppleby, Esq

BARTON UPON IRWELL, a village, a chapelry, a township a sub district, and a district in Lancashire The village stands on the river Irwell, adjacent to the Manchester and Liverpool railway, in the vicinity of Patricroft station, 5 miles W of Manchester It has a post office, of the name of Barton under Manchester, and it finds employment for many of its inhabitants in a silk mill and three spinning mills at Patricroft. An aqueduct here, across the Irwell, with three arches in the line of the Bridgewater canal, was the earliest structure of its kind in England. The chapelry includes the village, and was constituted in 1843 Pop in 1861, 3,204 The property is divided among a few The living is a p curacy in the diocese of Manchester Value, £150 * Patrons, the Bishop of Manchester, the Vicar of Eccles and others. The church is modern There are a fine Roman Catholic chapel of 1868 two Methodist chapels, and two public schools. The township includes two hamlets, and is in the parish of Eccles Acres, 10,530 Real property, £47,264 Pop in 1851, 12,687, in 1861, 14,216 Houses, 2,788 The sub-district bears the name of Barton, and is conterminate with the township The district comprehends also the sub district of Worsley, containing the townships of Worsley and Clifton in the parish of Eccles, and the sub district of Stretford, containing the township of Stretford in the parish of Manchester, and the townships of Flixton and Urmstone in the parish of Flixton Acres, 23,279 Poor rates in 1866, £11,141 Pop in 1861, 39,038 Houses, 7,462 Marriages in 1866, 318, births, 1,459,—of which 86 were illegitimate, deaths, 994,—of which 390 were at ages under 5 years, and 14 at ages above 85 years Marriages in the ten years 1851-60, 3,546, births, 11,780 deaths, 7,725 The places of worship in 1851 were 10 of the Church of England, with 6,626 sittings, 5 of Independents, with 1,562 s, 1 of Unitarians, with 339 s, 10 of Wesleyan Methodists, with 3,863 sittings, 1 of New Connexion Methodists with 200 s, 4 of Primitive Methodists, with 476 s, 5 of the Wesleyan Association, with 1 239 s, 1 of the New Church with 212 s, 1 of Roman Catholics, with 117 s, and 2 undefined, with 397 s The schools were 19 public day schools, with 2 960 scholars, 40 private day schools with 1,396 s., 43 Sunday schools, with 6,475 s, and 4 evening schools for adults, with 136 s

BARTON WESTCOT, a parish in Woodstock district, Oxford on a tributary of the Cherwell river 2¾ miles W of Heyford r station, and 4½ SSW of Deddington Post town, Sandford under Oxford Acres, 650 Real property, £1 679 Pop, 302 Houses, 70 The property is divided between two The living is a rectory in the diocese of Oxford Value, £230 * Patron, Mrs Seagrave The church has some Norman features, and was restored in 1856

BARUGH, a hamlet in Orton parish, Westmorland, near Orton and the Lune

BARUGH, a township in Darton parish, W R Yorkshire, 2 miles NW of Barnsley It includes the hamlets of Gawber and Higham Acres, 1,419 Real property, £4 383 Pop 1 771 Houses, 355

BARUGHS AMBO a township in Kirkby Misperton parish N R. Yorkshire, 4 miles SW of Pickering It consists of the hamlets of Great and Little Barugh Acres, 1,433 Real property, £2,094 Pop, 318 Houses, 60 A well preserved Roman camp is at Great Barugh.

BARUM See BARNSTAPLE

BARWAY See BARRAWAY

BARWE See BARROW UPON HUMBER and BARROW UPON SOAR.

BARWELL, a township in Blaby district and a parish in Blaby, Hinckley, and Market Bosworth districts, Leicester The township lies 2 miles NNE of Hinckley r station and 6¾ NE of Nuneaton and has a post office under Hinckley Acres, 2,200 Real property, £6,589 Pop, 1,353 Houses, 304 The parish includes also the hamlet of Potters Marston and the chapelry of Stapleton Acres, 3,950 Real property, £10,069 Pop, 1,613 Houses, 361 The property is subdivided The living is a rectory, united with the p. curacies of Marston and Stapleton, in the diocese of Peterborough. Value, £865 * Patron, Rev R Titley The church is ancient, and was recently restored. There are Wesleyan and Primitive Methodist chapels, and charities £22.

BARWICK, a parish in Yeovil district, Somerset, on the verge of the county, 2 miles S of Yeovil r station It includes the hamlet of Stoford, and its post town is Yeovil Acres, 784 Real property, £2,064 Pop, 458. Houses, 89 Barwick House is the seat of J Newman, Esq There are two flax mills The living is a rectory in the diocese of Bath and Wells Value £100 Patron, J Newman Esq The church is early English

BARWICK or BERWICK IN THE BRAKES, a parish in Docking district Norfolk 4 miles SSW of Burnham-Westgate r station, and 9 WNW of Fakenham Post town, Burnham, under Lynn Acres, 1,278. Real property, £1,321 Pop, 26 Houses, 5 Barwick House is the seat of D Hoste, Esq The living is a vicarage, united with the rectory of Stanhoe, in the diocese of Norwich. The church is in ruins

BARWICK HALL, a hamlet in Roothing Abbots parish, Essex, 6½ miles SW of Dunmow Pop 97

BARWICK IN ELMETT, a township in Tadcaster district and a parish in Tadcaster and Hunslet districts, W R. Yorkshire. The township lies 2½ miles N of Garforth r station, and 8 ENE of Leeds, includes the hamlets of Barrowby Crosgates Barnbow, Hiddle, Morwick Potterton, Schoies, and Stanks, and part of Winmoor, and has a post office under South Milford Acres, 6,400 Real property, £9,721 Pop, 1 804 Houses, 386 The parish includes also the township of Roundhay Acres, 8,030. Real property, £15,432 Pop, 2,374 Houses 496 The property is not much divided. Traces of a castle, said to have been the residence of Edwin, King of Northumbria, occur on Hall Tower hill A monastery founded about 730, stood somewhere in the parish. The living is a rectory in the diocese of Ripon Value, £770 * Patron, the Duchy of Lancaster The church is good, and there are charities £32. The chapelries of Manston and Roundhay are separate benefices The work house of Tadcaster district is in Barwick township

BARWISE a hamlet in Hoffe and How township, Appleby St Lawrence parish, Westmoreland

BASCHURCH, a township, a parish, and a sub district, in the district of Ellesmere Salop The township lies on the river Perry, near the Ellesmere canal and the Shrewsbury and Chester railway, 8 miles NW of Shrewsbury, and has a station on the railway, and a post office‡ under Shrewsbury The parish includes also the townships of Little Ness, Birch, Boreatton or Bratton, Eyton Fennemere, Merehouse, or Murhouse, Newtown Prescott, Stanwardine in the-Wood, Stanwardine in the Fields, Walford, Weston Lullingfeld, and Yeaton Acres, 8,273 Real property, £15,791 Pop, 1,553 Houses, 320 The property is subdivided There are traces of a Roman camp The living is a vicarage in the diocese of Lichfield Value, £293 * Patron, the Lord Chancellor The church is ancient The vicarage of Weston Lullingfield is a separate benefice Harris's school has an endowed income of £324, and other charities have £17 —The sub district comprises four parishes Acres, 21 283 Pop, 3 435 Houses, 712

BASCOTE, a hamlet in Long Itchington parish, Warwick 2 miles NNW of Southam

BASFORD a township in Wybunbury parish Cheshire, on the North-western railway 2½ miles SSE of Crewe It has a station on the railway Acres, 642 Real property, £820 Pop, 60 Houses, 12

BASFORD a village a parish, a sub district and a district in Notts The village is called also Old Basford It stands on the river Leen, adjacent to the Nottingham and Mansfield railway, in a luxuriant valley 3 miles NNW of Nottingham, and has a station of the name of Basford, on the railway, and a *post office* ‡ of the name of Old Basford, under Nottingham It has undergone great recent increase, is a chief seat of the cotton hose and lace manufactures, has cotton and corn mills, bleaching and dyeing works, is the seat of the court of the honour of Peverel, and contains a jail for the honour, with attached bowling green, which is much frequented by persons from Nottingham The parish includes also New Basford, Bagthorpe, Carrington, Sherwood, Mapperley, Two mile House, Bagnall, White Moor Place, and part of the hamlet of Daybrook Acres, 2,720 Real property £27,795 Pop, 12,185 Houses, 2,489 The property is much subdivided The living is a vicarage, united with the p curacy of Cinderhill, in the diocese of Lincoln Value, £260 Patron, the Lord Chancellor The church is early English was renovated in 1860, at a cost of about £3,000, and has a new lofty tower in three storeys The p curacies of New Basford, Cinderhill, and Carrington are separate benefices. There are fourteen dissenting chapels, and a free school

The sub-district comprises the parishes of Basford, Beeston, and Wollaton Acres, 6,500 Pop, 15,935 Houses, 3,303 —The district comprehends also the sub-district of Bulwell, containing the parishes of Bulwell, Bilborough, Strelley, Nuthall, and Hucknall Torkard, the sub district of Arnold, containing the parishes of Arnold, Lambley, Linby, Papplewick Calverton, and Woodborough, and the extra parochial liberty of Newstead Priory, the sub district of Carlton, containing the parishes of Gedling, Colwick, and West Bridgford, and part of the parish of Burton Joyce, the sub district of Wilford, containing the parishes of Wilford, Ruddington, Bradmore, Bunny, Gotham, Thrumpton, Barton in-Fabis, and Clifton with Glapton the sub district of Greasley, containing the parishes of Greasley, Eastwood, Kirkby in-Ashfield, Selston, and Annesley, the extra parochial tract of Felley, the extra parochial tract of Codnor Park, and part of the parish of Heanor,—the two last electorally in Derby, and the sub district of Ilkeston containing the parishes of Cossall, Trowell, and Ilkeston, and part of the parish of Heanor,—the two last electorally in Derby Acres, 88,039 Poor rates in 1866, £26,560 Pop in 1861, 73,285 Houses, 15 276 Marriages in 1866, 566, births, 2,971,—of which 256 were illegitimate, deaths, 1,703,—of which 807 were at ages under 5 years, and 37 were at ages above 85 years. Marriages in the ten years 1851–60, 5,781 births, 27,183, deaths, 15,848 The places of worship in 1851 were 43 of the Church of England, with 14,585 sittings, 4 of Independents with 1,371 s, 23 of Baptists, with 5,358 s, 1 of Quakers, with 300 s., 1 of Unitarians, with 100 s, 29 of Wesleyan Methodists, with 6,946 s, 7 of New Connexion Methodists, with 2,023 s, 19 of Primitive Methodists, with 2,816 s, 3 of the Wesleyan Association, with 782 s, 5 of Wesleyan Reformers, with 1,095 s, 6 of Latter Day Saints, with 562 s, and two undefined, with 84 s The schools were 48 public day schools, with 3,305 scholars, 115 private day schools, with 3,330 s., 117 Sunday schools, with 13,449 s., and 14 evening schools for adults, with 3[illegible]2 s. The workhouse is in Basford.

BASFORD, a township in Cheddleton parish, Stafford, 3 miles S of Leek Real property, £3,123. Pop., 428 Houses, 76 Charles Cotton, the comic poet, born in 1630, was a native

BASFORD (New), a village and a chapelry in Basford parish, Notts The village stands 1 mile SSE of Old Basford, and 2 NNW of Nottingham, and has a post-office under Nottingham The chapelry was constituted in 1847 Rated property, £4,590 Pop, 3,241 Houses, 699 The property is much subdivided. The living is a p curacy in the diocese of Lincoln Value, £130 Patron alternately the Crown and the Bishop The church was built in 1860, is of brick, with stone dressings, and has windows of stained glass

BASFORD (Old) See Basford, Notts.

BASHALL EAVES, or Beckshalgh, a township in Mitton parish W R. Yorkshire, on the western verge of the county, 2¼ miles WNW of Clitheroe It includes the hamlet of Pagefold, and was a seat of the Talbots and the Lacys Pop, 259

BASILDEN, or Basildon, a parish in Bradfield district, Berks, on the river Thames, and on the Great Western railway, 1 mile SSE of Goring station, and 7¾ WNW of Reading Post-town, Pangbourne, under Reading Acres, 3,083 Real property, £4,875 Pop, 712 Houses, 148 The property is divided among a few Basilden Park was the seat of the Viscounts Fane from 1718 till 1766, passed then to the baronet family of Sykes, and was recently purchased by T Morrison, Esq The house contains a fine collection of works of art The railway crosses the Thames a short distance above the church The parish had two churches at Domesday, and afterwards the right of a weekly market. The living is a vicarage in the diocese of Oxford. Value, £200 * Patron, the Rev W Sykes. The church is ancient There is a dissenting chapel

BASILDON, a chapelry in Laindon parish, Essex, 2 miles NNW of Pitsea r station, and 4 SE of Billericay Post town, Laindon, under Billericay Acres 1,627 Real property, £1,927 Pop, 160 Houses, 25 The living is annexed to Laindon rectory in the diocese of Rochester

BASING, or Old Basing, a village and a parish in Basingstoke district, Hants The village stands adjacent to the Basingstoke canal and the Southwestern railway, 2 miles NW of Basingstoke, and has a post office, of the name of Old Basing, under Basingstoke The parish includes also Water End. Acres, 5,104 Real property, £5,974 Pop, 1,193 Houses, 232 The property is all in one estate Ethelred I was defeated here, in 871, by the Danes. A very early castle, adjacent to the village, was held by the family of De Port from the Conquest till the time of Richard II, passed then, by marriage, to the Poynings, and went, in the time of Henry VI, to the Paulets Sir William Paulet, created Marquis of Winchester by Edward VI, rebuilt the castle in a style of great magnificence, and gave sumptuous entertainment in it to Queen Elizabeth John the fifth marquis, garrisoned it in defence of Charles I, maintained it against a siege, by successive parliamentary leaders, during two years and was eventually beaten by storm, under Cromwell's own leading, with results which made the place a ruin, and gave the victors about £200,000 worth of plunder Only an ivy clad gateway, and a few walls and mounds of the castle now remain, and even a subsequent but smaller mansion built near it, has passed away Many balls, skeletons, and other relics of the conflict have been found and a neighbouring field bears the name of Slaughter close Many ancient entrenchments are in the vicinity, and one, called Winklesbury Circle, about 1,100 feet in diameter, with a flint formed vallum, was used by Cromwell as a surveying post preparatory to his attack The living is a vicarage, united with the vicarage of Up Nately, in the diocese of Winchester Value, not reported Patron, Magdalene College, Oxford The church is late perpendicular, was repaired, in 1519, by Sir John Paulet, and contains tombs of the Paulets, including the six Dukes of Bolton, descendants of the fifth Marquis of Winchester Charities, £51

BASINGFIELD See Bassingfield

BASINGSTOKE, a town, a parish, a sub district, a district, a hundred, and a division in Hants The town stands on a headstream of the river Loddon, and on the Southwestern railway, 15½ miles SSW of Reading, and 45¼ SW by W of London A canal goes from it to the Thames, five roads from the S and the W meet at it to proceed to London, and two branch railways go off from its vicinity, the one to Reading, the other to Andover and Salisbury The town dates from the Saxon times, and was a royal possession and a market town at Domesday It consists of several streets, and contains neat well-built houses. The town hall is a handsome edifice of 1832, and cost £9,695 The corn exchange was built in 1865, at a cost of upwards of £3,000. The parish church is late perpendicular large, and handsome, consists of nave, chancel, and side aisles with a square tower, was built chiefly in the reign of Henry VIII, by Bishop Fox, was recently repaired and new seated, and contains a parochial library and the monument of Thomas Warton. An hospital for aged priests, founded in 1261 by Walter de Merton, adjoined the churchyard, but has disappeared. A picturesque ruin known as the Holy Ghost chapel, founded in the time of Henry VIII, by the first Lord Sandys, stands adjacent to the railway station, shows characters of very late perpendicular, with debased and Italian details, and is believed to occupy the site of some previous religious edifice or edifices, dating back to the times of the Saxons. A burying ground around it, now disposed as a new cemetery, contains two funeral chapels in decorated Gothic, each with tower and spire about 70 feet high, founded in 1857, and contains also some interesting ancient monuments. The town has four dissenting chapels, a grammar school with endowed income of £158, a blue-coat school with £170, other charities with £607, a mechanics' institute, a head post-office,‡ 3 banking-offices, and 5 chief inns, and it is a seat of petty sessions and a polling place. A weekly market is held on Wednesday, and fairs, on Easter Tuesday, Whit Wednesday, the last Thursday of May, 23 Sept, 11 Oct., and the last Thursday of Nov. The manufacture of druggets and shalloons was once extensive, but malting and the corn trade are now the chief employments. The town sent members to parliament in the times of Edward I and II, was chartered by James I and Charles I, and is now governed by a mayor, four aldermen and twelve councillors. John de Basingstoke, a celebrated Greek scholar of the 13th century, Sir James Lancaster, the eminent navigator in the time of Elizabeth, Richard White, the author of a History of Britain, in the time of James I, and the brothers Joseph and Thomas Warton, the former head master of Winchester, the latter the well known poet were natives of Basingstoke, and Thomas Warton, the father of these Wartons, and Sir George Wheeler the Eastern traveller, were vicars.—The parish is politically conterminate with the town and comprises 4,036 acres. Real property £17,603. Pop., 4,654. Houses, 945. The living is a vicarage in the diocese of Winchester, and, till 1864, was united with Basing and Up-Nately. Value, £574.* Patron, Magdalene College, Oxford.

The sub district comprises the parishes of Basingstoke, Worting, Eastrop, Basing, Tunworth, Weston Patrick, Upton Gray, Mapledërwell, Up Nately, Nately Scures, and Newnham, and the extra parochial tracts of Andwell and Weston Corbett. Acres, 19,884. Pop., 7,784. Houses, 1,577. The district comprehends also the sub district of Bramley, containing the parishes of Bramley, Sherborne St John, Sherfield upon-Loddon, Hartley Westpall, Stratfield Turgis, Silchester, Pamber, West Sherborne, and Stratfieldsaye,—the last partly in Berks, and the sub district of Dummer, containing the parishes of Dummer, Nutley, Woodmancott, Popham, North Waltham, Church Oakley, Steventon, Deane, Wootton St. Lawrence, Cliddesden, Farleigh Wallop, Ellisfield, Winslade with Kempshot, Herriard, Bradley, and Preston Candover. Acres, 73,802. Poor rates in 1866, £13,979. Pop in 1861, 17,429. Houses, 3,516. Marriages in 1866, 120, births 580,—of which 32 were illegitimate, deaths, 293,—of which 89 were at ages under 5 years, and 15 at ages above 85 years. Marriages in the ten years 1851-60, 1,001, births, 5,139, deaths 3,234. The places of worship in 1851 were 37 of the Church of England, with 6,913 sittings, 8 of Independents, with 1,0[illegible] s., 1 of Baptists with 100 s., 1 of Quakers, with 1[illegible] s., 8 of Primitive Methodists, with 927 s., and 1 of Lady Huntingdon's Connexion with 325 s. The schools were 27 public day schools, with 1,958 scholars, 19 private day schools, with 373 s., 20 Sunday schools, with 1,513 s., and 3 evening schools for adults, with 26 s. The workhouse is in Basing, was erected at a cost of £7,500, and has capacity for 400 inmates.—The hundred comprises seventeen parishes, and is cut into the two parts of Lower Half and Upper Half. Acres, 18,961 and 14,103. Pop. in 1851, 4,211 and 2,969. Houses, 840 and 631.—The division comprehends the hundreds of Basingstoke, Lower and Upper Bermondspit, Lower and Upper, and Holdshott, Lower. Acres, 70,906. Pop. in 1851, 13,560, in 1861, 12,790. Houses, 2,616.

BASINGSTOKE CANAL, a canal from Basingstoke in Hants to the Wey and Arundel canal in Surrey. It goes eastward, past Odiham and across the river Blackwater, to the border of Surrey in the vicinity of Ash, then goes 3¾ miles northward to the Chobham hills, near Farnborough, then proceeds east-north eastward, in the route of the Southwestern railway, to the Wey and Arundel canal about 3 miles from the latter's junction with the Thames. Its length is 37 miles, and it makes a total descent of 195 feet, with 29 locks, and passes, near Odiham, through a tunnel of ¾ of a mile. It was completed in 1796, at a cost of £180,000, and it is navigable by vessels of nearly 50 tons burden.

BASINGTHORPE. See BASSINGTHORPE.

BASINGWERK, a ruined Cistertian abbey in Holywell parish, Flint, on the coast of the estuary of the Dee, 1 mile NE of Holywell. The abbey was founded in 1131, by Ranulph, Earl of Chester, and was a beautiful structure in early English. The ruin comprises only the south transept of the church, with parts of the out buildings, and it stands on a gentle eminence, with very pleasing view, but is marred both by a neglected state of its own interior, and by the neighbourhood of smelting works and mean houses. A castle stood near it, on the margin of Watt's dyke, wielding command over a wide country, but has all disappeared excepting mere vestiges. The abbey is called also Dinas Basing and Greenfield.

BASLOW, a village, a township, and a chapelry in Bakewell parish, Derby. The village stands on the river Derwent, in the northern vicinity of Chatsworth, 3½ miles NE of Bakewell r. station. It has a post office‡ under Chesterfield, and a good inn, and it forms a pleasant centre to tourists for visiting Chatsworth and some of the most picturesque parts of the Peak district. A neat small Italian villa is at its east end.—The township is united to Bubnell, under the name of Baslow with Bubnell. Acres, 2,360. Real property, £4,004. Pop., 903. Houses, 191.—The chapelry includes the township, but is more extensive. Rated property, £6,129. Pop., 2,400. The property is divided among a few. The living is a p. curacy in the diocese of Lichfield. Value, £115.* Patron, the Duke of Devonshire. The church stands at the village, and is neat and commodious. The churchyard contains some interesting slabs and stone coffins. There are a Unitarian chapel, two public schools, and charities £10.

BASON BRIDGE, a station on the Glastonbury branch of the Bristol and Exeter railway, the first of two between Highbridge and Glastonbury, in the valley of the Brue, Somersetshire.

BASSALEG, or BASSALLEG, a village and a parish in Newport district, Monmouth. The village stands in the vale of the Ebbw, at the junction of the Western Valleys and the Sirhowy railways, adjacent to Tredegar Park, 3 miles WNW of Newport, and it has a station at the railway junction, and a post office under Newport. A priory of Black monks, a cell to the abbey of Glastonbury, was founded here about 1110, by Robert de Haya, but went into decay before the general dissolution. The parish includes also the hamlets of Duffryn, Craig, and Rogerstone. Acres, 6,957. Real property, £10,811. Pop. 2,169. Houses, 435. The property is all in one estate. Traces of a Saxon camp, called Craeg y Saesson, occur on the brow of a hill about a mile from the village, and traces of a British one, called Pen y Park Newydd, occur about a mile further. The living is a vicarage in the diocese of Llandaff. Value, £318. Patron, the Bishop of Llandaff. The church is an ancient structure, with an embattled tower. There are chapels for Independents and Baptists, and charities £23.

BASSENTHWAITE, a village, a parish, and a lake in Cockermouth district, Cumberland. The village stands on the E side of the lake, opposite Bassenthwaite L. r. station, 5 miles NNW of Keswick, and has a post office under Windermere. The parish is divided into two constablewicks, High side around the village and Low side or Hawes Acres, 6,930 Real property, £1 5o8 Pop, 570 Houses, 120 The property is much subdivided The surface is highly diversified and picturesque, ranging from the summit of Skiddaw to the meadows on the lake. Lead ore has been found, and a mine of antimony worked. The living is a vicarage in the diocese of Carlisle Value, £150 Patrons, the Dean and Chapter of Carlisle The church is old but good, and there are charities £14 and some land.—The lake is in the basin of the Derwent river, commences 3 miles NW of the foot of Derwent water, extends 4½ miles north north westward, with a mean breadth of ¾ of a mile, and has a surface elevation of 210 feet above the level of the sea Its bosom is not gemmed with any island, its head is flat and open, but looks away to the mountains round Derwent water, its W side is flanked by a range of wooded fells, mostly rising from the water's edge, its foot is screened by vale and slope, going up at 3 miles distance to Binsey hill, and its E side is flanked by the grand skirts and shoulders of Skiddaw, crowned, at 2½ miles' distance, by that mountain's summit Pike and perch abound in the lake, and salmon pass through it to the Upper Derwent

BASSETLAW, a wapentake in the N of Notts. It includes East Retford borough and fifty four parishes, and is cut into the divisions of Hatfeld, North Clay, and South Clay Acres of Hatfield div, 116,806 Pop in 1851, 24,621, in 1861, 26,093 Houses, 5 658 Acres of North Clay div, 45,714 Pop. in 1851, 10,357, in 1861, 10,183. Houses, 2,290 Acres of South Clay div., 40,314. Pop in 1851, 8,806, in 1861, 8,072 Houses, 1,766

BASSETT HOUSE AND THE KNOLL, an extra parochial tract in Blaby district Leicestershire, 7¼ miles SE of Leicester Pop, 14 Houses, 3

BASSETT STREET, a hamlet in South Stoneham parish, Hants, 3 miles N of Southampton

BASSETT WOOTTON See WOOTTON BASSETT

BASSILDON See BASILDON

BASSINGBOURNE, a village and a parish in the district of Royston and county of Cambridge The village stands 3 miles NNW of Royston r station, has a post office under Royston, and was formerly a market town The parish includes also the hamlet of Kneesworth Acres 4,223. Real property, £10,396 Pop, 2,213 Houses, 415 The property is much subdivided. The living is a vicarage in the diocese of Ely Value, £224 * Patrons the Dean and Chapter of Westminster The church is of the 14th century There are an Independent chapel, a British school, and charities £21

BASSINGFIELD, a hamlet in the parishes of Holme Pierrepont and West Bridgford, Notts, 4 miles SE of Nottingham. It has a post office under Nottingham. Pop, 53

BASSINGHAM, a parish and a sub district, in the district of Newark and county of Lincoln The parish lies on the river Witham, 3 miles S of Swinderby r station, and 8½ NE of Newark, and has a post office‡ under Newark. Acres 1,940 Real property, £6,395 Pop, 928 Houses, 191 The property is much subdivided. The living is a rectory in the diocese of Lincoln. Value, £183 * Patron, Corpus Christi College, Oxford The church was restored in 1861 There are two Methodist chapels a national school, and charities £29 —The subdistrict contains nine parishes Pop., 3,802

BASSINGHAM Norfolk See BESSINGHAM

BASSINGTHORPE, a parish in Grantham district, Lincoln, on the Great Northern railway, 2 miles SSE of Great Ponton station, and 3 NNW of Corby It includes the hamlet of Westby, and its post town is Corby, under Grantham. Acres, 1,790 Real property, £2,017 Pop, 154 Houses, 31 The living is a vicarage in the diocese of Lincoln Value, £230 Patron, the Earl of Dysart

BASSINGTON, a township in Eglingham parish, Northumberland, on the river Alne, 3 miles NW of Alnwick. Acres, 234 Pop., 9 Houses 2

BASTEAD, a hamlet in Wrotham parish, Kent 11 miles WNW of Maidstone

BASTON, a parish in Bourn district, Lincoln, 3½ miles NNW of Market Deeping, and 3 E by S of Braceborough r station It has a post office under Market Deeping Acres, 3,520 Real property, £5,897 Pop, 787 Houses, 183 The property is much subdivided The living is a vicarage in the diocese of Lincoln Value, £231 Patron, the Lord Chancellor The church is tolerable, and there are charities £14.

BASTWICK, a hamlet in Repps parish, Norfolk, on the North river 5½ miles NE of Acle It was formerly a parish, and has a ruined church, and it occasions Repps to be called Repps with Bastwick

BASWICK, or BERKSWICK, a township in Stafford district, and a parish in Stafford and Penkridge districts, Staffordshire The township is united to two other tracts, under the name of Baswick, Milford, and Walton, it lies on the Worcester canal, near the Northwestern and the Trent Valley railways, 2 miles SE of Stafford, and it contains the post office of Walton under Stafford Real property, £4,015 Pop, 660 Houses, 123 The parish contains also the township of Brockton and that of Acton Trussel and Bednell Acres, 6,603 Real property, £10,197 Pop, 1,555 Houses, 302 The property is divided among a few The living is a vicarage, united with the p. curacy of St Thomas, in the diocese of Lichfield. Value, £238.* Patrons J N Lane, Esq, and the Rev C Inge. The church is good, and the p curacy of Acton Trussel with Bednell is a separate benefice Charities, £15

BATCHACRE, a hamlet in Adbaston parish, Stafford, 5¼ miles SW of Eccleshall

BATCHCOTT, a township in Richard's Castle parish, Salop, on the verge of the county, 4½ miles SSW of Ludlow

BATCHPOOL, a township in Worfield parish, Salop 2 miles NE of Bridgnorth.

BATCHWORTH, or BATCHWORTH HEATH, a hamlet in Rickmansworth parish, Herts, on the verge of the county, 2 miles SSE of Rickmansworth. It has a post office of the name of Batchworth Heath, under Watford

BATCOMBE, a parish in Dorchester district, Dorset, 2 miles ESE of Evershot r station, and 3½ NW of Cerne Abbas It includes Newland tything and its post town is Cerne under Dorchester Acres, 1,109 Rated property, £1,035 Pop, 184 Houses, 37 The property is divided among a few The living is a rectory, annexed to the rectory of Frome Vauchurch, in the diocese of Salisbury The church is old and small

BATCOMBE, a parish in Shepton Mallet district, Somerset, near the East Somerset railway, 3 miles N of Bruton It has a post office under Bath. Acres, 3 229 Real property, £4,006 Pop, 713 Houses, 172. The living is a rectory, united with the vicarage of Upton Noble, in the diocese of Bath and Wells Value, not reported.* Patron, the Rev J Brown. The church was restored in 1844. There are two Wesleyan chapels

BATCOMBE, a tything in Nyland parish, Somerset, 5½ miles NW of Wells Pop. 11

BATES ISLAND, a small island in Earsdon parish, Northumberland nearly opposite Hartley, 4½ miles SSE of Blyth. Here are remains of a chapel and a hermitage. Here also is a small harbour, made by Lord Delaval, for sheltering fishermen in storms.

BATH, a city and a district in Somerset. The city stands on the river Avon the Fosse way, Akeman street, and the Great Western railway, 11¾ miles ESE of Bristol, and 106¾ W by S of London Its site is partly the bottom of a valley, partly the slopes and shoulders of encircling hills The Avon is navigable to it from the sea, the Kennet and Avon canal goes from it into the navigation of the Thames, and the Great Western railway, in its main line, its branches, and its connexions, gives it communication with all parts of the kingdom

History —The city owes its origin and its name to its famous thermal springs An old tradition says that the springs were discovered, and the city founded, by Bladud, son of Lud, king of Britain, about the year 863 B C., and a statue of Bladud with an inscription embodying the tradition was erected in the Pump room so late as 1630 But the first appreciators of the springs, and the real founders of the city, were most probably the Romans. These made the place one of their most important stations, called it Aquæ Solis or Calidæ, surrounded it with walls, nearly on the lines of the streets now called Lower Borough-walls, Westgate Buildings Sawclose, and Upper Borough-walls, built at it a temple to the goddess Minerva, and a manufactory of weapons for the legions, and constructed, around its springs a magnificent suite of baths, with sudatories, tesselated floors, and ornamental columns. The substruction of the station walls have frequently been laid open, fragments of the temple were found, during excavations, in 1869, and the remains of the baths, in remarkable preservation, at a depth of from 11 to 20 feet below the present surface, were discovered, at the razing of the old abbey house, in 1755. The Romans dedicated the springs to Apollo Medicus, and erected a statue in honour of him, early in the third century, and they probably maintained the baths in high fame till the end of their times

After their expulsion the place remained several years in comparative tranquillity, but during the protracted wars between the Southern Britons and the Saxons it was the scene of many obstinate contests Prince Arthur defended it for a time against successive armies but at length was overcome in its neighbourhood, and compelled to abandon it The Saxons made it their own, and called it Hat-Bathum or "hot baths" and Accemannes-cester or "the sick man's city Christianity was introduced in the sixth century, and led to the erection of religious houses by the Saxon kings A nunnery, on the site of the temple of Minerva, was founded in 676, by King Osric, destroyed by the Danes, rebuilt, about 775, by King Offa, and changed into a Benedictine abbey, in 973, by King Edgar That monarch was crowned, by Archbishop Dunstan, in the church, and a number of the kings, from Athelstane downward, occasionally resided here, and struck coins. The partisans of Robert, Duke of Normandy, fighting against William Rufus assaulted the city, and burned it to the ground. John de Villula, Bishop of Wells, bought it from Henry I, re erected the abbey church and made it the seat of his diocese The troubles in the time of King Stephen broke heavily upon it, and the whole city is said to have then been destroyed by fire It passed back, in 1193, to the Crown, and was then made a free borough, and began to rise in wealth and importance The abbey became very rich, and the monks did good service by introducing woollen manufacture Leland, who visited Bath in the reign of Henry VIII, says that it then had four gates, and that the walls which surrounded it contained many Roman antiquities, which he supposed to have been collected and set up by Norman architects Queen Elizabeth visited it in 1591, and granted then a charter to the burgesses, with powers for the improvement of the town In the early stages of the dissensions under Charles I, the city was fortified for the King, at an expense of £7 000, but on the retreat of the Marquis of Hertford into Wales, it was seized by the parliamentary forces under Sir William Waller The royalist army removed to the adjacent Lansdown hill, erected breastworks there and drew the parliamentarians into a battle, which ended in their defeat. The city was now recovered by the royalists, and it remained in their possession two years till June 1645, but was then, through treachery, surrendered to the parliamentarians Charles II, under advice of his physician, and attended by a numerous court, visited the place in 1663, and is thought to have then given rise, by his example, to the drinking of the waters In the reign of James II, the inhabitants closed their gates against the Duke of Monmouth, putting a stop to his career, and obliging him to fall back on his fate at Sedgemoor

The city as yet was comparatively insignificant, its buildings covered little more than fifty acres of ground and the accommodations and attractions for visitors to its medicinal waters were few and mean Some organization was given to it, as a watering place, in consequence of two visits of Queen Anne, before and after her accession to the throne, and a great and permanent one was effected by Beau Nash, the "King of Bath," who appeared here about 1703, and died in 1761 The first pump room was erected in 1706, and an officer appointed in charge of it Amusements were multiplied and regulated, the roads leading to the city were repaired, the streets were better paved, cleansed, and lighted, pleasure grounds and gardens were laid out, and spacious streets and places, with large ornate houses, were constructed. An architect, of the name of Wood, even formed the grand design of rebuilding the entire city on a uniform plan, and, though defeated in this, was so encouraged by the proprietors of the soil, as to make magnificent additions He first planned several streets, then in 1729 began Queen square in 1740 the North parade, and in 1754 the Circus, and in 1769 his son designed the Royal crescent Bath now was the summer rendezvous of persons of all classes, and even the occasional resort of members of the Royal family Fielding and Smollett linked it with the stories of their heroes, Lord Chesterfield was often at it, the great Chatham took to it for the healing of his gout, and Anstey, in his famous sarcastic "New Bath Guide, satirised its follies

Structure —Bath is strikingly beautiful Its site, in the hollow and up the sides of a sort of amphitheatre is grandly conducive to picturesque effect Its building material, the white oolite, so well known as Bath stone, and found in great abundance in neighbouring quarries, gives fine scope for architectural details Its street arrangement, compact in the old parts at the centre, outspread at the suburbs, and presenting a mixture of garden and grove, crescent and terrace, up the ascents of the encircling hills, tier above tier, to a commanding height over the valley, is unique and charming Good views of the city are obtained from Camden and Lansdown crescents, which can be reached by an easy walk from the railway station, and the best is obtained from Beechencliff, a steep eminence of upwards of 360 feet above the Avon, overhanging the railway, and accessible by a walk of ten minutes from the station, up Holloway, the Roman Fosse way, and taking the path to the left Camden-crescent, on the elevated acclivity of Beacon hill, is an elliptical range, of uniform design, with Corinthian columns and central portico. Lansdown crescent, Somerset place, Cavendish crescent, Cavendish place and St. James's square, are situated in the northern portion of the city, and form a splendid group. The Royal crescent and Marlborough buildings, a little lower, also command noble views, and the former is a fine semicircle of thirty houses, all uniform, with Ionic columns and surmounting cornice The Circus, still lower, has fronts, with Doric, Ionic, and Corinthian columns, double and in successive order, crowned by a decorated battlement Queen square, further down, but still on high ground, measures 316 feet by 306 and has four façades, all uniform and ornamental, each after a different design The North and South parades, east of the Abbey church are elegant ranges of buildings, with terraces nearly 1,800 feet long and 52 feet broad. Pulteney bridge, leading eastward from High street to Bathwick, is a fine structure of three arches, crowned on each side with houses, and Pulteney street, on a line with it, built about 1770 by the Hon William Pulteney, is in some respects the finest street in the city Green Park buildings and Norfolk crescent, in the SW, also are elegant Milsom street contains the finest shops, and may be called the Regent street of Bath

Public Buildings —The Railway station stands on the right bank of the Avon, and is a handsome edifice in the Tudor style An elegant viaduct takes the railway diagonally across Pulteney road, and a stone bridge and an ingeniously constructed skew one take it twice across the Avon, above and below the station Nine other bridges two of them stone two iron, three suspension, and two pedestrian, bestride the Avon The guild hall, in High street, was built in 1768-75, has a tetrastyle composite portico, includes court rooms, public offices, and a spacious banqueting room, and contains portraits of Frederick Prince of Wales and his consort George III and Queen Charlotte, the Earl of Chatham and Earl Camden The markets adjoin the guild hall, were reconstructed in 1863, in a manner of much elegance and convenience, and have a central dome, 40 feet in diameter The new gaol, at Twerton, was built in 1842, at a cost of about £23 000, and has capacity for 93 male and 24 female prisoners Beckford's tower, on the summit of Lansdown hill, was built by William Beckford, the author of "Vathek" who died in 1844, is 130 feet high, and commands an extensive view A walled garden was originally around it, and this is now a public cemetery, with Byzantine gateway Lansdown tower, 2½ miles beyond Beckford's tower, is on the battlefield of Lansdown, and was erected in 1720 by Lord Lansdown, the poet, to the memory of his grandfather, Sir Bevil Granville, who fell in the battle A handsome drinking fountain, contiguous to the Abbey and the markets, facing the High street, with sculptural representation of Rebecca at the Well, was constructed in 1861 Other buildings will be noticed in the subsequent paragraphs.

Baths—The baths are situated near the centre of the city The pump room was rebuilt in 1797, bears on its front a Greek motto, signifying "Water the best of elements," and is a handsome erection, 85 feet long, 48 feet broad, and 34 feet high, adorned with Corinthian portico and colonnade, and lighted by a double range of windows At the west end is an orchestra gallery, and at the east end, a handsome marble statue of Beau Nash. The King's or principal bath adjoins the pump-room, measures 66 feet by 41, is open to the sky, except a colonnade on one side, contains about 364 tons of water, and is filled daily, to a height of 4 feet 7 inches, with water rising directly from the spring in its centre, and bearing in temperature throughout the bath from 114° to 100° The Queen's bath is attached to the King's, derives its waters from it, slightly lessened in temperature, and measures 25 feet by 25 Private baths, in Stall street, draw supplies from a cooling reservoir connected with the King's bath, and contain excellent arrangements for baths of various kinds and various temperatures. The Cross bath, so called from an ancient cross which stood in it till 1745, is situated about 150 yards from the King's bath, yields 12 gallons per minute at 109°, and is used as a swimming bath by the less affluent classes The tepid swimming bath is in a neat building, from a design by Desimus Burton, measures 65 feet by 25, and is supplied from the King's at a temperature of 88° The hot bath, 40 yards SW of the King's, was built at the time of the finest extensions of the city, is an elegant structure, and has a spring of its own, giving constant supply at about 117° The royal private baths adjoin the hot bath, are remarkable for comfort and convenience, and comprise seven large baths, lined with steps for descending into them The Kingston baths, in Church-street, occupy the site of the Roman baths, have sudatories and various other conveniences, and are the property of Earl Manvers All the other baths belong to the borough, and are under the management of the town council The waters contain carbonic acid, sulphate and muriate of soda, sulphate and carbonate of lime, and minute quantities of silica and oxide of iron They act as a stimulant, and are regarded as beneficial against gout, rheumatism, paralysis, biliary obstructions, and cutaneous disorders, but may be injurious where there are inflammatory symptoms

Ecclesiastical Affairs—The benefices within the city are the rectory of St Peter and St Paul, or the Abbey, the r of St Michael, the r of Walcot, with Margaret c, the c of St. Thomas, and the c of St. Stephen, the r of St Saviour's, the r of Trinity, with the c of Avon Street chapel, the r of Bathwick, with the c of Wooley, the v of Widcombe with the c of St Matthew's, the v of Lyncombe, the r of St. James, with the c of Corn street chapel, the c of St John Baptist, the c of St John's chapel, the c of St Mary Magdalene, the c of Octagon chapel, the c of the Penitentiary chapel, the c of Christ Church, the c of Portland chapel, the c of All Saints, the c. of Queen Square chapel, and the c. of Laura chapel All are in the diocese of Bath and Wells The value of St Peter and St. Paul is £750,* of Walcot, £600, of St Saviour's, £390, of Trinity, £350, of Bathwick, £209, of Widcombe, £300, of Lyncombe, £235, of St James, £155, of the Penitentiary chapel, £200, and of the rest, not reported The patrons of St Peter and St. Paul, of St Michael, of Widcombe, of Lyncombe, and of St James, are Simeon's Trustees, of Walcot, also now Simeon's Trustees, of St Saviour's, the Rev Dr Stamer, of Trinity, the Rev S H Widdrington, of Bathwick, Lord W Powlett, of St John's chapel, Trustees, of St Mary Magdalene, the Lord Chancellor, of Octagon chapel the Proprietor, of the Penitentiary chapel, the Committee, of Portland chapel, the Rev T L Hill, and of Christ church and All Saints, the Rector of Walcot

The places of worship within the borough, in 1851, were 23 of the Church of England, with 20,575 sittings, 2 of Independents, with 1 430 s, 5 of Particular Baptists, with 2,304 s., 1 of Quakers, with 300 s, 1 of Unitarians, with 300 s, 1 of Moravians, with 300 s, 5 of Wesleyan Methodists, with 2,436 s, 1 of Primitive Methodists, with 432 s, 1 of the Wesleyan Association with 180 s., 2 of Wesleyan Reformers, with 891 s, 3 of Lady Huntingdon's Connexion, with 1,070 s, 1 of the New Church, with 300 s, 1 of Brethren, with 40 s, 3 of isolated congregations, with 1,220 s, 1 of Latter Day Saints, with 250 s, 1 of the Catholic and Apostolic Church, with 230 s, 3 of Roman Catholics, with 270 s, and 1 of Jews, with 40 s.

The Abbey church was cleared and remodelled in 1834, at a cost of nearly £11,000, and again was much renovated in 1869 It is one of the latest specimens of perpendicular English It was built on the site, and partly with the materials, of the previous pile, was commenced in 1499, stopped in 1539, and completed in 1616, yet is of uniform character It is cruciform, has a central tower, 162 feet high, and measures 210 feet in length 72 in breadth, 78 in height, and 126 along the transepts Its west front has a splendid window of seven lights, flanked by decorated turrets, its tower is well composed, and has octagonal, panelled, surmounting turrets at the corners, and its interior is remarkably light and elegant, in uniform perpendicular, but much crowded with tasteless monuments Traces of either an old Norman apse or a Roman temple can be observed on the outside of the east end The most interesting of the monuments are, in the nave, those of Bishop Montague, Beau Nash, the Hon William Bingham, James Quin, Herman Katencamp Col. Champion, John Malthus, and Sarah Fielding in the south transept that of Lady Waller in the north transept, those of Fletcher Partis, Sir R. H Bickerton, Dr Sibthorp, James Timesz Grieve, and Mary Frampton, and in the chancel, those of Lady Miller, Mrs Frazer, Col Walsh, and the artist Hoare—St. James's church is a neat structure, rebuilt in 1768, and has a new tower in the Italian style, surmounted by an elegant lanthern St Michael's church was preceded, on the same site, by three other churches, and is an elegant edifice, with a pierced spire 182 feet high. St Saviour's church was built in 1832, is an elegant edifice, in the decorated English style, with graduated and pinnacled buttresses, and has a tower of three stages, embattled and 120 feet high Trinity church was built in 1822, is in florid Gothic, and has a beautiful memorial window to William West Jones, Esq, put up in 1859 St. Mark's or Lyncombe church was built in 1832, is in the perpendicular style, and has a tower Widcombe church is the oldest in the city, has been partially restored, and has an ivy clad tower St Matthew's church was built in 1847, is a large edifice, in the decorated English style, and has a fine tower 155 feet high St Mary Magdalene's chapel was renovated from a state of ruin about 1820, and preserves the character of ancient early English, with embattled tower Christ church was built in 1798, is in the later English style, and has a handsome altar piece. Queen Square chapel was built in 1735, and is externally Doric, internally Ionic. Margaret chapel in Brock Street, is a commodious structure, in the early English style All Saints' chapel, near Lansdown Crescent, was erected in 1794 and is a good specimen of the decorated style. St. Stephen's church was built in 1845, and is in the decorated style with a tower of three stages St John Baptist's church was opened in 1864, and completed in 1868 and has a tower and spire 200 feet high Several of the dissenting places of worship are very handsome structures The Argyle Independent chapel is in the Roman style, and was enlarged in 1862, the Percy Independent chapel is in the Byzantine style, and was built in 1854, the New King street Wesleyan chapel, decorated Gothic 1847, the Moravian chapel, Roman, 1845, the New Jerusalem church, Roman Ionic, 1844, the South Parade Roman Catholic church, florid Gothic, 1863. The Abbey new cemetery was opened in 1844, the Lansdown new cemetery, in 1848, the Bathwick, in 1856, the Lower Bristol road and the upper Bristol road, in 1862, the Roman Catholic in 1859

Schools and Institutions —The schools within the borough, in 1851, were 16 public day schools, with 5,564 scholars, 113 private day schools, with 1,959 s, and 34 Sunday schools, with 5,095 s The free grammar school was founded and endowed with lands by Edward VI, and it numbers amongst its pupils Prynne, the two Lysonses Sir S Smith, and other distinguished men The Blue coat school, for 60 boys and 60 girls, is a new edifice in Upper Borough Walls The Walcot parochial school is a building in the Italian style, erected in 1841 at a cost of £1,700 The Art school, at Hetling House, was established in 1854 The Lansdown Proprietory college, on the ascent of Lansdown hill, was changed in the latter part of 1863, into a college for the daughters of military officers, was built in 1858, is in the Gothic style of the geometric period contains one school of 3,500 square feet, lighted by traceried windows, and another school of 2,100 feet, and has a lofty central tower The Wesleyan college, on the same ascent higher up was erected in 1850, is in the Tudor style, and has a tower 90 feet high Grosvenor college, in Grosvenor place was established in 1837 for the sons of noblemen and gentlemen The Bath Proprietory college occupies the building at the end of Pulteney-street, formerly the Sydney hotel The Somersetshire college is in the Circus

The royal, literary, and scientific institution, a little east of the Abbey, occupies the site of the old assembly rooms retains their portico, and has a large library, and a rich museum the last antiquarian and scientific, and free to the public The Athenæum, in Orange grove, was originally a mechanics institution The Bath and West of England society for the encouragement of agriculture, the arts manufactures, and commerce was established in 1777 The Commercial and Literary institution occupies a part of the post office building The city contains a greater number of booksellers and circulating libraries, in proportion to its population, than any other town in the kingdom It may be regarded also as the cradle of English geology, and it boasts a remarkable number of eminent literary men as natives or as residents Among the natives have been Gildas the historian John Hales the professor of Greek, B Robins the mathematician, R. L. Edgeworth, Terry the comedian, and Hone the author of the "Every day Book," and among the residents have been physicians, chemists, naturalists, historians, divines, artists, and popular writers, too numerous to be named The house No 13 New King street, was the residence of Herschel, at the time of his making the observations which led to the discovery of the planet Uranus

Charities —The Bath general hospital was founded in 1712 for the use of the diseased poor from all parts of the kingdom who may be benefited by the Bath waters, it comprises a suite of new buildings erected in 1861 at a cost of £18 000, together with an older adjoining suite, it contains accommodation for 86 male and 48 female patients and it is supported partly by endowment and partly by subscription The patients within it are accommodated with baths upon the premises supplied from the springs. The united hospital was founded in 1826 by the amalgamation of the city infirmary and the casualty hospital, is a spacious building with sick wards, lecture room, anatomical museum, and library, near the Cross bath, and, besides receiving in-patients, gives relief to vast numbers of out patients St John's hospital was founded in 1180 by Bishop Fitz Jocelyne, escaped the dissolution under Henry VIII, was given by Queen Elizabeth to the mayor and commonalty of the city, rebuilt in 1728 by Wood, and has an income returned at £214, but valued at £8,328 St Catherine's hospital, or the Blackberries, was founded in the reign of Edward VI Bellott's hospital, for poor persons using the waters, has an income of £76, and St Mary Magdalene's hospital for idiots, founded before 1332, has £118 Partis College, on Newbridge hill, for 30 reduced gentlewomen, was founded by Mrs Partis, and completed in 1827, and is a capacious range of building, forming three sides of a quadrangle There are also an eye infirmary, a penitentiary, lying in hospitals, almshouses, and other benevolent institutions, either liberally supported or well endowed

Amusements —Bath was at one time the gayest place in England, and it continues to possess the means of splendid and numerous amusements The assembly rooms, in the vicinity of the Circus, were erected in 1791 at a cost of £20 000, and contain a lofty vaulted octagon reception room, and a ball room 105 feet long 43 feet wide, and 42 feet high The theatre, in Beaufort square, is an elegant edifice of 1863, on the site of a previous one built in 1805 and burnt in 1862, reputed one of the best out of London The race course, on Lansdown is an oval 1½ mile round, and the grand stand on it was improved in 1859 The Victoria Park, immediately west of the Royal crescent and the Circus, is an ornate enclosure of about 22 acres, was thrown open to the public in 1830, at a cost of £4,000 raised by subscription, contains horticultural and botanic gardens, and has at the entrance an obelisk in honour of the Queen, and higher up a colossal bust of Jupiter by the self taught artist Osborne The Sydney gardens, at the end of Pulteney street, comprise 16 acres, were laid out in 1795, and used to be called the "Vauxhall" of Bath The walks and drives around the city may be endlessly varied, and abound with interesting objects charming close views, and brilliant prospects

Trade —Bath is a favourite residence of annuitants and a fashionable resort of wealthy strangers Hence arises its principal trade Rents are moderate, coal is abundant, the markets are well supplied, all the wants of taste and society are readily ministered to, and in a full season, from Christmas till the end of May, about 14,000 persons, in addition to the permanent population, are present A manufacture of coarse woollen cloth, called Bath coating, was at one time carried on, but has long been extinct Weekly markets are held on Wednesday and Saturday, and fairs on 14 Feb and 10 July The city has a telegraph station a head post office,‡ five banking offices, a savings bank, and nine chief hotels and it publishes four weekly newspapers The savings bank, originally founded in 1815, now occupies a handsome edifice in the Italian style built in 1842 Paper and carpet making is carried on in the neighbourhood

The Borough.—The city formerly consisted of the parish of St Peter and St Paul, the parish of St. James the parish of St. Michael and the part of the parish of Walcot south of Charlcombe, but it now comprises also the parish of Bathwick the parish of Lyncombe and Widcombe, and all the rest of the parish of Walcot except Soper's farm The extent from N to S is about 3 miles, from E to W, about 2 miles, in area, 3,534 acres The city is divided into 7 wards is governed by a mayor, 14 aldermen, and 42 councillors, has a corporate income of about £23 000, is a seat of courts, a polling place, and the head quarters of militia, and has sent two members to parliament since the time of Edward I Direct taxation in 1857, £45,527 Electors in 1868 3 230 Pop. in 1841, 50,800, in 1861 52,528. Houses 8,017 Real property in the three parishes St Peter and St Paul, St James, and St Michael, in 1860, £69 880

The District —The district of Bath comprehends the sub district of Abbey, containing the parishes of St Peter and St Paul, St James, and St Michael, all within the city, the sub district of Lyncombe, conterminate with the parish of Lyncombe and Widcombe, also within the city, the sub districts of Walcot and Lansdown, embracing, in nearly equal portions, Walcot within the city, the sub district of Bathwick, containing Bathwick parish within the city, and the parishes of Bathampton Claverton, and Monckton Combe, the sub district of Batheaston, containing the small part of Walcot without the city, and the parishes of Batheaston, Bathford, St Catherine Swainswick, Langridge, Woolley, Charlcombe, and Weston, and the sub district of Twerton, containing the parishes of Twerton, Dunkerton, Combhay, Wellow, Charterhouse Hinton, South Stoke, and Englishcombe Acres, 30,321 Poor rates in 1866, £30,950 Pop in 1861, 65,336 Houses, 11,223. Marriages in 1866, 654, births, 1,699,—of which 123 were illegitimate deaths, 1,523,—of which 433 were at ages under 5 years, and 53 at ages above 85 years Marriages in the ten years 1851-60 6,314, births, 17,614, deaths, 15,224 The places of worship in 1851 were 50 of the Church of England, with 26 332 sittings, 5 of Independents, with 1,710 s, 10 of Baptists with 3 473 s., 1 of Quakers, with 300 s, 1 of Unitarians, with 300 s., 12 of Wesleyan Methodists, with 3 228 s, 4 of Primitive Methodists, with 808 s, 1 of the Wesleyan Association, with 180 s, 9 of Wesleyan Reformers, with 1,780 s, 4 of Lady Huntingdon's Connexion, with 1,160 s, 1 of Moravians, with 300 s., 2 of the New Church, with 440 s, 1 of Brethren, with 140 s, 4 undefined, with 1,268 s, 1 of Latter Day Saints, with 200 s, 1 of the Catholic and Apostolic church, with 230 s, 3 of Roman Catholics, with 270 s, and 1 of Jews, with 40 s The schools were 62 public day schools, with 6 856 scholars, 136 private day schools, with 2,630 s, 59 Sunday schools, with 6,972 s, and 1 evening school for adults, with 2 s. The workhouse is on Odd Down in the parish of Lyncombe and Widcombe

BATH AND WELLS, a diocese comprehending all Somerset except Bedminster Acres, 1,043,059 Pop, 422,527 Houses, 83 600 The see sprang from a college at Wells, founded in 704 by King Ina, was constituted there, in 905, by Edward the Elder, was removed to Bath, in the time of William Rufus, by John de Villula, was for some time designated of Bath only, and altogether administered there, but in the 13th century, after long contention, was reconstituted of both Bath and Wells, with cathedral at each It numbers among its bishops, Lord Chancellor Burnell, Lord Treasurer De la March, Viceroy Drokensford, Lord Keeper Beckington, Lord Chancellor Stillington, Cardinals De Castello and Wolsey, Henry VIII's confidant Clerk, President Bourne, Montague, Laud Ken, and Baron Auckland The bishop's palace is at Wells The dignitaries and officials are a dean, four canons, three archdeacons, a sub dean, a chancellor of the diocese, a chancellor of the church, a treasurer, forty four prebendaries, and three minor canons The income of the bishop is £5,000, of the dean, £1,000, of one of the canons, £30, of two of the archdeacons, £65 and £250, of the chancellor of the church, £31, of the treasurer, £65, and of six of the prebendaries aggregately £86

The diocese is divided into the archdeaconries of Wells, Bath and Taunton The archdeaconry of Wells comprises seven deaneries, that of Bath comprises two deaneries, each in two districts, and that of Taunton comprises four deaneries. Many of the livings in the several deaneries have recently been raised in status,—chiefly p curacies raised to vicarages, and they are named according to their present rank in the separate articles on them in the Gazetteer, but all will be named here as they ranked in 1861

The deanery of Wells contains the rectories of Binegar Dinder, and Litton, the vicarages of Wells, Wookey, Pilton, Westbury, and East Harptree, and the p curacies of Coxley, Easton, Henton, Horrington North Wootton and Theale The deanery of Axbridge contains the rectories of Axbridge, Allerton, Badgworth, Biddisham, Blagdon, Bleadon, Breane, Christon, Hutton, Locking, Loxton, Lympsham, Rowberrow, Rodney Stoke, Shipham, Uphill and Weston super Mare, the vicarages of Banwell, Berrow, East Brent, South Brent, Burnham, Cheddar, Bishop Compton, Congresbury, Kewstoke, Weare, Wedmore, Winscombe and Worle, and the p. curacies of Churchill, Highbridge, Mark, Puxton, Blackford-Wedmore, Christ Church Weston, Trinity-Weston, and Emmanuel Weston The deanery of Carey contains the rectories of Alford with-Hornblotton, Ansford, Babcary, North Barrow, Batcombe, Blackford, Bratton, North Cadbury, South Cadbury, Charlton Musgrove, Compton Paunce foot, Croscombe, Cucklington with-Stoke Trister, Ditcheat, Holton, Keinton Mansfield, Kilmington, Kingweston, Lamyatt, East Lydford, West Lydford, Maperton Milton Clevedon, Penselwood, Pylle, Shepton Mallett, Sparkford, Sutton Montague, Weston Bamfylde, Wheathill, and Yarlington, the vicarages of Barton St. David, Castle Carey, Doulting, Evercreech, and East Pennard, and the p. curacies of South Barrow, North Brewham, South Brewham, Bruton, Lovington, Pitcombe, Redlynch, Shepton Montague, Stoke Lane, Wincanton, and Wyke Chamflower The deanery of Frome contains the rectories of Babington, Beckington with Standerwick, Berkley, Cameley, Camerton, Combe Hay, Dunkerton, Elm, Farley Hungerford Foxcot, Hemington with Hardington, Laverton, Mells, Merston-Bigot, Holcombe, Nunney, Orchardleigh, Radstock, Road with Wolverton, Stratton on the Fosse, Tellisford, Wanstrow, Whatley, and Writhlington, the vicarages of Buckland Dinham, Chewton Mendip, Cloford, Frome, Wellow, Kilmersdon, Midsomer Norton, and Norton St Philip and the p curacies of Ashwick, Chilcompton, Christ Church Frome, Trinity Church Frome, Hinton Charterhouse, Coleford, Lullington, Vobster, Clandown, Downside, Paulton, Rodden Chantry, Emborough Stone Easton, Farrington, and Witham Friary The deanery of Ilchester contains the rectories of Ilchester, Aller, Brimpton, Charlton Mackrell, East Chinnock, Middle Chinnock, Chiselborough, High Ham, Hardington, Kingsdon Lufton, Limington, Norton sub-Hamden, Odcombe Pendomer, North Perrot, Pitney, Podimore Milton, Thorne Coffin, and Yeovilton the vicarages of Charlton Adam, Chilthorne-Domer, Compton, Dundon, Haslebury Plucknett, Huish Episcopi with-Langport, Martock, Montacute, Northover, Somerton, and Long Sutton, and the p curacies of Nether Ham, Ash, Muchelney, West Chinnock, Stoke sub Hamden, and Tintinhull The deanery of Merston contains the rectories of Abbas Combe, Ashington, Barwick, West Camel, North Cheriton, Chilton-Canteloe, Closworth, East Coker, West Coker, Corton Denham, Goathill, Horsington, Kingston or Pitney, Pointington, Rimpton, Sandford Orcas, Stowell, Sutton Bingham, and Trent, the sinecure rectory of Socke, the vicarages of Charlton Canfield, Henstridge, Merston Magna, Milborne Port, Mudford, and Queen Camel, and the p curacy of Hendford. The deanery of Pawlet contains the rectories of Bawdrip Cossington, Greinton, and Huntspill, the vicarages of Pawlet and Woollavington with Puriton, and the p curacy of All Saints Huntspill. The deanery of Glastonbury contains the rectory of Street, the vicarages of Butleigh, Middlezoy, Meare, Moorlinch, Othery, Shapwick, and Weston Zoyland, and the p curacies of Burtle, Glastonbury St John, Glastonbury St. Benedict, Codney, Chilton on Polden with Edington, Catcott, and West Pennard

The deanery of Bath, in its Bath district, contains the rectories of St. Peter and St Paul, St. James, St Michael Walcot, St Saviour, Trinity, Bathwick, Claverton, Farmborough, Freshford, Marksbury Priston, Stanton Prior, and Timsbury, the vicarages of Lyncombe Widcombe, Bathampton, Englishcombe, and Weston, and the p curacies within the city The deanery of Bath, in its Keynsham district, contains the rectories of Barnett, Charlcombe, Kelston, Langridge, Newton St Loe, North Stoke, Saltford, and Swainswick, the vicarages of Batheaston, Bathford, Corston, Keynsham, South Stoke, and Twerton, and the p curacies of Brislington, Combe Down, Monkton Coombe, Queen Charlton, and Woolley The deanery of Chew, in its Chew Magna district, contains the rectories of Butcombe, Chelwood, Chew Stoke, Clutton, Compton-Martin Hinton Bluett Norton Malreward, Ubley, and Winford the vicarages of Chew Magna, Compton Dando, High Littleton, Stowey, Stanton Drew, and West Harptree, the p curacies of Dundry, Nempnett, and Whitchurch, and the donatives of Barrow Gurney and Publow The deanery of Chew, in its Portishead district, contains the rectories of Portishead Brockley, Chelvey Clapton, Kingston Seymour, Nailsea, Walton-in Gordano with Weston in Gordano Wraxall and Wrington, the sinecure rectory of Backwell, the vicarages of Backwell, Clevedon, Easton in Gordano, Long Ashton, Portbury, Tickenham and Yatton, and the p curacies of Burrington, Cleeve in Yatton, Christ Church Clevedon, East Clevedon, Flax Bourton, Kenn-in Yatton, Christ Church Nailsea, and Redhill Wrington

The deanery of Taunton contains the rectories of Angersleigh, Ashbrittle, Bathealton, West Bagborough, Cheddon Fitzpaine, Combe Florey, Heathfield, Kittesford, Lydeard St. Lawrence, West Monkton, Norton Fitzwarren, Oake, Orchard Portman, Runnington, Staple Grove, Stawley, and Thorn-Falcon, the vicarages of Bradford, Creech St Michael, North Curry, Halse, Kingston, Bishops Lydeard, Milverton, Wivehead, Pitminster, Stamford Arundell St Mary Magdalene Taunton, and Wellington, and the p curacies of Ash Priors, Bishops Hull, Corfe, Cothelstone, Hillfarrance, Otterford Ruishton, St. Gregory Stoke, St Mary Stoke, St James Taunton, Trinity Taunton St. Margaret Thorn, Thurlbere, Trull, and Wilton. The deanery of Bridgewater contains the rectories of Aisholt, Chilton, Charlinch, Chedzoy, Crowcombe, Dodington, Enmore, Fiddington Goathurst, Holford Kilve, Otterhampton, East Quantoxhead, Spaxton, and Thurloxton, the vicarages of Bridgewater, Cannington, Kilton, Stringston, Lyng, Over Stowey North Petherton, Stockland Gaunts, Stogursey, Nether Stowey and Wembdon the p curacies of Eastover Bridgewater, Trinity Bridgewater, Broomfield Purrow-Bridge, Michaelchurch, North Newton and Northmoor Green, and the donatives of Durleigh and Durston. The deanery of Crewkerne contains the rectories of Pearcrocome Buckland St Mary, Chaffcombe, Cricket Malherby, Cricket St Thomas, Curry-Mallet, Donyatt, Dowlish Wake with Dowlish West, Drayton, Earnshill, Fartham Hatch Beauchamp, Hinton St. George, East Lambrook in Kingsbury-Episcopi, Puckington, Seaborough, Seavington St Michael, Shepton Beauchamp, Staple Fitzpaine with Bickenhall, Stocklinch-Magdalene, Stocklinch Ottersea, South Brayton Wayford, White Staunton, and Winsham, the vicarages of Ashill, Chard, Combe St. Nicholas, Curry-Rivell, Fivehead Ilminster Ilton, Isle Abbots, Isle-Brewers, Kingsbury Episcopi, White Lackington, Merriott, Misterton South Petherton, and Swell, and the p curacies of Barrington, Broadway Tatworth, Chillington Crewkerne, Cudworth Courland, Dinnington, Hambridge, Kingstone, Knowle, Lopen, and Seavington St Mary The deanery of Dunster contains the rectories of Brompton Ralph, Brushford, Chipstable, Clatworthy, Elworth, Exford, Exton, Hawkridge, Huish Champflower, Luxnor, Luckham Monksilver Nettlecombe, Oare Porlock West Quantoxhead, Raddington, Sampford Brett, Selworthy, Skilgate Stock Pero Tolland, Treborough Withycombe, and Wootton Courtney, the vicarages of Brompton Regis Carhampton Old Cleeve, Cutcombe St Decumans, Dulverton, Minehead, Stogumber, Timberscombe, Winsford, and Wiveliscombe, and the p curacies of Bicknoller, Dunster, Fitzhead Leighland in Old Cleeve Upton, Williton in St Decumans Withypool and Withiel Florey

BATHAMPTON a parish in Bath district, Somerset, on the river Avon and the Great Western railway 1½ mile NE of Bath It has a station on the railway, and a post office under Bath Acres, 931 Real property £3,526 Pop, 382 Houses, 71 The property is not much divided. A series of suburban villas extends onwards to Bath The living is a vicarage in the diocese of Bath and Wells Value and patron, not reported The church is perpendicular English, has a fine west door, contains effigies of a knight and his lady of the time of Edward III, and was repaired in 1858

BATHAMPTON, Devon See BAMPTON

BATHAMPTON (GREAT and LITTLE), two tythings in Steeple-Langford parish, Wilts, 5½ miles NW of Wilton

BATHEALTON, a parish in Wellington district Somerset, near the Western canal, 4½ miles WNW of Wellington r station and 5½ from Wellington It has a post office under Wellington, Somerset Acres, 941 Real property, £1,481 Pop, 135 Houses, 26 The property is divided among a few The living is a rectory in the diocese of Bath and Wells Value, £226 * Patron, the Rev E Webber The church is good

BATHEASTON, a parish and a sub-district in Bath district, Somerset The parish lies on the river Avon, near the Fossé way, 1½ mile N by E of Bathampton r station, and 2½ NE of Bath It has a ferry to Bathampton, and a post office under Bath Acres, 1,863 Real property, £11,106 Pop, 1,648 Houses, 353 The property is much subdivided Lines of houses and numerous villas make the south western part suburban to Bath The manor belonged to the Saxon kings, and the church was early appropriated to Bath abbey Solsbury hill, 600 feet high, has traces of a circular camp supposed to have been used by the Saxons in their siege of Bath The living is a vicarage united with the p curacy of St Catherine, in the diocese of Bath and Wells Value, £298 * Patron, Christ Church college Oxford The church is perpendicular English, was partly rebuilt in 1860, and contains a tablet to the Rev J Conybeare, the Anglo Saxon scholar, who was several years vicar There are a church at St Catherines, Wesleyan and Moravian chapels, a national school, and charities £35 —The sub district comprises Soper's farm and eight parishes Acres, exclusive of Soper's farm, 9,810 Pop, 6,989 Houses, 1,374

BATHERM (THE), a stream of Devon, 8 miles long, falling into the Exe a little below Bampton

BATHERTON, or BARTHERTON, a township in Wybunbury parish Cheshire 2 miles S of Nantwich Acres, 404 Real property, £690 Pop, 24 Houses, 4

BATHFORD, a village and a parish in Bath district, Somerset. The village stands adjacent to the river Avon and to the Great Western railway 2 miles E by N of Bathampton station, and 3½ ENE of Bath, and it has a post office under Bath. The parish includes also the hamlets of Shockerwick and Warley Acres, 1,820 Real property £5,329 Pop, 892 Houses, 186 The property is divided among a few An old ford on the Avon at the village gave rise to the name Bathford, and an elegant viaduct, of one flat arch takes across the railway a little below Hampton cliffs, in the vicinity are picturesque, and command remarkably fine views Some interesting Roman remains have been found in the parish Bathford House is a chief residence. The living is a vicarage in the diocese of Bath and Wells Value, £395 * Patrons, the Dean and Chapter of Bristol The church is very good

BATH FORUM, a hundred in Somerset. It lies round Bath, and includes fourteen parishes Acres, 11,562 Pop, 9,213 Houses 1,874

BATHLEY, a township in North Muskham parish, Notts, 3½ miles NW by N of Newark Pop 234 Houses, 54 There is a Wesleyan chapel

BATHLEY, Norfolk. See BALE

BATHUMPTON See BAMPTON, Devon

BATHURST, a manor in Warbleton parish, Sussex, 5 miles NNE of Hailsham It belonged to the family of Bathurst, who were expelled from it in the wars between the houses of York and Lancaster, and it retains vestiges of their castle, which was demolished at the time of the expulsion

BATHWICK, a parish and a sub district in Somerset.

The parish lies on the left bank of the Avon, within the borough of Bath, and is intersected by the Kennet and Avon canal, and by the Great Western railway Acres, 573 Real property, £43,868 Pop., 5,266 Houses, 836 At the beginning of last century, the parish contained only a few scattered houses, and was marshy, but now it contains some of the finest streets and decorations of Bath, including Great Pulteney street, Laura place and the Sydney gardens The living is a rectory, united with the curacy of Woolley, in the diocese of Bath and Wells Value, £209 Patron, Lord W Powlett The church is in the decorated English style, with a tower 120 feet high was built in 1829, and contains a monument to Mackinnon, who figured at Culloden. Laura chapel is a separate charge There is a proprietary college, with about 100 pupils.—The sub district includes also other parishes beyond the borough Acres, 3,452 Pop, 7 132 Houses, 1,201

BATLEY, a town, a township, and a sub district in the district of Dewsbury, and a parish in the districts of Dewsbury and Hunslet, W R Yorkshire The town adjoins the Leeds and Manchester railway, 1¾ mile N by E of Dewsbury, and has a station on the railway, and a post office‡ under Leeds It is remarkable only as a seat of manufacture, but evinces much public spirit, and has a lecture hall, with mechanics' institution, erected in 1853 Pop, 7,206 Houses, 1,480 The township includes also the hamlets of Brownhill, Brookroyd, Carlinghow, Clark Green, Havercroft, Chapel-Fold, Healey, Staincliffe, White Sce, Kelpin-Hill, Capas Height, Purlwell, and New Roadside, and part of the hamlet of Batley Carr Acres, 2,140 Real property, £38,795 Pop., 14,173 Houses, 2,956 The sub district is conterminate with the township The parish includes also the townships of Morley, Gildersome, and Churwell Acres, 6,416 Real property, £69,308 Pop, 25,278 Houses, 5,260 The property is subdivided. The manufacture of cloths, carpets, and other fabrics from "shoddy," or the reduced substance of old woollen rags, is here carried on to a great extent, and there are upwards of twenty two factories The living is a vicarage in the diocese of Ripon Value, £300 * Patrons, Earl Cardigan and Earl Wilton The church is later English The p curacy of St Thomas is a separate charge, constituted in 1868 The vicarages of Morley and Gildersome, and the p curacy of Staincliffe, also are separate There are a handsome Independent chapel of 1856, an elegant Wesleyan chapel of 1861, four other dissenting chapels, a Roman Catholic chapel, an endowed grammar school, a workhouse, and charities £237.

BATLEY CARR, a hamlet and a chapelry in Batley and Dewsbury parishes, W R. Yorkshire The hamlet stands ¾ of a mile S of Batley, and has a post office under Dewsbury The chapelry was constituted in 1842 Rated property, £6,505 Pop, 3,859 Houses, 796 The property is much subdivided The living is a vicarage in the diocese of Ripon Value, £150 Patron the Vicar of Dewsbury The church is good.

BATSFORD, or BATTISFORD, a parish in the district of Shipston on Stour, and county of Gloucester, near the Stratford railway and the Fosse way, 2 miles NW of Moreton Post town, Moreton in the Marsh Acres, 932 Real property, £2,075 Pop, 130 Houses, 22 The property is not much divided Batsford Park is the seat of Lord Redesdale The living is a rectory in the diocese of Gloucester and Bristol Value, £370.* Patron, Lord Redesdale The church was rebuilt in 1862

BATSON, a hamlet in Malborough parish, Devon, 4½ miles SSW of Kingsbridge

BATTEL. See BATTLE

BATTLEFLEY See BALTERLEY

BATTERSLY, a township in Ingleby Greenhoe parish N R. Yorkshire, under the Moors, 5 miles E by S of Stokesley Acres, 1,020 Real property £575 Pop, 119 Houses, 20

BATTERSEA, a parish in the districts of Wandsworth and Croydon, Surrey The main body of it, or Battersea proper, is a sub district of Wandsworth suburban to London, on the river Thames and on the West End and Southwestern railway, opposite Chelsea, and the rest, consisting of Penge hamlet, lies in Croydon district, detached from the main body, 8 miles distant Acres of the main body, 2,177 of land and 166 of water, of the entire parish 3,153 Real property, £158,897 Pop of the main body in 1841, 6,616, in 1861, 19,600 Houses, 3,125 Pop of the entire parish in 1841, 6,887, in 1861, 24,615 Houses, 3,793 The manor was known to the Saxons as Petersey, signifying Peter's Island, belonged to the abbey of St. Peter at Westminster, was granted, in 1627, to the family of St John, and passed, in 1763, to the Spencers The old mansion on it was the residence of the famous Viscount Bolingbroke, and a haunt of the poet Pope, but has been entirely demolished, yet is commemorated in the neighbouring localities of Bolingbroke Terrace and Bolingbroke garden Battersea Fields, within the manor, along the Thames, were long notable as a marshy tract, producing a great variety of indigenous plants, and were the scene, in 1829, of the duel between the Duke of Wellington and Lord Winchelsea, but are now partly disposed in a fine new public park, and partly covered with streets and buildings The park comprises 185 acres, lies almost all below the level of high water, was purchased at a cost of £246 517, and laid out in 1852 58, at a further cost of £66,373, and is disposed in walks, drives, ornamental plantations, and a fine sheet of water A suspension bridge, across the Thames, at the upper end of the park, measures 347 feet between the towers and 705 between the abutments, is remarkably light and elegant, and was erected, in 1857, after designs by Mr T Page, at a cost of £85,319 The West End railway to Sydenham is carried across, in the vicinity, on a substantial, tasteful, segment-arched bridge, constructed by Mr Fowler, and opened in 1860, to the Victoria station in Pimlico; goes ¾ of a mile south southeastward to Battersea station, then runs 2½ miles west-south westward, parallel to the Southwestern railway, and past Battersea Rise to New Wandsworth station Battersea New Town adjoins the two railways where they mutually approach Battersea Old Town stands on the Thames below the park, and Battersea Rise is a hill covered with villas. Both Battersea and Battersea Rise have post offices‡ under London S W The living of Battersea is a vicarage in the diocese of Winchester Value, £992 * Patron, Earl Spencer The parish church is a commodious but inelegant structure, built in 1777 The vicarages of Christchurch, St George, and St John-with St Paul, are separate benefices Value of C, not reported, of St G, £290,* of St J, £430 * Patron of all, the Vicar of B C church was built in 1849, at a cost of £5,000, and is in the decorated English style, St G's church was built some years later, St J's, in 1863, St. P s, in 1869 The vicarages of Penge and Upper Penge also are separate benefices A handsome Independent chapel, in the Lombardic style, was built in 1867, at a cost of £4,488 There are several other dissenting chapels, the training national school, a free school with £160 a year and charities £121 See LONDON

BATTISFORD See BATSFORD

BATTISFORD a parish in Bosmere district, Suffolk, 2 miles W by S of Needham r station Post town, Needham Acres, 1,542 Real property, £2,662 Pop., 504 Houses, 103 The property is subdivided. An hospital of knights of St John of Jerusalem was erected here in the reign of Henry II, and given, at the dissolution, to Sir Richard Gresham The living is a vicarage in the diocese of Norwich Value, £400 Patron, the Rev E Paske The church is good.

BATTLE, a parish in the district and county of Brecon on the river Yscar, 3 miles NW of Brecon r station Post town, Brecon Acres, 1 544 Real property, £1,393 Pop., 118 Houses, 30 The surface is diversified, and commands fine views The manor belonged to the priory of Brecon Here was the scene either of the battle between Robert Fitzhamon and Rhys ap Tudor, or the battle at the invasion of Brecknockshire by Bernard Newmarch The living is a vicarage in the diocese of St David Value, £73 Patron, Col J V Watkins. The church is a low building, situated on an eminence

BATTLE, a small town, a parish, a sub district, a district, and a hundred, in Sussex. The town was called by the Saxons Epiton, signifying "heath land," and took its present name from the great battle of the Conquest, in 1066, commonly called the battle of Hastings. It stands in a fine valley, three fourths encircled by wooded hills, in the vicinity of the Tunbridge Wells and Hastings railway, 7 miles NW of Hastings, and it has a station on the railway, a head post office,‡ two banking offices, and two chief inns. The principal street runs up a rising ground, and is confronted, at a brief distance, by Battle Abbey, standing on the site of King Harold's camp, and on the spot where his standard was taken. This edifice was founded by the Conqueror, in commemoration of his victory, it contained his sword, his coronation robe, and the roll call of the knights who followed him from Normandy, and it was very richly endowed, and gave its abbots a seat in parliament. It passed at the dissolution to Sir Anthony Browne, continued with his descendants, the Lords Montacute, till the time of the fourth Lord, and was sold then to Sir Thomas Webster, and in 1857 to Lord Harry Vane. The buildings were converted into a mansion by Sir Anthony Browne, and, though still retaining a number of the original apartments, are so greatly changed as to present outwardly very little of their ancient character. The grand gateway still stands, and is chiefly late decorated English, of very beautiful workmanship, and a long range to the right of it was used till 1794 as the town hall, but has been allowed to go to ruin. A spot about ½ a mile distant on the road to Hastings commands the best view of the abbey, and at the same time affords a good comprehensive notion of the battle field of the Conquest. The petty sessions court house and county police station are a handsome edifice of 1861. The parish church is partly Norman, and was restored in 1869. There are three dissenting chapels, a mechanics' institute, a school with endowed income of £68, other charities with £80, and a workhouse built at a cost of £5,000. Extensive powder mills, of great note, are situated to the SW, and the walk to them, and the walks generally through the environs, are charming. A weekly market is held in the town on Tuesday, and fairs are held on Whit Monday, 6 Sept., and 22 Nov.

The parish contains also the hamlet of Netherfield. Acres, 7,880. Real property, £14,313. Pop., 3,293. Houses, 583. The living is a vicarage in the diocese of Chichester. Value, £500. Patron, Lord H Vane. The vicarage of Netherfield is separate.—The sub district comprises the parishes of Battle, Brightling, Dallington, Penhurst, and Ashburnham. Acres, 20,476. Pop., 5,494. Houses, 1,001.—The district comprehends also the sub-district of Ewhurst, containing the parishes of Ewhurst, Sedlescomb, Whatlington, and Mountfield, and the sub district of Bexhill, containing the parishes of Bexhill, Hollington, Catsfield, Crowhurst, and Westfield. Acres, 54,000. Poor rates in 1866, £1,118. Pop. in 1861, 12,680. Houses, 2,394. Marriages in 1866, 103, births, 421,—of which 35 were illegitimate, deaths, 204,—of which 60 were at ages under 5 years, and 5 at ages above 85 years. Marriages in the ten years 1851–60, 962, births, 4,?16, deaths, 2,292. The places of worship in 1851 were 15 of the Church of England, with 3,799 sittings, 3 of Baptists, with 590 s., 1 of Unitarians, with 350 s., 10 of Wesleyan Methodists, with 1,195 s., and 1 of Freethinking Christians, with 25 s. The schools were 14 public day schools, with 1,046 scholars, 15 private day schools, with 303 s., and 16 Sunday schools, with 1,149 s. The hundred of Battle is in the rape of Hastings, and consists of the parishes of Battle and Whatlington. Acres, 9,135. Pop., 3,635. Houses, 632.

BATTLE BARROW, a village in Burgate township, Westmorland, 1 mile NE of Appleby.

BATTLE BRIDGE, a village in Retrendon parish, Essex, 6½ miles E of Billericay. It has a post office under Chelmsford.

BATTLE BRIDGE, a chapelry in Islington parish, London, near the Regent's canal, and the terminus of the Great Northern railway. It was constituted in 1839. Pop., 17,489. Houses, 1,886. The living is a vicarage, united with p. curacy of St Matthias, in the diocese of London. Value, £300. Patron, the Vicar of Trinity.

BATTLEBURN, a hamlet in Kirkburn parish, E R Yorkshire, 3½ miles SW of Great Driffield.

BATTLEDEN. See BATTLESDEN.

BATTLEFIELD, a parish and a sub district in the district of Atcham, Salop. The parish lies adjacent to the Crewe and Shrewsbury railway, 1½ mile S by E of Hadnall station, and 3 NNE of Shrewsbury. Post town, Hadnall under Shrewsbury. Acres, 850. Rated property, £939. Pop., 81. Houses, 17. The property is divided among a few. Here was fought the battle in 1403, in which Harry Hotspur was slain, and Douglas captured. The living is a vicarage in the diocese of Lichfield. Value, £233. Patron, A. W Corbet, Esq. The church was erected by Henry IV to commemorate his victory over Hotspur, is chiefly perpendicular English, and was restored in 1861. A fair is held on 2 Aug.—The sub-district comprises five parishes, two chapelries, and an extra parochial tract. Acres, 11,554. Pop., 1,881. Houses, 39?.

BATTLE HALL. See NASH, Kent.

BATTLESBURY, an ancient British camp, 2 miles E of Warminster, Wilts. It crowns an abrupt eminence almost inaccessible on two sides, has ramparts rising 60 feet, occupies fully 23 acres, and commands a very extensive view.

BATTLESDEN, a parish in Woburn district, Beds, on Watling street, 3 miles SSE of Woburn, and 4½ NE of Leighton Buzzard r. station. Post town, Woburn. Acres, 1,123. Real property, £1,981. Pop., 143. Houses, 31. The manor belonged, in the time of Edward III., to the Firmbands, passed, in the time of Elizabeth, to the Duncombes, was purchased, in 1706, by the Bathursts,—to whom it gives the title of Baron, and is now the property of the Turners. The living is a rectory, united with the rectory of Potsgrove, in the diocese of Ely. Value, £509.* Patrons, the Trustees of the late Sir G P Turner, Bart. The church is good.

BATTRAMSLEY, a tything in Boldre parish, Hants, in the New Forest, 6½ miles NE of Ringwood. Real property, £1,888. Pop., 302.

BATTRIX, a hamlet in Bowland Forest township, Slaidburn parish, W R Yorkshire, 11 miles SW of Settle.

BATTYEFORD, a chapelry, with a village, in Mirfield parish, W R Yorkshire, 2 miles WSW of Dewsbury r. station. It was constituted in 1841, and its post town is Dewsbury. Rated property, £8,000. Pop., 3,115. Houses, 704. The property is much subdivided. The living is a p. curacy in the diocese of Ripon. Value, £150.* Patron, the Vicar of Mirfield. The church is good, and there is an Independent chapel.

BAUDOC. See BALDOCK.

BAUGHCOTT, a hamlet in Tugford parish, Salop, 6½ miles SE of Church Stretton.

BAUGHURST, a village and a parish in Kingsclere district, Hants. The village stands near the Roman Port way to Silchester, 5½ miles S of Aldermaston r. station, and 7 NNW of Basingstoke, and has a post office under Basingstoke. The parish includes also the tythings of Ham and Inhurst. Acres, 1,675. Real property, £1,210. Pop., 56?. Houses, 98. The property is subdivided. The living is a rectory in the diocese of Winchester. Value, £188.* Patron, the Bishop of Winchester. The church is a recent erection of brick and stone, with a lofty spire. There are two dissenting chapels.

BAULDOXFEE, a tything in Eling parish, Hants, 3 miles W of Southampton. Real property, £2,?19. Pop., 331.

BAULKING. See BALKING.

BAUMBER, or BAMBURGH, a parish in Horncastle district, Lincoln, on the Wolds, 4 miles NW by N of Horncastle r. station. It has a post office of the name of Baumber, under Horncastle. Acres, 3,200. Real property £4,052 Pop, 393 Houses 85 Sturton Hall is the seat of the Liveseys. The living is a vicarage, annexed to Sturton Magna. The church is good, and there is a Wesleyan chapel

BAUNTON, a parish in Cirencester district, Gloucester, on the Churn river and the Fosse way, 2 miles N of Cirencester r station Post town, Cirencester Acres, 1,340 Real property £1,596 Pop, 122. Houses, 29 The property is all in one estate The living is a vicarage in the diocese of Gloucester and Bristol Value, £67 Patron, Miss Masters. The church is very good.

BAUNTON, Devon See BAMPTON

BAUSELEY, or BALASLEY, a township in Alberbury parish, Montgomery, 10 miles NE of Welshpool Pop, 404 Houses, 83.

BAVANT TIFIELD See TIFIELD BAVANT

BAVERSTOCK, a parish in Wilton district, Wilts, on the river Nadder and on the Salisbury and Yeovil railway, near Dinton station, 4 miles W of Wilton It includes the hamlet of Hurdcott, and its post town is Barford St. Martin, under Salisbury Acres, 1,168. Real property, with Barford St. Martin, £5 984 Pop, 168 Houses, 34 The property is divided among a few The living is a rectory in the diocese of Salisbury Value, £296 * Patron, Exeter college, Oxford The church is good

BAVINGTON (GREAT), a township in Kirkwhelpington parish, Northumberland, 4 miles E of Watling street, and 10½ N of Corbridge Acres, 1,565 Pop, 61 Houses, 15 Bavington Hall is the seat of C C Shafto, Esq There is an English Presbyterian church

BAVINGTON (LITTLE), a township in Thockrington parish, Northumberland, 1½ mile S of Great Bavington, and 9 N of Corbridge Acres, 1,702 Pop., 67 Houses, 15 Limestone, freestone, and whinstone are quarried

BAWBURGH, a parish in Forehoe district, Norfolk, on the river Yare, 5½ miles W of Norwich r station Post town, Colney, under Norwich Acres 1,440 Real property, £3,604 Pop., 433 Houses, 92 The property is divided among a few The living is a vicarage in the diocese of Norwich Value, £120. Patrons, the Dean and Chapter of Norwich The church has a round tower, an old font, and a brass of 1531, and is good. St Walstan was a native

BAWCOMBE, a hamlet in West Alvington parish, Devon, 6½ miles SE of Modbury

BAWDER, a stream of N R Yorkshire running 10 miles eastward to the Tees, 3½ miles NW of Barnard Castle

BAWDESWELL, a parish and a sub district in the district of Mitford, Norfolk. The parish lies a little N of the Wensum river, 3 miles E by S of Elmham r station, and 3½ W by S of Reepham, and has a post office under Thetford. Acres, 1,196 Real property, £2,740 Pop, 515 Houses, 127 The property is much sub divided Bawdeswell Hall is a chief residence The living is a rectory in the diocese of Norwich Value, £208 Patron, Rev H Lombe The church is recent, and there are chapels for Wesleyans and Primitive Methodists, and an endowed school with £20 —The sub-district comprises eight parishes Pop., 3,333

BAWDRIP, a parish in Bridgewater district, Somerset, 3 miles NE of Bridgewater r station It has a post office under Bridgewater Acres, 1,880 Real property, £5,001 Pop., 472 Houses, 93 The property is divided among a few The living is a rectory in the diocese of Bath and Wells Value, £360 * Patron, E Page, Esq The church is ancient and cruciform There are Independent and Wesleyan chapels, and charities £6

BAWDSEY, a village and a parish in Woodbridge district, Suffolk The village stands near the mouth of the Deben river, 9 miles SSE of Woodbridge r station, has a post-office under Woodbridge, and was once a market town The parish comprises 1,741 acres of land, and 325 of water Real property, £3,090 Pop, 423 Houses, 101 The coast is defended by Martello towers Bawdsey Haven, in the mouth of the Deben, gives shelter to small craft Bawdsey Hall is on the coast. Bawdsey Sand is a shoal, about 5 miles distant, 4 miles long, and ⅜ of a mile broad, with 10 feet and upwards of water The living is a vicarage in the diocese of Norwich Value, £193 * Patron, the Lord Chancellor The church is a small, neat, recent structure, and was preceded by a fine early Saxon edifice, the reduced tower of which, now 60 feet high still stands There are a Wesleyan chapel, and national schools

BAWSEY, a parish in Freebridge Lynn district, Norfolk, 1½ mile NNW of Middleton r station, and 3 ENE of Kings Lynn Post town, Lynn Acres, 1,090 Real property, £549 Pop., 32 Houses, 5 The living is a rectory in the diocese of Norwich Value, £55. Patron, A Hammond, Esq The church is in ruins.

BAWTRY, a small town, a chapelry, and a sub-district in the district of Doncaster, W R Yorkshire The town stands on the verge of the county on the river Idle, and on the Great Northern railway, 8 miles SE of Doncaster Part of it is low, and used to be subject to inundation, but part is high, and contains a market place It has a station on the railway, a head post office,‡ a banking office, a hotel, a good supply of water, a church, and two dissenting chapels, Independent and Wesleyan The church is later English, consists of Roche abbey limestone, was built in 1350, and has a tower, added in 1712 A weekly market is held on Thursday, and fairs on Holy Thursday and 22 Nov An hospital for a priest and certain poor was founded in the neighbourhood about 1316 A farm house, a mile distant, occupies the site, and was formed of the materials of a palace of the Archbishops of York, inhabited by Cardinal Wolsey and Archbishop Sandys Bawtry-Hall is a seat of Lord Houghton Acres of the town, 244 Real property, £3,514 Pop, 1,011 Houses, 229 —The chapelry includes also the township of Austerfield Pop, 1,400 Houses, 318 The living is a p. curacy in the diocese of Lincoln Value, £500. Patron, Trinity College, Cambridge —The sub district comprises six parishes, and part of three others Acres, 31,765. Pop, 5,623 Houses, 1,202

BAXBY See THORNTON ON THE HILL.

BAXENDEN, a large village in Whalley parish, Lancashire, on the East Lancashire railway, 1½ mile N of Haslingden It has a post office under Accrington, a r station, two cotton mills, and a colliery

BAXTERLEY, a parish in Atherstone district, Warwick, 2 miles ENE of Kingsbury r station, and 3½ W by S of Atherstone Post town, Kingsbury under Tamworth Acres, 874 Real property, £2,115 Pop 273 Houses, 54 The property is divided among a few Baxterley Hall is the seat of Apsley Smith, Esq Coal is largely worked The living is a rectory in the diocese of Worcester Value, £202 Patrons, the Lord Chancellor and another The church is not good

BAXTON MOOR, a hamlet in Whitwell parish, Derby, 11 miles ENE of Chesterfield

BAYARD LEAP, an extra-parochial tract in Sleaford district, Lincoln, 5½ miles NW of Sleaford Pop, 18 Houses, 3

BAYCLIFF, a hamlet in Hill Deverill parish, Wilts, 5 miles W by S of Heytesbury

BAYDEN, a chapelry in Llangonoyd parish, Glamorgan, 5½ miles NW by N of Bridgend r station Post town, Bridgend Pop 339 The living is a p curacy, annexed to the vicarage of Llangonoyd, in the diocese of Llandaff The church is in ruins

BAYDON, a parish in the district of Hungerford and county of Wilts, on the verge of the county, 3½ miles WSW of Lambourne, and 7 SSE of Shrivenham r station It has a post office under Hungerford Acres, 3 080 Real property, £2,882 Pop, 350 Houses, 81 The property is subdivided The living is a vicarage in the diocese of Salisbury Value, £110 Patron the Rev A Meyrick The church was repaired in 1850 There is a Wesleyan chapel

BAYFIELD a parish in Erpingham district Norfolk, 2 miles W of Holt, and 7 E by N of Walsingham r station Post town Holt, under Thetford. Acres. 7..

Real property, with Glandford, £1 60. Pop, 30 Houses 4 The living is a rectory in the diocese of Norwich Value, £150 Patron, Major E Jodrell There is no church

BAYFORD, a parish in the district and county of Hertford, on the river Lea, near the Hatfield and Hartford railway, 3 miles SbW of Hertford It has a post office under Hertford Acres, 1,632 Real property, £2,138 Pop, 297 Houses, 61 The property is not much divided The manor belonged, before the Conquest, to Earl Tosti the Dane, and passed afterwards to the Knightons, the Fanshaws, and the Bakers Bayfordbury, the present seat of the Bakers, contains the portraits of the Kit-Cat club, brought hither from Barnes Elms The living is a vicarage in the diocese of Rochester, and till 1867 was annexed to Essendon Value, £100 Patron, W R. Baker, Esq The church was built in 1802 There is a national school

BAYFORD, a hamlet in Stoke Trister parish, Somerset, 1 mile E of Wincanton. It has a post office under Bath, and it forms a curacy with Cucklington rectory

BAYFORD, a farm house, originally a castle, near Sittingbourne, Kent The castle is said to have been erected by King Alfred, as a counter fortress to Castle Rough, about a mile distant, and it became the seat of successively the Nottinghams, the Cheneys, and the Lovelaces. The moat and a piece of wall still exist

BAYHAM, a hamlet in Frant parish, Sussex on the verge of the county, on the river Tun, 4 miles ESE of Tunbridge Wells A Premonstratensian abbey was removed hither, in 1200, from Ottcham or Otham, and largely endowed by Robert de Thurnham and Ela de Sackville, was given at the dissolution, to Cardinal Wolsey, passed afterwards to the Montagues, and was purchased, in 1714, by the ancestor of Marquis Camden The Marquis has now a villa here, amid beautiful grounds, and takes from the place the title of Viscount The ruins of the abbey, comprising the church and some contiguous buildings, in a state of tolerable preservation, stand in the grounds, and show interesting features of decorated early English and some decorated additions

BAY HORSE, a station on the Preston and Lancaster railway, 5¾ miles N by W of Garstang, Lancashire

BAYLHAM, a parish in Bosmere district, Suffolk, on the river Gipping and the Eastern Union railway, 1 mile NNW of Claydon station, and 7 NW by W of Ipswich Post town, Claydon under Ipswich Acres 1,332 Real property, £2,276 Pop, 327 Houses, 65 The property is all in one estate The living is a rectory in the diocese of Norwich Value, £256 Patron, W Downes, Esq The church is old but good

BAYNARDS, a r station in Surrey, on the Guildford and Horsham railway, 6¼ miles NW of Horsham

BAYNESS, a hamlet in Fylingdales parish, N R Yorkshire 9 miles S of Whitby

BAYNTON, a tything in Edington parish, Wilts

BAYONS MANOR, the seat of the D Eyncourts in Tealby parish, Lincoln, 4¼ miles E of Market Rasen

BAYSTON HILL, a chapelry in the parishes of Condover and St Julian Salop, on the Shrewsbury and Hereford railway, 1 mile N of Condover station, and 3¼ S of Shrewsbury It was constituted in 1844, and it has a post office under Shrewsbury Pop., 605 Houses, 134 The living is a vicarage in the diocese of Lichfield Value, £110 * Patron the Vicar of St Julian

BAYSWATER, a suburb of London, and a chapelry in Paddington parish and Marylebone borough, Middlesex The suburb adjoins Hyde Park, Kensington Gardens, and the Great Western railway, 3½ miles W of St Paul's and has a post office under London W and a r station It was called originally Baynard's water and it took the first part of its name from Baynard an associate of William the Conqueror who held it of Westminster abbey,—and the second part from copious springs which long supplied the greater part of the metropolis with water The same Baynard gave his name to Baynard Castle now extinct, and to the ward of Castle Baynard The suburb is now a fashionable richly built part of London and contains some fine streets, terraces crescents, and squares, of recent erection The extensive tea gardens, belonging to the famous herbalist Sir John Hill, satirized by Garrick, were here St George's burial-ground, fronting Hyde Park, contains the graves of Lawrence Sterne, Sir Thomas Picton and Mrs Radcliffe —The chapelry bears the name of St Matthews Bayswater, and was constituted in 1858 Pop, 5,513 Houses, 783 The living is a vicarage in the diocese of London Value, not reported. Patron, the Rev C Smalley A United Presbyterian church was built at Westbourne grove, in 1862, after designs by W G Habershow, and consists of nave, aisles, and transept, in the decorated English style, with tower and spire A lecture hall was built in the same locality, in 1861, after designs by A Billing and exhibits a highly embellished façade of four stories in the Venetian renaissance style The hall itself is in the rear, measures 70 feet in length, 30 in width, and 27 in height, and is lighted from above

BAYTHORNE END, a locality on the N verge of Essex, on the river Stour, adjacent to Baythorne Park, 4 miles SE of Haverhill. It has a post office under Halstead

BAYTON, a parish in the district of Cleobury Mortimer and county of Worcester, on the verge of the county, 6 miles W by S of Bewdley r station It has a post office under Bewdley Acres, 1,960 Real property, £2 597 Pop, 447 Houses, 100 The property is divided among a few The living is a vicarage, annexed to the vicarage of Mamble, in the diocese of Hereford The church is good

BAYVIL, a parish in the district of Cardigan and county of Pembroke, on the river Nevern, 3½ miles ENE of Newport, and 5½ SW of Cardigan r station Post-town, Newport under Haverfordwest. Acres, 1,344 Real property, £1 195 Pop, 118 Houses, 29 The property is divided among a few The living is a vicarage, united with the vicarage of Moylgrove, in the diocese of St. David's Value, £224 Patron, the Lord Chancellor The church is good

BAYWORTH, a hamlet in Sunningwell parish, Berks, 3 miles N of Abingdon Here was formerly a church in which many private marriages were celebrated before the marriage act

BEACHAMPTON, a parish in the district and county of Buckingham, on the river Ouse, 2¼ miles SW of Stoney-Stratford, and 4½ SW by W of Wolverton r station Post-town Stoney Stratford Acres, 1,492 Real property, £2,592 Pop, 272 Houses, 58 The property is divided among a few The manor belonged to the Bennets, one of whom was made a baronet in 1627, and figured as a great friend to University college, Oxford The living is a rectory in the diocese of Oxford Value £379 * Patron, Caius college, Cambridge. The church is a plain structure, and contains monuments of the Bennets A school has an endowed income of £48, and other charities £178

BEACHAMWELL. See BEECHAMWELL.

BEACHBOROUGH, the seat of the Brockman family, on the SE coast of Kent, 2½ miles NNE of Hythe A hill adjacent to the mansion commands very extensive views, insomuch that a bonfire on it can be seen from the coast of France, and is crowned by a summer house, which overlooks the views, and is accessible to strangers

BEACHINGSTOKE See BEECHINGSTOKE

BEACHLEY, a chapelry in Tidenham parish Gloucester, at the influx of the river Wye to the Severn adjacent to the South Wales railway, 2 miles SE of Chepstow Post town, Chepstow Rated property, £958 Pop, 229 The property is divided among a few Beachley Lodge is a fine seat Here is the Aust ferry across the Severn which was considered an important military pass in the times of war, and here was the termination of Offa's Dyke, which can still be traced The living is a p. curacy in the diocese of Gloucester and Bristol Value, £16 Patron, the Vicar of Tidenham The church is very good

BEACHY HEAD a promontory on the coast of Sussex, at the end of the South Downs 2½ miles SSW of Eastbourne. Its summit has an altitude of 575 feet above sea level, and commands a view from Hastings to the Isle of Wight, and across the channel to France Its front and sea skirts are precipitous, and pierced with caverns, the resort of multitudes of sea fowl. Shipwrecks here and in the vicinity used to be frequent and dreadful, but have been less numerous since the erection of the Belle Toute lighthouse in 1831 This stands on a projecting skirt of the promontory, and shows a revolving light at the height of 285 feet above the sea, flashing every 2 minutes, and visible at the distance of 22 miles On the 30th of June, 1690, the combined English and Dutch fleets of 56 sail, under Lord Torrington, were defeated within sight of Beachy Head, by the French fleet of 82 sail, under the Count de Jourville

BEACON, a locality 1 mile from Camborne, Cornwall, with a post office under that place

BEACON HILL, any eminence, with conspicuous summit, formerly used for a beacon fire or a signal post, and still retaining its ancient name. Eminences, called Beacon Hills, occur in Cornwall, Devon, Somerset, Wilts, Hants, Notts, Oxford, Cumberland, and other counties, and nearly all of them command extensive views

BEACONSFIELD, a small town, a parish, and a sub district, in the district of Amersham, Bucks The town stands on an eminence anciently used for beacon fires, 3 miles NE of Woburn Green r station, and 5¾ S by W of Amersham It has a post office,‡—B Bucks, and is a seat of petty sessions, and a polling place It consists of four streets, which meet at the centre in a spacious market place, and it contains the parish church and three dissenting chapels The church is built of flint and squared stones, comprises nave, chancel, and side aisles, with a western tower, belonged to an Augustinian monastery, founded at Burnham, in 1165, by Richard, Earl of Cornwall, and contains the remains of Edmund Burke, whose seat was in the neighbourhood, and a marble monument to the poet Waller, who owned the manor, is in the churchyard A weekly market recently ceased, but fairs are held on 13 Feb and 10 May —The parish includes also part of Coleshill hamlet. Acres, 4,541 Real property, with the rest of Coleshill, £9,619 Pop, 1,662. Houses, 342 The property is divided among a few The living is a rectory in the diocese of Oxford Value, £545 Patron, Magdalene College, Oxford. Charities, £114 —The sub district comprises two parishes and a chapelry Acres, 9,401 Pop, 3,092 Houses, 656

BEACONSTHORPE See BACONSTHORPE

BEACON WALKS See EXMOUTH

BEADLAM, a township in Helmsley parish, N R. Yorkshire, 2½ miles E of Helmsley Acres, 1,405 Real property, £1,200 Pop, 145 Houses, 30

BEADNELL, a village, a township, and a chapelry in Bambrough parish, Northumberland The village stands on the coast 3¾ miles ENE of Chathill r station, and 5½ SE of Bambrough, and has a post office under Chathill, and a small harbour The township comprises 743 acres Pop., 311 Houses, 66. The chapelry includes the township, but is more extensive, and was constituted in 1851 Rated property, £1,371 Pop, 577 Houses, 115 The property is not much divided The living is a vicarage in the diocese of Durham Value, £79 * Patron, the Vicar of Bambrough. The church is a handsome Gothic edifice

BEADONWELL, a hamlet in Frith parish, Kent, 4½ miles E of Woolwich

BEAFORD, a parish in Torrington district, Devon, on the river Torridge, 5 miles SE of Torrington, and 6¼ WSW of Umberleigh r station It has a head post office, designated Beaford, North Devon Acres, 3,203. Real property £2,702 Pop, 630 Houses, 133. The property is subdivided The living is a rectory in the diocese of Exeter Value, £315 * Patron, the Rev C Wood The church is an old fashioned edifice with a low tower There are chapels for Baptists and Bible Christians

BEAGHALL, or BEAL, a township in Kellington parish W R. Yorkshire, 4 miles E of Pontefract It includes Kellingley hamlet Acres, 1,757 Real property, £3 977 Pop, 468 There is a Wesleyan chapel

BEAKSBOURNE, or BEKESBOURNE, a parish in Bridge district, Kent, on the Canterbury and Dover railway, 2¾ miles SE of Canterbury It is a member of the cinque port liberty of Hastings, and has a station on the railway, and a post office under Canterbury Acres, 1,115 Real property, £2,393 Pop, 475 Houses, 92 The property is divided among a few Beaksbourne House is the seat of Dr C T Beke The living is a vicarage, in the diocese of Canterbury Value, £187 * Patron, the Archbishop of Canterbury The church is perpendicular English was restored in 1843, and contains the monument of Hooker, who became vicar in 1595 The parsonage has been much modernized, yet contains features which were in it in Hooker's time

BEAL, a township in Kyloe chapelry, Northumberland, on the Northeastern railway, opposite Holy Island, 7 miles SE of Tweedmouth It includes Lowlin, and has a station on the railway, and a post office‡ under Berwick It was the residence of the famous Irish female saint, Begogh

BEAL, Yorkshire See BEAGHALL.

BEALBY See BIFLBY

BEALE, or BEULT (THE), a river of Kent. It rises near Ticehurst, on the border of Sussex, and runs 15 miles northward to the Medway, in the vicinity of Yalding

BEALINGS a station on the East Suffolk railway, 3 miles WSW of Woodbridge.

BEALINGS (GREAT), a parish in Woodbridge district Suffolk, on a branch of the Deben river, and on the East Suffolk railway, near Bealings station, 2¼ miles W by S of Woodbridge Post town, Little Bealings, under Woodbridge Acres, 1,029 Real property, £2,091 Pop, 338 Houses 88 The property is divided among a few, and much of it belongs to Lord Henniker The living is a rectory in the diocese of Norwich Value, £250 * Patron, Lord Henniker The church is good

BEALINGS (LITTLE), a parish in Woodbridge district, Suffolk, on a branch of the Deben river and on the East Suffolk railway at Bealings station, 3 miles WSW of Woodbridge It has a post office under Woodbridge. Acres, 764 Real property, £1 142 Pop, 278 Houses, 62 The property is divided among a few The living is a rectory in the diocese of Norwich Value, £140 * Patron, F Smythies, Esq The church is tolerable

BEALTHANNIG See BARDNEY

BEAMDUNE See BAMPTON, Devon

BEAM HEATH, a tract in Nantwich and Alvaston townships, in the vicinity of Nantwich, Cheshire It consists of enclosed waste lands, managed by trustees under a private act of parliament

BEAMHURST a village in Checkley parish, Stafford, 3½ miles NW of Uttoxeter

BEAMINSTER.—pronounced Bemminster—a small town, a parish, a sub district, and a district in Dorset The town stands on the river Birt, near the confluence of its headstreams, among high environing hills, 4¾ miles NW of Powerstock r station, and 6 NNE of Bridport It is a place of considerable antiquity, but it was burnt to the ground by the troops of Prince Maurice in 1644, and again much destroyed by fire in 1684 and in 1781, and it now presents a modern and neat appearance It has a post office‡ under Bridport, a banking office, a hotel, a townhall, a church, a chapel of ease, an Independent chapel, a Wesleyan chapel, a free school, and almshouses with £173, and other charities with £90 and is a polling place for the county The church is later English and large, contains tombs of the Strodes of Parnham has a tower nearly 100 feet high, with curious sculpture on the western side, and was restored in 1862 A weekly market is held on Thursday and a fair on 19 Sept. A good trade exists in double Dorset or mould cheese, and the manufacture of sail cloth, sacking, and pottery is carried on The Rev T Hood, father of Lords Hood and Bridport, was master of the free school, and Bishop Sprat the poet, and Russell who defended Warton's History, were natives

The parish includes also the tything of Langdon, and the hamlets of Axknoll, Marsh, Meerhay, North Mapperton, Parnham, and Wansley Acres, 5,118 Real property £13,632 Pop, 2,614 Houses, 590 The property is much subdivided The manor belongs to the prebends of Beaminster Prima and Beaminster Secunda in the cathedral of Salisbury Parnham House, formerly the seat of the Strodes now the seat of Sir Henry Oglander, Bart, is an old Tudor edifice, and contains a fine hall, with gallery of portraits The living is a vicarage in the diocese of Salisbury Value, £246 Patron, the Bishop of Salisbury —The sub district comprises the parishes of Beaminster, Mapperton Hook, North Poorton, and Poorstock Acres, 11 901 Pop., 4,112 Houses, 912 The district comprehends also the sub district of Netherbury, containing the parishes of Netherbury, Stoke Abbott Broadwinsor, Burstock, Bettiscombe, Pilsdon, and Marshwood, the sub district of Evershot, containing the parishes of Evershot, Melbury Osmond, Melbury Sampford, Wraxall, Rampisham, East Chelborough, West Chelborough, Halstock, and Corscombe, and the sub district of Misterton, containing the parishes of Cheddington, South Perrot, Mosterton, Misterton, and Seaborough,—the two last electorally in Somerset. Acres, 53 764 Poor rates in 1866, £10,116 Pop in 1861, 13,587 Houses, 2 913. Marriages in 1866, 72, births, 420 —of which 20 were illegitimate, deaths, 219,—of which 71 were at ages under 5 years, and 10 at ages above 85 years Marriages in the ten years 1851-60, 1,020, births, 4,465, deaths, 2,821 The places of worship in 1851 were 31 of the Church of England, with 6,893 sittings, 7 of Independents, with 1,482 s, 1 of Baptists, with 194 s, 9 of Wesleyan Methodists, with 758 s, and 1 of Primitive Methodists, with 65 s The schools were 24 public day schools, with 1,286 scholars, 24 private day schools, with 523 s, 35 Sunday schools, with 2,127 s, and 2 evening schools for adults, with 25 s The workhouse is in Stoke Abbott

BEAMINSTER FORUM AND REDHONE, a hundred in Bridport division, Dorset It contains nine parishes of Beaminster district, three other parishes, and part of another Acres, 31,922 Pop in 1851, 9,950 Houses, 2,032

BEAMISH, a township in Tanfield chapelry, Chester-le Street parish, Durham, on the river Tipeth, near Stanhope railway, 6 miles SW of Gateshead Acres, 4 120 Real property, £6,757, of which £2,900 are in coal mines Pop, 2,074

BEAMSLEY, a township in Addingham and Skipton parishes W R Yorkshire, 6 miles E by N of Skipton Acres, 1 586 Real property £2,733 Pop, 264 Houses, 55 Here is an hospital, founded in the reign of Elizabeth by Margaret Countess of Cumberland, for 13 poor women, the income of which is £375

BEANACRE, a tything in Melksham parish, Wilts. Pop 257

BEANE (THE), a river of Herts It rises in the vicinity of Lnshden, and runs about 13 miles southward, past Yardley, Aston, Great Watton, and Stapleford to the Lea at Hertford

BEANLEY, a township in Eglingham parish, Northumberland, on the river Breamish, 7 miles NW of Alnwick Acres, 2,311 Pop 116 Houses, 23 The earls of Dunbar anciently held it on the tenure of maintaining a road into Scotland A cross stands on Hedgeley moor, at a short distance from the village, erected to the memory of Sir Ralph Percy, who fell in 1461 in a battle with the Yorkists

BEANTON See PARSTON, Oxford

BEARD, a township in Glossop parish, Derby, in the High Peak, near the river Etherow and the Peak railway 5 miles NW of Chapel le Frith It comprises the hamlets of Beard, Thornsett, Whitle, and Ollersett, and includes the village of New Mills Acres, 5,014 Real property, £15,623 —of which £1,150 are in mines Pop, 1,522 Houses, 310

BEARDON, a village 5½ miles N of Launceston, Cornwall

BEARD'S HILL a hamlet in St Peter's parish, Kent, 2 miles NE of Ramsgate

BEAR FOREST See BERE FOREST

BEAR GREEN, a locality 4½ miles S of Dorking Surrey, with a post office under Dorking

BEARL, a township in Bywell St. Andrew parish, Northumberland, 5 miles E of Corbridge Acres, 421 Pop, 58 Houses, 10

BEARLEY, a parish in Stratford on Avon district, Warwick, on the Stratford branch of the Oxford and Birmingham railway, and near the Birmingham canal, 4 miles NNW of Stratford It has a station on the railway, and a post office under Stratford on-Avon Acres, 810 Real property, £1,348 Pop, 238 Houses, 54 The living is a vicarage in the diocese of Worcester Value, £62 Patron, King's College, Cambridge The church is old

BEARN ROCK, or BEARN-BACK, a rugged islet below Worle Hill in the vicinity of Weston super-Mare, Somerset An exciting and productive sprat fishery is carried on at it from the middle of October till Christmas

BEARSE, a tract in the district of Chepstow and county of Gloucester, recently incorporated with St Briavels parish, and previously extra parochial

BEARSTED, or BERSTED, a parish in Maidstone district, Kent, on a tributary of the Medway river 2¼ miles E by S of Maidstone r station It has a post office under Maidstone Acres, 610 Real property, £2,036 Pop, 638 Houses, 132 The property is divided among a few Some lands here were held by the Bertie family before the reign of Henry II The living is a vicarage in the diocese of Canterbury Value, £191 * Patrons, the Dean and Chapter of Rochester The church is perpendicular English, and has a tower with three rude figures, said to refer to the name Bearsted There is a large national school

BEARSTONE, a township in Woore chapelry, Mucklestone parish, Salop, 6 miles NE of Market Drayton Pop, 101

BEARSWOOD GREEN, a hamlet in Hatfield parish, W R Yorkshire 2 miles SW of Thorne

BEARWARDCOTE, a township in Etwall parish, Derbyshire, near Icknield street and the Birmingham and Derby railway, 6 miles SW of Derby Pop, 32 Houses, 4

BEARWOOD, a chapelry in Hurst and Wokingham parishes, Berks, 2¼ miles S of Wokingham r station It was constituted in 1846, and its post town is Wokingham Pop, 814 Houses, 169 The living is a rectory in the diocese of Oxford Value, £180 * Patron, J Walter, Esq The church is handsome

BEATHWAITE GREEN, a hamlet in Levens township Heversham parish, Westmoreland near the river Kent, 3 miles N of Milnthorpe Here are Levens church and a Wesleyan chapel

BEAUCHAMP COURT, a farm house near the river Arrow 1 mile N of Alcester, Warwick It was once the seat of the Grevilles and the Beauchamps, Earls of Warwick, and was the birth place of Fulke Greville, Lord Brooke

BEAUCHAMP HATCH See HATCH BEAUCHAMP

BEAUCHAMP ROOTHING See ROOTHING BEAUCHAMP

BEAUCHIEF ABBEY an extra parochial liberty and a chapelry in the district of Ecclesall Bierlow, and county of Derby The liberty lies on the verge of the county, 3 miles NNW of Dronfield, and 4 SSW of Sheffield r station and its post town is Dronfield, under Sheffield Acres, 780 Real property, £1 038 Pop, 122 Houses 2 A Premonstratensian abbey was founded here, in 1183, by Robert Fitz Ranulph one of the murderers of Thomas a Becket The chapelry is conterminate with the liberty, and is a donative in the diocese of Lichfield Value, not reported Patron, E P Burnell Esq The church is a small building, erected about 1660, and has a tower which belonged to the abbey

BEAUDESERT, a parish in Stratford on Avon dis

trict, Warwick, in the eastern vicinity of Henley in Arden, near the Stratford canal 4½ miles W by S of Hatton r station Post town, Henley in Arden, under Birmingham Acres, 1,285 Real property, £2,563 Pop, 172 Houses, 40 A small village, of the same name as the parish, was formerly a market town A strong castle was erected here by Thurstane de Montfort, soon after the Conquest, but was completely destroyed in the wars of the Roses The living is a rectory in the diocese of Worcester Value £320 * Patron, the Lord Chancellor The church has a Norman chancel an early English nave, and a perpendicular tower Richard Jago, born in 1715, the author of "Edge-Hill" and other poems, was a native

BEAUDESERT PARK, a seat of the Marquis of Anglesey in Cannock chase, Stafford, 4 miles NW of Lichfield The Marquis takes from it the title of Baron The mansion is a stately old Tudor edifice, and the park is large and noble Castle Hill camp, within the grounds, was the site of an ancient royal hunting seat, and commands a very extensive view

BEAUFORT, a village in Aberystruth parish, Monmouth, and a chapelry in Aberystruth and Bedwelty parishes, Monmouth, and Llangattock and Llangunider parishes Brecon The village stands adjacent to the Merthyr and Abergavenny railway, near the source of the Ebbw y Fawr river, 2½ miles ENE of Tredegar, and has a r station, and a post office‡ under Tredegar It comprises a very dirty straggling street about a mile long, and extensive ironworks with seven furnaces The chapelry was constituted in 1846 Pop, 5,880 Houses, 1,212 The living is a p curacy in the diocese of Llandaff Value, £150 Patron, alternately the Crown and the Bishop.

BEAULIEU, or BEWLEY, a village, a parish, and a liberty, in the district of New Forest Hants. The village stands at the head of a creek, 4 miles SE of Lyndhurst Road r station, and 7 NE of Lymington. It has a post office† under Southampton, carries on some sack making and ship building, and has fairs on 15 April and 4 Sept It is a quaint old fashioned place, and was formerly of more note than now The creek at it goes 4½ miles south south eastward to the Solent, is navigable hither, and receives, at the head, a streamlet of 5 miles, coming from the vicinity of Lyndhurst, and called variously the Beaulieu and the Exe —The parish comprises 9,480 acres of land, and 2,560 of water Real property, £4,820 Pop, 1,176 Houses, 238 The property all belongs to the Duke of Buccleuch A Cistertian abbey was founded here, in the neighbourhood of the village, in 1204, by King John, had the privilege of sanctuary, and gave shelter to Margaret of Anjou and to Perkin Warbeck. The abbot's house, the refectory, the cloister walls, the dormitory, and the ruins of the sacristy, fratry, and chapter house still remain The abbot's house was moated by a Duke of Montague, to protect it from French privateers, and is still maintained as a seat of the Duke of Buccleuch The refectory is now the parish church, measures 125 feet by 30½, and shows the characters of late early English An hospital of the Knights Templars, of earlier date than the abbey, stood about ½ a mile distant, on a rising ground commanding an extensive view, and the ruins of it have been converted into farm buildings The living is a rectory in the diocese of Winchester Value £140 * Patron, the Duke of Buccleuch There are two Baptist chapels.—The liberty comprises the parishes of Beaulieu and Exbury Acres, 13,106 Pop, 1,549 Houses, 304

BEAUMANOR, a liberty in the parish of Barrow upon Soar, Leicester, 3 miles W of Mount Sorrel Acres, 1,210 Real property, £2,161 Pop, 137 Houses, 19 Beaumanor Park is the seat of W P Herrick, Esq, and the mansion is a splendid recent edifice, in the Tudor style, after a design by Railton

BEAUMARIS, a town, a parish and a sub district in the district of Bangor and county of Anglesey The town stands on the west side of Beaumaris bay at the NE end of the Menai strait, 2½ miles geographically, but 7 by road, N by E of Bangor, and 5½ NE of Llanfair r station It was the Welsh Porth-Wygyr and Bonover, and it acquired consequence from a castle erected by Edward I to secure his conquests It is well built, and comprises two long streets, Watergate and Castle street, together with a third leading to the west. It has a post-office‡ under Bangor, three hotels, a number of good lodging-houses, a county hall and court house, a county jail, a neat town hall, with elegant assembly room, a bath house a custom house, a church, four dissenting chapels, a free grammar school, almshouses, and other charities. The jail has capacity for 42 male and 7 female prisoners The church is a handsome structure, partly perpendicular English and contains an ancient monument, probably of Sir Henry Sydney and monuments of the Bulkeley family and of Lady Beatrice Herbert The grammar school was founded in 1609, by D Hughes and has £617 from endowment, and a fellowship and exhibition at Oxford The castle of Edward I, in a state of ruin, stands within the grounds of Sir R W B Bulkeley, Bart., adjacent to the upper end of the town, and has a picturesque appearance. It was garrisoned in 1643 for Charles I, and made a considerable defence, but surrendered in 1646, to General Mytton The outer wall has ten low round towers, the main structure is nearly quadrangular, with a large round tower at each corner, and the banqueting hall, the state rooms, the domestic apartments, and a small chapel, with finely groined roof, can still be traced A bardic meeting was held in 1832 in the ruined banqueting hall and chapel attended by Her Majesty, then Princess Victoria, and her mother the Duchess of Kent The surrounding grounds have been converted by the owner into a pleasant promenade

The town is much and increasingly frequented for sea bathing, and it offers many attractions to visitors,—fine bathing ground charming walks, pleasant recreations, and most magnificent views Ferries are open to Bangor and Aber, and steamers ply to Liverpool and Carnarvon A weekly market is held on Saturday, and fairs on 13 Feb, Holy Thursday, 19 Sept, and 19 Dec. The port has jurisdiction over Conway, Amlwch, Holyhead Aberffraw, Rhydpoint, and some smaller sub ports, and the craft belonging to it, at the close of 1867, comprised 133 small sailing vessels of aggregately 4,406 tons, and 168 larger ones of aggregately 14,921 tons, while the vessels which entered it during that year, counting repeated voyages, were 27 sailing vessels from the colonies and foreign countries of aggregately 6,370 tons, 1 074 sailing vessels coastwise of aggregately 18,350 tons, and 778 steam vessels coastwise of aggregately 313,606 tons The chief imports are timber, coal, and provisions, and the chief exports copper ores, slate and marble The town was made a borough by Edward I, it is governed by a mayor four aldermen and twelve councillors, is the seat of the assizes for Anglesey, and of quarter sessions, is the election town and the head-quarters of the militia and, along with Amlwch Holyhead and Llangefni, sends a member to parliament Its borough boundaries include Beaumaris parish and parts of six adjoining parishes Direct taxes, in 1857, £3,986 Electors in 1868, 563 Pop, 2 558 Houses, 541 —The parish comprises 440 acres of land, and 780 of water Real property, £6,443 Pop, 2,210 Houses, 466 The living is a vicarage, annexed to the rectory of Llandegfan in the diocese of Bangor —The sub district comprises eleven parishes and five parochial chapelries Acres, 35,370 Pop, 13,139 Houses, 2 953 See BARON HILL

BEAUMARIS BAY, the expansion of sea at the NE end of the Menai strait. It extends 12 miles north eastward from Bangor to Great Orme's Head, measures 7½ miles, across the entrance, east north eastward from Trwyn Dhu Point to Great Orme's Head, expands, in the NE, into the estuary of the Conway river, and is mainly occupied, in the upper part, opposite and around Beaumaris, by the Lavan Sands A safe capacious harbour on it, called Friar's Road, adjoins Beaumaris has anchorage in from 4 to 6 fathoms and is entered, round Puffin's Island, by two channels marked with buoys

BEAUMONT, a parish in Carlisle district, Cumberland, on the river Eden, the Roman wall, and the Carlisle and Silloth railway, in the vicinity of Burgh station 5 miles NW of Carlisle Post town, Burgh by Sands, under Carlisle Acres, 1,470 Real property, £2,306 Pop 237 Houses, 56 The property is subdivided. The living is a rectory, annexed to the rectory of Kirk Andrews upon Eden in the diocese of Carlisle The church is small and plain

BEAUMONT, a village in the parish of St Peter Jersey, 2 miles NE of St Aubin It has a post office under St Heliers Pop, 285

BEAUMONT CHASE, an extra parochial tract in Uppingham district, Rutland, 1½ mile from Uppingham. It commands some fine views Pop, 31 Houses, 4

BEAUMONT CUM MOZE, a parish in Tendring district, Essex, near the head of an inlet of the North sea, between the Naze and Harwich 4½ miles S of Wrabness r station, and 10 E of Colchester It has a post office, of the name of Beaumont, under Colchester Acres, 3,261, of which 215 are water Real property, £4,349 Pop, 490 Houses 109 The property is divided among a few Beaumont Hall is a chief residence The living is a rectory in the diocese of Rochester Value £652 * Patron, Wadham College, Oxford. The church is good, and there is a Wesleyan chapel

BEAUMONT LEYS an extra parochial tract in Barrow upon Soar district, Leicestershire, near the Leicester and Swannington railway, 2 miles N of Leicester Acres, 1,210 Real property, £1,955 Pop, 31 Houses, 6

BEAUPRE CASTLE, the ancient seat of the Bassett family, in Glamorganshire, on the river Thaw, 3 miles SE of Cowbridge It occupies the site of an early Welsh fortress, enlarged by the Normans, and is itself a curious mixture of Gothic and Greek architecture, designed by a native artist of the name of Twrch

BEAUSALL, a hamlet in Hatton parish, Warwickshire, 4 miles NW of Warwick It includes Brown-Lloyd Green, Old Park, Old Folly, New Folly, and Waste Green. Real property, £2,378 Pop, 273 Houses, 59

BEAU-VALE, a manor in Greasley parish, Notts, 7 miles NW of Nottingham It belonged anciently to the Cantilupes, and had a Carthusian priory founded by one of that family in the time of Edward III Some fragments of the ancient manor house, and some tottering walls of the priory, connected with the offices of a farm yard still remain

BEAUVOIR TOWN, or DE BEAUVOIR TOWN, a chapelry in West Hackney parish London, near Kingsland Road, 2½ miles N by E of St Pauls The living is a p curacy in the diocese of London Value, not reported Patron, R B De Beauvoir, Esq who built the church

BEAUWORTH, or BEAWORTH, a parish in Alresford district, Hants, 4¾ miles S of Alresford r station, and 6½ ESE of Winchester Post town, Cheriton, under Alresford Acres, 1 214 Real property, £1,194 Pop 127 Houses 23 A leaden box containing about 700 coins of William the Conqueror and William Rufus was found here in 1833 The parish is a resort of sportsmen. The living is a p curacy, annexed to the rectory of Cheriton in the diocese of Winchester

BEAWORTHY, or BEWORTHY, a parish in Okehampton district, Devon, 6 miles SW of Hatherleigh, and 9 W of Okehampton r station Post town, North Lew under Exbourne North Devon Acres 3,806 Real property, £1 122 Pop, 238 Houses, 52 The land is hilly and boggy The manor belongs to the representatives of the late Sir W Molesworth The living is a rectory in the diocese of Exeter Value £140 Patron Edwin Force, Esq The church is a neat small edifice, with a low square tower There is a chapel for Bible Christians

BEAZLEY END, a village 4½ miles N of Braintree, in Essex

BEBBANBURY See LAMBOROUGH

BEBINGTON, two townships and a parish in Wirrall district, Cheshire The townships are styled Higher and Lower, they lie on the river Mersey, and on the Birkenhead and Chester railway, 2½ and 3½ miles S by E of Birkenhead, they have a station, of the name of Bebington, on the railway, and a post office of the same name, under Birkenhead, and they have had great recent increase of houses and inhabitants from their situation on the Mersey, in immediate communication with Liverpool Acres of Higher Bebington, 1,084, of which 135 are water Real property, £14,790 Pop, 2,036 Houses, 336 Acres of Lower Bebington, 1,542, of which 490 are water Real property, £10,035 Pop, 2,485 Houses, 465 The parish includes also the townships of Tranmere, Storeton, and Poulton cum Spittle Acres, 6,437, of which 1,060 are water Real property, £66,922 Pop in 1841, 6,008, in 1861, 15,105 Houses, 2,549 The property is much subdivided Excellent building stone, with notable geological peculiarities is extensively quarried The living is a rectory, with St Mark's chapelry, in the diocese of Chester Value, £670 * Patron, the Rev G R. Feilden The parish church is partly Norman, partly mixed English, and St Mark's was built in 1866 The p curacy of Christchurch is a separate benefice, in the patronage of the Rev G Troughton and its church was built in 1859 The vicarages of Rock Ferry and Tranmere also are separate benefices. There are four dissenting chapels, two national schools, a workhouse, and charities £53

BEBSIDE, a township in Horton parish, Northumberland, on the Blyth railway, 2½ miles W of Blyth It has a r station, and extensive iron works Pop, 53

BECCANLEY See BECKLEY, Sussex.

BECCLES, a town, a parish, and a sub district, in Wangford district, Suffolk The town stands on the river Waveney, and on the Eastern Counties railway amid pleasant environs, 8½ miles W of Lowestoft It belonged anciently to Bury abbey, and suffered severely, in 1586, from fire It is now well built, and comprises several streets, which diverge from a spacious market place The town hall was built in 1839 and is used as a court house. The corn exchange was formerly the theatre. The assembly room is a handsome building, with a public library attached The house of correction is a substantial and commodious structure but is now used only as a police station The parish church is later English, consists of nave, chancel and aisles, altogether 148 feet long and 61½ feet wide, was renovated in 18.., and has a tower, 92 feet high, built about 1515, detached a short distance from the SE corner, and commanding a fine view of the surrounding country Another church or a chapel, connected with an hospital for lepers founded in the time of Edward III, stood at Endgate A new cemetery has been formed comprising 5 acres, beautifully laid out, and containing two chapels. The town has chapels for Independents, Baptists, and Methodists, a free grammar school with income of £184, another free school with £197, further charities with £290, a head post-office,‡ a railway station, two banking offices and two chief inns A weekly market is held on Friday and a fair also is held on Whit Monday The Waveney is navigable hence to the sea, making Beccles a sub port to Yarmouth a good coal, corn, and malt trade is carried on, and a weekly newspaper is published The town was incorporated by Queen Elizabeth, is governed by a mayor, four aldermen, and twelve councillors, possesses a common of about 900 acres, and has a corporate income of about £2,200, and is a polling place for East Suffolk The parish is conterminate with the borough Acres 1,892 Real property, £16 381 Pop, 4,266 Houses, 981 The living is a rectory in the diocese of Norwich Value, £370 Patron the Rev E Holland The sub district comprises thirteen parishes Acres, 18,181 Pop, 7,221 Houses 1,558

BECCONSALL See HESKETH WITH BECCONSALL

BECCOTT, a hamlet in Arlington parish, Devon

BECHAN a river of North Wales It rises on the Berwyn mountains, near the boundary between Montgomery and Merioneth, and runs 16 miles south ... t ward, past Llanwddon, Llwydiarth Park, and Pont-Dolanog to the Einion, 1¾ mile below Meifod

BECHTON See BETCHTON

BECK, a name of Saxon origin signifying "a brook," also a name of Scandinavian origin, signifying "a beacon stone" or "beacon tower"

BECK, a village in Arthuret parish, Cumberland, 2 miles W of Longtown

BECK, a village on the eastern border of Cumberland, 3½ miles NW of Kirkoswald

BECKBURY a parish in Shiffnal district, Salop, on a tributary of the Severn, 4¼ miles SW of Albrighton r station, and 5½ S by E of Shiffnal It has a post office under Shiffnal Acres, 1,343 Real property, £2,140 Pop, 297 Houses, 66 The property is divided among a few. The living is a rectory in the diocese of Hereford Value, £300 Patron, the Lord Chancellor The church is good.

BECKENHAM, a village and a parish in Bromley district, Kent The village stands on a small tributary of the Ravensbourne river, close to a junction of several railways, 3 miles SE of the Crystal Palace, and 2 W of Bromley, has stations on the railways, and a post office under London, SE, and is rapidly becoming a suburb The parish comprises 3,875 acres Real property, in 1865, about £40,000 Pop in 1861, 2,124, in 1865, about 3,500 The property is subdivided. Beckenham Place is the seat of A Cator Esq, Kelsey Park, of P R Hoare, Esq, Old Manor House, of H Fortescue, Esq, and Langley Park, of C Goodheart, Esq Beckenham was the residence of Brandon, Duke of Suffolk, when visited by Henry VIII, and Clay-Hill here was the residence of Edward King, author of the "Munimenta Antiqua," who died in 1807 The living is a rectory in the diocese of Canterbury Value, £900 * Patron, J Cator, Esq The church was built about the beginning of the 16th century, has a lofty white spire, rebuilt in 1796, and contains monuments of the Styles, the Burrells, the Hoares, and others and a tablet to Captain Hedley Vicars, who fell at Sebastopol. The ancient lich gate, for setting down corpses at funerals, still stands The p curacies of B St Paul and Shortlands are separate charges, both of them constituted in 1868 There are endowed national schools with £42 a-year, and other charities £68 Dr Assheton prolocutor in convocation who died in 1711 was rector

BECKERING HOLTON See HOLTON BECKERING

BECKERMET, a township in the parishes of St. Bridget Beckermet and St John Beckermet, Cumberland, on the river Ehen, adjacent to the Whitehaven and Furness railway, in the vicinity of Braystones station 3 miles S of Egremont It has a post office under Whitehaven Real property, with Calder, £2,188 A property in the neighbourhood, called Wotobank was the scene of the tragical subject of Mrs Cowley's "Edwina" The lady of a proprietor was killed on the grounds by a wolf, and found in a mangled state on a bank, when her husband exclaimed in horror, "Wo to this bank!"

"Wo to thee, bank! the attendants echoed round,
And pitying shepherds caught the grief fraught sound,
Thus to this hour, through every changing age,—
Through every year's still ever varying stage,—
The name remains"

BECKERMET ST BRIDGET, a parish in Whitehaven district, Cumberland, on the coast and on the Whitehaven and Furness railway, from Beckermet township south eastward to the vicinity of Calder Bridge. Post town Beckermet, under Whitehaven Acres, 5 025, of which 377 are water Rated property £3,909 Pop, 657 Houses, 126 The property is much subdivided Freestone is quarried The living is a vicarage, united to the p curacy of Calder Bridge, in the diocese of Carlisle Value, £127 Patron, Captain Irwin The church is old and lonely, and now used merely for marriages and burials, and a new church at Calder Bridge is attended by the inhabitants

BECKERMET ST JOHN, a parish in Whitehaven district Cumberland, on the coast and on the Whitehaven and Furness railway from Beckermet township north westward to the vicinity of Nethertown station Post town, Beckermet, under Whitehaven Acres 2,732 Rated property, £2,563 Pop., 492 Houses, 100 The property is much subdivided. The living is a vicarage in the diocese of Carlisle Value, £96 * Patron, H Gaitskell, Esq The church is modern.

BECKETSBURY, an ancient camp on Westridge, Gloucester, 1 mile N of Wootton under Edge It occupies about 4 acres, has a double trench, and is planted with beech

BECKETT, a tything in Shrivenham parish, Berks in the vicinity of the Great Western railway, 5 miles SW of Faringdon Pop, 23 Houses, 6 It was formerly called Becote, belonged once to the Earls of Evreux, then to the priory of Noion in Normandy, was seized, and made an occasional residence, by King John, and passed afterwards to a family who took from it the name of De Beckote It now belongs to Viscount Barrington The present mansion on it superseded a large ancient manor-house, is a fine edifice in the Tudor style, and contains some interesting paintings and the chess pieces of Charles I

BECKFOOT, a hamlet in Bingley township and parish, W R Yorkshire

BECKFOOT, Westmoreland. See BARBON

BECKFORD, a village and a parish in Winchcomb district, Gloucester The village stands near the Ashchurch and Evesham railway, 7 miles SW of Evesham, and has a r station, and a post office under Tewkesbury The parish includes also the hamlets of Bangrove, Didcote, and Grafton Acres, 2 650 Real property, £2 454 Pop, 478 Houses, 103. The property is divided among a few Beckford Hall is the seat of Hattil Foll, Esq The manor was given, in the time of Henry I, to the abbey of St Martin in Normandy, and passed, after the suppression first to Eton college, next to Fotheringhay, next to Sir Richard Lee The living is a vicarage, united to the p curacy of Aston under Hill, in the diocese of Gloucester and Bristol Value, £317 * Patron, the Rev Dr Timbrill The church is Norman, was recently restored, and has a lofty tower, crowned with pinnacles Charities, £47

BECK HALL See BILLINGFORD, Norfolk

BECKHAM (EAST), a parish in Erpingham district, Norfolk 4 miles WSW of Cromer, and 14 E by N of Walsingham r station Post town, Lower Sherringham, under Norwich Acres, 782 Real property, £608 Pop, 73 Houses, 17 The living is a sinecure in the diocese of Norwich, and the church has been long in ruins

BECKHAM (WEST), a parish in Erpingham district, Norfolk, 5 miles WSW of Cromer, and 13 E by N of Walsingham r station Post town, Lower Sherringham, under Norwich Acres, 785 Real property £1,477 Pop, 329 Houses, 42 The property is divided among a few The living is a vicarage in the diocese of Norwich Value £61 Patrons, the Dean and Chapter of Norwich The church is early English, and had formerly a round tower, surmounted by an octagonal lanthern

BECKHAMPTON a tything in Avebury parish, Wilts, on the Downs 6 miles W of Marlborough. Here are several barrows, two large Druidic stones, and a ruined ancient chapel Pop, 155

BECKINGHAM, a parish in the district of Newark and county of Lincoln, on the river Witham, 3½ miles N of Claypole r station, and 5 E of Newark. It includes the hamlet of Sutton, and has a post office under Newark Acres, 2,200 Real property, £4,200 Pop, 431 Houses 105 The property is not much divided The living is a rectory, united with the p curacies of Stragglesthorpe and Fenton, in the diocese of Lincoln Value, £697 * Patron, the Rev G Marsland The church was recently restored There is a Wesleyan chapel

BECKINGHAM, a parish in Gainsborough district, Notts, on the Lincoln and Doncaster railway 2½ miles W by N of Gainsborough It has a post office under Gainsborough, and a r station Acres, 3,010 Real property, £5,727 Pop, 450 Houses, 104 The property is much subdivided The living is a vicarage in the diocese of Lincoln. Value, £110 Patron, the Prebendary of Southwell The church is good, and there are Wesleyan and Primitive Methodist chapels and charities £21 Dr William Howell, the historian, was a native

BECKINGTON, a village and a parish in Frome district, Somerset. The village stands near the river Frome and the East Somerset railway, 3 miles NE of Frome, and has a post office‡ under Bath. It was formerly a place of some importance, carrying on woollen manufactures, but has suffered greatly from the decline of the clothing trade The parish includes also the hamlet of Rudge. Acres, 1 830 Real property, £5,243 Pop 1,036 Houses, 229 The property is much subdivided The living is a rectory, united with the rectory of Standerwick, in the diocese of Bath and Wells Value, £540 * Patron, S L Sainsbury, Esq The church was restored in 1861, and it contains monuments of the Seymours and the poet Daniel There are a Baptist chapel, national, British, and boarding schools, and charities £23 Thomas Beckington, Bishop of Bath and Wells, who figured in the legislation against the Wickliffites, was a native, and Kuish, one of the editors of the Polyglott Bible was rector

BECKJAY, a township in Clungunford parish, Salop, 9 miles WNW of Ludlow Pop, 73

BECKLEY, a village and a parish in Headington district, Oxford The village stands on the line of the Roman road from Alcester to Wallingford on an eminence overhanging the south side of Otmoor, 3 miles SE of Islip r station, and 5 NE of Oxford, and has a post office under Oxford It was the burial place of the British saint, Donanverdh, the hereditary property of king Alfred, and the site of the castellated palace of Richard King of the Romans The parish includes also the hamlets of Studley and Horton cum Studley Acres, 4 370 Real property, £1,888 Pop, 749 Houses, 165 The surface is hilly Various fragments of Roman pottery have been found A Benedictine priory was founded at Studley, in the time of Henry II, by Bertrand de St Walery, passed, at the dissolution, to the Crokes, and was converted into a dwelling house in 1587 The living is a vicarage in the diocese of Oxford Value, £112 Patron, the Rev T L Cooke The church is an interesting structure of the 14th century, and has remains of very curious frescoes, a font with ancient stone desk, and tombs of the Crokes There are almshouses with £92, and other charities £7

BECKLEY, a parish and a sub district in the district of Rye, Sussex. The parish adjoins the river Rother, on the border of the county, 6 miles NW of Rye r station, it was known to the Saxons as Beccanlen, and it has a post office under Staplehurst Acres, 5,316 Real property, £7,113 Pop, 1 292 Houses, 273 The property is subdivided There were formerly extensive iron works The living is a rectory in the diocese of Chichester Value, £851 * Patron, University college, Oxford. The church is very good There is a Wesleyan chapel A fair is held on Easter Thursday —The sub district comprises six parishes. Acres, 23,073 Pop, 5,574 Houses, 1 160

BECK (LITTLE), a hamlet in Egglesbarnby township, N R Yorkshire, 3½ miles SW of Whitby

BECK ROW, a watch or hamlet in Mildenhall parish, Suffolk 3 miles NW of Mildenhall Pop, 684 Houses, 151 There are two Methodist chapels

BECKS, a village in Marshfield parish, Gloucester

BECKSHALGH See BASHALL EAVES

BECKSIDE, a village 8½ miles SSE of Ravenglass, in Cumberland

BECKUPMONDS See BECCARMONDS

BECKWITH, a hamlet in Pannal parish, near Lower Harrogate W R Yorkshire

BECKY (THE) a streamlet of Devon rising on the east side of Dartmoor forest, and running 4 miles north eastward to the river Wrey, 1½ miles SE of Moreton Hampstead A fall occurs in it about 3 miles from its source, about 80 feet in descent down a granite precipice This makes a grand appearance after heavy rains, and has accompaniments which always look romantic, even when the water shrinks into mere tricklings among the rocks. A cottage belonging to the Earl of Devon is adjacent. The valley of the stream is the Houndtor Combe, overhung by the Houndtor mountain, capped with rocks resembling the colonnade of a ruined temple, and it both contains very striking scenery within itself, and looks out on some most interesting views

BECONTREE a hundred in Essex It is bounded on the W by the river Roding,—on the S by the Thames, measures 8 miles by 5½ and contains nine parishes Acres, 38,826 Pop in 1851, 46,777, in 1861, 73,023 Houses, 12,606

BECOTE. See BECKETT

BEDALE, a small town, a township, a parish, a sub district, and a district in N R Yorkshire The town stands on a small tributary of the Swale, adjacent to the Northallerton and Leyburn railway, near the Leeming Roman way, 8 miles SW by W of Northallerton It consists chiefly of one street, and has a head post office,‡ a railway station, a banking office, two chief inns, petty sessions, court house, and assembly rooms, a parish church, a Wesleyan chapel, two endowed schools, alms houses, a workhouse, and charities £247 The church is early English, and large, has a square embattled tower, so strong as to have been used for defence in the Border forays, contains ancient monuments to the Earl of Arundel and others, modern ones to Admiral Sir J P Beresford and Henry Peirse, Esq, and beautiful memorial windows to Mr and Mrs. Monson and others, and was renovated in 1855 A weekly market is held on Tuesday, and fairs on Easter Tuesday, Whit Tuesday, 6 July, 11 Oct, and the Monday week before Christmas The circumjacent country is highly cultivated, and has a character for producing excellent riding horses Bedale Hall, an elegant mansion, and Bedale Grange, another chief residence, are adjacent A castle was built by Brian Fitzalan, Earl of Arundel, on a spot now within the grounds of Bedale Hall, but has disappeared

The township includes the town, and comprises 1,613 acres Real property, £7,064 Pop., 1,157 Houses, 233 The parish contains also the townships of Firby, Crakehall Aiskew, Langthorne, and Rands Grange in the district of Bedale, and the township of Burrell cum Cowling in the district of Leyburn Acres, 7,551 Real property, £19,637 Pop, 2,860 Houses, 620 The property is not much divided The living is a rectory in the diocese of Ripon Value, £1,936 * Patrons, Trustees of Lord Beaumont, and of Harry Monson de la Poer Beresford, Esq The vicarage of Crakehall is a separate benefice The sub district comprises the parishes of Kirkby Fleetham Scruton, and Burneston, and parts of the parishes of Bedale, Catterick, Hornby, Kirklington, and Pickhill Acres, 25,210 Pop, 6 000 Houses 1,309 The district includes also the sub district of Masham, containing the parish of Well, and parts of the parishes of Masham and Thornton Watlass Acres, 45,585. Poor rates in 1866, £3,573 Pop in 1861, 8,650 Houses, 1,929 Marriages in 1866, 54, births, 227,—of which 13 were illegitimate, deaths, 149,—of which 35 were at ages under 5 years, and 11 at ages above 85 years Marriages in the ten years 1851-60, 586, births, 2,580, deaths, 1,758 The places of worship in 1851 were 12 of the Church of England, with 4 268 sittings 2 of Baptists, with 406 s., 16 of Wesleyan Methodists, with 2,446 s 5 of Primitive Methodists, with 508 s, 1 of Wesleyan Reformers, with 100 s, and 1 of Roman Catholics, with 60 s. The schools were 20 public day schools, with 931 scholars, 19 private day schools, with 345 s, 23 Sunday schools, with 1,333 s, and 1 evening school for adults, with 20 s

BEDANFORD See BEDFORD

BEDBURN (THE) a stream of Durham. It rises on Egglestone Common, and runs 10 miles north eastward to the Wear below Happy Land Park

BEDBURN (NORTH), a township in Auckland St Andrew parish, Durham near the Weardale railway and the river Wear, 5½ miles NW of Bishop Auckland

Acres, 2,036 Real property, £6,112,—of which £2,908 are in mines. Pop, 1,771 Houses, 335. There is a Wesleyan chapel

BEDBURN (SOUTH), a township in Auckland St. Andrew parish, Durham, on the Bedburn rivulet, 3½ miles from the Weardale railway, and 7½ W of Bishop Auckland Acres, 6,765 Real property, £2,920 Pop, 332. Houses, 61

BEDCESTER a hamlet in Fontmell Magna parish, Dorset, 3 miles S by W of Shaftesbury

BEDDAU GWYR ARDUDWY, a group of ancient graves on Michnant hill, Merioneth, 3 miles NE of Festiniog, and 14 WNW of Bala The men of Ardudwy made an incursion into the vale of Clwyd, carried off thence a number of maidens whom they intended to marry, and were pursued by the warriors of the vale to Michnant hill, and all there put to the sword The graves on the spot are the graves of these men, they were about 36 in number, arranged in a regular order, and they long continued to be each from 2 to 3 feet high, with a small stone at the head and another at the feet, but they have ceased to be distinguishable, and only two head stones are standing

BEDDGELERT, or BETHGELERT, a village in the district of Festiniog and county of Carnarvon, and a parish partly also in Merioneth The village stands at the confluence of the Colwyn and the Gwynnant rivers, near Aberglaslyn pass, 6 miles S of the summit of Snowdon, and 12 SE of Carnarvon, and is connected by railway, near completion in 1869, with the Cambrian at Port Madoc It nestles in a deep romantic vale, engirt by lofty mountains, amidst the grandest scenery in Wales, presents very strong attractions to tourists, artists, and anglers, was anciently noted as a resting place of pilgrims, and has a post office‡ under Carnarvon, a large excellent hotel, comfortable lodging houses, a parish church and two dissenting chapels The church is early English, measures 80 feet by 30, and belonged originally to an Augustinian priory The priory is thought by some to have been older than Owen Gwynedd, who began to reign in 1137, by others, to have been founded by Llewelyn the Great A romantic tradition asserts that Llewelyn founded it to commemorate the preservation of an infant child in its cradle from an intruding wolf, the animal being killed there by a watchful hound, and the hound itself killed immediately after through mistake by the master, and this tradition is the subject of the late Hon W R. Spencer's ballad of "Prince Llewelyn and his Greyhound Gelert," but it probably was borrowed from some one of similar old stories current in England, in Ireland, in France, in Persia, and in other countries. Fairs are held at the village on 10 April, 10 Aug, 21 and 27 Sept, and 13 Oct —The parish includes the hamlet of Llwynllinon the lordship of Nanthnynant, and the hamlet of Nantmor, and the two former contain the village of Beddgelert Acres, 26,716 Rated property, £2,187 Pop, 1,375 Houses, 275 The property is subdivided Titanium and copper ores are found Moel Hebog mountain, overhanging the village on the W, has a recess which was a hiding place of Owen Glendower, and yielded up from a bog in 1784, a very curious brass Roman shield Some pretty cascades occur on the Colwyn, a few hundred yards from the village, and the pass to the S, noticed in our article ABERGLASLYN teams with interest The principal scene of Southey's poem of "Madoc" is laid in the parish The living is a vicarage in the diocese of Bangor Value, £189 Patron, John Priestley, Esq

BEDDINGHAM, a parish in Lewes district, Sussex, on the river Ouse and on the South Coast railway, near Glynde station, 2½ miles SE of Lewes It has a post office under Lewes Acres, 2,915 Real property, £2,857 Pop, 334 Houses, 59 The property is divided among a few The manor is mentioned in the will of King Alfred, and had a monastery in the beginning of the 9th century The living is a vicarage, united with the vicarage of West Firle in the diocese of Chichester Value, £480 Patrons, the Bishop and the Dean and Chapter of Chichester alternately The church was restored in 1858

BEDDINGTON, a village and a parish in Croydon district, Surrey The village stands on the river Wandle, near the Southeastern and the Wimbledon and Croydon railways, 2½ miles W of Croydon, and it has a station on the latter railway, and a post office under Croydon London S The parish includes also the place called Beddington Corner and the hamlet of Wallington Acres, 3,909 Real property, £12,060 Pop, 1,556 Houses, 311 The property is divided among a few The manor belonged to the Carews from 1360 till 1860 Beddington House, on the manor, now the seat of the Rev A. H Bridges, is chiefly a brick edifice of 1709, but includes a great hall, with very rich open roof, visited by Queen Elizabeth, and contained interesting family portraits, a curious trophy of arms, and an elaborately-formed door lock An orangery here, destroyed in 1739, sprang from pips imported by Sir Francis Carew, the brother in law of Sir Walter Raleigh, the first pips planted in England At Woodcote, in the southern part of the parish, many Roman remains have been found The living is a rectory in the diocese of Winchester Value £1,212 * Patron, the Rev A. H Bridges The church shows Norman traces, was founded before the Conquest, and rebuilt of flint in the time of Richard I, was renovated and extended, at a cost of £3,000, in 1850, and was again repaired in 1869 The p curacy of Wallington is a separate charge, formed in 1867

BEDDINGTON CORNER, a locality in Beddington parish, Surrey, 2 miles N of Beddington village It has a post office under Mitcham, London S

BEDEWIND See PEDWIN (GREAT).

BEDFIELD, a parish in Hoxne district, Suffolk, 4 miles NW of Framlingham r station. It has a post office under Wickham Market. Acres, 1,268 Real property, £2,469 Pop, 415 Houses, 88 The property is subdivided. The living is a rectory in the diocese of Norwich Value, £256 * Patron, Earl Stradbroke The church is old but good

BEDFONT (EAST), a village and a parish in Staines district, Middlesex. The village stands adjacent to the Southwestern railway, near Feltham station, 3½ miles ENE of Staines, and has a post office of the name of Bedfont, under Hounslow The parish includes also the hamlet of Hatton Acres 1,856 Real property, £6,497 Pop, 1,150 Houses, 237 The property is divided among a few The living is a vicarage in the diocese of London Value, £288 * Patron, the Bishop of London The church is ancient, has a Saxon porch, and has been enlarged and improved There is a national school

BEDFONT (WEST), a hamlet in Stanwell parish Middlesex, on King's river, 1½ mile W by N of East Bedfont

BEDFORD, a town, two sub districts, and a district in Bedfordshire The town stands on the river Ouse, in a pleasant fertile valley, 47½ miles NNW of London The Ouse is navigable hence to the sea, the Hitchin and Leicester railway, deflecting from the Great Northern at Hitchin comes 105 miles hither, and goes away to the NW, the Bletchley and Bedford railway, 16 miles long comes northeastward from the Northwestern at Bletchley, the Bedford and Cambridge, 29½ miles long goes east north eastward to the Great Eastern, and the Bedford and Northampton, 26 miles long authorized in 1865, goes west north westward to Northampton

Bedford was known to the Saxons as Bedanford or Bedicanford, signifying 'the lodging or fortress at the ford' Cuthwulf defeated the Britons near it in 571 The Danes attacked it in 911 and 921, and burned it in 1010 A castle was built at it, near the river, soon after the Conquest, figured in the wars of the Barons, was taken, in 1138, by King Stephen, taken, in 1216 by Fulk de Brent, and destroyed in 1224, by Henry III Nothing of the castle remains except a portion of the entrenchments, and the site of its keep is occupied by a bowling green Hugh de Bellemont, son of the Earl of Leicester, was made Earl of Bedford by King Stephen, but fell from his allegiance, and was degraded Ingel

-am de Coucy was raised to the earldom by Edward III John Plantagenet, third son of Henry IV, was made Duke of Bedford by Henry V but died without issue The Russel family were raised to the dukedom in 1694, and have their chief seat at Woburn Abbey Three men who have shed great lustre upon Bedford were Sir W Harpur, some time Lord Mayor of London, who died in 1574, S Palmer the nonconformist, and John Bunyan the author of the "Pilgrim's Progress The first and the second were natives, and the third was born at Elstow, 1½ mile to the S, and achieved at Bedford the chief experiences of his remarkable life

The town consists of a principal street, nearly a mile long, several intersecting streets, and some suburbs, has undergone great recent improvement, and considerable increase, contains many old substantial houses, and some handsome new ones, and presents altogether a pleasing appearance The bridge across the Ouse, connecting High street and Mary street, occupies the site of one which stood nearly 600 years, has five arches, and was built in 1813, at a cost of £15,000 The town hall contains apartments for the sessions and the assizes. The county jail, on the site of the prison in which Bunyan wrote his Pilgrim's Progress, was rebuilt in 1849, at a cost of £23,000, is of three stories, and has capacity for 243 male and 29 female prisoners The work house was erected as a house of industry in 1795, at a cost of £5,000, and changed to its present form, at a further cost of £1,800 The county lunatic asylum was built in 1812, at a cost of £13,000, and was a substantial brick structure, but has been taken down, and a new edifice instead of it has been built at Stotfold. The county infirmary was founded in 1803, is a brick edifice, with stone front, and contains 100 beds The corn exchange in St. Paul's square, is a very commodious building Remains of an interesting edifice of the 11th century, with window tracery and other decorations, stand at the foot of a yard leading out at High street, and now form part of the George Inn A meadow, called King's mead, belonging from old times to the town, lies about 2 miles distant, on the right bank of the Ouse, and contains a sulphuretted saline spring Extensive water works and drainage works were formed in 1868

The town, as defined by its borough boundaries, comprises 2,200 acres, and it is divided into two wards and five parishes The wards are Eastern and Western, and the parishes are St Cuthbert, St. Peter, St Paul, St Mary, and St John. St Cuthbert is wholly in the Eastern ward, each of the other parishes is partly in both wards, and St Paul includes the chapelry of Trinity All the livings are in the diocese of Ely St Cuthbert, St Peter, St Mary, and St John are rectories, St Paul is a vicarage, and Trinity is a vicarage The value of St Cuthbert is £145,* of St Peter, £204,* of St Paul, £230,* of St Mary, £273,* of St John, £149,* of Trinity, £75 The patron of St Cuthbert and St Peter is the Lord Chancellor of St Paul, the Rev W C Fitzgerald, of St Mary, Balliol College, Oxford, of St John, the Corporation of the borough of Bedford, and of Trinity, the Vicar of St Paul St Cuthbert's church was rebuilt in 1847, and is in the Norman style St Peter's is Norman and early English, and was recently enlarged. St Paul's is early and decorated English, and has a handsome tower and octagonal spire Trinity church was built in 1840, and made a separate charge in 1860 St. Mary's is later English with a Norman tower St John's is later English A Wesleyan chapel, in the Florentine Gothic style, was built in 1866 The Bunyan chapel was rebuilt in 1849, on the site of the "Old Meeting, in which John Bunyan preached from 1671 till 1688 and has a tablet to him on its side, and his chair in the vestry There are eight other dissenting chapels An extra mural cemetery of 18 acres, with two conjoined chapels, was opened in 1855 A monastery seems to have been founded on the bank of the Ouse, to the W of the town pretty early in the Saxon times and a chapel, probably connected with it was the burial place of King Offa and was swept away in an inundation Caldwell priory, near this, was founded in the time of King John, for brethren of the order of the Holy Cross, and some vestiges of it remain. A Franciscan friary an hospital of St Leonard, and an hospital or priory of St John the Baptist, stood in the S part of the town, and the last was endowed in the time of Edward II, and still exists as a public charity

The charities and the educational appliances of Bedford are remarkably rich and numerous A bequest by Sir William Harpur, in the time of Edward VI of some property in Bedford and of 13 acres of land within the parish of St. Andrew Holborn in London, has increased in yearly value from £40 to upwards of £17,000, and is disbursed, under parliamentary regulation, in supporting a grammar-school, a commercial school, a preparatory English school, a national school, a girls' school, an infant school, and numerous almshouses, and in giving university exhibitions to scholars, apprentice fees for boys and girls, and marriage portions to maidens The grammar-school furnishes the highest education to free boarders and scholars, the other schools are conducted with signal efficiency, and all are accessible to the children of all classes of the townspeople The school buildings were considerably enlarged in 1861, and they form a handsome range, in the Tudor style Other charities exist, to the amount of about £790 a year and include schools and alms houses Scientific, artistic philanthropic, and religious societies are numerous The Literary and Scientific institution was established in 1846, includes a reading room and a museum, and was amalgamated, in 1864 with a public library dating from 1830, and now containing upwards of 8,000 volumes The working men's institute is a neat building of 1866, and contains a reading room and a library The Bedford Rooms are a fine edifice, with tetrastyle Grecian portico, and include an assembly room, 72 feet long, 32 wide, and 28 high, used for lectures, concerts, and public meetings

Bedford is the marketing centre of a great agricultural district, and carries on considerable manufacture of lace and a large manufacture of agricultural implements, but otherwise has little trade Weekly markets are held on Monday and Saturday, and fairs on the first Tuesday in Lent, 21 April, 6 July, 21 Aug, Old Midsummer day 12 Oct, 17 Nov, and 19 Dec The town has a head post office,‡ two railway stations with telegraph two banking offices and three chief inns it publishes three newspapers and it is the political capital of the county, the seat of assizes and sessions, the head quarters of the militia, and the head of an excise collection It is a borough by prescription was chartered by Henry II, is governed by a mayor, six aldermen, and eighteen councillors, and sends two members to parliament Real property, in 1860, £49,424 Direct taxes in 1857, £7,392 Electors in 1868 1108. Pop., in 1841, 9,178, in 1861, 13,413 Houses, 2,752

The two sub districts of Bedford are called Bedford and Kempston and Bedford and Cardington The former comprises the eastern ward of the borough and the parishes of Kempston, Wootton, Biddenham, Bromham, Oakley, and Clapham Acres, 18,351 Pop., 11,921 Houses, 2,487 The latter comprises the western ward of the borough and the parishes of Cardington, Elstow, Wilshamstead Cople, Willington, Goldington and Renhold Acres, 18,376 Pop, 11,731 Houses, 2,376 —The district comprehends also the sub district of Barford, containing the parishes of Great Barford, Ravensden, Wilden, Colmworth and Roxton, the sub district of Turvey, containing the parishes of Turvey Steventon, and Stagsden the sub district of Harrold, containing the parishes of Harrold, Pavenham, Felmersham Odell, Chellington, and Carlton the sub district of Sharnbrook, containing the parishes of Sharnbrook, Knotting, Souldrop Bletsoe, Thurleigh, and Milton Ernest and the sub district of Riseley, containing the parishes of Riseley, [illegible] Keysoe [illegible] and Yelden Acres, 97,920 Poor rates in 1866, £22,747 Pop in 1861, 38,072 Houses 7,923 Marriages in 1866, 297, births, 1,170,—of which 81 were illegitimate deaths, 721 —of which 230 were at ages under 5 years, and 24 at ages above 85 years Marriages in the ten years 1851-60, 2,926, births, 12,026, deaths, 7,399 The places of worship in 1851 were 43 of the Church of England, with 13,791 sittings, 12 of Independents, with 4,029 s., 14 of Baptists, with 3,648 s, 16 of Wesleyan Methodists, with 3,253 s, 5 of Primitive Methodists, with 906 s 2 of Moravians, with 640 s, 1 of the Catholic and Apostolic church, with 80 s, 1 of Jews, with 20 s., and 4 undefined, with 1,357 s. The schools were 43 public day schools, with 3,786 scholars, 27 private day schools, with 428 s, 73 Sunday schools, with 6,701 s, and 7 evening schools for adults, with 235 s

BEDFORD, a township and a chapelry in Leigh parish Lancashire. The township lies on the Tyldesley and Kenyon branch railway, 1 mile ENE of Leigh, and has a station on the railway Post town, Leigh, under Manchester Acres, 2,438 Real property, £11,144. Pop, 6,558 Houses, 1,323 The property is much subdivided. There are cotton and silk mills, an iron foundry, collieries, and brickfields The chapelry is conterminate with the township, and was constituted in 1842 The living is a vicarage in the dio. of Manchester Value, £300 * Patron, the Vicar of Leigh. The church is recent, and there are Methodist and Roman Catholic chapels and a national school

BEDFORD CIRCUS. See EXETER.

BEDFORD LEVEL, an extensive marshy flat, in Norfolk, Suffolk, Huntingdon, Northampton, Lincoln, and Cambridge. It includes about 63 000 acres in Norfolk 30,000 in Suffolk, 50,000 in Huntingdon, Peterborough fen in Northampton, the parts of Holland in Lincoln and nearly all the isle of Ely in Cambridge, and comprises altogether about 400 000 acres. It was anciently covered with forest, was disforested by the Romans, and intersected by a Roman road, was afterwards brought into a state of high cultivation, was laid waste, in the 13th century, by repeated inundations of the sea, and settled into a mixture of morass and lake in some places 20 feet deep, and in some parts navigated by boats. Repeated attempts were made to drain it, especially in the reign of Henry VI and in the early part of the reign of Charles I, but without success Another and better attempt was begun in 1619 by the fourth Earl of Bedford A company was then formed to effect and maintain drainage, was incorporated in 1664, and has continued to act till the present day Great cuts, called the Old and New Bedford rivers, Bevil's river, Sam's cut Peakirk, South eau Sixteen Feet counter, South Holland drain, and North Level drain were formed, numerous small cuts also were made, old embankments were strengthened and improved, new embankments were thrown up, and extensive tracts of pasture and corn land were reclaimed

The Bedford Level was divided, in 1695, into the North, Middle, and South Levels The North has its drainage by the Nen, the Middle and the South, by the Ouse, and the three, in some great respects, have competing interests The first was put under separate management from the others in 1753, and the second also has recently been proposed to be put under separate management from the third One of the earliest and chief works of the corporation was a sluice across the Ouse at Denver, about 12 miles above Lynn This consists of folding doors set in strong brick work and so constructed as to be opened by the fresh water when the tide runs out and shut by the salt water when the tide comes in, and it was formed entirely with a view to drainage, and possessed the advantage that the banks above it did not require to be strong enough to resist the weight and surge of the sea water, or high enough to prevent an overflow by an unusually high tide But the sluice was soon supposed to be injurious to navigation, particularly by occasioning a choking of Lynn harbour, and it gave rise to sharp controversy It was subject, however, to a gradual undermining of its brick work by the action of the tides, it suddenly "blew up" in 1713, it lay in ruin till 1750, and it then, in spite of strong opposition, was rebuilt The numerous and extensive works on the Middle and South Levels, till this time and later, failed to make the drainage good, and were accompanied by increasing obstruction to the navigation of the Ouse An opinion gained ground that the bad state of both drainage and navigation arose from the width, shallowness, and circuitousness of the river's course from Eau Brink to Lynn, and would be corrected by the forming of a straight cut between these points Such a cut was authorized by an act of 1795, but not completed till 1821, and it answered the expectations of its promoters. Other works, connected with it, were authorized by subsequent acts, and have been found highly beneficial A chief of these bears the name of the Middle Level drain, is about 11 miles long, and perfectly straight, was completed in 1852, at a cost of upwards of £400,000, has its outfall into Eau Brink cut, about 3 miles above Lynn by a sluice which cost £30,000, and was formed entirely for drainage, without reference to navigation This drain, though made solely for the benefit of the Middle Level, traverses the fen territory of Marshland which lies between Wisbeach and Lynn, forms no part of the Bedford Level, and was reclaimed, about the beginning of the present century, from a state of swamp, into a state of fertile corn land. On the 4th of May 1862, the sluice "blew up," the drain was swept by the tide, and the banks, which had been constructed to resist only the fresh water from above, threatened to give way Vigorous attempts were made to form a dam across the drain, but they failed, and on the 12th, under the weight of a high spring tide, the west bank broke to the extent of about 210 feet, allowing the roaring surge to pour, with spreading flood, over the adjoining lands, and for the next eleven days, at every tide, the inundation continued to go on till nearly 10,000 acres became submerged The remedy required only the reconstruction of the sluice and the reparation of the breach in the bank, there being a complete system of drainage throughout the lands themselves, yet it was a work of great difficulty and much expense

BEDFORD RIVERS (NEW and OLD) two of the finest drains of the Bedford Level They go 21 miles north eastward, from Earith in Hunts to Salter's Lode near Downham in Norfolk, and run nearly parallel to each other, about a mile asunder The New river was cut about 1650, and is 100 feet wide, while the Old was cut earlier, and is 70 feet wide

BEDFORDSHIRE, or BEDS, an inland county, bounded on the NW by Northampton on the NE by Huntingdon, on the E by Cambridge on the SE and the S by Herts, and on the SW and W by Bucks Its length southward is 35 miles, its greatest breadth, 23½ miles, its circuit, about 145 miles, and its area 295 582 acres The general aspect is diversified and pleasing The surface in the centre, called the vale of Bedford, is prevailingly flat and luxuriant, in the SW, hilly, a portion of the Chilterns, commanding extensive views, on the flanks of the vale of Bedford and in the N, hillocky and rolling, and in other parts a mixture of swells and flats The chief rivers are the Ouse, the Ivel, the Hiz, the Ousel, and the Lea The prevailing rocks in the S up to Houghton Regis and Barton in the-Clay, are chalk, those of a belt about 7 miles broad, east north eastward from Eaton Bray and Leighton Buzzard are upper greensand and gault, those of a belt of similar but more irregular breadth immediately N of this, are lower greensand, those of the tracts further N and NE, including most of the vale of Bedford, are middle oolite, variously coral rag, calcareous grit, and Oxford clay and those of a small tract along the Ouse N of Bedford, and of another small tract continuous with this in the extreme NW are lower oolite, variously forest marble, Bradford clay and fuller's earth Chalk, under the name of clunch is burnt for lime freestone is quarried at Tattenhoe, a little ironstone is found, fuller's earth, of economical value, was formerly raised in Aspley Guise, and a few grains of gold were once obtained at Pulloxhill Mineral springs occur at Bedford, Bletsoe, Bromham, Clapham, Cranfield, Milton Ernest Odell, and Turvey The climate is mild and genial, the prevailing winds south westerly

The soil is very various and mixed, and occasionally di

versity of husbandry A very thin soil lies on most of the chalk hills, a mixed sand prevails from Woburn to the vicinity of Biggleswade, a rich gravelly loam lies along much of the Ouse and the Ivel, and a clayey soil, often very fertile, prevails throughout the vale of Bedford and the N About 84,000 acres are in tillage, some small tracts are in market gardens, about 168,000 acres are pasture and a considerable extent, but not so large as formerly, is woodland The system of agriculture was much improved through the exertions of the late Duke of Bedford. The average size of farms is less than 200 acres The chief crops raised are wheat, barley, turnips, oats, and beans Large quantities of vegetables, butter, and cheese, are sent to market The cattle are of a mixed breed, and estimated at 200,000 The produce in wool is reckoned at 4,250 packs Husbandry employs a larger proportion of the population than in almost any other tract of equal extent in England Manufactures are confined chiefly to pillow lace, straw plat, rush mats, and agricultural implements The Great Northern railway traverses the eastern district, northward from Hitchin, and sends off a branch to Potton The Midland railway, deflecting from the former at Hitchin, goes north westward, through the centre of the county, to ward Leicester The Northwestern railway impinges on the county at Leighton Buzzard, and sends off thence a branch eastward to Luton The Bletchley and Bedford railway strikes off from the Northwestern at Bletchley, goes north eastward to Bedford, and is prolonged thence to Cambridge The Bedford and Northampton railway was in progress, but not completed, at June 1869 The turnpike roads have an aggregate of about 240 miles and are under eleven trusts, and the revenue from them, as reported in 1859 was £5,163

Bedfordshire contains 122 parishes, parts of 3 other parishes, and 2 extra parochial tracts, and is divided into the borough of Bedford and the hundreds of Barford, Biggleswade Clifton, Flitt, Manshead Redbornestoke, Stodden, Willey, and Wixamtree The registration county differs from the electoral one includes 10 parishes of Bucks, and 1 parish and parts of 2 others of Herts, excludes 1 parish to Herts, 3 parishes to Northampton, and 7 parishes to Huntingdon, comprises 305,36[illegible] acres, and is divided into the districts of Bedford, Biggleswade, Ampthill, Woburn Leighton Buzzard, and Luton. The county town is Bedford, and the market towns are Bedford Dunstable Ampthill, Biggleswade, Harrold, Leighton Buzzard, Luton, Potton, Toddington, and Woburn The chief seats are Woburn Abbey Luton Hoo, Oakley House, Silsoe Park, Hawnes House, Ampthill House Old Warden Park, Battlesden Park, Chicksand Priory, Milton Bryant, Sutton Park, Aspley Guise, Bromham House, Bushmead Priory, Colworth House, the Hasels, Henlow Grange, Hexton Hall, Houghton Regis Hinwick House, Hovbury Park Ickwellbury, Moggerhanger, Southhill, Stockwood Stratton, Tempsford and Turvey Real property in 1815, £364,277, in 1843, £517,474, in 1860, £619 326

The county is governed by a lord lieutenant, a high sheriff, about 36 deputy lieutenants and 160 magistrates It is in the Home military district, and in the Norfolk judicial circuit The assizes and quarter sessions are held at Bedford The police force includes 82 men for the county and 13 for Bedford borough The only prison is the county jail at Bedford The crimes, in 186[illegible], were 116 in the county and 34 in the borough the persons apprehended, 109 in the county and 21 in the borough, the number of depredators or suspected persons at large, 699 in the county and 98 in the borough, the houses of bad character 114 in the county and 14 in the borough The county exclusive of the borough, sends two members to parliament, and the electors in 1868 were 4,845 It was formerly in the diocese of Lincoln, but is now in the diocese of Ely, and it constitutes an archdeaconry, comprising six deaneries The poor rates for the registration county, in 18[illegible] were £73,870 Marriages in 186[illegible] 1,168,—of which [illegible] were not according to the rites of the Established church, births, [illegible],—of which [illegible] were illegitimate deaths, 3,104,—of which 1,[illegible] were at ages under 5 years, and 67 at ages above 85 years The places of worship within the electoral county in 1851 were 133 of the Church of England, with 42,557 sittings, 19 of Independents, with 5,827 s, 55 of Baptists, with 14,902 s., 3 of Quakers, with 622 s, 3 of Moravians, with 810 s, 78 of Wesleyan Methodists, with 16,786 s, 18 of Primitive Methodists, with 2,490 s, 1 of Brethren, with 500 s, 11 of isolated congregations, with 3,021 s 1 of the Catholic and Apostolic church, with 80 s, 3 of Latter Day Saints, with 240 s, 1 of Roman Catholics, with 21 s, and 1 of Jews, with 20 s The schools were 120 public day schools, with 9,863 scholars, 157 private day schools, with 3,140 s., 243 Sunday schools, with 24,753 s, and 22 evening schools for adults, with 652 s Pop in 1801, 63,393, in 1821 84,052, in 1841, 107,936 in 1861, 135 287 Inhabited houses, 27,422, uninhabited, 753, building, 139

The territory now forming Bedfordshire was inhabited, in the primitive times, by the tribe called Cassii. It became part of the Roman Britannia Superior afterwards part of the Britannia Prima, afterwards, in 310, part of the Flavia Cæsariensis It belonged, in the time of the heptarchy, to the kingdom of Mercia and became subject, in 827, to the Saxons And it first took the name of Bedford in the reign of Alfred the Great Icknield street crosses its southern extremity eastward over the chalk hills Watling street crosses its south western extremity north westward through Dunstable and near Battlesden A Roman road coming in from Baldock, traverses the eastern extremity to Potton. British, Roman, Saxon, and Danish remains occur near Dunstable, near Sandy, near Hexton at the Maiden Bower, at Tottenhoe, Arlesby, Biggleswade, Bradford, and other places Earth works, ruins, or other vestiges of ancient castles may be seen at Bedford, Risinghoe, Cainhoe, Bletsoe, Ridgmont, Meppershall Puddington, and Thurleigh An old cross stands at Leighton Buzzard, a famous priory stood at Dunstable, 14 other monastic houses stood in other places, and some of the old existing churches, particularly those of Luton, Elstow, Eaton Bray, Felmersham, and Puddington exhibit interesting features of ancient architecture

BEDFORD STREET See BRIGHTON

BEDGRALOE, a hamlet in Wales parish, W R Yorkshire 2 miles SSE of Rotherham

BEDGWYN See BEDWYN (GREAT)

BEDHAMPTON, a village and a parish in Havant district, Hants The village stands on Langston harbour adjacent to the South Coast railway, 1 mile W of Havant, and it has a post office under Havant, commands a charming sea view, and is noted for its fine springs The parish comprises 2,416 acres of land and 190 of water Real property, £4,182 Pop, 576 Houses, 11[illegible] The property is divided among a few The manor once belonged to a dowager Countess of Kent, who took a nun's vow in grief for the death of her husband, afterwards married Sir Eustace Dabrieschescourt founded a chantry in penance for her marriage, and died here in 1411 The living is a rectory in the diocese of Winchester Value, £323 * Patron E Daman, Esq The church is a small old, substantial edifice with painted steeple

BEDHURST, a tything in Compton Abbas parish, Dorset, 8 miles NNW of Dorchester

BEDICANFORD See BEDFORD

BEDINGFIELD, a parish in Hoxne district, Suffolk, 4 miles SSE of Eye r station, and 5[illegible] N by E of Debenham Post town, Thrandon, under Eye Acres, 1,753. Real property, £2 973 Pop, 321 Houses, 6[illegible] The property is divided among a few Bedingfield Hall is the seat of J J Bedingfield Esq The living is a rectory in the diocese of Norwich Value, £300 Patron, J J Bedingfield Esq The church is good

BEDINGHAM, a parish in Loddon district, Norfolk, 4 miles NW of Bungay r station Post town, Topcroft under Bungay Acres, 1,[illegible]49 Real property, £[illegible],171. Pop, 25[illegible] Houses, [illegible] The property is divided among a few Bedingham Hall is a chief residence The living is a vicarage in the diocese of Norwich Value £15[illegible] Patron the Impropriators The church is good

BEDLINGTON, a township, a parish, and a sub district, in the district of Morpeth, Northumberland The township lies on the river Blythe and on the Morpeth and Tynemouth railway, 5 miles SE of Morpeth, it includes an irregularly built village, chiefly of one spacious street, about a mile long, commanding a fine seaward view, and it has a station on the railway, and a post-office‡ under Morpeth, and is a seat of petty sessions. The monks of Durham, at the Conquest, when fleeing to Lindisfarne with the remains of St Cuthbert, rested a night here The parish includes also the townships of North Blyth, Chambois, Choppington, Netherton, and East and West Sleakburn, and, prior to October 1844, it formed part of the county of Durham Acres, 9,011, of which 523 are water Real property, £45,326, of which £29,937 are in mines Pop in 1841, 3 155, in 1861, 8 328 Houses, 1,490 The property is not much divided The manor belonged anciently to the Crown and passed to the Bishops of Durham The inhabitants are employed chiefly in the coal-trade, in quarrying works, in iron works and in chain and nail making The living is a vicarage in the diocese of Durham Value, £600 * Patrons, the Dean and Chapter of Durham The church was repaired and enlarged in 1818. The vicarages of Chambois and Choppington are separate charges. There are chapels for Presbyterians, Baptists, Wesleyans, and Primitive Methodists There is also a mechanics' institution The Rev J Woodmas, the expositor of Chrysostom, was vicar from 1696 to 1710 —The sub district comprises three parishes, two parochial chapelries, parts of three other parishes, and part of another parochial chapelry Acres, 50,622 Pop., 15,577 Houses, 2,822.

BEDLINGTONSHIRE, a hundred in Northumberland, conterminate with Bedlington parish

BEDMINSTER, a suburban town, a parish, a sub district, and a district in Somerset. The town is a southern suburb of Bristol, separated from the city by the river Avon, connected with it by two bridges, included within the borough, and traversed, from within a furlong of the terminus, by the Bristol and Exeter railway It comprises Redcliffe Crescent, a considerable number of streets, and some outskirts, has a receiving post office‡ of Bristol in North Street, and contains Bristol jail, a dispensary, four churches, five dissenting chapels, a Roman Catholic chapel, and remains of an hospital One of the churches is partly an ancient building, in a mixed style of architecture, another is a spacious pointed modern edifice, with a tower, erected about 1835, at a cost of £8,673, another is a large middle pointed edifice, of nave, aisles, and polygonal apsidal chancel, with tower and spire, erected in 1861, at a cost of £7,636, and one of the dissenting chapels, belonging to the Independents, is a large and handsome edifice, with a Grecian front The town is a polling place and a seat of petty sessions Pop in 1851 17,698 —The parish includes also the tythings of Bishport and Knowle Acres, 4,161 Real property, £58,280, of which £3,102 are in mines. Pop in 1841 17,862,—of whom 17,402 were within the borough of Bristol, in 1861, 22,346 Houses, 3,856 Coal is extensively worked Veins of strontian occur in the vale of the Avon The living is a vicarage in the diocese of Gloucester and Bristol Value, £450 Patron, the Bishop of Gloucester and Bristol The p. curacy of St Luke, and the vicarages of St Paul and St Peter are separate benefices, the first in the patronage of Trustees the second and the third in the patronage of the Bishop of Gloucester and Bristol. Value of St Luke, £400, of St Paul, £300,* of St. Peter, £300 * —The sub district is conterminate with the parish —The district comprehends also the sub district of Long Ashton, containing the parishes of Long Ashton, Dundry, Winford, Barrow Gurney, Backwell, Flax Bourton, and Wraxall, the sub district of Yatton, containing the parishes of Yatton, Tickenham, Nailsea, Chelvey Brockley, Kingston Seymour, Kenn, and Clevedon, and the sub district of St George, containing the parishes of Walton in Gordano, Weston in Gordano, Easton in Gordano, Clapton, Portishead, Portbury, and Abbots Leigh Acres, 57,068 Poor rates in 1866, £22,487 Pop in 1861, 41,257 Houses, 7,454 Marriages in 1866, 348, births, 1,794,—of which 61 were illegitimate, deaths, 966,—of which 424 were at ages under 5 years, and 36 at ages above 85 years Marriages in the ten years 1851-60, 2,825, births, 13,749, deaths, 7 875 The places of worship in 1851 were 28 of the Church of England with 10 505 sittings, 14 of Independents with 2,635 s 5 of Baptists, with 600 s. 2 of Quakers, with 290 s, 8 of Wesleyan Methodists, with 3,783 s, 1 of the Wesleyan Association, with 200 s, 3 of Wesleyan Reformers, with 942 s. 2 of Bible Christians, with 340 s, and 2 undefined, with 225 s The schools were 33 public day schools with 3,086 scholars 63 private day schools, with 1,057 s, and 36 Sunday schools, with 2,589 s The workhouse is in Long Ashton

BEDMONT, a locality 3 miles SW of St Albans, Herts It has a post office under Hemel-Hempstead.

BEDNALL See ACTON-TRUSSELL.

BEDS See BEDFORDSHIRE

BEDSTONE, a parish in the district of Knighton and county of Salop, on a tributary of the river Teme, and on the Craven Arms and Knighton railway, between Hopton Heath and Bucknell r stations, 4½ miles NE by E of Knighton Post town, Bucknell, under Aston on Clun Shropshire Acres, 776 Rated property, £739 Pop, 164 Houses, 26 The property is all in one estate The living is a rectory in the diocese of Hereford Value, £230 * Patron, E Rogers, Esq The church is good

BEDWARDINE-ST JOHN, a parish in the district and county of Worcester, on the river Severn, partly within the borough of Worcester It includes a western suburb of Worcester, the places called Boughton and Wick Episcopi or Upper and Lower Wick, and the reputedly extra parochial tract of Henwick Acres, 3,775 Real property, £19,548 Pop, 2,974 Houses, 653 The property is not much divided The living is a vicarage in the diocese of Worcester Value, £635 Patrons, the Dean and Chapter of Worcester The church is partly Norman and good. A school has an endowed income of £36, and other charities £60

BEDWARDINE ST MICHAEL a parish in the district and county of Worcester, adjacent to Bedwardine St. John, and within Worcester city Acres, 12 Real property, £5,359 Pop, 570 Houses, 100 The living is a rectory in the diocese of Worcester Value, £90 Patrons, the Dean and Chapter of Worcester The church was recently rebuilt. Charities, £113

BEDWAS, a village and two hamlets in Newport district, Monmouth, and a parish partly also in Cardiff district, Glamorgan The village stands near the Rhymney railway 2 miles NNE of Caerphilly, and has a r station The hamlets lie around the village, bear the names of Lower and Upper Bedwas, and jointly comprise 4,207 acres. Pop. of L. B, 422 Houses, 88 Pop of U B, 597 Houses, 115 The parish includes also the Glamorgan hamlet of Van Post town, Caerphilly, under Cardiff Acres, 5,032 Real property, exclusive of Van, £3,808 Pop, 1,081 Houses, 214 The property is much subdivided The living is a rectory united with the vicarage of Ruddry in the diocese of Llandaff Value, £380 * Patron, the Bishop of Llandaff The church is good.

BEDWELL PARK the seat of Sir Culling Eardley, Bart 3 miles ESE of Hatfield, Herts.

BEDWELTY, or BEDWELTY, a village, a sub district, and a parish in Abergavenny district Monmouth The village stands between the Rhymney and the Sirhowey rivers, near the Rhymney railway, not far from Bargoed station, 7½ miles W by S of Pontypool, it has a post-office under Newport Monmouth, and fairs on 15 April, 3 July, and 7 Oct, and is a polling place.—The sub district bears the name of Rock Bedwelty, and is conterminate with Ishlawrcoed hamlet Pop, 2,862 Houses, 584 —The parish includes also Tredegar sub-district, comprising the hamlets of Uchlawrcoed and Manmoel, extends many miles along the Rhymney and Sirhowey rivers and the Rhymney and Western Valleys railways, and contains the populous iron work towns of

Tredegar, Ebbwvale, and Sirhowey Acres, 16,210 Real property, £132,645,—of which £13,674 are in mines and £56,500 are in iron works. Pop in 1801, 1,434, in 1831 10,637, in 1861, 31,510 Houses, 5,724 The property is much subdivided. Very extensive coal works and iron works are carried on, and have, within the present century, drawn enormous increase of population An old document, written when there was but one place of worship in the parish, records that one sermon in the month at it was allowed by the bishop on application of the inhabitants The living is a vicarage in the diocese of Llandaff Value, £150 * Patron, the Bishop of Llandaff The church is a plain old building, repaired in 1809 The chapelries of Tredegar and Rhymney are separate benefices and there are chapels for Independents and Calvinistic Methodists Charities, £41

BEDWIN, or BEDWYN (GREAT), a small old town and a parish in the district of Hungerford and county of Wilts. The town stands on the Kennet and Avon canal adjacent to the Hungerford and Devizes railway, near Wans Dyke 5 miles SW of Hungerford, and has a station on the railway It is supposed to have been the Leucomagus of the Romans, and it was the Bedgwyn or Bedewind of the Saxons. It was the residence of Cissa, the Saxon viceroy of Wilts and Berks and the scene in 675 of a desperate battle between the forces of Wessex and those of Mercia. It enjoyed the privileges of a city under the Saxons, and retained them after the Conquest It was a borough by prescription, and sent two members to parliament from the time of Edward I till disfranchised by the act of 1832. It has an old fashioned market house, which has ceased to be used, an ancient church, and a dissenting chapel The church is cruciform, mixedly Norman and English, and built of flint, was restored in 1854, has a fine central tower, shows curious sculpturings on its round pillars and rich Norman decorations on its obtusely pointed arches, and contains interesting monuments of the Stokes and the Seymours The town has a post office under Hungerford and fairs on 23 April and 26 July Dr Willis, a physician of the 17th century who founded a philosophical society at Oxford, the germ of the Royal Society of London was a native —The parish includes also the tythings of Crofton and Wolfhall, East and West Grafton Martin, Wexcombe, and Wilton Acres, 10,420 Real property, £10,955 Pop 2,763 Houses 435 The property is divided among a few The manor belonged once to the Earl of Clare, and belongs now to the Marquis of Ailesbury Castle Hill, about a mile S of the town, takes name from an ancient entrenchment in which large quantities of Roman bricks and tiles have been found Chisbury, on Wans Dyke, 1½ mile N by E of the town, is a very fine Saxon camp of 15 acres with rampart 45 feet high, and encloses an ancient chapel, in decorated English, now used as a barn. The living is a vicarage in the diocese of Salisbury, and, till 1864, was united with another charge Value £212 Patron, the Marquis of Ailesbury The vicarages of East Grafton and Savernake Forest are separate benefices There is a Wesleyan chapel at Wilton Charities, £37

BEDWIN, or BEDWYN (LITTLE) a parish in the district of Hungerford and county of Wilts on the Kennet and Avon canal and on the Hungerford and Devizes railway near Wans Dyke 1½ mile NE of Bedwin r station, and 3½ SW by S of Hungerford It includes the hamlet of Chisbury and has a post office under Hungerford Acres 3,233 Real property £3,796 Pop, 496 Houses, 117 The property is not much divided The living is a vicarage in the diocese of Salisbury Value, £250 * Patron, the Marquis of Ailesbury The church is ancient partly Norman and built of flint consists of nave, aisles, and chancel, with a tower, and contains the tomb of a Hungerford

BEDWORTH a town and a parish in Foleshill district Warwick The town stands adjacent to the Coventry canal and the Coventry and Nuneaton railway, 3½ miles S of Nuneaton, and has a station on the railway, a post office under Nuneaton, and two chief inns. It carries on a manufacture of gauze ribbons, and a large trade in coals, lime, and bricks, and has a fair on Whit Wednesday Pop, 3,963 Houses, 888.—The parish comprises 2,157 acres Real property, £15,345, of which £2,700 are in mines Pop, 5,656 Houses, 1,239 The property is much subdivided The living is a rectory in the diocese of Worcester Value, £562 * Patron the Lord of the Manor The church is a modern edifice with square embattled tower, and was enlarged in 1850 There are three dissenting chapels, two free schools, and very extensive alms houses, the last in the form of three sides of a cloistered quadrangle, in later Gothic, built in 1840, at a cost of £8,500 The alms houses have £1,176 of income, and other charities £29

BEDWYN See BEDWIN

BEEBY, a parish in Barrow upon-Soar district, Leicester, on an affluent of the river Wreak, 4 miles SE of Syston r station, and 5½ NE of Leicester Post town, Hungarton, under Leicester Acres, 1,020 Real property, £2,620 Pop, 119 Houses, 26 The property is divided among a few Beeby House is a chief residence. The living is a rectory in the diocese of Peterborough Value, £282 * Patron, Earl Shaftesbury The church is good.

BEECH, a township in the parishes of Stone and Swinnerton, Stafford, 4½ miles NW of Stone Pop, 120

BEECHAMWELL a parish in Swaffham district, Norfolk, 4½ miles S of Narborough r station, and 5 SW of Swaffham It has a post office under Swaffham Acres, 3,730 Real property, £2,289 Pop., 356 Houses, 66 The property is divided among a few Beechamwell Lodge and Beechamwell Warren are chief residences. There are two livings, Beechamwell All Saints and Beechamwell St John and St Mary, both rectories, in the diocese of Norwich B. All Saints is united to the rectory of Shingham, and has no church B St John and St. Mary is a separate benefice Value, £191 * Patron, J Fielden, Esq The church is good, and has a fine tower

BEECHBURN, a station on the Stockton and Redcar railway, ¾ of a mile N of Crook in Durham Brancepeth Park and Mendon Hill, 845 feet high, are in its neighbourhood

BEECHEN CLIFF See BATH

BEECH HILL, a chapelry in Stratfieldsaye parish Berks, 6 miles S by W of Reading It has a post office under Reading Acres, 915 Real property, £1,455 Pop., 260 The chapelry was constituted in 1857 The living is a vicarage in the diocese of Oxford Value, £150 Patron, Mrs Forbes There is a Baptist chapel

BEECHING STOKE a parish in Devizes district, Wilts, on the river Avon, 2 miles S of the Kennet and Avon canal, and 6 ESE of Devizes r station It has a post office under Devizes Acres, 830 Real property, £1,893 Pop, 180 Houses, 44 The property is divided among four The living is a rectory in the diocese of Salisbury Value, £293 * Patron G W Heneage, Esq The church is tolerable

BEECHWOOD, a village 4½ miles WSW of Coventry, in Warwick, near a tunnel of its own name, 180 feet long, on the Northwestern railway

BEEDING See BEEDING (UPPER)

BEEDING (LOWER), a parochial chapelry in Horsham district, Sussex, in St Leonard's forest, on the Mid Sussex railway, near Faygate station, 5 miles ENE of Horsham It has a post office under Horsham Acres 9,675 Real property £5,166 Pop, 1,149 Houses, 172 There are several good residences Many cottages, occupied by labourers employed in the reclamation of waste land, have been erected since 1841 The lands of Bewbush and Holmbush belong ecclesiastically to Upper Beeding A large brown pottery manufactory is near Holmbush The living is a vicarage, united with the p curacy of Pollard Oak in the dio of Chichester Value, £135 * Patron, W F Hubbard, Esq The church was built in 1839, and enlarged in 1862 There are a chapel of ease and a national school

BEEDING (UPPER) a parish in Steyning district Sussex on the river Adur, near Bramber r station, and 1½ mile E of Steyning It has a post office, of the name of Beeding, under Hurstperpoint Acres 3,847 Real property, £5,356 Pop, 553 Houses, 118 The property is subdivided A small Benedictine priory was founded here about 1075, belonged to the alien monastery of Salmur, and passed to Magdalene college, Oxford. The living is a vicarage in the diocese of Chichester Value, £112 Patron, Magdalene college, Oxford. The church is good, and there is a national school

BEEDON, or BUDON, a parish in Wantage district, Berks, 2½ miles S of East Ilsley, and 6½ N by E of Newbury r station It includes the tything of Stanmore, and has a post office of the name of Beedon Hill, under Newbury Acres, 2,004 Real property, £2,251 Pop, 317 Houses, 66 The property is divided among a few The living is a vicarage in the diocese of Oxford Value, £126. Patron, Sir J Reade, Bart. The church is good

BEEFORD, a township in the district of Driffield, and a parish in the districts of Driffield, Skirlaugh, and Bridlington, E R Yorkshire. The township lies on the Beverley and Barmston drain, 4½ miles SSE of Lowthorpe r station, and 7 ESE of Great Driffield, and has a post office‡ under Hull Acres, 3,470 Real property, £5,021 Pop., 808 Houses, 183 The parish includes also the townships of Dunnington and Lissett Acres, 5,461 Real property, inclusive of Little Kelk, £8,452 Pop., 1,006 Houses, 221 The property is much subdivided The living is a rectory, united with the p. curacy of Lissett, in the diocese of York. Value, £779 * Patron, the Archbishop of York The church is perpendicular English, with a fine tower, and has an oaken screen, ancient stalls, and a brass of 1472 There are an Independent chapel, and two Methodist chapels

BEE HILL, an isolated eminence on the southern border of Rutland, in the vicinity of Lyddington It has a roundish outline, stands detached from hills to the N of it, and commands a fine view

BEELAH (THE) See BEILEAU (THE)

BEELEIGH, a hamlet in the parish of St. Peter in Maldon, Essex, 1 mile W of Maldon A Premonstratensian abbey was founded here, in 1180, by Robert de Mantell, and given, at the dissolution, to Sir John Gate. Bourchier, Earl of Essex, and his wife were buried in the church, and this, measuring 36 feet by 18, and having groined arches, still stands, and is used as a farm office.

BEELEY, a township chapelry in Bakewell parish, Derby, on the river Derwent, adjacent to Chatsworth Park, 1¾ mile N of Rowsley r station, and 3½ E by S of Bakewell Post town, Rowsley, under Bakewell Acres, 3,250 Real property, £1,134 Pop, 420 Houses, 74 The property is divided among a few Millstone grit is quarried on Beeley moor The living is a p curacy in the diocese of Lichfield Value, £98 Patron, the Duke of Devonshire. The church is tolerable Charities, £7

BEELSBY, a parish in Caistor district, Lincoln, 5 miles E of Caistor, and 6½ W of Waltham r station Post town, Caistor Acres, 2,189 Real property, £3,692 Pop, 181 Houses, 33. The property is divided among a few The living is a rectory in the diocese of Lincoln Value £450 Patron, the Collegiate Church of Southwell The church is good

BEENHAM, or BEENHAM-VALLENCE, a parish in Bradfield district, Berks, adjacent to the Kennet and Avon canal and to the Berks and Hants railway, 1¼ mile N of Aldermaston station, and 8½ WSW of Reading It has a post office, of the name of Beenham, under Reading Acres, 1,890 Real property, £2,548 Pop, 505 Houses, 105 The property is much subdivided Beenham House and Beenham Lodge are chief residences The living is a vicarage in the diocese of Oxford Value, £250 * Patron, Mrs Bushnell. The church was chiefly rebuilt in 1860 There are a Primitive Methodist chapel and a national school Stackhouse, the author of the 'History of the Bible,' was vicar

BEEN HILL See SUTTON Surrey

BEER, a village and a tything in Seaton parish, Devon The village stands on the coast, in a romantic cove, 1½ mile SW of Axmouth, has a post-office under Axminster, carries on fishing and lace making, and was noted, in former days, for smuggling It was the birthplace of the notorious Jack Rattenbury, sometimes called the Rob Roy of England, and it produced the wedding dress of Queen Victoria in 1839 The cove around it is a fine subject for the pencil Beer Head, projecting on the west, is crowned by two natural towers, and Beer quarry, about a mile inland, is a labyrinth of excavations, about ¼ of a mile long, and about 300 feet below the surface of the ground The tything includes the village, and forms a curacy with the vicarage of Seaton in the diocese of Exeter Pop, 1,157 Houses, 260 The church consists of nave, chancel, and aisles There are an Independent chapel, and charities £210.

BEER, a tything in High Ham parish, Somerset, 1 mile N of Langport Pop., 45

BEER, in CANNINGTON, Somerset See EDSTOCK and BEER

BEER ALSTON, a small ancient town, formerly a borough, in Beer Ferris parish, Devon It stands on an eminence overlooking the rivers Tamar and Tavy 5 miles NW of Bickleigh r station, and 6 S by W of Tavistock It has a post office under Tavistock, a chapel of ease, and chapels for dissenters, and it long had a weekly market It was given by William the Conqueror to a branch of the Alençon family, whence it took the name of Beer Alençon, corrupted into Beer Alston, and it passed to successively the Ferrers, the Champernouns, the Blounts, the Maynards, and the Edgcumbes It was a borough by prescription, and it sent two members to parliament from the time of Elizabeth till disfranchised by the act of 1832 Many of its inhabitants are employed in neighbouring lead and silver mines. Pop., about 1 600

BEER CHARTER, a hamlet in Braunton parish, Devon

BEER CROCOMBE, a parish in Langford district, Somerset, on Chard canal, 4½ miles NNW of Ilminster, and 6 SSE of Durston r station. Post town, Isle Abbots, under Taunton Acres, 871 Real property, £1,[illegible]34 Pop, 175 Houses 32 The property is divided among a few The living is a rectory in the diocese of Bath and Wells Value, £195 Patron, the Earl of Egremont. The church is good

BEER FERRIS, BEER FERRARS, or BEER TOWN, a parish in Tavistock district, Devon, between the rivers Tamar and Tavy upwards from their confluence, 4 miles W of Bickleigh r station, and 7 N by W of Plymouth It contains the town of Beer Alston and the village of Beer Town, the former of which has a post office under Tavistock Acres, 6,833, of which 950 are water Real property, £9,981 Pop, 2,847 Houses, 581 The property is subdivided A great part belongs to the Earl of Mount Edgcumbe, and the manor of Ley was long held by a family of its own name, one of whom was created Earl of Marlborough, but belongs now to Sir T Drake, Bart Much of the surface is picturesque, and many spots command fine prospects Silver and lead mines are worked and several kinds of rare minerals are found The living is a rectory in the diocese of Exeter Value, £700.* Patron, the Earl of Mount Edgcumbe. The church is decorated and perpendicular English, and very picturesque, consists of nave, aisle, chancel, and transepts, and contains monuments of the Ferrers and the Champernouns, and one to Lieutenant Major Bayley, who fell at the storming of Sebastopol There is a chapel of ease at High Cross, Beer Alston, and there are chapels for Independents, Wesleyans, U Free Methodists, and Bible Christians. Charities, £66 Stothart, the artist and antiquary, was killed at Beer Ferris.

BEER HACKETT, a parish in Sherborne district, Dorset on the Dorchester and Yeovil railway, near Yetminster station, 5 miles SE by S of Yeovil It includes the hamlet of Knighton, and its post town is Yetminster, under Sherborne Acres, 903 Rated property, £1,021 Pop, 96 Houses, 1[illegible] The property is much subdivided. The living is a rectory in the diocese of Salisbury Value, £201 Patrons, Sir J Munden and W Helyar, Esq The church needs repair

BEERHALL See AXMINSTER.

BEER REGIS See BERE REGIS

BEER-TOWN See BERE REGIS

BEES (ST), a small town, a township, and a sub district, in the district of Whitehaven, and a parish in the districts of Whitehaven and Bootle, Cumberland. The town stands on the coast, adjacent to the Whitehaven and Furness railway, 4 miles S of Whitehaven Its site is a narrow vale, watered by a streamlet, near the shore It has a station on the railway, a post office‡ under Whitehaven, and two hotels. It sprang from a religious house, founded about the year 650 by St Bega an Irish female Culdee. Her institution was destroyed by the Danes, and a Benedictine abbey was erected on the site of it, in the time of Henry I, by William des Meschines The abbey property was given at the dissolution, to Sir Thomas Chaloner, passed to the Wybergs and the Lowthers, and now belongs to the Earl of Lonsdale The church, retaining much of its original masonry, in combination with reconstructions at various periods till 1810, still stands It is a cruciform pile of red freestone, mixedly late Saxon, Norman, early and late English, with a low square central tower, and has some fine carvings. The nave and transept are used as the parish church, and the choir was fitted up as a lecture hall for the clerical college, established in 1817, for students not going to Oxford or Cambridge. A new lecture room was built in 1863. A grammar school, near the church, was founded in 1587 by Archbishop Grindal, and has an endowed income of £125, and a fellowship and scholarships at Oxford and Cambridge Other charities, £46 The poet Wordsworth, pointing to the origin of the town, and alluding doubtless more to the present than to the prior character of its church, says,—

"When Bega's voice, that instrument of love,
Was glorified and took its place above
The silent stars, among the angelic quire,
Her chantry blazed with sacrilegious fire,
And perished utterly but her good deeds
Had sown the spot that witnessed them with seeds
Which lay in earth expectant, till a breeze
With quickening impulse answered their mute pleas,
And lo! a statelier pile,—the Abbey of St Bees!"

The township includes the town, and comprises 1,758 acres of land and 187 of water Real property, £4,829 Pop, 1 031 Houses, 206 —The sub district includes also the townships of Preston Quarter, Sandwith, Rottington and Lowside Quarter, and the chapelry of Hensingham Acres, 10,407 Pop, 8,681 Houses, 1,659 —The parish includes likewise the town, township, or sub district of Whitehaven, the townships of Ennerdale, Kinniside, Weddicar, and Wasdale Head, and the chapelries of Nether Wasdale and Eskdale. Acres, 71,332, of which 2,972 are water Real property, £151,370,—of which £25 015 are in mines, and £22,358 are in railways. Pop in 1841, 19,687 in 1861, 23 901 Houses, 4,660 The surface is very diversified, and contains much of the admired scenery of the Lake country Cill Foot and Linethwaite mansions are in the vicinity of the town, and a number of other fine residences are in other parts St Bees Head, a large bold promontory, overhangs the Irish sea 2½ miles NW of the town, forms the most westerly ground of Cumberland, and is surmounted by a lighthouse, showing a fixed light 333 feet high, visible at the distance of 23 miles Coal, lime, and freestone are extensively worked and lead and iron ores are found Several vestiges of ancient works occur along the coast, appearing to be remains of fortifications raised by the Romans against incursions of the Irish and the Scotch The living is a p curacy in the diocese of Carlisle Value, £163.* Patron the Earl of Lonsdale The chapelries of Ennerdale, Hensingham Loweswater, Eskdale, Wasdale Head and Nether Wasdale and the four chapelries of Whitehaven, are separate benefices There are dissenting chapels of ten denominations See WHITEHAVEN

BEESANDS a fishing village in Stokenham parish, 2½ miles from Stokenham village, Devon

BEESBY See HAWERBY

BEESBY IN-THE MARSH, a parish in Louth district, Lincoln, 3 miles NNE of Alford r station Post town, Alford Acres, 1,180 Real property, £1,822 Pop, 174 Houses, 34 The property is divided among a few The living is a rectory in the diocese of Lincoln. Value, £207 Patron, Rev H P Mason The church is good

BEESON, a hamlet in Stokenham parish, Devon

BEESTHORPE a hamlet in Caunton parish, Notts, 5½ miles NW of Newark Pop, 43 Beesthorpe Hall here is a mansion of the time of James I

BEESTON, a hamlet in the parishes of Sandy and Northill, Beds, 2½ miles NNW of Biggleswade Pop of the Sandy portion, 364 Houses, 81 Pop of the Northill portion, inclusive of Hatch, 252 Houses, 55

BEESTON, a township in Bunbury parish, Cheshire, on the Crewe and Chester railway, 10¾ miles SE by E of Chester It has a r station, a Wesleyan chapel of 1836, and a Prim Methodist chapel Acres, 1,957 Real property, £2,786 Pop., 355 Houses 70 Beeston Castle here crowns an isolated sandstone rock, 366 feet high, and commands a charming view of the vale of Cheshire, and over the Mersey to Liverpool The castle was built, as a fortress, in 1228, by Ranulph de Blundeville, became a royal garrison between Henry III and his barons, was dismantled, in 1645 by order of parliament, and is now an extensive and picturesque ruin

BEESTON, a parish in Basford district, Notts, on the Midland railway, adjacent to the river Trent, 3¼ miles SW of Nottingham It contains the hamlet of Beeston Rylands and has a station on the railway and a post-office‡ under Nottingham. Acres, 1,440 Real property, £11,307 Pop, 3,195 Houses, 698 The property is subdivided There are a large silk mill, and considerable manufacture of lace and hosiery A canal, called the Beeston cut, goes off here from the river Trent to Nottingham The living is a vicarage in the diocese of Lincoln Value, £300 * Patron, the Duke of Devonshire The church is a handsome structure of 1844, conjoined to the chancel of an old previous pile A handsome parsonage was built in 1860 There are two Baptist chapels, two Methodist chapels, a public library, a national school, and charities £24

BEESTON, a township chapelry in Leeds parish, W R Yorkshire, on the Leeds and West Riding railway, within the borough of Leeds, 2¼ miles SSW of the town of Leeds It has a station on the railway, and a post office under Leeds. Acres, 1,535 Real property, £8,607,—of which £2,100 are in mines Pop, 2 547 Houses, 537 Extensive coal mines here were worked from the time of Charles II, but have become partly exhausted There are woollen and iron manufactures The living is a p curacy in the diocese of Ripon Value, £189 * Patron, the Vicar of Leeds The church is very old and there are two Methodist chapels.

BEESTON, or BEESTON NEXT LITCHAM, a parish in Mitford district, Norfolk, 2 miles N of Fransham r station, and 6¼ NE of Swaffham It includes Little Bittering, and its post town is Great Dunham, under Swaffham Acres, 2 075 Real property £4 491 Pop 615 Houses, 140 The property is much subdivided Beeston Hall is the seat of the Rev C B Barnwell The living is a rectory in the diocese of Norwich Value, £450 * Patron, the Rev C B Barnwell The church is very good, and has a conspicuous tower and spire. Charities, £51

BEESTON REGIS, a parish in Erpingham district, Norfolk, on the coast 3 miles WNW of Cromer, and 18 N by N of Walsingham r station Post town, Cromer, under Norwich Acres 957, of which 135 are water Real property, £839 Pop, 196. Houses, 46 Beeston Hall is the chief residence Some remains exist of a small Augustinian priory, founded in the 13th century by Lady Margery de Cressy The living is a rectory in the diocese of Norwich Value, £133. Patron, the Duchy of Lancaster The church is decorated English, with square embattled tower and has a painted rood screen

BEESTON RYELANDS See BEESTON, Notts.

BEESTON ST ANDREW, a parish in St Faith district, Norfolk, 4½ miles NNE of Norwich r station Post town, Rackheath, under Norwich Acres, 626 Real property, £1,201 Pop, 37 Houses, 5 The living is a rectory in the diocese of Norwich Value, £190 Patron, the Rev H Baufather The church is in ruins

BEESTON ST LAWRENCE, a parish in Tunstead district, Norfolk, 3½ miles ENE of Coltishall, and 10½ NE of Norwich r station Post town, Coltishall under Norwich Acres, 519 Real property, £1,020 Pop, 50 Houses, 7 The property is divided between two Beeston Hall is the seat of Sir J H Preston, Bart. The living is a rectory in the diocese of Norwich Value, £200 Patron, Sir J H Preston, Bart. The church is good, has a round tower, and contains some handsome monuments of the Prestons There is a Wesleyan chapel

BEETHA, or BELO (THE), a stream of Westmoreland It issues from Lily Farm, 5 miles E of Kendal, and runs 14 miles south westward, past Bridgend, End Moor, and Beetham, to the river Kent, ¾ of a mile W of Milnthorpe It makes a fall at Beetha mill

BEETHAM, a township and a parish in Kendal district, Westmoreland The township lies on the river Beetha, 1½ mile S of Milnthorpe Acres, 7 101, of which 1,885 are water Real property, with Tarleton, £6,095 Pop, 776 Houses, 160 The parish extends down both sides of the river Kent to Morecambe bay, includes the townships of Tarleton, Haverbrack, Witherslack, and Methop with Ulpha, is traversed by the Lancaster and Carlisle and the Lancaster and Ulverston railways, and contains the village of Arnside, with a station on the latter railway and a post office under Milnthorpe Acres, 17,449, of which 4,177 are water Real property, £11,449 Pop, 1,510 Houses, 289 The property is much subdivided. The surface is diversified, hilly, and picturesque Slate and limestone occur, and paper-making is carried on Beetham Hall, formerly the seat of the Betham family, now the property of the Earl of Derby, was a fine castellated mansion, but is now in ruins Cappleside House also was a great mansion, with 117 feet of frontage, but is likewise in ruins The towers of Arnside and Helslack, supposed to have been erected to guard the bay of Morecambe, make a conspicuous figure, but are also in ruins The living is a vicarage in the diocese of Carlisle. Value £159 * Patron, the Duchy of Lancaster The church is a neat edifice, and contains monuments of the Betham and Wilson families, and a manuscript history of the parish, written by the vicar Hutton The p curacy of Witherslack is a separate benefice A grammar school founded by Dean Barwick, has an endowed income of about £40, and other charities have about £472

BEETLEY, a parish in Mitford district, Norfolk 2 miles WSW of Elmham r station, and 4 N by W of East Derehnm Post town, Elmham, under Thetford Acres, 1 770 Real property, £2,570 Pop, 363 Houses, 82 The property is divided among a few The living is a rectory, annexed to the rectory of East Bilney, in the diocese of Norwich The church is good

BEFCOTE, a hamlet in Gnosall parish, Staffordshire, 5½ miles WSW of Stafford

BEGBROOKE, a parish in Woodstock district Oxford, near the Oxford canal, the Oxford and Rugby railway, and the Oxford and Wolverhampton railway 1½ mile SW of Woodstock Road r station, and 2½ SE by S of Woodstock Post town, Bladon, under Woodstock. Acres 623 Real property £1,437 Pop, 101 Houses, 17 The property is divided among a few A small portion of it once belonged to the abbey of Godestow The living is a rectory in the diocese of Oxford. Value, £170 * Patron, Brasenose college, Oxford The church has some Norman details, and is very good

BEGELLY, a township, a parish and a sub-district in Narberth district, Pembroke. The township lies near the Pembroke and Tenby railway, 5 miles S by E of Narberth and has a post office under Narberth, and a r station Acres, 2,447 Rated property, £2,430 Pop, 770 Houses, 160 The parish includes also the chapelry of Williamston Acres, 3,878 Real property, £4,082, of which £820 are in mines. Pop, 1,311 Houses, 288 The property is divided among a few Begelly House is the seat of J Child, Esq Coal and culm are mined The living is a rectory, united with the p curacy of Williamston, in the diocese of St. David's Value, £216 * Patron, Lord Milford The church is early English and good, and there is a Calvinistic Methodist chapel The sub district comprises five parishes. Acres, 13,038 Pop, 4 318 Houses, 907

BEGGARMONDS, a hamlet in Buckden township Arncliffe parish, W R Yorkshire, 11 miles NNE of Settle

BEGGAR'S BRIDGE, a handsome, one arched bridge on the river Esk 1½ mile W of Egdon, N R Yorkshire The erection of it is ascribed to a romantic love incident, and the scene around it is often visited by pleasure parties.

BEGGAR'S ISLAND See ANTONY

BEGGARY (THE), a streamlet of Beds, running 4½ miles eastward, past a place of its own name, to the river Ouse, 2 miles S of St Neots.

BEGGERIDGE, a hamlet in Wellow parish, Somerset.

BEGUILDY, or LLANFIHANGEL BEGUILDY, a township and a parish in Knighton district, Radnor The township lies on the river Teme, 8 miles NW of Knighton r station Real property, £2,210 The parish consists of two divisions, Lower and Upper, and includes the townships of Creebyther, Medwalled, Beguildy, and Pennant, and part of the borough of Knucklas, and its post town is Felindre, under Knighton Acres, 16,645 Real property, £6,868 Pop., 1,203 Houses, 214 The surface is hilly, and most of it is moor or pasture The living is a vicarage in the diocese of St. David's Value, £164 Patron, the Bishop of St David's Charities, £17

BEIGHAM, a hamlet in Frant parish, Kent, 2½ miles W of Lamberhurst. A small Premonstratensian monastery was founded here in 1200, and given, at the dissolution to Cardinal Wolsey, in aid of his colleges

BEIGHTON, a parish and a sub district in the district of Rotherham and county of Derby The parish lies on the river Rother and on the Eckington and Sheffield railway, 3 miles N of Eckington, contains a charmingly situated village of its own name, and has a station on the railway, and a post office under Sheffield Acres, 3,070 Real property, £8 864,—of which £4,000 are in mines Pop 1,284 Houses, 263 Medicinal waters which have been long in repute are at Birley and scythes and sickles are manufactured at Hackenthorpe The living is a vicarage in the diocese of Lichfield Value, £312 * Patron, Earl Manvers. The church was partly restored, partly rebuilt, in 1869 There are a Wesleyan chapel, and charities £34 —The sub district, in addition to Beighton parish in Derby, comprises two parishes and part of another in Yorkshire Acres, 10,656 Pop, 3,279 Houses, 675

BEIGHTON, a parish in Blofield district Norfolk, 2 miles SW of Acle, and 3 NNE of Buckenham r station It has a post-office under Norwich Acres, 1,015 Real property, £2,995 Pop, 365 Houses, 72 The property is divided among a few The living is a rectory in the diocese of Norwich Value, £363 Patron, R Fellowes, Esq The church is decorated English, and was recently restored There is a national school

BEIGHTON, Suffolk. See BRYTON

BEILBY See BIELBY

BEIN See BEN

BEIN Y PHOI, a mountain summit in the Isle of Man 1 750 feet high, 2 miles S of Snea Fell, and 7½ SSW of Ramsey

BEKESBOURNE. See BEAKSBOURNE

BEL. See BAL

BELAN POINT a headland in Carnarvonshire, at the SW entrance of the Menai strait, near the ferry to Anglesey, 3½ miles SW of Carnarvon Belan Fort here is the bathing station of Lord Newborough

BELAUGH a parish in Aylsham district Norfolk on the river Bure, 1½ mile SE of Coltishall and 7½ NNE of Norwich r station Post town, Hoveton, under Norwich

wich. Acres, 854 Real property £1,437 Pop, 154. Houses, 37 The property is all in one estate Belaugh Hall is the chief residence The living is a rectory, united with the vicarage of Scottow, in the diocese of Norwich Value, £411 * Patron the Bishop of Norwich The church has a brass of 1471, an ancient circular font, and a square pinnacled tower, and is very good

BELBANK. See BELLBANK.

BELBROUGHTON, a manor, a parish, and a sub district, in the district of Bromsgrove, Worcester The manor lies 4½ miles S by E of Stourbridge r station, and 6 NW of Bromsgrove, and has a post office‡ under Stourbridge and fairs on the last Monday of April and the second Monday of Oct The parish includes also the manors of Fairfield, Bromhull, and Brian's Bell, and the village of Hartle Acres, 4,605 Real property, £11,450 Pop, 1,995 Houses, 405 The property is much subdivided. An extensive manufacture of scythes, hay knives and many kinds of edge tools, is carried on. The living is a rectory in the diocese of Worcester Value, £1,214 * Patron, St John's college, Oxford. The church is old but good, and there are Wesleyan and Primitive Methodist chapels A school has an endowed income of £10, and other charities £24 The sub district comprises five parishes and part of a sixth Acres, 15,584 Pop, 4,867 Houses, 1,053

BELBURY RING, an ancient camp 2½ miles SW of Steeple Langford Wilts, occupying 17 acres, fortified by double and triple ramparts, and enclosing a still older work

BELBY, a township in Howden parish, E R York shire, near the Selby and Hull railway, 1 mile E by N of Howden Acres, 679 Real property, £829 Pop, 44 Houses, 6

BELCHALWELL See BELLCHALWELL

BELCHAMP NORTHWOOD an extra parochial tract in Sudbury district, Essex, contiguous to Belchamp Walter Pop, 12 Houses, 3

BELCHAMP OTTON, a parish in the district of Sudbury and county of Essex, on a small affluent of the river Stour 4 miles NE of Yeldham r station, and 5 W by N of Sudbury Post town, Belchamp St Paul, under Halstead. Acres, 1,603 Real property, £2,961 Pop, 375. Houses 81 The property is divided among a few The living is a rectory in the diocese of Rochester Value, £446 * Patron, the representatives of the late Rev E H Dawson The church is good, and there are charities £21

BELCHAMP-ST PAUL, a parish in the district of Sudbury and county of Essex, on the river Stour, 6 miles WNW of Sudbury r station It has a post office under Sudbury, and a fair on 11 Dec Acres, 2,557 Real property, £4 209 Pop, 832 Houses, 179 The property is divided among a few The parish is a meet for the East Essex hounds The living is a vicarage in the diocese of Rochester Value, £240 * Patrons, the Dean and Chapter of St Paul's The church is very good

BELCHAMP WALTER, a parish in the district of Sudbury and county of Essex, on a small affluent of the river Stour, 4 miles W of Sudbury r station It has a post office under Sudbury Acres, 2,125 Real property, £4 310 Pop, 768 Houses, 152 Belchamp Hall is the seat of the Raymonds and contains an interesting collection of pictures. The living is a vicarage, annexed to the vicarage of Pulmer, in the diocese of Rochester The church is a neat high edifice and contains a brass of 1591 and tombs of the Raymonds

BELCHFORD or BELSHFORD, a parish in Horncastle district, Lincoln, on the Wolds, 4½ miles NNE of Horncastle r station Post town, Horncastle Acres 2,390 Real property £3,885 Pop, 638 Houses, 148 The manor belongs to R Vyner, Esq The living is a rectory in the diocese of Lincoln Value, £125 * Patron, the Lord Chancellor The church is good, and there are two Methodist chapels and a national school.

BELFORD, a small town a township, a parish, a sub district, and a district, in Northumberland The town stands on a gentle eminence about a mile W of a station of its own name on the North eastern railway, 15½ miles SSE of Berwick It is neatly built, contains a church two dissenting chapels, and a workhouse, has a head post office,‡ a market place, and two chief inns, and is a seat of petty sessions The church was lately rebuilt, is in the early English style, and has a lofty tower A weekly market is held on Wednesday, fairs, on Tuesday before Whitsunday and 23 Aug, and races, in September —The township includes the town, and comprises 2,698 acres Pop., 1,067 Houses, 204 —The parish includes also the townships of Ross, Elwick, Easington, Easington Grange Middleton, and Detchant. Acres, 11,604, of which 2,224 are water Real property, £11,901 Pop., 1,724 Houses 329 The property is divided among five Belford Hall is the seat of the Rev J D Clark Coal, lime, and freestone occur Traces of an ancient chapel are on a rising ground near the town, and remains of a very strong Danish camp, encompassed by a deep ditch are not far distant. The living is a vicarage in the diocese of Durham Value, £147 * Patron, the Rev J D Clark.—The sub district and the district are coextensive, and contain the parishes of Belford and Bambrough, the extra parochial tracts of Monk's House and Fern Islands, and part of the parish of Ellingham. Acres, 41,753 Poor-rates in 1866, £4,548 Pop in 1861, 6 200 Houses, 1,221 Marriages in 1866, 41, births, 174,—of which 17 were illegitimate, deaths, 120,—of which 24 were at ages under 5 years, and 4 at ages above 85 years Marriages in the ten years 1851-60, 198, births, 2,007, deaths, 1,072 The places of worship in 1851 were 6 of the Church of England with 1,920 sittings, 1 of the Church of Scotland, with 500 s, 2 of the United Presbyterian Church, with 730 s, 3 of the Presbyterian Church in England, with 1,027 s, and 1 of Roman Catholics, with 70 s The schools were 10 public day schools, with 606 scholars, 8 private day schools, with 363 s, and 13 Sunday schools, with 678 s

BELGRAVE, a township and a parish in Barrow upon Soar district, Leicester The township lies on the river Soar, the Fosse way, and the Midland railway, 1½ mile NNE of Leicester, and has a post office under Leicester It gives the title of Viscount to the Marquis of Westminster Real property, £9,333. Pop., 1,510 Houses, 341 The parish includes also the township of South Thurmaston and the chapelry of Birstall Acres, 3,450 Real property, with North Thurmaston, £18,943 Pop, 2,808 Houses 625. Belgrave House and a half-share of the manor belong to Isaac Harrison, Esq The living is a vicarage, united with the p curacy of Birstall, in the diocese of Peterborough Value, £146 * Patron, the Bishop of Lichfield The church is later English, but has a Norman door, and contains monuments and a curious font There are chapels for Baptists, Wesleyans, and Primitive Methodists, a national school, town lands worth £90 a year, and other charities £36

BELGRAVE, a sub district of St George Hanover Square district, London It includes Buckingham palace and part of the parish of St. George Hanover Square. Acres, 580, of which 55 are water Pop, 55,113 Houses, 6 613

BELGRAVIA, the southern wing of the West End of London It is bounded, on the N, by Knightsbridge, on the E, by Grosvenor Square, on the SE, by Ebury Street, and on the W, by Sloane Street It stands on ground, originally marshy, belonging to the Marquis of Westminster, and was built chiefly in 1826-52 It includes Belgrave and Eaton squares, has generally large, regular, elegant houses, and is highly fashionable

BELIDDEN, an amphitheatre on the coast of Cornwall, about 1½ mile NNE of the Lizard It consists of a recess in cliffs, banked above by sloping turf and is thought by some antiquaries to have been used by the ancient Britons as a temple

BELLAN a township in Ruabon parish, Denbigh, 5½ miles E of Llangollen Pop, 138

BELLASIS, a hamlet in Stannington parish, Northumberland, near the river Blyth, 4½ miles S of Morpeth

BELLASIZE, a township in Eastrington parish, E R Yorkshire, near the Selby and Hull railway, 4½ miles E of Howden It includes the hamlets of Greenoak and Bennetland Acres, 1,348 Real property, £2,176 Pop, 281 Houses, 60

BELLBANK, a township in Stapleton parish, Cumberland, 7½ miles N of Brampton. Real property, £832 Pop, 111 Houses, 17

BELLBANK, a township in Bewcastle parish, Cumberland, 9½ miles NNE of Brampton Here are coal and iron works. Real property, £1,851 Pop, 415 Houses, 81

BELL BUSK, a hamlet in Cold Coniston township, Gargrave parish, W R Yorkshire, adjacent to the Midland railway, 6¾ miles WNW of Skipton It has a station on the railway, and a post office under Leeds

BELLCHALWELL, a parish in Sturminster district Dorset, 3 miles S of Sturminster, and 6¼ WNW of Blandford r station. Post town, Turnworth, under Blandford Acres, 1,308 Real property, with Fifehead Neville, £3,188 Pop, 158 Houses, 37 The property is divided among a few The living is a rectory in the diocese of Salisbury Value, not reported Patron, Lord Rivers The church has a Norman porch and a square tower, and is very good

BELLEAU, a village and a parish in Louth district, Lincoln The village stands near the Boston and Great Grimsby railway, in the vicinity of Claythorpe station, 4 miles NW by N of Alford The parish includes also the chapelry of Claythorpe, and its post town is Alford Acres, 1,344 Real property, £1,947 Pop, 214 Houses, 33 The property is divided among a few The name Belleau is derived from some fine springs of water arising from chalk rocks Ruins exist of a monastery, comprising two gateways and part of a turret. The lands were given, in the time of Cromwell, to Sir Henry Vane The living is a rectory, united with Aby, in the diocese of Lincoln. Value, £300 * Patron, Lord Willoughby d Eresby The church is an ancient edifice, with a small tower, and contains a fine effigies of a crusader

BELLEAU, or BEELAH (THE), a stream of Westmoreland It rises on Stanemoor, near the boundary with Yorkshire, and runs 8 miles westward to the Eden in the vicinity of Musgrave

BELLE ISLE, or CURWEN'S ISLE, an island in Windermere, Westmoreland, near the centre of the lake, opposite Bowness. It measures about 1½ mile in circuit, and upwards of 30 acres in area, is all disposed in landscape garden, and contains the mansion of Henry Curwen, Esq,—a circular four storey edifice, with Ionic-style portico, built in 1776 A baronial fortalice once stood on the site of the mansion belonged in the time of Charles I, to the family of Phillipson, and was garrisoned and defended, at that time, for the Crown

BELLERBY, a township chapelry in Spennithorne parish, N R Yorkshire, 1¼ mile N of Leyburn r station It has a post office under Bedale Acres, 2,540 Real property, £3,038 Pop, 391 Houses 90 Bellerby Park is the seat of J C Chaytor, Esq The living is a vicarage in the diocese of Ripon Value, £78 Patron J C Chaytor Esq

BELL HOUSES, a hamlet in Ecclesfield parish, W R Yorkshire, 5½ miles W of Rotherham

BELLIENSE, a village in St Martin parish, Guernsey

BELLINGDON, a hamlet in Chesham parish, Bucks, 2 miles NNW of Chesham Pop, 173

BELLINGHAM, a town, a township, a parish, a sub district, and a district in Northumberland The town stands on the left bank of the North Tyne, at the mouth of Hareshaw burn, adjacent to the Border Counties railway, 16 miles NNW of Hexham It has a station on the railway, a post office‡ under Hexham, a town hall, a church, a U Presbyterian chapel, a R Catholic chapel, and three public schools, is of small extent, but of local importance, a seat of county courts, and a polling place, and has had much recent change in connexion with iron works and the railway Markets are held on Saturdays, and fairs on the Wednesday before Good Friday, and on certain Saturdays of May, July, Aug, Sept, Oct, and Nov The church is of the 13th century, was recently restored, and has a finely groined stone roof. A fall of 30 feet, on the Hareshaw burn, is in the neighbourhood —Pop of the township, 860 Houses, 172 —The parish includes also the townships of Charlton East Quarter, Charlton West Quarter, Tarretburn, Nook, and Leemailing Acres, 20,211 Real property, £5,952 Pop, 1,662 Houses, 335 The property is subdivided The manor belonged, in the time of Richard II and Henry IV, to the De Bellinghams, passed to the Earls of Derwentwater, went to Greenwich Hospital and was sold to the Duke of Northumberland. The royalties were leased, in 1864, to Sir W Armstrong, for working ore Hesleyside, the seat of the Charlton family since the time of Edward VI, stands on a rising ground, on the right bank of the Tyne, 1¾ mile above the town The present mansion was built about the middle of last century, and occupies the site of a previous one of elaborate character, destroyed by fire Much of the parish is moor and sheep-walk, and many parts of it have cairns, tumuli, and Druidical stones Game is plentiful, and coal, ironstone, and limestone are worked The living is a rectory in the diocese of Durham Value, £200 Patron, Greenwich Hospital

The sub district comprises the parishes of Greystead, Falstone, and Thorneyburn, the townships of Bellingham, Charlton E Q, Charlton-W Q., and Tarretburn in Bellingham parish the townships of Rochester, Otterburn and Troughend in Elsdon parish and the extra parochial tract of Ramshope Pop, 4,247 Houses, 716 The district includes also the sub district of Kirkwhelpington containing the parishes of Corsenside, Wark, Thockrington, and Kirkharle, the parochial chapelry of Birtley, and parts of the parishes of Kirkwhelpington and Bellingham Acres, 235,861 Poor rates in 1866, £4,326 Pop in 1861, 7,080 Houses, 1,308 Marriages in 1866, 42 births, 239,—of which 29 were illegitimate, deaths, 126,—of which 37 were at ages under 5 years, and 8 at ages above 85 years Marriages in the ten years 1851-60, 263, births, 1,737 deaths 969 The places of worship in 1851 were 12 of the Church of England, with 2 248 sittings, 2 of the United Presbyterian church, with 680 s 5 of the Presbyterian church in England, with 1,444 s, 1 of Wesleyan Methodists with 123 s., 1 of Primitive Methodists, with 200 s, and 1 of Roman Catholics, with 54 attendants The schools were 15 public day schools, with 672 scholars, 8 private day schools, with 195 s, and 15 Sunday schools, with 554 s The workhouse is in Bellingham township

BELLISTER, a township in Haltwhistle parish, Northumberland, on the South Tyne, near the Newcastle and Carlisle and the Alston railways, 1 mile S of Haltwhistle. Acres, 983 Pop, 117 Houses, 27 Bellister Castle now a crumbling mass of ruin, was the seat of the Blenkinsops

BELLMANGATE, a hamlet in the township and parish of Guisbrough, N R Yorkshire.

BELLOWS CROSS a hamlet in Chettle parish, Dorset 2 miles W of Cranborne

BELL STREET See AVENING

BELLS YEW GREEN, a locality 4 miles from Tunbridge Wells, with a post office under that place

BELL TOUT See BEACHY HEAD.

BELLURIAN COVE a cove on the SW coast of Cornwall, 5½ miles NNW of the Lizard The rock of it is a conglomerate containing fragments of greywacke limestone and appears to have been surmounted by hornblende slate Mullion island about a mile in circuit, and of very curious outline, lies in the offing, and presents a striking appearance as seen in the descent to the cove

BELMISTHORPE, a hamlet in Ryhall parish, Rutland, on the river Wash 2½ miles NNE of Stamford It once belonged to the celebrated Lady Godwin Pop 121

BELMONT, a chapelry in Bolton le Moors parish, Lancashire, 3¾ miles E of Chorley r station It was constituted in 1851, and has a post office under Bolton Rated property, £4,005 Pop, 1,033 Houses, 202 There are cotton mills and print works The living is a vicarage in the diocese of Manchester Value, £120 * Patron, the Rev C Wright The church is good

BELMONT, a chapelry in the parish and county of Durham, on the Durham and Sunderland railway, 2 miles ENE of Durham It was constituted in 1852, it contains the Durham suburb of Gilesgate Moor or Gilligate, and the villages of Broomside and Carrville, and its post town is Durham Rated property, £6,840 Pop, 3,337 Houses, 676 The property is divided among a few Coal is worked Belmont Hall, Ravensflat and the Grange are chief residences The living is a vicarage in the diocese of Durham Value, £150 * Patron, alternately the Crown and the Bishop The church was built in 1857, and is in the early decorated English style There is a Wesleyan chapel

BELMONT, an estate in Herefordshire, on the river Wye, 2½ miles WSW of Hereford. A large Roman Catholic church and a wing of a Benedictine monastery containing 40 chambers, were built here in 1859 The church is cruciform, in the early English style very richly decorated, and is surmounted by a tower, intended to be terminated in a spire 210 feet high

BELO (The) See Beetha (The)

BELPER a town, two chapelries, a sub district, and a district in Derbyshire The town is in Duffield parish, and stands in a pleasant situation, on the river Derwent and on the Midland railway, 7½ miles N of Derby It was an inconsiderable village till 1777, but has risen to importance by means of manufactures, and was visited, in 1832, by Queen Victoria and the Duchess of Kent It comprises several regular streets and contains some interesting buildings. A handsome bridge of three arches spans the river An old chapel, built by John of Gaunt, is used as a school house The head church, erected in 1824, at a cost of £12,603, is a fine edifice, in the decorated style, with a high tower surmounted by pinnacles Christ Church, in Bridge street, was erected in 1854 A cemetery, with entrance offices and two chapels, in the late decorated style, was opened in 1859 There are chapels for Independents, Baptists, Wesleyan Methodists, Primitive Methodists, Un Free Methodists, and Unitarians There are also alms houses and a workhouse the latter in the Tudor style, and erected at a cost of £7,530 The town has a head post office,‡ a railway station with telegraph, a banking office, and four chief inns, and is a seat of petty sessions and a polling-place A weekly market is held on Saturday, and fairs on 28 Jan, 12 May, and 31 Oct Cotton works, belonging to the Messrs Strutt, employ upwards of 2,000 persons. Hosiery work and nail making also are carried on, and an extensive pottery and coal works are in the neighbourhood. Bridge Hill House, the residence of J H Strutt, Esq and Green Hall are fine mansions. The town gives the title of Baron, created in 1856, to the elder branch of the family of Strutt Acres, 3 078 Real property, £18,081 Pop, 9,509 Houses, 1,976.

The chapelries are Belper and Bridge Hill, were constituted in 1846 and 1845, and jointly comprise most of the town Pop 6 106 and 2,839 Houses, 1,309 and 563 Both are vicarages in the diocese of Lichfield Value of the former £300 * of the latter, £150.* Patron of the former the Vicar of Duffield, of the latter, alternately the Crown and the Bishop —The sub district is conterminate with the town —The district comprehends also the sub-district of Ripley containing the parishes of Pentrich and South Wingfield, the chapelry of Heage, and part of the parish of Crich, the sub district of Alfreton, conterminate with the parish of Alfreton, the sub district of Wirksworth, containing parts of the parishes of Wirksworth, Duffield, Ashover, and Kirk Ireton, the sub district of Horsley, containing the parishes of Horsley Morley, and Denby, the chapelry of Holbrook, and part of the parish of Kirk Hallam, and the sub district of Duffield containing the parishes of Mackworth, Allestree Quarndon Kedleston, and Kirk Langley, and parts of the parishes of Duffield and Mugginton Acres, 66 590 Poor rates in 1866 £15,542 Pop in 1861, 51,711 Houses, 10,535 Marriages in 1866 517, births 1,959,—of which 142 were illegitimate, deaths, 1 199,—of which 507 were at ages under 5 years, and 20 at ages above 85 years Marriages in the ten years 1851-60, 4,217, births 17,197, deaths, 10,106 The places of worship in 1851 were 30 of the Church of England, with 12 745 sittings, 8 of Independents, with 2 445 s. 12 of Baptists, with 2,931 s, 2 of Unitarians, with 776 s, 39 of Wesleyan Methodists with 9,036 s, 1 of the Methodist New Connection, with 100 s, 8 of Primitive Methodists, with 3,072 s., 13 of Wesleyan Reformers, with 2,290 s, 1 undefined, with 150 s, and 1 of Latter Day Saints, with 46 attendants The schools were 51 public day schools, with 4 515 scholars, 72 private day schools, with 1,556 s, 93 Sunday schools, with 10,405 s, and 5 evening schools for adults, with 171 s.

BELPH, a hamlet in Whitwell parish, Derby, 11 miles NE of Chesterfield

BELSAR HILLS, eminences in Cambridgeshire in the vicinity of the river Ouse, 8 miles E of St Ives They were occupied by William the Conqueror's camp when he menaced the Isle of Ely, and they took their name from his general Belasis

BELSAY, a township in Bolam parish, Northumberland, on the river Blyth, 9½ miles SW of Morpeth It has a post office under Newcastle upon Tyne Acres, 2,516 Pop, 384 Houses, 74 Belsay Castle, the *ancient seat of the Middletons, now the property of Sir* C M L Monck, Bart, is an old tower, with additions made by Sir C Middleton in 1628 The pile measures 56½ feet from N to S, and 47½ from E to W, has four projecting turrets, three of them round, the other square, terminates in a corbelled parapet, and contains, on the first floor, a solar 43 feet long, 21½ wide, and 17 high

BELSFORD, a hamlet in Harberton parish, Devon, 1 mile SW of Totnes Pop, 53

BELSHFORD See Belchford

BELSTEAD a parish in Samford district, Suffolk, near the Eastern Union railway, 3½ miles SW of Ipswich Post town, Ipswich Acres, 1 022 Real property £1,549 Pop, 292 Houses, 57 The property is divided among a few. The living is a rectory in the diocese of Norwich Value, £370 * Patron, the Rev F J Lockwood The church is tolerable, and there is an Independent chapel.

BELSTONE, a parish in Okehampton district, Devon on the headstreams of the Taw and Okement rivers, 2 miles SE of Okehampton r station, and 20 W by N of Exeter It includes the hamlet of Prestacott, and its post town is Okehampton Acres, 1,500 Real property, £1,205 Pop., 181 Houses, 41 The property is not much divided The surface lies within Dartmoor, and partakes of its striking scenery Belstone Cleave, on the course of the Okement river, shows wild massings of rock, with impetuous current of the stream The glen of St Michael of Halstock has the influx of the Black Avon from the uplands of Yes Tor, and contains Chapel Ford, named from an extinct ancient chapel of St Michael Belstone Tor, about 1½ mile above the ford, has on its W side a Druidic circle of 17 stones, the highest not more than 2½ feet above ground Some of the inhabitants are employed in woollen manufacture The living is a rectory in the diocese of Exeter Value, £154 * Patron, the Rev H G Fothergill The church is a small edifice of nave and chancel, with a very low tower, has Norman work and a fine old carved screen, is traditionally said to have been built by Baldwin de Brionis and was repaired in 1855 There is an Independent chapel

BELSWAINS a hamlet in Herts, on the North western railway 2 miles SSE of Hemel Hempstead.

BELTHORPE See Bishop Wilton

BELTINGE a hamlet in Herne parish, Kent, 6½ miles NNE of Canterbury

BELTINGHAM, a chapelry in Haltwhistle parish, Northumberland on the South Tyne, adjacent to the Newcastle and Carlisle railway, near Bardon Mill station,

4 miles W of Haydon Bridge. Post town, Bardon Mill, under Carlisle. Statistics not separately reported A market was formerly held here, and there is a very old and large yew in the churchyard. The living is a p. curacy in the diocese of Durham Value, £87 Patron, the Vicar of Haltwhistle The church is good

BELTISLOE, a wapentake in the parts of Kesteven, Lincoln It contains Basingthorpe parish 16 other parishes, and part of another Acres, 51,216 Pop in 1851, 8,816 in 1861, 8,289 Houses, 1,707

BELTOFT, a hamlet in Belton parish, Thorne district, Lincoln, 2 miles NE of Epworth. Pop, 139

BELTON, a parish in Loughborough district, Leicester 4½ miles NNE of Swannington r station, and 6 WNW of Loughborough Its statistics include the extra parochial tract of Grace Dieu, and its post town is Sheepshead, under Loughborough. Acres, 1,900 Real property, £5,259 Pop, 781 Houses, 161 The property is divided among a few The living is a vicarage in the diocese of Peterborough Value, £179 * Patron, the Marquis of Hastings The church is a fine old edifice, with tower and spire, and contains a monument of Roesia de Verdun the founder of Grace Dieu nunnery There are two dissenting chapels, a Roman Catholic chapel, a national school, and a great annual horse fair

BELTON a parish in Grantham district, Lincoln, on the river Witham, adjacent to the Great Northern and the Grantham and Boston railways, 2 miles NNE of Grantham. It contains a village of its own name, and has a post office under Grantham Acres, 1,709 Real property, £2,514 Pop, 142 Houses, 33 The property belongs all to Earl Brownlow, and gives him the title of Baron Belton Hall, the Earl's seat, stands in a park of 5 miles in circuit, and is an edifice, in the shape of the letter H, erected in 1689 after designs by Wren, and considerably modernized by Wyatt The living is a rectory in the diocese of Lincoln Value, £430 * Patron Earl Brownlow The church is ancient and good, and contains monuments of the Custs and the Brownlows, and a rich eight-sided font An ornamental cross is in the village and an ornamental tower on a height in the park. There is an endowed school

BELTON, a parish in the district of Thorne and county of Lincoln, in the Isle of Axholme, 1½ mile N of Epworth, and 3 miles SE of Godnow Bridge r station. It includes the hamlets of Beltoft, Carrhouse, Mosswood, Sandtoft, Westgate, and Woodhouse, and has a post office under Bawtry Acres, 8,530 Real property, £12,403 Pop, 1,871 Houses, 307 The property is much subdivided The living is a vicarage in the diocese of Lincoln Value, not reported * Patron, J Brunyee, Esq The church is handsome. There are three dissenting chapels, and charities £40 A fair is held on 25 Sept

BELTON, a parish in Uppingham district, Rutland on the river Eye, 4 miles WNW of Uppingham, and 5 WSW of Manton r station It contains a village of its own name, and has a post office under Uppingham Acres 2,380 Real property, £2,411 Pop 441 Houses, 93 The living is a vicarage, annexed to the rectory of Wardley, in the diocese of Peterborough The church is old but good, and has a square embattled tower There are a Baptist chapel and a free school Poors lands yield £83 a year, and other charities £20.

BELTON, a parish in Mutford district, Suffolk, on the East Suffolk railway and the Waveney river, 3 miles SW by W of Yarmouth It has a station on the railway, and includes the hamlet of Browston, and its post town is Yarmouth Acres, 2,030 Real property, £3,460 Pop, 516 Houses 114 The property is much subdivided The living is a rectory in the diocese of Norwich. Value, £362 * Patron, the Bishop of Norwich. The church is old but good, and has a round tower, which was rebuilt in 1849

BELVIDERE, a station on the North Kent railway 13¼ miles W of London Bridge Belvidere House in its vicinity, near the Thames, is the seat of Sir Culling Eardley, Bart, and contains a choice collection of pictures

BELVIDERE, Berks See VIRGINIA WATER.

BELVOIR, an extra parochial tract in the district of Grantham and county of Leicester, on the verge of the county near the Grantham canal, 7 miles W by S of Grantham Acres, 170. Real property, £1,780 Pop, 171 Houses, 18 Belvoir Castle here is the seat of the Duke of Rutland, and one of the most magnificent structures in the kingdom. The original building was a fortress erected soon after the Conquest by Robert de Todeni, standard bearer to William, and was several times burned down or otherwise destroyed The present pile is a modern, castellated, hollow quadrangle, restored by Wyatt, measuring 252 feet along the east front, and containing a noble apartment called the Regent's gallery, 127 feet long filled with the choicest productions of art It stands on an isolated and perhaps artificial hill, and commands a view of 30 miles, over a picturesque extensive vale, called the vale of Belvoir The Prince Regent, afterwards George IV, visited it in 1814, and Crabbe, the poet, lived in it as chaplain A great fire destroyed part of it in 1816, including a famous picture gallery, with damage estimated at £120,000 A priory of black monks stood near it, founded about 1076, by Robert de Todeni, and was given, at the dissolution, to Thomas, Earl of Rutland, and Robert Turwhit

BEMBRIDGE, a village and a chapelry in Brading parish, Isle of Wight. The village stands on the E side of Brading harbour, 2¼ miles ENE of Brading It has a post office under Ryde, and is a coast guard station It rose from obscurity about 1826, acquired some handsome houses and a hotel, and made strong claims to become a fashionable watering place, but has not met so much favour as its situation and other advantages deserve. The chapelry was constituted in 1827 Acres, not separately returned. Real property, £3,788 Pop, 783 Houses, 179 The tract of 2½ miles by 1¼, between Brading harbour and the Channel, bears the name of Isle of Bembridge and the termination of it on the NE is called Bembridge Point A ridge of hill, across its neck, called Bembridge Down, has an altitude of 355 feet, commands a very gorgeous view, was the scene of a rebuff of the French in 1546, and is crowned by a granite obelisk, 70 feet high, erected in 1849 to the memory of the late Lord Yarborough The rocks present a fine study to the geologist, and lignite, fuller's earth, and red ochre are found. The Bembridge ledge, and other ledges run off from the E coast into shoals, and the Bembridge floating lights are situated to the ENE, and show two lights 18 and 26 feet above deck and 43 feet apart A railway, 2 miles long, was authorised in 1864, to be formed from Yar Bridge to Bembridge Point, with pier and landing place The living is a p curacy in the diocese of Winchester Value, £100 * Patron, the Vicar of Brading The church was built in 1845, and is in the early English style

BEMERSLEY, a township in Norton-in the Moors parish, Stafford, 2 miles NE of Burslem. It includes part of Whitfield ville. Pop, 258 Houses, 45

BEMERTON, a chapelry in Fugglestone-St Peter parish, Wilts, 1½ mile W by N of Salisbury r station Post town, Salisbury Rated property, £1,336. Pop, 109 The property is subdivided The living is a rectory, annexed to the rectory of Fugglestone, in the diocese of Salisbury The old church had windows of decorated English and a font of early English, and was restored by George Herbert, the poet. The present church was built in 1861, is in the transition style from first to second pointed, and consists of nave, aisles, chancel, and porch with northeastern square tower, but presents a very irregular outline. George Herbert, who died in 1633, John Norris, the poet and metaphysician who died in 1711, and Archdeacon Cox the traveller and historian, who died in 1828, were rectors.

BEMMINSTER See BEAMINSTER.

BEMPSTONE, a hundred in Somerset. It contains Burnham and six other parishes Acres, 25,698 Pop in 1851, 8,129, in 1861, 8 389 Houses, 1,804

BEMPTON, a parish in Bridlington district, E R. Yorkshire on the coast and on the Hull and Scaborough railway, 4½ miles N of Bridlington It has a station on the railway, and its post town is Bridlington, under Hull Acres, 2,093, of which 163 are water Real property, £3,708 Pop, 346 Houses, 70 The property is much subdivided The living is a donative in the diocese of York Value, £51 Patron, H Broadley, Esq The church has a nave of four bays with round pillars, and a chancel rebuilt in 1829 There is a Wesleyan chapel

BEN, a prefix in Celtic names, signifying "a hill" or "mountain." It is sometimes written Bein, Bhein, or Pen, but in the last case is significant more of a projection or of a headland than of a summit

BENACRE, or BINACRE, a parish in Blything district, Suffolk, on the coast, 5¾ miles NNE of Wangford, and 5½ S of Carlton Colville r station Its post town is Kessingland, under Wangford. Acres, 1,660 Real property, £3 040 Pop, 212 Houses, 48. The property is not much divided Benacre Hall is the seat of Sir E S Gooch, Bart A lake of about 100 acres, called Benacre Broad, abounding in pike and other fish, lies about ¼ a mile from the sea. A stone vessel, containing about 900 Roman silver coins, some of them of the Emperor Vespasian, was found at the mending of a road in 1786 The living is a rectory united with the rectory of Easton Bavents and the vicarage of North Hales, in the diocese of Norwich Value, £440 Patron, Sir F S Gooch, Bart The church has a fine perpendicular font and is good

BENAIGHN, a township in Llannefydd parish, Denbighshire 5½ miles NW of Denbigh.

BENBOULE, a village 3¼ miles NE of Wadebridge, Cornwall

BENDALL, a village in the S of Derbyshire, 5½ miles ENE of Burton upon Trent.

BENDISH See BARTON BENDISH

BENDON, a quondam mansion, now a farm house, ¾ of a mile W of Axmouth, Devon It shows well the architectural features of the 16th century, and was long a seat of the Erle family, including Lord Chief Justice Erle and Sir Walter Erle

BENEDICT (ST) See CAMBRIDGE, HUNTINGDON, and LINCOLN

BENEFIELD, a parish in Oundle district, Northampton, adjacent to Rockingham forest, 3 miles W of Oundle r station It consists of two divisions, called Upper End and Lower End, and embraces an extra parochial tract in Rockingham forest and it has a post office under Oundle Acres, 5,100 Real property £6,068 Pop, 527 Houses, 110 The property is divided among a few The manor belongs to J W Russell, Esq Nine holes, called the Swallows occasionally suck up and absorb land floods. The living is a rectory in the diocese of Peterborough Value, £531 * Patron, J W Russell, Esq The church was recently restored, and is good A school has an endowed income of £10, and other charities £33

BENENDEN, a village and a parish in Cranbrook district, Kent The village stands 3 miles SE of Cranbrook, and 5 S of Staplehurst r. station, and has a post office under Staplehurst It is a place of great antiquity, contains several good old houses and presents a pleasant appearance It once was noted for cloth manufacture, and it has a fair on 15 May The parish comprises 6,508 acres Real property, £7,274 Pop, 1,662 Houses, 309 The property is divided among a few Ponds and springs abound A beacon stood near the village during the civil wars forming part of a line of communication between Tenterden and London The living is a vicarage in the diocese of Canterbury Value £112.* Patron, G Hardy, Esq The church was restored in 1862, at a cost of £6,000 There are a recent school church, a Baptist chapel a neat national school of 1861, an endowed school with £11 a year, and charities £60

BENET (ST) See LONDON

BENFIELDSIDE, a township and a chapelry in Lanchester parish, Durham The township lies on the river Derwent and on a branch of the Northeastern railway 4 miles N of Cold Rowley and has a r station It is a watering place, and has coal mines, and its post town is Medomsley, under Gateshead Acres, 1,834 Pop, 4,026. Houses, 728 The chapelry was constituted in 1847 Pop., 9,223 Houses, 1,575 The living is a vicarage in the dio. of Durham Value, £300 * Patron, al the Crown and the Bishop The church is good, and there are two Methodist chapels and a R Catholic one

BENFLEET, a station on the London and Southend railway, on the south coast of Essex, 6 miles W of Southend

BENFLEET (NORTH), a parish in Billericay district Essex, 2½ miles NE of Pitsea r station, and 3 W by S of Rayleigh It has a post office under Chelmsford Acres 2,418 Real property £3 225 Pop, 285 Houses, 56 The property is divided among a few The living is a rectory in the diocese of Rochester Value, £700 * Patron, Emmanuel College, Cambridge The church is good

BENFLEET (SOUTH), a parish in Rochford district, Essex, on the coast, including part of Canvey island, and on the London and Southend railway, at Benfleet station, 4 miles SSW of Rayleigh. It has a post office under Chelmsford Acres 3,361, of which 305 are water. Real property, £3,756 Pop, 573 Houses, 125 The property is much subdivided A strong castle was built here by the famous Danish pirate, Hastings, and taken and destroyed by Alfred the Great The waters on the coast were celebrated for oysters The living is a vicarage in the diocese of Rochester Value, £235 * Patrons, the Dean and Chapter of Westminster The church is a fine structure of the time of Henry VII

BENGAL, a hamlet, 1 mile W of Towcester, Northampton Pop, 39

BENGEO, a parish in the district and county of Hertford, on the river Rib and on Ermine street adjacent to the Hertfordshire railway, 1 mile N of Hertford, and partly within Hertford borough. Post town Hertford Acres, 3,047 Real property, £8,150 Pop, 1,791 Houses, 355 The living is a rectory in the diocese of Rochester Value, £620 * Patron, A Smith, Esq There are an old church now disused, a new church built in 1855, two chapels of ease, a Calvinistic chapel, three national schools, a reformatory, four alms houses, and other charities £15

BENGEWORTH ST PETER, a parish in Evesham district Worcester on the river Avon, and the Ashchurch and Evesham railway, with a r station, 1¼ mile SW of Evesham Post town, Evesham Acres, returned with Evesham Real property, £6,720 Pop, 1,259 Houses, 254 The property is not much divided A castle here belonged to the Beauchamps, and was destroyed in 1156 by the Abbot of Evesham The living is a vicarage in the diocese of Worcester Value, £158 * Patron, the Rev W Harker The church occupies the site of the Beauchamps castle, and is a substantial edifice with a handsome tower and spire A school endowed by John Deacle a native of Bengeworth and an alderman of London, has an income of £276, and other charities have £86

BENGLOG (FALLS OF), three cataracts on the stream at the outlet of Llyn Ogwen Carnarvon 4½ miles NE of the summit of Snowdon, and 10 SSE of Bangor They occur in a rocky chasm, have an aggregate descent of about 100 feet and are overhung by massive mountains

BENHADLAF (ISAF and UCHAF), two townships in the parish of Llanrhaiadr yn Mochnant on the mutual border of Denbigh and Montgomery, 10 miles SW of Chirk Real property, £4,205 and £2,471 Pop., 207 and 100

BENHADLAN a township in Llanarmon parish, Denbigh, 6½ miles SSW of Llangollen

BENHALL, a parish in Plomesgate district, Suffolk, adjacent to the Ore river and the East Suffolk railway, 1½ mile SW of Saxmundham It has a post-office, of the name of Benhall Green, under Saxmundham Acres, 2 156 Real property £3 816 Pop, 678 Houses 153 The property is divided among a few The manor belonged to successively the Uffords, the De la Poles, and the Dukes Benhall Lodge is the seat of the Rev E Hollond The living is a vicarage in the diocese of Norwich Value £173 Patron, the Rev E Hollond

The church is good, and has a brass of 1548 An endowed school has £28

BENHAM (MARSH), a tything in Speen parish, Berks, 1¼ mile W of Newbury Benham Place here belongs to Earl Craven Pop, 316

BENHILTON See SUTTON, Surrey

BENIARTH, a township in Bettws yn Rhos parish, Denbigh, 3¾ miles SSW of Abergele Pop, 90

BENJIE TOR, a summit in Dartmoor forest, Devon, overhanging the river Dart, 5 miles WNW of Ashburton It has a rugged rocky character, and commands a wild, striking view over Dartmoor and away to the Isle of Portland

BENNETLAND, a hamlet in Bellasize township, Eastrington parish, E R Yorkshire, 5 miles E by N of Howden. Pop, 82

BENNET'S (ST). See HORNING

BENNETTS END, a township in Cainham parish, Salop, 3¼ miles ESE of Ludlow Pop, 309

BENNETT'S HOUSES, a hamlet in Hawarden township and parish, Flint

BENNINGBOROUGH, a township in Newton upon Ouse parish, N R Yorkshire, on the river Ouse, 1¼ mile WSW of Shipton r station, and 7 NW of York Acres, 1,070 Pop, 88 Houses, 15 Benningborough Hall here is a fine mansion

BENNINGHOLME AND GRANGE, a township in Swine parish, E R Yorkshire, 7 miles E by S of Beverley Acres, 1,280 Real property, £2,460 Pop, 106 Houses, 15

BENNINGTON, a village and a parish in the district and county of Hertford The village stands near the river Beane, and near a branch Roman way, 5 miles ESE of Stevenage, and 6 from Stevenage r station It has a post office under Stevenage, and was formerly a market town, and has still a fair on 10 July The parish comprises 2,908 acres. Real property, £4,784 Pop, 637 Houses, 133 The property is divided among a few The manor belonged to the Benstedes, the Cæsars, and the Earl of Essex, and belongs now to the Proctors An ancient palace of the kings of Mercia stood here, and either that, or a castle which succeeded it, is now indicated by an intrenched eminence Bennington Place, to the east, is a fine seat The living is a rectory in the diocese of Rochester Value, £635 * Patron, the Rev J E Pryor The church contains some ancient monuments, and is good. There are a Wesleyan chapel and a national school

BENNINGTON, a parish and a sub-district in Boston district, Lincoln The parish lies on the Wash, 3 miles SSE of Sibsey r station, and 5 ENE of Boston It includes an allotment in the East Fen, and has a post office under Boston Acres, 7,195, of which 4,405 are water Real property, £7,025 Pop, 588 Houses, 133 The property is much subdivided The living is a rectory in the diocese of Lincoln Value, £805 * Patron the Earl of Ripon The church has a perpendicular clerestoried nave, a fine tower, and a sculptured octagonal font There are a Primitive Methodist chapel, an endowed school with £90 a year, five alms houses, and some other charities —The sub district comprises four parishes parts of three others, and the East Fen allotment of Boston. Acres, 50,285 Pop, 6,572 Houses, 1 340

BENNINGTON, a sub-district in Newark district, Notts. It contains six parishes and an extra parochial tract electorally in Lincoln and five parishes and part of another electorally in Notts Acres, 22,643 Pop, 4 606 Houses 1 051

BENNINGTON GRANGE, an extra parochial tract in the district of Newark and county of Lincoln, adjacent on the south to the parish of Long Bennington Pop, 13 Houses, 3

BENNINGTON (LONG), a village and a parish in the district of Newark and county of Lincoln The village stands on the river Witham, 3¾ miles W by S of Hougham r station, and 8 NW by N of Grantham, consists of one long street, and has a post office under Grantham The parish, inclusive of Bennington Grange, comprises 4,420 acres. Real property, £8,142. Pop, 1,066. Houses, 255 The property is subdivided Freestone and lime are worked A Cistertian priory, with local endowment, was founded here, before 1175, by Ralph de Filgeiis, given to the abbey of Savigney in Normandy, transferred, by Richard II, to the Carthusians of St Ann, near Coventry, conveyed by Henry V to the priory of Mountgrace, and given, at the dissolution, to the dean and chapter of Westminster Remains of a moat, which surrounded its farm house, are in Bennington Grange The living is a vicarage united with the p curacy of Foston, in the diocese of Lincoln Value, £463 * Patron, the Duchy of Lancaster The church is good, and there are two Wesleyan chapels, a national school, and charities £21

BENNIWORTH, a parish in Horncastle district, Lincoln, on the Wolds, 5¾ miles ENE of Wragby, and 8½ E of Wickenby r station Post town, Donington, under Louth Acres, 2,994 Real property, £4,224 Pop., 431 Houses, 83. The property is divided among a few A British urn was found The living is a rectory in the diocese of Lincoln Value, £506 * Patron, G F Heneage, Esq The church has a Norman porch, and is good There is a Wesleyan chapel

BEN RHYDDING, a hydropathic establishment, with a r station, in Wharfdale, W R Yorkshire, on the slope of Rombald's Moor, adjacent to the Leeds and Ilkley railway, 5 miles W of Otley It was erected in 1846, at a cost of nearly £30,000, and is an imposing pile, amid extensive and pleasant grounds

BENRIDGE a township in Mitford parish, Northumberland, 2 miles WNW of Morpeth Pop. 49

BENRIDGE a hamlet in Ponteland parish, Northumberland, 6¾ miles SSW of Morpeth Pop, 30

BENSHAM, a chapelry in Gateshead parish, Durham, 1¼ mile SSW of G r station It was constituted in 1845 Pop, about 3,600 The living is a vicarage Value, £430

BENSINGTON or BENSON, a village and a parish in the district of Wallingford and county of Oxford The village stands on the river Thames, 1¾ mile NNE of Wallingford r station, is a considerable place, and has a post office ‡ of the name of Benson, under Wallingford It occupies the site of a town of the ancient Britons, which was taken from them, in 572, by the West Saxons, held by the latter till 775, and surrendered then to the Mercians The parish includes also the hamlets of Fifield, Roke, and Crowmarsh Battle or Preston-Crowmarsh Acres, 2,922 Real property, £6,352 Pop, 1,169 Houses, 282 The property is divided among a few A very ancient manor house is in the hamlet of Fifield A Maison Dieu was founded in the time of Henry VI, by William de la Pole, Duke of Suffolk, and given to the University of Oxford The living is a vicarage in the diocese of Oxford Value, £250 * Patron, Christ Church college, Oxford The church is partly ancient, variously late pointed Norman and decorated, has a modern tower, contains a Norman font and two brasses, and is very good There are national and British schools, and charities £80

BENSON See BENSINGTON

BENSON-KNOT, a hill 2 miles ENE of Kendal, Westmoreland It rises abruptly, is not easily climbed, has an altitude of 1,098 feet above the level of the sea and commands an extensive and magnificent view

BENTFIELD, a hamlet in Stansted Mountfitchet parish, Essex, near the Eastern Counties railway, 3¼ miles NE of Bishop Stortford Acres, 740 Real property, £3,410 Pop 529 Houses 121

BENTHALL, a township in Alberbury parish, Salop 9 miles WNW of Shrewsbury

BENTHALL a parish in Madeley district Salop, near the river Severn, 2 miles NE of Much Wenlock r station Post town Much Wenlock, under Wellington Acres 821 Real property, £1,704 Pop, 439 Houses, 102 The property is all in one estate Lime spars are found, and potteries are carried on The living is a p curacy in the diocese of Hereford Value £93 Patron, the Vicar of Much Wenlock The church is good

BENTHAM, a hamlet in Badgeworth parish, Gloucestershire 4½ miles E of Gloucester Pop, 236

BENTHAM, two hamlets, a township, a parish, and a sub district in the district of Settle, W R. Yorkshire The hamlets are distinguished as High and Low High Bentham lies on the river Wenning, and on the Midland railway, 12 miles WNW of Settle, and has a station on the railway, a post-office‡ under Lancaster, a chapel of ease, a grammar school, a weekly market on Monday, and fairs on 5 Feb, 22 June and 25 Oct —The township includes the hamlets Acres, 7,642 Real property, £8,673 Pop, 2,342 Houses 465 —The parish includes also the township of Ingleton Acres, 25,500 Real property, £16,283 Pop, 3,589 Houses, 727 The property is much subdivided Large portion of the surface is upland. Many of the inhabitants are employed in factories and some in potteries The living is a rectory in the diocese of Ripon Value, £452.* Patron, Rev E. Sherlock. The church is at Low Bentham, and is ancient The p curacy of Ingleton, and that of Ingleton-Fells or Chapel le Dale are separate benefices. There are three dissenting chapels, two endowed schools, six alms houses, and other charities £58 —The sub-district comprises two parishes and part of a third Acres, 31,652 Pop, 5,436 Houses, 1,104

BENTLEY, a village, a parish, and a liberty in Alton district, Hants. The village stands adjacent to the Alton and Farnham railway, 5½ miles NE of Alton, and has a station on the railway, and a post office under Farnham.—The parish comprises 2,258 acres Real property, £4,717 Pop, 721 Houses, 140 The property is divided among a few The pavements of a Roman villa have been found at Powderham The living is a rectory in the diocese of Winchester Value, £700 * Patron, the Archdeacon of Surrey The church is Norman, with a small tower, and there are a Wesleyan chapel, and charities £17 —The liberty is conterminate with the parish

BENTLEY, a township in Wolverhampton parish, Stafford, near the Northwestern railway, 2 miles W by N of Walsall Acres, 1,600 Real property, £4,327, of which £1,270 are in mines, and £500 are in iron works Pop, 346 Houses, 68 The inhabitants are employed largely in collieries and iron works. Bentley Hall belonged to Col. Lane, who sheltered Charles II after the battle of Worcester, and was the seat of the late Hon E Anson

BENTLEY, a township in Worfield parish, Salop, 1 mile NE of Bridgnorth

BENTLEY, a parish in Samford district, Suffolk, at the junction of the Eastern Counties railway with the Hadleigh branch, 6 miles SW of Ipswich It has a station on the railway, and a post office under Ipswich Acres, 2,801 Real property, £3,725 Pop, 453. Houses, 95 The property is divided among a few The Tollemaches had a seat here before the Conquest The living is a vicarage in the diocese of Norwich Value, £152 * Patron, the Rev C E P Keene The church is good and there are national schools

BENTLEY a hamlet in Shustoke parish, Warwick, 3 miles SW of Atherstone Acres, 1,830 Real property, £2 719 Pop., 233 Houses 50 It includes Bentley Park, and forms a chapelry annexed to the vicarage of Shustoke The church was built in 1841

BENTLEY a hamlet in Rowley parish, E R York shire, 2 miles SSW of Beverley Acres, 1,037 Pop, 57 Houses, 11

BENTLEY, W R. Yorkshire See Arksey

BENTLEY (Fenny), a parish in Ashborne district, Derby, in Dovedale, 2½ miles N of Ashborne r station It has a post office under Ashborne Acres, 1 036 Real property £2,023. Pop, 305 Houses 61 The manor belonged to the Beresfords and the Cottons, and belongs now to Sir W Fitzherbert, Bart The living is a rectory in the diocese of Lichfield Value £124 Patron the Bishop of Lichfield The church was repaired in 1850, and contains a curious old monument of the Beresfords

BENTLEY GRANGE, a hamlet in Emley township and parish, W R Yorkshire, 6½ miles ESE of Huddersfield

BENTLEY (Great) a village and a parish in Tendring district, Essex The village stands near the Tendring Hundred railway, 8 miles SE by E of Colchester, and has a post office under Colchester, a railway station, and an annual fair The parish comprises 3 188 acres Real property, £5,380 Pop 1,033 Houses, 235 The property is subdivided. The living is a vicarage in the diocese of Rochester Value £360 * Patron, the Bishop of Rochester The church is very good, and there are a Wesleyan chapel and a national school

BENTLEY (Hungry), a liberty in Longford parish, Derby, 4½ miles S of Ashborne Real property, £1,611 Pop, 82 Houses 12

BENTLEY (Little), a parish in Tendring district, Essex, 2¾ miles NNE of Bentley r station, and 7½ E of Colchester It has a post office under Colchester Acres, 2 012 Real property, £3,453. Pop, 458 Houses, 101 The property is much subdivided. The living is a rectory in the diocese of Rochester Value, £650 * Patron, Emmanuel College, Cambridge The church is good

BENTLEY-PAUNCEFOOT, or Bentley (Lower and Upper) a township in Tardebigg parish, Worcester, 3½ miles SSE of Bromsgrove Pop, 238. Houses, 43

BENTLEY PRIORY, the seat of the Marquis of Abercorn, in the parish of Harrow on the Hill, Middlesex, 3 miles WNW of Edgeware It occupies the site of a small priory, and contains some antiques and fine paintings Queen Adelaide, after a residence of some months, died here in 1849

BENTON See Benton (Long)

BENTON CASTLE, an ancient fortress on Milford haven Pembrokeshire, on a beautiful small promontory, 3 miles NNE of Pembroke

BENTON (Little), a hamlet in Walker township, Long Benton parish, Northumberland, adjacent to the Northeastern railway, ½ a mile S of Long Benton. The manor belonged to the Scropes, the Fitzhughs, and others, and belongs now to the Bigges

BENTON (Long), a township, a parish, and a sub district in the district of Tynemouth, Northumberland The township lies on the Northeastern railway, and on the Blyth and Tyne railway, near the Roman wall, 3 miles NNE of Newcastle upon Tyne, and has stations on the railways, and a post office under Newcastle upon Tyne The village consists of one long street, and stands on rock, dry, healthy, and pleasant Pop, 2,222 Houses, 472 The parish includes also the townships of Walker, Killingworth, and Weetslade, and lies partly on the Tyne Acres, 9,040, of which 110 are water Real property, £39,372, of which £12,541 are in mines, £500 in quarries, and £2 000 in iron works. Pop. in 1841, 8,711, in 1861, 13,304 Houses, 2,415 The property is not much divided The manor belonged formerly to the De Merlays, and passed partly to the Brandlings The inhabitants are employed mainly in extensive collieries, quarries, foundries, copperas works, and gunpowder works, The living is a vicarage in the diocese of Durham Value £353 Patron Balliol College Oxford The church is very good The vicarage of Walker and the p curacy of Killingworth are separate benefices There are several dissenting chapels, and a national school —The sub district is conterminate with the parish

BENT'S GREEN a hamlet in Ecclesall Bierlow township W R Yorkshire, 2 miles SW of Sheffield

BENTWICHEN, a hamlet in North Molton parish, Devon.

BENTWORTH, a village and a parish in Alton district, Hants The village stands 3½ miles WNW of Alton r station, and has a post office under Alton The parish comprises 2,658 acres Real property, £4,091 Pop, 647 Houses, 123 The property is subdivided The manor was inherited from his father by George Wither the poet and was sold by him, at the outbreak of the civil war to raise a troop of horse The living is a rectory in the diocese of Winchester Value, £760 * Patron the Rev Mr Mathews. There is a dissenting chapel

BENTY GRANGE, a village 5½ miles SW of Bakewell Derby

BENWELL, a township and a chapelry in St. John parish, Northumberland The township lies on the river Tyne, the Roman wall, and the Newcastle and Carlisle railway, 2 miles W of Newcastle upon Tyne Acres, 1,346 Pop, 1,771 Houses, 350 Here are collieries, the oldest in England, one of which, in the beginning of last century, took fire from a candle, and burned for nearly thirty years Benwell is believed to have been the Condercum of the Romans, and urns, coins, inscriptions, and other Roman remains have been found Benwell tower belonged at one time to Tynemouth priory, and afterwards to the Shaftoes Benwell High Cross, to the E was named from a cross that formerly stood at it The chapelry is more extensive than the township, and was constituted in 1842 Pop, 4,323 Houses, 749 The living is a p curacy in the diocese of Durham Value, £150 * Patron, the Vicar of Newcastle. The church is a Gothic structure with a tower, built at a cost of £1,607

BENWICK, a chapelry in Doddington parish, Cambridge, in the Isle of Ely, 4½ miles NW of Chatteris r station, and 6¼ SW of March Post town, Doddington, under March Acres, 3,096 Real property, £7,040 Pop, 773 Houses, 162 The living is a rectory The church is recent There are two dissenting chapels.

BEOBRIDGE, a township in Claverley parish, Salop, 4½ miles SE of Bridgnorth Pop, 61

BEOFERLIC See BEVERLEY

BEOLEY, a parish in Kings Norton district, Worcester, on the verge of the county, 2½ miles NE of Redditch r station. Post town, Redditch, under Bromsgrove Acres, 4,480 Real property, £6 809 Pop., 682 Houses, 151 An ancient castle, of which very slight traces remain, belonged successively to the noble families of Mortimer, Beauchamp, and Holland Beoley Hall is the seat of Capt R Mole The parish is a meet for the North Warwick hounds. The living is a vicarage in the diocese of Worcester Value, £73 Patron, W Holmes, Esq The church is ancient There is a Wesleyan chapel.

BEPTON, a parish in Midhurst district, Sussex, 2½ miles SW of Midhurst r station, and 5½ ESE of Petersfield. Post town, Midhurst Acres, 1,224 Real pro ... troo, Prince of Wales Dr Cowper, chaplain to George II, and father of Cowper the poet, was rector The living is a rectory in the diocese of Chichester Value £127 Patron, the Earl of Egmont

BERDEN, or BERDON, a parish in the district of Bishop Stortford, and county of Essex, 4½ miles NW of Elsenham r station, and 6 N by W of Bishop Stortford It has a post office under Bishop Stortford Acres, 1,771 Real property, £2,856 Pop, 414 Houses, 82 The property is divided among a few A small Augustinian priory was founded here in the reign of Henry III, was given, at the dissolution, to Henry Parker, and passed to the hospitals of Christchurch, Bridewell, and St. Thomas The living is a vicarage in the diocese of Rochester Value, £170 * Patron, Christ's Hospital The church is ancient The Rev Joseph Mede, author of the "Clavis Apocalyptica," was a native.

BERDENESTAPLE See BARNSTAPLE

BERDWICK, a hamlet in the parish of Wick with-Abson, Gloucester

BERE ALSTON See BEER-ALSTON

BERECHURCH, a parish in Colchester district, and within Colchester borough Essex, near the river Roman, 2 miles S by W of Colchester r station Post town Colchester Acres, 1,450 Real property, £1,880 Pop, 112 Houses, 19 The property is divided among a few The living is a vicarage in the diocese of Rochester Value, £110 Patron, T White, Esq The church is good

BERE FERRIS See BEER FERRIS

BEREFORD See BARFORD, Beds

BERE FOREST an ancient royal hunting ground in Hants, on the SE border of the county, 4½ miles NNW of Havant It was divided into two walks, east and west, and it contained about 16,000 acres All has been enclosed, great part has been cleared and cultivated, and only 1,417 acres are now under wood The surface is comparatively level, yet presents some good pieces of scenery See WATERLOOVILLE.

BERE HACKET See BEER HACKET

BERE REGIS, a small ancient town, a parish, a sub district, and a hundred in Dorset The town stands on the Bere rivulet, adjacent to a vast tract of barren heath, 1¼ mile N of the river Piddle, 5½ miles N by W of Wool r station, and 8 SSW of Blandford Forum It dates from the time of the Romans, was a residence of Queen Elfrida and of King John, and suffered severely from fire in 1634, in 1788, and in 1817 It is now a poor place, consisting chiefly of thatched cottages It has a post office‡ under Blandford, and two inns, and, till lately, was a market town It was constituted a free borough by Edward I, but never sent representatives to parliament The parish church at it is a large ancient edifice, with a square tower, contains a round figured font, and numerous monuments of the Turbervilles and others, and was entirely restored and repaired in 1835 There are chapels for Independents and Methodists a free school with £30, and other charities with £16 Remains of King John's palace are seen in a field opposite the church, and the manor house of the Turbervilles, an ancient irregular structure, with armorial bearings, stands at the outlet toward Wool Cardinal Morton, who figured prominently in the time of Henry VII, and Bishop Turberville of Exeter, were natives Pop of the town, 1,336 Houses, 278

The parish includes also the tything of Shitterton and the hamlet of Milborne Stileham, and is chiefly in the district of Wareham, but partly in that of Blandford Acres, 8,894 Real property, £7,602 Pop, 1,624 Houses, 338 The property is divided among a few Half of the manor belonged to the Turbervilles from the time of the Conquest, and the other half was given by Henry III to Simon de Montfort, Earl of Leicester, given again to the king's brother Edmund and given by Henry VIII to the Turbervilles. Woodbury-Hill, ½ a mile east of the town, was the site of a Roman camp, has still a circular entrenchment of 10 acres, formed by three ramparts and ditches, commands a very extensive view, and is the scene of an annual fair, formerly very famous, on 18 Sept and the five following days The surrounding tract has many barrows. The neighbouring downs are a resort of sportsmen The living is a vicarage, united with the vicarage of Winterborne-Kingston, in the diocese of Salisbury Value, £330 * Patron, Balliol College, Oxford —The sub district is in the district of Wareham, and comprises seven parishes, besides the greater part of Bere Regis Acres, 33 833 Pop, 4,749 Houses, 988 —The hundred comprises only the parishes of Bere Regis and Winterborne Kingston, and is partly in the division of Wareham, partly in that of Blandford Acres 11,402 Pop, 2,213 Houses, 447

BERESFORD HALL, the ancient seat of the Beresfords, afterwards of the Cottons, on the NE verge of Stafford in Dovedale, 4½ miles SSE of Longnor A fishing house was built here, in 1674, by Charles Cotton, the poet and angler, adorned with panel portraits of himself and "his worthy father, Izack Walton, who used to angle here, but the building is now a mere shell, bereft of its decorations

BERETHREN CASTLE See ASHERTON

BERGH APTON See BURGH APTON

BERGHILL, a township in Whittington parish, Salop, 4½ miles E of Oswestry Pop., 328

BERGH-MATTISHALL. See BURGH MATTISHALL

BERGHOLT (EAST), a parish in Samford district, Suffolk, on the river Stour, and on the Eastern Union railway, midway between the Manningtree and the Bentley stations, 9 miles SW of Ipswich. It has a post-office under Colchester Acres, 3,063 Real property, £8,450 Pop, 1 397 Houses, 339 The property is much subdivided Ackworth House is the seat of Sir Thomas Seaton The living is a rectory in the diocese of

Norwich. Value, not reported Patron, Emmanuel College, Cambridge. The church is excellent, and there are three dissenting chapels, a Benedictine nunnery and chapel, a police station, an endowed school with £70 a year, and other charities with £112. J Constable, the painter, born in 1776, was a native

BERGHOLT (WEST), a parish in Lexden district, Essex, on the river Colne, near the Eastern Counties railway, 4 miles NW of Colchester It has a post office under Colchester Acres, 2 273 Real property, £4 238 Pop 906 Houses, 198. The property is subdivided A circular entrenchment here is thought to have been the site of the residence of the British king, Cunobeline The living is a rectory in the diocese of Rochester Value £600 * Patron, W F Hobbs, Esq The church is good

BERIDEN (THE), a stream of Norfolk. It rises near New Buckenham, and runs about 12 miles northward to the Yare, in the vicinity of Norwich.

BERKELEY, a small town, a parish, a sub district, and a hundred, in Gloucester The town stands on a pleasant eminence, in the vale of Berkeley, on the Little Avon river about a mile from the Severn, 2½ miles W of Berkeley Road r station and 6½ NNE of Thornbury It was a place of importance in the times of the Saxons, and figured at Domesday as a royal domain and a free borough An ancient religious house at it was suppressed, in the reign of Edward the Confessor, through some villany of Earl Godwin and conferred upon the Earl The manor connected with it, which is one of the largest in the kingdom, was given by William the Conqueror to his follower Roger de Berkeley, forfeited by that gentleman's grandson for his adherence to King Stephen, and given by Henry II to Robert Fitz Hardinge, governor of Bristol, who assumed the title of Baron de Berkeley The town consists principally of four streets contains a market house, a church, an Independent chapel, a Wesleyan chapel, a free school and charities £194, has a head post office‡ and two chief inns, and is a seat of petty sessions and a polling place The church is a spacious structure, partly early English, of the time of Henry II, partly of later character in renovations, and contains some curious monuments of the Berkeley family, and the ashes of Dr Jenner The tower belonging to it stands detached, and was built in the latter part of last century Dean Swift's well known epitaph on "Dicky Pearce, the Earl of Suffolk's fool is in the churchyard A market is held on the first Wednesday of every month, and fairs on 14 May and 1 Dec Trade is carried on in coal, timber, corn, malt, and cheese, and is facilitated by the vicinity of the Severn, and the Berkeley and the Gloucester canal The town has nominally a corporation, but is really governed by the county magistrates. Dr Jenner, who introduced the practice of vaccination, was a native Real property, £2,785 Pop, 1,011 Houses, 196

The parish includes also the tythings of Hamfallow, Hinton Breadstone Alkington and Ham, and the chapelry of Stone Acres, 15,740 of which 2 820 are water Real property, £33 284 Pop, 4,3[illegible] Houses, 875 The property is not much divided Great portion of the surface is rich dairy land Strontian and agates are found in the rocks Berkeley Castle, close to the SE side of the town was founded, soon after the Conquest, by Roger de Berkeley, and got important additions in the reigns of Henry II, Edward II and Edward III It was the scene of the murder of Edward II, by a red hot iron being driven through his body, at the instigation of his queen, and it sustained a siege of nine days, in 1645, from the parliamentarian forces but was obliged to surrender A small apartment, called K Edward's room now lit with windows but then lit only from arrow slits, is shown as the place where Edward II was murdered

"Mark the year and mark the night
When Severn shall re-echo with affright
The shrieks of death through Berkeley's roof shall ring,
Shrieks of an agonizing king"

The outline of the castle is not far from being circular The entrance is under a massive arch, adorned with rich Norman carvings The main body is an irregular court, with vestiges of a moat. The chief buildings are an ancient keep, flanked by three semicircular towers, and a square tower of more recent date A portion of the pile has been modernized, and contains numerous family portraits, some paintings by the Italian masters and the cabin furniture of the Navigator Drake The castle was formerly the residence of the Earls Berkeley, whose title dates from 1679, but is now the seat of Lord Fitzhardinge The living is a vicarage in the diocese of Gloucester and Bristol Value, now £750 * Patron, Lord Fitzhardinge The p curacy of Stone is a separate charge.—The sub district contains Berkeley parish and three other parishes, and is in the district of Thornbury Acres, 21,186 Pop, 5,396 Houses, 1 094 The hundred is cut into two divisions, Lower and Upper The Lower division contains Elberton parish, three other parishes, and parts of two others Acres, 13,393 The Upper division contains Berkeley parish, seventeen other parishes, and part of another Acres, 57,190 Pop of both, 24,453 Houses, 5,441

BERKELEY, or BERKLEY, a parish in Frome district, Somerset, on the Great Western railway, 2 miles ENE of Frome It includes part of the tything of Old Ford, and its post town is Frome Acres 1,927 Real property, with Standerwick, £3,351 Pop, 386 Houses, 86 The property is divided among a few Berkeley House is the seat of E Dickinson, Esq The living is a rectory in the diocese of Bath and Wells. Value, £410 * Patron, Sir C Mordant, Bart The church is good

BERKELEY AND GLOUCESTER CANAL, a ship canal in Gloucestershire It opens from the Severn, at a point about 2½ miles N of Berkeley, and goes 16½ miles north eastward, somewhat parallel with the Severn, to Gloucester It was completed in 1827, and is navigable for vessels of 300 tons A cut connects it with Berkeley

BERKELEY ROAD, a station on the Bristol and Birmingham railway, 22½ miles NNE of Bristol

BERKELEY (VALE OF), a rich strip of dairy land in Gloucestershire It extends from the southern vicinity of Gloucester, along the course of the Berkeley and Gloucester canal, to its junction with the Severn and thence past Berkeley, down the left side of the Severn, to Aust Its length is 23 miles, and its mean breadth, about 4 The soil of the upper part is clayey, that of the lower part is deep rich loam, and nearly all is disposed in grass for the produce of the dairy About 5,000 lbs. of butter are made weekly, and about 1,200 tons of cheese, chiefly double Gloucester, are made annually

BERKESWELL or BERKSWELL, a parish in Meriden district, Warwick on the Birmingham and Stafford railway, 6 miles W of Coventry It has a station on the railway, and a post office under Coventry Acres, [illegible] Real property, £10 872 Pop, 1,624 Houses, 363 The property is much subdivided Berkeswell House is the seat of T Walker, Esq The living is a rectory, united with the vicarage of Barston, in the diocese of Worcester Value £976 * Patrons the Misses Shirreff The church is Norman There are a well endowed school with £50 a year, recent alms houses with £150, and other charities £45

BERKHAMPSTEAD, a town a sub district, and a district in Herts. The town is chiefly in the parish of Great Berkhampstead, but includes part of that of Northchurch It stands in a deep rich valley on the Bulbourne river and on the Grand Junction canal adjacent to the Northwestern railway, 23 miles NW of London It perhaps occupies the site of the Roman station Durobrivæ and it was a residence of the kings of Mercia William the Conqueror made oath at it to maintain the ancient laws of the kingdom Robert, Earl of Mortaigne, got it from the Conqueror and erected at it a strong castle on the site of the Mercian palace Henry I took it from the earl, in punishment of rebellion and made it the centre of a royal domain Henry II kept his court at it King John gave it for a time to Jeffrey Fitz Piers Earl of Essex, but resumed it at the earl's death and made it again Crown property Richard, king of the Romans, got it from Henry III, and died at it The castle now belongs to the Prince of Wales as Duke of Cornwall, and gives him the title of Baron The "honour" connected with it includes numerous manors in Herts, Bucks, and Northampton

The town comprises one street about a mile long and five others leaving this at right angles The houses are chiefly of brick, and not regularly aligned, but many are handsome The railway passes on an embankment overlooking the town and the valley, and a communication comes from it over the canal. The remains of the castle are at the N end of Castle Street, and consist of detached portions of massive walls, with a double moat on the NW side, and a triple one on the other side The chief public buildings are a new market house, a grand town hall, a church, three dissenting chapels, a grammar school, a free school, a workhouse, and almshouses The church is a spacious, ancient, cruciform structure, of mixed styles with a central square embattled tower, has a number of side chapels, and contains tombs of the Torringtons, the Cornwallises, the Incents the Waterhouses, and others, and some brasses The grammar school was founded by Dean Incent, in the time of Henry VIII, underwent recent restoration, has an endowed income of about £1,300, and was intended originally for the education of 144 boys, but now educates only 24 The free school was founded, in 1727, by Thomas Bourne, and has an endowed income of £279 There were anciently three monastic hospitals The town has a head post-office,‡ a railway station, a banking office, and three chief inns A weekly market is held on Thursday, and fairs on Shrove Monday, Whit Monday, 5 Aug, 29 Sept, and 11 Oct Straw platting and the manufacture of wooden utensils are carried on Berkhampstead sent two members to parliament in the time of Edward III, and got a new charter from James I, conferring privileges some of which are still enjoyed. It is now a seat of petty sessions and a polling place Axtel the Puritan and Cowper the poet were natives The town's limits are those for registration of births and deaths Pop., 3,631 Houses, 738.

The sub district contains the parishes of Great Berkhampstead, Berkhampstead St Mary, and Little Gaddesden, and part of the parish of Pitstone Acres, 9,474 Pop, 5,733 Houses, 1,178 The district comprehends also the sub district of Tring, containing the parishes of Tring, Wigginton, Aldbury, Puttenham, and Marsworth, and part of the parish of Pitstone Marsworth and Pitstone are electorally in Bucks Acres of the district, 24 583 Poor rates in 1866, £6,506 Pop. in 1861, 13,204 Houses, 2,725 Marriages in 1866, 105, births, 456,—of which 30 were illegitimate, deaths, 253 —of which 106 were at ages under 5 years, and 7 at ages above 85 years. Marriages in the ten years 1851–60, 845, births, 4,286, deaths, 2,750 The places of worship in 1851 were 12 of the Church of England, with 4,035 sittings, 1 of Independents, with 314 s, 13 of Baptists, with 4,264 s 1 of Quakers, with 200 s, and 2 of Wesleyan Methodists, with 370 s The schools were 12 public day schools, with 859 scholars, 12 private day schools, with 320 s, 23 Sunday schools, with 2,368 s, and 1 evening school for adults, with 29 s

BERKHAMPSTEAD (GREAT), or BERKHAMPSTEAD ST PETER, a parish, containing most of the post town of Berkhampstead, in the district of Berkhampstead, Herts Acres, 4,250 Real property, with Friesden, £13,300 Rated property of B alone £12 538 Pop, 3,585 Houses 738 The property is much divided Berkhampstead Place is a chief residence The living is a rectory in the diocese of Rochester Value £434 * Patron, Prince of Wales Dr Cowper, chaplain to George II, and father of Cowper the poet, was rector

BERKHAMPSTEAD (LITTLE), a parish in the district and county of Hertford, 4 miles ESE of Hatfield r station, and 4½ SW of Hertford It has a post office under Hertford Acres, 1,689 Real property, £3 025 Pop, 450 Houses, 93 The property is subdivided. Berkhampstead House is a chief residence The observatory tower commands a fine view The living is a rectory in the diocese of Rochester Value, £249 * Patron the Marquis of Salisbury The church is very good Charities, £15 Bishop Ken was a native

BERKHAMPSTEAD ST MARY, or NORTHCHURCH, a parish in Berkhampstead district, Herts, on the Northwestern railway and the Grand Junction canal, averagely 1 mile NW of Berkhampstead, but including part of that town It has a post office, of the name of Northchurch, under Berkhampstead. Acres, 3,880 Real property, £7,454 Pop, 1,638 Houses, 334 The property is subdivided. An ancient structure, now used as a farmhouse, was originally part of a small priory The living is a rectory in the diocese of Rochester Value, £794 Patron, the Prince of Wales The church is decorated English, and cruciform There is a chapel of ease at Broadway, a beautiful edifice, built in 1854 There are also a Baptist chapel, and charities £30

BERKING See BARKING, Essex.

BERKLEY See BERKELEY, Somerset.

BERKS, or BERKSHIRE, an inland county, within the basin of the Thames It is bounded on the N, by Gloucester, Oxford and Bucks, on the E, by Surrey, on the S by Herts, and on the W, by Wilts Its outline is irregular, and has been compared by some to that of a lute, by others to that of a slipper or a sandal. Its boundary, in a tortuous line along the N, from its most westerly extremity to its most easterly one, is the Thames Its greatest length is 48 miles, its greatest breadth, 29 miles, its mean breadth, about 14 miles, its circuit, about 165 miles, its area, 451,210 acres Its surface presents few abrupt or bold elevations. A series of downs, a continuation of those in the N of Wilts goes eastward across its broadest part, and attains, at White Horse hill, an altitude of 893 feet above the level of the sea. Most of the other tracts are distinguished by soft, gentle, luxuriant beauty The chief streams are the Thames, the Kennet, the Ledden, the Lambourn, and the Ock. A small tract on the SE border, round Finchampstead and Sunninghill, consists of Bracklesham and Bagshot beds A large tract across all the S, from the western border in the southern vicinity of Hungerford, past Newbury and Wokingham, to the eastern boundary at Old Windsor, consists of London clay and plastic clay A broad tract all across, from the western border at Hungerford and the neighbourhood of Ashbury, to the Thames from the vicinity of Reading to Moulsford, consists of chalk A considerable belt N of this, and all across, consists of upper greensand and gault. A narrow belt, further N, consists of lower greensand Two belts still further N, the second lying all along the Isis or Thames to a point below the vicinity of Kennington, consist of oolite, the former of the upper series, the latter of the middle. The minerals and the fossils do not possess much interest, and mineral waters are scarce Peat exists in considerable quantity on low grounds of the Kennet, and in small quantity on some high lands of the Thames, and has been extensively burned for its ashes

About 260,000 acres are arable, 76,000 meadow, 55,000 parks and sheep walks 30,000 wood and 29,000 waste The soils are exceedingly various, ranging from strong stiff loam to a mixture of sharp sand and peat The vale of the White Horse is the most fertile tract, and the vale of the Kennet vies with it, and perhaps is better cultivated The state of agriculture and the condition of the farmer are middle rate Wheat, oats, barley, turnips, and beans are the chief crops grown, but buckwheat, vetches, pease, potatoes, rape, carrots, hops, flax, and artificial grasses also are cultivated Much land on the Thames and around Faringdon is devoted to the dairy The sheep walks are depastured by a native breed called the Notts, and by mixtures of them with the Southdowns, the Wiltshires and other breeds The cattle are mostly of the long horn or common country breed The draught horses are good and strong, but not tall Hogs and poultry are numerous in the dairy tracts, and from the proximity of London yield much profit to the farmer The native breed of hogs is highly esteemed and a mixed breed at Sunninghill Park is pre eminently good. Wood lands prevail much in the E, and get prominence there from Windsor forest Oak and beech are the chief trees in the woods Osiers are grown in watery places for baskets, and alders for rake handles and other uses Fine trout and other fish abound in most of the streams. Manufactures are of small note Woollen cloth, sacking, and sail cloth were formerly made in large quantity, but have ceased to be of any consequence Paper is made in the vale of the Kennet Much malt is manufactured for the London market and the Kennet and Windsor ales are in repute The Thames is navigable along all the N boundary and the Kennet, by means of cuts, for 30 miles, from Reading to Hungerford The Berks and Wilts canal goes across all the N, from the vicinity of Abingdon up the vale of the White Horse; and the Kennet and Avon canal completes the navigation of the Kennet from Newbury to Hungerford. The Great Western railway enters at Maidenhead, sends off a branch thence into Bucks towards High Wycombe, passes on to Twyford, sends off a branch thence across the Thames to Henley, passes on to Reading is joined there by a line coming up from the South western at Guildford passes up the Thames to Didcote, sends off thence a branch to Oxford, with sub branch to Abingdon, and goes away westward to Wilts in the vicinity of Shrivenham Minor lines also come to Windsor, the Staines line comes westward into junction with the Reading and Guildford at Wokingham, a line goes southward from Reading toward Basingstoke another line goes westward from Reading to Hungerford, and recently formed branches go from the Great Western to Wallingford and Faringdon The roads have an aggregate of about 1,620 miles

Berks contains 146 parishes, parts of 14 others, and three extra parochial tracts, and is divided into the boroughs of Abingdon, Maidenhead, Newbury, Reading, Wallingford, and Windsor, and the hundreds of Beynhurst, Bray, Charlton, Compton Cookham, Faircross, Faringdon, Ganfield Hormer Kintbury Eagle, Lambourn, Moreton Ock Reading, Ripplesmere, Shrivenham, Sonning, Theale Wantage, and Wargrave The act of 1844, for consolidating detached parts of counties, severed from Berks places amounting to 6,510 acres, and annexed to it places amounting to 1,515 acres The registration county excludes 4,100 acres of the electoral county, includes 113,464 acres of adjoining electoral counties, comprises altogether 564 717 acres, and is divided into the districts of Newbury, Hungerford, Faringdon Abingdon, Wantage, Wallingford, Bradfield, Reading, Wokingham Cookham, Easthampstead, and Windsor The county town is Reading, and the market towns are Reading, Abingdon, Faringdon, Newbury, Wantage, Wokingham, Maidenhead East Ilsley, Lambourn, Hungerford, Wallingford, and Windsor The chief seats are Windsor Castle, Wytham Abbey, Ashdown Park, Coleshill House, Pullingbear Park Sandleford Priory, Beckett Park, Basildon Park, Beenham House, Bear Place Stanlake Warfield House, Lockinge Park, Abbey House Aldermaston Bagor House Barton Court Benham House, Bear Wood Bill Hill, Binfield, Bisham Abbey Besselsleigh, Buckland Bussock, Castle Priory, Chaddleworth, Chilton House, Culham Court, Donnington Castle, Englefield House East Hendred, Hall Place, Hayward Lodge, Holme Park Hungerford Park, Kingston Lisle Luckley House Lambourn Place Maidenhead House, Midgham, Old Windsor, Padworth, Purley House, Shaw House Silwood, Slubbing Sunninghill Park Swallowfield House, Temple House, Titness Park, Wasing Lodge, West Court, White Knights, Winkfield Park, Woodley Lodge and Woolley Park Assessed property in 1815 £613 781 real property, in 1843, £967,175, in 1851, £977 836, in 1860 £1,021,914

Berks is governed by a lord lieutenant a high sheriff, 40 deputy lieutenants, and about 150 magistrates It is in the home military district and in the Oxford judicial circuit The Lent assizes are held at Reading the summer assizes at Abingdon Quarter sessions are held on 31 Dec and 8 April at Reading, and on 1 July and 14 Oct at Abingdon The police force includes 114 men for the county and 62 for the boroughs There are county jails at Reading and Abingdon, and a reformatory school at Reading The crimes, in 1864, were 223 in the county and 106 in the boroughs, the persons apprehended, 140 in the county and 91 in the boroughs, the known depredators or suspected persons at large, 662 in the county and 730 in the boroughs the houses of bad character, 64 in the county and 96 in the boroughs. Three members are sent to parliament by the county, exclusive of the boroughs, two by Reading, one by Windsor, one by Abingdon, and one by Wallingford The electors of the county, exclusive of the boroughs, in 1868, were 5 066 Berks is in the diocese of Oxford, and constitutes an archdeaconry, comprising four deaneries The poor rates for the registration county in 1863 were £124 426 Marriages in 1866, 1 529,—of which 213 were not according to the rites of the Established church births, 6 738,—of which 439 were illegitimate, deaths, 4,024,—of which 1,392 were at ages under 5 years, and 160 at ages above 85 years The places of worship within the electoral county in 1851 were 206 of the Church of England with 56,679 sittings, 34 of Independents, with 8,412 s , 41 of Baptists, with 8,222 s , 5 of Quakers, with 944 s , 1 of Unitarians, with 220 s , 72 of Wesleyan Methodists, with 10,034 s , 53 of Primitive Methodists, with 5 948 s , 4 of Lady Huntingdon's Connexion, with 730 s , 1 of Brethren, with 70 s 10 of isolated congregations, with 1,078 s., 2 of Latter Day Saints, with 300 s and 6 of Roman Catholics with 1,192 s The schools were 218 public day schools, with 16,584 scholars, 289 private day schools, with 6,065 s 245 Sunday schools, with 13,972 s , and 10 evening schools for adults, with 392 s Pop , in 1801, 110,480, in 1821, 132,639, in 1841, 161,759, in 1861, 176 256 Inhabited houses, 35 761, uninhabited, 1 355, building, 208

The territory now forming Berks was inhabited, in the ancient British times, by two tribes whom the Roman invaders called Bibroci and Attrebatii It became part of the Roman Britannia Prima It next formed part of the Saxon kingdom of Wessex and was then called Berrocscire It was the scene of frequent conflicts with the Danes, and it afterwards figured in the struggle between the Empress Matilda and Stephen, in the quarrels between King John and his nobles and in the war between Charles I and his parliament The chief events in its history will be found noted in the articles ABINGDON, MAIDENHEAD, WALLINGFORD WANTAGE and WINDSOR British, Roman and Saxon remains chiefly barrows and camps, occur at Little Coxwell, Sinodun, Letcombe, Uffingham, the White Horse hill Ashbury Ashdown, Speen, Binfield Castleacre, Hardwell, and Wantage Ickneild street traverses the county southwestward from Streatley to the southwestern vicinity of Newbury, and sends off branches along the hills An ancient road went from Speen to Silchester, another, called the Devil's Causeway, went by Old Windsor to Staines, and some others have left traces Ruined castles occur at Faringdon, Donnington, and Wallingford, and ancient mansions at Aldermaston, Appleton, Ockholt, Cumnor, and Wytham Abbeys stood at Abingdon, Bisham, Bradfield, Faringdon, and Reading priories at Bisham, Cholsey Hurley, Faringdon Reading Sandleford and Wallingford, preceptories at Bisham and Brimpton, and colleges at Shottesbrook Wallingford, and Windsor Interesting ancient churches, Norman or otherwise occur at Avington, Bucklebury Cumnor, Englefield, Shottesbrook, Uffington and Welford Berkshire gives the title of Earl to the Earl of Suffolk

BERKS AND HANTS RAILWAY, a railway from Hungerford in Berks to Devizes in Wilts It is 25 miles long and was opened in Nov 1862 and it was authorised in 1863, to be extended, 13 miles, to Westbury

BERKSHIRE See BERKS

BERKSHIRE ISLAND a wooded island in Windermere Westmoreland on the W side, near Ferry point

BERKSWELL See BARKSWELL

BERKSWICH See BASWICH

BERLING See BIRLING, Northumberland

BERMERSLEY See BEMERSLEY

BERMONDSEY, a parish and a district in Southwark borough, Surrey The parish lies on the right bank of the Thames, below London bridge, between Southwark proper and Rotherhithe, and is in the postal district of London S E, and traversed by the Greenwich railway Acres, 688, of which 27 are water Real property, £155,629 Pop. in 1841, 34,947, in 1861, 58,355 Houses, 8,220 Large portion of the surface is covered with compact town, suburban to London A quondam island or "eye," belonging to a Saxon chief Beormund, seems to have given rise to the name Bermondsey, originally Beormund's-eye, then Bermundesye A Cluniac abbey was founded here, in 1082, by Aylwin Child of London, endowed with the surrounding manor by William Rufus, made the prison and the death place of the widowed queen of Edward IV, given, at the dissolution, to Sir Robert Southwell, and sold, the same year, to Sir Thomas Pope. A magnificent mansion speedily superseded the abbey church, and was afterwards inhabited by Thomas Ratcliffe, Earl of Sussex, who died here in 1583 A gate of the abbey and some other remains were standing within the present century, but the only memorial of it now is the name of Abbey street. Two ancient hospitals, dedicated to St Saviour and St Thomas, stood adjacent A chalybeate well, some distance SE of the abbey's site, came into repute about 1770, and though now built over, is commemorated in the name of the Spa road Numerous watercourses or mill streams, rising and falling with the tidal current of the Thames, early attracted manufacturers of the classes requiring their aid, but gave rise to noxious effluvia, and were converted into sewers under the sanitary regulations consequent on the ravages of Asiatic cholera The suburb was long one of the filthiest seats connected with London, but has, of late years, been greatly improved One part of it, called Jacob's Island the scene of Bill Sykes's death in "Oliver Twist," is still pre eminently bad. The chief employments are leather working, ship building, and hat-making, but other employments are numerous A tract on the S is disposed in very productive market gardens

The living is a rectory in the diocese of Winchester Value, £300 * Patron, Mrs Pam The church is a plain structure of 1680 on the site of one which stood at the Conquest and it has, among its communion plate, a richly chased silver salver supposed to be of the time of Edward II, and to have belonged to the Cluniac abbey Three chapelries, all vicarages St James, Christ Church, and St Paul, were constituted in respectively 1840, 1845, and 1846 Value of each, £300 Patron of St. James, the Rector, of Christ Church and St Paul, alternately the Crown and the Bishop St. James church was built in 1829, at a cost of £21,412, and is a handsome structure, with an Ionic portico and a tower, after designs by Savage Christ Church was built in 1848, at a cost of £4,570, and is in the Romanesque style The total places of worship in 1851 were 5 of the Church of England, with 5 313 sittings 2 of Independents, with 1 500 s., 7 of Baptists, with 1,980 s, 2 of Wesleyan Methodists, with 1,072 s, 2 of the Wesleyan Association, with 370 s, 1 undefined, with 70 s, and 1 of Roman Catholics, with 1,250 s There is also a convent of the Sisters of Mercy The schools in 1851 were 13 public day schools, with 3 081 scholars 132 private day schools, with 3,277 s, 14 Sunday schools, with 3,237 s, and 5 evening schools for adults, with 252 s. One of the public schools has an endowed income of £213, another has £98, and other charities have £179

The district is conterminate with the parish, and is divided into St. James, St Mary Magdalene, and Leather Market Poor-rates in 1866, £25,638 Marriages in 1866, 617 births 2 897 —of which 79 were illegitimate, deaths, 1,623,—of which 801 were at ages under 15 years, and 20 at ages above 85 years Marriages in the ten years 1851-60, 4,341, births 21,152, deaths 13,228 St. James sub district is conterminate with St James chapelry Acres, 454, of which 27 are water Pop, 25,154 Houses, 3,630 St. Mary Magdalene sub district extends from the parish boundary, crossing Swan-street, near the Kent road, along the E side of Swan street and Pages-walk and the S side of the Grange road, Star corner, and Bermondsey-street to Crucifix lane, thence along the parish boundary to Artillery street, Church street, and Russell street to Dockhead, thence to Gedling-street and the Neckinger road to the Spa road, and along the Spa-road, Grange road, and Upper Grange-road, and thence along the parish boundary to Swan street. Acres, 142 Pop., 16,505 Houses, 2,195 Leather Market sub district commences at the parish boundary, crossing Swan street, near the Kent-road, and comprises the space in a line to run from that point and encompassing the W side of Swan street, Pages-walk, Grange road Star corner, Bermondsey street, into Snows fields, and following the parish boundary there into Crosby row, crossing Long lane, Baalzephon street, and the New road up to Swan-street again Acres, 92 Pop., 16,696 Houses, 2,393

BERMONDSPIT, a hundred in Basingstoke division, Hants. It is cut into lower half and upper half The lower half contains Candover parish and four other parishes Acres, 10,156 Pop. in 1851, 1,318 Houses, 249 The upper half contains Bentworth parish and eight other parishes Acres, 15,816 Pop, 2,430 Houses, 450

BERNE, a quarter in Whitchurch Canonicorum parish, Dorset, 4½ miles WNW of Bridport Pop 878

BERNE, Surrey See BARNES

BERNERS ROOTHING See ROOTHING BERNERS

BERNESLEY See BARNSLEY, Yorkshire

BERNICIA the northern part of the ancient Saxon kingdom of Northumbria It extended from the Tyne to the Forth, took its name from the river Brennich, which is the part of the Till above Wooler, and was a kingdom by itself separate from Deira or the southern part of Northumbria, from the time of Ida in 547 to that of Eanred in 841

BERNISTON See BARNARDISTON

BERNOLDSWICK. See BARNOLDSWICK

BERNWOOD, an ancient forest around Brill, on the borders of Bucks and Oxford See BRILL

BERRACH, a hamlet in Llanfihangel Aberbythych parish, Carmarthen, 2 miles SW of Llandilofawr

BERRICK PRIOR, a liberty in Newington parish Oxford, 4 miles NNE of Wallingford Pop, 181

BERRICK-SALOME a parish in the district of Wallingford and county of Oxford, adjacent to the Chiltern hills, 4 miles NE by N of Wallingford r station Post town, Brightwell, under Wallingford Acres 675 Real property, £971 Pop, 141 Houses, 36 The living is a p curacy, annexed to the vicarage of Chalgrove, in the diocese of Oxford Charities, £12

BERRIER AND MURRAH, a township in Greystoke parish, Cumberland, 8 miles W of Penrith Acres, 2,604 Real property, £1,248 Pop, 109 Houses, 19

BERRIEW, or ABER RHIW, a township and a parish in the district and county of Montgomery The township lies on the canal, at the influx of the river Rhiw to the Severn, 3½ miles NW of Montgomery, and 5½ SSW of Welshpool r station It has a post office‡ of the name of Berriew, under Shrewsbury, is a seat of petty sessions, and carries on some woollen manufacture Real property, with Allt, £2,398 The parish includes also the townships of Allt, Brincanisir Brithdir Ifrydd, Garthmill, Keel, Keelcochwyn Llandinir, Lunior, Penthryn, Trewstwelin, Vaynor Issa, and Vaynor Ucha Acres, 12,010 Rated property, £11,938 Pop, 2,155 Houses, 414 The property is much subdivided Vaynor Park is a chief residence Some fine scenery occurs on the Severn, and there are some ancient British remains The living is a vicarage in the diocese of St Asaph Value, £356 * Patron the Bishop of St. Asaph The church is good. A school has £93 from endowment, and other charities £52

BERRINGTON, a township in Kyloe chapelry Northumberland, 5½ miles S of Berwick-upon-Tweed Pop, 316

BERRINGTON, a hamlet in Chipping Campden

parish, Gloucester, near Chipping Campden Pop, 155 Houses, 42

BERRINGTON, a parish in Atcham district, Salop, on the river Severn, and the Severn V railway, with a r station, 4½ miles SE of Shrewsbury It has a post office under Shrewsbury Acres, 3,520 Real property £8,9?0 Pop, 772 Houses 112 The property is divided among a few The living is a rectory in the diocese of Lichfield Value £393 * Patron, Lord Berwick. The Atcham workhouse is here

BERRINGTON, a hamlet in Tenbury parish, Worcester, on the river Teme, 2 miles WNW of Tenbury Pop, 234 Houses, 4[illegible]

BERRINGTON AND EYE, a station on the Shrewsbury and Hereford railway 3½ miles N of Leominster, Hereford. Berrington Park adjacent is the seat of Lord Rodney, and a meet of the Hereford hounds.

BERROCSCIRE See BERKS

BERRON, a township in Llannefydd parish, Denbighshire, 5½ miles NW of Denbigh.

BERROW, a parish in Axbridge district, Somerset, on a bay of its own name, on Bristol channel 4 miles NNW of Highbridge r station and 9½ WSW of Axbridge Post-town, Burnham, under Bridgewater Acres 6 568, of which 4 410 are water Real property, with Brean, £7,994 Pop., 459 Houses, 112 The property is divided among a few A great extent of sand called Berrow flat, is alternately covered and abandoned by the tide, and this forms most of Berrow bay, which is simply an open narrow belt extending 8 miles northward from the mouths of the Parret and the Brue The living is a vicarage in the diocese of Bath and Wells Value, £186 * Patron the Archdeacon of Wells. The church is good

BERROW, a parish in Upton on Severn district Worcester, 5½ miles SW of Upton r station, and 7 W of Tewkesbury It has a post office under Ledbury Acres, 2,?50 Real property, £3,069 Pop, 453 Houses, 94 The property is much subdivided. The parish is a meet for the Ledbury hounds The living is a vicarage in the diocese of Worcester Value, £100 Patrons, the Dean and Chapter of Worcester The church is very good

BERRY BROW a village on the Huddersfield and Sheffield railway, 2 miles SSE of Huddersfield, W R Yorkshire It has a station on the railway, a post-office under Huddersfield, and two Methodist chapels

BERRY EDGE, a village on the NW border of Durham, ½ a mile E of Leadgate, and 5½ WSW of Swalwell It has a post-office under Gateshead See CONSETT

BERRY GREEN a hamlet 2 miles W of Bishop Stortford, Herts

BERRY HEAD, a headland at the south side of the entrance of Tor bay, Devon, 6 miles NE of Dartmouth It is square shaped, and consists of hard, smooth, flesh coloured limestone Its summit is crowned with traces of a Roman camp, and ruins of two large military stations constructed at the close of last century, and its north front is much quarried, and falls abruptly into deep water, with moorage for vessels, like a quay See ASH HOLE

BERRYMEAD See ACTON, Middlesex

BERRYNARBOR a village and a parish in Barnstaple district, Devon The village stands on an eminence, on the coast, 2½ miles E of Ilfracombe, and 9 N of Barnstaple r station It has a post office under Ilfracombe and contains a richly sculptured mansion of the time of Edward IV The parish comprises 4,958 acres. Real property, £6,235 Pop, 775 Houses, 184 The property is divided among a few Bowden farm house was the birthplace of Bishop Jewel. A small cromlech occurs about ½ a mile from the shore The living is a rectory in the diocese of Exeter Value £715 * Patrons, the Bishop of Exeter and others The church has a Norman and an early English chancel, a perpendicular nave and a decorated, high, massive tower, and is in tolerable condition There is an Independent chapel

BERRY POMEROY, a village and a parish in Totnes district Devon The village stands 1¾ mile E by N of Totnes r station The parish includes also Bridgetown, a suburb of Totnes, on the river Dart, and its post town is Totnes Acres, 4,525 Real property, £8,990 Pop 1,065 Houses, 222 The property, with small exception, belongs all to the Duke of Somerset Berry-Pomeroy Castle, on a rock, in a beautiful dell, surrounded with wooded heights, in the neighbourhood of the village, was built by Ralph de Pomeroy, a follower of the Conqueror, inhabited by his descendants till 1549, conveyed then to Protector Somerset, enlarged soon after, with magnificent additions at a cost of upwards of £20,000, inhabited, for the last time, by Sir Edward Seymour, in the time of James II and traditionally said to have been destroyed by lightning. The ivy-mantled walls of it, the great gateway, a round tower, a Tudor front of Protector Somerset's addition, and part of a Jacobean court of the time of Charles I, are still standing shattered and unroofed, and form, with the accompaniments of the dell and the woods, a very romantic object. The living is a vicarage in the diocese of Exeter Value, £360 Patron the Duke of Somerset The church is an ancient structure of nave, chancel, and aisles, and contains a handsome screen and tombs of the Seymours. John Prince, author of the "Worthies of Devon, was vicar for 42 years, and lies interred in the church

BERSHAM, a township and a chapelry in Wrexham parish, Denbigh The township lies on the river Clywedog, near Wat's Dyke, 1 mile W of Wrexham r station. Post town, Wrexham Acres, 1,901 Real property, £6,725 Pop, 3,073 Houses, 625 The Wrexham workhouse is here, and iron, lead, and coal works are carried on —The chapelry bears the name of Bersham Drelincourt or Berse-Drelincourt and is a p curacy in the diocese of St. Asaph Value, £90 * Patron, the Bishop of St Asaph There are a Calvinistic Methodist chapel and an endowed school

BERSTED See BEARSTED

BERSTED (NORTH), a tything in South Bersted parish, Sussex

BERSTED (SOUTH), a village and a parish in Chichester district, Sussex. The village stands 1 mile N of Bognor r station, and 1 from the coast and has a post-office under Bognor The parish extends to the shore, and includes Bognor and the tythings of North Bersted and Sampney Acres, 3,008 of which 152 are water Real property, £15,460 Pop., 3,123 Houses, 623 The property is much subdivided The living is a vicarage in the diocese of Chichester Value, £214 * Patron, the Archbishop of Canterbury The church was built in 1405, consists of chancel, nave, and aisles, has a tower with large buttresses, and an obtuse shingled spire, and contains a tomb of Sir R Hotham, the founder of Bognor The p curacy of Bognor is a separate benefice

BERT (THE) See BRIT (THE)

BERTHLWYD, a hamlet in Llangathen parish, Carmarthen, 3½ miles W of Llandilofawr

BERWICK, a district on the river Tweed and on the coast, in the extreme north of Northumberland. All of it, except the parish of Berwick upon Tweed, prior to the act of 1844, was a detached part of Durham It comprehends the sub-district of Berwick upon Tweed, containing Berwick upon Tweed parish and Tweedmouth parochial chapelry, the sub district of Norhamshire, conterminate with the parish of Norham, and the sub district of Islandshire containing the parish of Holy Island, and the chapelries of Kyloe and Ancroft. Acres, 57,975 Poor rates in 1866, £10,513 Pop. in 1861, 21,862 Houses, 3,5?? Marriages in 1866, 157, births, 677,—of which 61 were illegitimate, deaths, 491 – of which 161 were at ages under 5 years, and 11 at ages above 85 years. Marriages in the ten years 1851–60 873, births, 7,357, deaths, 4,380 The places of worship in 1851 were 10 of the Church of England, with 4,[illegible]3 sittings 2 of the Church of Scotland, with [illegible]98 s. 3 of the Presbyterian Church in England, with 1,320 s., 6 of the United Presbyterian Church, with 3,910 s, 1 of Independents, with 400 s, 1 of Baptists, with 350 s, 1 of Wesleyan Methodists, with 380 s, 5 of Primitive Methodists, with 701 s, 2 of Roman Catholics with 155 s, and 1 undefined, with 60 s. The schools were 25 public day schools, with 2,534 scholars, 31 private day schools, with 1,281 s, 34 Sunday schools with 2,713 s, and 1 evening school for adults, with 21 s See BERWICK UPON-TWEED

BERWICK, a hamlet in Llanelly parish, Carmarthen, in the vicinity of Llanelly Real property, £8,500,—of which £3,545 are in mines Pop., 1,809 Houses, 346

BERWICK, a village 4½ miles SE of Bridport, in Dorset.

BERWICK, a township in Atcham parish, Salop, on the river Severn, 3½ miles ESE of Shrewsbury

BERWICK, a village and a parish in Lewes district, Sussex. The village stands near the river Cuckmere, 1 mile S of a station of its own name on the South Coast railway, and 7 miles SE of Lewes. The parish comprises 1,097 acres, and its post town is Alfriston, under Lewes Real property, £1,591 Pop., 169 Houses, 34 The property is divided among a few The living is a rectory in the diocese of Chichester Value, £362.* Patron, J Ellman, Esq The church is good.

BERWICK BASSETT, a parish in Marlborough district, Wilts, 6 miles S by E of Wootton-Bassett r station, and 6½ NW of Marlborough. Post town, Winterbourne Bassett, under Swindon. Acres, 1,388 Real property, £1,643 Pop., 171 Houses, 33 The property is divided among a few The living is a vicarage, united in 1866 with Winterbourne Monkton, in the diocese of Salisbury Value, £300 Patron, the Bishop of S.

BERWICK (GREAT and LITTLE), a township in St. Mary Shrewsbury parish, Salop, on the river Severn, 2 miles NW of Shrewsbury Berwick House here is the seat of the Hon H W Powys Little Berwick is also a chapelry Pop, 825 The living is a p curacy in the diocese of Lichfield. Value, £54 Patrons, the Earl of Tankerville and others The church was repaired in 1859

BERWICK HALL See BARWICK HALL

BERWICK HILL, a township in Ponteland parish, Northumberland, 6½ miles S by W of Morpeth Acres, 1,604 Pop., 98 Houses, 20

BERWICK IN ELMET See BARWICK IN ELMET

BERWICK-IN THE BRAKES See BARWICK, Norfolk

BERWICK (LITTLE) See BERWICK (GREAT and LITTLE)

BERWICK PRIOR See BERRICK PRIOR

BERWICK-ST JAMES, a parish in Wilton district, Wilts, on an affluent of the river Wiley, 2¾ miles NNW of Wishford r station, and 5¼ WSW of Amesbury Post town, Winterbourne Stoke, under Salisbury Acres, 2,487 Real property, with Stapleford, £4,662 Pop, 252 Houses, 53 The property is divided among a few The living is a vicarage in the diocese of Salisbury Value, £54 Patron, Lord Ashburton The church is early English, has a Norman doorway, and is very good

BERWICK ST JOHN, a parish in Tisbury district, Wilts, at the source of the Ebell river, under White Sheet hills, near Cranborne Chase, 4¾ miles S of Tisbury r station, and 5½ E by S of Shaftesbury It has a post office under Salisbury Acres, 3,669 Real property, with Alvediston and Tollard-Royal, £7,280 Pop, 499 Houses, 98 The property is divided among a few Winkelbury camp, or Vespasian's camp, on a lofty ridge in the SW, is an entrenchment of 12½ acres, engirt by a single ditch and by a rampart 39 feet high, and commands a very extensive view The living is a rectory in the diocese of Salisbury Value, £562 Patron, New College, Oxford The church is a cruciform structure of the time of Henry VII, has a low, square, central, ornamented tower, was restored in 1861-2, and contains two ancient effigies of crusaders, and monuments of the Grove family and others There is a Baptist chapel.

BERWICK ST LEONARD, a parish in Tisbury district, Wilts, 1 mile E of Hindon, and 2¾ NNW of Tisbury r station Post town, Hindon, under Salisbury Acres, 970 Real property, with Hindon, Chicklade, and Fonthill-Gifford, £5,111 Pop 40 Houses, 8 The property is divided among a few Remains of the old manor house, the seat of the Howes from 1629 to 1735, where the Prince of Orange slept in 1668 on his way to London, are now part of a suite of farm buildings. The living is a rectory, united with the p curacy of Sedghill, in the diocese of Salisbury Value, £374 Patron, the Marquis of Westminster The church was recently restored.

BERWICK SALOME See BERRICK SALOME

BERWICK STREET See WESTMINSTER.

BERWICK UPON TWEED, a town, a parish, and a sub district, in the district of Berwick, Northumberland. The town stands on the left bank of the Tweed adjacent to the junction of the Northeastern and the North British railways, 64 miles by road, and 67¼ by railway, N by W of Newcastle upon Tyne Its site is a gentle declivity, sloping to the river, about ½ a mile from the sea. A tract of about 8 square miles around it, and including it, was formerly a peculiar jurisdiction, neither in England nor in Scotland, but, by a recent act, was incorporated with Northumberland The environs are diversified and beautiful, present picturesque views, especially along the Tweed and on the coast, and comprise charming walks and drives.

The town dates from ancient times, but comes obscurely into record, and probably was founded by the Saxon kings of Northumbria. It was taken, in 880, by Gregory of Scotland, given, in 1020, by the Cospatricks to Malcolm IV, and figured, in the early part of next century, as a place of mark, the capital of Lothian, and one of the first four royal boroughs of Scotland It was taken from the Scots, in 1174, by Henry II, restored to them by Richard I, ravaged by King John, taken, in 1272, by Edward I, who crowned Baliol at it in 1292, taken again, in 1295, by Edward, and made his capital of Scotland, retaken, in 1297, by the Scots under Wallace, while its castle remained with the English, made the scene, in 1305, of the exposure of half of the body of the executed Wallace, the place, in 1310, of the winter residence of Edward II and his queen, the place, in 1314, of the mustering of the English army before the battle of Bannockburn, taken again, in 1318, by the Scots under Bruce, retaken, in 1333, by the English after the battle of Halidon Hill, surprised and recaptured, in 1353, by the Scots, recaptured, next year, by the English, surprised again, in 1377, by seven Scotchmen, and held eight days against 7,000 archers and 3,000 cavalry, recovered by the Percys, and used by them, in 1406, against the Crown, taken promptly from them through the astounding effect of cannon shot, the first ever fired in England, attempted, in 1422, by the Scots, ceded to them, in 1461, by Margaret of Anjou after the battle of Towton, re ceded, in 1482, to the English, and declared, in 1551, a neutral territory, independent of both England and Scotland It was visited in 1603, by James I on his way to England, in 1633 and 1639, by Charles I, and taken, in 1648, by Cromwell

Many fortifications, at different periods, were raised round the town, and the latest walls, together with small portions of more ancient works, are still standing The original walls comprehended a circuit of nearly 2¾ miles, and included the present suburb of Castlegate, and a tower belonging to them, used as a watch tower, with commanding outlook on the surrounding country, and called the Bell tower, still exists. The present walls comprehend a circuit of about 1⅝ mile, were built in the time of Elizabeth, and consist of a broad rampart, formed of earth, faced with masonry, and defended on the land sides by five bastions, but they were dismantled in 1822, and are now disposed in a pleasant promenade The castle or citadel stood contiguous on the W, on high ground stooping precipitously to the Tweed, it dates from the same remote times as the town, long possessed much military strength, went into disrepair in the time of Elizabeth, contributed much building material for the town in the time of Cromwell, and has now all disappeared except the dilapidated exterior western wall The Countess of Buchan was shut up in it, in a wicker cage, four years, by Edward I, for putting the crown on the head of Robert Bruce at his coronation

The town presents a mixed appearance of the ancient and the modern Two chief lines of street intersect it, the one from N to S, the other from E to W and divide it into four nearly equal parts The town hall at the foot of High street, was built about 1755 by Dodd, and has a tetrastyle Doric portico, and a steeple 150 feet high The jail, on the E side of Wallace green, was erected in 1849, at a cost of £8 000, is in the Tudor style, and has capacity for 16 male and 7 female prisoners. The corn exchange was built in 1858, at a cost of about £5,000 The barracks were built in 1719, and enclose a quadrangle of 217 feet by 121 The railway station occupies the site of the castle, is a castellated structure 190 feet long and has all its offices on the east side The railway viaduct over the Tweed is 216 feet long, has twenty-eight semicircular arches, each 60 feet in span, is 124 feet high, from foundation to roadway, and commands a superb view The carriage bridge was built in 1609-1634 is 924 feet long but only 17 feet wide, and has 15 arches, gradually diminishing in span The harbour pier was constructed in 1810, at a cost of £40,000, runs nearly ½ a mile into the sea, and is crowned at the end by two fixed lights, the upper one bright, 44 feet high, and seen 11 miles off,—the lower one red, and seen when the bar has 10 feet water The parish church was built in the time of Cromwell, on the site of a previous edifice in which David Bruce was married to the sister of Edward III , was restored and enlarged in 1855, and is a plain neat structure, without a tower St Mary's church was built in 1858 A recently erected United Presbyterian church is a handsome edifice. There are eleven other places of worship, a national grammar school, with endowed income of £159, a school, with £1.., a freemen's academy other public schools, a dispensary, a workhouse, altered and enlarged, assembly rooms, in which concerts, &c are held, and a public subscription library A nunnery was founded by David I, a friary in 1270, and a priory at some other period, but all have disappeared.

The town has a head post office‡ of the name of Berwick, a telegraph station four banking-offices, and four chief inns, and it publishes three weekly newspapers A weekly market is held on Saturday and a fair on the last Friday of May Iron working, the trades connected with a seaport, and various kinds of manufacture on a small scale are carried on The adjacent fisheries were once worth £15,000 a year, but have decreased in value to £4,000 The town is a head port, and has Alnmouth, Belford, and Holy Island as sub ports. The harbour is rocky and suffers much from a shifting bar, but has good anchorage within The vessels belonging to the port at the commencement of 1868 were 14 small ones, of aggregately 502 tons, and 16 larger ones, of aggregately 1,651 tons The vessels which entered, in 1867, from the colonies and foreign countries, were 31 British, of aggregately 5,660 tons, and 57 foreign, of aggregately 6,862 tons, and those which entered coastwise were 372 sailing vessels, of aggregately 19,762 tons The customs, in the same year, amounted to £6,179 The chief imports are timber iron, bones, hemp, and tallow, and the chief exports, corn, wool, salmon, and provisions The town held various charters amid its shifting fortunes, but became permanently incorporated by charter of James VI , and now, as a borough, both municipal and parliamentary, includes also the rural parts of its own parish and the townships of Tweedmouth and Spittal on the right bank of the Tweed It is governed by a mayor six aldermen, and eighteen councillors, and it sends two members to parliament Acres, as a borough, 8,767 Direct taxes in 1857, £5,759. Electors, in 1868, 816 Pop as a borough, in 1841, 12 689, in 1861, 13,265 Houses 1,883 Stevenson, the writer on commerce, was a native

The parish comprises 7 606 acres of land and 589 of water Rated property, £33 541 Pop 8 613 Houses, 1 2.9 The living is a vicarage in the diocese of Durham Value £353 * Patrons, the Dean and Chapter of Durham St Mary's is a separate benefice, a vicarage of the value of £150, also in the patronage of the Dean and Chapter of Durham —The sub district comprises all the borough together with Ord township Acres, 11,335 Pop 14 127 Houses 2,135.

BERWYN, a station on the Ruabon and Corwen railway 3 miles W of Llangollen

BERWYN MOUNTAINS, a range of mountains in Merioneth and Montgomery It begins near Berwyn r station, and extends 20 miles south-westward to the sources of the rivers Dee and Dyfi A summit at its north eastern extremity, Moel Ferna, has an altitude of 2,108 feet above the level of the sea, another, 4 miles SW of this, Cader Ferwyn, has an altitude of 2,563 fee , and two others, 1½ mile and 4 miles SW of the road pass from Bala to Llanfyllin, have altitudes of 2,027 and 2,104 feet.

BERWYN RIVER, a streamlet of Cardigan It issues from Llyn-Berwyn, the "Verwin's rushie lin" of Drayton, and runs about 6 miles west-north westward, along a romantic mountain vale, to the Teifi, a little below Tregaron

BESCABY, an extra parochial tract in Melton-Mowbray district, Leicester, 5½ miles NE of Melton Mowbray Pop , 26 Houses, 4

BESCAR LANE, a station on the Southport and Manchester railway, 4 miles ESE of Southport, Lancashire.

BESCOT, a station on the South Staffordshire railway, 1½ mile S of Walsall. Bescot Hall, in the vicinity, is an old moated edifice, on the site of an ancient seat of the Hillarys and the Mountforts, and commands a fine view

BESFORD a township in Shawbury parish, Salop; near the river Roden, 3½ miles SE of Wem. Acres, 1,310 Pop , 167

BESFORD, a chapelry in St Andrew-Pershore parish, Worcester, on the river Avon and on the Birmingham and Gloucester railway, 2 miles WSW of Pershore Post town, Pershore Acres, 1,300 Real property, £2,025 Pop ,164 Houses, 34. Besford Court here is the seat of Sir T G S. Sebright, Bart The living is a p curacy, annexed to the vicarage of St. Andrew Pershore, in the diocese of Worcester The church is old, and has a tower

BESKABY See BESCABY

BESKERTHORPE. See BISCATHORPE.

BESSECAR, a hamlet in Cantley parish, W R. Yorkshire, 2 miles SE of Doncaster

BESSELS GREEN, a hamlet in Orpington parish, Kent. Here is a Baptist chapel.

BESSELSLEIGH, a parish in Abingdon district, Berks, 3½ miles NNW of Abingdon r station Post-town, Abingdon Acres, 893 Real property, £950 Pop , 92 Houses, 22. The manor belonged anciently to the Leighs, passed by marriage to the Bessels or Bessels, passed again by marriage to the Fettiplaces, was purchased by William Lenthall, Esq , speaker of the Long Parliament, and belongs now to his descendants The living is a rectory in the diocese of Oxford Value, £280 * Patron K J W Lenthall, Esq The church is a small building with chancel and belfry

BESSIES COVE, a romantic rocky recess, on the S coast of Cornwall, a little E of Cudden point, 7 miles ESE of Penzance A precipice flanks it pierced with caves, and crowned by an abode of fishermen

BESSINGBY, a parish in Bridlington district E Yorkshire, on the Hull and Scarborough railway, 1½ mile SW of Bridlington Post town, Bridlington, under Hull Acres 1,230 Real property £2 275 Pop ,70 Houses, 12 The manor house is an old brick building in the form of the letter L The living is a vicarage in the diocese of York. Value, £59 Patron, H Hudson, Esq The church was built in 1766 and has an ancient font

BESSINGHAM or BASSINGHAM a parish in Erpingham district, Norfolk, 4½ miles SW of Cromer, and 13 east of Walsingham r station Post town, Cromer, under Norwich Acres, 514 Real property, £856. Pop., 133. Houses, 34 The property is divided among a few The living is a rectory in the diocese of Norwich Value, £131 Patron F E Alden, Esq The church has a round tower, but is bad The moat yard, near it, is a fosse girt tumulus of about ½ an acre

BESTHORPE, a parish in Wayland district, Norfolk on the Roman road and the Norfolk railway, 1 mile E of Attleborough Post town, Attleborough Acres, 2 134

Real property £3,966 Pop., 554 Houses, 114 The property is divided among a few The living is a vicarage in the diocese of Norwich Value, £250 Patron, the Earl of Winterton The church is good

BESTHORPE, a township chapelry in South Scarle parish, Notts, on an affluent of the river Trent, 2½ miles E by N of Carlton r station, and 7 N by E of Newark upon Trent. It has a post office under Newark Acres, 510 Real property, £2 475 Pop, 338 Houses, 65 The property is subdivided Besthorpe Hall was built in the time of James I, and has a pointed roof and a tower The living is a p curacy, annexed to the vicarage of South Scarle in the diocese of Lincoln The church is good, and there are Independent and Methodist chapels a free school, and charities £9

BESTWOOD HALL, a farm house 4½ miles N of Nottingham, on a tract of 3,700 acres, once a royal domain and deer park, but now under cultivation

BESWICK, an extra parochial tract in Manchester borough, Lancashire, 1 mile NE of the Manchester and Sheffield railway depôt Acres, 60 Real property, £2,280 Pop, 851 Houses, 171 See BRADFORD and MANCHESTER.

BESWICK, a township chapelry in Kilnwick parish, E R. Yorkshire, 1½ mile NW of Lockington r station, and 6½ N by W of Beverley It includes the hamlet of Wilfholme, and has a post office under Beverley Acres, 1,593 Real property, £2,286 Pop, 252. Houses, 47 The property is divided among a few The living is a p curacy in the diocese of York. Value, £65 Patron, the Master of Archbishop Holgate's grammar-school. The church is good.

BETCHCOTT, a township in Smethcott parish, Salop

BETCHTON, a township in Sandbach parish, Cheshire, 2 miles SE of Sandbach. Acres, 2,594 Real property, £6,722 Pop., 798 Houses, 152 There are extensive salt works and a Methodist chapel.

BETCHWORTH, a village and a parish in Reigate district, Surrey The village stands on the river Mole, ¾ of a mile S of the Reigate and Reading railway, and 2½ miles W by S of Reigate, and it has a station on the railway, and a post office under Reigate The parish includes also the village of Brockham Acres, 3,726 Real property £7,196 Pop, 1,389 Houses, 264 The property is divided among a few Betchworth Park with the manor of West Betchworth, belonged to Lord Maltravers, who was made Earl Marshal by Richard II, passed by marriage, in 1437, to Sir Thomas Brown, went by purchase, in 1690, to Abraham Tucker, author of "the Light of Nature," who lived and died here, and is now united to Deepdene Park, the property of the family of Hope It contains a noble avenue of chestnuts and limes, nearly 1,000 feet long, contains also some shapeless ruins of Betchworth Castle, which was fortified and embattled by Sir Thomas Brown. Broome House, adjacent to the railway station, is the seat of Sir Benjamin Brodie. Brockham Lodge, in the neighbourhood of Brockham, is the seat of Mr W Bennet, and was the residence of Captain Morris, the song writer, who preferred the "sweet shady side of Pall Mall" to the woods of Betchworth The living is a vicarage in the diocese of Winchester Value, £200 * Patrons, the Dean and Chapter of Windsor The church was renovated and much altered in 1850, retains some interesting ancient parts, Norman and perpendicular, and has on the chancel floor a fine brass of W Wardysworth, vicar, 1533 Brockham-Green vicarage is a separate benefice. There are an Independent chapel, and £75 of charities.

BETHANIA a locality 2½ miles from Festiniog, in Merioneth, with a post office under Carnarvon

BETHEL, a locality 5½ miles W of Llangefni, in Anglesey, with a post office under Bangor

BETHFLKING See BALKING

BETHERSDEN, a village and a parish in West Ashford district, Kent The village stands 2 miles S of Pluckley r station, and 5½ WSW of Ashford, and has a post office under Staplehurst, and a fair on 31 July The parish comprises 6,345 acres Real property, £5,127 Pop, 1,124 Houses 237 The property is much subdivided. The manor belonged to the Grensteads, and passed to the Lovelaces A marble here, now little worked, and consisting almost wholly of minute fresh water shells, was formerly in great request for monumental sculptures and the decoration of cathedrals. The living is a vicarage in the diocese of Canterbury Value, £165 * Patron, the Archbishop of Canterbury The church is of Tudor date, and in good condition There are Baptist and Wesleyan chapels, a national school, and an education charity

BETHESDA, a village in Llandwrog parish, Carnarvonshire, on the coast, 5 miles SW of Carnarvon

BETHESDA a hamlet in Llanllechid parish, Carnarvon, 4½ miles SE of Bangor It has a post office‡ under Bangor, and has recently become populous in connexion with the neighbouring slate quarries

BETHGEILRT See BEDDGELERT

BETHNAL GREEN, a part of Tower Hamlets borough London, on the Eastern Counties railway, 2 miles NE by E of St Paul's It was formerly a hamlet in the parish of Stepney but was constituted a separate parish in 1743, and is now also a registration district It lies within the postal town delivery, and has receiving houses in Green street and in Bethnal Green road. Acres, 760 Real property, £166,220 Pop in 1841, 74,088, in 1861, 105,101 Houses, 14,731 Part is densely edificed, part consists of airy streets, and part is variously brick land, market garden, open field, and a portion of Victoria Park The whole, as a parish, is cut into four divisions, and as a district into four sub-districts, called Town, Church, Green, and Hackney Road. The inhabitants are chiefly journeymen silkweavers, who work in their own houses for the master weavers in Spitalfields The Columbia Buildings are a fine group of industrial dwellings and grand quadrangular market, with a massive tower, erected in 1864–9 by Miss Coutts. Bonner's Fields, in the E, were one of the assembling places of the Chartist rioters of 1848, took their name from an old mansion removed in 1851, said to have been the palace of Bishop Bonner Pepys in his diary, 26th June 1663, records going to Sir W Rider's house, at Bethnal Green, and says that the house "was built by the Blind Beggar so much talked of and sung in ballads,' and this "beggar' is said to have been the son of Simon de Montfort, Earl of Leicester, in the time of Henry III Sir T Gresham resided in Bethnal Green, and Ainsworth, the lexicographer, kept a school in it. The parish church is a plain brick structure built in 1746 Another church a handsome Grecian edifice, with a tower, was built in 1828, at a cost of £17,630, another, with traceried window and a good tower, was built in 1864, and ten others were built in 1840–50 The parochial living is a rectory, and each of the others is a vicarage in the diocese of London. The patron of all is the Bishop Value of the rectory, £500, * of St James the Great, £400, * of St Paul, £200, of each of the others £300 * or £300 The Jews Episcopal chapel, attached to the London society for promoting Christianity among the Jews, also is a separate charge Value, £300 * Patrons, Trustees. An Independent chapel was built in 1866, at a cost of £8,000 The total places of worship in 1851 were 13 of the Church of England, with 14,851 sittings, 14 of Independents, with 4,085 s, 6 of Baptists, with 1,637 s, 1 of Unitarians, with 250 s., 3 of Wesleyan Methodists, with 1,060 s, 1 of Primitive Methodists, with 250 s., 1 of Lady Huntingdon's Connexion, with 200 s, and 2 mixed and undefined, with 280 s The schools were 35 public day schools, with 8,237 scholars, 92 private day schools, with 2,277 s. 39 Sunday schools, with 9,786 s and 3 evening schools for adults, with 48 s One public school, together with an almshouse, has an endowed income of £808, and another has £157 There are four almshouses and a lunatic asylum, the latter founded before 1570 and the charities altogether have a yearly value of £560 The work house stood formerly in the Town sub district, but is now in the Green sub-district Poor rates in 1866, £33,461 Marriages in 1866, 2,099, births, 4,881 — of which 119 were illegitimate, deaths, 3,840,—of which

1,900 were at ages under 5 years, and 36 at ages above 85 years. Marriages in the ten years 1851-60, [illegible],671; births, 37,729; deaths, 21,733

BETLEY, a village and a parish in Newcastle under Lyme district, Stafford. The village stands on the verge of the county, near the Northwestern railway, 3½ miles N of Madeley station, and 6½ NW by W of Newcastle under Lyme. It has a post-office‡ under Crewe, and fairs on 30 April, 31 July, and 29 Oct, and was once a market town. It consists of one wide street, and is a pleasant, healthy place. The parish comprises 1,435 acres. Real property, £3,991. Pop, 850. Houses, 184. Betley Mere, a fine lake near the village, belongs to the Earl of Wilton. Betley Court, an elegant mansion, is the seat of Francis Twemlow, Esq, and Betley Hall, a fine old residence, is the seat of George Tollett, Esq. The living is a vicarage in the diocese of Lichfield. Value, £150.* Patron, G Tollett, Esq. The church consists of nave, chancel, and tower,—the nave ancient, the chancel built in 1610, the tower in 1713, and contains neat mural monuments of the Egertons and the Tolletts. There are a Wesleyan chapel, and charities £15

BETSHANGER. See BETTESHANGER

BETSOME, a hamlet in Southfleet parish, Kent, 3¼ miles SW of Gravesend. Pop, 188

BETTERTON, a tything in East Lockinge parish, Berks, near the Berks and Wilts canal, 2¼ miles SE by E of Wantage. Pop, 17

BETTESHANGER, or BETSHANGER, a parish in Eastry district, Kent, 3½ miles SSW of Sandwich r station, and 4 W of Deal. Post town, Northbourne, under Deal. Acres, 397. Real property, £1,700. Pop, 43. Houses, 6. Betteshanger Park belonged formerly to the Lors family and belongs now to Sir Walter James, Bart. The living is a rectory in the diocese of Canterbury. Value, £166. Patron, Sir W C James, Bart. The church is Norman, and has been restored

BETTISCOMBE, a parish in Beaminster district, Dorset, 5 miles W of Beaminster, and 6½ NW of Bridport r station. Post town, Broadwinsor, under Bridport. Acres, 667. Real property, with Pilsdon, £1,796. Pop, 76. Houses, 12. The living is a rectory in the diocese of Salisbury. Value, £180.* Patron, R. B Sheridan, Esq. The church was rebuilt in 1862, and in the early perpendicular style

BETTISFIELD, a township in Hanmer parish, Flint, with a station on the Cambrian railway, 4¼ miles NE of Ellesmere. It has a post office under Whitchurch. Acres, 2,234. Real property, £2,961. Pop, 361. Houses, 71. Bettisfield Hall is a seat of Sir John Hanmer, Bart, the descendant of Speaker Hanmer of Queen Anne's time, the editor of Shakespeare

BETTON, a township and a chapelry in St. Chad parish, Salop, 3½ miles SSE of Shrewsbury. The township is a conjoint one, bearing the name of Betton and Alkmere. Pop, 48. The chapelry is called Betton Strange. Acres and pop. returned with the parish. Rated property, £1,050. The property is divided among a few. Betton Strange House is the seat of G Scott, Esq, and Betton Hall the seat of the Norcops. The living is a vicarage in the diocese of Lichfield. Value, not reported. Patron, G Scott, Esq. The church is good

BETTWS, an ancient British topographical name, signifying variously a seat or a subordinate chapel, and a pleasant place between hill and vale

BETTWS, a parish in Newport district, Monmouth, on the Crumlin canal, near the Avon-llwyd railway, 2½ miles NW of Newport. Post town, Newport, Monmouth. Acres, 1,132. Real property, £1,236. Pop, 84. Houses, 15. The property is divided among a few. The living is a p curacy annexed to St Woollos, Newport, in the diocese of Llandaff. The church is bad

BETTWS, a parish in Bridgend district, Glamorgan, on the river Ogmore, 5½ miles N of Bridgend r station. Post town, Bridgend. Acres, 5,080. Real property, £1,3[illegible]7. Pop, [illegible]1. Houses, 77. The property is divided among a few. Coal is worked. The living is a p curacy, annexed to the vicarage of Newcastle, in the diocese of Llandaff. The church is good. There is a Unitarian chapel. Dr Price, the nonconformist divine, was a native

BETTWS, a parish in Llandilofawr district, Carmarthen, 3 miles SSE of Llandebie r station, and 8 S of Llandilofawr. Post town, Cross Inn, under Llanelly. Acres, 6,465. Real property, £3,844,—of which £760 are in mines. Pop, 1,547. Houses, 320. The surface is hilly, and includes the Bettws mountains, which are an offset of the Black mountains. The living is a vicarage in the diocese of St David's. Value, £98. Patron, the Bishop of St David's. There is a Calvinistic Methodist chapel

BETTWS, a township in Llanfawr parish, Merioneth, in the vale of Edernion, 1½ mile NE of Bala. Pop, 232. Fairs are held on 16 March, 22 June, 12 Aug, 16 Sept, and 12 Dec. There is a Calvinistic Methodist chapel

BETTWS, or BETTWS CEDEWEN, a village and a parish in Newtown district, Montgomery. The village is in Ucheldre township, and stands on the river Bechan 2½ miles above its influx to the Severn, and 3½ N by E of Newtown r station. The parish includes the townships of Ucheldre, Dolforwyn, Garthgellin, and Llanwnda, and its post town is Newtown, Montgomery. Acres, 5,305. Real property, £4,619. Pop, 730. Houses, 146. The property is divided among a few. The surface is undulating and upland, and part of it is pretty fertile. Gregynog was the seat of the Blayneys. A ruined ancient castle in Dolforwyn township is conjectured to have been built by the British in the time of the Romans, and the name of it, the latter part of which signifies "a maiden," is said to have suggested to Leland and Milton the tale of "the Maiden Sabrina." Some curiously wrought brazen and earthen vessels have been found near the castle. A vast hill camp, called Pen y Gaer, is in the neighbourhood of the village. The living is a vicarage in the diocese of St. Asaph. Value, £211.* Patron, the Lord Chancellor. The church belonged to a Cistertian nunnery, founded in the 13th century, has a tower built, in 1531, by John of Meredith, and contains a monument to him. There are chapels for Baptists and Methodists, and charities £24

BETTWS, or BETTWS Y CRWYN, a parish in the district of Knighton and county of Salop, on the river Teme and on Offa's Dyke, adjacent to Wales, 8 miles NW of Knighton r station, and 10 SE of Newtown. It contains the townships of Beguildy and Trebrodier, and part of the township of Kevencalanog, and its post town is Knighton. Acres, 8,664. Real property, £3,065. Pop, 520. Houses, 97. The property is divided among a few. The surface is upland, and includes a range called the Bettws hills. The living is a vicarage in the diocese of Hereford. Value, £57. Patron, Earl Powis. The church is tolerable

BETTWS ABERGELE, or BETTWS YN RHOS, a hamlet and a parish in St Asaph district, Denbigh. The hamlet stands 3½ miles SW of Abergele r station, and 9 W of St Asaph, has a post office, of the name of Bettws Abergele, under Rhyl, and is occasionally a seat of petty sessions. The parish includes the townships of Bennarth, Bodlyman, Cilcen, Denhenfryn, Maesgwig, Trellan, and Trofarth. Acres, 6,262. Real property, £3,720. Pop, 838. Houses, 193. The property is divided among a few. The surface lies high, is to a great extent uncultivated, and commands, from some points, grand views of the coast and the sea. The living is a vicarage in the diocese of St Asaph. Value, £399.* Patron, the Bishop of Llandaff. The church is good. There are four dissenting chapels and an endowed school with £44 a year

BETTWS BLEDDRWS, a parish in Lampeter district, Cardigan, with a station on the Manchester and Milford railway, 3 miles NNE of Lampeter. Post town, Lampeter, under Carmarthen. Acres, 2,216. Real property, £1,123. Pop, 222. Houses, 41. The property is divided among a few. The living is a rectory in the diocese of St David's. Value, £143.* Patron, the Bishop of St. David's. The church has a tower and spire, and is good. There are chapels for Baptists and Calvinistic

Methodists David ap Gwylim, who flourished in the middle of the 14th century, and whose writings were published in 789, and have mainly contributed to fix the modern literary dialect of Wales, was a native

BETTWS CEDEWEN See BETTWS, Montgomery

BETTWS CLYRO, or CAPEL BETTWS, a chapelry in Clyro parish, Radnor, on the river Wye, 3½ miles N of Hay r station Post town, Hay, under Hereford. Real property, £1,853 Pop, 188 Houses, 38 The living is a p curacy, annexed to the vicarage of Clyro, in the diocese of St. David's

BETTWS DISSERTH, a parochial chapelry in the district of Builth and county of Radnor, on the river Edwy, 7 miles SW of New Radnor, and 12 W of Kington r station Post-town, New Radnor Acres, 1 885 Real property, £810 Pop, 130 Houses, 19 The property is divided among a few The living is a p curacy, annexed to the rectory of Disserth, in the diocese of St David's The church is excellent

BETTWS EVAN, or BETTWS-JEUVAN, a hamlet and a parish in Newcastle in Emlyn district, Cardigan The hamlet stands on elevated ground, midway between Cardigan bay and the river Teifi, 5 miles N by W of Newcastle in Emlyn r station The parish includes also the hamlet of Llynnchel, and its post-town is Newcastle in Emlyn, under Carmarthen. Acres, 2,640 Real property, £1,537 Pop., 419 Houses, 101 The property is much subdivided The living is a p. curacy, annexed to the vicarage of Penbryn, in the diocese of St David's The church is good

BETTWS GARMON, a hamlet and a parish in the district and county of Carnarvon The hamlet stands on an eminence, adjacent to the rivulet Gwrfai, amid grand scenery of crag and lake and mountain, 3 miles ESE of Griffith's Craig r station, and 5 SE of Carnarvon, and it has fairs on 15 May and 3 Dec The parish comprises 2,759 acres, and its post town is Carnarvon Real property, £749 Pop, 94 Houses, 21 The property is divided among a few The surface is largely mountainous, and lies immediately W of Snowdon. Green pastures below the hamlet contrast finely with bold crags and rugged heights above A spring on the hill-side, called St Garmon's well, about a mile W of the hamlet, has considerable medicinal repute. The living is a vicarage in the diocese of Bangor Value, £90 Patron, the Bishop of Llandaff The church is good.

BETTWS GWERFIL GOCH, a hamlet and a parish in Corwen district, Merioneth. The hamlet stands near the river Alwen, 4 miles NW of Corwen r station, and has a post office under Corwen The parish comprises 2,650 acres Real property, £695 Pop, 242 Houses, 59 The property is divided among a few The living is a rectory in the diocese of St Asaph Value, £124 Patron, the Bishop of St. Asaph The church is early English, and tolerable

BETTWS-JEUVAN See BETTWS EVAN

BETTWS LEIKI, or BETTWS LLEUCE, a parochial chapelry in Tregaron district, Cardigan, on the river Ayron 5 miles WSW of Tregaron r station, and 18 NW of Llandovery Post town, Llandewy Brevi, under Carmarthen. Acres, 2,312 Real property, £2,393 Pop., 349 Houses, 72 The property is much subdivided. The living is a vicarage in the diocese of St David's Value, £50 Patron, the Incumbent of Llandewy Brevi The church needs repair

BETTWS NEWYDD, a parish in Abergavenny district, Monmouth, near the river Usk 2½ miles E of Nantyderry r station, and 3½ N by W of Usk It has a post office under Newport, Monmouth Acres, 1,122 Real property, £1 057 Pop, 129 Houses, 27 The property is divided among a few The living is a p curacy, annexed to the vicarage of Llanarth, in the diocese of Llandaff The church is bad

BETTWS-PENPONT See PENPONT

BETTWS Y COED, a village, a parish, and a sub district, in the district of Llanrwst and county of Carnarvon The village stands at the terminus of the Llanrwst railway, 3½ miles S of Llanrwst, has a post office under Llanrwst, a r station with telegraph, and an inn, and is a resort of anglers and artists A curious picturesque bridge, called Pont y Pair, spans the Llugwy here, over a cataract which is notable as a salmon leap The parish comprises 3,537 acres Real property, £1,417 Pop, 509 Houses, 103 The property is all in one estate Some fine scenery, with several good waterfalls occurs in the vales and on the hills The living is a vicarage in the diocese of Bangor Value, £101 Patron, the Bishop of Bangor The church is ancient and good, and contains a monument of Gryffydd, grandnephew of the last Llewelyn There are an Independent chapel and a Calvinistic Methodist chapel.—The sub district comprises four parishes and part of another Acres, 35,118 Pop, 2,735 Houses, 578

BETTWS Y CRWYN See BETTWS, Salop

BETTWS YN RHOS. See BETTWS ABERGELE.

BEULAH, a locality 9 miles from Builth in Breconshire, with a post-office under Builth

BEULAH SPA, a mineral well 2 miles ENE of Mitcham, in Surrey Its water somewhat resembles that of Epsom, and was once in high repute, but buildings which were raised in connection with it went into decay, and the site was advertised for sale in 1857

BEULT (THE) See BEALE (THE)

BEVERCOATES, a parish in East Retford district, Notts, 2½ miles NW of Tuxford, and 3½ from Tuxford r station. Post-town, Tuxford, under Newark. Acres, 790 Real property, £799 Pop, 48. Houses, 7 The living is a vicarage, annexed to the vicarage of West Markham, in the diocese of Lincoln. The church is in ruins

BEVERE, an island in the Severn, 2½ miles N of Worcester It is supposed to have been a resort of beavers, was a retreat of the inhabitants of Worcester during the plague of 1637, and is now a good and favourite bathing place It contains a mansion, commands a fine view of the Abberley and the Malvern hills, and has a post office, of the name of Bevere Green, under Worcester

BEVERLEY, a town, four parishes, a sub district, and a district in E R. Yorkshire The town stands on the Hull and Scarborough railway, at the E foot of the Wolds, about a mile W of Hull river, 8½ miles NNW of Hull The country to the E is flat, but the parts adjacent are fertile and well wooded All was anciently swampy, then covered with forest, then cleared for fuel and for cultivation Lakes frequented by beavers, in the swampy epoch, are supposed by many to have given rise to the name Beverley in the form of Bever Lac The town, however, may possibly have been the Petuaria of Ptolemy, with Roman origin, dating from the second century, and it was known to the Saxons as Beoforlic and Beverloga. John, Archbishop of York, commonly called St John of Beverley, founded a monastery at it in 700, and died and was buried here in 721 The Danes destroyed the monastery in 867 King Athelstane, after his great victory of Brunanburgh in 938, found the church of the monastery partly restored, richly endowed and extended it, as a collegiate church or minster, and gave it the right of sanctuary for a mile round the town, marked by four stone crosses, set up at the principal approaches. William the Conqueror, in 1069, encamped in the neighbourhood, and issued strict orders to his army to respect the property of the church The principal part of the town, together with the church, was destroyed by fire in 1186 Edward I, during his wars against Scotland, in 1299-1316, frequently visited Beverley, and carried the standard of St. John at the head of his army Henry IV visited the town in 1399, Edward IV marched through it in 1471, and Charles I alternately took post in it and was dislodged in 1639 and 1642 The town early acquired a right of prize and toll over the shipping of the Humber, and, in later times, it struggled hard against the transfer of that right to the rising port of Hull Many a legend exists respecting alleged miracles, in the old times, in the minster, and a monkish pretence runs through old history that the standard of St John together with the standards of St Peter of York and St. Wilfrid of Ripon, had much to do with the vic tories of the English arms An old ballad, speaking of the battle of the "Standard" in 1138 and putting a speech into the mouth of the Scottish king, says,—

"The holy cross,
That shines as bright as day,
Around it hung the sacred banners
Of many a blessed saint,
St. Peter and John of Beverley,
And St Wilfrid there they paint.
'Oh had I but yon holy rood
That there so bright doth show,
I would not care for yon English host,
Nor the worst that they could do'"

The town consists of several streets, and is well built. The principal street is nearly a mile long, and terminates in an ancient gateway, called the North Bar The guild hall is a handsome edifice, new fronted in 1832, and contains apartments for the corporation and for sessions. The county house of correction was erected at a cost of £42,000, and afterwards enlarged, and contains accommodation for 166 male and 21 female prisoners The market cross is a modern erection, more curious than useful There are also a corn exchange and assembly-rooms. One of Athelstane's crosses still stands on an eminence to the N There were anciently a monastery of black friars, a monastery of grey friars, and an establishment of knights-hospitallers, and two gateways of the first may still be seen on the NE of the minster There are a grammar school with eight scholarships at Cambridge, and a library, a blue coat school, a mechanics institution, a dispensary, three hospitals, for 6, 12, and 32 widows, a work house, and almshouses. The charities amount annually to £3 825, of which £1,559 are from minor estates The parish churches of St Martin and St Nicholas are extinct and there are now the parish churches of St Mary and St John, a handsome chapel of ease erected in 1841, eight dissenting chapels and a Roman Catholic chapel St Mary's church is cruciform with a central tower, was originally Norman and early English, but now exhibits early decorated and perpendicular additions, has a very fine seven light west window, between two beautiful octagonal pierced turrets, and contains an octagonal font of 15[illegible], and some interesting monuments A resolution was taken in 1859 to restore this edifice, and was carried out in 1865 St. John's church, or the minster, as it now stands, is supposed to have been completed in the early part of the reign of Henry III It consists of nave, choir, presbytery, transepts, central lantern, and two western towers, and is altogether 332 feet long It shows a mixture of styles yet is considered equal in variety of composition, correctness of detail, and elegance of execution to any of the great English cathedrals Mr Rickman says "The north porch of Beverley minster is, as a panelled front, perhaps unequalled The door has a double canopy, the inner an ogee, and the outer a triangle with beautiful crockets and tracery, and is flanked by fine buttresses breaking into niches, and the space above the canopy to the cornice is panelled, the battlement is composed of rich niches, and the buttresses crowned by a group of four pinnacles Of perpendicular fronts the same author says, "By far the finest is that of Beverley minster What the west front of York is to the decorated style, this is to the perpendicular with this addition, that in this front nothing but one style is seen all is harmonious Like York minster, it consists of a very large west window to the nave and two towers for the end of the aisles. This window is of nine lights and the tower windows of three lights The windows in the tower correspond in range nearly with those of the aisles and clerestory windows of the nave the upper windows of the tower are belfry windows Each tower has four large and eight small pinnacles, and a very beautiful battlement The whole front is panelled and the buttresses, which have a very bold projection, are ornamented with various tiers of [illegible] work, of excellent composition, and most delicate execution The doors are uncommonly rich, and have the hanging feathered ornament, the canopy of the great centre door runs up above the sill of the window, and stands free in the centre light with a very fine effect. The gable has a real tympanum, which is filled with fine tracery The east front is fine, but mixed with early English The chief monuments are a magnificent altar tomb of Henry Percy, fourth Earl of Northumberland, an altar-tomb of George Percy, grandson of Hotspur, a splendid altar tomb of two daughters of Earl Puch, called the "Maiden Tomb," and a monument to Major General Bowes, who fell at the assault of one of the forts of Salamanca

Beverley has a head post office,‡ a telegraph station, four banking offices, and two chief inns, and publishes two weekly newspapers. A weekly market is held on Saturday, a fortnightly cattle market, on Wednesday, fairs, four times a year, and races on the Hurn pastures, in June Waggons, carts, carriages, agricultural implements, artificial manures, whiting, and leather are manufactured in large establishments A canal goes to the river Hull Beverley is a seat of quarter sessions, the place of election for the east riding, and the head quarters of the east riding militia. The town sent two members to parliament once in the time of Edward I, received a charter from Elizabeth, and has sent two members to parliament from her time until now It is governed by a mayor, six aldermen, and eighteen councillors. The municipal borough consists of the parishes of St Mary, St Martin, and St Nicholas, while the parliamentary borough includes also the greater part of the parish of St. John Acres of the m borough, 2,228, of the p. borough, 9,168 Direct taxes in 1857, £6,517 Electors in 1863, 1,474 Pop of the m borough in 1841, 7,574 in 1861, 9,654 Houses, 2,156 Pop of the p borough in 1841, 8,671, in 1861, 10,868. Houses, 2,403 Beverley gives the title of Earl to the Percys, and it numbers among its distinguished natives Alfred, the ancient biographer, eight archbishops of York, Alcock and Fisher, bishops of Rochester, Green, bishop of Lincoln, Julia Pardoe, author of the "City of the Sultan," and Mary Woolstonecroft or Godwin

St Mary's parish comprises 570 acres Real property, £12,648 Pop, 3,331 Houses, 831 St. Martin's parish comprises 760 acres. Real property, £10,509 Pop, 4,413 Houses, 958 St. Nicholas' parish comprises 898 acres Real property, £5,526 Pop, 1,410 Houses, 337 St John's parish includes the townships of Thearne, Weel, Molescroft, Storkhill and Sandholme, Woodmansey with Beverley Parks, and Tickton with-Hull Bridge within the borough, and the township of Eske and part of the township of Aike, without the borough Acres, 8,280 Real property, £17,903 Pop., 1,315 Houses, 261 St Mary's is a vicarage St Nicholas a rectory, and St Martin's and St John's vicarages in the diocese of York St Mary and St. Nicholas form one living, of the value of £289,* in the gift of the Lord Chancellor St John and St Martin, with Tickton chapelry, form also one living, of the value of £420,* in the gift of Simeon's Trustees The sub district comprises the parishes of St Mary, St Martin, St. Nicholas, Bishop Burton, Cherry Burton Walkington and Skidby, most of the parish of St John, and part of the parish of Rowley Acres, 24,639 Pop 13 007 Houses 2,554 The district comprehends also the sub district of South Cave, containing the parishes of Newbald and Brantingham and parts of the parishes of South Cave, Elloughton, and Rowley the sub district of Leven containing the parishes of Routh and Wawne, and part of the parish of Leven and the sub district of Lockington containing the parishes of Lockington, Etton, South Dalton, Holme on the Wolds, Lund, Scorborough and Leckonfield with Arram, and parts of the parishes of Kilnwick and St John Acres, 78 434 Poor rates in 1866, £8,621 Pop. in 1861, 21,029 Houses, 4 450 Marriages in 1866, 169, births, 681,—of which [illegible] were illegitimate, deaths, 357,—of which 133 were at ages under 5 years, and 20 at ages above 85 years Marriages in the ten years 1851-60, 1,547, births, 6,507, deaths, 3,331 The places of worship in 1851 were 29 of the

Church of England, with 7,475 sittings, 5 of Independents, with 1,068 s, 5 of Baptists with 1,090 s, 20 of Wesleyan Methodists, with 3,655 s, 11 of Primitive Methodists, with 1,407 s., and 1 of Roman Catholics, with 63 s. The schools were 24 public day schools, with 1,894 scholars, 39 private day schools, with 994 s, and 36 Sunday schools, with 2,456 s

BEVERLEY AND BARNSTON CUT, a great drain along the low flat country of E. R Yorkshire from the Hull river, in the vicinity of Hull, north north westward to the vicinity of Beverley, and thence northward and north eastward to the sea at Barnston Its length, irrespective of branches, is 24 miles.

BEVERLEY PARKS. See WOODMANSEY

BEVERSBROOK, a tything in Calne and Hillmarton parishes, Wilts, 2 miles NE of Calne

BEVERSTONE, a village and a parish in Tetbury district, Gloucester The village stands 1½ mile WNW of Tetbury, and 6½ SSW of Brimscomb r station, and has a post office under Stroud. The parish comprises 2,360 acres Real property, £2,818 Pop, 1,0 Houses, 34. The property is not much divided A castle was erected here, in the time of Edward III, by Thomas, Lord Berkeley, was repeatedly besieged, and finally taken and burned, in the parliamentary wars, and is now a mass of ruin. Roofing stone is quarried The living is a rectory, united with the p curacy of Kingscote, in the diocese of Gloucester and Bristol Value, £590 * Patron, the Crown The church is a small ancient edifice of nave and chancel, and has a stone pulpit.

BEVIL S RIVER, a cut in the fens of the Isle of Ely, Cambridge It commences at the boundary, 6 miles SE of Peterborough, and goes 4¾ miles north westward to the Twenty Foot river

BEVINGTON, chapelry in Liverpool parish, in the northern part of Liverpool borough Pop, 14,331 Houses, 2,161 It was constituted in 1845, and is a vicarage in the diocese of Chester Value, £300 Patron, alternately the Crown and the Bishop

BEVOIS, a village in Hants, on the river Itchin, 2 miles N of Southampton It stands on the estate of Bevois Mount, and has a post-office of the name of Bevois Hill, under Southampton Bevois Mount contained the castle and the tomb of Sir Bev s of Hampton, was purchased, in the early part of last century, by the great Earl of Peterborough, was, in his time, a resort of Pope and Swift, and became afterwards the residence of the poet Sotheby,—who sang it in the sonnet entitled "Farewell to Bevois Mount"

BEWALDETH AND SNITTLEGARTH, a township in Torpenhow parish, Cumberland, near the foot of Bassenthwaite water, 6 miles ENE of Cockermouth Real property, £1,343 Pop, 95 Houses, 14.

BEWBUSH. See BEEDING (LOWER)

BEWCASTLE, a township and a parish in Longtown district, Cumberland The township lies in an upland tract, between the rivers Line, Kirkbeck, and Irthing, 6½ miles NNW of Rosehill r station, and 10 NE of Brampton Real property, £1,918 Pop, 152 Houses, 27 Here was a Roman station, garrisoned by part of the second Roman legion, to protect the workmen employed in building the Roman wall Here also was a Norman castle, repaired by Bueth, a Norman baron, lord of the manor, immediately after the Conquest, and called from him Bew castle The structure was square, each front about 87 feet long was occupied by a border garrison in the time of Elizabeth and demolished by parliamentary forces in 1641, and the ruin of it, in one part about 40 feet high, is still standing Many Roman coins and inscriptions have been found The right of fair and market was acquired in the time of Edward I but has long been in disuse The parish includes also the townships of Nixons, Bailey, and Bellbank, and its post town is either Gilsland or Brampton under Carlisle Acres, 30,000 Rated property, £8,693 Pop., 1,091 Houses, 205 The property is much subdivided The manor was given, in the time of Charles I, to Sir Richard Graham, and it remains now with his descendant Sir F U Graham of Netherby Large portion of the surface is wild and waste Coal, limestone, and lead are found. The living is a rectory in the diocese of Carlisle. Value, £120 Patrons, the *Dean and Chapter of Carlisle* The church is small and good, on a rising ground within the fossé which surrounds the station An ancient obelisk, a single block, 14 feet high, with sculptures and inscriptions which were but lately deciphered, stands in the churchyard There is an English Presbyterian chapel.

BEWDLEY a town, a borough and a sub-district in the district of Kidderminster, Worcester The town stand on a rising ground, on the right bank of the river Severn, and on the Severn valley railway, 3 miles WSW of Kidderminster It was originally an extra parochial liberty, but was united, in the time of Henry IV, to the parish of Ribbesford. It lay anciently within the marches of Wales, but was annexed, in the time of Henry VIII, to the county of Worcester It belonged to the Beauchamps, but became afterwards a royal domain A palace was erected at it by Henry VII for his son Arthur, who was married here by proxy, and the palace was occupied by Charles I, suffered much in the war with his parliament, and was subsequently taken down and erased The surrounding scenery is remarkably fine, and has been supposed by some to have given rise to the name Bewdley, as a corruption of the French Beaulieu. A Roman camp is on the neighbouring hill Basall or Wasall, and an isolated mound of red sandstone, called the Devil's Spade full, the subject of a curious legend, is in a hollow The town has wide streets, and, in general, is well built. Wribbenhall, on the other bank of the Severn, is a suburb, with some good streets, and is reached by a handsome stone bridge, erected in 1797 The town hall is a neat edifice of 1818, and the market place behind it has side arcades and an open area Bewdley church is a spacious structure, with a tower, and Ribbesford church is an ancient building, with Norman porch and low tower There are chapels for Baptists, Methodists, Quakers, and Unitarians, a grammar school with endowed income of £44, a literary institution, with free library, and almshouse and other charities, with income of £234 The town has a railway station, a head post-office,‡ a banking office, and two chief inns A weekly market is held on Saturday and fairs on 23 April, the Monday before 26 July, and 11 Dec. Large employment formerly arose from the carrying trade on the Severn, but was severely and permanently damaged by the formation of the Stourport and Stourbridge canal Manufactures are carried on in combs, leather, and malt John Tombes the opponent of Baxter and Richard Willis, an artizan's son who rose to be Bishop of Winchester, were natives

The borough was constituted by Edward IV, reconstituted by James VII, constituted again, on its original basis, after a long lawsuit, in the time of Anne, and reconstituted, on its present basis, by the reform bill It now, as a municipal borough, includes most of the parish of Ribbesford, and as a parliamentary borough, includes also the rest of that parish, and the hamlets of Wribbenhall, Hoarstone, Blackstone, Netherton, and Lower Mitton, in the parish of Kidderminster It is governed by a mayor, four aldermen, and twelve councillors, and it sends one member to parliament. *Direct taxes* in 1857, £4,060 Real property in 1860, £11,160 Electors in 1868, 361 Pop. of the m borough in 1841, 3,400, in 1861, 2,905 Houses, 686 Pop of the p borough in 1851, 7,318, in 1861, 7,084 Houses, 1,598 —There are five ecclesiastical charges within the borough,—Bewdley Ribbesford, Far-Forest, Wribbenhall, and Lower Mitton The Bewdley one is a vicarage, in the diocese of Hereford, income not reported, patron, the Rector of Ribbesford. The other four will be separately noticed —The sub district comprises three parishes, one of them electorally in Salop and one electorally in Stafford Acres, 9,021 Pop, 4,142 Houses, 911

BEWERLEY, a township in Ripon parish, W R Yorkshire, on the river Nidd, adjacent to Pateley Bridge, 11 miles NW of Ripley It includes part of the village of Greenhow Hill Acres, 5,872 Real property,

£4,973, of which £1 051 are in mines Pop, 1,297 Houses, 238 The inhabitants are chiefly employed in lead mines Bewerley House is the seat of the Yorkes.

BEWHOLME See NUNKEELING

BEWICK, a hamlet in Aldbrough township and parish E. R. Yorkshire, 7 miles SSE of Hornsea.

BEWICK (NEW and OLD), two townships in Eglingham parish, Northumberland, on Hatchope burn, 7½ and 6¾ miles SE of Wooler Acres, 1,125 and 5,487 Pop, 77 and 204 Houses 16 and 35 Two ancient British camps, and the Cateran s or Robber s hole, are here

BEWLEW CASTLE, a hamlet in Bolton chapelry, Morland parish, Cumberland, 3½ miles NW of Appleby

BEWLEY See BEAULIEU

BEWORTHY See BEAWORTHY

BEWSBOROUGH, a hundred in the lathe of St. Augustine Kent. It contains Buckland parish, and fourteen other parishes Acres, 15,857 Pop in 1851, 3,654 Houses, 680

BEWSY HALL, the seat of Lord Lilford, on Sankey canal, 1 mile NW of Warrington, Lancashire

BEXHILL, a village, a parish, a hundred, and a sub-district, in Sussex. The village stands on a rising-ground, in the neighbourhood of the sea and of the South Coast railway, 5 miles WSW of Hastings It has a station on the railway, a post office‡ under Hastings and an inn, and a fair is held at it on 1 July It contains some good houses, commands some chalybeate springs, enjoys a very salubrious air, is surrounded by charming environs, with fine extensive views, and has, for some time, been coming into favour as a watering place —The parish includes also the liberty of Sluice, and extends some distance on the shore Acres, 8,811, of which 817 are water Real property, £11,799 Pop., 2,084 Houses, 409 The property is subdivided The sea is receding from the coast, and has left to view a submarine forest. Lignite is found The living is a rectory in the diocese of Chichester Value, £989 * Patron, the Bishop of Chichester The church has a Norman nave and an early English chancel, and is good A subordinate church, St Mark s, is a rectory and a separate charge, of the value of £286, also in the patronage of the Bishop There are a Wesleyan chapel and two national schools.—The hundred is conterminate with the parish The sub district comprises four parishes, and is in Battle district. Pop., 4,312 Houses 644

BEXINGTON, a hamlet in Abbotsbury parish, Dorset, 1¼ mile W by S of Abbotsbury It was anciently a distinct parish, and the ruin of its church still stands near the shore

BEXLEY, a village, a parish and a sub district, in the district of Dartford, Kent. The village stands on the Cray river, and on the Lee and Dartford railway, 3 miles W of Dartford, has a r station with telegraph, a post office under London SE, and a fair on 13 Sept, and gave the title of Baron to the Vansittarts The parish includes Bexley Heath and three hamlets Acres, 5,025 Real property, £25,284 Pop, 4 944 Houses 1,002 The property is much subdivided The manor belonged, in the Saxon times, to the see of Canterbury, was alienated, by Cranmer, to Henry VIII, granted, by James I, to Sir John Spielman, sold by Spielman to Camden the antiquary, and bequeathed by Camden to University college, Oxford, for maintaining a professorship of history The living is a vicarage in the diocese of Canterbury Value, £ 2 * Patron, Viscount Sydney The church is chiefly early English, with later windows The vicarage of Bexley Heath and the p curacy of Lamorbey are separate benefices. There are a national school, an infant school alms houses with £100 a year and other charities £104 —The sub-district comprises four parishes Acres, 12,9 3 Pop, 13,026

BEXLEY HEATH a village and a chapelry in Bexley parish, Kent The village stands 1¼ mile NW of Bexley r station is modern pleasant large, and rapidly increasing, and has a post office under London SE a market house, a police station, a church with lofty spire, three dissenting chapels, a public library and reading room The chapelry was constituted in 1866 Pop, 2 989 The living is a vicarage. Value, £160 Patron, Viscount Sydney

BEXTON, a township in Knutsford parish, Cheshire, 1 mile SW of Knutsford Acres, 621 Real property, £1 306 Pop, 66 Houses, 13

BEXWELL a parish in Downham district, Norfolk, 1 mile E of Downham Market r station Post town, Downham Acres, 1 177 Real property, £2,073 Pop, 94 Houses, 16 The property is divided among a few The living is a rectory in the diocese of Norwich Value, £375 * Patron, the Bishop of Norwich The church is good

BEYNHURST, a hundred in Berks It extends 7 miles along the Thames, below Henley, and contains Bisham, and four other parishes. Acres, 12,099 Pop, 3,407 Houses, 684

BEYTON, or BEIGHTON, a parish in Stow district, Suffolk, 2 miles SSE of Thurston r station, and 5 ESE of Bury St Edmunds It has a post office under Bury St Edmunds Acres, 625 Real property £1 531 Pop, 360 Houses, 84 The property is subdivided The living is a rectory in the diocese of Ely Value, £175 * Patron, the Lord Chancellor The church is good.

BEYWORTH, a suburb of Petworth, in Sussex

BIBRACTE See BRAY

BIBRIDGE, a hamlet in Kirkharle township and parish, Northumberland, 10 miles SE of Otterburn

BIBURY, a village, a parish, and a sub district, in the district of Northleach, Gloucester The village stands on the river Colne, near Icknield street, 5½ miles S of Northleach, and 7½ NE of Cirencester r station, and has a post-office under Swindon —The parish includes also the tythings of Ablington and Arlington, and the chapelry of Winson Acres 6,800 Rated property, £6,898 Pop, 1,080 Houses, 234 The property is divided among a few Bibury House was built by the Sackvilles, is the seat of Lord Sherborne and commands a fine view along the Colne A very interesting old manor house, built in 1590, and belonging to the family of Coxwell is at Ablington The living is a vicarage in the diocese of Gloucester and Bristol Value, £1,023 * Patron, Lord Sherborne The church belonged to the abbey of Osney, shows features of Saxon, Norman, early English, and decorated, and is in very good condition There are a Baptist chapel, national and British schools, a police station, and charities £10 —The sub district comprises ten parishes and the greater part of Bibury parish Acres, 31,193 Pop, 5,642 Houses 1,147

BICESTER—popularly BISTER—a town, two townships, a parish, a sub district, and a district in Oxford The town stands in a rather flat situation, on Akeman street, and on the Oxford and Bletchley railway, near the ancient Alcester, 12 miles NNE of Oxford It was called by the Saxons Burenceaster or Bernaceaster, was probably built, in the time of Birinus, from the ruins of Alcester, and was a frontier garrison of the West Saxons against the Mercians An Augustinian priory dedicated to St Edburgh, was founded at it, in 1182, by Gilbert Basset, baron of Hedingdon, and given at the dissolution, to Charles Duke of Suffolk Both parties, in the civil war of the time of Charles I, inflicted damage on it and the royalists, in 164 , were defeated in a skirmish here A fragment of the priory, now a dwelling house, still exists, a spring called St Edburgh's well, formerly held in high repute for medicinal virtue is in the neighbourhood, and a path, called Edburg balk, a corruption of St Edburgh s walk, leads from the priory to the well Numerous ancient coins and other relics have been found The town is neat contains many recently rebuilt houses and has of late years been much extended by new streets and buildings The parish church is spacious was erected in 1400, on the site of the priory church has a seemingly Saxon arch early English and decorated parts, and a perpendicular tower, was recently restored and adorned, at a cost of £3 00, and has a brass and many tombs There are three dissenting chapels, a cemetery of 1861, large national schools, a workhouse built at a cost of £4,610, and charities £217 A handsome county court house was erected in

1864 The town has a head post office,‡ a railway station, a banking office, and two chief inns, is a seat of petty sessions, and publishes two weekly newspapers A weekly market is held on Friday, and fairs on Easter Friday, the first Friday of June and of July, 5 Aug., the Friday before and the Friday after 11 Oct, and the second Friday after 11 Oct, and the Friday after 11 Dec Manufactures in clothing sacking, and pale ale are carried on. Pop., 2,798 Houses, 620

The two townships are called Bicester Market End and Bicester Kings End B Market End contains most of the town and includes Wretchwick hamlet Acres, 1,040 Pop, 2,711 Houses 593 B Kings End lies to the N, had formerly a market, which was removed to B-Market End, and contains Bicester House and the site of Bigenhall. Acres, 1,540 Pop., 338. Houses, 64 —The parish consists of the two townships. Acres, 2,580 Real property, £10,498 Pop, 3,049 Houses, 657 The property is not much divided. The hunting establishment of T T Drake, Esq, the master of the Bicester hounds, is at Stratton Audley, 2 miles N of the town. The living is a vicarage in the diocese of Oxford Value, £270 * Patrons, the Trustees of the late Sir G P Turner —The sub-district contains the parishes of Bicester, Stratton Audley, Caversfield, Fringford, Newton Purcell, Shelswell, Hethe, Cottesford, Tusmore, Hardwick, Stoke-Lyne, Launton, Merton, Ambrosden, Piddington and Boarstall, the last electorally in Bucks Acres, 33,949 Pop, 8,115 Houses, 1,749 The district comprehends also the sub-district of Bletchington, containing the parishes of Bletchington, Ardley, Bucknell, Middleton Stoney, Chesterton, Wendlebury, Weston-on the Green, Charlton upon Otmoor, Oddington, Noke, Islip Kirtlington, Lower Heyford, Upper Heyford, Somerton, Fritwell, and Souldern Acres, 64,127 Poor rates in 1866, £9,410 Pop in 1861, 15 555 Houses, 3,378 Marriages in 1866, 80, births, 562,—of which 43 were illegitimate, deaths, 299,—of which 100 were at ages under 5 years, and 16 at ages above 85 years Marriages in the ten years 1851–60, 1,095, births, 5 371, deaths, 3,277 The places of worship in 1851 were 33 of the Church of England, with 7,635 sittings, 9 of Independents, with 973 s., 2 of Baptists, with 150 s, 14 of Wesleyan Methodists, with 1,519 s, 2 of Primitive Methodists, with 110 s, and one of Roman Catholics, with 170 s The schools were 26 public day schools, with 1,073 scholars, 26 private day schools, with 534 s, 52 Sunday schools, with 2,320 s, and 1 evening school for adults, with 15 s

BICKENHALL, a parish in Taunton district, Somerset, near the Chard canal and the Chard and Taunton railway, 5 miles SE of Taunton Post town, Staple Fitzpaine, under Taunton Acres, 1,004 Real property, £1,475 Pop, 229 Houses, 44. The property is all in one estate The living is a rectory, united to the rectory of Staple Fitzpaine, in the diocese of Bath and Wells The church is good

BICKENHILL, a parish in Meriden district, Warwick, on the Northwestern railway and the Warwick canal, 2 miles NW of Hampton-Junction r station and 8 SE of Birmingham It comprises Church, Middle, Lynden, and Marston quarters, and has a post-office under Birmingham Acres, 3,771 Real property, £6,674 Pop, 714 Houses, 170 The property is divided among a few The living is a vicarage in the diocese of Worcester Value, £222 * Patron, the Earl of Aylesford The church is old but good There are a chapel of ease, a national school, and charities £6

[BIC]KER, a parish in Boston district Lincoln, 1½ mile SW of Swineshead r station, and 8 WSW of Boston It includes the hamlets of Frist and Gauntlet, and part of the tract of Copping-Syke, and has a post office under Spalding Acres, inclusive of the extra parochial tract of Ferry Corner, 3,720 Real property, £8,002 Pop, 832 Houses, 166 The property is much subdivided The living is a vicarage in the diocese of Lincoln Value, £440 * Patrons, the Dean and Chapter of Lincoln The church was once cruciform, has a transition Norman nave and a central tower, and contains a Norman font There are two Methodist chapels, a free school, and charities £116

BICKERSTAFFE, a township chapelry and a sub district in the district of Ormskirk, Lancashire. The chapelry is in Ormskirk parish, lies on the Ormskirk and St. Helen's railway, near Blague-Gate station, 3½ miles SE of Ormskirk, was constituted in 1843, and has a post-office under Ormskirk Acres, 6,353 Real property, £10,733, of which £1,320 are in mines Pop, 1,637 Houses, 289 The property is divided among a few The township gives the title of Baron to the Earl of Derby Many of the inhabitants are colliers. The living is a p curacy in the diocese of Chester Value, £150 * Patron, the Earl of Derby The church is good The sub district includes also two other townships and two other parishes Acres, 11,335 Pop, 2,826 Houses, 485

BICKERSTONE. See BIXTON

BICKERTON, a township and a chapelry in Malpas parish, Cheshire The township lies 4 miles S of Beeston r station, and 5 NE of Malpas, and has a post-office under Whitchurch Acres, 1,755 Real property, £2,062 Pop, 379 Houses, 82 Bickerton hill commands a fine view, and has yielded some Roman coins The chapelry is more extensive than the township, and was constituted in 1843 Pop, 1,357 Houses 276 The living is a p curacy in the diocese of Chester Value, £120 * Patrons, the Rectors of Malpas

BICKERTON, a township in Rothbury parish, Northumberland, adjacent to the river Coquet, 4½ miles WSW of Rothbury Acres, 505 Pop, 22. Houses, 4

BICKERTON, a township in Bilton parish, W R. Yorkshire, 3½ miles NE by E of Wetherby Acres, 1,080 Real property, £1,405 Pop, 149 Houses, 30

BICKFORD, a village in Penkridge township and parish, Stafford

BICKINGTON, a parish in Newton Abbot district, Devon, on the Lemon rivulet, 3½ miles NE of Ashburton, and 4 W of Newton-Junction r station It has a post office under Newton Abbot Acres, 1,375 Real property, £1,876 Pop., 294 Houses, 60 The surface abounds with large limestone rocks. There is a large serge manufactory The living is a vicarage in the diocese of Exeter Value, £220 Patrons, the Dean and Chapter of Exeter The church is an old edifice, with square tower, and there is a small Wesleyan chapel

BICKINGTON ABBOTS See ABBOTS BICKINGTON

BICKINGTON (HIGH), a parish and a sub-district in Torrington district, Devon The parish lies on the river Taw, and on the North Devon railway, 2 miles NW of the Portsmouth Arms r station, and 7½ E of Torrington Post town, Atherington under Barnstaple Acres, 4,194. Real property, £3,384 Pop., 738 Houses, 150 The property is subdivided The manor belongs to A D Bassett, Esq A weekly market was held for some time prior to 1725. The parish is a resort of sportsmen The living is a rectory in the diocese of Exeter Value, £475 * Patron, the Rev S Palmer The church is an ancient edifice of nave, chancel, north aisle, and south transept. There are chapels for Baptists and Bible Christians, and charities £12 —The sub-district comprises five parishes Acres, 17,455. Pop, 2,937 Houses, 574

BICKLEIGH, a parish in Tiverton district, Devon, on the river Exe, 4 miles S of Tiverton r station Post-town, Tiverton Acres, 1,835 Real property, £2,141 Pop, 254 Houses, 55 The property is divided among three The manor belonged anciently to the Bickleighs, and passed to the Courteneys, and then to the Carews. The living is a rectory in the diocese of Exeter Value, £420 * Patron, Sir W P Carew The church is a neat structure of nave south aisle, chancel, and western tower, and contains some handsome monuments of the Carews Charities, £28 Bamfylde Moore Carew, born in 1690, the son of a rector of the parish, and popularly known as "King of the Beggars, was a native

BICKLEIGH, a parish in Plympton St Mary district, Devon, on the Cat water and on the South Devon and Tavistock railway, near Dartmoor forest, 6 miles NNE of Plymouth. It has a station on the railway and its post-town is Tamerton, under Plymouth Acres, 2 323 Real property, £2,070 Pop, 402 Houses, 73 The property is all in one estate Very beautiful and romantic scenery lies along the Cat water The living is a vicarage, annexed with the p curacy of Sheepstor, in the diocese of Exeter Value, £253 * Patron, Sir M Lopes, Bart. The church excepting the tower, was rebuilt in 1839 and it contains the tomb of Sir Nicholas Slanning, whose death forms the catastrophe of Mrs. Bray's novel of "Fitz of Fitzford"

BICKLEY, a township in Malpas parish, Cheshire, near Cholmondeley Castle, 3½ miles NE of Malpas. Acres 2,0?5 Real property, £2,790 Pop., 397 Houses, 73 About a quarter of an acre of the surface, covered with trees, sank suddenly with a thundering noise, on 18 June 1657, into a deep subterranean flood, long since dried up, leaving a chasm, called the Barrel Fall. Two metal tablets, inscribed with a decree of the Emperor Trajan, were found in 1812, and conveyed to the British museum There is a Wesleyan chapel

BICKLEY, a chapelry, with a r station, in Bromley parish, Kent, 1½ mile E of Bromley Pop, 473 Living, a vicarage The church was built in 1865, at a cost of £10 000 There are many fine villas

BICKMARSH AND LITTLE DORSINGTON, a hamlet in Welford parish, Warwick, on Icknield street, 6 miles SSE of Alcester Acres, 1,340 Real property, £1 275 Pop., 50 Houses 11

BICKNACRE, a hamlet in Woodham-Ferris and Danbury parishes, Essex, 5½ miles SE of Chelmsford Real property, £957 Pop, 304 A priory of black canons was founded here, in the time of Henry III, by Maurice Jeffrey, and a portion of it, with arches, still stands

BICKNOLLER a parish in Williton district, Somerset adjacent to the Watchet and Taunton railway, near Williton station, 4 miles SE of Watchet It has a post-office under Taunton Acres, 1,390 Real property, £2 614 Pop, 345. Houses, 67 The property is divided among a few The surface includes part of the Quantock hills, and contains points which command extensive views. Two Roman camps, called Trendle's and Turk's castles, and a beacon, are near the church, and very many Roman coins and other relics have been found The living is a vicarage in the diocese of Bath and Wells. Value, £124 Patron, the Vicar of Stogumber The church is good

BICKNOR,—anciently BYKENORE—a parish in Hollingbourn district, Kent, 3¾ miles SSW of Sittingbourne r station, and 7 ENE of Maidstone Post town, Stockbury under Sittingbourne. Acres 631 Real property, £653 Pop, 53 Houses, 8 The property is divided Bicknor Place is the seat of T Whitehead, Esq The living is a rectory in the diocese of Canterbury Value, £11? Patron the Lord Chancellor The church is small, and very early Norman

BICKNOR (ENGLISH), a parish in the district of Monmouth and county of Gloucester, on the verge of the county, at the river Wye 3¼ miles N of Coleford, and 6¼ SW of Mitcheldean Road r station It includes two places, called Mailscot and New Weir, formerly extra parochial, and its post town is Coleford Acres, 2 377 Real property, £3,280 Pop., 592 Houses, 125 The property is divided among a few Bicknor Court the seat of Col. Woosnam, stands on a cliff overhanging the Wye, and commands a fine view Much of the land is disposed in cyder orchards and in meadows. Coal, ironstone and limestone are worked The living is a rectory in the diocese of Gloucester and Bristol. Value £500 * Patron, Queen's College, Oxford. The church stands within the fosse of an ancient fortification, and is good Charities £5

BICKNOR (WELSH), a parish in the district of Monmouth and county of Hereford within a loop of the river Wye opposite English Bicknor, 1¼ miles S by W of Ross r station Post town, Goodrich, under Ross Acres 8 ?92 Real property £1,572 Pop., 80 Houses, 18. The property is all in one estate The living is a rectory in the diocese of Hereford Value, £159 * Patron, Rev F Armich Blake The church was rebuilt in 1859 A recumbent stone figure in the previous church is said to have been monumental of the Countess of Salisbury, who nursed Henry V at Courtfield, a mansion about half a mile off

BICKTON, a tything in Fordingbridge parish, Hants, 5½ miles N of Ringwood Real property, £1,067 Pop, 237

BICTON, a parish in St Thomas district, Devon, on the river Otter, near the coast, 4 miles WSW of Sidmouth, and 7½ S by E of Whimple r station It includes the hamlet of Yettington, and its post town is Budleigh Salterton, under Exeter Acres, 1,294 Real property, £2,114 Pop., 166 Houses, 34 The property all belongs to the Hon Mark Rolle, son of Lord Clinton. The manor was given by William the Conqueror to W Porto, went through various families to Sir Robert Dennys, and passed, by marriage, to Sir Henry Rolle, the ancestor of Lord Rolle. Bicton House, the family seat, is an elegant mansion, in one of the finest parks in England The gardens were noted by the late Mr Loudon as among the best he had ever seen, an arboretum in the park is one of the choicest and largest in the kingdom, and there is a noble avenue of araucaria, oak, and beech. The jail for the county was provided in terms of the tenure of the estate, and stood in the parish till 1518 The living is a rectory in the diocese of Exeter Value, £220 Patrons, the Heirs of Lord Rolle The church is a handsome edifice, recently erected by Lady Rolle The previous church was a curious old structure, and part of it is now a mausoleum, connected by a cloister with the ancient tower

BICTON, a chapelry in St. Chad and St Alkmond parishes, Salop, on the river Severn, and on Watling street, near the Shrewsbury and Oswestry railway 3 miles NW by W of Shrewsbury It was constituted in 1853, and it has a post office, of the name of Bicton Heath, under Shrewsbury Rated property, £4,650 Pop, 569 Houses, 128 The property is divided among a few The living is a vicarage in the diocese of Lichfield Value, £140 Patron, the Vicar of St Chad The church is good

BICTON, a township and a parochial division in Clun parish, Salop. The township lies 4½ miles SSW of Bishops Castle The parochial division bears also the name of Ediclift, and comprises the townships of Bicton, Ediclift, Whitcott Keysot, and Shadwell

BIDACOTT, a hamlet in Chittlehampton parish, Devon, ½ a mile from Chittlehampton

BIDBOROUGH, a parish in Tunbridge district, Kent, adjacent to the Southeastern railway, 2½ miles NW by N of Tunbridge Wells Post town, Tunbridge Wells Acres, 1,299 Real property, £1,621 Pop, 210 Houses, 46 The property is divided among a few There are some mineral springs The living is a rectory in the diocese of Canterbury Value, £227 * Patron, Mrs Deacon The church has a Norman porch, and is in good condition Charities, £23

BIDCOMBE, BRIMSDON, or COLD KITCHEN HILL, an eminence of much beauty, with a solitary peak, on the west border of Wilts, 4½ miles SW of Warminster It has many tumuli, entrenchments, and other memorials of the ancient inhabitants, is the subject of a poem in imitation of Denham's "Cooper's Hill," and commands a magnificent view over Wilts and Dorset, and away to the Welsh mountains

BIDDENDEN, a village and a parish in Tenterden district, Kent The village stands 4 miles S of Headcorn r station, and 5½ NE of Cranbrook, and has a post office under Staplehurst, and fairs on 6 April and 8 Nov The parish comprises 7 208 acres. Real property, £6 933. Pop., 1 412 Houses, 281 The property is much subdivided The manor belonged, in the time of Edward III, to Sir Walter Manney, and passed to the Hendens The living is a rectory in the diocese of Canterbury Value, £136 * Patron, the Archbishop of Canterbury The church has features from early English to late perpendicular, and was restored in 1857 National schools have £20 a year from an old endowment a curious charity, furnishing a distribution of stamped cakes to all comers on Easter Sunday, has £30, and other charities have above £70

BIDDENHAM, a parish in the district and county of Bedford, on the river Ouse, 2 miles W of Bedford r station It has a post office under Bedford. Acres, 1,780 Real property, £2,752 Pop, 350 Houses, 71 The property is divided among a few The living is a vicarage in the diocese of Ely Value, £100 * Patron Lord Dynevor The church is Norman, in good condition

BIDDESCOTE. See BITTERSCOTE.

BIDDESHAM See BIDDISHAM.

BIDDESTONE, or BIDSTON, a parish—formerly two parishes, St. Peter and St. Nicholas—in Chippenham district, Wilts, 3 miles N by W of Corsham r station, and 4 W of Chippenham. Post town, Chippenham Acres of B St. Peter, 127, of B St Nicholas, returned with Slaughterford Real property of both, £3,226 Pop. of B. St. P, 34 Houses, 5 Pop, of B St N, 407 Houses, 89 The property is much subdivided The living is a rectory, united with the vicarage of Slaughterford, in the diocese of Gloucester and Bristol. Value, £102 Patron, Winchester College The church of St Peter was perpendicular English, but has been taken down The church of St Nicholas is Norman, has a picturesque bell turret, and was well repaired in 1850 There is a Baptist chapel Edmund Smith, the translator of Longinus, and author of the tragedy of Phœdra and Hippolytus, died in the parish, and his tomb is in St Nicholas church.

BIDDICK (NORTH), a hamlet in Washington and Whitburn parishes, Durham, 4½ miles SSE of Gateshead. Pop., 371

BIDDICK (SOUTH), a township in Houghton-le-Spring parish, Durham, on the Durham Junction railway, 6 miles WSW of Sunderland. Acres, 343. Pop, 48 Houses, 11

BIDDISHAM, a parish in Axbridge district, Somerset, on the river Axe, 3 miles W by S of Axbridge, and 5 SE of Weston super Mare Junction r station Post-town, Axbridge, under Weston-super Mare Acres, 574 Real property, £1,740 Pop, 147 Houses, 29 The property is much subdivided The living is a rectory in the diocese of Bath and Wells Value, £152 * Patron, the Bishop of London. The church is tolerable

BIDDLESDON, or BITTLESDON, a village and a parish in the district of Brackley, and county of Bucks. The village stands on the verge of the county, 3¼ miles NE of Brackley r station It was formerly a market town, but is now a small secluded place. The parish comprises 1,630 acres, and its post town is Brackley Real property, £2,718 Pop, 169 Houses, 29 The property is divided among a few Biddlesdon House is the seat of G Morgan, Esq The manor was held some time by William the Conqueror, passed to Robert de Mappershall, and then to Ernald de Bosco, was given by the latter to the Cistertian Monks of Gerndon, for founding an abbey on it, and went at the dissolution, to Thomas, Lord Wriothesley Considerable remains of the abbey stood about the year 1700, but have all disappeared. The living is a vicarage in the diocese of Oxford. Value, £69 Patron, G Morgan, Esq The church is a modern edifice adjoining Biddlesdon House

BIDDLESFORD, a hamlet in Arreton parish, Isle of Wight, 2 miles SE of Newport.

BIDDLESTONE, a township in Alwinton parish Northumberland, in the basin of the Coquet river, under the Southeastern Cheviots, 7½ miles NW of Rothbury Pop, 198 Houses, 33 The manor belonged anciently to the Vissards, but was given by Edward I to Sir W de Selby, and belongs still to his descendants. James I, when on his way to London, in 1603, was entertained here, and knighted five of the Selbys. Here is a Roman Catholic chapel

BIDDULPH, a parish in the district of Congleton and county of Stafford, on the Stoke and Congleton railway, around Gillow Heath station, 3 miles SSE of Congleton It consists of the four hamlets of Over Biddulph or Overton, Nether Biddulph, Middle Biddulph, and Knypersley, and its post town is Congleton Acres, 5,635 Real property, £14,544, of which £4,622 are in mines Pop, 3,468 Houses, 692 The property is much subdivided Biddulph Hall, a picturesque Tudor edifice, was anciently the seat of the Biddulph family, but is now mainly a ruin, and partly a farm-house. Knypersley Hall is the seat of J Bateman, Esq The land is largely moorish and hilly, and a peak of it, called Mow Cop, 1,091 feet high, commands fine prospects, even to the Mersey A tract, called Biddulph Moor, is inhabited by a sort of gipsey tribe, a people of peculiar habits, said to have descended from a Saracen, who came to England in the train of a Crusader Coal, ironstone and limestone are extensively worked, and several kinds of manufacture are carried on Remains of a Druidical temple, known as the Bride Stones, and of three curious artificial caves, are on the N border The living is a vicarage, united with the p curacy of Knypersley, in the diocese of Lichfield. Value, £122 Patron, J Bateman, Esq The parish church is a substantial edifice, with a tower, and Knypersley church is a structure of 1849, in the early English style. Another church, in the Norman style, was built, in 1863, at Biddulph Moor, and forms a separate charge There are a Wesleyan chapel, and charities £22.

BIDEFORD, a town, a parish, a sub-district, and a district, in Devon The town stands on the river Torridge, 5 miles above its influx to the sea, and at the terminus of the Bideford extension of the North Devon railway, 9 miles SW of Barnstaple, and 42 miles by road but 48½ by railway NW by W of Exeter Its site is chiefly a hill side on the left bank of the river, amid pleasant environs, and commands delightful views of the river's vale The place was given, soon after the Conquest, to Richard de Granville, a Norman knight, remained with his descendants till 1750, and was then sold by one of the heirs of William Granville, third Earl of Bath, to J Cleveland, Esq of Tapley It gave the title of Baron, in the time of Queen Anne, to Lord Lansdown. Forts were erected at it, on both sides of the river, by the parliamentarians, in the civil war, but they were taken for the king by Colonel Digby, in 1643, and one of them, called Chudleigh fort, a small battlemented structure, is still standing The plague raged here in 1646 and 1680 and three aged female inhabitants were put to death on a charge of witchcraft in 1682 The French privateers, in the time of Queen Anne, captured so many valuable vessels, engaged in the town's commerce, in their crossing the bay off the river's mouth, that they called it the Golden bay The streets are wide and airy, some new good houses have taken the place of old mean ones, and there are a noble mansion and a series of villas in the outskirts. A bridge of 24 arches and 677 feet long, erected in the early part of the 14th century, forms the approach on the NE, was widened in 1864-5, at a cost of about £4,000, and is a favourite promenade The town hall is an ornamental edifice of 1850, and serves for courts, town business, and concerts The parish church was recently rebuilt, superseded an early English structure and is large and handsome The Independent chapel was rebuilt in 1859, and is a very fine edifice The Wesleyan chapel is large and was much improved in 1865 There are also chapels for Baptists and Bible Christians, a free grammar and other public schools, a working men's club established in 1864, a dispensary, alms houses, and a workhouse,—the last built in 1836 at a cost of £3,645 The charities amount yearly to £577, but include £135 for keeping the bridge in repair The quay adjoins the bridge, is upwards of 1,200 feet long, admits vessels of 500 tons at high water, and forms an agreeable walk The Bideford extension railway joins the North Devon at Fremington Pill is 6 miles long, and was opened in 1855, and a line from it to Appledore and Westward Ho, 4 miles long, was authorised in 1866 The town has a head post office,‡ a railway station with telegraph, two banking offices, two chief inns, two weekly markets, and two annual fairs, publishes a weekly newspaper and is a seat of sessions and a polling place Ship building sail making, rope making, and pottery work are carried on, and a large saw mill was created in 1835 The port is a bonding one, and formerly had a large foreign commerce, but is now engaged chiefly in the coasting trade The vessels belonging to it, at the beginning of 1868, were 56 small ones, of aggregately 1,854 tons, and 75 larger ones, of aggregately 9,104 tons. The vessels entering coastwise, in 1867, counting repeated voyages were 710 sailing vessels, of aggregately 29,878 tons, and 99 steam vessels, of aggregately 7,230 tons, clearing coastwise, 100 sailing vessels, of aggregately 6,715 tons, and 99 steam vessels, of aggregately 7,230 tons, entering from the British colonies, 6 vessels of aggregately 1,550 tons, entering from foreign countries, 9 vessels, of aggregately 2,493 tons, clearing for the British colonies, only 1 vessel, of no more than 53 tons, and clearing for foreign countries, 2 vessels, of jointly 507 tons. The customs in 1867 amounted to £3,147 The chief exports are oak bark, corn, earthen ware, tiles, sailcloth, cordage and linens, and the chief imports, timber, coal, and lime A steamer sails regularly to Ilfracombe, Lynmouth, and Bristol The town sent members to parliament in the times of Edward I and II, but not since, was incorporated by Queen Elizabeth and is now governed by a mayor, four aldermen, and 12 councillors. Sir P Grenville, the naval hero, Dr John Shebbeare, author of the "Adventures of a Guinea," and Abraham and Benjamin Donne, the mathematicians, were natives, Strange, the philanthropist, died here of the plague in 1646, and Hervey, the author of "Meditations," was for some time curate, and wrote here part of his works.

The parish is conterminate with the borough Acres, 3,155 Real property, £18,170 Pop in 1841, 5,211, in 1861, 5,742 Houses, 1,188 The living is a rectory in the diocese of Exeter Value, £633.* Patron, Sir G S Stucley, Bart —The sub district includes also the parish of Landcross. Acres, 3,527 Pop., 5,851 Houses, 1,209 —The district comprehends likewise the sub-district of Northam, containing the parishes of Northam, Abbotsham, and Littleham, the sub district of Parkham, containing the parishes of Parkham, Monkleigh, Buckland Brewer, and Alwington, the sub district of Bradworthy containing the parishes of Bradworthy, West Putford, East Putford, Bulkworthy, and Newton St. Petrock, and the sub district of Hartland containing the parishes of Hartland, Welcombe, Clovelly, and Woolfardisworthy and the extra parochial tract of Lundy Island. Acres, 73 450 Poor rates in 1866, £9,806 Pop in 1861, 17 790 Houses 3,702 Marriages in 1866, 151, births, 607,—of which 46 were illegitimate, deaths 329,—of which 87 were at ages under 5 years, and 25 at ages above 85 years. Marriages in the ten years 1851-60, 1,375, births, 5,620, deaths, 3,553 The places of worship in 1851 were 22 of the Church of England, with 6,993 sittings, 5 of Independents, with 1 235 s., 6 of Baptists, with 1 150 s, 18 of Wesleyan Methodists, with 3,364 s, 15 of Bible Christians, with 1 695 s, and 1 undefined, with 200 s The schools were 18 public day schools with 1,709 scholars, 47 private day schools, with 952 s, and 45 Sunday schools, with 3,555 s

BIDFIELD, a tything in Bisley parish, Gloucester, 3¼ miles E of Stroud

BIDFORD, a village, a parish, and a sub district, in the district of Alcester, Warwick The village stands on the river Avon, 3¾ miles SSE of Alcester r station, and 7 W S W of Stratford on Avon, and has a post office under Bromsgrove It was once a market town, and it consists chiefly of one long street One of the houses in it was the old Falcon inn, traditionally said to have been a haunt of Shakspeare, for drinking ale and playing at shovel board An absurd story is current that the poet and some of his companions engaged here in a drinking contest with a party of the natives, that he and his companions lay down after it under a crab tree in the neighbourhood and slept there from Saturday evening till Monday morning, and that, being urged on awakening to go back and renew the contest, he exclaimed, "No, I have had enough, I have drunk with

"'Piping Pebworth dancing Marston,
Haunted Hillbro, hungry Grafton,
Dudging Exhall, papish Wicksford,
Beggarly Broom, and drunken Bidford'"

The parish includes also the hamlets of Barton, Broom and Marlcliff Acres, 3,240 Real property, £8,167 Pop, 1,565 Houses, 370 The manor was held by William the Conqueror, was given, by the Empress Maud, to the monks of Bardsley, and passed to the Clarkes, the Danets, and the Skipwiths Bidford Grange House was a picturesque old edifice, with unequal gables The scenery, over much of the surface, is richly beautiful, and has fine spots on "the smooth flowing Avon" Blue flagstone is quarried. The living is a vicarage in the diocese of Worcester Value, £213 Patron, the Rev T Boultbee The church was mainly rebuilt in 1835, and is in the Norman style, with a tower There are two Methodist chapels, a working men's institute, a national school, and charities £107 —The sub district comprises four parishes Acres 9,230 Pop, 2,749 Houses, 643.

BIDSTON See BIDDESTONE.

BIDSTONE a township and a parish in Wirrall district, Cheshire. The township lies on the Hoylake railway, 3 miles W N W of Birkenhead, and has a railway station Acres, 1,689 Real property, £3,062 Pop, 282 Houses, 48 —The parish includes also the townships of Moreton cum Lingham, Claughton cum Grange, and Saughall Massey or Saughan Massie, and its post town is Birkenhead Acres, 4,243 Real property, £20,130 Pop, 2,154 Houses, 323 The property is subdivided. Bidstone Hill commands a fine view of the surrounding country, the Mersey, and the Irish sea A lighthouse, 50 feet high, stands on the hill, showing a fixed light, elevated 300 feet above high-water, visible at the distance of 23 miles, and leading, when in line with Leasowe light, through the Horse channel at the Mersey's mouth, and a telegraph was adjacent, communicating eastward with Liverpool, and westward, through a chain, with Holyhead Water works for Birkenhead, and a cemetery with two chapels, were being formed in Bidstone in 1862 The living is a vicarage in the diocese of Chester Value, £98 * Patron, the Bishop of Chester The church is excellent. Claughton and Moreton are separate benefices A school has an endowed income of £15, and other charities £5

BIELBY, or BEALBY, a township in Hayton parish, E R. Yorkshire, on the Pocklington canal, 3½ miles S by W of Pocklington Acres, 1,220 Real property, £1,944 Pop, 268 Houses, 50 It forms a curacy united to the vicarage of Hayton

BIERLEY, a chapelry in North Bierley township, Bradford parish, W R Yorkshire Pop in 1861, about 3,000 Post town, Bradford The living is a vicarage in the diocese of Ripon Value, £130 * Patron, Mr Wilson The church is good. See BIERLEY (NORTH)

BIERLEY (EAST), a hamlet in Hunsworth township Bradford parish, W R Yorkshire, adjacent to the Leeds and Halifax railway, 3 miles SE by S of Bradford

BIERLEY-LANE See BIERLEY (NORTH)

BIERLEY (NORTH) a township in Bradford parish, W R. Yorkshire, on the Lancashire and Yorkshire railway, 2 miles SE of Bradford It includes the village of Wibsey, the hamlets of Bierley Lane, Carr Lane Hill top, Odsall Moor, Woodhouse Hill, and Holly Hall, and the populous districts of Low Moor and Slack Acres, 3,090 Real property, £35,133, of which £1,137 are in mines and £13,884 in iron works Pop in 1841, 9,512 in 1861, 12,503 Houses, 2,663 There are numerous good residences, three churches, five dissenting chapels, and three national schools.

BIERTON WITH BROUGHTON a parish in Aylesbury district, Bucks, on the Aylesbury railway, near the Aylesbury canal, 1½ mile NE of Aylesbury It has a post office, of the name of Bierton, under Aylesbury Acres, 2,470 Real property, £5,312 Pop., 691 Houses, 149 The property is divided among a few The living is a vicarage, united with the vicarage of Quarrendon in the diocese of Oxford Value, £310 * Patrons, the Dean and Chapter of Lincoln The church is a structure of the 12th century, with tower and spire, was recently well repaired, and contains a piscina, and a curious monument of 1616 to Samuel Pope and his thirteen children There are chapels for Baptists and Methodists, a national school, and charities £40

BIESTON a township in Wrexham parish, Denbigh, near Wrexham Acres, with Gourton, 844. Pop, 104 Houses, 22.

BIGA (THE), a streamlet of Montgomery It rises on the NE side of Plinlimmon, and runs 5 miles eastward to the Clewydog at Aber Biga.

BIGBURY, a village, a parish, and a bay in Kingsbridge district, Devon The village stands on the right side of the river Avon, 1½ mile from the bay, 3½ S of Modbury, and 8 S of Ivybridge r station The parish includes also the hamlet of St. Ann s Chapel, and its post town is Modbury, under Ivybridge. Acres, 3 167, of which 265 are water Real property, £3,758. Pop, 497 Houses, 109 The property is divided among a few The living is a rectory in the diocese of Exeter Value, £658 * Patron, —Livingston, Esq The church is perpendicular English, with tower and spire, and is good There are chapels for Baptists and Bible Christians —The bay extends from Bolt Tail to Stoke Point, measures 7½ miles across the entrance, and 3¾ thence to the head, receives the rivers Avon and Ferne, is beset with rocks, and very dangerous in navigation, has several coves in its coast, and presents a variety of picturesque views

BIGBY, a parish in Caistor district, Lincoln, 2½ miles SSF of Barnetby r station, and 4 F of Glanford Brigg It includes the hamlets of Kettleby and Kettleby Thorp, and has a post office under Brigg. Acres, 3,410 Real property, £4,916 Pop., 249 Houses, 44 The property is divided among a few The living is a rectory in the diocese of Lincoln Value, £708 * Patron, V D Elwes, Esq The church is early English, in good condition. There is a free school Roman coins and fragments of a Roman pavement have been found

BIGGAR, a hamlet in Walney chapelry, Dalton in Furness parish, Lancashire

BIGGEN (NEW), a township in Shotley parish, Northumberland, at the verge of the county, on the river Derwent, 8 miles SF of Corbridge Pop., 56

BIGGES QUARTER, or CARLISLES QUARTER, a township in Long Horslev parish, Northumberland, 6 miles NW by N of Morpeth Acres, 2,869 Pop, 259 Houses, 58.

BIGGIN, a township and a chapelry in Ashborne district, Derby The township is in Wirksworth parish, and lies near the Cromford and High Park railway, 7½ miles SW of Bakewell r station Acres, 595 Real property, £1,153 Pop, 133 Houses, 28 The chapelry was constituted in 1848 Post town, Ashborne Pop, 399 Houses, 84 The living is a vicarage in the diocese of Lichfield Value £40 * Patron, the Duke of Devonshire The church is modern There are two Primitive Methodist chapels and a national school

BIGGIN, a township in Kirk Fenton parish, W R Yorkshire, near the North Midland railway, 6½ miles WNW of Selby Acres, together with Little Fenton, 2,250 Pop, 142 Houses, 28 Teasel, for the use of fullers, was first cultivated here

BIGGIN, a hamlet in Oundle parish, Northampton, 2 miles WNW of Oundle

BIGGIN, Warwick See NEWTON and BIGGIN

BIGGIN (LOW), a hamlet in Kirkby-Lonsdale township and parish, Westmoreland, 2 miles NW of Kirkby Lonsdale

BIGGLESWADE a town a parish, a sub district, a district, and a hundred, in Beds. The town stands in a fertile valley on the right bank of the river Ivel, adjacent to the Great Northern railway, 10½ miles ESE of Bedford and 41 NNW of London It was anciently called Bykleswade It suffered destruction of 150 houses by fire in 1785, and it now contains many neat modern houses The town hall is recent and handsome The county court house also is recent The parish church is early English, with late chancel, was originally collegiate, and contains some very interesting brasses There are chapels for Independents, Baptists, and Methodists, a free school, with endowed income of £51, other charities, with £1 ;4, and a workhouse, erected at the cost of £4,850 The town has a head post office,‡ a railway station with telegraph, a banking office, and three chief inns, and is a seat of petty sessions and a polling place A weekly market is held on Wednesday, and fairs on 14 Feb, Easter Saturday, Whit Monday, 2 Aug, and 8 Nov A good trade exists in corn, timber, and coals and is aided by the Ivel being navigable hence to the Ouse, and the manufacture of thread lace and straw plait is carried on Some Roman relics, several armour clad human skeletons, and about 300 gold coins of Henry VI have been found in the neighbourhood The environs are pleasant, and contain some handsome villas and mansions Pop of the town, 1,027 Houses, 838

The parish includes also the hamlets of Holme and Stratton Acres, 4,310 Real property, £14,741 Pop, 4,631 Houses, 920 The property is not much divided At Stratton Park, about a mile SF of the town, the Cottonian Library was preserved, after being removed from Connington, in the time of the civil war The living is a vicarage in the diocese of Ely Value, £347 * Patron, the Bishop of Ely —The sub district contains the parishes of Biggleswade, Edworth, Astwick, Stotfold Arlsey, Henlow, Clifton, Langford, Warden, Southill, Campton, Meppershall, and Upper Stondon, and the extra parochial tracts of Chicksands Priory and Shefford Hardwick Acres, 31,910 Pop, 16,113. Houses, 3,102 —The district includes also the sub-district of Potton, containing the parishes of Potton, Tempsford, Blunham, Northill, Sandy Everton, Cockayne-Hatley, Wrestlingworth, Sutton, Eyworth and Dunton Acres of the district, 58,041 Poor-rates in 1866, £16,506 Pop in 1861, 25,393. Houses, 5,021 Marriages in 1866, 180, births, 990,—of which 90 were illegitimate, deaths, 641,—of which 231 were at ages under 5 years, and 10 at ages above 85 years Marriages in the ten years 1851-60, 1,694, births, 9,007 deaths 5,244 The places of worship in 1851 were 24 of the Church of England, with 8,074 sittings, 2 of Independents, with 506 s, 10 of Baptists with 3 504 s, 11 of Wesleyan Methodists, with 2 565 s, 1 of Primitive Methodists, with 110 s 1 of Latter Day Saints, with 140 s, 1 of Roman Catholics, with 21 s, and 2 undefined, with 350 s. The schools were 23 public day schools, with 1,753 scholars, 23 private day schools, with 448 s, 34 Sunday schools, with 3,529 s, and 6 evening schools for adults, with 168 s —The hundred contains only thirteen parishes and part of another Acres, 27,672 Pop, 12,371 Houses, 2,488

BIGHTON, a parish in Alresford district Hants, 2 miles NF of Alresford r station, and 7½ SW of Alton It has a post office under Alresford Acres 2,004 Real property, £2,404. Pop., 299 Houses, 65 The property is all in one estate Remains of a Roman villa have been found at Bighton Woodshot in the NW The living is a rectory in the diocese of Winchester Value, £310 * Patron, the Rev J T Maine The church is Norman, small and good

BIGLANDS AND GAMBLESBY, a township in Aikton parish Cumberland, on the river Wampool, 3 miles N of Wigton Pop, 205 Houses, 42 Here is a mineral spring

BIGNALL END a township in Audley parish, Stafford 3 miles WSW of Kidsgrove r station, and 4 NW of Newcastle under-Lyne Real property, £2,393, of which £800 are in mines Pop., 737 Houses, 152

BIGNOR, a parish in Chichester district, Sussex, 4½ miles SW of Pulborough r station, and 4½ S by E of Petworth. It includes the detached hamlet of Buddington, surrounded by the parish of Lasebourne, and its post town is Bury, under Petworth Acres, 1,115 Real property, £1,458 Pop, 167 Houses, 31 The property is divided among a few Bignor Park is the seat of J H Hawkins, Esq, contains some interesting antiquities and works of art, and commands striking views of the Weald and the South Downs. It was long annexed to

Arundel Castle, and once the property of Nicholas Turner, Esq, and, in the latter connection, was the residence of Mrs. Charlotte Smith, author of the "Old Manor House," and Mrs Dorset, author of the "Peacock at Home." Three very fine tesselated pavements, believed to have belonged to three apartments of a Roman villa, were discovered in 1811, in Oldbury hill, and the villa is thought to have stood at the "Ad decimum," or station of the tenth milestone on the Roman road from Chichester The living is a rectory in the diocese of Chichester Value, £143 Patron, Lord Leconfield The church is early English, and has long lancet windows and chancel

BIKINACRE. See BICKNACRE

BILBANK See BELLBANK.

BILBOROUGH, a parish in Basford district, Notts, on the Nottingham canal, 3 miles W of Radford r station, and 4 NW of Nottingham It includes the hamlet of Broxtow, and its post town is Wollaton, under Nottingham Acres, 1,090 Real property, £1,798 Pop, 232 Houses, 47 The property is divided between two Coal was formerly worked The living is a rectory in the diocese of Lincoln Value, £273 Patron, T W Edge Esq The church is tolerable.

BILBROOK, a hamlet in Old Cleeve parish, Somerset, 3¼ miles ESE of Dunster

BILBROUGH, a parish in Tadcaster district, W R Yorkshire, 3 miles WSW of Copmanthorpe r station, and 4 NE of Tadcaster It has a post office under York Acres, 1,360 Real property, £3,386 Pop, 216 Houses 40 The property is divided chiefly among three The living is a rectory in the diocese of York Value, £274 Patron T Fairfax, Esq The church contains the remains of Thomas, Lord Fairfax, the celebrated parliamentary general Charities, £14

BILBURY RING See BELBURY RING

BILBY, a hamlet in Barnby Moor township, Notts, 4½ miles WNW of East Retford Pop, 43

BILDESTONE, or BILSTON, a village and a parish in Cosford district, Suffolk. The village stands 6 miles NNW of *Hadleigh r station*, and has a post-office‡ under Ipswich. It was formerly a market town and still has fairs on Ash Wednesday and Holy Thursday The parish comprises 1,420 acres Real property £3,769 Pop, 733 Houses, 164 The property is divided among a few The living is a rectory in the diocese of Ely Value, £346.* Patron, the Rev J Cedge The church is later English, and stands apart from the village A spired tower was built in the centre of the village in 1864 There are a Baptist chapel and a national school

BILEIGH See BEELEIGH

BILHAM, a township in Hooton Pagnell parish, W R Yorkshire, 6½ miles WNW of Doncaster It includes Bilham ow hamlet, and yields coal, lime, and fine sand for founders Acres, 518 Real property, £1,224 Pop, 6- Houses, 14 Bilham House here commands an extensive and brilliant view

BILHAM ROW See BILHAM

BILLERICAY, a small town, a chapelry, and a district in Essex The town stands on an eminence, near the site of a Roman station 4½ miles S of Ingatestone r station and 9 SSW of Chelmsford It commands a fine view of the surrounding country away to Kent and the Nore, and it is of ancient origin and has been much improved. It has a head post office,‡ a banking office, one chief inn, a church two dissenting chapels, an endowed school, a public reading room, and a workhouse, and is a seat of petty sessions, and a polling place. The church is a brick building, partly as old as the time of Edward III, and has a tower, of previous date, much decayed A weekly market is held on Tuesday, fairs are held on 2 Aug and 7 Oct, and brewing, brick making and country business are carried on Rated property £5,972 Pop, 1,390 Houses, 218 — The chapelry is conterminate with the town, and is in the parish of Great Burstead The living is a vicarage in the diocese of Rochester Value, £-20 Patron, the Bishop of Rochester

The district comprehends the sub district of Brentwood, containing the parishes of East Horndon, West Horndon, Childerditch, Little Warley, Ingrave, South Weald, and Shenfield, the sub district of Great Burstead, containing the parishes of Great Burstead, Little Burstead, Hutton, Mountnessing Dunton Ramsden Crays, Ramsden Bellhouse, the liberty of Lee Chapel, and most of the parish of Laindon, and the sub district of Wickford, containing the parishes of Wickford, Downham, Nevendon, Vange, Pitsea, Bowers Gifford and North Benfleet, and the chapelry of Basildon. Acres, 50,345 Poor-rates in 1866, £7,426 Pop in 1861, 15,031 Houses, 2,748 Marriages in 1866, 65, births 440,—of which 22 were illegitimate, deaths, 299,—of which 73 were at ages under 5 years, and 13 at ages above 85 years Marriages in the ten years 1851-60, 804, births, 4,192, deaths, 2,974 The places of worship in 1851 were 18 of the Church of England with 2,751 sittings, 6 of Independents, with 1,716 s, 3 of Wesleyan Methodists, with 140 s, and 2 of Roman Catholics, with 390 s The schools were 17 public day schools, with 841 scholars, 24 private day schools, with 358 s, 18 Sunday schools, with 934 s, and 1 evening school for adults, with 9 s

BILLESDON, a township, a parish, a sub district, and a district in Leicestershire. The township lies 3½ miles NE of the Via Devana, 6 NE of Glen r station, and 8½ E by S of Leicester It has a post office‡ under Leicester, and fairs on 23 April, 5 July, and the first Monday of Oct An old market cross stands in it, and the making of earthenware and hosiery is carried on Real property, £4,639 Pop, 909 Houses, 195 —The parish includes also the townships of Goadby and Rolleston Acres, 4,430 Real property, £8,526 Pop, 1,085 Houses, 233 The property is much subdivided. A camp of 18 acres, with ditch and rampart, occurs at Billesdon Coplow, was the site of a Roman temple, and commands a fine view The living is a vicarage, including the p. curacies of Goadby and Rolleston, in the diocese of Peterborough Value, £279 * Patron H Greene, Esq The church has a steeple, which was rebuilt in 1862. There are chapels for Baptists and Wesleyans, a free school, alms houses, other charities £69, and a workhouse Villiers, first Duke of Buckingham, is said to have received his early education here

The sub district and the district are co extensive, and contain the parishes of Billesdon, Skeffington Tugby, Alexton, Loddington, Withcote, Ouston, Tilton, Lowesby, Hungerton, Scraptoft, Humberstone, Evington, Thurnby, Houghton on the Hill, Galby, Kings Norton Carlton Curlieu, Burton Overy, Glenn Magna, and Wistow, the parochial chapelry of East Norton, the extra parochial tracts of Noseley and Launde, and part of the parish of Rothley Acres, 50,721 Poor rates in 1866, £7,068 Pop in 1861, 7,272 Houses, 1,571 Marriages in 1866, 47 births 201,—of which 7 were illegitimate, deaths, 82,—of which 18 were at ages under 5 years, and 1 at ages above 85 years Marriages in the ten years 1851-60, 431, births, 2,035, deaths 1,135 The places of worship in 1851 were 32 of the Church of England, with 5,090 sittings, 2 of Independents, with 160 s, 1 of Lady Huntingdon's Connexion, with 170 s, 3 of Baptists, with 600 s, 9 of Wesleyan Methodists, with 1,040 s, and 1 of Primitive Methodists, with 30 s The schools were 15 public day schools with 519 scholars, 20 private day schools, with 237 s, 25 Sunday schools, with 901 s, and 1 evening school for adults, with 14 s

BILLESLEY, a parish in Stratford on Avon district Warwick near the Stratford and Birmingham canal, 4 miles WNW of Stratford r station Post town, Stratford on Avon Acres, 750 Real property, £736 Pop, 35 Houses, 6 The property is divided among a few The living is a rectory in the diocese of Worcester Value £300 Patrons, M Miles, Esq, and Rev T Higgins The church is good

BILLING (GREAT), a parish in the district and county of Northampton near the river Nen 1½ mile N of Billing Road r station and 4 ENE of Northampton It has a post office under Northampton Acres, 1 290

Real property, £2,850 Pop, 425 Houses, 90 The property is divided among a few The manor belonged formerly to the O'Briens, Earls of Thomond, and belongs now to the Elweses The living is a rectory in the diocese of Peterborough Value, £495 * Patron, Brasenose College, Oxford. The church is very good and there are a Wesleyan chapel, a parochial school, and charities £39 Sir J Wake, the diplomatist of James I, was a native

BILLING (LITTLE), a parish in the district and county of Northampton, on the river Nen, adjacent to Billing Road r station, 3 miles E by N of Northampton. Post town Great Billing, under Northampton Acres, 856 Real property, £1,639 Pop, 76 Houses, 15. The manor belonged to the Longuevilles, and their seat on it is now a farm house. The living is a rectory in the diocese of Peterborough Value, £340 * Patron, Earl Brownlow The church has a curious old font.

BILLINGBEAR, the seat of Lord Braybrooke, 3¼ miles NE of Wokingham, Berks

BILLINGBOROUGH, a parish in Bourn district Lincoln, 3 miles E of Folkingham, and 7 S of Heckington r station It has a post office‡ under Folkingham. Acres, 2,020 Real property, £6,704 Pop, 1,149 Houses, 261 The property is divided among a few The living is a vicarage in the diocese of Lincoln. Value, £295 * Patron, Earl Fortescue The church is decorated English, and has a fine tower and spire There are Baptist and Wesleyan chapels, an endowed school with £32 a year, and charities £41

BILLINGE, a village, two townships, and a chapelry in Wigan parish, Lancashire The village stands 2 miles S of Orrel r station and 4½ SW by W of Wigan, and has a post office under Wigan The townships are called Billinge Chapel-End and Billinge Higher End Acres of B. Chapel End, 1,129 Real property, £11,309, of which £7,580 are in mines Pop 2,015 Houses, 389 Acres of B Higher End 1,519 Real property, £5,616, of which £2,000 are in mines and £641 in quarries Pop, 1,051 Houses, 204 Billinge Hill here is 633 feet high, has a beacon on the top, and commands a view on one side to Ingleborough, on another to the Welsh mountains Some of the inhabitants are employed in cotton mills The chapelry consists of the two townships, and is a p curacy in the diocese of Chester Value, £403 * Patron, the Rector of Wigan The church is good. There are a Roman Catholic chapel, a national school, and charities £117

BILLINGFORD, a parish in Mitford district, Norfolk, on the river Wensum, 1½ mile ESE of Elmham r station, and 3½ SSW of Foulsham. It has a post office under Thetford Acres, 1,820 Real property, £2,337 Pop., 354 Houses, 74. The manor belongs to the Earl of Leicester An hospital for poor travellers was founded at Beckhall here, in the time of Henry III, by William Beck. The living is a rectory in the diocese of Norwich Value, £360 * Patron, the Earl of Leicester The church is good There are a Primitive Methodist chapel and a national school

BILLINGFORD, or PIPLESTON, a parish in Depwade district, Norfolk, on the river Waveney, 1 mile E of Scole, and 2 SE of Diss r station Post town Scole Acres 1,820 Real property, £1,589 Pop, 199 Houses 43 The property is not much divided The manor belonged to Sir S Burley the Black Prince's favourite, executed in 1388 The living is a rectory, united with the rectory of Little Thorpe, in the diocese of Norwich Value, £264. Patron, G Wilson, Esq The church is good.

BILLINGHAM, a township and a parish in Stockton district, Durham The township lies on the Billingham river, and on the Clarence and Hartlepool railway, 3 miles NNE of Stockton-on Tees and has a station on the railway, and a post office under Stockton-on Tees Acres, 3,139, of which 339 are water Real property, £4,908. Pop., 931 Houses, 187 The parish includes also the townships of Cowpen Bewley, Newton Bewley, and Wolviston Acres, 11,691, of which 2,328 are water Real property, £13,525 Pop 2,166 Houses, 426 The property is divided among a few Billingham Grange is a chief residence Coal is worked A great battle was fought in the parish, in 900, by Eardulph king of Northumbria The living is a vicarage in the diocese of Durham Value, £210 * Patrons, the Dean and Chapter of Durham The church is late Saxon and transitional Norman, has a tower 141 feet high, and contains a chancel screen and three brasses Church land yields £52 a year, and other charities £38 The rectory of Wolviston and the vicarage of Haverton-Hill are separate charges There are a Wesleyan chapel and national schools.

BILLINGHAM RIVER, a stream of Durham, rising near Great Stainton, and running 11 miles eastward, past Thorpe and Billingham, to the Tees, 2½ miles below Stockton

BILLINGHAY, a parish in Sleaford and Boston districts, and a sub district in Sleaford district, Lincoln The parish lies on Billinghay Skirt 3½ miles WSW of Tattershall r station and 8½ NE of Sleaford It includes the township of Dogdyke, and the hamlet of Walcott, and has a post office‡ under Sleaford. Acres, 7,630 Real property, £17,794. Pop, 2,217 Houses, 477 The property is much subdivided Billinghay Skirt is a cut 5 miles long, from the Sleaford canal to the river Witham The living is a vicarage, united with the p curacy of Walcott in the diocese of Lincoln Value, £280 * Patron, Earl Fitzwilliam The church has Norman arches, and is good There are chapels for Independents, Baptists, Wesleyans, and Primitive Methodists —The sub district comprises five parishes, parts of two other parishes, and an extra parochial tract Acres, returned with Sleaford sub-district Pop, 5,423 Houses, 1,100

BILLINGLEY, a township in Darfield parish, W R Yorkshire, on the North Midland railway, near Darfield station, 6½ miles ESE of Barnsley Acres, 861 Real property, £1,224 Pop, 192 Houses, 40

BILLING ROAD, a station on the Blisworth and Peterborough railway, adjacent to the river Nen, 4 miles E of Northampton

BILLINGSHURST, a village, a parish, and a sub district in Petworth district, Sussex The village stands on the Roman Stane street, adjacent to the Mid Sussex railway, near the Arun and Wey canal, 7 miles SW of Horsham, and has a station on the railway, a post office‡ under Horsham, and fairs on Whit Monday and 8 Nov It probably got its name from being a settlement of the great Saxon tribe of Billing.—The parish is divided into East and West Billingshurst Acres, 6,758 Real property, £6,234 Pop, 1,495 Houses, 296 The property is much subdivided. Gratwick House is the seat of R Bascoby, Esq The living is a vicarage in the diocese of Chichester Value, £170.* Patron, Sir C Goring, Bart The south side of the church is very early Norman, the rest, chiefly perpendicular English There are two dissenting chapels, a national school, and charities £7 —The sub district comprises three parishes. Acres, 21,072 Pop, 4,245 Houses, 832

BILLINGSIDE, a township in Lanchester parish, Durham, on a branch of the Tyne and Stanhope railway, 12 miles SW of Gateshead. Acres, 283 Pop, 10 Houses, 2.

BILLINGSLEY, a parish in Bridgnorth district Salop, on a small affluent of the Severn, 3½ miles WSW of Hampton Loade r station and 5½ S of Bridgnorth It has a post office under Bridgnorth Acres, 1,285 Real property, £1,951 Pop, 144 Houses 26 The property is all in one estate Coal and ironstone have been worked The living is a rectory in the diocese of Hereford Value, £195 Patron, the Duke of Cleveland The church is good Dr Thomas Hyde, who co operated in Walton's Polyglott, was a native

BILLINGTON, a chapelry in Leighton Buzzard parish, Beds, on the river Ouse and the Leighton and Luton railway, 2 miles SE of Leighton Buzzard Post town, Leighton-Buzzard Acres, returned with the parish Real property, £2,345 Pop, 484 Houses, 102 The property is divided among a few The living is a rectory in the dio of Ely Value, £280 * Patrons the Inhabitants The church is good. There is a Wesleyan chapel

BILLINGTON a liberty in Bradley parish, Staffordshire, 2 miles SW of Stafford Billington Bury here is an ancient British camp and commands a fine view

BILLINGTON, a sub district in Blackburn parish and district, Lancashire It comprises the township of Billington Langho and three other townships. Acres, 5,550 Pop. 1 717 Houses, 338

BILLINGTON LANGHO, a township chapelry in Blackburn parish, Lancashire, on the Blackburn and Clitheroe railway, 5½ miles NNE of Blackburn It has a station, of the name of Langho, on the railway, and its post town is Whalley, under Blackburn Acres, 2 060 Real property, £4,719 Pop, 1,058 Houses, 205 The inhabitants are chiefly cotton weavers The living is a p. curacy in the diocese of Manchester Value, £120 Patron, the Vicar of Blackburn The church is ancient. There are a Roman Catholic chapel, a national school, and charities £38

BILLISBORROW See BILSBORROW

BILLOCKBY a parish in Flegg district, Norfolk, on the river Bure, 3 miles NE of Acle, and 7 NE of Buckenham r station Post town Acle, under Norwich. Acres, 389 Real property, £967 Pop., 46 Houses, 14 Billockby Hall is the seat of the Lucas family The living is a rectory in the diocese of Norwich. Value, £100 Patrons, the Lucas family

LILLSBOROUGH See BILSBORROW

BILLY QUAY, a village in Heworth chapelry Durham, on the river Tyne, 3½ miles E of Gateshead Here are works of the Arkendale Mining Company, a ship yard and several manufactories

BILLY ROW See CROOK and BILLY ROW

BILNEY, a railway station in Norfolk, on the Lynn and Dereham railway, 7 miles ESE of Kings Lynn

BILNEY (EAST), a parish in Mitford district Norfolk, 3 miles WSW of Elmham r station, and 5 NNW of East Dereham It has a post office under Swaffham Acres, 544 Real property, £1 004 Pop, 198 Houses, 43 The property is divided among a few The living is a rectory, united with the rectory of Beetley in the diocese of Norwich Value, £642 Patron, W Collison, Esq The church is good Bilney, the martyr, burned at Norwich in 1531, was a native

BILNEY (WEST) a parish in Freebridge Lynn district, Norfolk, on the Lynn and Dereham railway, at Bilney station, 7 miles ESE of Kings Lynn Post town, East Winch, under Lynn Acres, 2,750 Real property, £2,439 Pop, 253 Houses, 50 The living is a vicarage in the diocese of Norwich Value £60 Patron, J Dalton, Esq The church is ancient Charities, £6 and a fuel allotment

LILSBORROW, a township in Garstang parish, Lancashire 4½ miles SE of Garstang Acres, 812 Real property, £1,455 Pop, 176 Houses, 37 There are a Wesleyan chapel, and an endowed school with £48 a year

BILSBY, a parish in Spilsby district, Lincoln, adjacent to the East Lincoln railway, 1 mile E of Alford It includes the hamlets of Asserby and Thurlby, and its post town is Alford Acres, 2 820 Real property, £5,111 Pop, 572 Houses, 122 The property is much subdivided. The living is a vicarage in the diocese of Lincoln Value, £193 * Patron, J Mason, Esq The church is good Charities, £7

LILSDALE, a mountain vale a township, a hamlet, two constablewicks, and a chapelry in Helmsley district, N R Yorkshire The vale begins about 5 miles SE by S of Stokesley, and extends 11 miles southward to Rievaulx, 3½ miles NW of Helmsley Its head is overhung by Whinston and Botton Head, mountains 2 300 and 1,485 feet high, and its sides are flanked by other heights, and cut by lateral vales The view at its head is very magnificent, and the scenery in some other parts of it is grand —The township is called Bilsdale Midcable, the hamlet, Bilsdale Kirkham, the constablewicks Bilsdale East-side and Bilsdale High West side, and all are in the vale or on its sides —The chapelry also is called Bilsdale Midcable, and it includes all the Bilsdales, and likewise the hamlets of Crossett, Chapelgate, Chapgate, and Urra and the constablewick of Raisdale, and is in the parish of Helmsley The nearest railway station to it is Stokesley, and the nearest post towns, Stokesley, under Northallerton, and Helmsley, under York Acres, 18 971 Real property £4,018 Pop., 738. Houses 126 The property is not much divided The living is a p curacy in the diocese of York Value, £130 Patron, the Vicar of Helmsley The church is good, and there is a Quakers chapel

BILSDALE WEST SIDE, a township in Hawnby parish, N R Yorkshire on the W side of Bilsdale vale 8 miles NW by N of Helmsley It includes part of the hamlet of Laskill Gate Acres, 4,014 Real property, £2,429 Pop, 162 Houses, 28

BILSFORD a hamlet in Buckland Brewers parish, Devon, 6½ miles W of Torrington

BILSHAM, a tything in Yapton parish, Sussex, 3 miles SW of Arundel

BILSINGTON a parish in East Ashford district, Kent, on the Military canal, and partly in Romney marsh, 3 miles ENE of Ham street r station, and 6 SSE of Ashford It has a post office under Ashford, and a fair on 5 July Acres, 2 843 Real property £4,057 Pop, 360 Houses, 75 The property is divided among a few The manor of Bilsington Inferior was given to the Earls of Arundel, in the time of Edward III, on the tenure of serving the king as butler at Whitsunday, and belongs now to the Cosways A priory of Augustinian canons was founded on Bilsington Inferior, about 1253, by John Mansell, provost of Beverley, and the manor connected with it was held by a tenure similar to that of Bilsington Inferior Remains of the priory still stand, partly appropriated into a farm house, on high ground, commanding a good view over the marsh The living is a vicarage in the diocese of Canterbury Value, £52 Patron, W Cosway, Esq The church is good

BILSTHORPE, a parish in Southwell district, Notts, in Sherwood forest, 5¾ miles NW of Southwell r station Post town, Kirklington, under Southwell Acres, 1,572 Real property, £1 703 Pop, 197 Houses 44 The property is much subdivided The manor was given by William the Conqueror to G de Gaunt, and passed to the Foljambes, the Broughtons, and others The old manor-house stood near the church, and is said to have given shelter, for a short time to Charles I The living is a rectory in the diocese of Lincoln Value, £300 * Patron, the Earl of Scarborough The church is small, and contains several interesting monuments

BILSTON, a town, a township, three chapelries, and a sub district, in Wolverhampton parish and district, Stafford The town is within Wolverhampton borough, 2¾ miles SE of Wolverhampton town, and 2¾ NW of Wednesbury The Birmingham and Fazeley canal passes near, the Stour Valley railway passes within a mile, the London and Northwestern railway also passes near, the Birmingham and Wolverhampton, and the Oxford and Wolverhampton railways pass through, and all these railways have stations for it at the most convenient points The place was at one time a royal manor, of little note, it continued, till a modern period, to possess only a few private houses and it burst into importance, and rapidly acquired bulk, as a centre of the hardware trade The town occupies an elevated position, and is nearly 2 miles long Few of the houses are handsome, many are substantial, but many also are poor and dismal Smoke from furnaces and other works continually obscures the air, and incessant noise and bustle banish all repose Strangers who can admire the blaze of upwards of fifty smelting furnaces will think the environs grand but those who love a clear atmosphere and quietude will feel appalled. Cholera attacked 3,568 of the inhabitants, and carried off 742, in 1832, and again carried off 723 in 1849, and it so roused attention to sanitary measures as to occasion much improvement Extensive schools, built in 1832, and known as the Cholera schools, are now a dissenting chapel Other extensive schools, called St Leonard's and St Mary's, the former a tasteful erection of 1858, at a cost of £2,500, have apartments for 1,000 persons, in which lectures are delivered occasionally from October till March. A suite of baths and wash houses, of ornamental character, was built in 1853 at a cost of £2,700 St Leonard's church, at the northwestern extremity of the town, was rebuilt in 1827, is a neat Grecian edifice, with low tower, and contains a splendid altar piece St Mary's church, at the other end of the town, was built in 1829 at a cost of £7,223, and is in the later English style, with a fine tower St Luke's church, in Pinfold street was built at a cost of £4,825, is in the early English style, and consists of nave, aisles, and chancel, with tower and spire. There are chapels for five denominations of dissenters, and for Roman Catholics. The new Independent chapel is a highly ornamental structure of 1864, and one of the Methodist chapels is a very fine edifice A new cemetery was recently opened at a brief distance into the country The town has a head post office,‡ a banking office, and four chief inns, and is a seat of petty sessions and a polling place. Markets are held on Mondays and Saturdays. Great trade is carried on in coal, iron, and stone from the neighbourhood, metal casting, in all its branches, and the manufacture of japanned and fancy iron goods in vast variety, are highly prominent, and brass-working, bell making, malting, and rope making also are carried on The hardware articles produced are too numerous to be mentioned, but include trays, waiters, iron buckets, hurdles, pattens, keys, buckles, locks, bridle bits, screws, chains, boilers, and weighing machines Area of the town, 1,730 acres Real property, £139,980, of which £32,528 are in mines, £44,590 in iron works, and £1,200 in quarries Pop., in 1841, 20,181, in 1861, 24,364 Houses, 4,631 —The township and the sub district are conterminate with the town —The chapelries are St Leonard, St. Mary, and St Luke, and were constituted in 1841, 1843, and 1845 Pop, 7,457, 9,040, and 4,902 Houses, 1,417, 1,703, and 935 St Leonard is a p curacy, and the others are vicarages, in the diocese of Lichfield Value of St. Leonard, £635,* of St Mary, £300,* of St Luke, £300 * Patrons of St Leonard, Resident Householders, of St Mary, the Bishop of Lichfield, of St Luke, alternately the Crown and the Bishop Charities, £38.

BILSTON, Suffolk See BILDESTONE.

BILSTONE, a township in Norton juxta Twycross parish, Leicester, adjacent to the Ashby de la Zouch canal, 3 miles NW of Market Bosworth Acres, 570 Real property, £1,279 Pop, 116 Houses, 25

BILTON, a village and a parish in Rugby district Warwick The village stands adjacent to the Rugby and Leamington railway, 1¼ mile SW of Rugby, and has a post office under Rugby The parish comprises 2 243 acres Real property, £6,505 Pop, 1,096 Houses, 225 New Bilton forms a suburb of Rugby Bilton Hall was purchased by Addison, in 1711, prior to his marriage with the Countess of Warwick, appears to have been mainly built about the time of James I, but probably received some additions under Addison, retained some pictures and other objects which he placed in it, was bequeathed by his daughter and heiress to the Hon John Simpson, and remains in possession of that gentleman's family Bilton Grange is a magnificent Tudor mansion, erected about 1840, after designs by Pugin belonged to Capt J Hibbert, and was often announced for sale between 1860 and 1865 The living is a rectory in the diocese of Worcester Value, £678 * Patron the Rev R O Assheton The church is a neat Gothic structure, with graceful octagonal spire The vicarage of New Bilton is a separate charge, constituted in 1868 Value, £150 * A school has an endowed income of £20, and other charities £71

BILTON, a hamlet in Lesbury parish, Northumberland, adjacent to the Northeastern railway, at the junction of the branch to Alnwick, 18½ miles N of Morpeth It has a station at the railway junction Pop, 121

BILTON, a township, a parish, and a sub district in the district of Tadcaster, W R Yorkshire The township lies on the York and High Harrogate railway, near Hammerton station, 5 miles ENE of Wetherby and has a post-office under York Acres, 1,420 Real property, £2,606 Pop, 242 Houses, 44 The parish includes also the townships of Bickerton and Tockwith Acres, 4,150 Real property, £6,894 Pop, 926 Houses, 201 A Cistertian nunnery was founded here, at Synningthwaite, about 1,160, by Bertram de Haget The living is a vicarage in the diocese of York. Value £300 * Patron, the Prebendary of Bilton Tockwith was made a separate benefice in 1867 There are two Wesleyan chapels and an endowed school —The sub district comprises two parishes and two parts Pop, 1,493

BILTON, or BILTON IN HOLDERNESS, a township chapelry in Swine parish, E R. Yorkshire, 3 miles N of Marfleet r station, and 4 NE of Hull Post town, Coniston, under Hull Acres, 1,120 Real property, £1,784 Pop 102 Houses, 16 The property is all in one estate. The living is a vicarage in the diocese of York Value, £150 * Patron, Viscount Downe The church is excellent

BILTON WITH HARROGATE, a township and two chapelries in Knaresborough parish and district, W R. Yorkshire The township lies on the North Midland railway, 2 miles W of Knaresborough, and contains the post town of Harrogate Acres, 4,800 Real property, £29,286 Pop, 4,563 Houses, 905 The two chapelries are Bilton and Harrogate Bilton was constituted in 1828 Pop, 407 Houses, 91 The living is a vicarage in the diocese of Ripon Value, £154 Patron, W Sheepshanks, Esq A school has an endowed income of £30 Harrogate, town and chapelry, will be noticed in the article HARROGATE.

BIMPTON See BRIMPTON

BINACRE See BENACRE

BINBROOK, a village, a parish, and a sub district in the district of Louth, Lincoln The village stands on the river Ancholme, at the foot of the Wolds, 7 miles ENE of Market Raisen r station, and has a post office‡ under Market Raisen It was formerly a market town, and a place of some note, but has considerably decayed The parish consists of two quondam parishes, Binbrook-St Gabriel and Binbrook St Mary, united by act of parliament and is held by some to include the hamlet of Orford which others regard as extra parochial Acres, 6,070 Real property, £8,082 Pop, 1,334 Houses, 277 The property is divided among a few The manor belongs to C Turnor Esq There are extensive rabbit warrens The living is a rectory and a vicarage—St Mary a rectory, St Gabriel a vicarage—in the diocese of Lincoln Value, £291 Patron, the Lord Chancellor The church of St M is bad, and that of St G is in ruins There are three Methodist chapels, a temperance hall, a national school, a reading room, a police station, and a church estate £83 —The sub-district contains fourteen parishes and two extra parochial tracts Pop, 4,468

BINCHESTER, a township in St Andrew Auckland parish, Durham, on the river Wear, adjacent to the Weardale railway 2 miles N by E of Bishop Auckland Acres, 500 Real property, with Newfield, £3,473,—of which £2,294 are in mines Pop, 33 Houses, 5. The manor has belonged to the Wren family since the time of James I, and their mansion on it, a venerable building with wings, appears to have been built about the beginning of that king's reign. A spot on the brow of an eminence, commanding an extensive view, and now enclosed and cultivated, was the Roman station Binovium or Vinovium, and has yielded a great variety of Roman relics The extent of the station was probably about 30 acres The Roman Watling street passed either through it, or close on its western side

BINCOMBE, a parish in Weymouth district, Dorset, on the river Wey, on the Southwestern railway, and on the downs, 4½ miles S by W of Dorchester r station. Post-town, Dorchester Acres, 977 Real property, £1,035 Pop, 191 Houses, 41 The property is divided between two Good stone is quarried, and there is a mineral spring Numerous barrows are on the downs The living is a rectory united with the rectory of Broadway, in the diocese of Salisbury Value £437 * Patron, Caius College, Cambridge The church is old but good, and has a tower

BINDERTON, a parish in Westhampnett district, Sussex, 3¼ miles N by W of Chichester r station. Post town, Chichester Acres, 1,790 Real property, £1,139 Pop 109 Houses, 16 Binderton House is the seat of the Teasdales The living is a p. curacy, annexed to the rectory of West Dean, in the diocese of Chichester The church is in ruins

BINDON, a hamlet in Wool parish, and a liberty in Cerne, Wareham, and Wimborne divisions, Dorset The hamlet lies on the river Frome, and on the Southwestern railway, ½ a mile E of Wool station, and 5 W by S of Wareham A Cistertian abbey was founded here, in 1172, by Robert de Newburgh, was given, at the dissolution to Thomas, Lord Poynings, descended to the Earl of Suffolk, and was sold to the family of Weld. The remains of it, in foundation walls of the church, have been cleared out, and include part of the tomb of one of the abbots, and some features of the grounds connected with it, in canals, fish ponds, and shady walks, and thick wood have been restored to their original state. The materials of the buildings were carried off for the construction of Lulworth Castle, the seat of Lords Suffolk and the Welds Bindon Hill, in the vicinity, towards the coast, has sand cliffs, succeeded by snowy precipices.—The liberty includes the parishes of Wool and Chaldon-Herring, and parts of three other parishes, but its limits, in some directions, are not defined

BINEGAR, a parish in Shepton Mallet district, Somerset, at the eastern end of the Mendip hills, 4 miles N of Shepton-Mallet r station, and 5 NW of Wells Post town, Shepton Mallet. Acres, 1,216 Rated property, £1,919 Pop, 309 Houses, 70 The property is subdivided The living is a rectory in the diocese of Bath and Wells Value not reported Patron, the Bishop of Bath and Wells The church was rebuilt in 1859 A fair is held on the Wednesday and Thursday of Whit sun week

BINES GREEN, a locality 3½ miles N of Steyning, Sussex, where a fair is held on 12th June

BINFIELD, a small village and a parish in Easthampstead district, Berks The village stands in Windsor forest 2½ miles N of Bracknell r station, and 3½ NE of Wokingham, and has a post office under Bracknell The parish comprises 3,207 acres Real property, £7,341 Pop, 1,371 Houses, 270 The property is much subdivided. Binfield House, Binfield Park, and Pope's Wood are chief residences The last was the early home of the poet Pope, who described it as

"My paternal cell,
A little house, with trees a row
And, like its master, very low"

The present house is mainly reconstruction and enlargement but includes the room which is believed to have been the poet's study Here Pope wrote great part of his early poems, and in the adjoining grounds stood a tree now destroyed, bearing the inscription by Lord Lyttelton "Here Pope sung" The Roman road, called the Devil's highway, passed near the village and an entrenchment there bears the name of Cæsar's camp. The living is a rectory in the diocese of Oxford. Value, £623 * Patron, the Lord Chancellor The old church was of the time of Edward III, had a picturesque square tower was restored and enlarged in 1848, and further enlarged in 1859 The new church was built in 1867, and is in the early English style There are a national school, and charities £52

BINFIELD, a hundred in Oxford in the extreme SE, extending from the Chilterns to the Thames. It contains seven parishes and part of another Acres, 21,900 Pop, 9,598 Houses, 1,962

BINFIELD HEATH, a hamlet in Binfield hundred, Oxford, 2½ miles N of Sonning, and 3½ SSW of Henley on Thames. It has a post office under Henley on Thames

BINGFIELD, a township in St John Lee parish, Northumberland, on Watling-street and on the river Erringburn, 5½ miles N by W of Corbridge Acres 2,047 Pop, 93 Houses, 18 Here are a mineral spring and a chapel of ease

BINGHAM, a small town a parish, a sub-district, a district, and a wapentake in Notts. The town stands near the Fosse way, on the Nottingham and Grantham railway, in the vale of Belvoir, 9 miles E of Nottingham. It consists chiefly of two streets, parallel to each other, and is well built It has a post-office‡ under Nottingham, a railway station, two chief inns, a church, two dissenting chapels, a free school, and a workhouse, and is a seat of petty sessions and a polling place The church is early and decorated English, large, and cruciform, has a square tower, highly sculptured, and a lofty spire, contains a monument to White, the first editor of the "Ephemeris," and was anciently connected with a small college or guild. A weekly market is held on Thursday, and fairs on the Tuesday and Wednesday before 13 Feb, on Whit-Thursday and on 8 and 9 Nov —The parish is stated in the Census to include likewise part of the hamlet of Newton Acres, 3,054 Real property, £9,609 Pop, 1,918 Houses, 416 The property is not much divided The living is a rectory in the diocese of Lincoln Value, £1,503 * Patron, the Earl of Chesterfield Archbishop Abbot and Bishops Hanmer and Wren were for some time rectors, and Archbishop Cranmer, the astronomer White, Colonel Hutchinson, and Lord Howe were natives of the parish or of its vicinity

The sub-district contains the parishes of Bingham, Whatton, Elton, Granby, Langar, Shelton, Sibthorpe, Flintham, Kneeton, East Bridgford, Car Colston, Screveton, Hawksworth, Thoroton, Orston, Scarrington, Barkestone, and Plungar,—the two last electorally in Leicester, and contains also the chapelry of Flawborough Acres, 31,695 Pop, 7,879 Houses, 1,703 The district comprehends likewise the sub district of Ratcliffe on Trent, containing the parishes of Ratcliffe on-Trent, Shelford, Tythby Cropwell Bishop, Colston Basset, Owthorpe, Kinoulton, Hickling, Widmerpool, Stanton on-the Wolds, Plumtree, Tollerton, Cotgrave, and Holme-Pierrepont, and the extra-parochial tract of Lodge on the Wolds Acres of the district, 68,139 Poor rates in 1866, £8,968 Pop in 1861, 15,670 Houses, 3,391 Marriages in 1866, 84, births, 444,—of which 46 were illegitimate, deaths, 255,—of which 93 were at ages under 5 years, and 8 at ages above 85 years Marriages in the ten years 1851-60, 1 000, births, 5,161, deaths, 3,006 The places of worship in 1851 were 36 of the Church of England, with 7,814 sittings, 1 of Independents, with 274 s, 2 of Baptists, with 100 s., 22 of Wesleyan Methodists, with 3,634 s, 14 of Primitive Methodists, with 1,405 s, 4 of Independent Methodists with 330 s, 1 of Roman Catholics, with 60 s, and 1 undefined, with 246 s The schools were 29 public day schools, with 1,579 scholars, 32 private day schools, with 704 s, 56 Sunday schools, with 3 207 s, and 1 evening school for adults, with 38 s —The wapentake is mainly identical with the district, but less extensive, and it is cut into two divisions, north and south Acres, 24,930 and 29,831 Pop 13,553 Houses, 2,955

BINGHAM MELCOMBE, the seat of the Bingham family in Dorset, on an affluent of the Piddle river, 9 miles NE of Dorchester It was the birth place of Sir Richard Bingham, who fought at the siege of St. Quintin, and has a monument in Westminster abbey

BINGHAM TOWN, a suburb of Gosport, in Hants It is now, and contains some genteel residences

BINGLEY, a town, a township, a parish, and a sub district in the district of Keighley, W R Yorkshire The town stands on an eminence, amid wooded environs, with picturesque views, adjacent to the river Aire, the North Midland railway, and the Leeds and Liverpool canal, 6 miles NW of Bradford It is named among the places given by William the Conqueror to his followers, and it had an ancient castle, which has disappeared It now consists chiefly of one long street, partly brick, and partly stone, and it has undergone much recent improvement, in connection with manufactures. It has a post-office, under Leeds, a railway and telegraph station, two chief inns, a parish church, Independent Baptist and Methodist chapels, a free grammar school, and a new and handsome mechanics' institute, and is a seat of petty sessions and a polling place The church is a plain structure of the time of Henry VIII The grammar school dates from 1529, was recently re built, and has an estate yielding £250 a year A weekly market was formerly held on Tuesdays, and fairs are now held on 25 Jan the first Tuesday of April, 25 Aug, and the second Tuesday of Oct Industry is carried on in the extensive manufacture of worsted yarn, and in iron founding, tanning, and malting Pop, 5,238. Houses, 1,158 —The township bears the name of Bingley with Micklethwaite and contains also the hamlets of Beckfoot, Cottingley, Cross Flatts, Cross Roads, Cullingworth, Eldwick, Faweather, Gilstead, Hainworth, Harden, Priest Thorpe, Riddlesden, and Ryshworth Real property, £35,525 Pop, 13,254 Houses, 2,525 —The parish includes likewise the township of Morton Acres, 13,892 Real property, £44,258 Pop., 15,367 Houses, 3,226 The pro perty is subdivided Riddlesden Hall was anciently the seat of the Maudes A large treasure in Roman coins was found in Morton The living is a vicarage in the diocese of Ripon Value, £500 * Patron, the Bishop of Ripon A new chapelry, called Holy Trinity, was con stituted in 1868 The vicarages of Cullingworth and Morton also are separate charges —The sub district is conterminate with the parish

BING WESTON, a quarter in Worthen parish, Salop, 2 miles WSW of Worthen.

BINHAM, a village and a parish in Walsingham dis trict, Norfolk. The village stands 4 miles NE of Wal singham r station, and 5 SE of Wells, and has a post office under Wells, Norfolk, and a fair on 26 July It is pleasant and picturesque, much visited in summer by parties at the watering places, and retains the shaft of an ancient cross A Benedictine abbey was founded here, in 1104, by Peter de Valoines, and the church of it still stands, and is used as the parish church The nave has two pure early Norman arcades, the west front is very fine early English, with magnificent window, and the stalls, seats, and font are good perpendicular —The parish comprises 2,242 acres. Real property, £3,402 Pop, 512. Houses, 130 The property is subdivided. The living is a vicarage in the diocese of Norwich Value, £103 Patron, T T Clarke, Esq Charities, £25

BINHAM, a hamlet in Old Cleeve parish, Somerset, 2 miles W of Watchet

BINHAMY See STRATTON, Cornwall

BINLEY, a tything in St Mary Bourne parish, Hants, 6¼ miles NNE of Andover Pop, 138

BINLEY, a parish in Foleshill district, Warwick, on the river Sow, adjacent to the Northwestern railway, 2½ miles E of Coventry It includes the liberty of Earns ford, and its post town is Coventry Acres, 2,470 Real property, £2,356 Pop, 196 Houses, 51 The manor belongs to Earl Craven, and Binley Hall is the seat of the Lloyds The living is a donative in the dio cese of Worcester Value, £52. Patron, Earl Craven The church was built by the sixth Lord Craven, and is a Grecian structure, with a medallioned roof Charities, £6 Wagstaffe, the nonjuring bishop, was a native

BINNEL BAY, a wide curve at the western end of the Undercliffe, on the S coast of the Isle of Wight, 3¼ miles WSW of Ventnor

BINNINGTON, a township in Willerby parish, E R Yorkshire, on the Hartford river, and on the York and Scarborough railway, 8 miles SW by S of Scar borough Acres, 910 Real property, £1,000 Pop, 90 Houses 16

BINOVIUM See BINCHESTER

BINSCOE, a village in West Tanfield parish, N R Yorkshire, 3½ miles SE of Masham

BINSCOMB a tything in Godalming parish, Surrey, 1 mile N of Godalming

BINSEY, a small village and a parish in the district of Abingdon and county of Oxford The village stands on the right bank of the Isis, near the West Midland railway 1¼ mile NNW of Oxford It was originally called Thorney, from a profusion of thorns around it, and it afterwards took the name of Binsey, signifying the Island of Prayer, from its being a retreat of nuns and a great resort of pilgrims. A rude church was con structed adjacent to it, about the year 730, by St Fride swide, and this, together with a reputed holy well, drew crowds of pilgrims for ages, insomuch that 24 inns stood in the neighbourhood for their accommodation The parish comprises 470 acres, and its post town is Oxford Real property, £1,002 Pop, 67 Houses, 15 The property is divided among a few The living is a vicar age in the diocese of Oxford Value £90 Patron, Christ Church College, Oxford The church is an an cient brick building without a tower

BINSEY, a hill 3 miles NNE of the foot of Bassen thwaite water, in Cumberland

BINSTEAD, a small village and a parish in the Isle of Wight The village stands on the coast of the Solent, amid charming environs, 1¼ mile W by N of Ryde. The parish comprises 1,140 acres of land and 335 of water, and its post town is Ryde Real property, £2,775 Pop, 486 Houses, 105 The manor be longed, at the Conquest, to William Fitz Stur, and passed to the Bishops of Winchester Several picturesque villas, one of them belonging to Lord Downes, stand near the village and on the coast. Quarr Abbey House is the seat of Admiral Sir Thomas J Cochrane Remains of a Cistertian abbey, called Quarr abbey, founded in 1132, by Baldwin de Redvers, afterwards Earl of De von, stand at a farmstead, 5 furlongs west of the village, and, though fragmentary and mutilated, show some in teresting features A siliceous limestone, containing many fossils, and well suited for building, has been ex tensively quarried since at least the time of William Rufus. The living is a rectory in the diocese of Win chester Value, £80 * Patron, the Bishop of Winches ter The church was rebuilt in 1842, is in the early English style, and embodies some sculptured stones of a previous Norman edifice.

BINSTEAD, or BINSTED, a parish and a sub district in the district of Alton, Hants The parish lies 2¼ miles SSW of Bentley r station, and 4 NE by E of Al ton, contains the hamlets of Issington, Weck, Westcote, and Wheatley, and has a post office under Alton Acres, 6,833 Real property £7,101 Pop, 1,195 Houses, 231 Binstead Hill is the seat of the Coult hards The living is a vicarage, united with the vic arage of Kingsley, in the diocese of Winchester Value, not reported * Patrons, the Dean and Chapter of Win chester The church is ancient, has a low embattled tower and a spire, and contains several monuments There is a Primitive Methodist chapel —The sub-district comprises eight parishes and an extra parochial tract Acres, 27,452 Pop, 4,806 Houses, 980

BINSTED, a parish in Westhampnett district, Sus sex, 1½ mile N of Yapton r station, and 2 W by S of Arundel Post town, Arundel Acres, 1,056 Real property, £1,176 Pop, 110 Houses, 19 Binsted House is a chief residence The living is a rectory in the diocese of Chichester Value, £150 * Patron, J Bones, Esq The church was repaired in 1869

BINTON, a parish in Stratford-on Avon district, Warwick, on the river Avon, 4 miles W by S of Strat ford on Avon r station Post town, Stratford on Avon Acres, 1,260 Real property, £1,695 Pop, 250 Houses, 54 The property is divided among a few Paving stone is quarried, and needles and fish hooks are made The living is a rectory in the diocese of Worces ter Value, £140 * Patron, the Marquis of Hertford The church is decayed

BINTREE, or BYNTRY, a parish in Mitford district, Norfolk, 3 miles NE of Elmham r station, and 2½ WNW of Reepham It has a post-office under Thet ford Acres, 1,455 Real property, £2,853 Pop, 406 Houses, 90 The property is divided among a few The living is a rectory, united with the rectory of Themelthorpe, in the diocese of Norwich. Value, £462 Patron Lord Hastings The church is good, and there are a Baptist chapel, and charities £17

BIRBECK, a stream of Westmoreland, running from Shap Fells to the river Lune

BIRBECK FELLS, a township in Orton and Crosby Ravensworth parishes, Westmoreland, on the Birbeck stream, and on the Lancaster and Carlisle railway, 4 miles SSE of Shap Real property, £1,054 Pop, 200 Most of the surface is wild moor and mountain

BIRBURY See BIRDINGBURY

BIRCH, a township in Bischurch parish, Salop, 7½ miles NW of Shrewsbury Pop, 22.

BIRCH, a hamlet in Warrington parish, Lancashire, in the vicinity of the Runcorn Gap and St Helen's railway 5½ miles W of Warrington

BIRCH, a parish in Lexden district, Essex, 3½ miles SE of Marks Tey r station and 5 SW of Colchester It comprises two ancient parishes, Great Birch and Little Birch, and has a post office under Colchester Acres, 3 069 Real property, £4,318 Pop, 940 Houses, 189 The property is divided among a few Birch Hall is the seat of C G Round, Esq There are remains of a small castle The living is a double rectory in the diocese of Rochester Value, £469 * Patron, alternately the Bishop of Rochester and C G Round, Esq The church of Great Birch is good, and that of Little Birch is in ruins

BIRCH, Hereford See BIRCH (MUCH)

BIRCH, or BIRCH IN RUSHOLME, a hamlet and a chapelry in Manchester parish, Chorlton district, Lancashire The hamlet stands 1¼ mile NW of Levenshulme r station and 2½ S by E of Manchester The chapelry includes the hamlet, was constituted, conterminate with Rusholme township, in 1838, and was reconstituted, on a smaller scale, in 1854 Post town, Levenshulme under Manchester Pop, 2,043 Houses 344 The property is much subdivided The living is a rectory in the diocese of Manchester Value, £160 * Patron, Sir J W H Anson Bart The church is good

BIRCH or BIRCH ST MARY, a chapelry in Bury and Middleton parishes, Lancashire near the Lancashire and Yorkshire railway, 2 miles WNW of Middleton It was constituted in 1842 and its post town is Middleton, under Manchester Pop., 3,773 Houses, 747 The living is a vicarage in the diocese of Manchester Value, £150 * Patron the Rector of Middleton The church is a Gothic structure built in 1828, at a cost of £4 000 There is a large national school.

BIRCHALL See BIRCHOLT

BIRCHAM See BIRCHAM (GREAT)

BIRCHAM CLIFFE, a hamlet in Lindley cum Quarmby township, Huddersfield parish, W R Yorkshire, 2 miles NW of Huddersfield

BIRCHAM (GREAT) a parish in Docking district, Norfolk, 3 miles S of Docking, and 9½ W by N of Fakenham r station It has a post office, of the name of Bircham, under Rougham. Acres, 3 606 Real property £2 453 Pop, 489 Houses, 86 The property mostly belongs to the Marquis of Cholmondeley The living is a rectory in the diocese of Norwich Value, £514 * Patron A Hamond, Esq The church is good

BIRCHAM (NEWTON), a parish in Docking district, Norfolk, 2 miles S of Docking and 9½ W by N of Fakenham r station Post town, Bircham, under Rougham Acres 1 123 Real property, £959 Pop, 118 Houses, 20 The property is divided among a few The living is a rectory, united with the rectory of Bircham Tofts, in the diocese of Norwich Value, £434 * Patron, the Marquis of Cholmondeley The church is good

BIRCHAM TOFTS, a parish in Docking district, Norfolk 3 miles S by E of Docking and 9 W by N of Fakenham r station Post town Bircham, under Rougham Acres, 1 131 Real property, £919 Pop, 165 Houses 25 The living is a rectory annexed to Bircham Newton

BIRCH AND BALDWIN HIF a township in Ellesmere parish, Salop in the neighbourhood of Ellesmere Pop 65

BIRCHANGER, a parish in the district of Bishops Stortford and county of Essex on the Eastern Counties railway, 2 miles NE of Bishops Stortford Post town, Bishops Stortford Acr 1 091 Real property £2 050 Pop, 358 Houses, 80 The property is divided among a few An hospital was founded here, by Richard de Newport, in the time of King John The living is a rectory in the diocese of Rochester Value, £218 * Patron New College, Oxford. The church is good.

BIRCHER, a township in Yarpole parish, Hereford 4½ miles NNW of Leominster Pop, 207

BIRCHES, a township in Great Budworth parish, Cheshire 3 miles ESE of Norwich Pop., 9

BIRCHES, a locality on the river Severn, in Salop 3 miles W by N of Madeley A landslip here, in 1773 changed the course of the river for several hundred yards.

BIRCHETTS GREEN, a village in Wargrave and Hurley parishes, Berks, 4 miles WNW of Maidenhead

BIRCHFIELD, a chapelry in Handsworth parish, Stafford, 3 miles N of Birmingham It has a post office under Birmingham Pop, about 2 000 Living, a vicarage Value, £300 The church was built in 1863

BIRCH (GREAT) See BIRCH and BIRCH (MUCH)

BIRCHGROVE, a station with telegraph on the Swansea Vale railway, 4½ miles NNE of Swansea.

BIRCHGROVE, a place with a post office under East Grinstead, in Sussex

BIRCHILLS, a station on the South Stafford railway 1½ mile NNW of Walsall

BIRCHINGTON, a village and a parish in Thanet district, Kent The village stands adjacent to the Kent Coast railway, 3½ miles W by S of Margate, and has a station on the r, and a post office under Margate It occupies a gentle declivity with extensive prospects by sea and land, and is about ¾ of a mile long The parish is within the Cinque port liberty of Dover, and comprises 1,680 acres of land, and 390 of water Real property, £8,885 Pop, 813 Houses, 186 The property is divided among a few The manor belonged from the beginning of the 15th century, to the family of Quex and passed by marriage, in the time of Henry VII, to the Crispes. One of its owners, a distinguished puritan, in 16?7, was carried off from it to the Continent, by the royalist captain Golding and long kept prisoner at Ostend and Bruges. William III frequently rested at the manor house on his excursions to Holland The present mansion is modern, bears the name of Great Quex, and is the seat of H P Cotton Esq Two towers stand in the park, and are good sea marks, and one of them contains a fine peal of bells The living is a p curacy, annexed to the vicarage of Monkton, in the diocese of Canterbury The church consists of nave chancel, and aisles, with tower and spire, and on the north side of it is a chapel of the manor, containing some fine monuments and ancient brasses There are chapels for Baptists and Wesleyans, and a national school

BIRCHLEY See BILLINGE

BIRCH (LITTLE) a parish in the district and county of Hereford, 3½ miles ESE of Tram Inn r station, and 6 S of Hereford Post town, Birch, under Ross Acres, 967 Real property, £1,948 Pop, 336 Houses, 78 The property is much subdivided The living is a rectory in the dio of Hereford Value, £160 Patron, the Rev S Thackwell The church was rebuilt in 1869

BIRCH (LITTLE), Essex. See BIRCH

BIRCH (MUCH or GREAT) a parish in the district and county of Hereford 3 miles SE of Tram Inn r station, and 6½ S of Hereford It has a post office, of the name of Birch, under Ross Acres, 1 297 Real property £2 221 Pop, 496 Houses 103 The property is much subdivided The Living is a vicarage in the diocese of Hereford Value, £106 Patron, I G Symons, Esq The church is very good Charities, £7

BIRCHOLT, or BIRCHALL a parish and a franchise in Kent The parish is in East Ashford district and lies 2½ miles N of Smeeth r station, and 4½ E by S of Ashford Post town, Smeeth under Ashford Acres, 238 Real property, £470 Pop, 60 Houses, 7 The property is divided between two The living is a rectory in the diocese of Canterbury Value, £40 Patron, E Knatchbull Hugessen, Esq The franchise, called also a barony, is in the lathe of Shepway, and contains four parishes and part of another Acres 10,482 Pop, 2,271 Houses 461

BIRCHOVER, a township in Youlgreave parish, Derby, 1 mile N of Winster Real property, £1,152. Pop., 51 A rocking stone of about 20 tons is here

BIRCH VALE, a place with a r station in Hayfield chapelry, Derby, ¾ mile W of Hayfield

BIRCHWOOD, a village in Alfreton parish, Derby

BIRDALL See RAISTHORPE and BIRDALL

BIRDBROOK, a parish in the district of Risbridge and county of Essex, on the Halstead railway, 2½ miles SE of Haverhill It has a station on the railway Post town, Bumpstead Steeple, under Halstead Acres, 2,386 Real property, £4,047 Pop, 643 Houses, 143. Birdbrook Hall was formerly a seat of Sir W B Rush. Baythorn House was built in 1668 A Roman camp occurs at Watson Bridge, and a large tumulus at Ford Meadow, and a number of Roman urns, coins, and other relics have been found The living is a rectory in the diocese of Rochester Value, £600 * Patron, Clare Hall, Cambridge The church is a neat substantial edifice, and contains the remains of Martha Blewitt, who was the wife of successively nine husbands, and died in 1681

BIRDENBURY See BELDENBURY

BIRDFORTH, a chapelry and a wapentake in N R Yorkshire The chapelry is in Coxwold parish, and lies 3 miles ENE of Sessay r station, and 5 NNW of Easingwold Post-town, Coxwold, under Easingwold Acres, 601 Real property, £935 Pop, 40 Houses, 8 The property is divided between two The living is a p curacy in the diocese of York Value, £94 Patron, the Archbishop of York. The church is tolerable —The wapentake includes seventeen parishes and parts of six others Acres, 103 177 Pop in 1851, 14,462, in 1861, 14,072 Houses, 3,012

BIRDHAM, a parish in Westhampnett district, Sussex, on Chichester harbour, and on the Arundel and Portsmouth canal, 4 miles SW of Chichester r station It has a post office under Chichester Acres 1,948 of which 140 are water Real property, £3,762. Pop, 436 Houses, 99 The property is subdivided The living is a rectory in the diocese of Chichester Value, £396 * Patrons, the Dean and Chapter of Chichester The church is good, and there is a national school

BIRDINGBURY, or BIRBURY, a parish in Rugby district, Warwick, on the river Leam, adjacent to the Leamington and Rugby railway, 7 miles SW by W of Rugby It has a station on the railway, and its post town is Leamington Hastings, under Rugby Acres, 1,180 Real property, £1,568 Pop, 18 Houses, 46. The property is divided among a few The manor belonged formerly to the Wheelers, and belongs now to Sir T Biddulph, Bart The living is a rectory in the diocese of Worcester Value, £120 Patron, Sir T Biddulph, Bart The church is good

BIRDLIP, a hamlet in Brimpsfield parish, Gloucestershire, near Whitcombe Park, 5¼ miles SE by E of Gloucester It is a meet for the Cheltenham hounds, and has fairs on 8 May and on the Tuesday before the second Thursday of Sept Birdlip Hill, in the vicinity, is crossed by Ermine street, and commands a noble view

BIRDRIDDING, a hamlet in Coverham parish, N R Yorkshire, 4½ miles SW of Middleham

BIRDSALL, a parish in Malton district and E R Yorkshire, 1¾ mile SW of North Grimston r station, and 5½ S by E of New Malton Post town, North Grimston under Malton Acres, 3,972 Real property £3,750 Pop, 355. Houses, 53 The property is divided among a few Birdsall Hall, formerly a seat of Lord Middleton, is the chief residence The living is a vicarage in the diocese of York Value, £40 Patron, the Marquis of Hertford The church is a handsome edifice, built in 1814 by Lord Middleton Henry Burton the famous puritan divine who died in 1648, was a native

BIRDS GREEN, a hamlet in the parishes of Beauchamp Roothing and Willingale Doe, Essex, 9½ miles SSW of Dunmow

BIRDSMOORGATE, a locality 8 miles from Crewkerne, in Somerset, with a post office under Crewkerne

BIRDWELL, a hamlet in Worsbrough township, Darfield parish, W R Yorkshire, near the Sheffield and Doncaster railway 4 miles SSE of Barnesley It has a post office under Barnesley, and a station, jointly with Hoyland, on the railway

BIRDWELL-FLAT, a hamlet in Swinton township, Wath upon Dearne parish, W R Yorkshire, 4½ miles NNE of Rotherham

BIRKBY, a township in Cross Canonby parish, Cumberland, on the coast and on the Carlisle railway, 1 mile NE of Maryport. Acres, 871, of which 143 are water Real property, £906 Pop, 157 Houses, 25

BIRKBY a township in Muncaster parish, Cumberland, in Eskdale, 2½ miles E of Ravenglass. Real property, £906. Pop., 119 See BARNSCAR.

BIRKBY, a township and a parish in Northallerton district N R Yorkshire The township lies on the Great Northern railway, 1½ mile SSE of Cowton station, and 6 NNW of Northallerton Real property, £1,263 Pop, 87 Houses, 15 The parish includes also the townships of Hutton Bowville and Little Smeaton, and its post town is East Cowton, under Northallerton Acres, 3,619 Real property, £4,166 Pop, 298 Houses, 51 The living is a rectory in the diocese of York Value, £233 * Patron, Rev W R Holmes The church is very good

BIRKDALE, a township chapelry in North Meols parish, Lancashire, on the coast, and on the Southport railway, 1½ mile S of Southport. It has a r station, several streets, good residences, and boarding houses, and, in 1869, had greatly increased in pop, and was about to have a sewerage system and public gardens Post town, Southport Acres, 5,670, of which 3,435 are water Pop. in 1861, 1,286 Houses, 237 The living is a vicarage in the diocese of Chester Value, £350 * Patrons, Trustees. The church is recent, and has a spire.

BIRKDALE, a hamlet in Dufton parish, Westmoreland, 9 miles NE of Appleby Pop, 13

BIRKDALE, a hamlet in Muker chapelry, in the vicinity of Muker, N R Yorkshire

BIRKENHEAD, a seaport town, a township, and seven chapelries, in the district of Wirrall, Cheshire. The town stands on the Mersey, opposite Liverpool, about a mile by water W of Liverpool, and 14¾ by railway NNW of Chester The place was anciently called Lircheved, Birkete, Birket wood, and Birkenhedde, and took its name from being engirt by forest A Benedictine priory was founded at it, about the year 1170 by Hamon de Massey, baron of Dunham Massey, sent its priors to sit in the parliaments of Chester as nobles of the palatinate and, in 1282, acquired the right to maintain a ferry, still known as the Monks ferry, across the Mersey to Lancashire A fine crypt and some interesting ruins of the priory still exist The greater part of the priory estate was bestowed by Henry VIII on Ralph Worsley, and passed to successively the Powells, the Clevelands, and the Prices In 1753, there were three ferry boat houses, one at Woodside for Birkenhead, one at Seacombe, about a mile further down the river, and one at Rock ferry, 1¼ mile further up, but these were only conveniences for the dwellers inland, and the travellers to Chester Even so late as 1801, Birkenhead had only 110 inhabitants, and 20 years later, only 200 The first move towards a town was the purchase, in 1824, by Mr Laird, father of the celebrated shipbuilder, of several acres of land on the shore of the Wallasey Pool an inlet from the Mersey The pool and the land adjoining it were speedily seen to be excellently suited for docks, and measures were soon adopted for converting the place into a great port The town, once begun, made astonishingly rapid progress, and, though it has suffered some checks, it now enjoys every prospect of a steady and accelerating increase

Birkenhead is well aligned and well built, and it had the singular advantage of being all planned before the building operations for it were well begun T C Thornburn Esq., C E, reported to us in 1865 —" Length of streets laid out, 54 miles, scavenged, 43, adopted, 40 Area of Birkenhead Park, 190¾ acres, of which 92 are la 1 out in ornamental ground, lakes, and grass, 14½ occupied by roads and drives, and 77 laid out in building ground. Cost of land, £61,028, of formation, £78,654 Hamilton-square occupies 6 or 7 acres, is edificed with stone fronts, and presents a very grand appearance The market house is one of the finest in England, cost £30,000, exclusive of the site, and is 430 feet long, and 131 wide The post office is an ornamental edifice, in the Corinthian style The free public library and the theatre were built in 1864, and the former is in the Florentine style The working man s hall was built in 1865, at a cost of from £4,000 to £5,000 A ragged school was then in contemplation, the sum of £7,000 having been given for it by Wm Jackson, Esq, M P St Mary s church is an elegant structure, in the decorated English style, built in 1819, and the churchyard includes the burial ground and ruins of the ancient priory Holy Trinity is an edifice in the Norman style St Anne s, built of the red sandstone of the district, makes a fine appearance St. James' is in the early English style, and is built of beautiful white Storeton stone St John's, in the decorated style, was built in 1845, and has a fine tower and spire St Paul s was built in 1863, and St. Peter s partly in 1868 Upwards of thirty non established places of worship are within the town (including Claughton and Oxton), and some of them are very beautiful and ornamental structures There are two Roman Catholic churches, the older one, a Grecian edifice, the other, opened in 1862, in the early French Gothic style, from designs by Pugin There is also a convent, in the Italian style, built in 1863, at a cost of £10,000. St Aidan s theological college, under the principalship of the Rev Dr Baylee, forms a fine pile of Tudor architecture, with good internal arrangements, and furnishes about one in eighteen of the candidates for orders in the Established church A court house, two banks, gas works, water works, working men's houses, an abbatoir, and an extensive new cemetery, also draw attention A handsome infirmary, built at an expense of upwards of £5 000 and presented to the town by Mr John Laird, M P, was opened in 1863. A street railway runs from Woodside ferry by the Park to Oxton, a distance of about 3 miles, an outward railway giving communication with the country, will be noticed in the next article, and other railways, from the docks to the West Cheshire line, from Hooton to Parkgate, and from Hooton to Queensferry, with branches to the Holyhead and to the Buckley, have been projected.

The harbour of Birkenhead is magnificent The docks were commenced in 1844, on a vast plan which was approaching completion in 1869 The water area of them is 168 acres, the lineal quay space, about 10 miles and the cost will be upwards of £3,000 000 The west float has a quayage of 2 miles, 210 yards, the east float, 1 mile, 1 566 yards the Egerton dock, 771 yards, the Morpeth dock, 1,290 yards, the Morpeth basin, a tidal one, 703 yards, the low water basin, also a tidal one, 1,300 yards, and a dock, north of this, 482 yards Two side basins and two large graving docks branch from the west float, a system of railways encompasses the east float, passages ample and well contrived, communicate among the docks, the passage from the river to the Morpeth dock is so contrived that it can be used as a graving dock a system of sluices, for scouring away deposits is connected with the low water basin an extensive building contains the machinery for the sluices, and has a tower 200 feet high, and bridges, cranes, coal hoists, sheds, warehouses, and other appliances are plentiful and well placed A landing stage, at Woodside ferry, 800 feet long and 80 feet wide constructed in 1862 rests on pontoons similar to the Liverpool stages rising and falling with the tide, is connected with the piers by two iron bridges, and gives every accommodation to passenger traffic Another landing stage, in the low water basin 1,000 feet long and 50 feet wide, is of similar construction and serves for vessels at all states of the tide The cost of the dock works in 1868 was £220,618

The commerce of Birkenhead is, in all respects, a branch of that of Liverpool, and chiefly devoted to coal, guano, and grain The Cunard Company recently obtained accommodation for their steamers in the harbour, and other sea going steamship companies are expected to follow their example. Very extensive trade is carried on in ship building and engineering The works of the Messrs. Laird Brothers employ from 3,000 to 4,000 men, and have paid £720 000 in wages in six years. The Canada works have paid £500,000 in eight The Britannia works also are extensive, and have acquired their magnitude through the skill and enterprise of their proprietor, James Taylor, Esq, the inventor of the steam lifts and the elephant The town has a head post office,‡ a telegraph station, two banking offices, and fourteen chief inns, publishes three newspapers, and is a seat of petty sessions and a polling place. Markets are held on Tuesdays and Saturdays, and fairs on the last Tuesday of Feb. and April and on 3 July and 8 Oct —Acres of the township, 1,265, of which 365 are water Real property in 1860, £235,548, of which £64,601 are in railways Pop in 1841, 8,223 in 1861, 36,212. Houses, 4,609 The township, with Claughton, Oxton, Tranmere, and part of higher Bebington, was, in 1861, made a parliamentary borough, sending one member to parliament Electors in 1866, 4,563 Pop, 51,649 Houses, 7,189

The chapelries are St Mary, St James, Trinity, St Anne, St John, St. Paul, and St Peter The first is the oldest, and was formed out of Bidstone parish, the next four were formed out of the first, and St Paul was formed out of Bebington Trinity was constituted in 1841, St. Anne, in 1847, St Paul, in 1858, St John, in 1859, St. Peter, in 1867 There is also a Mariners' church All the livings are p curacies in the diocese of Chester Value of St Mary, £153, of Trinity, £300, of St Anne £159,* of St. John, £300,* of St Peter, £300, of the others, not reported Patrons of St. John, the Church Patronage Society, of St Anne the Rev A. Knox of the others Trustees

BIRKENHEAD RAILWAY, a ramified railway connecting Birkenhead with Chester and with the NE of Cheshire It existed prior to August 1859, under the names of the Chester and Birkenhead railway, and the Birkenhead Lancashire, and Cheshire Junction It consisted then of a main line from Chester to Grange Lane, a line from Grange Lane to Monks ferry, a line from Grange Lane to Bridgend, all at Birkenhead, and a main line from the station at Chester to the Northwestern railway at Lower Walton, Runcorn, and the aggregate length of it was a little upwards of 33 miles A branch from Hooton to Helsby, 5¾ miles long, and a branch to Tranmere Pool, ¾ mile long, were opened in July, 1863, and a line from Hooton to Parkgate, 5 miles long, was opened in October, 1866

BIRKENSHAW, a railway station, two hamlets, and a chapelry in Birstall parish, W R Yorkshire The station bears the name of Birkenshaw and Tong, and is on the Gildersome branch of the Leeds and Halifax railway, 4½ miles SE of Bradford The hamlets are Birkenshaw and Birkenshaw bottom, and stand near the r station, within Gomersal township, and the former has a post office under Leeds The chapelry bears the name of Birkenshaw cum-Hunsworth, and was constituted in 1842 Pop, 3,633. Houses, 756 The inhabitants are chiefly employed in collieries and woollen mills The living is a p curacy in the diocese of Ripon Value, £150 * Patron, the Vicar of Birstall The church was built in 1829 There are a U Free Methodist chapel, a mechanics institute, and a national school

BIRKBY AND AUSTHWAITE, a township in Millom parish, Cumberland, in Eskdale, 6½ miles ENE of Ravenglass Real property, £710 Pop, 114 Houses 19 Birker Fell here forms part of the S screen of the Esk, and is streaked by a streamlet which makes a sudden romantic fall, over a naked precipice, between cliffs

BIRK HILL, a hill on the E side of Ulles water, Westmoreland, immediately N of Place Fell A short streamlet descends its N side to the lake, and makes a cascade, called Scalea Force

BIRKIN a township in Pontefract district, and a parish in Pontefract and Selby districts, W R York shire The township lies on the river Aire and on the Selby canal, 3¾ miles NE of Knottingley r station, and 7¼ SW of Selby Acres, 2,064 Real property, £3,515 Pop, 168 Houses, 35 The parish contains also the townships of Hurst Courtney, Temple Hurst, Chapel Haddlesey, and West Haddlesey, the last of which has a post office under Selby Acres, 5,509 Real property, £9,438 Pop., 821 Houses, 184 The living is a rectory, with Chapel Haddlesey chapelry, in the diocese of York Value, £1,008 * Patron, the Rev T Hill The church is ancient. There are three Wesleyan chapels

BIRKLE See BIRTLE

BIRKLEY See BIRTLEY, Northumberland

BIRK RIGG, a hill in Furness Lancashire, 1½ mile W of Morecambe bay, and 3 E of Dalton It commands a very extensive and magnificent panoramic view

BIRK RIGGS, a hamlet in High Abbotside township, Aysgarth parish, N R Yorkshire, 1 mile NE of Hawes

BIRKS AND COLSTERDALE, a hamlet in East Witton parish, N R Yorkshire, 3¼ miles SE of Middleham

BIRKS BRIDGE, a one arched bridge over the river Duddon, at the E base of Birker Fell, in Cumberland It spans a romantic rocky chasm, supposed to represent the "Fairy Chasm' of Wordsworth

BIRKSCLUGH. See BRISCOE.

BIRKWITH a hamlet in Horton-in-Ribblesdale parish, W R Yorkshire, 7½ miles N of Settle

BIRKWOOD, a hamlet in Crofton parish, W R Yorkshire, 3½ miles SE of Wakefield

BIRLEY, a parish in the district and county of Hereford, on an affluent of the river Lugg, adjacent to Watling street, 3¾ miles NW of Dinmore r station, and 4 ENE of Weobley Post town, Weobley Acres, 1,004 Real property, £1,482 Pop, 190 Houses, 35 The property is divided among a few The living is a vicarage, annexed to the vicarage of King s Pion, in the diocese of Hereford The church is very good.

BIRLEY CARR, a hamlet in Ecclesfield township and parish, W R Yorkshire, 4½ miles N of Sheffield

BIRLING, or BERLING, a township in Warkworth parish, Northumberland, on the river Coquet and on the coast, 8½ miles SE of Alnwick Acres, 826 Pop, 83 Houses, 14

BIRLING, or BYRLING, a parish in Malling district, Kent, adjacent to the river Medway, 2¾ miles WSW of Snodland r station, and 6 NW of Maidstone It has a post office under Maidstone Acres 1,883 Real property, £3,277 Pop, 662. Houses, 111 The property is subdivided The manor belonged formerly to the Mammots, the Says, and the Nevilles, and belongs now to the Earl of Abergavenny Comfort, now a farm house, and Birling place, now represented only by a fragment, were seats of the Nevilles A range of chalk heights, called Birling Hills, occupies the W The living is a vicarage in the diocese of Canterbury Value, £158 Patron, the Earl of Abergavenny The church is perpendicular English, in good condition, and contains the remains, but no monuments, of some of the Nevilles

BIRLING GAP, a depression and an artificial cut in the bold high coast of Sussex, 1½ mile W of Beachy Head The cut was made to afford means of escape to shipwrecked mariners, and was for some time, defended by an arch and portcullis, vestiges of which still exist.

BIRLINGHAM, a parish in Pershore district, Worcester, on the river Avon, 1½ mile E of Defford r station, and 2¼ SSW of Pershore It has a post-office under Pershore Acres, 1,210 Real property, £3,847 Pop., 353 Houses, 74 The property is divided among a few Birlingham Court is the seat of the Porter family The living is a rectory in the diocese of Worcester Value, £205 * Patron, the Rev R L Landor The church is mainly modern, but has an old tower, and includes an ancient Saxon arch Charities, £12

BIRMINGHAM, a division of Hemlingford hundred, Warwick It takes name from the town of Birmingham but does not include any of that town or borough, adjoins it on the E and NE, and contains five parishes and part of another Acres, 24,281 Pop, 16,234 Houses, 3 216

BIRMINGHAM, a great town the fourth in point of population in England, at the NW angle of Warwickshire, adjacent to Worcestershire and Staffordshire, 83 miles SSE of Manchester, 97 SE by S of Liverpool, and 112 NW of London It is all, as a borough, in Warwickshire, but, as to its suburbs, it extends into Worcestershire and Staffordshire It stands on Icknield street, which gives name to a street, a road, and a square, on the streams Rea, Tame, and Cole, and on an ample system of railways and canals which give it communication with all parts of the kingdom The main lines of the Northwestern and the Midland railways, together with the South Stafford, the Stour Valley, and other subordinate lines, have a central station in it, and the Great Western, with branches radiating through the west of England and into Wales, has another station The chief canals are the Staffordshire, the Warwick, and the Worcester, the last of which was, in 1865, about to be converted into a railway

History -An early name of the place was Bromwycham, signifying "house of broom village," and alluding probably to the existence around it of an extensive heath, and the present name arose from that of the lords of the manor after the Conquest, but upwards of one hundred and fifty varieties of the names, or of the spellings of them, have been traced. A Roman station, called Bremenium, was supposed to have been here, but this is now set aside as fabulous The original village is believed to have existed as part of the Saxon kingdom of Mercia, but was too obscure to be noted on a map It is conjectured to have begun the working of iron at a very early period, but the earliest authentic mention of it is in the pages of Leland who describes it as a town of smiths Birmingham makes very little figure in early history Some of the inhabitants followed the lords of the manor, in the time of Henry III, to the battle of Evesham, and most, in the time of Charles I, were warm partizans in the cause of the parliament. They furnished 15,000 sword blades to the parliamentarian army, they seized the king s personal effects on occasion of his making a halt at Aston Hall, they confronted and fought a royalist force of 2,000 men sent to punish them, and they suffered then a discomfiture which cost them a good number of lives, and a destruction of property to the value of £30 000 The town was nearly depopulated by the plague in 1665, but it rose to a population of 15,032 at the end of the next 35 years, and it thenceforth became so devoted to industry as to grow rapidly in prosperity and consequence No public question, for a long time, disturbed it. In 1791, a politico religious riot occurred, with the effect of destroying several lives and about £50,000 worth of property, in 1831, the famous political union, with Thomas Attwood at its head, assisted greatly to compel the passing of the reform bill, and in 1839, chartist riots broke out, and were quelled only by a large detachment of London police, and the arrival of a considerable body of soldiers Since that time, the town has been one of the quietest in the kingdom The Duke of York publicly visited it in 1765, the Duchess of Kent and the Princess Victoria, in 1830, Prince Albert in 1844, 1849, and 1855, Queen Victoria, in 1849, 1852 and 1858, the Duke of Cambridge, in 1857, and Louis Kossuth, in 1852 and 1857 The British Association held their meetings in it in 1839, 1849, and 1865, and the Social Science Association held their first meeting in it in 1857

Site and Streets —Part of the town stands on comparatively low ground, but much stands on a hill, nearly in the form of a crescent This hill is part of the watershed between the eastern and the western seas, and rises 115 feet in 1,000 yards from the side of the Rea, and one portion of it, nearly in the centre of the borough, occupied by St. Philip's church, is 475 feet above low water mark at London bridge The town is compact, and, including the suburbs, extends about 4 miles by 6 The streets are very numerous, generally short and irregular and give an aggregate length of nearly 200 miles New street is the most brilliant High street and Bull street are conspicuous, and many others are full of good shops, and have a lively appearance The houses are in general well-built, chiefly of brick most of the more recent faced with Roman cement and plaster, but many, especially in the principal streets are now built of stone An almost fourfold increase in the total of houses has taken place since the beginning of the century, and this has made a very great change in the general aspect of the town Spots formerly occupied by villas, gardens, orchards and bare common are now covered by busy streets and places formerly distant from the town and altogether rural, are now disposed in pleasant suburbs

Public Buildings —The town hall, at the top of New-street was built in 1832-1850, at a cost of nearly £50,000 The material of it is Anglesey marble, and the style Roman Corinthian, after the model of a peripteral Grecian temple The basement of it is 23 feet high, the columns 36 feet high and 3½ feet thick, the capitals, 4 feet high The chief apartment can accommodate 3,000 persons sitting or 6,000 standing, is elegantly decorated, and contains a magnificent organ, which cost about £3,500. The exchange, built in 1862-5, on a site adjoining the grammar school, with a frontage of 186 feet toward Stephenson place and 63 feet toward New street, is of stone, after designs by Mr E. Holmes, in a very mixed Gothic style, four stories high with a central entrance tower, 100 feet high. The public offices, in Moor-street, were built in 1806, and greatly extended in 1861 and 1865 New corporate buildings and assize courts were projected in 1869, at a cost of £125,500 A new post office, with government grant of £21,850, was projected in 1869 Two large banking offices and a club house were built in 1869 The borough gaol, at Winson green, was erected in 1845-9 at a cost of £30,000, and has capacity for 391 male and 85 female prisoners Three sets of public baths are in Kent street, in Woodcock street, and in Northwood street. The cavalry barracks, in Great Brook street, were built in 1793, and possess extensive accommodation The temperance hall was built in 1860, at a cost of about £2 300 is a neat edifice in the Italian style and has a room which will accommodate 800 persons. The central railway station, in New street, was opened in 1854, presents a handsome front, in the Italian style 312 feet long and has a magnificent interior, spanned by a semicircular roof of glass and corrugated iron, resting only on massive side pillars, and 1,100 feet long 212 feet wide, and 80 feet high A bronze statue of Nelson by Westmacott, in 1809, a very fine work is in the Bull Ring, a Sicilian marble statue of Thomas Attwood, by Thomas, is at the top of Stephenson Place a bronze statue of Sir Robert Peel, by Hollins, is at the top of New street, a Sicilian marble statue of Joseph Sturge, by Thomas, with fountains and emblematical figures is at the Five Ways, Edgbaston, and a colossal marble bust of Mendelssohn, by Hollins, is in the town hall Three other statues were completed in 1868, one of James Watt, by Hollins, one of Sir Rowland Hill, by the same artist and one of the late Prince Consort, by Foley, but the two latter, though intended for the open air, have been placed within public buildings

Ecclesiastical Affairs —The parish of Birmingham, the parish of Edgbaston, and a populous portion of the parish of Aston, are within the borough The rectories of St. Martin, St Philip St George, St Thomas, and All Saints, the vicarages of St Peter, St Matthias, St Mary, St. Bartholomew, St. Mark, St Paul Christ Church, St Luke, Bishop Ryders, St Stephen, St Jude Ladywood, St Barnabas St David, and the p curacy of Immanuel are in Birmingham parish all in the diocese of Worcester Value of St. Martin, £1 018,* of St Philip, £300 * of St George £550,* of St Thomas, £480, of All Saints £270 of St Peter £330 of St Matthias, £225, of St. Mary, £320 * of St Paul, £275 * of Christ Church £370, of St. Stephen, £300,* of St Jude £300,* of Ladywood, £300,* of the others, not reported Patrons of St Martin, St. George, St. Thomas All Saints St Matthias St Mary, St Mark, St Luke, Bishop Ryders, St Davids, Immanuel, and St. Barnabas, Trustees of St Philip and Christ Church, the Bishop of Worcester, of St Stephen and St Jude, the Bishop and the Crown alternately, of St Paul, the Rev G B F Latimer, of St Bartholomew and Ladywood, the Rector of St Martin, and of St. Peter, the Rector of St Philip. The other livings within the borough are noted in the articles EDGBASTON and ASTON

The places of worship, in 1865, were 35 of the Church of England, and about 91 of other denominations, and many of them were recent structures. Those in 1851, according to the Census, were 25 of the Ch of England, with 30,843 sittings, 1 of Presbyterians, with 700 s , 12 of Independents, with 6,607 s , 1 of Lady Huntingdon's, with 200 s. 9 of P Baptists, with 6,749 s , 1 of G Baptists, with 568 s , 2 of Quakers, with 744 s , 5 of Unitarians, with 3,084 s , 13 of W Methodists, with 7,814 s , 3 of New C Methodists, with 1,338 s , 3 of Prim Methodists, with 656 s , 1 of the W Association, with 600 s , 2 of W Reformers with 270 s , 1 of Welsh C Methodists, with 132 s , 1 of the New Church with 500 s , 1 of Brethren, with 100 attendants, 3 of isolated congregations, with 1,300 s , 1 of Latter Day Saints with 1 600 s , 2 of the Cath and Ap Church, with 600 s , 4 of R Catholics, with 1,549 s , and 1 of Jews with 360 s According to returns, in 1865, the Church of England provides 36,000 sittings.

St Martin's church, in the Bull Ring, dates from the 13th century, underwent exterior restoration in 1854, at a cost of about £6,000 has a handsome spire, rebuilt at the Restoration, and contains four curious ancient monuments of the Lords de Birmingham St. Philips church, in an elevated open area of about four acres, was built in 1715 by Archer, a pupil of Vanbrugh, is in the Italian style, with tower and cupola, and has a very handsome interior, with about 1,800 sittings. St Georges church, in Tower street, was built in 1822, by Rickman, at a cost of £12,735, is in the decorated English style, consists of nave, chancel, and side aisles, with pinnacled tower 114 feet high, and contains a fine altar-piece and 1,959 sittings St Thomas' church, at Holloway Head, was built in 1829, at a cost of £14,222, is in the Ionic style, with an almost semicircular front, and a tower 130 feet high, crowned by cupola and cross, figures conspicuously in distant views of the town, and contains about 2,100 sittings All Saints church, at Birmingham Heath, was built in 1833, at a cost of £3,817 St Peters church, in Dale End, was built in 1827, at a cost of £19,000, is in the Doric style, with an octagonal turret, after the model of the choragic monument of Lysicrates, and contains an altar-piece of the Ascension, and 1 903 sittings St. Matthias church, in Farm street, was founded in 1855, is in the middle pointed style, consists of nave aisles, chancel, and north and south chapels, and contains 1,151 sittings St Marys church, in St Marys square, was built in 1774, and is an octagonal brick edifice, with small stone spire. St Bartholomew's church, in Masshouse lane, was built in 1749, and is a very plain brick structure, but contains a good altar piece St. Marks church, in King Edward street, was built in 1841, at a cost of £3 100 and is in the mediæval style St Pauls church, in St Pauls square, was built in 1779, has a very beautiful spire erected in 1823, and is adorned with a window of stained glass, which cost £440 Christ church, in New street, was built in 1805-1815 at a cost of about £26 000, is in the Roman Doric style, with lofty portico and spire, and contains a carved mahogany altar piece, and about 1,500 sittings. St Lukes church, in Bristol road, was built in 1842, at a cost of £3 700 is in the Norman style, with a tower, and contains about 1,200 sittings. Bishop Ryders church in Gem street, was built in 1838, at a cost of £4,500, and is a neat structure of brick and stone with a lofty tower St Stephens church, in Newtown Row was built in 1844, at a cost of £3,320 and is in the Gothic style St Judes church, in Hurst street was built in 1851, at a cost of about £2 500, and is in the early English style Ladywood church, or St Johns Ladywood, was built in 1854, is in the decorated geometric style, consists of nave, chancel and aisles, with north western tower and contains 1,250 sittings St Barnabas church, in Tyndal street North, was built in

1860, at a cost of about £3,000, is in the decorated English style, and presents to the street a good wide window of seven lights, and a neat broach spire. St. David's church, Nelson street, is decorated Gothic, was built in 1864, and cost about £5,000. Selly Oak church was built in 1861, and is in the early decorated English style, with tower and spire, 150 feet high. St Gabriel's church, in Barn-street, was built in 1869, at a cost of £4,200. A church for Heath street was projected in 1869, at a cost of £5,000. Immanuel church, in Broad street, has superseded the former Magdalen chapel. Other churches are noticed in the articles ASTON, ASHTED, DERITEND, BROMWICH CASTLE, BORDESLEY, SALTLEY, LOZELLS, EDGBASTON, and KINGS NORTON.

The Presbyterian church, in Broad street, was founded in 1848, and is an elegant edifice, in the Italian style, with tower and belfry. The Independent chapel, in Carr's lane, noted for the ministry of the Rev. Angell James, was rebuilt in 1820, has an imposing front, in the Grecian style, and contains about 2,100 sittings. The Independent chapel, in Steelhouse lane, was built in 1818, and is a fine brick edifice, with neat spacious interior. The Independent chapel, in Francis street, Edgbaston, was built in 1856, at a cost of upwards of £7,000, and is in the decorated geometric style, with nave, transepts, tower, and spire. The Moseley Independent chapel was built in 1862, is in an adaptation of the early English style, after designs by Mr E. Holmes, consists of red brick, with blue and white brick work in patterns, and Bath stone dressings, and contains about 1,000 sittings. The Baptist chapel, in Graham street, was built in 1824, and is a large massive edifice, with Doric portico. The Baptist chapel, in Bradford street, was originally an amphitheatre, converted to its present use, in 1849, at a cost of £1,200, and is a large edifice of cemented brick. The Baptist chapel, in Heneage street, was built in 1840, at a cost of upwards of £4,000, and is very neat and commodious. The Baptist chapel, in Bristol road, was built in 1861, after designs by Cranston, at a cost of about £7,000, is in the early decorated English style, has a tower and spire 130 feet high, and contains about 900 sittings. The Quakers meeting-house, in Bull street, was rebuilt in 1806, and is in plain Italian style, with massive portico. The Unitarian chapel, in Moor-street, a massive re-erection of 1802, on the site of Dr Priestley's, was sold in 1861 to the Roman Catholics. A chapel in lieu of this, in Broad street, stands over the canal, is called the church of the Messiah, was built in 1862, after designs by Bateman, at a cost of £15,000, and is in the geometric style, with large windows and a spire about 150 feet high. The Methodist chapel, in Cherry street, was rebuilt in 1823, and is a spacious structure, and several of the other Methodist chapels are handsome buildings, especially one in Martin street, in decorated Gothic, designed by Mr Chamberlain, and one at the Lozells, also Gothic, designed by Mr Bland. The Church of the Saviour, in Edward street, not connected with any sect, was built in 1847, shows a plain exterior, but has a tastefully decorated and very beautiful interior. The Roman Catholic cathedral, in Bath street, was built in 1838, after designs by Pugin, at a cost of about £20,000, is in the Gothic style, with two front towers, each 180 feet high, is interiorly cruciform, and richly embellished, and contains an elaborately carved Flemish pulpit of the 16th century, and relics of St Chad. The bishop's house, also designed by Pugin, nearly opposite the cathedral, is a fine specimen of the 15th century domestic Gothic. The Oratory, in Hagley road, Edgbaston, was built in 1852, is a large edifice in the Italian style, and is the residence of a body of priests and laymen living under the rule of St. Philip Neri, of Florence. The convent in Hunters lane, within a mile of the centre of the town, is occupied by "sisters of mercy," and includes a richly ornamented chapel. The Jews synagogue in Blucher street was built in 1856, at a cost of about £10,000, is in the Byzantine style, designed by H. I. Thomason, shows in front a triple arched portico, and is divided interiorly by two arcades, each of seven arches.

Schools and Colleges.—The schools within the borough in 1851 were 66 public day schools, with 13,082 scholars, 388 private day schools, with 9,151 s., and 63 Sunday schools, with 21,406 s. The free grammar school, in New street, was erected in 1834, after designs by Barry, at a cost of £67,000, is of Derbyshire stone, and in a mixed style of Gothic and Tudor, and has a quadrangular form, 174 feet in front, 125 feet in the flanks, and 65 feet high. The endowment for it belonged originally to the guild of the Holy Cross founded in 1383, was conveyed to the school, in 1552, by Edward VI., and now yields about £13,000 a year, with a prospect of rapid increase. About 255 boys commonly are taught in the classical department, about 215 in the commercial, and there are ten exhibitions of £50 each, for four years, at Oxford and Cambridge. The Birmingham and Edgbaston proprietory school, in Hagley road, was founded in 1838, is a handsome edifice, in the Tudor style, and gives a classical and commercial education to the sons and nominees of shareholders. The blue coat school, in St Philip's churchyard, was built in 1724, enlarged in 1794, is a noble building, and gives free education to commonly about 140 poor boys and 60 girls. The Protestant Dissenters charity school, in Graham street, was established about 1700, is a handsome Tudor edifice, and gives clothing and training to about 35 poor girls. The free industrial school, in Gem street, was built in 1850, is a neat brick edifice, and has commonly an attendance of about 220 children. There are also a boys' reformatory school at Saltley, a girls reformatory at Smethwick, and industrial schools in Penn street and Vale-street.

The diocesan training college, at Saltley, was built in 1852, is a plain yet tasteful edifice, in the domestic style of the 13th century, and trains schoolmasters for the dioceses of Worcester, Lichfield, and Hereford. Queen's college, in Paradise street, opposite the town hall, is an edifice in the Gothic style, was chartered in 1843, 1847, and 1852, affords instruction in medicine and surgery, in arts, in laws, in civil architecture and engineering, and in theology, comprises rooms for 70 resident students, lecture halls, chemical laboratory, engineering workshops, model room, museums, libraries, and a chapel, and possesses a variety of endowments, scholarships, and prize funds. Sydenham college, in Summer-lane, was established in 1851, gives a complete course of medical and surgical education, and contains libraries, laboratories, museums, and all other requisite appliances. Spring Hill college, a theological seminary of the Independent body, has been removed to Moseley, and will be noticed in our article on MOSELEY.

Arts and Literature.—The Birmingham and Midland Institute was incorporated by act of parliament in 1854, has magnificent buildings, designed by F. M. Barry, contiguous to the town hall, in the Roman style, founded in 1855, promotes literature and industrial science, possesses museums and reading rooms, and maintains lectures and periodical meetings. A free public library, and a public gallery of art are attached to the institute. The school of art dates from 1842, occupies a wing of the institute, and is attended by upwards of 600 students, paying fees to the annual amount of nearly £600. The society of artists have a building in New-street, with elegant Corinthian portico, and a large room surmounted by a cupola, and maintain exhibitions of modern paintings every autumn, besides classes for studying figure drawing. The old library, in Union street, was erected in 1798, and contains upwards of 40,000 volumes. Other public libraries, of various character, exist in connection with institutions, schools, churches, and chapels, a lending free library is in Constitution Hill, and a new free library was contemplated, in 1865, in Deritend. The botanic garden, in Westbourne road, Edgbaston, was opened in 1829, is charmingly laid out, and contains a great number of choice plants, both tender and hardy. There were, in 1865, four weekly newspapers, one daily, one on five days of the week, and a monthly periodical, a kind of local Punch.

Amusements.—The theatre, in New street, was rebuilt in 1821, at a cost of about £14,000, is a handsome edi face in the Ionic style, with medallions of Shakespeare and Garrick, underwent a complete renovation in 1825, and is capable of accommodating 2,000 persons. Another theatre, in Broad street, is an edifice in the pointed style of the 14th century, and has accommodation for upwards of 2 000 persons. A grand musical festival is held in the town hall every third year, for the benefit of the general hospital, and generally attracts crowds of strangers. Concerts of a high order also are often given there; balls, lectures, and other entertainments here are not infrequent, and popular concerts are given there every Monday evening, and organ performances every Thursday. Holder's concert hall measures 116 feet by 72, gives entertainments in all kinds of music, and is open every evening. Day's concert hall, erected in 1862, is an ornamental edifice in the Italian style, and contains a splendid concert room 130 feet long, 64 feet wide, and 50 feet high, capable of accommodating 2,000 persons. The Museum concert hall is also a large and handsome building. Assembly and concert rooms are attached to the Royal hotel. Bingley hall, in Broad street, was erected in 1850 at a cost of about £6,000, is a plain, large, brick building, in Roman Doric, and serves both as an amphitheatre, and for exhibitions of cattle, pigs, and poultry. There are three public parks, Adderley park, at Saltley, opened in 1856; Calthorpe park, in Pershore road, opened in 1857, and Aston park, noticed in our article on ASTON.

Hospitals and Asylums.—The general hospital, in Summer lane, is an extensive brick building, commenced in 1766, opened in 1779, extended in 1830 and in 1857, and about to be remodelled in 1865, contains extensive wards for sick inmates, ranges of offices and apartments for officials, and a committee room, with interesting portraits and busts, ministers in the course of a year, on the average, to nearly 4,000 in patients, and nearly 20,000 out patients, makes an annual expenditure of about £10 000, and is supported partly from endowment, partly from the profits of the triennial musical festivals in the town hall, and mainly by annual subscriptions and other voluntary contributions. The Queen's hospital, in Bath row, was founded in 1840, is a handsome structure of centre and two wings, with a portico, contains 200 beds, besides fever wards, ministers annually to about 2,000 in patients and nearly 7,000 out patients, and is supported mainly by voluntary contributions. The dispensary, in Union street, was erected in 1808, but dates from 1794, ministers yearly to upwards of 6,000 persons, and is supported by subscriptions. The lying-in hospital, in Broad street, Islington, was founded in 1812, contains 20 beds, and ministers yearly to about 1,130 midwifery cases. The eye infirmary, in Temple row, was founded in 1824, has wards for in door patients, and gives relief yearly to about 3,000 cases. The children's hospital, founded in 1862, is in Steelhouse lane, and has accommodation for in and out door patients. There is also a homœopathic hospital in the Old Square. The lunatic asylum, at Birmingham Heath, was founded in 1847, and opened in 1850, is a neat Tudor edifice, within pleasant grounds of about 20 acres, and has accommodation for nearly 400 patients. The licensed victuallers asylum, in Bristol road, is a handsome Tudor edifice of 1849, and serves as a home for decayed licensed victuallers and their widows. The institution for the blind at Edgbaston, is a large, fine Tudor edifice, built in 1852, at a cost of upwards of £10,000, stands attached to play grounds and gardens of about two acres, and has accommodation for upwards of 100 blind boarders. There are also an institution for the deaf and dumb, a magdalen asylum, a number of suites of alms houses, and a variety of other benevolent institutions.

Cemeteries.—The general cemetery, at Key Hill, comprises nearly eleven acres, was, in great part, excavated from rock, is tastefully laid out with walks and shrubberies, has a chapel in the centre, and contains some fine monuments. The Church of England cemetery, near it, was opened in 1848, comprises about nine acres, and has a beautiful cruciform church in the later English style, with tower and spire. The borough cemetery, at Witton, was recently formed at a cost of about £75,000, comprises 105 acres, and has two fine chapels in the decorated English style, each with lofty tower and spire,—also a smaller one for Roman Catholics.

Districts.—The parish of Birmingham forms a registration district, divided into the sub districts of St Martin, St Philip, St George, St Thomas, All Saints, St Peter, St Mary, St. Paul, and Ladywood. The poor law administration is under a local act. Acres, £2,660. Poor rates in 1866, £130,604. Pop in 1851, 138 215, in 1861, 212,621. Houses 42 389. Marriages in 1866, 2,358, births, 8,980,—of which 441 were illegitimate, deaths, 6,096,—of which 2,830 were at ages under 5 years, and 49 at ages above 85 years. Marriages in the ten years 1851–60, 20,172, births 78 720, deaths, 54,239. The workhouse is on the Dudley road, at Birmingham Heath, was erected in 1852, at a cost of £11,176, is an imposing edifice, in the Tudor style, on grounds of nearly fifteen acres, contains accommodation for 1,666 inmates, and includes an asylum for children and a large chapel. The board room and offices are at the corner of Paradise street and Suffolk street, were built at a cost of £5 100, and are in the Italian style. Workhouse schools for boys were founded in 1869. The portions of the borough not within the parish of Birmingham are in the districts of ASTON and KINGS-NORTON, which see. The town is salubriously situated, escapes much disease in consequence of the dryness of its soil and air, and had no cases of indigenous cholera in the terrible visitations of 1832 and 1850.

Markets and Trade.—Markets are held on Monday, Thursday, and Saturday, a hay market on Tuesday, corn and cattle markets on Tuesday and Thursday, and fairs for three days, commencing on Whit Thursday, and on the Thursday nearest to 29 Sept. The market hall, extending from the Bull Ring to Worcester street, is open every day, was constructed at a cost of about £67,261, is in the Grecian style of architecture, with arched entrances and Doric supports, measures 365 feet in length, 108 feet in width, and 60 feet in height, has accommodation for 600 stalls, and contains a grand ornate fountain, upwards of 13 feet high, constructed at a cost of fully £400. The corn exchange, in High street, was built in 1847, at a cost of £6,000, and is divided interiorly into three compartments by rows of Doric pillars, and covered with a glazed roof. Smithfield market, on the site of the ancient residence of the lord of the manor, was constructed in 1816, covers several acres, and is divided into three departments, for the several kinds of beasts. The general trade of the town, intrinsic, inward, and outward, is connected chiefly with its manufactures, and possesses vast facilities in the ramifications of railway and canal. The post office‡ has, in the town and suburbs, 22 receiving houses and a large number of pillar and wall letter boxes, and at each of 10 of the receiving houses are a money order office and a savings bank. Telegraph offices are at the railway stations, and at the exchange. The banking offices are Lloyds & Co.'s (which has absorbed Moilliet and Co.'s), the Birmingham bank, the Birmingham Town and District bank, the Birmingham and Midland bank, the Birmingham Joint Stock bank, and branches of the bank of England and the National Provincial bank. Chief hotels are Nock's Royal, the Stork, the King's Head, the Union, the Swan, the Hen and Chickens, the Queen's (at the North Western station), and a new hotel at the Great Western station.

Manufactures.—Leland, in the time of Henry VIII., said of Birmingham,—"There be many smithes in the towne, that used to make knives, and all manour of cuttinge tools, and many lorimers that make bittes, and a great many naylors, so that a great part of the towne is maintained by smithes." Camden, in the time of Elizabeth, described it as "swarming with inhabitants, and echoing with the noise of anvils." It made swords by the thousand in the time of Charles I., reached great improvement in metal working in the time of Charles II., began to make fire arms after the Revolution, and has gone on thence till the present day improving its old trades and adding new ones with an ingenuity, a force, and a magnitude unrivalled in the world It has been stimulated much by the abundance of coal and iron ore in its neighbourhood, but stimulated far more by its own genius, and, while attaining the highest excellence and the greatest breadth in the working of metals, it has become prominent also in dealing with other materials The largest establishments are for iron and brass founding, for the rolling, stamping, plating, and drawing of metals, for iron roofs and girders, steam engines and railway waggons, lamps and gasometers, galvanized iron and metallic bedsteads, and for glass blowing, coach making, and brewing Trades employing large numbers of workpeople are for tools, machines, steel pens, steel toys, keys, locks, screws, bolts, files, buckles, fire irons, bridle bits, iron chains, awl blades, axle trees, and nails Trades of a prominent kind on small objects, either useful or fanciful, are very numerous and exceedingly various The trades in buttons, in buckles, and in locks alone, have each many different branches. The gun trade is of great extent, and includes many departments Glass working, besides crown and sheet window glass, plate glass, stained glass, chandeliers, candelabra, lustres, and similar objects, produces such things as beads, bugles, buttons, hour-glasses, and many kinds of toys Gold and silver plating and electro plating consume annually large supplies of the precious metals For gold and silver goods there is an assay office in the town. Jewellery of all kinds, and many sorts of silver and gold toys, are made Papier mache, enamelled and japanned, is a staple trade Bone, whalebone, ivory, and pearl are largely worked Chemicals, and articles requiring chemical manipulation, are extensively manufactured. Some of the chief establishments worth visiting are, for iron foundry, the Soho works and Mr Clifford's rolling mills, for brass foundry the show-rooms of the Messrs Winfield in Cambridge street, for steel pens, the works of Mr Joseph Gillott, in Graham street, for buttons, the Regent works, in Regent street, for fire arms, the establishments of Messrs. Westley, Richards & Co, in High street, Messrs Cooper & Goodman, Woodcock street, and Messrs Tipping and Lawden on Constitution hill, for glass, the establishment of the Messrs. Osler, in Broad street, for electro-plate and silver, the establishment of Messrs Elkington & Co, in Newhall street, and for papier mâche, the show rooms of Messrs J Bettridge & Co, in Barr street At Small Heath, near the town, is the small arms factory, built and fitted at a cost of more than £60,000, for making rifles by machinery The factory is the only one of its kind in England except the government factory at Enfield, and the works of the London armoury company

The Borough —Birmingham was incorporated so late as 1838, and it acquired the right of sending two members to parliament by the reform act of 1832, and the right of sending a third by the bill of 1867 Its borough boundaries, as already noted, include the parishes of Birmingham and Edgbaston, and a populous portion of the parish of Aston, yet they exclude the considerable suburbs of Handsworth and Kings Norton as well as some smaller ones The extreme is 5¾ miles, the mean breadth, 3 miles, and the area, 7,831 acres The borough is divided into twelve wards—nine of them conterminous with the sub districts of Birmingham registration district the other three Edgbaston, Duddeston cum Nechells, and Deritend and Bordesley It is governed by a mayor, fifteen aldermen, and forty eight councillors, it has a court of quarter sessions, a recorder, and a stipendiary magistrate, and is a polling place for the northern division of the county There are also a bankruptcy court and a county court The police force consists of 377 men, costing £25,289 a year, of which £5,508 is repaid by the imperial treasury The number of indictable offences committed in 1863 was 883, of persons apprehended, 600, of known depredators and suspected persons at large, 3 534, of houses of bad character, 939 Direct taxes in 1864 about £200 000 Electors in 1868, 15,497 Population in 1801, 73 670, in 1821, 106,722, in 1841, 182,922, in 1861, 296,076, in the middle of 1868 (Registrar General's calculation), 327,834 Houses in 1861, 50 060 Some of the most distinguished names connected with the local history of Birmingham are John Baskerville, James Watt, Dr Priestley, Hutton, the historian, and Murdoch, the inventor of gas, and two of the most distinguished natives were Bishop Smallbroke and Cary, the translator of Dante

BIRMINGHAM CANALS, artificial lines of navigation radiating from Birmingham, and giving it water communication with most parts of the kingdom The old Birmingham canal was formed in 1768-9, is 22½ miles long, with several branches, rises 132 feet, by means of 21 locks, goes through Warwickshire and Staffordshire, through the very heart of the mining district to the Stafford and Worcester canal near Autherley, and opens a communication through the Severn with Shrewsbury, Gloucester, and Bristol, through the Trent with Gainsborough, Hull, and London, and through canal junction with the Staffordshire Potteries Manchester, and Liverpool The Fazeley canal was formed in 1783 is 20½ miles long rises 248 feet, by means of 44 locks, goes through Warwickshire and Staffordshire to Wyrley and Essington canal near Whittington, and the Coventry near Fazeley, and leads the way to Manchester, Hull Oxford, and London These two canals were soon amalgamated under the name of the Birmingham and Fazeley canal, and this was leased, under an act of 1846, to the London and North Western railway Two other canals from Birmingham, the Warwick and Birmingham canal and the Worcester and Birmingham canal, will be noticed in their proper alphabetical places

BIRMINGHAM RAILWAYS, lines of railway radiating from Birmingham, and giving it railway communication with most parts of the kingdom These are nine, the Birmingham and Derby, the Birmingham and Gloucester, the Birmingham and Oxford, the Birmingham and Wolverhampton, the Birmingham, Wolverhampton, and Stour Valley, the North Staffordshire, the South Staffordshire, the London and Birmingham, and the Manchester and Birmingham, but the first and the second have been amalgamated with the Midland, the third and the fourth with the Great Western, and the other five with the London and North Western, and they will be noticed in the articles on these heads

BIRNSTON See BARNSTON, Essex

BIRSTALL, a village in Dewsbury district, and a parish in Dewsbury and Bradford districts, W R Yorkshire The village stands at the terminus of a branch of the Leeds and Dewsbury railway, 7 miles SW of Leeds has a post office‡ under Leeds, and is a polling place The parish includes the townships of Gomersal, Heckmondwike, Liversedge, Wike, Cleckheaton Hunsworth, Drighlington, and Tong Acres, 13,696 Real property, £132,020,—of which £25,594 are in mines, and £2,710 in quarries Pop in 1841, 29,723, in 1861, 43,507 Houses, 9,237 The property is much subdivided Many of the inhabitants are employed in numerous factories, or in handicrafts connected with them, and not a few are miners of coal and ironstone. The living is a vicarage in the diocese of Ripon Value, £480 * Patron, the Bishop of Ripon The church was erected in the time of Henry VIII, and was not long ago enlarged The chapelries of Birkenshaw, Whitechapel, Cleckheaton, Gomersal, Wike, Heckmondwike, Liversedge, Roberttown Drighlington, Tong, and Tong Street are separate benefices. There are several dissenting chapels, and charities £119 Dr Priestley was a native

BIRSTALL or BURSTALL, a chapelry in Belgrave parish Leicestershire, on the river Soar 2 miles NW of Sileby r station, and 3½ N by E of Leicester Post town, Belgrave under Leicester Acres, 1,230 Real property, £3 862 Pop, 40? Houses, 295 The property is divided among a few Birstall House is the seat of the Worswicks. The living is a p curacy, annexed to the vicarage of Belgrave in the diocese of Peterborough The church is modern There are Baptist and Wesleyan chapels and a national school

BIRSTALL DRUB, a hamlet in Gomersal township Birstall parish, W R. Yorkshire

BIRSTWITH a township and a chapelry in Hampsthwaite parish W R Yorkshire. The township lies on the river Nidd, and on the Nidd Valley railway, 3 miles WSW of Ripley It includes the hamlets of Wreakes, Brigg, and Swarcliffe, and has a station on the railway, and a post office under Ripley Acres 1 670 Real property, £2 401 Pop, 655 Houses 146 —The chapelry is not quite so extensive as the township, and was constituted in 1857 Pop., 640 Houses, 142 The living is a vicarage in the diocese of Ripon Value, £200 Patron, F Greenwood Esq The church was built in 1857 There are two Methodist chapels

BIRT, or BRIT (THE), a river of Dorset It rises a little N of Beaminster, and runs 9 miles southward to the channel at Bridport harbour

BIRTHORPE, a hamlet in Sempringham parish Lincoln, 2½ miles E by S of Folkingham. Acres, 390 Real property, £940 Pop, 65 Houses, 11

BIRTHWAITE, a village in Windermere parish, Westmoreland, now absorbed in the village of WINDERMERE which see

BIRTLE, a township, a chapelry, and a sub-district, in the district of Bury, Lancashire The township bears the name of Birtle cum Bamford, is in Middleton parish, and lies near the Manchester and Rossendale railway, 2½ miles NE of Bury Acres, 1,388 Real property £7,900,—of which £300 are in mines Pop, 2,350 Houses, 404 The inhabitants are employed chiefly in cotton and woollen manufactures and in calico printing The chapelry consists of part of this township and part of Bury parish and was constituted in 1848 Pop, 2,135. Houses, 353 The living is a vicarage in the diocese of Manchester Value, £180 Patron, the Rector of Middleton The church was built in 1840 There are three dissenting chapels.—The sub district comprises parts of two parishes Pop, 4,758

BIRTLE, a hamlet in Lunedale township, Romald Kirk parish, N R Yorkshire, 5½ miles NW of Barnard Castle

BIRTLE CUM BAMFORD See BIRTLE, Lancashire

BIRTLES, a township chapelry in Prestbury parish, Cheshire, 2¾ miles W by N of Macclesfield r station Post town, Alderley, under Congleton Acres 460 Real property, £980 Pop, 73 Houses, 11 Birtles Hall is the seat of T Hibbert, Esq A Roman urn and some other Roman relics have been found The living is a p curacy in the diocese of Chester Value, £50 Patron, T Hibbert, Esq

BIRTLEY, a township and a chapelry in Chester le Street parish, Durham The township lies on the Team Valley railway, 5 miles S by E of Gateshead, and has a post office‡ under Fence Houses, and a r station Acres, 1,392 Real property, £11,539,—of which £1,450 are in mines, and £6,500 in iron works Pop, 2,246 Houses, 385 The property is divided among a few Coal is worked, and there is a brine spring The chapelry was constituted in 1850 Pop, 3,888. Houses, 710 The living is a vicarage in the diocese of Durham Value, £300* Patron, the Rector of Chester le Street. The church was built in 1848 There are Wesleyan and Roman Catholic chapels, and a literary institute.

BIRTLEY, or BIRKLEY, a parochial chapelry in Bellingham district, Northumberland, on the North Tyne river and on the Border Counties railway, near Wark station, 5 miles SE of Bellingham It was disjoined in 1765 from the parish of Chollerton, it includes the township of Broomhope and Buteland, and its post town is Wark, under Hexham Acres 6,720 Rated property, £3,425 Pop 404 Houses, 80 The property is divided among six. Coal and other useful minerals occur The living is a vicarage in the diocese of Durham Value, £192 Patron, the Duke of Northumberland The church is not good

BIRTSMORTON, a parish in Upton on Severn district, Worcester under the Malvern hills, 5½ miles SW of Upton on Severn r station, and 7 WNW of Tewkesbury Post town, Burrow under Salbury Acres, 1,268 Real property, £2,101 Pop, 259 Houses 63 The property is much subdivided The manor was long held by the ancient Cornish family of Nanfans, and the manor house a very ancient edifice, moated round, and now a farm house, was the birthplace of the Right Hon W Huskisson The living is a rectory in the diocese of Worcester Value, £430* Patron C Filson, Esq The church contains several curious ancient monuments and was repaired in 1839 There are a Wesleyan chapel, a parochial school, and charities £20

BISBROOK, a parish in Uppingham district, Rutland, 1½ mile E of Uppingham, and 2 NW of Seaton r station Post town, Uppingham Acres 720 Real property, £2,031 Pop, 266 Houses, 58 The property is divided among a few The living is a vicarage in the diocese of Peterborough. Value, £252. Patron, the Duke of Rutland The church is good.

BISCATHORPE, or BESKERTHORPE, a parish in Louth district, Lincoln, on the river Bain, 8 miles WSW of Louth r station Post town Donington, under Louth Acres, 1,050 Real property, £1,370 Pop, 90 Houses, 11 The property is divided among a few The living is annexed to Gayton le Wold

BISCOTT, a chapelry in Luton parish Beds, 3 miles NW of Luton It was formed in 1866 Pop., 781 Living, a p curacy Value £200 Patron, J S Crawley, Esq

BISCOVAY or PAR a chapelry in St Blaze and Tywardreath parishes Cornwall, on the coast and on the Cornwall railway, 1¼ mile S of Par station, and 5 SSW of Lostwithiel It has a post office, of the name of Biscovay, under Par station It was constituted in 1845 Rated property, £3,237 Pop, 2,327 Houses, 433 The property is divided among a few The living is a vicarage in the diocese of Exeter Value, £150 Patron, alternately the Crown and the Bishop The church is good

BISHAM, or BYSHAM MONTAGUE,—anciently BUSTLEHAM,—a parish in Cookham district, Berks, on the river Thames, 2 miles W by N of Cookham r station, and 4 NW of Maidenhead It has a post-office, of the name of Bisham under Maidenhead Acres 2,520 Real property, £5,491 Pop, 605 Houses, 130 The property is divided among a few Bisham Abbey is the seat of G Vansittart, Esq A pointed doorway, an octagonal tower, and a hall are part of an ancient monastic edifice and the rest of the mansion is of the ancient style of the Tudor architecture The hall was tastefully restored in 1859, and has at one end a dark oak gallery at the other, a beautiful ancient lancet window The scenery of the grounds of the mansion is very fine, and has engaged the pencil of some eminent artists A preceptory of Knights Templars was early founded here, passed, in the reign of Stephen, to other knights, was converted into an Augustinian priory in 1338 by Montacute, Earl of Salisbury, was changed into a Benedictine abbey, a short time before the dissolution, by Henry VIII was afterwards given, by that king, to his repudiated wife, Anne of Cleves, was conveyed by her to Sir Philip Hobby, in exchange for his house in Kent, and was for three years the residence, under its owner's guardianship of the Princess Elizabeth, afterwards Queen Elizabeth The barn of the priory, the old moat round the garden, and the spring which supplied the Princess Elizabeth's bath, still remain There was an extensive copper factory at Temple mills, but it was recently converted into a paper factory The living is a vicarage in the diocese of Oxford Value, £156* Patron G Vansittart, Esq The church shows some traces of Norman architecture, but was destructively modernized about 1810, and restored in better taste a few years ago and it contains some grand monuments of the Hobbys. Many persons of high historical note, especially Earls of Salisbury, Neville the king maker, the famous Marquis of Montague, and Edward the last Plantagenet, were buried in the abbey, but the monuments of all have disappeared The vicarage of Stubbings is a separate charge There is a national school

BISHAMPTON, a parish in Pershore district, Worcester, in the vale of Evesham, 4 miles N by W of Fladbury r station, and 4½ NE of Pershore Post town, Pershore Acres 2,110 Real property, £2,510 Pop 409 Houses, 105 The property is much subdivided The living is a vicarage in the diocese of Worcester-

Value, £103 * Patron, the Bishop The church was about to be rebuilt in 1869 There is a Baptist chapel

BISH MILLS, a hamlet in Bishops Nympton parish, Devon

BISHOP AND CLERKS, a group of rocks 2 miles W of Ramsey Island, and 4 SW of St David's Head, in Pembroke A lighthouse stands on one of them built in 1839, with a red revolving light, 144 feet above high water level, seen every 20 seconds The Nimrod steamer was wrecked on these rocks in February 1860, when all on board perished

BISHOP AUCKLAND, a town, a township, and a sub-district, in the district of Auckland, Durham The town stands on an eminence about 140 feet high, between the rivers Wear and Gaunless, near their point of confluence, and adjacent to the Weardale railway, 10¾ miles NNW of Darlington It took its name from the vicinity of the Bishop of Durham's palace, conjoined with ancient abundance of oak woods, and it was formerly a borough by prescription It has pleasant environs, and is well built and neat It has a post office‡ under Darlington, a railway station, two banking-offices, two chief inns, a spacious town hall, a church, seven non established chapels, a grammar school, two other endowed schools, a workhouse and alms houses, is a seat of petty sessions and a polling place, and publishes two weekly newspapers The town hall stands in the centre of the town, adjoining the church; was built in 1862, at a cost of about £8,500, has a groined principal entrance, surmounted by a neat stone balcony, is crowned by angle roofs with iron pallisading, and with a spire 100 feet high, and contains a large music hall, and offices for the Board of Health. The church is modern, and ranks as a chapel to the charge of Auckland St. Andrew A Wesleyan chapel, in modified Italian style, was built in 1866 The other non established chapels are for Independents, Presbyterians, Quakers, two Methodist bodies, and Roman Catholics The grammar-school was founded by James I, and has £38 from endowment, and one of the other endowed schools was founded by Bishop Barrington, and has £367 The episcopal palace stands on the NE side of the town, in a fine park of 800 acres, on the river Gaunless, with charming views, was built by Bishop Cosins, on the site of a previous one by Bishop Beck, underwent restoration and extension, with fine entrance Gothic gateway and screen, by Bishop Barrington, after designs by Wyatt, and contains several valuable old paintings, by the Italian masters Newton Cap bridge in the vicinity, over the river Wear was built in 1390, and has two arches, the one circular and 101 feet in span, the other pointed and 91 feet in span A weekly market is held in the town on Thursday, and fairs on Holy Thursday and the following day, on 1 June, and on the Thursday before 11 Oct. Pop 6,480 Houses, 1,186 —The township includes most of the town extends into the country, and is in the parish of St Andrew Auckland Acres, 1,919 Real property, £18,061,—of which £2,300 are in mines Pop, 7,279 Houses, 1,333 Coal and limestone are worked, and cotton manufactures are carried on Extensive engineering and edge tool works were established in 1862, and have branches at Bedburn —The sub district comprises twenty three townships and a parochial chapelry Acres 23,545 Pop., 34,878 Houses, 6,612

BISHOP BRIDGE, a hamlet in Glentham parish, Lincoln, on the river Ancholme, 4½ miles WNW of Market Raisen Pop, 61

BISHOP BURTON, or LOUTH BURTON, a parish in Beverley district, E R. Yorkshire, on the Wolds, 3 miles W of Beverley r station It has a post office, of the name of Bishop Burton under Beverley Acres, 3 970 Real property, £7,778 Pop, 499 Houses, 102 The property is divided among a few A residence of the Archbishops of York was formerly here Bishop Burton Hall is the seat of the Watts The living is a vicarage in the diocese of York Value, £100 * Patrons, the Dean and Chapter of York The church commands a fine view, and is good There are a Baptist chapel, an endowed school with £20, and almshouses with £72

BISHOPDALE, a township in Aysgarth parish N R Yorkshire, 4½ miles SE of Askrigg Acres, 4,805 Real property, £1,925. Pop, 87 Houses, 17 The surface is an upland vale, traversed by a rivulet of 8 miles, tributary to the Ure The vale is picturesque, and the rivulet makes a fine fall, called Foss Gill

BISHOPDOWN See BISHOPSDOWN

BISHOPHILL See YORK

BISHOPLEY See NEWLANDSIDE.

BISHOP MIDDLEHAM, a township and a parish in Stockton district Durham The township lies on the river Skern, 2¾ miles SE of Ferryhill r station, and 8½ SSE of Durham, and has a post-office under Ferryhill Acres, 2,023 Real property, £2,941 Pop, 432 Houses, 100 The parish contains also the townships of Mainsforth, Cornforth, Thrislington, and Garmondsway-moor Acres, 5,971 Real property, £7,233 Pop., 2,272 Houses, 475 The property is subdivided The manor was once a seat of the Bishops of Durham The living is a vicarage in the diocese of Durham Value, £285 * Patron, the Lord Chancellor The church is good, and there are charities £32

BISHOP MONKTON, a township chapelry in Ripon parish, W R Yorkshire, adjacent to the Northeastern railway, 1½ mile NE of Wormald Green station, and 4 SSE of Ripon It has a post office under Ripon Acres, 2,089 Real property, £3 734 Pop, 444 Houses, 112 The property is subdivided. The living is a p curacy in the diocese of Ripon Value, £100. Patrons, the Dean and Chapter of Ripon The church is good

BISHOP MORCHARD, or MORCHARD BISHOP, a village, a parish, and a sub district, in Crediton district, Devon The village stands 2¼ miles ENE of a station on the North Devon railway, called Morchard Road, and 6½ miles NW of Crediton, and has a post-office‡ of the designation of Morchard Bishop, North Devon, and a fair is held at it on the Monday after 9 Sept —The parish includes also several small hamlets Acres, 7,088. Real property, £8,361 Pop, 1,658 Houses, 362 The property is subdivided The manor formerly belonged to the Bishops of Exeter Barton House is a fine edifice The living is a rectory in the diocese of Exeter Value, £533 * Patron, Rev R Bartholomew The church consists of nave, chancel, and aisles, with a tower, is a neat structure, was not long ago repaired, and contains several monuments There are chapels for Independents and Bible Christians —The sub district contains ten parishes. Acres 27,659 Pop, 4,569 Houses, 961

BISHOP MORLEY'S COLLEGE, an extra parochial tract within Winchester city, Hants Pop., 23 Houses 9

BISHOP NORTON, a township and a parish in Caistor district Lincoln The township lies on the river Ancholme, near Ermine street, 6 miles SSE of Kirton Lindsey r station, and 7½ WNW of Market Rasen Real property, £4,019 Pop, 364 Houses, 82 —The parish includes also the township of Atterby, and its post town is Glentham, under Market Rasen Acres, 4,210 Real property, £5,373 Pop, 459 Houses, 104 The living is a vicarage in the diocese of Lincoln Value, £135 * Patron, the Prebendary of Bishop Norton The church is good. There are two Methodist chapels

BISHOP ROCK, an insulated rock of the Scilly Isles westward of the main group, and 7 miles distant from Hugh Town It is nearly covered at high water A cast iron light house was nearly completed on it in 1850, but was then swept away by a gale, and a granite light house was then planned, took two years to be founded, and was successfully completed

BISHOP RYDER See BIRMINGHAM

BISHOPSBOURNE, a parish in Bridge district, Kent, adjacent to the Dover and Canterbury railway, near Adisham station, 4 miles SE by S of Canterbury It has a post office under Canterbury Acres, 2,002 Real property, £2,739 Pop, 416 Houses, 75 The property is divided among a few The manor belonged once to the Archbishops of Canterbury, and afterwards to the Colepeppers and the Auchers Bourne Park is the seat of M Bell, Esq Some Saxon barrows, on the higher ground, were opened in 1844 The living is a rectory in the diocese of Canterbury Value, £700 * Patron, the Archbishop of Canterbury The church is perpendicular English, was restored in 1843, has a modern east window of five lights, with armorial bearings, and contains the monument of Hooker exhibiting his bust, in a square cap and gown Hooker was rector from 1595 till his death in 1600, and the parsonage, though greatly modernized, retains parts which probably were in it in Hooker s time

BISHOPS BURTON See BISHOP BURTON

BISHOPS CANNINGS, a village, a parish, and a sub district, in the district of Devizes, Wilts The village stands on the Kent and Avon canal, 1½ mile S of Wans Dyke, and 3 NE of Devizes r station, and has a post office under Devizes —The parish includes the tythings of Bourton, Easton, Chittoe Coate, and Horton, and the chapelry of St James or Southbroom Acres, 12,641 Real property, £11,114 Pop 4,062 Houses, 750 The property is subdivided The manor belonged, till the time of Henry VII, to the ancient family of Canynge The living is a vicarage in the diocese of Salisbury Value £395 * Patrons, the Dean and Chapter of Salisbury The church is early English, with Anglo Norman interior, is supposed to have been built about the same time as Salisbury cathedral, was interiorly renovated in 1829, and contains an organ which cost £440 the gift of William Baley, a native, who went round the world with Captain Cook. The chapelries of Chittoe and Southbroom are separate charges —The sub district contains seven parishes and parts of two others. Acres, 22,892 Pop 3,812 Houses, 854.

BISHOPS CASTLE, a small town, a parish, a sub-district, and a division in Clun district, Salop The town stands on a declivity, 3 miles W of the river Onny, 4½ E of Offa s Dyke, and 9½ WSW of Church Stretton. Railways from the Shrewsbury and Hereford line, by way of Bishops Castle to the Oswestry and Newtown line, were authorized in 1861, and a branch from the Craven Arms station to Bishops Castle was opened in 1866 A castle of the Bishops of Hereford once stood here, but was long ago destroyed. The town is irregularly built, and presents a poor appearance It has a head post office,‡ a banking office, two chief inns, a town hall, a market house, a church, two dissenting chapels, a free school with £13, and other charities with £13 The church occupies the site of one burnt in the civil wars, was, with the exception of its old square tower, rebuilt in 1861, is in the early pointed style, and comprises nave chancel, aisles, transepts, and vestry A weekly market is held on Friday, and fairs on the second Monday of Jan, the Friday before 13 Feb, 20 March, the Friday after 1 May, the second Monday of June, 5 July, 9 Sept the second Monday of Oct, and 13 Nov The town sent two members to parliament till disfranchised by the act of 1832, it possesses a corporation, but not regulated by the municipal corporation act, and it is a seat of petty sessions and a polling place. Real property, £6,872 Pop, 1,778 Houses, 383 The parish extends beyond the borough liberties, and includes the townships of Broughton Colebatch, Woodbatch, and Lee-with Oakeley Acres, 5 C13 Real property, £11,512 Pop, 2,083 Houses, 434 The property is divided among a few The manor belongs to the Earl of Powis Bishops Mote, on a high hill, a mile W of the town, is an ancient entrenchment of nearly an acre The living is a vicarage in the diocese of Hereford Value, £300 * Patron, the Earl of Powis —The sub district contains four parishes and the greater part of two others Acres, 16,834 Pop, 2,924 Houses, 593 —The division is part of Purslow hundred and contains eight parishes and part of another Acres 36,394 Pop, 4,652 Houses 908

BISHOPS CAUNDLE See CAUNDLE BISHOP

BISHOPS CHIFFTON See CHIFFTON BISHOPS

BISHOPS CLEEVE a township in Winchcombe district and a parish in Winchcombe and Tewkesbury districts, Gloucester The township lies 1½ mile E of Cleeve r station and 3 N by E of Cheltenham, and has a post office under Cheltenham. Real property, £3,950 Pop, 703 Houses, 154 —*The parish includes also the hamlets of Gotherington*, Woodmancote, Stoke Orchard, and Southam and Brockhampton Acres, 8 150 Real property, £15,107 Pop, 1,970 Houses 486 The property is much subdivided. The Cleeve hills, along the E, have a crescent shaped ancient British camp, and the *race-ground of the Cheltenham races, and exhibit brilliant scenery of cliff and wood* There are mineral springs The living is a rectory in the diocese of Gloucester and Bristol Value, £2,000 * Patron, the Rev W I Townsend. The church exhibits features from early Norman downward is cruciform and large, and *has a central tower, of modern construction* The parsonage was at one time the residence of the Bishops of Worcester There are Independent and Baptist chapels and a national school

BISHOPS CLIST a locality in Clist St Mary parish, Devon, 2¼ miles NNE of Topsham, with a post-office under Exeter *It was anciently the site of the seat of* the Bishops of Exeter, and of an hospital founded by Bishop Stapleton.

BISHOPS COURT, the seat of the Bishop of Sodor and Man, in Kirkmichael parish, Isle of Man, 3½ miles WSW of Ramsey. It is a Gothic edifice, restored *by Bishops Wilson and Murray*, and stands amidst extensive, ornate picturesque grounds

BISHOPSDOWN, a hamlet in Caundle Bishop parish, Dorset, 4½ miles SSE of Sherborne Pop, 73

BISHOPS FEE a liberty in St Margaret s parish within the borough of Leicester

BISHOPS FONTHILL, a *parish in Tisbury district*, Wilts, 2 miles ENE of Hindon, and 3 N of Tisbury r station Post town, Hindon under Salisbury Acres, 1,735 Real property, with Chilmark and Rudge, £5,008 Pop, 187 Houses, 43 The property is divided among a few The living is a rectory in the diocese of Salisbury Value, £246 Patron the *Bishop of Winchester* The church is early English, and in fair condition Charities, £11

BISHOPS FROME, a township and a sub district in Bromyard district and a parish in Bromyard and Ledbury districts, Hereford The township lies on the river Frome, 4 *miles S of Bromyard, and 5½ N of Ashperton* r station, and has a post office under Worcester Real property, £2,329 The parish includes also the townships of Halmonds Frome, Leadon, Walton, Stanford-Regis, and Eggleton Acres, 4,550 Real property, £11,367 Pop, 1,014 Houses, 215 The property is much subdivided. The living *is a vicarage in the diocese* of Hereford Value, £608 * Patron, the Rev J Hopton The church was built in 1862, is in the Norman style, and consists of nave, chancel, north aisle, and vestry, with a tower —The sub district contains seven parishes and the greater part of another Acres, 22,305 Pop, 4,439 *Houses*, 911

BISHOPSGATE, a hamlet on the N border of Surrey adjacent to the Great Park of Windsor, near Virginia water It lies amid charming scenery, and was the place where the poet Shelley wrote his "Alastor"

BISHOPS HAMPTON See HAMPTON LUCY

BISHOPS HATFIELD See HATFIELD BISHOPS

BISHOPS-HULL a parish in Taunton district, Somerset, adjacent to the Bristol and Exeter railway, 1½ mile W of Taunton It has a post office under Taunton Acres, 1,341 Real property, £10 567 Pop, 1,614 Houses 321 The property is subdivided The living is a vicarage in the diocese of Bath and Wells Value, £292 Patron, the Rev W P Williams St John's is a separate vicarage, formed in 1864 There are an Independent chapel, a national school and charities £60

BISHOPSIDE (HIGH and LOW), a township in Ripon parish, W R Yorkshire on the river Nidd, 11 miles WSW of Ripon It includes the town of Pateley Bridge, and the hamlets of Fell Beck, Raikes, Smelthouse Waths, Whitehouses and Wilsill Acres, 5,813 Real property, £4,180 Pop, 2 032 Houses, 439

BISHOPS ITCHINGTON a parish in Southam district Warwick, on the river Itchin and on the Oxford and Rugby railway, 2 miles SSE of Harbury station, and 3¾ SW of Southam It has a post office under Rugby Acres, with Chapel Ascote, 3,026. Real property, £4,586 Pop, 593 Houses, 131 The property is divided among a few The living is a vicarage, united with the p curacies of Chadshunt and Gaydon in the diocese of Worcester Value, £416 * Patron, the Bishop of Lichfield The church is good, and there is an Independent chapel, a national school, and charities £22

BISHOPS LAVINGTON See LAVINGTON (WEST)

BISHOPS LYDEARD, a village, a parish, and a sub district, in the district of Taunton, Somerset. The village stands near the Quantock hills, adjacent to the Taunton and Watchet railway, 5 miles NNW of Taunton, and has a station on the railway, a post office‡ under Taunton, and a fair on 5 April The parish includes the tythings of Lydeard Punchardon, Town, Church, East Bagborough, Quantock Hill, East Coombe, Cames Ash, Ash Week, and Free, and the hamlet of Kenley Bottom Acres, 4 686 Real property, £9,086 Pop, 1,459 Houses, 292. The property is divided among a few The living is a vicarage in the diocese of Bath and Wells Value, £120 * Patrons, the Dean and Chapter of Wells The church has a very beautiful tower, in perpendicular English, of the time of Henry VII, and was repaired in 1860 There are two sculptured crosses in the churchyard, an Independent chapel, a parochial school, a petty sessions court house ten alms houses with £120 a year, and other charities £40. The Rev F Warre, who became vicar in 1836, is known for learned local researches.—The sub district contains nine parishes Pop, 4 030 Houses 811

BISHOPS NYMPTON, a village and a parish in South Molton district, Devon The village stands 3½ miles SE of South Molton, and S ENE of South Molton Road r station, and has a post office under South Molton, and fairs on the third Monday of April, and on the Wednesday before 25 Oct The parish includes also the hamlets of Bish Mills, Ash Mills, and Newton Acres, 9,579 Real property, £6,476 Pop, 1,198 Houses, 248 The property is subdivided A fine old mansion at the village was formerly the seat of the Bassetts and others, and is now the seat of A Fisher, Esq A large mansion, called the Parsonage, is believed to have been a residence of the Bishop of Exeter Limestone abounds, and there is a large woollen factory The living is a vicarage in the diocese of Exeter Value, £296 * Patron, the Bishop of Exeter The church is a fine ancient edifice, of nave, chancel, and south aisle, with a pinnacled tower about 100 feet high, was restored in 1869 and contains an elegant screen and a rich monument of the Pollard family There are chapels for Wesleyan Methodists and Bible Christians

BISHOPS OFFLOW, or BISHOPS OFFLEY a township in Adbaston parish, Stafford 3¾ miles W of Eccleshall It includes Outlands hamlet Real property, £1,519 Pop, 200 Houses, 46

BISHOPS SPARKFORD, a tything in St. Faith parish, within the city of Winchester, Hants Real property, £802 Pop, 191

BISHOPS STORTFORD, or BISHOP STORTFORD, a town, a parish, a sub district, and a district in Herts. The town stands on the river Stort and on the Eastern Counties railway, 12 miles ENE of Hertford, and 32¼ NNE of London. A castle was built here by William the Conqueror, and given to the Bishops of London, but was resumed and destroyed by King John Bishop Bonner used the ruin as a gaol, and burnt a martyr on Goose green The town stands partly on the side of a hill consists principally of four streets, in the form of a cross and contains many respectable buildings It has a head post office,‡ a railway station with telegraph, three banking offices, two chief inns, a market house, two churches, three dissenting chapels, several public schools, alms houses, and a workhouse The market house was built in 1828, has a handsome Ionic front, and contains a large public hall The parish church is later English, spacious and elegant, and has a lofty tower and spire Newtown church was built in 1859, and is in the early English style The Independent chapel was built in 1860 and is in the Italian style. The Wesleyan chapel in the Gothic style, was built in 1867 The diocesan training college for sixty school mistresses, was erected in 1851, at a cost of £12 000 The grammar school was founded in 1579, and counts among its pupils Sir H Chauncey, the county historian The workhouse cost £11,585, and can accommodate 400 persons. A church estate yields £107 a year, and other charities £66 A weekly market is held on Thursday and fairs on Holy Thursday, the Thursday after Trinity Sunday, and 11 Oct. Malting is extensively carried on in numerous malt houses A railway from the Eastern Counties line at Bishops Stortford, to the Braintree branch at Braintree, was opened in May 1869, and was to be joined, at Dunmow, by a branch from the Epping The river Stort has been made navigable from Bishops Stortford to the Lea at Roydon Pop of the town, 4,673 Houses, 903 The parish comprises 3,241 acres Real property, £25,743 Pop, 5,390 Houses, 1,049 The living is a vicarage in the diocese of Rochester Value, £419 Patron, the Precentor of St Paul s Newtown vicarage is a separate benefice, in the patronage of the Vicar Value, £300 Hockerill vicarage also is a separate benefice. See HOCKERILL

The sub district contains the parishes of Bishops Stortford, Great Hadham, Little Hadham, and Farnham,—the last electorally in Essex. Acres, 12 385 Pop, 7,982 Houses, 1,598 The district comprehends also the sub district of Braughing, containing the parishes of Braughing, Albury, Furneux Pelham, Stocking Pelham, and Brent-Pelham, the sub district of Sawbridgeworth, containing the parishes of Sawbridgeworth, Thorley, Great Hallingbury, and Little Hallingbury,—the two latter electorally in Essex, and the sub district of Stansted containing the parishes of Stansted Mountfitchet, Birchanger, Elsenham, Henham, Ugley, Berden, and Manuden,—all electorally in Essex Acres, 53 689 Poor rates in 1866, £13,855 Pop. in 1861, 20,212 Houses, 4 186 Marriages in 1866, 132, births, 631,—of which 56 were illegitimate, deaths, 382,—of which 114 were at ages under 5 years, and 17 at ages above 85 years Marriages in the ten years 1851–60, 1,115 births, 6,368, deaths, 3,633 The places of worship in 1851 were 22 of the Church of England, with 7,018 sittings, 11 of Independents, with 3 540 s, 3 of Baptists with 199 s, 1 of Quakers, with 200 s, 5 of Wesleyan Methodists with 620 s. 1 of Primitive Methodists, with 70 s, and 1 undefined, with 60 s. The schools were 20 public day schools, with 2,413 scholars, 31 private day schools, with 588 s, and 26 Sunday schools, with 2,171 s

BISHOPS SUTTON, a parish and a hundred in Hants. The parish is in Alresford district, lies on the river Arle, 1¼ mile SE of Alresford r station, and 8½ SW of Alton, and has a post office under Alresford Acres, 3 510 Real property, £3,916 Pop, 507 Houses, 111 The property is divided among a few The manor was early acquired by the Bishops of Winchester, and had a palace of theirs, which is now traceable in nothing but the alleged site of their kennel. The living is a vicarage, united with the p curacy of Ropley, in the diocese of Winchester Value, £350 * Patron, Mrs Deacon The church is partly Norman, partly decorated, and contains a good brass of the 15th century —The hundred is in Alton division, and consists of lower half, containing Bishops Sutton and two other parishes, and upper half, containing Bighton and two other parishes. Acres, 10,373 and 6,992 Pop, 1,615 and 1,074 Houses, 320 and 203

BISHOPS TACHBROOK, a parish in the district and county of Warwick, on an affluent of the river Avon near the Fosse way 2¼ miles SW of Leamington r station, and 3½ SE of Warwick It includes the hamlet of Tachbrook Mallory and a place called the Asps, and its post town is Whitnash, under Leamington Acres, 3,446 Real property, £4 413 Pop., 603 Houses, 140 The property is divided among a few The living is a vicarage in the diocese of Worcester Value, £313 * Patron, the Bishop of Lichfield The church shows Norman

traces, and contains some fine monuments A school has an endowed income of £10, and other charities £5

BISHOPS TAWTON, a village, a parish, and a sub district, in the district of Barnstaple, Devon The village stands on the river Taw, near the North Devon railway 2 miles S by E of Barnstaple, and has a post office under Barnstaple It was the seat of the see of Devonshire, from the division of the see of Sherborne in 905 till the removal of the bishops to Crediton, and it possesses some remains of the episcopal palace The parish includes Newport, the suburb of Barnstaple Acres, 4,263 Real property, £9,742 Pop, 1,857 Houses, 380 The property is divided among a few The manor belonged to the Bishops of Devonshire, but was conveyed, in 1550, to the Russell family, and belongs now to the Duke of Bedford The living is a vicarage in the diocese of Exeter Value, £440 * Patron the Dean of Exeter The church is an ancient edifice of nave, aisle, and chancel, with low square tower, was partially restored in 1849, and contains monuments of the Bourchiers Earls of Bath The p curacy of Newport is a separate benefice — The sub district contains eight parishes Acres 26 709 Pop, 6,307 Houses, 1,305

BISHOPS-TEIGNTON a village and a parish in Newton Abbot district Devon The village stands on the river Teign, near the South Devon railway, 2 miles W by S of Teignmouth, and has a post office under Teignmouth The parish includes also the hamlets of Coombe and Luton Acres, 4,748, of which 365 are water Real property £7 593 Pop, 974 Houses, 279 The property is divided among three The manor of Bishops Teignton belongs to the Comyns family, that of Luton to Lord Clifford A mansion and a sanctuary were built in the parish by Bishop Grandison, and remains of the former exist in a barn at Radaway The living is a vicarage united till 1866 with Luton ch, in the diocese of Exeter Value, £215 * Patron, the Rev W R Ogle The parish church is a neat Gothic edifice of nave, chancel, and aisles, with a tower and spire erected in 1815 and the church of Luton is a Gothic structure of nave and chancel A school has an endowed income of £4, and other charities £12

BISHOPSTOKE, a village and a parish in Winchester district, Hants The village stands on the river Itchen, about a mile E of a station of its own name on the Southwestern railway, whence the branches go off toward Gosport and Salisbury and 6½ miles NNE of Southampton It is large and well built, includes a new cheese market a square enclosure with sheds in 3 acres, constructed in 1852, and has a post office under Winchester A hotel with posting establishment adjoins the railway station The parish comprises 3 360 acres Real property, £5,342 Pop, 1,390 Houses, 251 The property is divided among a few The manor was held, in the time of Edward VI, by Bishop Bale The villa and fine gardens of the Garnier family noticed by Bolton are here The living is a rectory in the diocese of Winchester Value £467 * Patron, the bishop of Winchester The church was built in 1825, and has a western tower There is a Wesleyan chapel

BISHOPSTOKE, Gloucester See STOKE BISHOP

BISHOPSTON, a chapelry in Horfield parish, Gloucester Pop to in, Bristol Statistics, not separately returned The living is a vicarage in the diocese of Gloucester and Bristol Value, £150 Patron, the Bishop The church is a plain building

BISHOPSTON or LLANDILO FERWALLT, a parish in Swansea district, Glamorgan, near Bishopston Road r station and 5 miles SW by W of Swansea It includes Kittle Hill village, and has a post office under Swansea Acres 2 287 Real property, £2 101 Pop, 419 Houses 93 The property is much subdivided The manor belonged to the Bishops of Llandaff Interesting features of limestone rock occur in a wooded glen, and lead ore has been worked The living is a rectory in the diocese of St Davids Value £238 * Patron, the Bishop of Llandaff The church has an embattled tower, and is good J Davies, author of the "Celtic Researches," was rector

BISHOPSTONE, a hamlet in Stone parish, Bucks, 2 miles SSW of Aylesbury Pop, 274

BISHOPSTONE, a tything in Montacute parish, Somerset 3½ miles WNW of Yeovil Pop 257

BISHOPSTONE, a parish in Weobly district, Hereford, near the river Wye, and the Hereford and Brecon railway, 7 miles WNW of Hereford It has a post office under Hereford Acres, 776 Real property, £1,518 Pop, 288 Houses, 67 The property is divided among a few A fine tessellated pavement and other Roman remains have been found The living is a rectory in the diocese of Hereford, and till 1865 was united with Yazor Value, £180 * Patron, Rev C H Davenport The church is ancient and cruciform, was recently restored, and contains several beautiful monuments Charities, £49

BISHOPSTONE, a parish and a hundred in Lewes district Sussex The parish lies on the Newhaven railway, 9 miles SSE of Lewes, and has a post office under Lewes, and a r station Acres, 1,937, of which 108 are water Real property, £1,995 Pop 322 Houses, 73 The property is divided among a few The living is a vicarage in the diocese of Chichester Value £85 Patron, the Bishop of London The church is Norman and early English, has a tower of four stages, was recently restored, and possesses high interest to artists and antiquaries The Rev J Hurdis, author of the "Village Curate," was a native, and his monument is in the church —The hundred is in the rape of Pevensey, and consists of the parishes of Bishopstone and Denton Acres, 2,945 Pop, 528 Houses, 108

BISHOPSTONE, a parish in Highworth district, Wilts, on the verge of the county, 2¾ miles S of Shrivenham r station, and 6 E of Swindon It has a post-office under Shrivenham Acres, 4,452 Real property, £4,513 Pop, 710 Houses, 147 The property is subdivided The living is a vicarage in the diocese of Gloucester and Bristol Value, £208.* Patron, the Bishop of Gloucester and Bristol The church is tolerable A school has an endowed income of £59 and other charities £60

BISHOPSTONE, a village, a parish, and a sub-district in the district of Wilton, Wilts The village stands on an affluent of the river Avon, 3½ miles SSW of Wilton r station, and 4½ SW of Salisbury —The parish includes also the hamlets of Throope, Croucheston, Faulston, Hamston, Netton, and Pitts and its post-town is Bishopstone, under Salisbury Acres, 4,452 Real property, with Stratford Toney, £6,047 Pop 685 Houses, 136 The property is subdivided The living is a rectory and a vicarage in the diocese of Salisbury Value, £806 * Patron, the Earl of Pembroke The church is cruciform, shows features of many styles and periods, but is mainly of the time of Henry VI he longed to the priory of Monkton Farleigh, and contains two stone coffins, which are supposed to hold the remains of bishops Charities, £10 —The sub district contains eleven parishes and an extra parochial tract Acres, 31,479 Pop, 4,904 Houses 1,035

BISHOPSTONE Monmouth. See BISHTON

BISHOP STORTFORD See BISHOPS STORTFORD

BISHOPSTOWE See AUSTIS COVE

BISHOPSTROW, a parish in Warminster district Wilts, on the Great Western railway, 1¾ mile SE of Warminster Post town Warminster Acres, 1,015 Real property, £2,031 Pop, 258 Houses, 52 The property is divided among a few Bishopstrow House is the seat of the Temple family Many Roman coins have been found The living is a rectory in the diocese of Salisbury Value, £220 * Patron, Sir F D Astley, Bart The church is good

BISHOPS WALTHAM a small town, a parish, a sub district and a hundred, in Droxford district Hants The town stands at the source of the river Hamble, and at the terminus of a branch of the Gosport Junction railway, 3½ miles NNE of Botley, and 9½ SE of Winchester It figured at Domesday as a considerable village, was mentioned by Leland as a "praty tounlet," and is now a neatly built market town It has a post office‡ under Southampton a banking office, two chief inns, a church, a chapel, a free school, and the ruins of an episcopal palace, and is a polling place. The church is ancient and large, built of brick, stone, and flint, the chancel possibly erected by William of Wykeham, the rest chiefly in perpendicular English, of the 17th century The palace was originally built by Bishop Henry de Blois, brother of King Stephen, underwent much alteration by subsequent bishops, particularly by William of Wykeham, who died in it, was a parallelogram of two courts, with square towers at the angles, and suffered demolition in the civil war Henry II held a great council in it in 1182, Richard Cœur de Lion was grandly entertained in it after his coronation at Winchester, and Bishop Poynet made it over to the Marquis of Winchester in the time of Edward VI The chief parts of it now standing are a ruined tower of early date, and the front of the great hall 65 feet long possibly the work of Wykeham A large pond lies in front of it, receiving brooks from the neighbourhood, and discharging the Hamble river A park of 1,000 acres lay around it, devoted to the chase, but is now under cultivation Waltham Chase lay to the SE, well stocked with deer till the beginning of the 17th century, infested then by a notorious gang of deer stealers known as the Waltham Blacks, and now a rough common of about 2,000 acres. The manor belonged to the Bishops of Winchester from the earliest times and, though alienated by Bishop Poynet along with the palace, came back to them at the Restoration A terra-cotta pottery was established in 1861 Fairs are held on the second Friday of May, on 30 July, and on the Friday before 18 Oct The Royal Albert infirmary stands on a neighbouring hill, was founded in 1864, and has, over the entrance, a fine terra cotta statue of the late Prince Consort — The parish includes the tythings of Ashton, Curdridge, and West Hoe, and the hamlets of Dean and Dundridge Acres, 7 388 Real property, £11,099 Pop, 2,267 Houses, 473 The living is a rectory in the diocese of Winchester Value, £915 * Patron the Bishop of Winchester The p curacy of Curdridge is a separate charge A free school has £41, and other charities £95 —The sub district contains the parishes of Bishops Waltham, Durley, and Upham Acres, 12,714 Pop, 3,267 Houses, 689 —The hundred consists of lower half, containing the parishes of Bishops Waltham and Durley, and upper half, conterminate with the parish of Droxford Acres, 16,849 Pop, 4,872 Houses, 977

BISHOPS WICKHAM See WICKHAM BISHOPS

BISHOPSWOOD, a chapelry in Brewood parish, in the vicinity of Brewood, Stafford It was constituted in 1851 and its post town is Brewood under Stafford Rated property, £5,051 Pop., 588 Houses, 139 The property is divided among a few The living is a vicarage in the diocese of Lichfield Value, £150 * Patron, the Vicar of Brewood. The church is fair

BISHOPSWOOD, a chapelry in Walford and Ruardean parishes, Hereford on the river Wye, 3¼ miles SSW of Ross r station It was constituted in 1845, and its post town is Walford under Ross. Acres and property, not reported. Pop 403 Houses, 100 The property is much subdivided, and there are iron works The living is a p curacy in the diocese of Hereford Value, £35 Patron J Partridge, Esq The church is good.

BISHOPSWORTH See BISHPORT

BISHOPS WYCKS See WYCKS BISHOPS

BISHOP-THORNTON, a township chapelry in Ripon parish, W R Yorkshire, 3½ miles NW of Ripley r station, and 5¼ SW by S of Ripon Post town, Ripley, Yorkshire Acres, 3,027 Real property, £4,211 Pop., 541 Houses, 106 The living is a p curacy in the diocese of Ripon Value, £85 Patrons, the Dean and Chapter There are Wesleyan and R Catholic chapels

BISHOP THORPE, or THORPE UPON OUSE, a village and a parish in the district and county of York The village stands on the left bank of the river Ouse, 1¾ mile E by N of Copmanthorpe r station and 3½ S by W of York, and has a post office, of the name of Bishop Thorpe, under York —The parish comprises 760 acres Real property, £3,286 Pop, 452 Houses, 88 The property is subdivided. The manor belongs to the see of York, and Bishop Thorpe palace on it is the seat of the Archbishops The palace was erected, in the reign of John by Archbishop Walter de Grey, was altered or enlarged by Archbishops Sharpe, Dawes, Gilbert, and others, and, as it now stands, was chiefly the work of Archbishop Drummond, who died in 1766 The gateway and the front are in the pointed style, after designs by Atkinson, the former surmounted by a crocketted turret the latter adorned with a fine entrance canopy, the chief apartments are elegant, and have good paintings, engravings, and other works of art, and the chapel, which adjoins the dining room has an antiquely carved pulpit, a floor of black and white marble, and windows of stained glass,—one of them embellished with the arms of the Archbishops, from the Reformation to the Revolution The grounds include only about six acres but are tastefully laid out. The living is a vicarage in the diocese of York Value, £300 * Patron, the Archbishop of York The church was rebuilt in 1768, and again in 1842, has three painted windows the mullions of one of which belonged formerly to Cawood Castle, and contains the tomb of Archbishop Drummond

BISHOPTON, a township and a parish in Stockton district, Durham The township lies 2 miles SSW of Stillington r station, and 5½ WNW of Stockton upon Tees and has a post office under Stockton Acres, 2,102. Real property, £3,077 Pop, 342 Houses, 80 —The parish includes also the townships of Little Stainton and East and West Newbiggin Acres, 4,031 Real property, £4,699 Pop, 448 Houses, 99 The property is subdivided There are vestiges of an entrenchment, supposed to have surrounded the mansion of Roger de Conyers, who, in the time of King Stephen, resisted and overcame William Cumyn, an insurrectionary and devastating pretender to the see of Durham. The living is a vicarage in the diocese of Durham Value, £250 * Patron not reported The church is excellent

BISHOPTON, a township in Ripon parish, W R Yorkshire, 2¾ miles WNW of Ripon Acres, 375 Real property, with Sutton and Clotherholme, £3,037 Pop, 81 Houses, 18

BISHOPTON, a hamlet and a chapelry in Old Stratford parish, Warwick The hamlet lies adjacent to the Stratford and Avon canal, 2 miles NW of Stratford on Avon Pop, 51 — The chapelry is a p curacy in the diocese of Worcester, in the patronage of the Vicar of Stratford, the statistics not reported

BISHOP WEARMOUTH See WEARMOUTH BISHOP

BISHOP WILTON, a village, a township and a parish in Pocklington district, E R Yorkshire The village stands on a brook in the Wolds, 3 miles NE of Fangfoss r station, and 4½ N of Pocklington, and has a post office under York The township includes the village, and is united to Belthorpe, under the name of Bishop Wilton with Belthorpe Acres 4,970 Real property, £4,778 Pop., 658. Houses, 141 The parish includes also the townships of Bolton and Youlthorpe with Gowthorpe Acres, 7,204 Real property, £7,238 Pop., 910 Houses, 189 The property is divided among a few The scenery is picturesque Remains exist of a moated palace built, in the time of Edward IV by Bishop Neville An ancient Beacon, called the Wilton Beacon, crowns an eminence about a mile NE of the village The living is a vicarage in the diocese of York Value, £148.* Patron, Sir T Sykes, Bart. The church consists of nave, aisles, north chapel and chancel, with west tower and octagonal spire and was repaired in 1859 There are chapels for Wesleyan Methodists and Primitive Methodists

BISHPORT, or BISHOPSWORTH, a chapelry in Bedminster parish, Somerset, near Wans Dyke and the Bristol and Exeter railway, 3 miles SW of Bristol It has a post office of Bishopsworth under Bristol Pop, 1,606 Houses, 337 The living is a vicarage in the diocese of Gloucester and Bristol Value, £300 * Patron, the Bishop The church was built in 1842 There are an Independent chapel and a national school

BISHTON, a hamlet in Tidenham parish, Gloucester, 1 mile NE of Chepstow Pop 42

BISHTON a township in Colwich parish, Stafford, 2 miles NW of Rugeley Pop, 173

BISHTON, or BISHOPSTONE, a parish in Newport district, Monmouth; on the South Wales railway, 1¼ mile E of Llanwern station, and 5½ E by S of Newport Post town, Magor, under Chepstow Acres, 1,211 Real property, £1,462 Pop, 188 Houses, 36 The property is divided among a few The living is a vicarage in the diocese of Llandaff Value, £111 Patron, the Archdeacon of Llandaff The church is good.

BISLEY, a decayed small town, a parish, a sub district, and a hundred in Gloucester The town stands 1¾ mile N of the Cheltenham and Great Western Union railway, in the neighbourhood of the Sapperton tunnel, and 3½ miles E of Stroud. It has a post office under Stroud, is a polling place, and long carried on a considerable manufacture of woollens, which now is nearly extinct A weekly market used to be held on Thursday, but now is merely nominal Fairs are held on May 4 and 12 Nov —The parish includes also the tythings of Avenis, Pidfield, Bussage, Chalford, Oakridge, Steanbridge, Througham, and Tunley Acres, 8,033 Real property, £14,277 Pop, 4,692 Houses, 1,166 The property is much subdivided The manor belonged anciently to the Mortimers, and was held by Edward Duke of York, afterwards Edward IV A common of 1,200 acres was given by Roger Mortimer, Earl of March, to the poor of the parish, but has been much curtailed by enclosure Roman remains have been found at Custom Scrubs, and a Roman pavement and vault at Lillythorne The living is a vicarage united with the p curacy of France Lynch, in the diocese of Gloucester and Bristol Value, £527 * Patron, the Lord Chancellor The church is decorated English, of the time of Edward IV, was recently restored, and contains an ancient Norman font, a monument of a crusader, supposed to be one of the Nottingham family, and a brass of Catherine Sewell A stone cross, believed to be of the 13th century, octagonal and finely panelled, is in the churchyard The vicarages of Bussage, Chalford, and Oakridge are separate benefices There are four dissenting chapels, endowed schools with £56, and other charities with £242 —The sub district is conterminate with the parish, and is in the district of Stroud —The hundred contains seven parishes Acres, 27,003 Pop, 18,183 Houses, 4,163

BISLEY, a parish in Chertsey district, Surrey near the Basingstoke canal and the Southwestern railway, 3½ miles WNW of Woking station, and 4 SE of Bagshot Post town, Chobham, under Farnborough station Acres, 930 Real property, £1,496 Pop, 313 Houses, 73 The manor belongs to the Sumners A boys' refuge farm school, connected with a farm of 58 acres, was built in 1869, at a cost of £5,775 The living is a rectory in the diocese of Winchester Value, £183 * Patron, J Thornton, Esq The church is ancient Charities, £10

BISPHAM, a township in Croston parish, Lancashire, near the river Douglas 2 miles E of Rufford station, and 6 NE of Ormskirk Acres, 926 Real property, £1,740 Pop, 277 Houses, 49 A free grammar school here, founded in 1692, has an income of £162

BISPHAM a township and a parish in Fylde district, Lancashire The township bears the name of Bispham with Norbreck, lies on the coast, and on the Blackpool railway, 1¼ mile N of Blackpool and has a post office of Bispham under Preston, and a r station Acres, 2,621, of which 357 are water Real property £3 307 Pop, 437 Houses 88 The parish includes also the township of Layton with Warbreck, which contains the town of Blackpool and the village of South Shore Acres, 5,865, of which 1,827 are water Real property, £20,555 Pop, 4,011 Houses, 819 The property is much subdivided The living is a vicarage in the diocese of Manchester Value £2 5 * Patron, the Rev C Hesketh The church is modern The chapelries of Blackpool and Southshore are separate benefices. There are an Independent chapel and a free school

BISS (THE), a stream of Wilts It rises near Edington, and runs 7 miles north north westward, through Trowbridge to the Avon, 1¼ mile below Bradford.

BISSICK, a locality in Ladock parish, Cornwall, 5½ miles NE of Truro A fair is held on 9 May

BISTER See BICESTER

BISTERN See BARTLEY, Hants.

BISTERN AND CROW, a tything in Ringwood parish, Hants, 1 mile SE of Ringwood Pop, 98 It forms a curacy, annexed to the vicarage of Ringwood

BISTERN CLOSES an extra parochial tract in Ringwood district, Hants, contiguous to Ellingham parish, 2 miles SW of Ringwood

BISTRE, a township and a chapelry in Mold parish, Flint The township lies 1 mile N of Llong r station, and 2 E of Mold It includes part of Buckley hamlet, which has a post-office under Flint Real property, £3,189 Pop, 1,733 Houses, 372 The chapelry is more extensive than the township, and was constituted in 1844 Pop, 2,347 Houses, 501 The living is a p curacy in the diocese of St Asaph Value, £150 * Patron, the Vicar of Mold The church was built in 1841, sank and became shattered from undermining in coal-works, and was restored in 1861

BITCHFIELD, a parish in Grantham district Lincoln, on the Great Northern railway, 2 miles SE of Great Ponton station and 3 NW of Corby Post town, Corby, under Grantham Acres, 1,344 Real property, £2,017 Pop, 159 Houses, 32 The living is a vicarage in the diocese of Lincoln Value, £174 Patron, the Bishop of Lincoln The church is good

BITCHFIELD, a township in Stamfordham parish, Northumberland, near the river Blyth, 9 miles SW of Morpeth Pop, 10

BITTADON, a parish in Barnstaple district, Devon, 3½ miles SSE of Ilfracombe, and 5½ N by W of Barnstaple r station Post town, Ilfracombe Acres, 1,018 Real property £597 Pop, 65 Houses, 11 The property is divided among four The living is a rectory in the diocese of Exeter Value, £83 Patron, W A Yeo Esq The church is small but good, and contains some fine monuments of the Chichester and Acland families

BITTERING (LITTLE), a parish in Mitford district, Norfolk, 3 miles N by E of Wendling station, and 5 NW of East Dereham Post town, Litcham, under Swaffham Acres 398 Rated property £384 Pop, 30 Houses, 3 The property is all in one estate The living is a rectory in the diocese of Norwich Value, £100 Patron, James Dover, Esq

BITTERLEY, a township and a parish in Ludlow district, Salop The township lies under the Clee hills, 4 miles NE of Ludlow, and is connected by railway with Ludlow station The parish includes also the townships of Cleeton, Hill upon Cott, Middleton, and Snitton, with parts of Henley and Hopton, and its post town is Ludlow Acres, 6 591 Real property, £7,872 Pop, 972 Houses, 189 The property is divided among a few The Clee hills here exhibit grand scenery, command noble views, and contain abundance of coal and ironstone The living is a rectory, united with the p curacy of Middleton, in the diocese of Hereford Value, £8 5 * Patron, the Rev C Walcot The church contains a carved oak pulpit a carved oak screen, and an ancient stone font, and is in tolerable condition A stone cross with graduated pedestal, and hexagonal shaft, crowned by tabernacled niches, is in the churchyard A grammar-school has £34 and other charities £26

BITTERN, a village, a tything, and a chapelry in South Stoneham parish Hants The village stands on the left side of the Itchen river near Bittern Road r station, and 2 miles NE of Southampton and has a post office under Southampton The tract around it was long held by the Bishops of Winchester, and had a residence of theirs —The tything is united to Pollack, under the name of Bittern and Pollack Real property, £8 404 Pop, 1,7?3 Houses, 3?7 Bittern manor is the seat of Mrs Stuart Hall Remains of the Roman station Clausentum, including walls of flint and small stones with Roman grouting, are in the grounds This station was connected by roads with Winchester Porchester, and the ferry to the Isle of Wight, and probably was intended to defend the approach to them and it became the head-quarters of Tetricus, one of the British usurpers after Gallienus. Numerous coins and medals, chiefly of Claudius and Constantine, and numerous inscriptions, chiefly relating to Tetricus, have been found, and many of the inscriptions may be seen on the spot The chapelry is less extensive than the tything, and was constituted in 1853 Pop 1 603 Houses, 338 The living is a vicarage in the diocese of Winchester Value, £200 * Patron the Bishop of Winchester The church stands on an eminence, at the village, and is a handsome structure in the decorated style, with a lofty spire. There is a Wesleyan chapel

BITTERSCOTE, or BIDDESCOTE, a liberty in Tamworth parish, Stafford, 1 mile SE of Tamworth Acres, 330 Pop, 62 Houses, 13

BITTESBY, a liberty in Claybrooke parish, Leicester, on the Midland railway, 3 miles WNW of Lutterworth Real property, £1,226 Pop, 12 House, 1

BITTESWELL, a parish in Lutterworth district, Leicester, near Watling street, 1 mile NNW of Lutterworth, and 2 ESE of Ullesthorpe r station It has a post office under Lutterworth Acres, 2 630 Real property, £4,384 Pop, 439 Houses, 105 The property is subdivided There is a mineral spring The living is a vicarage in the diocese of Peterborough. Value, £428 * Patrons, the Haberdashers' Company and Christ s Hospital, London The church is good, and there are an endowed school, six alms houses, and other charities £69

BITTISCOMBE a hamlet in Upton parish, Somerset, 4½ miles ENE of Dulverton

BITTIESTON See BIDDIESDON

BITTON, a village a parish, and a sub district, in the district of Keynsham, and county of Gloucester The village stands near the confluence of the Boyd and the Avon, adjacent to the Julian way, 2 miles NE of Keynsham r station, and 6 SE of Bristol, and it has a post office under Bristol —The parish includes also Hanham chapelry and Oldland hamlet, with Kingswood village Acres, 7,156. Real property, £28,319, of which £1,594 are in mines Pop, 9,630 Houses, 2,032 The property is much subdivided. Coal and iron ore are worked, and the workers at them, in last century, were noted for vicious character, and for reclamation by the preaching of Wesley and his associates Traces of many Roman antiquities have been found The living is a vicarage in the diocese of Gloucester and Bristol. Value, £390 * Patron, the Bishop of Gloucester and Bristol The church is partly Norman, partly perpendicular English, and has a good tower The vicarages of Hanham, Oldland, and Kingswood are separate benefices There are a Wesleyan chapel, national schools, and charities £26 —The sub district comprises three parishes Acres, 8,267 Pop, 5,071 Houses, 1,063

BIX, a parish in Henley district Oxford, under the Chiltern hills, 2¾ miles NW of Henley on Thames r station Post town, Henley on Thames. Acres, 3,075 Real property, £3,018 Pop, 392 Houses, 83 The area comprises two quondam parishes, Bixbrand in the N and Bixgibwen in the S The living is a rectory in the diocese of Oxford Value, £487 * Patron, the Earl of Macclesfield

BIXLEY, a parish in Henstead district, Norfolk, near the Eastern Union railway, 3 miles SE by S of Norwich Post town, Norwich Acres, 760 Real property £1 814 Pop, 161 Houses 31 The property is divided among a few Bixley Hall is a handsome edifice built, about the middle of last century, by Sir Edward Ward The living is a rectory, united with the rectory of Earls Framingham, in the diocese of Norwich. Value, £603 Patron, the Rev C D Brereton The church is ancient and good, contains monuments of the Wards, and formerly had an image of St Wandegisilus, to which pilgrimages were made.

BIXTON, or BICKERSTONE, a quondam parish a rectory, now incorporated with Burnham Broom, in Norfolk

BLABY, a village, a parish, and a district in Leicestershire The village stands on a branch of the river Soar and on the Union Canal, 4½ miles S of Leicester, and has a station on the S Leicester railway, and a post office under Leicester Pop, 1,023. Houses, 244 The parish includes also the chapelry of Countesthorpe Acres, 3,300 Real property, £7,524 Pop, 1,998 Houses, 463 The property is subdivided Worsted and stocking manufactures are carried on The living is a rectory, united with the p. curacy of Countesthorpe, in the diocese of Peterborough. Value, £350 * Patron, the Lord Chancellor The church is very good There are Baptist and Wesleyan chapels, a fine national school, and a cemetery with two chapels of 1862 —The district comprehends the sub district of Wigston, containing the parishes of Blaby, Kilby, Foston, Wigston-Magna, and Oadby, and part of the parishes of St Margaret Leicester and Aylestone, and the sub district of Enderby, containing the parishes of Enderby, Whetstone, Cosby, Narborough, Glenfield, Thurlaston and Croft, the extra parochial tracts of Kirby Frith, Glenfield Frith, Leicester Forest East, Leicester Forest West the Knoll and Bassett House, and parts of the parishes of Aylestone and Barwell Acres 34,207 Poor rates in 1866, £8,122 Pop. in 1861, 14,171 Houses, 3,120 Marriages in 1866, 93, births, 483,—of which 40 were illegitimate, deaths, 262,—of which 128 were at ages under 5 years, and 8 at ages above 85 years Marriages in the ten years 1851-60, 939, births, 5 193, deaths, 3,046 The places of worship in 1851 were 17 of the Church of England, with 5,181 sittings, 6 of Independents with 1 834 s, 6 of Baptists, with 1,498 s, 5 of Wesleyan Methodists, with 661 s, 4 of Primitive Methodists, with 474 s, 2 of the Wesleyan Association, with 185 s, 1 of Wesleyan Reformers, with 60 s, and 1 undefined, with 230 s The schools were 14 public day schools, with 922 scholars, 45 private day schools with 832 s 31 Sunday schools, with 2,895 s and 2 evening schools for adults, with 31 s The workhouse is in Enderby, was built at a cost of £4,400 and can accommodate 350 persons

BLACKATON, a hill, 5½ miles WNW of St Germans, in Cornwall

BLACKAWTON, a village, a parish, and a sub district, in the district of Kingsbridge, Devon The village stands 4 miles W of Dartmouth and 6 S by W of Totnes r station, and has a post office under Totnes The parish includes Street chapelry, and extends to the coast Acres, 5,646, of which 60 are water Real property with East Allington, £11,644 Pop, 1 229 Houses 252 The property is much subdivided The living is a vicarage, united with the p curacy of Street, in the diocese of Exeter Value £129 * Patron, Sir H P Seale, Bart The church is perpendicular English, and contains a carved oak pulpit and screen, and several neat monuments The chapel at Street is an erection of 1836, and there are Wesleyan chapels at the village and at Street, and charities £16 The sub district comprises three parishes Acres, 12,408 Pop, 2,571 Houses, 538

BLACK BANK, a railway station in Cambridgeshire on the Peterborough and Ely railway, 5 miles NW by N of Ely

BLACKBERRY See BRACKBURY

BLACKBOROUGH, a parish in Tiverton district Devon, on the W side of Black Down 4½ miles SE of Tiverton Junction r station, and 6 ENE of Cullompton It has a post office under Cullompton Acres, 508 Pop, 76 Houses, 16 The manor belongs to the Earl of Egremont The living is a rectory in the diocese of Exeter Value, £140 Patron, the Earl of Egremont The church is modern, consists of nave and chancel, with tower and octagonal spire, and stands conspicuously on an eminence

BLACKBOURN a hundred in Suffolk It lies between Norfolk on the N, Hartismere hundred on the E and Thedwastre hundred on the W, and contains Great Ashfield parish thirty two other parishes, and part of another Acres 63 557 Pop. 15 703 Houses, 3 302

BLACKBOURNE, a hundred in the lathe of Scray,

Kent It contains Appledore parish and four other parishes. Acres 17,79[illegible]. Pop, 2,987 Houses, 500

BLACKBOURTON, a parish in Witney district, Oxford, 6 miles SW of Witney r station It has a post office under Faringdon Acres, 1,300 Real property, £2,973 Pop, 200 Houses 61 The living is a vicarage in the diocese of Oxford Value, £148 Patron, Christ Church, Oxford. The church is early English, and contains a stone pulpit and monuments of the Hungerfords and Sir A Hopton Maria Edgeworth was a native

BLACKBOYS, a locality 7 miles SW of Mayfield, and 8½ NE of Lewes in Sussex It has a post office under Hurst Green, and a fair on 6 Oct

BLACKBROOK, a hamlet in Parr township, near Prescot, Lancashire

BLACKBROOK, a suburb of Kidderminster

BLACK BROOK, a stream of Leicestershire, running 9 miles north eastward to the Soar opposite Barrow

BLACK BULL, a station with telegraph on the North Staffordshire railway, 6 miles N of Stoke

BLACKBURN, a town, a township a parish, a sub district a district, and a hundred in Lancashire. The town stands on the river Blackwater, 9 miles E by S of Preston, and 12½ N by W of Bolton The Leeds and Liverpool canal passes through it, and railways go from it N, S, E and W The country around it possesses little scenic interest, yet is sheltered by hills on the NE and NW, and it lay for ages wild and barren, but has been much improved by cultivation All of it was given by William the Conqueror to Hubert de Lacy and it was divided among that baron's followers and descendants. The town is large was very prosperous up to the juncture of the cotton distress in 1862, and has owed most of its importance to modern manufactures The older streets are irregularly built but extensive improvements have been made since 1850, many of the houses now are good and neat and the suburbs contain a number of villas The market place is surrounded by ornate public buildings, and by other lofty, well built houses, with good shops The town hall faces two sides of the market place, was built in 1856, at a cost of £30,000, and is in the Italian style, with Doric and Corinthian decorations The exchange stands opposite the town-hall, was built in 1862-5, is in the pointed style, with chief entrance under an ornate octagonal tower, and has a principal apartment 140 feet by 53 The county court house was built in 1863 The public park comprises about 50 acres, and is picturesque and tasteful The water works were constructed at a cost of more than £70,000 The infirmary was completed in 1865, at a cost of about £25,000, and is in the Italian style The workhouse was built in 1864, at a cost of nearly £30,000 The mechanics institute and the free public library are on a large scale The Reform club and the Conservative club were built in 1863 St Mary's church originated in the Saxon times and belonged to Whalley abbey, was rebuilt in 1824 and re decorated in 1857, and is in the pointed style of the 14th century St John's church was built about 1790, and is in the Grecian style St Peters church is transition Norman Trinity church was built in 1846 has a lofty tower of 1855, and is in the decorated English style The United Presbyterian church is a handsome edifice of 1863 Two Independent chapels of 1810 and 1858 also are handsome Two Roman Catholic chapels of 1820 and 1865 are ornamental, and a convent of 1851 is elegant The places of worship in 1851 were 12 of the Church of England, 17 of Dissenters, and 3 of Roman Catholics The ultra mural cemetery was opened in 1857 and has three chapels There are an endowed grammar school with £120 a year, a charity school for educating and clothing 90 children, 14 national schools and 15 other public schools

The manufactures of Blackburn arose about the year 1650 The first of note was "Blackburn checks" the next was "Blackburn greys" the next, about 1765, was calicoes and this, after being taken up by the power looms, was followed by low priced muslins Cotton mills and print works are numerous, and employ a large proportion of the inhabitants The value of cotton goods produced prior to 1862 exceeded £2,000,000 a year The cotton spinning was much advanced by an invention of James Hargrave, a native, originally a carpenter, and the cotton printing was introduced by the family of Sir Robert Peel Some woollen cloth also is made, considerable industry is carried on in breweries foundries and machine-works, particularly in the manufacture of weaving machinery, and much business is done in connexion with neighbouring factories, corn mills paper mills, and collieries. Weekly markets are held on Wednesday and Saturday, and fairs on the Wednesday before 2 Feb, on every alternate Wednesday thence till Michaelmas, and on Easter Monday 11 and 12 May, 29 Sept, and 17 Oct The town has a head post-office,‡ a telegraph station, four banking offices, and three chief inns, and publishes four weekly newspapers It is a seat of courts and a polling place, it was constituted, by the act of 1832, a parliamentary borough sending two members to parliament, and it was made municipal in 1851, with government by a mayor, twelve aldermen, and thirty six councillors Acres, 3,610 Real property in 1860 £170,703 Direct taxes in 1857, £26,354 Electors in 1865, 1,894 Pop in 1841, 36 629, in 1861, 63,126 Houses, 11,306 Robert Bolton, the compiler of the Liturgy, who died in 1631, was a native

The township and the sub district are conterminate with the borough The parish includes also nineteen other townships in the district of Blackburn and the townships of Walton le Dale, Cuerdale, and Samlesbury, in the district of Preston It was originally part of Whalley parish, and it measures 14 miles in length, 10 miles in breadth, and 45,269 acres in area Real property, £314,105 Charities, £526 Pop in 1841, 71,711 in 1861, 110,349 Houses, 20,139 Parts of the surface are embellished, and have Witton Park, Woodfold, Feniscowles, and other seats, but much is poor or waste land, with clay soil A ridge of high ground goes across it, and culminates, at an altitude of about 630 feet, on Billinge hill Sandstone abounds and coal and alum stone occur The living is a vicarage in the diocese of Manchester Value, £593.* Patron, the Bishop of Manchester The separate vicarage of St Thomas and p curacies of Christ Church, St John, St Paul, St Michael, Trinity Church, and St. Peter with St Luke are in the town, and the chapelries of Great Harwood Samlesbury, Walton le Dale Balderston, Lower Darwen, Over Darwen St James, Over Darwen Trinity, Over Darwen St John, Langho, Mellor, Salesbury Tockholes Witton, Feniscowles, Hoddlesden, Higher Walton, and Bamber Bridge are in the other parts Value of St Thomas, £300, of each of the others in the town, £300 * Patron of St Thomas, the Bishop of Manchester of Christ Church, the Bishop and others, of all the rest, the Vicar of Blackburn The chapelries not in the town are separately noticed

The district comprehends Blackburn sub district, conterminate with the borough, Billington sub district, containing Billington Langho, Dinkley, Salesbury, and Wilpshire townships in Blackburn parish, Mellor sub-district, containing Mellor Balderstone, Osbaldeston, Clayton le Dale, and Ramsgreave townships in Blackburn parish, Witton sub district, containing Witton, Pleasington, Livesey, and Tockholes townships in Blackburn parish, Darwen sub district, containing Lower Darwen, Over Darwen, and Eccleshill townships in Blackburn parish, and Yate and Pickupbank township in Whalley parish, Harwood sub district, containing Great Harwood, Little Harwood, and Rishton townships in Blackburn parish, and Clayton le Moors chapelry in Whalley parish, and Oswaldtwistle sub district, containing Oswaldtwistle and Church Kirk townships in Whalley parish Acres, 43,569 Poor rates in 1866, £39,712 Pop in 1841 75,089 in 1861, 119,942 Houses 21,883 Marriages in 1866, 1,291, births, 5,171,—of which 277 were illegitimate, deaths, 3 913,—of which 2,063 were at ages under 5 years, and 29 at ages above 85 years Marriages in the ten years 1851-60, 10,180, births, 42,610, deaths 27,750 The places of worship in 1851 were 23 of the Church of England, with 18,988 sittings, 1 of the United Presbyterian church with 800 s, 16 of Independents, with 8,163 s, 7 of Baptists, with 1,109 s, 2 of Quakers, with 600 s, 9 of Wesleyan Methodists, with 4,363 s, 3 of Primitive Methodists, with 1,507 s, 6 of the Wesleyan Association, with 1,686 s, 1 of Wesleyan Reformers, with 700 s, 1 of the New Church, with 151 s, 1 of Latter Day Saints, with 100 s., and 6 of Roman Catholics, with 2,445 s The schools were 52 public day schools, with 7,000 scholars, 33 private day schools with 1,341 s, 76 Sunday schools, with 21,375 s, and 15 evening schools for adults, with 408 s —The hundred was anciently called Blackburnshire, extends 24 miles along the boundary with Yorkshire, goes westward to the vicinity of Preston, and south eastward beyond Haslingden, and is cut into two divisions, higher and lower Acres of the h division, 87,190 Pop in 1851, 116,544 Acres of the l division, 79,773 Pop in 1851, 57,981 Pop of both divisions in 1861, 188,129 Houses, 36,208

BLACKBURN, a hamlet in Kimberworth township, W R Yorkshire, 1 mile W of Rotherham.

BLACKBURN RAILWAYS, railways in Lancashire connecting Blackburn with places to the N, to the W, to the S, and to the E They are the Blackburn, Clitheroe, and Northwestern Junction, the Blackburn and Preston the Blackburn, Darwen, and Bolton and the Blackburn, Burnley, Accrington, and Colne Extension, but all are incorporated with the LANCASHIRE and YORKSHIRE, and will be noticed under that head

BLACKBURN RIVER, a stream of Cumberland, falling into the South Tyne, 2 miles above Alston

BLACKBURTON, Oxford See BLACKBOURTON

BLACK BURTON, Yorkshire See BURTON IN LONSDALE.

BLACKBURY, a hamlet in Colyton Rawleigh parish, Devon, 4½ miles WSW of Colyton A Roman camp is in its neighbourhood

BLACK CALLERTON, a township in Newburn parish, Northumberland, 6 miles NW of Newcastle Acres, 1,377 Pop, 172 Houses 32

BLACK CARTS WITH RYEHILL, an extra parochial tract in Hexham district, Northumberland, near the Roman wall, 8½ miles NW of Hexham Pop, 19 Houses, 3

BLACK CHAPEL, a chapelry in Great Waltham parish, Essex, on the river Chelmer, 4½ miles N of Chelmsford r station Post town, Great Waltham, under Chelmsford Statistics with the parish The living is a p. curacy in the diocese of Rochester Value, £80 Patrons, Trustees

BLACK COMBE, a mountain in the S of Cumberland, between Duddon sands and the sea, 6½ miles SSE of Ravenglass It consists chiefly of clay slate, rises to the altitude of 1,919 feet, and commands a panoramic view to Yorkshire, Scotland, Ireland, the Isle of Man, and Wales

"This height a ministering angel might select,
For from the summit of Black Combe (dread name
Derived from clouds and storms!) the amplest range
Of unobstructed prospect may be seen
That British ground commands."

BLACK COUNTRY (THE), a tract of mines and iron works in the S of Stafford, and on the N verge of Warwick It extends chiefly from Wolverhampton to Birmingham, south eastward 13 miles, and from Dudley to Walsall, north eastward, 7 miles. "The name is eminently descriptive, for blackness everywhere prevails The ground is black the atmosphere is black, and the underground is honey combed by mining galleries stretching in utter blackness for many a league. The scene is marvellous, and to one who beholds it for the first time by night, terrific

BLACKDEN, a township in Sandbach parish, Cheshire, on the Northwestern railway, 6½ miles SSE of Knutsford Acres, 735 Real property, £1,261 Pop, 157 Houses, 31

BLACKDOWN, a hamlet in Kidderminster Foreign, in the neighbourhood of Kidderminster, Worcester

BLACKDOWN a village in Broadwinsor parish, Dorset, 5½ miles WNW of Beaminster It forms a curacy, annexed to the vicarage of Broadwinsor

BLACK DOWN, the highest summit of the Mendip Hills, in Somerset, 3 miles NE of Axbridge It has an altitude of 1,100 feet above the level of the sea, is crowned by a mark of the Sappers and Miners, and commands a very extensive and brilliant view

BLACK DOWN, an upland ridge on the mutual border of Somerset and Devon, around the sources of the Axe, the Otter, and the Culme rivers It is chalky and bleak, and its highest point has an altitude of 1,160 feet above the level of the sea, and is crowned by a column, erected by the inhabitants in honour of Wellington

BLACK DOWN, a hill ridge in the NW of Dorset, a continuation eastward of the Somerset and Devon Black Down It rises to the altitude of 817 feet above the level of the sea, is crowned by a monument to Admiral Sir Thomas Hardy, and has a number of large marl pits, which have sometimes been regarded as Druidical

BLACK DOWN, a high ridge on the E border of Hants, between Liphook and Petersfield. It commands a picturesque view of the neighbouring parts of Sussex, toward Midhurst and Petworth

BLACK DOWN, a barren eminence in the Isle of Wight, 3½ miles NW of Ventnor

BLACK DOWN, a tything in Crewkerne parish, Somerset, 6½ miles SW of Crewkerne

BLACKENHALL See BLAKENHALL

BLACKENHURST, a hundred in Worcester, cut into two divisions, lower and upper The lower division contains Abbots Morton parish, two other parishes, and part of another Acres, 6,887 The upper division contains Badsey parish and six other parishes Acres, 9,673 Pop of both, 3,643 Houses 767

BLACKER, a hamlet in Worsbrough township, Darfield parish, W R Yorkshire, 2 miles S of Barnesley

BLACKER, a hamlet in Darton township and parish, W R Yorkshire, 3½ miles NW of Barnesley

BLACK FORCE, a cascade on Fell Head, Westmoreland, within the basin of the Lune, 6 miles SSW of Orton It occurs at the head of a wild chasm, approached from Borrow Bridge, and consists in the fall of a streamlet from such a giddy height as to be all reduced to spray before reaching the bottom

BLACKFORD, a hamlet in Stoke St Milborough parish, Salop, 8 miles NE of Ludlow

BLACKFORD, a chapelry in Wedmore parish, Somerset between the rivers Axe and Brue, 2¾ miles N by E of Edington Road r station, and 4½ S of Axbridge It has a post office under Weston super Mare Pop, 677 Houses, 147 The chapelry was constituted in 1844 The manor belonged to H Saxey, and was given by him to Bruton hospital The living is a vicarage in the diocese of Bath and Wells Value, £300 * Patron, the Vicar of Wedmore The church is modern

BLACKFORD a parish in Wincanton district, Somerset, 4½ miles W SW of Wincanton r station and 5 N by W of Milborne Port Post town, North Cadbury, under Bath Acres, 578 Real property, with Compton and Pauncefoot, £2,839 Pop, 164 Houses, 37 The living is a rectory in the diocese of Bath and Wells Value, £177 * Patron, B H Hunt, Esq The church is early English, with a fine Norman entrance arch There are a Wesleyan chapel and a national school

BLACKFORD, a manor in Selworthy parish, Somerset, 3¾ miles W of Minehead Pop, 15

BLACKFORDBY, a chapelry in Ashby de la Zouch and Seal parishes Leicester 2 miles NW of Ashby de la Zouch r station Post town, Ashby de la Zouch Acres 1,117 Real property, £3,061 Pop, 615 Houses 129 The church was recently rebuilt There are a Wesleyan chapel and a national school

BLACK FRIARS, an extra parochial spot in St Alphage parish, Canterbury city, Kent

BLACK FRIARS, an extra-parochial tract within Leicester borough, Leicestershire. Pop, 1,173 Houses, 257

BLACKGANG CHINE, a grand chasm on the S coast of the Isle of Wight, down the seaward face of St Catherine's Hill, 5½ miles W of Ventnor The crest of the hill above it is 709 feet high, and the precipices on its flanks are, in some parts, 400 feet deep It commences in two large separate convergent fissures, it then goes down in a deep declivitous, crumbling gorge, and it terminates by flinging a tiny streamlet over a precipice of 40 feet upon the beach The shore below it is strewn with massive fragments of fallen rock, the whole chasm is so black, naked, shattered, and profound as to strike the mind with awe, and it flings back from the vibrations of even a light gale a reverberating sound like thunder The approach to it is enclosed and leads through a toy shop, and there are an hotel and good lodging houses in the neighbourhood The Clarendon West Indiaman was wrecked opposite the chine in October 1836, when all on board, except three seamen, perished

BLACK HAMBLETON, a mountain near the north-western extremity of the river Derwent's basin, N R Yorkshire, 9 miles NW of Helmsley It has an altitude of 1,400 feet, and commands a magnificent view

BLACK HEAD, a headland on the SE coast of Cornwall, dividing Mevagissey bay from St. Austell's bay It is 153 feet high

BLACK HEAD, a promontory on the S coast of Cornwall, 6 miles NE of the Lizard It is bare and sombre, but possesses interest for beautiful serpentine

BLACKHEATH, a hamlet, five chapelries, and a hundred in Kent The hamlet is in the parishes of Greenwich, Lewisham, Lee, and Charlton, lies on Watling street and on the North Kent railway, adjacent to Greenwich Park, 6 miles ESE of London Bridge, and has a station on the railway, and a post office‡ under Greenwich, London, SE The village is a polling place, and has a public library, public rooms, and an excellent bath The rural tract is elevated plain, and commands very fine views Many barrows, seemingly of the British Roman period have been opened on it along the line of Watling street, and a cavern, called the Point, about 150 feet long, with four irregular chambers, supposed to have been artificially formed as a retreat during the struggles between the Saxons and the Danes occurs on the ascent above Greenwich Park The vicinity of the tract to London occasioned it to be the scene of some memorable transactions, and its freedom from damp and smoke has long made it a favourite resort of London citizens The Danes encamped here in 1011 Wat Tyler, at the head of 100,000 followers, encamped here in 1381 Henry IV met the Emperor Paleologus here in 1400 Henry V was welcomed here, with great pomp, by the London magistrates and chief citizens, in 1415 on his return from Agincourt The Emperor Sigismund was received here by Henry in 1416, and conducted hence in state to Lambeth Jack Cade raised his banner here, on one of the old barrows, in 1450 Henry VI encamped here in 1452, to oppose the Duke of York Edward IV was received here by the London citizens, in 1471, on his coming from France Lord Audley, with his Cornish troops, took post here in 1497, and was beaten by the Earl of Oxford Cardinal Campejo, the papal legate was met here, in 1519 by the Duke of Norfolk And Henry VIII met here Anne of Cleves, in 1539 and conducted her hence to Greenwich Palace Two other famous scenes here are depicted by Shakspeare and Sir Walter Scott Montague House, the residence of Queen Caroline, stood here but has been demolished Brunswick House the ... of Lord Chesterfield, afterwards occupied by the Duchess of Brunswick, and Lord Lyttleton's Villa, the residence of General Wolfe, are adjacent to Greenwich Park ... houses called the Bastile and the Mince Pie House, built by Sir John Vanbrugh, are on Maze hill Morden college founded in 1695 by Sir John Morden, for decayed merchants, a brick quadrangle and considerable grounds, and now supporting upwards of 70 inmates, is on the S side A grammar school founded and endowed in 1652 by the Rev Abraham Colfe, is within Lewisham Park Lodge was once the residence of the Princess Sophia of Gloucester, and is now occupied by Prince Arthur —The chapelries are St. John All Saints Blackheath Park, St Germans, and Dartmouth, the last annexed to Lewisham vicarage, the others, separate charges Value of All Saints, £300, of the others, not reported. Patron of St John, W Angerstein, Esq, of All Saints the Vicar of Lewisham, of Blackheath Park, J Cator, Esq There are chapels for Independents and Wesleyans, a large proprietary school and a natural history society —The hundred is in the lathe of Sutton at-Hone, and contains the parishes of Lee, Lewisham, Charlton, and Eltham Acres, 16,206 Pop in 1851, 121,753, in 1861, 157,696 Houses, 26,559

BLACKHEATH, a hundred in Surrey, cut into two divisions, first and second The first division contains Alford parish and six other parishes Acres, 20 910 The second division contains Albury parish and three other parishes. Acres, 23,722. Pop of both, 10,473 Houses 2,059

BLACK HEATH, a wild open tract in the centre of Wilts, immediately S of the Ridge way and in the northern part of Salisbury plain, SE of Market Lavington

BLACKHEDDON a township in Stamfordham parish, Northumberland, on an affluent of the river Blyth, 11 miles SW of Morpeth Acres, 1,019 Pop, 63

BLACKHILL, a village in Lanchester parish, Durham, 1 mile W of Shotley Bridge It has a post office under Gateshead, a large saw-mill, a large forge, two Methodist chapels, and a Roman Catholic chapel

BLACKHOW-TOPPING, an eminence among the eastern moors of N R Yorkshire, near the Pickering and Whitby railway, 9 miles NE by N of Pickering Here are numerous tumuli and other ancient works

BLACKLAND, a parish in Calne district, Wilts, near the Roman road, 1½ mile SE of Calne r station, and 7 ESE of Chippenham Post town, Calne, under Chippenham Acres, 637 Real property £1,004 Pop, 54 Houses, 12 The property is divided among a few Blackland House was formerly the seat of the Maundrells, and is now the seat of the Fenners The living is a rectory in the diocese of Salisbury Value £160 Patron the Rev James Mayo The church was repaired in 1853

BLACKLAND, a tything in Calne parish, Wilts, within Calne borough

BLACK LANE, a station on the Bolton and Rochdale railway Lancashire 3 miles W by S of Bury

BLACK LEAD MINE MOUNTAIN See BORROWDALE Cumberland

BLACKLEY, a village, two chapelries and a sub district in Manchester parish and district, Lancashire The village stands on the river Irk, near the Manchester and Leeds railway, 3 miles N of Manchester and has a post-office under Manchester, and a police station The chapelries are B and B-St Andrew Acres, 1,7.. Real property, £10,955 Pop, 4 112 Houses 833 The property is subdivided Many of the inhabitants are employed in cotton manufactures and in extensive dye works The livings are rectories Value of B £152 P church was rebuilt in 1833, and is in the early English style, with a fine tower St A church was built in 1866 There are two Wesleyan chapels a Roman Catholic chapel a mechanics institution, a Church institute, public schools, and a reformatory —The sub district includes also Harpurhey township

BLACKLOW HILL, a small wooded eminence, near Guy's Cliff, 1½ mile N of Warwick A stone cross on it commemorates that Piers Gaveston, Earl of Cornwall, the minion of Edward II, was beheaded here in 1312 The hill commands a delightful and diversified view

BLACKMANSTONE a parish in Romney Marsh district, Kent, 5 miles ESE of Hamstreet r station Post town, New Romney Acres, 293 Real property, £52. Pop, 8 Houses, 2 The living is a rectory in the diocese of Canterbury Value, £44 Patron, the Archbishop

BLACKMILL, a village in Glamorgan, 5½ miles WNW of Llantrissant It has a post office under Bridgend

BLACKMOOR a chapelry in Selborne parish, Hants, constituted in 1867 Pop 448 Living, a p curacy Value, £180 Patron, Sir R Palmer

BLACKMOOR, Hereford See BLAKEMERE

BLACKMOOR FOOT, a hamlet in Leathwaite township, Almondbury parish, W R. Yorkshire, in the vicinity of Huddersfield.

BLACKMOOR VALE, the valley of the Cale river, on the mutual border of Somerset and Dorset, south south eastward from Wincanton toward Sturminster It is flanked by hill ranges, often 4 miles asunder, and has a rich tenacious, marshy soil, notable as pasture land, and for the vigorous growth of oaks. It was originally called White Hart forest, from an incident in a hunt by Henry III

BLACKMORE, a tything in Melksham parish, Wilts, 2 miles NE of Melksham Pop., 279

BLACKMORE, a parish in Ongar district Essex 3½ miles ESE of Chipping Ongar r station, and 4 NW by W of Ingatestone It has a post office under Ingatestone, and a fair on 21 Aug Acres, 2,576 Real property, £4,802. Pop, 644 Houses, 144 The property is divided among a few An Augustinian priory was founded on the site of the manor house, by the De Sampfords, in the time of Henry II, passed, under Cardinal Wolsey, to his colleges at Oxford and Ipswich, and afterwards to Waltham abbey, and was given, at the dissolution, to John Smith The living is a vicarage in the diocese of Rochester Value, £83 Patrons, the Representatives of the late C A Crickett, Esq The church belonged to the priory, and is ancient, small, and good Charities, £54

BLACK MOUNTAINS, a wild, high mountain ridge on the E border of Brecknock, extending 16 miles southward from the valley of the Wye near Hay to the valley of the Usk below Crickhowel Its highest point is Pen Cador Fawr, 2,545 feet high, 4½ miles SE of Talgarth.

BLACK NOTLEY See NOTLEY (BLACK)

BLACK PARK, a township in Whitchurch parish, Salop, 2 miles NE of Whitchurch Pop 97

BLACKPILL, a locality on the coast of Glamorgan, on the W side of Swansea bay, 2 miles N of Mumbles. It has a post office under Swansea, and a r station.

BLACK PILL See PWLL DDU

BLACKPITS, a village 3 miles from Rochdale, in Lancashire It has a post office under Rochdale, several large mills, and a national school

BLACKPOOL a small village on the coast of Devon, 3 miles SSW of Dartmouth

BLACKPOOL, a town and a par chapelry in Bispham parish, Lancashire The town is in Layton with Warbreck township, and stands on the coast, at the termini of two branch railways, from Poulton st and from Lytham, 18 miles WNW of Preston It was not long ago an obscure place, but is now a fashionable watering resort It stands on a ridge of low clay cliffs, overlooks a fine bathing beach, provided with machines, commands charming views, along the coast and across the sea, to Wales and the Lake district, and consists of well built houses, ranged in an irregular terrace about two miles long It has a post office under Preston, a telegraph, a police station, a number of hotels, a newsroom, a library, an athenæum, a theatre three churches five dissenting chapels, and a R Catholic chapel The church of the chapelry was built in 1821, and has been twice enlarged The other two churches are recent ones, for the South shore and Claremont Park parts of the town beyond the chapelry The R Catholic chapel is a handsome Gothic edifice The ruin of a mansion, the seat of Sir Thomas Tyldesley and the retreat of the Pretender in 1715 while the measures were in progress for the rebellion, stood at the west end of the town A handsome pier, upwards of 500 yards long, was built in 1863 Pop of the town in 1851, 1,664, in 1861, 3,506 Houses, 634 The chapelry was constituted in 1860 Pop, 1,957 Houses, 387 The living is a vicarage in the diocese of Manchester Value, £340 * Patrons, Five Trustees Southshore and Claremont Park or Christchurch are p curacies Value of the former, £200 Patron, Col Clifton

BLACK PRINCE'S CHANTRY See CANTERBURY

BLACKRAKE, a hamlet in Carlton Highdale township, N R Yorkshire, 7 miles SW of Middleham

BLACKROCK, a ferry station on the river Severn, near Portskewet r station, 4 miles SW of Chepstow, in Monmouth There is an inn here, and the width of the ferry, at full tide, is about 2½ miles

BLACK ROCK, a reef in the mouth of the Mersey, 3 miles NNW of Liverpool A lighthouse stands on it, a round white tower, built in 1830 at the cost of £35,000, with a revolving minute light, twice bright and once red, 88 feet high, showing also a fixed light at a lower elevation when there is 12 feet water in the channel

BLACKROCK, a locality 7 miles from Abergavenny in Monmouth, with a post office under Abergavenny

BLACKROD, a village and a township chapelry in Bolton le Moors parish Lancashire The village stands on elevated ground near the river Douglas and the Bolton and Preston railway, 4½ miles SSE of Chorley, and it has a joint station with Horwich on the railway, and a post office of its own under Chorley Its site is supposed to have been occupied by the Roman station Coccium, on Watling street, and many Roman relics have been found The chapelry comprises 2,367 acres Real property, £14,264, of which £7,711 are in mines Pop, 2 911 Houses, 546 The property is not much divided. The inhabitants are chiefly cotton spinners and colliers A fire in a colliery here was extinguished by drawing into it the river Douglas The living is a vicarage in the diocese of Manchester Value, £400 * Patron, the Vicar of Bolton The church is good, and there is a Wesleyan chapel A free grammar school has £140 a year, besides sums for three exhibitions at Pembroke college, Cambridge, and other charities have £101

BLACK SAIL a foot pass from Wastdale Head, up Mosedale, to the head of Ennerdale, in Cumberland

BLACKSLADE, a hamlet in the parish of Widecombe in the Moor, Devon

BLACKSOLE See WROTHAM

BLACKSTAKES, a roadstead in the river Medway, above Sheerness, in Kent It has from 3 to 5 fathoms water, and is used by wind bound ships

BLACKSTONE, a hamlet in Kidderminster Foreign, Worcester, on the river Severn, 2 miles below Bewdley A picturesque range of cliffs, called the Blackstone rocks, here flanks the Severn

BLACKSTONE EDGE, a range of high hills, along the mutual border of Lancashire and Yorkshire, 6 miles ENE of Rochdale

BLACKTAIL, a shoal, with a beacon, on the coast of Essex, extending off, from the mouth of the Thames, past Shoeburyness to the Maplin sand.

BLACKTHORN, a hamlet in Ambrosden parish, Oxford, on Akeman street, 3 miles SE by E of Bicester It has a post office under Bicester Acres, 2,280 Real property, £3 108 Pop, 376 Houses 83

BLACKTOFT, a township and a parish in Howden district, E R Yorkshire The township lies on the river Ouse, nearly opposite the influx of the Trent, 3 miles S by E of Staddlethorpe r station, and 7 ESE of Howden, and it includes the hamlet of Staddlethorpe, and has a post office under Howden Real property, £3,280 Pop, 120 Houses, 80 The parish contains also the township of Scalby Acres, 3,813 Real property, £4,733 Pop, 534 Houses, 107 The property is divided among a few The living is a vicarage in the diocese of York Value, £220 * Patrons, the Dean and Chapter of Durham The church is very good

BLACK TOR, a rocky hill in Dartmoor forest, Devon, 6½ miles ESE of Tavistock It has a picturesque appearance, and overhangs an ancient British town.

BLACK TORRINGTON See TORRINGTON (BLACK)

BLACKWALL, a hamlet in Poplar parish and Tower Hamlets borough, Middlesex, on the Thames, at the influx of the Lea, 4½ miles E of St Paul's A railway goes to it from Fenchurch street, is 4 miles long, runs 4,464 yards on viaduct, has stations at Chadwell, Stepney, Limehouse, the West India docks, and Poplar, and sends off a junction line, through Bow common to the Eastern Counties railway Blackwall contains the West India docks, opened in 1802, the East India docks, opened in 1803, and the Brunswick wharf for packets, opened in 1840,—all splendid works, replete with interest, and it carries on a vast amount of iron ship building amid accompaniments which strike a stranger with astonishment The Blackwall reach of the Thames, extending down the E side of the Isle of Dogs to the mouth of the Lea, has a depth of from 13 to 23 feet, and is encumbered with a shelf in the upper part, with shoals off the West India docks and at Leaness, and with one or two shifting shoals See LONDON

BLACKWATER (THE), a river of Essex It rises 3 miles ESE of Saffron Walden, and runs past Braintree Coggeshall, Witham, and Maldon, to the North sea at Mersea island It makes great folds in its course yet goes prevailingly south eastward to Braintree, east by south ward thence to Coggleshall, southward thence to Maldon and east by northward thence to the sea Its length is about 40 miles, and its last reach, below Maldon, to the length of 10 miles, is estuary of the mean width of 1¾ mile It bears the name of the Pant for some distance below its source, and it receives the Chelmer at Maldon

BLACKWATER (THE), a river of Dorset and Hants It rises near Cranborne, in Dorset, and runs 15 miles south south eastward to the Stour, a little above Christ church, in Hants.

BLACKWATER (THE) a river of Surrey, Hants, and Berks It rises near Farnham, traces the boundary first between Surrey and Hants, then between Hants and Berks, and goes altogether about 18 miles northward and west north westward to the Loddon near Swallow field

BLACKWATER, a village on the SW border of Hants, on the Blackwater river, 2 miles NW of Christchurch The seat of the Earl of Malmesbury, a fine mansion possessing valuable paintings, is adjacent

BLACKWATER, a village in Yateley parish, on the NE border of Hants, on the Blackwater river, adjacent to the Reading branch of the South Eastern railway, 3½ miles NNW of Farnborough station It has a station on the railway, a post office under Farnborough station, and a Baptist chapel Sandhurst and Wellington colleges are in the vicinity

BLACKWATER, a hamlet in the Isle of Wight, 2 miles S by E of Newport It has a post office under Newport

BLACKWEIR, a locality 1½ mile from Cardiff, in Glamorgan with a post office under Cardiff

BLACKWELL, a parish and a sub-district in the district of Mansfeld and county of Derby The parish lies on the verge of the county, 2½ miles NE of Alfreton r station Post town, Normanton, under Alfreton Acres, 1,700 Real property, £2,705, of which £400 are in mines Pop, 517 Houses, 101 The property is divided among a few, and coal is worked The living is a vicarage in the diocese of Lichfield Value, £90 Patron the Duke of Devonshire. The church was built in 1826 There are a P Methodist chapel and an endowed school —The sub dis. comprises four parishes Pop, 4 552

BLACKWELL, a township in Bakewell parish, Derby, on the river Wye, 3½ miles SW of Tideswell Acres 1 071 Real property £921 Pop, 37 Houses, 7

BLACKWELL, a township in Darlington parish Durham, on the river Tees, near the Croftbridge railway 1½ mile SW by S of Darlington Acres, 1,479 Real property, £3 578 Pop, 336 Houses, 62 Blackwell Grange is the seat of the Allan family and was the death place of George Allan, the antiquary There is a Wesleyan chapel

BLACKWELL a hamlet in Tredington parish, Worcester, adjacent to the Moreton and Stratford on Avon railway, 2½ miles NW by N of Shipston upon Stour Real property £1 272 Pop, 20. Houses 51

BLACKWELL a station on the Birmingham and Bristol railway, 2 miles NE of Bromsgrove station

BLACKWELL (HIGH and LOW) two townships in St Cuthbert parish Cumberland, near the Carlisle and Lancaster railway, 2½ and 2 miles S of Carlisle Acres. 2 459 and 941 Real property, £4 801 and £2,329 Pop, 341 and 183 Houses, 59 and 34 The manor was given, in the time of Edward III, by the heiress of Sir John le Wigton, to Sir Robert Parvinge

BLACKWOOD, a village in the W of Monmouth 16 miles NW of Newport It has a post-office‡ under Newport, Monmouth, and a r station with telegraph

BLACKWOOD AND CROWBOROUGH, a township in Horton parish, Stafford, 4 miles W of Leek Real property £2 996 Pop, 590 Houses, 122

BLACKWORTH See BACKWORTH

BLACON CUM CRABHALL, a township in the parishes of Holy Trinity, St Oswald, and Backford, Cheshire, near the Ellesmere canal and the Chester and Holyhead railway, 2 miles WNW of Chester Acres, 1,115 Real property, £1 927 Pop, 69 Houses, 13

BLACON HILL, a hill 4½ miles SE of Dawtry, in Notts It has vestiges of a Danish camp

BLADINGTON See BLEDINGTON

BLADON, a village and a parish in Woodstock district Oxford The village stands adjacent to the S end of Blenheim Park, 1½ mile ENE of Handborough r station, and 2 S of Woodstock and it has a post office under Woodstock Pop, 395 Houses, 87 The parish includes also the hamlet of Hensington Acres, 1 350 Real property, £2,857 Pop, 665 Houses, 128 The manor belongs to the Duke of Marlborough The living is a rectory, united with the p curacy of Woodstock, in the diocese of Oxford Value, £329 * Patron, the Duke of Marlborough The church was built in 1804, was remodelled and enlarged in 1862, and is in a very early pointed style There are two Methodist chapels, a mixed school, and charities £231 Dr Griffith, who defended Basing House, was rector

BLAEN, a prefix of Welsh names, signifying "the upper part," "the end," "the extremity," "the point"

BLAEN AERON, a township in Caron ys Clawdd parish, Cardigan, 4 miles NE of Tregaron Real property, £834 Pop, 276 Houses, 54 Here are two dissenting chapels

BLAENAN, a hamlet in Llanfihangel Ar Arth parish, Carmarthen, 10 miles SW of Lampeter

BLAENAU See BRAENEY

BLAENAVON, a village, a chapelry, and a sub district in the district of Abergavenny, Monmouth The village stands on the Avon Llwyd river, at the terminus of the Eastern Valleys railway 6 miles NNW of Pontypool, and it has a post office‡ under Pontypool Extensive iron works and iron mines are adjacent, the former begun in 1790, the latter worked by horizontal shafts The chapelry includes the village, comprises parts of the parishes of Llanover, Llanfoist, and Llanwenarth, and was constituted in 1860 Pop 5 876 Houses, 1,105 The living is a p curacy in the diocese of Llandaff, and since 1864 has included Capel Newydd Value, £290 * Patron Thomas Hill, Esq There are two Baptist chapels.—The sub district also comprises parts of three parishes Acres, 7,988 Pop, 7 114 Houses, 1,376

BLAEN CARON, a township in Caron ys-Clawdd parish, Cardigan, in the vicinity of Tregaron Pop, 99 Houses 23

BLAENGILLSYRCH, a township in Llanwrin parish, Montgomery, near the river Dovey, 2 miles N of Machynlleth

BLAEN CWENT See ABERYSTWITH

BLAENGWRACH a chapelry in Glyncorrwg parish, Glamorgan, in the Vale of Neath, on the Vale of Neath railway at Glyn Neath station, 9 miles NE of Neath Post town, Glyn Neath under Neath Acres 3 031 Real property £820 Pop, 250 Houses, 55 The scenery is fine Aberpergwm is a chief residence Many of the inhabitants are employed in copper and iron mines The living is a p curacy, annexed to the p curacy of Glyncorrwg, in the diocese of Llandaff There is an Independent chapel Dr A Rees, the author of the "Cyclopedia" was a native

BLAENHONDDAN, a hamlet in Cadoxton parish,

Glamorgan, in the Vale of Neath, 2½ miles NE of Neath It includes the village of Cadoxton Real property, £11,461, of which £6,550 are in mines, and £200 in iron works Pop, 1,661 Houses, 311 The inhabitants are chiefly employed in copper mines

BLAENLLYNFI, a quondam borough town in Cathedine parish, Brecon, near Llynsavaddan lake, 7½ miles NW of Crickhowel Remains stand here, low broken walls and a deep fosse, of a castle which is thought to have been the residence of Prince Hwgan earl, in the 10th century, and was afterwards the seat of the Norman lord of Welsh Talgarth

BLAENPLNAL, or LLANPENAL, a chapelry in Llanddewy Brefi parish, Cardigan, on the river Aeron 4 miles NW of Tregaron r station, and 26 SW of Llanidloes. Post town, Tregaron, under Carmarthen Acres, 4,105 Real property, £1,115 Pop, 522 Houses, 107 The property is much subdivided The living is a p. curacy in the diocese of St David's Value, £84 Patrons, the Earl of Lisburne and R Price, Esq The church is good

BLAENPORTH, a parish in the district and county of Cardigan, on the coast 6 miles NW by N of Newcastle Emlyn r station It includes part of the village of Aberporth, which has a post office under Cardigan Acres, 3,518, of which 30 are water Real property, £2 017 Pop, 732 Houses, 180 The property is much subdivided Traces of two ancient camps are on the coast, and a mound represents a castle of great strength, thought to have been built by Gilbert Earl of Clare, and which was besieged and taken in 1116 by Gryffydd ap Rhys, and afterwards demolished There is a mineral spring The living is a vicarage in the diocese of St. David's Value, £37 * Patron, alternately the Earl of Lisburne and J V Lloyd, Esq The church is very bad

BLAENSAWTHE, or BLAENSAWDDE, a hamlet in Llanddeusaint parish, Carmarthen, under the Black Mountains, 7½ miles S by E of Llandovery Real property, £758 Pop, 214

BLAEN Y FFOS, a locality 6 miles from Cardigan, with a post office under Cardigan

BLAGDON, a tything in Cranborne parish Dorset, 3½ miles N of Cranborne Pop, 36

BLAGDON, a township in Stannington parish, Northumberland, near the river Blyth and the North eastern railway, 7 miles S of Morpeth It was held, in the time of Henry III, by John de Plessis, passed in 1567, to the Fenwicks, and afterwards to the Whites, and now contains Blagdon Park, the seat of Sir M. W Ridley, Bart

BLAGDON, a hamlet in Paington parish, Devon, 5 miles E by N of Totnes

BLAGDON, a tything in Pitminster parish, Somerset, 3½ miles S of Taunton It has a post office under Taunton

BLAGDON, a parish and a sub district in Axbridge district, Somerset The parish lies under the Mendip hills 6 miles NE by E of Axbridge, and 7 SE of Yatton r station, and has a post office, of the name of Blagdon Somerset and a fair on the last Friday of Aug Acres, 3,595 Real property, £6,649 Pop, 1,089 Houses, 233 The property is subdivided Some ruins at Reghillbury are said to be remains of an ancient palace Lapis calaminaris is found The living is a rectory in the diocese of Bath and Wells Value, £512 * Patron, W Fripp, Esq The church is modern and there is a Methodist chapel An endowed school has £18 a year, and other charities £21 Dr John Langhorne was rector —The sub district comprises seven parishes and a ville Acres, 22,1,6 Pop 5,620 Houses 1,176

BLAGDON HILL See BLACK DOWN, Dorset

BLAGRAVE, a tything in Lambourn parish, Berks, in the vicinity of Lambourn Pop, 196 Houses, 39

BLAGUE GATE, a station on the St Helen's and Ormskirk railway, Lancashire, between Rainford Junction and Ormskirk

BLAIDES, a hamlet in Melbecks township, Grinton parish, N R Yorkshire, 4½ miles W of Reeth

BLAINA, a village, with iron works, in Ebbw Vale, Monmouth, on the Western Valleys railway, 2 miles SSE of Nantyglo It has a station on the railway, and a post office‡ under Tredegar A church in the Norman style, was built here in 1845 The circumjacent tract of country is highly picturesque

BLAINEY WITH DUFFRYN, a parcel in Llangunider parish, Brecon, 4½ miles WNW of Crickhowel Real property, £5,985, of which £1,356 are in quarries Pop, 3,045 Houses, 635

BLAISDON, a parish in Westbury on Severn district, Gloucester, on the Gloucester and Hereford railway, 2 miles SE of Longhope station, and 4 N of Newnham Post town, Longhope, under Newnham Acres, 900 Real property, £1,656 Pop, 282 Houses, 58 The property is divided among a few The living is a rectory in the diocese of Gloucester and Bristol Value, not reported * Patron, H Crawshay, Esq The church is early English There is a national school

BLAISE CASTLE, the seat of J S Harford, Esq, in Henbury parish, Gloucester, in a picturesque limestone ravine 4 miles NNW of Bristol The house is modern, and contains a fine collection of pictures The grounds are beautiful both naturally and artificially, and have a lofty tower which commands a brilliant view across the Severn into Wales

BLAKE FELL, a lofty broad based mountain, between Ennerdale lake and Lowes water, in Cumberland

BLAKEHALL, a r station 1¾ mile S of Ongar, in Essex

BLAKELLY See BLACKLEY

BLAKEMERE, or BLACKMOOR, a parish in Weobley district, Herefordshire, adjacent to the river Wye and to the Hereford and Brecon railway, 2¾ miles SW of Moorhampton station, and 10 W by N of Hereford Post town, Peterchurch, under Hereford Acres, 1,127 Real property £1,450 Pop, 175 Houses, 36 The property is subdivided The living is a vicarage, annexed to the vicarage of Preston on Wye, in the diocese of Hereford The church is good

BLAKEMORE VALE See BLACKMOOR VALE

BLAKENEY a chapelry in Awre parish, Gloucester, on the W side of the Severn and on the South Wales railway, near Gatcombe station, and 3½ miles S by W of Newnham It has a post office‡ under Newnham, and fairs on 12 May and 12 Nov Real property, £4,159 Pop, 1,079 Houses, 211 The living is a vicarage in the dio of G and B Value, £232 Patrons, the Haberdashers' Company The church is modern There are Independent and Baptist chapels and two public schools

BLAKENEY, a small seaport and a parish in Walsingham district Norfolk. The seaport stands on a natural harbour of its own name, 5½ miles NNW of Holt, and 7¼ E of Wells r station, and has a post-office under Thetford. It was anciently called Snitterley, and it got the right to a market in the time of Henry III A Carmelite monastery was founded at it about 1295, and given, at the dissolution, to William Rede, and some remains of the edifice, including several fine arches, are still standing John de Baconsthorpe who was styled "the resolute and subtle doctor," held a place in the monastery and rose to be head of the English Carmelites The parish church, on an eminence a little S of the town, is a curious flint structure, in early and in later English, has a lofty embattled tower which serves as a mark to mariners in taking the harbour, and contains a fine ancient font, three sedilia, and remains of a screen and stalls There are chapels for Baptists and Methodists. The harbour has a dangerous shifting bar, yet serves well both for commerce and for shelter About 60 vessels, aggregately nearly 4,000 tons, belong to the port The chief export is corn the chief imports are coal, timber, iron, hemp, tar and tallow, and a considerable fishery is carried on —The parish comprises 1 865 acres, of which 235 are water Real property, £3 260 Pop 961 Houses, 264 The property is not much divided The living is a rectory, united with the p curacy of Glandford and the rectory of Cockthorpe in the diocese of Norwich Value £506 * Patron, Lord Calthorpe

BLAKENHALL, or BLACKENHALL, a township in Wybunbury parish, Cheshire, near the Northwestern railway, 5½ miles S by E of Crewe Acres 1,541 Real property £2,201 Pop, 236 Houses 32

BLAKENHAM (GREAT), a parish in Bosmere district, Suffolk, on the river Gipping, and on the Eastern Union railway ½ a mile NNW of Claydon station, and 3½ SSE of Needham Market. It has a post office under Ipswich Acres, 869 Real property, £1,759 Pop 291 Houses, 57 The manor belonged to the abbey of Bec in Normandy, and passed, in the time of Henry VI, to Eton college The living is a rectory in the diocese of Norwich Value, £166 Patron, Eton college The church is good, and there is a Baptist chapel

BLAKENHAM (LITTLE), a parish in Bosmere district, Suffolk, 1¾ mile WSW of Claydon r station and 4¾ miles S by E of Needham Market Post town, Great Blakenham under Ipswich Acres, 1 054 Real property, £1 633 Pop 146 Houses, 34 The property is divided among a few The living is a rectory in the diocese of Norwich Value £280 * Patron, the Rev J Jackson. The church is good

BLAKESALL, a hamlet in Wolverley parish, Worcester, 3½ miles N of Kidderminster

BLAKESLEY, a village and a parish in Towcester district, Northampton The village stands 4½ miles W by N of Towcester r station, and 6 S of Weedon, and has a post office under Towcester Pop, 523 Houses, 108 —The parish includes also the hamlet of Woodend and part of the hamlet of Foxley Acres, 2,840 Real property, £7,318 Pop, 777 Houses, 195 The property is much subdivided Blakesley Hall belonged anciently to the Knights of St. John, and is now the seat of J W Wight, Esq The living is a vicarage in the diocese of Peterborough Value, £170 * Patron, J W Wight, Esq The church contains a brass of 1416 and is good. There are two Baptist chapels, a free school for boys, and charities £242

BLAKESTONE. See BLAXTON

BLAKEWELL, a hamlet in Chittlehampton parish, Devon, about a mile from Chittlehampton village It has a chapel for Bible Christians.

BLAKEWELL a hamlet in Marwood parish, Devon

BLANANLLYN, a village in Kilrhedin parish, Carmarthen 4½ miles S of Newcastle Emlyn

BLANCHLAND a village and a township chapelry in Shotley parish, Northumberland The village stands in a deep narrow green vale, flanked by heathy hills, on the N side of Derwent river 6 miles SSW of Riding Mill r station, and 9 SSE of Hexham, and has a post office‡ under Carlisle, and a fair on 24 Aug A premonstratensian abbey was founded here, in 1165, by Walter de Bolbeck, raised to the rank of a mitred abbey in the time of Edward I, given, at the dissolution, to John Bellow and John Broxholm, passed, by purchase, to Bishop Crewe, and was bequeathed by him, along with other estates, for charitable purposes The tower of it was formed in 1752 into a chapel, which continues to be the church of the chapelry and the gateway and some other parts also are still standing —The chapelry or township bears also the name of Shotley High Quarter, and comprises 3,728 acres Rated property, £535 Pop, 474 Houses 95 Much of the surface is moor and morass. Lead ore occurs in considerable abundance, and has long been mined The living is a p curacy in the diocese of Durham Value, £193 * Patron, the Trustees of Bishop Lord Crewe

BLAND, a hamlet in the township and parish of Sedbergh W R Yorkshire

BLANDFORD, a sub district, a district and a division in Dorset The sub district contains the parishes of Blandford Forum, Blandford St Mary, Bryanstone, Langton Long Blandford Tarrant Crawford Tarrant Keynston, Durweston, Stourpaine Stepleton Iwerne, Iwerne Courtney, Pimperne, Tarrant Gunville Tarrant Hinton Tarrant Launceston Tarrant Monkton, Tarrant Rawston and Tarrant Rushton and the extra parochial tract of Hinford Acres 31,530 Pop 8 542 Houses 1,697 The district includes also the sub district of Milton Abbas, containing the parishes of Milton Abbas Turnworth, Hilton, Stickland Winterborne, Houghton Winterborne, Milborne St Andrew, Winterborne Clenstone, Winterborne Whitechurch, Winterborne Kingston, Winterborne Thomson, Winterborne-Zelstone Anderson, Almer, Spetisbury, and Charlton Marshall, and part of Bere Regis Acres of the district, 57,731 Poor-rates in 1866, £10,152 Pop. in 1861, 14,827 Houses, 2,878 Marriages in 1866, 91, births, 447 —of which 34 were illegitimate, deaths, 297,—of which 92 were at ages under 5 years, and 13 at ages above 85 years Marriages in the ten years 1851–60, 993, births, 4,314, deaths, 2,550 The places of worship in 1851, were 33 of the Church of England, with 7,773 sittings, 7 of Independents, with 1,801 s, 9 of Wesleyan Methodists, with 1,048 s, 4 of Primitive Methodists, with 280 s, and 1 of Roman Catholics, with 200 s. The schools were 26 public day schools, with 1 895 scholars 29 private day schools, with 789 s, 37 Sunday schools with 2 361 s, and 2 evening schools for adults, with 23 s The workhouse is in Blandford Forum, and was erected at a cost of £1,200 —The division contains the hundreds of Cogdean and Rushmore, parts of the hundreds of Bere Regis, Coombs Ditch Cranborne, Loosebarrow, Monckton up Wimborne, Piddletown, Pimperne, and Whiteway, and part of the liberty of Dewlish Acres, 51 373 Pop, 12,211 Houses 2,265 Blandford gives the title of Marquis to the Duke of Marlborough

BLANDFORD FORUM, or CHIPPING BLANDFORD, a town and a parish in Blandford district Dorset. The town stands on the river Stour, and on the Dorset Central railway, 10 miles NW by W of Wimborne Minster It dates from remote times, but was damaged by arms in the civil war, and by fire in 1579, 1677, 1684, 1713, and 1731,—suffering in the last of these years a demolition of all its houses except forty, and it now presents as modern and sprightly an appearance as any town in the county It comprises two main streets, meeting in a spacious market place, and consists chiefly of red brick houses, with high roofs and ornamented fronts The town hall is a handsome edifice of Portland stone with Doric columns and entablature The corn exchange was built in 1855 and is a commodious structure The chief bridge across the Stour is a substantial structure of six arches The parish church built after the fire of 1731, is a handsome Grecian edifice, with a tower A pump, under a portico, adjacent to the church, was erected in 1760, as a memorial of the fire The Independent chapel was built in 1868, and is in the early English style A high roofed ancient mansion, near the parish church, is the only existing house which dates prior to 1731 A farm house in the outskirts beyond East street, includes remains of Damorey Court, the seat in the time of Edward II, of Roger D Amorie, constable of Corfe Castle Bryanstone Park, the seat of Lord Portman terminates one of the streets The town has a head post office‡ of the name of Blandford, a railway station, two banking offices, three chief inns, two dissenting chapels, five endowed schools, almshouses, and charities, including the schools and the almshouses to the yearly amount of £1,085 A weekly market is held on Saturday, and fairs on 7 March, 10 July, and 8 Nov The manufacture of very fine point lace was formerly carried on and was followed by a manufacture of shirt buttons The town is a borough by prescription, but sent members to parliament only under Edward I and Edward III it was incorporated by James I, and is now governed by a mayor or bailiff, four aldermen, and twelve councillors, and it is a seat of petty sessions and a polling place Pop of the borough, 1,521 Houses, 296 —The parish comprises 862 acres Real property, £5 937 Pop 3 900 Houses, 731 The living is a rectory and a vicarage in the diocese of Salisbury Value, £300 * Patrons the Dean and Chapter of Winchester Archbishop Wake Archbishop Lindsay, Bishop Lisle, Dean Ryves, Creech Pitt, and Bastard the poets, Sagittary the physician, L Wake the founder of the corporation of the sons of the clergy, and John A. James the author of the "Anxious Inquirer, were natives. Races were formerly run, but have been discontinued.

BLANDFORD PARK, the seat of Lord Churchill in Oxford, adjacent to the Oxford and Worcester railway, 6 miles WNW of Woodstock It belonged to the first Lord Clarendon, and was then called Cornbury Park. The Earl of Leicester, the favourite of Queen Elizabeth, died at it

BLANDFORD ST MARY, a parish in Blandford district, Dorset, on the river Stour, adjacent to the Dorset Central railway, ½ a mile S of Blandford Forum It has a post-office under Blandford Acres, 1,583 Real property, £2 747 Pop 409 Houses, 77 The property is divided among a few The living is a rectory in the diocese of Salisbury Value, £313 * Patron, Worcester College, Oxford The church was built by Governor Pitt, grandfather of the great Earl, and contains several monuments of his family Dr Brown Willis, the antiquary, was a native

BLANKNEY, a parish in Sleaford district, Lincoln, 6 miles SW of Stixwould r station, and 9 N of Sleaford It includes the hamlet of Linwood and has a post-office under Sleaford Acres, 6,000 Real property, £7,324 Pop, 560 Houses, 90 The property is divided among a few Blankney Hall is the seat of H Chaplin, Esq Much of the surface was formerly a waste, over which travellers were guided by the Dunston pillar, but is now good turnip land. The living is a rectory in the diocese of Lincoln Value, £821 * Patron, H Chaplin, Esq The church is good, and there is a national school.

BLASKENWELL a tything in Corfe Castle parish, Dorset, in the vicinity of Corfe Castle

BLASTON, two parishes—B St Giles and B St. Michael—in the district of Uppingham and county of Leicester, 3 miles N of Medbourne Bridge r station, and 5½ W by S of Uppingham Post town Hallaton, under Uppingham Acres, 1,267 Real property, £2 404 Pop of B St Giles, 25 Houses, 6. Pop of B St Michael, 63 Houses, 15 The property is subdivided B. St Giles is a donative rectory in the diocese of Peterborough Value, £213 Patron, the Rev G O Fenwicke. The church is good B St Michael is a p curacy, annexed to the rectory of Hallaton Charities, £10

BLATCHINGTON, or BLETCHINGTON (EAST), a parish in Lewes district, Sussex, on the Newhaven branch of the South Coast railway, and on the coast, 1 mile NNW of Seaford Post town, Seaford, under Lewes Acres, 821, of which 66 are water Real property, £1,004 Pop, 128 Houses, 28. The property is divided among a few A strong battery is here for the defence of the coast The living is a rectory in the diocese of Chichester Value, £200 * Patron, the Rev N R Dennis The church is good.

BLATCHINGTON, or BLETCHINGTON (WEST), a parish in Steyning district, Sussex, near the South Coast railway, 2½ miles NW of Brighton Post town, Brighton Acres, 876 Real property, £805 Pop., 59 Houses, 10 The living is a rectory, annexed to the vicarage of Brighton, in the diocese of Chichester

BLATCHINWORTH, a township and a sub district in the district of Rochdale, Lancashire The township bears the name of Blatchinworth with Calderbrook lies on the Manchester and Leeds railway, 5 miles NE of Rochdale, contains seven hamlets and Littleborough village,—the last with a post office‡ under Manchester and a r station, and has romantic scenery numerous good residences, a church, five dissenting chapels, an endowed school eight cotton mills, twelve woollen mills two collieries, and rich quarries Real property, £14,551, of which £1,020 are in mines. Pop, 4 860 Houses, 980 —The sub district is conterminate with the township.

BLATHERWICK, or BLATHERWYCKE, a parish in Oundle district, Northampton on an affluent of the river Nen, 5 miles ESE of Seaton r station, and 6 NW by N of Oundle It comprises the ancient parishes of Holy Trinity and St Mary Magdalene, united in 1448, and has a post office under Wansford Acres, 1,975 Real property, £2,141 Pop., 189 Houses, 41 The property is divided among a few Blatherwick Hall is the seat of S O Brien, Esq The living is a rectory in the diocese of Peterborough Value, £394 * Patron, S O'Brien, Esq The church has a brass of Sir H Stafford, of 1548, and is good

BLAUNAY a township in Nantglyn parish, Denbighshire, 4½ miles SW of Denbigh Pop, 128

BLAWITH, a township-chapelry in Ulverston parish, Lancashire, on the river Crake, 4 miles NW of Foxfield r station, and 6½ N of Ulverston Post town, Newby Bridge, under Newton-in Cartmel Acres, 2,620 Real property, £1 032 Pop., 193 Houses, 39 The property is much subdivided. Much of the surface is upland moor The living is a p curacy in the diocese of Carlisle Value, £63. Patrons, Messrs Petty and Postlethwaite The church is an edifice of slatestone and red sandstone, in the pointed style, and was built in 1862 Charities, £10

BLAXHALL, a parish in Plomesgate district, Suffolk, on the river Alde, 2 miles NE of Wickham Market Junction r station, and 5 SSW of Saxmundham It has a post office under Wickham Market. Acres 1,975 Real property £2,746 Pop, 589 Houses, 122 The property is divided among a few The living is a rectory in the diocese of Norwich Value, £498 * Patron, the Rev A N Bates The church was restored in 1863 There are a free school, and charities £18

BLAXTON, or BLAKESTONE, a township in Finningley parish, W R. Yorkshire, 5 miles NE of Bawtry Acres, 1,640. Real property, £2,702 Pop, 153 Houses 32

BLAYDON a small town in Winlaton township and parish, Durham, on the river Tyne, and on the Newcastle and Carlisle railway, 4 miles W of Newcastle on-Tyne It was not long ago a small village, but it acquired importance from a large manufacture of articles in fire clay, and from transit communication, by river and by railway, with neighbouring iron works and collieries, and it is now a considerable, well built place, with regular streets running N and S It has a post office‡ called Blaydon on Tyne, a station with telegraph on the railway, two chief inns, a mechanics institute, a handsome church, much improved in 1869, and three Methodist chapels Axwell Park, the fine seat of Sir W A Clavering, Bart., is in the vicinity

BLAYNE, a hamlet in Llandebie parish, Carmarthen, 4½ miles S of Llandilo fawr

BLAYNEY, or BLAENYAU a parcel in Llanfihangel Cwmdû parish, Brecon, under the Black Mountains, 5½ miles NNW of Crickhowel Pop., 140

BLAZEY (ST), a small town and a parish in St. Austell district, Cornwall The town stands under an amphitheatre of wooded heights 1 mile NNW of Par r station, and 4 ENE of St Austell It took its name from Blaise, Bishop of Sebaste in Armenia, who is said to have landed at Par in the third century, and to have suffered martyrdom in 316 It has a post office‡ under Par station, and an inn, and is a centre of traffic for the neighbouring mines, and fairs are held at it on 2 Feb and 1 July The parish includes also Par harbour Acres 1 797 Real property, £28,514, of which £21,505 are in mines, and £1,0?? in canal Pop., 4,224 Houses, 876 The property is divided among a few Granite and slate are quarried, tin and iron ores are worked, and there is a large iron foundry Much scenery within the parish and in the neighbourhood is picturesque and romantic. Prideaux, the seat of Sir Coleman Rashleigh, Bart, an ancient edifice, with granite stairs, is on a height above the town and Prideaux Warren, the remains of an ancient earth work, is on an adjacent height The living is a vicarage in the diocese of Exeter Value, £120 * Patron, — Carlyon, Esq The church has an effigies of St. Blaise, and is good There are Wesleyan Methodist Primitive Methodist, and United Free Methodist chapels The vicarage of Biscovey or Par is a separate benefice R. Allen, who brought oolite stone into use was a native

BLEABERRY FELL, a mountain ridge on the E side of the upper part of Derwent water, in Cumberland

BLEABERRY TARN a lakelet, between High Stile and Red Pike, on the left flank of Buttermere vale, in Cumberland.

BLEABERRY-TARN, a lakelet on high ground, between Eskdale and Miterdale, 6½ miles NE of Ravenglass, in Cumberland

BLEADON, a parish in Axbridge district, Somerset, on the river Axe, and on the Bristol and Exeter railway, 2 miles S of Weston super Mare Junction station, and 4½ SE of Weston super Mare It includes the hamlets of Oldmixon and Shiplet, and has a post office under Weston super Mare Acres, 2,795 Real property, £6,617 Pop 623 Houses, 131 The property is subdivided Remains of an ancient British camp are on Bleadon Hill, and bones, coins, and armour have been found The living is a rectory in the diocese of Bath and Wells Value, £469 * Patron, the Bishop of Winchester The church was repaired in 1830 M Casaubon was for some time rector

BLEAN, a parish, an ancient forest, and a district, in Kent The parish is called also Blean Church St. Cosmus and St Damian in the Blean, lies on the Whitstable railway, 2 miles NW by N of Canterbury, and has a post office, of the name of Bleau, under Canterbury Acres, 2,260 Real property, £4,414 Pop, 626 Houses, 130 The property is subdivided Much of the land in the north is under coppice The living is a vicarage in the diocese of Canterbury Value, £523 Patron, Eastbridge Hospital The church is small — The forest belonged anciently to the Crown, extended from the vicinity of Herne to the vicinity of Chatham, was given away piecemeal, both before and after the Conquest, till nearly all was alienated, and lost gradually the character of a forest till it became known only as the Blean Wild boars abounded in portions of it so late as the Reformation, and the yellow pine marten is still occasionally found —The district comprehends the sub district of Herne, containing the parishes of Herne Reculver, and Chislett, the sub district of Whitstable, containing the parishes of Whitstable, Swalecliff, and Seasalter, and the sub district of Sturry containing the parishes of Sturry, Blean, Westbere, Heath, St. Dunstan, and St Stephen or Hackington the villes of St Gregory and Staplegate, and the precincts of Archbishop's Palace and Christ Church Acres, 32,221 Poor-rates in 1866, £8,099 Pop in 1861, 16,161 Houses, 3,291 Marriages in 1866 124, births 673,—of which 20 were illegitimate, deaths, 345 —of which 122 were at ages under 5 years, and 6 at ages above 85 years Marriages in the ten years 1851-60 1,048, births 5,245, deaths, 2,820 The places of worship in 1851 were 14 of the Church of England with 6,324 sittings, 3 of Independents, with 757 s, 7 of Wesleyan Methodists, with 780 s, 1 of Primitive Methodists, with 57 s, and 1 of French Protestants, with 30 s The schools were 9 public day schools, with 673 scholars, 41 private day schools, with 885 s, and 16 Sunday schools, with 1,366 s The workhouse is in Herne

BLEANGATE, a hundred in the lathe of St Augustine Kent It contains Herne parish and seven other parishes Acres, 21,231 Pop, 6,509 Houses, 1,234

BLEAN (High and Low), two hamlets in Painbridge township W R Yorkshire, 1 mile SW of Askrigg

BLEASBY, a hamlet in Legsby parish, Lincoln, 4½ miles N of Wragby It was formerly a parish Pop, 127

BLEASBY, a parish, with a village and a r station, in Southwell district, Notts, on the river Trent and on the Midland railway, 3 miles SSE of Southwell It includes the hamlets of Gibsmere, Notown, and Goverton and its post town is Thurgarton, under Southwell Acres, 1,550 Real property, £2,803 Pop, 332 Houses, 72 The property is subdivided Bleasby Hall is the seat of the Kelhams The parish is a meet for the Rufford hounds The living is a vicarage, united with the vicarage of Morton, in the diocese of Lincoln Value, £188 * Patron, Southwell College Church The church is ancient and very good

BLEASDALE, or ADMARSH, a chapelry in Lancaster parish, Lancashire, among the hills 5 miles ENE of Garstang r station It has a post office of the name of Bleasdale, under Garstang Acres, 8,490 Real property, £2,418 Pop, 372 Houses, 62 Most of the area was formerly forest, belonging to the Crown Bleasdale Tower is the seat of W J Garnett, Esq Bleasdale Fell is 1,709 feet high The living is a p curacy in the diocese of Manchester Value, £80 * Patron, the Vicar of Lancaster The church was built in 1837 There are an endowed school, a reformatory, and charities £44

BLEA TARN, a lakelet at the head of Watendlath, in Cumberland 6½ miles S by E of Keswick

BLEA TARN, a hamlet and a lakelet in Warcop parish, Westmoreland. The hamlet lies on the E side of Patterdale, 6 miles NNE of Ambleside The manor was given, in the time of Henry II, by John Tailbois, to Byland abbey in Yorkshire, and a cell to that abbey was built on it The lakelet lies high, and sends a stream let, jointly with that from Angle tarn, to the head of Ulleswater

BLEA TARN a lakelet in Little Langdale, Westmorland, in a deep rocky hollow, at a high elevation, 5½ miles W of Ambleside Wordsworth made its basin the home of the Solitary in his "Excursion," and described it as

> " Beneath our feet a little lowly vale —
> A lowly vale, and yet uplifted high
> Among the mountains, even as if the spot
> Had been, from earliest time, by wish of theirs
> So placed to be shut out from all the world."

BLEA WATER, a lakelet in Bampton parish Westmoreland on high ground on the W side of Mardale, 6½ miles SW of Bampton

BLECHINGDON See BLETCHINGTON

BLECHINGLEY See BLETCHINGLEY

BLECHYNDEN, a coast guard station on Southampton water Hants, adjacent to the Southwestern railway, 2 miles WSW of Southampton

BLEDDFA, or LLYTHYAUCH, a parish in Knighton district, Radnor, on the river Lug and in Radnor forest, 5 miles SW of Knighton r station Post town, Knighton, Radnorshire Acres, 2,740 Real property, £2,473. Pop, 250 Houses, 46 The surface is hilly, and to a considerable extent waste. The living is a rectory in the diocese of St David's. Value, £181 Patron, the Bishop of St David's The church is tolerable

BLEDINGTON, or BLADINGTON, a parish in Stow on the Wold district Gloucester, on the verge of the county and on the Oxford and Worcester railway, 2½ miles S of Addlestrop station and 4 SE of Stow on the Wold Post town, Stow on the Wold, under Moreton in the Marsh Acres, 1,110 Real property, £2,868 Pop, 396 Houses, 91 The property is divided among a few The living is a vicarage in the dio of G and Bristol Value, £88 Patron Christ Church, Oxford The church is ancient There is a Wesleyan chapel

BLEDISLOE, a tything and a hundred in Gloucester The tything is in Awre parish, 2 miles SE of Newnham The hundred contains the parishes of Awre Alvington, and Lydney Acres, 16,741 Pop, 4,781 Houses, 877

BLEDLOW, a village and a parish in Wycombe district, Bucks The village stands in a romantic ravine, called the Glyde, on the verge of the county, adjacent to the Thame and Maidenhead railway, 2 miles SW of Princes Risborough and has a station on the railway, and a post office under Tring —The parish includes also a liberty called Bledlow Ridge Acres 4,130 Real property, £4,891 Pop 1,130 Houses, 232 The property is subdivided The living is a vicarage in the diocese of Oxford Value, £175 * Patron, Lord Carrington The church is early English, has interesting features, injured by white wash, and stands on the brink of the ravine at the village

BLEDLOW RIDGE is a separate charge, a p. curacy constituted in 1868, and in the patronage of trustees Its church was previously a chapel of ease There are a Primitive Methodist chapel, a public school, and charities £59

BLEINE See BLAN AND BLEINE

BLELHAM TARN, a lakelet in the extreme N of Lancashire, near Windermere lake, 3½ miles SSW of Ambleside sula The medicinal leech abounded in it, but has been exterminated

BLENCARN, a township in Kirkland parish, Cumberland, 8½ miles SE of Kirkoswald Here are a mineral spring and an endowed school

BLENCOGO, a township in Bromfield parish, Cumberland near the Carlisle and Maryport railway, 4½ miles WSW of Wigton Acres, 1,697 Real property, £2,649 Pop, 218 Houses, 37 Boucher, who supplemented Johnson's Dictionary, was a native

BLENCOW (GREAT), a township in Dacre parish, Cumberland, 4½ miles WNW of Penrith It has a station on the Cockermouth railway, and a post office under Penrith, both of the name of Blencow Real property, £674 Pop, 99 Houses, 13. Here is a free grammar school, with £191

BLENCOW (LITTLE), a township in Greystoke parish, Cumberland, 4½ miles WNW of Penrith It has a post office, of the name of Blencow, under Penrith Real property, £674 Pop 99 Houses, 13 Here is a free grammar school, founded in 1596, with income of £191, at which the first Lord Ellenborough was educated

BLENDON, a hamlet in Bexley parish, Kent, 3½ miles E of Dartford It has a post office under Bexley Heath, London S E Pop, 122

BLENDWORTH, a parish in Catherington district, Hants, on the border of Bere forest 2 miles NW of Rowlands Castle r station, and 7 SSW of Petersfield Post town, Rowlands Castle, under Havant Acres, 2,304 Real property, £3,499 Pop, 219 Houses, 45 The property is divided among a few Blendworth House is the seat of Sir W W Knighton, Bart. The living is a rectory in the diocese of Winchester Value, £220 * Patron, the Rev M Ward The church is a handsome recent edifice, in the decorated style, with lofty tower and spire A school has £19 from endowment.

BLENG (THE), a stream of Cumberland It rises on Hay Cock, 2½ miles NE of Wastwater, and runs 6 miles south westward to the vicinity of Gosforth, then goes 2½ miles thence eastward to the Irt

BLENHEIM PARK, an extra parochial tract, the seat of the Duke of Marlborough, in Woodstock district, Oxford, on the river Glyme and on Akeman street, immediately W of Woodstock Acres, 2,940 Real property, £2,400 Pop., 118 Houses 22. This was a royal demesne, containing the ancient palace of Woodstock was given to the great Duke of Marlborough, along with the parliamentary grant of £500,000 for decorating the grounds and building a mansion, and took its present name from his victory of Blenheim on the Danube on 2 Aug 1704 The park is entered from Woodstock by a triumphal arch, it has much diversity of surface and was laid out by "Capability Brown, it abounds with fine old trees, and displays groups of wood so arranged as to represent the battle of Blenheim, and it contains a lake of 260 acres, spanned by a fine three arched bridge,—a column 134 feet high, surmounted by a colossal statue of the great Duke,—a curious old house, called High Lodge, once inhabited by the profligate Earl of Rochester, as ranger of the park —a spring called Rosamund's Well, traditionally said to have supplied the bath of the 'Fair Rosamund during her residence in the "Bower,'—and traces of Akeman street, together with spots in which remains of Roman buildings have been found. The gardens possess great wealth of plants, and contain the Temple of Health, in memory of George III,—the Cascade artificially constructed but looking entirely natural,—the Fountain, modelled after that of the Piazza Navona at Rome,—and some fine specimens of statuary and architecture, modelled after the antique The mansion was founded in 1705, but not completed till after the great Duke's death It was designed by Vanbrugh, and is esteemed his master piece and it cost about £300 000 It consists of a centre and two wings, connected by colonnades, forms three sides of a square, enclosing a court, measures 384 feet along the front, and is in the Grecian style, faulty and very heavy, yet shows such skilful combination of porticoes, colonnades, and towers as to look highly imposing The chief apartments are the hall, 67 feet high, with ceiling allegorically representing the battle of Blenheim, the great dining-room, thick with pictures by Rubens and Vandyke, the saloon, with walls and ceiling decorated by La Guerre, the library, 183 feet long with marble statue of Queen Anne by Rysbrach, and the chapel, with marble monument of the great Duke and his Duchess by Rysbrach, and with a Lombard pulpit in Derbyshire spar The collection of paintings and of objects of vertu is one of the largest and choicest in Britain, insomuch that Waaggen says,—"If nothing were to be seen in England but Blenheim, with its park and treasures of art, there would be no reason to repent the journey to this country "

BLENKINSOP, a township in Haltwhistle parish, Northumberland, on the Newcastle and Carlisle railway, and on the Roman wall 3 miles W of Haltwhistle Acres, 4,910 Pop, 1 4 Houses, 90 Haltwhistle Castle is the ruin of a strong square tower, the ancient seat of the Blenkinsops, noted for their Border feuds, and Blenkinsop Hall is the seat of J Coulson, Esq, the descendant of the Blenkinsops A Roman altar was found in 1720, and an inscription to Ceres in 1816 Coal is worked

BLENNERHASSET AND KIRKLAND, a township in Torpenhow parish, Cumberland, on the river Ellen, near the Carlisle and Maryport railway, 4 miles WNW of Ireby Real property, £1,372 Pop., 234 Houses, 46 Here is an Independent chapel.

BLESTIUM See MONMOUTH

BLETCHINGLLY, or BLECHINGLEY a village and a parish in Godstone district, Surrey The village stands on an eminence, adjacent to one of the sources of the Medway river, near the Roman vicinal way, and near a branch of the Southeastern railway, 3 miles E of Redhill Junction station, and 5 E by N of Reigate and it has a post office‡ under Redhill It claims to have been a place of ancient importance, is said to have once possessed seven churches, contains some picturesque old houses, and sent members to parliament from the time of Edward I till disfranchised by the act of 1832 It formerly had a weekly market, and still has fairs on 10 May 22 June, and 2 Nov The parish includes also the hamlet of Ham Farm Acres, 5 585 Real property, £7,513. Pop, 1,691 Houses, 292 The property is much subdivided. The manor belonged at one time to the Clares, and passed to the Mordaunts, the Howards, and others A castle on it, belonging to Gilbert de Clare, Earl of Gloucester, was destroyed in 1263, by the royal forces, but was afterwards restored, and the foundations of it may still be seen in a field south of the village. Earl Godwin is often said to have retreated to Blechingley, after the overwhelming of his fine Kentish manors by the sea, and to have lived here in great state, but he does not appear to have had any property here Pendhill, the seat of C Manning, Esq, between the village and neighbouring chalk hills, is thought to have been designed by Inigo Jones Traces of a Roman villa, under White Hill, were discovered in 1813, and very many Roman coins have been found The living is a rectory in the diocese of Winchester Value, £1 200 * Patron, H Chawner, Esq The church is early English, with traces of Norman, consists of nave, south aisle, and double chancel, with a tower, had once a wooden spire, 160 feet high, and contains some splendid monuments There are an Independent chapel, a free grammar school, a charity school, an orphanage for 100 girls, four alms houses for widows, and a workhouse. The orphanage was built and endowed, by the Duchess of Leeds, in 1866 and, together with one for 100 boys at Hellingly, cost upwards of £70,000 Archbishop Herring and Bishop Thomas were rectors

BLETCHINGTON, Sussex See BRATCHINGTON

BLETCHINGTON, or BLECHINGDON, a parish and a sub district in the district of Bicester, Oxford The parish lies near Akeman street, the Oxford canal, the river Cherwell, and the Oxford and Rugby railway, 2 miles NE of Woodstock Road station, and 6 SW by W of Bicester, and it has a post office under Oxford. Acres, 2,540 Real property £4,631 Pop, 650 Houses,

142 Bletchington Park is the seat of Viscount Valentia, was partly rebuilt near the end of last century and occupies the site of a house which was held for the king, and surrendered to the parliament, in the civil war A striped marble is found here, which has been used in ornamental architecture The living is a rectory in the diocese of Oxford Value, £356 * Patron, Queen's College, Oxford Charities, £55 Dr Fairclough was a native The sub district comprises seventeen parishes. Acres, 20,178 Pop, 7,440 Houses, 1,629

BLETCHLEY, a township and a parish in Newport Pagnell district, Bucks The township lies adjacent to Watling street, and on the Northwestern railway, at the junction of the branches to Bedford, Oxford, and Banbury, 14 miles, by railway, E of Buckingham, and it has a station on the railway, and a head post office‡ of the name of Bletchley Station Acres, 1,180 Real property £1,700 Pop, 426 Houses, 97 The parish includes also the hamlet of Water Eaton and part of the township of Fenny Stratford Acres 3,150 Real property, with the rest of Fenny Stratford £8 843. Pop, 1,653 Houses, 361 The property is divided among a few The original head manor was Water-Eaton, and was given by William the Conqueror to Geoffry, bishop of Constance in Normandy The living is a rectory in the diocese of Oxford Value, £456 * Patron, Joseph Bennitt, Esq The church is a handsome Gothic structure, with a tower, and contains the tomb of Lord Grey de Wilton, who died in 1442 and a curious tablet to Dr Sparke, who was rector in 1616

BLETCHLEY, a township in Moreton Sea parish, Salop, 3½ miles W of Market Drayton Pop, 101

BLETHERSTON, a parish in Narberth district, Pembroke, on the South Wales railway, at Clarbeston Road station, 5 miles N W by W of Narberth Post town, Wiston, under Narberth Acres 2,366 Real property, £1,900 Pop, 254 Houses, 56 The property is subdivided The living is a p curacy, annexed to the vicarage of Llawhaden in the diocese of St David's. The church is not good

BLETHVAUGH See BLEDDFA

BLETSOE, a parish in the district and county of Bedford, on the river Ouse, and on the Midland railway, 1½ mile SSE of Sharnbrook r station, and 6 NNW of Bedford It has a post office under Bedford Acres, 2,239 Real property £4,021 Pop, 412 Houses, 80 The property is all in one estate, and belonged once to the Pateshulls and the Beauchamps An old castle now a farm house, was the seat of the ancestors of Lord St John of Bletsoe The living is a rectory in the diocese of Ely Value, £310 * Patron, Lord St John The church contains tombs of the St John family and of Frances Countess of Bolingbroke Charities, £13

BLEWBERRY, a village in Wantage district, and a parish in Wantage and Wallingford districts, Berks. The village stands near the Ridge way and Icknield street, 2½ miles WSW of Wallingford Road r station, and 4 NE by N of East Ilsley, and it has a post office under Wallingford, and a fair on the Thursday after 29 Sept Pop, 539 Houses, 152 The parish includes also the hamlet of Upton with Nottingham fee liberty, and the liberty of Aston Upthorpe Acres, 6,814 Real property, £8,071 Pop, 1 111 Houses, 231 The property is divided among a few The ancient manor house was engirt by moat and earthen rampart Blewberry Hill has barrows and an ancient camp The living is a vicarage in the diocese of Oxford, and till 1866 was united with Upton and Aston Upthorpe Value £161 * Patron, the Bishop of Oxford The church is old but good There are a Wesleyan chapel a free school for 30 boys and 30 girls, and a large amount of charities

BLEYNE, a hamlet in Llannon parish, Carmarthen, 7 miles NNE of Llanelly

BLICKLING, a parish in Aylsham district Norfolk, on the river Bure, near the line of the projected railway to Cromer, 1½ mile NNW of Aylsham and 12½ E by N of Fakenham r station Post town, Aylsham, under Norwich Acres, 2,125 Real property £2,606 Pop, 392 Houses, 80 The property is chiefly in one estate The manor belonged anciently to the Crown, was given by the Conqueror to the bishops of Norwich, and passed to the Dagworths, the Erpinghams, the Falstofs, the Boleyns, the Hobarts, and the Suffields The mansion on it, in the time of Henry VIII, was the birthplace of Anne Boleyn whence she married the king and the present mansion, Blickling Hall a seat of the Marquis of Lothian, was built in 1625 by Sir Henry Hobart, and is a fine specimen of Tudor architecture. The library measures 127 feet by 21, and contains upwards of 10,000 volumes, and the various rooms are enriched with numerous family portraits and other interesting pictures, and with statues of Queen Anne Boleyn and Queen Elizabeth. The grounds comprise about 1,000 acres, and contain statues from Oxnead Hall, a pyramid on a base of 45 feet square over the remains of John Earl of Buckinghamshire and a fine lake, in form of a crescent, about a mile long. Charles II and his queen visited the hall in 1671, and an old distich says, -

> " Blickling two monarchs and two queens has seen,
> One king fetched thence, another brought a queen "

The living is a rectory, united with the rectory of Erpingham, in the diocese of Norwich Value £521 * Patron, the Dowager Lady Suffield The church has a sculptured octagonal font, contains monuments and brasses of the old proprietors of the manor and of others and is in fair condition

BLIDESLOE. See BLIDISLOE

BLIDWORTH, a village, a parish, and a sub district, in Mansfield district, Notts. The village stands in Sherwood forest, 4 miles E of Kirkby r station, and 5 SE of Mansfield, and has a post office under Mansfield The parish includes also the hamlets of Bottoms, Fishpool, and Rainworth Acres, together with Haywood Oaks and Lindhurst extra parochial tracts, 6,610 Real property, £6,694 Pop 1,166 Houses, 250 The property is subdivided The manor belongs to the Archbishop of York A hollowed block of rock is regarded by some as a Druidical altar The living is a vicarage in the diocese of Lincoln Value, £253 * Patron, alternately the Bishop of Manchester and the Prebendary of Oxton The church is Norman, and was repaired in 1839 There are a Wesleyan chapel and a national school — The sub district includes also two extra parochial tracts Acres 6 610 Pop, 1,188 Houses, 253

BLINDBOTHILL, a township in Brigham parish, Cumberland 2 miles W of Cockermouth Real property, £1,206 Pop, 116 Houses, 19

BLINDCRAKE, ISELL and REDMAIN, a township in Isell parish, Cumberland, 3 miles NNE of Cockermouth Real property £3 920 Pop 335 Houses, 72

BLINDLEY HEATH, a chapelry in Godstone parish, Surrey, near the Southeastern railway S of Godstone station, and 5¾ miles N by W of East Grinstead It has a post office under East Grinstead The statistics are returned with the parish The living is a vicarage in the diocese of Winchester Value £173 * Patron, the Vicar of Godstone There is a national school

BLIND TARN a mountain lakelet in Furness Lancashire, on the S side of Dow crag, under Walney scar 3 miles W of Coniston

BLISLAND, a parish in Bodmin district, Cornwall, on the border of the moors, 4 miles NNE of Bodmin, and 5½ N of Bodmin Road r station Post town, Bodmin Acres, 6,335 Real property, £3 0[illegible] Pop, 5[illegible] Houses, 121 The property is divided among a few Granite, schist, stream tin, and other minerals are found The living is a rectory in the diocese of Exeter Value £ [illegible] Patron, the Rev [illegible] The church has a fine brass of 1410 and is good There is a Wesleyan chapel A fair is held on 25 Sept

BLISWORTH, a village and a parish in Towcester district, Northampton The village stands on the Grand Junction canal, 1 mile SSW of the Northwestern railway, at the junction of the line to Northampton and Peterborough, and 4½ SSW of Northampton and it has a station of its own name, at the railway junction and a post office under Northampton — The parish comprises

1,980 acres Real property, £1,314 Pop, 1,022 Houses, 199 The property is divided among a few The Blisworth tunnel on the canal SSE of the village is 1¾ mile long The Blisworth cutting on the railway goes through hard blue limestone, is 2 miles long with a mean depth of 50 feet, and, though not the largest work of its kind on the line, was the most difficult Building stone is quarried, and some iron ore is found The living is a rectory in the diocese of Peterborough Value, £351 * Patron, the Rev W Berry The church is ancient and of mixed architectural character, has a brass of 1503, and was recently restored There are a Baptist chapel, a free school, and charities £25

BLITHBURY, a hamlet in Mavesyn Ridware parish, Stafford, on the river Blithe, 2 miles NE of Rugeley Pop, 114 See Abbots Bromley

BLITHE, or Blythe (The), a river of Stafford It rises 3 miles E of Lane End, and runs about 22 miles south south eastward, past Leigh, Chartley, Blithbury, and Kings Bromley to the Trent, 7 miles above Burton

BLITHE, or Blythe (The), Suffolk See Blythe (The)

BLITHE BRIDGE, a hamlet in Kingston parish, Stafford, on the river Blithe, 4½ miles SW of Uttoxeter See also Blyth Bridge

BLITHE MARSH a village in Cheadle district, Stafford, on the river Blythe, 3½ miles WSW of Cheadle It has a post office under Stone

BLITHFIELD, a township and a parish in Uttoxeter district, Stafford The township lies on the river Blithe, 2 miles W by S of Abbots Bromley, and 3¼ ENE of Colwich r station It includes the hamlet of Admarston, and its post town is Abbots Bromley under Rugeley Real property, £3,526 —The parish includes also the liberty of Newton Acres, 3,193 Real property, £5,952 Pop, 338 Houses, 75 The property is divided among a few Blithfield House is the seat of Lord Bagot, forms a large quadrangle with towers and pinnacles and contains some interesting portraits The living is a rectory in the diocese of Lichfield Value, £388.* Patron, Lord Bagot The church has monuments and brasses of the Bagots, the Bromptons, and others, and is good An endowed school has £35, and other charities £35

BLOCKHOUSE, an extra parochial tract in Worcester city Acres, 13 Pop., 1,671 Houses, 329

BLOCKHOUSE FORT, a regular fortification, commanding the entrance to Portsmouth harbour It has bastions and a moat, is bomb proof and casemated, and is armed with 36 guns of the largest calibre, placed level with the water

BLOCKLEY, a village and a parish in the district of Shipston on Stour, and county of Worcester The village stands in a south eastern projection of the county, on the Fosse way, adjacent to the Oxford and Worcester railway, 3¼ miles NW of Moreton in the Marsh, and has a station on the railway, a post office‡ under Moreton in the Marsh, a church, a Baptist chapel, a Primitive Methodist chapel, and national and British schools. It is an ancient place, and had once a monastery, founded before 855, and a palace of the bishops of Worcester —The parish includes also the hamlets of Aston-Magna, Dorne Ditchford, Draycott, Northwick, and Paxford Acres, 7 870 Real property, £16,092. Pop, 2 596 Houses 580 The property is much subdivided The manor belongs to the see of Worcester There are stone quarries silk mills, and corn mills. Traces of the Fosse way exist, and many Roman coins and other Roman relics have been found The living is a vicarage in the diocese of Worcester Value £762 * Patron the Bishop of Worcester The church is partly Norman, has a modern tower, and contains two brasses of the 15th century The vicarage of Aston Magna is a separate benefice

BLODWELL, a township in Llanyblodwell parish, Salop, 5½ miles SSW of Oswestry Pop, 384 Blodwell Hall is the deserted seat of the Tanats, descendants of Linion, a prince of Powys.

BLOFIELD, a village, a parish, a sub district a district, and a hundred in Norfolk The village stands near the Yarmouth railway and the river Yare, 1 mile NE of Brundall r station, and 7 E of Norwich, and it has a post office under Norwich, and is a seat of petty sessions —The parish comprises 2,831 acres Real property, £7,548 Pop, 1,155 Houses, 265 The property is subdivided The living is a rectory in the diocese of Norwich Value £896 * Patron, Caius College, Cambridge. The church is good An endowed school has £10, and other charities £75 —The sub district contains the parishes of Blofield, Brundall, Postwick, Great Plumstead Little Plumstead, Witton Bradeston, Strumpshaw, Buckenham, Hassingham, Lingwood Burlingham St Edmund, Burlingham St Andrew, Hemblington, and Woodbastwick, and part of the parish of Thorpe St Andrew Acres 17,816. Pop, 5,787 Houses, 1 144 —The district comprehends also the sub-district of South Walsham, containing the parishes of South Walsham St. Mary, South Walsham St Lawrence, Burlingham St. Peter, Ranworth, Panxworth, Upton, Fishley Acle, Beighton, Moulton, Halvergate, Tunstall, Wickhampton Freethorpe Southwood, Cantley, Limpenhoe, and Reedham Acres of the district, 44,178 Poor rates in 1866 £6,904 Pop in 1861, 11,521 Houses, 2,859 Marriages in 1866, 77, births, 364,—of which 36 were illegitimate, deaths 238 —of which 73 were at ages under 5 years, and 7 at ages above 85 years Marriages in the ten years 1851-60, 811, births, 3,410, deaths, 2,330 The places of worship in 1851 were 33 of the Church of England, with 5,537 sittings 2 of Independents, with 350 s, 3 of Baptists, with 370 s, 2 of Wesleyan Methodists, with 232 s, and 8 of Primitive Methodists, with 835 s The schools were 16 public day schools, with 793 scholars, 27 private day schools, with 454 s, 23 Sunday schools with 1,009 s, and 1 evening school for adults, with 24 s The workhouse is in Lingwood —The hundred comprises twenty four parishes and part of another Acres, 19,594 Pop, 6,280 Houses 1,265

BLO NORTON, or Norton Belleau, a parish in Guiltcross district, Norfolk, at the verge of the county on the river Waveney, 5½ miles S by E of Harling Road r station, and 9½ ESE of Thetford Post-town, Garboldisham, under Thetford Acres, 1,132. Real property £2,395 Pop 370 Houses, 87 The property is much subdivided The living is a rectory in the diocese of Norwich Value £336 Patron the Rev C. H Browne The church is very good There are Independent and P Methodist chapels, and charities £97

BLOOMFIELD, a village in Tipton parish, Worcester Here is a Wesleyan chapel

BLOOMSBURY, or St George Bloomsbury, a parish, which is also a sub district, in the district of St Giles Middlesex, in Finsbury borough about 1¼ mile WNW of St. Paul's, London Acres, 122 Real property, with St Giles in the Fields, £299,540 Pop in 1851, 16 981, in 1861, 17,392 Houses, 1,990 It was originally part of St Giles in the Fields parish, and was separately constituted in 1729 It includes Bloomsbury square, Russell square, Woburn square, and part of Torrington square, together with intermediate and adjacent streets. Part of it shows the architecture of the time of Queen Anne, and much consists of houses which were fashionable residences till about 1828 It contains the British museum, and the buildings or offices of several metropolitan institutions A sitting statue of Fox, 9 feet high, by Westmacott, is in Bloomsbury square, and a statue of the Duke of Bedford, also by Westmacott, is in Russell square St George's church, adjacent to New Oxford street, was built in 1731, at a cost of £9,790 is in a mixed style of Doric and Corinthian and has a steeple, modelled after Pliny's account of the tomb of Mausolus, crowned by a statue of George II The French Episcopal chapel, in Bloomsbury street, was built in 1845, and is noted for the use of the Anglican liturgy in French The Baptist chapel, adjacent to this, was built in 1848, and has a circular window 18 feet in diameter, and towers with spires 117 feet high The living is a rectory in the diocese of London Value, £783.* Patron the Lord Chancellor Christ church, in Woburn square, is a separate benefice, with income of £500, in the patronage of the Rector Bedford chapel and the French Episcopal chapel also are separate incumbencies. S Jenyns and T Hook were natives, and Richard Baxter, Sir H Sloane Dr Radcliffe, Akenside, Romilly, Lawrence Lord Mansfield, and Lord Chancellor Loughborough were residents

BLOOMSBURY, a suburb of Birmingham, in the NE of the borough It has a station, jointly with Nechells, on the Birmingham and Derby railway

BLOORE WITH TYRLEY AND HALES, a township in Drayton Tyrley parish, Stafford, near the Birmingham and Liverpool Junction canal 3 miles E of Market-Drayton Pop in 1841, 561 Houses, 103 An action was fought on Bloore Heath in 1459, between the Lancastrians and the Yorkists, and is commemorated on the spot by a cross

BLORE, a township and a parish in the district of Ashborne and county of Stafford The township bears the name of Blore with Swinscoe, and lies on the river Dove, 4 miles NW of Ashborne r station Acres, 1,250 Real property, £2,523 Pop, 248 Houses, 54 The parish includes also the township of Calton in Blore, and is sometimes called Blore Ray Post town, Ashborne Acres 3,730 Real property, £3,443 Pop, 320 Houses, 71 The property is divided among a few The living is a rectory in the diocese of Lichfield Value, £170 * Patron, C Shore, Esq The church is old but good, and contains some curious monuments of the Bassets Charities, £17

BLORENGE, a mountain at the head of the Avon Llwyd valley, Monmouth, 2½ miles SW of Abergavenny It consists of old red sandstone, capped by carboniferous and millstone grit, has an altitude of 1,170 feet, and figures grandly in the scenery of north western Monmouth

BLOWICK, a beautiful small bay in Ulles water, Westmoreland, at the foot of Place fell, about a mile N of Patterdale inn.

BLOWICK (HIGHER and LOWER) two hamlets in North Meols parish Lancashire, near the coast, 6½ miles NNW of Ormskirk.

BLOWTY, a township in Llangadfan parish, Montgomery 6½ miles WNW of Llanfair Pop, 85

BLOW WELLS profound pits near Stallingborough in Lincoln, 1½ miles NW of Great Grimsby They afford an inexhaustible supply of water, and are popularly regarded as unfathomable

BLOXHAM a village, a parish, a sub district, and a hundred in Oxford. The village stands 3½ miles SW of Banbury r station, and has a post office‡ under Banbury The parish is shown in the Census as including the chapelry of Milcombe Acres, 4,240 Real property, £10,902 Pop, 1,667 Houses 369 Bloxham Grove is occupied by the Rev G Warriner The living is a vicarage in the diocese of Oxford. Value, £290 * Patron, Eton College The church is a fine edifice of mixed styles, from Norman to late English, has a very beautiful crocketed spire, 195 feet high, was restored in 1865, at great cost and contains monuments of the Griffiths and the Thorneycrofts The vicarage of Milcombe is a separate benefice There are a Wesleyan chapel built in 1858 a Baptist chapel, a very large middle class school in the collegiate style, enlarged in 1864, an endowed school with £30 a year, and charities £390 —The sub district contains six parishes, and is in Banbury district Acres, 18,771 Pop 6,216 Houses, 1,490 —The hundred contains eleven parishes and parts of two others Acres 29 770 Pop, 8,985 Houses, 2,111

BLOXHOLME or BLOXHAM, a parish in Sleaford district, Lincoln, 5½ miles N of Sleaford r station Post town, Digby under Sleaford Acres, 1,298 Real property, £1,970 Pop 115 Houses, 23 The property is all in one estate The living is a rectory, united with the vicarage of Digby, in the diocese of Lincoln Value, £245 * Patron, the Right Hon R A C H Nisbet The church is good

BLOXWICH, a village, a chapelry, and a sub district in Walsall district Stafford The village stands on the Wyrley and Essington canal adjacent to the Walsall and Stafford railway, 2½ miles NNW of Walsall and has a station on the railway, and a post office‡ under Walsall The chapelry is in Walsall parish, and was constituted in 1842 Rated property, £17,509 Pop in 1841 3,831, in 1861, 7,315 Houses, 1,424 The property is much subdivided The living is a vicarage in the diocese of Lichfield Value, £300 * Patron, the Inhabitants The church is very good, and there are chapels for Wesleyans and Roman Catholics The sub district includes also Pelsall township in Wolverhampton parish Pop, 9,237 Houses, 1,800

BLOXWORTH, a parish in Wareham district, Dorset, 3 miles ESE of Bere Regis, and 5 NNW of Wareham r station It has a post office under Blandford Acres, 2 776. Real property, £1,661 Pop, 264 Houses, 50 The property is all in one estate Part of the surface is heath, and there are vestiges of a Danish camp The living is a rectory in the diocese of Salisbury Value, £230 * Patron, the Rev G Pickard Cambridge The church is very good

BLUBBERHOUSES, a township in Fewston parish, W R Yorkshire 7½ miles N by W of Otley It has a post office under Otley Acres, 3,527 Pop, 87 Houses, 15 Here is a small church, built in 1851

BLUE ANCHOR, a hamlet in Old Cleeve parish, Somerset on Bridgewater bay 2 miles W of Watchet It occupies a rising ground, with a brilliant prospect, and is a small watering place with a hotel

BLUE GILL a profound ravine on High street mountain, Westmoreland, adjacent to the ascent of the highest summit from Troutbeck 7½ miles NNE of Windermere

BLUE JOHN MINE, a chambered cave in the Man Tor, Derby about a mile WNW of Castleton It is entered by steeply descending stairs, contains a chamber, 60 feet wide and 150 feet high, called Lord Mulgrave's dining room, has, further in, another chamber, called the Variegated cavern, and beyond this a profound gulf, overlooked by a rail guarded ledge, makes a magnificent display of stalactites and crystals, and yields a vast quantity of beautiful spar It is visited under the direction of guides and shown with Bengal lights and blasts

BLUE PITS, a village in Rochdale parish Lancashire, 2½ miles SSW of Rochdale It has a r station with telegraph, Castleton Moor church built in 1862, and a Wesleyan chapel also built in 1862

BLUNDESTON a parish in Mutford district, Suffolk, near the coast, 2½ miles ENE of Somerleyton r station and 3½ NW by N of Lowestoft It has a post office under Lowestoft Acres, 1,678 Real property, £3,306 Pop, 664 Houses, 136 The property is much subdivided The manor belongs to F H Reeve, Esq The living is a rectory, united with the rectory of Flixton, in the diocese of Norwich Value, £617 * Patrons Executors of T Morse, Esq The church is old There are a Wesleyan chapel a national school, and charities £8

BLUNHAM, a village and a parish in Biggleswade district, Beds The village stands on the river Ivel, near the Cambridge and Bedford and the Great Northern railways, 6½ miles E of Bedford, and has a station on the former railway and a post office under St Neots It was once a market town Pop, 647 Houses, 147 The parish includes also the hamlet of Muggerhanger Acres 3,300 Real property £7,206 Pop., 1,150 Houses, 243 The property is much subdivided Blunham House and Blunham Park are chief residences and the former is the seat of Sir C G Payne, Bart The living is a rectory in the diocese of Ely Value, £731 * Patron Countess Cowper The church is Norman and good The vicarage of Muggerhanger is a separate benefice There are two dissenting chapels, a national school for boys, and an industrial school for girls

BLUNSDON (BROAD) a chapelry in Highworth parish Wilts, 3½ miles SE of Cricklade, and 4 N of Swindon r station It includes the tything of Bury Blunsdon, and has a post office under Swindon Acres, 2,260 Rated property £2,194 Pop, 800 Houses, 158 The property is divided among a few The living is a rectory in the diocese of Gloucester and Bristol Value, £300 * Patron, the Bishop of G and B The church is good

BLUNSDON ST ANDREW, or LITTLE BLUNSDON, a parish in Highworth district, Wilts, 3½ miles SSE of Cricklade, and 3½ NNW of Swindon r station Post town, Broad Blunsdon under Swindon Acres, 1,422 Real property with Broad Blunsdon and Bury Blunsdon, £5,853 Pop, 84 Houses, 16 The property is divided among a few Blunsdon Castle Hill has a camp, commonly regarded as Roman The living is a rectory in the diocese of Gloucester and Bristol Value, £305 Patron, H Calley Esq The church is fair

BLUNTISHAM, a township and a parish in St Ives district, Huntingdon The township lies on the river Ouse, 3 miles SE of Somersham r station, and 4½ NE of St Ives, and has a post office under St Ives Real property, £4,961 The parish includes also the hamlet of Earith Acres, 3,423. Real property, £9,747 Pop, 1,351 Houses, 314 The property is much subdivided The manor was given, in 1015, to Ely abbey Bluntisham House is the seat of the Tebbuts. Part of the land is fen The living is a rectory in the diocese of Ely Value, £1,010 * Patron, the Bishop of Peterborough The church is early English, terminates, in the east, in a half hexagon, and has a screen, a piscina, and an octagonal font There are chapels for Independents Baptists, Wesleyan Methodists, Primitive Methodists, and Quakers An endowed school has £83 a year, other charities £138 Dr Knight, author of Lives of Erasmus and Dean Colet, was rector

BLURTON AND LIGHTWOOD FOREST, a township chapelry in Trentham parish, Stafford, on the North Stafford railway, adjacent to the Grand Trunk canal, 1 mile SE of Trentham r station and 5 SE by E of Newcastle under Lyme Post town, Trentham, under Stoke upon Trent. Acres, 2,210 Real property, £6,985 Pop, 2,857 Houses, 594 The property is divided among a few The living is a vicarage in the diocese of Lichfield, and till 1866 was united with Redbank Value, £400 * Patron, the Duke of Sutherland The church is good

BLYBOROUGH, a parish in Gainsborough district Lincoln, 2¾ miles SSE of Northorpe r station and 9 ENE of Gainsborough It has a post office under Kirton Lindsey Acres, 2,345 Real property, £2,911 Pop, 209 Houses, 41 The property is divided between two Blyborough Hall is the seat of C Luard, Esq There are some mineral springs The living is a rectory in the diocese of Lincoln Value, £519 * Patron, the Lord Chancellor The church is good

BLYFORD See BLYTHFORD

BLYMHILL, a parish in the district of Shiffnall, and county of Stafford, near Watling street, 5 miles NW by W of Brewood, and 5½ SE of Newport r station It has a post office under Shiffnall Acres, 2,925 Real property, £4,519 Pop, 591 Houses, 127 The property is divided among a few The parish is a meet for the Albrighton hounds The living is a rectory in the diocese of Lichfield Value, £450 Patron, Earl Bradford The church was repaired in 1859

BLYSOOG (THE), a stream of Cardigan It rises near the coast, WSW of Aberporth, and runs 5 miles southward to the Teifi at Llechryd

BLYTH (THE), a river of Northumberland It rises 2 miles E of Throckington, and runs about 24 miles eastward past Bradford Whalton, Kirkley, Stannington, and Bedlington, to the North sea at South Blyth

BLYTH, a sub district in the district of Tynemouth, Northumberland, on the S side of Blyth river, at the coast It contains South Blyth township, Newsham lordship and Horton and Cramlington chapelries Acres, 10,222 Pop., 12,989 Houses, 2,569

BLYTH, a village and a township in Worksop district, Notts, and a parish in Worksop and East Retford district, Notts and in Doncaster district, W R Yorkshire The village occupies a gentle ascent on the Ryton rivulet, 2½ miles W by S of Ranskill r station and 7 NNE of Worksop, and has a post office under Worksop. It was formerly a market town, and it still has fairs on Holy Thursday and 20 Oct The township includes also the hamlets of Norney and Oldcoates, and part of the hamlet of Ranby Real property, £4,721 Pop, 698 Houses, 167 The parish includes likewise the lordship of Hodsock and the townships of Styrrup, Barnby-Moor, Ranskill, Torworth, Austerfield, and Bawtry Acres, 17,110 Real property £31,057 Pop, 3,185 Houses, 784 Blyth Hall, in Blyth township, belonged formerly to the Mellishes and is now the seat of H H Walker, Esq Serlby Hall, 2 miles N of Blyth village, is the seat of Viscount Galway The country around these seats, as well without the parks as within, is so rich and ornate as to look all like a garden An hospital for a warden, three chaplains, and a number of leprous persons, was founded at Blyth Spittal, to the S of Blyth village, by William de Cressy Lord of Hodesac, but has all disappeared A Benedictine priory was founded at Blyth village, in 1088, by Roger de Busly, and given, at the dissolution, to Richard Andrews and William Ramsden, and a part of it, called the conventual nave, still stands connected with the nave of the parish church The living is a vicarage in the diocese of Lincoln Value, £751 * Patron, Trinity College, Cambridge The church is a noble edifice in successive characters from Norman to later English, has a very ancient tower, and contains an effigies and armorial bearings of the Mellishes The p curacy of Bawtry, with the p curacy of Austerfield, is a separate benefice There are four dissenting chapels, two public schools, and two alms houses

BLYTH AND TYNE RAILWAY, a finished railway in the SE of Northumberland The main part of it, 20 miles long, was authorized in 1852, and comprises a line from South Blyth, through a coal and mineral district, to Hayhole Tyne, for coal, and to Percy Main, on the North Shields railway, for passengers and goods Another part, opened in October 1860, includes a Tynemouth branch of 1½ mile to Dairy house, and a branch of 6 miles from South Blyth to the Northeastern near Morpeth Another part is an extension of 13¾ miles to Warkworth, another, opened in 1864 is an extension of 25 miles to Newcastle, and others, authorised in 1867, are lines and branches of aggregately 24 miles.

BLYTH BRIDGE, a station on the Stoke and Uttoxeter railway 5½ miles SE of Stoke

BLYTHBURGH a village and a parish in Blything district, Suffolk The village stands on the river Blythe 3½ miles NNE of Darsham r station, and 4½ ESE of Halesworth It was formerly a market town of some note, but it suffered severely from a fire and other events in the 17th century and went into decay A fair is still held at it on 5 April A priory of Black canons stood here, was given by Henry I to St Osyth's abbey in Essex and passed, at the dissolution, to Sir Arthur Hopeton, and some trifling remains of its buildings still exist —The parish includes also the hamlets of Hinton and Bulcamp, and its post town is Wenhaston, under Halesworth Acres, 4,116 Real property, £4,383 Pop, 832 Houses 125 The manor belongs to Sir J P Blois, Bart, and Henham Hall to the Earl of Stradbroke A battle between Anna king of East Anglia and Penda king of Mercia in which the former was slain, was fought at Bulcamp in 654 The living is a vicarage in the diocese of Norwich. Value, £8. Patron, Sir J R Blois, Bart The church is fine early English very much decayed, and has painted windows, a font, and remains of ancient monuments There are a Primitive Methodist chapel and the Blything workhouse

BLYTHE (THE), a river of Warwick It rises near Chadwick End, and runs about 12 miles northward, past Packington and Coleshill, to the Tame, 1½ mile below Coleshill

BLYTHE (THE), Northumberland. See BLYTH (THE)

BLYTHE, or BLITHE (THE), a river of Suffolk It rises near Wilby and runs about 15 miles eastward, past Heveningham Walpole, Halesworth, and Blythburgh, to the North sea at Southwold It is navigable to Halesworth

BLYTHE, or BLITHE (THE), Stafford See BLITHE.

BLYTHE HALL, the seat of the Dugdales, in Warwick, on the river Blythe, 1 mile NE of Coleshill.

Here i ıd S r William Dugdale, the antiquary, county his or an and author of the "Monasticon"

BLYTHFORD, or BLYFORD, a parish in Blything district Suffolk, on the river Blythe, 2½ miles E by S of Halesworth r station Post town, Halesworth Acres, 947 Real property, £1,518 Pop, 193 Houses 41 The living is a donative in the diocese of Norwich Value, not reported Patron, the Rev Jeremy Day The church has two Norman doors and a perpendicular English tower but is mainly decorated English

BLYTHING, a district and a hundred in the NE of Suffolk The district comprehends the sub district of Westleton containing the parishes of Carlton, Kelsale, Knodishall Aldringham, Leiston Theberton Middleton, Yoxford, Darsham, Westleton, Dunwich, Walberswick, Blythburgh, Thorington, and Bramfield, the sub district of Halesworth containing the parishes of Sibton, Peasenhall, Ubbeston, Heveningham, Huntingfield, Cratfield, Linstead Magna Linstead Parva, Chediston, Cookley, Walpole, Halesworth, Wissett, Rumburgh, and Spexhall, and the sub district of Wenhaston, containing the parishes of Holton, Wenhaston, Blythford, Westhall, Brampton, Stoven, Uggeshall, Sotherton, Wangford, Reydon Southwold, Easton Bavents, South Cove, Frostenden, Wrentham, Covehithe, Benacre, and Henstead Acres, 92 097 Poor rates in 1866, £10,746 Pop. in 1861, 26,828 Houses, 5,915 Marriages in 1866, 170, births, 841,—of which 59 were illegitimate, deaths, 480, —of which 172 were at ages under 5 years, and 18 at ages above 85 years Marriages in the ten years 1851-60, 1,951, births, 8,180, deaths, 5,530 The places of worship in 1851 were 47 of the Church of England, with 14,903 sittings 9 of Independents, with 2,149 s , 4 of Baptists, with 410 s , 1 of Quakers, with 200 s , 11 of Wesleyan Methodists, with 2,238 s and 16 of Primitive Methodists, with 2,109 s The schools were 26 public day schools, with 2,318 scholars, 64 private day schools, with 1,512 s , 50 Sunday schools, with 3,610 s , and 5 evening schools for adults, with 78 s The workhouse is in Blythburgh parish.—The hundred is mainly identical with the district, but not so extensive Acres, 87,941 Pop 23,343 Houses, 5,080

BLYTH (NORTH), a township in Bedlington parish Northumberland, on the river Blyth, at its mouth, opposite South Blyth Pop , 128

BLYTH (SOUTH), a seaport town a township and a chapelry in Earsdon parish, Northumberland The town stands on the S side of the river Blyth, at its mouth, and on the Blyth and Tyne railway 9 miles SE of Morpeth It was formerly a disagreeable place, of poor appearance, with narrow, irregular streets, but it has been much improved, and it now contains many good houses It has a post office,‡ of Blyth, Northumberland, a r station with telegraph, a bank, a church of 1863, two Presbyterian chapels, a Wesleyan chapel of 1866, a P Methodist chapel, and national schools. A weekly market is held on Wednesday, a large trade is carried on in coals and coasting, and much manufacturing industry is a foot in connexion with shipping The harbour has undergone great improvement since 1854 and not yet completed, costing nearly £50,000, and including docks, a quay of 1 400 feet, and a breakwater of about 3,000 yards. The depth of water over the bar, at full tides was formerly 16 feet and this has been increased Two fixed lights, put up in 1788, are 415 feet apart, and 26 and 48 feet high —The township comprises 1,190 acres Pop 1 953 Houses 327 The manor belongs to Sir M W Ridley, Bart —The chapelry is conterminate with the township and is a donative in the diocese of Durham Value, £93 Patron, Sir M W Ridley, Bart The church was built in 1751

BLYTON a village and a parish in Gainsborough district, Lincoln The village stands near the Manchester and Lincoln railway, 3 miles NE of Gainsborough, and has a station on the railway, and a post-office under Gainsborough The parish includes also the hamlet of Wharton Acres 2,880 Real property, £4 719 Pop, 779 Houses, 171 The property is divided among a few The living is a vicarage in the diocese of Lincoln Value, £399 * Patron, the Earl of Scarborough The church is good and there are two Methodist chapels, and a school with £20 of endowed income.

BOARDLEY See HETTON WITH BOARDLEY

BOARHUNT, a parish in Fareham district, Hants, on the N slope of Portsdown Hill, 2 miles NE of Fareham r station Post town, Fareham Acres, 1,938 Real property, £1,536 Pop , 267 Houses, 51 Portsdown Hill has an altitude of 447 feet, commands brilliant views, and is crowned by an obelisk to the memory of Lord Nelson The living is a donative, with Southwick, in the diocese of Winchester Value, not reported Patron, T Thistlethwaite, Esq The church is transition Norman, or possibly Saxon, but has been restored

BOARSHURST See SADDLEWORTH

BOARSTALL, or BORSTALL, a parish in the district of Bicester, and county of Bucks, in Bernwood forest, on the verge of the county, 6 miles SSE of Bicester r station Post town, Brill, under Tetsworth Acres, 3,080 Real property, £2,692 Pop , 255 Houses, 53 The property is divided among a few The manor was obtained, from Edward the Confessor, by the huntsman Nigel, for service done in the forest and is now held by his descendant, Sir T D Aubrey, Bart Boarstall Tower, the old manor house, played a conspicuous part in the civil war, and is now a picturesque ruin The living is a vicarage, annexed to the vicarage of Brill, in the diocese of Oxford The church was rebuilt in 1818, and contains monuments of the Aubreys

BOBBERSMILL, a locality 1¼ mile from Old Basford, and 2 from Nottingham, with a post office under Nottingham

BOBBING, a parish in Milton district, Kent, 1½ mile W by N of Milton and 2 NW of Sittingbourne r station Post town, Milton, under Sittingbourne Acres, 1,071 Real property, £2,720 Pop., 419 Houses, 83 The property is subdivided The manor belonged to the Savages, and afterwards to the Cliffords Bobbing Court, the seat of the Savages is now a ruin Bobbing Street, about a mile NE of the church, is on a branch of Watling street The living is a vicarage in the diocese of Canterbury Value, £... Patron the Rev G Simpson The church is ancient and good has a tower and spire, and contains a piscina and monuments of the Savages and the Tuftons. Titus Oates was vicar

BOBBINGTON, a parish in the district of Wolverhampton, and counties of Stafford and Salop 3½ miles W of the river Stour and the Stafford and Birmingham canal, 4½ miles E by N of Hampton Lode r station, and 8 WNW of Stourbridge It includes the hamlet of Halfpenny Green, and its post town is Enville, under Stourbridge Acres, 2,676 Real property, £4 130 Pop , 431 Houses, 87 The property is divided among a few The living is a vicarage in the diocese of Hereford Value, £97 Patron, W Whitmore, Esq The church is good An endowed school has £42, and other charities £31

BOBBINGWORTH, a parish and a sub district in Ongar district, Essex The parish bears also the name of Bovinger and lies 2½ miles NW of Ongar r station, and 5½ SE of Harlow Post town, Ongar Acres, 1,628 Real property, £2,471 Pop 334 Houses, 67 The property is divided among a few The living is a rectory in the diocese of Rochester Value, £393 * Patrons, J A Houblon and C Cure, Esqs The church is good —The sub district contains fifteen parishes Acres 17 465 Pop 5,46.. Houses, 1,11..

BOBS NOSE, or HOPE NOSE, a headland on the N side of the entrance of Torbay, Devon, 4 miles N of Berry Head The Orestone, Tor stone, Thatcher, and Shag rocks, with from 5 to 10 fathoms water round them, are near it

BOCKENFIELD a township in Felton parish, Northumberland 8 miles N of Morpeth Acres, 2,324 Pop , 127 Houses 23

BOCKHAMPTON See EASTBURY AND BOCKHAMPTON

BOCKHAMPTON (HIGHER and LOWER), two villages in Stinsford parish, Dorset 2 miles E of Dorchester They have a post office, of the name of Bockhampton, under Dorchester

BOCKING, a village, a parish, and a sub-district, in Braintree district, Essex The village stands on the left bank of Blackwater river, and on the Braintree railway, adjacent to Braintree, forms a suburb of that town, consists chiefly of one long street and is a seat of petty sessions A trade in baizes, called "bockings," was at one time prominent, and a manufacture of silk and crape is now carried on The parish includes also Bocking street and Bocking Church street, ¾ and 2 miles distant from Braintree, both with post offices under that town, and the former situated on the branch Roman road from Chelmsford Acres, 4,607 Real property, £15,156 Pop, 3,555 Houses, 768. The property is much subdivided The manor was given by Ethelred to the see of Canterbury, and belongs now to the corporation of the sons of the clergy The living is a rectory in the diocese of Rochester Value £923 * Patron the Archbishop of Canterbury The church is early English, had anciently three altars and five chantries, and contains some monuments and two brasses There are an Independent chapel, much improved in 1869, a charity school with £50, and other charities with £172 Dr Dale, the author of "Pharmacologia," was a native. The sub district contains five parishes Acres, 11,507 Pop., 5,281 Houses, 1,171

BOCKLETON, a parish in the districts of Tenbury and Bromyard, and counties of Worcester and Hereford, and a sub district in the district of Tenbury The parish lies 5 miles S of Tenbury r station, and 6 E by N of Leominster, and it includes the hamlet of Hampton Charles, and has a post office under Tenbury Acres, 3,229 Real property £2,588 Pop, 316 Houses, 74. The property is divided among a few The living is a vicarage in the diocese of Hereford Value, £127 * Patron, the Rev J J Miller The church is good — The sub district contains five parishes and parts of two others Acres, 17,777 Pop, 3,013 Houses, 648

BOCKLETON, a village in Stoke St Milborough parish, Salop, 6½ miles NE of Ludlow

BOCONNOC, a parish in Liskeard district, Cornwall, on affluents of the river Lerrin, 3 miles SW of Doublebois r station, and 4 NE of Lostwithiel Post town, Lostwithiel Acres, 2,003 Real property, £1,606 Pop, 323 Houses, 57 The manor belonged to the Courtenays, the Carminowes, and the Mohuns, was purchased by Governor Pitt, the grandfather of the great Earl of Chatham, and is now the property of Lady Grenville The old mansion on it was the headquarters of Prince Maurice, and for a short time the residence of Charles I,—who narrowly escaped being shot by an assassin on the grounds The present mansion was built by Governor Pitt, and improved by Lord Camelford, was the birthplace of the Earl of Chatham, is now the residence of the Hon G M Fortescue, and contains a bust of Lord Chatham, some fine paintings by Kneller Lely, and Reynolds, and two ebony chairs, made out of Queen Elizabeth's cradle The grounds are the finest in Cornwall, and contain an obelisk, 123 feet high, to the memory of Sir Richard Lyttleton Lead mines were formerly worked, but were not productive The living is a rectory, united with the rectory of Broadoak, in the diocese of Exeter Value, £378 * Patron, Lady Grenville

BOD, or BODE a prefix to Welsh or ancient British names signifying an abode or residence

BODAIOCH, a township in Tref Eglwys parish Montgomery, on the river Trannon, 4½ miles N of Llanidloes

BODDINGTON, a parish in Tewkesbury district, Gloucester, on the river Chilt, 4 miles SW by W of Cheltenham r station It includes the township of Barrow, and has a post office under Cheltenham Acres, 930 Real property, £1,670 Pop 392 Houses, 81 The manor belongs to Mrs. J E Blagdon and has a curious old moated mansion King Alfred fought his last battle with the Danes, in 893, "at the burg" The living is a p curacy, annexed to the vicarage of Staverton in the diocese of Gloucester and Bristol The church is ancient, and looks to be Norman, but is not really so

BODDINGTON, or BODINGTON, a parish in the district of Banbury and county of Northampton, near the Oxford canal, 3½ miles E by N of Fenny Compton r station, and 9 SW of Daventry It includes the villages of Lower and Upper Boddington, and has a post-office, of the name of Boddington, under Daventry Acres, 3,770 Real property, £6,265 Pop, 724 Houses, 161 The property is subdivided The living is a rectory in the diocese of Peterborough Value, £707 * Patron, Emmanuel College, Cambridge The church is handsome There are a Wesleyan chapel, an endowed school, and charities £47

BODEDERN, a village and a parish in the district and county of Anglesey The village stands 3 miles ENE of Valley r station, and 6½ E by S of Holyhead and has a post-office under Bangor It takes its name from Edern or Edeyrn, a bard of the 7th century, who resided at it and it is a seat of petty sessions and has fairs on 13 March, 16 April, 5 May, 9 June, Whit Tuesday, 16 Aug, 14 Sept., and 1 and 22 Oct —The parish comprises 4,235 acres Real property, £4,183 Pop, 1,054 Houses, 240 The property is divided among a few Presaddfed is an old mansion, once the residence of Sir John Bulkeley A well preserved cromlech is near this mansion The spinning of yarn is carried on in two mills. The living is a vicarage in the diocese of Bangor Value, £104 * Patron, Jesus College, Oxford The church is ancient, and very good, and contains tombs of the families of Presaddfed and Tre Jorweth There are chapels for Independents Baptists, Calvinistic Methodists, and Wesleyans Charities, £19

BODLIGAN, a township in St Asaph parish, Flint Pop, 54

BODEIGAR, a township in Llanbedr Dyffryn Clwyd parish, Denbigh 2 miles NE of Ruthin Pop, 93

BODELWIDDAN See BODLLEWYDDAN

BODENHAM, a village, a parish, and a sub district, in the district of Leominster Hereford The village stands near the river Lug, 2½ miles E of Dinmore r station, and 6½ SSE of Leominster, and it has a post office under Leominster, and was once a market town —The parish includes also the townships of Bowley, Bryan-Maund, Whitchurch Maund, and the Moor Acres, 5,260 Real property, £7,463 Pop., 1,096 Houses, 231 The property is divided among a few The living is a vicarage in the diocese of Hereford Value, £636 * Patron, John Arkwright, Esq The church is ancient and good, and has an incomplete spire There are a Wesleyan chapel, an endowed school with £90, and other charities with £94 —The sub district comprises six parishes, parts of two other parishes, and a chapelry Acres, 24,884 Pop, 4,021 Houses 846

BODENHAM, a village in Nunton parish, Wilts, 3 miles SSE of Salisbury It has a post office under Salisbury

BODEWRYD, an extra parochial chapelry in the district and county of Anglesey, 2¾ miles SW of Amlwch r station, and 12½ NE of Holyhead Post town, Amlwch, under Bangor Acres, 526 Real property, £1,687 Pop., 26 Houses, 4 The property is all in one estate The living is a vicarage in the diocese of Bangor Value, £70 Patron, Lord Stanley of Alderley The church has monuments of the Wynnes and is small

BODFACH, a township in Llanfyllin parish, Montgomery on the river Cain, ¾ of a mile NW of Llanfyllin Pop, 42 Bodfach House is an elegant mansion, the seat of Lord Mostyn and fine grounds, with a charming view

BODFARY See BODVARI

BODFARI or BODVARI, a village in St Asaph district, Flint, and a parish partly in that district and county, and partly in Ruthin district, Denbigh The village stands near the confluence of the rivers Clwyd and Wheeler, 2¾ miles E of Trefnant r station, and 4

NE of Denbigh and it has a post office under Rhyl, and is a good fishing station It is supposed to be the Roman Varis, and has yielded numerous Roman coins, urns, and other relics An ancient camp, supposed to be British and called Moel y gaer is on a neighbouring hill The parish includes also the township of Aberwheeler. Acres, 4,795 Real property, £5,874 Pop, 813 Houses, 187 The scenery of vale and hill is fine. The living is a rectory in the diocese of St Asaph Value, £296 Patron, the Bishop of Llandaff The church stands on a rising ground, and has a good tower and a carved oak pulpit Charities £6

BODFFIFIG a tything in Aberffraw parish, Anglesey

BODFELL HALL, a residence near Pwllheli, in Carnarvon It was the birthplace of Mrs. Thrale or Piozzi.

BODFFRIN, or BODVERN, a parish in Pwllheli district, Carnarvon, on the coast, 4½ miles N by W of Aberdaron and 14 WSW of Pwllheli r station Post town, Aberdaron, under Pwllheli Acres 511 Real property, £273 Pop, 50 Houses, 12 The living is a p curacy, united with Llaniestyn, in the diocese of Bangor The church has disappeared, but there are ruins of an ancient chapel

BODFUAN See BODVEAN

BODGADFAN, a township in Llangelynin parish, Merioneth, on the coast, 4½ miles N of Towyn Real property, £561 Pop, 211

BODGEDRWYDD, a tything in Aberffraw parish, Anglesey

BODGONWYCH, a township in Llangernieu parish, Denbigh, 9 miles NE of Llanrwst Pop, 78

BODGYNFEL, a township in Gwyddelwern parish, Merioneth 2 miles N of Corwen

BODHAM, a parish in Erpingham district, Norfolk, 3 miles E of Holt, 5¼ W of the line of the projected railway to Cromer, and 12 E of Walsingham r station Post town, Holt, under Thetford. Acres 1,688 Real property, £2 007 Pop, 316 Houses 71 The property is divided among a few The living is a rectory in the diocese of Norwich Value not reported Patron, T J Mott, Esq The church is very good.

BODIAM or BODIHAM, a village and a parish in Ticehurst district, Sussex The village stands on the river Rother, 3¾ miles ESE of Hurst Green, and 4 ENE of Robertsbridge r station, and it has a post office under Hurst Green, and a fair on 6 June The parish comprises 1,596 acres. Real property £2 495 Pop, 303 Houses, 60 The manor belonged to Sir Edward Dalryngrudge, who fought at Crecy and Poictiers, passed to the Lewknors and others, and now belongs to A E Fuller, Esq A grand strong castle on it was built by Dalryngrudge, stood out for the Crown against the parliamentarians in the civil war, was taken by the latter and dismantled, and is now a picturesque ruin, nearly square, with round towers at the angles, square towers in the middle of the sides, a great machicolated gateway, and remains of ancient defences and approach A modern mansion, called Bodiam Castle, stands in the vicinity The living is a vicarage in the diocese of Chichester Value, £250 * Patron, T Cubitt, Esq The church is early and decorated English

BODICOTT a chapelry in Adderbury parish Oxford, near the Oxford canal the Cherwell river and the Oxford and Rugby railway, 2 miles S of Banbury It has a post office under Banbury Acres, 1,080 Real property £4,334 Pop, 676 Houses 163. The property is much subdivided Bodicott House and Bodicott Grange are chief residences The living is a vicarage in the diocese of Oxford Value, £150 * Patron, New College, Oxford The church is good, and here are Baptist and Wesleyan chapels and a national school John Kersey the mathematician, was a native

BODIDDA, a township in Gyffin parish, Carnarvon, 1 mile SW of Conway Pop, 157

BODIDRIS, and BODIDRIS IFFLAM two townships in Llanarmon parish, Denbigh, 8 miles SE of Ruthin Pop 106 This belonged formerly to the Lloyds, and belong now to the Mostyns

BODICREF ABBOT and BODICREF VALL two townships in Llanarmon parish, Denbigh, 5½ miles ESE of Ruthin Pop 93 and 120

BODINGEN, a township in Ysceifiog parish, Flint, 3½ miles S of Holywell Pop, 18

BODINGTON See BODDINGTON, Northampton

BODINNOCK, a hamlet in Lanteglos-by Fowey parish, Cornwall, 5½ miles SSE of Lostwithiel

BODLES, a hamlet in Bentley with Arksey parish, W R Yorkshire, 2 miles N of Doncaster

BODLE STREET, a chapelry in four parishes, Sussex, 5 miles NE of Hailsham. It has a post office under Hurst Green Pop 763 Living, a rectory Value, £140 *

BODLITH, a township in Llansilin parish, Denbigh, 7¼ miles SE of Chirk

BODLLEWYDDAN, a chapelry in St. Asaph parish, Flint, on the verge of the county 3 miles W of St Asaph r station Post town, St Asaph, under Rhyl Pop, 653. The manor belonged at one time to the family of Humphries and was purchased from them in the time of Charles II, by Speaker Sir William Williams The present mansion on it the seat of Sir Hugh Williams, Bart, is a beautiful castellated edifice, amid tasteful grounds The living is a vicarage in the diocese of St Asaph Value, £200 Patron Sir H Williams Bart The church was built in 1856–60, by the Dowager Lady Willoughby de Broke as a memorial of her husband, stands on a conspicuous site, is a richly ornate cruciform structure in the decorated English style, comprises a nave of 66 feet, a chancel of 42½ feet, an octagonal vestry, and a tower and spire 202 feet high, and is said to have cost £60,000

BODLYMAN, a township in Bettws Abergele parish, Denbigh, 3½ miles SW of Abergele Pop, 131

BODLYN LAKE, a lake 6 miles NNE of Barmouth, in Merioneth Some cairns, standing stones, and other antiquities are near it

BODLYNGHARAD (ISAF and UCHAF) two townships in Llanfwrog parish, Denbigh, in the neighbourhood of Ruthin

BODMIN, a town, a parish, a sub district, and a district in Cornwall The town stands in a hollow between two hills near the centre of the county, 3½ miles WNW of Bodmin Road r station, and 22 SW of Launceston A hermitage of St Guron stood here about the beginning of the 6th century, and gave place, about 518 to a monastic cell founded by St. Petroc This is thought by some, but erroneously, to have become the first seat of the bishopric of Cornwall, was occupied by old British or Benedictine monks till 926, and gave place then to a Benedictine priory, founded by King Athelstan This was destroyed by Danish pirates in 981, yet continued to be a centre of monks till about 1120, and then was succeeded by an Augustinian monastery, founded by one Algar, and this passed, at the dissolution, to Thomas Sternhold one of the translators of the Psalms A Grey friary was founded by John of London, a merchant, and augmented by Edmund, Earl of Cornwall, was given, at the dissolution, to William Abbot, and passed, about twenty years after, to the corporation Part of the refectory was afterwards used as the town hall A lazar house was founded, at an early period, in the north western vicinity refounded and incorporated by Queen Elizabeth and endowed with property, yielding £140 a year which came to be transferred to the infirmary at Truro, and some remains of the building including several pointed arches, were not long ago standing No fewer than thirteen churches or free chapels were at one time in the town and its environs, and one of these, an ivy clad structure, called the chapel of St Thomas, still adjoins the chancel of the parish church while a tower, which belonged to another, called the chapel of the Holy Cross stands on a hill about ¼ a mile to the N The town was so populous in 1351 as to lose 1,500 persons in that year by pestilence, and it was one of the places which had authority to stamp tin, but it lost that privilege in 13-7 It owed its consequence mainly to the number and influence of its ecclesiastics and it sank suddenly at the Reformation, into much decay, but it revived during last century was then made the seat of the assizes for the county, and has since enjoyed some prosperity as a provincial metropolis Perkin Warbeck commenced his rebellion here, preparatory to his attack on Exeter, the Cornish and Devonish men also commenced their insurrection here in the time of Edward VI, and Fairfax took the town Powers were obtained, in 1864 and 1867, to make railways from Bodmin to the Cornwall railway, and to Wadebridge

The town consists chiefly of one long street, running E and W, and a good view of it is got from Beacon hill to the S The county hall contains two handsome court houses, grand jury room, indictment room, and other offices The mayoralty house, with judges lodging, was built in 1838 The county jail was rebuilt in 1859, at a cost of £40,000, and has capacity for 15. male and 42 female prisoners The county lunatic asylum, as also the jail, stands in the outskirts of the town The market house was opened in 1840, and is commodious The county militia barracks are a recent erection The parish church measures 151 feet by 63, was, save the tower and part of the chancel, rebuilt, in the perpendicular style, in 1472, has a square tower, formerly surmounted by a lofty spire, which fell by lightning in 1699, and contains a Norman font, some curiously carved old oak seats, and a large sculptured monument of Thomas Vyvyan, a prior who died in 1533 There are chapels for Wesleyans, Bible Christians, and Lady Huntingdon's Connexion The town has a head post office,‡ a banking office, a literary institution, and two chief inns There used to be annual races and occasional assemblies A weekly market is held on Saturday, and fairs on 25 Jan, the Saturday before Palm Sunday, the Tuesday before Whit Sunday, 6 July, and 6 Dec Bone lace was formerly made in considerable quantity, and shoe making is now carried on The mines of Restormel, Messer, Carnwinnan, Boconnoc Great Treveddoe, West Fortescue, Wheal Fortescue, and Wheal Maudlin are near enough to have some influence on the trade. The town was incorporated by Edward III, and it sent two members to parliament from the time of Edward I till 1867, but was reduced, by the act of that year, to the right of sending only one Its municipal boundaries comprise only the town but its parl boundaries comprise four parishes It is governed by a mayor, four aldermen, and twelve councillors, and it is the seat of all the assizes and quarter sessions for the county and of county courts Direct taxes in 1857, £2,481 Electors in 1868, 403 Pop of the m borough, 4,466, of the p borough, 6,381 Houses, 794 and 1,191

The parish comprises 6,191 acres Real property, £14,675, of which £11,940 are in the borough Pop, 4 809 Houses, 864 The property is not much divided Bodmin priory, on the site of the ancient monastery, passed from Thomas Sternhold to successively the Pescodes the Pashleighs, the Penningtons, and the Gilberts A trigonometrical station, 1 mile E of the town, is 645 feet high A monument to the late General Gilbert, 144 feet high, is on the Beacon to the S The living is a vicarage in the diocese of Exeter Value £350 * Patron, J F Basset, Esq —The sub district contains the parishes of Bodmin, Lanhydrock, Lanivet, and Withiel Acres, 16,317 Pop, 5,524 Houses, 1,222 —The district comprehends also the sub district of Lanlivery, containing the parishes of Lanlivery, Luxulion, St Winnow, and Lostwithiel, the sub district of St Mabyn, containing the parishes of St Mabyn, St. Tudy, Helland, Cardinham, Warleggon Temple, and Blisland, and the sub district of Egloshayle, containing the parishes of Egloshayle St Minver Lanhydron and St Kew Acres of the district, 89,091 Poor rates in 1866, £10,710 Pop in 1861, 19,691 Houses, 4,019 Marriages in 1866 100 births 605,—of which 42 were illegitimate deaths 395,—of which 93 were at ages under 5 years, and 25 at ages above 85 years Marriages in the ten years 1851-60, 1,498, births, 6 385, deaths, 4,025 The places of worship in 1851 were 24 of the Church of England, with 6,065 sittings, 29 of Wesleyan Methodists, with 3,9 7 s 1 of Primitive Methodists, with 40 attendants, 19 of the Wesleyan Association, with 3,697 sittings, 15 of Bible Christians, with 1 65 s, 1 of Lady Huntingdon's Connexion, with 301 s, 1 undefined with 30 s, and 1 of Roman Catholics, with 200 s The schools were 28 public day schools, with 1,234 scholars, 50 private day schools, with 893 s, 41 Sunday schools, with 2,152 s, and 1 evening school for adults, with 13 s. The workhouse is in Bodmin

BODMIN ROAD, a station on the Cornwall railway, 20¾ miles NE of Truro, and 27 W of Plymouth

BODNEY a parish in Swaffham district, Norfolk, on the river Wissey, 6½ miles W by S of Watton and 7 S by E of Swaffham r station Post town, Great Cressingham, under Thetford Acres, 2,605 Real property, £1,304 Pop, 117 Houses, 19 The property is divided among a few Bodney Hall was a retreat of French nuns after the first French revolution The living is a rectory, annexed to the rectory of Great Cressingham, in the diocese of Norwich The church is good

BODNOD, a township in Eglwys fach parish, Denbigh, 6½ miles N of Llanrwst Pop, 465

BODORGAN, a station on the Chester and Holyhead railway, 12 miles SE by E of Holyhead Bodorgan House, the seat of O A F Meyrick, Esq, 2¼ miles SSW of the station, is an elegant edifice

BODORLAS, a township in Corwen parish, Merioneth, in the vicinity of Corwen Pop, 177

BODORRYN, a township in Abergele parish, Denbigh Real property, £2,059 Pop, 139

BODOLN, an ancient seat of the Owens, near Bodorgan House, 2¾ miles SE of Aberffraw, in Anglesey

BODRACH a township in Llangerniew parish, Denbigh, 9 miles NE of Llanrwst Pop., 139

BODPAN, a township in Llanfyllin parish, Montgomery Pop, 77

BODRYDDAN, the seat of the Conways, 1¼ mile E of Rhuddlan, in Flint It was the residence of Dean Shipley the father in-law of Bishop Heber

BODUILLEIN, a township in Ruabon parish, Denbigh, 5½ miles N of Chirk Pop, 338

BODVACH See BODFACH

BODVARI See BODFARI

BODVEAN or BODVAEN a parish in Pwllheli district Carnarvon, 2½ miles SE of Nevin, and 4 WNW of Pwllheli r station It has a post office under Pwllheli Acres, 2,572 Real property, £1,434 Pop, 382 Houses, 84 The property is divided between two Bodvean Hall is the seat of Lord Newborough The living is a rectory in the diocese of Bangor Value, £198 Patron, the Bishop of Bangor The church is modern, and has monuments of the Wynnes There are a Calvinistic Methodist chapel, and a slightly endowed school

BODVEEN See BODFEAN

BODWRDDA See ABERDARON

BODWROG a parochial chapelry in the district and county of Anglesea, 4 miles S by W of Llanerchymedd, and 4 NNE of Ty Croes r station Post town, Gwindy, under Bangor Acres, 1,318 Real property, £1 053. Pop, 319 Houses, 78 The property is subdivided The living is a vicarage, annexed to the vicarage of Llandrygarn, in the diocese of Bangor The church is good

BODYDDON, a township in Llanfyllin parish, Montgomery Pop, 173

BODYHAM See BODIAM

BODYNWYDDOG, a township in Bryn Eglwys parish, Denbigh, 5¼ miles NW of Llangollen

BODYSCALLEN, an ancient seat of the Wynnes, now the property of the Mostyns, in the north eastern extremity of Carnarvon, near the Conway river 2½ miles NNE of Conway

BODYSGAW and BODYSGAWEN two townships in Llannefydd parish, Denbighshire, 5¼ miles NW of Denbigh

BODYVOL, a township in Llanfechan parish, Montgomery, 4½ miles E of Llanfyllin

BOGNOR a small town and a township chapelry in South Bersted parish, Sussex The town stands on the coast, 3¾ miles S of the South Coast railway, and 6½ SE

... of Chichester. It has a governing body under a local act, a head post office, a station with telegraph at the terminus of a railway, opened in 1864, to the South Coast line at Fastergate, and a pier, constructed chiefly of iron on the screw principle, 1,000 feet long with a head 10 feet across, opened in 1865. The town was changed from an obscure hamlet to a fashionable watering place, between 1790 and 1799, by Sir Richard Hotham, at a cost of about £60,000, and took, for a time, the name of Hothamston. It was frequented by Queen Charlotte and her children in the time of George III, and it then possessed a sort of exclusive character, but it afterwards became dependent on general public patronage. It comprises rows of brick houses, two squares open on one side to the sea, a crescent, a terrace, and several detached mansions, it possesses good lodging houses, several hotels, and excellent bathing conveniences, and it has a church of 1821, an Independent chapel of 1869, a Wesleyan chapel, a public school for 60 girls, a reading room, a circulating library, a people's institute, a small annual regatta, and occasional races. Markets are held thrice a week, and a fair on 5 July. The surrounding country is flat, and the Bognor rocks, famed by geologists and not long ago forming a line of low cliffs along the coast, are now visible only at low water.—Pop. of the town, 2,726. Houses, 457.—The chapelry was constituted in 1822. The living is a p. curacy in the diocese of Chichester. Value, £107.* Patron, the Archbishop of Canterbury. Bognor Lodge, built by Sir R. Hotham, is now the seat of Sir J. L. Harrington, Bart.

BOGTHORN, a hamlet in Keighley parish, W. R. Yorkshire.

BOKERLEY DITCH, an ancient British earthwork in the S of Wilts, extending from Cranbourne Chase, across Grim's Ditch to Tippet. It is thought to have been a territorial boundary of the Belgæ. Many relics have been found, and many barrows still occur around it.

BOLAM, a chapelry in Gainford parish, Durham, 5½ miles S of Bishop Auckland. It has a post office under Darlington. Pop., 190. The chapelry was constituted in 1867. Living, a p. curacy. Value, £150.

BOLAM, a township and a parish in Castle Ward district, Northumberland. The township lies between the rivers Blyth and Wansbeck, near the Devil's causeway, a branch of Watling street, and on the Morpeth and Scots Gap railway, near Angerton station, 8 miles W SW of Morpeth. Acres, 1,119. Pop., 102. Houses, 21.—The parish includes also the townships of Bolam Vicarage, Trewick, Gallow Hill, Shortflatt, Harnham, Bradford, and Belsay, the last of which has a post office under Newcastle on Tyne. Acres, 7,376. Real property, £7,682. Pop., 635. Houses, 133. The property is divided among a few. Bolam manor belonged anciently to the De Bolams, passed to the Horsleys, and went from them to Lord Decies. Harnham manor belonged, in the time of Charles II, to Colonel Philip Babington, governor of Berwick. Belsay Castle belonged formerly to the Middletons, and belongs now to the baronet family of Monck. A stone coffin was found in a tumulus on Bolam moor. Coal and limestone occur. The living is a vicarage in the diocese of Durham. Value, £273.* Patron, the Lord Chancellor. The church is ancient, in good condition, and contains the effigies of a Knight Templar, supposed to be Sir Walter de Bolam, and a tomb of the Middletons.

BOLAM VICARAGE, a township in Bolam parish, Northumberland. Acres, 189. Pop., 30. Houses, 4.

BOLAS MAGNA, or GREAT BOLAS, a township and a parish in Wellington district, Salop. The township lies on the river Tern, 2½ miles NNE of Crudgington station, and 6 NW of Newport, and has a post office, of the name of Great Bolas, under Wellington, Salop.—The parish includes also the township of Meeson. Acres, 2,... Real property, £4,069. Pop., 278. Houses, 61. The property is divided among a few. The living is a rectory in the diocese of Lichfield. Value, £301.* Patron, ... Hill.

BOLAS PARVA, or LITTLE BOLAS, a township in Hodnet parish, Salop, 6½ miles NW of Bolas Magna. Pop., 14.

BOLBECK, an extensive tract in Shotley parish, Northumberland, on the river Derwent, 7 miles S of Corbridge. It lay in commonage till 1765, and an act was then obtained for enclosing it.

BOLEBROUGH, a township in Llanllwchaiarn parish, Montgomeryshire, 2 miles SW of Montgomery.

BOLBURY. See BOLTBURY.

BOLD, two hamlets and a township in Prescot parish, Lancashire. The hamlets are Bold and Bold Heath, and the former stands adjacent to the Lincoln railway, 4 miles ESE of Prescot. The township includes also the hamlet of Maypole. Acres, 4,238. Real property, £8,151. Pop., 778. Houses, 137. The family of Bold, now represented by that of Bold Hoghton, were seated here from the Conquest till 1761, and they gave name to Bold street in Liverpool. The ancient mansion is now a farm house, and the modern one is Bold Hall. Bishop Barnes, who died in 1588, was a native.

BOLD, a hamlet in ... on Bitterell parish, Salop, 6½ miles NW of Cleobury Mortimer.

BOLDERSTONE, a locality 1½ mile from Rochdale, in Lancashire, with a post-office under Rochdale.

BOLDMERE, a chapelry in Sutton Coldfield parish, Warwick, near Sutton Coldfield. It was constituted in 1858, and its post town is Sutton Coldfield, under Birmingham. Pop., 918. Houses, 158. The living is a vicarage in the diocese of Worcester. Value, £134.* Patron, the Rector of Sutton Coldfield.

BOLDON, two villages and a parish in South Shields district, Durham. The villages are West and East Boldon, and the former stands in the southern vicinity of the Brandling Junction railway, 4½ miles NW of Sunderland, and has a post office under Gateshead, while the latter is about a mile to the E.—The parish comprises 3,934 acres. Real property, £8,637. Pop., 1,024. Houses, 211. The property is much subdivided. The manor has belonged, from time immemorial, to the see of Durham, and gives name to the "Boldon Book," an ancient survey of the diocese preserved in the cathedral. Limestone is abundant. The living is a rectory in the diocese of Durham. Value, £653.* Patron, the Bishop of Durham. The church is early English, and has several memorial windows put up in 1851. There are a chapel of ease, an Independent chapel, built in 1863, a Wesleyan Methodist chapel, a national school, and charities £14.

BOLDRE, a village and a parish in Lymington district, Hants. The village stands on the Lymington river, near the Lymington branch railway, 2½ miles N of Lymington, and has a post office under Lymington.—The parish includes also the tythings of South Baddesley, Battramsley, Pilley, and Walhampton, Sway and Walhampton. Acres, 11,950, of which 1,790 are water. Real property, exclusive of the parts within Lymington borough, £9,810. Pop., 2,842. Houses, 605. The property is much subdivided. Fully one half of the surface, comprising 180 acres in Wilverley walk, 635 in Rhinefield walk, 750 in Whitley Ridge walk, and 5,030 in Ladycross walk, is in the New Forest. Boldre Wood House is used as a lodge ... and Walhampton House belongs to the ... family. Many parts contain ... close scenery, and some spots command extensive ... views. ... parts within a line from East ... through Boldre church, to the west bank of Lymington river ... within Lymington parliamentary borough. The living is a vicarage, united with the cur. of Lymington, and ... 1861 to that of Brockenhurst, in the diocese of Winchester. Value, £331.* Patron, the ... The church stands on a hillock ... however, ... about a mile from the village, is early English, ... altered by restorations, has a singular ... and contains a well preserved ... a monument ... who represented Lymington in the time of Charles I, and the ... one of the ... "Forest Scenery," ... the ... place of Southey to his second wife, Caroline Bowles. ... at Boldre ... is a separate benefice, was constituted in 1840, and is in the patronage of the Bishop of Winchester, with income of £100.* The chapelries of Sway and Baddesley also are separate benefices. There is a Baptist chapel. A school, founded and endowed by Gilpin, has £57 a year. Gilpin was vicar during thirty years, and died in 1804.

BOLDRON, a township in Startforth parish, N. R. Yorkshire, 2 miles SW by S of Barnard Castle. Acres, 1,222. Pop., 178. Houses, 42.

BOLE, a parish in the district of Gainsborough, and county of Nottingham; on the river Trent and on the Manchester and Lincolnshire railway, 2½ miles SW of Gainsborough. Post town, Gainsborough. Acres, 1,250. Real property, £2,101. Pop., 238. Houses, 44. The property is all in one estate. The living is a vicarage in the diocese of Lincoln. Value, £130. Patron, the Bishop of Lincoln. The church is old. There are a Wesleyan chapel, and charities £6.

BOLEBROOK, an ancient seat of the Sackvilles in Hartfield parish, Sussex, 4½ miles E of East Grinstead. It was built of brick, in the 15th century, but is now a small ruin. It passed, for a time, to Lord G. Germaine, and gave him the title of Baron.

BOLEHALL AND GLASCOTE, a township in Tamworth parish, Warwick, in the south eastern outskirts of Tamworth town and borough. Real property, £7,087. Pop., 1,191. Houses, 252.

BOLEY HILL. See ROCHESTER.

BOLINGBROKE, a village, a parish, and a soke or wapentake in Lincoln. The village stands 3½ miles W by S of Spilsby r. station, and 7½ SE of Horncastle, and has a post office under Spilsby. A weekly market is held at it on Tuesday, and a fair on 10 July. It gives the title of Viscount to the family of St. John. The parish includes an allotment, called New Bolingbroke, in the West Fen, and also an allotment in Wildmore Fen, and is in Spilsby district. Acres 2,570. Real property, £4,591. Pop. 1,019. Houses, 205. The property is much subdivided. A castle was built here by William de Romara, Earl of Lincoln, was enlarged in the time of Queen Elizabeth, and was the focus of several struggles in the civil wars of Charles I., but was dismantled by the parliamentarians, and only the SW tower of it remains. Henry IV. was born in this castle, and hence was called Henry of Bolingbroke. The living is a rectory, united with the rectory of Hareby, in the diocese of Lincoln. Value, £373. Patron, Sir John J. Smith, Bart. The church is ancient, and suffered much in the civil war, but is now pretty good. There are two Methodist chapels, an endowed national school, and charities £12.—The soke is in the Parts of Lindsey, contains twenty seven parishes, and is cut into two sections, East and West. Acres, 26,840 and 29,388. Pop. 12,376. Houses 2,498.

BOLINGBROKE (NEW), a chapelry in Bolingbroke, Mavis Enderby, Ruthby, Asgarby, Miningsby, Revesby, and Hameston parishes, Lincoln, in the fens, 5½ miles SW of Bolingbroke, and 5½ NE of Langrick r. station. It has a post office under Boston. Pop. 947. Houses, 183. The living is a vicarage in the diocese of Lincoln. Value, £100.* Patrons, Trustees. The church is modern. There are two Methodist chapels.

BOLLAIT, a farm in St Buryan parish, Cornwall, 4½ miles SW of Penzance. Tradition alleges it to have been the battlefield of Athelstan's final victory over the Britons in 936. Two standing stones are on it, called the Pipers, 12 and 16 feet high, about a furlong apart, and may possibly be memorials of the fight. A stone circle, called the Merry Maidens, also is near.

BOLLIN (THE), a river of Cheshire. It rises near Macclesfield, and runs about 20 miles north westward, past Wilmslow, Morley, and Hale, to the Mersey, about a mile below Warburton.

BOLLIN-FEE, a township in Wilmslow parish, Cheshire, on the Bollin river, ¼ a mile NW of Wilmslow r. station, and 6 SW of Stockport. Acres, 2,004. Real property, £8,520. Pop., 2,143. Houses, 426. The inhabitants are chiefly employed in the silk and cotton manufacture. Bollin Hall is the seat of the Fitton family.

BOLLINGTON, a township in Bowden and Rostherne parishes, Cheshire, on the Bridgewater canal, near the river Bollin, 3 miles SW of Altrincham. It has a post-office under Manchester. Acres 631. Real property, £1,827. Pop., 277. Houses, 52. It forms a curacy, annexed to the vicarage of Rostherne. The church was built in 1851, and a national school, in 1857.

BOLLINGTON, a township, a chapelry, and a sub-district in Prestbury parish, Cheshire. The township lies near the river Bollin, the Macclesfield canal and the Macclesfield and Manchester railway, 3 miles N by E of Macclesfield, and has a post office‡ under Macclesfield. Acres, 1,184. Real property, £16,184, of which £1,373 are in freestone and slate quarries. Pop. 3,439. Houses, 1,108. The property is subdivided. The inhabitants are employed chiefly in quarries, collieries, and silk and cotton factories. The chapelry is conterminate with the township, and was constituted in 1835. The living is a p. curacy in the diocese of Chester. Value, £150.* Patron, the Vicar of Prestbury. The church was built in 1834, at a cost of £4,000, and is in the early English style. There are an Independent chapel in the early second pointed style, built in 1868, three other dissenting chapels, a Roman Catholic chapel, and two national schools. The sub district comprises five townships. Acres, 8,676. Pop., 10,357. Houses, 2,243.

BOLLOM, a hamlet in Clarborough parish, Notts, 1 mile N of East Retford. Pop., 103.

BOLNEY, a hamlet in Harpsden parish, Oxford, 2 miles S of Henley. It is said to have been formerly a parish. Bolney Court is the seat of the Maynes.

BOLNEY, a village and a parish in Cuckfield district, Sussex. The village stands 3½ miles SW by W of Cuckfield, and 5 W of Haywards Heath r. station, and has a post office under Cuckfield, and fairs on 17 May and 11 Dec. The parish comprises 3,540 acres. Real property, £4,112. Pop., 789. Houses, 157. The property is much subdivided. The northern portion is covered with wood, and lies within St Leonard's forest. Bolney common is famed for cherry trees, and commands noble views. Bolney Place and Colwood House are chief residences. The living is a vicarage in the diocese of Chichester. Value, £150.* Patron, the Bishop. The church was recently restored and enlarged.

BOLNHURST, a parish in the district and county of Bedford, 3 miles E by S of Sharnbrook r. station, and 6½ NNE of Bedford. Post town, Wilden, under Bedford. Acres, 2,160. Real property, £2,083. Pop., 348. Houses, 67. The property is divided among a few. The living is a rectory in the diocese of Ely. Value, £159.* Patron, the Rev. F. M. Harvey. The church is good. An endowed school has £12.

BOLSOVER, a small town and a sub district, in the district of Chesterfield, and a parish in the districts of Chesterfield and Mansfield, Derby. The town occupies the summit of a steep hill, 5½ miles E of Chesterfield r. station. It commands a splendid view, retains traces of fortifications which once surrounded it, and was formerly a place of note, but is now straggling and decayed. It has a post office‡ under Chesterfield, a nominal weekly market, and fairs on the last Friday of April and the first Friday of Oct. It formerly carried on a famous manufacture of steel buckles and spurs, and subsequently engaged in the making of tobacco pipes and fire bricks. Pop., 1,526. Houses, 350.—The parish includes also the hamlets of Oakley, Whaley, Oxcroft, Stanfree, Shuttlewood, Woodside, Woodhouse, and Glapwell. Acres, 6,000. Real property, £8,079. Pop., 1,629. Houses, 367. The property is divided among many. The manor belonged at the Conquest to Peveril of the Peak, passed to the Earl of Morton, afterwards King John, went, in the time of Henry III., to the Earl of Chester, and afterwards to Lord Abergavenny, was resumed, in 1243, by the Crown, passed to Roger Lovetot, the Ripards, the Sturys, the Earl of Richmond, and the Duke of Norfolk, reverted again to the Crown, went, in the time of Edward VI., to Sir John Byron, and afterwards to Lord Talbot and Sir Charles Cavendish, descended from the last to the Dukes of Newcastle, and passed from them, by marriage, to the Duke of Portland A Norman keep was built on it by the Peverils, and made a military figure in the troubles of the time of King John A palatial castle superseded this under Sir Charles Cavendish was besieged and partly demolished in the civil war, underwent partial reconstruction after the Restoration, was unroofed about the middle of last century, and is now a picturesque ruin The Duke of Newcastle three times entertained Charles I and his court here, and on one of these occasions, which was assisted by the genius of Ben Jonson, spent about £15,000 The riding house is still in good order, and the Tudor restoration of the Norman keep is used as the parsonage A yellow magnesian limestone is quarried in the parish, and was used in the construction of the new houses of parliament The living is a vicarage in the diocese of Lichfield Value, £111 * Patron, the Duke of Portland The church is Norman with later additions, has a fine early English spire, and contains splendid monuments of the Dukes of Newcastle and Portland, and a number of other monuments There are chapels for Independents and Methodists, and charities £103 One of the Dukes of Newcastle and his second duchess were noted for their writings, and the lady of the present vicar is known for a history of Etruria and several kindred works The castle contains a fine collection of Etruscan and other antiquities The sub district contains three parishes, with the exception of one of the hamlets of Bolsover Acres, 11,247 Pop, 2,402 Houses, 523

BOLSTERSTONE, a chapelry in Ecclesfield parish, W R Yorkshire, on the river Don, 1½ mile SW of Deepcar [illegible] station, and 8 NW by N of Sheffield. It has a post office under Sheffield. Real property, £2,996 Pop, 1,904 There are collieries coke works and chemical works Bolsterstone hill is 970 feet high The living is a p curacy in the dio of York Value, £119 * Patron, J R Wilson, Esq The church is plain There are a Roman Catholic chapel and a free school

BOLSTONE. See BOLTSTONE

BOLTBURY, a hamlet in Malborough parish, Devon, on the coast between Bolt Tail and Sewmill Cove, 4½ miles SW of Kingsbridge Boltbury Down here falls precipitously to the sea and a chasm, at the highest part of its sea-cliff, bears the name of Ralph's Hole, and was long the retreat of a noted smuggler

BOLTBY, a township in Felixkirk parish, N R Yorkshire, 5 miles NE of Thirsk Acres, 1,782 Real property, £2,970 Pop 3[illegible]6 Houses, 69

BOLT HEAD and BOLT TAIL, two headlands on the coast of Devon the former at the W side of the mouth of Salcombe haven, the latter 4½ miles NW by W of this, and 6 SSE of the mouth of the river Avon Bolt Head is 430 feet high, wild, desolate, and torn with fissures and caverns Bolt Tail is pierced at the shore by Ramillies Cove which is named from the wrecking of the Ramillies frigate at it in 1760 See BOLTBURY

BOLTON, a small town, two townships, and a parish in Wigton district Cumberland The town stands on the river Ellen, 6½ miles SSW of Wigton, consists of two parts, High and Low and has a dingy appearance A branch railway to it from the Maryport and Carlisle line, was opened on 26th December 1866 The townships are High Bolton and Low Bolton or Bolton wood and Quarry hill Acres of H B, 3,877 Pop, 330 Houses 6[illegible] Acres of L B, [illegible]1,570 Pop, 718 Houses, 119 The parish consists of the two townships, and its post-town is Ireby under Wigton Real property, £8,121, of which £[illegible] are in mines Pop, 1,048 Houses, 211 The property is much subdivided Coal, limestone and copper ore are worked A copper battle-axe was found [illegible] The living is a rectory in the diocese of Carlisle Value, £212 * Patron the Earl of Lonsdale The church is ancient, in tolerable condition, and was alleged by old superstition to have been built by a wizard

BOLTON, a township in Edlingham parish, Northumberland, on the river Alne, 4 miles NW of Alnwick Acres 2,043 Pop 154 Houses 31 The Earl of Surrey mustered his forces here before the battle of Flodden An hospital was founded here before 1225 by Robert de Roos, and became the property of the Collingwoods Some remains of antiquity have been found The township forms a curacy annexed to the vicarage of Edlingham

BOLTON, a chapelry in Morland parish Westmoreland, on the river Eden, and on the Eden Valley railway, near Kirkby Thore r station, and 4 miles NNW of Appleby It includes the hamlet of Bewley Castle, and has a post office under Penrith Acres, with Morland township, 5,149 Rated property, £2,223 Pop 390 Houses, 73 The property is much subdivided The living is a p curacy in the diocese of Carlisle Value £80 * Patron, the Vicar of Morland. The church is good, and there is a Methodist chapel

BOLTON, a township in Bishop Wilton parish, E R Yorkshire, 3 miles NW of Pocklington Acres, 904 Real property, £1,340 Pop, 127 Houses, 24 Bolton Hall is the seat of the Prestons.

BOLTON, a township in Calverley parish, W R Yorkshire, 2 miles NNE of Bradford It includes the hamlets of Hodgson Fold, Low Fold, and Out Lane, and part of the village of Frizinghall Acres 7[illegible]6 Real property, £3,604 Pop, 937 Houses, 216 The inhabitants are chiefly employed in the woollen factories

BOLTON, a town, two townships, three sub districts, and a district in Lancashire The town is in the parish of Bolton le Moors, and sometimes itself bears that name, it consists of the townships of Little Bolton, Great Bolton, and Haulgh, excepting the higher or detached part of the first, and it stands on the rivulets Croal, Bradshaw, and Tonge, 1½ mile NNW of their joint influx to the Irwell, and 11 NW of Manchester A canal connects it with Manchester and Bury, and railways go from it in six directions toward Manchester Bury Blackburn, Chorley, Wigan and Leigh It dates from the time of the Saxons, became a market town, by royal charter, in 1256, and made some figure at several points of history The manor belonged, in 1037 to Richard de Poictou, passed, in 1100, to Roger de Merlays, went afterwards to Ranulph de Blundeville Earl of Chester, belonged, in the time of Edward III, to the Ferrers, passed to the Pilkingtons till forfeited by Sir Thomas for his adherence to the cause of Richard III, was then given to Lord Stanley, who became Earl of Derby, and is now divided into four parts one belonging to the Earl of Derby, another to Lord Bradford another to S Freeman Esq and another to various parties The seventh Earl of Derby besieged and stormed the town in 1644, in the cause of Charles I, and was beheaded in it in 1651, in terms of a military sentence, after the battle of Worcester His Countess also acted as a heroine, and was the Charlotte de Tremouille who figures in "Peveril of the Peak" The town made a start in manufactures in 1337 when a number of immigrant Flemings settled in it and it displayed such vast enterprise in them during the sixty years preceding 1862 as to have become a great provincial town No fewer than about 400 dwelling houses and shops, besides warehouses factories, and other erections, were built in it during the year 1858

Much of the ground now occupied by the town, and by environing villages, was, not many years ago all bare or rural, without a single dwelling Part of the site is a hill, and this commands a good view of the valley below, studded with factories and print works The town presents strongly the aspect of a great seat of manufacture, yet has several long and broad streets, and contains many good private houses, and some fine public buildings The exchange, with free library was erected in 1825 The market hall a very fine structure, was built in 1855, at a cost of about £80,000 The new town-hall was in progress in 1866, at a cost of about £30,000 A public park of about [illegible] acres was opened in 1866, and cost about £60,000 A mechanics institute, a monument to the Earl of Derby of 1651, and several other public erections also are recent The water works were constructed at a cost of £[illegible],000 A spacious ornamental cemetery, at Tonge was opened in 1856 The grammar school dates from 1641 possesses £456 a year from en dowment, and had Ainsworth, the lexicographer, for both pupil and master. The Church of England institute was built in 1853, and is a fine edifice, with main frontage of 150 feet. Two other schools have endowed incomes of £82, and £21, and charities, additional to the schools have £1,017. There are numerous public schools, a temperance hall, assembly rooms, a theatre, and public baths. The places of worship, in 1851, were 36, with about 23,000 sittings, and twelve more were built prior to 1869, also two rebuilt and enlarged, giving an addition of about 12,000 sittings. St Peter's church, the mother one of Bolton le Moors, was erected in 142-, was a large structure, with very beautiful east and south windows, and, in March 1865, was about to be taken down and rebuilt. Holy Trinity church, in Bradford square, was built in 1825, at a cost of £13,413, and is a handsome edifice in the later English style, with a tower. St Paul's church, at end of Deansgate, was built in 1863. St. James' church in 1869, and each has a tower and spire. The Congregational chapel, at the junction of St George's road and Bath street, was built also in 1863, at a cost of £7,000, and is in the decorated English style, with a spire 130 feet high. The Wesleyan chapel, in Park street, was built in 1864, at a cost of £11,000, and is a very beautiful edifice, with fine carvings.

Textile manufactures in Bolton were greatly accelerated by the inventions of Arkwright, who resided here when a barber, and of Crompton, who, when a weaver, lived at Hall in the Wood, an old timbered seat of the Starkies in the neighbourhood, still extant. Cotton velvets and muslins began to be made about 1760, and muslins, cambrics, counterpanes, dimity, and ginghams came to be the chief productions. About 17,667 persons were employed, prior to the juncture of the cotton distress of 1862, in cotton mills, print works, and bleach and dye works, and about 5,514 were employed in iron foundries and engine works. The number of factories in 1865, was 70, and that of foundries 33, and one of the machine works has a brick chimney 368 feet high. Vast quantities of coal are mined in the neighbourhood, and the trade in them contributes to the local traffic. The town has a head post office,‡ two telegraph offices, three banking offices, and eight chief inns, is a seat of petty sessions and a polling place, and publishes two weekly newspapers. Markets are held on Monday and Saturday, fairs on 4 and 5 Jan, 30 and 31 July, and 13 and 14 Oct. The town was invested with the franchise by the act of 1832, and incorporated in 1848, and it sends two members to parliament, and is governed by a mayor, twelve aldermen, and thirty six councillors. Direct taxes, in 1857, £31,087. Electors in 1868, 2,293. Pop in 1841, 50,583, in 1861, 70,395. Houses, 13,129.

Little Bolton township includes a detached part called Higher End, not within the borough, and contains the villages of Horrocks Fold and Eagley Bank. Acres, 1,450. Real property, £78,877. Pop, 25,891. Houses, 5,128. Great Bolton township is wholly within the borough. Acres, 820. Real property, £137,070. Pop, 43,435. Houses, 7,767.—The three sub districts of Bolton, are Little Bolton, Bolton Eastern, and Bolton Western, and the first consists of the portion of Little Bolton township within the borough, while the other two are simply subdivisions of Great Bolton.—The district comprehends also Sharples sub district containing Sharples township and the detached part of Little Bolton township, Edgeworth sub district, containing Edgeworth, Entwistle, and Quarlton townships, Turton sub district, containing Turton, Bradshaw, and Longworth townships, Tonge with Haulgh sub district, containing Tonge, Haulgh, Breightmet, and Harwood townships, Horwich sub district containing Horwich and Lostock townships, Halliwell sub district, containing Halliwell and Heaton townships, Westhoughton sub-district, conterminate with Westhoughton township, Hulton sub district, containing Little Hulton, Middle Hulton, Over Hulton, and Farnworth townships, Farnworth sub district, containing Farnworth and Kersley townships, and Lever sub district, containing Great Lever and Darcy Lever townships and Little Lever chapelry. Acres, 43,896. Poor rates in 1866, £39,825. Pop in 1861 130,269. Houses, 24,941. Marriages in 1866, 1,311, births, 5,640,—of which 408 were illegitimate, deaths, 4,122,—of which 1,914 were at ages under 5 years, and 39 at ages above 85 years. Marriages in the ten years 1851-60, 11,232, births, 50,712, deaths, 32,924. The places of worship in 1851 were 26 of the Church of England, with 19,611 sittings, 2 of the Presbyterian Church in England, with 850 s., 14 of Independents, with 5,971 s, 2 of Baptists, with 640 s, 2 of Quakers, with 632 s, 2 of Unitarians, with 1,014 s, 22 of Wesleyan Methodists, with 8,150 s, 2 of New Connexion Methodists, with 600 s, 9 of Primitive Methodists with 1,690 s., 1 of the Wesleyan Association, with 300 s, 1 of Calvinistic Methodists, sittings not reported, 5 of the New Church, with 786 s, 1 of Brethren, with 70 s, 1 of Latter Day Saints, with 140 s, 2 undefined, with 700 s; 2 of Roman Catholics, with 600 s, and 1 of Jews, with 14 attendants. The schools were 58 public day schools, with 7,956 scholars, 92 private day schools, with 3,682 s, 103 Sunday schools, with 25,729 s, and 18 evening schools for adults, with 522 s. The new workhouse stands at Fishpool, and is a large ornamental edifice, with excellent arrangements.

BOLTON ABBEY, or EAST BOLTON, a township chapelry in Skipton parish, W R Yorkshire, on the river Wharfe, 6 miles ENE of Skipton r station. It includes the hamlet of Bolton Bridge, which has a post office under Skipton. Acres, 3,995. Real property, £1,816. Pop., 112. Houses, 23. The property is not much divided. The manor belongs to the Duke of Devonshire, and came to him from the Burlingtons. The scenery is picturesque, and includes soft reaches of valley, undulating slopes, precipitous cliffs, hanging woods, and the wild chasm of the Strid, overhung by the mountains of Simon's Seat and Barden Fell. An Augustinian priory was founded at Embsay, in 1121, by William de Meschines, and removed, 33 years afterwards, to the banks of the Wharfe here, by his lady, to commemorate the loss of their heir at the Strid. The story of its refounding is sung by Wordsworth in his "Force of Prayer" and "White Doe of Rylstone," and by Rogers in the "Boy of Egremond." The priory was given, at the dissolution, to Henry Clifford, Earl of Cumberland, and passed from his family in 1635, to the Burlingtons. Much of the original building, together with additions, in decorated and perpendicular English, is standing in a state of ruin, and the nave serves as the present church, contains monuments of Lady Margaret Neville, Lord Clifford, and Prior Marsden, and was repaired in 1859.

> 'In the shattered fabric's heart,
> Remaineth one protected part.
> A rural chapel neatly dressed
> In covert like a little nest.'

Bolton Park, originally a gate house of the priory, is an occasional seat of the Duke of Devonshire. The living is a rectory in the diocese of Ripon. Value £111.* Patron, the Duke of Devonshire. There is a school with endowed income of £104. See STRID (THE)

BOLTON AND LEIGH RAILWAY. See NORTH WESTERN RAILWAY.

BOLTON BRIDGE. See BOLTON ABBEY.

BOLTON BROW, a hamlet in Skircoat township, W R Yorkshire, 1 mile S of Halifax.

BOLTON BY BOWLAND, or WEST BOLTON, a parish in the district of Clitheroe and W R Yorkshire, on the river Ribble, at the verge of the county, 4 miles NNE of Chatburn r station, and 6 NE by N of Clitheroe. It includes the hamlet of Forest Beck, and has a post office, of the name of Bolton by Bowland, under Blackburn. Acres, 5,792. Real property, £6,242. Pop, 729. Houses, 152. Part of the surface lay within the ancient Bowland forest. Bolton Hall was formerly the seat of Sir R. Pudsey, gave shelter to Henry VI after the battle of Hexham, and is now the property of Mrs. A. Littledale. The living is a rectory in the diocese of Ripon. Value, £325.* Patron, Mrs A. Little dal The church is later English, was restored in 1850, and contains a tomb of Sir R Pudsey and his three wives and twenty five children There are an Independent chapel, a sessions court house, an endowed school with £31 a year charities £20, and a workhouse

BOLTON CASTLE, or CASTLE BOLTON a township chapelry in Wensley parish, N R Yorkshire, in Wensleydale, 5½ miles WNW of Leyburn r station Post town, Leyburn under Bedale Acres, 5,160 Real property £1,578 Pop 253 Houses, 54 Bolton Hall is the seat of Lord Bolton, and gives him his peerage title Bolton Castle is the ruined seat of Lord Chancellor Scrope built by him in the reign of Richard II at a cost of £12,000, forms a hollow quadrangle, with towers at the corners, was the prison of Mary Queen of Scots for two years before her removal to Tutbury, and sustained a siege by the parliamentarians near the end of the civil war The living is a p curacy, united with the p. curacy of Redmire in the diocese of Ripon Value, £115 Patron, the Rector of Wensley The church is ancient

BOLTON (EAST) See BOLTON ABBEY

BOLTON EASTERN See BOLTON, Lancashire

BOLTON FELL END a locality on the E border of Cumberland, 6½ miles from Brampton It has a post office under Carlisle

BOLTON (GREAT) See BOLTON, Lancashire

BOLTON HALL See BOLTON BY BOWLAND and BOLTON CASTLE

BOLTON (HIGH) See BOLTON Cumberland

BOLTON IN-COPELAND, a hamlet in Gosforth parish Cumberland, 5 miles N of Ravenglass

BOLTON LE-MOORS, a parish in the districts of Bolton, Wigan, and Chorley Lancashire It centres in the post town of Bolton, and contains the townships of Great Bolton, Little Bolton, Sharples Quarlton Edgworth, Entwistle, Longworth, Turton, Bradshaw, Haulgh, Tonge, Breightmet, Harwood, Lostock, Darcy-Lever, Blackrod Anglezarke, and Rivington, and the chapelry of Little Lever Acres, 30,062 Real property, £332 547, of which £29,3 6 are in mines, and £4,969 in quarries Pop in 1841, 73,905, in 1861, 97,215 Houses, 18,355 The living is a vicarage in the diocese of Manchester Value, £350 * Patron, the Bishop of Manchester The vicarages of Holy Trinity, St George, Christ Church and St John, and the p curacies of All Saints Emmanuel, St Mark, and St Paul, within the borough of Bolton, are separate benefices Value of Holy Trinity St George, Christ Church, and St John, each £300, of Emmanuel, 300,* of St Mark, £100, of St Paul, £150, of All Saints, £123 Patron of H T, the Bishop of Manchester, of St G and E the Vicar of Bolton of C and St J, alternately the Crown and the Bishop, of A S, T T ipping, Esq, of St M and St P, Trustees The vicarages of Astley Bridge, Belmont, Blackrod, Bradshaw, Little Lever, and Lever Bridge, and the p curacies of Harwood, Rivington, Tonge Turton, and Walmsley also are separate benefices See the articles on these places and BOLTON

BOLTON LE SANDS a township and a parish in Lancaster district Lancashire The township lies on the Lancaster and Kendal canal, and on the Lancaster and Carlisle railway, contiguous to the sands of Morecambe bay 4 miles N by E of Lancaster, and it has a station on the railway and a post office under Lancaster Acres 1,771 Real property, £4 220 Pop, 632 Houses, 146 —The parish contains also the townships of Over Kellet Nether Kellet and Slyne with Hest Acres, 7,905 Real property, £1 ,502 Pop, 1,713 Houses 347 The property is much subdivided The living is a vicarage in the diocese of Manchester Value £187 * Patron, the Bishop of Manchester The church is modern and very good The vicarage of Over Kellet is a separate benefice An endowed school has £35, other charities £101

BOLTON (LITTLE) See BOLTON Lancashire

BOLTON (LOW) See BOLTON, Cumberland

BOLTON PERCY a township and a parish in Tadcaster district W R Yorkshire The township lies on the river Wharfe, and on the York and North Midland railway, 3½ miles ESE of Tadcaster and it has a station on the railway, and a post office under Tadcaster Acres, 2,170 Real property, £5,516 Pop 292 Houses, 51 —The parish contains also the townships of Appleton Roebuck, Colton and Steeton Acres, 7,148 Real property, £13,402 Pop, 1,118 Houses 237 The property is divided among a few The manor belonged to the Percys of Topcliffe, and afterwards to the Beaumonts The living is a rectory in the diocese of York. Value, £1,540 * Patron the Archbishop of York The church is perpendicular English was erected in 1423, consists of nave, aisles, chancel, and north chapel, with a handsome tower and contains three beautiful stalls a well preserved piscina, a monument to Lord Fairfax, the famous parliamentary general, and a memorial window of 1860 to Sir W M Milner, Bart There are a Wesleyan chapel, three public schools, and charities £34

BOLTON PRIORY See BOLTON ABBEY

BOLTON UPON DEARNE, a village and a parish in Doncaster district, W R Yorkshire The village stands on the river Dearne near the North Midland railway, 1½ mile NE of Wath and Bolton station, and 7 N by E of Rotherham and has a post office under Rotherham —The parish includes also the hamlet of Goldthorpe Acres, 2,213 Real property £1,443 Pop, 579 Houses, 112 The property is subdivided The living is a vicarage in the diocese of York Value, £88 Patron, Mrs Hirst The church is good, and there are a Wesleyan chapel, a national school, and charities £19

BOLTON UPON SWALE, a chapelry in Catterick parish, N R Yorkshire, on the river Swale, 2¾ miles SW of Cowton r station, and 5½ ESE of Richmond Post town, Catterick Acres, 578 Real property, £1,578 Pop, 105 Houses, 23. The property is not much divided The living is a p curacy in the diocese of Ripon Value, £100 * Patron, the Vicar of Catterick The church is good and contains a monument of Henry Jenkins, a native of Ellerton in the neighbourhood, who died in 1370 at the age of 169 An endowed school at Scorton has £231, and other charities £18

BOLTON (WEST) a village in Alnwick district, Northumberland on the river Alne, 5½ miles W of Alnwick It has a post office under Alnwick

BOLTON (WEST), Yorkshire See BOLTON BY BOWLAND

BOLTON (WESTERN) See BOLTON Lancashire

BOLTON WOOD See BOLTON, Cumberland

BOLVENTOR a chapelry in Alternon and St. Neot parishes, Cornwall 7 miles N of Liskeard r station and 9 SW of Launceston Post town, Alternon, under Launceston Pop 344 Houses, 67 It was constituted in 1849 The living is a p curacy in the diocese of Exeter Value, £75 * Patron, Francis Rodd, Esq The church is very good

BOMBY, a hamlet in Bampton parish, Westmoreland, on the river Lowther 3½ miles NW of Shap

BOMERE HEATH a locality 3 miles from Shrewsbury, in Salop with a post office‡ under Shrewsbury

BONBUSK, a hamlet in Cuckney township Norton Cuckney parish Notts, 5½ miles SW of Worksop

BONBY, or BONDBY, a parish in Glanford Brigg district, Lincoln on the river Ancholme, 1½ miles NNW of Barnetby r station and 6 N of Brigg Post town, Worlaby, under Brigg Acres, 2 410 Real property £3,742 Pop. 471 Houses 101 The property is divided among a few An alien priory was founded here in the time of King John and given to the Chartreux house at Beauvale in Notts, in the time of Henry IV The living is a vicarage in the dio of Lincoln Value £233 * Patron, the Earl of Yarborough The church is old but good There are two Methodist chapels

BONCHURCH, a village and a parish in the SE of the Isle of Wight The village stands on the coast, at the eastern part of the Undercliff, 1 mile E of Ventnor, and has a post office under Ventnor, and an excellent hotel It is charmingly situated, among picturesque scenery and has a number of fine, scattered private residences The parish contains part of Nettlecombe tything Acres, 618, of which 70 are water

Real property, £3,452 Pop, 561 Houses, 80 The property is much subdivided The name Bonchurch is a corruption of Boniface Church, and arose from a legend respecting St Boniface, the apostle of Central Germany St Boniface Down rises behind the village to an altitude of 785 feet above the level of the sea, and commands a grand prospect. Parts of the acclivities and of the coast are highly romantic The living is a rectory in the diocese of Winchester Value, £140 * Patron, H B Leeson Esq, M D The church was built in 1848, and is a plain edifice in the Norman style. The previous church, now disused, still stands The Rev William Adams, author of the "Shadow of the Cross," and John Sterling, whose life was written by Hare and Carlyle, lie interred in the churchyard, Miss Elizabeth Sewell, Author of "Amy Herbert" the Rev James White, author of the "Eighteen Christian centuries," and Edmund Peel, author of the "Ian Island, are residents in the parish, and Admiral Hobson was a native.

BONDARY, or PARSON'S ROAD, an extra parochial tract in the district of Ashby-de la Zouch and county of Derby, 2 miles N of Ashby de la Zouch. Pop, 52 Houses, 9

BONDEBY See BONBY

BONDGATE See AISMUNDERBY

BONDINGTON a hamlet in Dunster parish, Somerset Pop, 16

BONDLEIGH, or BUNDLEY, a parish in Okehampton district Devon, on the river Taw, 2 miles NNW of North Tawton, and 4½ WSW of Morchard Road r station Post town, North Tawton, North Devon Acres, 1,784 Real property, £1,600 Pop., 279 Houses, 58 The manor belongs to the Earl of Egremont The living is a rectory in the diocese of Exeter Value, £232 * Patron, Heirs of E of Egremont The church is ancient, partly Norman, with a lofty square tower There are chapels for Baptists and Bible Christians

BONDS See LARNACRE WITH BONDS

BONE END a village on the southern verge of Bucks, on the river Thames, 3 miles E of Great Marlow It has a post office under Maidenhead

BONEHILL, a liberty in Tamworth parish Stafford, adjacent to the Coventry canal, 1¾ mile SW of Tamworth Pop, 299 Houses, 66 Bonehill House is a seat of the Peels

BONGATE See APPLEBY, Westmoreland

BONIFACE (ST) See BONCHURCH

BONINGALE, or BONINGHALL, a parish in Shiffnall district Salop on the verge of the county 1½ mile E by W of Albrighton r station and 5½ SE of Shiffnall Post town, Albrighton, under Wolverhampton Acres, 1,003 Real property, £2,198 Pop, 187 Houses, 38 The property is divided among a few The living is a rectory in the diocese of Lichfield Value, £200 Patron, C T Whitmore, Esq

BONNEN GATE, a village in Strickland Kettle township, Westmoreland, 3½ miles NW of Kendal

BONNE NUIT BAY, a bay on the N side of Jersey, 3 miles E by S of Rondnez point, and 1¾ SW of the Dnouilles It has a horse shoe form, of about ⅓ of a mile in diameter, and the cliffs above it command a fine view

BONNINGTON, a parish in East Ashford district, Kent, on the military canal in Romney Marsh, 3 miles SSW of Smeeth r station, and 6½ SE by S of Ashford Post town, Bilsington, under Ashford Acres, 1,109 Real property £1,900 Pop, 187 Houses, 39 The property is much subdivided The living is a rectory in the diocese of Canterbury Value, £225 Patron, T Papillon, Esq The church is good

BONNINGTON, the old seat of the Boys family in Kent, near Goodnestone, 7½ miles ESE of Canterbury Two distinguished members of the family were Sir John Boys, of military celebrity and Lieutenant Governor Boys of Greenwich hospital, notable for escape in the "Luxembourg"

BONNINGTON SUTTON See SUTTON BONNINGTON

BONOVER. See BEAUMARIS

BONRON, a township in Gwyddelwern parish, Merioneth, 2 miles N of Corwen

BONSALL, or BONTESHALL, a village and a parish in Ashborne district, Derby The village stands near the river Derwent and the Cromford canal 1½ mile W of Matlock Bath r station, and 2 SW of Matlock, and it has a post office under Matlock Bath, and an ancient market cross —The parish includes also the hamlet of Slaley Acres, 2,464 Real property, £5,489 Pop 1,290 Houses, 305 The scenery is picturesque, and the rocks include much limestone and some valuable ores The inhabitants are employed chiefly in stocking making, comb making and the mining of zinc and lead Traces exist of the Roman road to Manchester The living is a rectory in the diocese of Lichfield Value, £220 * Patron, the Bishop of Lichfield The church is ancient has a tower and fine spire, and was beautifully restored in 1863 There are chapels for Baptists, Wesleyan Methodists, and Primitive Methodists An endowed school founded in 1704, has £90

BONSTEAD HILL, a township in Burgh by Sands parish, Cumberland, on the Carlisle and S lloth railway, 2 miles W by N of Burgh Pop, 74 Houses 14

BONT, a Welsh word used in topographical nomenclature, and signifying "a bridge" It is the same as Pont

BONT, a village in Llanwrtyd parish, Brecon, 12 miles W of Builth

BONT, a township in Llanfairtalhaiarn parish, Denbigh, 3½ miles SE of Ruthin. Pop, 80

BONTESHALL See BONSALL

BONTEYEN, a village in Llangeitho parish, Cardigan 8½ miles NW of Llanbedr

BONTHORPE, a hamlet in Willoughby parish, Lincoln, 3½ miles S of Alford Pop, 14.

BONT NEWYDD, a village in Llanbeblig parish, Carnarvonshire, in the eastern vicinity of Carnarvon

BONT NEWYDD, a village in Llanwnda parish, Carnarvonshire, adjacent to the Nantlle railway, 2½ miles S of Carnarvon It has a station on the railway and a post office under Carnarvon

BONTRHYDYFERE a village in Llanwrtyd parish, Brecon 11½ miles W of Builth

BONT UCHEL, a hamlet in Trepark township, Cyfylliog parish, Denbigh, 5½ miles W of Ruthin

BONVILLE COURT, the old seat of the Bonville family, now the property of J Longbourne, Esq, near Tenby, in Pembroke

BONVILSTON, or TRE SIMWN, a parish in Cardiff district, Glamorgan, 3½ miles SW by W of St Fagans r station, and 8 WSW of Cardiff It has a post office of the name of Bonvilston, under Cardiff Acres, 1,178 Real property, £1,583 Pop, 291 Houses, 55 The property is divided among a few Bonvilston Park is the seat of J J Bassett, Esq The living is a p curacy in the diocese of Llandaff Value, £53 Patron, J J Bassett, Esq The church is good Charities, £12

BONWEN See RHUGGATT AND BONWEN

BONWICK, a township in Skipsea parish E R Yorkshire, near the coast, 4½ miles NNW of Hornsea. Acres 745 Real property £537 Pop, 31 Houses, 2

BONWYSON, a township in Gwyddelwern parish Merioneth, 2½ miles N of Corwen.

BOODE, a hamlet in Braunton parish, Devon

BOOHAY, a hamlet in Brixham parish, Devon, 1½ miles NE of Dartmouth Pop, 23.

BOOKHAM (GREAT), a village and a parish in Epsom district, Surrey The village stands 2½ miles SW of Leatherhead r station, and 4 NW of Dorking has a post office under Leatherhead, and formerly had a fair The parish comprises 3,240 acres Real property, £6,616 Pop, 1,106 Houses, 211 The property is much subdivided Bookham Grove is the seat of the Dawnays, Eastwick House was formerly the seat of the Howards, and Polesden now the property of Sir Walter R. Farquhar, Bart, belonged to Sheridan The living is a vicarage in the diocese of Winchester Value, £340 * Patron Viscount Downe The church has a monument to Sheriff Slyfield, of the time of Queen Elizabeth, and is [illegible] Charities, £55 The rectory of Kinmore is a separate benefice

BOOKHAM (LITTLE), a parish in Epsom district Surrey, 3 miles SW of Leatherhead r station and 3¾ NW by W of Dorking Post town, Great Bookham, under Leatherhead Acres, 950 Real property, £2,187 Pop 219 Houses, 40 The property is divided among a few The living is a rectory in the diocese of Winchester Value, £156 * Patrons the Representatives of the Rev G P B Pollen The church is Norman, has a brass of 1590, and is good Charities, £65

BOOLEY, a township in Stanton upon Hine Heath parish Salop 4½ miles SE of Wem Pop, 117

LOON WOOD, a hamlet in Gosforth parish, Cumberland, 5½ miles N of Ravenglass.

BOOSELEY (UPPER and NETHER), two villages on the north [illegible] border of Staffordshire, 2 miles SW of Longnor

BOOTH, a hamlet in Knedlington township, E. R. Yorkshire, near the ferry over the river Ouse, 1¼ mile SW of H[illegible] Pop, 36

BOOTH, Lancashire See [illegible], ROUGHLEE, GOLDSHAW, BAR[illegible], and HIGHAM

BOOTHAM, a sub district in the district of York It comprises 12 parishes, parts of three other parishes, and two extra parochial tracts within the borough of York, and Huntingdon parish beyond Acres, 9,447 Pop, 14,125 Houses, 2 5[illegible]8

BOOTHBY, a hamlet in Welton in the Marsh parish, Lincoln, 5½ miles ENE of Spilsby Pop., 30

BOOTHBY, or BOOTHBY GRAFFO, a parish in the district and county of Lincoln, on the Wolds, 5½ miles SE of Swinderby r station, and 9 S of Lincoln Post town, Navenby, under Grantham Acres, 2,850 Real property £3,0[illegible] Pop, 218 Houses, 38 The property is divided among a few Here are remains of Somerton Castle, built in 1305 by Bishop Bec, and used as the prison of John of France after the battle of Poictiers The living is a rectory in the diocese of Lincoln Value, £[illegible] Patron J Fullerton, Esq The church was rebuilt in 1842 There is a national school

BOOTHBY GRAFFO, a wapentake in the parts of Kesteven, Lincoln It contains Boothby parish, twenty-five other parishes, and part of another Acres, 56,601 Pop in 1851 10,857 in 1861 11,797 Houses, 2 343

BOOTHBY PAGNELL, a parish in Grantham district, Lincoln adjacent to the Great Northern railway, 1½ mile ESE of Great Ponton station, and 5 SE of Grantham It has a post office, of the name of Boothby, under Grantham. Acres, 1,79[illegible] Real property, £2 431 Pop, 112 Houses, 22 The property is divided among a few Boothby House is a chief residence The parish is a meet for the Belvoir hounds. The living is a rectory in the diocese of Lincoln Value, £376 * Patron, T Lundell, Esq The church is good The erudite Bishop Sanderson was rector here for forty years

BOOTHEN, a township in Stoke upon Trent parish, Stafford, 1 mile from Stoke Pop, 253 Houses, 52.

BOOTHROYD, a hamlet in Dewsbury township, W R Yorkshire, 5½ miles W of Wakefield

BOOTHS (HIGHER), a township in Whalley parish, Lancashire on the Manchester and Accrington railway, near the Baxenden station, 5 miles SSW of Burnley Acres, 2,000 Real property, £21,03[illegible], of which £6 169 are in mines Pop [illegible] Houses, 908 The inhabitants are chiefly employed in cotton factories and in collieries

BOOTHS (LOWER), a township in Whalley parish Lancashire, 1¾ mile ENE of Baxenden r station, and 1 SSW of Burnley Acres, 630 Real property, £12 102 Pop 1,035 Houses, [illegible] The inhabitants are chiefly employed in cotton factories

BOOTHSTOWN, a hamlet in Worsley township, Lancashire, 7 miles WNW of Manchester It has a post office under Manchester

BOOTH TOWN, a hamlet in Northowram township, W R Yorkshire, 1 mile NE of Halifax It has a post office under Halifax

BOOTLE, a village, a parish, a sub district, and a district in Cumberland The village stands on a rivulet, not far from the Whitehaven and Furness railway about 1¾ mile from the shore, and 6½ S by E of Ravenglass, and it has a station on the railway, and a post office, under Whitehaven It consists chiefly of a single street, yet possesses interest for tourists in some charming environs, and is a polling place A market was formerly held, and there are fairs on 5 April and 24 Sept The parish comprises 6,652 acres of land and 494 of water Real property, £1,7[illegible] Pop, 901 Houses, 160 The property is much subdivided Part of the surface is Bootle Fell and part is the northern skirt and ascent of the Black Combe mountain Remains of a Roman camp are on Esk Meals common, and vestiges of a Benedictine nunnery, founded by a daughter of Henry de Boyvill, fourth lord of Millom, are at Seaton The living is a rectory in the diocese of Carlisle Value, £460 * Patron, the Earl of Lonsdale The church is partly ancient, of early English date, with Saxon vestiges, underwent repair in 1837, has a pinnacled tower, 90 feet high, built in 1862 and contains an octagonal font of red sandstone, and a brass of Sir Hugh Askew, who was knighted at the battle of Pinkie There are an Independent chapel, a free school, and a work house —The sub district contains the parishes of Bootle, Corney, Whitbeck, and Whicham, and part of the parish of Millom Acres, 62,932 Pop, 3,598. Houses, 6[illegible]0 The district comprehends also the sub district of Muncaster, containing the parishes of Muncaster, Drigg, Irton, and Waberthwaite, and parts of the parishes of Millom, and St Bees Acres of the district, 100 0o6 Poor rates in 1866, £2 41[illegible] Pop in 1861, 5,880 Houses, 1,093 Marriages in 1866, 48, births, 214,—of which 21 were illegitimate, deaths, 131,—of which 35 were at ages under 5 years, and 5 at ages above 85 years Marriages in the ten years 1851-60, 401, births, 1,739, deaths, 968 The places of worship in 1851 were 13 of the Church of England, with 3,179 sittings, [illegible] of Independents, with 20[illegible] s, 2 of Baptists, with 100 s, and 4 of Wesleyan Methodists, with 497 s The schools were 1[illegible] public day schools, with 631 scholars, 8 private day schools, with 1[illegible] s, and 12 Sunday schools, with 507 s

BOOTLE CUM LINACRE, a township and three chapelries in Walton on the Hill parish, Lancashire The township lies on the Mersey, the Liverpool and Southport railway and the Leeds and Liverpool canal, 3½ miles N by W of Liverpool, was, till lately, a much frequented watering place, but is now occupied, on all its river front by Liverpool docks, and has a post office‡ under Liverpool, and four railway stations Acres, 1,781 of which 610 are water Real property in 1860, £25,1[illegible] Pop. in 1851, 6 414 Houses, 1,049 Pop in 1869, about 15,200 —The chapelries are St Mary St John, and Christchurch, the two former p curacies, the latter a vicarage, in the diocese of Chester Value of St M, £[illegible]00, of C, £300 * Patron of St M, W S Millar, Esq, of St J and C, Trustees St M 's church was built in 1826, St J s in 1864, at a cost of £5,000 C church, in 1866, at a cost of £8 800, and all are handsome A Wesleyan chapel, in French first pointed style was built in 186[illegible] A Roman Catholic chapel was built in 1868 There are also United Presbyterian, Baptist and Welsh Methodist chapels a national school, and a Christian Association's reading and lecture rooms

BOOTON, a parish in St Faith district, Norfolk, 1½ miles SW of Aylsham, and 9 E of Elmham r station It has a post office under Norwich Acres, 1 040 Real property, £1,921 Pop, 24[illegible] Houses, 55 Booton Hall is the seat of P Parmeter, Esq The living is a rectory in the diocese of Norwich Value, £22[illegible] Patron W Elwin, Esq The church is ancient

BOOZE, a hamlet in Arkengarth Dale parish N R Yorkshire 3½ miles NW of Reeth

BORASTON, a township chapelry in Burford parish, Salop, at the verge of the county on the river Teme, the Kington canal, and the Tenbury railway 1 mile W of Tenbury Post town, Tenbury Rated property, £1 1[illegible]1 Pop, 235 Houses, 39 The property is subdivided among a few The living is a p curacy annexed to the rectory of Burford, in the diocese of Hereford The church is tolerable

BORDALE See BORROWDALE

BORDEAN, a tything in East Meon parish, Hants, 3½ miles W of Petersfield Pop, 109

BORDEN, a parish in Milton district, Kent, on the Chatham and Dover railway 1½ mile W of Sittingbourne It has a post-office under Sittingbourne Acres 2,132 Real property, £5,886 Pop, 1,023 Houses, 204 The property is divided among a few Many Roman coins, and foundations of two Roman buildings were discovered at Sutton Barn here in 1816 The living is a vicarage in the diocese of Canterbury Value, £290 * Patron, Rev F E Tuke The church has a Norman west door and a Norman tower, and includes some Roman bricks in its walls A charity for the poor, for widows, and for other purposes, has £1,227 a year, and other charities have £17 Dr Plot, the author of the county histories of Oxford and Stafford, was born at Sutton Barn, and a mural monument to him is in the church

BORDER COUNTIES RAILWAY, a railway in Northumberland It starts from the Newcastle and Carlisle railway immediately above Hexham, crosses the river Tyne, goes up the valley of the North Tyne, past Wark and Bellingham, to Keilder, and becomes united thence with the Border Union railway at Riccarton in Scotland, and through that with the North British railway at Hawick It was authorized in 1854, and completed in 1862 The length of it from Hexham to Keilder, is 33¾ miles and thence to Riccarton 8½ miles

BORDER UNION RAILWAY, a railway from Carlisle in Cumberland to Hawick in Scotland It starts from the Citadel station at Carlisle, goes northward to Longtown, sends off a branch thence south westward to Gretna, proceeds north north eastward to Newcastleton, sending off branches to Canobie and Langholm, and goes northward from Newcastleton, up the Liddel, past Riccarton, and down the Slitrig, into junction with the Hawick branch of the North British railway at Hawick Its main line is 44 miles long, its branches aggregately 10½ miles It was authorized in 1859, and completed in 1862

BORDESLEY, a hamlet in Aston parish, Warwick, within the south eastern part of the town and borough of Birmingham It contains the Birmingham stations of the Birmingham and Oxford and the Birmingham and Wolverhampton railways, and is traversed by those railways and by the Birmingham and Warwick canal Acres, with Deritend, 1,090 Real property, £90,544 Pop in 1851, 13,857, in 1861, 21,339 Houses, 4 413 Camp Hill here, contiguous to the canal and the Gloucester railway, was the scene of Prince Rupert's battle with the townsmen of Birmingham, and Bordesley Hall, near this, was burnt by the rioters in 1791 Streets and other thoroughfares are contiguous, and share in the general character and business of the town Two chapelries, Holy Trinity and St Andrew, are in B, the former a p curacy, the latter a vicarage, in the dio of Worcester Value of Holy Trinity, £300,* of St Andrew, £320 Patron of Holy Trinity, the Vicar of Aston, of St Andrew, alternately the Bishop and five trustees. Holy Trinity church was built in 1822, at a cost of £14,235 is a fine Gothic edifice, faced with stone, and has a grand eastern window and a beautiful altar piece St Andrew's church was built in 1844, at a cost of upwards of £4,000, is in the early decorated style, and consists of nave, spacious chancel, and north aisle, with tower and spire

BORDESLEY, a hamlet in Tardebigg parish, Worcester, near the Worcester and Birmingham canal, 5 miles E by S of Bromsgrove A Cistertian abbey was founded here, in 1138, by the Empress Maud, and given at the dissolution, to Lord Windsor, and the chapel attached to it is still standing Bordesley Park is the seat of the Dugdales

BORDWOOD FOREST, an ancient forest in the eastern part of the Isle of Wight, on the S side of Yar river, 1½ mile W of Sandown It was given by Henry V to Philippa Duchess of York, and was long a noble hunting ground, well stocked with deer and other game The last "Lady" of the Island, Isabella de Fortibus, had a hunting seat in it on a knoll, which still retains the name of Queen's Bower The best timber in the island was obtained from it, but now scarcely one large tree of it exists.

BOREATTON, or BRATTON, a township in Baschurch parish, Salop, on the river Perry, 9 miles NW of Shrewsbury Real property, £1,5?3 Pop, 32 Boreatton Hall and Boreatton Park are chief residences

BOREDALE, a glen 2½ miles long, in Westmorland, descending northward to the lower end of Martindale, and separated by Place Fell and Birk Fell from Ulles-water

BOREHAM, a village and a parish in Chelmsford district, Essex The village stands on the river Chelmer, near the Eastern Counties railway, 3¼ miles NE of Chelmsford, and it has a post office under Chelmsford, and was once a market town —The parish comprises 3 739 acres. Real property, £7,00? Pop, 989 Houses, 186 The property is divided among a few Boreham House is the seat of Sir J T Tyrell Bart Newhall belonged to Waltham abbey, and passed to the Shardelowes, the Butlers the Boleyns, Henry VIII, the Ratcliffes, the Villierses, Cromwell, Monk, the Cavendishes, and Olmius Lord Waltham A mansion on it was built by the Butlers in the time of Henry VII, inhabited by the Princess Mary, the Duke of Buckingham, Cromwell, and Monk, and demolished, all except the great hall, by Lord Waltham The hall is now a chapel, 96 feet by 50, retaining the arms of Henry VIII and Elizabeth and a convent is connected with it, first occupied by nuns who fled from Liege at the first French revolution, and used as a seminary for Roman Catholic ladies The living is a vicarage in the diocese of Rochester Value, £?3? * Patron, the Bishop of Rochester The church has a square Norman tower contains tombs of the Ratcliffes, Earls of Sussex, and is good The churchyard contains a mausoleum of the Walthams, after the model of the Temple of the Winds There are national schools, Butler's charity school with £156 a year, and other charities with £13

BOREHAM, a hamlet 1 mile SE of Warminster, in Wilts A church was erected here in 1865 Boreham House here is the property of Sir F D Astley, Bart An earthwork in the vicinity, called the Berries, is a vestige of a Roman station on the road from Old Sarum to Bath, and has yielded Roman pottery and many coins

BOREHAM STREET, or BOREHAM MANOR, a hamlet in Wartling parish, Sussex, on the river Ashburn, 4½ miles E of Hailsham It has a post office of the name of Boreham Street, under Hurst Green, and a fair is held at it on 21 Sept

BORE PLACE, the seat of the Streatfields in Chiddingstone parish, Kent, 6½ miles SSW of Sevenoaks It was formerly the seat of the Willoughbys, and of Chief Justice Read

BORESFORD AND ELDWARDINE, a township in Brampton Bryan parish, Hereford, 2 miles E by S of Knighton Pop, 110 Houses 20

BORESHILL, a locality 2 miles from Tenterden, in Kent with a post office under Staplehurst

BORINGDON the ancient seat of the Parkers, Earls of Morley, in Devon, on the Catwater, 5½ miles N of Plymouth The mansion was built about the middle of the 14th century, but is now reduced to a fragment used as a farm house The grounds contain a Roman camp, and command most brilliant views The Earls of Morley take from Boringdon the titles of Viscount and Baron

BORINGER See BOTTINGWORTH

BORLEY, a parish in the district of Sudbury and county of Essex, on the verge of the county, at the river Stour, 2½ miles NW of Sudbury r station Post town, Sudbury Acres, 776 Real property £1,?9? Pop., 190 Houses, 40 The property is divided among a few The living is a rectory in the diocese of Rochester Value £240 * Patron, the Rev Edward Bull The church stands on a rising ground, contains a monu ment to Sir Edward Waldegrave master of the wardrobe to Queen Mary, and is very good

FOPLEY, a hamlet in Ombersley parish, Worcester, on the river Severn 5½ miles WNW of Droitwich

BOROUGHBRIDGE, a small town, a township chapelry, and a sub district in the district of Knaresborough, W R Yorkshire The town stands on the river Ure, and on a branch of the Northeastern railway, 6½ miles LSE of Ripon It was formerly called Newborough, in contradistinction to the neighbouring small town of Aldborough, and it takes the latter part of its present name from a bridge built over the Ure at it soon after the Conquest, and now superseded by a modern bridge. A battle was fought in its vicinity, in 1322, between the forces of Edward II and those of the Earl of Lancaster Three rude monumental pillars, called the Devil's Arrows, somewhat obeliskal, and respectively 18, 22, and 31 feet high, stand about ¼ a mile to the south, and have been the subject of much discussion among antiquaries A neat, fluted, Doric column, seemingly of the 14th century, stood in the market place, and a quondam mansion of the Tancreds is now an inn The town has a post office‡ under York, a railway station two banking offices, and two chief inns, and carries on some trade in hardware It formerly had much business from traffic on the great North road, but has declined since the era of railways A weekly market is held on Saturday, and fairs on 27 April, 22 June 16 Aug, 23 Oct and 13 Dec The town was made a borough in the time of Mary, sending two members to parliament, but was disfranchised by the act of 1832 —The township or chapelry includes the town, is in the parish of Aldborough, and comprises 85 acres Real property, £2,302 Pop, 909 Houses, 215 The property is subdivided The living is a vicarage in the diocese of Ripon Value £300* Patron, the Vicar of Aldborough The church is a substantial modern building with a tower, and there are Baptist and Wesleyan chapels, a temperance hall, national schools, and charities £5 The sub district comprises three parishes and part of a fourth Pop, 5,061 Houses, 1,152

BOROUGHBRIDGE, a hamlet in the parishes of Lyng, Othery, and Weston Zoyland, Somerset, at the confluence of the rivers Tone and Parret, 5 miles NW of Langport It has a post office under Bridgewater Pop 93 A ruined chapel here crowns a seemingly artificial mound, and belonged to Athelney abbey

BOROUGH-FEN (VILLA), an extra-parochial tract in Peterborough district, Northampton, 5 miles N by E of Peterborough Acres, 5,160 Real property, £6,086 Pop 202 Houses 31

BOROUGH-GREEN, a hamlet in Ightham and Wrotham parishes, Kent, 6 miles ENE of Sevenoaks It has a post office under Sevenoaks, and a Baptist chapel

BOROUGH GREEN, Cambridge See Burrough Green

BOROUGH HILL an eminence in the vicinity of Daventry Northampton It was the scene of the Danish victory over the Saxons in 1006, and the place of Charles I's encampment before the battle of Naseby, and it has vestiges of a large ancient camp, and commands a fine view

BOROUGH ISLAND, an islet in Bigbury bay at the mouth of the river Avon in Devon

BOROUGH ROAD, a sub district in the district of St George Southwark, extending northward from the Borough road to Mint street, in Southwark Acres, 65 Pop, 16,613 Houses, 2,000

BOROUGH STREET, a hamlet 2¼ miles SE of Epsom, in Surrey, on the Roman road to Chichester

BORRAS HOVAH, a township in Wrexham parish, Denbigh near the river Dee, 2 miles NE of Wrexham Acres 351 Pop 49 Houses, 9

BORRAS RIFFRI, a township in Gresford parish, Denbigh adjacent to the Chester and Shrewsbury railway 3 miles N of Wrexham Acres, 552 Pop, 20 Houses 9

BORROW (THE) a stream of Westmoreland It rises on Hump Pike, and runs 8 miles south eastward to the Lune, 1½ mile below Orton r station It takes its name from a Roman camp at Castle Dykes, which commanded a wild pass through Shap fell

BORROWASH a village in Ockbrook parish, Derbyshire, on the Midland railway, near the Derby canal and the Derwent river, 4½ miles ESE of Derby It has a station on the railway, a post office under Derby, a Wesleyan chapel, a cotton and lace factory, and flour-mills Elvaston Castle, the seat of the Earl of Harrington, is near it

BORROW BRIDGE (HIGH and LOW), two localities on the Borrow river in Westmoreland, the former on the road from Shap to Kendal, the latter on that from Orton to Kirkby Lonsdale Both have inns, and Low Borrow Bridge has also a village, amid romantic scenery adjacent to a deep cutting on the Lancaster and Carlisle railway and is a noted resort of anglers for trout fishing

BORROWBY, a township in Leake parish, N R Yorkshire, 5 miles N of Thirsk It has a post office under Thirsk Acres 1,280 Real property, £2,098 Pop, 345 Houses, 83. There is a Wesleyan chapel

BORROWBY a township in Lythe parish, N R Yorkshire, 10 miles NW by W of Whitby Acres, 710 Real property, £7 6 Pop, 98 Houses, 19

BORROWDALE the glen of the Borrow river, also the village at Low Borrow Bridge, in Westmoreland

BORROWDALE, a chapelry and a vale in Crosthwaite parish, Cumberland The chapelry lies 7 miles S by W of Keswick r station, and 14 NW of Windermere, and contains the hamlet of Rosthwaite, which has a post office under Windermere Real property, £2,6?? Pop, 422 Houses 85 The living is a p curacy in the diocese of Carlisle Value, £90 * Patron, the Vicar of Crosthwaite The church stands near Rosthwaite, and was rebuilt in 1824 Another church, of recent erection stands at Grange, and is served by a p curate with a salary of £80 appointed by Miss Heathcote The are dissenting chapels at Rosthwaite and Grange —The vale commences in three heads Stonethwaite, Seathwaite, and Borrowdale Haws, coming down from the mountain passes out of Langdale, Wastdale, and Buttermere, is overhung, at the convergence of these, by the massive mountain range of Glaramara, and descends thence between lofty flanks, northward to the head of Derwent water The low grounds or bottoms of it have much diversity of width and contour, but comprise about 2,000 acres of good land, chiefly disposed in pasture "The mountains and hills around it have many outlines of base, form, and summit, but generally are so bold in character, so cloven with ravines, and so strikingly grouped together as to form a series of imposing pictures The depressions among them vary from gorge to glen, and from rocky mountain defile to green cultivated valley, and the lower parts, both bottom and slope, show much diversity of breadth and colour, rock and wood, wild nature and ornate culture The draining stream is called sometimes Borrowdale beck, sometimes Derwent river, and is the chief feeder of Derwent water Castle Crag a lofty wooded, and almost isolated eminence adjoining the stream near the foot, commands a glorious view of all the vale, was the site of successively a Roman camp, a Saxon fortalice, and a monastic castle, to command the pass toward the mountains, and has yielded Roman relics which are preserved in Keswick museum The Bowder stone, at the foot of a precipice, opposite Castle Crag, is a mass of fallen rock, 62 feet long, 36 feet high, and 84 feet in circumference with outline resembling that of a ship upon its keel, and is sung by Wordsworth The Black Lead Mine mountain, on a flank of the Seathwaite head vale, rises to the height of about 2,000 feet, and is famous for a plumbago mine and a group of yew trees The mine occurs about midway up its ascent ceased recently to be worked after having been worked for upwards of two centuries is the only plumbago mine in England, and sent all its produce to London The yew trees are lower than the mine four in number very old, and a sheet of copsewood Wordsworth, after noting a famous yew at Lorton, says,—

" Worthier still of note
Are those fraternal four of Borrowdale
Joined in one solemn and capacious grove
Huge trunks!—beneath whose sable roof
Of boughs, as if for festal purpose deck'd
With unrejoicing berries ghostly shapes
May meet at noontide,—Fear and trembling Hope
Silence and Foresight, Death the skeleton,
And Time the shadow,—there to celebrate,
As in a natural temple, scatter'd o'er
With altars undisturbed of mossy stone,
United worship, or in mute repose
To lie and listen to the mountain flood
Murmuring from Glaramara's inmost caves."

BORROWDON, or BURRADON, a township in Alwinton parish, Northumberland, near the river Coquet, 6½ miles NW of Rothbury Acres, 1,538 Pop, 144 Houses, 31

BORSTALL See BOARSTALL

BORTH, a village, a small watering place, in Cyfoeth y Brenin township, Cardigan, adjacent to the Newtown and Aberystwith railway, 8 miles NNE of Aberystwith It has a station on the railway, and a post office under Shrewsbury It stands close to the sea, and consists of a street of mean white houses Sandy beaches, called Borth sands, extend 4 miles from its vicinity northward to the estuary of the Dovey, and are overlooked by cliffs, commanding splendid sea views

BORTHIN, a hamlet in Llandyssil parish, Cardigan, 8 miles E of Newcastle Emlyn Pop, 263

BORVA See BUFFA

BORWICK, a township, with a r station, in Warton parish, Lancashire, on the Furness and Midland railway, near the Northwestern, 3 miles NNE of Carnforth Acres, 836 Real property, £1,765 Pop, 191 Houses, 35 Borwick Hall, the seat of the Standishes, gave lodging to Charles II on his way to Worcester

BOSBURY, a village and a parish in Ledbury district Hereford The village stands on the river Leddon, under the Malvern hills, 3 miles WNW of Colwall r station, and 4 N by W of Ledbury, and has a post office under Ledbury The parish includes the parochial divisions of Upleadon and Catley Acres, 4,759 Real property, £8,499 Pop, 1,090 Houses, 234 The property is much subdivided An old building, now used as a farm house, was once a seat of the Bishops of Hereford The parish is a meet for the Ledbury hounds The living is a vicarage in the diocese of Hereford Value £337 Patron, the Bishop of Hereford The church is ancient and good A grammar school has £90 from endowment, other charities £83

BOSCASTLE, a village and a sub district in Camelford district, Cornwall The village is in the parishes of Minster and Forrabury, stands ½ a mile from the coast, 5½ miles N of Camelford, occupies a romantic site on the sides of hills, overhanging two deep vales, and has a post office‡ under Camelford, a ruined ancient chapel, and a Methodist chapel It was once a market town, and still has fairs on the first Thursday of May 5 Aug, and 27 Nov Its name is a corruption of Botteaux Castle, and was taken from a baronial mansion, the seat of the Norman family of De Bottreaux, which stood on what is now a green mound The manor went, in the time of Henry VI by marriage, to Lord Hungerford, descended to the Earls of Huntingdon, passed to the Marquis of Hastings, who takes from it the title of Baron Botteaux, and was purchased by the late T R. Avery, Esq Boscastle Port, at the nearest part of the coast is the harbour of the village, lies in the debouch of a narrow, high flanked vale, has a small pier and breakwater, and carries on an export coasting trade in corn, slates, and manganese The scenery around the village is strikingly picturesque, and that on the coast, very grand The sub district comprises seven parishes Acres, 17,368 Pop, 2,429 Houses 530

BOSCAWEN, a manor in St. Buryan parish, Cornwall It has belonged, since the time of King John, to the Boscawens, who became Viscounts Falmouth in 1720, and gives them the title of Baron A famous Druidical circle of 16 stones, called the Nine Maidens, occurs on the farm of Boscawen Un

BOSCOBEL, an extra parochial tract in Shiffnall district, Salop on the verge of the county, in Brewood forest, 6 miles E by N of Shiffnall Acres, 600 Pop, 22 Houses 3 Boscobel House, then a seat of the Giffords, was the hiding place of Charles II, on 3 Sept, 1651, after the battle of Worcester The edifice was of timber, and is much altered, but still retains some of its original features, together with reminiscences of the king's retreat, and is shown to strangers An oak tree near it is said to be a scion of the oak in which the king sat concealed while his pursuers passed round and under it

BOSCOMBE, a parish in Amesbury district, Wilts, on an affluent of the river Avon, and on the Basingstoke and Salisbury railway, 1½ mile NE of Porton station and 4 SE of Amesbury It has a post-office under Marlborough Acres, 1,692 Real property, with Comeldon, Idmiston, Porton, and Winterbourne Gunner, £7,630 Pop, 148 Houses, 34 The property is divided among a few The living is a rectory in the diocese of Salisbury Value £330 * Patron, the Bishop of Salisbury The church is old but good, and there are almshouses, with endowed income of £21 Richard Hooker was rector from 1591 till 1595, and wrote here the first four books of his "Laws of Ecclesiastical Polity"

BOSCOMBE CHINE, a narrow water worn ravine on the coast of Dorset, 2 miles E of Bournemouth Boscombe Lodge, the seat of Sir Percy Shelley, Bart, is adjacent

BOSDEN See HANDFORTH

BOSHAM, a village, a parish, and a hundred in the SW of Sussex The village stands on Chichester harbour, 1 mile S of the South Coast railway, and 3½ W by S of Chichester, and it has a station on the railway, and a post office, of the name of Bosham Pound, under Chichester It was known to the Saxons as Posenham and it possessed importance for ages as a landing place, but is now inhabited chiefly by fishermen A monastic establishment was founded at it, in the 7th century, by a Scot named Dicul, and a collegiate church, in 1120 by Bishop Warlwast It belonged early to the see of Canterbury, was obtained, through guile, by Earl Godwin, had a seat of Harold, whence he sailed on his fatal visit to Duke William in Normandy, was given, at the Conquest, to the Archors, and passed, first to Bishop Warlwast, then to the Dean and Chapter of Chichester The parish includes the tythings of Broadbridge, Creed Old Fishbourne, Gosport, and Walton, and is in the district of Westbourne Acres, 3,830, of which 645 are water Real property, £8,136 Pop, 1,158 Houses, 236 The property is divided among a few The present manor house has an ancient moat, and probably occupies the site of the seat of Harold The living is a rectory in the diocese of Chichester Value, £220 * Patrons, the Dean and Chapter of Chichester The church possesses much interest for artists and antiquaries, is partly Saxon or Norman, and partly early English contains a Norman font and a monument to a daughter of Canute, and was restored in 1862 A colossal head, supposed by some to be for Woden or Jupiter, was found in the church yard, and is preserved in the palace garden at Chichester There are an Independent chapel and charities £91 Herbert de Bosham secretary to Thomas a Becket, and afterwards a cardinal, was a native —The hundred comprises five parishes, and is in the rape of Chichester Acres, 15,544 Pop, 2,722 Houses, 541

BOSHERSTON, a parish in the district and county of Pembroke, on the coast, 5 miles S by W of Pembroke, and 7½ S of New Milford r station It has a post office under Pembroke Acres, 1,660 Real property, £1,071 Pop, 251 Houses, 54 Limestone cliffs on the coast are pierced with caverns, and show very striking forms. The largest cavern, called Bosherston mere runs inland more than ¼ of a mile, terminates in a narrow vertical aperture, is lashed by the waves, in a storm, with tremendous noise and sometimes ejects from its terminal aperture, a column of foam 40 feet high, resembling the Iceland geysers The hermitage and well of St Govan, the Sir Gawaine of fable, the nephew of King Arthur, are in the vicinity of the mere The living is a rectory in the diocese of St Davids Value, not reported Patron the Earl of Cawdor

BOSKEDNAN, a locality 4 miles NNW of Penzance in Cornwall It commands an extensive view of wild country and of the ocean and has a Druidical circle 66 feet in diameter, with eight stones erect and three prostrate

BOSKENNA, a locality in St Buryan parish, Cornwall, 5 miles SW of Penzance It has a cromlech, is near the Boscawen Druidical circle, and is thought to have been the seat of an archdruid

BOSLEY, a township chapelry in Prestbury parish, Cheshire, adjacent to the Macclesfield canal and the North Stafford railway, 6¼ miles S by W of Macclesfield It has a station on the railway, and a post office under Congleton Acres, 3,160 Real property, £3,351 Pop, 461 Houses, 94 There is a large reservoir connected with the Macclesfield canal The living is a p curacy in the diocese of Chester Value, £110 * Patron the Vicar of Prestbury The church was recently rebuilt

BOSMERE a hundred in Fareham division, Hants It contains the parishes of North and South Hayling and Warblington Acres, 14,510 Pop, 3,235 Houses, 692

BOSMERE a lake a district, and a hundred in Suffolk The lake lies 1 mile SE of Needham Market, is an expansion of the river Gipping, covers about 30 acres and abounds with fish Bosmere Hall, the seat of the Hail family, is adjacent —The district comprehends the sub district of Needham Market, containing the parishes of Great Blakenham Baylham, Barking, Creeting St Mary, Creeting All Saints, Creeting-St Olave, Little Stonham, Earl Stonham, Darsley, Battisford, Ringshall, Great Bricett Wattisham, Offton, Nettlestead, Somersham Little Blakenham, Bramford, and Hoxton, and the sub district of Coddenham containing the parishes of Coddenham, Gosbeck Hemingstone, Ash-Bocking, Swilland, Henley, Akenham, Claydon, Barham, Ashfield with Thorpe, Framsden, Helmingham, Pettaugh, Winston, Debenham Mickfield, and Stonham Aspall, and the parochial chapelry of Crowfield Acres, 57,809 Poor rates in 1866 £3,370 Pop in 1861 16,174 Houses, 3,547 Marriages in 1866 121, births, 481, —of which 36 were illegitimate deaths 304 —of which 91 were at ages under 5 years and 11 at ages above 85 Marriages in the ten years 1851-60, 1,084, births, 5,231 deaths, 3,131 The places of worship in 1851 were 39 of the Church of England, with 6,823 sittings, 8 of Independents, with 3 0 5 s, 7 of Baptists, with 1,171 s, 1 of Quakers, with 200 s 1 of Wesleyan Methodists, with 84 s and 2 of Primitive Methodists, with 114 s The schools were 21 public day schools, with 1 169 scholars, 27 private day schools, with 697 s, 41 Sunday schools, with 2 103 s and 2 evening schools for adults with 63 s The workhouse is in Barham The hundred bears the name of Bosmere and Claydon, and is mainly identical with the district, but of less extent Acres 49,331 Pop, 13,125 Houses, 2,878

BOSSALL, a township and a parish in the district of York and N R Yorkshire The township lies on the river Derwent 3 miles S of Barton Hill r station, and 10 NE of York Acres, 1 0 [illegible] Pop 158 Houses, 31 The parish extends beyond the York and Scarborough railway, has there the h[illegible] post office of Flaxton Station, and includes the townships of Flaxton on the Moor Harton, Claxton Sand Hutton and Buttercrambe Acres, 9 117 Real property, £10,677 Pop, 1,07[illegible] Houses, 21[illegible] The property is [illegible] The living is a vicarage, united with the p curacy of Buttercrambe, in the diocese of York Value [illegible] Patrons, the Dean and Chapter of Durham The church is [illegible] some part of it [illegible], with a central tower The rectory of Flaxton and the [illegible] of Sand Hutton are separate benefices

BOSSENDEN, a wood 3½ miles WNW of Canterbury in Kent Here John Nicols [illegible] of Tra[illegible] who [illegible] crowds from the neighbouring [illegible] followed [illegible] to deliverance [illegible] Sir William

Courtenay, the knight of Malta, was shot in 1838, with eight of his followers

BOSSINEY, a village in Tintagel parish, Cornwall, in a bleak tract, 4½ miles NNW of Camelford Pop 87 It was once a market-town, and it sent two members to parliament from the time of Henry III till disfranchised by the act of 1832 It consists of mean cottages, and stands round a large barrow, on which the writ of election used to be read Sir Francis Drake, Sir Francis Cottington and other distinguished men represented it in parliament A singular cove, small, and murky, called Bossiney Hole is under the cliffs on the adjacent coast

BOSSINGHAM, a hamlet in Upper Hardres parish, Kent, 5½ miles S of Canterbury Pop, 149

BOSSINGTON, a tything in Porlock parish, Somerset, on the E side of Porlock bay Bossington hamlet, about a mile inland, is strikingly picturesque Bossington beacon, flanking the bay, is a ridge 801 feet high commands brilliant views, and has been adorned with paths and tasteful woods by its proprietor, Sir Thomas D Acland, Bart

BOSSINGTON, a parish in Stockbridge district, Hants, on the river Anton, and on the Roman road from Winchester to Sarum, adjacent to the Andover railway 3½ miles SSW of Stockbridge Post town, Broughton, under Winchester Acres, 615 Real property, £722 Pop, 4[illegible] Houses, 9 The property is all in one estate The living is a p curacy, annexed to the rectory of Broughton, in the diocese of Winchester The church was rebuilt in 1839, and is a handsome edifice, of stone and flint, in the early English style.

BOSTOCK, a township in Davenham parish Cheshire, on the Chester canal, near the Grand Junction railway, 2½ miles NW of Middlewich Acres, 1,111 Real property, £2,471 Pop, 1[illegible] Houses, 30 Bostock Hall is the seat of the France family

BOSTON, a town, a parish, a sub district, and a district in Lincoln The town stands on the river Witham, 5 miles from the Wash and 31 SE by E of Lincoln The Witham is navigable up to it, making it a seaport, canals, communicating with the Trent, give it inland navigation to almost every part of England, and railways diverging from a central station go north eastward, north westward, westward, and southward The Romans are supposed to have had a ferry a short distance below it, and a fort at the mouth of the Witham and are even thought, from some relics discovered in 1716, to have had buildings on the spot A monastery was built at it, in 654, by the Saxon, St Botolph, and destroyed by the Danes in 870, and this is believed to have given rise to the name Boston, written first Botolph's town afterwards Botonstow The monastery was rebuilt soon after 870 four priories, Augustinian, Dominican, Franciscan, and Carmelite, together with three colleges or hospitals, also were built, a castle of Ranulph Earl of Richmond likewise was erected, and, though these dated from only the 13th and following centuries, they indicate a large amount of early prosperity A tax levied in 1204 produced £780 from Boston and £836 from London The town suffered greatly from a fire in the time of Edward I, and from an inundation in 1285, it was made a staple port for the lead, wool leather, and other commodities in the time of Edward III, and it sent sixteen ships to the siege of Calais in the time of Edward III It afterwards suffered much decline from the silting up of its harbour and it continued, till recently, to suffer embarrassment from the same cause, in spite of modern improvements but it has experienced [illegible] from the enclosure of the neighbouring fens, and [illegible] the influence of the railways A portion of its inhabitants were leaders in the great Puritan emigration, went in 1630 to America, and there gave its name to what [illegible] the capital of New England

The town is cut [illegible] two parts east and west by the Witham, [illegible] built A long street, called Bargate, and a spacious market-place, are on the E side of the river, and [illegible] long street called High street nearly parallel [illegible] the river, is on the W side An elegant [illegible] of 55 feet, after a design by Rennie, spans the river, and was erected in 1804-7, at a cost of £22,000. Water works were formed in 1850. There are a guild hall, a market house and assembly rooms, a corn exchange, a theatre, and a freemasons' hall, —the last in the Egyptian style built in 1863. The ancient monasteries and castle have disappeared, but Hussey tower, built by William Lord Hussey, who was beheaded at Lincoln in the time of Henry VIII., is near St John's row. The parish church is decorated English, with grand interior, and had it been cruciform, would have rivalled most of the lesser cathedrals. It measures 282½ feet by 99, has a south porch and a south west chapel, contains an altar piece after Rubens, an ancient font, and monuments of the Tilneys, and has recently undergone complete restoration. The steeple of it is 262¾ feet high, was built after the model of the north west steeple of Antwerp cathedral, is a master piece of skill, and terminates in an octagonal lantern, which formerly was lighted up at night to guide seamen to the port. A white marble statue of the late Herbert Ingram is in the churchyard, and was set up in 1862. The chapel of ease in High street, was built in 1822. The Independent chapel in Red Lion street was rebuilt in 1869. The Wesleyan Centenary chapel is a spacious structure, and has an organ with 2,490 pipes and 49 stops. There are two chapels for Independents, three for Baptists, and one each for Unitarians, P. Methodists, New C. Methodists, Free Methodists, and Roman Catholics, a free grammar school, founded in 1551, two other endowed schools, with £130 and £65 a year, a mechanics' institute, two subscription libraries and news rooms, a dispensary, a drinking fountain, and a work-house.

The navigation up to the town has been improved by deepening the river, forming a canal, and enlarging the harbour, and it brings hither vessels of 300 tons. The craft belonging to the port at the beginning of 1868, were 83 sailing vessels under 50 tons, 57 sailing vessels above 50 tons, and 2 steam vessels of 106 tons. The various vessels which entered during 1867 were, coastwise, 563 of aggregately 27,070 tons, and from foreign countries, 30 of aggregately 4,074 tons. The chief export is corn, and the chief imports coals, timber, hemp, iron, and tar. Ship building, iron founding, rope making, sail making, and the making of agricultural implements are carried on. Weekly markets are held on Wednesday and Saturday, and fairs on 4 and 5 May, 5 Aug., 15 Sept., 18 Nov., and 11 Dec. The town has a head post office,‡ a telegraph station, 4 banking-offices, and three chief inns, and publishes two newspapers. It is a seat of quarter sessions and a polling place, was made a borough by Edward IV., is governed by a mayor, six aldermen, and eighteen councillors, and sends two members to parliament. Its municipal boundaries are conterminate with Boston parish, excepting the fen allotments, and its parliamentary boundaries comprise Boston and Skirbeck parishes, excepting Skirbeck fen allotment. Direct taxes in 1857, £20,306. Electors in 1868, 1,093. Pop. of the m. borough in 1851, 14,733; in 1861, 14,712. Houses, 3,210. Pop. of the p. borough in 1851, 17,518; in 1861, 17,893. Houses, 3,901. Boston the bibliographer, Fox the martyrologist, and Diamond the blind calculator, were natives. The town gives the title of baron to the Irby family.

The parish includes two allotments in respectively the East and West Fen. Acres, 5,220. Real property, £59,622. Pop., 15,078. Houses, 3,273. The property is much subdivided. The living is a vicarage, united with the p. curacy of St James, in the diocese of Lincoln. Value, £360.* Patrons, the trustees of H. Ingram, Esq. The chapel of ease is a separate charge, with income of £100, in the patronage of the Trustees of the Rev. P. Alpe.—The sub district comprises the parishes of Boston and Skirbeck, excepting the fen allotments of both. Acres, 7,950. Pop., 17,527. Houses, 3,838.—The district comprehends also the sub district of Kirton in Holland, containing the parishes of Frampton and Wyberton, and parts of the parishes of Kirton, Sutterton, Algarkirk, and Fosdyke; the sub district of Bennington, containing the parishes of Bennington, Butterwick, Wrangle, and Leake, parts of the parishes of Fishtoft, Freiston, and Leverton, and the East fen allotment of Boston; the sub district of Sibsey, containing the parish of Sibsey, the parochial townships of Carrington, West Ville, Thornton-le-Fen, Langrick Ville, and Frith Ville, the extra parochial tracts of Salt Pits and Lowlands' Marsh, and the West and Wildmore fen allotments of Boston, Skirbeck, Fishtoft, Freiston, and Leverton; and the sub districts of Swineshead, containing the parishes of Swineshead, Bicker, and Wigtoft, parts of the parishes of Kirton and Sutterton, the extra parochial tracts of North Forty Foot Bank, Drainage Marsh, Forty Foot Bridge, Gibbet-Hills, Pikes-Farm, Ferry Corner, Pelhams Lands and Harts Grounds, and the fen allotments of Sutterton, Algarkirk, and Fosdyke. Acres, 123,5?7. Poor rates in 1866, £21,334. Pop. in 1861, 37,969. Houses, 8,006. Marriages in 1866, 295; births, 1,118, —of which 96 were illegitimate; deaths, 608, —of which 170 were at ages under 5 years, and 24 at ages above 85 years. Marriages in the ten years 1851-60, 2,954; births, 12,042; deaths, 7,446. The places of worship in 1851 were 29 of the Church of England, with 12,691 sittings; 3 of Independents, with 1,385 s.; 7 of Baptists, with 2,044 s.; 1 of Unitarians, with 230 s.; 29 of Wesleyan Methodists, with 5,684 s.; 1 of New Connexion Methodists, with 729 s.; 11 of Primitive Methodists, with 1,285 s.; 1 of Wesleyan Reformers, with 50 attendants; 1 of Latter day Saints, with 103 at.; and 1 of Roman Catholics, with 340 sittings. The schools were 33 public day schools, with 3,111 scholars; 63 private day schools, with 1,423 s.; 53 Sunday schools, with 4,600 s.; and 2 evening schools for adults, with 20 s.

BOSTON, Lancashire. See ASHTON UNDER LYNE.

BOSTON DEEPS, the NW side of the Wash, leading up to the mouth of the Witham river, in Lincoln. It is divided on the landward side, from the shore, by Wainfleet and Friskney flats, and on the other side, from Lynn Deeps, by the Long Sand, Dog's Head, Leger, and Lynn Knock shoals. The part of it called the South Channel gives the best seaway, and has in some parts four fathoms of water, but is encumbered by a shifting bar.

BOSTON, SLEAFORD, AND MIDLAND COUNTIES RAILWAY, a railway in Lincolnshire, eastward from the Great Northern loop at Boston, to the Great Northern main at Barkstone, N of Grantham Junction. Its length is 28 miles. It was authorized in August 1853, and was opened from Sleaford to Grantham in June 1856, and from Boston to Sleaford in April 1859. A bill was lodged for the session of 1863 to obtain powers for connecting this railway with Freiston shore by means of railways and pier. See FREISTON.

BOSTON SPA, a village and a chapelry in Bramham parish, W. R. Yorkshire. The village stands on the river Wharfe, ¼ of a mile SW of Thorp-Arch r. station, and 3½ NW by W of Tadcaster, and has a post office‡ under Tadcaster. It consists of a single well built street, and has a fine bridge over the Wharfe, three hotels, a good church with a tower, built in 1814, and a Wesleyan chapel. A saline spring here was brought into notice in 1744, has been recommended by distinguished physicians, and draws invalids and other visitors to the village as a watering place. A pump room, hot and cold baths, and other kindred appliances are in operation; and a number of handsome residences are in the neighbourhood. The chapelry includes the village, and was constituted in 1852. Rated property, £5,040. Pop., 1,123. Houses, 251. The property is subdivided. The living is a vicarage in the diocese of York. Value, £150.* Patron, Christ Church, Oxford.

BOSWIDDY, a hamlet in St Erth parish, Cornwall, 3½ miles NE of Marazion.

BOSWORTH FIELD. See BOSWORTH (MARKET).

BOSWORTH (HUSBANDS), a village and a parish in Market Harborough district, Leicester. The village stands adjacent to the rivers Welland and Avon, the Union canal, and the Northwestern railway, 1 mile ENE of Welford station, and 6 WSW of Market Harborough, and has a post office‡ under Rugby, and a fair on 16 Oct.

—The parish comprises 3,870 acres Real property, £7,30 Pop, 901 Houses 211 The property is much subdivided Bosworth Hall is an ancient mansion, the seat of the Tunvilles The Union canal passes through a tunnel in the parish, 1 170 yards long The living is a rectory in the diocese of Peterborough Value, £...05 Patron, J W Lamb Esq The church is early English, with tower and spire, was rent by lightning to the extent of 30 feet, in 1755 but is now good There are chapels for Baptists Wesleyans, and Roman Catholics An endowed school has £15, other charities £77 Spencer, bishop of Norwich in the time of Richard II, was rector

BOSWORTH (MARKET), a village a township, a parish, a sub district, and a district in Leicester The village stands on an eminence ¾ of a mile E of the Ashby de la Zouch canal, 5½ miles W of Desford r station, 3 NE of Watling street and 11½ W by S of Leicester It has a post office‡ under Hinckley, a banking office, an inn a church, Independent, Baptist, and Primitive Methodist chapels, a grammar school, almshouses, and a workhouse, and is a seat of petty sessions and a polling place The church is early English, was recently restored, has a lofty handsome spire, and contains monuments of the Dixies The grammar school was founded in 1593, and rebuilt in 1827, has an endowed income of £250, with four scholarships at the universities, and had as a master, the Rev Anthony Blackwall, author of "Introduction to the Classics," —as an usher, Dr Samuel Johnson — and as pupils Dawes, author of "Miscellanea Critica," and Thomas Simpson the celebrated mathematician A weekly market is held on Wednesday, and fairs on 8 May and 10 July —The township includes also the hamlet of Coton Real property £7,003 Pop., ... Houses, 191 —The parish contains likewise the chapelries of Sutton Cheney, Shenton, Carlton and Barlestone Acres, 7,4-9 Real property, £17,670 Pop, 2,... Houses ...4 The property is much subdivided The manor belonged once to the Hastings family, and belongs now to Sir Alexander Dixie But Bosworth Field now a meadow adjacent to the canal, 2 miles S of the village was the scene of Richard III's defeat in 1485 by the Earl of Richmond, who mounted the throne as Henry VII, and a spring on it, at which King is said to have drunk during the battle and called Richard's well, was covered over in 1812 by R ...l, ... of Sutton House and bears an inscription ... Dr Parr This field was also the scene of the skirmish, in 1644 between the parliamentary and the royal forces The living is a rectory, united with the p curacies of Sutton Cheney, Shenton and Barlestone in the diocese of Peterborough Value, £903 * Patron, Sir A Dixie, Bart The vicarage of Carlton is a separate benefice

The sub district contains the parishes of Peckleton, Desford Newbold Verdon, Cadeby, Sibson Twycross, Orton on the Hill Norton juxta Twycross, and Congerstone, the extra parochial tract of Copsall Hall most of the parishes of Market Bosworth and Shackerstone, and parts of the parishes of Kirkby Mallory, Earwell, and Hinckley Acres 35 137 Pop, 7,185 Houses, 1,541 — The district includes also the sub district of Ibstock, containing the parishes of Thornton, Ratby and Markfield and parts of the parishes of Market Bosworth, Ibstock, Shackerstone, and Nailstone Acres of the district ...,26 Poor rates, £8 709 Pop in 1841, 13 600 in 1861 13,12... Houses, 2,911 Marriages 97 births ... —of which ... were illegitimate, deaths, 212 —of which ... were at ages under 5 years and 13 at ages above 85 years Marriages in the ten years 1851-60 ...7, births 4,3-7, deaths, 2,771 The places of worship in 1851 were 20 of the Church of England, with ... sittings ... of Independents with 154 s, 5 of Baptists, with ...64 s, ... of Wesleyan Methodists, with ... s and 7 of Primitive Methodists, with 587 s There were 31 public day schools with 1 801 scholars, 22 private day schools with 28 s, ... Sunday schools with 2,6..5 s, and 1 evening school for adults with 18 s.

BOTALLACK, a tin and copper mine in the western peninsula of Cornwall, 2 miles N of St Just, and 6 NNE of Land's End It is partly worked on the face of high cliffs, descends to a depth of 425 feet, runs out, in one level, 510 feet, under the sea, goes twice as far, in other levels, into the land, and is altogether as wonderful a work as the great pyramid of Egypt. Queen Victoria visited it in 1845 and the sons of Louis Philippe in 1851 The scenery above it is romantically grand and the cliffs consist of hornblende and clay slate, and contain a great variety of curious minerals

BOTANY BAY, a hamlet in Enfield parish, Middlesex, 3½ miles NE of Barnet

BOTCHERBY, a township in St Cuthbert parish, Cumberland, within the city of Carlisle Acres, 40... Pop, 176 Houses 37

BOTCHERGATE, a township in St Cuthbert parish, Cumberland, within the city of Carlisle Acres, 64... Pop 9,122 Houses 1,690

BOTCHESTON, a hamlet in Ratby parish, Leicester, 6 miles E by N of Market Bosworth Pop, with Newtown Unthank, 118 Houses, 20

BOTEGWEL, a township in Abergele parish, Denbigh Pop, 113

BOTESDALE, a village, a chapelry and a sub-district, in Hartismere district, Suffolk. The village stands 3 miles WNW of Mellis r station, and 7 WNW of Eye consists chiefly of one long street, has a post office‡ under Scole a banking office, an inn, a church, and a free grammar school, and is a polling place The church is later English, restored, and contains the remains and monuments of Sir Nicholas Bacon and Lord Chief Justice Holt The grammar school was founded in 1576, by Sir N Bacon, and has six exhibitions at Corpus Christi college, Cambridge A weekly market is held on Thursday, and a fair on Holy Thursday The name Botesdale is a corruption of Botolph's Dale Pop 680 Houses, 139 —The chapelry includes the village, lies in Redgrave parish, and is a p curacy, annexed to Redgrave rectory, in the diocese of Norwich —The sub district comprises seven parishes Acres, 15 081 Pop, 5,288 Houses 1,135

BOTHAL, a township and a parish in Morpeth district, Northumberland The township is called Bothal Demesne, and lies on the Wansbeck river, near the Northeastern railway, 3 miles E of Morpeth Acres, ...,027 Real property, £6,.95 Pop 642 Houses, 122 The parish includes also the townships of Oldmoor, Pegsworth, Longhirst and Ashington and Sheepwash, and its post town is Morpeth Acres 7 593 Real property, £5,510, of which £903 are in mines Pop, 1 2... Houses, 241 The property is divided among a few The manor belonged, in the time of Henry II, to the Bertrams, passed by marriage first to the Ogles, then to the Cavendishes and belongs now to the Duke of Portland Remains of a castle of the Bertrams, and of an ancient chapel of the Virgin still exist Coal is worked The living is a rectory, united with the rectory of Sheepwash, and the p curacy of Hebburn in the diocese of Durham Value, £1 377 * Patron, the Duke of Portland The church contains tombs of the Ogles A school is endowed with £2 a year

BOTHAMSALL a parish in East Retford district, Notts, on the river Meden, 5½ miles NNE of Ollerton and 6 WNW of Tuxford r station Post town, Walesby, under Newark Acres, 1,030 Real property £2 275 Pop, 2.. Houses 57 The property is all in one estate The living is a vicarage in the diocese of Lincoln Value, £52 Patron, the Duke of Newcastle The church is good

BOTHEL AND THREAPLAND, a township in Torpenhow parish Cumberland near the river Ellen, 4½ miles W of Ireby Real property, £3,1.2 Pop, 400 Houses, 9. Limestone abounds, and is worked

BOTHENHAMPTON, a parish in Bridport district, Dorset, adjacent to the river Brit and the southwestern railway, ¾ of a mile SE of Bridport Post town Bridport Acres, 823 Real property, £2,992 Pop, 546 Houses, 11. The property is divided among a few The living is a vicarage in the diocese of Salisbury.

Value, £95 * Patron, Sir H M Nepean, Bart The church is good

BOTH HERGESTS a township in Kington parish, Hereford, 2½ miles SW of Kington Pop, 163. Houses 35

BOTLEY, a tything in Cumnor and North Hinksey parishes, Berks, 2 miles W of Oxford It has a post office under Oxford Pop, 6.

BOTLEY a hamlet in Chesham parish Bucks, 1½ mile E of Chesham Real property, £3,298 Pop, 499

BOTLEY, a hamlet in Ullenhall chapelry, Warwick, 1½ mile NNW of Henley in Arden

BOTLEY, a village and a parish in South Stoneham district, Hants The village stands on the river Hamble, ½ a mile S of the Salisbury and Gosport railway and 4½ SW of Bishop's Waltham, and has a station on the railway, a post office‡ under Southampton, and a recently erected market house A considerable trade is done in flour and timber a fortnightly market is held on Tuesday, and fairs are held on the Tuesday before Shrove Tuesday, the Tuesday before Whit Monday, 23 July the Tuesday before 24th Aug and 13 Nov A mock trial at a public house here, followed by the hanging of a man in jest, with the effect of hanging him to death, gave rise to the proverbial phrase of "Botley assizes" An act was obtained in 1862 for constructing a railway, 3½ miles long in connexion with the Southwestern, from Botley to Bishops Waltham, the works to be completed within three years The parish comprises 1 817 acres of land and 70 of water Real property, £4,502. Pop, 860 Houses 181 The property is subdivided Botley Grange and Botley Hill are chief residences A farm here was held by the political writer William Cobbett The living is a rectory in the diocese of Winchester Value, £310 Patron, Rev J M Lee The church was built in 1836, and enlarged in 1859 There is an Independent chapel

BOTLEYS AND LYNE, a chapelry in Chertsey parish, Surrey, near the Chertsey branch of the Southwestern railway, 2 miles SW of Chertsey Post town, Chertsey Rated property, £6,211 Pop 494 Houses, 110 The property is divided among a few Botleys Park is the seat of R Gosling, Esq, and has richly wooded grounds The chapelry was constituted in 1849 The living is a p curacy in the diocese of Winchester Value £100 * Patron the Bishop of Winchester The church is good

BOTLOE, a hundred in the NW of Gloucester It adjoins Worcester and Hereford, is 12 miles long, and 8 broad, and contains eight parishes and part of another Acres, 26,811 Pop, 7,204 Houses, 1,536

BOTOLPH, or BOTTOLPHS, a parish in Steyning district, Sussex, on the river Adur, 1½ mile SSE of Steyning, and 1 S by E of Bramber r station Post town Steyning under Hurstperpoint. Acres, 910 Real property, £632 Pop, 54 Houses, 10 The property is all in one estate The living is a vicarage, annexed to the rectory of Bramber, in the diocese of Chichester The church is very good

BOTOLPH BRIDGE, or BOTTLE BRIDGE, a parish in the district of Peterborough and county of Huntingdon, near the river Nen and the Great Northern railway 2 miles SW of Peterborough Post town, Peterborough The statistics are returned with Orton Longville The manor belonged to the Draytons, the Lovells, and the Shirleys The living is a rectory, annexed to the rectory of Orton Longville in the diocese of Ely The church is in ruins

BOTOLPH CLAYDON, a hamlet in East Claydon parish Bucks, 3½ miles SW of Winslow

BOTOLPH (ST) See LONDON, CAMBRIDGE, COLCHESTER and LINCOLN

BOTOLPHS DALE See BOTESDALE

BOTOLPHS TOWN See BOSTON

BOTRUAL, a township in Llanfairtalhairn parish, Denbigh 4½ miles S of Abergele Pop, 106

BOTSWORTH See BOTTESFORD, Leicester

BOTTLGIR PACH an extra parochial tract in Llanrwst district Merioneth, 7 miles NW of Corwen

BOTTESFORD, a township and a parish in Glanford Brigg district, Lincoln The township lies 4 miles E of the river Trent, 3 S of Frodingham r station, and 7 W of Brigg Real property, £3,300 Pop 357 Houses, 39 The parish contains also the townships of Ashby Burringham, Yaddlethorpe, Holme, and part of East Butterwick and its post town is Ashby under Brigg Acres, 7,470 Real property with the rest of East Butterwick, £11 371 Pop, 1,616 Houses, 361 The property is much subdivided The living is a vicarage, annexed to Messingham, in the diocese of Lincoln The parish church is good, and there are a recent chapel of ease, two Methodist chapels, and a national school

BOTTESFORD or BOTSWORTH a village and a parish in the district of Grantham and county of Leicester The village stands in the vale of Belvoir near the Grantham canal and the Nottingham and Grantham railway, 7 miles WNW of Grantham, and it has a station on the railway, and a post office‡ under Nottingham The parish includes also the hamlets of Easthorpe and Normanton Acres, 5 010 Real property, £9 588 Pop, 1,115 Houses, 317 The property is much subdivided The manor was given at the Conquest to R de Todeni, and belongs now to the Duke of Rutland The living is a rectory in the diocese of Peterborough Value, £993 * Patron, the Duke of Rutland The church is large, cruciform, and very good, with a tower at the west end, and contains monuments to many of the Earls and Dukes of Rutland There are four dissenting chapels, two endowed hospitals for poor men and poor widows, with £479 and £133 a year and a school with £35

BOTTESLOW, a township in Stoke upon Trent parish Stafford, 2 miles E of Newcastle under Lyne Pop, 167 Houses, 31

BOTTISHAM a village, a parish, and a sub district, in Newmarket district, Cambridge The village stands on an affluent of the river Cam, 3½ miles NNE of Fulbourn r station, and 6½ ENE of Cambridge, and it has a post office under Newmarket and is a seat of petty sessions The parish includes also the hamlets of Lode and Longmeadow Acres, 4,700 Real property, £8,830 Pop, 1,508 Houses 332 The property is much subdivided Bottisham Hall is the seat of the Jenyns family Traces exist at Anglesey of an Augustinian priory founded in the time of Henry I The living is a vicarage in the diocese of Ely Value, £258 * Patron Trinity College Cambridge The church is early English, good, and beautiful The vicarage of Lode is a separate benefice There are chapels for Independents and Baptists, and two national schools --The sub district contains two parishes and most of another Acres, with Newmarket sub district, 25,323 Pop 3 373 Houses, 754

BOTTLE BRIDGE See BOTOLPH BRIDGE

BOTTOM HEAD See BOTTON HEAD

BOTTOMS, a hamlet in Blidworth parish, Notts, 5½ miles SE of Mansfield Pop, 230

BOTTON See WRAY WITH BOTTON

BOTTON FELL and BOTTON HEAD eminences on the eastern verge of Lancashire part of the backbone of England, 12 miles E of Lancaster

BOTTON HEAD or GREENHOE, a mountain at the head of Bilsdale, N R Yorkshire 6½ miles SE of Stokesley It has an altitude of 1,485 feet

BOTTOR ROCK, a fissured trap hill adjacent to Hennock village, and 3 miles W by N of Chudleigh, in Devon It towers conspicuously over a large tract of country and commands a magnificent view

BOTTREAUX See BOSCASTLE

BOTTWNOG a parish in Pwllheli district, Carnarvon 5½ miles SSW of Nevin, and 8 WSW of Pwllheli r station It has a post office under Pwllheli Acres, 157 Real property, £701 Pop, 138 Houses, 27 The property is much subdivided The living is a p curacy annexed to the rectory of Meyllteyrn, in the diocese of Bangor The church is very good, and there is a Calvinistic Methodist chapel An endowed school has £200 a year, and other charities have £6

BOTUS FLEMING, a parish in St. Germans district, Cornwall, near the Hamoaze 2 miles NW of Saltash r station Post town, Saltash Cornwall Acres 1,128 Real property, £1,329 Pop, 237 Houses 40 The property is divided among a few The manor belonged to the Flemings of Stoke Fleming The living is a rectory in the diocese of Exeter Value, £230 * Patron, not reported The church is good

BOWELL, a hamlet in Hayes parish, Middlesex, 4½ miles SE of Uxbridge Pop, 373

BOUGHROOD, or [illegible] a parish in the district of Hay and county of Radnor, on the river Wye, with a station on the [illegible] railway, 7 miles WSW of Hay Post town Llyswen under Hereford Acres 1,633 Real property £1,986 Pop, 292 Houses, 57 The property is all in one estate Boughrood Castle, on the site of an ancient baronial fortalice of which slight vestiges remain, is the seat of W de Winton, Esq The scenery is wooded, romantic, and picturesque The living is a vicarage in the diocese of St David's Value, £213 Patron the Bishop of St David's The church is good R Powell, a native, was vicar, and founded, at Brecon a charity which has £262 a year

BOUGHTON, a hamlet in Diddington and Southoe parishes, Huntingdon, 3½ miles N of St Neots Pop 51

BOUGHTON a hamlet in Asgarby parish Sleaford district, Lincoln, 2 miles E of Sleaford Pop, 22

BOUGHTON, a village in St. John Bedwardine parish, Worcestershire 2 miles SW of Worcester Boughton House here is the seat of the Isaacs

BOUGHTON a hamlet in Weekley parish, Northampton, 3½ miles NE of Kettering Boughton Park here belonged formerly to the Montagues, and belongs now to the Duke of Buccleuch and the mansion on it contains two cartoons of Raphael and other rare paintings

BOUGHTON, a parish in Brixworth district, Northamptonshire on an affluent of the river Nen, and on the Northampton and Market Harborough railway, 3 miles N of Northampton It contains Boughton Green, where a large fair is held on 24, 25, and 26 June, and has a post office under Northampton Acres, 1,5[illegible]0 Real property, £3,207 Pop, 37[illegible] Houses, 91 The property is divided among a few Boughton House is the seat of Col R H H Vyse The living is a rectory in the diocese of Peterborough Value £296 Patron, Col R H H Vyse. The church is modern and there are a Wesleyan chapel and a charity of 45 acres

BOUGHTON, a parish in Downham district Norfolk, 1½ mile N of Stoke Ferry, and 6 E by S of Downham r station Post town, Stoke Ferry, under Brandon Acres, 1,323 Real property £2,193 Pop, 238 Houses, 1[illegible] The property is divided among a few The living is a rectory in the diocese of Norwich Value, £100 * Patron Sir W J H B Folkes, Bart.

BOUGHTON, a parish in Southwell district Notts, 2 miles NE of Ollerton and 6 SW by W of Tuxford r station Post town Ollerton, under Newark Acres, 1 372 Real property £1 976 Pop, 39[illegible] Houses, 91 The property is divided among a few The living is a vicarage in the diocese of Lincoln, and till 1866 was annexed to Kneesall Value, £250 Patron, Southwell church There are two dissenting chapels

BOUGHTON, Kent See BOUGHTON UNDER BLEAN

BOUGHTON ALUPH, a parish in East Ashford district, Kent, adjacent to the river Stour and the Canterbury railway, 1½ mile WNW of Wye station, and 4 NNE of Ashford It contains Boughton Lees, which has a post office under Ashford Acres, 2 [illegible]18 Real property, £3,2[illegible]8 Pop, 17[illegible] Houses, 80 The property is divided among a few The manor belonged in the time of King John, to Mulch de Boughton The living is a vicarage in the diocese of Canterbury Value, £216 Patrons the [illegible] of Dr [illegible] The church is [illegible] and contains [illegible] of the [illegible] Charities £5

BOUGHTON BLEAN See BOUGHTON UNDER BLEAN

BOUGHTON (GREAT) a township and a district in Cheshire The township is in St Oswald parish and partly within Chester city, and lies on the Chester and Crewe railway 1 mile E of Chester Acres, 7[illegible]0 Real property [illegible] Pop [illegible] Houses, 281 — The district comprises Great Boughton poor law union, and Chester city, the latter being regulated, in poor law matters by a local act It comprehends the sub district of Tattenhall, containing the parishes of Tattenhall Handley, Waverton, Aldford, Harthill, Coddington, Farndon, and Tilston, the extra parochial tracts of Willington and Kingsmarsh, and parts of the parishes of Malpas Shocklach, Tarvin, and St Oswald, the sub district of Hawarden containing the parishes of Hawarden electorally in Flint Dodleston partly in Flint, Pulford, and Eccleston, the extra parochial tract of Shotwick Park and parts of the parishes of Shotwick and St Mary on the Hill, the sub district of Chester Castle, containing the parishes of Barrow Sutton Guilden, Christleton, St John Baptist, St Olave, and St Michael, the extra parochial tracts of Claverton, Priors-Hay Spittle Boughton, and Chester Gaol and Barracks and parts of the parishes of Tarvin, St Oswald, and St Mary on the Hill and the sub district of Chester Cathedral containing the parishes of Backford, Plemonstall, Thornton le Moors, Ince St Peter, St Bridget, St Martin, and Holy Trinity the extra parochial tracts of Stanlow, Little St John and Cathedral Precincts, and parts of the parishes of Stoke Shotwick, St Oswald, and St Mary on the Hill Acres 10[illegible]79[illegible] Poor rates, including Chester, £23,104 Pop in 1841, 49 097, in 1861, 58 501 Houses, 11,232 Marriages, 638, births, 1,674, —of which 1[illegible]1 were illegitimate, deaths, 1 238,—of which 3[illegible]6 were at ages under 5 years, and 30 at ages above 85 Marriages in the ten years 1851–60 5,423, births, 16,820, deaths, 12 874 The places of worship in 1851 were 47 of the Church of England with 18,120 sittings, 1 of the Presbyterian church in England, with [illegible]0 s, 6 of Independents, with 1,610 s 2 of Baptists, with 352 s, 2 of Quakers, with 600 s, 1 of Unitarians with 250 s., 21 of Wesleyan Methodists, with 2,746 s, 12 of New Connexion Methodists with 2 862 s, 20 of Primitive Methodists, with 1,[illegible]88 s, 1 of the Wesleyan Association with 77 s, 8 of Calvinistic Methodists, with 1,163 s, 3 undefined, with 310 s, 1 of Roman Catholics with 135 s, and 1 of Latter day Saints, with 250 attendants The schools were 66 public day schools, with 5 208 scholars 91 private day schools, with 2 143 s, and 76 Sunday schools, with 5 928 s The workhouse is in Holy Trinity parish

BOUGHTON GREEN See BOUGHTON, Brixworth, Northampton

BOUGHTON HILL See BOUGHTON UNDER BLEAN

BOUGHTON KETTERING See BOUGHTON, Weekley Northampton

BOUGHTON LEES See BOUGHTON ALUPH

BOUGHTON MALHERBE, a parish in Hollingbourne district, Kent on the verge of the Weald, 5 miles NNW of Pluckley r station, and 10 [illegible] of Maidstone Post town, Lenham under Maidstone Acres, 2,699 Real property, £2 94[illegible] Pop 40[illegible] Houses 70 The property is divided among a few The manor belonged, in the time of Henry III, to the Malherbe family passed to the Wottons of whom was Sir Henry Wotton, whose life was written by Isaac Walton, passed again to Sir Horace Mann, the correspondent of Walpole, and belongs now to the heirs of Earl Cornwallis The manor house bears the name of Boughton Place, was built by Sir Edward Wotton in the time of Henry VIII, and visited by Queen Elizabeth, and is now a farm house retaining some of the ancient rooms The materials of it are said to have been [illegible] Castle the baronial fortalice of the [illegible] some traces of which still exist [illegible] the church Chilstone Hall is the seat of J S Douglas Esq The living is a rectory in the diocese of Canterbury Value, £170 * Patrons the Heirs of Earl Cornwallis The church is decorated English, in good condition There are a Baptist chapel a national school and charities [illegible]

BOUGHTON MONCHELSEA, a parish in Maidstone district Kent [illegible] the Weald [illegible] S by E of Maidstone, and [illegible] NW of Staplehurst r station It has a post office under Staplehurst Acres, 2,29[illegible] Real property £[illegible] Pop, 1,190 Houses 2[illegible] The property is subdivided The manor belongs [illegible] to the Moncheleas of Swanscombe Kentish rag is extensively worked Remains of a hyena were found here, in a fissure, by the late Dr Buckland The living is a vicarage in the diocese of Canterbury Value £395 * Patrons, the Dean and Chapter of Rochester The church is very good There are a n school, and charities £9

BOUGHTON PLACE See BOUGHTON MALHERBE

BOUGHTON (SPITTLE), an extra parochial tract, in Great Boughton district, Cheshire, contiguous to St John Baptist parish within Chester city

BOUGHTON UNDER BLEAN, a village a parish, and a hundred in Faversham district, Kent The village stands on the edge of Blean forest, 3½ miles SE of Faversham r station, and has a post office,‡ of the name of Boughton, under Faversham, and a fair on the Monday after 29 June —The parish comprises 2,353 acres Real property, £8,904 Pop, 1,621 Houses, 323 The property is subdivided Nash Court, then held by the Hawkinses, who were Roman Catholics was demolished by a mob in 1715, and rebuilt in 1766 Boughton House is the seat of the Laggs. Boughton Hill, adjacent to the village, commands an extensive and brilliant view The living is a vicarage in the diocese of Canterbury Value, £300 * Patron the Archbishop of Canterbury The church comprises nave, aisle, three chancels, and a tower There are a Wesleyan chapel, a national school, and charities £74 —The hundred is in the lathe of Scray, and comprises four parishes Acres, 11,354 Pop, 2,930 Houses 581

BOULBY, a hamlet in Easington parish, N R. Yorkshire, 9 miles E of Guisborough Extensive alum works have been in operation here since 1615 An old edifice, now a farm house, was the seat of the Conyerses.

BOULDON, a township in Holdgate parish, Salop, 7½ miles NNE of Ludlow Pop, 64 Houses, 13

BOULEY BAY, a bay on the NE side of Jersey, immediately W of Rozel tower, and 3¾ miles SSW of the Droudles It has a half moon outline, and measures 1½ mile across the entrance

BOULGE, a parish in Woodbridge district, Suffolk, 3 miles NNW of Woodbridge r station Post town, Bredfield, under Woodbridge Acres 517 Real property, £962 Pop., 231 Houses, 43 The property is divided among a few The living is a rectory, united with the rectory of Debach, in the diocese of Norwich Value, £300 * Patron, H W Field, Esq The church is very good

BOULMER AND SEATON HOUSE, a township in Long Houghton parish, Northumberland, on the coast, 5½ miles E of Alnwick Acres, 391 Pop, 156 Houses, 27 The coast is diversified with Boulmer point and Boulmer bay, and the inhabitants are chiefly fishermen

BOULSDON AND KILLCOTT, a tything in Newent parish, Gloucestershire, 9 miles NW of Gloucester Real property, £2,341 Pop, 634 Houses, 137

BOULSTON, or BULSTON a parish in Haverfordwest district, Pembroke, on the river Cleddau, 4 miles SE by S of Haverfordwest r station Post town, Haverfordwest. Acres, 1,822, of which 160 are water Real property, £948 Pop 251 Houses, 54 The property is divided among a few The manor belongs to R J Ackland, Esq The living is a donative in the diocese of St Davids Value £25 Patron, R J Ackland, Esq The church contains monuments of the Wogans, and is good

BOULSTONE, or BOLSTONE, a parish in the district and county of Hereford adjacent to the Monmouth and Hereford railway, and to the river Wye, 1¼ mile S by W of Holme Lacy r station, and 5½ SSE of Hereford Post town, Holme Lacy, under Hereford Acres, 657 Real property, £812 Pop 61 Houses, 13 The property is not much divided The manor belongs to Sir E. F Stanhope Bart The living is a p curacy annexed to the vicarage of Holme Lacy in the diocese of Hereford The church has a square tower, and is good

BOULSWORTH a mountain on the mutual border of Lancashire and Yorkshire, part of the backbone of England 5½ miles ENE of Burnley Its altitude is 1,359 feet

BOULTHAM, a parish in the district and county of Lincoln, on the river Witham, the Roman road, and the Midland railway, 2 miles SSW of Lincoln Post town, Lincoln Acres, 1 210 Real property, £2,343 Pop, 95 Houses, 20 The property is divided among a few Boultham Hall is a chief residence The living is a rectory in the diocese of Lincoln Value, £126 Patron, R Ellison Esq The church is good

BOULTON, a township chapelry in St Peter parish, Derbyshire, on the Derby canal, 3 miles SE of Derby Post town Derby Acres, 1,210 Rated property, £1,500 Pop., 224 Houses 45 The property is subdivided The living is a vicarage in the diocese of Lichfield Value, £120 Patrons, the Landholders The church is partly Norman, and in good condition

BOUNDS GREEN, a locality in Middlesex, adjacent to the New river and to the Great Northern railway, 1 mile SE of Colney Hatch r station It has a post office under Colney Hatch London, N

BOUNTISBOROUGH a hundred in Winchester division, Hants It contains Godsfield, Itchin Abbas, and Itchin Stoke parishes Acres, 5,181 Pop 518 Houses 107

BOURG (LE), a village in St Clement parish, Jersey

BOURIDGE See BOVERIDGE

BOURN, a parish in Caxton district, Cambridge, on an affluent of the river Cam, 2 miles SSE of Caxton, and 3½ WNW of Lords Bridge r station It has a post office under Royston Acres, 4,065 Real property, £4,981 Pop, 893 Houses, 187 The property is divided among a few Bourn Hall is the seat of Earl Delawarr The manor belonged to Morcar, the Saxon, and passed to the Picots, and a castle on it was destroyed in the civil wars of the time of Henry III The living is a vicarage in the diocese of Ely Value, £161 * Patron, Christs College Cambridge Charities, £12

BOURN, a small town, a parish, a sub district, and a district in Lincoln The town stands on a flat tract, adjacent to the fens, at the terminus of the Bourn and Essendine railway 5½ miles S by E of Folkingham A large spring the source of a rivulet adjoins it, and two canal cuts for barges go from it to Boston and the river Glen A Roman pavement and other remains have been found and are thought to indicate that the place was edificed by the Romans A strong castle was built in the Saxon times, made long and vigorous resistance to William the Conqueror, and was given by William Rufus to Walter Fitzgilbert, but has disappeared An Augustinian abbey was founded in 1138 by Baldwin Fitzgilbert, but is known now only by its site The town suffered severely by fire in 1605 and 1637, and now consists chiefly of one street about 1½ mile long The Bull Inn is an edifice said to have been built by William, Lord Burleigh The Red Hall is a brick structure engirt partly by a morass, partly by a deep moat, long held by the Digby family, and latterly used as a ladies boarding school The town hall, in the market place, is a fine edifice of 1821 built at a cost of £3,600, and includes court rooms The parish church is partly Norman, consists of nave, side aisles, a short south transept, and a lofty chancel, had formerly two large west end towers, and was finely renovated in 1852 There are Independent and Wesleyan chapels, a free school two almshouses, other charities, and a workhouse The charities have an annual value of £813 and the workhouse was erected at a cost of £6,700 The town has a head post office,‡ two banking offices, and two chief inns, and is a seat of quarter and petty sessions and a polling place A weekly market is held on Thursday, and fairs on 7 March, 10 May 30 Sept, and 29 Oct Wool stapling, tanning, and malting are carried on The great Lord Burleigh and the notorious Dr Dodd executed for forgery, were natives Pop, 3,066 Houses, 610

The parish includes also the hamlets of Dyke, Cawthorpe, Dyke Fen, Tongue End and Bourn North and South Fens. Acres, 9,352 Real property, £21,221

Pop 3,739 Houses, 761 The property is not much divided The living is a vicarage in the diocese of Lincoln Value, £320 * Patrons, the Executors of the late J T Ostler, Esq —The sub-district comprises the parishes of Bourn, Haconby, Morton Edenham, Witham-on the Hill, Carlby, and Thurlby Acres, 39,106 Pop., 7,854 Houses, 1 509 —The district comprehends also the sub district of Deeping, containing the parishes of Baston, Langtoft, Market Deeping, and Deeping St James, and the extra parochial tract of Deeping Fen, the sub district of Corby containing the parishes of Corby, Irnham, Careby, Little Bytham Castle Bytham, Creeton, Swayfield, and Swinstead, and the sub district of Aslackby, containing the parishes of Aslackby, Kirk by Underwood Folkingham, Laughton, Horbling, Billingborough Sempringham, Dowsby, Pointon, and Dunsby Acres of the district 106,934 Poor rates in 1866, £9 700 Pop in 1861, 21,293 Houses, 4 402 Marriages in 1866, 145, births, 614,—of which 49 were illegitimate, deaths, 318,—of which 95 were at ages under 5 years and 15 at ages above 85 years Marriages in the ten years 1851-60, 1,540, births, 7,149, deaths, 4,049 The places of worship in 1851 were 29 of the Church of England with 9,510 sittings, 2 of Independents, with 450 s 6 of Baptists, with 1 034 s , 16 of Wesleyan Methodists with 2,500 s , 1 of Primitive Methodists, with 100 s. 2 of Wesleyan Reformers with 208 s , 1 of Latter Day Saints with 70 s , 1 undefined, with 150 s , and 1 of Roman Catholics, with 100 s. The schools were 26 public day schools with 1 143 scholars, 59 private day schools, with 1,071 s , 52 Sunday schools, with 3,249 s and 2 evening schools for adults, with 24 s

BOURN AND ESSENDINE RAILWAY, a railway in Lincoln 6½ miles long east north eastward from the Essendine station of the Great Northern railway to the town of Bourn It was opened in May 1860 A new branch now prolongs it to Spalding

BOURNE a hamlet in Piddletown parish Dorset, 5½ miles NE of Dorchester Sail cloth is manufactured

BOURNE Surrey See WRECCLESHAM

BOURNE, Hants See BOURNE ST MARY

BOURNE (EAST) See EASTBOURNE

BOURNE END, a village in Bovington parish, Herts, 2 miles ESE of Berkhampstead. It has a church, an Independent chapel and an industrial school

BOURNEMOUTH, a watering place in Christchurch parish, and two chapelries in Christchurch and Holdenhurst parishes, Hants The watering-place stands at the mouth of the Bourne rivulet, on Poole bay, 4 miles WSW of Christchurch r station, and 5 E of Poole It has a head post office,‡ and public conveyances run to it from Poole and Christchurch It is of recent origin, has no street, and includes villas, lodging houses, hotels a sanatorium, baths, a small infirmary of 1869 two churches, three dissenting chapels and a library and reading room The sanatorium is an Italian edifice, with accommodation for 40 patients St Peter's church was built in 1844, is in the early decorated style, and was altered and greatly enlarged in 1864 The churchyard contains the remains of Godwin the novelist, Mrs Godwin, better known as Mary Wolstonecraft, author of "A Vindication of the Rights of Woman," —and Mary Wolstonecraft Shelley widow of the poet Shelley The beach is one of the best in England the environs comprise churches, woods, open heaths, and variety of walks and drives, and the views inland, and to Purbeck and the Isle of Wight, are very fine A local newspaper is published every Saturday —The chapelries were constituted in 1845 and 1867 Pop , 1 940 and 350 The livings are vicarages in the diocese of Winchester Value, £350 and £150 * Patrons, Sir G Gervis, Bart , and Trustees

BOURNE (RIVER) a stream of Dorset and Hants It rises 2 miles SW of Kingston, and runs 4 miles south eastward to Poole bay at Bournemouth

BOURNE (RIVER) a stream of Warwick It rises 2 miles SW of Atherstone, and runs 8 miles west south westward to the Blythe, in the vicinity of Coleshill

BOURNE (RIVER), a stream of Hants and Wilts It rises near Easton in Wilts, goes 10 miles southward past Collingbourn, and through the border of Wilts, to Park House, then proceeds 10 miles south westward past Boscombe Porton, and the Winterbournes, to the Avon below Salisbury

BOURNE ST MARY, a tything and a parish in Whitchurch district, Hants The tything lies near the Southwestern railway, 3 miles NW of Whitchurch, and has a post office under Andover Pop , 384 The parish includes also the tythings of Binley, Egbury, Stoke, Swampton Tangier, and Week Acres, 7,678 Real property, £5,350. Pop , 1,188 Houses, 282 The property is much subdivided The living is a p curacy, annexed to the vicarage of Hurstbourne Priors, in the diocese of Winchester The church is good

BOURNE (WEST) See WESTBOURNE

BOURN MOOR, a township in Houghton le-Spring parish, Durham, 2 miles N of Houghton le Spring Acres, 500 Pop , 973 Houses, 198 Here are some brine springs.

BOURN NORTH AND SOUTH FENS. See BOURN, Lincoln

BOURNS (THE), a tract in the valley of the Avon, S of Amesbury, in Wilts.

BOURTON, a tything in Shrivenham parish, Berks, on the Wilts and Berks canal and on the Great Western railway, about a mile from Shrivenham station Real property £2 545 Pop , 328 Houses, 72 A church was built here in 1861, in the geometric style There are also a Baptist chapel, a neat free school, and six alms houses.

BOURTON, a hamlet in Buckingham parish, within Buckingham borough, 1 mile E of the town Acres, 1,360 Real property, £2,157 Pop 44 Houses, 9

BOURTON, a chapelry in Gillingham parish, Dorset on the verge of the county 2½ miles SW of Mere, and 3 NNW of Gillingham r station It has a post office under Bath Acres, 623 Real property, with Silton £5 415 Pop , 921 Houses, 210 The property is much subdivided The living is a p curacy in the diocese of Salisbury Value, £90 Patrons, Trustees The church is good

BOURTON, a township in Much Wenlock parish Salop, 3½ miles SSW of Wenlock Pop , 181

BOURTON a tything in Bishops Canning parish Wilts, 3½ miles NE of Devizes Real property, with Easton, £1,517 Pop , 216

BOURTON, a railway station in Somerset, on the Bristol and Exeter railway, at Flaxbourton, 5½ miles WSW of Bristol

BOURTON, Warwick See BOURTON UPON DUNSMOOR

BOURTON (BLACK) See BLACKBOURTON

BOURTON (FLAX) See FLAXBOURTON

BOURTON (GREAT and LITTLE), a chapelry in Cropredy parish, Oxford, 3 miles N of Banbury Acres 1,380 Real property, £4,035 Pop , 500 Houses 124 The living is annexed to Cropredy The church was built in 1863 There are two dissenting chapels

BOURTONHOLD, a hamlet in the parish and borough of Buckingham Real property, £1,223 Pop., 565 Houses 136

BOURTON ON THE HILL, a village and a parish in Shipston on Stour district, Gloucester The village stands on the side of a hill, commanding a delightful prospect, 2½ miles W of Moreton r station, and 4½ N by W of Stow on the Wold and has a post office under Moreton in the Marsh —The parish comprises 2,900 acres Real property, £5,613 Pop , 500 Houses, 125 The property is divided among a few The living is a rectory, united with the rectory of Moreton in the Marsh in the diocese of Gloucester and Bristol Value, £675 * Patron, Lord Redesdale The church is good, and there are school charities £112

BOURTON ON THE WATER, a village and a parish in Stow on the Wold district, Gloucester The village stands on the river Windrush, and on the Fosse way, at the terminus of the Bourton on the Water railway 4 miles SSW of Stow on the Wold, and has a post office‡ under Moreton in the Marsh. The parish comprises 2,282 acres. Real property, £6,188. Pop., 1,011. Houses, 234. The property is much subdivided. Many Roman antiquities, one of them a curious gold signet, have been found in the vicinity of the village, and there was formerly a paved aqueduct. The living is a rectory, united with the p. curacies of Clapton and Lower Slaughter, in the diocese of Gloucester and Bristol. Value, £470.* Patron, Wadham College, Oxford. The church is Grecian, and has a lofty tower, surmounted by a cupola. There are a Baptist chapel and two public schools.

BOURTON ON THE WATER RAILWAY, a railway in Oxford and Gloucester, 6¼ miles long, westward, from the Chipping Norton junction of the West Midland railway to the village of Bourton on the Water. It was authorized in June 1860, and opened in March 1862.

BOURTON UPON DUNSMOOR, a parish in Rugby district, Warwick, on the river Leam, and on the Leamington and Rugby railway, 1 mile SSE of Birdingbury station, and 5½ SW by W of Rugby. It includes the hamlet of Draycott, and has a post office, of the name of Bourton under Rugby. Acres, 2,520. Real property, £3,186. Pop., 332. Houses, 77. The property is divided among a few. Bourton Hall is the seat of B. Shuckburgh, Esq. The parish is a meet for the North Warwick hounds. The living is a rectory in the diocese of Worcester. Value, £350.* Patron, B. Shuckburgh, Esq. The church was repaired in 1859. Charities, £19.

BOUT, a village in Eskdale, Cumberland, 7 miles ENE of Ravenglass. It has an inn, and is in the vicinity of waterfalls and other attractions on the way up Eskdale to the mountain passes into Wastdale Head, Langdale, and Duddon vale.

BOUTHROP. See Leach Martin (East).

BOVENEY, a chapelry in Burnham parish, Bucks, on the River Thames, near the Great Western railway, 2 miles W of Eton. Post town, Dorney, under Windsor. Acres, 480. Rated property, £857. Pop., 172. Houses, 31. The property is divided among a few. The living is a p. curacy, annexed to the vicarage of Burnham, in the diocese of Oxford. The church is good.

BOVENHILL, a hamlet in Tettenhall parish, Stafford, 1 mile NW of Wolverhampton. Pop., 17.

BOVERIDGE, or Bouridge, a tything in Cranborne parish, Dorset, 1¼ mile NE by N of Cranborne. Pop., 174. It has a chapel of ease and an almshouse, and is a curacy with Cranborne. Boveridge House is the seat of the Brounckers.

BOVERTON, a hamlet in Lantwit Major parish, Glamorgan, on the Julian way, 4½ miles S of Cowbridge. It has a post office under Cowbridge. It disputes with other places the claim of being the Roman Bovium, and it has traces of a baronial fortalice which belonged first to the lords of Cardiff, then to the family of Seys.

BOVEY BROOK, or Wrey River, a stream of Devon. It rises in Dartmoor forest, 6 miles SW of Moreton Hampstead, and runs about 18 miles first north-eastward to the vicinity of Moreton, next south-eastward to the Teign, 4 miles SW of Chudleigh. It traverses much romantic scenery, and is notable for trouting.

BOVEY HEATHFIELD. See Bovey (South).

BOVEY (North), a parish in Newton Abbot district, Devon, on the Bovey brook, on the E border of Dartmoor, near the Moreton Hampstead railway, 1½ mile SW of Moreton Hampstead. Post town, Moreton Hampstead, under Exeter. Acres, 5,654. Real property, £2,901. Pop., 513. Houses, 103. The property is subdivided. The ancient lords of the manor had the power of inflicting capital punishment. Most of the surface is thickly strewn with fragments of rock. The living is a rectory in the diocese of Exeter. Value, £2?3.* Patron, the Earl of Devon. The church is very old, but good.

BOVEY (South), or Bovey Tracey, a village and a parish in Newton-Abbot district, Devon. The village stands on Bovey brook, and on the Moreton Hampstead railway, 6½ miles NW of Newton, and has a post office under Newton Abbot, and a r. station with telegraph. It was formerly a market town, and still has fairs on Easter Monday, Holy Thursday, and the first Thursday of July and Nov. Part of an ancient cross stands in an open space in it, and an ancient wayside monument is built into one of its houses. Cromwell made a night attack on a part of Lord Wentworth's brigade here, in 1646, and captured 400 troopers and 7 standards. The parish comprises 7,212 acres. Real property, £8,229. Pop., 2,080. Houses, 413. The property is much subdivided. The manor belonged anciently to the Traceys, one of whom, Sir William Tracey, was the leader in the assassination of Thomas a Becket, and belongs now to the Earl of Devon. A reach of valley adjacent to the village bears the name of Bovey Heathfield, has a low flat bottom, seeming to have been once a lake, and contains deposits of porcelain clay, and beds of lignite called Bovey coal. The clay is worked in an interesting pottery close to the village, and the lignite is used as fuel at the pottery, in lime kilns, and by the poor. A great ridge of hills flanks the valley, and culminates picturesquely in the Bottor rock. The living is a vicarage in the diocese of Exeter. Value, £450.* Patron, the Crown. The church is perpendicular English, with a square tower, and was renovated in 1859. A chapel of ease, a beautiful structure, stands adjacent to the pottery. There are chapels for Baptists and Wesleyans, and a free school. The Devon house of mercy was erected here in 1868, includes a lofty chapel, in the first pointed style, and has accommodation for seventy-two inmates and eight sisters.

BOVEY TRACEY. See Bovey (South).

BOVINGDON, a parish in Hemel Hempstead district, Herts, on the verge of the county, near the North-western railway and the Grand Junction canal, 2½ miles SW of Boxmoor r. station, and 3½ SSE of Berkhampstead. It has a post office under Hemel Hempstead. Acres, 3,958. Real property, £6,087. Pop., 1,1?5. Houses, 2?1. The property is divided among a few. The living is a vicarage in the diocese of Rochester. Value, not reported. Patron, the Hon. G. D. Ryder. The church is good, and there are a chapel of ease, two Independent chapels, a Wesleyan chapel, three industrial schools, and charities £14.

BOVISAND, a small bay in Devon, on the E side of Plymouth sound, opposite the Breakwater, 3 miles SSE of Plymouth. Here is a coast guard station, a granite battery, and a great water reservoir for ships.

BOVIUM. See Bangor Iscoed and Boverton.

BOW, a village, a parish, and a sub-district in the district of Crediton, Devon. The village stands on the slope of a hill, near the Okehampton railway, 7½ miles W by N of Crediton, and has a post office‡ of Bow, North Devon, and a r. station. It was formerly a market town, and it still has fairs on Holy Thursday and 22 Nov. The parish is called also Nymet Tracey. Acres, 2,740. Real property, £3,466. Pop., 904. Houses, 205. The manor belonged anciently to the Traceys. Colleton House and Gratton House, now the seats of the Sandersons and the Wreyfords, are fine modern mansions. The living is a rectory, united with the rectory of Broad Nymet, in the diocese of Exeter. Value, £430. Patron, F. Vandermeulen, Esq. The church stands about a mile from the village, and has a low square tower. There are an Independent chapel and a free school. The sub-district comprises eight parishes. Acres, 19,402. Pop., ?,316. Houses, 735.

BOW, a parish and a sub-district in Poplar district, Middlesex. The parish is called also Stratford le Bow, lies on the river Lea and on the North London and Eastern Counties railways, within Tower Hamlets borough, in the eastern suburbs of London, 4 miles ENE of St Pauls, includes the village of Stratford, the hamlet of Old Ford, and part of Victoria Park, and has a station of Bow on the North London railway, a station of Stratford on the Eastern Counties railway, and post offices of Bow,‡ Bow Road,‡ and Old Ford, under London E. Acres, 809. Real property, £78,400. Pop. in 1851, 4,626; in 1861, 11,590. Houses, 1,81?. The name Bow alludes to a bow-shaped three-arched bridge across the Lea, built by Matilda, the queen of Henry I, and not taken down till 1831, and the name Stratford alludes to a ford in the Lea, on the line of the Roman road or "stratum" to Luxton A new bridge, in lieu of the ancient one, with one oblique arch of 70 feet, was erected in 1839, at a cost of £11,000 Bow was once famous for cream and cakes, it also carried on an extensive manufacture of porcelain, and it had a notable annual fair which became so great a nuisance, that it was suppressed by parliament It now has dye houses, large breweries, and the East London waterworks, and takes a character from the proximity of the India docks. The parish was formerly a chapelry to Stepney, and became parochial in 1717 The living is a rectory in the diocese of London Value, £349 * Patron the Bishop of London The church was built in the time of Henry II, presents a curious mixture of Norman and early English, and has a low tower and an eight-sided corner turret The vicarage of Old Ford is a separate benefice A Baptist chapel, in the Byzantine style, at a cost of nearly £7,000 was built in 1867 There are other dissenting chapels, two endowed schools with £27 and £234, and charities £170 —The sub district contains also the parish of Bromley St Leonard Pop, 35,667

BOW AND ARROW CASTLE, a rude pentagonal tower on the coast of Dorset, on a sea girt crag 300 feet high, 1½ mile NNE of Portland Bill It is said to have been built by William Rufus, and it was taken, in 1142, by the Earl of Gloucester for the Empress Matilda A bridge connects it with the mainland, and gives force to a charming local view

BOWBANK, a hamlet in Lunedale township Romaldkirk parish N R Yorkshire, 10 miles WNW of Barnard Castle

BOW BEECH, a locality 4 miles from Eden Bridge on the W border of Kent, with a post office under Eden Bridge

BOW BRICKHILL See Brickhill (Bow)

BOWBRIDGE, a hamlet in Low Abbotside township, N R Yorkshire, 1 mile W of Askrigg.

BOWBRIDGE, a hamlet in Stroud parish, Gloucester, on the Thames and Severn canal, 1 mile from Stroud It has a post office under Stroud

BOW-BROOK, an affluent of the river Cale tracing part of the boundary between Dorset and Somerset

BOWCOMBE, a hamlet in Carisbrooke parish, Isle of Wight, 2½ miles SW of Newport Pop, 93 Bowcombe vale around it, formerly displayed much beauty but has suffered by destruction of its wood Bowcombe down on the W, shows traces of a Roman road commands a rich and extensive view, and was ascended in 1618, for sake of its prospect, by Charles I when Prince of Wales

BOW COMMON, a chapelry in the parishes of Lime House Stepney, Bromley St Leonard, and All Saints Poplar, Middlesex, on the Blackwall Extension railway, within Tower Hamlets borough on the eastern side of London, 3 miles E by N of St Pauls It was constituted in 1858 Pop, 2 077 Houses 279 The living is a vicarage in the diocese of London Value, £150 * Patron the Rev A B Cotton

BOWDEN, Cheshire See Bowdon

BOWDEN, Devon See Pettisnallor

BOWDEN EDGE a township in Chapel le Frith parish, Derby, 1 mile NE of Chapel Real property, £4 299 Pop, 1 297 Houses 241 Bowden Hall an old seat here is now a farm house

BOWDEN (Great), or Bowden Magna, a village and a parish in Market Harborough district Leicester The village stands on an eminence near the river Welland, and the Northwestern railway 1 mile NE of Market Harborough, and has a post office of the name of Great Bowden under Rugby —The parish includes also the town and chapelry of Market Harborough Acres, [illegible]120 Real property [illegible] Pop 3 [illegible]7 Houses, 777 The property is subdivided The living is a vicarage in the diocese of Peterborough Value, £8[illegible] Patron Christ Church College Oxford The church is good, and there are charities £-7 The p[illegible] curacy of Market Harborough is a separate benefice

BOWDEN HILL, a chapelry in Laycock parish, Wilts 3½ miles SSE of Chippenham It was constituted in 1868 Pop, about 400 Living a vicarage

BOWDEN (Little), or Bowden Parva a parish in Market Harborough district and county of Northampton, ½ mile S of Market Harborough It includes the hamlet of Little Oxenden, and its post town is Market Harborough under Rugby Acres, 1,670 Real property, £4 492 Pop 486 Houses 105 The property is subdivided The living is a rectory in the diocese of Peterborough Value, £400 * Patron, the Rev T W Barlow The church is good, and there are charities £70

BOWDEN MAGNA See Bowden (Great)

BOWDEN PARVA See Bowden (Little)

BOWDER STONE See Borrowdale, Cumberland

BOWDON, or Bowden, a village, a township, and a parish in Altrincham district, Cheshire The village stands on the Roman road from Kinderton, adjacent to the Manchester, Knutsford, and Northwich railway near the river Bollin, ½ of a mile SW of Altrincham, and it has a station on the railway, with refreshment rooms and telegraph, and a post office under Manchester It enjoys fine air and charming environs, and is a favourite resort of ruralizing parties from Manchester —The township includes the village, and comprises 6_8 acres. Real property, £14,322 Pop 1 827 Houses 301 —The parish contains also the townships of Altrincham, Bagguley Timperley, Hale, Ashley, Dunham Massey, Carrington, Partington, and Bollington Acres, 17,971 Real property, £9[illegible] 900 Pop 14 822 Houses, 2,779 The property is not much divided The manor belonged to the priory of Birkenhead, and was given, by Henry VIII, to the see of Chester Dunham Park is the seat of the Earl of Stamford, and has fine grounds The living is a vicarage in the diocese of Chester Value, £460 * Patron, the Bishop of Chester The church stands on elevated ground, was rebuilt after the model of the previous one, in the later English style, in 1860, at a cost of about £12,000, and comprises nave, chancel aisles, transepts, chapel, and vestry with a tower The p curacy of St John is a separate charge, constituted in 1866 Patron, the Bishop of C The church was completed in 1867, at a cost of £5,[illegible], and is in the early English style, and cruciform The chapelries of Altrincham, Carrington, Dunham Massey, Ringway, and Timperley, are separate benefices There are numerous dissenting chapels, numerous public schools, and charities £1[illegible]4

BOWENT RIVER, or College Burn, a stream of Northumberland It rises among the Central Cheviots adjacent to the boundary with Scotland, and runs 7 miles northward to the river Glen, in the vicinity of Kirk Newton It is rich in trout and pebbles.

BOWER ASHTON a hamlet in Long Ashton parish Somerset 2½ miles SW of Bristol It has a post office under Bristol

BOWER CHALK, a parish in Wilton district, Wilts, near Cranborne Chase, [illegible] miles S of Dinton r station and 7½ SW of Wilton Post town Broad Chalk, under Salisbury Acres, 2,[illegible] Real property, with Broad Chalk, £9,512 Pop 4[illegible]6 Houses, [illegible] The property is divided among a few The living is a vicarage annexed to the vicarage of Broad Chalk, in the diocese of Salisbury The church is tolerable

BOWERDALE, a glen 2 miles long, descending to the middle of the W side of Haweswater in Cumberland

BOWER (East and West), two hamlets in Bridgwater parish Somerset

BOWER HINTON-WITH-HURST a hamlet in Martock parish Somerset, 2 miles NE of South Petherton Pop [illegible]

BOWERMAN'S NOSE, an isolated rock 3½ miles SW of Moreton Hampstead, in Devon It rises fully 40 feet high and looks like a colossal statue of a man

BOWERS GIFFORD, a parish in Billericay district, Essex, on the Tilbury and Southend railway 1½ mile E of Pitsea station, and 7 SE of Billericay It includes part of Canvey island, and has a post office under Chelmsford Acres, 2,60[illegible] Real property, £3,768

Pop, 259 Houses, 48 The property is divided among a few Bowers Hall is the seat of Mrs Curtis Much of the land is marshy The living is a rectory in the diocese of Rochester Value, £564 * Patron, the Rev Horace Roberts The church is tolerable

BOWES, a village, a township, and a parish in the district of Teesdale, and N R Yorkshire The village stands on the river Greta and on the Roman road to Brough, adjacent to the South Durham and Lancashire Union railway, 4 miles SW of Barnard Castle, and has a station on the railway, a post office under Darlington, and an inn It consists chiefly of one long street and formerly was a market town The Roman station of Lavatrae occupied its site, and many Roman inscriptions have been found here, one of them narrating the reparation of a bath for the first Thracian cohort —The township includes also the hamlets of Bowes Cross, Gallow Hill, Low Field Mellwater, Sleightholme, Stoney-Keld, Applegarth Forest, and part of Tan Hill Acres, 16,090 Real property, £7,405 Pop, 760 Houses, 154 —The parish contains also the township of Gilmonby Acres, 18,331 Real property, £8,890 Pop, 849 Houses 169 The property is much subdivided Bowes House is the seat of T Harrison, Esq A quadrangular tower, 75 feet by 60, and about 53 feet high part of a castle, built by Allan Niger, first Norman Earl of Richmond, stands on the crown of a hill defended by a deep ditch, and is supposed to have been constructed of materials taken from the Roman station A Roman aqueduct, formed for bringing water nearly 2 miles to the Roman baths at the station, was recently discovered A natural bridge in limestone rock 16 feet in span, crosses the Greta bears the name of God's bridge, and is occasionally used as a carriage road Much of the parish consists of the dreary mountainous tract of Stainmoor The living is a p curacy in the diocese of Ripon Value, £90 Patron, T Harrison, Esq The church is an humble ancient building, partly Norman, and the churchyard contains the grave and monument of the two lovers commemorated in Mallet's pathetic ballad of "Edwin and Emma" A class boarding school at Bowes, now extinct, is said to have been the Dotheboys Hall of Dickens' "Nicholas Nickleby" A grammar school, founded in 1693, has an endowed income of £201, other charities, £5

BOWES CROSS, a hamlet in Bowes parish, 1¾ mile E of Bowes village, N R Yorkshire

BOW FELL a mountain on the mutual border of Cumberland and Westmoreland, at the head of Borrowdale, Eskdale, and Langdale, 8 miles WNW of Ambleside It has an altitude of 2,914 feet above the level of the sea, and figures grandly in the background views from Windermere and Esthwaite water

BOW HILL, a hill 5 miles NNW of Chichester, in Sussex It has a height of 702 feet, and commands a fine view

BOWLAND BRIDGE, a locality at the boundary between Westmorland and Lancashire on the Winster river 6½ miles WNW of Kendal

BOWLAND FOREST, an ancient forest on the mutual border of Lancashire and W R Yorkshire It included the parishes of Mitton and Slaidburn, and part of the parish of Whalley and belonged to the honour of Clitheroe It contained wild deer so late as 1812, but is now enclosed and cultivated The family of Parker, of Browsholme Hall, have long held the office of hereditary forester

BOWLAND FOREST (HIGH), a township in Slaidburn parish, W R Yorkshire, on the river Hodder 10 miles NW of Clitheroe It includes the hamlets of Dunsop and Battrix Acres, with Low Bowland Forest, 18,048 Real property £2,920 Pop, 167 Houses, 25

BOWLAND FOREST (LOW), or WHITEWELL a township in Whalley parish W R Yorkshire, on the river Hodder, 7 miles WNW of Clitheroe A portion of it, including Harrop Fold hamlet, lies detached from the rest Real property £3,715 Pop, 319 Houses, 50

BOWLAND (LITTLE), a township in Whalley parish, Lancashire under Bleasdale, 7 miles NW of Clitheroe Acres, with Leagram township, 7 699 Real property, with Leagram, £3,206 Pop, 123 Houses, 19

BOWLD, a hamlet in Idbury parish, Oxford, 5½ miles NNW of Burford Pop, 39

BOWLEES BURN, a stream of Durham, running 5 miles southward to the Tees, 2½ miles above Middleton in Teesdale

BOWLEY, a township in Bodenham parish, Hereford, 1½ miles SE of Leominster Pop., 206

BOWLING, a village, a township, two chapelries and a sub district in the parish and district of Bradford, W R Yorkshire The village stands adjacent to the Bradford and Halifax railway, 1½ mile SSW of Bradford, and has a station on the railway The Bowling Iron Works, which furnished many supplies to Government during the war in the Crimea, are adjacent The township includes also the village of Dudley Hill Acres 1,545 Real property, £36,691, of which £250 are in mines, and £6,300 in iron works Pop in 1841, 8 918, in 1861, 11,494 Houses, 3,160 The property is divided among a few Bowling Hall is the seat of the Sturge family, and was the head quarters of the Earl of Newcastle, in 1642 on occasion of his victory over Fairfax on Adwalton Moor The inhabitants are employed variously in the iron works in the cloth trade in stone quarries, and in coal and iron mines. The chapelries are Bowling St John, constituted in 1844, and Bowling St Stephen, constituted in 1860 Pop, 8,488 and 1,297 The living of St J is a vicarage, that of St S a p curacy in the dio of Ripon Value of St John, £175,* of St Stephen, £120 * Patron of St J, the Vicar of Bradford, of St S, C Hardy, Esq The church of St J is good, and that of St S was built in 1861, and is in the early decorated style, with tower and spire An Independent chapel, in the Romanesque style, was built in 1865, and there are other dissenting chapels —The sub district is conterminate with the township

BOWLING BANK, a locality 6 miles from Wrexham in Denbigh, with a post office under Wrexham

BOWLING GREEN, an extra parochial tract in Guildford borough Surrey

BOWLING GREEN HOUSE, a seat on the N side of Putney Heath, about 1 mile S of Putney in Surrey It was for some years the residence, then the death place, of William Pitt

BOWMONT WATER, a stream of Northumberland It rises among the Cheviots, within Scotland, and runs about 14 miles chiefly among the Cheviots, and about one half in Northumberland, to a confluence with the College Burn in the vicinity of Kirk Newton and there forms the Glen It is rich in landscape and in fine trout

BOWNESS, a small peninsula adjacent to Bassenthwaite village, on the E side of Bassenthwaite water, in Cumberland

BOWNESS, a hamlet and a crag near the middle of the N side of Ennerdale water, in Cumberland

BOWNESS, a village a township, and a parish in Wigton district, Cumberland The village stands on the Solway Frith, adjacent to the Port Carlisle terminus of the Carlisle and Silloth railway, 11½ miles WNW of Carlisle, and has a post office under Carlisle Its site is occupied by the Roman station Tunnocelum, at the western termination of Severus wall, many of the houses are believed to have been built of materials of the wall and the station, some vestiges of the wall can still be traced, and a Roman road went hence to Maryport The township includes also Port Carlisle Real property, £3,146 Pop, 484 Houses 107 The parish contains also the townships of Langland, Drumburgh, and Anthorn Acres, 17 047, of which 6,633 are water Real property £9,705 Pop, 1,321 Houses, 251 The property is much subdivided The living is a rectory in the diocese of Carlisle Value, £393 * Patron, the Earl of Lonsdale The church is tolerable Charities £21

BOWNESS, a small town in Undermilbeck township, Windermere parish, Westmoreland, on a small bay of Windermere lake, opposite Belle Isle, 1½ mile SSW of Windermere village It has a post office‡ under Windermere, three fine hotels, a handsome grammar school built in 1836 and the parish church of Windermere,—a long, low, ancient edifice with a square tower. It has been much improved and extended since the opening of the Windermere railway in 1847, contains many new neat houses, and is a grand centre of tourists visiting the lakes. A good quay and small pier are at it; steam boats ply from it on the lake, and some trade is carried on in the exporting of slate. Pop., about 1,100.

BOWOOD, a tything in Netherbury parish, Dorset, 2 miles SW of Beaminster.

BOWOOD, a hamlet in Harpford parish, Devon.

BOWOOD, an extra-parochial liberty in Calne district, Wilts, in Pewsham forest, 2 miles SW of Calne. Acres, 962. Real property, £1,013. Pop., 10. Houses, 18. Bowood House here, the seat of the Marquis of Lansdowne, is an edifice in the Italian style, with Doric portico, partly designed by Adams, and contains a rich collection of pictures. The grounds show much beauty, both natural and artificial, and have splendid gardens, a fine lake, and a mausoleum.

BOWSCALE, a township in Greystoke parish, Cumberland, on the river Caldew, under Souter fell, 9 miles NE of Keswick. Acres, 2,560. Pop., 32. Houses, 7. Part of the surface is mountainous, and bears the name of Bowscale fell. An elevated lakelet here, called Bowscale tarn, is fabled to contain two immortal fish; and Wordsworth, in his "Feast of Brougham Castle," represents these as waiting on the "shepherd" Lord Clifford,—

> "Both the undying fish that swim
> In Bowscale tarn did wait on him,
> The pair were servants of his eye
> In their immortality."

BOW STREET, a village in Tir-y-Mynach township, Cardigan, 4 miles N of Aberystwith. It has a station on the W. railway, and a post office under Shrewsbury.

BOWTHORPE, a parish in Forehoe district, Norfolk, on the river Yare, 3½ miles W of Norwich. Post town, Colney under Norwich. Acres, 645. Pop., 21. Houses, 4. The living is a donative, annexed to the vicarage of Earlham, in the diocese of Norwich. The church was desecrated in the 17th century.

BOWTHORPE, Yorkshire. See MENTHORPE.

BOWTHWAITE, a hamlet in Fountains-Earth township, but in Malzeard parish, W. R. Yorkshire, in the vicinity of Ripon.

BOWTOR, a hill in Dartmoor, Devon, 6½ miles S of Okehampton.

BOX, a hamlet in Minchinhampton parish, Gloucester, ½ a mile W of Minchinhampton.

BOX, a village and a parish in Chippenham district, Wilts. The village stands on the Box river, adjacent to the Great Western railway, 5 miles NE by W of Bath, and has a station on the railway and a post office‡ under Chippenham. It contains numerous old houses, and an ancient market cross, and is supposed to occupy the site of Roman baths. Numerous Roman relics have been found in the vicinity, and a Roman pavement and other remains are in the parsonage garden.—The parish includes also the hamlets of Wadswick, Box-Quarry, Ashley, Kingsdown, Washwell, and Middle-hill, and the ... of Hazelbury. Acres, 4,517. Real property, £1..., of which £1,125 are in quarries. Pop., 2,051. Houses, 40.. The property is subdivided. The surface is a picturesque assemblage of hill and dale. Box Hill has ... quarries of Bath stone, one of them subterranean. Box tunnel, in the course of the railway, is ... yards long, and in some parts 300 feet below the surface, and was formed at a cost of £100,000. The living is a vicarage in the diocese of Gloucester and Bristol. Value, £... Patron, the ... The church is ... of the ..., and contains the tomb of ... The ... school, with £75 from endowment ... charities ...

BOX AND STOCKBRIDGE, a hundred in the rape of Chichester, Sussex. It contains Westbourne parish

and twelve other parishes. Acres, 21,365. Pop., 4,710. Houses, 915.

BOXFORD, a village and a parish in Newbury district, Berks. The village stands on the river Lambourn, 4½ miles NW of Newbury r. station, and has a post office under Newbury.—The parish includes Westbrook and ... ing. Acres, 2,760. Real property, £4,811. Pop., 6.6. Houses, 143. The property is subdivided. The living is a rectory in the diocese of Oxford. Value, £761.* Patron, the Rev. Mr. Wells. The church is good. There are two Methodist chapels and a parochial school.

BOXFORD, a village and a parish in Gosford district, Suffolk. The village stands on an affluent of the river Stour, 4½ miles WSW of Hadleigh r. station, and 6 ... SE of Sudbury, and has a post office‡ under Colchester, and fairs on Easter Monday and 21 Dec.—The parish includes also the hamlet of Hadleigh. Acres, 1,820. Real property, £4,174. Pop., 980. Houses, 206. The property is subdivided. The living is a rectory in the diocese of Ely. Value, £710.* Patron, the Crown. The church is good, and there are an Independent chapel, an endowed grammar school, and charities £58.

BOXGROVE, a village, a parish, and a sub-district in Westhampnett district, Sussex. The village stands 2 miles NNE of Drayton r. station, and 3½ NE by E of Chichester.—The parish includes also the hamlets of Crocker Hill and East Hampnett, the tythings of Halnaker and Strettington, and part of the hamlet of Seabeach, and has a post office under Chichester. Acres, 3,676. Real property, £5,249. Pop., 600. Houses, 155. The property is divided among a few. The manor was given by Henry I. to Robert de Haye; passed to the Poynings, the Delawarrs, and the Morleys; and belongs now to the Duke of Richmond. Halnaker House, built by Sir Thomas West, Lord Delawarr, in the time of Henry VIII., is now a mass of ruin. Goodwood, the seat of the Duke of Richmond, is a great feature. See GOODWOOD. A priory was founded at Boxgrove by Robert de Haye; made a cell to the Benedictine abbey of Lessay, in Normandy, and allowed to retain its endowments at the suppression of the monasteries. The living is a vicarage in the diocese of Chichester. Value, £457.* Patron, the Duke of Richmond. The church consists of the chancel, aisles, transepts, and central tower of the ancient priory; is all rich early English, except the tower, which is Norman; and contains tombs of the Poynings, the Delawarrs, and the Morleys,—also three others, probably of Henry I.'s queen Adeliza and her two daughters. An endowed school has £56, almshouses, £11.., and other charities £13.—The sub-district comprises seven parishes. Acres, 16,732. Pop., 3,032. Houses, 761.

BOX HILL, a railway station and a hill in Surrey. The station is on the Red Hill and Reading branch of the South-eastern railway, ½ a mile S of Burford Bridge, and 1½ ENE of Dorking. The hill adjoins the station; rises over the Mole river, has an altitude of 445 feet above the river's level, and commands a noble view from the south downs of Sussex to the N of London. Its N side is mainly steep, and all verdureless; its W side, to the extent of about 230 acres, is covered with box; it is ascent, from the main road, is provided with seats; and its summit is crowned with a cottage of its proprietor, H. T. Hope, Esq.

BOX HILL WELLS. See BOX.

BOX LANE. See BOX MOOR.

BOXLEY, a village and a parish in Hollingbourn district, Kent. The village stands at the foot of a range of chalk hills, 2 miles NE by N of Maidstone, has a post office under Maidstone, and was once a market town. The parish includes part of Penenden Heath, and comprises 5,745 acres. Real property, £11,577. Pop., 1,470. Houses, ... The property is much subdivided. The manor was given by Richard I. to ... and passed, after the ... to Sir Thomas Wyatt, and belongs now to the ... of ... The abbey was founded in 1146 by William d'Ypres, Earl of Kent; stood 1½ mile WSW of the village; was Cistercian; and was dedicated, and well endowed, but at ...

and an automaton crucifix, which attracted crowds of pilgrims, and were publicly burnt at the Reformation, and is now all gone except the foundations. Boxley Abbey mansion adjacent is the seat of Major M. G. Best. Boxley House is the seat of Mrs Mercer, and Boxley Park is the seat of E. Lushington Esq. A deep chalk cavern called Sowenth occurs at Grove, and was worked so early as 1630. Fulling mills stood on the neighbouring rivulets, and have been succeeded by paper mills. A Roman urn and several other Roman relics have been found in the neighbourhood of Grove. The living is a vicarage in the diocese of Canterbury. Value, £331.* Patron, the Dean and Chapter of Rochester. The church is decorated English, and contains the remains of the poet Sir ... and tombs of the Wyatts and others. There is a national school.

BOX MOOR, a chapelry in Hemel Hampstead parish, Herts, on the Grand Junction canal and the North Western railway, 2½ miles NW by N of Kings Langley. It has a station on the railway, from which omnibuses run to Hemel Hampstead, and a post office‡ of the name of Box-Moor, Hertfordshire. It was constituted in 1841. Rated property, with Hemel Hampstead, £25,772. Pop., 3,813. Houses, 787. The property is much subdivided. The scenery in the neighbourhood of the station is very rich and beautiful, and the moor, whence the name is taken, is at some distance. The railway, north ward from the station, passes over an embankment, with fine views, crosses the Box Lane viaduct, and runs parallel with the canal. The living is a vicarage in the diocese of Rochester. Value, £160. Patron, the Vicar of Hemel Hampstead. The church is good.

BOX QUARRIES. See Box, Wilts.

BOX RIVER, a stream of the NW of Wilts. It rises on the border of Gloucester, N of Marshfield, runs 4½ miles eastward, past West Keynton, and across Akeman street, to Castle Combe, then goes 6 miles southward past Slaughterford and Lwridge, to Box village, then goes 3 miles south-westward, somewhat parallel with the Western railway, to the river Avon at Bathford.

BOXTED, a parish in Lexden district, Essex, on the river Stour, 2 miles ESE of Nayland, and 5½ N of Colchester r. station. It has a post office under Colchester. Acres, 3,082. Real property, £5,019. Pop., 935. Houses, 210. Boxted Hall is the seat of the Poleys. The living is a vicarage in the diocese of Rochester. Value, £110.* Patron, the Bishop of Rochester. The church has a curious monument of Sir J. Poley, and is very good. Charities, £10.

BOXTED, a parish in Sudbury district, Suffolk, on the river Stour, 8 miles NNW of Sudbury r. station. Post town, Hartest under Bury St Edmund. Acres, 1,307. Real property, £1,698. Pop., 192. Houses, 35. Boxted Hall is a ... of residence. The living is a rectory, annexed to the rectory of Hartest, in the diocese of Ely. There are charities £11, and a fair is held on Whit Tuesday.

BOX TREE, a quarter in Tamworth parish, Warwick. Pop., 538.

BOX TUNNEL. See Box, Wilts.

BOXWELL WITH LEIGHTERTON, a parish in Tetbury district, Gloucester, on the Cotswolds, 4½ miles ESE of Wotton under Edge, and 5½ E of Charfield r. station. It has a post office of the name of Leighterton, under Wotton under Edge. Acres, 2,260. Real property, £2,693. Pop., 257. Houses, 56. The property is divided among a few. Boxwell Court is the seat of the Rev. R. W. Huntley. About 45 acres are covered with box trees. An ancient nunnery stood at Boxwell, and is said to have been destroyed by the Danes. The living is a rectory in the diocese of Gloucester and Bristol. Value, £350.* Patron, the Rev R. W. Huntley. The church is ancient, and has a very ancient font. There is also a very ancient chapel at Leighterton.

BOXWORTH, a parish in the district of St Ives and county of Cambridge, 3 miles WSW of Long Stanton r. station, and 6 SSE of St Ives. Post town, Long Stanton under Cambridge. Acres, 2,521. Real property, £2,946. Pop., 317. Houses, 61. The property is divided among a few. The living is a rectory in the diocese of Ely. Value, £419.* Patron, G. Thornhill, Esq. The church has a monument of Sanderson, the blind professor of mathematics, and is good.

BOYATT, a tything in Otterbourne parish, Hants, 4½ miles S of Winchester. Pop., 160.

BOYCE COURT, the seat of the Drummond family, once the property of the Earls of Essex, in Gloucester, on the Hereford canal, 2 miles NNW of Newent.

BOYCOTT, a hamlet in Stowe parish, Bucks, 2 miles NW of Buckingham. Acres, 310. Pop., 20. Houses, 5.

BOYCOTT, a township in Pontesbury parish, Salop, 8 miles SW of Shrewsbury. Pop., 33.

BOYDEN. See BAYDEN.

BOYLESTONE, a parish in the district of Uttoxeter, and county of Derby, on an affluent of the river Dove, 3½ miles N by W of Scropton r. station, and 7 S of Ashborne. Post town, Cubley under Derby. Acres, 1,360. Real property, £2,660. Pop., 268. Houses, 61. The property is divided among a few. The living is a rectory in the diocese of Lichfield. Value, £261.* Patron, the Rev. Tem... Hall. The church is very good.

BOYNE HILL, a chapelry, with a railway station, in Bray parish, Berks, on the Great Western railway, in the southern vicinity of Maidenhead. Post town, Maidenhead. Pop., 1,071. The living is a vicarage in the diocese of Oxford. Value, £120.* Patron, the Bishop of Oxford. The church was built in 1857, and is in the Gothic style and ornate. There are national schools.

BOYNTON, a parish in Bridlington district, E. R. Yorkshire, on the Bridlington river, near the Bridlington railway, 3 miles WNW of Bridlington. It has a post office under Hull. Acres, 2,690. Real property, £3,320. Pop., 123. Houses, 21. The property all belongs to Sir G. Strickland, Bart. Boynton Hall is the baronet's seat, and a pavilion above it commands most beautiful views. The living is a vicarage in the diocese of York. Value, £141. Patron, Sir G. Strickland, Bart. The church is modern, but has an old tower.

BOYTHORPE. See Boythorpe.

BOYTON, a parish chiefly in Launceston district, Cornwall, and partly in Holsworthy district, Devon, on the Bude canal and the river Tamar, 5 miles N by W of Launceston r. station, and 17 NNW of Tavistock. It includes Northcott hamlet, and has a post office under Launceston, and a fair on the third Monday of Aug. Acres, 4,956. Real property, £2,651. Pop., 470. Houses, 93. The property is divided among a few. Bradridge, the old seat of the Hoblyns and Beardon, also an old seat, are now farm houses. Manganese mines were worked, but have been discontinued. The living is a vicarage in the diocese of Exeter. Value, £120.* Patron, the Rev. F. G. Dingar. The church is good. Agnes Best, a martyr of the time of Mary, resided at Northcott.

BOYTON, a parish in Woodbridge district, Suffolk, on the river Ade, near Hollesley bay, 4 miles WSW of Orford, and 7 SE of Melton r. station. Post town, Hollesley under Woodbridge. Acres, 1,563. Real property, £1,968. Pop., 294. Houses, 75. The property is divided among a few. The living is a rectory in the diocese of Norwich. Value, £365.* Patrons, Mrs Warner's Trustees. The church is very good, and there are almshouses for eight men and eight women.

BOYTON, a parish in Warminster district, Wilts, on the river Wiley, adjacent to the Great Western railway, 1½ mile NW of Codford station, and 2½ SE of Heytesbury. It includes Corton township, and its post town is Upton Lovel under Bath. Acres, 3,936. Real property, £3,338. Pop., 410. Houses, 91. The property is divided among a few. The manor belonged, in the time of Henry II, to the Giffords, and passed to the Lamberts. The mansion on it was built in 1618, by Thomas Lambert, was occupied in the present century by Aylmer Lambert, who collected here upwards of 30,000 specimens of plants, and is now the seat of the Rev. Arthur Fane. A pit in the neighbourhood of the grounds, called Chapel Hole, is popularly believed to have swallowed up a church. The living is a rectory in the diocese of Salisbury. Value, £519.* Patron, M...

dalen College, Oxford. The church dates from the latter part of the 12th century, was restored in 1860 at a cost of upwards of £2,000, and contains grand monuments of the Giffords, and several new memorial windows.

BOYTON, Norfolk. See [illegible].

BOZAH, a hamlet in Stockbury parish, Kent, 7½ miles SE of Rochester.

BOZEAT, a parish in Wellingborough district, Northampton, on the verge of the county, 4 miles SE by E of Castle Ashby r. station, and 6½ S of Wellingborough. Post town, Easton Maudit, under Northampton. Acres, 2,4[illegible]. Real property, £3,37[illegible]. Pop., 9[illegible]5. Houses, 211. The property is subdivided. The living is a vicarage, [illegible] to the rectory of Strixton, in the diocese of Peterborough. Value, £275.* Patron, Earl Spencer. The church is good. Charities, £22.

BRABOURNE, two villages, a parish, and a sub-district in East Ashford district, Kent. The villages are East Brabourne and Brabourne Lees. East Brabourne stands 3 miles NNE of Smeeth r. station, and 6 E of Ashford, has a post office under Ashford, and was once a market town. Brabourne Lees is a mile to the west, and also has a post office under Ashford.—The parish comprises 3,499 acres. Real property, £4,697. Pop., 743. Houses, 1[illegible]. The property is much subdivided. The manor belonged to Aymer de Valence, and passed to the Scotts and the Honeywoods. Much of the land is [illegible]. Large barracks stood near Brabourne Lees, but have been removed. The living is a vicarage, united with the rectory of Monks Horton, in the diocese of Canterbury. Value, £320. Patron, the Archbishop of Canterbury. The church is early English, contains monuments of the Scotts, and is in good condition. A [illegible] stood in the church in Evelyn's time, 50 feet in length. There are two Baptist chapels, and charities £5.—The sub-district contains seven parishes. Acres, 11,6[illegible]. Pop., 4,032. Houses, 794.

BRABOURNE-LEES. See BRABOURNE.

BRACEBRIDGE. See BAYSTRIDGE.

BRACEBOROUGH, a parish in Stamford district, Lincoln, on the river Glen, and on the Bourne and Essendine railway, [illegible] miles NE of Essendine, and 3¼ SW of Bourne. It includes Shillingthorpe hamlet, and has a spa, of the name of Braceborough Spa, on the [illegible] post town is Thurlby, under Bourne. Acres, 2,2[illegible]. Real property, £2,628. Pop., 2[illegible]0. Houses, 50. The property is divided among a few. The living is a rectory in the diocese of Lincoln. Value, £10[illegible].* Patron, the Lord Chancellor. The church is good. There is a private lunatic asylum.

BRACEBRIDGE, a parish in the district and county of Lincoln, on the river Witham, 2 miles S of Lincoln r. station. Post town, Lincoln. Acres, 1,182. Real property, £6,373. Pop., [illegible]. Houses, 87. The property is [illegible] subdivided. The living is a vicarage in the diocese of Lincoln. Value, £203.* Patron, Mrs Bromhead. The county lunatic asylum is here, and a new chapel for it was built in 18[illegible].

B[illegible]LBY, a parish in Grantham district, Lincoln, 4[illegible] WNW of [illegible]kingham, and 6 SE of Honington [illegible] Ropsley, under Grantham. Acres, [illegible] property, £1,3[illegible]. Pop., 168. Houses, 37. The living is a [illegible] in the diocese of Lincoln. Value, [illegible].

B[illegible], a parish in Shrewsbury district, Salop, on the Shrewsbury and Hereford railway, 1 mile S of Shrewsbury. [illegible] within Shrewsbury borough, [illegible] Nesten and [illegible], and part of [illegible], and contains the [illegible] Kingsland [illegible] Shrewsbury. Pop., 1,[illegible]. Houses, [illegible]. The living is a vicarage in the diocese of Hereford. Value, £2[illegible]. Patron, [illegible]. The church [illegible] cost [illegible].

B[illegible], a [illegible] W. R. Yorkshire, [illegible] Liverpool and Leeds canal, [illegible] WNW of [illegible] and [illegible] WSW of Skipton. Post town, [illegible] Skipton. Acres, [illegible] property, £[illegible]2. Pop., 1[illegible]. Houses,

20. The property is divided among a few. An old house here was a retreat of Henry VI. Limestone is worked. The living is a vicarage in the diocese of Ripon. Value, £120. Patron, J. T. Hopwood, Esq. The church is very good.

BRACKERIDGE, a hamlet in Meon-Stoke parish, Hants.

BRACKEN, a township in Kilnwick parish, E. R. Yorkshire, 6 miles SW by S of Great Driffield. Acres, 460. Real property, £1,008. Pop., 31. Houses, 6.

BRACKENBER, a hamlet in Shap parish, Westmoreland.

BRACKENBOROUGH, a parish in Louth district, Lincoln, on the East Lincoln railway, 2 miles N of Louth. Post town, Louth. Acres, 890. Real property, £931. Pop., 59. Houses, 11. It is a meet for the South Wold hounds.

BRACKENFIELD, a township-chapelry in Morton parish, Derby, 2 miles SW of Stretton r. station, and [illegible] NW of Alfreton. Post town, Alfreton. Real property, £3,4[illegible]. Pop., 317. Houses, 77. The property is divided among a few. The living is a vicarage in the diocese of Lichfield. Value, £80.* Patron, G. Turbutt, Esq. The church was built in 1856. There are a Primitive Methodist chapel and a national school.

BRACKENFOOT, a hamlet in Kirton township, W. R. Yorkshire, 5½ miles W of Wetherby.

BRACKEN-HILL, a hamlet in Roos parish, E. R. Yorkshire, 5½ miles N of Patrington.

BRACKENHILL, Cumberland. See BRACONHILL.

BRACKENHOLM-WITH-WOODHALL, a township in Hemingbrough parish, E. R. Yorkshire, on the river Derwent, adjacent to the Selby and Hull railway, 4 miles NW of Howden. Acres, 1,[illegible]. Real property, £1,950. Pop., 10[illegible]. Houses, 19.

BRACKENTHWAITE, a township in Lorton chapelry, Cumberland, between Grasmoor Pike and Loweswater, 5 miles S of Cockermouth r. station. Acres, 2,478. Real property, £1,17[illegible]. Pop., 11[illegible]. Houses, 2[illegible].

BRACKENTHWAITE, Yorkshire. See BRACKENFOOT.

BRACKLESHAM BAY, a small bay on the coast of Sussex, [illegible] miles NW of Selsey Bill, and 6¾ SSW of Chichester. Very rare fossil shells are found in [illegible] masses of clay on the shore.

BRACKLEY, a small town, two parishes, a sub-district, and a district in Northampton. The town stands on a descent at the confluence of two head-streams of the river Ouse, adjacent to the Banbury and Bletchley railway, 9¾ miles ESE of Banbury. It was a place of note in the times of the Saxons, was nearly destroyed by the Danes, rose again to importance, and was walled and had a castle. Tournaments were held in its vicinity, at Bayards Green, in 1249 and subsequent years; and the barons met at it, in 12[illegible]4, to treat with King John. The town consists mainly of a single street, nearly a mile long, and contains some good houses, chiefly built of stone. An ancient cross, 28 feet high, or [illegible] stood in its centre, and was taken down in 1[illegible]. The town-hall, an elegant [illegible] structure, occupies the site of the cross, and was erected in 170[illegible] by the Duke of Bridgewater, at a cost of £2,000. St. John's hospital, now a ruin, was founded in the time of Henry I, by Robert le Bossu, Earl of Leicester, for [illegible] and six fellows, passed to Magdalene College, Oxford, and was a retreat of the [illegible] of that college during the contests between King John and the barons. The chapel of it still shows interesting architectural features, [illegible] once had tombs of several noblemen; and the hall has been rebuilt, and contains 1[illegible]5 blazoned shields of nobles and distinguished men. Another hospital, dedicated to St. Leonard, stood in the town, but has disappeared. St. Peter's church is chiefly early English, and has a lofty tower and a Norman font. St. James' church [illegible] place, some years ago, to a cemetery chapel in connexion with its burying ground. There are three dissenting chapels, a free grammar school, [illegible] almshouses, and a workhouse,—the last erected at a cost of £[illegible],000. The town has a head post office,‡ a railway station with telegraph, two banking offices, and two chief inns. A weekly market is held on Wednesday, and fairs on the Wednesday after 25 Feb., 19 April, the Wednesday after 22 June, the Wednesday after 11 Oct., and 11 Dec. A great wool trade flourished in the reign of Edward III., and for some time before and after, but the chief trade now is in lace and shoes. The town claims to have been incorporated by Henry III.; it sent two members to parliament from the time of Edward VI. till disfranchised by the act of 1832, and it still has nominally a corporation, but is not regulated by the Corporation act. It is a polling place, has a building of 1851 for police station and petty sessions, and it gives the title of Viscount to the Earl of Ellesmere. Samuel Clarke, the famous orientalist, a contributor to Walton's "Polyglot," was a native. Pop., 2,239. Houses, 497.

The two parishes are St. Peter and St. James, and they jointly include all the town. Acres of St. Peter, 3,717; of St. James, 420. Real property of St. Peter, £4,713; of St. James, £2,551. Pop. of St. Peter, 1,615. Houses, 354. Pop. of St. James, 768. Houses, 154. The property is subdivided. The livings are conjoint—St. Peter a vicarage, St. James a p. curacy—in the diocese of Peterborough. Value, £359. Patron, the Earl of Ellesmere.—The sub-district contains also the parishes of Kings-Sutton, Newbottle, Aynho, Croughton, Hinton-in-the-Hedges, Steen, Evenly, Whitfield, Mixbury, Finmere, Westbury, and Turweston,—the two last electorally in Bucks, the previous two electorally in Oxford. Acres, 31,630. Pop., 7,656. Houses, 1,657.—The district includes also the sub-district of Sulgrave, containing the parishes of Sulgrave, Helmdon, Morton-Pinkney, Eydon, Culworth, Thorpe-Mandeville, Chacombe, Greatworth, Marston-St. Lawrence, Thenford, Farthinghoe, Radstone, Syresham, and Lillingstone,—the last electorally in Bucks,—and part of Wappenham. Acres of the district, 58,719. Poor-rates in 1866, £9,908. Pop. in 1861, 13,471. Houses, 3,010. Marriages in 1866, 101; births, 435,—of which 29 were illegitimate; deaths, 250,—of which 90 were at ages under 5 years, and 12 at ages above 85. Marriages in the ten years 1851-60, 989; births, 4,435; deaths, 2,848. The places of worship in 1851 were 27 of the Church of England, with 6,600 sittings; 2 of Independents, with 432 s.; 5 of Baptists, with 1,116 s.; 1 of Quakers, with 107 s.; 6 of Primitive Methodists, with 1,192 s.; 1 of Wesleyan Reformers, with 100 s.; and 2 of Moravians, with 290 s. The schools were 27 public day schools, with 1,238 scholars; 19 private day schools, with 388 s.; and 32 Sunday schools, with 2,138 s.

BRACKNELL, a village, a chapelry, and a sub-district, in the district of Easthampstead, Berks. The village stands adjacent to the South-western railway, 3 miles W of Ascot race-course, and 4 E of Wokingham. It has a station on the railway, and a post-office,‡ of the name of Bracknell, Berkshire, and is a polling place. Fairs are held at it on 25 April, 22 Aug., and 1 Oct. It consists of one fine, long, open street; and there are several large mansions in its neighbourhood. The chapelry includes the village, is in the parishes of Warfield and Winkfield, and was constituted in 1851. Pop., 1,007. Houses, 202. The living is a p. curacy in the diocese of Oxford. Value, £65. Patron, the Bishop of Oxford. The church is a graceful structure of 1851 in the early English style. There are an Independent chapel, a literary institute, and national schools.—The sub-district contains five parishes. Acres, 20,614. Pop., 6,165. Houses, 1,203.

BRACON-ASH, a parish in Henstead district, Norfolk, 2¼ miles NNW of Swainsthorpe r. station, and 7 SW of Norwich. It has a post-office under Norwich. Acres, 971. Real property, £1,895. Pop., 271. Houses, 43. The property is divided among ten. Bracon Hall is the seat of the Rev. P. Berney. The living is a rectory in the diocese of Norwich. Value, £245. Patron, the Rev. T. Berney. The church is very good; and there is a national school.

BRACONDALE, a hamlet in Trowse parish, Norfolk; within the county of the city of Norwich.

BRACTON. See BRATTON CLOVELLY.

BRADBOURNE, a township in Ashborne district, and a parish in Ashborne and Bakewell districts, Derby. The township lies on an affluent of the river Dove, 5 miles NNE of Ashborne r. station. Real property, £2,733. Pop., 141. Houses, 28. The parish contains also the townships of Brassington, Ballidon, and Aldwark, the hamlet of Lea Hall, and the chapelry of Atlow; and its post town is Brassington, under Wirksworth. Acres, 6,253. Real property, £13,609. Pop., 1,187. Houses, 248. The property is subdivided. Bradbourne Hall is a chief residence. Tissington Hall is the seat of Sir William Fitzherbert, Bart. Limestone is abundant. Roman coins have been found. The living is a vicarage, united with the p. curacy of Ballidon, in the diocese of Lichfield. Value, £110. Patron, the Duke of Devonshire. The church has a Norman tower, and is good. The chapelries of Brassington and Atlow are separate benefices. Charities, £21.

BRADBOURNE PARK, the seat of the Twisden family in East Malling parish, Kent, 3¾ miles WNW of Maidstone. A younger brother of the learned Sir Roger Twisden settled here in the time of Charles II., and was himself made a baronet. Paper mills are on a stream which runs through the grounds.

BRADBURY, a township in Sedgefield parish, Durham, on the North-eastern railway, 10 miles N of Darlington. It has a station on the railway, and commands fine views. Acres, 2,043. Real property, £2,100. Pop., 174. Houses, 32.

BRADBY, or BRETBY, a chapelry in Repton parish, Derby, near the river Trent and the Birmingham and Derby railway, 3 miles E by N of Burton-upon-Trent. Post town, Repton, under Burton-upon-Trent. Real property, £2,712. Pop., 32?. Houses, 56. The manor belonged formerly to the Mowbrays and the Berkeleys, and belongs now to the Earl of Chesterfield. Bradby Park is the Earl's seat; and the grounds of it contain the site of a castle of the Mowbrays, and a strong mansion which was garrisoned for Charles I. and taken down in 1780. The living is a donative in the diocese of Lichfield. Value, £80. Patron, the Earl of Chesterfield.

BRADDAN. See KIRK-BRADDAN.

BRADDEN, a parish in Towcester district, Northampton, on the river Tove, 3 miles W of Towcester r. station, and 7 SW by W of Blisworth. Post town, Towcester. Acres, 1,000. Real property, £1,500. Pop., 1?0. Houses, 39. The property is divided among a few. Bradden House is the seat of the Rev. C. Ives. The parish is a resort of sportsmen. The living is a rectory in the diocese of Peterborough. Value, £227.* Patron, the Rev. C. Ives. The church was rebuilt in 155?. Bishop Van Mildert was for some time rector. Charities, £17.

BRADDONS, a ridge of heights sheltering the north side of Torquay, in Devon. It is crested, toward the town, with a series of beautiful villas.

BRADEL. See BRADLE.

BRADEN, an ancient forest around Bradenstoke in Wilts.

BRADENSTOKE. See BRADFORD, Wilts.

BRADENHAM, a parish in Wycombe district, Bucks, on the Chilterns, 3½ miles NW by N of High Wycombe r. station. Post town, High Wycombe. Acres, 1,001. Real property, £1,?38. Pop., 185. Houses, 35. The property is divided among a few. Bradenham House belonged formerly to Lord Windsor, and was visited by Queen Elizabeth in 1566; was the death-place, in 1848, of D'Israeli, the author of "Curiosities of Literature," and is now the seat of the Rev. John Graves. The living is a rectory in the diocese of Oxford. Value, £2?4.* Patron, the Rev. John Graves. The church is good.

BRADENHAM (EAST), a parish in Swaffham district, Norfolk, on the river Wissey, 3½ miles S of Wendling r. station, and 7 SW of East Dereham. Post town, West Bradenham, under Thetford. Acres, 2,340. Real property, £3,246. Pop., 3?9. Houses, 86. The property is divided among a few. The manor belongs to Henry S. Adlington, Esq. The living is a rectory in the [illegible] of Norwich Value, £278 * Patron H S [illegible] Esq The church is of flint Charities £11

BRADENHAM (WEST), a parish in Swaffham district, Norfolk, on the river Wissey, 3½ miles S by W of Wendling r station, and 5½ SW by W of East Dereham Post town, Shipdham under Thetford Acres, 1,682 Real property, £3,019 Pop, 387 Houses, 83 The manor of West Bradenham belongs to W Haggard, Esq that of Bradenham Hall to B Girling, Esq The living is a vicarage in the diocese of Norwich Value, £290 * Patron the Bishop of N The church is ancient, and was restored in 1857 There are a national school, and charities £24

BRADENSTOKE, a hill in Lyneham parish, Wilts, adjacent to the Wilts and Berks canal and to the Great Western railway, 3½ miles SW by W of Wootton Basset. An Augustinian abbey was founded here, in 1142 by Walter D'Evreux given at the dissolution to Richard Pexel, and sold by his heirs to the Methuens of Corsham Remains of it still stand, showing features of decorated English and are used as a farm house

BRADESTON, a parish in Blofield district Norfolk on the Yarmouth railway and the river Yare, ½ a mile E of Brundall r station and 4 WSW of Acle Post town, Blofield, under Norwich Acres, 716 Real property, £ 183 Pop, 133 Houses, 31 The living is a rectory, annexed to the rectory of Strumpshaw, in the diocese of Norwich

BRADFIELD a village, a parish, and a district in Berks The village stands on an affluent of the river Thames, 3 miles NW by W of Theale r station and 7½ W of Reading, and has a post office‡ under Reading The parish comprises 4 384 acres Real property, £6,558 Pop 1,167 Houses, 200 The property is divided among a few Bradfield Hall is a chief residence The surface contains rich close scenes and commands fine views The living is a rectory united with the p[illegible] of Trinity in the diocese of Oxford Value £788 * Patron, the Rev T Stevens The church was restored and enlarged in 1848 There are two chapels of ease and a P Methodist chapel St Andrew's college is a handsome edifice of 1850, and was endowed in 1859 and chartered in 1862, as a foundation school for 16 foundation boys and 153 commoners An abbey was founded here before the close of the 7th century, by King Ina Bishop Lloyd was sometime rector — The district comprehends the sub district of Bucklebury containing the parishes of Bradfield Bucklebury Frilsham Yattendon Stanford Dingley Basildon Ashampstead Streatley and [illegible]ring — the last electorally in Oxford the sub district of Mortimer, containing the parishes of Stratfield Mortimer Beenham Vallence, Aldermaston, Padworth, Ufton [illegible]stead Bannister, Sulhampstead Abbots, and Burghfield and the sub district of Tilehurst containing the parishes of Tilehurst Englefield, Tidmarsh, Sulham, [illegible] Pangbourn Whitchurch and Maple Durham, — the two last electorally in Oxford Acres 62 16[illegible] Poor rates in 1866 £11 962 Pop in 1861, 13,771 Houses, 3 323 Marriages in 1866 8[illegible], births, 478 — of which [illegible] were illegitimate deaths 266, — of which 72 were at ages under 5 years, and 13 at ages above 85 years [illegible] in the ten years 1851-60 874 births 5 015 [illegible] The places of worship in 1851 were 27 of the Church of England, with [illegible] sittings [illegible] of Independents, with 825 2 of Baptists, with 121 s 3 of Wesleyan Methodists with 214 s 5 of Primitive Methodists, with 772 s, and 3 of Lady Huntingdon's Connexion, with 560 s The schools were 23 public day schools with 1 075 scholars 25 private day schools with [illegible] and 18 Sunday schools, with 800 s The workhouse is in Bradfield and cost £7 [illegible]

BRADFIELD a parish in Tendring district, Essex, [illegible] of the Stour and on the Harwich branch of the Eastern Union railway 3 miles [illegible] S of Manningtree It has a station on the railway and a post office under Manningtree Acres, 2 719 of which 600 are water Real property £5 057 Pop 914 Houses 212 The property is subdivided [illegible] is a residence The living is a vicarage annexed to the rectory of Mistley in the diocese of Rochester The church is good Speaker Grimston, of the time of Charles II was a native

BRADFIELD a parish in Tunstead district Norfolk here the line of telegraph from Norwich to Cromer 2½ miles NNW of North Walsham r station and 17 N by E of Norwich Post town, North Walsham, under Norwich Acres 777 Real property £1,220 Pop, 226 Houses, 46 The property is all in one estate The living is one part a rectory and one part a donative in the diocese of Norwich Value of the rectory £165 * Patron, Lord Suffield The donative is annexed to the rectory of Antingham St Mary The church was repaired in 1859 There is an Independent chapel

BRADFIELD a village, two hamlets, a township a chapelry and a sub district, in Ecclesfield parish, W R Yorkshire The village stands on an affluent of the river Don 4 miles W by S of Oughty bridge r station, and 7 NW by W of Sheffield and it has a post office under Sheffield and fairs on 17 June and 9 Dec The hamlets are Nether Bradfield and Bradfield Dale The township includes also the hamlets or divisions of Bolsterstone, Brightholmlee Dungworth, Laurest Green Holdsworth, Midhope Moorwood, Onesacre Oughtibridge with Gate, Smallfield Stannington, Storrs, [illegible] hill, Wigtwizzle and Worrall Acres, 33,730 Real property, £16,4[illegible] Pop 9 089 Houses 1,696 Much of the surface is moor hill, and mountain and one summit called Bradfield Point, has an altitude of 1,21[illegible] feet above the level of the sea Traces of a Saxon camp exist, and Roman remains have been found — The chapelry comprises only part of the township, and is a rectory in the diocese of York Value, £200 * Patron the vicar of Ecclesfield The church is early English There are two dissenting chapels and an endowed school — The sub district is conterminate with the township

BRADFIELD a hamlet in Uffculme parish Devon 3½ miles NE of Cullompton The manor has belonged to the family of Walrond since the time of King John The mansion dates from the reign of Elizabeth and was recently restored

BRADFIELD COMBUST, or BURNT BRADFIELD, a parish in Thingoe district Suffolk, [illegible] miles SSW of Thurston r station, and 5½ SSE of Bury St Edmunds Post town, Bury St Edmunds Acres 918 Real property £1 424 Pop 173 Houses 38 The property is subdivided Bradfield Hall was the seat of Arthur Young the writer on agriculture An edifice belonging to Bury abbey, stood in the parish, and was burned in 1327 The living is a rectory in the diocese of Ely Value, £180 * Patron, the Rev H Hasted The church was restored in 18[illegible]

BRADFIELD ST CLARE a parish in Thingoe district, Suffolk, 7 miles S by W of Thurston r station and 5½ SE by S of Bury St Edmunds Post town, Bury St Edmunds Acres, 1,128 Real property, £1 788 Pop, 273 Houses 51 The property is divided among a few The living is a rectory in the diocese of Ely Value, £275 Patrons, W [illegible] and G J Lewin, Esqs The church is good

BRADFIELD ST GEORGE a parish in Thingoe district Suffolk 3½ miles SSW of Thurston r station, and 4½ SE of Bury St Edmunds Post town Bury St Edmunds Acres, 1 981 Real property £2,238 Pop 427 Houses 110 The property is much divided The living is a rectory, united with the rectory of Rushbrook in the diocese of Ely Value £570 Patron the Marquis of Bristol The church has a spire, seen over a wide extent of country

BRADFORD, a parish in Holsworthy district, Devon on the river Torridge 7½ miles NE of Holsworthy and 10 S by W of Bideford r station Post town, Black Torrington under Highampton, North Devon Acres, 2 4[illegible] Real property £2 100 Pop, 444 Houses [illegible] The property is chiefly divided among four Dunsland has been a baronial mansion, belonged at the Conquest, to Ralph de Cahiho, passed to the Arscotts and the Bickfords, and belongs now to the Coham[illegible] [illegible] There are traces of a fortified camp, supposed to have been formed by the famous Hengist. The living is a rectory in the diocese of Exeter. Value, £608.* Patrons, the Rectors of East Down, Bratton Fleming, and Goodleigh. The church is cruciform, and has a tower and some monuments, but is, or recently was, in very bad condition. Charities, £14.

BRADFORD, a township and a chapelry in Manchester parish, Lancashire. The township lies adjacent to the Manchester and Sheffield railway, 1¼ mile E of Manchester, and has a post office under Manchester. Acres, 279. Pop., 3,523. Houses, 707. The chapelry extends into Beswick township, bears the name of Bradford-cum-Beswick, and was constituted very recently. The statistics are not reported. The living is a rectory in the diocese of Manchester, with a parsonage, and in the patronage of the Bishop. The church was built in 1862, at a cost of £6,000; and is in the early English style, and cruciform. There are Wesleyan and Free Methodist chapels, large schools built in 1864, at a cost of £3,000, and a police station.

BRADFORD, a township in Bolam parish, Northumberland, on the river Blyth, 10 miles WSW of Morpeth. Acres, 1,033. Pop., 18. Houses, 5.

BRADFORD, a township in Bamborough parish, Northumberland, in the vicinity of the Northeastern railway, 2½ miles ESE of Belford. Acres, 526. Pop., 19. Houses, 8.

BRADFORD, a village and a parish in Wellington district, Somerset. The village stands on the river Tone, 2¾ miles NE of Wellington r. station, and 3½ WSW of Taunton; and has a post office under Taunton.—The parish comprises 1,783 acres. Real property, £4,488. Pop., 562. Houses, 110. The property is divided among a few. The living is a vicarage in the diocese of Bath and Wells. Value, £120.* Patron, A. Adair, Esq. The church was repaired in 1858. There are an Independent chapel and a national school.

BRADFORD, a town, a parish, two sub-districts, a district, and a hundred in Wilts. The town stands on the river Avon, on the Kennet and Avon canal, and on the Great Western railway, 3½ miles NW by N of Trowbridge. It was known to the Saxons as Bradenford, and it is now sometimes called Bradford-on-Avon. A battle was fought at it in 652, between Cenwalf and Cuthred; and St. Dunstan, in 951, was elected here to the see of Worcester. Its site is partly a hollow, partly slopes and acclivities, encompassed by hills. The older portion is on the N side of the river, and rises in a series of terraces, to a crowning point with an extensive view. Many curious old houses are in it; and one called the Duke's House, an edifice full of windows, formerly a residence of the Pierreponts, Dukes of Kingston, is in the near vicinity. Two bridges span the river; the upper one a very ancient structure, with 9 arches; the lower a more modern structure, with 4. An ancient square edifice with a pyramidal roof, supposed variously to have been a chapel, an almonry, and an ecclesiastical toll-house, and now used as a lock-up prison, stands on one of the piers of the upper bridge. Structures of the 14th century, arising out of a monastery founded in 705 by St. Aldhelm, and given in 1001 by King Ethelred to the great nunnery at Shaftesbury, and now used as offices of a farm-stead, are at the skirt of Jew's Harp hill. The parish church is Norman and early English; consists of nave, north aisle, chancel, and chapel, with western tower and small spire; contains many curious tombs and a fine altar piece; and has been partly modernized. Christ Church was built in 1841, is in the perpendicular style, and has a tower and lofty spire. There are chapels for Independents, Baptists, Wesleyan Methodists, Primitive Methodists, and Lady Huntingdon's Connexion, a free school, with £53 a year; another school, in a very handsome edifice of 1860; and two alms-houses and other charities, with jointly £138 a year. The town has a head post office‡ of the name of Bradford-on-Avon, a railway station with telegraph, a banking office, and three chief inns. A weekly market is held on Monday; and a fair on Trinity Monday. An important woollen manufacture was long carried on, but has greatly declined.

The town never was incorporated, but it sent members to parliament in the time of Edward I.; and it therefore is called a borough. Pop., 4,291. Houses, 1,036.

The parish includes also the chapelries of Holt, Atworth, and Limpley-Stoke, and the tythings of Trowle, Winsley, South Wraxall, and Leigh and Woolley; and it is sometimes called Bradford-on-Avon and Great Bradford. Acres, 11,310. Real property, £33,751. Pop., 8,032. Houses, 1,964. The property is subdivided. Much of the surface consists of fine chalk hills. The living is a vicarage, united with the rectory of Westwood, in the diocese of Salisbury. Value, £602.* Patrons, the Dean and Chapter of Bristol. Christ Church is a separate benefice, a p. curacy, of the value of £150,* in the patronage of the Vicar. The p. curacies of Holt, Atworth with South Wraxall, and Winsley with Limpley-Stoke also are separate benefices.—The two sub-districts are Bradford Northwestern and Bradford Southeastern. They divide Bradford parish between them; and the former contains also the parish of Monkton Farleigh, while the latter contains the extra-parochial tract of Little Chalfield and Cottles, and the parishes of Great Chalfield, Broughton Gifford, Winkfield with Rowley, Westwood with Iford, and Freshford,—the last electorally in Somerset.—The district consists of these two sub-districts. Acres, 19,800. Poor-rates in 1866, £6,165. Pop. in 1861, 10,117. Houses, 2,411. Marriages in 1866, 75; births, 307,—of which 17 were illegitimate; deaths, 190,—of which 43 were at ages under 5 years, and 8 at ages above 85. Marriages in the ten years 1851–60, 759; births, 3,218; deaths, 2,383. The places of worship in 1851 were 14 of the Church of England, with 4,892 sittings; 4 of Independents, with 1,132 s.; 5 of Baptists, with 1,072 s.; 5 of Wesleyan Methodists, with 1,064 s.; 3 of Primitive Methodists, with 286 s.; and one of Lady Huntingdon's Connexion, with 200 s. The schools were 16 public day schools, with 1,178 scholars; 25 private day schools, with 337 s.; 22 Sunday schools, with 2,255 s.; and 2 evening schools for adults, with 54 s. The workhouse is in Westwood.—The hundred includes only Bradford and four other parishes. Acres, 17,126. Pop., 9,422. Houses, 2,205.

BRADFORD, a town, a township, a parish, two sub-districts, and a district in W. R. Yorkshire. The town stands at the junction of three fine valleys, amid a diversified, picturesque, hilly country, within the basin of the river Aire, 9 miles W by S of Leeds. It is at similar distance from Keighley, Halifax, Huddersfield, Dewsbury, and Wakefield, and at shorter distances from a number of populous villages; and it maintains crowded intercourse with them all. A canal goes from its centre to the Leeds and Liverpool canal; a railway to Idle, 2¼ miles, was authorised in 1866; and branch railways go northward, eastward, and southward, passing speedily into lines which ramify toward all parts of the kingdom. The town is mentioned in some old records, but does not seem to have made any figure in ancient times. It was described by Leland, in the reign of Henry VIII., as a "pretty quick market town," with a parish church and a chapel, and "standing much by clothing." It took part with the parliament against Charles I.; twice repulsed a large body of the king's troops; and was stormed and taken by the Earl of Newcastle. Serious riots took place in it, in 1812, resulting in the execution of 17 men; and a strike of its operatives occurred in 1825, continuing ten months, and producing much misery.

The town is chiefly built of fine freestone; and contains many very handsome edifices, both private and public. It includes narrow, ill-constructed streets, but has recently undergone great improvement. It is extending in all directions, and it possesses such suburbs, or goes so nearly into adjacent villages, as to be practically a town 5 miles. It looks, from the neighbourhood, to be full of factories; it contains some of the finest warehouses in the kingdom; and it may be pronounced to show an aggregate of architectural character equal to that of any manufacturing town of its size. Very great improvements were made up to 1866; and other great ones were then in progress. St. George's Hall [illegible] centre of the town, covers an area of 1,600 yards, [illegible] fronts to three several streets, has a western elevation 77 feet high with rusticated basement, surmounted by Corinthian columns and pilasters, contains a [illegible] hall, 76 feet long and 54 feet high, lighted by 16 arched windows, and was erected in [illegible] 3 at a cost of £13,000. The new exchange is in the Venetian Gothic style, has a chief entrance under a tower [illegible] 150 feet high, contains a great hall in [illegible] of nave and aisles, 80 feet by [illegible], and was built in [illegible] at a cost of about £30,000. The court house, at Hall Ings, is a neat and convenient structure, with lock-ups [illegible], and was built in 1834, at a cost of [illegible]. The debtors' prison, a well contrived and well managed suite of buildings and yards, was superseded, [illegible] the passing of the County Court act, by one in [illegible]. The county court house, in Manor row, was built in 1861, at a cost of nearly £4,000, and is in the [illegible] style, with a frontage of 70 feet in length. The [illegible] barracks stand in the midst of a drill ground [illegible] acre, were erected in 1861, and comprise a drill room of 77 feet by 60, and several other spacious apartments. The theatre and opera house was erected in 1867, and is an ornamental edifice. Peel's monument, in Peel place, shows a fine statue of Sir Robert Peel in bronze. The office of the Old bank, erected in [illegible] is a handsome edifice in the Gothic style. Several [illegible] of [illegible] houses, of recent erection, are splendid [illegible] extensive. One of these, that of Messrs Milligan [illegible] and Co, adjoins St George's hall, and is not [illegible] inferior to that pile in magnificence; another, [illegible] of Messrs John Foster and Son, called Foster's buildings, is equally beautiful and imposing; another, that of Mr Hastings, in [illegible] street, is in a style which [illegible] termed the eclectic Gothic; another, that of Mr [illegible] built in 1862, has a height of four or five [illegible], with 18 windows in the length; and others, [illegible] in 1863-5, are similarly splendid.

The town and its suburbs, till a recent period, were [illegible] provided with established places of worship. [illegible] there were here in 1840; but several were soon [illegible] erected, and a plan was subsequently formed [illegible] the Church Building Society to erect ten more within [illegible] years, and was well advanced in 1863 toward completion. The parish church, or St Peter's, is perpendicular English, of the time of Henry VI, has a square tower, of a later date, buttressed to the top and crowned with pinnacles, underwent recently entire interior renovation, including the construction of a fine oaken roof, [illegible] contains a beautiful, canopied, sculptured font, a monument to the mathematician Sharpe, who died in 1742, a rich sculptural monument by Flaxman to the [illegible] of the [illegible], and many other monuments. Christ church was built in 1814, and is a plain [illegible] with low pinnacled tower. St James' [illegible] was built in 1838, and is a handsome edifice. St [illegible] church, at Broomfields, the fourth of the ten of the Church Building Society, was erected in 1862, is in [illegible] English style, has a south transept and a [illegible] tower, and contains 750 sittings. St [illegible] church, near Hopper lane, West gate, the fifth [illegible], was built in the same year, is also in the decorated English style, with 700 sittings, has a western [illegible] 74 [illegible] and was to have likewise a tower [illegible] feet high. All Saints church, at Horton [illegible], was opened in the early [illegible] of [illegible] [illegible] Gothic [illegible] under [illegible] at [illegible] £10,000. St Michael and All Angels [illegible] built in 1863, and is [illegible] [illegible] Independent chapel, in Horton lane, was [illegible] 18[illegible] [illegible] style, and [illegible] above [illegible] chapels, in Manningham lane and [illegible] were built about the same time, at cost [illegible] £7,000; several dissenting chapels were [illegible] 186[illegible] and [illegible] others [illegible] [illegible] places of worship, in 1851, were 12 of the Church of England, with 10,02[illegible] sittings, [illegible] of the United Presbyterian church, with 1,3[illegible] s.; 6 of Independents, with [illegible] [illegible] Particular Baptists, with 2,8[illegible] s.; 2 of General Baptists, with 600 s.; 1 of Quakers, with 1,400 s.; 1 of Unitarians, with 400 s.; 1 of Moravians, with 2[illegible] s.; 12 of Wesleyan Methodists, with 7,070 s.; 1 of New Connexion Methodists, with 773 s.; 5 of Primitive Methodists, with 1,950 s.; 3 of the Wesleyan Association, with 1,440 s.; 3 of Wesleyan Reformers, with [illegible] s.; 1 of Brethren, with 100 s.; 1 of Latter Day Saints, with 400 s.; and 1 of Roman Catholics, with [illegible] s.

The free grammar school dates from the time of Edward VI, was rebuilt in 1830, is a spacious and elegant structure, containing a good library, has an endowed income of £131, and entitles its scholars to be candidates for the Hastings exhibitions in Queen's college, Oxford. New schools, in connexion with St James' church, were built in 1860. There were, within the borough, in 1851, 27 public day schools, with 5,91[illegible] scholars; 85 private day schools, with 3,[illegible]33 s.; and [illegible] Sunday schools, with 16,077 s. There are a [illegible] exhibition, a mechanics' institute, a public library, a philosophical society, a temperance hall, and, in the neighbourhood, [illegible] training schools for Independents, Baptists, and Wesleyans. There are also cavalry barracks, an infirmary, a fever hospital of 1860, a dispensary, a workhouse, two large ornate cemeteries, and a grand recent [illegible].

The town has a head post office, two telegraph stations, two banking offices, and six chief inns. Markets are held on Mondays and Thursdays; and fairs on 3 March, 17 June, and 9 Dec. Manufactures of worsted yarn and worsted stuffs have long been carried on; manufactures of damask, [illegible], and mixed worsted and silk goods are now extensive; manufactures of cotton fabrics engage attention; alpaca manufacture was introduced, and is carried on, at Saltaire, 4 miles distant; and extensive iron works, together with abundant supplies of iron ore and coal, exist at Bowling and Low Moor, in the neighbourhood. The town is a seat of sessions, and a polling place, and publishes three weekly newspapers. It was incorporated in 1847, and [illegible] a mayor, fourteen aldermen, and forty-two councillors; and it sends two members to parliament. Its municipal and parliamentary limits are co-extensive, and comprise the townships of Bradford, Bowling, Horton, and Manningham. Direct taxes in 1857, £[illegible]098. Electors in 18[illegible], 5,1[illegible]. Pop. in 1841, 66,715; in 1861, 106,218. Houses 2[illegible]. Dr John Sharpe, the archbishop, Abraham Sharpe, the mathematician, [illegible] representatives, and Dr Scoresby, the arctic navigator and scientific writer, was for some time vicar.

The township consists of the central parts of the borough. Acres, 1,680. Real property, £[illegible]6,518; of which £2,[illegible] are in mines, £1,9[illegible] in quarries, £11,067 in railways, and £12,885 in gas-works. Pop. in 1841, [illegible]; in 1861, 48,640. Houses 10,288. The parish is 1[illegible] miles long, and [illegible] in mean breadth, and comprises the townships of Bradford, Bowling, Horton, Manningham, North Bierley, Thornton, Clayton, Allerton, Wilsden, Shipley, Heaton, Idle, Eccleshill, and Haworth,—the last in the district of Keighley, the rest in that of Bradford. Acres, 34,146. Real property, £580,[illegible]; of which £10,[illegible] are in mines, £5,881 in quarries, and £18,684 in iron works. Pop. in 1841, 105,257; in 1861, 1[illegible]. Houses, 3[illegible],021. The surface is a picturesque diversity of hill and vale. Some of the seats are Bowling Hall, W. Walker, Esq.; Manningham House, S. C. Lister, Esq.; Horton House, Mr Thorpe; and [illegible] Hall, W. [illegible] Cunnett, Esq. The living is a vicarage in the diocese of Ripon. Value, £601.* Patrons, Simeon's Trustees. The vicarages of Christchurch, St James, St John, St John Bowling, and St Paul Manningham, and the p. curacies of St Thomas, St [illegible], St Jude, St Andrew, St Michael and All Angels, and St Stephen Bowling, within the borough, are separate benefices. Value of [illegible] and St [illegible], each £200;* of St James, £[illegible]; of St John, £[illegible];* of St John Bowling, £175;* of St [illegible], £150;* of St [illegible] and St Luke, each £300; of St Jude, £200;* of St Andrew, £100; of St Stephen, £1[illegible]. Patron of C[illegible], St J[illegible] Bowling, St Paul, and [illegible], the Vicar of B[illegible]; of St James, [illegible] Wood, [illegible]; of [illegible], [illegible] Brethren and Preston and the Vicar of [illegible]; of St Paul, J. Hollings, Esq.; of St T[illegible], St M[illegible], and St Luke, [illegible] the bishop, of St Stephen, C Hardy, Esq. The rectory of Haworth the vicarages of Pudsey, Buttershaw, Oxenhope, Shipley, Denholme, and Wilsden, and the p curacies of New Leeds, Horton, Bankfoot, Cullingworth, Wibsey, Low Moor Clayton, Eccleshill, Lister-Dyke, Heaton, and Thornton, also are separate benefices

The two sub districts are Bradford East End and Bradford West End and the former comprises the part of Bradford township eastward of Broad Stones, Church Bridge, and Market-street, while the latter consists of the rest of the township — The district comprehends also the sub-district of Bowling, conterminate with the township of Bowling, the sub district of Horton, containing the townships of Horton and Manningham, the sub district of Thornton, containing the townships of Thornton and Clayton, the sub district of Wilsden, containing the townships of Wilsden and Allerton, the sub district of Shipley, containing the townships of Shipley and Heaton, the sub district of North Bierley, conterminate with the township of North Bierley, the sub district of Idle, containing the townships of Eccleshill, Idle and Bolton, the sub district of Pudsey, conterminate with the township of Pudsey, the sub district of Calverley, conterminate with the township of Calverley with Farsley, the sub district of Drighlington, containing the townships of Drighlington and Tong, and the sub district of Cleckheaton containing the townships of Cleckheaton, Wike, and Hunsworth Acres, 40,331 Poor rates in 1863 £37,163 Pop in 1841, 132,161, in 1861, 196,475 Houses, 41,822 Marriages in 1866 2,294, births, 8,417,—of which 614 were illegitimate, deaths, 5,951,—of which 2,871 were at ages under 5 years, and 57 at ages above 85 Marriages in the ten years 1851-60, 18,1?3, births, 74,843, deaths, 48,609 The places of worship in 1851, were 32 of the Church of England with 23 42? sittings, 1 of the United Presbyterian church, with 630 s, 17 of Independents, with 10,615 s, 15 of Baptists, with 7 760 s., 1 of Quakers with 1,000 s 2 of Unitarians, with 440 s, 3 of Moravians with 1,131 s, 43 of Wesleyan Methodists, with 17,301 s, 3 of New Connexion Methodists, with 1,197 s 18 of Primitive Methodists, with 4,122 s, ? of the Wesleyan Association, with 1,827 s, 10 of Wesleyan Reformers, with 1,184 s., 5 undefined, with 668 s, 3 of Latter day Saints, with 590 s, and 1 of Roman Catholics, with 330 s The schools were 66 public day schools with 10 798 scholars, 188 private day schools, with 7,427 s., 161 Sunday schools, with 32 645 s, and 52 evening schools for adults, with 1,479 s Workhouses are in Bradford and Idle townships

BRADFORD, LEEDS, AND HALIFAX RAILWAY See LEEDS, BRADFORD and HALIFAX RAILWAY

BRADFORD, WAKEFIELD, AND LEEDS RAILWAY, a railway connecting the three towns from which it takes its name, by junctions with the Leeds, Bradford, and Halifax at Leeds and Ardsley and with the Lancashire and Yorkshire It is 10 miles long, and was authorized in 1854, and opened in 1857 It is the shortest line between Leeds, Bradford, and Wakefield, affords the most direct route from Leeds and Bradford by way of the Great Northern, to London, and accommodates an extensive coal district.

BRADFORD ABBAS, a village, a parish, and a sub district, in Sherborne district, Dorset The village stands on the river Yeo, adjacent to the South western railway, 2½ miles ESE of Yeovil station, and 3½ SW by W of Sherborne, and has a post office under Sherborne The parish comprises 1,130 acres Real property, £3,055 Pop, 585 Houses, 134 The property is all in one estate The living is a vicarage, united with the rectory of Clifton Maybank, in the diocese of Salisbury Value, £479 * Patron Winchester college The church is good An endowed school has £94, and other charities £23 The sub district comprises thirteen parishes. Acres, 12,830 Pop, 3,372 Houses, 738

BRADFORD CUM BESWICK See BRADFORD, Manchester

BRADFORD DOWN, a range of hill in Dorset immediately W of Dorchester The summit of it, 3 miles from the town commands an extensive view

BRADFORD EAST END See BRADFORD, Yorkshire

BRADFORD (GREAT) See BRADFORD Wilts

BRADFORD (NORTH) a hundred in Salop It is cut into the three divisions,—Drayton, containing eight parishes and parts of two others, Wem, containing three parishes and part of another, and Whitchurch, also containing three parishes and part of another Acres, 120 093 Pop, 27 279 Houses 5 713

BRADFORD NORTHWESTERN See BRADFORD, Wilts

BRADFORD ON AVON See BRADFORD Wilts

BRADFORD PEVERELL, a village and a parish in Dorchester district Dorset The village stands on the river Frome, under Bradford Down, near the Roman road to Ilchester and near the Dorchester and Yeovil railway, 3 miles NW by W of Dorchester —The parish includes also the hamlet of Muckleford, and its post town is Stratton, under Dorchester Acres, 2,700 Real property, £2 658 Pop, 361 Houses, 75 The property is divided among a few Roman antiquities have been found The living is a rectory in the diocese of Salisbury Value, £229 * Patron, Winchester College The church is good Charities, £5

BRADFORD ROAD, a chapelry in Manchester parish Lancashire, in the eastern suburbs of Manchester It was constituted in 1837, and reconstituted in 1850 Pop, 10,5?0 Houses, 2 043 The living is a rectory in the diocese of Manchester, of the value of £300, in the patronage of trustees

BRADFORD (SOUTH), a hundred in Salop It is cut into the two divisions of Newport, containing eight parishes and part of another, and Wellington, containing eighteen parishes Acres, 86,818 Pop, 18,620 Houses, 9 ?2?

BRADFORD SOUTHEASTERN See BRADFORD, Wilts

BRADFORD (WEST), a township in Mitton parish W R Yorkshire, on the river Ribble 2 miles N of Clitheroe Acres, 1,700 Real property, £2,157 Pop 289 Houses, 73

BRADFORD WEST END See BRADFORD Yorkshire

BRADGATE, a hamlet in Kimberworth parish, W R. Yorkshire, 1 mile W of Rotherham

BRADGATE PARK See BROADGATE PARK

BRADHOLME, a hamlet in Thorne parish, W R Yorkshire

BRADIFORD, a village in Pilton parish, Devon

BRADING—anciently BRERDING, or BRERDYNGE—a small town and a parish in the Isle of Wight The town stands on the I of W railway, at the head of Brading haven, 3½ miles S by E of Ryde, and has a r station, a post office under Southampton, and an inn It is a very ancient, but decayed place, and consists chiefly of one long street, dejected and half ruinous It was long a market town It formerly sent members to parliament, it still is governed by a small corporation, and it possesses a common seal, with the words, "The Kings town of Brading" The town hall and market house is a half-timbered structure, given up to neglect A massive iron ring fastened to the ground, in an open space, is a relic of the barbarous sport of bull baiting The parish church was originally built in 704, by Wilfrid of York, is, to a considerable extent, transition Norman, and contains an effigies of Governor Cherowin who died in 1441, and two ancient monuments of the Oglanders The churchyard has the grave of Leigh Richmond's "little Jane," and the tomb of Mrs Berry, with the inscription beginning, "Forgive blest shade, the tributary tear," set to music by Dr Calcott There is an Independent chapel Some business is done in corn and fishing, small vessels come up at high water to the quay and fairs are held on 12 May and 2 Oct —The parish contains also the villages of Bembridge and Sandown and the hamlet of Alverstone Acres, 10,107, of which 543 are water Real property, £19 819 Pop, 3,?0? Houses, 7?6 The property is much subdivided Nunwell, NW of the town, amid richly wooded grounds ...

the seat of Sir H. Oglander, Bart., the descendant of [illegible] Okelandre, who came from Normandy with the Conqueror. [illegible] down S and W of Nunwell, commands a brilliant view. Brading Haven, is only partly in the parish, goes out to the sea by a narrow mouth at Bembridge point, covers about 800 acres, looks like a [illegible] at high water and like a muddy swamp at low, yields prodigious quantities of excellent cockles, and was formerly noted for an oyster bed. Several strenuous attempts have been made to reclaim it from the tide by means of an embankment across its mouth, but without success. The living is a vicarage in the diocese of Winchester. Value, £250.* Patron, Trinity College, Cambridge. The p. curacies of Bembridge and Sandown are separate benefices. Legh Richmond was for some time curate, and wrote here his "Young Cottager," "Dairyman's Daughter," and "Negro Servant."

BRADLE, a tything in Church Knowle parish, Dorset, 1 mile W of Corfe Castle. Pop., 180. Houses, [illegible]

BRADLE, Gloucester. See BROADWELL.

BRADLEY, a tything in Cumnor parish, Berks, 4½ miles NNW of Abingdon. Pop. 8. Houses, 1.

BRADLEY, a hamlet in Frodsham township and parish, Cheshire, 1 mile ESE of Frodsham. Pop., 77.

BRADLEY, a township in Malpas parish, Cheshire, 2 miles SE of Malpas. Acres, 837. Real property, £1,037. Pop., 110. Houses, 22.

BRADLEY, a parish in Ashbourne district, Derby, 2½ miles E by S of Ashbourne r. station. Post town, Ashbourn. Acres, 2,374. Real property, £3,[illegible] Pop., 250. Houses, [illegible] The property is divided among a few. The parish is a resort of sportsmen. The living is a rectory in the diocese of Lichfield. Value, £259.* Patron, the Bishop of Lichfield. The church is ancient [illegible] Osborne's charities for Bradley and many other places in the county yield £65 a year.

BRADLEY, a hundred in Gloucester. It lies in the [illegible] part of the county, and contains Aston Blank parish, sixteen other parishes, and parts of two others. Acres, 2[illegible]. Pop., 7,9[illegible]. Houses, 1,225.

BRADLEY, a parish in Basingstoke district, Hants, 6 miles WNW of Alton r. station, and [illegible] S of Basingstoke. Post town, Preston Candover, under Micheldever station. Acres 960. Real property, £860. Pop., 116. Houses, 25. The property is divided among a few. The living is a rectory in the diocese of Winchester. Value, £250.* Patron, [illegible] Esq. The church is good, and there are charities £20.

BRADLEY, a hamlet in Holt chapelry, Leicester, 2¾ miles NW of Rockingham. A small Augustinian priory was founded here, in the time of King John, by Robert de Bundy, and given, at the dissolution, to Thomas Nevill.

BRADLEY, a parish in Caistor district, Lincoln, 2½ miles SW of Great Grimsby r. station. Post town, Grimsby. Acres, 1,523. Real property, £1,200. Pop., 108. Houses 19. The manor belongs to Sir J. Nelthorpe, Bart. The living is a rectory in the diocese of Lincoln. Value, £1[illegible].* Patron, Sir J. Nelthorpe, Bart.

BRADLEY, a chapelry in Wolverhampton parish, Stafford, constituted in 1867. Pop., about 1000. Living, a vicarage. Value, £150. The church was completed in [illegible] at a cost of £[illegible],000, and is in the early English style.

BRADLEY, a hamlet in Burslem parish, Stafford, in the vicinity of Burslem. It is rich in minerals.

BRADLEY, a parish in the district and county of Stafford, 2 miles SE of Haughton r. station, and 3 SW of Stafford. It includes the liberties of Billington and Woollaston, and its post town is Church Eaton, under Stafford. Acres, [illegible]376. Real property, £5,7[illegible]. Pop., [illegible] Houses, 12[illegible]. The property is much subdivided. The living is a vicarage in the diocese of Lichfield. Value, £7[illegible]. Patron, the Duke of Sutherland. The church is very good. A free school has [illegible], £12, and other charities £10.

BRADLEY, a chapelry in Himbleton parish, Worcester, 5½ miles ESE of Droitwich. Pop., [illegible]. Houses, 62. The living is a rectory. Value, £270. Patron, the Bishop of Worcester. The church was built in 1865.

BRADLEY, a hamlet in Huddersfield township, W. R. Yorkshire, on the Manchester and Leeds railway, 2 miles NE by E of Huddersfield. It has a station on the railway, a church of 1861, and a large cotton factory.

BRADLEY, Salop. See WYKE AND BRADLEY.

BRADLEY, West Gloucester. See LINWELL and BRADLEY.

BRADLEY AND MOXLEY, a railway station in Staffordshire, on the Birmingham and Wolverhampton railway, 1½ mile SE of Bilston.

BRADLEY FIELD. See UNDERBARROW.

BRADLEY FOLD, a station on the Bolton and Rochdale railway, Lancashire, 2¾ miles E by N of Bolton.

BRADLEY (GREAT), a parish in Risbridge district, Suffolk, on the verge of the county, 5 miles SE of Dullingham r. station, and 6 N of Haverhill. It has a post office under Newmarket. Acres, 2,29[illegible]. Real property, £3,36[illegible]. Pop., 4[illegible]. Houses, 99. The property is divided among a few. The living is a rectory in the diocese of Ely. Value, £407. Patrons, the Trustees of the Rev. W. S. P. Wilder. The church is substantial.

BRADLEY GREEN, a village in Biddulph parish, Stafford, 5¾ miles N of Burslem.

BRADLEY HAVERSTOE, a wapentake in the parts of Lindsey, Lincoln. It contains Bradley parish and thirty-two other parishes. Acres, 8[illegible]. Pop., 10,771. Houses, 2,2[illegible].

BRADLEY IN THE MOORS, a parish in Cheadle district, Stafford, near the Uttoxeter canal, 1½ mile WSW of Alton r. station, and 4 ESE of Cheadle. Post-town, Alton, under Stafford. Acres 650. Real property, £1,014. Pop. 43. Houses, 11. The property is all in one estate. The living is a vicarage in the diocese of Lichfield. Value, £58. Patron, the Earl of Shrewsbury. The church is good.

BRADLEY (LITTLE), a parish in Risbridge district, Suffolk, on the verge of the county, 5 miles N of Haverhill, and 6 SE by S of Dullingham r. station. Post town, Great Bradley, under Newmarket. Acres, 957. Real property, £1,[illegible]01. Pop., 28. Houses, 7. The property is all in one estate. The living is a rectory in the diocese of Ely. Value, £25. Patrons, F. B. and C. F. Foster. The church has a brass of Day the printer who died in 1584, and four other brasses.

BRADLEY (LOWER and UPPER). See BRADLEY-BOTH.

BRADLEY (MAIDEN). See MAIDEN BRADLEY.

BRADLEY MANOR, a hamlet in Bilston township, Stafford, 1½ mile from Bilston. It has a post office, of the name of Bradley, under Bilston.

BRADLEY MILLS, a hamlet in Dalton township, Kirkheaton parish, W. R. Yorkshire, 2 miles NE of Huddersfield.

BRADLEY (NORTH), a tything, a parish, and a sub-district in Westbury district, Wilts. The tything lies on an affluent of the river Avon, adjacent to the Great Western railway, 2 miles S of Trowbridge, and has a post office under Trowbridge. Real property, £5,917. Pop., 955. Houses 231. The parish includes also the tything of Southwick. Acres, 4,030. Real property, £8,0[illegible]8. Pop., 21[illegible]. Houses, [illegible]. The living is a vicarage in the diocese of Salisbury. Value, £[illegible]. Patron, Winchester College. The church was built in the 12th century, and was recently restored, and a new one, to be in the early transition style, with chapel and tower in the perpendicular style, was formed in 1862. Road Hill vicarage is a separate charge. There is a Baptist chapel. An asylum for poor, founded by archdeacon Daubeny, and a school have £1[illegible].—The sub-district includes also part of Steeple Ashton parish. Acres, 6,070. Pop., 2,71[illegible]. Houses, 577.

BRADLEYS BOTH, or BRADLEY (LOWER and UPPER), a township in Kildwick parish, W. R. Yorkshire, on the Leeds and Liverpool canal, and on the North Midland railway, 2½ miles SSE of Skipton. Acres 1,5[illegible]. Real property, £2,5[illegible]1. Pop., [illegible]12. Houses, 1[illegible]1.

BRADLEY (WEST), a parish in Wells district, Somerset, on the Somerset and Dorset railway, near West Pennard station, 4 miles ESE by S of Glastonbury. It includes the hamlet of Lottisbrook, and its post town [illegible]

East Pennard under Shepton Mallet Acres, 62 Real property, £1 [illegible] Pop, 136 Houses, 31 The living is a p curacy, annexed to the vicarage of East Pennard, in the diocese of Bath and Wells.

BRADMERE POOL a pond in the NE of Dartmoor, Devon, [illegible] miles NW of Moreton Hampstead It occupies about 3 acres, is said to be unfathomable, continues full to the lip in the greatest droughts and is thought by some to have been artificial and Druidical An elliptical mound contiguous to it is also thought to have been Druidical, and a cromlech, called the Spinsters Rock, with three supporting stones 7 feet high, and an incumbent stone 15 feet long and 10 feet broad, is about 100 yards distant.

BRADMORE, a parish in Basford district, Notts, 5½ miles SE of Beeston r station, and 7 S of Nottingham Post town, Bunny under Nottingham Acres, 1,560 Real property, £2,[illegible] Pop, 290 Houses, [illegible] Many of the inhabitants are stocking makers The living is a vicarage annexed to the vicarage of Bunny in the diocese of Lincoln The church was long ago burnt, and has not been rebuilt

BRADMORE, Middlesex See HAMMERSMITH

BRADNEY a township in Worfield parish, Salop, [illegible]½ miles NE of Bridgnorth

BRADNINCH, a precinct in Exeter city Devon, contiguous to the parish of St. Paul Pop 91 Houses 10

BRADNINCH, a small town and a parish in Tiverton district, Devon The town stands on an eminence, 1 mile N of Hele station, and 2 SW of Collumpton It was anciently called Braines and it gave the title of Baron under that name to the Dukes of Cornwall It dates from the Saxon times, and is thought by some to be older than Exeter It was the head quarters of King Charles and his army on two occasions in 1644, and the head quarters of Fairfax s army in October 1645 It was almost entirely destroyed by fire in 16[illegible]5, and it is now a poor place, consisting chiefly of one street It sent members to parliament from the time of Edward II till that of Henry VII, and was long a market town It has a post office under Collumpton, and fairs are held at it on the first Wednesday of April and the third Wednesday of Sept The town hall was built in the time of Henry VI, and repaired in 1838 An old jail, with capacity for two male and two female prisoners, was restored in 1835, and is still in use The parish church is later perpendicular English, was recently restored, and contains a fine screen of 1528, and an old painting of the crucifixion There are Baptist and Wesleyan chapels, and charities £70 —The parish includes also the hamlet of Hele. Acres, 4,3[illegible]1 Real property £8,[illegible]6[illegible] Pop 1,796 Houses, 388 The property is much subdivided The manor belongs to the Duchy of Cornwall Bradninch House is an interesting old mansion, formerly the seat of the Sainthill family, now the seat of G Pearse, Esq The living is a vicarage in the diocese of Exeter Value, £18[illegible] Patrons, the Dean and Canons of Windsor

BRADNOP, a township in Leek parish Stafford, 2 miles SE by E of Leek Real property, £1,513 Pop, 451 Houses, 85 The inhabitants are chiefly employed in copper mines

BRADNOR See RATTON, BRADNOR and RUSHOCK

BRADOCK See BOCONNOC Cornwall

BRADON, a parish in Langport district, Somerset near the Chard canal, 3 miles N by E of Ilminster and 5 SW of Langport r station It includes the tythings of North and South Bradon, and its post town is Isle Abbots under Taunton Acres, [illegible]90 Real property, returned with Isle Brewers and Puckington Pop 39 Houses 11 The living is a sinecure rectory in the diocese of Bath and Wells Value, £10[illegible] Patron, the Earl of Egmont The church is in ruins

BRADON FOREST an ancient forest, once occupying the greater part of the N of Wilts. It was known to the Saxons as Bradene or Bradun, overrun by Ethelwold in 905, and held, in the time of Henry II by Bernard of York Bradon Pond in it, 4 miles E of Malmsbury, measures ¾ of a mile by [illegible], and is the largest sheet of water in the county

BRADPOLE, a parish in Bridport district, Dorset, on the Bridport railway, 1 mile NE of Bridport Post town, Bridport Acres, 966 Real property, £5,321 Pop, 1,[illegible]1[illegible] Houses 270 The property is divided among a few The living is a vicarage, united with the p. curacy of St Andrews, in the diocese of Salisbury Value, £265 * Patron, the Lord Chancellor The church was built in 1860 is in the early English style, and consists of nave chancel and vestry with bell turret The Bridport workhouse is in Bradpole

BRADSHAW, a township and a chapelry in Bolton le Moors parish Lancashire The township lies on the Bolton and Blackburn railway, adjacent to the Oaks station, 3 miles NE of Bolton, and has a post office under Bolton Acres, 1,080 Real property, £3,77[illegible] Pop, 792 Houses, 146 Bradshaw Hall was the seat of John Bradshaw, who presided at the trial of Charles I, and is now the seat of T Hardcastle, Esq There are two cotton mills, a bleaching mill and quarries —The ch is more extensive than the township and was constituted in 1853 Pop, 1 968 Houses, 378 The living is a vicarage in the diocese of Manchester Value, £1[illegible]0 * Patron, the Vicar of Bolton The church is tolerable

BRADSHAW, a village and a chapelry in Ovenden township, Halifax parish, W R Yorkshire The village stands 1 mile NW of Halifax —The chapelry was constituted in 1842, and its post town is Halifax Pop., 2,171 Houses 4[illegible]7 The living is a p curacy in the diocese of Ripon Value £150 Patron, the Vicar of Halifax The church was built in 1839

BRADSHAW EDGE, a township in Chapel en le Frith parish Derby, 1 mile W of Chapel en le Frith Real property £7 [illegible]0 Pop., 2,518 Houses, 455

BRADSHAW LEACH, a station on the Bolton and Wigan railway, Lancashire, 8¾ miles WSW of Bolton Pennington Hall, in the vicinity, is the seat of J Bradshaw, Esq

BRADSOLE, or ST RADIGUND a ruined Premonstratensian abbey in Polton parish, Kent on high ground commanding a good view, 3 miles NW of Dover It was founded, in 11[illegible] by Jeffrey Earl of Perth, and given, at the dissolution, to the Archbishop of Canterbury The principal gateway nearly all remains, much covered with ivy and the chapel and some other parts are now used as a farm house

BRADSTONE a parish in Tavistock district, Devon, on the river Tamar 4¼ miles SSE of Launceston r station, and 8 NW by N of Tavistock Post-town Launceston Acres, 1 2[illegible]7 Real property £1 [illegible]35 Pop, 142 Houses, 23 The property is divided between the Bradshaws and the Kellys The manor house, an old Tudor edifice belongs to the former, and is now tenanted by a farmer The living is a rectory in the diocese of Exeter Value, £204 * Patron, the Bishop of Exeter The church is perpendicular English, consists of nave aisles and chancel, with a tower, and is in tolerable condition

BRADWALL a township in Sandbach parish, Cheshire, on the Manchester and Birmingham railway 2 miles NNW of Sandbach Acres, 2,063 Real property £3 784 Pop 157 Houses, 66 Bradwall Hall is the seat of the Lathams

BRADWELL, a parish in Newport Pagnell district Bucks, on the Newport Pagnell railway, 3 miles [illegible] of Stony Stratford It has a post office under Stony Stratford, and a railway station Acres, 892 Real property £3,[illegible]2 Pop 1,[illegible]8 Houses, [illegible]38 The living is a vicarage in the diocese of Oxford Value £1[illegible] Patron, the Lord Chancellor The old church is early English, and New Bradwell church, annexed to Stantonbury, is recent Charities £20

BRADWELL, a township in Hope parish Derby under the Peak, 2 miles SE of Castleton It has a post office under Sheffield Real property, £2,[illegible] Pop 1 304 Houses 2[illegible]7 Some of the inhabitants are cotton workers, but more are employed in lead and calamine mines A stalactite cavern includes numerous chambers and extends upwards of 400 yards Traces of a Roman camp or Norman fort [illegible] castle, and Roman tiles, coins, and other relics have been found there The township has a school church, Wesleyan Primitive Methodist and Unitarian chapels, and charities £8

BRADWELL, a parish in Mutford district Suffolk, on the East Suffolk railway, near Belton station, 3 miles SW by S of Great Yarmouth Post-town, Yarmouth Acres 2,38[illegible] Real property, £4 482 Pop, 28[illegible] Houses, 80 The property is subdivided The living is a rectory in the diocese of Norwich Value, £632 * Patron, J Walker, Esq The church has a curious ancient font and is good

BRADWELL, a village a parish, and a sub district, in the district of Maldon, Essex The village stands near the point of the peninsula between the Blackwater estuary and the sea, 5½ miles by water, but 12 by road, E of Maldon station, and has a post office under Maldon, and a fair on 24 June It is thought by Camden to occupy the site of the Roman Othona and the Saxon Ithancestre The parish is sometimes called Bradwell next the Sea and comprises 4 734 acres of land, and 5 321 of water Real property, £8,151 Pop, 1,094 Houses 217 The property is divided among a few Bradwell Lodge is a chief residence There are decoys for wild fowls. The living is a rectory in the diocese of Rochester Value, £1,624 * Patron, W J Warner, Esq The church is good, and there are charities £109 —The sub district contains five parishes Acres, 25,887 Pop, 2 8[illegible]3 Houses, [illegible]79

BRADWELL, Oxford See BROADWELL

BRADWELL ABBEY, an extra parochial tract in Newport Pagnell district, Bucks, on the Northwestern railway contiguous to Bradwell parish 3½ miles SE by E of Stony Stratford Acres 650 Real property, £750 Pop, 14 Houses, 3 A small Black priory was founded here in the time of Stephen by a Lord of Wolverton, and given at the dissolution to Arthur Longfield, and is [illegible] house.

BRADWELL NEXT COGGESHALL, a parish in Braintree district, Essex, on the river Blackwater, 2 miles W of Coggeshall, and 4 [illegible] of Braintree station Post town, Coggeshall, under Kelvedon Acres, 1 1[illegible] Real property, £2,0[illegible]8 Pop, 273 Houses, 67 The property is divided among a few The [illegible] belonged formerly to the Maxeys The parish is a resort of sportsmen The living is a rectory in the diocese of Rochester Value, £2[illegible] * Patron [illegible] [illegible] [illegible], Esq The church contains monuments of the Maxeys and is good Charities, £23

BRADWELL NEAR THE SEA See BRADWELL, Maldon, Essex

BRADWORTHY, a village, a parish and a sub district in Bideford district Devon The village stands [illegible] 7 miles NNW of Holsworthy and 12 SW of Bideford r station, and it has a post office under Holsworthy, North Devon, and fairs on 10 June, and [illegible] Sept The parish includes also the [illegible] of [illegible] Derworthy [illegible], and [illegible] Acres, 9,[illegible]5[illegible] Real property [illegible] Pop 981 Houses 1[illegible] A considerable portion of the surface is [illegible] and common Many traces of Roman settlement [illegible] The living is a vicarage, united with the p[illegible] of [illegible] in the diocese of [illegible] Value £2[illegible] * Patron, the Crown The church [illegible] and a lofty tower The sub district contains [illegible] parishes Acres, 17,2[illegible]7 Pop, 911 [illegible]

BRAFFERTON, a township in Great Aycliffe parish, Durham, on [illegible] and on the North eastern railway, [illegible] N of Darlington Acres, 2,09[illegible] Real property, £21[illegible] Pop, 2[illegible] Houses, 4[illegible] There is a Methodist chapel

BRAFFERTON, a village, a [illegible] and a [illegible] parish in [illegible] district, N R Yorkshire The village stands on the river [illegible] to the Boroughbridge [illegible] and [illegible] NE [illegible] has a station [illegible] contiguous to [illegible] village,

which has a post office under York The township comprises 1,920 acres Real property, £1,600 Pop 199 Houses, 42 The parish includes also the townships of Helperby and Thornton Bridge Acres, 4,5[illegible]3 Real property £7 562 Pop, 901 Houses, 214 The property is subdivided The living is a vicarage in the diocese of York Value, £30[illegible] * Patron, the Lord Chancellor The church is good and there are charities £27

BRAFFORDS a village in Swanland township, E R Yorkshire 7 miles W of Hull

BRAFIELD a parish and a sub district in Hardingstone district Northampton The parish is called also Brafield on the Green and lies 1½ mile S [illegible] of Billing Road r station, and [illegible] S of Northampton Post-town Little Houghton under Northampton Acres, 1,950 Real property £2,442 Pop, 4[illegible]4 Houses 108 The property is divided among a few The living is a vicarage, annexed to the vicarage of Little Houghton, in the diocese of Peterborough The church was restored in 18[illegible] There are a Baptist chapel a national school, and charities £[illegible] —The sub district contains seven parishes Pop, 3 [illegible]

BRAICH MELYN, a hamlet in Llanllechid parish Carnarvon 3½ miles SE of Bangor

BRAICH Y DINAS or DINAS PENMAEN, an ancient British fort on the NE coast of Carnarvon on the summit of Penmaenmawr 4½ miles WSW of Conway It had capacity for 20 000 men possessed more strength than any other British post in Snowdonia and was the station of the [illegible] Welsh army during the negotiation between Prince Llewelyn and Edward I

BRAICH Y PWLL, a headland at the south western extremity of Carnarvon, 2½ miles N of Bardsey island It is the Canganum Promontorium of Ptolemy, and commands a very grand view

BRAIDLEY a hamlet in Carlton Highdale township, N R Yorkshire, 9 miles SW of Middleham

BRAILES two hamlets, a parish, and a division in Warwick The hamlets are Upper and Lower Brailes they lie [illegible] miles ESE of Shipston on Stour, and about [illegible] NE [illegible] of Moreton r station, they have post office‡ of the name of Brailes under Shipston on Stour and one of them was formerly a market town, and has still a fair on Easter Thursday The parish includes also the hamlets of Chelmscott and Winderton, and is in the district of Shipston on Stour Acres, 5,220 Real property, £10,[illegible]48 Pop, 1,[illegible]7 Houses, 30[illegible] The property is divided among a few The manor belonged, before the Conquest, to Edwin Earl of Mercia, was given by the Conqueror, to Henry de Newburgh and passed to the Beauchamps Brailes House is now the seat of the Sheldons Brailes Covert is a meet of the Warwick hounds Some parts of the surface are hilly and have fine views The living is a vicarage in the diocese of Worcester Value, £311 * [illegible] Esq The church is partly early English partly perpendicular, and is in good condition There are a Quakers chapel, a Roman Catholic chapel and school an endowed school with £[illegible] a year a national school a literary and reading room and charities £68 —The division contains fifteen parishes [illegible] Acres 35 2[illegible] Pop 7 [illegible] Houses, [illegible]

BRAILSFORD a parish and a sub district in Ashbourne district Derby The parish lies on [illegible] of the [illegible] [illegible] W of Duffield r station and [illegible] S[illegible] of Ashbourne and it includes the hamlet of [illegible] [illegible] which has a post office under Derby Acres [illegible],2[illegible]6 Real property £[illegible] Pop, 7[illegible]3 Houses [illegible] The property is [illegible] The living is a rectory in the diocese of Lichfield Value, £[illegible]73 * Patron Earl Ferrers The church is [illegible] and there are two Methodist chapels [illegible] —The sub district contains [illegible] parishes and parts of three others Pop, 3 [illegible]

BRAINES See BRAUNTON, Devon

BRAINSHILL [illegible] a parish in [illegible] and county of Hertford [illegible] river [illegible] NW of Hertford [illegible] Post town Hertford Acres, 1 [illegible]10 Real property, £1 807 Pop, 1[illegible] Houses, 45 The property is divided among [illegible]

a few. Braintfield Place is the seat of the Lessays. The living is a rectory in the diocese of Rochester. Value, £207.* Patron, Abel Smith, Esq. The church is good. Thomas a Becket was rector.

BRAINTREE, a small town, a parish, a sub-district, and a district in Essex. The town stands on the river Blackwater, on the Roman road to Colchester, and on the Blackwater Valley and Bishops Stortford railway, 6½ miles north-north-westward from the Witham Junction of the Eastern Counties railway, and 12 miles NNE of Chelmsford. It arose, in the Roman Catholic times, from thoroughfare of pilgrims into Suffolk and Norfolk, fell fast into decay after the Reformation, and revived under the influence of trade. The manor was known, at the Conquest, as Great Rayne or Branchetr n, and belonged till the time of Edward VI., to the Bishops of London. The town is straggling, occupies a rising ground, and connects on the N with Bocking. The streets, for the most part, are narrow, and many of the houses are old and timbered. A corn exchange was built in 18 9. The parish church stands on a high mound thought to have been the site of an ancient camp, is later English and spacious, with a tall spire, was enlarged, prior to the Reformation, with the proceeds of three plays acted in it, and contains the tomb of Dr Collins, physician to Peter the Great. The site of the former church, and some vestiges of a palace of the Bishops of London, are ½ a mile distant. The town has a head post office,‡ a railway station with telegraph, two banking offices, two chief inns, four dissenting chapels, a mechanics' institute, a free school, and some charities, and it is a seat of petty sessions and a polling place, and publishes a weekly newspaper. The Independent chapel is a large and handsome edifice, built in 1832, and the free school has £18 a year from endowment, and educated Ray the naturalist. A weekly market is held on Wednesday, and fairs on 8 May and 2 Oct. A considerable woollen trade sprang up in the time of Elizabeth, but went into decay, and a trade in silk and crape is now carried on. Dawes, the archbishop, and Tusser, the agricultural poet, were born in the neighbourhood. Pop., 4,305. Houses, 980.

The parish comprises 2,213 acres, of which 58 lie detached within Stisted. Real property, £10,324. Pop., 4,620. Houses, 1,0 1. The property is much subdivided. The living is a vicarage in the diocese of Rochester. Value, £300.* Patron, Rev. C. T. Cartwright. The sub-district contains the parish of Braintree, Rayne, Black Notley, White Notley, and Cressing. Acres, 10,4 3. Pop., 6,600. Houses, 1,500. The district comprehends also the sub-district of Bocking, containing the parishes of Bocking, Panfield, Stisted, Pattiswick, and Bradwell-next-Coggeshall, and the sub-district of Finchingfield, containing the parishes of Finchingfield, Wethersfield, Shalford, and Great Saling. Acres, 38,652. Poor-rates in 1866, £10,187. Pop. in 1861, 17,170. Houses, 3,839. Marriages in 1866, 135; births, 578,—of which 34 were illegitimate; deaths, 339,—of which 105 were at ages under 5 years, and 13 at ages above 85. Marriages in the ten years 1851-60, 1,233; births, 5,391; deaths, 3,603. The places of worship in 1851 were 14 of the Church of England, with 5,924 sittings; 8 of Independents, with 4,7 0 s.; 2 of Baptists, with 810 s.; 1 of Quakers, with 210 s.; and 1 of Wesleyan Methodists, with 250 s. The schools were 19 public day schools, with 1,500 scholars; 50 private day schools, with 1,174 s.; 22 Sunday schools, with 2,455 s.; and 2 evening schools for adults, with 47 s. The workhouse is in Bocking.

BRAISEWORTH, or BRISEWORTH, a parish in Hartismere district, Suffolk, 2 miles SSW of Eye r. station, and 3½ SE of Mellis. Post-town, Eye. Acres, 720. Real property, £1,317. Pop., 164. Houses, 30. Braiseworth Hall is a chief residence. The living is a rectory in the diocese of Norwich. Value, £149. Patron, Sir E. Kerrison, Bart. The church was built in 1857.

BRAISHFIELD, or BRASFIELD, a chapelry in the parishes of Mitchelmersh, Romsey, and Hursley, Hants, on the Anton river, and the Andover railway, 3½ miles N of Romsey r. station. It was constituted in 1855, and it has a post office under Romsey. Pop., 452. Houses, 100. The living is a vicarage in the diocese of Winchester. Value, £50.* Patron, the Rector of Mitchelmersh.

BRAISTY WOOD, a hamlet in Hartwith with Winsley township, W. R. Yorkshire, 4½ miles W of Ripley.

BRAITHWAITE, a township in Crosthwaite parish, Cumberland, on the Cockermouth and Penrith railway, 3 miles W of Keswick. It has a railway station, a post office under Windermere, and an inn. Pop., 326. Houses, 67. The surface commands splendid prospects. The inhabitants are employed chiefly in lead mines and woollen manufactures.

BRAITHWAITE, a hamlet in Keighley parish, W. R. Yorkshire, in the vicinity of Keighley.

BRAITHWAITE, a hamlet in Kirk-Bramwith parish, W. R. Yorkshire, 4½ miles W of Thorne.

BRAITHWAITE, Mid Cumberland. See MIDDLESCEUGH WITH BRAITHWAITE.

BRAITHWELL, a village and a township in Doncaster district, and a parish in Doncaster and Rotherham districts, W. R. Yorkshire. The village stands 2½ miles SSE of Conisbrough r. station, and 4¾ W by N of Tickhill, and has a post office under Rotherham. The township includes also the hamlet of Micklebring. Acres, 1,990. Real property, £2,734. Pop., 422. Houses, 99. The parish contains also the township of Bramley. Acres, 2,904. Real property, £4,581. Pop., 7 7. Houses, 177. The property is much subdivided. Roman coins and arms have been found. The living is a rectory in the diocese of York. Value, £330.* Patron, the Lord Chancellor. The church is early English. There are two Wesleyan chapels, and charities £21.

BRAKES, a township in Leintwardine parish, Hereford, 1½ miles W of Ludlow. Pop., 179. Houses, 25.

BRAMALL. See BRAMHALL.

BRAMBER, a village, a parish, and a rape in Sussex. The village stands on the river Adur, and on the Roman road from Dover to Winchester, adjacent to the Horsham and Shoreham railway, ½ a mile SE of Steyning, and has a station on the railway. It consists now of only a few cottages, but it was long a place of importance, and a market town. It was known to the Saxons as Brymmburgh, signifying "a fortified hill," and it was a borough by prescription, and sent two members to parliament till disfranchised by the act of 1832. One of its representatives, for a time, was the famous Wilberforce.—The parish includes the village, and is in the district of Steyning, and its post town is Steyning, under Hurstperpoint. Acres, 854. Real property, £1,123. Pop., 119. Houses, 26. The manor belonged, before the Conquest, to the Saxon kings, was given, by the Conqueror, to William de Braose, passed to the Howards, and belongs now to the Duke of Norfolk. A Roman castellum seems to have been here, and remains of a Roman bridge have been observed. A Saxon royal fort succeeded the castellum, a Norman keep was added to the fort, and a great baronial castle arose out of these, a moated, irregular parallelogram, 560 feet by 280, and was held by the parliamentarian troops during the civil war, and went soon afterwards into decay. Little of it now remains except a fragment of a lofty barbican tower, and a mound representing the keep. The tower has a Norman window, and the mound commands an extensive and very striking view. The living is a rectory, united with the vicarage of Botolph, in the diocese of Chichester. Value, £160. Patron, Magdalene College, Oxford. The church stands close to the castle, shows some Norman features, and seems once to have been cruciform, with a central tower.—The rape extends quite across the county from Surrey to the channel, is bisected, in the southern part, by the Adur, measures 21 miles by 9, and contains the hundreds of Brightford, Burbeach, East Easwrith, Fishergate, Patching, Singlecross, Steyning, Tarring, Tipnoak, West Grinstead, and Windham and Ewhurst. Acres, 117,443. Pop. in 1851, 3 ,995; in 1861, 35,1 7. Houses, 6,58 .

BRAMBLE CHINE, a small ravine on the NW coast of the Isle of Wight, at Colwell bay, 2 miles SW of Yar-

[illegible] of oyster shell [illegible] fossil state, is [illegible] the same position [illegible]

FRAMBLETYE HOUSE, a ruin 2½ miles SE of East Grinstead, in Sussex. It possesses [illegible] interest [illegible] notoriety through Horace Smith's [illegible]. The house was built, in the time of James I., [illegible] Compton, and belonged in 1683 to [illegible] Richards, who fell from a [illegible] charge of [illegible]

BRAMCOTE, a village and a parish in the district of Shardlow, and county of Nottingham. The village stands [illegible] of the county and near the Nottingham canal and the Erewash river, 1½ mile ENE of [illegible] station, and 5 W by S of Nottingham, and has a post office under that town.—The parish comprises 1,070 acres. Real property, £2,700. Pop., [illegible] Houses, 147. The property is divided among a [illegible] House is the seat of the Sherwins. The [illegible] Druidical monument 50 feet high, [illegible] Much of the surface [illegible] and [illegible] is found. A number of the inhabitants [illegible] and hosiery trades. The living is a [illegible] annexed to the vicarage of Attenborough, in the [illegible] Lincoln. The church was built in 1862 in [illegible] decorated English style, and consists of nave [illegible] chancel and vestry, with a tower and spire 130 feet high. The previous church contained monuments of the [illegible]. There is a Wesleyan chapel, a national school, and charities £40.

BRAMCOTE, a hamlet in Pulkington and Wolvey parishes, Warwick, in the vicinity of the Ashby de la Zouch canal, 4 miles SE of Nuneaton. Pop., 73.

BRAMDEAN, a parish in Alresford district, Hants; 4 miles SSE of New Alresford r. station, and 8½ E by S of Winchester. It has a post office under Alresford. Acres, [illegible] Real property, £1,825. Pop., 282. Houses, [illegible] The property is subdivided. The parish is [illegible] of stone [illegible]. A Roman pavement was found [illegible] discovered. The living is a rectory in the diocese of Winchester. Value, £261.* Patron, the Lord Chancellor. The church is Norman, with an early English chancel, and has been restored.

BRAMERTON, a parish in Henstead district, Norfolk, near the river Yare, 2½ miles SSW of [illegible] station, and [illegible] SE of Norwich. It has a post office under Norwich. Acres, 725. Real property, £1,810. Pop., 3[illegible] Houses, 60. The property is divided among a few. Bramerton Hall is the seat of R. Fellowes, Esq. The living is a rectory in the diocese of Norwich. Value, [illegible] Patron, R. Fellowes, Esq. The church is very good. There are an endowed school, and other charities, £4.

BRAMFIELD, a parish in Blything district, Suffolk, on the East Suffolk railway, near the river Blythe, 2 miles S of Halesworth. It has a post office under Saxmundham. Acres, 2,716. Real property, £5,100. Pop., [illegible] Houses, 1[illegible] The property is much subdivided. Bramfield Hall is the seat of Col. Robinson. The living is a vicarage in the diocese of Norwich. Value, £1[illegible] Patron, the Lord Chancellor. The church is early English, with lancet windows, and has a rich [illegible] round tower stands detached. [illegible] Independent and Methodist chapels, [illegible] school with £29 a year. An ancient [illegible] which fell in 1843 is mentioned in the ballad [illegible] —

"[illegible] Bramfield oak
[illegible]
[illegible] Halesworth cross
[illegible]"

BRAMHOPE. [illegible]

BRAMFORD, a parish in Bosmere district, Suffolk, [illegible] and on the Eastern Union railway, [illegible] NW of Ipswich. It has a station on the railway, and a post office under Ipswich. Acres, 3,22[illegible] Real property, £[illegible] Pop., 1,[illegible] Houses, 2[illegible] [illegible] mill, chalk pits, and extensive manure and cement works. The living is a vicarage, united with the p. curacy of Burstall, in the diocese of Norwich. Value, £79.* Patrons, the Dean and Chapter of Canterbury. The church was restored in 18[illegible] There are an Independent chapel, a national school, and charities £23.

BRAMFORD SPEKE. See BRAMPFORD SPEKE.

BRAMHALL, or BRAMALL, a township in Stockport parish, Cheshire, on the Manchester and Macclesfield railway, 2½ miles S of Stockport. It has a station on the railway. Acres, 3,250. Real property, £7,819. Pop., 1,615. Houses, 331. Bramhall House, now the seat of the Davenports, belonged formerly to the Bramhalls, is a fine timbered edifice of the 15th century, partly modernized, and contains portraits of Sir A. Legh and many ancient interesting objects. There are a cotton mill, a silk mill, a police station, and Independent and Wesleyan chapels.

BRAMHAM, a township, a parish, and a sub-district, in Tadcaster district, W. R. Yorkshire. The township bears the name of Bramham cum Oglethorpe, lies 2½ miles SW of Newton Kyme r. station, and 4 W of Tadcaster, and has a post office, of the name of Bramham, under Tadcaster. Acres, 3,971. Real property, £6,007. Pop., 1,331. Houses, 267.—The parish contains also the township of Clifford cum Boston. Acres, 5,152. Real property, £15,152. Pop., 3,481. Houses, 721. The property is much subdivided. Bramham Park, now the property of G. Lane Fox, Esq., belonged formerly to the Lords Bingley, was built in the time of Queen Anne, consists of centre and wings, in the Greco-Italian style, contained till recently a portrait of Queen Anne given by her in acknowledgment of her being entertained, and was visited by George IV. The proprietor of it has abandoned it as a residence, but maintains the grounds around it in good order, and resides in a handsome neighbouring mansion. Bramham Moor has large remains of Watling street, and is a resort of sportsmen. Excellent limestone is quarried, and coal is found. Sir Thomas Rokeby, in 1408, on the part of Henry IV., fought and defeated the Earl of Northumberland at Bramham. The living is a vicarage in the diocese of York. Value, £3[illegible]0.* Patron, Christ Church, Oxford. The church consists of nave, aisles, and chancel, with tower and short spire, and has a fine pointed doorway. The vicarages of Boston Spa and Clifford are separate benefices. [illegible] college, a fine building amid ornate grounds, is an educational institution for young gentlemen. There are two Methodist chapels, an endowed school, and charities £28.—The sub-district contains three parishes, parts of three others, and an extra-parochial tract. Acres, 17,659. Pop., 4,950. Houses, 1,058.

BRAMHOPE, a township-chapelry in Otley parish, W. R. Yorkshire, on the Leeds and Thirsk railway, 2 miles S of Arthington station, and 3½ SE by E of Otley. Post town, Otley. Acres, 1,290. Real property, £2,077. Pop., 312. Houses, 83. The manor belongs to [illegible] Dyneley, Esq. The living is a p. curacy in the diocese of Ripon. Value, £[illegible] Patrons, Trustees. The church is plain. There are a Wesleyan chapel and a church school.

BRAMINGHAM (GREAT and LITTLE), two hamlets in Luton parish, Beds; 3½ miles N of Luton.

BRAMLEY, a parish and a sub-district in Basingstoke district, Hants. The parish lies on the Reading and Basingstoke railway, 4½ miles N by E of Basingstoke, and has a post office under Basingstoke. Acres, 2,25[illegible] Real property, £2,[illegible]5. Pop., 467. Houses, 9[illegible] The property is divided among a few. The living is a vicarage in the diocese of Winchester. Value, £385.* Patron, Queen's College, Oxford. The church is ancient, has a brass of 1508, and a monument to Dr. Shaw, the oriental traveller, and is in good condition.—The sub-district contains eight parishes. Acres, 21,[illegible] Pop., 5,00[illegible] Houses, 1,021.

BRAMLEY, a parish in Hambledon district, Surrey, on the Guildford and Horsham railway, [illegible] miles S by E of Guildford. It has a post office under Guildford, and a r. station. Acres, 4,008. Real property, £5,[illegible]08. Pop., 1,129. Houses, 219. The property is much subdivided. The manor house is an old edifice with pic turesque gables, now occupied by a farmer The living is a vicarage in the diocese of Winchester Value, £100 Patron the Lord Chancellor The church is partly Norman and has a good early English chancel

BRAMLEY, a village and a township-chapelry in Leeds parish, W R Yorkshire The village stands adjacent to the Leeds, Bradford, and Halifax railway, near the Leeds and Liverpool canal, 4 miles NW by W of Leeds, and it has a station on the railway and a post office‡ under Leeds —The chapelry comprises 2 331 acres Real property, £27,[illegible]24 Pop, 6,690 Houses, 1,[illegible]57 The property is much subdivided Cloth manufacture is carried on, and excellent stone is quarried The living is a p curacy in the diocese of Ripon Value, £239 * Patron, the Vicar of Leeds The church was rebuilt in 1863, at a cost of £[illegible],000 There are four dissenting chapels a Roman Catholic chapel, an endowed school with £23 a year, and charities £73

BRAMLEY, a township in Braithwell parish, W R Yorkshire, 4 miles S by W of Conisbrough station, and 5¾ W by S of Tickhill Real property, £1,817 Pop., [illegible] Houses 78 Bramley Grange belonged to Roche Abbey, and passed to the family of Spenser

BRAMLEY [illegible], a hamlet in Thruscross township, Fewston parish W R Yorkshire, 9 miles W of Ripley

BRAMPFORD SPEKE, a village and a parish in St Thomas district, Devon The village stands on the river Exe, near the Bristol and Exeter railway, 4 miles N of Exeter, and has a post office under Exeter The parish includes also the hamlet of Cowley-Bridge Acres, 1,642 Real property £3,200 Pop, 194 Houses 87 The property is subdivided The manor belonged anciently to the family of Espek or Speke, and belongs now to Sir S H Northcote, Bart The living is a vicarage united with the rectory of Cowley, in the diocese of Exeter Value, £216 * Patron the Lord Chancellor The church is very ancient, consists of nave, north aisle, chancel, and south chapel, with western square tower and has been completely restored Charities, £15

BRAMPTON, a small town, a township, a parish, a sub-district, and a district, in Cumberland The town stands in a deep narrow vale, near the confluence of the rivers Irthing and Gelt, 1¼ mile N of Milton r station 2 S of the Roman wall and 9 ENE of Carlisle It is thought by Camden to occupy the site of the Roman station Bremeturacum, it rose early to some importance, as a seat of population, and a centre of strength, it sustained much damage during the wars in the time of Edward II, it was occupied, in 1715 by the troops of the Pretender, and in 1745 by those of Prince Charles Edward It is long, and irregularly built, and has few modern houses. The town hall is an octagonal structure, resting on piazzas, and was erected in 181[illegible] The parish church is a spacious edifice of 1788 built in lieu of an ancient one about a mile distant The grammar school near the church, occupies the site of an hospital, founded in 1688 The workhouse was erected at a cost of £1 2[illegible]0 There are chapels for Presbyterians, Independents and Methodists The town has a post office‡ under Carlisle and two chief inns, and is a seat of petty sessions, and a polling place A weekly market is held on Wednesday and fairs on 20 April, Trinity Wednesday, the second Wednesday of Sept and 2[illegible] Oct Some cotton manufacture and extensive brewing are carried on A mineral railway goes to Tindal fell and a railway to [illegible] town was [illegible] in 18[illegible] Pop, 2 37[illegible] Houses, 51[illegible]

The township extends into the country Real property £10 742 Pop 2,[illegible] Houses, [illegible] The parish contains also the townships of Easby and Naworth Acres, 1[illegible],970 Real property, £1[illegible] 571 Pop 3,5[illegible] Houses, 7[illegible] The property is much subdivided The manor belongs to the Earl of Carlisle Naworth Castle is the Earl of Carlisle's seat, and was formerly that of the Dacre family Freestone is quarried A famous Roman inscription, noticed by Camden, is still visible on a rock overhanging the Gelt An ancient camp occurs on [illegible] hill, with very extensive views The living is a vicarage in the diocese of Carlisle Value, £[illegible] * Patron the Earl of Carlisle —The sub district contains the parishes of Brampton, Farlam, Nether Denton and Upper Denton, the extra parochial tract of Midgeholm and part of the parish of Lanercost Pop, [illegible],301 Houses, 1,0[illegible]7 The district comprehends also the sub district of Walton containing the parishes of Walton and Irthington, and part of the parish of Lanercost and the sub district of Hayton containing the parishes of Hayton, Cumrew, Cumwhitton, and Castle Carrock, the extra parochial tract of Geltsdale, and part of the parish of Wetheral Acres 95,178 Poor rates in 1866, £1[illegible] 188 Pop in 1861 10 [illegible] Houses, 2 179 Marriages in 1866, [illegible] births, 307,—of which 33 were illegitimate, deaths, 19[illegible],—of which 42 were at ages under 5 years, and 12 at ages above 8[illegible] Marriages in the ten years 1851-60 41[illegible], births, 3,211, deaths, 1,83[illegible] The places of worship in 1851, were 12 of the Church of England with 2,[illegible]57 sittings, 1 of the Presbyterian church in England with 200 s, 1 of Independents, with 2[illegible]0 s, and 1[illegible] of Wesleyan Methodists with 1,2[illegible]0 s The schools were 11 public day schools, with [illegible]2 scholars, 7 private day schools, with 392 s, and 15 Sunday schools, with 1 [illegible]03 s

BRAMPTON, a parish in Chesterfield district, Derby, 3½ miles W by N of Chesterfield r station It includes the village of Cutthorpe, and has two post offices, of the names of Old Brampton and New Brampton under Chesterfield Acres 8,[illegible]2[illegible] Real property, £10 141 Pop., 4 927 Houses, 1 05[illegible] The property is much subdivided Brampton Hall is the seat of the D[illegible] Coal and iron ore are found, and pottery ware, lace and stockings are manufactured The living is a vicarage in the diocese of Lichfield Value, £300 * Patron the Bishop of Lichfield The parish church is tolerable St Thomas's church is a Gothic structure with a tower, was erected in 18[illegible]2, at a cost of £2,930 and is served by a rector, with income of £300,* appointed by the bishop There are chapels for Independents, Wesleyans and Primitive Methodists an endowed school, two national schools and charities £71

BRAMPTON, a parish in the district and county of Huntingdon, on the river Ouse, near the Great Northern railway, 1½ mile WSW of Huntingdon It has a post office under Huntingdon Acres, 2 411 Real property £7,[illegible]47 Pop, 1 2[illegible]0 Houses [illegible] The property is divided among a few Brampton Park belonged to Sir John Barnard, who sat in the parliament which restored Charles II, was the birthplace of Samuel Pepys, secretary to the admiralty under Charles II and James II, and became the seat of Lady O[illegible] Sparrow The mansion was mostly rebuilt in 1820, and contains some fine family paintings The living is a vicarage in the diocese of Ely Value, £100 * Patron, the Bishop of [illegible] The church is later English, in very good condition; and has a monument to Sir John Barnard Charities, £[illegible]

BRAMPTON, a township in Torksey parish Lincoln on the river Trent, 7 miles S by E of Gainsborough Acres 790 Real property £1,[illegible]70 Pop 92 Houses, 1[illegible]

BRAMPTON, a parish in Aylsham district, Norfolk, on the river Bure and on the line of the projected railway from Norwich to Cromer, 2 miles SE of Aylsham and 11 N of Norwich Post town Aylsham, under Norwich Acres [illegible]21 Real property, £1,2[illegible]0 Pop, 1[illegible] Houses [illegible] The property is divided among a few Some Roman coins, urns, and other antiquities have been found The living is a rectory in the diocese of Norwich Value, £160 Patron, the Rev H [illegible] Marsham The church has a round tower, surmounted by an octagonal lanthorn and is very good

BRAMPTON, a parish in Blything district Suffolk on the East Suffolk railway [illegible] miles NE by N of Halesworth It has a station on the railway, and its post town is Great [illegible] under [illegible] Acres 2 00[illegible] Real property £3 [illegible]16 Pop, [illegible]10 Houses [illegible] Brampton Hall is the seat of the Rev G O Leman The living is a rectory in the diocese of Norwich Value, £[illegible]34 * Patron the Rev G O Leman The church is good and there are town lands £[illegible]

BRAMPTON, a township in Long Marton parish Westmoreland 2 miles N of Appleby Real property [illegible] 972 Pop., 301 The manor belonged to the Veteriponts, the Greystocks, the Lancasters, and the Burtons

BRAMPTON, a station on the Northampton and Market Harborough railway, 4½ miles N of Northampton

BRAMPTON, or BRAMPTON ASH, a parish in the district of Market Harborough and county of Northampton, near the Market Harborough and Belmont railway, 4 miles E by S of Market Harborough Post town, [illegible]barston, under Rugby Acres, 2,2[illegible] Real property, £3 2[illegible] Pop., 107 Houses 21 The property is divided among a few The living is a rectory in the diocese of Peterborough Value, £400 * Patron, Earl Spencer The church has two brasses and is good. Charities £6 Bishop Cumberland was some time rector

BRAMPTON ABBOTS, a parish in Ross district, Hereford on the river Wye, and on the Hereford and Gloucester railway, 1½ mile N of Ross Post town Ross Acres 1,152 Real property, £2,901 Pop 257 Houses, 49 The property is divided among a few Brampton Abbots House is the seat of the Garrolds The living is a rectory in the diocese of Hereford Value, £245 * Patron, the Bishop of Hereford The church is very good

BRAMPTON-ASH See BRAMPTON, Northampton

BRAMPTON BIERLOW, a village a township and a chapelry in Wath upon Dearne parish, W. R. Yorkshire The village stands adjacent to the South Yorkshire railway and to the Dove and Dearne canal, 2½ miles WNW of Wath r station, and 5 N of Rotherham The township includes also the hamlets of Coley Lane Cartwood Hoober New Mill, and West Melton, and part of the hamlet of Elsecar which has a post office under Rotherham Acres, 3 074 Real property £[illegible],221, of which £2,700 are in mines Pop., 1 938 Houses 374 The property is divided among a few There are iron foundries.—The chapelry was constituted in 1850, and is less extensive than the township Pop 1 733 Houses, 341 The living is a vicarage in the diocese of York Value, £150 Patron, the Vicar of Wath The church is very good There are an Independent chapel, a well endowed national school, and charities £76

BRAMPTON BRYAN, a village and a township in the district of Knighton and county of Hereford, and a parish partly also in the county of Radnor The village stands on the river Teme, 3 miles ESE of Knucklas r station and 10 W by S of Ludlow, and has a post-office, of the name of Brampton Bryan Herefordshire, and a fair on 21 and 22 June It dates from remote times, and had a castle built by the Normans or Brian de Brampton, held long by the Harleys and being besieged and destroyed by the royalists in the civil war.—The township includes the village Pop 158 Houses 29.—The parish contains also the townships of Boresford and Pedwardine and the lordship of Stanage Acres 5,51[illegible] Real property, with Pilleth and Coxall £6 [illegible] Pop 430 Houses 8[illegible] The property is divided among a few Brampton Park is the seat of the Earl of Oxford Coxwall Knoll has vestiges of a camp which was occupied by Caractacus [illegible] and has [illegible] by O Scapula The living is a rectory in the diocese of Hereford Value £300 * Patron, Lady Langdale The church was injured in the civil war and had long a ruined tower, but was beautified in 1870 by the erection of a new [illegible] and it contains the monuments of Lord Treasurer Harley, the founder of the Harleian library Charities £1[illegible]

BRAMPTON CHAPEL, a parish in Brixworth district, Northamptonshire, on an affluent of the river Nen, and on the Northampton and Market Harborough railway, adjacent to Brampton station, 4½ miles NNW of Northampton It has a post-office under Northampton Acres 1 230 Real property £2 11[illegible] Pop., 170 Houses 33 The church has been [illegible] remodelled

BRAMPTON CHURCH, or BRAMPTON MAGNA, a parish in Brixworth district, Northamptonshire, on an affluent of the river Nen, adjacent to the [illegible] W by S of Brampton r station and [illegible] miles NNW of Northampton Post town, Brampton, under Northampton Acres, 1 100 Real property £[illegible] Pop., 158 Houses 3[illegible] The property is not much divided Brampton Lodge is a chief residence The living is a rectory in the diocese of Peterborough Value, £316 Patron, Corpus Christi College, Oxford The church is decorated English and in good condition Charities, £25

BRAMPTON CROFTSEND, a village in Long Marton township and parish, Westmoreland, 3 miles N of Appleby

BRAMPTON-EN-LE-MORTHEN, a township in Treeton parish, W. R. Yorkshire, near the North Midland railway, 5 miles SE of Rotherham Acres, 1,0[illegible]0 Real property £1 511 Pop. 116 Houses 29

BRAMPTON (LITTLE), a township in Hopesay parish, Salop, 3½ miles SE of Bishops Castle It has a post office of the name of Little Brampton, Shropshire Pop 44

BRAMPTON (LITTLE), Hereford. See BODD[illegible] and LITTLE BRAMPTON

BRAMPTON MAGNA See BRAMPTON CHURCH

BRAMPTON (NEW and OLD) See BRAMPTON Derby

BRAMSHALL, a parish in Uttoxeter district Stafford on the North Stafford railway, 2 miles W of Uttoxeter It has a station on the railway, and includes the hamlet of Dunsdale, and its post town is Uttoxeter, under Derby Acres, 1 276 Real property, £1 [illegible] Pop 193 Houses, 35 The property is divided among a few The living is a rectory in the diocese of Lichfield Value £200 * Patron the Dowager Lady Willoughby de Broke The church is good, and there are church lands yielding £10 a year

BRAMSHALL (LITTLE) a hamlet in Uttoxeter parish Stafford contiguous to Bramshall parish

BRAMSHAW, a parish in the district of New Forest, and counties of Hants and Wilts, 5 miles SSW of Dunbridge r station, and 6½ NNW of Lyndhurst It includes the hamlets of Bramshaw and Furzley, and has a post office under Lyndhurst Acres [illegible],51[illegible] Real property, with West Wellow £3,194 Pop., 16[illegible] Houses, 16[illegible] The property is subdivided Bramshaw House is a chief residence The Hants portion amounting to 1 [illegible] acres, is all in the New Forest The living is a vicarage in the diocese of Salisbury Value £1[illegible] Patrons the Dean and Chapter of Salisbury The church has a neat, ancient, modernized structure, said to have been built by the Conqueror, and has a [illegible] brick, ivy clad tower

BRAMSHILL (GREAT and LITTLE) two tythings in Eversley parish, Hants, 3½ miles N by E of Winchfield Real property, £1 428 Pop. 171 Houses, [illegible] Bramshill House was built by the eleventh Lord Zouch as a residence for Prince Henry, son of James I, is now the seat of Sir William Cope and exhibits interesting features, both external and internal of the age in which it was erected The grounds around it are extensive and picturesque Abbot, archbishop of Canterbury, accidentally killed a man while shooting in the park and the Duke of Wellington once thought of it instead of Strathfieldsaye

BRAMSHOTT, a village and a parish in the district of Farnborough, and county of Hants The village stands near the verge of the county, 1 mile NW of Liphook r station, and 4 W of Haslemere, and has a post office under Liphook The parish is intersected by the Guildford and New Portsmouth railway and includes the hamlet of Liphook which has a head post office Acres, 6 676 Real property, £[illegible] Pop., 1 [illegible] Houses 280 The property is divided among a few Foley House is the seat of J [illegible] Esq. Some hundreds of Roman coins were found in 1741 in the bed of Woolmer pond, 1½ mile W of Liphook The living is a rectory in the diocese of Winchester Value, £78[illegible] Patron Queen's College, Oxford The church is ancient [illegible] early English [illegible] central tower [illegible] Norman [illegible] interesting brasses

BRAMWITH (KIRK), a parish in Doncaster district, W. R. Yorkshire, on the Stainforth and Keadby canal, and on the Doncaster and Keadby railway, [illegible] NE by N of Doncaster It has a station of the name of Bramwith, and includes the hamlets of

Fruthwaite and Hawkhouse Green, and part of the hamlet of Kirkhouse Green, and its post town is Stamforth, under Rotherham Acres, 1,260 Real property £2,[illegible] Pop, 226 Houses 54 The property is much subdivided The living is a rectory in the diocese of York Value £517 * Patron the Duchy of Lancaster The church is good

BRAMWITH (SAND), a hamlet in Stanforth township, Hatfield parish, W R Yorkshire, contiguous to Kirk Bramwith parish

BRAN (THE), a stream of Carmarthen It rises on the mountains at the boundary with Brecon, and runs about 11 miles south south eastward, past Trecastle, to the Towy, below Llandovery

BRANAR See MAIGHALAD and PLANAI

BRANCASTER, or BRANCESTER a village and a parish in Docking district, Norfolk The village stands on a small bay of its own name 4 miles NNW of Stanhoe r station and 6 E by N of Hunstanton, and has a post office,‡ of the name of Brancaster, under Lynn It occupies the site of the Roman station Branodunum, held by Dalmatian horse for repelling Saxon invaders, and it has furnished coins, urns, knives, and other Roman relics. It possesses a quay for vessels, and is a coast guard station, and there is a malt house adjacent to it, 312 feet long The parish comprises 3,672 acres of land, and 2,105 of water Real property £1,80[illegible] Pop., 1,002 Houses 243. The property is much subdivided The living is a rectory in the diocese of Norwich Value, £821 * Patron, the Rev C Birch The church is good, and there are a Wesleyan chapel and charities £91

BRANCEPETH, a township in Durham district and a parish in Durham and Auckland districts, Durham The township lies on the river Wear and on the Durham and Bishop Auckland railway 4 miles SW of Durham, and has a station on the railway, and a post office under Durham Acres 4,[illegible]15 Real property, £7,1[illegible]0, of which £3,597 are in mines Pop 1,[illegible]93 Houses, 266 The parish contains also the townships of Stockley Willington, Brandon and Byshottles, Tudhoe Hedley Hope, Helmington Row, and Crook and Billy Row Acres, 22,525 Real property, with Cornsay township, £77,151, of which £12,781 are in mines. Pop, 15 71[illegible] Houses, 2,893. The property is not much divided Brancepeth Castle was erected, in the reign of Stephen, by the family of Bulmer, passed to the Nevills and the Russells, and belongs now in right of his wife, to Viscount Boyne. It was rebuilt in 1821, but retains much of its prior appearance, and is a massive and splendid edifice A suite of rich armour, said to have been taken from David Bruce of Scotland at Nevill's Cross, is in the entrance hall, and a fine collection of antiquities and paintings is in the rooms The grounds and the adjacent country are picturesque Coal beds and sulphur springs occur, and coal and stone are worked The living is a rectory in the diocese of Durham Value £511 * Patron, R D Shafto, Esq The church is ancient and cruciform, has an early English tower and later English chancel and clerestory and contains an ancient stall work and chancel screen an ancient carved chest and a fine canopied font The rectories of Willington and Crook and the vicarage of Tudhoe, are separate benefices There are three dissenting chapels, a R Catholic Chapel, and charities £[illegible]2

BRANCH AND DOLE a hundred in the S of Wilts It contains Berwick parish fourteen other parishes and part of another Acres 3[illegible],76[illegible] Pop, 7,[illegible]48 Houses, 1,[illegible]

BRANCHESTER See BRANCASTER

BRANCHTHLIN See BRANSTEE

BRANDENBURGH HOUSE, a quondam mansion in Middlesex on the Thames adjacent to Hammersmith It was built, in the time of Charles I, by Sir Nicholas Crispe, at a cost of £23,000 sold by Crispe's heir to Prince Rupert passed to Mrs Margaret Hughes Bubb Dodington and the Margrave of Brandenburg-Anspach, became the residence and death place of the queen of George IV, and was soon after, razed to the ground

BRANDESBURTON, or BRANDSBURTON, a village, a township a parish and a sub district, in the district of Skirlaugh E R Yorkshire The village stands 6 miles E of Lockington r station, and 8 NE of Beverley and has a post office under Beverley It is a seat of petty sessions, and has a fair on 14 May —The township comprises 4,562 acres Real property, £6,798 Pop, 781 Houses 1[illegible]5 The parish includes also the township of Moor Town Acres, 5 060 Real property, £7,275 Pop, 811 Houses, 1[illegible]9 The property is divided among a few The manor was bequeathed in 1601, by Lady Dacres, to Emmanuel hospital, Westminster Brandesburton moor is a meet for the Holderness hounds The living is a rectory in the diocese of York Value £895 * Patron, St John's College Cambridge The church is ancient, and has two brasses of 13[illegible] There are an Independent chapel and an endowed school, and the latter has £25, other charities £1[illegible] —The sub district contains three parishes and parts of four others. Acres 12 8[illegible] Pop, 1,616 Houses 30[illegible]

BRANDESTON, a parish in Plomesgate district, Suffolk, on the river Deben 3½ miles SW of Framlingham r station and 5 NW by N of Wickham Market It has a post office under Wickham Market Acres, 1,224 Real property, £2,690 Pop, 46[illegible] Houses, [illegible]7 The property is divided among a few Brandeston Hall is a chief residence The living is a vicarage in the dio of Norwich Value, £[illegible]00 * Patron, C Austin, Esq The church is good There is an Independent chapel.

BRANDESTONE, or BRANDISTONE a parish in St Faith district, Norfolk 3 miles SE of Reepham, 6 W of the projected railway from Norwich to Cromer, and 11 NW by N of Norwich Post town, Foxley, under Norwich Acres 764 Real property, £1,40[illegible] Pop 181 Houses 3[illegible] The property is divided among five Brandeston Hall belonged formerly to the Atthills The living is a rectory in the diocese of Norwich Value, £150 * Patron, Magdalen College Oxford The church is good, and there are a national school, and charities £2[illegible]

BRANDISTONE Northampton See BRANSTON

BRANDLING RAILWAY, a railway in the N of Durham It connects the towns of Gateshead South Shields, and Sunderland, and makes a junction with the Newcastle and Carlisle railway, was opened in September 1839, took its name from the projector, Robert W Brandling, Esq of Low Gosforth, and is now incorporated with the Northeastern railway

BRANDON, a hamlet in Hough on the Hill parish, Lincoln, 7½ miles N of Grantham Pop, 11[illegible]

BRANDON a township in Eglingham parish, Northumberland, on the river Breamish, 8 miles SSE of Wooler Pop, 134 Houses, 22

BRANDON, a small town and a parish in the district of Thetford and partly in the county of Norfolk, but chiefly in the county of Suffolk The town stands on the Little Ouse river, adjacent to the Norfolk railway, 6 miles by road and 7½ by railway, NW by W of Thetford It has a head post office ‡ a railway station with telegraph, a banking office, three chief inns a parish church, four dissenting chapels, a free grammar school, and nine almshouses The church stands about ½ of a mile distant, is an ancient quadrangular edifice, of flint and stone, and has a Norman porch, a fine tower, and two cupolas A weekly market is held on Thursday, and fairs on 14 Feb, 11 June and 2[illegible] Nov A good grain trade is carried on and a manufactory of gun flints formed the sole source for the supply of these to government prior to the use of percussion caps The town gave name to the Dukes of Suffolk and the title of Baron to the Earls of Macclesfield, and it gives the title of Duke to the Dukes of Hamilton Lord Mayor Fyre of London who built Leadenhall market was a native Pop, 2 203 Houses 512 The parish comprises 6,759 acres Real property £7,0[illegible]1 Pop 2 21[illegible] Houses, 51[illegible] The property is subdivided Brandon Park is the seat of E Bliss Esq About 2 100 acres are fen, and there are extensive and productive rabbit warrens The living is a rectory, united with the rectory of Wangford in the diocese of Ely Value, £500 * Patron T F Cartwright Esq

BRANDON AND BRETFORD, a township in Wolston parish, Warwick, on the river Avon, and on the [illegible] Rugby railway, 5 miles E of Coventry. It has a station, of the name of Brandon, on the railway. Real property, £4,044. Pop, 31[illegible]. Houses, 1[illegible]. Here [illegible] castle, built soon after the Conquest, a small convent of [illegible] nuns, founded by [illegible] de Clinton, and given to Kenilworth priory, and a chapel [illegible] St Edmund, founded by the Turvilles, [illegible] of Wolston. Some traces of the castle still exist. Brandon Hall is the seat of the [illegible] family.

BRANDON AND BYSHOTTLES, a township in Brancepeth parish, Durham, near the Durham and Bishop Auckland railway, 3 miles SW by W of Durham. It has a station, of the name of Brandon. Acres, [illegible]. Real property, £11,[illegible], of which £5,812 are in mines. Pop, 1,[illegible]. Houses, 270. Brandon hill here has an altitude of 875 feet, is crowned with a tumulus, 120 yards in circumference and 24 feet high, and commands an extensive view.

BRANDON HILL. See Bristol.

BRANDON (Little), or Brandon Parva, a parish in Forehoe district, Norfolk, on the river Yare, 2 miles NNE of Hardingham station, and 5 NW by N of Wymondham. Post town, Wymondham. Acres, 97[illegible]. Real property, £1,886. Pop, 208. Houses 41. The property is subdivided. The living is a rectory in the diocese of Norwich. Value £281. Patron, Isaac Preston, Esq. The church was restored in 1861. An endowed school has £12, and other charities, £18.

BRANDSBURTON. See Brandesburton.

BRANDSBY WITH STEARSBY, or Bransby with Stearsby, a parish in Easingwold district, N R Yorkshire, [illegible] miles S of Ampleforth station, and 4 ENE of Easingwold. It has a post office, of the name of Brandsby, under York. Acres, 3,0[illegible]. Real property, £[illegible],071. Pop, 284. Houses, [illegible]. The property is divided among four. Brandsby Hall is the seat of [illegible] Cholmeley, Esq. The living is a rectory in the diocese of York. Value, £[illegible]28. Patron, [illegible] Cholmeley, Esq. The church is good, and there are a Roman Catholic chapel, and charities £7.

BRANDSHEL, a liberty in the parishes of Hitchenden, Great Missenden, and Little Missenden, Bucks, 3½ miles NNE of Wycombe.

BRANDWOOD HIGHER END and BRANDWOOD LOWER END, two hamlets in Spotland township, Lancashire, 4½ miles N of Rochdale.

BRANDY STREET, a hamlet in [illegible] parish, [illegible], 3½ miles W of Macclesfield. Pop, 2[illegible].

BRANFIELD. See Bramfield.

BRANKSEA. See Brownsea.

BRANKSTON. See Branxton.

BRANNOCKSTOWN. See Braunton.

BRANODUNUM. See Brancaster.

BRANSBURY, a tything in Barton Stacey parish, Hants, 4½ miles SE of Andover. Pop, 81.

BRANSBY, a hamlet in Stow parish, Lincolnshire, [illegible] NW of Lincoln. Acres 2[illegible]0. Real property, £673. Pop, [illegible]. Houses 1.

BRANSBY WITH STEARSBY. See Brandsby with Stearsby.

BRANSCOMBE, a village and a parish in Honiton district, Devon. The village stands on the coast 4[illegible] miles E of Sidmouth, and 5 S by E of Honiton station, and has a post office under Sidmouth. It is a straggling but very pleasant place, and contains many memorials of [illegible]. The parish comprises [illegible] acres of land [illegible]. Real property, £4,[illegible]. Pop, [illegible]. Houses 1[illegible]. The property is subdivided. The manor belonged, before the Conquest, to the Dean and Chapter [illegible] or [illegible], [illegible] of the village, [illegible] in the time of [illegible], of the [illegible] family, and the [illegible] of the [illegible] [illegible] the [illegible] of [illegible] College in [illegible]. The cliffs, at [illegible], [illegible] about the vicinity of the village, are [illegible] picturesque bulk. A small bay below the village, [illegible] the [illegible] of [illegible] mouth, [illegible] or calcedonies. The living is a vicarage in the diocese of Exeter. Value, £1[illegible]. Patrons, the Dean and Chapter of Exeter. The church is cruciform, and partly Norman, partly English, has a central tower in disrepair, and contains an ancient monument with two kneeling effigies.

BRANSDALE, a mountain vale in N R Yorkshire. It commences at the S side of Botton Head mountain, 7 miles SE by S of Stokesley, and extends 12 miles south south eastward to the southern vicinity of Kirkby Moorside.

BRANSDALE EAST SIDE, a hamlet in Kirkby Moorside parish, N R Yorkshire, in Bransdale, 9 miles N by E of Helmsley. Acres, 2,7[illegible]0. Pop, 134.

BRANSDALE WEST SIDE, a township in Kirkdale parish, N R Yorkshire, in Bransdale, 8 miles N of Helmsley. Acres, 4,905. Pop, 7[illegible]. Houses 14.

BRANSFORD, a chapelry in Leigh parish, Worcestershire, on the river Teme, adjacent to the Malvern railway, 4[illegible] miles SW by W of Worcester. It has a station, of the name of Bransford Road, on the railway, and its post town is Powick, under Worcester. Acres 1,[illegible]. Real property, £[illegible],118. Pop, 27[illegible]. Houses 5[illegible]. The property is much subdivided. The living is a vicarage in the diocese of Worcester, annexed to [illegible] Earl Somers. The church is good.

BRANSGORE, a chapelry in Christchurch parish, Hants, near the river Avon, and the Christchurch branch railway, [illegible] miles NNE of Christchurch. Post town, Christchurch. Statistics returned with the parish. The living is a p. curacy in the diocese of Winchester. Value £73. Patron, T [illegible]esson, Esq.

BRANSIL CASTLE, a ruin on the eastern verge of Herefordshire, under the Malvern hills, in the vicinity of Ledbury. The castle was doubly trenched, and had a tower at each angle, and the ruin commands a fine view.

BRANSON. See Branston, Lincoln, and Branstone.

BRANSTON, Branstone, or Braunston, a parish in Melton Mowbray district, Leicester, 7 miles N of [illegible] station, and 8 NNE of Melton Mowbray. It has a post office under Grantham. Acres, 9[illegible]0. Real property, £2,603. Pop, 297. Houses, 57. The property is divided among a few. The living is a rectory in the diocese of Peterborough. Value £250. Patron, the Duke of Rutland. The church is very good.

BRANSTON, or Branson, a parish in the district and county of Lincoln, [illegible] miles SE of Lincoln station. It includes a fen allotment, and has a post office under Lincoln. Acres, [illegible]. Real property, £[illegible]. Pop, 1,[illegible]. Houses, 2[illegible]3. The property is much subdivided. The living is a rectory in the diocese of Lincoln. Value £[illegible]77. Patron the Rev. B Curtois. The church is pretty good, and there are two Methodist chapels, a Church school, and charities £2[illegible].

BRANSTONE, or Branson, a township in Burton upon Trent parish, Stafford, on [illegible] the Grand Trunk canal, and the Midland railway, 2 miles SW of Burton upon Trent. It has a post office under Burton upon Trent. Acres, 1,[illegible]. Real property, £4,[illegible]. Pop, [illegible]. Houses, 111.

BRANSTREET HILL, a mountain 2½ miles S of the head of Haweswater, in Westmoreland.

BRANSWELL. See Brauncewell.

BRANT (The), a stream of Lincolnshire. It rises a little SW of Normanton, and runs [illegible] to the river Witham [illegible] miles SSW of Lincoln.

BRANTBROUGHTON. See Broughton (Brant).

BRANT FELL, an eminence [illegible] mile [illegible] of Bowness, in Westmoreland. It commands one of the noblest and most comprehensive views of Windermere.

BRANTFIELD. See [illegible].

BRANTHAM, a parish in Samford district, Suffolk, on the river Stour, and on the [illegible] railway, 2 miles NNE of Manningtree station, and [illegible] SSW of Ipswich. It has a post office under Manningtree. Acres, [illegible]482, of which [illegible] are water. Real property, £[illegible]. Pop, [illegible]. Houses, [illegible]. The property is subdivided among a few. The living is a rectory in the diocese of Norwich. Value [illegible]. Patron, Emmanuel College, Cambridge. The church is good.

BRANTHWAITE, a township with a r station, in Dean parish Cumberland on the Cleator railway, 5 miles SE of Workington Real property £2 529 Pop., 231 Houses, 58 Stone is quarried, and there are paper and woollen mills, and a Methodist chapel

BRANTINGHAM, a township and a parish in Beverley district, E R Yorkshire The township lies 2½ miles N by E of Brough station, and 11 W by N of Hull Real property, £2 720 Pop, 231 Houses, 55 —The parish contains also the townships of Ellerker and Thorpe-Brantingham, the latter of which has a post office under Brough Acres, 3,632, of which 592 are water Rated property, £6,749 Pop 572 Houses 124 The property is divided among a few The living is a vicarage united with the p curacy of Ellerker, in the diocese of York. Value £255 * Patrons, the Dean and Chapter of Durham The church is fair

BRANTINGTHORPE. See BRUNTINGTHORPE.

BRANTON, a township in Eglingham parish, Northumberland, 9½ miles SSE of Wooler Acres, 1,1 7 Pop, 106 Houses, 19 Here is a dissenting chapel

BRANTON, a hamlet in Cantley parish, W R Yorkshire, 2 miles SE of Doncaster

BRANTON GREEN See DUNSFORTH (UPPER)

BRANTWOOD, a villa, with charming grounds, on the E side of Coniston water, in Lancashire A seat in the grounds was the poet Wordsworth s favourite point for viewing the lake, and bears the name of Wordsworth s seat

BRANXTON, a parish in Glendale district, Northumberland, on the skirts of the Cheviots and the river Till, 3 miles ESE of Cornhill station, and 9 NW by N of Wooler Post town, Etal, under Coldstream. Acres, 1,487 Real property, £2 3 2 Pop, 255 Houses, 41 The property is divided between two Here is the field of the battle of Flodden fatal to James IV of Scotland, fought in 1513 See FLODDEN The living is a vicarage in the diocese of Durham Value, £234 Patrons, the Dean and Chapter of Durham The church is good Stockdale, the poet, was a native

BRASCOTE a hamlet in Newbold Verdon parish, Leicester, 2 miles ESE of Market Bosworth Pop, 40 Houses, 10

BRASHFIELD See BRAISHFIELD

BRASIL BANK, a sea bank of the mouth of the Mersey in Lancashire on the N side of the Rock channel, 1 mile W of the lighthouse

BRASSACOTT a hamlet in North Petherwin parish, Devon, 5½ miles NW of Launceston

BRASSINGTON, a township-chapelry and a sub district, in the district of Ashborne, Derby The chapelry is in Bradbourne parish, lies 4 miles W by N of Wirksworth, and 7 WSW of Cromford r station, and has a post office under Wirksworth Real property £6 5 2 Pop 713 Houses 163 The property is subdivided Brassington Hall is a chief residence Slate tiles, from a peculiar kind of grey clay, are manufactured The living is a vicarage in the diocese of Lichfield Value £55.* Patron, the Rev J B Littler The church is partly Norman, and was repaired in 1858 There are three dissenting chapels and a free school — The sub-district contains three parishes parts of three others and an extra parochial tract Pop, 4,470.

BRASS KNOCKER, a locality 2½ miles from Bath, with a post office under Bath

BRASTED, a village and a parish in Sevenoaks district Kent The village stands on the river Darent, 4 miles WNW of Sevenoaks and 5½ N of Edenbridge station, and has a post office under Sevenoaks, and fairs on Ascension day and 25 Sept —The parish comprises 4 1 acres Real property, £ 87 Pop 1,1 2 Houses 212 Brasted Park is the seat of William Tipping Esq and was once the retreat of Louis Napoleon The land lies on the edge of the Weald, and has fine views Pig iron ills are on the Darent The living is a rectory in the diocese of Canterbury Value, £673 Patron the Archbishop of Canterbury The church internally is chiefly early English, externally, of various characters. There are a Calvinist chapel, a national school, and charities £31

BRATHAY (THE), a stream of Westmoreland and Lancashire It rises on the Stake mountain, and runs 9 miles east south eastward to the head of Windermere. It traverses Great Langdale expands into Elter water, makes a fall of about 20 feet, a little below that lake and is joined by the Rothay, a few yards from Windermere Char and trout enter its mouth from Windermere, and all the char go up the Brathay, while all the trout go up the Rothay

BRATHAY a chapelry in Hawkshead parish Lancashire, on Brathay river and Windermere lake, 2 miles SW of Ambleside, and 7½ by road from Windermere r station Post town, Ambleside, under Windermere It was constituted in 1853. Pop, 212 Houses, 40 Brathay Hall is the seat of G Redmayne, Esq The scenery around Brathay Bridge, taken in connexion with its perspectives, is surpassingly rich The living is a vicarage in the diocese of Carlisle Value, £142 Patron G Redmayne Esq The church is a recent erection, on a wooded knoll, in the neighbourhood of Brathay-Bridge

BRATOFT, or BRAYTOFT, a parish in Spilsby district, Lincoln, on the East Lincoln railway 1 mile SW of Burgh station, and 4½ E by S of Spilsby Post town Burgh, under Boston Acres, 1,811 Real property £3 073 Pop, 280 Houses, 57 The property is much subdivided The living is a rectory in the diocese of Lincoln Value, £255 * Patron, the Lord Chancellor The church comprises nave and aisles, with clerestory, contains an ancient font, and has, over the chancel arch, a contemporary painting of the defeat of the Armada

BRATTLEBY, a parish in the district and county of Lincoln, on the Wolds, 4½ miles NE of Saxilby r station and 7 NNW of Lincoln Post town, Hackthorn, under Lincoln Acres 1,229 Real property, £1,920 Pop 153 Houses 28 The property is all in one estate The living is a rectory in the diocese of Lincoln Value, £ 60 Patron, Balliol College, Oxford The church is good

BRATTON, a chapelry in Westbury parish Wilts 3 miles ENE of Westbury r station It has a post office under Westbury Rated property £4 190 Pop, 744 Houses, 170 The property is much subdivided Bratton Castle, on the crown of a hill is an ancient camp of 23 acres, partly defended by a double rampart in some parts 35 feet high, and said to have been constructed by the Danes. The White Horse, on the S slope below the camp is a colossal figure similar to the White Horse of Berks probably ancient, and originally of rude design but remodelled in 1778 The living is a vicarage in the diocese of Salisbury Value £300 * Patron, the Vicar of Westbury Charities, £3

BRATTON, a township in Wrockwardine parish Salop, 2 miles W of Wellington

BRATTON, North Salop See BOLLATION

BRATTON CLOVELLY a village, a parish and a sub district, in the district of Okehampton Devon The village stands 8 miles WSW of Okehampton r station and 12 N by W of Tavistock, is large and scattered, and has a post office under Lew Down, North Devon The parish comprises 8 316 acres Real property, £6,0 4 Pop, 70 Houses, 147 The property is much subdivided The manor bore anciently the name of Bracton and was the birthplace of Henry de Bracton, the eminent lawyer of the time of Edward I An ancient earthwork called Broadbury Castle defended by vallum and fosse is on an eminence about 3 miles N of the village About 2,000 acres of the land are common The living is a rectory in the diocese of Exeter Value, £41 * Patron the Bishop of Exeter The church is a fine edifice of the 15th century with a lofty tower, and has a handsome font — The sub-district contains five parishes. Acres, 23 663 Pop, 2 5 Houses, 4

BRATTON FLEMING a parish in Barnstaple district Devon, on an affluent of the river Taw, 6 miles NE of Barnstaple r station Post town Shirwell under Barn staple Acres, 5,847 Real property, £[illegible] 549 Pop, 688 Houses, 1[illegible] The property is much subdivided The manor belonged anciently to the Fleming family, passed to the Dillons, and belongs now to Sir Arthur Chichester Part of the surface is hilly Six standing stones occur at Nighiscott, and are supposed to have been part of a Druidical circle The parish is a meet for the North Devon hounds The living is a rectory in the diocese of Exeter Value £[illegible] Patron Caius College, Cambridge The church is perpendicular English, consists of nave, chancel, and north aisle, with a tower, and was restored in 1861 There is a small Baptist chapel

BRATTON SEYMOUR, or BRATTON ST MAUR, a parish in Wincanton district, Somerset, 2[illegible] miles NW of Wincanton r station, and [illegible] SE of Castle Cary Post town, Wincanton, under Bath Acres, 1,0[illegible] Pop, 80 Houses 21 The living is a rectory in the diocese of Bath and Wells Value, £161 Patrons, Sir M Lopes and J Hodges Esq, alternately The church stands on a green eminence overhanging a dell

BRAUGHIN, a village, a parish, a sub district and a hundred in Herts The village stands on the river Quin, adjacent to Ermine street and to the Buntingford railway, 3½ miles SE by S of Buntingford, and has a station on the railway, and a post office under Ware It was a domain of the Saxon kings, was known to the Saxons as Brochung, and to the Normans as Brachinges, and was long a place of considerable importance, and a market town It has now a fair on Whit Monday Vestiges of the Roman Ad Fines are at Campwood in its neighbourhood The parish includes also part of the hamlet of Puckeridge Acres, 4,300 Real property £7,000 Pop, 1,18[illegible] Houses 240 The property is divided among a few The living is a vicarage in the diocese of Rochester Value, £2[illegible]0 Patrons the heirs of the late Rev W [illegible]owe The church contains monuments of the Brograves and is good There are an Independent chapel, an almshouse and charities £2[illegible] —The sub district is in Bishop Stortford district, and contains five parishes Acres, 1[illegible],246 Pop, 2,912 Houses, [illegible] The hundred contains thirteen parishes Acres, [illegible] Pop, 20,[illegible]31 Houses 4,121

BRAUNCEWELL WITH DUNSBY, or BRANSWELL-WITH-DUNSBY, a parish in Sleaford district, Lincoln, 4½ miles NNW of Sleaford r station Post town, Sleaford Acres, 3,470 Real property, £4,828 Pop, 112 Houses 18 The property is divided among a few The living is a rectory, united with the vicarage of Anwick in the diocese of Lincoln Value, £71[illegible] Patrons alternately the Marquis of Bristol and Mrs [illegible] Robinson The church is good

BRAUNSTON, Leicester See BRANSTON

BRAUNSTON, or BRANTSTONE, two villages and a parish in Daventry district, Northampton The lower village stands at the junction of the Oxford and the Grand Junction canals, 2½ miles NW of Daventry, and 4 SW of [illegible] r station, and has a post office‡ under Rugby The Braunston village [illegible] ¾ of a mile to the [illegible] Braunston parish comprises [illegible] 930 acres Real property £8[illegible] Pop 1,[illegible]28 Houses 2[illegible] The property is much subdivided The Grand Junction canal here passes through a tunnel 1[illegible] mile long The living is a rectory in the diocese of Peterborough Value £[illegible]7 Patron Jesus College, Oxford The church was rebuilt in 1849 There are a Baptist and Wesleyan chapels, an endowed national school and charities £2[illegible] Bishop [illegible] was sometime rector

BRAUNSTON, or BRANSTON, a parish in Oakham district Rutland, on the river Gwash, 2[illegible] miles SW of Oakham r station It has a post office under Oakham Acres [illegible] Real property, £2,[illegible] Pop [illegible] Houses 101 Braunston Lodge is a chief residence The living is a [illegible] curacy annexed to the vicarage of Hambleton in the diocese of Peterborough There are a Baptist chapel and charities [illegible]

BRAUNSTONE, a chapelry in Glenfield parish Leicester, on the river Wreak and the Union canal, adjacent to the Midland railway [illegible] miles, 2 miles SW of Leicester Post town Leicester Acres 1,610 Real property, £[illegible] 018 Pop 197 Houses 37 Braunstone Frith, [illegible] extra-parochial liberty adjoining on the NE, is included in the returns, and contains Braunstone Hall, formerly belonging to the Hastings family, and now the seat of C Winstanley, Esq The living is a p curacy, annexed to the rectory of Glenfield in the diocese of Peterborough

BRAUNSTON (LITTLE) See BRAUNSTON Northampton

BRAUNTON, a village, a parish, a sub district and a hundred in Devon The village stands near the mouth of the river Taw, 5 miles WNW of Barnstaple r station is a considerable place, with several streets and many shops, and has a post office under Barnstaple It was originally called Brannock's town, and took that name from St Brannock, a prince of Calabria, who came hither in the year 300 [illegible] The parish comprises 10,173 acres of land and 1,[illegible]0 of water Real property £11,236 Pop, 2,[illegible] Houses 472 The property is much subdivided There are several manors and one of them belonged in Edward the Confessor's time to the Crown, and was afterwards given to St Peter's, Exeter St Brannock's House at the upper end of the village, Franklin's Cottage, a short distance thence, and a number of other places command magnificent views An extensive tract between the village and the sea, called Braunton Field, is noted for fertility A tract of blown sand on the coast, called Braunton Burrows, has witnessed many shipwrecks, and possesses two lighthouses 933 feet apart, erected in 18[illegible], with fixed lights 86 and 40 feet high, for directing vessels over Barnstaple bar An ancient chapel, called St Anne's, is embedded in the burrows, and remains of another ascribed to St Brannock crown a neighbouring hill The living is a vicarage in the diocese of Exeter Value £4[illegible]0 Patron, the Bishop of Exeter The church is early English in a [illegible] condition, and was proposed to be restored in 1860 There are chapels of Independents and Methodists A school has £7[illegible] from endowment, and other charities £23 [illegible] the missionary was a native —The sub district is in the district of Barnstaple, and contains seven parishes Acres [illegible] Pop 6,937 Houses 1,47[illegible] —The hundred contains [illegible] parishes Acres, 71,152 Pop 14,7[illegible] Houses 10[illegible]

BRAWBY, a township in Salton parish N R Yorkshire, on the river Rye, [illegible] miles NNW of New Malton A fair is held on the Monday after 11 July Acres, [illegible],080 Real property £1,[illegible]73 Pop, 215 Houses 42

BRAWDY, a parish in Haverfordwest district, Pembroke, on the coast [illegible] miles E of St David's and 9 NW by N of Haverfordwest r station Post town, Roch, under Haverfordwest Acres, [illegible]491 of which 60 are water Real property, £[illegible]103 Pop 614 Houses, 133 The property is much subdivided The living is a vicarage united with the vicarage of Hays Castle in the diocese of St David's Value £115 Patron, the Bishop of St David's

BRAWITH See KNAYTON WITH BRAWITH

BRAXTED (GREAT), a parish in Witham district, Essex on the river Blackwater adjacent to the Eastern Counties railway, 2[illegible] miles ENE of Witham Post town Witham Acres 2,0[illegible]1 Real property £[illegible] Pop 384 Houses 86 [illegible] Braxted [illegible] stood at [illegible] the time of Edward [illegible] The living is a [illegible] in the diocese of Rochester Value, £[illegible] Patron, Corpus Christi College, Cambridge The church [illegible] some Norman portions, and is good Charities, 1[illegible]

BRAXTED (LITTLE), a parish in Witham district, Essex on the river Blackwater, adjacent to the Eastern Counties railway [illegible] of Witham Post town Witham Acres 5[illegible] Real property, £1[illegible]7 Pop 111 Houses 2[illegible] The property is divided among a few The living is a [illegible] in the diocese of Rochester Value £115 Patron [illegible] Sir W [illegible] Bush The church is good [illegible] £7

BRAY, a village, a parish, a sub-district, and a hundred in Cookham district, Berks. The village stands on the Thames, near the Great Western railway, 1½ mile S by E of Maidenhead; and has a post office under Maidenhead. It occupies the site of the Roman station Bibracte, and is now within the liberty of Windsor forest.—The parish consists of the four divisions of Bray, Maidenhead, Touchen, and Water Oakley; and contains part of the borough of Maidenhead. Acres, 9,102. Real property, £26,694. Pop., 4,801. Houses, 9[illegible]8. The property is much subdivided. Bray Wick Lodge and Bray Grove are chief residences. Ockwells is an old seat; and Cresswells, formerly Filberts, was the place of Nell Gwynne's residence. Jesus Hospital, founded in 1627 by William Goddard for 44 persons, is a picturesque brick quadrangle with an old chapel. Monkey Island, about a mile SE of the village, contains a decayed fishing house, built by the third Duke of Marlborough, the drawing room of which was grotesquely decorated with paintings of monkeys. The living is a vicarage, united with the p. curacy of Touchen End, in the diocese of Oxford. Value, £500.* Patron, the Bishop of Oxford. The church is early English and decorated, has a much later square tower, and was repaired and altered in 1859. Boyne Hill vicarage is a separate benefice. There are a chapel of ease built in 1861, a Wesleyan chapel, two national schools, an endowed hospital, forming a square of [illegible]0 houses with a chapel, and other charities £43. Archbishop Laud had a farm in the parish; and Simon Aleyn, notable for having repeatedly changed his creed from popery to protestantism, and from protestantism to popery, was vicar in four reigns, and died in 1588. An old ballad represents him as saying,—

"And this is law, I will maintain
Until my dying day, sir,
That, whatsoever king shall reign,
I'll be the vicar of Bray, sir."

The sub-district contains four parishes. Acres, 16,462. Pop., 6,714. Houses, 1,320.—The hundred is of less extent than Bray parish. Pop., 2,935. Houses, 580.

BRAYBROOKE, a village and a parish in the district of Market Harborough and county of Northampton. The village stands near the Leicester and Bedford railway, 3 miles SSE of Market Harborough; and has a post office under Market Harborough. It gives the title of Baron to the family of Neville Griffin.—The parish comprises 3,060 acres. Real property, £4,923. Pop., 438. Houses, 99. The property is divided among a few. The manor belonged to the Griffins, ancestors of Lord Braybrooke, and had a castle. The living is a rectory in the diocese of Peterborough. Value, £600.* Patron, the Rev. J. W. Field. The church contains effigies of Sir T. Latimer and Sir N. Griffin, and is good. There are a baptist chapel and charities £21. Robert de Braybrooke, Lord Chancellor at the beginning of the 14th century, was a native.

BRAYDON, a hamlet in Purton parish, Wilts, 4½ miles S by W of Cricklade. Acres, 1,478. Pop., 19. Houses, 11.

BRAYE. See ARDLEY and EATON BRAY.

BRAYFIELD (COLD), a parish in Newport Pagnell district, Bucks, on the river Ouse, 3½ miles E of Olney, and 7 W by S of Oakley station. Post town, Turvey, under Bedford. Acres, 630. Real property, £1,2[illegible]0. Pop., 99. Houses, 18. The property is divided among a few. The living is a p. curacy annexed to the vicarage of Lavendon, in the diocese of Oxford. The church is good.

BRAYFORD, a hamlet in Charles parish, Devon; 9 miles E NE of Barnstaple. It has a baptist chapel.

BRAY (HIGH). See HIGHBRAY.

BRAYSTONES, a hamlet in Lowside Quarter township, St Bees parish, Cumberland; on the Whitehaven and Furness railway, 3 miles S of Egremont. It has a station on the railway.

BRAYTHORN, a hamlet in Stainburn township, Kirkby Overblow parish, W. R. Yorkshire; 3½ miles NE of Otley.

BRAYTOFT. See BRATOFT.

BRAYTON, a village in Aspatria parish, Cumberland; adjacent to the Carlisle and Maryport railway, 2 miles E by N of Aspatria. It has a station on the railway. Brayton Hall, in the vicinity, is the seat of Sir W. Lawson, Bart.

BRAYTON, a township and a parish in Selby district, W. R. Yorkshire. The township lies on the Selby canal, between the rivers Ouse and Aire, and on the Leeds and Selby railway, 1½ mile SSW of Selby. Acres, 1,790. Real property, £2,976. Pop., 367. Houses, 80. The parish contains also the townships of Gateforth, Hambleton, Thorpe Willoughby, Burn, and Barlow; and its post town is Selby. Acres, 10,820. Real property, £15,983. Pop., 1,794. Houses, 3[illegible]6. The property is much subdivided. The living is a vicarage in the diocese of York. Value, £355.* Patron, the Archbishop of York. The church is of various dates and character, from Norman downward; consists of nave, aisles, and chancel, with lofty west steeple; shows much beautiful Norman work; is in very good condition; and contains a fine sculptured font of 1861. The chapelries of Gateforth and Barlow are separate benefices. There are a Wesleyan chapel, and charities £11.

BREADSALL, a parish in Shardlow district, Derbyshire; on the Little Eaton canal and the Midland railway, 2½ miles NNE of Derby. It has a post office under Derby. Acres, 2,410. Real property, £4,111. Pop., 592. Houses, 135. The property is divided among a few. A fine building stone is quarried. A small priory was founded by the Dethicks in the time of Henry III.; was given, at the dissolution, to the Duke of Suffolk; passed to Sir John Bentley, to Erasmus Darwin, and to Sir Francis Darwin; was purchased, in the present century, by Francis Morley, Esq.; underwent, in 1861, extensive restoration; and is now a beautiful specimen of pointed architecture, with a tower 70 feet high, commanding a view to Lichfield cathedral. The living is a rectory in the diocese of Lichfield. Value, £5[illegible].* Patron, Sir [illegible] H. Crewe, Bart. The church is decorated English in good condition. There are a Wesleyan chapel, an endowed national school, and charities £70. Hutton, the abridger of Poole's "Synopsis," was rector; and Dr Darwin, the naturalist, was a resident.

BREADSTONE, a tything in Berkeley parish, Gloucester; 2 miles NE of Berkeley. Pop., 12[illegible]. Houses, [illegible].

BREAGE, or St BREACA,—pronounced Braig,—a village, a parish, and a sub-district in the district of Helston, Cornwall. The village stands on the coast, [illegible] miles W of Helston, and 6½ S by E of Crowan Road r. station; and has a post office under Helston, and a fair on 19 June. It is said to have been founded by the Irish St Breaca. The parish comprises 7,036 acres of land and 105 of water. Real property, £12,212; of which £4,883 are in mines. Pop., 5,173. Houses, 1,0[illegible]7. Much of the property belonged formerly to the Godolphin family, and belongs now to the Duke of Leeds. Godolphin mansion is now used as a farm house. Godolphin hill and Tregonning hill rise to altitudes of 4[illegible]3 and [illegible]6 feet, consist of granite, and are rich in minerals. China clay is worked out of part of Godolphin hill, and sent to neighbouring ports for shipment. Huel Vor or Wheal Vor tin mine is in the same hill, has been worked in lodes 30 feet wide, extends upwards of 1½ mile under ground, and has yielded, at times, clear profits of £10,000 in [illegible] months. The living is a vicarage, with Germoe, in the diocese of Exeter. Value, £[illegible]. Patron, the Crown. The church contains [illegible] monuments of the Godolphins. The vicarages of Godolphin and [illegible] of Cury and Gunwalloe are separate benefices. Charities, £8. Lord Treasurer Godolphin was a native.—The sub-district includes also the parish of Germoe. Acres, 8,[illegible]18. Pop., 6,18[illegible]. Houses, 1,2[illegible].

BREAKSEA POINT. See ATHAN (St).

BREAM, or BREAME, a tything in Newland parish, and a chapelry in Newland and West Dean parishes, Gloucester. The tything lies in Dean forest, [illegible] NW of Lydney r. station, and 3[illegible] SSW of Coleford. Pop., 824. Houses, 151. The chapelry was constituted in

1854, and its post town is Lydney. Pop 2,083. Houses, 401. The property is much subdivided. The living is a vicarage in the diocese of Gloucester and Bristol. Value, £200.* Patron, the Bishop. The church was partly rebuilt in 1861. There are two Methodist chapels. National schools were built in 1862.

BREAMORE, or BROMORE, a parish and a liberty in Fordingbridge district, Hants, on the river Avon, and on the Salisbury and Dorset railway, 7 miles S of Salisbury. It includes Outwick, and has a post office under Salisbury, and a r station. Acres, 2,651. Real property, £4,081. Pop 565. Houses 115. The manor belongs to Sir Charles Hulse, Bart. Breamore House, the baronet's seat, was burnt down in 1856. A priory of black canons was founded in the time of Henry I, by Baldwin, Earl of Devon, and given, at the dissolution, to the Marquis of Exeter. The living is a donative in the diocese of Winchester. Value, £410. Patron, the Rev. J. N. Palmer. The church is ancient and good. Charities, £11.—The liberty is in Ringwood division, and conterminate with the parish.

BREANT, a parish in Axbridge district, Somerset, on the river Axe and on the coast, 4 miles SW by S of Weston super Mare Junction r station, and 8 W of Axbridge. Post town, Lympsham under Weston super Mare. Acres, 3,167, of which 2,000 are water. Real property, £2,350. Pop 145. Houses 27. The property is divided among a few. Brean Down is 300 feet high, and projects into a promontory 1½ mile long, westward from the mouth of the river Axe. Cliffs with abundance of sea plants, are on the coast, and a great extent of sandy beach lies below. An act was passed in 1862 for the construction of harbour, piers or jetties, at Brean Down, and for the formation of a railway thence to the Bristol and Exeter railway. The living is a rectory in the diocese of Bath and Wells. Value, £210.* Patron, W. Wales, Esq. The church is good.

BREARLEY, a hamlet in Addle parish, W. R. Yorkshire, 4½ miles ESE of Otley.

BREARLEY. See BRIERLEY.

BREARTON, a chapelry in Knaresborough parish, W. R. Yorkshire, 3 miles NW of Knaresborough. It became a separate charge in 1866. Pop, 275. Living, a vicarage. Value, £200. The church was built in 1839.

BREASTON, Durham. See BRIERTON.

BREASTON, a chapelry in Wilne parish, Derbyshire, on the Derby canal and the Midland railway, ½ a mile NW of Sawley station, and 8 ESE of Derby. Post town, Sawley, under Derby. Real property, £3,592. Pop, 709. Houses, 161. The property is much subdivided. The living is a rectory, united with the rectory of Risley, in the diocese of Lichfield. Value, £390. Patron, the Bishop of Lichfield. The church is good, and there are two Methodist chapels, and charities [illegible].

BREATHING HILLS, a hamlet in [illegible] Knowle parish, Lincoln, 2 miles W of Grantham.

BRECHFA, a parish in the district and county of Carmarthen, on the river Cothy, 8 miles NW by W of Llandilo r station, and [illegible] NE of Carmarthen. Post town, Llanarthney, under Carmarthen. Acres, [illegible]. Real property, [illegible]. Pop 122. Houses, 26. The property is subdivided. The living is a rectory in the diocese of St Davids. Value, £72. Patron, the [illegible]. The church is good. Fairs are held on the [illegible] 13 May, and on 3 [illegible] Oct.

BRECKENBROUGH. See NEWBY [illegible].

BRECKLES, a parish in Wayland district, Norfolk, [illegible] miles N by W of [illegible] station, and [illegible] of Watton. Post town, [illegible] under [illegible]. Acres, 1,810. Real property, £1,[illegible]. Pop, 12[illegible]. Houses, [illegible]. The property is all in one [illegible]. The living is a vicarage in the diocese of Norwich. Value, £[illegible]. [illegible] The church [illegible].

BRECKLES (LITTLE), [illegible] parish, Norfolk, [illegible] SSE of Watton. [illegible]

BRECKNOCK, or BRECON, a town, two parishes, a sub district, and a district in Brecknockshire. The town stands at the confluence of the Honddu and the Usk, 18 miles E by S of Llandovery, and 19½ WNW of Abergavenny. A canal connects it with Abergavenny and the sea, a railway connecting it with Merthyr-Tydvil, was opened in 1863; another railway, to connect it with Hereford, and with junction lines N and S, was opened in 1863, and another, to connect it with Neath and with the Central Wales, was opened to Brecknock in 1864. It was anciently called Brycheiniog, and is now sometimes called Aberhonddu. The ancient Britons had a port or town on its site; the Romans built a station at Caer Bannau, on the Via Julia Montana, in its western neighbourhood, and the native princes long continued to make it a centre of strength, and were called from it Princes of Brycheiniog. Bernard de Newmarch, a Norman baron, obtained from the English crown, in 1092, a grant of a large tract around it, took possession of this by force of arms, and built at the town, in 1094, a strong castle to maintain his power. The castle passed to the Braoses and the Bohuns, and was eventually resumed by the Crown, and, together with strong walls and other fortifications which were erected around the town, it was used for ages to repress the turbulence of the native tribes, and both it and the town walls were dismantled by the towns people in the civil war of the 17th century, to avert the horror of the siege. The keep of the castle was made the prison of Morton, Bishop of Ely, under charge of the crafty Duke of Buckingham, and became the scene of the intrigue of these two dignitaries to dethroning Richard III and enthroning Henry VII, and hence is called the Ely tower. Buckingham's motive for joining in the intrigue is alleged to have been resentment of what he thought too small reward from Richard, and therefore is he represented as saying,—

> "And is it thus? Repays he my deep service
> With such contempt? Made I him king for this?
> O let me think on Hastings and be gone
> To Brecknock while my fearful head is on."

The town lies in the heart of the grandest part of South Wales. The tract around it is an assemblage of hills and mountains, picturesque by nature and embellished by art, with the two Alpine peaks, called the Brecknock beacons, culminating 6 miles to the SSW. The town consists chiefly of three streets on the left bank of the Usk, and the flat suburb of Llanfaes on the right bank, and is altogether about a mile long. The remains of the ancient castle, consisting of two square towers in the garden of the castle hotel, not older than the time of Edward III, and of the lofty mound on which the keep stood, are on an eminence in an angle between the Honddu and the Usk. The original structure is said to have been built of materials from the Roman station of Caer Bannau, and the complete castle is [illegible] long, of about 300 feet by 200 [illegible] Benedictine priory, comprising an embattled gate [illegible], the refectory and part of the cloisters, [illegible] a little N of the castle. The priory was founded in 1090 by Bernard de Newmarch [illegible] for his violence, and [illegible] subject to Battle Abbey. A mansion [illegible] Marquis of Camden, stands adjacent to the [illegible] was built out of the [illegible] Sir [illegible] Price, whose son [illegible] Sir [illegible] Charles I was sheltered here by Sir H. Price after the battle of Naseby, and George IV [illegible] in 1821, on [illegible] return from Ireland. The priory walls [illegible] and picturesque [illegible] to the public, [illegible] town walls. [illegible] the [illegible] and [illegible] on [illegible] Castle, the [illegible] built [illegible] of the town [illegible]

Llanfaes suburb, has seven arches, and commands a fine view. The county hall was built in 1843, at a cost of £12,000; has a tetrastyle Doric portico; and contains an Ionic crown court, 60 feet long, 45 feet wide, and 35 feet high. The county jail was enlarged in 1858, and a new one was projected in 1869, to cost £6,300. There are a borough hall, a market house, extensive barracks, a theatre, an infirmary, and a workhouse. A statue of the Duke of Wellington, 8 feet high, on a pedestal of 10 feet, was placed in 1851, on the Bulwark. St John's church was originally the church of the Benedictine priory, was entirely rebuilt in the 13th century, and much altered afterwards, is cruciform, with a massive tower, shows the characters of early English in the chancel and transepts, of decorated English in the nave, and of decorated and perpendicular in the tower, measures 62 feet by 29 along the chancel, and 136½ by 28½ along the nave, has a wooden screen dividing the chancel from the transept, and a large circular Norman font, with intersecting arches, and contains numerous monuments, some of them remarkable. St Mary's church was originally Norman, has a tower in good perpendicular English, and was enlarged in 1858. St David's church fell down in 1852, was rebuilt in 1860, is in the early decorated style, and consists of nave and chancel, with tower and spire. Christ's college was originally the chapel of a Dominican friary, was changed, in 1531, into a seat of learning, under a dean and nineteen prebendaries, is now attached to the diocesan college of Lampeter, has an antique stone cross and monuments of several bishops, and includes buildings in the monastic style of imposing aspect, erected in 1861, at a cost of £10,000. There are chapels for Independents, Baptists, Calvinistic Methodists, and Roman Catholics, a grammar school at which Jones, the county historian was educated, a theological academy for Independents, and an endowed day school, alms houses, and an hospital, possessing jointly, with other charities, an income of £517.

The town has a head post office,‡ four banking offices, and three chief inns, is the seat of assizes and of quarter sessions for the county, and publishes a weekly newspaper. Markets are held on Wednesday, Friday, and Saturday, and fairs on the first Wednesday of March, 4 May, 5 July, 9 Sept., and 17 Nov. Races are run in September. The chief trade has connexion with agriculture, and with the manufacture of iron and the smelting of copper and tin. The town has sent a member to parliament since the time of Henry VIII., was chartered, in 1556, by Mary, and is governed by a mayor, a recorder, four aldermen, and twelve councillors. The municipal and the parliamentary boroughs differ in extent, and the one measures 3½ miles by two, exclusive of a portion, about 10 miles distant, in the parish of Llywel. Direct taxes in 1857, £3,621. Real property in 1860, £26,4[illegible]3. Electors in 1868, 29[illegible]. Pop. of the m. borough, 5,2[illegible]. Houses, 1,1[illegible]. Pop. of the p. borough, 5,639. Houses, 1,227. The notorious Dr. Dodd was at one time prebendary of St. Mary's, and Mrs. Siddons and Charles Kemble were natives. The town gives the title of Baron to the Marquis of Camden. Two extraparochial tracts, called Christ's College and Castle Inn, are included in the town.

St John's parish consists of the lower division or chapelry of St Mary, and the upper division which includes the hamlet of Venny Vach. St David's also consists of a lower division, or Llanfaes, and an upper division. Acres of St John, [illegible],637, of St David, 2,7[illegible]. Both are vicarages in the diocese of St David's, and St John's has united to it the p. curacy of St Mary. Value of St John, £160, of St David, £141. Patron of St John, not reported, of St David, the Bishop and Dean and Chapter of St David's.—The sub-district contains also the parishes of Llanspyddid, Aberyscir, Battle, Llanddew, and Cantref and part of the parish of Llandefailog-fach. Acres, [illegible]1,018. Pop., 7,[illegible]. Houses, 1,[illegible].—The district comprehends also the sub-district of Merthyr-Cynog, containing the parishes of Merthyr-Cynog, Garthbrengy, and Llanfihangel-Nant-Bran, and the chapelry of Llanfihangel-Fechan; the sub-district of Devynnock, containing the parishes of Devynnock, Llandilo-vane, Llywel, and Traianglas; the sub-district of Penkelly, containing the parishes of Llansaintffraed, Llansaintffraed, Llanhamlach, and Llanthetty; and the sub-district of Llangorse, containing the parishes of Llangorse, Llangasty-Talyllyn, Cathedine, Llansantffraed, Llanfihangel-Talyllyn, Llanywern, Talachddu, Llandefalley, Llanvillo, Llandefaelog-Tre'r-graig, and Llanfihangel-Talyllyn, and part of the parish of Gwenddwr. Acres, 196,793. Poor rates in 1866, £10,6[illegible]2. Pop. in 1861, 17,279. Houses, 3,[illegible]. Marriages in 1866, 1[illegible]1; births, 526,—of which 41 were illegitimate; deaths, [illegible],—of which 84 were at ages under 5 years, and 18 at ages above 85 years. Marriages in the ten years 1851-60, 1,324; births, 5,182; deaths, [illegible],7[illegible]. The places of worship in 1851 were 41 of the Church of England, with [illegible]290 sittings; 14 of Independents, with 3,712 s.; 12 of Baptists, with 2,[illegible]29 s.; 19 of Calvinistic Methodists, with 2,619 s.; 5 of Wesleyan Methodists, with [illegible] s.; and 1 of Roman Catholics, with 150 s. The schools were 20 public day schools, with 1,[illegible]8 scholars; 21 private day schools, with [illegible]11 s.; 62 Sunday schools, with 3,[illegible] s.; and 1 evening school for adults, with 13 s.

BRECKNOCK BEACONS. See ARTHUR'S CHAIR.

BRECKNOCK CANAL AND RAILWAYS. See BRECON CANAL and RAILWAYS.

BRECKNOCKSHIRE, BRECONSHIRE, or BRECON, an inland county of South Wales. It is bounded on the NW by Cardigan, on the N and NE by Radnor, on the E by Hereford and Monmouth, on the S by Monmouth and Glamorgan, and on the W by Carmarthen. Its outline is not far from being roughly triangular, with the sides toward the NE, the S, and the W. Its length, from N to S, is 38 miles; its greatest breadth, from E to W, 32 miles; its circumference, about 108 miles; and its area, [illegible]60,158 acres. The greater part of the surface is mountainous and wild. A region of hills, coming in from Cardigan, occupies most of the NW and the N, to the vicinity of the Irvon river, culminating in Drygarn, 2,071 feet high, and many of them well clothed with wood and heather. A barren chain, called Mynydd Eppynt, commences at the western boundary, 3 miles above Trecastle, and extends north-eastward, across the county, to Builth, presenting abrupt acclivities to the NW, and gradual ones to the SE. A series of mountain masses and ridges, intersected by narrow valleys, occupies all the southern half of the county, culminating successively, from W to E, in the Fan-Gihirych mountain, the Capellante mountain, the Brecknock beacons, and Pen-y-cader-fawr, respectively 2,[illegible]96, 2,394, 2,862, and 2,[illegible]45 feet high, and exhibiting a great variety of form and character. The valleys are larger and more level than in some other parts of Wales, and, together with the slopes of the hills and the skirts of the mountains give a great aggregate of ground to decoration and the plough.

The chief rivers are the Usk, the Wye, and the Irvon; and the minor ones, the Tawe, the Taf, the Cilieni, the Tarell, the Ysgir, the Hepste, the Honddu, the Cray, the Senni, the Tarell, the two Grwyneys, the Crawnon, the Llech, the Dulas, the Camlais, and the Wevery. Picturesque falls occur on the Hepste, the Crawnon, and the Llech. The chief lake is the Llyn Savaddan, the largest in South Wales; and the chief others Llyn-y-Fan-fawr and Llyn-y-Cwm. Mineral springs are at Builth and Llanwrtyd. All the district in and the NW, to within 7 miles of Builth, consists of lower silurian rocks. A tract in the N around Builth, together with two narrow belts thence to the SSW, are upper silurian. A very great tract across all the centre of the county, and filling more than half of its area, is old red sandstone. A narrow belt along all the southern border of the tract, is carboniferous limestone and shale; and some parts adjacent, mixed with that belt, and S of it to the boundary, belong to the coal measures, which constitute the great coal field of Monmouth and Glamorgan. Limestone is similarly scarce in the silurian regions. Excellent freestone is worked at Penderyn. Clay is quarried for hearths and [illegible], and pennant stone for [illegible]

Limestone, coal, and iron are worked in the S. Some lead, copper, and tripoli are found.

The soils are exceedingly various, and range in fertility from the poorest to the richest. That in the best parts of the N is stiff clay loam; that of the vale of Usk, a sandy loam; that of the vale of Wye, a good, brown, gravelly [illegible]. About 210,000 acres are in cultivation, and about 150,000 are waste. Great improvements have been effected through the exertions of the Brecon Agricultural Society. Field crops are raised in sufficient quantity for home consumption; butter, cheese, timber, wool, and cattle are exported; and some hops and orchard produce are grown. The leases are various, and the [illegible] are [illegible] than in most other parts of Wales. [illegible] cattle have generally superseded the old Welsh [illegible] in the lowlands, and a hardy race of small [illegible] sheep depastures the uplands. Leather and coarse woollens are manufactured, to a small extent, for the English market; and the iron works in the S [illegible] large business. The Brecon canal [illegible] traffic [illegible] from the centre of the county. One railway goes from Brecon to Merthyr Tydvil, another goes from Brecon towards Hereford, another goes from the latter at [illegible], past Builth, toward Llanidloes, another goes from Brecon toward Neath, and two others were in course of formation in 1869 from the last at Devynnock toward Llandovery and toward Garth.

The county contains sixty-five parishes, part of another [illegible], and three chapelries; and is divided into the six hundreds of Builth, Crickhowell, Devynnock, Merthyr, Pencelly, and Talgarth. The registration county [illegible] parts of Hereford and Radnor, but gives off larger parts to [illegible], Carmarthen, and Glamorgan; amounts to [illegible] acres; and is divided into the districts of Builth, Brecknock, Crickhowell, and Hay. The market towns are Builth, Brecknock, Crickhowell, and Hay; and the chief seats are Brecknock Priory, Dinas, Buckland, Llwyn[illegible], Llangoed Castle, Gwernyfed, Castell [illegible], [illegible], Penbont, Pennoyre, and Abercam[illegible]. Real property in 1815, £146,734; in 1843, £193,472; in 1860, £[illegible],959. The county is governed by a lord lieutenant, a high sheriff, and about forty-five magistrates. It is in the Home military district, and the South Wales judicial circuit; and it forms an archdeaconry in the diocese of St Davids. The assizes are held at Brecknock in Lent and summer; and quarter sessions on 1 Jan., [illegible] April, 2 July, and 15 Oct. The police force consists of 34 men for the county at large, and four for Brecknock borough. The number of crimes committed in 1864 was [illegible]; and of persons apprehended, [illegible]; of known depredators or suspected persons at large, 110; of houses of bad character, 53. The only prison is the county jail at Brecknock. One member is sent to parliament for Brecon borough, and one for the rest of the county. [illegible] number of county electors in 1868 was [illegible]. Pop. in 1801, 32,325; in 1821, 43,826; in 1841, [illegible]; in 1861, [illegible]. Inhabited houses, 12,013; uninhabited, [illegible]; building, [illegible].

The territory [illegible] possession of Brecknockshire after [illegible] of the Silures, and [illegible] part of the province of [illegible] Secunda. It was once called Garth [illegible], and it took its present name from a Welsh prince called Brychan, who lived in the 5th century. Most part of it came under the power of the Normans [illegible] of [illegible] prince of Brecknock, in [illegible] in 109[illegible]; but [illegible] among the mountains [illegible] two centuries longer, till the [illegible]. Most of it was long swayed by the [illegible] Castle; and all of it, more or less, was [illegible] the [illegible] attacks of Owen Glendower. [illegible] Henry Grey, [illegible] Fitzalan, [illegible] and [illegible]. [illegible] roads [illegible] from [illegible], [illegible] Brecknock, Castle [illegible], [illegible] old churches, or [illegible].

BRECON. See BRECKNOCK and BRECKNOCKSHIRE.

BRECON AND HEREFORD RAILWAY. See HEREFORD, HAY, and BRECON RAILWAY.

BRECON AND MERTHYR TYDVIL RAILWAY, a system of railway between Brecon and Merthyr Tydvil in South Wales. It was authorized in 1859, and opened in 1863. It includes a line of 12½ miles from the Brecon canal in Llanthetty parish to Merthyr Tydvil, and a line of 1⅝ mile, continuous with the former, from Merthyr Tydvil, into junction with Dowlais railway, which communicates with the Taff Vale; and it includes also an extension from Talybont to Brecknock.

BRECON CANAL, a canal south-eastward from the centre of Brecknockshire and Brecknock to the Monmouth canal near Pont-y-Pool in Monmouth. It was formed in 1811, at a cost of £170,000; is 33 miles long; has capacity for barges of 25 tons, falls 68 feet, with eight locks, in the first 18½ miles to Clydach; and goes thence, on a level, past Abergavenny, to the Monmouth canal.

BRECONCHILL, a hamlet in Coverham parish, N. R. Yorkshire, 2 miles SW of Middleham.

BRECONHILL, or BRACKENSHILL, a township in Arthuret parish, Cumberland, on the river Line, 1½ miles [illegible] N of Longtown. Acres, [illegible]525. Real property, £2,[illegible]01. Pop., 3[illegible]0. Houses, [illegible]1.

BREDBURY, a township chapelry in Stockport parish, Cheshire, adjacent to the Peak Forest canal, 2 miles ENE of Stockport r. station. Post town, Stockport. Acres, 2,521. Real property, £15,07[illegible], of which £1,8[illegible] are in mines. Pop., 3,408. Houses, 676. The living is a vicarage in the [illegible] of Chester. Value, £160.* Patron, alt. the Crown and the Bishop. The church is good; and there are an Independent chapel, and charities £16.

BREDE (THE), a stream of Sussex. It rises 2 miles E of Penhurst, and runs 12 miles east-south to the Rye.

BREDE, a parish in Rye district, Sussex, on the river Brede, 4 miles W by N of Winchelsea r. station, and 5 ENE of Battle. It has a post office of the name of Brede Hill, under Staplehurst; and a fair is held in it on Easter Tuesday. Acres, 4,840. Real property, £6,793. Pop., 1,05[illegible]. Houses, 214. The property is subdivided. The manor belonged anciently to the Attefords, and passed, in the time of Henry IV., to the Oxenbridges. The manor house, called Brede Place, shows interesting ancient features, commands a fine view, and is now occupied by a farmer. There is an iron foundry. The living is a rectory in the diocese of Chichester. Value, £1,02[illegible].* Patron, T. Frewen, Esq. The church was enlarged in the early part of the 16th century, by Sir Goddard Oxenbridge, contains a monumental effigies of him, and fine buoyant traceries introduced by him, and is in good condition. There is a Wesleyan chapel.

BREDE HILL. See BREDE.

BREDENBURY, or BRIDENBURY, a parish in Bromyard district, Hereford, 3 miles WNW of Bromyard, and 7 E by N of Leominster r. station. Post town, Bromyard, under Worcester. Acres, 5[illegible]5. Real property, £726. Pop., 52. Houses, 11. Bredenbury House is the chief residence, and there is an ancient camp. The living is a rectory in the diocese of Hereford. Value, £11[illegible]. Patron, E. Higginson, Esq.

BREDFIELD, a parish in Woodbridge district, Suffolk, near the East Suffolk railway, 3 miles N of Woodbridge. It has a post office under Woodbridge. Acres, 1,067. Real property, £2,3[illegible]0. Pop., 4[illegible]. Houses, 99. The property is subdivided. Bredfield Hall is the chief residence. The living is a rectory in the diocese of Norwich. Value, £2[illegible].* Patron, the Lord Chancellor. The church is old but good. There are an Independent chapel, a [illegible] school, and charities £5.

BREDGAR, a parish in Milton district, Kent, among the chalk hills, 3 miles SSW of Sittingbourne r. station. It has a post office under Sittingbourne. Acres, 1,727. Real property, [illegible]876. Pop., [illegible]47. Houses, 117. The property is much subdivided. Bedgar House is a chief residence. The living is a vicarage in the diocese of Canterbury. Value, £130.* Patron, Sir [illegible] Dering, Bart. The church is perpendicular English, with a com[illegible] ous Norman doorway under the tower, has Roman bricks in its walls, contains a brass of 1508, and is in good condition. A chantry or small college was founded in it, in the time of Richard II, by Robert de Bredgar. There are a Wesleyan chapel, built in 1809, and charities £28.

BREDHURST, a parish in Hollingbourn district, Kent, 3 miles SSW of Rainham r. station, and 4½ SE of Chatham. Post town, Rainham, under Sittingbourne. Acres 600. Real property, £709. Pop., 117. Houses, 23. The property is divided among a few. The living is a vicarage in the diocese of Canterbury. Value, £101. Patron, the Archbishop of Canterbury. The church is old but good.

BREDICOT, a parish in Pershore district, Worcestershire, on the Birmingham and Gloucester railway, 3¼ miles E of Worcester. Post town, Spetchley, under Worcester. Acres, 397. Real property, with Churchill, £1,570. Pop., 53. Houses, 13. The property is all in one estate. The living is a rectory, united with the vicarage of Tibberton, in the diocese of Worcester. Value, £200.* Patrons, the Dean and Chapter of Worcester. The church is good.

BREDON, a village in the district of Tewkesbury, and a parish in the districts of Tewkesbury and Winchcombe, and county of Worcester. The village stands on the river Avon, adjacent to the Birmingham and Gloucester railway, 3½ miles NE of Tewkesbury, and has a station on the railway, and a post office under Tewkesbury. Eanulf, grandfather of King Offa, got a grant of it from Ethelbald, king of Mercia, and founded at it a monastery, which was transferred, before the Conquest, to the see of Worcester. The parish includes also the hamlets of Norton by Bredon, Hardwick with Mitton, Kinsham, and Westmancote, and the chapelry of Cutsdean. Acres, 5,818. Real property, £11,608. Pop., 1,553. Houses, 366. Bredon hill separates the vales of Cotswold and Evesham, has an altitude of 900 feet, commands an extensive prospect, has traces of a Roman camp with a double trench, and is a meet for the Worcester hounds. Wellshill Hall is the ancient seat of the Hanfords. The living is a rectory, united with the p. curacies of Norton and Cutsdean, in the diocese of Worcester. Value, £2,300.* Patron, the Duke of Portland. The church occupies the site of the ancient monastery, is an old and interesting edifice of different periods, chiefly early English, has a central tower, surmounted by a graceful spire, and was restored in 1845. The remains of Dr. Prideaux, bishop of Worcester in the time of Charles I., lie in the chancel; a rich monument of Giles Reed, of date 1611, is in a south chapel; and several ancient monastic tombs are in the churchyard. There are a Baptist chapel, a free school with £130 a year, and charities £300.

BREDON ON THE HILL. See BREEDON ON THE HILL.

BREDWARDINE, a village and a parish in the district of Hay, and county of Hereford. The village stands on the river Wye, adjacent to the line of the Hereford and Brecon railway, 7½ miles E by N of Hay, and has a post office under Hereford. The parish comprises 2,245 acres. Real property, £3,117. Pop., 420. Houses, 93. The property is divided among a few. Bredwardine Castle, now a ruin, was the seat of the Bredwardine family, one of whom was Archbishop of Canterbury in 1349. The living is a vicarage, united with the rectory of Brobury, in the diocese of Hereford. Value, £370.* Patron, the Rev. N. D. H. Newton. The church is an old structure, of nave and chancel, with a tower, and is in good condition. A charity to the poor, bequeathed by George Jarvis, Esq., who died in 1793, yields £1,255 a year.

BREDY (THE), a stream of Dorset. It rises on the downs in Little Bredy parish, and runs 8 miles westward to the sea at Bridport.

BREDY (LITTLE), a parish in Dorchester district, Dorset, on the downs at the source of the Bredy stream, 5 miles SSW of Grimstone and Frampton r. station, and 6¾ W by S of Dorchester. It has a post office under Dorchester. Acres, 1,636. Real property, with Kingston Russell, £2,193. Pop., 199. Houses, 41. The property is all in one estate. Stone is quarried. The living is a p. curacy, annexed to the rectory of Long Bredy, in the diocese of Salisbury. The church is good.

BREDY (LONG), a parish in Dorchester district, Dorset, on the downs, near the source of the Bredy stream, 1¾ miles SW of Grimstone and Frampton r. station, and 8 W of Dorchester. It includes the hamlet of Upper Kingston, and its post town is Little Bredy, under Dorchester. Acres, 2,117. Real property, £3,067. Pop., 250. Houses, 55. The property is divided among a few. The living is a rectory, united with the p. curacy of Little Bredy, in the diocese of Salisbury. Value, £52?.* Patron, R. Williams, Esq. The church is good. Charities, £8.

BREEDON ON THE HILL, a village and a township in the district of Shardlow and county of Leicester, and a parish in the districts of Shardlow and Ashby de la Zouch, and counties of Leicester and Derby. The village stands at the base of a high limestone rock, near the verge of the county, 4 miles N of Swannington r. station, and 5 NE by N of Ashby de la Zouch, and has a post office, of the name of Breedon, under Ashby de la Zouch. A small monastery of Black canons, subject to the priory of St. Oswald in Yorkshire, was founded here in 1144 by Ferrers, Earl of Nottingham, and given, at the dissolution, to the Shirleys. —The township includes also the hamlets of Wilson and Tonge. Acres, 3,010. Real property, £3,19?. Pop., 89?. Houses, 222.—The parish contains also the townships of Staunton Harrold and Worthington, and the liberty of Newbold. Acres, ?,?10. Real property, £11,797. Pop., 2,417. Houses, 5?2. The property is divided among a few. The manor belongs to the Earl of Stamford. Limestone is worked. The living is a vicarage in the diocese of Peterborough. Value, £205. Patron, the Earl of Stamford. The church surmounts the limestone rock at the village, contains tombs of the Shirleys, and is good. The p. curacy of Worthington is a separate benefice. There are two Wesleyan chapels, an endowed school with £?1 a year, and a vicarage augmentation charity £2?1.

BREEM. See BREAM.

BREHAM, or BRAHER, one of the Scilly islands, in the NW of the group, 2½ miles NW of Hugh Town. It is 2 miles long, rugged, wild, and high, and inhabited chiefly by fishermen. It contains some Druidical remains. Pop., 11?.

BREHON, an islet, ¾ of a mile long, separated by a narrow strait from the W side of Sark, in the Channel Islands.

BREIDDON HILL, or CRAIG BREIDDEN, a triple crested eminence on the E border of Montgomery, overhanging the river Severn, 6¼ miles NNE of Welshpool. It is crowned with an ancient camp, and with a pillar to Rodney; and has been thought by some to be the place where Ostorius Scapula finally overthrew Caractacus.

BREIGHTMET, a township in Bolton le Moors parish, Lancashire, 2½ miles E of Bolton. Acres, 970. Real property, £6,627, of which £1,504 are in mines. Pop., 1,062. Houses, 295. Cotton manufacture is carried on; and there are a church of 185?, a Wesleyan chapel, and an endowed school with £26 a year.

BREIGHTON CUM GUNBY, a township in Bubwith parish, E. R. Yorkshire, on the river Derwent, near the Selby and Hull railway, 4½ miles NW of Howden. Acres, 2,030. Real property, £1,823. Pop., 207. Houses, 43. Part of the land is common.

BREINTON, a parish in the district and county of Hereford, on the river Wye, and on the Hereford and Brecon railway, 2½ miles W by S of Hereford. It includes the hamlet of Warham and a part of Hereford city, and its post town is Hereford. Acres, ?,629. Real property, £3,221. Pop., 308. Houses, 83. The property is subdivided. The living is a vicarage in the diocese of Hereford. Value, £250. Patron, the Bishop of Hereford. The church is tolerable, and there are charities £17.

BRELISWORTH. See BLAISWORTH.

BRELADE (ST), a parish in the SW of Jersey. It [illegible] of St Aubin, which has a post office [illegible], and includes also the village of Com[illegible]. [illegible] Houses, 3[illegible]. The scenery is beautiful, [illegible] handsome villas. St Brelade bay, [illegible] St Aubin, has a horse shoe outline, [illegible], and shows charming features. [illegible] rectory in the diocese of Winchester. [illegible] £15[illegible] Patron, the Governor of Jersey. The [illegible] W side of the bay, and is a small [illegible] of the 12th century. A little chapel in the [illegible] some remains of frescoes, but [illegible] modern [illegible], and is used as an [illegible]. St Aubin's chapel is a separate charge.

BREMBLE. See BREMHILL.

BREMENIUM. See BIRMINGHAM.

BREMETENRACUM. See BRAMPTON, Cumberland.

BREMHILL, or BREMBLE, a village and a parish in Calne district, Wilts. The village stands on the Roman [illegible] to Bath, near the Wilts and Berks canal, [illegible] miles [illegible] of the Great Western railway, and [illegible] by N of Chippenham; and has a post office, of the name of Bremhill, [illegible] Chippenham.—The parish includes also the [illegible] of La[illegible], Studley, Spirthill, Charlcott, [illegible]. Acres, [illegible]. Real property, £7,78[illegible]. Pop., 1,[illegible]57. Houses, 252. The property is divided [illegible]. [illegible] House belonged formerly to the Hungerfords, and is now occupied by a farmer. A [illegible] pillar, surmounted by a female figure, in [illegible] of the time of Edward IV, is at Wick Hill [illegible] the village, and some other points, com[illegible] views. The living is a vicarage in the dio[illegible] of Salisbury. Value, £[illegible]. Patron, the Bishop [illegible]. The church [illegible] edifice, in very [illegible], has a finely carved rood loft, and con[illegible] of the Baytons and the Hungerfords. [illegible] crosses are adjacent, and several epitaphs [illegible] are from the pen of the poet Bowles, [illegible], and died here in 1850. There are [illegible] Primitive Methodist chapels, a Moravian [illegible] Tytherton Grange, and a charity by [illegible] £107.

BREMILHAM, or COWAGE, a parish in Malmesbury [illegible], Wilts, on the river Avon, near Akeman street, [illegible] W of Malmesbury, and 9 WSW of [illegible] station. Post town, Malmesbury, under [illegible]. Acres, [illegible]. Real property, with West[illegible] £335. Pop., 29. Houses, 5. The [illegible]. The living is a rectory in [illegible] of Gloucester and Bristol. Value, £121. [illegible] Hon and Rev R [illegible]. The church [illegible].

[illegible], a village, a parish, a sub district, and [illegible]. The village stands [illegible] miles S [illegible] k Wood r station, and [illegible] of Tunbridge [illegible], and has a post office under Staplehurst. Some [illegible] houses are in it, and a clump of trees, [illegible], figures conspicuously over many [illegible].—The parish includes also the hamlets of M[illegible] [illegible] Rosse's Pond, Hen[illegible]s, Parsons [illegible]. Acres, [illegible],780. Real property, [illegible]. Pop., 2,811. Houses, [illegible]30. The property is [illegible] similar to [illegible]. The living is a vicarage in the dio[illegible]. Value, £7[illegible]. Patron, [illegible]. The church is old, cruciform, and [illegible] tower [illegible] vicarage [illegible] Baptist chapel, [illegible] chapel [illegible] 217.—The sub district [illegible] parishes, and is in the district [illegible]. Acres, 1[illegible]. Pop., [illegible]. Houses, [illegible] of [illegible] and part of [illegible]. Acres, [illegible]. Houses, 81.

BRENDON, a parish in Barnstaple district, Devon [illegible] extremity of the county [illegible] to the [illegible] of Lynton and [illegible] town, Lynton, under Barnstaple. Acres, 6,793. Real property, £1,570. Pop., 2[illegible]. Houses, 57. The manor belonged, in the time of Edward the Confessor, to Ailward Tochetone; was given by William the Conqueror to Ralph de Pomeroy, passed to the Beaples and the Chichesters, and belongs now to F W Knight, Esq. Much of the surface is sheep walk and deer preserve. The vale of Brendon is narrow, deep, and picturesque. The parish is a meet for the North Devon hounds. Major Wade, a leader in the insurrection under the Duke of Monmouth, was made prisoner at Farley farm. The living is a rectory in the diocese of Exeter. Value, £200. Patron, F W Knight, Esq. The church is a structure partly of 1738, mainly of 1[illegible]28.

BRENDON HILLS, a range of hills in Somerset, 7 miles SSW of Watchet. It is several miles long, and 1,210 feet high, consists of loose, shelly limestone, and was recently discovered to contain a valuable vein of carbonate of iron. The Ebbw Vale company are working the vein, and have constructed a railway to it from Watchet. A British camp, called Elworthy Barrows, is on the W point of the range, and British urns have been found.

BRENKLEY, a township in Dinnington parish, Northumberland, [illegible] miles W of the Northeastern railway, and 7[illegible] N by W of Newcastle upon Tyne. Acres, 983. Pop., 51. Houses, 10.

BRENNICH (THE), the part of the river Till above Wooler, in Northumberland. It gave name to the Saxon kingdom of Bernicia.

BRENNING (THE), a stream of Cardigan, falling into the Teifi near Tregaron.

BRENSON, or BRENSTON, a hamlet in Newchurch parish, Isle of Wight, 1½ mile S of Newchurch. The Dairyman's Cottage, immortalized by Legh Richmond, is adjacent.

BRENT. See BRENT (SOUTH), Devon.

BRENT (THE), a stream of Herts and Middlesex. It rises near Barnet, and runs 16 miles south south westward past Hendon and Hanwell, to the Thames at Brentford.

BRENT, or BRAINT (THE), a stream of Anglesey. It rises near Llanddaniel, and runs 6 miles south south westward to the Menai strait, below Aberm[illegible].

BRENT (EAST), a village and a parish in Axbridge district, Somerset. The village stands near the Bristol and Exeter railway, 2 miles N by E of Highbridge station, and 6 WSW of Axbridge; and has a post office under Weston super Mare. The parish includes also the hamlets of Rooksbridge and Edingworth. Acres, 3,037. Real property, £10,[illegible]. Pop., 7[illegible]7. Houses, 176. The property is much subdivided. Brent knoll, on the southern border, is a conical hill 583 feet high, commands an extensive view, and is crowned with vestiges of a doubly entrenched Roman camp. Roman coins and other relics have been found near, and King Alfred is said to have fought with the Danes at Battleborough at the foot of the hill. The living is a vicarage in the diocese of Bath and Wells. Value, £902.* Patron, the Bishop of Bath and Wells. The church is an interesting edifice, with a spire 140 feet high, and has several windows of ancient painted glass. There are a Methodist chapel and a national school; and the church was anciently a cell to Glastonbury abbey.

BRENT ELEIGH, or BRENT ILLEIGH, a parish in Cosford district, Suffolk, near the river Brett, [illegible] miles NE by N of Sudbury r station. Post town, Lavenham, under Sudbury. Acres, 1,617. Real property, £2,[illegible]. Pop., 228. Houses, [illegible]. The property is divided among a few. Brent Eleigh Hall belonged to the Shelters, and passed to [illegible]. The living is a rectory in the diocese of Ely. Value, £[illegible]. Patron, Mrs Brown. The church shows Norman features, has a later English tower, and is good; and there are charities £9[illegible]. A market was formerly held in the parish.

BRENTFORD, a town, three chapelries, a sub district, and a district in Middlesex. The town stands at the [illegible] of the river Brent to the Thames, 7½ miles W by S of London. The Grand Junction canal unites here with the Brent, and accompanies it to the Thames. The Southwestern, the Great Western and the Metropolitan railways communicate with the town in various ways and have stations for it with telegraph and the Great Western connects here likewise with large docks for heavy traffic by water to London The town is ancient, and took its name from a ford, on the line of a great thoroughfare, across the Brent It was the scene, in 1016, of a destructive overthrow of the Danes, by Edmund Ironside, and, in 1642, of a still more important overthrow of the parliamentarians by the royalists A chapter of the garter was held at it in 1445, and six martyrs were burnt in it in 1558 The "Two Kings of Brentford" have done great service with all sorts of poets and poetasters, from William Cowper to Tom D'Urfey John Lowin the landlord of the "Three Pigeons" here, in the time of Ben Johnson, was a famous actor, and performed in Shakspeare's own company The town is described by the poet Gay as a "tedious town, for dirty streets and white legged chickens known," and by the poet Thomson as "Brentford town — a town of mud " It now comprises one long principal street, and contains some good houses A bridge connects the lower end of the town, across the Thames, with Kew, and another bridge, erected in 1825 on the site of a very ancient one, crosses the Brent The town-hall and market house is a handsome brick and stone edifice St Lawrence' church is at the end of the town, near the bridge St George's church was rebuilt, excepting the tower, in 1764 has been several times renovated, presents a light and pleasing appearance, and contains a splendid altar piece, a large font and monuments of the Clitherows Dr W H Ewin, Sarah Howell, and the father of John Horne Tooke St Paul's church was built in 1868, and is in the decorated English style, and highly ornate There are two Independent chapels, two Baptist chapels, a Wesleyan chapel, a Roman Catholic chapel, literary club and reading rooms, British schools built at a cost of about £3,000, three national schools, a dispensary, a workhouse built at a cost of £9,000 the Grand Junction waterworks, with a chimney 150 feet high, extensive foundries, nurseries, brickfields tile and pottery works saw mills, maltings, a brewery, a soap manufactory, a weekly market on Tuesday, and fairs of three days in May and three days in Sept The town has post-offices of Brentford† and Old Brentford, under London W, a banking office, two chief inns, and a police station is a seat of sessions and county courts, and the place of election for Middlesex, and comprises part of Isleworth parish and all its own three chapelries. Sion House, a seat of the Duke of Northumberland, Osterley Park, the seat of the Earl of Jersey, Boston House, the seat of Col Clitherow and many handsome villas are in the neighbourhood Pop of the town in 1861, 9,021 Houses, 1,902

The chapelries are St Lawrence or New Brentford, a township of Hanwell parish, St George Old Brentford in Ealing parish, and St Paul Old Brentford, also in Ealing Pop of St L, 11,995, of St G 2,591, of St P, 4 109 The livings are vicarages in the diocese of London Value of St L, £233,* of St G, £300,* of St P, £300 Patron of St L, the Rector of Hanwell of St G, the Vicar of Ealing, of St P, alternately the Crown and the Bishop John Horne Tooke was incumbent of St George —The sub district includes also the rest of Ealing parish Acres 4 034 Pop, 13,958 Houses, 2 723 —The district comprehends likewise the sub district of Twickenham, conterminate with Twickenham parish the sub district of Chiswick, conterminate with Chiswick parish, the sub district of Isleworth, containing the parishes of Isleworth and Heston and the sub district of Acton, containing the parishes of Acton, Hanwell, Perivale and Great Greenford Acres, 23 105 Poor-rates in 1866, 29 605 Pop in 1861 50,316 Houses 9 402 Marriages in 1866, 453 births, 2 030, — of which 101 were illegitimate deaths 1,245,—of which 483 were at ages under 5 years, and 31 at ages above 85 Marriages in the ten years 1851-60 2,995, births 11 307, deaths, 9,009 The places of worship in 1851 were 17 of the Church of England, with 11,757 sittings 10 of Independents, with 2 927 s, 3 of Baptists, with 610 s, 1 of Quakers, with 160 s, 3 of Wesleyan Methodists, with 1,206 s 2 of Primitive Methodists, with 178 s, 1 of Latter Day Saints, with 80 s, 1 undefined with 10 s and 2 of Roman Catholics with 250 s The schools were 3 public day schools, with 4,252 scholars 116 private day schools, with 2,308 s, 27 Sunday schools, with 3,126 s, and 1 evening school for adults with 8 s

BRENTFORD END, a hamlet in Isleworth parish, Middlesex, 1 mile WSW of Brentford A chapel, with fraternity of All Angels, was founded here by Somerset chaplain of Henry VI, and given, in the time of Edward VI, to the Duke of Somerset

BRENTFORD (New and Old) See Brentford

BRENTINGBY a chapelry in Wyfordby parish, Leicester on the river Wreak, the Oakham canal, and the Midland railway 2 miles E of Melton Mowbray Post town, Melton Mowbray Pop, 54 The living is a p curacy, annexed to the rectory of Thorpe Arnold, in the diocese of Peterborough

BRENT KNOLL See Brent (East)

BRENT MILL, a hamlet in South Brent parish, Devon

BRENTON See Brent Tor

BRENT PELHAM, a parish in Bishop Stortford district, Herts, on the verge of the county, 5 miles E of Buntingford r station It has a post office under Buntingford Acres, 1,601 Real property, £2,120 Pop, 280 Houses 60 The property is divided among a few The living is a vicarage, united with Furneux Pelham in the dio of Rochester Value, £320 * Patron the Treas of St Paul's The church was recently restored

BRENTSIDE, a hamlet in Middlesex, on the river Brent 3 miles N by W of Brentford It has a post office under Ealing London W

BRENT (South), a village and a parish in Totnes district, Devon The village stands on the river Avon, adjacent to the South Devon railway, 6 miles W of Totnes, and has a station, of the name of Brent, on the railway, and a post office, of the same name, under Ivy Bridge It was formerly a market town, and it still has large fairs on the last Tuesday of April and Sept —The parish comprises 9,374 acres. Real property, £8,417 Pop 1,205 Houses, 249 The property is much divided The manor once belonged to the abbey of Buckfastleigh but has been disencumbered The surface is diversified, and includes the striking eminence of South Brent Tor Micaceous iron ore, used for the sanding of manuscript, is found The living is a vicarage in the diocese of Exeter Value, £832 * Patron, the Rev N Cole The church is old and large, consists of nave chancel, and aisles, and has a Norman tower There are chapels for Independents and Baptists parish lands, yielding £14 a year, and other charities £23

BRENT (South), a village and a parish in Axbridge parish Somerset The village stands under Brent Knoll, adjacent to the Bristol and Exeter railway, 3 miles N by E of Highbridge station and 7½ W of Axbridge, and has a post office under Weston super Mare —The parish includes also the hamlet of Week Acres 3,126 Real property, £10 ,94 Pop, 905 Houses, 200 The property is much subdivided The manor belonged formerly to the abbots of Glastonbury The living is a vicarage in the diocese of Bath and Wells Value, £518 * Patron, the Archdeacon of Wells The church is partly Norman and contains a large monument to a Somerset of 1663 There are a Bible Christian chapel a national school, and charities £8

BRENT TOR, or BRENTON, a parish in Tavistock district, Devon, on the river Lyd 4 miles N by W of Tavistock r station Post town, Tavistock Acres, 1,212 Real property £832 Pop, 123 Houses 28 The manor belonged formerly to the abbey of Tavistock, and belongs now to the Duke of Bedford A remarkable eminence here, bearing the same name as the parish starts abruptly from an elevated down, has an altitude of 1,100 feet is seen at a great distance, and serves as a mark for vessels entering Plymouth harbour It s form is conical, its surface rock , and its mineral structure a subject of much discussion among geologists A mine of manganese was long worked, but has been abandoned The living is a vicarage in the diocese of Exeter Value £60 Patron the Duke of Bedford The church surmounts a precipice on the crown of the Tor, is a curious weather worn structure 37 feet by 1[illegible], and is said to have been built by a merchant who, overtaken by a storm at sea, vowed to erect a church on the first point of land he saw

BRENT TOWN, a village in Preston parish, Kent, in the vicinity of Faversham

BRENT WITH WRINGTON, a hundred in Somerset It contains the parishes of East Brent, South Brent, Wrington and three others. Acres, 22,787 Pop, 4,7[illegible] Houses 1 015

BRENTWOOD, a small town a chapelry, and a sub district in Billericay district, Essex The town stands adjacent to the Eastern Counties railway, near Watling street, 5¾ miles NE by E of Romford Its name is a corruption of Burnt Wood, and was derived from the burning long ago of a circumjacent forest Some Roman antiquities have been found in it The town was at one time, a seat of assizes, and has of late been extended and improved The town hall was built in 1864, and is in the Italian style, with Corinthian portico The county lunatic asylum is an edifice in the Tudor style The grammar school was founded in 1557, by Sir Anthony Browne, and has an endowed income of £1[illegible] The old church is early English, was built in 1221 and is now used for a national school The new church is a Gothic structure, with a handsome square tower, and was built in 1835 The Roman Catholic chapel was built in 1861, is formed of Kentish rag with bath stone facings consists of nave, aisles, and chancel with a tower and spire 110 feet high and was [illegible] of Lord Petre whose seat near Ingrave is about 2 miles to the S There are chapels for Independents and Wesleyans The town has a head post office,‡ a railway station with telegraph, a banking office, and two chief inns, and is a seat of petty sessions The weekly market has ceased but fairs are held on 18 July and 15 Oct Pop, 2,811 Houses, 532 —The chapelry includes the town and is in South Weald parish Acres, 730 Real property, £[illegible] Pop, [illegible] Houses, 553 The property is much subdivided The living is a p curacy in the diocese of Rochester Value £124 * Patron C J Tower Esq —The sub district contains six parishes Acres, 11[illegible]8 Pop 8 167 Houses 1 378

BRENZETT, a parish in Romney Marsh district, Kent 2 miles SE by E of Appledore r station, and 4½ WNW of New Romney Post-town, Appledore under Staplehurst Acres, 1,862 Real property, £3,153 Pop 270 Houses, 57 The property is divided among a few The living is a vicarage in the diocese of Canterbury Value, £91 Patron, the Rev W Brockman The church belonged anciently to Guisnes abbey in Artois, has some Norman portions, and is in good condition There is a Wesleyan chapel

BREOCK (St), a parish in St Columb district, Cornwall on the river Camel including part of the town of Wadebridge and 10 miles NW of Bodmin Road r station Post town Wadebridge, Cornwall Acres, 8,257, of which 2[illegible] are water Real property, £[illegible] Pop. 1,[illegible] Houses, 192 The property is divided among a few The manor belonged once to the Arundells, and passed to the [illegible] An eminence called the [illegible] is crowned by a circular [illegible] and commands a fine view A [illegible] trade is carried on by railway with Bodmin and Camelford The living is a rectory in the diocese of Exeter Value, £[illegible] * Patron the Rev G S Prideaux The church is [illegible], contains some old monuments and [illegible] There are chapels for Independents, Bible Christians, and Wesleyans The [illegible] the Ordnance survey

BREEDING. See [illegible]

[illegible] See [illegible]

BRERETON, a chapelry in [illegible], Stafford, adjacent to the Trent Valley railway 1 mile SE of Rugeley It was constituted in 1843, and it has a post office under Rugeley Pop, 1,3[illegible] Houses 231 Coal is worked The living is a vicarage in the diocese of Lichfield Value £10[illegible] * Patron, the Vicar of Rugeley The church is in the early English style, and has a fine spire There is a Wesleyan chapel

BRERETON CUM SMETHWICK, a parish in Congleton district, Cheshire, on the river Croke, 2 miles SE of Holmes Chapel r station, and 3 NE by N of Sandbach It has a post office, of the name of Brereton, under Congleton, and is a seat of petty sessions. Acres, 4 501 Real property £7,80[illegible] Pop 592 Houses 104 The property is subdivided Brereton Hall was built by Sir W Brereton, the parliamentary leader, and is now the seat of the Howards The living is a rectory in the diocese of Chester Value, £691 * Patron, Mrs. E Lloyd The church is later English, and good, and there are three dissenting chapels A school has £8, and other charities £1[illegible]

BRESSINGHAM or BRISSINGHAM, a parish in Guiltcross district, Norfolk on the verge of the county 2½ miles W of Diss, and 1 from Diss r station Post town, Diss Acres, 3 [illegible] Real property £[illegible] Pop, 596 Houses, 13[illegible] The property is much subdivided The manor belonged formerly to the Pillingtons There are remains of a large conduit, constructed by Sir Richard de Boyland The living is a rectory in the diocese of Norwich. Value, £[illegible] * Patron C Pidwell, Esq The church is old but good, and has a lofty tower A school has £13 and other charities £23

BRET, or BRETTON (THE), a river of Suffolk It rises near Bradfield Combust, and runs 17 miles south south eastward, past Lavenham and Hadleigh, to the Stour, 3¾ miles E of Nayland

BRETBY, Derby See BRADBY

BRETBY Yorkshire See [illegible]

BRETFORD See BRANDON and BRETFORD

BRETFORTON a parish in Evesham district Worcester, on the West Midland railway 2 miles WNW of Honeybourne station and 3½ E of Evesham Post town, Evesham Acres, 1,68[illegible] Real property, £3,161 Pop, 565 Houses, 123 The property is divided among a few The living is a vicarage in the diocese of Worcester Value £182 * Patron, the Rev C Morris The church is good There is a national school

BRETHERDALE, a township in Orton parish, Westmoreland 4 miles SW of Orton Pop 82

BRETHERTON, a township chapelry in Croston parish, Lancashire, on the Douglas river, 1 mile E of Croston r station, and 9 SSW of Preston It has a post office under Chorley Acres, 2,40[illegible] Real property £1,48[illegible] Pop, 77[illegible] Houses 140 The property is not much divided The living is a rectory in the diocese of Manchester Value £1[illegible]0 * Patron, the Rector of Croston The church is a recent structure, in the early English style There are an Independent chapel a Wesleyan chapel, and an endowed school, the last founded in 1654, and having £112 a year

BRETON (THE) See BRET

BRETTEL LANE, a hamlet in the SW of Stafford, adjacent to the West Midland railway 1½ mile NNE of Stourbridge It has a station on the railway a post office‡ under Brierley Hill, several [illegible], and some glass works

BRETTENHAM a parish in Thetford district, Norfolk, on the [illegible] and the little Ouse river, 1½ mile S of the Norfolk railway, and 3½ E of Thetford Post town Thetford Acres 1,0[illegible] Real property £88[illegible] Pop 72 Houses 11 The property is all in one estate, belonging to Sir W P [illegible], Bart The living is a rectory in the diocese of Norwich Value, £200 Patron the [illegible] The ancient church was burnt in 16[illegible] and is now a [illegible] The present church is [illegible] small [illegible], with some [illegible]

BRETTENHAM a parish in Cosford district, Suffolk on the [illegible], 3½ miles NNW of Bildeston and 7 SW by W of Stowmarket r station Post-town, Bildestone, under Ipswich. Acres, 1,558. Real property, £3,001. Pop., 420. Houses, 85. The property is divided among a few. Brettenham Hall belonged formerly to the Wenyeves, and passed to the Bendes. Some vestiges in the parish are supposed to mark the site of the Roman station of Combretonium. The living is a rectory in the diocese of Ely. Value, £377.* Patron, the Lord Chancellor. The church is good.

BRETTON, a township in Hawarden parish, Flint, near Saltney marsh, 3 miles SE by E of Hawarden. Acres, 733. Real property, £1,609. Pop., 208. Houses, 40.

BRETTON, a sub-district in Wakefield district, W. R. Yorkshire. It contains West Bretton township, two other townships, and a chapelry. Acres, 9,923. Pop., 5,057. Houses, 1,004.

BRETTON (Monk), a township and a chapelry in Roystone parish, W. R. Yorkshire. The township is also called Burton, lies on the Barnesley canal, 1 mile from Cudworth r. station, and 2 NE of Barnesley, includes the villages of Burton Grange, Cliff Bridge, Littleworth, Old Mill, and Smithies, and has a post office, of the name of Monk Bretton, under Barnesley. Acres, 2,050. Real property, £6,923. Pop., 1,918. Houses, 407. A Cluniac monastery was founded at Burton Grange, in the time of Henry II., by Adam Fitz Swain. The chapelry is more extensive than the township. Pop., 2,439. Houses, 520. The living is a p. curacy in the diocese of York. Value, £150.* Patron, the Vicar of Royston. The church was built in 1839. There are a school church, three Methodist chapels, a national school, six alms houses, and other charities £36.

BRETTON (West), a township-chapelry in Sandal Magna and Silkstone parishes, W. R. Yorkshire, 3 miles SW of Crigglestone r. station, and 6 SW by S of Wakefield. Post town, Bretton, under Wakefield. Acres of the Sandal Magna portion, 870. Pop., 132. Houses, 32. Acres of the Silkstone portion, 980. Pop., 372. Houses, 71. Real property, £1,783. Bretton Hall is the seat of W. B. Beaumont, Esq. The living is a p. curacy in the diocese of Ripon. Value, not reported. Patron, W. B. Beaumont, Esq.

BRETT-SAMPFORD. See Sampford Brett.

BREWARD (St.), or Simonward, a parish in Camelford district, Cornwall, on the river Lark, under Brown Willey mountain, 7 miles N by E of Bodmin, and 8½ N by W of Bodmin Road r. station. Post-town, St. Tudy, under Bodmin. Acres, 9,237. Real property, £2,960. Pop., 765. Houses, 143. The property is subdivided. The surface is prevailingly moorish upland, and rugged; but encloses fine scenes, and commands fine prospects. Brown Willey and Rough Tor mountains figure conspicuously in the landscape. Hanter Gantick, 1 mile S of the church town, is a deep romantic valley, sometimes called the Cornish Valley of rocks. Granite is quarried, and slate is found. The living is a vicarage in the diocese of Exeter. Value, £200.* Patrons, the Dean and Chapter of Exeter. The church is partly Norman, and in fair condition.

BREWERY FIELD, a chapelry in Leeds parish, W. R. Yorkshire, in the part of the parish within Hunslet district. It was constituted in 1851. Post town, Leeds. Rated property, about £10,000. Pop., 6,859. Houses, 1,580. The property is much subdivided. The living is a vicarage in the diocese of Ripon. Value, £300.* Patron, alternately the Crown and the Bishop.

BREWHAM LODGE, an extra-parochial tract in Wincanton district, Somerset, on the east border of the county, 4½ miles ENE of Bruton. It was a hunting seat of King John, and belongs now to the Hoares. Pop., 8.

BREWHAM (North), a parish in Wincanton district, Somerset, adjacent to the Wilts and Somerset railway, 3 miles NE of Bruton. Post town, South Brewham, under Bath. Acres, 2,026. Real property returned with South Brewham. Pop., 321. Houses, 73. The living is annexed to South Brewham, and the church is used as a barn.

BREWHAM (South), a parish in Wincanton district, Somerset, on the Wilts and Somerset railway, 2½ miles NE by N of Bruton. It has a post office under Bath. Acres, 2,671. Real property, with North Brewham and Eastrip, £5,314. Pop., 519. Houses, 121. The property is subdivided. The living is a vicarage, with North Brewham, in the diocese of Bath and Wells. Value, £102. Patron, Sir H. Hoare, Bart. The church is good, and there are a Wesleyan chapel and a national school.

BREWHOUSE YARD, an extra-parochial tract in Radford district, Notts, contiguous to Nottingham. Real property, £... Pop., 165. Houses, 24.

BREWOOD, a small town, a parish, and a sub-district, in Penkridge district, Stafford. The town stands near Watling-street, the river Penk, and the Birmingham and Liverpool canal, 2½ miles WNW of Four Ashes r. station, and 1½ SW by S of Penkridge, and has a post office‡ under Stafford. It formerly had a weekly market, and still has fairs on the third Tuesday of March, May, and Nov., and on 19 Sept. Some trade is carried on in malting and lock making. The parish includes also the liberties of Chillington, Somerford, Engleton, Horsebrook, Coven, Kiddermore Green, and Huttons and Gunston. Acres, 11,839. Real property, £21,634. Pop., 3,399. Houses, 723. The property is divided among a few. Chillington Hall, a fine mansion, is the seat of the Giffards. Two nunneries, Cistertian and Benedictine, were founded in the parish, the former in the reign of Richard I. or of John, and came to be known as the White Ladies and the Black Ladies; and they figure under these names in the narrative of Charles II.'s concealment in the neighbouring locality of Boscobel, after the battle of Worcester. The living is a vicarage in the diocese of Lichfield. Value, £470.* Patron, the Bishop of Lichfield. The church is later English, with a handsome spire, and was renovated in 1833. The vicarages of Bishopswood and Coven are separate benefices. There are chapels for Independents, Methodists, and Roman Catholics. A grammar school, founded by Dr. Knightley in the time of Queen Elizabeth, and at which Bishop Hurd and Sir T. Littleton were educated, has £412 a year from endowment, and other charities have £47.—The sub-district contains two parishes and parts of three others. Acres, 20,782. Pop., 5,529. Houses, 1,17..

BREWOOD FOREST, an ancient forest on the mutual border of Stafford and Salop, around Brewood.

BRIADUN. See Bradon Forest.

BRIAN'S BELL, a hamlet in Belbroughton parish, Worcester, 1½ miles S of Stourbridge.

BRIAN'S PUDDLE. See Aff Puddle.

BRIANSTON. See Bryanstone.

BRIAVELS (St.), a village, a parish, and a hundred, in Gloucester. The village stands near Offa's Dyke and the river Wye, 4 miles SSW of Coleford, and 5 NW of Woolaston r. station, and has a post office‡ under Coleford. It formerly was a market town, and it long made a figure as a defensive post against the Welsh. A castle was built at it, in the time of Henry I., by Fitzwalter, Earl of Hereford, enlarged and strengthened at several periods, and governed by distinguished peers from the reign of King John till that of George III. The entrance-gateway, two huge round towers flanking the gateway, a long pile of building behind, and some interesting features in the interior still remain. Tradition says that King John was either a guest or a prisoner in the castle, and that he wrote on it,—

> "St. Briavel's water and Whyral's wheat
> Are the best bread and water King John ever eat."

The parish includes also the places called the Fence, the Hearse, Mork, Stowe, Hewelsfield, and part of Hudnolls, sometimes deemed extra-parochial; and is in the district of Chepstow. Acres, 5,10.. Real property, £6,18.. Pop., 1,261. Houses, 275. The manor belongs to the Duke of Beaufort. Roman coins have been found at Chanwell. The living is a vicarage in the diocese of Gloucester and Bristol. Value, £18.. Patrons, the Dean and Chapter of Hereford. The church was recently restored. There are an Independent chapel and a national school.—The hundred contains other parishes, and part of another. Acres, ...12. Pop., 25,217. Houses, 5,765.

[illegible] a parish in [illegible] district, Suffolk, 2½ [illegible] by N of [illegible] station, and [illegible] W of Needham [illegible] station. Post town [illegible] under Ipswich. Acres 91[illegible]. Real property, £1,43[illegible]. Pop 207. Houses [illegible]3. The property is divided among a few. An Augustinian priory was founded here, in 1110, by Ralph Fitz [illegible], was annexed to the monastery of Nob[illegible] in France, and given, in the time of Henry VI, to King's College, Cambridge. The living is a vicarage in the diocese of Norwich. Value, £[illegible]. Patron, King's College, Cambridge. The church [illegible] very good. [illegible] held on 5 [illegible].

BRICETT (LITTLE), a hamlet in Offton parish, Suffolk, [illegible] miles ESE of Bildeston. Pop, 2[illegible]. It was formerly a [illegible] and [illegible], but has no church.

BRICHDEN. See BRINGTON.

BRICKENDON, a liberty in All Saints parish, Herts, [illegible], S of H[illegible]. Acres, 1,[illegible]20. Real property, £[illegible]3. Pop, [illegible]. Houses 104. [illegible] Bury [illegible] belonged formerly to Waltham abbey, and is now the seat of R Hine, Esq.

BRICKET WOOD, a railway station in Herts, on the Watford and St Albans railway, 2 miles NNE of Watford.

BRICKHILL, a hamlet in Lockbourn parish, Hants, 3½ miles NW of [illegible]bridge.

BRICKHILL (BOW), a village and a parish in Newport Pagnell district, Bucks. The village stands near Watling street, the river Ouzel, the Grand Junction canal, and the Bletchley and Bedford railway, 2 miles E of Fenny Stratford station. The parish comprises 1,3[illegible] acres, and its post town is Fenny Stratford, under Bletchley station. Real property, £2,80[illegible]. Pop., [illegible]. Houses, 12[illegible]. The property is divided among a few. The surface includes Bow Brickhill eminence, 683 feet high, and is partly common. Some of the inhabitants are lace and straw plait makers. The living is a rectory in the diocese of Oxford. Value £[illegible]70.* Patron, Queen's College, Cambridge. The church stands conspicuously on a steep eminence above the village. Charities, £52.

BRICKHILL (GREAT), a village and a parish in Newport Pagnell district, Bucks. The village stands near Watling street, the river Ouzel, and the Grand Junction canal, 3 miles SSE of Fenny Stratford, and 4 SE of Bletchley station, and has a post office under Bletchley station. The parish comprises 2,370 acres. Real property, £3,920. Pop. 590. Houses 117. The property is divided among a few. The manor, with Great Brickhill House, belongs to Sir P D P Duncombe, Bart. The living is a rectory in the diocese of Oxford. Value £425.* Patron, Sir P D P Duncombe, Bart. The church contains monuments of the Duncombes, the Pannefoots, and others. There are a Baptist chapel, a Wesleyan chapel, a free school, and charities £55.

BRICKHILL (LITTLE), a village and a parish in Newport Pagnell district, Bucks. The village stands near Watling street and the Bletchley and Bedford railway, 2 miles SE of Fenny Stratford station. It formerly had a weekly market, and was, at one time, a seat of assizes. The parish comprises 1,3[illegible] acres, and its post town is [illegible] Brickhill, under Bletchley station. Real property, £2,4[illegible]. Pop., 423. Houses, 93. The property is divided among a few. The living is a vicarage in the diocese of Oxford. Value, £119. Patron, the Bishop of Oxford. The church was restored in 1865. There are a national school and charities £77. A popular rhyme says, respecting the three Brickhill villages,—

"[illegible] stand three Brickhills all in a row,
Great Brickhill, Little Brickhill, and Brickhill of the Bow."

BRICKLEHAMPTON, a chapelry in St Andrew [illegible] parish, Worcester, near the river Avon, 3½ miles SSW of [illegible] station, and [illegible] SE of [illegible]. Post town, [illegible]. Acres 810. Real property £1,[illegible]. Pop. 157. Houses, [illegible]. The property is divided among a few. The living is annexed to the vicarage of [illegible] in the diocese of Worcester. The church is very good.

BRICKLETON, a tything in [illegible] parish, Hants, [illegible] miles N of Andover. Pop. [illegible].

BRICKLEY [illegible]. See [illegible] WALTHAM.

BRICKWALL PARK, the seat of the Frewen family, near Northiam, in Sussex. The mansion has a three-gabled timber front, of the time of Queen Elizabeth; was visited by that monarch, in 1573 on her way to Rye; was the birthplace of Accepted Frewen, the hot opponent of Cromwell, and afterwards Archbishop of York; and contains some interesting pictures and old curiosities.

BRICKWORTH, an old modernized mansion, 6 miles SE of Salisbury, in Wilts, long the seat of the Eyres, and now belonging to the Earl of Ilchester.

BRIDE, or BRIT (THE), a river of Dorset. It rises in the northern vicinity of Beaminster, and runs 8 miles southward to the Channel at Bridport harbour.

BRIDE, Isle of Man. See KIRK BRIDE.

BRIDEKIRK, a township and a parish in Cockermouth district, Cumberland. The township lies near the river Derwent and the Cockermouth railway, 2 miles NNW of Cockermouth. Acres, 916. Real property £1,608. Pop., 125. Houses, 2[illegible]. The parish contains also the townships of Papcastle, Little Broughton, Great Broughton, Ribton, Dovenby, and Tallentire; and its post town is Cockermouth. Acres, 9,[illegible]. Real property, £19,993. Pop., 2,870. Houses, 608. The property is subdivided. The manor belonged to Gisburn abbey, and was given, at the dissolution, to the Tolsons. Bridekirk Hall is the seat of the Dykes family. Freestone and limestone are quarried. The living is a vicarage in the diocese of Carlisle. Value, £240.* Patron, F L B Dykes, Esq. The church is ancient and good, has a Norman doorway, and contains a curious, carved square font, about 2 feet high, supposed to have been Roman. Great Broughton chapelry, formerly a curacy, was made a separate charge in 1863. Charities, £122. Sir Joseph Williamson, secretary of state to Charles II, and Thomas Tickell, the poet, were natives.

BRIDELL, a parish in the district of Cardigan and county of Pembroke, near the river Teifi and the Carmarthen and Cardigan railway, 3 miles S by E of Cardigan. Post town, Cardigan. Acres 2,179. Real property, £1,65[illegible]. Pop 3[illegible]. Houses, 73. The property is divided among a few. The living is a rectory in the diocese of St David's. Value £110. Patron, the freeholders of the parish. The church is ancient, in tolerable condition; and a St Catherine's cross is in the churchyard. There is a dissenting chapel.

BRIDENBURY. See BREDENBURY.

BRIDE (ST). See LONDON.

BRIDES (ST), a parish in Haverfordwest district, Pembroke, on the S side of St Bride's Bay, 7½ miles WNW of Milford, and 9 W of Johnston r. station. Post town, St Ishmaels under Milford. Acres, 1,[illegible]83. Real property, £2,006. Pop 151. Houses, 30. Gold Top road, or Little Haven, near the church, has anchorage for small craft. The living is a rectory in the diocese of St David's. Value £1[illegible].* Patrons, alternately Sir W P L Phillips and Mrs B Allen.

BRIDES (ST), Glamorgan. See BRIDES SUPER [illegible] (ST).

BRIDE'S BAY (ST), a large bay in Pembroke. It faces the W, is flanked on the N side of the entrance by Ramsey island, on the S side by Skomer island, goes 10½ miles inland, and is [illegible] miles wide at the widest part, and 6½ near the head. It is replete with dangers from westerly winds, and has no one perfect refuge, but is otherwise safe, and gives anchorage for small craft in Solvach creek near St David's, and in Goodhope road near St Bride's.

BRIDE'S MAJOR (ST), a hamlet and a parish in Bridgend district, Glamorgan. The hamlet stands between Ogmore river and the Bristol channel, 3½ miles S by W of Bridgend r. station, and has a post office under Bridgend. Real property, £1,[illegible]23. Pop. 351. Houses, 71. The parish contains also the hamlets of [illegible] and Southerndown. Acres, 6,[illegible]2, of which 600 are water. Real property, £[illegible],13[illegible]. Pop. 52[illegible]. Houses 1[illegible]8. The property is divided among a few. The Witchele [illegible] are on the coast. The living is a vicarage united with the vicarage of Wick, in the diocese of Llandaff. Value, £17[illegible].* Patron, F Turberville, Esq The church is ancient and good, and contains monuments of the Butlers and the Wyndhams There is a Calvinistic Methodist chapel See Dunraven Castle

BRIDES MINOR (St), a township and a parish in Bridgend district, Glamorgan The township lies on the river Ogmore, and on the South Wales railway, 2½ miles N by W of Bridgend Acres, 1,829 Real property, £1 035 Pop, 534 Houses, 110 The parish includes also the hamlet of Ynysawdre, and its post town is Bridgend Acres, 2,217 Real property, £1,283 Pop, 879 Houses, 176 The property is divided among a few Remains of Ogmore Castle, which belonged to the duchy of Lancaster, are in Ynysawdre Coal is worked The living is a rectory in the diocese of Llandaff Value, £176 * Patron the Earl of Dunraven

BRIDES NETHERWENT (St), a parish in Chepstow and Newport districts, Monmouth, on the Julian way, 2 miles N by E of Magor r station and 6½ E by S of Caerleon It includes the hamlet of Llandevenny, and its post town is Magor, under Chepstow Acres, 1,032 Real property, £1,399 Pop, 171 Houses, 37 The property is divided among a few The living is a rectory in the diocese of Llandaff Value, £178 Patron, F Perry Esq The church is good

BRIDESTOW, a village and a parish in Okehampton district, Devon The village lies in a pleasant valley near Dartmoor, 6 miles SW of Okehampton, and 11 N by E of Tavistock r station, was formerly called Bridgetstow and has a post office of the name of Bridestow, North Devon, and fairs on the first Wednesday of June and 29 July The parish comprises 5,661 acres Real property £3 995 Pop, 832 Houses 176 The property is divided among a few Millaton House is the seat of J G Newton, Esq, and contains a collection of natural history objects from Dartmoor, and Leawood was long the seat of the Calmady family and is now the seat of S C Hamlyn, Esq There are extensive lime works The living is a rectory united with the p curacy of Sourton, in the diocese of Exeter Value, £424 * Patron, the Bishop of Exeter The church is very old, has a curious Norman gateway, and was restored in 1866 There are chapels for Independents, Wesleyans, and Bible Christians, and a fine school of 1863

BRIDES SUPER ELY (St), a parish in Cardiff district, Glamorgan, on the river Ely and the South Wales railway, 2 miles WNW of St. Fagans station, and 6 W by N of Cardiff It has a post office, of the name of St Brides, under Cardiff Acres, 676 Real property, £935 Pop 122 Houses 28 The property is subdivided The living is a rectory, united with the rectory of Michaelstone super Ely in the diocese of Llandaff Value, £195 * Patron, Mrs Traherne The church is good

BRIDES WENTLLOOGE (St), a parish in Newport district, Monmouth, on the coast and on the South Wales railway, adjacent to the mouth of the river Usk, 1½ mile E by N of Marshfield station, and 4 SSW of Newport Post town, Newport, Monmouth Acres 3,094, of which 1 690 are water Real property, £3,073 Pop., 241 Houses, 47 The property is divided among a few The living is a vicarage, united with the vicarage of Coedkernew, in the diocese of Llandaff Value, £120 * Patron, the Bishop of Llandaff The church is good, and there is an Independent chapel

BRIDFORD, or BRIDGEFORD, a parish in St Thomas district, Devon, on the river Teign 4 miles E by N of Moreton Hampstead r station, and 9 SW of Exeter Post town, Moreton Hampstead under Exeter Acres 4 114 Real property, £2,946 Pop, 576 Houses, 112 Lead mines were not long ago worked, but have been relinquished The living is a rectory in the diocese of Exeter Value £305 * Patron, Sir L. V Palk Bart The church is a small old structure, with turreted tower, and has a fine screen

BRIDGE, a village, a parish a district, and a hundred in Kent The village stands on Watling street, and on the Little Stour river, near the Bekesbourne station of the Canterbury and Dover railway, 3 miles SE of Canterbury, and has a post office under Canterbury The parish comprises 1,161 acres Real property, £3,239 Pop, 89 Houses, 119 The manor belonged to an ancient priory, on the ground now occupied by the church, and passed to the Dutch family of Brennus Bridge Hill House was the seat and death place of the Baron de Montesquieu, grandson of the famous president The living is a vicarage annexed to the vicarage of Patrixbourne, in the diocese of Canterbury The church is Norman and early English, and contains a remarkable monumental effigies, supposed to be of a steward of the archbishop and some singular carvings, representing the creation and fall of man There are a Wesleyan chapel, a literary institute, and a national school The artist Jansen resided much at Bridge, and painted here his portrait of the lady popularly called the "Star in the East"

The district comprehends the sub district of Barham, containing the parishes of Barham, Bridge, Patrixbourne, Bekesbourne, Bishopsbourne Kingstone, Womenswould, Adisham, Ickham, Wickhambreux, Stodmarsh, Littlebourne and Fordwich and the sub district of Chartham, containing the parishes of Chartham, Waltham, Petham, Upper Hardres Lower Hardres Nackington, Thanington, Milton Chapel, and Harbledown, the extra parochial tracts of Mint and St Nicholas Hospital, and part of the parish of Holy Cross Westgate Acres, 47,394 Poor rates in 1866, £6,219 Pop in 1861, 11,316 Houses, 2,308 Marriages in 1866, 55, births, 344,—of which 9 were illegitimate, deaths, 200,—of which 54 were at ages under 5 years, and 7 at ages above 85 Marriages in the ten years 1851-60, 690, births, 3,579, deaths, 2,041 The places of worship in 1851, were 23 of the Church of England, with 5,659 sittings, 1 of Independents, with 160 s, 7 of Wesleyan Methodists, with 680 s and 2 of Primitive Methodists with 50 s The schools were 29 public day schools with 1,054 scholars, 17 private day schools, with 277 s, and 18 Sunday schools, with 530 s The workhouse is in Bridge, and cost £5,000 —The hundred bears the name of Bridge and Petham is in the lathe of St. Augustine, and contains eight parishes Acres, 13,369 Pop, 3,909

BRIDGE-CASTERTON See CASTERTON (GREAT)

BRIDGEEND See BRIDGEND

BRIDGEFOOT, a station on the Cleator railway, in Cumberland 4 miles ESE of Workington

BRIDGEFORD See BRIDFORD

BRIDGEFORD (EAST and WEST) See BRIDGFORD

BRIDGEFORD (GREAT and LITTLE), two hamlets in Seighford parish, Staffordshire, 3½ and 4 miles NW by N of Stafford Pop, 134 and 93

BRIDGEGATE, a village in Abson parish, Gloucester, 9 miles E of Bristol

BRIDGE (GREAT), a locality on the Walsall and Dudley railway, in Stafford, 2 miles NNE of Dudley It has a station on the railway, and a post office under Tipton

BRIDGEHAM See BRIDGHAM

BRIDGEHAMPTON See BRIDGHAMPTON

BRIDGE HEWICK, a township in Ripon parish, W R Yorkshire, 2 miles E of Ripon Acres 867 Pop, 89 Houses, 18

BRIDGE HILL, a chapelry, with a village, in Duffield parish, Derby near the river Derwent and the Midland railway and included in Belper It was constituted in 1845 Post town, Belper Pop 2 859 Houses, 553 The living is a vicarage in the diocese of Lichfield Value, £150 * Patron, alternately the Crown and the Bishop

BRIDGEHOUSES, a village, suburban to Sheffield, W R Yorkshire

BRIDGEMERE, a township in Wybunbury parish, Cheshire on the verge of the county near the North western railway, 6½ miles SSE of Nantwich It has a post office under Nantwich Acres, 1,097 Real property £1,595 Pop., 187 Houses, 37

BRIDGEN, a hamlet in Bexley parish, Kent, 3½ miles W of Dartford Pop 138

BRIDGEND, a hamlet in Horbling parish, Lincoln, 4½ miles ENE of Folkingham Pop, 46 A Gilbertine priory was founded here, in the time of king [illegible] by a London citizen of the name of Godwin and [illegible] at the dissolution, to Edward Lord Clinton

BRIDGEND, a hamlet in St Dogmells parish Pembroke, in the vicinity of Cardigan

BRIDGEND, a hamlet on the Yealm estuary in Devon, [illegible] to Newton Ferrers 6½ miles SE of Plymouth

BRIDGEND, a small town a sub-district and a district in Glamorgan The town is in the parishes of Coyty and Newcastle, and stands on the river Ogmore, and on the South Wales railway 20 miles W of Cardiff It is a [illegible] place, and consists of three parts,—Bridgend proper, Oldcastle and Newcastle The latter two are on opposite sides of the river, and took their name from [illegible] fortresses The Oldcastle fortalice has disappeared but remains of the Newcastle one, consisting of [illegible] walls and a Norman doorway still exist. The town hall is a recent handsome structure A parish church, on a conspicuous site is in the Newcastle sec[illegible] and a chapel of ease is in Oldcastle There are [illegible] dissenting chapels a dispensary and a work[illegible] —the latter erected at a cost of £4,[illegible]00 A railway goes north via [illegible] up the river, and a branch goes to Porthcawl harbour The town has a head post office,‡ a railway station with telegraph a banking office and three [illegible] is a seat of petty sessions and a polling-place, and publishes a weekly newspaper A weekly market is held on Saturday and fairs on 2[illegible] Feb, 1 April, Holy Thursday, 6 June, and 17 Nov Woollen manufacture and a corn trade are carried on, and iron works, coal [illegible], and stone quarries are in the neighbourhood Dr Price and his nephew Mr Morgan, men of science, were [illegible] The population of the town is not returned, but that of the two parishes in which it lies is

The sub-district contains the parishes of Coyty, Newcastle, Laleston, Merthyr-Mawr, Tythegston, Newton Nottage, Pyle, Kenfigg, Ewenny, Wick, St Brides Major and St Andrew Minor Acres 33,498 Pop, 11,[illegible] Houses, 2,2[illegible]9 The district comprehends also the [illegible] district of Maesteg containing the parishes of [illegible], Llangeinor, Llandyfodwg, Llangonoyd, Llandilo, [illegible] St Brides Minor, and part of Llangynwyd, and the sub-district of Cowbridge, containing the parishes of Cowbridge Llangan, St Mary Hill, Llanblethian, Ystradowen, Llansannor, Penllin St Hilary, St Mary Church, Flemingston, Llanmaes-Brewes, St Athan, Gileston, Llantwit Major, Llandow St Donats Marcross, Monknash, Llanmihangel, Llandough, Llanilltyd, [illegible] and Colwinston [illegible] the extra-parochial tracts of Nash and Stembridge Acres, 1[illegible]9,51[illegible] Poor rates in 1863 £17,402 Pop in 1861, 2[illegible],4[illegible] Houses [illegible]2 Marriages in 1866, 2[illegible]7, births, [illegible],034,—of which [illegible] were illegitimate, deaths [illegible]9[illegible],—of which 2[illegible]9 were at ages under 5 years and 31 at ages above 85 Marriages in the ten years 1851-60, 2,[illegible], births 8,001, deaths [illegible] The places of worship in 1851 were 40 of the Church of England, with [illegible] sittings, 1[illegible] of Independents, with 4,65[illegible] s, 14 of Baptists, with 2,47[illegible] s, 1[illegible] of Calvinistic Methodists with 4,[illegible] s, 11 of Wesleyan Methodists, with 1,820 s and 1 of Unitarians, with [illegible] The schools were 20 public day schools, with 2,519 scholars 25 private day schools, with 77[illegible] s, 70 Sunday schools with 4,9[illegible] s, and 2 evening schools for adults with 41 s

BRIDGENORTH See BRIDGNORTH

BRIDGERULE, a parish in Holsworthy district Devon, on the river Tamar and the Bude canal 4 miles [illegible] of Holsworthy and 1[illegible] SW by S of Bideford r station It has a post office under Holsworthy Acres, [illegible] Real property, £2,[illegible] Pop, 410 Houses 87 [illegible] 1,01[illegible] acres, is on the right side of the Tamar, and [illegible] in Cornwall The manor was [illegible] by William the Conqueror, to Ruald Adobed, [illegible] Ruald or Rub Adobel, and it is named [illegible] from him and from a bridge over the Tamar The living is a vicarage in the diocese of Exeter Value, £[illegible] Patron, the [illegible] The church [illegible] English and [illegible] a [illegible] state but has a good porch There is a [illegible] Curtis [illegible]

BRIDGE SOLLARS, a parish in Weobly district, Herefordshire on Offa's dyke, the river Wye and the Hereford and Brecon railway 1½ mile WNW of Credenhill station, and 6 WNW of Hereford Post town, Bishopston under Hereford. Acres, 768 Real property, £1,[illegible] Pop, [illegible]2 Houses, 10 The property is divided among a few The living is a vicarage in the diocese of Hereford Value, £100 Patron the Lord Chancellor The church is early decorated English, and good

BRIDGET (St) See CHESTER

BRIDGET BECKERMET (St) See BECKERMET (St BRIDGET)

BRIDGETOWN See BERRY POMEROY

BRIDGE TRAFFORD a township in Plemonstall parish Cheshire 4½ miles NE of Chester Acres, 401 Real property, £719 Pop, 5[illegible] Houses 10

BRIDGEWATER, or BRIDGWATER, a town, a parish a sub-district and a district in Somerset The town stands in a level, well wooded country on the river Parret, contiguous to the Bristol and Exeter railway 6 miles SSE of Bridgewater bay, and 39½ SSW of Bristol It dates from remote times, and was anciently called Burgh Walter It took that name from Walter de Douay, a Norman baron, to whom the Conqueror gave the manor, and it may have obtained its present name either by corruption of the ancient one, or from a bridge across the Parret William de Briwere or Bruer became owner of it in the time of Henry II, and founded at it a stone bridge instituted an hospital and built a strong large, moated castle The last gave the place military consequence, and drew on it the scourge of the civil wars The barons seized it in the revolt against Henry III, the royalists garrisoned it in support of Charles I, and the parliamentarians under Fairfax, besieged it, captured it, and laid it desolate The castle mounted 40 guns against Fairfax, and, soon after being taken by him, was demolished The Duke of Monmouth took special post in the town, was received and proclaimed as king mustered his forces on the Castle field and marched hence to his fate at Sedgemoor Many of his partisans, who fell into the hands of the victors, were afterwards treated cruelly or put to death here by Judge Jeffries and his [illegible] Kirke

The town stands chiefly on the right bank of the Parret was almost entirely rebuilt after the damage done to it by Fairfax is now a neat place principally of red brick houses, and contains some good streets The part of it on the right bank is suburban and inferior, and bears the name of Eastover An iron bridge of one arch, on the site of the ancient stone one connects the main body with the suburb and a bridge with an arch of 100 feet in span, takes across the railway The castle stood in King's square, and a fragment of it exists in West Water gate The ancient hospital stood on the ground now occupied by St John's church and was upheld for a community of Augustinian monks and for the entertainment of pilgrims An ancient monastery of Grey Friars, probably originating with the same founder as the hospital stood in Silver street and an arched doorway of it still exists. A house in Mill street, of Tudor architecture, was the birthplace of Admiral Blake. The town hall has a great cistern over it for supplying the town with water and contains three pieces of tapestry, which were formerly at Enmore Castle. The market house is a handsome modern structure with a lofty portico and is surmounted by a dome St Mary's church is a large edifice of red stone, partly of the 14th century, but principally of the 15th It has a slender spire rising 120 feet from the tower and 174 from the ground, and contains an altar piece after Guido, and a monument, of 1624, to Sir Francis Kingsmill Trinity church is a modern Gothic structure [illegible] at a cost of £3,2[illegible] St John's church, with its tower, is a handsome edifice of bath stone built in 1844 at a cost of £10,000 The tomb of Oldmixon the historian who was a native of the town is in the churchyard of St Mary and a memorial stone over the victims of the cholera is in that of St John A new Catholic chapel was built in 18[illegible], at a cost of

£5,000. There are also chapels for Baptists, Quakers, Unitarians, Wesleyans, P. Methodists, Free Methodists, Brethren, and R. Catholics, two endowed schools, six other public schools, a school of art and literature and science institution, a workhouse, built at a cost of £9,000, an infirmary, alms houses, and other charities.

The town has a head post office,‡ a railway station with telegraph, three banking offices, and three chief inns, is a seat of assizes and sessions, a polling place, a bonding port, and a coast guard station, and publishes three weekly newspapers. Weekly markets are held on Tuesday and Saturday, and fairs on the second Thursday in Lent, 24 June, 2 3, and 4 Oct, and 28 Dec. The chief manufactures are Bath bricks, red bricks, coarse pottery, and iron ware. The Bath brickworks are the only ones in the world, and produce bricks to the value of about £13,000 a year. The Parret is navigable up to the town for vessels of 200 tons, rises, at the mouth, in spring tides, to 36 feet, and, like other rivers in the Bristol channel and the Severn frith, flows in a solid upright wave of great velocity. This is usually 5 or 6 feet high, but sometimes, after a westerly gale, 9 feet high, and is liable to do great damage to shipping. A canal 12½ miles long, cut in 1811, goes from the town to Taunton, and is continued thence to Chard, and a project has long been entertained of forming a railway from it down to Stolford on Bridgewater bay. The vessels registered at Bridgewater port, at the beginning of 1863, were 72 small sailing vessels of aggregately 2,803 tons, 57 larger sailing-vessels of 10,040 tons, and 5 steam vessels of 264 tons. The vessels that entered in 1867 counting repeated voyages, were 14 British vessels from foreign ports of 2,330 tons, 33 foreign vessels from foreign ports, of 4,021 tons, 10 British vessels and 2 foreign, from British colonies, of 3,9?? tons, 3,823 sailing vessels, coastwise, of 172,896 tons, and 447 steam vessels, coastwise, of 18,021 tons. The amount of customs in the same year, was £6 373. Chief exports are Bath bricks, and chief imports, timber, tallow, hemp, wine, and coal. The town was constituted a borough by King John, is governed by a mayor, six aldermen, and eighteen councillors, and sends two members to parliament. The borough is of the same extent parliamentarily as municipally, and consists chiefly of part of Bridgewater parish, but includes small portions, with two houses, in Durleigh and Wembdon parishes. Direct taxes in 1857, £5 868. Real property in 1860, £34 554, of which £2 378 were in the canal. Electors in 1868 679. Pop in 1861, 11 320. Houses, 2,123. The town gave the titles of Earl, Marquis, and Duke to the Egertons.

The parish includes also the hamlets of East Bower, West Bower, Dunwear, Horsey, Hamp, and Haygrove. Acres, 4,315, of which 190 are water. Real property, exclusive of the borough, £15,963. Pop in 1811, 10 4?6, in 1861, 12,120. Houses, 2,274. The living is a vicarage, united with the rectory of Chilton, in the diocese of Bath and Wells. Value, £325.* Patron, the Lord Chancellor. Trinity and St John are separate benefices, vicarages, of the value of £200 and £300,* the former in the patronage of the Vicar, the latter in that of the Bishop.

The sub district contains the parishes of Durleigh, Wembdon, Chedzoy, Chilton Trinity, and the greater part of Bridgewater. Pop, 15,6?1. Houses, 2,9??.—The district comprehends also the sub district of Middlezoy, containing the parishes of Middlezoy, Othery, Lyng, Weston Zoyland, and parts of Durston and North Petherton, the sub district of Huntspill, containing the parishes of Huntspill, Pawlett, Puriton, Bawdrip, Woolavington, Cossington, and part of Shapwick, the sub district of Polden Hill, containing the parishes of Moorlinch, Greinton, Ashcott, and the greater part of Shapwick, the sub district of North Petherton, containing the parishes of Lyng?, Goathurst, Enmore?, Thurloxton, St Michael Church, and part of North Petherton, and the sub district of Stowey, containing the parishes of Over Stowey, Nether Stowey, Aisholt, Lydeard?, Stockland Bristol, Otterhampton, Cannington, Charlinch, and Spaxton. Acres, 93,277. Poor rates in 1866,

£21,638. Pop in 1851, 34,420. Houses, 7,019. Marriages in 1866, 263, births 1,07?,—of which ?? were illegitimate, deaths, 6?2,—of which 212 were at ages under 5 years and 27 at ages above 85. Marriages in the ten years 1851-60, 2,570. Births, 11 113, deaths, 6,181. The places of worship in 1851 were 43 of the Church of England, with 13,591 sittings, 11 of Independents, with 3 020 s., 7 of Baptists, with 873 s., 1 of Quakers, with 330 s., 1 of Unitarians, with 250 s., 11 of Wesleyan Methodists, with 1,66? s., 1 of Primitive Methodists, with 234 s., 1 of Bible Christians, with 13? s., 1 of Brethren with 98 s., 1 of Latter Day Saints with 38 s., and 3 of Roman Catholics with 370 s. The schools were 23 public day schools with 2,656 scholars, 6? private day schools, with 1,0?2 s., and 58 Sunday schools, with 4,107 s.

BRIDGEWATER BAY, an expansion of the S.E. side of Bristol channel. It is the Vexala Æstuarium of the Romans. It commences between Hurlstone point and Brean down, which are 2? miles apart, and goes inward 9 miles to the mouth of the Parret river. Most of it has a depth of from 10 to ? fathoms at high water, and great part of it is dry at low water. The Gore and the Culver sands are part of its bottom, Steep island lies at its head at the mouth of the Parret estuary, and lights at Burnham, N.E. of that island, guide the fair way into the estuary.

BRIDGEWATER CANAL, a canal in Lancashire and Cheshire. It was cut by Brindley, for the first Duke of Bridgewater in 1758-65. It goes from Manchester west south westward, past Stretford, Altrincham, and Preston Brook, to Runcorn Gap, on the Mersey, sends off a branch from Stretford, west north westward to Barton, Worsley, and Leigh, and makes a junction, at Preston Brook, with the Grand Trunk canal. It measures 27 miles from Manchester to Runcorn Gap, and goes all the way on a level, but falls to the Mersey 82½ feet by ten locks. The branch to Leigh is 11 miles, goes on a higher level, and crosses the Irwell on a lofty viaduct. An embankment, 9,700 feet long, 17 feet high, and 112 feet wide at the base, is on the line near Bollin.

BRIDGFORD (EAST), a village and a parish in Bingham district, Notts. The village stands on the Fosse way and on the river Trent, 2½ miles N of Bingham station, and 9½ E N E of Nottingham, and has a post office under Nottingham. It occupies the site of the Roman Margidunum, and is sometimes called Bridgford on the Hill. The parish comprises 1 910 acres. Real property, £3,430. Pop, 1 078. Houses, 238. The property is subdivided. A ferry is on the Trent at the village. Gypsum is found. Roman coins and other Roman relics have been got on Castle hill. The living is a rectory in the diocese of Lincoln. Value, £702.* Patron, Magdalene College, Oxford. The church is of various dates and character, from early English onward, and was restored in 1852. There are three dissenting chapels, a fine national school of 18?? and charities £18.

BRIDGFORD (WEST), a township and a parish in Basford district, Notts. The township lies on the Grantham canal, near the Midland railway, 2 miles SE of Nottingham. Pop, ?? Houses, ?? The parish contains also the township of Gamston, and includes part of the village of Bassingfield, which has a post office under Nottingham. Acres, 1 720. Real property, £?,??0. Pop, 390. Houses, 7?. The property is divided between two. The living is a rectory in the diocese of Lincoln. Value, £?55. Patron, J. Musters, Esq. The church is good, and there is an endowed school, with £27 a year.

BRIDGHAM, a parish in Guiltcross district, Norfolk, on the Little Ouse river, near the Norfolk railway, 2½ miles SW of Harling road station, and ? N. by E of Thetford. It has a post office under Thetford. Acres, 2,092. Real property, £1,600. Pop, 329. Houses, 72. The property is divided among a few. The manor belongs to Sir ? Fitzherbert, Bart. The living is a rectory in the diocese of Norwich. Value, £395. Patron, the Lord Chancellor. The church has a Norman porch, and is good. There is a Wesleyan chapel.

BRIDGEHAMPTON, a tything in Yeovilton parish, Somerset, 2 miles E by N of Ilchester. Real property, £1,197. Pop. 112. Houses, 23.

BRIDGING, a locality near Bexley in Kent, with a post office under Bexley Heath, London S.E.

BRIDGNORTH, a town, two parishes, a sub-district, a district, and a division in Salop. The town stands on the river Severn, adjacent to the Severn Valley railway, 13½ miles SW by W of Wolverhampton; and a railway from it to Wolverhampton and other places in Staffordshire was authorised in 1866. The town was founded by the Princess Ethelfleda, and was anciently called Brugge or Brigge. A castle is thought to have been built at it by the Saxons, and either this was renovated or a new one erected, of great strength, in 1102, by Robert de Belesme, Earl of Shrewsbury. Henry I speedily took the castle, and made it a royal fortress. Henry II [illegible] it, and [illegible], escaped death beneath its walls. Thomas a Becket lodged in it. John made it a visit. Edward I came to it fresh from his fields of victory. Edward II took refuge in it from the alarms of pursuit. Henry IV rendezvoused his forces at it. Charles I came to it at the commencement of the great disasters of his reign, and pronounced the promenade connected with it the finest walk in his kingdom. The parliamentarians in 1645 laid siege to it, obtained possession of it at the end of three weeks, by capitulation, and then dismantled it, and blew up its fortifications. A large portion of the town was burned to the ground during the siege. Henry IV is represented as saying, in reference to his friends,—

"On Wednesday next, Harry, thou shalt set forward
On Thursday, we ourselves will march.
Our meeting is Bridgnorth; and Harry, you
Shall march through Gloucestershire, by which account,
Our business valued some twelve days hence
Our general forces at Bridgnorth shall meet."

The town is divided by the Severn into two portions, called the Upper and the Lower. The Upper portion is on the [illegible] bank, on the [illegible] and summit of a [illegible] sandstone rock, rising 180 feet above the level of the river, and presents a remarkably picturesque appearance. The houses rest on the [illegible] rock, and in some instances, have cellars hewn out of it; a hollow [illegible] deep, goes down the slope of the rock to the river; and a railed terrace, cut along the [illegible] of the [illegible] above [illegible], and around the castle's site, and commands splendid views. The High-street is spacious, and once had [illegible] at Chester. Extensive street improvements have been made since 18[illegible]. A large fragment of the castle [illegible] exists, inclining seventeen degrees from the perpendicular, in consequence of undermining at the siege preceding its demolition. A handsome bridge, with six arches, crosses the Severn. The town hall, in the middle of High-street, was built in 1646. The agricultural hall is in the Gothic style, and was built in 1857. The market hall is a [illegible] of coloured brick, erected in 18[illegible]. [illegible] Century, was the birthplace of Bishop Percy. St. Mary's church was originally founded at Quatford in the time of William [illegible] by Roger Earl of Shrewsbury, but was soon removed to the castle at Bridgnorth, made collegiate or [illegible] and [illegible] exempt [illegible] John [illegible] in the time of Edward III. The present edifice is in the [illegible] style [illegible] cupola, and was erected in 1792. St Leonard's [illegible] decorated English, was [illegible] of nave, chancel, and north and south aisles, [illegible] tower, has a handsome [illegible], and a carved oak pulpit, and [illegible] the place [illegible]. There are chapels for Independents, Baptists, and Methodists, a free grammar school, with [illegible] exhibitions at Oxford, a blue [illegible] school, an hospital, an alms-house, with [illegible] £277 a year, a [illegible] institute, a [illegible] library, [illegible] his Dinner [illegible] house, and a public library, with about 6,000 volumes.

The town has a head post office,‡ a railway station with telegraph, two banking offices, and two chief inns, is a seat of sessions and a polling-place, and publishes a weekly newspaper. A market is held on Saturday; and fairs on the third Monday of Jan., Feb., March, Aug., and Sep., on the second Monday of June, July and Dec., and on 1 May and 29 Oct. Much business is done in agricultural produce; and manufactures are carried on in carpets, rugs, and worsteds. The town was chartered by Henry II; sent two members to parliament from the time of Edward I till 1867, was reduced, in that year, to the right of sending only one; and is governed by a mayor, four aldermen, and twelve councillors. The municipal borough includes the two town parishes, part of Quatt, and most of Quatford. The parliamentary borough includes also the parishes of Astley Abbots, Tasley, and Oldbury, the rest of Quatford parish, and Romsley [illegible] in Alveley parish. Direct taxes in 1857, £4,006. Electors in 1865, 658. Pop. in 1861 of the m. borough, 6,2[illegible]. Houses, 1,270. Pop. of the p. borough, 7,6[illegible]. Houses, 1,570. Francis Moore, the physician, and Stedman, the divine, were natives.

The two parishes are St. Mary or Low parish and St. Leonard or High parish. Acres of St. Mary, 531. Real property, £8,189. Pop., 2,6[illegible]3. Houses, 567. Acres of St. Leonard, 590. Real property, £[illegible],957. Pop., 3,011. Houses, 631. St. Mary is a rectory, St. Leonard a p. curacy, in the diocese of Hereford. Patron of both, T. Whitmore, Esq. Value of St. Mary, £250;* of St. Leonard, £308.* The sub-district includes also the parishes of Tasley and Oldbury, and the greater part of Quatford. Acres, 3,382. Pop., 6,240. Houses, 1,294. The district comprehends also the sub-district of Worfield, containing the parishes of Worfield, Quatt, Alveley, and Claverley, and the sub-district of Chetton, containing the parishes of Chelmarsh, Glazeley, Deuxhill, Billingsley, Sidbury, Middleton Scriven, Neenton, North Cleobury, Burwarton, Loughton, Stanton, [illegible], Monkhopton, Acton Round, Upton-Cressett, Morville, and Astley Abbots, part of Quatford, and the greater part of Chetton. Acres, 69,[illegible]. Poor rates in 1866, £8,732. Pop. in 1861, 1[illegible],9[illegible]. Houses, 3,29[illegible]. Marriages in 1866, 85; births, 4[illegible],—of which 30 were illegitimate; deaths, 213,—of which 53 were at ages under 5 years, and 13 at ages above 85. Marriages in the ten years 1851-60, 915; births, 4,517; deaths, 2,9[illegible]. The places of worship in 1851 were 20 of the Church of England, with 6,1[illegible]2 sittings; 1 of Independents, with 400 s.; 2 of Baptists, with 530 s.; 5 of Wesleyan Methodists, with 3[illegible]9 s.; 1 of Primitive Methodists, with 28 s.; 1 Catholic and Apostolic, with 200 s.; and 3 of Roman Catholics, with 2[illegible] s. The schools were 15 public day schools, with 1,1[illegible] scholars; 10 private day schools, with 317 s.; 19 Sunday schools, with 1,202 s.; and 1 evening school for adults, with 12 s. The workhouse is in St Leonard.—The division is in Brimstree hundred; and contains Worfield and Claverley parishes, and part of Bobbington. Acres, 18,973. Pop., [illegible]. Houses, 713.

BRIDGWATER. See BRIDGEWATER.

BRIDLINGTON,—pronounced BURLINGTON,—two small towns, a township, a parish, a sub-district, and a district in E. R. Yorkshire. The towns are Bridlington [illegible] Bridlington Quay. Bridlington [illegible] stands on a gentle declivity, at the [illegible] river, [illegible] to the Hull and Scarborough railway, about [illegible] of a mile from the sea, 6 miles WSW of Flamborough Head, and [illegible] NNE of Hull. A Roman [illegible] probably [illegible] its site, and a Roman road [illegible] from it, across the Wolds, toward York. An Augustinian priory was founded at it in the time of Henry I, by Walter de Gant; and [illegible] in the [illegible] of Edward II, to [illegible] his son by [illegible]. The [illegible] belonged to it, and at the dissolution was [illegible] by the inhabitants. The town was [illegible] Henrietta Maria, queen of Charles I, [illegible] to the neighbouring [illegible] Hill [illegible], the parliamentarians [illegible] under Admiral [illegible] now consists chiefly of one long [illegible], but possesses interest for the beauty of its [illegible] and for its priory church, now the parish church [illegible] 200 feet long, [illegible] early English choir of seven bays, an early English transept, a magnificent reredos, and five chapels in one range, but now consists chiefly of the nave, 185 feet long, 68 feet wide, and 96 feet high, in the best geometrical decorated English, contains a hexagonal stone pulpit, and a tall Purbeck marble font, and has an east window, constructed in 1861. A gatehouse of the priory is used as the town hall, and some cells have been used as a prison and a school. A market house, with a corn exchange, was built in 1856. There are here or at B. Quay chapels for Independents, Baptists, Wesleyan Methodists, Primitive Methodists, and U. Free Methodists, a grammar school, founded in 1637, an endowed school for girls, charities, including the two schools, to the amount of £402 a year, a workhouse, two subscription libraries, a small museum, and five chief inns. The town has a post office‡ under Hull, a railway station with telegraph, and two banking offices, and is a seat of county courts and a polling place. A weekly market is held on Saturday, a fortnightly cattle market on Tuesday, and fairs on the Monday before Whitsunday and 21 Oct. Bridlington is the scene of three of Montgomery's sonnets.

Bridlington Quay stands on the shore, on a fine bay, ¾ of a mile from Bridlington, is a seaport, a sea bathing resort, and a coast guard station, and has a post office‡ under Hull. It comprises a spacious principal street, descending to the harbour, and some other streets, and is well built, and lively. The Victoria public rooms are a Tudor edifice, with embattled tower, built at a cost of £8,000, and include promenade, exhibition, billiard, and news rooms. The church is a structure in the early English style, built in 1840. There are hot and cold sea water baths, and races are run in October. The bathing accommodation on the beach is very good, the sands firm, and the views and walks delightful. A spring within high water mark gives a copious supply of the purest water, intermittent springs are in the neighbourhood, and a chalybeate spring, of similar quality to the springs of Scarborough, is about ¼ of a mile distant. The harbour has two piers extending far into the sea, and is defended by a cross battery, and the bay is a commodious anchoring place, sheltered by Flamborough Head and the Smithic sand. The port is under Hull, and has a considerable trade in corn, malt, and manures. The seats of Boynton, Thorpe Hall, Bessingby, Sewerby, and Sledmere Park, and some beautiful villas are in the neighbourhood. An improvement at Bridlington Quay was projected in 1864, to comprise the erection of a sea wall from the North pier to the esplanade, and the making of a promenade, with terraced-walks, and a flight of stone steps to the beach, and estimated to cost £35,000. A sea fight between three American vessels under Paul Jones and two British ones took place in the vicinity in 1779.

The township includes the two towns, and comprises 3,060 acres of land and 67 of water. Real property, £21,738. Pop., 5,775. Houses, 1,303. The parish includes also the townships of Buckton, Hilderthorpe with Wilsthorpe, Sewerby with Marton, Speeton, and Grindall, and the hamlet of Easton. Acres, 13,276. Real property, £35,636. Pop., 6,838. Houses, 1,551. The property is much subdivided. The living is a vicarage in the diocese of York. Value, £218.* Patrons, Simeon's Trustees. Bridlington Quay, Speeton, and Sewerby with Marton and Grindall are separate benefices, the first a vicarage of value £150,* in the patronage of the vicar of Bridlington. William de Newburgh, the monkish historian, Thomas Newman, commemorated by a tablet in the churchyard, and Kent, the landscape gardener, were natives, and several men of note were connected with the priory. The sub-district contains the parishes of Bessingby, Carnaby, Boynton, Flamborough, Rudston(?), the greater part of Bridlington, and part of Fraisthorpe. Pop., 8,518. Houses, 1,921. The district comprehends also the sub-district of Skipsea, containing the parishes of Burton Agnes, Barmston, and parts of Skipsea, Ulrome(?), Lissett(?), and Beeford; and the sub-district of Hunmanby, containing the parishes of Hunmanby, Argam, Rudston, Flixton(?), Wold Newton, Burton Fleming, Reighton, and part of Bridlington. Acres, 67,484. Poor rates in 1866, £10,623. Population in 1861, 14,371. Houses, 3,079. Marriages in 1866, 93; births, 456,—of which 17 were illegitimate; deaths, 292,—of which 121 were at ages under 5 years, and 5 at ages above 85. Marriages in the ten years 1851-60, 1,053; births, 4,718; deaths, 2,913. The places of worship in 1851 were 24 of the Church of England, with 4,790 sittings; 2 of Independents, with 610 s.; 2 of Baptists, with 360 s.; 26 of Wesleyan Methodists, with 4,1?? s.; and 11 of Primitive Methodists, with 1,500 s. The schools were 17 public day schools, with 1,270 scholars; 42 private day schools, with 881 s.; 26 Sunday schools, with 1,702 s.; and 1 evening school for adults, with 7 s.

BRIDPORT, a town, a parish, a sub-district, a district, and a division in Dorset. The town stands on a gentle eminence, between the rivers Bride and Asker, a little above their confluence, and at the terminus of a branch railway, surrounded by hills, 1½ mile N of the Bride's mouth, 9½ by railway WSW by Maiden Newton, and 15 by road W of Dorchester. It had a mint and 120 houses at the time of the Conquest; was occupied by both the royalists and the parliamentarians, but not contested by either during the civil war; made a riotous outburst at the time of the Duke of Monmouth's landing at Lyme; and had an ancient priory, dedicated to St. John the Baptist. It consists of three spacious airy streets, contains many handsome houses, and commands from its summit-ground many fine vista views. The town hall occupies the site of an ancient chapel, was built in 1786, and is a handsome edifice of brick and Portland stone. The parish church is cruciform, chiefly later English, has a central, square, pinnacled tower, was restored in 1860, at a cost of upwards of £3,000, and contained a monument to a kinsman of Queen Philippa, and some other interesting monuments. St. Andrew's church, near the northern entrance to the town, is a new, small, beautiful edifice. There are chapels for Independents (a new one,) Baptists, Quakers, Unitarians, Methodists, and Roman Catholics, a free school, with £30 a year, alms-houses with £73, other charities, with £97, and a mechanics' institute. Bridport Harbour is at the mouth of the Bride, 1½ mile distant, has a post office of its own under Bridport, some cottages, and an inn, and takes its name from a basin enclosed by a double wooden pier, flanked by picturesque cliffs, and capable of admitting vessels of 200 tons.

Bridport has a head post office,‡ a railway station with telegraph, two banking offices, and two chief inns, is a seat of sessions, a coast guard station, and a bonding port, and publishes a weekly newspaper. Markets are held on Wednesday and Saturday, and fairs on 6 April, Holy Thursday, and 11 October. Manufactures are carried on in shoe thread, twine, cordage, sailcloth, and fishing nets. The cordage was at one time a great staple, supplied nearly all the royal navy in the time of Henry VIII., and became so identified with the work of the hangman as to be popularly called "the Bridport dagger." The vessels registered at the port at the beginning of 1868 were 9 of 1,430 tons; and those which entered in 1867, counting repeated voyages, were 3 of 155 tons from British colonies, 15 British of 2,747 tons and 5 foreign of 640 tons from foreign countries, and 60 sailing vessels of 10,427 tons coastwise. The customs in 1867 were £2,803. The chief exports are cheese, butter, and the local manufactures; and the chief imports hemp, flax, tallow, timber, wines, spirits, coal, and slate. The town was chartered by Henry III.; sent two members to parliament from the time of Edward I. till 1867; was reduced in 1867 to the right of sending only one; and is governed under the new act by a mayor, six aldermen, and eighteen councillors. The borough includes all Bridport parish, and parts of Burton-Bradstock, Bothenhampton, Walditch, Allington, Bradpole, and Symondsbury parishes. Acres, 636. Direct taxes in 1857, £3,770. Electors in 1868, 70?. Pop. in 1861, 7,719. Houses, 1,551. The town gave the title of Baron and Viscount to the family of Hood.

The parish comprises 62 acres. Real property, £1?,102. Pop., 4,617. Houses, 9?2. The property is much silk twist. The living is a rectory in the diocese of Salisbury. Value, £250.* Patron, the Earl of Ilchester. The sub-district includes also the parishes of Allington and Bradpole. Acres, 1,623. Pop., 8,00[illegible]. Houses, 1,[illegible]. The district comprehends also the sub-district of Whitchurch-Canonicorum, containing the parishes of Whitchurch-Canonicorum, Chideock, Symondsbury, Wootton-Fitzpaine, and Charmouth Lewston, and the parochial chapelry of Stanton St. Gabriel; and the sub-district of Burton-Bradstock, containing the parishes of Burton-Bradstock, Loders, Askerswell, Chilcombe, Litton-Cheney, Puncknowle, Swyre, Bothenhampton, and Walditch, and the parochial chapelry of Shipton-George. Acres, 53,1[illegible]7. Poor rates in 1866, £8,6[illegible]. Pop. in 1861, 1[illegible],82[illegible]. Houses, 3,520. Marriages in 1866, 12[illegible]; births, [illegible]71,—of which 31 were illegitimate; deaths, 357,—of which 12[illegible] were at ages under 5 years, and 16 at ages above 85. Marriages in the ten years 1851-60, 1,[illegible]; births, [illegible]; deaths, 3,529. The places of worship in 1851 were 2[illegible] of the Church of England, with [illegible]932 sittings; 6 of Independents, with 2,1[illegible]0 s.; 1 of Baptists, with [illegible] s.; 1 of Quakers, with 250 s.; 1 of Unitarians, with 474 s.; 6 of Wesleyan Methodists, with 1,459 s.; and 1 of Latter Day Saints, with 140 attendants. The schools were 23 public day schools, with 1,504 scholars; 3[illegible] private day schools, with 69[illegible] s.; 32 Sunday schools, with 2,[illegible]31 s.; and 3 evening schools for adults, with 32 s. The workhouse is in Bridport. The division contains the hundreds or liberties of Beaminster, Beaminster-Forum and Redhone, Broadwindsor, Godderthorne, Haydor, Loders and Bothenhampton, Powerstock, and Whitchurch-Canonicorum; and parts of the hundreds or liberties of Eggardon, Frampton, Uggescombe, and Cerne, Totcombe and Modbury. Acres, 87,104. Pop. in 1851, 24,67[illegible]; in 1861, 23,848. Houses, [illegible],051.

BRIDPORT HARBOUR. See BRIDPORT.

BRIDPORT RAILWAY, a railway in Dorset, from the Great Western system at Maiden-Newton, west-south-westward, to Bridport. It was opened in November 1857, is [illegible] miles long, and has a station at Powerstock.

BRIDSTOW, a parish in Ross district, Hereford, on the River Wye, adjacent to the Monmouth and Hereford railway, 1 mile W by N of Ross. Post town, Ross. Acres, 2,19[illegible]. Real property, £5,506. Pop., 717. Houses, 143. Wilton Castle here is an old seat of the Lords Grey de Wilton, burnt in the civil wars, and now only a ruin. The living is a vicarage in the diocese of Hereford. Value, £276.* Patron, the Bishop of Hereford.

BRIDY. See BRIDY.

BRIERCLIFFE, a township and a chapelry in Whalley parish, Lancashire. The township bears the name of Briercliffe-with-Extwistle, and lies near the East Lancashire railway, 3 miles NE by E of Burnley. Post town, Burnley. Acres, 4,180. Real property, £[illegible],222. Pop., 1,[illegible]2. Houses, 263. There are quarries and cotton mills. The chapelry was constituted in 18[illegible]2. Pop., [illegible]. Houses, 303. The living is a vicarage in the diocese of Manchester. Value, £250.* Patrons, Hulme's Trustees. The church was built in 1840. There are two Baptist chapels and a national school.

BRIERDEAN, or BRIERDON, a township in Earsdon parish, Northumberland, on the Blyth railway, [illegible] miles NNW of North Shields. Acres, [illegible]35. Pop., [illegible]07. Houses, [illegible]. Coal and limestone are worked. A terrible colliery disaster occurred here in March, 1860.

BRIERFIELD, a station on the East Lancashire railway, 2[illegible] miles NE of Burnley.

BRIERLEY, a township in Felkirk parish, W. R. Yorkshire, adjacent to the Barnsley canal and the North Midland railway, [illegible] miles NE of Barnsley. It includes the hamlet of Grimethorpe, and has a post-office under Barnsley. Acres, 2,610. Real property, £3,6[illegible]. Pop., [illegible]. Houses, 10[illegible]. Most of the inhabitants are colliers.

BRIERLEY, a village in Sedgley parish, Stafford, 3[illegible] miles NE of Dudley.

BRIERLEY, Hereford. See BROADWARD AND BRIERLEY.

BRIERLEY HILL, a town and a chapelry in Kingswinford parish, Stafford. The town stands on the river Stour, the Dudley and Stourbridge canal, and the West Midland railway, 2[illegible] miles NNE of Stourbridge; and has a station on the railway and a head post-office.‡ It lies in a hilly tract of great mineral wealth, forms a street about a mile long, carries on industry in coal mines, clay fields, brick works, potteries, glass works, iron rolling mills, boiler works, chain and spade factories, and malting establishments, and publishes a weekly newspaper. The church at it is a structure in [illegible] time, built in 17[illegible], and enlarged in 182[illegible] and 1837, with a tower which commands an extensive view; and there are chapels for Independents, Baptists, Wesleyan Methodists, and Primitive Methodists. The chapelry includes the town, and was constituted in 1842. Pop., 10,7[illegible]. Houses, 2,[illegible]60. The living is a rectory, united with the p. curacy of Harts Hill, in the diocese of Lichfield. Value, £300.* Patron, the Rector of Kingswinford.

BRIERLEY, or ST. ANNE'S IN THE GROVE, a chapelry with a village, in Halifax parish, W. R. Yorkshire, near the Manchester and Leeds railway, 3[illegible] miles ESE of Halifax. Post town, Halifax. Rated property, £15,[illegible]7. Pop., 6,570. The property is subdivided. The living is a p. curacy in the diocese of Ripon. Value, £160.* Patron, the Vicar of Halifax. The church is tolerable.

BRIERTON, or BIERTON, a township in Stranton parish, Durham, near the Hartlepool railway, 3[illegible] miles SW by S of Hartlepool. Acres, [illegible]45. Real property, £[illegible]12. Pop., 30. Houses, 4.

BRIERY COTTAGES. See GRETA MILLS.

BRIERYHURST, or BRIERYHURST, a township in Wolstanton parish, Stafford, adjacent to the North-western railway, 2 miles NNE of Newcastle-under-Lyne. Real property, £5,157, of which £400 are in mines. Pop., 4,072. Houses, 798. The working of coal and iron ore is carried on.

BRIESTFIELD, or BRIESTWHISTLE, a hamlet in Lower Whitley township, Thornhill parish, W. R. Yorkshire, 6¾ miles E of Huddersfield.

BRIGG. See GLANFORD-BRIGG.

BRIGGE. See BRIGG-NORTH.

BRIGHAM, a township and a parish in Cockermouth district, Cumberland. The township lies on the river Derwent, and on the Cockermouth and Workington railway, 2 miles W of Cockermouth, and has a station on the railway. Real property, £4,30[illegible]. Pop., [illegible]0[illegible]. Houses, 122. The parish contains also the town and chapelry of Cockermouth, and the townships of Blindbothel, Graysouthen, Setmurthy, Eaglesfield, Mosser, Buttermere, Whinfell, and Embleton; and its post-town is Cockermouth. Acres, 22,[illegible]87. Real property, £46,112. Pop., 7,874. Houses, 1,[illegible]. The property is much subdivided. The surface is greatly diversified, ranging from soft valley to bold high mountain, and contains much brilliant scenery. Limestone, freestone, slate, and coal are worked. The living is a vicarage in the diocese of Carlisle. Value, £190. Patron, the Earl of Lonsdale. The church is ancient, but English, in good condition. The chapelries of Cockermouth, Lorton, Mosser, Setmurthy, Wythop, Embleton, and Buttermere are separate benefices. There are an Independent chapel and charities £142.

BRIGHAM, a township in Foston-on-the-Wolds parish, E. R. Yorkshire, near the Hull and Scarborough railway, 1½ miles SE of Great Driffield. Acres, 1,170. Real property, £1,[illegible]48. Pop., 111. Houses, 2[illegible].

BRIGHOUSE, a village and a chapelry in Hipperholme-cum-Brighouse township, Halifax parish, and a sub-district in Halifax district, W. R. Yorkshire. The village stands on the river Calder, adjacent to the Manchester and Leeds railway, 3[illegible] miles ESE of Halifax, and has a station with telegraph on the railway, a post-office under Normanton, and fairs on 13 May and 12 Oct. Trade is carried on in cotton, woollen, and worsted manufactures, in [illegible] and [illegible] making, and in the working and exporting of building stone. Rastrick Hall, the seat of the Thornhills, is in the vicinity. The chapelry includes the village, and was constituted in

1842 Rated property, £11,660 Pop 4,562 Houses, 947 The property is much subdivided The living is a p curacy in the diocese of Ripon Value, £250 * Patron, the Vicar of Halifax The church is a modern Gothic edifice built at a cost of £3,515 There is a chapel of ease, two Methodist chapels, and an endowed grammar school with £119 a year —The sub district consists of parts of the parishes of Halifax and Dewsbury Acres, 5,514 Pop, 9,992 Houses 2,107

BRIGHSTONE See BRIXTON, Isle of Wight.

BRIGHTFORD, a hundred in the rape of Bramber, Sussex It contains the town of Worthing and seven parishes Acres, 10,319 Pop, 8,678 Houses, 1,603

BRIGHTHAMPTON, a hamlet in Bampton parish, Oxford, 4 miles E of Bampton Acres, 410 Real property £1,033 Pop, 89 Houses, 21

BRIGHTHELMSTONE See BRIGHTON

BRIGHTHOLMLEE, a hamlet in Bradfield chapelry, W R Yorkshire, 6½ miles NW of Sheffield

BRIGHTLEY, a hamlet in Okehampton parish, Devon, near Okehampton

BRIGHTLEY, a hamlet in Chittlehampton parish, Devon, 2½ miles from Chittlehampton

BRIGHTLING, a parish in Battle district Sussex, in the Weald 4 miles WSW of Robertsbridge r station, and 6½ NW of Battle It has a post office under Hurst Green Acres, 4,613 Real property, £3,794 Pop, 661 Houses, 132 The property is subdivided Brightling Down is 646 feet high, commands an extensive panoramic view, and is crowned by an observatory Rosehill Park is the seat of O Meyrick, Esq, and Socknersh, the seat of John Halloway, Esq The living is a rectory in the diocese of Chichester Value, £563 * Patron, the Rev B Hayley The church is tolerable A school has £22 from endowment, and other charities £18

BRIGHTLINGSEA, a village and a parish in Lexden district Essex The village stands on the estuary of the Colne, opposite Mersea island, at a terminus of the Tendring Hundred railway, 8 miles SE by S of Colchester, is a sub port to Colchester, and a member of the cinque port of Sandwich and has a post office‡ under Colchester, and a recently erected temperance hall Fairs are held on the first Thursday of June and 15 Oct, and a large trade is carried on in the fishing of sprats and oysters The parish comprises 3,560 acres of which 470 are water Real property, £7,081 Pop, 2,585 Houses, 589 The property is subdivided The living is a vicarage in the diocese of Rochester Value, £213 * Patron, the Bishop of Peterborough The church has a tower nearly 100 feet high, serving as a sea-mark, and contains brasses of a merchant, a nun and W Beriffe, 1579 There are a chapel of ease in Gothic architecture, and chapels for Independents, Wesleyans, and Swedenborgians

BRIGHTON, a town a parish, and a district on the coast of Sussex The town stands on swell, slope, and cliff, under the South Downs, 18 miles W by N of Beachy-Head, 21 E by N of Selsea Bill 8 SW by W of Lewes, 27 E of Chichester, and 50½ S of London The sea before it forms a great slender bay, bounded by Beachy Head and Selsea Bill and gives an open view past the latter, to the Isle of Wight One railway goes direct to London, another goes to Lewes, and thence to Kent, and a third goes to Chichester and Portsmouth, and thence to the west

Name and History —The name popularly is always Brighton but anciently was Brighthelmstone and continues so in all legal and parochial documents, and was derived from some person of the name of Brighthelm supposed probably, to have been an Anglo Saxon bishop of Selsea The place is thought to have been a scene of Druidical worship, and, from the discovery at it of Roman coins and other Roman relics, is concluded to have been occupied by a Roman station The manor belonged, in the time of Edward the Confessor, to Earl Godwin, descended to his son Harold, who fell in the battle of Hastings, was given, by the Conqueror to William de Warrene, and was given, soon after, in gift to the priory of Lewes The town or what was so considerable at the end of the 16th century, as to become then the seat of a market, and consisted of two parts,—one on the beach, inhabited by fishermen,—the other on the cliffs, inhabited by landsmen The Flemings, the French and the Spaniards made attacks on the town, or descents in its neighbourhood, through a period of three centuries, and continually checked its prosperity A block house for arms and ammunition, and encompassing strong walls, with four gates were erected for its defence, in the times of Henry VIII and Elizabeth, but were gradually destroyed by the sea Even the lower part of the town itself underwent assaults from the billows and eventually disappeared Charles II fled hither from his overthrow at Worcester, spent a night in a small inn, still existing in West street, and embarked in the neighbourhood for Fecamp in Normandy The town declined till about 1750, and had then only about 800 inhabitants, chiefly poor fishermen Dr Russell, a distinguished physician, drew attention to it, at that time, as a desirable bathing place, and some persons of influence and fashion soon began to visit it from London Dr Johnson, with Mrs Thrale and Fanny Burney, was here in 1770, and the Prince of Wales, afterwards George IV first came in 1782, and then founded a permanent summer residence in 1784 Brighton suddenly underwent a change of fortune and it has gone on increasing, steadily and rapidly, from that time till the present, so as to be now the greatest watering place in the world

Streets and Places —The town extends three miles, from Hove on the W to Kemp Town on the E, and presents such an imposing frontage to the sea as cannot be rivalled by any other town All of it, with small exception, is modern, and much is handsome, elegant or grand Some parts stand on slopes, descending from the skirts of the South Downs, some on low flat grounds, at the bottom, and some on cliffs, immediately overhanging the sea The central portion includes the Steyne named from the "stane" or rock on which the fishermen of the old time used to dry their nets, and contains some houses of the last century, the pavilion or palace built by George IV, and two large enclosures thickly planted with shrubs The western portion includes the early fashionable extensions, exhibits a prevailing character of comparative stillness or uniformity, and contains the fine localities of Regency-square, Brunswick sq, Brunswick terrace, and Adelaide crescent The eastern portion includes the later extensions, displays a richer style, and contains streets, squares, crescents, and terraces, edificed with as splendid houses as almost any in the kingdom Kemp Town here surmounts a cliff nearly 200 feet high, was commenced in 1821, on the estate of Thomas Read Kemp, Esq and includes a crescent 800 feet across with wings 350 feet each The streets, for the most part, are spacious, and intersect one another at right angles, the higher places have chiefly gardens or shrubbery, and command fine views, and the prevailing aspect of its over residences, shops, and thoroughfares, is similar to that of the best part of London

Public Buildings —A sea wall for resisting the encroachment by the sea, extends nearly a mile westward from Kemp-Town was built at a cost of about £100,000, and diminishes upwards from a thickness of fully four teen feet to a thickness of about two feet A chain pier, situated at the west end of the sea wall, extends 1,014 feet into the sea, was constructed in 1822, by Captain Brown, at a cost of £30,000, suffered much injury from storms in 1824 and 1833, but has since been repaired and strengthened, is divided by four towers, into four spans, of 255 feet each has [illegible] the roadway, expands at the head into a platform 80 feet square, and is used as a public promenade A west pier, on iron supports, was opened in 1866, is 1,115 feet long, and has promenading space for fully 2,000 persons The Pavilion or palace of George IV underwent alterations and changes till 1817, assumed a fantastic character, with domes minarets, cupolas, and spires, alleged to resemble the Kremlin at Moscow, was occasionally visited by William IV and Victoria, was sold in 1850, to the town authorities of Brighton, for 53,000, and is now used for all sorts of occasions for public entertainment the entrance h ll . . . , magnificent, the banqueting room . . . is 60 feet by 42 the music room is of similar size, the rotunda is 55 feet in diameter . . . the Queen's . . . is 162 feet long The stables connected with the pavilion are in the Moorish style, with a vast glazed dome lighting a circle of about 250 feet, and was formed, in 1867, into a concert hall and rooms The house in which Mrs Fitzherbert resided is adjacent A bronze statue of George IV by Chantry, erected in 1828 at a cost of £3 000, and a fountain, called the Victoria, are in the Steyne The town hall is a handsome modern erection, 144 feet long and 11 feet broad with three double porticoes raised at a cost of £30,000, and contains a principal apartment 85 feet by 35 and various committee, magistrates and assistants rooms The market house stands on the site of the old town hall, was built in 1830 and is in the form of a T County court offices in Gothic style, were built in 18 . The assembly rooms are at the Old Ship hotel The theatre was enlarged and remodelled in 1866 and now accommodates an audience of about 1 900 The railway terminus is an elegant and commodious structure, and has a Roman portico surmounted by an illuminated clock The water works are supplied from wells in the chalk pumped by powerful engines, sending the water to reservoirs at levels which command the highest houses, they are managed on a capital of £250,000, and considerable additions to them were in progress in 1865 A grand hotel was erected in 1864 nine storeys high at a cost of £170 000 The cavalry barracks can accommodate 623 men the infantry barracks, about 400 The sewage of the town was carried further out to sea in 1867, and was decided, in 1870, to be diverted landward

Churches —The places of worship within the parliamentary borough in 1851 were 24 of the Church of England and 38 of other denominations and of the latter, 6 belonged to Independents, 7 to Baptists 1 to Quakers 1 to Presbyterians, 2 to Wesleyan Methodists, 1 to Primitive Methodists 1 to United Free Methodists 1 to Bible Christians 1 to Lady Huntingdon's Connexion, 2 to French Protestants, 1 to German Protestants 1 to the Catholic Apostolic Church 2 to Roman Catholics, 1 to Jews 2 to mission congregations and 7 of some what iso lated character but several of the 38 were only rooms or halls. St Nicholas' church on an eminence, in the NW of the town, dates from the time of Edward III has always served as a landmark for fishermen was rebuilt in 1853 . . . memorial of the Duke of Wellington, who habitually attended it while a pupil of the vicar . . . early English style, . . . the original perpendicular screen and . . . circular Norman font, and has, in the churchyard . . . cross about 18 feet high dedicated to the Duke of Wellington and inscribed round the shaft with the names of his chief victories The churchyard contains monumental stones of Captain Tettersell, the preserver of Charles II, Phoebe Hessell, who fought . . . and Mrs Crouch the actress St Peter's church, at the head of the Steyne was built in 1828 after designs by Sir Charles Barry, at a cost of £20 000, is in the later pointed style with windows of . . . nave, aisles and . . . tower . . . St Paul's church, in West street, on the edge of the Downs . . . was built in 1847, by Mr Carpenter, . . . St Paul . . . St James' church . . . was built in 1850 . . . at a cost of £5,000 . . . St Mary Magdalene's was built in 1862 and . . . St Michael's was built . . . early geometric style, and cost £6,670 . . . also built also in 1862, is in the early decorated style and cost £3 550 Other established churches are All Souls, Christ Church St John's St Stephen's St Mary's, St George's, All Saints . . . , St Margaret's, St Martin's, and St Mark's Some of the dissenting places of worship are spacious and handsome The Roman Catholic church, in Upper North street was built in 1862, consists of nave, aisles chancel Lady chapel and side chapels and has a tower and spire 143 feet high

Schools and Institutions —There were within the borough, in 1851, 32 public day schools, with 5 094 scholars 210 private day schools, with 4,3 6 s , and 24 Sunday schools with 3 932 s Brighton college, in the east, was founded in 1848 and forms a quadrangle, with chapel and cloisters The proprietary grammar school was erected in 18 . The military school . . . attended Grimm's blue coat school has £78 from endowment and Dean's . . . school has £303 The county hospital in Kemp Town, was founded in 1828, has since acquired two wings, called the Adelaide and the Victoria, and contains accommodation for 150 patients The asylum for the blind, close by the county hospital, was built in 1861, is in the Venetian Gothic style, and forms nearly a square edifice, in red and black brick The town museum was opened in November 1861, occupies a spacious suite of rooms in the N wing, of the Pavilion, and contains collections of antiquities natural history . . . and miscellaneous curiosities. There are a . . . proprietary college, a . . . school for . . . a literary and scientific institution, a natural history society, an art society, a young men's literary union, numerous reading rooms and libraries, and a variety of benevolent and miscellaneous institutions Two cemeteries lie to the N of the town the one opened in 1851 and belonging to a private company, the other opened in 1859, on ground given to the town by the Earl of Bristol, and called the parochial cemetery

Means of Health . . . —The climate differs, as to warmth in the higher and lower parts, and in the . . . is of equal . . . and healthy . . . for children and . . . and suitable for . . . sheltered . . . . . . the season, . . . from July to October and another for repose . . . October till April The bathing beach is partly sand and . . . with machines divided into groups for respectively ladies and gentlemen Bathing establishments with every variety of baths and also a large public swimming bath, are in the town A charming park which is called the German Spa, furnishing artificial mineral waters similar to those of the most celebrated continental spas, is in a narrow valley running up to the hill from the East cliff A long public promenade . . . a lower promenade, for the inhabitants of Kemp Town is reached by a tunnel through the rocks, pleasure boats are in constant waiting for hire, regattas, concerts, lectures, and all other sorts of entertainment are frequent, the theatre is . . . in brisk service, harriers hunts and fox hunts are made almost daily over the neighbouring downs races are run in August, and excursions can be made, in . . . direction to many . . .

Trade —A large . . . is carried on . . . till Christmas . . . from May till July, and a general fishery . . . to the supply of the . . . by about . . . boats . . . and commerce . . . more than nominal The retail trade is extensive A weekly market is held on Thursday and a . . . Thursday . . . a head post office . . . post-office receiving offices in . . . Victoria road, Kemp Town, and West . . . telegraph offices on . . . four banking offices . . . many hotels, inns . . . houses, . . . 20,000 visitors . . . weekly . . . published on Wednesday and Saturday and . . . newspapers . . . on Monday, Wednesday, Thursday, Friday, and Saturday Onenibuses run from the railway station to Hove and Kemp Town, and an omnibus runs to Shoreham

The Borough —The town is governed under a charter of 1854, by a mayor, a recorder 12 aldermen, and 36 councillors, and under the act of 1832, sends two members to parliament The municipal borough is conterminate with the parish of Brighton The parliamentary borough consists of the parishes of Brighton and Hove and comprises 3 192 acres A police force is maintained consisting of 101 men and costing annually about £7,255 The number of crimes committed in 186-, was 311, of persons apprehended 1 018 of known depredators and suspected persons at large 1,013, of houses of bad character, 263 Direct taxes in 18-7, £74,2-7 Real property in 1860 £-52,877 Borough income in 1861, £-9,491 Electors in 1868, 6 652 Pop in 1831 41,-94, in 1861 87,317 Houses, 13,983 Bishop Kidder was a native

The Parish —The parish comprises 1 980 acres of land and 310 of water Real property, £161,217 Pop, 77 693 Houses, 12 727 The property is much subdivided Fully one half of the land is rural, chiefly down pasture The living is a vicarage united with the rectory of West Blatchington, in the diocese of Chichester Value not reported * Patron, the Bishop of Chichester The parish church is St Nicholas, and the other nineteen churches are all separate charges Value of St John's £90, of the Chapel Royal, £--, of All Souls and St Mary's, £100, of St. James', £130, of All Saints, £200, of Christ Church, £420, of St. Stephen's, £425, of the others, not reported Patron of St Peter's, All Souls' Christ Church St John's, St Paul's, St Stephen's, All Saints, St Michael's, St Mary Magdalene's and the Chapel Royal the Vicar, of St James', the Trustees of the late N Kemp, Esq, of St Mary's, the Rev H V Elliott of St George's, L Peel, Esq, of Trinity, the Trustees of the late Rev R Anderson, of St Margaret's, Mrs W M Du Pre, of St Mark's the Trustees of St Mary's Hall

The District —The district is conterminate with the parish, forms a poor law union under a local act and is divided into the Palace, St Peter, and Kemp Town Poor rates in 1866, £37 050 Marriages in 1866 902, births 2 754,—of which 174 were illegitimate deaths, 1,886,—of which 650 were at ages under 5 years and 43 at ages above 85 Marriages in the ten years 1851-60, 6,181, births, 22 438, deaths, 15 737 Of the places of worship and the schools returned in 1851 as in the borough, all the places of worship, 29 public day schools 189 private day school, and 23 Sunday schools were in the district

BRIGHTON (NEW), a village and a chapelry in Wallasey parish Cheshire The village stands within Liscard township on the coast at the mouth of the Mersey near the Lighthouse, 3½ miles N by W of Birkenhead It enjoys a salubrious climate, commands fine bathing grounds and is much frequented as a summer watering place It has a post office‡ under Birkenhead, three good hotels, numerous lodging houses and a [illegible] establishment for convalescents a life-boat station reading rooms assembly rooms, a church, and a Wesleyan chapel The church was built in 1856, at a cost of about £3 000, and is in the early English style with a tower and spire The chapelry includes the village and was constituted in 1861 Pop 2,404 Houses, 367 The living is a vicarage in the diocese of Chester Value, £600 * Patron, the Bishop

BRIGHTON PLACE a farm house, 1 mile E of Sutton Valence, in Kent, long the seat of the Wottons, the birthplace of Sir Henry Wotton, afterwards the residence of Horace Mann

BRIGHTON RAILWAY See LONDON, BRIGHTON, and SOUTH COAST RAILWAY

BRIGHTON, UCKFIELD, AND TUNBRIDGE WELLS RAILWAY See UCKFIELD and TUNBRIDGE WELLS

BRIGHTSIDE a village, a chapelry, a township, and a sub district, in Sheffield parish W R Yorkshire The village stands adjacent to the Sheffield and Rotherham railway, 2½ miles NE of Sheffield, and has a station on the railway, and a post office under Rotherham The chapelry was constituted in 1854 Pop, 10 101 Houses, 2,101 The living is a vicarage in the diocese of York Value, £-00 * Patron, alternately the Crown and the Archbishop One church was built in 1851, and another, at a cost of nearly £12,000, in 1869 The township bears the name of Brightside Bierlow, and includes Bridgehouses, Nursery, and Wicker which are suburbs of Sheffield,—as also the villages of Crabtree, Grimesthorpe, and Neepsend Acres, 2,-10 Real property, £85 768, of which £1 66- are in mines and quarries Pop 29 818 Houses 6 213. There are cutlery works, rolling mills, a chapel of ease, two Methodist chapels, a library, national schools, and charities £41 —The sub district is conterminate with the township

BRIGHT WALTHAM, BRIGHT WALTON, or BRICKLETON, a parish in Wantage district, Berks near the downs, 7 miles S of Wantage and 8½ NW of Newbury r station It has a post office under Wantage Acres, 2,0-8 Real property, £3,312 Pop, 430 Houses, 91 The living is a rectory in the dio of Oxford Value £700 * Patron, J R Hinman, Esq The church and a school are recent and there is a Wesleyan chapel

BRIGHTWELL, a parish in Wallingford district, Berks near the river Thames and the Great Western railway, 2½ miles W N W of Wallingford r station and 3½ E of Didcot It has a post office under Wallingford Acres, 2,024 Real property, £-,503 Pop, 70- Houses 158 The property is divided among a few The manor belongs to the Bishop of Winchester An ancient castle stood here, and was destroyed about the time of Henry II The living is a rectory in the diocese of Oxford Value, 674 * Patron, the Bishop of Winchester The church was repaired in 1858 and there are a national school, and charities £25 Godwin, author of a work on Jewish and Roman antiquities, Bernard, the astronomer, and Wintle, the orientalist were rectors

BRIGHTWELL a parish in Woodbridge district, Suffolk, 3 miles S by E of Bealings r station and 6½ E by S of Ipswich Post town, Bucklesham, under Ipswich Acres 965 Real property £831 Pop, 81 Houses, 14 The property is divided among a few The living is a vicarage united with the p curacy of Foxhall in the diocese of Norwich Value, £112 Patron Sir J Shaw Bart The church is good

BRIGHTWELL BALDWIN, or BRITWELL BALDWIN a parish in Henley district, Oxford 2¼ miles W by N of Watlington, and 8 NNE of Wallingford Road r station It includes the liberty of Cadwell and its post town is Cuxham, under Tetsworth Acres, 1,660 Real property, £2,151 Pop 277 Houses, 57 Brightwell house is the seat of F J Austen, Esq The parish is a resort of sportsmen The living is a rectory in the diocese of Oxford Value, £386 * Patron, Mrs L S Norton The church is fine decorated English, with a perpendicular tower and contains tombs of the Carletons There are a national school, and charities £28 Bishops Westfaling and Paul were rectors

BRIGHTWELL PRIOR, or BRITWELL PRIOR, a chapelry in Newington parish, Oxford under the Chilterns 1¼ mile SW of Watlington, and 7½ NW by N of Wallingford Road r station Post town, Britwell-Salome under Wallingford Real property, £806 Pop, 43 Houses, 6 The manor belonged formerly to the Wells, and Brightwell House is now the seat of H Lowndes, Esq An ancient priory stood here, and a nunnery of St Clare was set up for some time by French Nuns who fled from the first revolution The living is a p curacy, annexed to the rectory of Newington, in the diocese of Oxford The church is Norman in the nave, and early English in the chancel, and has a decorated font

BRIGHTWELL SALOME or BRITWELL SALOME, a parish in Henley district, Oxford, on Icknield street, under the Chilterns, 1¼ mile SW of Watlington, and 8 NW by N of Wallingford Road r station It has a post office of the name of Britwell Salome, under Wallingford Acres 871 Real property, £1 312 Pop, 217 [illegible] The south-eastern part toward the Chil terns, rises into Brightwell downs and has an ancient camp. The living is a rectory in the diocese of Oxford Value, £440.* Patron, the Marquis of Lansdowne The church is partly Norman, and has two brasses.

BRIGHTWELLS BARROW, a hundred in the E of Gloucester. It adjoins Oxford and Wilts, is 9½ miles long, and contains Fairford parish, ten other parishes, and part of another. Acres, 26,790 Pop, 8,030 Houses, 1,708

BRIGMERSTON, a hamlet in Milston parish Wilts, on the river Avon, 3½ miles N of Amesbury Pop, 38. It belongs to C E Rendall, Esq, and forms a curacy with Milston.

BRIGNALL, a parish in Teesdale district and N R Yorkshire, on the Tees, at the influx of that river, 3½ miles SE of Barnard Castle r station. It contains [illegible] of Greta Bridge which has a post office under Darlington. Acres, 2,037 Real property, £2,102 Pop, 1[illegible] Houses, 3[illegible] The property is all in one estate. A Roman camp is adjacent to Greta Bridge, and a Roman road went thence to the Tees at Piercebridge, and to Leswick at Catterick bridge. The scenery is picturesque, and ranks up to Scargill cliff and woods, sung by Scott in his "Rokeby". Brignall banks themselves are thus sung in that poem:—

O Brignall banks are wild and fair,
And Greta woods are green,
And you may gather garlands there
Would grace a summer queen

The living is a vicarage in the diocese of Ripon Value, £350 Patron, the Lord Chancellor The church is old and [illegible].

BRIGSLEY, a parish in Caistor district Lincoln, 3 m [illegible] of Holton le Clay r station, and [illegible] S by W of Great Grimsby Post town, Waltham, under Grimsby [illegible] Real property £1,647 Pop, 1[illegible] Houses, 35 The property is subdivided. The living is a rectory in the diocese of Lincoln Value, £60. Patron, Southwell Collegiate Church The church is good

BRIGSTEER, a hamlet in the township of Levens and Helsington, Westmoreland, 3½ miles SSW of Kendal

BRIGSTOCK, a village and a parish in Thrapston district, Northampton The village stands on a rivulet at the river Nen, near Rockingham forest 6 miles NNW of Thrapston station and 7½ NE of Kettering It has a post office‡ under Thrapston, and fairs on 25 April, 4 Sept, and 22 Nov, and was once a market town The parish comprises 5,900 acres Real property, £8,11[illegible] Pop, 1,[illegible] Houses, 266 The property is divided among a few Brigstock Park belonged formerly to the Montagues The living is a vicarage united with the curacy of Stanion in the diocese of Peterborough Value, £[illegible] Patron, the Duke of Cleveland The church is partly Norman, and good, and there are Independent and primitive Methodist chapels, an endowed school with £20 a year, and charities £65

BRILL, a village, a parish, and a sub district, in the district of Thame and county of Bucks. The village stands on an eminence, within the ancient Bernwood forest 2½ miles S of the Julian way, and 7 NNW of Thame r station It has a post office‡ under Thame, and fairs on the first Wednesday of May and the Wednesday before old Michaelmas day, and was formerly a market town. It was a summer residence of the Saxon kings. Edward the Confessor had a hunting-lodge adjacent to it, Henry II kept his court here in 1160, attended by Becket and others in 1162 King John spent his Christmas here in 1205, Henry III held his court here in 1224, and Sir G Gerard under Charles I placed a force here in 1642, and repelled an attack by Hampden The parish comprises 2,900 acres Real property, £5,873 Pop, 1,432 Houses, 321 The property is much subdivided The manor was given by the Conqueror to Nigel [illegible], and has descended from him to Sir J D Aubrey, Bart Stone is quarried, yellow ochre is found, and clay has been worked into pottery here since the time of the Romans, but ceases to be so. [illegible] A mineral spring in the immediate neighbourhood of the village has some medicinal repute, and a hotel stands adjacent to it for the accommodation of visitors. A grove near the village is probably a relic of Bernwood forest Muswell or Muzzle hill is crowned by an ancient camp and a hermitage, and commands a fine view The living is a vicarage, united with the vicarage of Boarstall in the diocese of Oxford Value £101.* Patron, C S Ricketts, Esq The church is partly Norman and good, and there are two Independent chapels, a Wesleyan chapel, a national school, four alms houses, poors' lands £120 a year, and some other charities —The sub district contains eleven parishes Acres, 20,720 Pop 5,646 Houses 1,237

BRILLEY, a parish in the district of Presteigne and county of Hereford, and a sub-district partly also in the county of Radnor The parish lies on the verge of the county near the river Wye and the Hereford and Brecon railway 5½ miles NNE of Hay Post town, Whitney under Hereford Acres, 3,792 Real property £4,182 Pop, 517 Houses 101 The living is a vicarage, united with the rectory of Michaelchurch in the diocese of Hereford Value, £350.* Patron, the Bishop of Worcester A school has £50 from endowment and other charities £6 —The sub district contains seven parishes Acres, 1[illegible] Pop, 2,687 Houses, 109

BRIMFIELD, a village and a parish in the district of Tenbury and county of Hereford The village stands near the river Teme and the Leominster canal 1½ mile E of Woofferton r station and 5 S by E of Ludlow, and has a post-office under Ludlow —The parish includes also the hamlet of Wyson Acres 1,542 Real property, £3,681 Pop, 665 Houses, 131 The property is much subdivided The living is a rectory in the diocese of Hereford Value £165.* Patron the Bishop of Hereford The church is a plain good edifice, with a [illegible] modern tower, and there is a dissenting chapel

BRIMHAM, a hamlet in Hartwith with Winsley township W R Yorkshire, 8½ miles WNW of Ripley Brimham Rocks are a group of shattered crags of romantic character and antiquarian interest Two of the rocks, called the Cannons, are perforated, another, called the Rock Idol, is supposed to have been a Druidical, and several others are great rocking stones, two of them computed to weigh 100 tons each and moveable by hand

BRIMINGTON, a chapelry or parish, with a village of its own name, in Chesterfield district, Derby, near the Chesterfield canal and the North Midland railway, 2 miles NE of Chesterfield The village is modern and well built, and has a post office under Chesterfield Real property in the parish, £3,778 Pop, 1,808 Houses, 370 The property is divided among a few Brimington Hall is a chief residence The living is a rectory in the diocese of Lichfield Value £300.* Patron, the Vicar of Chesterfield The church was built in 1808, and rebuilt, all except the tower in 1847 There are three Methodist chapels, a mechanics' institute, a national school, and charities £3.

BRIMPSFIELD, a parish in Cirencester district, Gloucester, on Ermine street, 6½ miles S of Cheltenham r station It includes the hamlets of Birdlip and Caudle Green, and has a post office under Stroud Acres 2,311 Real property, £3,239 Pop 1,201 Houses 270 The property is divided among a few A castle belonging to the Giffords stood here, and was destroyed by Edward II A Benedictine priory here was a cell to Fontenay abbey in Normandy, and was given by Henry VI to Eton college The living is a rectory, united with Cranham in the diocese of G and Bristol Value £410.* Patron, J Goodrich, Esq The church is very good There are a Baptist chapel and a national school

BRIMPTON, a parish in Newbury district, Berks, on the rivers Enborne and Kennet 1½ mile SW of Woolhampton r station, and 6 ESE of Newbury It has a post office under Reading Acres, 1,692 Real property, £3,[illegible] Pop, [illegible] Houses, 1[illegible] The property is divided among a few A preceptory of the Knights Templars, afterwards of the Knights Hospitallers, was here The living is a vicarage in the diocese of Oxford Value, £8[illegible] Patron, the Rev G [illegible] The church is good, and there are charities £81

BRIMPTON, a parish in Yeovil district, Somerset, adjacent to the Yeovil and Exeter railway, 2 miles W by S of Yeovil. It includes the hamlets of Alvington and Houndstone, and its post town is Yeovil. Acres 46[illegible]. Real property, with Westcombe, £3,014. Pop, 1[illegible]5. Houses, [illegible]. The property is much subdivided. The manor once belonged to the Sydenhams, and Brimpton House now belongs to the Earl of Westmorland. The living is a rectory in the diocese of Bath and Wells. Value, £170.* Patron, Mrs. L. Morris. The church is good.

BRIMSCOMBE, a hamlet in Minchinhampton parish, and a chapelry in Minchinhampton and Rodborough parishes, Gloucester. The hamlet stands adjacent to the Thames and Severn canal, and to the Great Western Union railway, 3 miles ESE of Stroud, and has a station on the railway, a post office under Stroud, and a hotel. The chapelry includes Chalford and other hamlets, and was constituted in 1840. Rated property, £[illegible],809. Pop, 1,430. Houses, 322. The property is much subdivided. The living is a vicarage in the diocese of Gloucester and Bristol. Value, £300.* Patron, D. Ricardo, Esq. The church was built in 1839. There are two Methodist chapels and a national school.

BRIMSLADE. See SAVERNAKE (SOUTH).

BRIMSTAGE, a township in Bromborough parish, Cheshire, 2 miles W of Spital station, and 4 NE of Great Neston. Acres, 1,012. Real property, £1,[illegible]22. Pop, 185. Houses, [illegible].

BRIMSTONE, a village in Wiston Castle parish, Pembroke, 6½ miles N of Haverfordwest.

BRIMSTREE, a hundred in Salop. It adjoins Staffordshire, and is cut into the three divisions of Bridgnorth, Brewood, and Shiffnal. Acres, 62,[illegible]. Pop, 13,12[illegible]. Houses, 2,610.

BRINCAMISH, a township in Church-Stoke parish, Montgomeryshire, [illegible] miles NW of Montgomery. Pop, 50.

BRINCHIL. See BRINSUCHIL.

BRINCLIFFE EDGE, a hamlet in Ecclesall Bierlow township, W. R. Yorkshire, 1½ mile SW of Sheffield.

BRIND, a hamlet in Wressell parish, E. R. Yorkshire, on the Selby and Hull railway, 2 miles NNW of Howden.

BRINDLE, a parish and a sub-district in Chorley district, Lancashire. The parish lies on the Leeds and Liverpool canal, and on the Preston and Blackburn railway, near Bamber-bridge station, 5 miles N by E of Chorley, and has a post office under Chorley. Acres, 2,935. Real property, £6,401. Pop, 1,[illegible]01. Houses, 2[illegible]5. The manor belongs to Lord Cheetham. There is a cotton factory, print works, chemical works, brick works, and quarries. The living is a rectory in the diocese of Manchester. Value, £515.* Patron, the Duke of Devonshire. The church is good; and there are a chapel at B. Heath, built in 1861, a Roman Catholic chapel, a large boarding school, a workhouse, and charities £31.—The sub-district includes also part of Leyland parish. Acres, 10,[illegible]88. Pop, 6,021. Houses, 1,112.

BRINDLEY, a township in Acton parish, Cheshire, 4½ miles WNW of Nantwich. Acres, 1,[illegible]90. Real property, £1,77[illegible]. Pop, 227. Houses, 41.

BRINDLEY FORD, a locality with recently erected iron works, on the north border of Staffordshire, in the Biddulph valley, 4 miles N of Burslem. A chapel was erected here in 1861, in plain Gothic style, with about [illegible]00 sittings.

BRINDLEYS, an extra-parochial tract in Howden district, E. R. Yorkshire, 2 miles N of Howden.

BRINGHURST, a township and a parish in the district of Uppingham and county of Leicester. The township lies on the river Welland, ¾ of a mile SW of Great Easton, and 2 W of Rockingham r. station. Pop, 1[illegible]. Houses, 2[illegible]. The parish contains also the townships of Drayton and Great Easton; the latter of which has a post office under Uppingham. Acres, 3,[illegible]. Real property, £7,50[illegible]. Pop, 82[illegible]. Houses, 18[illegible]. The living is a vicarage, united with the p. curacy of Great Easton, in the diocese of Peterborough. Value, £211. Patrons, the Dean and Chapter of Peterborough. The churches are good; and there are three dissenting chapels.

BRINGTON, or BRUNINGTON, a parish in the district of Thrapston and county of Huntingdon, on an affluent of the river Ouse, 6 miles N by W of Kimbolton, and 6[illegible] ESE of Thrapston r. station. Post town, Kimbolton, under Thrapston. Acres, 1,190. Real property, £1,290. Pop, 191. Houses, 41. The property is much subdivided. The living is a rectory, united with the p. curacies of Bythorn and Old Weston, in the diocese of Ely. Value, £[illegible]02.* Patron, Clare College, Cambridge.

BRINGTON, or BRINTON, two villages and a parish in Brixworth district, Northampton. The villages are Great Brington and Little Brington; and the former stands 1 mile N of the latter, in the western vicinity of Althorp Park, [illegible] miles NNE of Weedon r. station, and 7 NW of Northampton, and has a post office under Northampton. The parish includes also the hamlet of Nobottle. Acres, 3,[illegible]. Real property, £6,17[illegible]. Pop, 80[illegible]. Houses, 170. The property is divided among a few. The living is a rectory in the diocese of Peterborough. Value, £[illegible]34. Patron, Earl Spencer. The church contains some fine monuments of the Spencer family, has a fine set of open benches of the 15th century, and is good. There are Baptist and Wesleyan chapels, an endowed school, and a poors' estate £225 a-year. Archbishop Chicheley was rector.

BRINGHYFIELD, a township in Llanbadarn-fawr parish, Radnorshire, [illegible] miles WNW of Radnor. Pop, 2[illegible]4.

BRININGHAM, a parish in Walsingham district, Norfolk, [illegible] miles SW of Holt, and 7 ENE of Walsingham r. station. It has a post office under Thetford. Acres, 1,011. Real property, £2,413. Pop, 206. Houses, 51. The property is subdivided. The living is a vicarage in the diocese of Norwich. Value, not reported. Patron, the Rev. S. Brereton. The church is tolerable.

BRINKBURN, a parochial chapelry, consisting of the townships of B. South side, B. High ward, and B. Low ward, in Rothbury district, Northumberland, on the river Coquet, 4½ miles SE by E of Rothbury, and 7 WSW of Longhorsley r. station. Post town, Long Horsley, under Morpeth. Acres, 3,[illegible]78. Real property, £2,[illegible], of which £[illegible]00 are in iron works. Pop, 220. Houses, 43. The manor belonged to a priory of Black canons, founded here in the time of Henry I. by William de Bertram, Lord of Mitford; was given, at the dissolution of monasteries, to the Earl of Warwick; and passed to the Cadogans. Remains of the priory, including most of the walls of the church, still exist. The church is transitional Norman, cruciform, with low square tower, narrow plan, and gloom; an interesting relic of the age in which it was built. A branch of Watling-street intersected the chapelry; and traces of a Roman station and bridge can still be seen. Some persons suppose Brinkburn to be the Brunanburgh where Athelstane, in 938, defeated the Danes. Coal and lime abound.

BRINKELY. See BRINKLEY.

BRINKHILL, a parish in Spilsby district, Lincoln, 3 miles WSW of Alford r. station, and 5½ NNW of Spilsby. Post town, Ulceby. Acres, 780. Real property, £1,339. Pop, 177. Houses, 37. The living is a rectory in the diocese of Lincoln. Value, £137. Patron, Col. Cracroft. The church is good; and there are a Wesleyan chapel, and charities £8.

BRINKLEY, a parish in Newmarket district, Cambridge, 3 miles E of Six Mile Bottom r. station, and 5½ S by W of Newmarket. It has a post office under Newmarket. Acres, 1,5[illegible]0. Real property, £2,257. Pop, 317. Houses, 66. The property is divided among a few. Brinkley Hall is a chief residence. The living is a rectory in the diocese of Ely. Value, £2[illegible]1.* Patron, St John's College, Cambridge. The church is old but good. There is an endowed school with £[illegible] a-year.

BRINKLOW, a village and a parish in Rugby district, Warwick. The village stands on the Fosse way and the Oxford canal, 1½ mile SW of Shilton r. station, and [illegible] NW of Rugby. It has a post office under Coventry; is said to have been anciently a market town. The parish comprises 2,1[illegible] acres. Real property, £[illegible]. Pop, 7[illegible]. Houses, 170. The property is much subdivided. The manor belonged anciently to the Mow-

Brays, and [illegible] castle of the m, but passed to the Stonehouses and the Sergeaves. Traces of a Roman camp exist, and some Roman relics have been found. The living is a rectory in the diocese of Worcester. Value, £225.* Patron, the Lord Chancellor. The church is variously early and decorated English, was restored in 1862, and comprises nave, aisle, chancel with a tower. There are chapels for Independents and Primitive Methodists. A school has £7 from endowment, and other charities have £31. The family of [illegible], the antiquary, were residents.

BRINKWORTH, a village and a parish in Malmesbury district, Wilts. The village stands on a headstream of the Avon, 3½ miles WNW of Wootton Bassett r. station, and 5½ ESE of Malmesbury; and has a post office under Chippenham [illegible] is a polling place. The parish includes also the tything of Grittenham. Acres, 5,434. Real property, £10,618. Pop. 1,273. Houses, 280. The property is subdivided. The living is a rectory in the diocese of Gloucester and Bristol. Value, £598.* Patron, Pembroke College, Oxford. The church is early English, with a square tower, and there are an Independent chapel, and charities £26. Crisp, the antiquary, was rector.

BRINNINGHAM. See BRININGHAM.

BRINNINGTON, a township in Stockport parish, Cheshire, adjacent to the Peak Forest canal, 2 miles NE of Stockport. Acres, 75[illegible]. Real property, £18,101. Pop., [illegible],546. Houses, 1,10[illegible]. Many of the inhabitants are [illegible].

BRINSCOMBE, a hamlet in Weare parish, Somerset.

BRINSLEY, or BRINSLEY, a hamlet and a chapelry in Greasley parish, Notts. The hamlet lies on the river Erewash, the Nottingham canal, and the Midland railway, near [illegible], 5 miles SE by S of Alfreton, and has a post office, of the name of Brinsley, under Alfreton. Pop. 1,1[illegible], chiefly stocking makers and colliers. The chapelry till very recently was annexed to the vicarage of Greasley, but is now a separate benefice. The living is a vicarage in the diocese of Lincoln. Value, £133. Patron, the Duke of Newcastle. The church was built in 18[illegible]. There are two Wesleyan chapels.

BRINSOP, a parish in Weobly district, Herefordshire, on [illegible] on an affluent of the river Wye, 2 miles [illegible] of Credenhill r. station, and 5½ NW of Hereford. Post town, Bishopstone, under Hereford. Acres, 1,6[illegible]. Real property, £1,0[illegible]2. Pop. 115. Houses, 2[illegible]. The property is divided among a few. The living is a vicarage in the diocese of Hereford. Value, £[illegible]. Patron, the Bishop of Hereford. The church is old but good, and contains two monuments of the Dauncys.

BRINSWORTH, a township in Rotherham parish, W. R. Yorkshire, adjacent to the North Midland railway, 2 miles SW by S of Rotherham. Acres, 1,0[illegible]0. Real property, £3,1[illegible]7. Pop., 777. Houses, 151.

BRINTON, a parish in Erpingham district, Norfolk, 3½ miles SW by W of Holt, and [illegible] of Walsingham [illegible]. It has a post office [illegible] Thetford. Acres, 6[illegible]. Real property, £1,015. Pop., 177. Houses, [illegible]7. The property is divided among a few. The living is a [illegible] annexed to the rectory of Thornage, in the diocese of Norwich. The church is good.

[illegible]

[illegible] SOP, [illegible] in Doncaster [illegible] Yorkshire, [illegible] NW [illegible]

[illegible] parish [illegible] Cumberland [illegible] station [illegible]

[illegible]

BRISLEY, a parish in Mitford district, Norfolk, 3 miles W by S of Elmham r. station, and 5½ NNW of East Dereham. Post town, East Bilney, under Swaffham. Acres, 1,201. Real property, £2,700. Pop. 362. Houses, 85. The property is subdivided. The living is a rectory united with the vicarage of Gateley, in the diocese of Norwich. Value, £[illegible]56.* Patron, Christ's College, Cambridge. The church is good.

BRISLINGTON, a parish in Keynsham district, Somerset, on the river Avon and the Great Western railway, 2½ miles SE of Bristol. It has a post office under Bristol. Acres, 2,30[illegible]. Real property, £9,397. Pop., 1,45[illegible]. Houses, 215. The property is divided among a few. Brislington House is a large and well arranged lunatic asylum. Brislington tunnel on the line of the railway, goes through the shale and sandstone of the coal measures, is 3,145 feet long, and has four ventilating shafts. The living is a vicarage in the diocese of Bath and Wells. Value, £179. Patron, [illegible] Esq. The church is good, and was not long ago enlarged. There are a national school and charities £1[illegible].

BRISONS, or [illegible] (THE), two dangerous rocks, between 60 and 70 feet in height, about [illegible] of Cape Cornwall, 4 miles N of Land's End, in Cornwall. The brig New Commercial was wrecked here, in a [illegible] in January, 1851.

BRISSINGHAM. See BRESSINGHAM.

BRISTOL, a city, with special jurisdiction, on the mutual border of Gloucester and Somerset. It includes eighteen town parishes, and an extra-parochial tract forming the district of [illegible] of the parishes of Clifton and St Philip and St Jacob Out, part of the parish of St. James and St Paul Out, and part of the tything [illegible] of Stoke Bishop in the [illegible] of Clifton, and part of the parish of Bedminster, in the district of Bedminster. It stands on the river Avon, at the influx of the Frome, 6 miles in direct distance from the Avon's mouth, 11½ WNW of Bath, and 118 by railway W of London. The Avon [illegible] nearly 30 feet, was partly diverted past [illegible] in a deep new cut in 1804-9, with [illegible] a great floating harbour, and gives it, for large sea-borne vessels, all the characters of a seaport. A [illegible] and the Kennet and Avon canal at Bath, and [illegible] Exeter, London, Wales, and Gloucester.

History.—Bristol is supposed to have been founded by Brennus, the alleged king of the Britons, and was called by these people Caer Oder, the "city of Oder," or perhaps the "city of the Chasm," in allusion to the gorge through which the Avon flows at Clifton. It must also have been adopted and improved by the Romans, and is thought, by some antiquaries, to be the Roman Abona, on the Julian way. It is mentioned by a writer of the sixth century, and again by one of the seventh, as a fortified town, and is thought to have been a meeting place, in 603, of St. Augustine with the bishops of the primitive church; and it was known to the Saxons as [illegible] signifying "the pleasant city." Harold set sail from it, in 1063, to invade Wales, and coins were struck at it both in his reign and that of the Conqueror. [illegible] then [illegible] and this was seized in 1088 [illegible] head quarters by the [illegible] for the crown [illegible] kept here after his defeat [illegible] Prince Henry [illegible] the abbey of St. Augustine [illegible] King [illegible] Bristol [illegible] the people by [illegible] in 12[illegible] [illegible] and a palace [illegible] [illegible] father [illegible] from [illegible] and two [illegible] towards, joined [illegible] and [illegible] city [illegible] in 12[illegible] [illegible] to Bristol, and gave the citizens a charter The Earl of Kent, acting for Queen Isabella in 1326, captured the city, and put its governor to death Edward III constituted it a county within itself, made it a centre of traffic for wool, and sent twenty two ships from it to the siege of Calais. Henry, Duke of Lancaster, while acquiring the mastery against Richard II, assailed Bristol, captured the castle, and put its governor, the Earl of Wilts, and two of his knightly assistants to death The citizens, in the reign of Henry V, acted valiantly in his cause Henry VI visited the city in 1446, his queen Margaret, in 1459, Edward IV, in 1461, and Henry VII in 1487 Baldwin, the subject of Chatterton's "Bristowe Tragedy," was executed on occasion of Edward IV's visit, and the citizens made a costly display of dress on occasion of Henry VII's visit, and were fined for it by the king Sebastian Cabot sailed from Bristol in 1497, in the remarkable voyage which took him to Labrador about a year before Columbus saw the American mainland Henry VIII made Bristol the seat of a bishopric, and gave his own sword to the mayor as a symbol of authority, and the sword is still preserved Elizabeth visited the city in 1574, and she was received with great pomp, and lodged on St Augustine's back Four ships went from Bristol, in 1588 against the Armada. The parliamentarians, in 1642, garrisoned the city, strengthened the castle, and erected batteries on Priors and St Michael's hills,—the last of which is still called "the Fort" Prince Rupert, next year, carried the place by storm, entering it through a breach near Berkeley square Charles I then visited it, and lodged in Small street Fairfax, in 1645, stormed Priors Hill fort, compelled Rupert to surrender, and afterwards destroyed the castle Charles II visited the city in 1663, and Queen Anne, in 1702 and 1710 Edmund Burke sat for Bristol, and made here some of his grandest speeches A riot, of three days continuance, occurred in 1831, in resentment of the recorder, Sir C Wetherell, having voted against the Reform bill, involved a destruction of property to the value of about £70,000, and occasioned wounds or death to several hundred individuals

Site, Streets and Environs—The site of Bristol is diversified in both form and elevation Some of it consists of eminences, rising high above the level of the neighbouring streets, and much is a variety of slope, declining chiefly to the Avon The city proper, or ancient city, is on the right bank of the river, intersected by long and ramified reaches of the floating harbour, the Clifton suburb, itself almost a city, is on the same bank, further down, but almost conjoined with the city proper by recent buildings, and the Bedminster suburb is on the left bank, separated from the ancient city only by the river Brandon Hill between the ancient city and Clifton, rises to the height of 250 feet, is laid out as a public park, has two guns from Sebastopol on its summit, and commands a fine view of Bristol and to the south The ground to the north west is naturally romantic, has been richly embellished by architecture and other arts, and includes brilliant scenes and charming walks, but will be noticed separately in our account of Clifton The country to the south, behind Bedminster, rises gradually, in a series of swells and eminences, till it attains, in Dundry Hill at a distance of 4 miles, an elevation of about 700 feet Interesting points to the north west, on or near the river are, on the left bank Nightingale Valley Ashton Court and Leigh Court, and on the right bank, Henbury cottages, Blaise Castle, Kingsweston Park, and Penpole Point The ancient city shows more resemblance than perhaps any other place in Britain to some of the old towns of Belgium and Germany Some of the streets here are very narrow, lanes, courts, and alleys are numerous, and many of the houses are curious ancient structures with overhanging upper stories numerous windows and fronting gables, but these interesting relics are fast disappearing under modern improvements The central point is at the intersection of High street from the south east, Broad street from the north west, Corn street from the south west, and Wine street from the north east, and one of the most striking of the picturesque old thoroughfares is Maryport street, opening into High street The more modern parts of the city, on all sides of the ancient one, contain spacious streets, many of them well aligned, and some parts are distinguished by elegant houses

Public Buildings.—The castle stood on the isthmus between the Avon and the Frome, commanding the entrance to the town from the east, occupied about an acre of ground, and is commemorated in the name of Castle street now built on its site, but has left scarcely a vestige except a crypt, which was converted into a forge Two of the city gateways, and part of the walls of the 17th century, are still standing, and one of the gateways, adjoining St John's church has two ancient statues said to be those of Brennus, the supposed founder of the city, and his brother Belinus The ancient High cross had figures of eight kings, with other decorations, and is now at Stourhead, and a partial restoration of it, effected in 1851 is now to be seen at the entrance of College green Colston's house, in Small street, where Charles I lodged, has a hall in perpendicular architecture, with a fine timber roof Canynge's house, once the masonic hall, in Redcliffe street, has also a perpendicular hall, and rich, light, wooden roof Red lodge, near Park-street, long occupied by the learned Dr Pritchard is a curious old edifice with interior porch, carved staircase, and elegant ceilings The Bishop's palace, adjoining the cloisters of the cathedral, was burnt in the riots of 1831, and some remains of it are yet standing The college gate, a little west of the cathedral comprises an elaborate Norman gateway and a fine perpendicular superstructure, in excellent preservation, and is probably part of the original edifice of Fitzhardinge's abbey Ancient crypts under the houses in High street forming the store houses of the merchants in the middle ages the Back hall, built in the 15th century, Bartholomew's gateway, in Christmas street, and the perpendicular door of the Guard house, also are interesting structures

The Guild hall in Broad street, was originally built in the time and style of Richard II, was rebuilt, in 1843, in the same style is 117 feet long and 45 and 75 feet high, has statues of Edward III, Queen Victoria, and others, between the windows and contains apartments for the several law courts Colston's Hall was inaugurated in 1867 cost till then about £25,000 and would cost about £15,000 more for completion, and includes a very splendid music hall, with accommodation for about 3 000 persons The Council house, in Corn street was built in 1827, at a cost of upwards of £14 000, and is a chaste pedimented structure The Exchange also in Corn street, was built in 1781, at a cost of £50,000 is an edifice of the Corinthian order, 100 feet long and 118 feet wide, includes a peristyle, capable of containing 1,440 persons, and is used chiefly by the corn merchants The commercial rooms, in the same street, nearly opposite the Exchange, were built in 1811, are surmounted by statues representing Bristol, Commerce and Navigation, serve as the general exchange and contain a reading room The Custom house, in Queen square, was burnt in the riots of 1831 but re erected on the same site, and is a neat and appropriate structure The Excise office was burnt at the same time and has been succeeded by a new Inland Revenue office The Post office adjoins the Exchange, and has receiving offices in North street, West-street, Redcliffe, Redland Hotwells, and Clifton

The Railway station occupies an eminence rising from Temple meads adjacent to the Avon, serves for at once the Great Western the Exeter and the Gloucester railways and is a handsome structure in the Tudor style A proposal was raised unsuccessfully in 1861 to extend the railway lines to the centre of the city, and it was renewed in 1864 with every prospect of success The Bank of England's office, adjoining the Guildhall, is a modern edifice, adorned with Ionic columns The West of England and South Wales bank, built in 1858, is on the model of the Library of St Mark in Venice, the lower story Doric, with five arched arcades and embler[illegible] ornaments, the upper storey being, with ornate [illegible], and ten emblematic female figures, the entablature [illegible] by a richly sculptured frieze. The National Provincial bank, in Corn street, was founded in 185[illegible], and is [illegible] an ornamental edifice with sculptural [illegible]. The [illegible] Insurance office, in the same street, was founded in the same year, and is in the Corinthian style. The City Hotel, in Broad street, was built in 18[illegible], and measures 110 feet by 136 feet. The gaol was built in 1820, partially burnt in the riots of 18[illegible], afterwards rebuilt, and has capacity for 1[illegible] male and 42 female [illegible]. The [illegible] Bridewell was entirely destroyed in the riots, and afterwards rebuilt, in larger and better [illegible], [illegible], and has capacity for 76 male and 29 female prisoners. A stone bridge of three arches, the centre one [illegible], with a span of 55 feet, connects the [illegible] of the city with Redcliffe, and, in terms of an act passed in 18[illegible], was widened and much altered. [illegible], opened in 1827, connects [illegible] of St Stephen and St Augustine, and leads to Clifton; and two iron bridges, each [illegible] of 100 feet in span, connect the city with [illegible]. The chain suspension bridge formerly over the Thames at Hungerford market in London, and erected there in 1845 by Brunel at a cost of £110,000, was removed to Clifton in 1862. A bronze equestrian statue of William III., by Rysbrach, at a cost of £1,800, is in the centre of Queen's square. A large market place is behind the exchange; another of less extent is in [illegible] street, and another is in Nicholas street. The [illegible], the Merchants', and the Coopers' halls, [illegible]. The theatre, in King street, was erected in 17[illegible], and is [illegible] and commodious. A new theatre was [illegible] in 18[illegible], is convenient and elegant, and has seats for [illegible]. The Assembly room in Princes street, has [illegible] decorations, and is spacious. The [illegible], at the head of Park street, have a Corinthian [illegible], are intended for public assemblies [illegible] of all kinds, and include a grand hall 117 feet by 55 [illegible], and 47 feet high.

Ecclesiastical Affairs.—The see of Bristol was erected in 15[illegible], and [illegible] with property from the dissolved monasteries. Its territory was taken from the dioceses of Salisbury and Worcester, and included Bristol, great part of Dorset, and part of Gloucestershire. Paul Bush[illegible], provincial of the Bons Hommes, was the first bishop, and Trelawney, Bo[illegible], Butler, Secker, Conybeare, Newton, and [illegible] have been [illegible] followed. The see was [illegible], in 18[illegible], to that of Gloucester; and the two now form one diocese, under the name of Gloucester and Bristol. The chapter of each remains distinct; and that of Bristol comprises a dean, an archdeacon, a chancellor, four canons, [illegible] honorary canons, and three minor canons. The income of the archdeacon is £200, and that of each of the minor canons, £1[illegible]. The divisions [illegible] of Bristol archdeaconry will be noticed in the article GLOUCESTER AND BRISTOL.

The livings within Bristol city are the rectories of [illegible] with St Ewens, St John Baptist with St [illegible], St Mary le Port, St Michael, St Peter, St Stephen, and St Werburgh; the vicarages of St Augustine, St Mary Redcliffe, All Saints, St George, [illegible], St Nicholas with St Leonard, St Philip and St Jacob, St Thomas, Temple, St Andrew [illegible], St Barnabas, St Clement, St James, St Jude, St Luke, St Paul, St Simon, Trinity, Emmanuel, St [illegible], and St Matthias; and the p. curacies of St Mark and St Silas. Value of Christ Church, £[illegible], of St John Baptist, £[illegible], of St Andrew, St Thomas, St Jude, and St Matthias, £1[illegible], of St [illegible], St [illegible], and St Simon, £[illegible], of St Luke, £203, [illegible] of St Peter, £2[illegible], of St Stephen, £2[illegible], of St [illegible], £70, of St Augustine, £[illegible]10, of [illegible], £2[illegible], of All Saints, £1[illegible], of St [illegible], of St [illegible], £[illegible], of St Philip and St Jacob, £[illegible]78, of St Thomas, £120, of Temple, £[illegible], of St Clement, £[illegible], of St James, £[illegible], of [illegible] St Mark and St Silas not reported, of St Paul, £[illegible], of [illegible], £400, of St [illegible], £19[illegible]. Patron of Christ Church, the Rev. James Robertson, of St John Baptist, St Mary le Port, St Michael, St Peter, St Philip and St Jacob, Temple, St Clement, St James, St Paul, Trinity, Emmanuel, St [illegible], St Mark, and St Silas, Trustees, of St Stephen and St Werburgh, the Lord Chancellor, of St Augustine, All Saints, St George, and St Nicholas, the Dean and Chapter of Bristol, of St Mary Redcliffe, St Thomas, St Barnabas, and St Andrew, the Bishop of Gloucester and Bristol, of St Jude, St Simon, and St Matthias, alternately the Crown and the Bishop, of St. Luke, the vicar of St Philip and St Jacob. The living within the city but not within the district will be found noticed in the articles BEDMINSTER, CLIFTON, PHILIP AND JACOB OUT (STS.), and JAMES AND PAUL OUT (STS.).

The places of worship within the city, in 1864, were the cathedral, 22 parish churches, 25 other places of worship belonging to the Established church, 1 of Presbyterians, 15 of Independents, 9 of Baptists, [illegible] of Brethren, 1 of Moravians or United Brethren, 1 of Friends, 1 of Welsh Calvinistic Methodists, 1 of the New Christian church or Swedenborgians, 9 of Wesleyan Methodists, [illegible] of the Methodist Free church, 2 of Bible Christians, 1 of the Methodist New Connexion, 3 of Primitive Methodists, 2 of Unitarians, 6 of Roman Catholics, 1 of Jews, the Seamen's floating chapel, and 11 places of the Bristol City Mission. There were also 4 convents.

The Cathedral stands on the south side of College green, and was the church of the Augustinian abbey, founded by Robert Fitzharding. The nave was taken down in the 16th century, and measured 118 feet in length and 70 feet in breadth; but a new nave, 117 feet by 5[illegible], with ornate W. front, and with two towers 130 feet high, was being built in 1868-9. The pile, besides the nave, consists of an aisled, four-bayed choir, 175 feet long, 73 feet wide, and 13[illegible] feet high, a transept, 128 feet long and 43 feet high, an ambulatory and lady chapel, opening into the choir, and a central, two storey, pinnacled tower 133 feet high. It was built mostly in the former half of the 14th century, is chiefly late [illegible] rich decorated English, passing into perpendicular, and underwent extensive restoration in 1860 and 1861. It abounds in monuments, both ancient and modern, many of the ancient ones with stellated Spanish canopies, and many of the modern ones highly interesting either in themselves or for their associations. The chief are those of Abbot David, 1234, Thomas Lord Berkeley, 124[illegible], Maurice Lord Berkeley, 1281, Thomas Lord Berkeley, 1321, Abbot Knowle, 1332, Maurice, Lord Berkeley, 1[illegible]68, Abbot Newland, 1515, Abbot Gwilyn, 15[illegible], Bishop Bush, 1558, Sir Henry Newton and his lady, 1599, Sir John Young, 1603, Sir P. Codrington, 1615, Sir C. Vaughan, 1630, Sir John Newton, 1660, Sir R. N. Cradock, the judge, who, however, with his lady, was buried in Yatton church, Mrs. Mason, with epitaph by her husband and Gray, Mrs. Draper, Sterne's Eliza, by Bacon, Lovel, the tragedian, with epitaph by Coleridge, Bishop Butler, with epitaph by Southey, Dr. Lowth, editor of the Hebrew Bible, Catherine Vernon, by [illegible], [illegible] Crawford, by Chantrey, Mrs. Middleton, by Baily, Elizabeth Stanhope, by Westmacott, Maria Elwyn, by Chantrey, and Robert Southey, by Baily. The chapter house has a Norman vestibule, is a beautiful vaulted, enriched late Norman apartment, 4[illegible] feet long, 25 feet wide, and 2[illegible] feet high, and was, not long ago, tastefully renovated and [illegible].

The church of St Mary Redcliffe crowns a knoll of red sandstone a short distance west of the railway station, takes the name of Redcliff from its site, and is a finer edifice than the Cathedral, one of the grandest parish churches in England, the pride of Bristol and the Western lands. The date of its foundation is controverted; but it was mostly built under the direction of George Codwin, [illegible], [illegible] which are estimated [illegible] to have cost £40,000. It is English, of all periods, with ornaments of the most [illegible] and delicate description, consists of nave, transept, and choir, all aisled, south porch, [illegible] house, and lady chapel; and has a rich western tower, with the stump of a spire which was once [illegible] finished The nave is 128 feet long, 52 wide, and 51 high, the choir 60 feet long, 52 wide, and 53 high, the transept, 117½ feet long and 47 wide, the Lady chapel, 38 feet long and 23 wide, and the tower, 200 feet high A muniment room, above the north entrance contains fragments of the coffer in which Chatterton pretended to find the Rowley manuscripts The church contains effigies of William Canynge, John Lamington, and John Jay, canopied monuments of the brothers Mede of the 15th century, altar tombs of Robert Lord Berkeley and Sir John Inlyne, and the armour of Admiral Sir William Penn, father of the founder of Pennsylvania

Christ Church occupies the site of a previous church dating from 1003, and is a modern Grecian structure, with handsome tower and spire The church of St John the Baptist is in a line with the city wall, was built, traditionally, in 1397, by Walter Frampton, and contains effigies of its founder, an altar tomb of a Bristol merchant of Henry VII's reign, and a well preserved ancient hour glass The church of St Mary le Port is perpendicular English St Peter's church was built in 1130, has been much altered and contains a brass of 1431, and its churchyard contains the remains of the poet Savage, who was sent to the city prison for debt after writing his "London and Bristol delineated and died there in 1743 St. Stephen's church was built, in 1472 by John Shipward, is perpendicular English, with an elegant square tower, 133 feet high, has a richly ornate porch, contains a recessed canopied tomb and two fine effigies, and has a chantry, founded by Edward Blanket, who invented the article of bed furniture which bears his name St Werburgh's church was rebuilt in 1761, has a tower of 1385, is in the later English style, and contains a brass of 1546, and a monument of Robert Thorne, the founder of the grammar school All Saints' church is an ancient structure in Norman and perpendicular English, has a tower of 1716, and contains a monument, by Rysbrach, of Edward Colston, a merchant of the city, who spent about £70,000 in local benefactions. St Nicholas church is a modern edifice with tower and spire, but has a crypt of 1503, with a stone coffin of 1311 The church of St Philip and St. Jacob is in a mixed style, in both body and tower, but presents curious features, interesting to an architect, was recently repaired, and contains an ancient figure erroneously ascribed to the eldest son of the Conqueror, and a Norman font Temple church which belonged originally to the Knights Templars, presents a mixture of Norman and early English has a tower 114 feet high leaning 2½ feet out of the perpendicular, and contains two brasses of 1395 St Thomas church excepting the tower, was rebuilt in 1793 St Silas' church and the Penitentiary church were built in 1867, at a cost of £5,000 and £2 200

St Andrew's church, Montpelier, was built in 1845, and is in the style of the 13th century St James church was originally the church of a Benedictine priory founded by Robert, Earl of Gloucester, son of Henry I, was made parochial in 1347 is a very curious specimen of Norman, with a tower added in 1371, was recently restored and contains an ancient monument, said to be that of its founder St Bartholomew's church in Union street, was built in 1861, and is a structure of Pennant stone, with freestone dressings, in the early decorated style Emmanuel church near the goods station of the Great Western railway was built in 1863, at a cost of £3 190, and is an edifice in plain early decorated English St Paul's church, Portland square is a conspicuous edifice, and contains a monument to Col Vassall The Mayor's chapel St Mark's church or the chapel of the Gaunts was founded in 1230 in connexion with Gaunts' hospital of Bon Hommes, has a tower of 1487, was at one time collegiate, but became the chapel of the Mayor, is a gem of pointed architecture—the reredos perpendicular, the rest early English or decorated and contains four very fine sedilia, and monuments of Sir Maurice de Gaunt, Sir Henry de Gaunt, Sir Robert de Gourney Sir Maurice Berkeley, Bishop Salley of Llandaff, John Carr, and Sir J. K. Haberfield The Poyntz chapel, a small chantry, now used as a vestry adjacent to the Mayor's chapel, is rich perpendicular English, has a fan tracery roof, with some Spanish encaustic enamelled tiles of the age of Charles V, and contains the remains of Captain Bedloe, the associate of Titus Oates in the Popish plot An edifice in Merchant street, once a Dominican priory now used as a den, school, includes the ancient dormitory 86 feet by 25, with a roof of the 14th century, and the lesser hall, 49 feet by 24½ Several of the dissenting places of worship are handsome edifices, and one of the finest, a Wesleyan chapel, on the latter containing about 1,000 sittings, was founded and completed in the short space of three months in 1851 An act of parliament for an ultra mural general cemetery was passed in 1837 and the area of all the churchyards of the city at that time, including the sites of the churches, was only 14 acres The new cemetery, on the Bristol road, was opened in the beginning of 1856 and was enlarged in 1862, is highly ornamental, and has two funeral cruciform chapels, with belfries about 100 feet high, to the Episcopal chapel

Education—There were, in 1851 within the city, 77 public schools, with 11,881 scholars 209 private day schools, with 6,345 s., and 91 Sunday schools, with 14,128 s Thirteen of the public day schools were supported by endowments, 45 by religious bodies, and 19 by subscription Five of the endowed ones were collegiate and grammar schools, 8 of the next class were National Four were Roman Catholic and 5 of the subscription class were ragged schools 2 orphan schools, 1 for the blind and 1 for the deaf and dumb The city grammar school was founded, in 1532, by Robert Thorne has been reformed in management, under authority of the Court of Chancery possesses five exhibitions and two scholarships at Oxford, and is attended by about 300 pupils Henry VIII's college grammar school is near the Cathedral Colston's hospital for the education and maintenance of 120 boys, was founded in 1708, has an income of upwards of £2,500, had Chatterton as a scholar for seven years and is now located in the quondam episcopal palace at Stapleton Colston's free schools in Temple parish and in Pile street, each for 40 boys were founded at the same time as the hospital Queen Elizabeth's or Carr's hospital was founded in 158 , for the education of poor boys after the manner of Christ's hospital in London, has an income of £6 000, and is an edifice in the castellated Tudor style, 400 feet long at Brandon Hill rebuilt in 1847, by Fosters The Red Maids school, for educating maintaining, and clothing 44 girls, was founded in 1627 by Alderman Whitson has now an income of about £600, and now admits 120 scholars, and possesses a handsome school house in the Tudor style with a tower, erected in 1837 The Bristol Fine Arts' Academy, in Queen's road, was built by subscription in 1857 is in the Italian style and contains statues of Flaxman and Reynolds The Bristol School of Art held in the same building, is attended by upwards of 2 000 pupils The Baptist college at Stokes Croft, for training young men for the ministry, was founded in 1770, has some income from endowment is associated with the memory of Hall and Foster and other distinguished men and contains a collection of heathen idols, the only complete copy in existence of Tyndale's New Testament published in 1525, and an original miniature portrait of Oliver Cromwell

Science and Literature—The British Association and the Royal Agricultural Society have visited Bristol The Philosophical and Scientific Institute in Park street, was opened in 1825, is a handsome Corinthian edifice with circular portico, erected by Cockerell, at a cost of £11,000, and contains a theatre for lectures, a library, and an excellent museum The Athenæum, in Corn street, was erected in 1854 has a library of 7,000 volumes, and contains a lecture hall, reading rooms, refreshment rooms, and other spacious apartments The City Library in King street, was founded in 1613, is a handsome building with emblematic figures in front, and has about 6,000 volumes The Bristol Library Society, founded in 1772, and possessing some 10 000 volumes, is now located in a portion of the late Bishop's College, Queen's road.

[illegible] also a law library and a [illegible] library [illegible] neighbourhood likewise contain some [illegible] antiquities, [illegible] present an interesting field for [illegible]

[illegible]—The General Hospital at the side of [illegible], was erected in 1858, after a design by [illegible] at a cost of about £15,000 has a warehouse [illegible], includes towers, rooms [illegible] and colonnades for exercise, the con[illegible] accommodation for 170 patients. The Royal Infirmary [illegible] Marlborough street, was built in 1785, is a [illegible] with accommodation for 200 patients [illegible] by subscription. Muller's orphan [illegible] Ashley Down, which provides for and edu[illegible] orphans, was erected at intervals from 1835 [illegible] an aggregate cost of £[illegible] 000. The orphan [illegible] at the bottom of Ashley Hill, has about [illegible] was instituted in 179[illegible] and is supported by [illegible] Temple hospital has an income [illegible] hospital, £1,600, Stephens almshouses [illegible] almshouses, £345, Fosters' [illegible] there are a seamen's hospital, [illegible] and several [illegible], and a number of [illegible] institutions. The endowed charities are es[illegible] at [illegible] 2,000 a year, and the subscription charities, [illegible] 5,000.

Trade and [illegible]—A mart for the sale of Eng[illegible] at Bristol in the 11th century, a great [illegible] carried on in the time of Edward III [illegible] both inland and commercial, of [illegible] character, has long been flourish[illegible] markets are held on Wednesday, Friday, and Saturday, a weekly cattle market on Thursday, [illegible] fairs, [illegible] March, the Thursday before 25 July, and [illegible] Newspapers are published daily, and four [illegible] Wednesday, Thursday, and Saturday. Manu[illegible] carried on in glass, soap, starch, refined [illegible], malt liquors, drugs, dyes, woollen, [illegible] cotton, [illegible], leather, brushes, tobacco pipes, [illegible] chemicals, cocoa, copper, brass, tin, [illegible] cables, anchors, engines, machin[illegible] building. A sugar factory in Temple street [illegible] perhaps the best looking structure of [illegible] in the kingdom. The Great Western cotton [illegible] 1840, are conspicuous, but were [illegible] the cotton famine. There [illegible] banking [illegible] of [illegible] is the head [illegible] of the West of England and South Wales bank [illegible] and of all grades.

C[illegible]—The harbour consists of floating docks, [illegible] 1804-[illegible] by changing the course of the Avon, and [illegible] the old channel, at a cost of £[illegible]00,000, [illegible] a length of 2[illegible] miles, has undergone [illegible] its original formation, and includes a [illegible] mile long and several graving docks [illegible] at [illegible]ham, and the berths of the [illegible] timber ships, the sailing smacks, and [illegible] respectively at the [illegible], [illegible] bridge. [illegible] at [illegible] station at Pill. The [illegible] at the port on [illegible] December, 1867, [illegible] of aggregately 1,712 tons, [illegible] of aggregately 52,304 tons, [illegible] vessels, of aggregately 583 tons, and 27 [illegible] of aggregately [illegible] 702 tons. The [illegible] in 1867, including repeated voyages, [illegible] 5,5[illegible] [illegible] tons [illegible] and 6[illegible] coasters [illegible] and those which cleared [illegible] of [illegible] tons, 107 [illegible] 7[illegible] coasters, of 461,813 tons. The [illegible] customs in 186[illegible] £1,[illegible], and in 1867 [illegible] 7 [illegible] imports [illegible] fruit, [illegible] oil, metals, tobacco, wool, [illegible] chief exports, coal [illegible] other [illegible] tobacco [illegible] spirits, iron, tin, [illegible] coast [illegible] salt, [illegible] pro-duce, provisions, cattle, and Irish linens, and the chief exports, groceries, wines, spirits, and the articles of local manufacture. Steamers ply to all the chief ports of Monmouth, South Wales, and Devon and Cornwall, to Liverpool and London, to Dublin, Wexford, Waterford, and Cork, and to Cadiz, Charente, Bordeaux, and [illegible] The "Great Western" steam ship, the first steamer which crossed the Atlantic, and the still larger steam ship the "Great [illegible]" were built at [illegible].

The Borough.—The city, as defined by its borough boundaries, comprises 4,671 acres, and measures 4 miles by 3. It was first chartered by Henry III., has sent two members to parliament since the time of Edward I., and is governed by a mayor, sixteen aldermen, and forty-eight councillors. Assizes are held in spring and summer. The police force consists of 30[illegible] men, and is maintained at a cost of about £17,000. The number of indictable offences committed in 1863 was [illegible]31, persons apprehended, 291, convicted summarily, 2,006, depredators and suspected persons at large, 774, of houses of bad character, 172. The water supply comes from the Mendip hills, a distance of 15 miles, amounts at the reservoir, to nearly a million of gallons a day, and is conveyed in pipes which cross the Avon through a tubular arch. Municipal revenue, £48,483. Property and assessed taxes, in 185[illegible], £132,[illegible]. Real property in 1860, £[illegible]03,07[illegible]. Electors in 1865, 11,[illegible]. Pop. in 1841, 123,135, in 1861, 154,093. Houses, 23,[illegible].

Eminent Citizens.—William Botoner, who wrote an itinerary of the city in the reign of Henry VI., Norton, the alchemist, who died in 1477, Grocyne, Greek professor at Oxford and friend of Erasmus, Sebastian Cabot, who discovered Labrador, T. White, the founder of Sion college, Elliott, who discovered Newfoundland, Fowler, the printer, who died in 1679, Archbishop Matthew, 162[illegible], Bishop Thomas, 1[illegible]59, Child, the composer, 1697, Admiral Sir W. Penn, 1670, Lewis, the author of a "Life of Wickliffe," 17[illegible]1, Chatterton, 1770, Sir W. Draper, Mrs Robinson, the "English Sappho," 1800, [illegible], author of "Memoirs," 1831, Sir Thomas Lawrence, the poet Southey, the sculptor Bailey, and a number of other persons known to fame, were either natives or residents of Bristol. Sir H. Davy made his first scientific appearance here under Dr Beddoes, the poets Coleridge and Wordsworth resided here for a time, and found their first patron in the native publisher, Joseph Cottle, Hannah More kept a school with her sister in Park street and died at Clifton, and Robert Hall spent in Bristol both his early and his closing years. The city gave the title of Marquis to the family of Hervey.

The District.—Bristol poor law district excludes Clifton, Bedminster, and some other parts of the borough, is administered under a local act, and is divided into five sub districts. The [illegible] St James sub district, conterminate with St James In parish, St Augustine sub district, containing St Augustine and St Michael parishes, St Paul sub district, containing St Paul In[illegible] St Philip and St Jacob In parishes, St Mary Redcliffe sub district, containing St Mary Redcliffe, Temple and St Thomas parishes, and Castle Precincts sub district, containing Castle Precincts extra parochial tract and St Nicholas, St Stephen, St [illegible], St Werburgh, All Saints, St Ewen, St John, St Peter, Christ Church, and St Mary le Port parishes. Acres of the district 1,840. Poor rates in 1866, £[illegible]. Pop. in 1841, 6[illegible],266, in 1861, 6[illegible],0[illegible]7. Houses, [illegible],10[illegible]. Marriages in 1866, 1,35[illegible], births, 2,219,—of which 10[illegible] were illegitimate, deaths, 1,800,—of which [illegible]07 were at ages under 5 years, and [illegible] at ages above 85. Marriages in the ten years 1851-60, 12,[illegible], births, 21,8[illegible], deaths, 17,[illegible]. The Bristol workhouse is a new structure, on the site of the old French prison, at [illegible], about 2½ miles from the city. The borough lunatic asylum stands near the workhouse, and is a handsome edifice in the Tudor style, built in 18[illegible], at a cost of upwards of £[illegible]40,000, and contains accommodation for [illegible]00 patients.

BRISTOL AND EXETER RAILWAY, a railway from Bristol south south westward, through Somerset and part of Devon, to Exeter. It was authorised in 1836, and opened partially in 1841 and totally in 1844 It has a length of 107 miles, but includes in this a branch of 4 miles to Clevedon, one of 1½ mile to Weston super Mare, one of 20¼ miles to Yeovil, and one of 5 miles to Tiverton It commences in a junction with the Great Western at Bristol, goes south westward to the deflection of its branch to Weston, proceeds southward to a point some miles past Bridgewater, goes thence south westward to Exeter, and forms there a junction with the South Devon It is on the broad gauge, has [illegible] embankments and 127 bridges and passes, near Beam Bridge, through a tunnel 3,300 feet long The cost of constructing the main line was £23 676 per mile

BRISTOL AND GLOUCESTER RAILWAY, a railway in Gloucestershire, north north-eastward, from Bristol to Gloucester, now incorporated with the MIDLAND RAILWAY which see

BRISTOL AND PORTISHEAD RAILWAY, a railway from the Bristol and Exeter at Bedminster west north westward to Portishead, with works at Portishead It comprises a railway line, 10 miles long, opened in 1867 and a pier at Portishead, and other works there, required to be completed in 1870

BRISTOL AND SOUTH WALES UNION RAILWAY, a railway from Bristol, north north-westward, through Gloucestershire, to the Severn at the New Passage ferry and connected by a junction in Monmouthshire, on the other side of the ferry, with the South Wales railway It was authorised in July 1857 and opened to the South Wales junction, in 1863 It forms one line of 11½ miles on the Gloucestershire side of the Severn, and one line about three quarters of a mile, on the Monmouthshire side It is on the broad gauge, and was estimated to cost £300,000

BRISTOL CHANNEL, the outer part of the estuary of the Severn It is bounded, on the left by Somerset and Devon, on the right by Monmouth, Glamorgan, Carmarthen, and Pembroke It commences in King Road, at the mouth of the Avon, goes south westward, to the [illegible] side of Bridgewater bay, and proceeds thence westward to the ocean Its width at King Road, is about 5 miles, at other parts, throughout its central reaches from 8 to 22 miles, and at its mouth, between Hartland Point through Lundy Island, to St Govan's Head, about 40 miles Its length from King Road to Lundy Island, is nearly 80 miles Its depth in the upper part, between extensive shoals, called the English Grounds and the Welsh Grounds, is from 5 to 10 fathoms, in the part at Cardiff, between the islands called the Steep and Flat Holms, from 5 to 8 fathoms, in the part opposite Nass Point, from 13 to 15 fathoms, and in the open part between Bideford and Carmarthen bays, from 30 to 40 fathoms The tidal rise is greater than anywhere else on the British coasts and runs into the mouth of the rivers with a high, upright rapid wave, locally called a bore often dangerous to shipping but is considerably modified by the strength and direction of the winds

BRISTOL PORT AND PIER RAILWAY, a railway from the port of Bristol, 5¾ miles, to the Old Channel at the mouth of the Avon It was authorised in July 1862, and opened in March 1865 A dock [illegible] feet long and 85 feet wide, was in course of formation at its terminus in 1869 and is for the accommodation of such large vessels as cannot readily go up the Avon to Bristol See AVONMOUTH

BRISTOL ROAD See BIRMINGHAM

BRISTON or BURSTON, a village and a parish in Erpingham district Norfolk The village stands on the river Bure, [illegible] miles SSW of Holt, and [illegible] of Aylsham [illegible] and has a post office under Thetford, a fortnightly stock market and a cattle fair on 25 May The parish comprises 2,75[illegible] acres Pop 93[illegible] Houses 232 The property is subdivided The living is a vicarage in the diocese of Norwich Value £ 17[illegible] Patron Lord Hastings The church is decorated and perpendicular English, and had formerly a round tower There are chapels for Independents, Wesleyans and Primitive Methodists, a national school and charities £9

BRIT (THE) See BRIT and BRIDE (THE)

BRITAIN See SUMMARY

BRITAIN (LITTLE), a hamlet in Exhall parish, Alcester district, Warwick, 2 miles SE of Alcester

BRITANNIA See INTRODUCTION

BRITANNIA BRIDGE, a tubular viaduct over the Menai strait between Carnarvon and Anglesey, on the line of the Chester and Holyhead railway 1 mile SW of the Menai bridge, and 2 W by S of Bangor station It was designed by Mr Robert Stephenson, was commenced in 1846 and opened in 1850, and cost £621 865 The channel, at its site is 1 100 feet wide, is swept by a very rapid tide, ordinarily rising 20 feet and is beset, in the middle, by a rock called the Britannia rock, which is bare to the height of 10 feet at low water, and covered to the same height by full tide This rock gave name to the bridge, and afforded a main facility for constructing it The bridge consists of two abutments at the ends, two towers, 230 feet distant from the abutments, a central tower on the Britannia rock, 460 feet distant from the other towers and two vast wrought iron tubes, or tunnels placed side by side, and resting on the abutments and the towers Each abutment is 176 feet long, each of the nearer towers, 62 feet broad, the central tower, 45½ feet broad and the total roadway 1,841 feet long The approaches are ornamented by two colossal Egyptian statues of lions couchant, each 25 feet long, and 12 feet 8 inches high, the two nearer towers measure 62 feet by 52½ at the base, taper to 55 feet by 32 at the top, and rise 190 feet above high water level, the central tower has similar measurements of base and taper and rises 230 feet from its foundation on the rock, and the bottom of the roadway is elevated 101 feet above the level of high water The two tubes or tunnels consist of plates, rivets and angle irons, are flat in the bottom and arched in the top, have an exterior height increasing from 22¾ feet at the ends to 30 feet in the centre are four feet lower in the interior than in the exterior, and each 14 feet wide and possess a total computed weight of about 10,000 tons The trains going W invariably pass through one line of tube, and those going E invariably pass through the other The bridge as seen from a distance, looks very [illegible] and even as seen close at hand possesses none of the picturesqueness of its beautiful neighbour the suspension bridge, yet, on close inspection, impresses the mind with a sense of vastness and power

BRITFORD, or BURFORD, a village, a parish and a sub district in Alderbury district, Wilts The village stands adjacent to the Salisbury and Southampton canal near the Bishopstoke and Salisbury railway 1¼ mile SE of Salisbury, and has a fair on 12 Aug The parish includes also the tything of East Harnham and the hamlet of Longford, and its post town is Salisbury Acres 3,118 Real property £[illegible],030 Pop 873 Houses 157 The property is divided among a few The manor belonged anciently to King Harold and belongs now to the Earl of Radnor Longford Castle the seat of the Earl, occupied by Viscount Folkestone, was built about 1591 by Sir Thomas Gorges is a curiously constructed edifice of triangular form, with an inner court, and possesses a very fine picture gallery The living is a vicarage in the diocese of Salisbury Value, £291 Patrons the Dean and Chapter of Salisbury The church is cruciform and contains a [illegible] mausoleum of the Bouveries, and a curious, sculptured altar tomb usually, but erroneously said to be that of the Duke of Buckingham who was beheaded by Richard III East Harnham [illegible] is a separate [illegible] The parish contains Alderbury workhouse The sub district comprises five parishes, a tything, a [illegible] and an extra parochial tract Acres, [illegible] Pop, 5,[illegible]33 Houses 955.

BRITHDIR, a hamlet in Gelligaer parish, Glamorgan, on the river Rumney at the verge of the county, 8 miles SE of Merthyr Tydvil Real property £37,323 of which £1[illegible] are in mines, and £[illegible]844 in iron works Pop 3,870 Houses 68[illegible] The inhabitants are employed chiefly in the iron works and in collieries The hamlet forms a curacy with Gelligaer

BRITHDIR, a township in Berriew parish, Montgomeryshire, 1½ miles NW of Montgomery. Pop., 155.

BRITHDIR, a township in Llanrhaiadr-yn-Mochnant parish, Montgomery, 4½ miles N of Llanfyllin. Pop., 252.

BRITHDIR, a township in Llanidloes parish, Montgomery, near Llanidloes.

BRITHDIR ISAF AND BRITHDIR UCHAF, two townships in Dolgelley parish, Merioneth, near Dolgelley. Pop., 427 and 110.

BRITHERSTOW. See B[illegible].

BRITISH CHANNEL. See CHANNEL (THE).

BRITON. See [illegible], Northampton.

BRITON FERRY, a village and a parish in Neath district, Glamorgan. The village stands at the mouth of the Neath river, the end of the Neath canal, and the [illegible] of a short branch of the South Wales railway, 2½ miles SSE of Neath; and has a head post office.‡ Large docks were formed here in 1861 and previous years, aided by £20,000 from the Vale of Neath Railway Company; they comprise a tidal and floating area of 27 acres, and are provided with Armstrong's hydraulic machinery; and they will afford shipping accommodation to the mineral districts of Aberdare and Merthyr Tydvil, nearer than that at Cardiff. The village is likewise the port of Neath, has undergone much recent increase, and promises soon to be an important town. The parish bears also the name of Llansawel, and comprises 1,593 acres. Real property, £8,040, of which £2,410 are in iron works. Pop., 3,781. Houses, 627. The manor belonged formerly to the Mansells, and belongs now to the Earl of Jersey. The local scenery and the distant views are very fine. The view from a hill including a great part of the basin and screens of Bristol channel, and that from the churchyard is celebrated by Mason. The living is a vicarage in the diocese of Llandaff. Value, £124. Patron, the Earl of Jersey. The church is good, quaint, and pretty.

BRITON FERRY ROAD, a railway station in South Wales, on the Aberdare and Swansea railway, between Neath Abbey and Swansea.

BRITTAL LANE. See BRETTEL LANE.

BRITTENTON, a hamlet in [illegible] parish, Oxford, [illegible] miles SE of Witney. Pop., 102.

BRITTON. See BRETTON.

BRITWELL, a liberty in Burnham parish, Bucks, 3½ miles NE of Maidenhead. Pop., 94.

BRITWELL, Oxford. See BRIGHTWELL.

BRIVAELS (ST.). See BRIAVELS (ST.).

BRIXHAM, a town, a parish, and a sub-district, in Totnes district, Devon. The town stands at the south [illegible] point of Torbay, 2½ miles [illegible] of a station on the Dartmouth railway called Brixham Road, and [illegible] of Dartmouth. It is a seaport under Dartmouth, a coast-guard station, and a seat of petty sessions; and it has a head post office,‡ (designated Brixham, South Devon,) a banking office, and three chief inns. It consists of two parts, lower and upper; and extends full [illegible] mile [illegible]. It is irregularly built, but [illegible]; and had it been well ordered, would have been one of the most charming places in the county. The parish church, in the upper part, is [illegible] of the 15th century, repaired [illegible] of about 1700, and contains several monuments, one of [illegible] Judge Buller. Another church, in the lower town, is a plain but commodious structure, built in 1816, and enlarged in 1830. Independents, Baptists, and Wesleyans have chapels [illegible] [illegible], Middle, and Fore streets. A free school has £78 a year from endowments; and other charities have [illegible]. A small [illegible] and [illegible] [illegible] [illegible]. [illegible] [illegible] [illegible] [illegible] [illegible] [illegible]. [illegible] is done in ship-building, [illegible] about 1,000 [illegible], of between 30 and [illegible] tons [illegible] [illegible] trawling, and [illegible] 100 boats in [illegible] about 100 schooners and [illegible] of [illegible] about 18,000 tons, carry on [illegible] [illegible] [illegible] [illegible]. The exports are chiefly [illegible], [illegible], [illegible], and [illegible]; the imports, coal, [illegible], and fruit coastwise, and cattle from the Channel Islands and France. The appearance of the fish market on every week-day evening is very striking; and a peculiar mode of selling at it is the subject of a famous picture by Collins. The pier was built in 1808. The harbour is a refuge for vessels in stormy weather; and a breakwater was recently formed to increase the security of the anchorage. The Prince of Orange landed here in 1688, and the Duke of Clarence visited the place in 1823. A pillar, commemorative of the Prince of Orange's landing, and enclosing part of the stone on which he first stepped, is on the pier; and a tablet, commemorating the Duke of Clarence's visit, is inserted in the pier wall. A spring on the outskirts of the upper town was long celebrated for ebbing and flowing; but in consequence of changes on the ground near it, has lost its intermittent property. Pop. of the town, 4,590. Houses, 928.

The parish includes also the hamlets of Lupton, and Woodhush. Acres, 5,740, of which 143 are water. Real property, £16,475. Pop., 5,984. Houses, 1,247. The property is much subdivided. A fourth of the manor was purchased many years ago by twelve of the fishermen, and the shares of these were afterwards divided. A magnificent view of Torbay is obtained from Furzeham. Traces of an ancient camp are at Berryhead. A large bone cave was recently discovered, containing bones and flint objects of a kind involved in recent geological discussions, and noticed in Sir Charles Lyell's new work on the Antiquity of Man. The living is a vicarage, united with the vicarage of Churston Ferrers, in the diocese of Exeter. Value, £491.* Patron, the Crown. Lower Brixham is served by a vicar, with salary of £207,* appointed by the Crown. The sub-district consists of the parishes of Brixham and Churston Ferrers. Acres, 8,517. Pop., 6,730. Houses, 1,390.

BRIXHAM ROAD. See BRIXHAM.

BRIXTON, a village and a parish in Plympton St. Mary district, Devon. The village stands near the river Yealm, 3 miles SSW of Plympton r. station, and 4½ ESE of Plymouth; and it has a post office under Plympton, and is a seat of petty sessions. Acres, 2,01[illegible] of land, and 85 of water. Real property, £5,102. Pop., 691. Houses, 13[illegible]. The property is divided among a few. The manor was long held by a family of its own name, and belongs now to [illegible] W. [illegible]ott, Esq. Remains of a mansion of the time of Henry VII. are at Hareston. The living is a vicarage in the diocese of Exeter. Value, £107. Patrons, the Dean and Canons of Windsor. The church is decorated English, with a lofty tower, and in good condition. Charities, £30.

BRIXTON, a metropolitan suburb, five chapelries, a sub-district, and a hundred, in Surrey. The suburb is in Lambeth parish, 2 miles SSW of St. Paul's, London; extends about 2 miles southward from the vicinity of Kennington; is partly in [illegible] [illegible] with other suburbs; has a r. station, with telegraph, on the London Chatham and Dover railway, and a station on the line from Ludgate Hill; has also post offices‡ of Brixton East,‡ B[illegible] Hill, [illegible] Road, North B[illegible], and [illegible] Hill, under London S; and contains Drouet's establishment for pauper children, Bailey's [illegible] [illegible] [illegible], and the county house of correction. The chapelries are St. Matthew, constituted in 1824; [illegible] [illegible] [illegible] [illegible], B. St. John [illegible] [illegible]; B. Christ church, in 1856; [illegible] in 18[illegible]; and B. St. Jude, in 1868. Pop. of [illegible] 10,3[illegible]; of B. St. John, 1,907; of B. C., 3,77[illegible]. The livings of St. M., St. J., and C. are vicarages, [illegible] of St. [illegible], in the diocese of London. Value of St. M., £70[illegible]; of St. John, £250;* of C., [illegible]; of St. Jude, not reported. Patron of St. M., [illegible]; of St. John, [illegible]; of C., [illegible]. [illegible] [illegible] [illegible] St. Matthew's church is [illegible] [illegible] [illegible]; and [illegible] [illegible] St. Jude's church [illegible] [illegible] [illegible] [illegible] was built in 1863. There are chapels for [illegible] and [illegible] Lady Huntingdon's Connexion.

ion, and Methodists The sub district is in Lambeth district, and conterminate with the chapelry of Brixton St Matthew as it was originally constituted Acres, 1,445 Pop, 20,067 Houses, 3,223 The hundred is cut into two divisions, Eastern and Western The E division comprises Lambeth parish seven other parishes, and part of two others Acres, 22,186 Pop in 1851, 314,515 The W division comprises Wandsworth parish, [illegible] other parishes and part of another Acres, 7 699 Pop in 1851, 9 552 Pop of the entire hundred in 1861 409,701 Houses 62 763.

BRIXTON, or BRIGHSTONE, a village and a parish on the SW coast of the Isle of Wight The village stands on a brook, ¾ of a mile NNE of Grange chine, and 6 SW of Newport and has a post office under Newport and an inn The parish includes also the hamlet of Limerstun, and part of the hamlet of Chuton Acres, 3,251, of which 100 are water Real property, £3,806 Pop, 690 Houses, 123 The property is divided among a few The land was formerly part of the manor of Swainston The Hon A Court Holmes residence of Westover adjoins the village A slight adjacent encurvature of the sea bears the name of Brixton bay the coast is cut with a series of chines, presenting picturesque features and the interior, at the distance of 1¾ mile, is a range of hills, called Mottiston, Brixton, and Limerston downs The living is a rectory in the diocese of Winchester Value, £515 * Patron, the Bishop of Winchester The church was rebuilt on the site of an ancient previous one in 1852, and is variously of Norman early English decorated, and perpendicular character The parsonage is a picturesque edifice, and was the home of Bishop Ken two years as rector, and the asylum of the old age of William Wilberforce

BRIXTON DEVERILL, a parish in Warminster district, Wilts, on a head stream of the river Wiley, and on the Roman road to Salisbury, 5 miles S of Warminster r station Post town Longbridge Deverill, under Warminster Acres, 2,470 Real property, £2 076 Pop, 225 Houses, 47 The property is divided among a few Alfred halted here a night on his march against the Danes The living is a rectory in the diocese of Salisbury Value, £480 * Patron, the Bishop of Salisbury The church was repaired in 1863

BRIXTON DOWN See BRIXTON, Isle of Wight

BRIXTON HILL, BRIXTON RISE, AND BRIXTON ROAD See BRIXTON, Surrey

BRIXWORTH, a village a parish a sub district, and a district, in Northamptonshire The village stands adjacent to the Northampton and Market Harborough railway 7 miles N of Northampton, and has a station on the railway, and a post office‡ under Northampton It was formerly a market town under the Fitz Simons, and it still has a fair on Whit Monday Here are a workhouse built at a cost of £5,800 and the kennels of the Pytchley hounds The parish comprises 3,110 acres Real property, £7 636 Pop, 1,2[illegible]3 Houses, [illegible] The property is subdivided Brixworth Hall belonged formerly to the Nicholses and passed to the Woods Some of the inhabitants are lace makers, and some quarriers The living is a vicarage in the diocese of Peterborough Value £300 * Patron, the Bishop of Peterborough The church shows fine features of very early Norman with additions of later character has a curious staircase leading to the tower, is supposed to have been built on the foundations of a Roman basilica, and was restored in 186[illegible] There are a Wesleyan chapel an endowed school with £50 a year, and charities £38

The sub district contains the parishes of Brixworth, Holcot, Scaldwell, Lamport, Haselbeech, Maidwell, Draughton Faxton Old or Wold, Walgrave, and Hannington Acres, 19,135 Pop, [illegible] Houses [illegible] — The district comprehends also the sub district of Spratton, containing the parishes of Spratton, Ravensthorpe, Holdenby East Haddon Cold Ashby, Naseby, Thornby, Guilsborough, Cottesbrook, and Great Creaton, and the sub district of Moulton containing the parishes of Moulton, Overstone, Boughton, Pitsford, Harlestone, Harlestone Church Brampton, and Chapel Brampton, and the extra parochial tract of Althorp Acres, [illegible] Poor rates in 1866, £14 667 Pop in 1861 15,859 Houses, 3,[illegible]60 Marriages in 1866 7[illegible] births, 47[illegible],—of which 31 were illegitimate deaths, 2[illegible],—of which 97 were at ages under 5 years, and 7 at ages above 85 Marriages in the ten years 1851-60, 1,0[illegible], births, 4 71[illegible], deaths 3,078 The places of worship in 1851 were 30 of the Church of England, with 6 907 sittings 6 of Independents, with 1,[illegible]50 s, 10 of Baptists, with 2 150 s, 7 of Wesleyan Methodists, with 1,392 s, and 2 undefined, with 260 s The schools were 28 public day schools, with 1 573 scholars, 31 private day schools, with 477 s, and 42 Sunday schools, with 2,3[illegible] s

BRIZE NORTON See NORTON BRIZE

BROAD BLUNSDON See BLUNSDON (BROAD)

BROADBOTTOM, a suburb of Mottram, in Mottram parish, Cheshire, 3 miles W of Glossop It has Mottram r station and a post office under Manchester

BROADBRIDGE, a tything in Bosham parish, Sussex, 3½ miles W of Chichester Broadbridge Heath here is a meet for the Horsham hounds

BROADBURY CASTLE See BRATTON CLOVELLY

BROAD CAMPDEN See CAMPDEN (BROAD)

BROADCAR, a hamlet in Shropham parish, Norfolk, 3½ miles N of East Harling It was anciently a parish

BROADCARR, a hamlet in Nether Hoyland township Wath upon Dearne parish, W R Yorkshire 4½ miles S of Barnesley

BROAD CHALK, a village and a parish in Wilton district, Wilts The village stands in the vale of Chalk, near Cranborne Chase, 1 mile S by E of Dinton station, and 7½ SW of Wilton, and has a post office under Salisbury It was for some time the residence of John Aubrey, the antiquary The parish includes also the hamlets of Knighton and Stoke Farthing Acres, 6,904 Real property, with Bower Chalk, £9,812 Pop, 79[illegible] Houses, 16[illegible] The property is divided among a few The manor belonged once to the Gawens and was given to Wilton Abbey An ancient camp, of [illegible] acres, occurs at Bury Orchard, and a barrow, called Gawens barrow, is near the camp The living is a vicarage, united with the vicarage of Bower Chalk, in the diocese of Salisbury Value, £[illegible] * Patron, King's College, Cambridge The church belongs to the time of Henry VIII with a Norman doorway on the west, and is in good condition There is an Independent chapel, and the foundation stone of a new one, to be in the Gothic style, was laid in 1862

BROAD CLIST a village a parish, and a sub district in St Thomas district, Devon The village stands on the river Clist, adjacent to the Bristol and Exeter railway, 5 miles NNE of Exeter, and has a station on the railway a post office‡ under Exeter, and fairs on the first Monday of April and Sept It was burnt, in 1001 by the Danes. The parish includes also the hamlets of Dag and Westwood Acres, 9,158 Real property £14 [illegible] Pop, 2 318 Houses 468 The property is divided among a few The manor belonged, at Domesday to the Crown, was given by Henry I to the Nonants, has passed to the Ferdinands, the [illegible], and [illegible], and belongs now to Sir T D Acland, Bart Killerton, on which is Killerton House, the seat of Sir T D Acland, belonged [illegible] to a family of its own name passed through several hands, and was purchased about the middle of the 17th century by the Aclands Columbjohn, now also the property of Sir T D Acland, belonged at one time to the Earls of Devon, and passed through several families A mansion on it built by the Aclands of Devon and afterwards supplanted by a new one, was garrisoned, during the civil war, for Charles I and became the headquarters of Fairfax, when his army was stationed at Silverton The living is a vicarage in the diocese of Exeter Value, £497 Patron, Sir T D Acland The church is later English, has a lofty tower and was restored in 183[illegible] There is a domestic chapel in the park of Killerton House A suite of alms houses has £24 a year, and other charities £17 —The sub district contains four parishes Acres, 14,[illegible] Pop, [illegible] Houses, [illegible]13

BROADFIELD, an extra-parochial tract, formerly a parish, in Royston district, Herts, 2½ miles [illegible] W of Buntingford. Acres, 620. Real property, £59[illegible]. Pop., 19. Houses, 6. It still ranks as a rectory, annexed to the rectory of Cottered, in the diocese of Rochester.

BROADFIELD, a tything in Wrington parish, Somerset, 8 miles SW of Bristol. Pop., 575. Broadfield Down here possesses fine [illegible] and [illegible] views, and has, on its NW shoulder, an ingenious seat, now [illegible] Dr Buckland.

BROADGATE, or BRADGATE PARK, an extra-parochial tract in Barrow-upon-Soar district, Leicestershire, [illegible] miles NW of Leicester. Acres, 1,1[illegible]. Real property, £1,0[illegible]. Pop., [illegible]. Houses, 1. The land is chiefly forest. It was part of the manor of Groby, belonged to the successive Earls of Leicester, the Earls of [illegible], and the Lords Grey of Groby, and was the birth-place of Lady Jane Grey. A large and splendid mansion stood on it, and some portions of the ruins of it still remain, along with a chapel containing a fine monument of the Greys.

BROAD GREEN, a hamlet in Broadwas parish, Worcestershire, 5½ miles WNW of Worcester. Pop., 113.

BROAD GREEN, a village on the Liverpool and St Helens railway, Lancashire, 4½ miles E by N of Liverpool. It has a station on the railway, and a post-office under Liverpool. It is wholly modern, and includes several villas.

BROAD HAVEN, a village on the coast of Pembroke, on St Bride's bay, [illegible] miles WSW of Haverfordwest. It is frequented for sea-bathing, presents a pleasant appearance, has a fine, firm, sandy beach, and commands splendid coast views.

BROAD HAVEN, a small bay on the south coast of [illegible], between Stackpole and St Govan's heads, [illegible] miles S of [illegible] W of Pembroke.

BROADHEATH, a hamlet in Hallow parish, Worcestershire, [illegible] mile NW of Worcester. Pop., [illegible]

BROADHEATH, a station on the Manchester and Warrington railway, [illegible] miles SW of Manchester. It serves for Altrincham.

BROADHEMBURY, a village and a parish in Honiton district, Devon. The village stands [illegible] 5 miles ESE of Cullompton station, and 6 NW of Honiton, and has a post-office under Honiton. It was formerly a market-town, and it still has a fair on the second Monday of Dec. The parish includes also the hamlets of Colliton, [illegible], [illegible], and Kerswell. Acres, 4,703. Real property, £7,901. Pop., 817. Houses, 161. The property is subdivided. The manor belonged anciently to the Fovington family, was given to Dunkeswell abbey, and passed, in the time of Elizabeth, to the family of Drewe. A Cluniac abbey stood at Kerswell, and was subordinate to Montacute priory, in Somerset. An ancient entrenchment, called Hembury fort, crowns a bold spur of highland, commands an extensive prospect, comprises an oval area, engirt by three well-preserved lofty ramparts, seems to have been formed [illegible] but was occupied by the Romans, and is [illegible] by [illegible] antiquaries to have been the Roman [illegible] Moridunum. The living is a vicarage in the diocese of Exeter. Value, £20[illegible]. Patrons, the D[illegible] and Chapter of Exeter. The church is [illegible], consists of nave, chancel, and south aisle, with [illegible], and has an ornamental screen, and [illegible] monuments of the [illegible] family. There are an Independent chapel and charities £60. [illegible]

BROADHEMPSTON, a village and a parish in Newton-Abbot district, Devon. The village stands [illegible] miles [illegible] of Dartmouth, 2 [illegible] the South Devon railway, [illegible] N of Totnes, and has a post-office under [illegible]. The parish comprises 2,0[illegible] acres. Real property, £4,148. Pop., 6[illegible]. Houses, 1[illegible]. The property is [illegible]. The manor belonged formerly to the Champernownes [illegible], now to [illegible] Esq. The living is a vicarage in the diocese of Exeter. Value, £11[illegible] from the crown. The church consists of nave, chancel, and aisles, and has an ornamental screen. There are chapels for Independents and Wesleyans.

BROADHINTON, a parish in Marlborough district, Wilts, 1½ miles SE of Wootton-Bassett station, and 6 SSW of Swindon. Post-town, [illegible] under Swindon. Acres, 3,650. Real property, £2,826. Pop., 637. Houses, 111. The property is divided among about sixty. The living is a vicarage in the diocese of Salisbury. Value, £302. Patron, St Nicholas Hospital, Salisbury. The church is old but good, and has a square embattled tower. The vicarage of Broad Town is a separate benefice. A school has £42 from endowment, and other charities have £[illegible]. Sir John Glanville, the eminent lawyer, was a native.

BROADHINTON, a liberty in Hurst parish, Berks, 4 miles NW by W of Wokingham. Acres, 1,710. Pop., [illegible]31. Houses, 1[illegible].

BROADHOLME, a township in Thorney parish, Notts, on the verge of the county, adjacent to the Fossdyke, 7 miles W of Lincoln. Acres, 560. Real property, [illegible],057. Pop., 11[illegible]. Houses, [illegible]. A small nunnery was founded here, in the reign of Stephen, by Agnes de Camville, and given, at the dissolution, to Elizabeth, to John [illegible] and William Huber.

BROADLEY, a hamlet in St Enoder parish, Cornwall, on the river Towy, [illegible] miles NW of Kidwelly. Pop., [illegible]21.

BROADLANDS, the seat of Viscount Palmerston in Hants, on the river Anton, 1 mile S of Romsey. The house is of white brick, with stone dressings, was designed by [illegible] Brown, and contains a good collection of pictures and some antique statuary. The park is small but beautiful [illegible].

BROADLANDS, a seat of lace manufacture in the vicinity of Newport, Isle of Wight. The [illegible] of Alexandra, Princess of Wales, were [illegible] there.

BROADLAND, a township in Haward[illegible] parish, Hunt, 1 mile S of [illegible]. Acres, 73[illegible]. Pop., 77. Houses, 13. Here is the seat of [illegible].

BROADLAND, a hamlet in North Curry parish, Somerset, 7 miles E of Taunton.

BROAD MARSTON, a hamlet in Pebworth parish, Gloucester, [illegible] miles N of Chipping-Campden. Pop., [illegible]50.

BROADMAYNE, or BROADMAYNE, a parish in Dorchester district, Dorset, 2 miles S of the Southwestern railway, and [illegible] of Dorchester. It has a post-office under Dorchester. Acres, 2,[illegible]10. Real property, £1,0[illegible]. Pop., [illegible]00. Houses, 97. The property is much subdivided. The living is a rectory, annexed to the rectory of West Knighton, in the diocese of Salisbury. The church is not good.

BROADNYMET, a chapelry in North Tawton parish, Devon, 1 mile W of Bow, and 6 W of [illegible]. Acres, [illegible]. Pop., returned with the parish. The living is a sinecure rectory in the diocese of Exeter. The church is [illegible], [illegible] and [illegible], but has gone to ruin.

BROADOAK, or BRADOCK, a parish in Liskeard district, Cornwall, 2 miles SSW of Doublebois station, and [illegible] NE by E of Lostwithiel. It includes West Taphouse hamlet, and its post-town is Lostwithiel. Acres, [illegible]. Real property, £1,[illegible]. Pop., [illegible]. Houses, 5[illegible]. The property is divided among a few. The manor was [illegible] Doublebois [illegible], [illegible] Broad [illegible] of the [illegible] in 164[illegible], of the parliamentary [illegible] by the [illegible] under Hopton. The living is a rectory, annexed to the rectory of [illegible], in the diocese of Exeter. The church is good and [illegible].

BROADOAK, [illegible] of Matthew Henry, in [illegible] Hantshire, [illegible] 6½ miles SSW of [illegible].

BROADOAK, [illegible], a hamlet in Sheffield parish, W. R. Yorkshire, [illegible] miles SW of Sheffield.

BROADOAK, [illegible] in Symondsbury parish, Dorset, near Bridport. A church was built here in 18[illegible].

BROADOAKSHAM, a hamlet in [illegible] parish, Devon, 7 miles S of [illegible].

BROADOYD HEAD, a hamlet in Dent [illegible] and parish, W. R. Yorkshire, [illegible] miles NW of [illegible].

BROADSIDE, a township in Alnwick parish, Northumberland Pop, 123

BROADSOUND, a belt of sea among the Scilly Isles, NW of St Agnes It is obstructed by the Crim shoal, and is dangerous to vessels from its tidal currents

BROADSTAIRS, a village and a chapelry in St Peter parish, Thanet, Kent The village stands on the coast, adjacent to the Kent Coast railway, 2½ miles N by E of Ramsgate, and has a station on the railway a post office‡ under Ramsgate, and two hotels It is an ancient place was the scene of a fierce battle, in 853, between the Saxons and the Danes, had extensive fortifications, pierced by a sea gate, with a portal and some part of which remains took its name from the "broad stairs" which led up from the sea gate, possessed, a little above the fortifications, a Lady chapel, of so high repute that ships lowered their top sails in going past it and sent, about the middle of last century a number of vessels to the cod fisheries of Iceland and the Northern seas Its old pier was swept away by a storm in 1808, and its present pier is a rough picturesque, timber structure The village is now frequented as a bathing place, has good accommodations and a fine sandy beach, and commands splendid views. It is also a coast guard station The chapelry includes the village extends into the country, and was constituted in 1850 Rated property £4,628 Pop, 1,378 Houses, 300 The property is much subdivided Old coins have been found in the cliffs, and a spermaceti whale 61 feet long came ashore in 1762 The living is a rectory in the diocese of Canterbury Value £230 Patron, the Vicar of St Peter The church was built in 1828, and has a tower added in 1852 A Baptist chapel includes a portion of the old Lady chapel There is also a Wesleyan chapel

BROADSTONE, a township in Munslow parish, Salop, 6½ miles SE of Church Stretton Pop, 210. It forms a curacy with Munslow

BROADTOWN, a hamlet in Broad Hinton parish, and a chapelry in Broad Hinton and Cliffe Pypard parishes, Wilts The hamlet lies 1¼ mile NW of Broad Hinton village, and 3 SE of Wootton Bassett r station The chapelry includes the hamlet, and was constituted in 1846 Post town, Broad Hinton, under Swindon Pop, 473 Houses, 98 The living is a vicarage in the diocese of Salisbury Value £100 * Patrons, the Vicars of Broad Hinton and Cliffe Pypard alternately

BROADWARD, a township in Clungunford parish, Salop 8 miles W of Ludlow Pop, 18

BROADWARD AND BRIERLEY, a township in Leominsterout parish, Hereford, 1¼ mile S of Leominster

BROADWAS a parish in Martley district, Worcestershire, on the river Teme, 1½ mile NNW of Bransford Road r station and 6 W of Worcester It includes the hamlet of Broadgreen, and has a post office under Worcester Acres, 1,160 Real property £2,347 Pop, 311 Houses, 63 The living is a rectory in the diocese of Worcester Value, £253 * Patrons, the Dean and Chapter of Worcester The church is partly Norman

BROAD WATER, the lake of Bassenthwaite, in Cumberland See BASSENTHWAITE

BROADWATER, a hundred in Herts It lies around Bennington and Datchworth, and contains twenty two parishes Acres 59,511 Pop, 19,800 Houses, 3,777

BROADWATER, a village a parish and a sub district, in Worthing district, Sussex The village stands near the South Coast railway, 1 mile N of Worthing, and has a post office under Worthing It was formerly a market town, under the Camois family, who had a castle adjacent to it and it still has fairs on 22 June and 29 Oct The parish includes also the township and town of Worthing Acres, 2,960, of which 320 are water Real property, £32,153 Pop 6,460 Houses, 1,188 The property is much subdivided Offington, anciently the seat of the Lords Delawarr, now the seat of J T Dunbury Esq, is about ½ a mile W of the village The living is a rectory in the diocese of Chichester Value £800 Patron the Rev F K Ha[illegible]t The church is cruciform and was restored in 1854 The vicarage of Christchurch and the p curacies of Worthing and St George are separate benefices Charities £27 —The sub district contains five parishes Pop, 8,957

BROADWATER, a chapelry in Frant parish, Sussex, near Tunbridge Wells Pop, 577 Living a p curacy Patron, Lord Abergavenny The church was built in 1866 and is in the French late first pointed style

BROADWAY, a village and a parish in Weymouth district, Dorset The village stands on the river Wey, near the Weymouth railway, 3½ miles N by W of Weymouth, and has a fair on the Wednesday before 18 Sept The parish includes also Little Moor hamlet, and part of Nottington hamlet and its post town is Radipole, under Weymouth Acres, 1,020 Real property, £5,072 Pop, 611 Houses, 133 The property is much subdivided Stone is quarried The living is a rectory, annexed to the rectory of Lincombe, in the diocese of Salisbury The church is good, and there are charities £9

BROADWAY, a village and a parish in Chard district, Somerset The village stands near the Chard canal, and near the Chard, Ilminster, and Taunton railway 2 miles NW of Ilminster r station, took its name from a Roman way across its site, and through Neroche forest, and has a fair on 1 Sept The parish includes also the tythings of Capland and Rapps, and its post town is Ilminster Acres, 2,072 Real property, £2,861 Pop, 431 Houses, 89 The property is much subdivided The living is a p curacy in the diocese of Bath and Wells. Value, £107 Patron, the Rev Dr W Palmer The church is ancient and cruciform There are an Independent chapel, and charities £23

BROADWAY, a village, a parish, and a sub district, in Evesham district, Worcester The village stands 3½ miles W of Campden r station, and 5½ SE by S of Evesham, and has a head post office ‡ The parish comprises 4,800 acres Real property, £10,343 Pop, 1,500 Houses 361 The property is much subdivided. The Broadway hills were the quarters of the royalists after the battle of Evesham, and command a fine view Stone is quarried The living is a vicarage in the diocese of Worcester Value, £240 * Patrons, Trustees The church was built in 1839, and there are chapels for Independents, Wesleyans, and Roman Catholics A school has £74 from endowment, and other charities, £27 The sub district contains sixteen parishes seven of them electorally in Gloucester Acres, 28,570 Pop, 6,870 Houses, 1,511

BROADWELL, a hamlet in Leamington Hastings parish, Warwick, 3½ miles NE of Southam Pop 220

BROADWELL, or BRADLE, a parish in Stow on the Wold district, Gloucester, on the Fosse way, 1½ mile NNE of Stow on the Wold and 2 miles WNW of Adlestrop station It has a post office under Moreton in the Marsh Acres, 1 600 Real property, £3,713 Pop, 398 Houses, 92 The property is much subdivided Broadwell House is the seat of Lord Leigh The living is a rectory, united with the rectory of Adlestrop in the diocese of Gloucester and Bristol Value, £615 * Patron, Lord Leigh The church is good, and there are a national school and charities £16

BROADWELL or BRADWELL, a village in the district of Witney, and a parish in the districts of Witney and Faringdon, and county of Oxford The village stands on Akeman street, 4 miles NNE of Lechlade and 8½ SW of Witney r station The parish includes also the hamlet of Filkins, the chapelry of Holwell, and the township of Kelmscott, and its post town is Clanfield, under Faringdon Acres, 5,871 Real property, £7 630 Pop 1 103 Houses 255 The property is divided among a few Filkins is the seat of the Colstons and Broadwell Grove belonged formerly to the Thomonds, and belongs now to the Harveys The living is a vicarage united with the p curacy of Kelmscott, in the diocese of Oxford Value, £207 Patron, the Rev T T Woodman The church is cruciform and good has a fine spire, and contains monuments of the Colstons There are a free school and charities £3 The vicarages of Holwell and Filkins are separate benefices

BROADWINSOR, a village and a parish in Beaminster district, Dorset The village stands 3 miles WNW of

Leominster, and 5 S of Crewkerne r station, and has a post office‡ under Pridport, and a f ir on T i its Monde The parish includes also the tythings of Chi Bhay, Dib lerond Drimpton and Little Wimson Acres, 6,214 Real property, £11,810 Pop, 1 535 Houses, 311 The living is a vicarage, united with the p cu acy of Bla kdown in the diocese of Salisbury Value, £ 58 * Patron, the Bishop of Salisbury The church is an cient, and has a tower There are an Independent chapel an endowed school, with £23 and other chari ties with £18 Thomas Fuller, author of the ' History of the Holy War,' was vicar

BROADWOOD KELLY, a parish in Okehampton dis trict Devon 5½ miles E by N of Hatherleigh and 6 WSW of Lapford r station Post town, Winkleigh North Devon Acres 2,663 Real property, £2,023 Pop, 312 Houses, 73 The property is much divided The manor belongs to E Clare, Esq The living is a rectory in the diocese of Exeter Value, £278 * Pa tron, the Rev Mr Hole The church stands on elevated ground, consists of nave, chancel, and aisles, and was repaired in 1836

BROADWOOD WIDGER, a village, a parish, and a sub district, in the district of Holsworthy, Devon The village stands on the acclivity of a hill, 6 miles NE by E of Launceston r station, and 11 NNW of Tavistock The parish comprises 8,780 acres, and its post town is Launceston Real property, £4,?43 Pop, 815 Houses, 1?6 The property is divided among a few About 1 500 acres are open woodland The living is a vicarage, united with the p curacy of Week St Germans, in the diocese of Exeter Value £148 Patrons, the Dean and Chapter of Bristol The church is an old edifice, and dilapidated, and there are chapels for Wesleyans and Bible Christians —The sub district contains four parishes, and part of another Acres, 22,1?7 Pop in 1851, 2,461 Houses, 438

BROBURY, a parish in Weobly district Hereford, on the river Wye, adjacent to the Hereford and Brecon railway, at Kinnersley station, 8½ miles E by N of Hay Post town, Bredwardine, under Hereford Acres, ?69 Real property £819 Pop, 70 Houses, 17 The pro perty is divided among a few Brobury scar is a bold rural object, amid the fine scenery of the Wye The living is a rectory, annexed to the vicarage of Bredwardine, in the diocese of Hereford The church is small and plain

BROCARDS, or BROCKHILLS CASTLE, an ancient camp on ground commanding a pass of Watling street about a mile SSW of Church Stretton, in Salop

BROCK, a station on the Lancaster and Preston rail way 2 miles S by E of Garstang in Lancashire Claughton Hall, a mansion of the time of Charles I is now a farm house and stone quarries are in the neighbourhood

BROCKAMIN, a hamlet in Leigh parish, Worcester shire, 4½ miles W of Worcester Pop 252

BROCKDISH, a parish in Depwade district, Norfolk, on the river Waveney, 3 miles SW by W of Harleston r station, and 6 E of Diss It has a post office under Scole Acres, 1 069 Real property, £2 304 Pop, 511 Houses, 117 The property is much subdivided The living is a rectory in the diocese of Norwich Value £2?? * Patron, Sir E Kerrison The church is ancient, and has a tower There are a Wesleyan chapel, and charities £17 Blomfield, the county historian, was rector

BROCKENHURST, a village and a parish in Lymington district Hants The village stands, embosomed in wood in the New Forest on the river Boldre, adjacent to the Southwestern railway, 4 miles N by W of Lym ington It has a station on the railway, and a post office under Lymington The parish lies wholly in the New Forest and comprises 2,950 acres Real property, £4,173 Pop, 1 0?? Houses, 20? The property is divided among a few Brockenhurst Park, Brockenhurst, ... the ... scenery ... the old ... is a meet for the New Forest ... Boldre Bridge, or W... House, was for the ... of ... Saxon ... in the vicinity, has several tumuli The living

is a vicarage in the diocese of Winchester Value £100 * Patron, J Morant, Esq The church crowns a knoll about ½ a mile S of the village, is variously Saxon, very early Norman late Norman and early English, has been much remodelled, and contains an ancient square Norman font of Purbeck marble An enormous yew tree, and a grand ivy clad oak are in the churchyard Charities, £24

BROCKET HALL, the seat and death place of the late Viscount Melbourne and the late Viscount Palmer ston, in Hatfield parish, Herts, on the river Lea, 2 miles N of Hatfield

BROCKFORD, a hamlet in Wetheringsett parish Suffolk, 2½ miles NW of Debenham Pop, 277 It forms a curacy with Wetheringsett

BROCKHALL a parish in Daventry district, North ampton, on Watling street the Grand Junction canal, and the Northwestern railway, 2½ miles N of Weedon station, and 4½ E of Daventry Post town Weedon Acres 861 Real property, £2,127 Pop, 51 Houses 9 The property is divided among a few Brockhall Park belonged formerly to the Fyners and the Thornhills, and belongs now to T R Thornton, Esq The living is a rectory in the diocese of Peterborough Value, £138 * Patron, T P Thornton, Esq The church is partly Norman, and in good condition

BROCKHAM, or BROCKHAM GREEN, a village and a chapelry in Betchworth parish, Surrey The village stands on the river Mole, 1½ mile SW of Betchworth r station, and 2 E of Dorking and has a post office of the name of Brockham Green, under Reigate The chapelry was constituted in 1848 Pop, 701 Houses, 117 The property is all in one estate The living is a vicar age in the diocese of Winchester Value, £110 * Pa tron, Col Goulburn The church is a neat edifice in the Norman style with a spire, and there are a baptist cha pel and a girls orphanage See BETCHWORTH

BROCKHAMPTON, a tything in Havant parish, Hants, near Havant Pop 109

BROCKHAMPTON, a parish in Ross district, Here ford, on the river Wye, 2½ miles NNE of Fawley r sta tion, and 5 N of Ross Post town How Caple, under Ross Acres, 785 Real property £1,50? Pop, 1?? Houses, 28 The property is divided among a few A Roman camp occurs about a mile north of the church The living is a vicarage in the diocese of Hereford Value, £74 Patrons the Dean and Chapter of Here ford The church is good

BROCKHAMPTON, a township or a parish and a sub-district, in Bromyard district Hereford The town ship lies 2 miles NE of Bromyard, and 9 NNW of Mal vern Link r station, is sometimes called Norton with Brockhampton, and has been regarded variously as a township partly of Bromyard parish and as itself a separate parish Post town, Bromyard, under Worcester Acres, 1 ?10 Pop, ?2? Houses 12? The place contains several good residences suburban to Bromyard The living is a p curacy annexed to the vicarage of Bromyard, in the diocese of Hereford —The sub district contains part of two parishes, eleven entire parishes, two of them electorally in Worcester and an extra parochial tract Acres, 21 812 Pop, 3,716 Houses, 761

BROCKHAMPTON Oxford See BROCKHAMPTON

BROCKHAMPTON, Gloucester See SOUTHAM AND BROCKHAMPTON

BROCKHAMPTON AND KNOWLE, a tything in Buckland Newton parish Dorset ... miles NE of Cerne Abbas Pop, 1?? Houses ??

BROCKHOLES a place in Honley chapelry W R Yorkshire at a railway junction, 4 miles SE by S of Huddersfield It has a r station with telegraph, and chapel of ease

BROCKHOLES, Lancashire See CLIMSALL AND BROCKHOLES

BROCKHURST a village in Monks Kirby parish, Warwick, 5½ miles NNW of Rugby

BROCKHURST, a manor in East Grinstead parish, Sussex near East Grinstead

BROCKHURST CASTLE See BROCARDS CASTLE

BROCKLEBANK, a township in Westward parish

Cumberland, 4 miles SE by E of Wigton Real property, £2,100 Pop, 118 Houses, 27 Brocklebank fell is a front of the mass of the uplands which extend southward in the Caldbeck fells and Skiddaw

BROCKLESBY, a parish in Caistor district, Lincoln adjacent to the Great Grimsby and Sheffield railway, 9 miles WNW of Great Grimsby It has a station on the railway and includes the hamlet of Little Limber, and its post town is Limber under Ulceby Acres, inclusive of Newsham extra parochial tract 5,850 Real property, £3,494 Pop 252 Houses, 47 Brocklesby Park is the seat of the Earl of Yarborough, and was visited by Prince Albert, in 1849, at the opening of Grimsby dock The mansion has a fine picture gallery, and the grounds have a mausoleum by Wyatt and a temple The living is a rectory, united with the vicarage of Kirmington, in the diocese of Lincoln Value, £179 * Patron Lord Yarborough The church is handsome

BROCKLEY, a parish in Bedminster district, Somerset, on the Bristol and Exeter railway, near Nailsea station, 8 miles SW of Bristol It has a post office under West Town Somerset Acres, 692 Real property, £1,729 Pop, 93 Houses, 19 The property is divided among three Brockley Hall is the seat of the Piggotts Brockley Combe is a rocky wooded hollow, about 300 feet flanked by hills, and was a favourite resort of the poet Coleridge Lead ore is found The living is a rectory in the diocese of Bath and Wells Value, £128 * Patrons, the Trustees of the late Rev W Piggott The church is pretty good, and there are charities £9

BROCKLEY, a parish in Thingoe district, Suffolk, on an affluent of the river Stour, 6½ miles SSW of Bury St Edmunds r station Post town, Lawshall, under Bury St Edmunds Acres, 1,565 Real property, £2,571 Pop, 390 Houses, 71 The property is much subdivided The living is a rectory in the diocese of Ely Value, £510 * Patron, the Rev Mr Cartwright The church is an ancient structure, with a small tower, and contains a handsome monument of the Spurges There are a Baptist chapel, and charities £62

BROCKLEY, a hamlet on the NW border of Kent, adjacent to the Croydon railway, 1 mile WSW of Lewisham It has a post office‡ under Lewisham London, S E, and had anciently a Premonstratensian monastery founded about the end of the reign of Henry II

BROCKLEY COMBE See BROCKLEY, Somerset

BROCKLEY HILL an eminence on the northern verge of Middlesex, in the line of Watling street, 2 miles NNW of Edgeware Many relics have been found here

BROCKLEY HILL, Kent See SYDENHAM

BROCKLEY WHINS, a railway station in the N of Durham, on the Pontop and Shields railway, 6 miles W of Gateshead

BROCKMANTON, a township in Puddlestone parish, Hereford 4½ miles E of Leominster Real property, £516

BROCKMOOR, a chapelry in Kingswinford parish, Stafford, adjacent to the West Midland railway ¾ a mile NW of Brierley Hill It was constituted in 1844, and its post town is Brierley Hill Pop, 3 544 Houses, 721 Most of the inhabitants are employed in coal and iron works The living is a vicarage in the diocese of Lichfield Value £150 * Patron, alternately the Crown and the Bishop The church is a neat structure, and there is a Wesleyan chapel

BROCKSFIELD See BROXFIELD

BROCKTHROP, or BROCKTHORPE a parish in Wheatenhurst district, Gloucestershire, under the wolds adjacent to the Gloucester and Bristol railway, 1½ mile NE of Haresfield station, and 4 S of Gloucester It has a post office, of the name of Brockthorpe, under Gloucester Acres 2 000 Real property £2,[illegible] Pop, 150 Houses, 40 The property is divided among a few The living is a vicarage, united with the vicarage of Whaddon in the diocese of Gloucester and Bristol Value £180 * Patrons, the Dean and Chapter of Gloucester two turns, and Sir J Neild Bart, one turn The church is early English in tolerable condition and has, in the cornice of the porch, a curious inscription relating to the execution of Charles I

BROCKTON, a township in Eccleshall parish, Stafford shire adjacent to the Stafford and Worcester canal, 1 miles SE of Stafford Acres, 1,690 Real property, £1,709 Pop 278 Houses, 51 Brockton House and Brockton Lodge belonged to the Chetwynds

BROCKTON a township in Longford parish, Salop, 2 miles SW of Newport Pop 125

BROCKTON a township in North Lydbury parish Salop 2 miles S of Bishops Castle Pop, 137

BROCKTON a township in Worthen parish, Salop, on the verge of the county, 9 miles N of Bishops Castle Pop 303

BROCKWEAR, or BROOKS WEIR, a village, on extra parochial ground, contiguous to Hewelsfield parish, in Gloucestershire, on the river Wye, 6 miles N of Chepstow Pop, 212 Here are a Moravian chapel built in 1832, and remains of an ancient camp

BROCKWELL, a locality about a mile W of Dulwich, on the NE border of Surrey, with a post office‡ under Dulwich, London, S

BROCKWORTH, a parish in the district and county of Gloucester, on Ermine street, in the vale of Gloucester 4 miles ESE of Gloucester It has a post office under Gloucester Acres, 1,847 Real property £4 605 Pop, 477 Houses 97 The property is divided among a few The grounds called the Court were the site of a Roman station, and have yielded Roman remains Cooper's Hill, a steep projection from neighbouring hills commands a brilliant view The parish is a meet for the Cotswold hounds The living is a vicarage in the diocese of Gloucester and Bristol Value £150 * Patron T C Davis Esq The church is perpendicular English with Norman arches under the tower John Theyer the antiquary, who died in 1673 was a native There are a national school and charities £45

BRODSWORTH, a township and a parish in Doncaster district, W R Yorkshire The township lies 4¼ miles W of N of Bessacar station, and 5½ NW by N of Doncaster and has a post office under Doncaster The parish includes also the hamlets of Pigburn and Scawsby Acres 3 170 Real property, £3,350 Pop 452 Houses, 87 The property is divided among a few Brodsworth Park belonged to the Earls of Kinnoul passed by sale to Peter Thellusson, Esq who died in 1798, bequeathing it to be under trustees for three generations, but through judgment of the Lord Chancellor, was inherited by his son, Lord Rendlesham Limestone is quarried The living is a vicarage in the diocese of York Value, £172 * Patron, the Archbishop The church is old There is a Wesleyan chapel a free school and charities £15

BROGDEN WITH ADMORGILL, a township in Barnoldswick parish W R Yorkshire adjacent to the Leeds and Liverpool canal and near the Midland railway, 9 miles SW by W of Skipton Acres 1,670 Pop 123 Houses 25

BROKEHAMPTON See BROCKHAMPTON

BROKE HOUSE or BROOK the old seat of the Willoughbys de Broke, 2 miles W of Westbury, in Wilts It belonged previously to the Cheyneys

BROKENBOROUGH, a parish in Malmesbury district, Wilts, on Akeman street 2 miles NW of Malmesbury, and 7½ W by S of Minety r station It has a post office under Chippenham Acres, 2,572 Real property £4 732 Pop 503 Houses, 99 The property is divided among a few The manor belonged to the Saxon kings, and passed to the Molines. Some Roman remains have been found The living is a vicarage annexed to the vicarage of Westport, in the diocese of Gloucester and Bristol The church is good

BROKEN END See UNDERBARROW

BROKENHAUGH, a quarter in Haydon parochial chapelry, Northumberland adjacent to the Newcastle and Carlisle railway, 6 miles WNW of Hexham Pop, [illegible]

BROM [illegible] See BROOM [illegible]

BROMBLOW See BROMLOW

BROMBOROUGH, a township and a parish in Wirrall district, Cheshire The township lies on the Mersey and on the Birkenhead and Chester railway 4½ miles S by E of Birkenhead, and has a station on the railway, and a post office under Chester. It had formerly a weekly market, and it adjoins the [illegible] on the [illegible]. Acres 2,600, of which 1,080 are water. Real property, £8,910. Pop., 1,001. Houses, 195. The parish includes also the township of Brimstage. Acres 3,612. Real property, £9,002. Pop., 1,279. Houses, 2[illegible]. The manor belongs to S. Mainwaring, Esq. Bromborough Hall is the seat of P. Rankin, Esq. Bromborough Pool, a creek of the Mersey, is occupied by the [illegible] floating gunpowder magazines, and has on its shore the establishment of Price's Patent Candle Company. A small priory was founded at Bromborough, about [illegible], by the Bleds. The living is a rectory in the diocese of Chester. Value, £250.* Patrons, the Dean and Chapter of C. The church was rebuilt, in the early English style in 18[illegible], at a cost of £5,000. There are two chapels of ease, a large national school built in [illegible] at a cost of £2,000, and charities £[illegible].

BROMBY, or B[illegible], a township in Frodingham parish, Lincoln, 7 miles WNW of Glanford Brigg. Real property, £1,6[illegible]. Pop., 20[illegible]. Houses, 8.

BROME, or BROOME, a parish in Hartismere district, Suffolk, 2 miles N of Eye r. station, and 3½ ENE of Mellis. It has a post office under Scole. Acres, 832. Real property, £2,0[illegible]. Pop., 231. Houses, 68. The property is divided among a few. Brome Hall belonged anciently to the Bretons, passed to the Cornwallis family, and is now the seat of Sir E. Kerrison, Bart. The old mansion, built about the middle of the 16th century, was recently taken down, and a new one erected on its site. The living is a rectory, united with the rectory of Oakley, in the diocese of Norwich. Value, £561.* Patron, Sir E. Kerrison, Bart. The church is very good. There are a national school and charities £18.

BROME, Norfolk. See BROOME.

BROMESBERROW. See BROMSBERROW.

BROME (SOUTH). See SOUTHBROOM.

BROMESWELL, a parish in Woodbridge district, Suffolk, on the river Deben, adjacent to the East Suffolk railway, near Melton station, 2½ miles NE of Woodbridge, [illegible] town, Melton, under Woodbridge. Acres, 1,5[illegible]3. Real property, £1,633. Pop., 210. Houses, 4[illegible]. The property is divided among a few. The living is a rectory in the diocese of Norwich. Value, £150.* [illegible] the [illegible] of Bristol. The church is good. There are a free school, and charities £[illegible].

BROMFIELD, a township and a parish in Wigton district, Cumberland. The township lies on an affluent of the river Waver, 2½ miles NW of Leegate station, and 6 W by S of Wigton; it includes the hamlets of Crookdale and Scales. Real property, £3,164. Pop., [illegible]11. Houses, 66. The parish contains also the townships of Blencogo, Langrigg and Mealrigg, Dundraw and Kelsick, and West Newton and Allonby; and has post offices of Langrigg, under Carlisle, and Allonby, under Maryport. Acres, 11,644, of which 573 are water. Real property, £1[illegible]. Pop., 2,2[illegible]0. Houses, 482. The property is much subdivided. The surface extends 9½ miles south-west, and to the coast, and borrows charm from a fine perspective of the Caldbeck and Skiddaw mountains. Some remains exist of Mungo Castle. The living is a vicarage in the diocese of Carlisle. Value, £270.* Patron, the Bishop of Carlisle. The church was [illegible] in 18[illegible]. The chapelries of Allonby and West Newton are separate benefices. A grammar school, founded in 1612, has an endowed income of £4[illegible]. Boarding [illegible] [illegible] is [illegible].

BROMFIELD, a hamlet in Denbigh, [illegible]. It lies round [illegible] and Cheshire, and contains [illegible] of four others. Acres, [illegible]. Real property, £18,[illegible]. Pop., in 1861, 3[illegible],[illegible]. Houses, 7,1[illegible]2.

BROMFIELD, a village, a township, and a parish in Ludlow district, Salop. The village stands near the confluence of the Onny and the Teme, adjacent to the Shrewsbury and Hereford railway, 2½ miles NW by N of Ludlow; [illegible], and a [illegible] Bromfield [illegible]. The [illegible] Lady Holter. Acres [illegible]. Acres, 5,112. Pop., [illegible]. Houses,

11[illegible]. The parish contains likewise the chapelry of Halford. Acres, 7,1[illegible]. Real property, £9,437. Pop., 702. Houses, 138. The property is divided among a few. Oakley Park, contiguous to the village, is a fine mansion. A small college of secular canons was founded in the time of Henry I., on the bank of the Teme below the influx of the Onny; became, in 1155, a Benedictine priory, subject to St. Peter's Abbey at Gloucester; and was given in the time of Mary to Charles Fox. The living is a vicarage in the diocese of Hereford. Value, £31[illegible].* Patron, R. C. W. Clive, Esq. The church adjoins some remains of the ancient priory, is an ancient structure of various dates, with a tower, and was repaired in 1850.

BROMFIELD. See BROOMFIELD.

BROMFORD LANE, a joint station with Oldbury, on the Birmingham and Wolverhampton railway, 5½ miles NW of Birmingham.

BROMHALL, a hamlet in Sunninghill parish, Berks. Here was a small Benedictine nunnery, founded before the time of King John, and given, at the dissolution, to St. John's college, Cambridge. Here also was the residence of Richard II.'s queen, Isabella.

BROMHALL. See BROOMHALL, Cheshire.

BROMHAM, a parish, with a village, in the district and county of Bedford, on the river Ouse, 2 miles SW of Oakley r. station, and 4 WNW of Bedford. Post town, Bedford. Acres, 1,798. Real property, £2,9[illegible]. Pop., 301. Houses, 67. The property is divided among a few. Bromham Hall is the seat of the Trevors. A bridge of 25 arches crosses the Ouse at the village. The living is a vicarage, united with the vicarage of Oakley, in the diocese of Ely. Value, £396. Patron, Trinity College. The church is very ancient, but good; has a square tower, and contains monuments of the Trevors and the Dyves. There is a free school.

BROMHAM, a village, a parish, and a sub-district in Devizes district, Wilts. The village stands 1 mile N of the Kennet and Avon canal, 1¾ S of the line of road to Bath, 2 miles N by E of Seend r. station, and 4 NW of Devizes; and has a post office under Chippenham, and an hostelry. The parish comprises 2,5[illegible] acres. Real property, £6,894. Pop., 1,[illegible]02. Houses, 31[illegible]. The property is divided among a few. The manor was held in the time of Edward the Confessor, by Earl Harold; belonged, in the time of Henry VI., to Lord St. Amand; and passed from him to the Bayntons. Bromham House was destroyed in 1645. Spye Park house was built in 1650 by the Bayntons, is an interesting embattled edifice, on the verge of a fine hill, was occasionally visited in the time of Charles II., by the witty but profligate Earl of Rochester, and is now the seat of J. Bayntun Starky, Esq. Sloperton Cottage, in the north, near Bowood Park, was long the residence and eventually the death place of the poet Moore. The living is a rectory in the diocese of Salisbury. Value, £[illegible]98.* Patron, the Rev. E. Edgell. The church is decorated English, richly sculptured; has a handsome spire; was restored in 18[illegible]; and contains tombs of the Bayntons, an elaborate tomb of a Beauchamp, and a monumental tablet to Dr. Sewell, who wrote "Season on the Seasons." The churchyard contains the grave of the poet Moore. There are a Baptist chapel, a Wesleyan chapel, and alms-houses, the latter with £20 a year. Bishop Ward, the Somersetshire [illegible] Collinson, and Dr. Season were natives. The sub-district contains this parish and parts of another. Acres, 13,003. Pop., 1,88[illegible]. Houses, 1,10[illegible].

BROMHILL. See BROMHOLM AND BROOMHILL.

BROMHOLM, a hamlet in Bacton parish, Norfolk, 4½ miles NE of North Walsham. It once had a noble and rich priory. See BACTON.

BROMLEY, a small town, a parish, a sub-district, and a district in Kent. The town stands on high ground, on the Ravensbourne river, adjacent to the Mid-Kent railway, 10 miles SE of St. Paul's, London. It commands good views to the N and SW, and is set in a rich and beautiful country with a [illegible] [illegible]; is a seat of petty sessions and a polling place; and has a railway station, a post office, [illegible] der London SE, and a town-hall, good inns, a church, three dissenting chapels, a college for clergymen's widows, a National school, and a literary institute. The church is chiefly perpendicular English, mainly rebuilt in 1829, and consisting of nave, chancel, and aisles, has, at the west end, an ancient embattled tower, surmounted by a cupola, and contains a Norman font, a brass of 1456, a monument of Dr Hawkesworth the essay writer of the "Adventurer," and the graves of Bishop Pearce, Bishop Porteus, and the wife of Dr Johnson. The college is a large brick structure, founded in 1666, by Bishop Warner, and renovated in 1765, gives residences and support to 40 widows, and has an income of £1,993. A drainage system for the town was projected in 1859.

The parish comprises 4,646 acres. Real property in 1860, £28,5.. Rental in 1860, £46,771. Rateable value in 1861, £28,705, in 1865, £37,810. Pop in 1861, 5,505, in 1865, 6,023. Houses in 1861, 1,080, in 1866, 1,338. The manor was given, in the 8th century, by Ethelbert, King of Kent, to the bishops of Rochester; continued with some slight interruptions, to be held by them till a few years ago; and belongs now to Coles Child, Esq. A palace was built on it, by one of the bishops, soon after the Conquest, underwent improvements by successive bishops, was visited by Walpole and Pope, and gave place in 1776 to a new palace, a plain brick mansion, now the residence of the present lord of the manor. The parish ceased, at the recent rearrangement of sees, to be in the diocese of Rochester; and the residence of the bishops was then fixed at Danbury in Essex. A chalybeate spring is in the palace grounds; and another spring was there till lately called St Blaize's well, had had anciently a small oratory, and was a resort of pilgrims, in the Romish times at Whitsuntide. An old moated mansion at the southern extremity of the town, belonged successively to the Bankwells, the Clarks, and the Simpsons, and some remains of it exist under the name of Simpsons place. Elmstow Lodge, Sickley Park, and Sundridge are in the neighbourhood. The living is a p. curacy in the diocese of Canterbury. Value, £160. Patron, the Bishop of Worcester. The vicarages of Elmstow, Bickley, and Bromley Common are separate benefices.

The sub-district contains the parishes of Bromley, Beckenham, Hayes, West Wickham, Keston, Downe, Cudham, and Knockholt. Acres, 23,118. Pop, 11,75.. Houses, 2,257. The district comprehends also the sub-district of Chislehurst, containing the parishes of Chislehurst, Farnborough, Chelsfield, Orpington, St Mary Cray, St Paul Cray, Foots Cray, and North Cray. Acres, 39,927. Poor-rates in 1866, £11,191. Pop in 1861, 20,368. Houses, 3,851. Marriages in 1866, 162; births, 87.,—of which 3. were illegitimate; deaths, 494,—of which 163 were at ages under 5 years, and 15 at ages above 8.. Marriages in the ten years 1851–60, 907; births, 5,414; deaths, 3,078. The places of worship in 1851 were 17 of the Church of England, with 5,489 sittings, 5 of Independents, with 1,010 s., 4 of Baptists, with 630 s., 10 of Wesleyan Methodists, with 1,23. s., and 1 of the Wesleyan Methodist Association, with 16 s. The schools were 20 public day schools, with 1,717 scholars, 24 private day schools, with 395 s., 17 Sunday schools, with 1,17. s., and 1 evening school for adults, with 19 s. The workhouse is in Farnborough. The hundred is in the lathe of Sutton at Hone, bears the name of Bromley and Beckenham, and contains only the parishes of Bromley and Beckenham. Acres, 8,5.1. Pop, 7,629. Houses, 1,452.

BROMLEY, a township in Worfield parish, Salop, 1 mile NE of Bridgnorth.

BROMLEY, a township in Eccleshall parish, Stafford shire, 5 miles NW of Stafford. Acres, 1,080. Real property, £7.1. Pop, 41. Houses, 4.

BROMLEY, a hamlet in Wortley township, Tankersley parish, W. R. Yorkshire, 7 miles SW of Barnsley.

BROMLEY, Northumberland. See Broomley.

BROMLEY ABBOTS. See Abbots Bromley.

BROMLEY BAGOTS. See Bagots Bromley.

BROMLEY COMMON, chapelry in Bromley parish, Kent, 2 miles from Bromley town and 1 station. It was constituted in 8.1, and has a post office under Bromley. Pop, 1,163. Houses, 247. The living is a vicarage in the diocese of Canterbury. Value, £1.. Patron, the Bishop of Worcester. The church was built in 184., and is a handsome edifice in the Gothic style.

BROMLEY CROSS, a station on the Bolton and Blackburn railway, Lancashire, 2 miles N of Bolton.

BROMLEY (Great), a village and a parish in Tendring district, Essex. The village stands 3 miles SSE of Ardleigh r. station, and 5½ E of Colchester; has a post office under Manningtree, and is a seat of petty sessions. The parish comprises 2,95. acres. Real property, £5,50.. Pop, .5.. Houses, 175. The property is subdivided. The living is a rectory in the diocese of Rochester. Value, £698.* Patron, W Gallam, Esq. The church has a brass of 14.2, and is good. Charities, £31.

BROMLEY HURST. See Abbots Bromley.

BROMLEY (King's), or Bromley Regis, a parish in Lichfield district, Stafford, on the river Trent, 2¾ miles E of Armitage r. station, and 5 N of Lichfield. It has a post office, of the name of King's Bromley, under Lichfield. Acres, inclusive of King's Bromley Hays, sometimes deemed extra-parochial, 3,97.. Real property, £7,381. Pop, 618. Houses, 148. The manor belonged in the Saxon times to Earl Leofric, after the Conquest to the Crown, and passed to the Agards and the Newtons. Bromley Hall is the seat of the Lane family. The living is a vicarage in the diocese of Lichfield. Value, £210. Patron, the Bishop of Lichfield. The church is later English, and has monuments of the Agards and the Newtons. A school has £10a from endowment, and other charities, £74.

BROMLEY (Little), a parish in Tendring district, Essex, 2½ miles SE of Ardleigh r. station, and 6½ E by N of Colchester. Post town, Great Bromley, under Manningtree. Acres, 1,541. Real property, £3,73.. Pop, 37.. Houses, 90. The property is subdivided. The living is a rectory in the diocese of Rochester. Value, £.1.* Patron, Wadham College, Oxford. Charities, £10.

BROMLEY REGIS. See Bromley (King's).

BROMLEY-ST LEONARD, a parish in Poplar district, Middlesex, on the river Lea, the Limehouse cut, and the North London and Eastern Counties railways, near Bow and Stratford stations, 3½ miles ENE of St Paul's, London. It has a post office, ‡ of the name of Bromley, under Bow, London E. Acres, 61.. Real property, £81,318. Pop, 24,077. Houses, 3,40.. Part of the land is disposed in market gardens. Many of the inhabitants are employed in chemical works, mills, a ... ash factory, a brewery, a distillery, and the East and West India docks. The limits include part of the city of London workhouse, and part of Tower Hamlets cemetery. A Benedictine nunnery, dedicated to St Leonard, was founded at Bromley, in the time of the Conqueror, by William, Bishop of London, and given, at the dissolution, to Sir Ralph Sadler. The living is a vicarage in the diocese of London. Value, £.00. Patron, J Walter, Esq. The church belonged to the nunnery, and has Norman traces. The vicarage of St Michael and the p. curacies of St Leonard's chapel, St Gabriel, and St Andrew are separate benefices. Value of St M., £300,* of St G and St A each £200. St M's church was built in 1866-8, and is in the early English style. St A's and St G's were built in 1869. There are a Wesleyan chapel, public schools, almshouses, and some charities.

BROMLOW, a township in Worthen parish, Salop, 9 miles N of Bishops Castle. Pop, 468.

BROMORE. See Blamore.

BROMPTON, a town and two chapelries in Chatham and Gillingham parishes, Kent. The town consists of two parts, New and Old, the former, adjacent to the London and Dover railway, 1½ mile E of Chatham, with a station on the railway, the latter on the brow of a hill, overlooking the Medway, 1 mile NE of Chatham, with a post office,‡ under Chatham. A grand naval hospital, barracks for the Royal marines light infantry, barracks and hospital for the infantry of the line, and barracks, with stables, for the Royal engineers ar. here, all within the extensive [illegible] dings which defend the [illegible] and [illegible] of [illegible] The [illegible] include a museum, containing models and [illegible]. A [illegible] gymnasium was erected in 1860, at a cost of upwards of £6,000. The new convict prison is here, and, at the census of 1861, had 1,[illegible]9 inmates. A fair is held on 22 May. The [illegible] are Old B[illegible] and New B[illegible]. Pop, 8,119 and 4 [illegible]. The livings are vicarages in the diocese of Rochester. Value £150* and £166. Old B[illegible] church is a neat edifice in the pointed style, with a spire. New B[illegible] church was built in 1866, at a cost of £5,600, and is in the early decorated style. There are chapels for Wesleyans and Roman Catholics.

BROMPTON, a suburb of London, a sub-district, in the parish and district of Kensington, Middlesex, between Knightsbridge and Chelsea, 3½ miles SW by W of St Paul's. It has post offices‡ under London, S W, and a large railway station of West Brompton [illegible] Acres, [illegible] Pop in 1851, 9,465, in 1861, 18,19[illegible]. Houses, 2,[illegible]2. The north eastern part is called Old Brompton and the south western part, New Brompton. [illegible] of the [illegible] is occupied by streets, terraces, crescents, and squares, chiefly of recent erection, and form a continuous town between [illegible] and Chelsea. A part, formerly [illegible], was famous, for nearly two hundred years, as a nursery garden. The consumption hospital in Fulham road was founded in 1846, has accommodation for 200 patients, and includes a beautiful chapel built in 1850. A cancer hospital was established in 1851 [illegible] a new building for it, with a principal front 130 feet long, was built in [illegible] at a cost of £7,000. Trinity church was erected in 1828, and the burying ground [illegible] it was formed out of [illegible] garden [illegible] to high [illegible] account by Miss [illegible]. The other churches are in Old Brompton, West Brompton, and Onslow square, and all are vicarages, in the diocese of London. Value of Trinity vicarage, £635, of West Brompton, £300, of the others, not reported. Patron of Trinity, the Bishop of London, of West Brompton, the [illegible] corporation of Brompton, of Old Brompton chapel, the Vicar of K[illegible], of St Paul's Onslow square, C. J. Freake, Esq. There are several dissenting chapels, and there is a Roman Catholic establishment with a spacious chapel. Henry Cromwell, William [illegible], Lord Count [illegible], A. Murphy, John Philpot Curran, Sir [illegible], the [illegible] W. Beloe, Charles Incledon, George Colman, and John Leech were residents.

BROMPTON, a township in Church-Stoke parish, Salop, [illegible] miles NW by W of Bishop Castle. Pop 119.

BROMPTON, a chapelry in Northallerton parish, N R Yorkshire, adjacent to the Northeastern railway, 1½ mile N of Northallerton. It has a station on the railway, and a post office under Northallerton. Acres, 3,562. Real property, £[illegible],070. Pop, 1,[illegible]. Houses, 316. The property is much subdivided. Here is Standard Hill, the scene of the victory over the Scots in 1138. The inhabitants are chiefly weavers. The living is a p. curacy in the diocese of York. Value, £120. Patrons, the Dean and Chapter of Durham. The church is good. There are Wesleyan and Primitive Methodist chapels.

BROMPTON, a township and a parish in Scarborough district, N R Yorkshire. The township lies near the [illegible] N by W of Ganton r. station, [illegible] S W by W of Scarborough, and it has a post [illegible] York [illegible] seat of petty sessions. Pop, 53[illegible]. [illegible] The parish contains also the townships of S[illegible], [illegible] and Snaiton. Acres, 10,180. Real property, £11,[illegible]. Pop, 1,484. Houses, [illegible]. [illegible] The manor was [illegible] Norman [illegible], had a seat of the [illegible] on an eminence, called Castle hill, and passed to the [illegible]. The living is a vicarage united with the [illegible] of S[illegible] in the diocese of York. Value, £[illegible]. Patron Sir [illegible]. The church [illegible] spacious and elegant. There are [illegible] Wesleyan [illegible] Brompton the [illegible], who wrote [illegible] of [illegible], was [illegible].

BROMPTON (HIGH). See [illegible]

BROMPTON (LOW). See B[illegible]

BROMPTON (NEW AND OLD). See BROMPTON, Kent and Middlesex.

BROMPTON PATRICK, a township and a parish in [illegible] district, N R Yorkshire. The township lies on the [illegible] of the river Swale, near the Northallerton and Leyburn railway, 4 miles NW by W of Bedal. Acres, 1[illegible]. Real property, £2,31[illegible]. Pop 205. Houses, 4[illegible]. The parish contains also the townships of Newton-le-Willows, Hunton, and Arrathorne, the first of which has a station on the railway, and the second a post office under Catterick. Acres, 5,7[illegible]. Real property, £10,035. Pop, 1,[illegible]16. Houses, 2[illegible]. The property is much subdivided. The living is a vicarage, united with the vicarage of Hunton, in the diocese of Ripon. Value, £200. Patron, the Bishop of Ripon. The church is good and there are charities £27.

BROMPTON POTTER, a township in Ganton parish, E R Yorkshire, on the York and Scarborough railway, 3 miles E of Sherburn. Pop, 1[illegible].

BROMPTON RALPH, a parish in Williton district, Somerset, 3½ miles WSW of Crowcombe Heathfield r. station, and 4 N of Wiveliscombe. Post town, Wiveliscombe, under Wellington, Somerset. Acres, 2,6[illegible]0. Real property, £3,49[illegible]. Pop, 436. Houses, 94. The property is divided among a few. There are traces of a Roman camp. The living is a rectory in the diocese of Bath and Wells. Value £[illegible]47*. Patrons, J [illegible] Esq and Miss E[illegible]ott. The church is old, and was enlarged in 1847. There is an Independent chapel.

BROMPTON REGIS, a village and a parish in the district of Tiverton, and county of Somerset. The village stands near the river Exe, 3½ miles NE of Dulverton and 10 N by W of Tiverton r. station, and has a post office under Tiverton. It was once a market town, and fairs are still held at it on 1 Aug and the second Thursday after 10 Oct. The parish comprises 8,[illegible]10 acres. Real property, £6,718. Pop, [illegible]. Houses, 1[illegible]2. The property is much subdivided. A priory of Black canons was founded at Barlinch, in the time of Henry II, by William de Tay. Building stone abounds. The living is a vicarage in the diocese of Bath and Wells. Value, £100.* Patron, Emmanuel College, Cambridge. The church was restored in 1853. There are [illegible] and Bible Christian chapels, and charities £1[illegible].

BROMPTON UPON SWALE, a township in [illegible] parish, N R Yorkshire, on the river Swale and the Richmond railway, 3½ miles E of Richmond. It includes the hamlet of [illegible], and has a post office under Richmond. Acres, 1,710. Real property, £3,1[illegible]8. Pop, [illegible]06. Houses, [illegible]. It forms a curacy with Easby.

BROMSBERROW, a parish in Newent district, Gloucester, on the verge of the county, [illegible] miles SE of [illegible] r. station. Post town, [illegible]. Acres, 1,8[illegible]. Real property, £3,206. Pop., 30[illegible]. Houses 51. The property is divided among a few. Bromsberrow Place belonged to the Yateses, and passed to the [illegible]. Bromsberrow Heath is a meet for the Ledbury hounds. The living is a rectory in the diocese of Gloucester and Bristol. Value, £339. Patron [illegible]. The church is [illegible] excellent, and has monuments of the Yateses. Charities £5.

BROMSGROVE or BROMESGROVE, a town, a parish, a sub-district, and a district, in Worcester. The town stands on the river Salwarp, [illegible], 1½ mile W of the Midland railway, near the Worcester and Birmingham canal, 12 miles NE by N of Worcester. It was anciently called [illegible] and sent two [illegible] to parliament in the time of Edward I, and it had, in the [illegible] of a corporate town, [illegible] recorder, alderman, and other officers. It consists chiefly of [illegible] about a mile long, and contains many good modern houses, with some [illegible], curious and quaint. It has a [illegible] post office‡ a railway station with [illegible] two banking offices, four chief inns, a [illegible] of [illegible], a parish church, a Baptist chapel of 18[illegible], other dissenting chapels, a Roman Catholic chapel, a grammar school, a free school, a literary and mechanics' institute, charities £300 a year, and a workhouse, and it is a seat of petty sessions and a polling place, and publishes a weekly newspaper. The church [illegible] chancel [illegible] Norman [illegible] has a [illegible] spire 1[illegible] feet high, was [illegible] in 1858, at a cost of £[illegible], and contains [illegible] monuments of the [illegible] of Shrewsbury and [illegible] of Councillor [illegible]. The Roman Catholic chapel was built in 18[illegible], is in the decorated English style [illegible] and [illegible] a conspicuous object to travellers entering the town. The grammar school dates from the time of Edward VI., has an endowed income of £[illegible], and holds [illegible] fellowships and scholarships [illegible] Worcester college, Oxford. A weekly market is held on Tuesday, a monthly market, toll free, on the first Tuesday after 6 Jan., 2[illegible] June, the second Tuesday of Dec., and the last Tuesday of the other months, and [illegible] on 24 June and 1 Oct. A considerable [illegible] and [illegible] manufacture was formerly carried on, but has ceased; and the chief manufacture now is nails. Real property, £[illegible],024. Pop. [illegible],262. Houses, 1,1[illegible]. The parish includes also the hamlet of Chadwick [illegible] the chapelry of C[illegible] Hill. Acres, 10,[illegible]68. Real property, £2[illegible],5[illegible]. Pop., 10,822. Houses, 2,[illegible]. The property is much subdivided. The Lickey hills, a little north of the town, are on the watershed between the Severn and the Trent, were not long ago reclaimed from wildness to cultivation, and command delightful views. A chalybeate spring is at Burnet green, and a petrifying spring at [illegible]. A Premonstratensian priory was founded, in the time of Henry I., at Dodsworth, and part of it is included in a farm house. The living is a vicarage in the diocese of Worcester. Value, £1,00[illegible].* Patrons, the Dean and Chapter of Worcester. The vicarages of [illegible] and C[illegible] Hill are separate benefices.

The sub-district contains the parishes of Bromsgrove and Stoke Prior. Acres, 1[illegible],783. Pop., 1[illegible],[illegible]11. Houses, 2,[illegible]31.—The district comprehends also the sub-district of [illegible]borough[illegible], containing the parishes of [illegible], Clent, Hagley, Pedmore, and [illegible], and part of the parish of Halesowen; and the sub-district of [illegible], containing the parishes of [illegible], Alvechurch, and Coston Hackett. Acres, [illegible]7,374. Poor rates in 1866, £11,711. Pop. in 1861, 26,207. Houses, 5,510. Marriages in 1866, 190; births, 1,02[illegible],—of which 87 were illegitimate; deaths, 558,—of which 2[illegible] were at ages under 5 years, and 16 at ages above 85. Marriages in the ten years 1851-61, 1,[illegible]3; births, 8,00[illegible]; deaths, 5,200. The places of worship in 1851 were 1[illegible] of the Church of England, with 6,747 sittings; 3 of Independents, with 900 s.; 1 of Baptists, with 310 s.; [illegible] of Wesleyan Methodists, with 1,731 s.; 9 of Primitive Methodists, with 1,[illegible]4 s.; and 1 of the Wesleyan Association, with 300 s. The schools were 16 public day schools, with 1,[illegible]84 scholars; 4[illegible] private day schools, with [illegible]2[illegible] s.; 26 Sunday schools, with [illegible],311 s.; and 3 evening schools for adults, with [illegible] s.

BROMSHALL. See B[illegible]SHALL.

BROMSTON, a hamlet in St. Peter parish, Kent, near Broadstairs.

BROMWICH (CASTLE), a chapelry in Aston parish, Warwick, on the Birmingham and Derby railway, adjacent to the Birmingham and [illegible] canal, 5[illegible] miles [illegible]NE of Birmingham. It has a station on the railway, and a post office under Birmingham. Pop., [illegible]. Houses, 12[illegible]. Castle Bromwich Hall is an old seat, and belongs to the Earl of Bradford. An ancient castle is supposed to have stood on an eminence, still called Castle hill. Traces of [illegible] entrenchments exist, and [illegible] have been found. The living is a [illegible] in the diocese of Worcester. Value, £[illegible]. Patron, the Earl of Bradford. There is a free school.

BROMWICH (LITTLE), a hamlet in Aston parish, Warwick; contiguous to Castle Bromwich. Pop., [illegible]. Houses, [illegible].

BROMWICH (WEST), a town, a parish, [illegible] sub-districts, in [illegible] Stafford. The town stands [illegible] the river Tame, on branches of the Birmingham canal, and on the Birmingham and Wolverhampton and [illegible] Valley railways, [illegible] Stafford [illegible], [illegible] miles NW[illegible], [illegible] of Birmingham. It [illegible], at the [illegible] rural valley [illegible] but is now [illegible] upwards of [illegible] with [illegible] industry [illegible] progress [illegible]. The High street [illegible] consists [illegible] many handsome streets [illegible] with [illegible] buildings, churches, &c. [illegible] and [illegible] shops [illegible]. St. George [illegible] in [illegible] street [illegible], a Wesleyan chapel, [illegible] a tasteful edifice, [illegible] about 708 persons, and serves for concerts, lectures, and public meetings. [illegible] market place [illegible] at the south end of High street, [illegible] supplied. The police station [illegible] erected in 18[illegible], [illegible] officers with [illegible] body of men. All [illegible] church, at [illegible] at the north-east side of the parish, is [illegible] structure, [illegible] nave, chancel, and aisles, with a tower, and contains [illegible] Norman font, two [illegible] and a memorial window of 18[illegible] to the late Earl of Dartmouth. Christ Church, in High street, was built in 182[illegible] at a cost of £18,[illegible], and is a [illegible] edifice [illegible] with [illegible] and [illegible] tower 11[illegible] feet high. Trinity church, in [illegible] road, was built in 18[illegible], at a cost of nearly £3,000, and is a [illegible] structure, in the early English style, with a [illegible] turret [illegible]. The church at Hill [illegible] was built [illegible] in 1841, and is a [illegible] brick structure, without tower. St. Peter's church [illegible] Oldbury lane, was built in 185[illegible], and is a neat stone edifice, with a small tower. An Independent chapel is a pleasing [illegible] structure [illegible], a Wesleyan chapel, [illegible] building of 18[illegible], raised at a cost of [illegible],[illegible]01; and the Roman Catholic chapel is an edifice in the early English style, with a turret at each angle. There are likewise, within the parish, two other Independent chapels, five other Wesleyan, two Baptist, six Primitive Methodist, and one New Connexion Methodist. All Saints' schools, in All Saints' street, were erected in [illegible] and form a handsome pile. The Temperance and [illegible] Institution [illegible] in High street, contains a [illegible] library and reading rooms, and [illegible] lectures during winter. The [illegible] in [illegible], was erected in 18[illegible], at a cost of about £[illegible], is in the Gothic style, and has capacity for 600 [illegible]. The new cemetery, on an eminence [illegible] the [illegible] was opened in 185[illegible], comprises [illegible] acres, and has two Gothic chapels. An infirmary, [illegible] was founded in 18[illegible].

The prosperity of the town [illegible] rich four mines of ironstone and coal. [illegible] are carried on in all the departments of [illegible] hardware, also in [illegible], [illegible], chemicals, bricks, cement, and paper. [illegible] gas works, [illegible] in 1825, and constructed at a cost of £1[illegible],000, [illegible] upwards of 150 miles of pipes, and supplies, in addition to West Bromwich itself, parts of Birmingham, Wednesbury, Darlaston, Walsall, [illegible], Tipton, and Great Bridge. Two stations of the Birmingham and Wolverhampton railway, of the names of West Bromwich and Swan village, [illegible] with telegraph, [illegible] stations of the [illegible] railway are within a mile of the [illegible]. Numerous branches of canals also give great facilities for traffic. A weekly market is held on Saturday; and [illegible]. There are a head post office, [illegible] banking office, [illegible] and three [illegible]. Pop. 17,[illegible]. Houses, 3,[illegible].

The parish contains 5,71[illegible] acres. Real property, £126,[illegible], of which £[illegible]5,5[illegible] are in mines, and £[illegible] in [illegible]. Pop. in 1841, 2[illegible]; in 1861, [illegible],7[illegible]. Houses, 8,1[illegible]. The [illegible] is [illegible] and some of it is in a state of [illegible] cultivation [illegible] manor belonged, in 1[illegible], to [illegible] 1[illegible] to [illegible] 1[illegible], to [illegible], and in 18[illegible]2 [illegible] of [illegible] on [illegible] was [illegible] of the present [illegible]. A [illegible] priory was founded [illegible] in the time of Henry [illegible] [illegible] Parliament [illegible] priory, is [illegible] of stone [illegible]

[illegible] of Al[illegible] [illegible] £[illegible] [illegible] Church [illegible]

[illegible] West Bromwich [illegible] [illegible] divided from [illegible] Dudley [illegible] parish, [illegible] Oldbury [illegible] Acres [illegible] Pop. [illegible] Houses [illegible] Marriages [illegible] [illegible] Congregational [illegible] Methodist [illegible] [illegible]

BROMYARD [illegible]

BROMYARD [illegible] [illegible] Hereford. [illegible] [illegible] Worcester [illegible] church [illegible] Norman [illegible] [illegible]

[illegible] Acres [illegible] Pop. in 1871 [illegible] Houses [illegible] Marriages [illegible] deaths, 246,—of which [illegible] 1851-60, 712, births, [illegible] [illegible] England [illegible] Wesleyans [illegible] Independents [illegible] Latter-Day Saints [illegible] schools, with [illegible] Sunday schools [illegible] The [illegible] Lancaster [illegible]

[illegible]

BRONCROFT [illegible] [illegible] Pop. [illegible] Houses [illegible]

BRONGYNTYN [illegible] [illegible]

BRONLLYS [illegible]

BRONWYDD [illegible] Pop. [illegible] Houses [illegible]

BRONSGROVE [illegible]

BRONIARTH [illegible]

BRONINGTON [illegible] Pop. [illegible] Houses [illegible]

[illegible]

[illegible] along the [illegible] of his relative, the poet [illegible]

BRONYGARTH, a township in St Martin's parish, Salop, [illegible] of Oswestry. It [illegible] Pop, 324

BRONYSCAWEN, an ancient camp in [illegible] Carmarthen [illegible] 13 miles [illegible] of Carmarthen [illegible] and some other early Roman coins were found here

BRONYWOOD, a township in [illegible] parish, Montgomeryshire, 2 miles [illegible] of Montgomery

BROOK, a parish in the Isle of Wight, on the SW coast 2½ miles WNW of Brixton. Post town, Brixton under Newport. Acres, 718. Real property, £1,[illegible] Pop, 156. Houses, 32. The manor belonged [illegible] to the Bowermans, and belongs now to C Seely, Esq. The manor house was built toward the close of last century, and occupies the site of a previous one in which Henry VII was entertained. The coast includes Brook Chine and Brook Point, at the latter of which are remains of a very curious mass of petrified trees. The living is a rectory in the diocese of Winchester. Value, £250. Patron, Mrs Cave. The church is a very [illegible] uninteresting structure, picturesquely situated, and was gutted by fire in December, 1862

BROOK, a hamlet in [illegible] parish, Hants, 7 miles SW of Romsey. Pop, 317

BROOK, a tything in Kings Somborne parish, Hants, 7 miles N of Romsey. Pop, 86

BROOK, a locality, with a strong mineral spring near Tavistock, in Devon

BROOK, a parish in East Ashford district, Kent, 2¾ miles SE of Wye [illegible] station, and 4 NE of Ashford. Post town, Wye, under Ashford. Acres, 552. Real property, £1,[illegible] Pop, 120. Houses, 21. The property is subdivided. The living is a [illegible] in the diocese of Canterbury. Value, £171. Patrons, the Dean and Chapter of Canterbury. The church tower is dilapidated

BROOK, Wilts. See [illegible]

BROOK, or [illegible] a hamlet in Stourton parish, Somerset, [illegible] miles SW of Mere. Pop, 235. Houses, 70

BROOKE, a parish in Loddon district, Norfolk, on an affluent of the river Yare, 4¾ miles WNW of Loddon, and [illegible] of [illegible] station. It has a post office under Norwich. Acres, 2,135. Real property, £4,115. Pop, 746. Houses, 168. The property is divided between two. Brooke Hall and Brooke House are the chief residences, and the former is an edifice in the Grecian style, built in 1830. The living is a vicarage in the diocese of Norwich. Value, £216.* Patron, the Lord Chancellor. The church is good, and there is a Baptist chapel. Charities, £150. Sir Astley Cooper was a native

BROOKE, a parish in Oakham district, Rutland, on the river Gwash, near the Syston and Peterborough railway, 2½ miles SSW of Oakham. Post town, Oakham. Acres, 1,560. Real property, £2,171. Pop, 112. Houses, 22. A small Augustinian priory was founded here in the time of Richard I, by Hugh Ferrers, made subordinate to the monastery of Kenilworth, and given at the dissolution, to Anthony Cope. The living is a vicarage, annexed to the vicarage of Oakham, in the diocese of Peterborough. Charities, £17.

BROOKEND, a locality 2 miles N of Berkeley, in Gloucester, with a post office under Berkeley

BROOKEND, a hamlet in Shenley parish, Bucks, near the Northwestern railway, 2½ miles WNW of [illegible] Acres, 1,620. Pop, 20[illegible] Houses, 18

BROOKEND, Leeds. See Thornton with Brookend

BROOKESBY, a parish in Melton Mowbray district, [illegible] on the river Wreak, and on the Syston and Peterborough railway, 2 miles [illegible] of the [illegible] and 5¾ WSW of Melton Mowbray. It has a station on the railway [illegible] town is [illegible] Acres, [illegible] Real property, with [illegible] £2,7[illegible] Pop, [illegible] Houses, [illegible] Brookesby Hall was formerly a seat of the Villiers [illegible] and was the birthplace of [illegible] [illegible] of [illegible] The [illegible] is [illegible] of the [illegible] not [illegible] The church [illegible] Villiers

BROOKFIELD, [illegible] Middlesex, near [illegible] Post town, [illegible] Pop, 4[illegible] Houses, [illegible] The living [illegible] in the diocese of London. Value, [illegible] the Bishop of London

BROOK GREEN, [illegible] Middlesex, adjacent to [illegible] south side of Hammersmith [illegible] in Hammersmith, London W; a Roman Catholic [illegible] almshouses

BROOKHAMPTON, a township in [illegible] parish, Salop, 3 miles [illegible] of [illegible] Pop, [illegible] Houses, [illegible]

BROOKHAMPTON, a hamlet in [illegible] parish, Oxford, on the river [illegible] miles N of [illegible] Pop, 113

BROOKHAMPTON, a township in [illegible] parish, Worcester

BROOKHILL, [illegible] Dartmouth [illegible] by hills 1½ mile SE [illegible] to A [illegible] Holdsworth, Esq, and belongs now to [illegible] Davenport, Esq. The [illegible] Walter Raleigh, [illegible] ments, and the grounds show [illegible] contain the foundations of [illegible]

BROOKHOUSE, a hamlet in Laughton-en-le-Morthen parish, W R Yorkshire, [illegible] miles SW of [illegible]

BROOKHOUSE, or [illegible] of the Earls of Warwick, [illegible] a [illegible] parish, [illegible] adjacent to [illegible] 3½ miles NE of [illegible]

BROOKING. See [illegible]

BROOKLSTONE, [illegible] Stafford, near Cheadle

BROOKLAND, a parish in Romney Marsh district, Kent, adjacent to the [illegible] 2½ miles [illegible] of Appledore station, and [illegible] It has a post office under [illegible] Acres, 1,[illegible] Real property, [illegible] Pop, 4[illegible] Houses, 90. The property is much subdivided. The living is a vicarage in the diocese of Canterbury. Value, £93. Patrons, the Dean and Chapter of Canterbury. The church is early English, and [illegible] Norman font, and the belfry was [illegible] and is constructed of timber. There is a Wesleyan chapel

BROOKLANDS, a railway station on the [illegible] of Cheshire, on the Manchester and [illegible] railway, 2¼ miles NE by N of [illegible]

BROOK (North), a locality [illegible] in Devon, with a post office [illegible] Exeter

BROOK (North and South), two tythings in Micheldever parish, Hants, [illegible] western railway, 7 miles NNE of Winchester. Pop, [illegible]

BROOKFORD, a [illegible] township and parish, W R Yorkshire, 6½ miles W of Wakefield

BROOKSTREET, a hamlet in South Weald parish, Essex, on Watling-street and the [illegible] the Eastern Counties railway [illegible] wood. A [illegible] was founded [illegible] before the [illegible] Brown [illegible]

BROOKSWITH. See [illegible]

BROOKTHORPE. See [illegible]

BROOKWOOD, a [illegible] near Woking [illegible] See [illegible]

BROOM, a [illegible] 2 miles SW of [illegible] It has a post [illegible] Pop, 287. Houses, [illegible]

BROOM, a township in [illegible] 2 miles [illegible] Real property, £1,634. Pop, 1[illegible] Houses, [illegible]

BROOM, a [illegible] 2 miles S of Alcester. Pop, [illegible]

[illegible] Worcester [illegible] station [illegible] Pop., 118. Houses [illegible] The living is a rectory [illegible] 1820. [illegible] The [illegible] brick structure [illegible]

[illegible] township [illegible] parishes, [illegible] Pop., 129.

[illegible] See [illegible]

[illegible] Pop., 13.

[illegible] district [illegible] Post town [illegible] property, £3,014. Pop. [illegible] property is [illegible] among a [illegible] the [illegible] charities [illegible]

[illegible] Suffolk. See [illegible]

[illegible] See [illegible]

[illegible] FIELD, [illegible] Chelmsford district, Essex, [illegible] Eastern Counties rail [illegible] It has a post office [illegible] Acres, 2,115. Real property, £3,724 [illegible] The church [illegible]

[illegible] district [illegible] under [illegible] Pop., 1,421 [illegible] property is [illegible] among [illegible] of [illegible] The church is good [illegible]

[illegible] FIELD [illegible] Bridgewater district [illegible] It has a post [illegible] Acres, [illegible] £4,075. Pop., 525. Houses, 91. [illegible] Broomfield Hall [illegible] of Bath and Wells [illegible] Charities, [illegible]

[illegible] See [illegible]

[illegible] township [illegible] Yorkshire [illegible] the Market Weigh [illegible] 3½ miles [illegible] Pop., 115. Houses [illegible] 1440 [illegible]

[illegible] Houses, 23 [illegible]

BROOMHILL, a [illegible] in [illegible] county of Kent and Sussex, on the coast, [illegible] miles [illegible] Acres, 3,081, of which [illegible] Pop., 10. Houses, 2 [illegible] of the [illegible] of New Romney, and has no church.

BROOMHILL, a [illegible] Bilbrook, [illegible] parish [illegible] Kidderminster.

BROOMHILL, Norfolk. See [illegible]

BROOMHOLM. See [illegible]

BROOMHOUSE AND [illegible] LAND, a township in [illegible] parochial chapelry, Northumberland, 3½ miles [illegible] of Bellingham. Pop., 115.

BROOMHOUSE, a hamlet in [illegible] township, Alnwick parish, Northumberland, 1 mile [illegible] of Alnwick. Pop., [illegible]

BROOMLEY, or BROOMLEYS, a township in Bywell St Peter parish, Northumberland, on the Newcastle and Carlisle railway, 4½ miles SE of Corbridge. Acres, 3,45[illegible] Pop., 478. Houses, 87.

BROOM LODGE. See [illegible] WALK.

BROOM PARK, a township in [illegible] parish, Northumberland, 5 miles W by S of Alnwick. Acres, [illegible] Pop., 77. Houses, 11.

BROOME PARK, the seat of Sir Henry C. Oxenden, [illegible] in Barham parish, Kent, 7½ miles SE of Canterbury. The house was built, about 1620, by a member of the Dixwell family, and was marked for architectural [illegible] The park contains some fine [illegible]

BROOM RIDGE, a hamlet in Ford parish, Northumberland, [illegible] miles NW of Wooler. The place [illegible] with [illegible] is thought to be the [illegible] where Athelstan, in 938, defeated the Scots and [illegible] the scene of [illegible] in 15[illegible] Henry Percy.

BROOM (South). See SOUTHBROOM.

BROOMSHIELDS [illegible] a hamlet in [illegible] parish, Northumberland, 5½ miles W of [illegible] Acres, [illegible] Pop., 10[illegible] Houses, [illegible] It is sometimes [illegible]

BROOM-WALK, [illegible] in [illegible] parish [illegible] New Forest, on the river Avon, 2½ miles N of [illegible] included [illegible] Lodge, and [illegible] acres.

BROSGELLYDD, a township in Gwyddelwern parish, Merioneth, 2 miles N of Corwen.

BROSELEY, a small town, a parish, and a sub-district in Madeley district, Salop. The town stands on the [illegible] Severn, and on the Severn Valley railway, adjacent to Coalport station, 7 miles SSE of Wellington. It [illegible] extends over a distance of 2 miles, in an irregularly built street, crossed at intervals by small [illegible] It is surrounded by a mining district, in which coal and ironstone are worked; it carries on manufactures of fire-brick, tile, and tobacco-pipes; and it has a post office under Wellington, Salop; a banking office, two chief inns, a town hall, a parish church, [illegible] chapels, and endowed charities £20. The church is [illegible] later English style, and was built in 1845 [illegible] £[illegible] with a lofty tower [illegible] A weekly market is held on Wednesday, and fairs on 2 [illegible] May, and [illegible] Oct. [illegible] is the neighbourhood [illegible] iron bridge, with one arch of 100½ feet in span, over the Severn, 2½ miles to the NNW. The parish comprises 1,12[illegible] acres. Real property, £[illegible]57[illegible], of which £[illegible]097 are in mines. Pop., 721 [illegible] 958. [illegible] is not included [illegible] The [illegible] with [illegible] Ford [illegible] sub-district [illegible] Acres, 7,847. Pop., [illegible]

BROTHERCROSS, a hundred in Norfolk [illegible] parishes. Acres, 22,8[illegible]2. Pop., [illegible] Houses, [illegible]

BROTHERTOFT. See [illegible]

[illegible] SWAITE, a hamlet in [illegible] in [illegible]land, 2 miles S [illegible] is [illegible] of [illegible] and 72 f[illegible] and [illegible] ninsses of [illegible]

PLOTHERTOFT, a chapelry in [illegible] parish, [illegible] 2 miles SSW of [illegible] station, and [illegible] NNW of [illegible] Post-town [illegible] Acres [illegible] Property, £1,867. Pop 124. Houses, 2[illegible] The living is [illegible] in the diocese of Lincoln. [illegible] £10[illegible] Patron [illegible] Charities, £13

PLOTHERTON, a township and a parish in Ponte[illegible] district, W R Yorkshire. The township lies on the river Aire, [illegible] the York and [illegible] railway, 3 miles NNE of Pontefract, and has a post office under [illegible] Milford. Acres, 798. Real property, £3,071. Pop 1,3[illegible] Houses, 306. The parish contains also the townships of Sutton and [illegible] Acres, 2,190. Real property, £5,283. Pop [illegible] Houses 326. The property is much subdivided. A plot of ground near the church was the site of a house in which Thomas de Protherton, son of Edward I, and ancestor of the Dukes of Norfolk, was born, while his mother was with a hunting party. Limestone of superior quality is raised. The living is a vicarage in the diocese of York. Value, £192.[illegible] Patrons, the Dean and Chapter of York. The church is [illegible] and there are three dissenting chapels, a national school, and charities £12.

PROTHERWICK, a township in W[illegible]worth parish, Northumberland, on the river Coquet, adjacent to the Northeastern railway, 6 miles SSE of Alnwick. Acres, 184. Pop [illegible] Houses, 2.

PROTTON, a township and a parish in Guisborough district, N R Yorkshire. The township lies on the coast, adjacent to Saltburn station, [illegible] miles NE[illegible] of Guisborough, and has a post office [illegible] Acres, 9,201, of which 319 are water. Real property, £2,[illegible] Pop [illegible] Houses, 70. The parish contains also the townships of Hilton and Skinningrove. Acres, 4,[illegible] Real property, £4,124. Pop [illegible] Houses, 105. The property is divided among a few. The living is a [illegible] in the diocese of York. Value, £300. Patron, the Archbishop. The church commands a [illegible] view.

PLOUGH, a small old town, a township, and a parish in East Ward district, Westmoreland. The town stands on Watling street and on the [illegible] Hilbeck, in the valley of the Eden, 2 miles NNW of [illegible] station, and 5 NNE of Kirkby Stephen. It occupies the site of the Roman station Verterae, was very anciently a place of importance, and now consists chiefly of one long street. It has a post office‡ under Penrith, an [illegible] of an ancient castle, a [illegible] church, three other places of worship, and a free school. The foundation of [illegible] founded in 1506. The castle [illegible] to the Conquest, was sacked in 1175, by William the Lion of Scotland, belonged for a time to the Viteripont[illegible] [illegible] Cliffords, suffered severe injury in 1521, [illegible] and was restored, in 1[illegible], by the celebrated Countess Anne Clifford. The [illegible] ancient edifice, [illegible] tower of 150 feet [illegible] and the stone pulpit, and [illegible] are held on the Thursday before Whitsunday [illegible] 12 Oct. —The township includes the town, and is [illegible] by the Hilbeck rivulet into Market [illegible] and Church Brough. Acres, [illegible] Real property [illegible] township, £[illegible] Pop, 840. Houses, 18[illegible] —The parish contains also the townships of [illegible] Stainmore [illegible] and [illegible] Sowerby, and is [illegible] Stainmore. Acres, 2[illegible],017. [illegible] Kirkby Stephen. [illegible] £12,[illegible] Pop, 1,[illegible] Houses, 300. The property is [illegible] Hall [illegible] Hall, once the seat of the [illegible] [illegible] an extensive [illegible] William the Conqueror [illegible] the boundary between [illegible] and Scotland [illegible] Stainmore [illegible] and a [illegible] a [illegible] beatified [illegible] the church, [illegible]

[illegible] Patrons the [illegible] College, Oxford. The p[illegible] of Stainmore is a separate benefice [illegible] £99. [illegible] Methodists [illegible]

PLOUGH, a hamlet and a township in [illegible] E R York-shire, on the [illegible] and Hull railway, [illegible] 10 miles W by S of Hull. It has [illegible] railway, and a post office ‡ [illegible] from [illegible] here on the Humber. [illegible] the seat of the [illegible] Ad[illegible]

PLOUGH, a township in Catterick parish, N R Yorkshire, on the river Swale, 5 miles [illegible] of Richmond. Acres, 1,682. Real property, [illegible] 1,950. Pop, 123. Houses, 2[illegible] An [illegible] hospital [illegible] about the [illegible] of [illegible] the seat of the Lawsons. The [illegible] chapel.

PLOUGH HILL, [illegible] Yorkshire. See D[illegible], LEPTON AND PLOUGH.

PLOUGH HILL [illegible] See PLOUGH AND SHAPTON.

PLOUGHALL, a township in [illegible] parish, Salop, 2 miles [illegible] of W[illegible] Pop, 90.

PLOUGHAM, a small village and a parish in West Ward district, Westmoreland. The village stands on the river Lowther, adjacent to [illegible] and near the Lancaster and Carlisle railway, 1½ mile SE of Penrith. It occupies the site of the Roman station Brocavum, and takes its name from the Saxon town of Burgham. The parish includes also the hamlets of Hornby, [illegible], and Woodside, and its post town is Penrith. Acres, 6,0[illegible] Real property, £4,1[illegible] Pop, 2[illegible] Houses, [illegible] The property is divided among a few. Brougham Castle stands [illegible] and belonged to the Norman family of Veteripont [illegible] the Cliffords, suffered desolation in the wars with the Scots, was restored by the Countess Anne, and [illegible] It comprised [illegible] [illegible] walls, enclosing a large [illegible] and extensive [illegible] striking still [illegible] [illegible] wherein [illegible] dining [illegible] from England [illegible] Wordsworth makes it the scene of a great festival at the restoration of the [illegible] Clifford:—

> "From town to town, from tower to tower,
> The red rose is a gladsome flower.
> Behold her how she smiles to-day,
> On this great throng, this bright array!
> Knight, squire, and yeoman, [illegible]
> We have them at the feast of Brougham."

Fine traces of Roman works are seen in the vicinity, and several [illegible] coins and coins have been found. A neat [illegible] stone obelisk, called the Countess' Pillar, [illegible] to the south, erected by the Countess Anne Clifford, to commemorate her parting [illegible] being by Wordsworth's Poems, Mr [illegible] Brougham Hall, the seat of Lord [illegible] on a [illegible] adjacent to the [illegible] [illegible] Lowther [illegible] a beautiful view to the [illegible] [illegible] Wordsworth [illegible] the [illegible] [illegible] connected with it [illegible] [illegible] proprietor, and was [illegible] of [illegible] The living [illegible] Carlisle. Value, £201.* Patron, Sir [illegible] [illegible] [illegible] Countess Anne Clifford.

PLOUGH AND SHAPTON, [illegible] parish [illegible] Lincoln [illegible] [illegible] Acres, [illegible] Real property, £1,252. Pop, 1[illegible] [illegible] [illegible] Houses, [illegible] and [illegible]

PLOUGH HALL, a [illegible] parish, Stafford-shire, 6 miles [illegible]

PLOUGHTON LANE. See [illegible]

PLOUGH SOWERBY, a township in [illegible] parish

[illegible] Houses, [illegible]

BROUGHTON, [illegible] in Newport Pagnell district, [illegible] Acres, 1,0[illegible] Houses, [illegible] The [illegible] The living is a [illegible] Value, [illegible] The church is [illegible]

BROUGHTON, [illegible] Welsh parish, [illegible] from [illegible] Acres, [illegible] £7,17[illegible] £7,897 in quarries [illegible] The [illegible]

BROUGHTON, a [illegible] in Hawarden [illegible] Flint, [illegible] SW of Chester. It has a [illegible] Broughton Hall on the railway, [illegible] property, £2,249. Pop. [illegible] Broughton Hall [illegible] The living [illegible]

BROUGHTON, [illegible] parish and a sub-district [illegible] The village stands on [illegible] probably [illegible] miles SW of [illegible] under Winchester, and a [illegible] of July. [illegible] property, [illegible] The property is [illegible] The living is a rectory, united [illegible] in the diocese of [illegible] The church [illegible] chapels for Independents, [illegible] school [illegible] Acres, [illegible] Houses, [illegible]

BROUGHTON, a parish in St Ives district, Huntingdon [illegible] W of [illegible] NE of Huntingdon. Post town, [illegible] under Huntingdon. Acres, 2,070 [illegible] Pop. 370. Houses, 82. The [illegible] The living is a rectory [illegible] Value, £280.* Patron, [illegible] The church was recently restored.

BROUGHTON, a township-chapelry [illegible] district, Lancashire. The chapelry is [illegible] Acres [illegible] Pop. [illegible] Houses, [illegible] The living is a p. curacy in [illegible] Value, £100. [illegible] contains [illegible]

[illegible]

[illegible] property, £60,[illegible]0. Pop., 9,8[illegible]5. Houses, 1,7[illegible]9. Broughton Hall belonged formerly to the Chorltons and the Stanleys, was [illegible] burnt in 1847 [illegible] Clowes. The [illegible] Broughton and Tower [illegible] [illegible] several streets straight, airy, and crossing one [illegible] at right angles, and the two are [illegible] The [illegible] was constituted in 1840. The living is a [illegible] in the diocese of Manchester. Value, £400.* [illegible] Trustees. There are [illegible] dissenting chapels, one of them built in 18[illegible], at a cost of £[illegible],000. The sub-district is conterminate with the chapelry.

BROUGHTON, a village and a parish in Glanford Brigg district, Lincoln. The village stands on Ermine street, probably on the site of a Roman station, near the river Ancholme, and the Grimsby railway, 3 miles NW of Glanford Brigg; and has a post office under Brigg. The parish includes also the township of Castlethorpe and the hamlets of Manby and [illegible]. Acres, 6,918. Real property, £10,320. Pop., 1,[illegible]0. Houses, 28[illegible]. The property is much subdivided. A nunnery was founded here in 11[illegible], by William [illegible]. The living is a rectory in the diocese of Lincoln. Value, £524.* Patron, [illegible] Dent, Esq. A new church was built in 18[illegible], and there are two Methodist chapels and a national school.

BROUGHTON, a parish in Kettering district, Northampton, on an affluent of the river Nen, near the [illegible] railway, [illegible] miles SW of Kettering. It has a post office under Wellingborough. Acres, [illegible] Real property, £3,[illegible]91. Pop., 738. Houses, 175. Most of the property is divided among three. The living is a rectory in the diocese of Peterborough. Value, £391.* Patron, the Duke of Buccleuch. The church is partly Norman, and was restored in 1851. There are a Methodist chapel, [illegible] school, and charities £13. [illegible] Bolton [illegible] was a native and rector.

BROUGHTON, a village and a parish in Banbury district, Oxford. The village stands on an affluent of the river Cherwell, 2[illegible] miles SW by W of Banbury station. The parish includes also the township of North Newington, which has a post office under Banbury. Acres, 1,9[illegible] Real property, [illegible] Pop. 641. Houses, 137. The property is divided among a few. The manor belonged to the [illegible] Broughtons, passed to the Wykehams and the Fiennes, and belongs now to Lord Saye and Sele. Broughton Castle, the mansion of the Fiennes, stands on low ground, is quadrangular, moated and defended by a tower, comprises structures of the 14th, the 15th and the 16th centuries, built respectively by the De Broughtons, the Wykehams, and the Fiennes, shows marks of injuries sustained during the civil wars, includes apartments where [illegible] death of Charles I was [illegible] and where Cromwell's officers were quartered [illegible] of [illegible] hall, and contains some interesting pictures and arms, and curious works of art. The living is a rectory in the diocese of Oxford. Value, £[illegible] Patron, the [illegible] The church is of the 14th century, with tower and spire, and contains several [illegible] monuments. There are an Independent chapel, an endowed school with £[illegible] a year, and charities £[illegible]

BROUGHTON, a parish in Wem district, Salop, on the [illegible] and Shrewsbury railway, [illegible] miles SSW of Wem. It includes the townships of [illegible] and [illegible] Post town, Shrewsbury. Acres, 880. Real property, £[illegible] Pop., [illegible] Houses, [illegible] The property is divided among a few. The living is a vicarage in the diocese of Lichfield. Value, £[illegible] Patron, [illegible] The church was rebuilt in 18[illegible] in the early [illegible] style, and consists of nave and chancel, with [illegible] turret [illegible]

BROUGHTON, a hamlet in Ladeshall parish, Stafford, 4[illegible] miles [illegible] of [illegible] station, and [illegible] of [illegible] Post town, [illegible] Acres [illegible] Pop., 21. Houses, 2. Broughton Hall is an old [illegible] The living [illegible] Value, [illegible] Patron, Sir H. D. Broughton, Bart. The church is [illegible]

BROUGHTON, a township in [illegible], in Craven, [illegible] parish [illegible] 3 miles SE of [illegible] Acres 2,180 Real property, £4,123 Pop, 57[illegible] Houses, 12[illegible] A cairn on the summit of [illegible] hill, is [illegible] to be monumental of a Danish chief

BROUGHTON, a township in Appleton-le-Street parish, N R Yorkshire, 2 miles NW [illegible] Malton Acres, [illegible] Real property, £1,3[illegible]7 Pop, 153 Houses, 27 An hospital was founded here, in the reign of [illegible] by the [illegible] St John There is a Wesleyan chapel

BROUGHTON, a hamlet in Monknash parish, Glamorgan, 5¼ miles SW of Cowbridge

BROUGHTON, a township in Bishops Castle parish, Salop, 1 mile NW of Bishops Castle Pop, 70

BROUGHTON, a township in Claverley parish, Salop, 4½ miles E of Bridgnorth Pop, 8[illegible]

BROUGHTON, a hamlet in Stoke St Mary parish, Somerset, 3¼ miles SE of Taunton Pop, [illegible]

BROUGHTON, a hamlet in Whitchurch parish, Warwick, 5½ miles S of Stratford-on-Avon Pop, [illegible]18

BROUGHTON, W R Yorkshire See BROUGHTON IN AIREDALE

BROUGHTON, Aylesbury, Bucks See BIERTON WITH BROUGHTON

BROUGHTON ASTLEY, a township and a parish in Lutterworth district, Leicester The township lies on the Midland railway, near the Fosse way, 5½ miles N by W of Lutterworth, and has a station on the railway Pop, 3[illegible] Houses, 77 The parish contains also the townships of [illegible]thorpe and Sutton in the Elms, and its post town is Cosby, under Lutterworth Acres 1[illegible]0 Real property, £[illegible],541 Pop, 78[illegible] Houses, 182 The property is much subdivided The living is a rectory in the diocese of Peterborough Value, £[illegible]1* Patron, [illegible] Esq The church is [illegible] There are a Baptist [illegible] and a national school, and charities £10

BROUGHTON BRANT, a parish in the district of Newark and county of Lincoln [illegible] 1[illegible] miles NE of [illegible] station, and 8 [illegible] It has a post office of the name of Brant Broughton under Newark Acres 2,[illegible] Real property, £[illegible],453 Pop, 7[illegible] Houses, 1[illegible] The living is a rectory in the diocese of Lincoln Value £[illegible]* Patron, Sir R Sutton Bart The church is decorated English There are Quaker and Wesleyan chapels, and a Church school

BROUGHTON CASTLE See BROUGHTON Oxford

BROUGHTON CHURCH, a parish in the district of Burton upon Trent and county of Derby, 2½ miles NNE of Sudbury r station, and 10 W by S of Derby It includes the hamlets of Sapperton and [illegible]hill, and has a post office of the name of Church Broughton, under Derby Acres, 2,27[illegible] Real property, £3,661 Pop 6[illegible]1 Houses, 1[illegible]1 The living is a vicarage in the diocese of Lichfield Value, £[illegible]28 Patron, William [illegible] Esq The church is ancient, and was recently repaired There are a Primitive Methodist chapel, an endowed school with £[illegible] a year, and charities £22

BROUGHTON CROSS, a station on the Cockermouth and Workington railway, 2½ miles W of Cockermouth, in Cumberland

BROUGHTON CUM BRETTINS See BROUGHTON Parva

BROUGHTON (Great), or BROUGHTON [illegible] a township [illegible] in Brigham parish, Cumberland, [illegible] miles N of [illegible] station, and 7 NE of Workington Post town, Cumberland, under Newton in Cartmel Acres, 2,[illegible]30 Real property, £[illegible] Pop, [illegible] Houses, 107 The property is subdivided Broughton [illegible], Broughton Hall and Broughton Lodge are chief residences The living is a p curacy in the diocese of Carlisle Value £[illegible]7* Patron, the Duke of Devonshire The church is good

BROUGHTON GIFFORD, a parish in Bradford district, Wilts, on the Great Western railway and the river Avon, near the Kennet and Avon canal, [illegible] SW of Melksham station, and 4 [illegible] of Bradford It has a post office under Melksham Acres, 1,677 Real property, £3,7[illegible]7 Pop, [illegible]21 Houses, 11[illegible] The property is divided among a few Broughton Gifford House is the seat of [illegible] family The living is a rectory in the diocese of Salisbury Value, £[illegible] Patron the Lord Chancellor The church is of the time of Henry VII, was recently restored, and has a [illegible] 1620 There are a Baptist chapel, a school with £[illegible], and other charities [illegible]

BROUGHTON (GREAT), a township and a chapelry in Brigham parish, Cumberland The township lies on the river Derwent, adjacent to the Cockermouth and Workington railway at Broughton Cross station, 3 miles W of Cockermouth It has a post office under Carlisle Acres, inclusive of Little Broughton, 2,[illegible]13 Real property, £[illegible]77, of which £2,3[illegible]2 are in mines Pop, 830 Houses, 18[illegible] The chapelry is more extensive than the township, includes Little Broughton, and was [illegible] constituted Pop, 1,1[illegible] The living is a vicarage in the diocese of Carlisle Value £100* Patron, the Vicar of Brigham The church is new There are chapels for Baptists, Quakers, and Wesleyans A school and alms-house have £[illegible] from endowment

BROUGHTON (GREAT and LITTLE), a division of Broughton township, [illegible] in Cleveland [illegible], N R Yorkshire

BROUGHTON HACKETT, a parish in Pershore district, Worcester, on the Midland railway, 1 mile N by E of Spetchley station, and 6 NNW of Pershore Post town, Spetchley, under Worcester Acres, [illegible]90 Real property, £782 Pop, 1[illegible]1 Houses, 3[illegible] The property is subdivided Blue limes [illegible] is quarried The living is a rectory in the diocese of Worcester Value, £[illegible] Patron the Lord Chancellor The church is very good

BROUGHTON HALL See BROUGHTON, Flint

BROUGHTON (HIGHER and LOWER) See BROUGHTON, [illegible], Lancashire

BROUGHTON IN AIREDALE, a village, a township, and a parish in Skipton district, W R Yorkshire The village stands [illegible] the Leeds and Liverpool canal and the North Midland railway, in the vicinity of [illegible] station, and 4 miles WSW of Skipton, and has a post office of the name of Broughton under Skipton It is thought to occupy a Roman station, and it was plundered by the Pictish and Scottish forces in the middle of the 14th century The township includes the village, and comprises 2,[illegible]0 acres Pop, 1[illegible]2 Houses, 86 The parish includes also the hamlet of Elslack Acres, 3,[illegible] Real property, £5,2[illegible] Pop, [illegible]71 Houses, [illegible] The property is divided between two Broughton Hall is the seat of the Tempest family The parish is noted for a fine breed of cattle The living is a vicarage in the diocese of Lincoln Value, £190 Patron, Christ Church College, Oxford The church has a Norman doorway, contains monuments of the Tempests, and is good

BROUGHTON IN FURNESS, or WEST BROUGHTON, a small town, a township, chapelry, and sub-district in the district of Ulverstone, Lancashire The town stands on the river Duddon, adjacent to the Furness railway, at the junction of the branch line to Coniston, 9 miles by road, NW by N of Ulverston It occupies a hill slope, is [illegible] houses, nearly in a regular square, and has of late years undergone great improvement It has a post office‡ under Ulverstone, a railway station with telegraph, two churches, and a common school A weekly market is held on Wednesday, and fairs on 27 April, 1 Aug, and 6 Oct A manufacture of woollen [illegible] used to be carried on, and a [illegible] in [illegible] slates and in iron and copper ores, from neighbouring mines, is now considerable The chapelry includes the township in Kirkby Ireleth parish, and comprises 7,[illegible] acres Real property, £[illegible]7 Pop, 1,1[illegible] Houses, [illegible] The property is much subdivided The manor belonged formerly to the Broughton family, and was forfeited, in 1[illegible]7, by Sir [illegible] Broughton, who joined [illegible] Broughton Tower, now the seat of J D Sawrey, Esq, crowns a [illegible] N of the town, includes part of the ancient mansion of the Broughtons, and commands a full and [illegible] view The living is a p curacy in the diocese of Carlisle Value, £103* Patron, J D Sawrey, Esq The church is [illegible], and there are two [illegible]

[illegible] the south [illegible] com [illegible] extra [illegible] on the Sheffield [illegible] Sheffield [illegible], a township in [illegible] N of [illegible] Houses, 129 [illegible] on the NW [illegible] 2½ miles N of Broughton [illegible]

[illegible] a parish in Melton Mowbray [illegible] on the verge of the county [illegible] Grantham canal, 6 miles NW [illegible] station [illegible] Acres, 2,11[illegible] Houses 107. The property [illegible] Lodge is the chief [illegible] in the diocese of Peterborough [illegible] W. H. Sawyer [illegible] and has very [illegible] and charities £17.

[illegible] Oxford, on the verge of the [illegible] Value, £[illegible] Patron, [illegible] is very good.

[illegible] See Broughton [illegible]

[illegible] See Broughton [illegible]

[illegible] (West), Lancashire. See Broughton [illegible]

[illegible] See Broughton, [illegible]

[illegible] See [illegible]

[illegible] in the North Sea, [illegible]

[illegible] a parish in Mitford district [illegible] a post office under [illegible] Acres, 2,6[illegible] Real property [illegible] Houses, 57. The property is all [illegible] diocese [illegible] The [illegible] North [illegible] 2 miles NW of [illegible]

Houses, 1[illegible]. The property is much [illegible] Living is a [illegible] of [illegible] Value, £15[illegible] Patron, the Bishop of Lichfield [illegible] is good.

BROWNSTON, a chapelry, with a village, in Modbury parish, Devon, near the South Devon [illegible] 3 miles N of Modbury [illegible], with the parish [illegible] Living is a p. curacy, annexed to the vicarage of Modbury, in the diocese of Exeter. The church [illegible] by the late Rev. Prebendary Oxenham, [illegible] specimen of modern Gothic.

BROWN GILLY, a hill, 6½ miles NW of Liskeard, in Cornwall. It is 1,100 [illegible] high.

BROWNHILL, a hamlet in [illegible] township [illegible] parish, W. R. Yorkshire, 6½ miles NW of Wakefield.

BROWNHILLS, [illegible] south of [illegible], on the Birmingham [illegible] railway, near Cannock Chase, [illegible] miles N [illegible] of Walsall. It has a station on the railway [illegible] Walsall.

BROWNLOW [illegible]

BROWNRIGG, a hill [illegible] the head of [illegible] from the head of [illegible] Dale, 9 miles [illegible] Yorkshire.

BROWNSEA, or BRANKSEA, an island and a chapelry in Studland parish, Dorset. The island lies in Poole harbour, 2 miles SSE of Poole, measures [illegible] in circuit, and forms a romantic group of [illegible] hillocks, with about 100 acres [illegible] the sea. It was [illegible] park, [illegible] now a village, a pier, a [illegible] road, and [illegible] the Stud [illegible] A castle on it was built in the time of Elizabeth, [illegible] one of the harbour [illegible] in the time of Charles I., [illegible] recently renovated and [illegible] The property was [illegible] for many years [illegible] Col. Waugh [illegible] its improving [illegible] but was put up for sale in 1859. [illegible] constituted in 185[illegible] island. Post town, Poole. Pop., 1[illegible]3. Houses, [illegible] Living is a [illegible] in the diocese of Salisbury. Value, £60.[illegible] Patron, [illegible] Esq. The church [illegible] in 1854, and is in the early decorated style, of [illegible] stone, with a square [illegible] tower.

BROWNSHALL, a hamlet and a hundred [illegible] Sturminster [illegible] Dorset. The hamlet is in [illegible] parish, [illegible] miles SE of Sherborne, [illegible] place. The hundred [illegible] and three other parishes. Acres, 11,56[illegible] Pop., 2,87[illegible] Houses, [illegible]

BROWNSHOLME, the seat of the Parkers, on the W border of W. R. Yorkshire, 4 miles NNW of Clitheroe. The house is in the Tudor style, and contains the great seal of the Commonwealth, and some [illegible] paintings and antiquities.

BROWNSIDE. See [illegible] and Brownside.

BROWNSOVER, a township-chapelry in Clifton-upon-Dunsmore parish, Warwick, on the Oxford canal, [illegible] adjacent to the Midland and the North-western railways, 2 miles N by E of Rugby. Post-town, Rugby. Acres, 87[illegible]. Real property, £[illegible] Pop., 7[illegible] Houses, 1[illegible]. Brownsover House is the seat of [illegible] The living is a p. curacy, annexed to the vicarage of Clifton-upon-Dunsmore, in the diocese of Worcester. [illegible] the tower of Rugby [illegible]

BROWNSTONE, [illegible] in Modbury parish, Devon [illegible] 3 miles NE of Modbury. [illegible] diocese of Exeter, [illegible]

BROWNSWELLS, [illegible] Middlesex [illegible] Hatch [illegible] NNW [illegible] Islington [illegible]

BROWN WILLY, a [illegible] the NE [illegible] Cornwall, [illegible] of Camelford [illegible] consists of [illegible] of [illegible] the highest point [illegible] Cornwall, [illegible] the [illegible]

[illegible] of its [illegible]

BROWSTON, a hamlet in Belton parish, Suffolk; 4½ miles SSW of Yarmouth. Pop., 61.

BROXA, a township in Hackness parish, N. R. Yorkshire; [illegible] NW of Scarborough. Acres, 150. Real property, £740. Pop., 71. Houses, 11.

BROXASH, a hundred in Hereford; [illegible] extends [illegible] from the [illegible] boundary to [illegible], and contains Bromyard parish, and twenty seven other parishes, and parts of two others. Acres, 78,997. Pop., 11,878. Houses, 2,433.

BROXBOURNE, or BROXBURN, a village, a township, and a parish in Ware district, Herts. The village stands on the verge of the county, on the New river, [illegible] W of the Eastern Counties railway, and 4½ N by W of Waltham Abbey; and it has a station with telegraph on the railway, a post office under Hoddesdon, and two inns. The township comprises the village, and comprises 1,9?3 acres. Real property, £5,[illegible]. Pop., 7?5. Houses, 1?4. The parish includes also part of the village and chapelry of Hoddesdon. Acres, 150?. Real property, with the rest of Hoddesdon, £11,923. Pop., 2,0?3. Houses, 541. The property is subdivided. The manor belonged to the Knights of St. John, and passed to the Cocks, the Monsons, and others. Broxbourne Bury is now the seat of the Bosanquets. And [illegible] Cock entertained James I. The living is a vicarage in the diocese of Rochester. Value, £3?1.* Patron, H. J. Smith, Esq. The church is later English, of the time of Henry VIII., consists of nave, chancel, aisles, and two small chapels, with a [illegible] steeple and [illegible] turret, contains an old [illegible] font, and many interesting [illegible] monuments, and was restored in 1857. The p. curacy of Hoddesdon is a separate benefice. A school has £20 from endowment, [illegible] £10[illegible], and other charities £72.

BROXFIELD, a township in Embleton parish, Northumberland; 2 miles NNE of Alnwick. Acres, [illegible]. Pop., 27. Houses, 5.

BROXHOLME, a parish in the district and county of Lincoln; adjacent to the Great Northern railway, [illegible] miles [illegible] of Saxelby station, and [illegible] NW of Lincoln. Post town, Saxelby under Lincoln. Acres, 1,24?. Real property, £2,593. Pop., 12?. Houses, 19. The living is a rectory in the diocese of Lincoln. Value, £273.* Patron, J. Robinson, Esq. The church is ancient.

BROXTED, a parish in Dunmow district, Essex; on the river Chelmer, [illegible] miles E of Elsenham r. station, and [illegible] NW of Dunmow. Post town, Great Easton, under Dunmow. Acres, ?,149. Real property, £4,131. Pop., 835. Houses, 21?. The living is a vicarage in the diocese of Rochester. Value, £170.* Patron, [illegible] de Beauvoir.

BROXTON, a township and a hundred in Cheshire. The township is in Malpas parish, and lies 4½ miles N of Malpas town, and about the same distance S of Tattenhall r. station. Acres, 2,128. Real property, £[illegible],290. Pop., 516. Houses, 11?. Broxton Hall here was the seat of the Dods, the Egertons and the [illegible], is now [illegible] a farm-house, and commands [illegible] prospects. The hundred lies around the township, marches with Flint and Denbigh, and is cut into two divisions, East and West. The E. division contains six parishes and parts of eight other parishes. Acres, 3?,13?. The W. division contains five parishes and parts of [illegible] other parishes. Acres, 1?,4?5. Pop. of both, 18,49?. Houses, ?,510.

BROXTOW, a hamlet and a hundred in Notts. The hamlet is in [illegible] parish, 3½ miles NW of Nottingham, and [illegible] parish. The hundred lies around the [illegible], extends 23 miles northward from the Trent, and [illegible] from Derby line, and is cut into two divisions, North and South. The N. division contains sixteen parishes. Acres, [illegible]. Pop. in 1861, 48,6??. The S. division contains [illegible] parishes. Acres, [illegible]. Pop. in 1861, 35,4?3. Pop. of both in 1861, 58,850. Houses, 1?,6?0.

BROYLE (THE), a [illegible] near [illegible] mile [illegible] of Cuckfield, in Sussex. It extends a considerable distance N and W, and is the [illegible] the Romans [illegible]; it has not been fully investigated.

BRUAN [illegible]. See [illegible], Brecon.

BRUCKEN HILL, a [illegible] in [illegible] field parish, W. R. Yorkshire; 4½ miles N of Sheffield.

BRUE (THE), a river of Somerset. It rises [illegible] on the [illegible], and runs about 30 miles west-south-westward, past [illegible] Castle Cary and Glastonbury, to Bridgewater bay, near the estuary of the Parret.

BRUEN-STAPLEFORD, a township in Tarvin parish, Cheshire; 6 miles E of Chester. Acres, 711. Real property, £1,[illegible]. Pop., 1?3. Houses, 2?.

BRUERA, or CHURTON HEATH, a chapelry in St. Oswald parish, Cheshire; on the river Dee, [illegible] N of [illegible], and 5½ S of Chester. Post town, Aldford, under Chester. Acres, 321. Real property, £217. Pop., [illegible]. Houses, 6. The living is a [illegible], and was separated from St. Oswald's in 18?3. Value, £?80. The church is Norman [illegible].

BRUERN, an extra-parochial tract in Chipping-Norton district, Oxford; 5 miles N of Burford. Acres, [illegible]. Real property, £1,[illegible]. Pop., 5?. Houses, [illegible]. A Cistercian abbey was founded here, in 1147, by Nicholas Basset; and given, at the dissolution, to Sir Anthony Cope. The buildings were [illegible] residence, and were destroyed by fire in last century. Old fish ponds connected with them still exist. The tract is [illegible] the [illegible] uplands.

BRUGGE. See BRIDGNORTH.

BRUGHAM, or BRUGAN (THE), a stream of Montgomery, running into the Severn at Llanidloes.

BRUISYARD, a parish in Plomesgate district, Suffolk; on the river [illegible] N of Framlingham station, and [illegible] NW of Saxmundham. Post town, Cransford, under Wickham Market. Acres, 1,12?. Real property, £1,7[illegible]. Pop., 22?. Houses, 61. The property is [illegible] among a few. The manor belongs to the Earl of Stradbroke. A chantry or college was removed hither, in 1354, from Campsey, changed after wards into a nunnery, and given at the dissolution, to Nicholas Hare. The living is a vicarage in the diocese of Norwich. Value, £60.* Patron, the Earl of Stradbroke. The church has two brasses.

BRUMBY. See BROMBY.

BRUMHILL. See BROMHILL and BROOMHILL.

BRUMPTON. See BROMPTON.

BRUMSTEAD, or BRUNSTEAD, a parish in Tunstead district, Norfolk; 1 mile N of Stalham, 3 SW of the coast, 6 SE of North Walsham r. station, and 16 NE of Norwich. Post town, Stalham, under Norwich. Acres, 789. Real property, £1,?00. Pop., 99. Houses, 22. The property is divided among a few. The manor belongs to Cubitt Burnaby, Esq. The living is a rectory in the diocese of Norwich. Value, £170. Patron, the Earl of Abergavenny. The church is [illegible].

BRUNANBURGH. See BRUNSWICK and BROOMRIDGE.

BRUNDALL, a parish in Blofield district, Norfolk; on the river Yare and the Yarmouth railway, [illegible] E of Norwich. It has a station on the railway, and its post town is Blofield, under Norwich. Acres, 51?. Real property, £[illegible]. Pop., 1?5. Houses, 1?. The property is [illegible]. Brundall House is the seat of [illegible] H. Harvey, Esq. The living is a rectory, annexed to the rectory of Witton, in the diocese of Norwich. The church is tolerable.

BRUNDISH, a parish in Hoxne district, Suffolk; 4 miles N by W of Framlingham, [illegible]. Post town, Framlingham, under [illegible]. Acres, 1,7?1. Real property, £2,740. Pop., 451. Houses, 9?. The living is a p. curacy, annexed to the vicarage of Tannington, in the diocese of Norwich. The church is [illegible].

BRUNDON. See BALLINGDON CUM BRUNDON.

BRUNE STEEGH. See [illegible].

BRUNSLEY. See [illegible].

BRUNSTON, a township in [illegible] parish, Salop; [illegible] of [illegible] Castle.

[illegible]

weekly market is held on Saturday, and fairs on 23 April and 17 Sept. [illegible]

[illegible] Acres [illegible] Real property, £11,[illegible] Pop., [illegible] Houses [illegible] The living is a vicarage in the diocese of [illegible] Value, 168 [illegible] Pop., 3,9[illegible] [illegible] hundred [illegible] eight [illegible] Acres, 12,[illegible] Pop., 4,209 Houses [illegible]22

[illegible] See [illegible]

LIYANMAUND, [illegible] Herefordshire [illegible] 8 miles NNW of [illegible] Pop., [illegible]

[illegible] Dorset, on the river [illegible] adjacent to the [illegible] Dorset railway [illegible] Post town, [illegible] Acres 1,512 Real property £1,254 Pop., 206 Houses, [illegible] The living is a rectory [illegible] annexed to the rectory of [illegible], in the diocese of Salisbury.

[illegible] Dorset, on the river [illegible] 7[illegible] miles SW of [illegible] Real property, £2,[illegible]29 Pop., 10[illegible]

[illegible] See [illegible]

[illegible] a town [illegible] Wrexham [illegible] SW of Wrexham, and has [illegible] Wrexham Acres, 2[illegible] Real property, £2[illegible] Pop., [illegible] Houses [illegible] 1,104 [illegible] The living is a p[illegible] curacy in the diocese of St Asaph Value, £2[illegible] Patron, the Vicar of Wrexham. There are several dissenting chapels.

[illegible] See [illegible]

[illegible] See [illegible]

[illegible] See [illegible]

[illegible] township in [illegible] parish [illegible] 2[illegible] miles SW of [illegible] Pop., [illegible]

[illegible] a township in [illegible] parish [illegible] miles SW of Oswestry Pop., 200

[illegible]

— Patron, C. W. C. Wynne. — The church is — . There is a Calvinist Methodist chapel. — Charities, £15.

BRYN — , a township in Llanelidan parish, Denbigh, 5½ miles S of Ruthin. Pop., 207.

BRYNEGLWYS, a parish in the district of Corwen, and county of Denbigh, 5 miles NE of Corwen r. station, and 11 WNW of Ruabon. It is divided into the townships of Bodynlliw, Llan —, Llwynhowell, Cwthwaen, and — ; and it has a post office under Corwen. Acres, 3,283. Real property, £ 737. Pop., 441. Houses, 89. The property is divided among a few. Much of the surface is upland. There is a mineral spring. The living is a vicarage in the diocese of St Asaph. Value, £103. Patron, Sir W. W. Wynn, Bart. The church is in fair ? and. There are Calvinistic Methodist and Wesleyan chapels. A school has £12 from endowment, and other charities £. .

BRYNELLEN, a township in Llanfair Caereinion parish, Montgomery, near Llanfair. Pop., 70.

BRYNELLTYN, a township in Llanfyllin parish, Montgomery, near Llanfyllin. Pop., 70.

BRYNFFYNNON, a township in — parish, Denbigh, near Abergele. Pop., 15.

BRYNFFYNNON, a village in Llanfair-is-Gaer parish, Carnarvon, 2 miles NE of Carnarvon.

BRYNFORD, a township in Holywell parish, and a chapelry in Holywell and Ysceifiog parishes, Flint. The township lies near the town and r. station of Holywell. Real property, £2,019, of which £700 are in mines. The chapelry was constituted in 1854. Post town, Holywell. Pop., 910. Houses, 190. The living is a rectory in the diocese of St Asaph. Value, not reported. Patron, the Bishop of St Asaph.

BRYNGLAS, a township in Llanfair Caereinion parish, Montgomery, 1 mile SW of Llanfair. Pop., 7 .

BRYNGWALDDAN, a township in Llangurig parish, Montgomery, 7 miles WNW of Llanidloes. Pop., 71.

BRYNGWRAN, a hamlet and a sub-district in the district and county of Anglesey. The hamlet stands 3½ miles N by W of Valley r. station, and 8 ESE of Holyhead, and has a post office under Holyhead, and fairs on Easter Monday, Holy Thursday, 11 Oct., and 24 Nov. The sub-district lies around the hamlet, and contains ten parishes, nine parochial chapelries, an extra-parochial tract, and a villa. Acres, 2-,09-. Pop., 5,746. Houses, 1,25-.

BRYNGWYN, a township in Dymeirchion parish, Flint, 3½ miles E of St Asaph. Real property, £1,500. Pop., 88.

BRYNGWYN, a parish in Abergavenny district, Monmouth, 2½ miles WNW of Raglan r. station, and 7 SE by E of Abergavenny. Post town, Raglan, under Newport, Monmouth. Acres, 1,18-. Real property, £2,131. Pop., 373. Houses, 72. The property is divided among a few. Bryngwyn House is the seat of the Hon. Col. Crawley. The living is a rectory in the diocese of Llandaff. Value, £200. Patron, the Earl of Abergavenny. The church is good. Charities, £10.

BRYNGWYN, a parish in the district of Hay and county of Radnor, on the river Arrow, 3½ miles WNW of the Hereford and Hay railway, and 6 NNW of Hay. Post town, Hay, under Hereford. Acres, 4,636. Real property, £2,112. Pop., 334. Houses, 65. The property is much subdivided. The living is a rectory in the diocese of St David's. Value, £201. Patron, the Bishop of St David's. The church is bad. Charities, £9.

BRYNGWYN (Isaf and Ucha), two townships in Cwm parish, Flint, on the verge of the county, 6 miles ESE of St Asaph. Real property, £1,002. Pop., 191 and —.

BRYNGWYNE, a hamlet in Llanfihangel Abergwili parish, Carmarthen, near Llandilofawr.

BRYNHAFOD, a hamlet in Llanelian parish, Carnarvon, 1 mile NW of Llandilofawr.

BRYNHEULOG, a township in Llandrillo parish, Merioneth. — .

BRYNHOWELL-WITH-KELNAHILL, a township in — parish, — , 2 miles SW of Ker—.

BRYNHALL, — property £1,110. Pop., 116. Houses, 21.

BRYNKINALT, a township in Chirk parish, Denbigh, on the river Dee, adjacent to the Shrewsbury and Chester railway, 1 mile NE of Chirk. Brynkinalt House here, the seat of Lord Dungannon, belonged to the Trevors, and was the scene of much of the early life of the mother of the first Duke of Wellington.

BRYNKIR, a station on the Carnarvonshire railway, 11 miles S of Carnarvon.

BRYNLLANFAIR, a locality in Llanfair-is-Gaer parish, Carnarvonshire, on the Menai strait, adjacent to the Carnarvon railway, 3 miles NNE of Carnarvon. It has a post office under Bangor.

BRYNLLWARCH, a township in Kerry parish, Montgomery, 2 miles SE of Newtown. Pop., 71.

BRYNLLYS. See BRONLLYS.

BRYNMAWR, a village in Llanelly and Llangattock parishes, Brecon, 1 mile SW of Crickhowell.

BRYNMAWR, a large seat of mining works, on the northern border of Monmouth, on the Merthyr and Abergavenny railway, in the vicinity of Nantyglo. It has a post office under Tredegar, a station, an inn, a school, and several chapels. A railway from it to Blaenavon was authorised in 1859.

BRYNPOLYN, a township in St Asaph parish, Flint, near St Asaph. Real property, £3,670. Pop., 75.

BRYNSADDLER, a locality, 2 miles from Llantrisant r. station, Glamorgan, with a post office under Cardiff.

BRYNSIENCYN, or BRYNSIENCYN, a village in Llanidan parish, Anglesey, 3½ miles NW of Carnarvon. It has a post office under Bangor and a — on 1— .

BRYNSIMON, a township in Llandinam parish, Montgomery, 2 miles SW of Montgomery.

BRYNTANGOR, a township in Llanrhaiadr parish, Denbigh, near Denbigh.

BRYNTEG-WITH-TAL-Y-GARTH, a township in Castle Caereinion parish, Montgomery, 3 miles NE of — . Real property, £1,-3-. Pop., 227. Houses —.

BRYN-Y-LLEDD, — , Carnarvon, near Llanelltyd. Real property, £21. Pop., 056.

BRYNYORKIN, a locality near to Caerwys, Flint. It belongs to the Yorkes, — built in — of 1610, the — of — Jones.

BRYNYPYS, a village in Towyn parish, Merioneth, near Towyn.

BRYNYWALL, a township in — parish, Flint, near Hawarden. Pop., 60.

BUBB-DOWN, a wood — in Dorset, adjacent to the Weymouth and Yeovil railway, 2 miles N by E of Evershot. It forms a conspicuous landmark, and commands a very extensive and beautiful view.

BUBBENHALL, or BOBENHULL, a parish in the district and county of Warwick, on the river Avon, 4 miles SW by S of Kenilworth r. station, and 5 SSE of Coventry. It has a post office under Kenilworth. Acres, 1,230. Real property, £2,—. Pop., 319. Houses, 7—. The property is divided among a few. The living is a vicarage in the diocese of Worcester. Value, £1—. Patron, the Bishop of Worcester. The church is good.

BUBNELL. See BASLOW.

BUBWITH, a hamlet in Wh— parish, Salop, near — . Post town, — , 1 mile NW of Whitchurch.

BUBWITH, a township, a parish, and a sub-district in Howden district, E. R. Yorkshire. The township lies on the river Derwent, and on the Selby and Market Weighton railway, 6½ miles NE by E of Selby; and has two inns in the town, a new — and Bubwith Bridge, Ho—, — post office under — . Acres, — . Real property, £2,5—. Pop., 34-. Houses, 123. The parish contains also the townships of Harlthorpe, Foggathorpe, Gribthorpe, Willitoft, Spaldington, and Breighton-with-Gunby. Acres, 10,171. Real property, £2,75—. Pop., 1,—. Houses, 303. The property is much subdivided. Many of the — and — , — the living is a — in the

[illegible]

... Norwich. Value, £117. [illegible] inhabitants. The church is [illegible] of 1471, [illegible] has a square tower and [illegible] beautiful [illegible] a number of curious and interesting monuments. There are Wesleyan [illegible] and [illegible] chapels, a national school, an alms-house for six women, and other charities £61.

LUCKENHAM TOFT [illegible] parish in the [illegible] district, Norfolk. The village stands [illegible] of about [illegible] miles SSE of Attleborough [illegible] and 7 SSW of Wymondham; and has a post office under Attleborough. Acres, [illegible]. Real property, [illegible]. Pop., 1,214. Houses, 25[illegible]. The property is divided [illegible]. The manor was given by the Conqueror [illegible] knights [illegible]. A castle was built on it, soon after the Conquest, and gave place to [illegible]. The living is a vicarage in the diocese of Norwich. Value, £10[illegible]. Patrons, the Inhabitants. The church belonged to the priory [illegible] plain [illegible]. There are [illegible] school and some charities.

LUCKENHAM PARVA. See LUCKENHAM [illegible].

LUCKENHILL, a township in Woolhope parish, Hereford. [illegible] Pop., 1[illegible].

LUCKFIELD [illegible] a parish in [illegible] district, Devon, on [illegible] the river [illegible] and the Exeter [illegible] 3 miles W of Honiton. It [illegible] Acres, 1,5[illegible]. Real property, £2,71[illegible]. Pop., [illegible]. Houses, [illegible]. The property is divided [illegible] and Hendle [illegible] Fort are [illegible] partly within the [illegible]. The living is a vicarage in the diocese of Exeter. Value, £120. Patrons, the Dean and Chapter of Exeter. The church is [illegible] and is in [illegible] condition.

LUCKRAST ABBEY. See LUCKRASTLEIGH.

LUCKRASTLEIGH, a village, a parish, and a sub-district in the district of Totnes, Devon. The village stands [illegible] Dartmoor, 2½ miles SW [illegible] Ashburton, and [illegible] from the South Devon railway [illegible] completion in 1869. It dates from old [illegible] formerly a market town, [illegible] and serge manufactures [illegible] employing about 1,0[illegible] hands, and has a [illegible] Newton Abbot [illegible] fairs on the [illegible] Thursday of [illegible]. The parish comprises 5,92[illegible] acres. Real property, £11,181. Pop., 2,4[illegible]. Houses, [illegible]. The property is [illegible] subdivided. The manor [illegible] [illegible] Sir [illegible] [illegible] [illegible] [illegible] 190 [illegible] the [illegible] [illegible] [illegible] [illegible] the diocese [illegible] [illegible] [illegible]

[illegible] long ago [illegible] The church [illegible] contains several [illegible] of [illegible] and [illegible] black [illegible] on the grave of [illegible] Thomas [illegible] There are chapels for Independents [illegible] and Wesleyans, and charities £77 The sub-district contains four parishes Acres, 10,610 Pop, 3,200 Houses, 852

BUCKHOLT (East and West), an extra-parochial tract in Stockbridge district, Hants, on the verge of the county, on the Roman road from Winchester [illegible] miles N of Dean [illegible] station and 5 SW by W of Stockbridge Acres, 1,271 Pop, 118 Houses, [illegible] Queenwood college is here

BUCKHORN WESTON, a parish in the district of [illegible] and county of Dorset on the verge of the [illegible] on the Salisbury and Yeovil railway, 3½ [illegible] WSW of Gillingham station and [illegible] of Wincanton [illegible] Post-town [illegible] Acres, 1,652 Real property with Kington Magna, £7,020 Pop, 509 Houses, 117 The living is a rectory in the diocese of Salisbury Value, £600* Patron, Lady Stapleton

BUCKHOW BANK See BUCK BANK

BUCKHURST, a hamlet in Chigwell and Loughton parishes, Essex, on the Eastern Counties railway [illegible] to Epping [illegible] 9¾ miles NE of Bishopsgate, London. It has a station, of the name of Buckhurst Hill, on the railway, and a post office of the name of Buckhurst, under Woodford, London, N E It was constituted in 1838 Pop, 902 Houses 117 The living is a rectory in the diocese of Rochester Value, £300* Patron, the Vicar of Chigwell The church is [illegible] and [illegible], and there is an independent chapel

BUCKHURST PARK, the seat of Earl Delawarr in Sussex, 6½ miles [illegible] of East Grinstead [illegible] gateway tower of the splendid, ancient, extinct mansion of the Sackvilles, is adjacent

BUCKINGHAM, a town, a parish, a sub-district, a district, and a hundred in Bucks The town stands on a bend of the river Ouse, [illegible] a mile [illegible] of the Buckinghamshire railway, 16 miles NW of Aylesbury The Buckingham [illegible] railway gives it communication in five directions, toward Banbury, Oxford, Aylesbury, Bedford, and London and a branch canal, of 10 miles, formed in 1801 goes from it, north-eastward, down the valley of the Ouse, to the Grand Junction canal and Stony Stratford The town dates from ancient times Remains of a Roman villa were discovered within 2 miles of it in 1837 The Roman general Aulus Plautius, on some spot near it, surprised and routed the Britons under the command of the sons of Cunobelin The Saxon saint, Rumbald, the subject of wondrous legends, was buried in it, and a shrine being erected over his grave, and afterwards [illegible], attracted for ages crowds of pilgrims Edward the Elder resided a short time in it in 918 and raised two forts for its defence The Danes ravaged it in 941, and [illegible] in 1010 A castle was built on an eminence, [illegible], soon after the Conquest, but [illegible] and has disappeared A great fire, in 1725, burned [illegible] 138 dwelling houses, and destroyed property to the amount of £38,000 The town had previously been the capital of the county but it then lost that character, and has never since acquired any great prosperity

Buckingham is one of the most uninteresting towns in the kingdom It consists chiefly of one long, irregular street, and is edificed mainly with [illegible] brick houses [illegible] and [illegible] give it [illegible] The town hall is a large brick structure of 1685 The [illegible] building of 1758, enlarged in 1839, and has [illegible] for [illegible] male and 3 female prisoners [illegible] on the [illegible] of the ancient castle, [illegible] of about £7,000 and has a [illegible] 150 feet high The Independent chapel was built in 1857 and is in the early English style There are [illegible] Wesleyan and Primitive Methodist chapels [illegible] was opened in 1810, and has two [illegible] grammar school [illegible] of a chantry, founded in 1268, by [illegible] Stratton, has [illegible] and is enclosed by [illegible] walls Another school has £31 from endowment [illegible] £22, and other charities [illegible] The workhouse cost £4,700, and has [illegible] for 500 persons Lambard's house, occupied [illegible] which was inhabited some time by Catherine of Arragon the first queen of Henry VIII, was built in 1611, occupied [illegible], by Prince Rupert, and gave quarter, for a night in 1645, to Charles I Another house, still extant, was visited by Queen Elizabeth The prebendary house, of the same date as Lambard's, is a curious edifice, with a crooked chimney

The town has a head post office,‡ a railway station with telegraph, three banking offices and two chief inns; is a seat of petty sessions and a polling place, and publishes a weekly newspaper Markets are held on Monday and Saturday, [illegible] fairs on 12 Jan, the last Monday of Jan, 7 March, the second Monday of April, 6 May, Whit Thursday, 10 July, the second Wednesday of Aug, 4 Sept, 2 Oct, the [illegible] after 11 Oct, 8 Nov, and [illegible] Dec The chief [illegible] lace making with bobbins; but straw plait making has [illegible] introduced, and [illegible] along tanning, [illegible] wool [illegible] carried on The town was made a borough by Henry VIII, is governed by [illegible] mayor, four aldermen, and [illegible] councillors, sent two members to parliament till 1867 and now sends only one Its m[illegible] limits are conterminate with the parish, and its p[illegible] limits include also the parishes of Maids Moreton, [illegible] Thornborough, [illegible] Radclive, Preston Bisset, Tingewick, and [illegible] Chackmore Real property in 1860 £42,927 Direct taxes in 1857 £5,436 Electors in 1868, 407 Pop of the m[illegible] borough, 3,849 Houses, 818 Pop of the p[illegible] borough, 7,721 Houses, 1,700 Bishop [illegible] of Buckingham [illegible], and Goode the translator of the Psalms, were natives The town has given the title of Duke to the families of successively Stafford, Villiers, Sheffield, and Grenville

The parish includes the precinct of Prebend End, the chapelry of Gawcott, and the hamlets of Lenborough, Bourton, and [illegible] Acres, 5,777 Real property, £18,347 Pop, 3,849 Houses, 818 The property is much subdivided Buckingham manor belonged anciently to the Giffards, Earls of Buckingham, passed to successively the Clares, the Audleys, and the Staffords, suffered forfeiture, and was given to Richard [illegible] in 1400, was restored to the Staffords in 1485, and forfeited again in 1521, passed to successively Lord Mounteagle, the Careys, and the Brian family, and was leased, [illegible], for 999 years, to the corporation Lenborough manor lay annexed to Buckingham manor till 1721, was held thence for nearly a century by the Crown, passed then to the Dormers, was purchased in 1718 by Edward Gibbon, Esq, the grandfather of the historian, and passed afterwards to the Coodriches Stowe, the grounds [illegible] residence of the Duke of Buckingham, is in the neighbouring parish of Stowe The living is a vicarage in the diocese of Oxford Value, £16 [illegible] Patron, the Bishop of Oxford The vicarage of Gawcott is a separate benefice

The sub-district contains the parishes of Buckingham, Padbury, [illegible], Addington, Steeple Claydon, and Middle Claydon Acres, 14,[illegible] Pop, 5,98[illegible] Houses, 1,291 The district comprehends also the sub-district of Tingewick, containing the parishes of Tingewick, Barton Hartshorn, Chetwode, Preston Bisset, Hillesden, [illegible] ford, [illegible] and [illegible] Gibbon, and the sub-district of Luckhampstead, containing the parishes of Luckhampstead, [illegible], Leckhampstead, Thornton, Thornborough, [illegible] Foscott, Akeley cum Stockholt, [illegible] Lillingstone Dayrell, Stowe, [illegible] and Water Stratford, and Radclive, and the extra-parochial tract of Lamport [illegible] Acres, 52,113 Pop [illegible] Poor rates in [illegible] £10,675 Pop in 1841, [illegible] Houses, 3,620 Marriages in [illegible], 92, births [illegible] —of which 23 were illegitimate, deaths, 211 —of which [illegible] were at ages under 5 years, and 8 at ages above 85 Marriages in the ten years 1851-60, 1,050, births, 4,190, deaths [illegible] of [illegible] 23 [illegible] Independ[illegible] [illegible] Baptists, with 210 s. [illegible] 7 of [illegible] Methodists, with [illegible] The schools were [illegible] public [illegible] 1114 [illegible] 23 private [illegible] schools [illegible] 25 [illegible] evening [illegible] The hundred is [illegible] but not quite so extensive [illegible] Pop. 10,641. Houses [illegible]

BUCKINGHAMSHIRE, an inland county [illegible] bounded on the N by Northamptonshire, on the [illegible] by Beds and Herts, on the [illegible] on the S and SW by Berks, and on [illegible] It has a somewhat irregular outline [illegible] sides, a [illegible] being N and S [illegible] the river Thames, dr[illegible] [illegible] Its greatest length [illegible] greatest breadth, 27 miles [illegible] 18 miles [illegible] circumference [illegible] miles [illegible] in the centre [illegible] on the south [illegible] of the Chiltern hills [illegible] about 16 miles [illegible] The chief [illegible] the Thame [illegible] Colne [illegible] northern boundary [illegible] a little [illegible] Aylesbury [illegible] Newport Pagnell [illegible] [illegible] spots, but [illegible] [illegible]

[illegible]

Stoke [illegible] the county [illegible] from [illegible] [illegible] of them larger [illegible] is [illegible] prises [illegible] acres [illegible] divided into [illegible] Amersham, Aylesbury, Buckingham, Eton, Newport Pagnell, Winslow, and Wycombe. The boroughs are Aylesbury, Buckingham, Great Marlow, and [illegible] [illegible] The market towns are Amersham, Aylesbury, [illegible] Buckingham, Chesham, [illegible] Stratford, Great Marlow, High Wycombe, [illegible] Olney, [illegible] Slough, Stony Stratford, [illegible] Winslow [illegible] Hampden, [illegible] Dropmore, [illegible] Clifton, [illegible] Lilies, Dinton, [illegible] Horsford, [illegible] Claydon, [illegible] Shardeloes, [illegible] Weston Underwood [illegible] Little [illegible] Hall, Newlands, [illegible] Bradenham [illegible] Wotton, and L[illegible] Property assessed in 181[illegible] in 1843, £827,806, in 1861, £87[illegible] in 18[illegible] £917,728.

The county is governed by a lord lieutenant, a high sheriff, [illegible] deputy lieutenants, and about 221 [illegible] It is in the Home [illegible] the Norfolk [illegible] The [illegible] sessions [illegible] at Aylesbury [illegible] prises [illegible] the county at large [illegible] for the boroughs of Buckingham and Wycombe [illegible] £10 [illegible] Aylesbury, and there is a borough [illegible] Buckingham. The number of crimes committed, in 18[illegible] of persons [illegible] 184 [illegible] persons [illegible] of houses of [illegible] 82 There [illegible] seats to parliament [illegible] at large [illegible] the four boroughs [illegible] 1868 [illegible] The county is in the diocese of Oxford [illegible] The [illegible] poor rates for the [illegible] The number of [illegible] ges, in 1866, was 1,0[illegible] of which 18[illegible] were not [illegible] rites of the [illegible] Church [illegible] of which 285 [illegible] of deaths 2,0[illegible] of which 1,160 were at ages under [illegible] years and [illegible] above 80. The places of worship in 1851 within the county proper were 22[illegible] of the Church of England [illegible] sittings [illegible] of Independents with 11,0[illegible] of Baptists with [illegible] of Quakers with 1,18[illegible] 81 of Wesleyan Methodists [illegible] of Primitive Methodists with 4[illegible] Reformers with 648 [illegible] Connexion with [illegible] 1,0[illegible] 11 of isolated congregations [illegible] of Roman Catholics with 27 [illegible] public day schools, with 13,713 scholars [illegible] day schools, with [illegible] 352 Sunday schools [illegible] 1,08[illegible] and 21 evening schools for adults [illegible] Pop. in 1801, 108,13[illegible] in 1821 [illegible] inhabited [illegible] building 25[illegible]

The territory [illegible] [illegible]

a the colleges at Aldbridge and Eton and [illegible] hospital at Newport [illegible] but there are also 14 other [illegible] and [illegible] other hospitals, which [illegible], [illegible] extent. Eight churches show ancient Norman features, and two others are good specimens of [illegible] English. The county gives the title of Duke to the family of Hampden Hobart.

BUCKINGHAMSHIRE RAILWAY, a railway of Buckinghamshire and Oxfordshire. It commences in a junction with the Northwestern at Bletchley, goes west-southwestward to Claydon, and thence [illegible] to Oxford; sends off two lines in the vicinity of Winslow and Claydon, the one southeastward to Aylesbury, the other northwestward and west-northwestward past Buckingham and Brackley, to Banbury; and forms junctions at Oxford and Banbury with the Oxford and Rugby railway. Twenty-one miles of it are single line, and the rest double. It was authorised in 1847 [illegible] then an amalgamation of two previous schemes, the Oxford and Bletchley, incorporated in 184[illegible], and the Buckingham and Brackley, incorporated in 1846, while the line to Aylesbury was not incorporated till 1[illegible]

BUCKISH MILLS, a hamlet in Parkham and Woolfardisworthy parishes, Devon, on the coast, [illegible] miles SW of Bideford. It has a Wesleyan chapel, and [illegible] it is a pleasing feature amid a range of cliffs and woods.

BUCKLAND, a village, a parish, and a sub-district in Faringdon district, Berks. The village stands 1[illegible] mile S of the river Isis, [illegible] NE by E of Faringdon station, and 13½ SW by W of Oxford, and has a post office under Faringdon. The parish includes also the hamlet of Carswell. Acres, 4,134. Real property, £5,720. Pop., 912. Houses, 171. The property is divided among a few. Buckland House is the seat of Sir P. Throckmorton, Bart., was built in 1757 after designs by Wood of Bath, and contains relics of Mary Queen of Scots and Charles I., some other curiosities, and some fine pictures. The living is a vicarage in the diocese of Oxford. Value, £310.* Patron, the Bishop of Gloucester and Bristol. The church is old but good. There are Baptist and Roman Catholic chapels, an endowed school with £42 a year, and charities £60.—The sub-district contains five parishes and four parts. Acres, 2[illegible]. Pop., 4,915. Houses, 1,033.

BUCKLAND, a parish in Aylesbury district, Bucks, between the Aylesbury and the Wendover canal, 2½ miles S of Marston Gate r. station, and 3 W NW of Tring. Post-town, Tring. Acres, 1,514. Real property, £2,614. Pop., 782. Houses, 1[illegible]. The property is divided among a few. The living is a p. curacy, annexed to the vicarage of Stoke Mandeville, in the diocese of Oxford. The church is ancient. There are a chapel of ease, Baptist and Methodist chapels, and a national school.

BUCKLAND, a parish in Winchcombe district, Gloucester, under the Cotswolds, 1¾ mile SW of Broadway, and 6¼ W SW of Campden r. station. It includes the hamlet of Laverton, and its post town is [illegible]. Acres, 2,270. Real property, £3,28[illegible]. Pop., [illegible]. Houses, 7[illegible]. The manor belonged formerly to the Greshams, and belongs now to Sir T. Phillipps, Bart. The living is a rectory in the diocese of Gloucester and Bristol. Value, £222. Patron, Sir T. Phillipps, Bart. The church is later English, has a [illegible] painted window of [illegible] and [illegible]. Charities [illegible]. The [illegible] school has £20 from endowment.

BUCKLAND, a parish in Royston district, Herts, near Ermine-street and the source of the [illegible] river, 3 miles N of [illegible] station. It [illegible] the [illegible] of Chipping, and [illegible] post town [illegible]. Acres, 1,552. Real property, [illegible]2,1[illegible]. Pop., [illegible]. Houses, [illegible]. The property is divided [illegible]. The living is a rectory in the diocese of [illegible]. Value, [illegible]. Patron, King's College, [illegible]. The church is good.

BUCKLAND, [illegible] Tewkesbury [illegible], near [illegible] Sub[illegible] and the Cheltenham [illegible], 3 miles SW by W of [illegible] station. [illegible] Acres, 97[illegible]. Real property, £5[illegible]. Pop., 1[illegible]. Houses, [illegible] [illegible]

cese of Canterbury. Value, £267. Patron, Sir J. [illegible] Tyrrell, Bart. The church has long been in ruin.

BUCKLAND, a parish in Dover district, Kent, on the river Dour, and on the Canterbury and Dover railway, 1¼ mile NW of Dover. Post town, Dover. Acres, 978. Real property, £6,[illegible]. Pop., [illegible]. Houses, 3[illegible]7. The property is subdivided. The surface is hilly. There are paper and corn mills. A lepers hospital was founded about 1150. The living is a vicarage in the diocese of Canterbury. Value, £18[illegible]. Patron, the Archbishop of Canterbury. The church is good; and there are a Wesleyan chapel and a national school.

BUCKLAND, a parish in Reigate district, Surrey, on the Reading and Reigate railway, [illegible] mile ESE of Betchworth station, and [illegible] W of Reigate. It has a post office under Reigate. Acres, 1,741. Real property, £2,71[illegible]. Pop., 369. Houses, 61. The property is divided among a few. Buckland House is a chief residence. The living is a rectory in the diocese of Winchester. Value, £[illegible].* Patron, All Souls College, Oxford. The church was rebuilt in 1860. Spencer, the biographer of Archbishop Chichele, was rector.

BUCKLAND, a village in Cheshunt parish, Herts, 2 miles SW of Royston.

BUCKLAND, a hamlet in Thurlstone parish, Devon, 3¾ miles W of Kingsbridge.

BUCKLAND, a mansion under [illegible] mile [illegible] in Brecon, on the river Usk, [illegible] miles NW by W of Crickhowell. It is the seat of J. P. Gwynne Holford, Esq.

BUCKLAND ABBEY. See BUCKLAND MONACHORUM.

BUCKLAND BEACON. See BUCKLAND-IN-THE-MOOR.

BUCKLAND BREWER, a village and a parish in Bideford district, Devon. The village stands 5 miles from the coast, and 1½ SSW of Bideford r. station, and has a post office under Bideford. It was formerly a market town, and it still has fairs on Whit-Tuesday and 2 Nov. The parish contains also the hamlets of Thelbridge, [illegible], and Galsworthy. Acres, 6,137. Real property, £4,653. Pop., 9[illegible]2. Houses, 178. The property is divided among three. The manor was held [illegible] the time of Henry III., to the [illegible], and belongs now to the Rolle family. The living is a vicarage, united with the p. curacies of East Putford and [illegible], in the diocese of Exeter. Value, £24[illegible].* Patron, the [illegible]. The church is large and ancient, has a Norman door and a lofty tower, and contains many ancient monuments. There are chapels for Baptists and Bible Christians.

BUCKLAND DENHAM, a village and a parish in Frome district, Somerset. The village stands near Frome river, 2½ miles NNW of Frome r. station, and has a post office under Frome. It formerly was a market town, and still has a fair on 10 Oct. The parish comprises 1,39[illegible] acres. Real property, £2,4[illegible]. Pop., 4[illegible]. Houses, 108. The property is divided among a few. The living is a vicarage in the diocese of Bath and Wells. Value, £181.* Patron, the Bishop of Bath and Wells. The church was [illegible] and is good. There are a Wesleyan chapel, a national school, and charities £11.

BUCKLAND (EAST), a parish in South Molton district, Devon, on an affluent of the river Taw, 5 miles NW by N of South Molton, and 7 NNE of [illegible] r. station. Post town, South Molton, North Devon. Acres, 1,3[illegible]. Real property, £1,1[illegible]. Pop., [illegible]. Houses, 23. The manor belongs to [illegible]. The living is a rectory, united with the [illegible], in the diocese of Exeter. Value, [illegible]. Patron, [illegible]. The church has [illegible] tower. There are a Wesleyan chapel, [illegible]

BUCKLAND EGG. See [illegible]

BUCKLAND DINHAM, [illegible] parish, Somerset, 5¾ miles S of Bridgwater. Real property, £2[illegible]7.

BUCKLAND FILLEIGH, a parish in Torrington district, Devon, [illegible] NW of [illegible], [illegible] Bideford r. station. Post town, Shebbear, under Highampton, North Devon. Acres, 3,[illegible]7. Real property,

£1 s 7 [illegible] The [illegible] a few [illegible] Ford Conten [illegible] seat of [illegible] is a rector [illegible] £218 [illegible] and contains [illegible]

BUCKLAND IN THE MOOR, a parish in Newton Abbot district, Devon, on the river Dart, [illegible] to [illegible] NW of Ashburton [illegible] of Newton [illegible] Ashburton under Newton Abbot. Acres [illegible] Real property, [illegible] Pop., 113. Houses [illegible] The property is [illegible] The manor, which [illegible] belongs to the family of [illegible] surrounding [illegible] and commands a brilliant panoramic view. The living is a [illegible] annexed to the vicarage of Ashburton, with [illegible] The church is small, and was recently repaired. [illegible]

BUCKLAND MINCHIN. See BUCKLAND ST. [illegible]

BUCKLAND MONACHORUM, a village, a parish, and a sub-district, in the district of Tavistock, Devon. The village stands near the river Tavy and near the [illegible] station of the Tavistock railway, [illegible] miles S by E of Tavistock; [illegible] one of the [illegible] of [illegible] Plymouth [illegible] was a market town, and still [illegible] fair on [illegible] Monday. The parish includes also the hamlet of Milton, and part of the [illegible] Acres, [illegible] Real property, [illegible] Pop., 1,454. Houses, 265. The property is [illegible] belongs to Sir [illegible] Massey [illegible] the abbey, a Cistercian [illegible] Sir Francis Drake, the famous [illegible] Abbey [illegible] and the Colwell [illegible] Ashburton [illegible] 7 [illegible] Cornwall, [illegible] during the [illegible] Small [illegible] copper mines and [illegible] The living is a vicarage in the diocese of Exeter. Value, £[illegible] The church [illegible] and [illegible] a chapel [illegible] to [illegible] and [illegible] £10 [illegible] Acres, 30,[illegible] Pop., 8,6[illegible] Houses, 1,4[illegible]

BUCKLAND NEWTON, [illegible] district, Dorset [illegible] Newton [illegible] N [illegible]

[illegible]

BUCKLAND DINHAM [illegible]

[illegible] and probably was [illegible] the church.

BUCKLAND RIPERS, a parish in Weymouth district, Dorset, [illegible] NW of Weymouth [illegible] It includes part of [illegible] Weymouth. Acres, 1,2[illegible] Real property, £1,[illegible] Pop., [illegible] Houses, 27. The property is divided among a few. The living is a rectory in the diocese of Salisbury. Value, £176. Patron, Q. H. [illegible] Esq. The church is good.

BUCKLAND ST. MARY, a village and a parish in Chard district, Somerset. The village stands 1½ mile [illegible] miles NW of Chard [illegible] station, and [illegible] of Ilminster, and [illegible] fairs on [illegible] and [illegible] Wednesday after 21 Sept. The parish comprises 3,404 acres. Real property, £[illegible] 7. Pop., 71[illegible] Houses, 1[illegible] The property is much subdivided [illegible] the [illegible] have been found [illegible] The living is a rectory in the diocese of Bath and Wells. Value, £[illegible] 43. Patron, [illegible] The church was rebuilt [illegible] at a cost of [illegible] £20,000, [illegible] consists of nave with [illegible] a south porch, and a massive western tower [illegible] marbles, [illegible] and [illegible] Baptist chapel.

BUCKLAND SORORUM, or BUCKLAND MINCHIN, [illegible] in Durston parish, Somerset, 4½ miles W of [illegible] A house of [illegible] was founded [illegible] in 11[illegible] by William [illegible] The property of it was given, in [illegible] to the Knights [illegible] and the [illegible] the sisters of the [illegible] dissolution, [illegible]

BUCKLAND TOUT SAINTS, a parish in Kingsbridge district, Devon, 2[illegible] miles N of Kingsbridge [illegible] Acres [illegible] Real property [illegible] The living [illegible] of [illegible] Exeter. The church was recently rebuilt [illegible]

BUCKLAND (WEST), a parish in South [illegible] district, Devon, [illegible] post [illegible] Acres, 1,77[illegible] Real property, £[illegible] Houses, 7[illegible] The [illegible] the diocese of Exeter. Value, £[illegible] [illegible] 18[illegible]

BUCKLAND (WEST), a parish in Wellington district, Somerset [illegible] of Wellington [illegible]

[illegible]

BUCKNELL [illegible]

[illegible] Newton [illegible]

[illegible] is divided [illegible]

[illegible] belonged to [illegible] [illegible] at the dissolution to John Winchcombe, commonly called Jack of Newbury; passed, by marriage, to the famous Lord Bolingbroke; [illegible] the [illegible] of Winchcombe, and [illegible] to the present [illegible] W. H. H. Hartley, Esq. A fine manor mansion was built on it by Jack of Newbury, and visited, in Lord Bolingbroke's time, by Swift; but has been destroyed. Bucklebury common is an elevated undulating tract, commanding fine views. The living is a vicarage, united with the p. curacy of Marlston, in the diocese of Oxford. Value, £173.* Patron, W. H. H. Hartley, Esq. The church is Norman, with low square tower and small spire, and contains monuments of the Winchcombes. There are an Independent chapel, and an endowed school with £[illegible]. The sub-district contains nine parishes. Acres, 23,919. Pop., [illegible]. Houses, 1,178.

BUCKLERS HARD, a village in Beaulieu parish, Hants, on Beaulieu creek, [illegible] miles ENE of Lymington. It was designed by the second Duke of Montagu to be a town, with sugar refineries in connection with his West India [illegible]; [illegible] had, at one time, several ship yards, but is now of little importance.

BUCKLESHAM, a parish in Woodbridge district, Suffolk, [illegible] miles S of Bealings r. station, and [illegible] E of Ipswich. It has a post office under Ipswich. Acres, 1,622. Real property, £[illegible]. Pop., 362. Houses, 7[illegible]. Many curious petrifactions are found. The living is a rectory in the diocese of Norwich. Value, £[illegible].* Patron, the Rev. L. W. [illegible]. The church is [illegible], and was repaired in 1842. There is a national school.

BUCKLEY, a chapelry in Hawarden parish, Flint, 2 miles NE by N of Hope r. station, and [illegible] of Mold. It has a post office under Mold. Its statistics are returned with the parish. The living is a p. curacy, annexed to the rectory of Hawarden. A railway from Buckley to Connah's Quay, 5 miles long, was formed under act of 1860, and was at first for minerals only, but was allowed in 18[illegible] for passengers also.

BUCKLOW, a hundred in Cheshire, separated by the river Mersey from Lancashire. It extends southward to Northwich, westward a little past Runcorn, and eastward [illegible] miles past Altrincham; contains eight parishes and parts of two others, and is cut into two divisions, East and West. Acres of the E. div., 58,098. Pop. in 1851, 26,298. Acres of the W. div., 15,[illegible]. Pop. in 1851, 28,552. Pop. of both in 1861, 6[illegible]. Houses, 11,[illegible].

BUCKMILL, a hamlet in Idle township, Calverley parish, W. R. Yorkshire, [illegible] miles NE of Bradford.

BUCKLAND MILLS, a chapelry in Woolfardisworthy parish, Devon, [illegible] [illegible] miles [illegible] station of Bideford. Post town, Bideford. Pop., 2[illegible]. The living is a p. curacy in the diocese of Exeter. Value, not reported.* [illegible], Mrs. [illegible]. The church is recent.

BUCKMINSTER, a village and a parish in Melton Mowbray district, Leicester. The village stands on the verge of the county, [illegible] miles NNW of [illegible] station, and [illegible] NE of Melton Mowbray. The parish includes also the chapelry of Sewstern, and its post town is Colsterworth, under Grantham. Acres, [illegible]. Real property, £2,8[illegible]. Pop., [illegible]. Houses, 1[illegible]. Buckminster Park is a fine Grecian mansion of 17[illegible], the seat of the Earl of Dysart. The living is a vicarage, united with the p. curacy of Sewstern, in the diocese of Peterborough. Value, £10[illegible].* Patron, the Earl of Dysart. The church is ancient, of various dates, and has a tower and spire. There are a Wesleyan chapel, and [illegible] [illegible], and charities £[illegible].

BUCKNALL, a parish in Horncastle district, Lincoln, on an affluent of the Witham river, 2½ miles [illegible] of Southrey r. station, and 6½ W of Horncastle. Post town, [illegible] under Horncastle. Acres, 2,471. Real property, £2,[illegible]. Pop., [illegible]. Houses, [illegible]. The property is divided among a few. The living is a rectory in the diocese of Lincoln. Value, £[illegible].* Patron, [illegible] [illegible]. The church is good; and there are two Methodist chapels, a free school, and charities £18.

BUCKNALL, a township and a parochial chapelry in Stoke-upon-Trent parish, Stafford. The township lies on [illegible] Bucknall Eaves. Bucknall lies on the [illegible] line of the North Stafford railway, 2 miles NE of Stoke-upon-Trent, [illegible]; and includes the hamlet of [illegible]ley. Pop., 1,1[illegible]. Houses, 2[illegible]. Bucknall Eaves lies about a mile [illegible]. Pop., 24[illegible]. Houses, 50. The parochial chapelry bears the name of Bucknall-cum-Bagnall, includes the township of Bagnall, and was constituted in 1807. Post town, Hanley, under Stoke-upon-Trent. Real property, £8,621, of which £[illegible] is in mines. Pop., 2,1[illegible]. Houses, 408. The property is much subdivided. The living is a rectory, [illegible] with the p. curacy of Bagnall, in the diocese of Lichfield. Value, £200. Patron, the Rev. [illegible] Powys. The church is [illegible].

BUCKNELL, a parish in Bicester district, Oxford, near the Oxford canal [illegible] railway, 2¾ miles NW of Bicester. Post town, Bicester. Acres, 1,670. Real property, £2,[illegible]. Pop., [illegible]. Houses, 55. The property is divided among a few. Bucknell House is the seat of [illegible]. The living is a rectory in the diocese of Oxford. Value, not reported.* Patron, New College, Oxford. The church is early English, with a Norman tower, and has a brass of 1638. Charities, £11.

BUCKNELL, a township and a parish in the district of Knighton; the former in the county of Salop, the latter partly also in the county of Hereford. The township is on the river Teme, adjacent to the Knighton railway, 4½ miles ENE of Knighton. It has a station on the railway, and a post office under Leintwardine. Acres, 2,720. Real property, £3,[illegible]. Pop., [illegible]. Houses, 10[illegible]. The parish includes also the townships of Bedstone and Coxall. Acres, [illegible],160. Real property of [illegible] [illegible] and Bucknell [illegible] £10,2[illegible]. Pop., 7[illegible]. Houses, [illegible]. The property is divided among a few. The living is a vicarage, united with the p. curacy of Buckton, in the diocese of Hereford. Value, £[illegible].* Patrons, the [illegible]' Company, London. The church is good. Charities, £1[illegible].

BUCKROSE, a wapentake in E. R. Yorkshire. It is bounded on the N and the W, above and below Malton, by the river Derwent; and contains twenty-eight parishes. Acres, 1[illegible]. Pop. in 18[illegible], 1[illegible]; in 1861, 1[illegible]. Houses, 2,[illegible].

BUCKS. See BUCKINGHAMSHIRE.

BUCKS GREEN, a hamlet in Rudgwick parish, Sussex.

BUCKSHAW, a hamlet in Holwell parish, Dorset, 4 miles S[illegible] of Sherborne. Pop., [illegible].

BUCKSTONE (THE), a famous rocking-stone in Gloucestershire, on the Kymin, [illegible] N of Coleford. [illegible] [illegible], consists of a [illegible] [illegible], and measures about 53 feet in circumference. It probably was [illegible] [illegible], from [illegible].

BUCKTHORPE. See [illegible].

BUCKTON, a township in the parochial chapelry of Kyloe, Northumberland, 3½ miles NNW of Belford. Pop., 18.

BUCKTON, a township in Bridlington parish, E. R. Yorkshire, on the coast, near the Bridlington railway, 3½ miles N of Bridlington. Acres, 2,047; of which 1[illegible] are water. Real property, £2,7[illegible]. Pop., 181. Houses, 31.

BUCKTON AND CONALL, a township in [illegible] parish, Hereford, on the river Teme, [illegible] miles [illegible] of [illegible]. Acres, 1,[illegible]. Pop., 1[illegible]. Houses, [illegible].

BUCKWORTH, a parish in the district and county of Huntingdon, [illegible] miles W of the Great Northern railway, and 7 NW of Huntingdon. Post town, [illegible], under Huntingdon. Acres, 1,[illegible]. Real property, £2,78[illegible]. Pop., [illegible]. Houses, [illegible]. The property is all in one estate. The living is a rectory in the diocese of Ely. Value, £3[illegible].* Patron, [illegible] [illegible]. The church is good.

BUDBROOKE, a parish and a sub-district in the district and county of Warwick. The parish lies on the Birmingham and Warwick canal, and on the Birmingham and Oxford railway, 1½ mile [illegible] of Warwick. It [illegible] the hill and Lower [illegible] property, £6,288. Pop., 492. [illegible] Park [illegible] the seat of Lord [illegible] [illegible] square tower [illegible] school has £30 from endowment [illegible] The sub-district contains [illegible] 13,413. Pop., 4,443. Houses, 938.

[illegible] BY [illegible] township in [illegible] parish, Notts [illegible] Ollerton. [illegible] Houses, 21.

BUDDINGTON, a hamlet in [illegible] parish, Sussex [illegible] Pop., 35.

[illegible] hamlet in [illegible] parish [illegible]

[illegible] BUDLES, a hamlet in St. Peter parish, Kent [illegible] of Ramsgate.

[illegible] a hundred in [illegible] division [illegible] parishes of Compton, Hursley [illegible] Acres, 14,190. Pop. in 1851, 2,0[illegible] [illegible] the upper half contains Ashley parish [illegible] and parts of two others. Acres, [illegible] Pop. [illegible] 2,270. Houses, 441.

[illegible] Cornwall. The village stands on [illegible] at the mouth of [illegible] Westward [illegible] of [illegible] Devon, and [illegible] great trade [illegible] shell-sand [illegible] Pop., 70[illegible] Houses, 10[illegible] The living [illegible] diocese of Exeter. Value, £120. [illegible]

[illegible] a village and a parish [illegible] Devon. The village stands [illegible] of the Cornwall Railway [illegible] Knowle [illegible] Saltash, Cornwall [illegible] property, £1,7[illegible] Pop., 1,270. [illegible] copper [illegible] constructed in 18[illegible] [illegible] church [illegible] The living is a [illegible] Plymouth. The church [illegible]

[illegible]

[illegible] a hundred in [illegible] Devon [illegible]

[illegible] Acres, [illegible] Houses, [illegible] It has [illegible]

[illegible] of different [illegible] alternating [illegible] A [illegible] from [illegible] Housele [illegible] to the [illegible] the South.

BUDLEIGH (EAST), a village, a parish, a sub-district and a hundred in Devon. The village stands on the river Otter, 2 miles from the coast, 3½ miles E of [illegible], and 5 WSW of Sidmouth; and has a post office under Exeter. Its large [illegible] consists chiefly of cob [illegible], and was once a market-town. The parish includes also the village of [illegible] Salterton, and the hamlets of Great and Little [illegible] Acres, [illegible] 77, of which 4[illegible] are water. Real property, £9,163. Pop., 2,4[illegible] Houses, 50[illegible] The property is divided among a few. The [illegible] of [illegible] belonged successively to the [illegible] and [illegible] families, and Hayes [illegible] now a farm house belonging to [illegible] was the birthplace and property of Sir Walter Raleigh. The living is a vicarage, united with the p. curacy of Salterton, in the diocese of Exeter. Value, £315. Patron, the Hon. Mrs. [illegible] The church is [illegible] English, consists of nave, aisles, and chancel, and contains the [illegible] and many monuments. The vicarage of [illegible] Raleigh [illegible] separate benefice. There are a chapel of ease and Baptist and Wesleyan chapels [illegible] Salterton, and an Independent chapel [illegible] Budleigh. Charities, £43.—The sub-district contains [illegible] three [illegible] parochial tract, and [illegible] district of St. Thomas. Acres, 12,021. Pop., 4,614. Houses, 1,0[illegible]2. The hundred contains twelve [illegible] parishes. Acres, 5[illegible]. Pop. in 1851, 23,178; in 1861, 22,797. Houses, 4,[illegible]21.

BUDLEIGH SALTERTON, a village [illegible] parish in Devon, on the coast, [illegible] east of the mouth of the [illegible] S of [illegible] Budleigh. [illegible] hotels [illegible] lodging houses [illegible] long age [illegible] is now [illegible] bathing-place. It [illegible] the shore [illegible] natives [illegible]

"[illegible] eyes
I never [illegible] sunny ray
[illegible] straight [illegible] then [illegible] arise
[illegible] large [illegible] grey,
And [illegible] with [illegible] eyes,
[illegible] through [illegible] bright transparence."

BUDLEIGH (WEST), a hundred in Devon. It contains [illegible] parish and six other parishes. Acres, 17,8[illegible] Houses, [illegible]

BUDNEY, a [illegible] in Whitchurch parish, Salop [illegible] Whitchurch.

BUDOCK, a parish in Falmouth district, Cornwall [illegible] Falmouth [illegible] Falmouth station [illegible] Acres, [illegible]4, of which [illegible] Real property, £10,671. Pop., 2,[illegible]5[illegible] Houses, [illegible] The living is a vicarage [illegible] in the diocese of Exeter [illegible] chapel [illegible] Charities, £1[illegible]

BUDOCK (ST.). See ST. BUDOCK (ST.)

BUDON. See [illegible]

BUDWORTH, a [illegible] district [illegible] Cheshire. It [illegible] Budworth [illegible] Acres, [illegible]

BUDWORTH (GREAT), a town, a township [illegible] and a parish in Northwich district, Cheshire. The township [illegible] Great [illegible] North[illegible] miles N of

Northwich; and has a post office under Northwich, and fairs on 15 Feb., 5 April, and 2 Oct. Acres, 842. Real property, £6,0[illegible]. Pop., 613. Houses, 1[illegible]8. The parish contains also the townships of Seven Oaks, Anderton, Crowley, Whitley Superior, Whitley Inferior, Barnton, Stretton, Appleton, Dutton, Aston by Budworth, Hoover Inferior, Tabley Inferior, Plumley, Pickmere, Little Leigh, [illegible]ton, Hartford, Winnington, Comberbach, Marbury, Marston, Wincham, Northwich, Castle Northwich, Lostock Gralam, Nether Peover, Allostock, Hulse, Pinches, Anderton, and Lach Dennis; and the chapelry of Witton cum Twambrooks. Acres, 35,920. Real property, £1[illegible] 201. Pop. in 1841, 17,103; in 1861, 18,152. Houses, 3,834. The property is much subdivided. Marbury Hall, Arley Hall, and Belmont House, are chief residences. Budworth mere and Pickmere are small lakes. Many of the inhabitants are employed in salt works. The living is a vicarage in the diocese of Chester. Value, £676.* Patron, Christ Church College, Oxford. The church is ancient; has an embattled tower; and contains monuments of the Pooles, the Warburtons, and the Leycesters. The chapelries of Antrobus, Barnton, Hartford, Little Leigh, Lostock, Lower Peover, Stretton, Tabley, Lower Whitley, Wallerscote(?), Witton, and Northwich, are separate benefices. Witton grammar school has £[illegible] from endowment, and other charities £172.

BUDWORTH (LITTLE), a parish in Northwich district, Cheshire; on an affluent of the river Weaver, near Delamere forest, 4 miles N by E of Tarporley, and 2½ SW by W of Hartford r. station. It has a post office under Tarporley. Acres, 2,752. Real property, £3,6[illegible]. Pop., 552. Houses, 122. The property is divided among a few. The living is a vicarage in the diocese of Chester. Value, £[illegible]. Patron, the Bishop of Chester. The ancient church belonged to St. Mary's nunnery in Chester; and the present one was built in 1798. Dodd's alms houses have £[illegible] from endowment, and other charities £62.

BUERSILL, a hamlet in Castleton township, Rochdale parish, Lancashire; 2 miles SE of Rochdale.

BUERTON, a township in Audlem parish, Cheshire; adjacent to the Birmingham and Liverpool canal, 7 miles S by E of Nantwich. Acres, 2,953. Real property, £4,410. Pop., 464. Houses, 93. There are two Methodist chapels, and charities £60.

BUERTON, Aldford parish, Cheshire. See PULFORD.

BUGBROOKE, a parish and a sub-district in the district and county of Northampton. The parish lies on Watling street, the Grand Junction canal, and the Northwestern railway, [illegible] miles SE of Weedon station, and 5½ W by S of Northampton; and has a post office under Weedon. Acres, 2,420. Real property, £5,301. Pop., 9[illegible]5. Houses, 213. The property is much subdivided. The living is a rectory in the diocese of Peterborough. Value, £[illegible]. Patron, the Rev. T. H. Harrison. The church is ancient; and has a screen and an octagonal font. There are a Baptist chapel, a national school, and charities £2[illegible]. The sub-district contains six parishes. Acres, 9,[illegible]. Pop., [illegible],15[illegible]. Houses, [illegible]65.

BUGLAWTON, a township-chapelry in Astbury parish, Cheshire; on the river Dane and the North Stafford railway, 1 mile NE of Congleton. Post town, Congleton. Acres, 2,[illegible]. Real property, £8,127. Pop., 2,074. Houses, [illegible]. [illegible] Hall is the seat of the Pearsons. There are several silk mills and a cotton mill. The living is a p. curacy in the diocese of Chester. Value, £100.* Patron, the Vicar of Astbury. The church is [illegible]. There are two Methodist chapels and a national school.

BUGLEY, a hamlet in Gillingham parish, Dorset; [illegible] miles NNW of Shaftesbury.

BUGSBY'S HOLE, a reach on the Thames [illegible] below Greenwich [illegible]. It has a post office under Greenwich, London, S.E. [illegible] has a [illegible] of the [illegible] to [illegible].

BUGSWORTH, a hamlet with [illegible], in Glossop parish, Derby; on the New Mills and Peak Forest railway, [illegible] miles NNW of Chapel-en-le-Frith.

BUGTHORPE, [illegible] a parish in Pocklington district, E. R. Yorkshire; on an affluent of the river Derwent, 4 miles NW of Garrowby r. station, and 6½ N by W of Pocklington. Post town, Stamford Bridge, under York. Acres, 1,[illegible]. Real property, £[illegible],381. Pop., 24[illegible]. Houses, 5[illegible]. The property is all in one estate. The living is a vicarage in the diocese of York. Value, £200. Patron, the Archbishop of York. The church was repaired in 18[illegible].

BUILDWAS, a parish in Madeley district, Salop; on the river Severn, and on the Severn Valley railway, at the junction of the branch to Much Wenlock, 3½ miles SE of the Wrekin, and 4 NW of Much Wenlock. It has a station on the railway at the junction; and its post town is Ironbridge, under Wellington, Salop. Acres, 2,128. Real property, £2,679. Pop., 2[illegible]0. Houses, 5[illegible]. The property is divided among a few. Buildwas Park is the seat of W. Moseley, Esq. A Cistertian abbey was founded in the parish in 1135, by Roger, bishop of Chester; and given at the dissolution to Lord Powis. The side aisles and the chapels of the abbey church have perished; but the nave, the transept, the tower, and the choir, and the chapter house, mostly remain, are in the Norman, and form a noble ruin. The living is a donative in the diocese of Lichfield. Value, £20. Patron, W. Moseley, Esq. The church was built in 1720.

BUILTH, a small town, a parish, a sub-district, a district, and a hundred in Brecon. The town stands on the river Wye, and on the Llanidloes and Brecon railway, 12 miles SW of New Radnor. It is sometimes called Llanfair-ym-Muallt. It occupies the site of the Roman station Bullaeum; it had a castle in the 11th century, said to have been built by Bernard Newmarch; and it was the favourite residence and the final retreat of the last Llewelyn. That prince was betrayed by the inhabitants, who continue to be reproached as "[illegible] of Builth;" and he was slain in a dingle 3 miles [illegible], thence called Cwm Llewelyn. The town consists chiefly of two principal streets, which form nearly right angles on the side of a steep declivity. The castle and the greater part of the town were destroyed by fire in 1690. The foundations of the keep, measuring about [illegible] feet in circuit, can still be traced. A bridge of six arches spans the Wye, and connects the town with Radnorshire. The parish church is [illegible], and has a [illegible] tower, and contains an ancient monument of a [illegible] removed from a previous church. There are [illegible] dissenting chapels and a [illegible] charity. [illegible] "The Park Wells," three mineral springs, severally saline, chalybeate, and sulphureous, are about 1 mile to the NW, and draw visitors from a distance to the town. The environs generally are picturesque, the climate salubrious, and the sport for anglers good. The town enjoys ready communication with all parts of Wales and England, from the intersection near it of the Central railway from Llanidloes to Brecon with the line from Knighton to Llandovery; and it has a station at the junction, and another station at the Wells. It has a post office,‡ a weekly market on Monday, and fairs on the third Monday of Feb., the Friday before 12 May, 27 June, 2 Oct., and 6 Dec.; and is a seat of petty sessions.—The parish includes the town, and comprises 712 acres. Real property, £2,[illegible]. Pop., 1,[illegible]. Houses, 226. The living is a vicarage in the diocese of St. Davids. Value, £[illegible].* Patron, Thomas, Esq.

The sub-district contains the parishes of [illegible], Llanganten, [illegible], Maes-Mynis, Llanddewi-Abergwesin(?), Alltmawr, Llangynog, and Crickadarn, the [illegible] and parts of Llanfihangel and Llanfihangel-Bryn-Pabuan, also the parish of Llanelwedd, [illegible] in Radnor. Acres, 27,789. Pop., 5,4[illegible]. Houses, [illegible]. The district comprehends also the sub-district of Llanwrtyd, containing the [illegible] of Llanafan-fawr, [illegible], [illegible], and [illegible] parochial chapelries of [illegible], Disserth, [illegible]. [illegible] and [illegible], and the sub-district of Abergwesyn, containing the parishes of Llanfihangel-Abergwesin, Llanddewi-Abergwesin, Llangammarch, Llanlleonfel, [illegible], and parts of the parishes of Llanafan-fawr and [illegible].

... Acres, 102,05[illegible] ... in 1861, ... Pop. in 1861, 6,8[illegible] Houses, 1,[illegible] Marriages in 1866, 61; births, 262,—of which 40 were illegitimate; deaths, 150,—of which 98 were at ages under 5 years, and 6 at ages above 85. Marriages in the ten years 1851-60, 577; births, ... deaths, ... The places of worship in 1851 were 20 of the Church of England, with 2,050 sittings; 12 of Independents, with 1,101 s.; ... of Calvinistic Methodists, with ... s.; 5 of Baptists, with 850 s.; and 1 of Primitive Methodists, with 20 attendants. The schools were 9 public day schools, with ... scholars; 8 private day schools, with 171 s.; 30 Sunday schools, with 1,736 s.; and 1 evening school for adults, with ... s.—The hundred contains twenty parishes. Acres, 97,607. Pop., 6,482. Houses, 1,203.

BULBOURN, a rivulet falling into the river Gade, near Berkhampstead, in Herts.

BULBRIDGE, a tything in Wilton parish, Wilts, near Wilton. Pop. 5[illegible]. It formerly was a parish, and it ranks as a rectory, annexed to the rectory of Wilton, in the diocese of Salisbury.

BULBY. See HAWTHORPE WITH DUNSBY.

BULCAMP, a hamlet in Blythburgh parish, Lincoln, ... miles SE of Baldesworth.

BULCOTE, a chapelry in Burton Joyce parish, Notts, between the Trent and the Nottingham railway, 1 mile NE of Burton Joyce r. station, and 4¾ NE of Nottingham. Post town, Burton Joyce, under Nottingham. Acres, 970. Real property, £1,1[illegible]. Pop., 136. Houses, 24. The property is divided among a few. The living is a perpetual curacy, annexed to the vicarage of Burton Joyce, in the diocese of Lincoln.

BULEY CASTLE, a ruined castle on the river Eden, 3½ miles NW of Appleby, in Westmoreland. It was built by Roland de ... and passed to the Vieuxponts ... bishops of Carlisle.

BULFORD, a parish in Amesbury district, Wilts, on the river Avon, 2 miles NNE of Amesbury, and 4½ N by W of Porton r. station. Post town, Amesbury, under Salisbury. Acres, 3,47[illegible]. Real property, with Durrington and Winton, £7,2[illegible]. Pop., 38[illegible]. Houses, 78. Bulford House is a chief residence. Some British ... and an ancient work, supposed to ... a ... barrow, large, ... within ... The living is a vicarage in the diocese of Salisbury. Value, £7[illegible]. Patron, ... The church is ... and ...

BULK, a township in Lancaster parish, Lancashire, adjacent to ... and the Carlisle railway, 2 miles NE of Lancaster. Acres, 1,14[illegible]. Real property, ... Pop., 1[illegible]. Bulk House is the seat of the Eskells.

BULKELEY, a township in Malpas parish, Cheshire, ... miles NE of Malpas. Acres, 91[illegible]. Real property, ... Pop., 1[illegible]. Houses, 38.

BULKINGTON, a village and a parish in Nuneaton district, Warwick. The village stands near the Coventry canal and the Trent Valley railway, 3 miles SE by S of Nuneaton, ... station on the railway, and post town under ... The parish includes also the hamlets of ... Barnacle, ... Ryton, Weston-in-Arden, Wolvey Heath, and ... Marston Jabbett. Acres, ... Real property, ... Pop., 1,8[illegible]. Houses, ... The property is much subdivided ... of the inhabitants are ... ribbon weavers. The living is a vicarage in the diocese of Worcester. Value, £[illegible]. Patron, ... The church is ... and there are ... chapels for ... and ... schools built in 18[illegible] ...

BULKINGTON, a tything in Keevil parish, Wilts ... Acres, ... Pop., 210. Houses, ...

BULKWORTHY, a parish in ... district, Devon ... miles ... of ... Acres, ... Real property, ... Pop., 1[illegible]. Houses, ... The property is ... The living is a ... annexed to the ... of ...

[illegible] ...

... curacy of ... and ... in the diocese of Exeter. The church was built by Lord Chief Justice Hankford.

BULLAM. See BULLHAM.

BULLBARROW, a chalk down 4 miles SW of Milton Abbas, in Dorset. It has an altitude of 927 feet above the sea, and is crowned by an ancient camp, a circular work with double ramparts, commanding a very extensive view.

BULL BAY, a small bay on the N coast of Anglesey, 1½ mile W of Amlwch. It has anchorage in five fathoms, but lies open to northerly winds.

BULLERS GREEN, a township in the parish and within the borough of Morpeth, Northumberland. Acres, 8[illegible]. Pop., 2[illegible]. Houses, [illegible].

BULLEY, a parish in Westbury-on-Severn district, Gloucestershire, 2 miles SW of Oakle-street r. station, and 5 WNW of Gloucester. Post town, Huntley, under Gloucester. Acres, [illegible]. Real property, £1,8[illegible]. Pop., 2[illegible]6. Houses, 47. The property is subdivided. The living is a p. curacy, annexed to the vicarage of Churcham, in the diocese of Gloucester and Bristol. The church has Norman parts.

BULLFA, a village in Carth parcel, Ystradyfodwg ... parish, Brecon ... miles ... of Neath.

BULLGILL, a station on the Maryport and Carlisle railway, in Cumberland, 4½ miles NE of Maryport.

BULLINGDON, a hundred in Oxfordshire, ... adjoining Berks below Oxford; extends 15 miles ... and ... towards Bucks; and contains twenty-three parishes and parts of two others. Acres, 44,393. Pop., 12,1[illegible]. Houses, 2,[illegible].

BULLINGHAM, a ... on the west border of Herefordshire, ... miles from Kington.

BULLINGHAM (LOWER), a township in St. Martin parish, Herefordshire, 1¾ mile S of Hereford. Acres, 1,100. Real property, £2,300. Pop., 177. Houses, 5[illegible].

BULLINGHAM (UPPER), or BULLINGHOPE, a parish in the county and district of Hereford, on the river Wye, 2 miles S of Hereford. Post town, Hereford. Acres, 698. Real property, £1,361. Pop., 8[illegible]. Houses, 19. The property is in one estate. The parish is ecclesiastically united with Lower Bullingham and Grafton townships. The living is a vicarage in the diocese of Hereford. Value, ... Patron, the Bishop of Hereford. The church is ...

BULLINGTON, a parish in Andover district, Hants, on an affluent of the river Test, 4 miles WNW of Micheldever r. station, and 4 S of Whitchurch. Post town, Sutton Scotney, under Winchester. Acres, 1,628. Real property, with Tufton, £3[illegible]. Pop., 171. Houses, ... The property is divided among a few. Bullington House is an old mansion ... a ... camp at ... Hill and Norton ... antiquities have been found ... The living is a vicarage, united with the vicarage of ... in the diocese of Winchester. Value, £60[illegible]. Patron, ... The church is good.

BULLINGTON, a chapelry in Goltho parish, Lincoln, 2 miles ... of Wragby ... and ... r. station. Post town, Wragby. Acres, ... Real property, £952. Pop., 4[illegible]. Houses, 6. A Gilbertine priory and convent were founded here in the time of ... by Simon Fitz-William ... at the dissolution, to the Duke of Suffolk. The living is annexed to ... in the diocese of Lincoln.

BULLOCKS HALL, a township in Warkworth parish, Northumberland, near to the North-eastern railway, 7 miles SE of Alnwick. Acres, ... Pop., 1[illegible]. Houses, 2.

BULLOCKS HILL, a ... in Sandbach parish, Cheshire, ... miles ... of Sandbach ...

BULL POINT, ... Devon, ... miles ... of ...

BULLS SAND, ... the north of the ... Spurn ... Yorkshire ... it ... fathoms ... distance of ...

BULLSCROSS, ... in Enfield parish ... Middlesex ... 2 miles W ... and the ...

LULLSHEAD HILL, [illegible] station [illegible] in Lanc[illegible], 2½ miles WSW of Alton [illegible] it [illegible] and [illegible].

LULLSMARL HILL, an eminence on the mutual border of Dorset and Somerset, 3 miles E of Milborne port. It commands extensive views both E and W.

LULLSLAUGHTER BAY, a small bay near St Govan's Head, on the south coast of Pembroke.

LULLSTON. See LOLLESTON.

LULWELL. See LULWORTH.

LULMAN'S WELL [illegible], a locality 2½ miles from Newcastle-on-Tyne, with a post office under that town.

LULMER, a parish and a sub-district in the district of Sudbury and county of Essex. The parish lies on the verge of the county, near the river Stour and the Sudbury railway, 2 miles WSW of Sudbury; and has a post office under Sudbury. Acres, 2,77[illegible]. Real property, £5,[illegible]. Pop., 709. Houses, 170. The property is [illegible] among a few. The living is a [illegible] united with the vicarage of [illegible] Walden, in the diocese of Rochester. Value, £41[illegible]. Patron, S. M. Raymond, Esq. The church is good. The sub-district contains nine parishes and an extra-parochial tract. Acres, 17,501. Pop., 4,553. Houses, 1,051.

LULMER, a township, a parish, a sub-district, and a wapentake in N. R. Yorkshire. The township lies on an affluent of the river Derwent, 3 miles WNW of Castle Howard station, and 6½ SW by W of New Malton. Acres, 1,430. Real property, £2,115. Pop., 84. Houses, 72. The parish contains also the townships of Hendersk[illegible]lf and Welburn, the latter of which has a post office under York. Acres, 3,800. Real property, £4,893. Pop., 1,077. Houses, 227. The property is divided among a few. The living is a rectory in the diocese of York. Value, £39[illegible]. Patron, Earl Fitzwilliam. The church is good. The sub-district is in the district of Malton, and contains four parishes and parts of two others. Acres, 21,222. Pop., 4,07[illegible]. Houses, 832. The wapentake contains thirty-three parishes and parts of seven others. Acres, 10[illegible],723. Pop. in 1851, 21,[illegible]; in 1861, [illegible]. Houses, [illegible].

LULMERSHIP COURT, a seat in the eastern vicinity of Reading, Berks. It was the residence of the prime minister Viscount Sidmouth, often visited by Pitt and Windham; and belongs now to [illegible] Webb, Esq.

LULPHAN, a parish in Orsett district, Essex, 4½ miles NW of Stanford-le-Hope r. station, and 6½ SSE of Brentwood. Post town, Orsett, under Romford, London, E. Acres, 1,607. Real property, £2,[illegible]12. Pop., 2[illegible]8. Houses, [illegible]7. The property is divided among a few. The living is a rectory in the diocese of Rochester. Value, £31[illegible]. Patron, J. S. Hurd, Esq. The church is tolerable.

LULSTON. See POLLESTON.

LULSTRODE PARK, a seat of the Duke of Somerset, 2¾ miles ESE of Beaconsfield, in Bucks. It belonged anciently to the Bulstrodes, passed to the Jeffreyses, was sold, about the end of the 17th century, to the Earl of Portland, and resold, in 180[illegible], to the Duke of Somerset. [illegible] mansion was built on it by Judge Jeffreys, and is described in Mrs Montagu's Letters. The present mansion was founded by the Duke of Somerset, stood long in an incomplete state, and was begun to be reconstructed in 18[illegible], on a new design, by [illegible]. An ancient entrenchment, enclosing 21 acres, is in the park.

LULVERHITHE, a hamlet within Hastings borough, Sussex, on the coast and on the Brighton railway, 2 miles west of Hastings. Pop., [illegible]. Houses, 1[illegible].

LULWELL, a village, a parish, and a sub-district in Basford district, Notts. The village stands in Sherwood forest, adjacent to the Midland railway, [illegible] miles NNW of Nottingham, and has a station on the railway, and a post office under Nottingham. The parish includes also the hamlet of Bampsh[illegible]. Acres, 1,210. Real property, £[illegible],7[illegible]2. Pop., 3,0[illegible]. Houses, 78[illegible]. The property is subdivided. [illegible]well Hall is the seat of the Rev. C. [illegible]. Limestone is worked; [illegible] printing, lace making, [illegible] making, brick making, and malting are carried on. The living is a rectory in the diocese of Lincoln. Value, £25[illegible]. Patron, the Rev. C. [illegible]. The church is new and has a square tower. There are chapels for [illegible], Wesleyans, [illegible] Wesleyans, [illegible] Ascension [illegible] 1[illegible] [illegible] The sub-district contains [illegible] parishes. Acres, 8,264. Pop., 7,8[illegible]2. Houses, 1,[illegible]71.

LULWICK, a [illegible] in Oundle district, Northamptonshire, on an affluent of the river [illegible], [illegible] miles [illegible] of Seaton r. station, and 7 NW by W of Oundle. It has a post office under Wansford. Acres, [illegible]. [illegible] Real property, £[illegible]. Pop., [illegible]. Houses, 7[illegible]. The property is [illegible]. [illegible] Hall is the seat of Thomas Tryon, Esq. The living is a rectory in the diocese of Peterborough. Value, [illegible]. Patron, T. Tryon, Esq. The church is [illegible] English, and has [illegible]. Charities, £3[illegible].

LULWICK SHORTLANDS, an extra-parochial tract in Oundle district, Northampton; contiguous to Lulwick. Pop., 6[illegible]. Houses, 1[illegible].

LUMPSTEAD HELION, a parish in the district of Risbridge and county of Essex, on the N verge of the county, [illegible] on the [illegible] and Haverhill railway, near Bartlow [illegible] station, [illegible] miles NNE of [illegible]. It has a post office under Newmarket. Acres, [illegible]. Real property, £4,210. Pop., 5[illegible]7. Houses, 1[illegible]. The property is divided among a few. [illegible] The living is a vicarage in the diocese of Rochester. Value, £17[illegible]. Patron, Trinity College, Cambridge. The church is good.

LUMPSTEAD STEEPLE, a parish in the district of Risbridge and county of Essex, on the [illegible] and Haverhill railway, near Bartlow station, [illegible] miles NE by E of [illegible]. It has a post office under [illegible]. Acres, 3,2[illegible]. Real property, £[illegible]. Pop., [illegible]. Houses, 23[illegible]. The living is a vicarage in the diocese of Rochester. Value, £22[illegible]. Patron, [illegible]. The church is [illegible]. There are an Independent chapel and national and British schools.

LUNPLEY, a township and a parish in the district of [illegible]. The township lies on the [illegible], near the Calveley station, 3½ miles SSE of [illegible]ley, and it has a post office [illegible] under [illegible]; and fairs on 11 and 12 [illegible], and 30 and 31 July. Acres, 1,140. [illegible]. Pop., 99[illegible]. Houses, 20[illegible]. The parish contains also the townships of [illegible], [illegible], [illegible], [illegible]ham, Calveley, [illegible], [illegible], Stapleford [illegible], Peckforton, and [illegible]. Acres, 13,[illegible]. Real property, £25,87[illegible]. Pop., [illegible]727. Houses, [illegible]. The manor belonged to Hugh Lupus, and passed to the [illegible]. A college [illegible] was founded here, in 1[illegible], by Sir Hugh de Calveley; and was purchased from the Crown in the time of Elizabeth, by Thomas Aldersey, of London, who gave the income for charitable uses. The living is a vicarage, united with the perpetual curacy of Peckforton and Calveley, in the diocese of Chester. Value, £117[illegible]. Patron, the [illegible] Company. The church is [illegible] English; has [illegible] and [illegible] was [illegible] restored in 18[illegible], and contains [illegible] of [illegible] of the 14th century, [illegible] commander against the Spanish armada. [illegible] of Tilstone and [illegible] There are seven dissenting chapels, two [illegible] schools, and charities £10.—The sub-district contains [illegible] and is [illegible]. Pop., 7,[illegible].

LUNCKTON, a hamlet in [illegible] parish, [illegible], [illegible] miles NW of Stoning[illegible]. Pop., 72. It unites [illegible] with [illegible].

LUNDLEY. See [illegible].

LUNCAY, a town, two parishes, and a sub-district, in Wangford district, Suffolk. The town [illegible] verge of the county, [illegible] river [illegible], on the [illegible] railway, [illegible] miles W of [illegible]. The name of [illegible] "[illegible]", [illegible] stronghold of the [illegible] of [illegible] sound [illegible] one of the [illegible] St [illegible] and thought to be [illegible]

[illegible] Martin [illegible] of Edward IV [illegible] views [illegible] of the [illegible] the Bungay [illegible]

> We [illegible] of Bungay
> [illegible]
> I [illegible] King of Cockaygne,
> [illegible]

[illegible] found [illegible] on a spot between [illegible] in 1163, by [illegible] Glanville [illegible] the [illegible] The town [illegible] in 1688, and [illegible] consists of spacious well [illegible] streets [illegible] houses [illegible] The corn [illegible] May [illegible] church [illegible] built in 1690 [illegible] and [illegible] chapels [illegible] Independents [illegible] Methodists [illegible] The grammar school [illegible] £54 from [illegible] The town lands yield £[illegible] for [illegible] The town [illegible] banking [illegible] petty sessions [illegible] The Waveney is navigable [illegible] corn [illegible] grain, flour, [illegible] malting [illegible] 702, of [illegible] 3,909 [illegible] Houses [illegible] the town [illegible] Acres [illegible] Real property £4,310 Pop. [illegible] Trinity [illegible] Houses [illegible] Value of St [illegible] Trinity [illegible] Value, £[illegible] the Duke of [illegible] parishes [illegible] Houses, 1,117

BUNNY, [illegible] of Notts, [illegible] of Nottingham [illegible] Acres [illegible] Pop., 273 Houses [illegible] The [illegible] living is a vicarage [illegible] The church [illegible]

BUNTINGFORD, a village [illegible] and a [illegible] Herts. The village [illegible] of Hertford [illegible]

[illegible] o 99 [illegible] The property [illegible] village, and [illegible] parish of [illegible] The living and [illegible] Pop., 681 [illegible] is a p. curacy, annexed to the vicarage of [illegible] in the diocese of [illegible] and [illegible] Acres 2,[illegible] Pop. [illegible] Houses 1,[illegible]

BUNWELL, a parish in Depwade district, [illegible] 2¼ miles [illegible] of New [illegible] and 4½ WSW of [illegible] station. It has a post office under [illegible] Acres 2,470 Real property £5,[illegible] Pop., 907 Houses, 212 The property is divided among a few. The living is a rectory in the diocese of Norwich. Value, £[illegible] Patron, Sir [illegible] Bart. The church [illegible] good. There are a P. Methodist chapel and a national school.

BURASTON. See B[illegible]

BURBACH. See B[illegible], Leicester.

BURBAGE, a village and a parish in Pewsey district, Wilts. The village stands near the Kennet and Avon canal, near the Reading and Devizes railway, in the neighbourhood of Savernake station, 6 miles SSE of Marlborough, is a straggling [illegible] place, and has a post office under Marlborough. The parish comprises 3,2[illegible] acres. Real property £5,51[illegible] Pop., 1,6[illegible] Houses 3[illegible] The property is divided among a few. The living is a vicarage in the diocese of Salisbury. Value £[illegible] Patron, the Bishop of Salisbury. The church has an edifice of 1[illegible] with an old tower and contains two memorial windows, the one to Bishop Denison [illegible] [illegible] the Curate [illegible] [illegible] a Wesleyan chapel [illegible] charities, £1[illegible]

BURBAGE, a chapelry in [illegible] parish, Derby, 1 mile S of Buxton. It was formed in 1804 [illegible] [illegible] Buxton [illegible] p. curacy. Value, £100

BURBACH, or BURBAGE, a [illegible] district, Leicester. The chapelry is in [illegible] on the verge of the county at Watling street, 1[illegible] miles [illegible] of Hinckley [illegible] Acres, [illegible]170 Real property £[illegible] Pop. 1,8[illegible] Houses [illegible] The property is much subdivided. Many of the inhabitants are stocking makers. The living is a p. curacy, annexed to the rectory of Aston Flamville, in the diocese of Peterborough. The church [illegible] There are chapels for Independents, [illegible] and Primitive Methodists, and a national school. The sub-district contains [illegible] parishes. Acres, 1[illegible] Pop., [illegible] Houses [illegible]

BURBEACH, a hundred in the rape of Bramber, Sussex. It contains [illegible] and [illegible] parishes and part of [illegible] Acres, 17,[illegible] Pop. in 1851, 2,[illegible] Houses [illegible]

BURBECK, a streamlet falling into the [illegible] in Whinfell, in Westmoreland.

BURBO FLATS, a sand bank off the mouth of the Mersey and the Dee, Lancashire and Cheshire. It is 7 miles long and from 2 to [illegible] broad, and is partly bare at low tide. The main channels to the Mersey are the [illegible] and the [illegible] Rock channel to the [illegible] [illegible] and the [illegible] low [illegible] channels.

BURBROOK, a streamlet falling into the [illegible] near [illegible], in Derby.

BURCOMBE, a parish in Wilton district, Wilts, on the [illegible] of the river Avon, adjacent to the Salisbury and Yeovil railway, 1½ mile W of Wilton. It [illegible] North [illegible] and [illegible] called South [illegible] post town is Wilton [illegible] Salisbury. Acres, 1,[illegible] Real property, £1,[illegible] Pop., 374 Houses [illegible] The living is a p. curacy in the diocese of Salisbury [illegible] Patron, St [illegible] [illegible]

BURCOT, a [illegible] in Dorchester parish, Oxford [illegible] miles [illegible] of Abingdon. Acres, 1[illegible] Real property, £1,[illegible] Pop., 17[illegible] Houses [illegible] It has [illegible] [illegible] Place.

BURCOTT, a hamlet in Wing parish, Bucks, 3½ miles SW of Leighton Buzzard. Pop., 17[illegible]

BURCOTT, a township in North [illegible] parish, Salop, on an affluent of the Severn, 2 miles NE of Bridgnorth.

BURCOTT, a tithing in St Cuthbert Out, within Wells, [illegible] Somerset, 1 mile W of Wells. Real property, £1,1[illegible]. Pop., 103.

BURDALE, a station on the Malton and Driffield railway, E. R. Yorkshire, [illegible] miles SE of New Malton.

BURDENS BALL, a tything in South Newton parish, Wilts, 2 miles N of Wilton.

BURDON, a hamlet in Highhampton parish, Devon, 4½ miles W of Hatherleigh. Burdon House here is the seat of C. Burdon, Esq.

BURDON, a township in Bishop Wearmouth parish, Durham, [illegible] the Durham and Sunderland railway, 4 miles S by W of Sunderland. Acres, 1,00[illegible]. Real property, £1,[illegible]. Pop., [illegible]. Houses, 13.

BURDON (GREAT), a township in Haughton-le-Skerne parish, Durham, near the Stockton railway, 2½ miles NE of Darlington. Acres, 588. Real property, £1,[illegible]. Pop., 101. Houses, 17.

BURDOSWALD, a locality in Lanercost parish, Cumberland, on the Roman wall, 4½ miles NE by E of Brampton. The Roman station Amboglanna was here, and many Roman inscriptions have been found.

BURE (THE), a river of Norfolk. It rises near Hindolveston, and runs about 42 miles, south-eastward, past Aylsham and Acle, to the Yare at Yarmouth. It receives the [illegible] and the Thurne in the parishes above and at Acle, and is navigable to Aylsham.

BURE, a tything in Christchurch parish, Hants, on the bay, 1 mile E of Christchurch. Real property, £4,327. Pop., 786.

BURES, a hamlet and a sub-district in the district of Sudbury. The hamlet is in the Essex part of Bures St Mary parish; lies on the river Stour, adjacent to the Sudbury railway, 5 miles SSE of Sudbury; and has a station on the railway, a post office‡ under Colchester, and a fair on Holy Thursday. Acres, 1,[illegible]0. Real property, £3,020. Pop., 623. Houses, 1[illegible]0. The sub-district contains, besides Bures St Mary parish, two parishes in Essex and four in Suffolk. Acres, 17,022. Pop., 5,612. Houses, 1,281.

BURES MOUNT, a parish in Lexden district, Essex, on the river Stour, adjacent to the Sudbury railway, near Bures station, 6 miles S by E of Sudbury. Post town, Bures, under Colchester. Acres, 1,[illegible]. Real property, £2,4[illegible]. Pop., 301. Houses, 5[illegible]. An ancient artificial mound here, about 80 feet high, and of unknown origin, has a base of nearly 1½ acre. The living is a rectory in the diocese of Rochester. Value, £400.* Patron, the Rev. P. [illegible].

BURES ST MARY, a parish in the district of Sudbury and counties of Essex and Suffolk, on the river Stour, and on the Sudbury railway, at Bures station, 5 miles SSE of Sudbury. It contains the hamlet of Bures, which has a post office under Colchester. Acres, [illegible],131. Real property, £9,201. Pop., 1,[illegible]. Houses, 369. The property is much subdivided. Edmund, king of East Anglia, is said to have been crowned here. The living is a vicarage in the diocese of Ely. Value, £27[illegible]. Patron, O. [illegible] Esq. The church has [illegible] and was restored in 18[illegible]5. There are a baptist chapel, a national school, and charities £10.

BURFA. See [illegible]STOPP.

BURFIELD. See BURGHFIELD.

BURFORD, a small town, a parish, and a sub-district in Witney district, Oxford. The town stands on the river Windrush, near Wychwood forest, 4½ miles SSW of [illegible] station, and 18 W by N of Oxford. It is a place of high antiquity. A synod was held at it in 70[illegible], in presence of the kings Ethelred and Berthwald, to correct [illegible] respecting Easter. A battle was fought in its vicinity, at Battle-edge, in 75[illegible], between Ethelbald, king of Mercia, and Cuthred of the West Saxons; [illegible] to him when Cuthred got his [illegible] the Mercian [illegible], [illegible] weight, was found, a number of years ago, [illegible] little below the surface, on the scene of action, and supposed to have been deposited there after the battle. Another was fought in the vicinity also, in 1649, between Fairfax and the royalists, when the latter were defeated, and some of them imprisoned in the church. The town contains many old houses, and is ill built, decayed, and dull. It has a post office‡ under [illegible], a banking office, two chief inns, a town hall, a parish church, Baptist, Quaker, and Wesleyan chapels, a free school, and alms-houses. The church is large, cruciform, and interesting; has a Norman central tower, other Norman portions, and some early English work; but is mainly perpendicular, of various dates; includes several large chapels, and a very rich south porch; and contains a number of curious monuments of Sir Lawrence Tanfield, Edmund Harman, and other persons. The charities, including schools and almshouses, amount annually to £319. A weekly market is held on Saturday; and fairs on the last Saturday of April, 5 July, 25 Sept., and the first Saturday of Dec. A considerable trade in saddlery, rugs, and other articles was formerly carried on; but has greatly declined. Heylin, the author of "Microcosmus," Needham, the author of "Mercurius Britannicus," and Beechey, the painter, were natives. The town gives the title of Earl to the Duke of St Albans. Pop., 1,435. Houses, 337.

The parish includes also the hamlets of Upton and Signett. Acres, 2,170. Real property, £[illegible],880. Pop., 1,649. Houses, 3[illegible]. A small priory, a cell to Keynsham abbey in Somerset, anciently stood near the town, and was given, at the dissolution, to Edmund Harman, and conveyed, by the Long Parliament, to the famous Speaker Lenthall. A mansion, in the Tudor style, and called Burford Priory, now occupies the site, and is the seat of Charles Greenaway, Esq. Quarries of fine building stone are in St Kitts, and supplied the materials for St Paul's cathedral. The living is a vicarage, united with the p. curacy of Fulbrook, in the diocese of Oxford. Value, £294.* Patron, the Bishop of Oxford.—The sub-district contains ten parishes, part of another, and an extra-parochial tract. Acres, 17,845. Pop., [illegible],819. Houses, 1,10[illegible].

BURFORD, a township and a parish in the district of Tenbury and county of Salop. The township lies on the river Teme and the Leominster canal, adjacent to the Tenbury railway, 1 mile W of Tenbury, and had formerly a market. Pop., 387. Houses, 88. The parish contains also the townships of Boraston, Greet, Nash, [illegible], Tilsop, Weston, Whitmore, and Whitton. Post-town, Tenbury. Acres, [illegible]. Real property, £10,[illegible]. Pop., 1,12[illegible]. Houses, 210. The property is subdivided. The living is a rectory of three portions in the diocese of Hereford; the first portion united with the p. curacies of Boraston and Nash, the second portion united with the p. curacy of Whitton, and all three in the patronage of Lord Northwick. Value of the first, £4[illegible];* of the second, £256;* of the third, £337.* The church was anciently collegiate, and has a brass of the 14th century. There are churches also in Boraston and Nash. Charities, £10.

BURFORD, Wilts. See BUTTFOLD.

BURG. See [illegible].

BURGAGE, a part of Southwell parish, Notts.

BURGATE, a parish in Hartismere district, Suffolk, 1½ mile NE of Mellis station, and 1¼ WNW of Eye. Post town, Mellis, under Scole. Acres, 2,076. Real property, £2,918. Pop., 359. Houses, 69. The property is divided among a few. The living is a rectory in the diocese of Norwich. Value, £560. Patron, the Bishop of Norwich. The church has a double canopied brass of 1409, and is in fair condition.

BURGATE (MIDDLE, NORTH, and SOUTH), three tithings in Fordingbridge parish, Hants, on the river Avon, from 1 to 2½ miles N of Fordingbridge. Real property, £1,9[illegible], £2,61[illegible], and £1,7[illegible]. Pop., 6[illegible], 12[illegible], and 609. Burgate House belongs to the family of Coven.

BURGEDIN, a township in Guilsfield parish, Montgomery, 2 miles N of Welshpool. Pop., 1[illegible]1.

[illegible] N[illegible] of South [illegible] [illegible] the S[illegible] [illegible] miles S[illegible] [illegible] [illegible] the town, and [illegible] post office. [illegible] [illegible] the early [illegible] [illegible] [illegible] [illegible] 7 [illegible]

BURGH [illegible] Burgh, [illegible] of [illegible] [illegible] a castle. [illegible] district, Suffolk, 3 [illegible] NW of Woodbridge [illegible] under Woodbridge. Acres, [illegible] £2,[illegible] Pop., 271. Houses, [illegible] The living is a [illegible] Norwich. Value, £247.* [illegible] Esq. The church is very good. Char[illegible]

BURGH-IN-THE-MARSH. See BURGH-IN-THE-MARSH.

BURGH SOLDENE. See [illegible]

BURGH ST. PETER. See BURGH ST. PETER, &c.

[illegible] See PEVENHAM.

[illegible] in [illegible] parish, Surrey, [illegible] New [illegible] 2 miles [illegible] A church was built here in 1850, [illegible] cost £967.

[illegible] See P[illegible]HAM.

BURGH-CUM-HARRINGTON, a parish in [illegible] 2 miles SSW of [illegible] 3 [illegible] and has a post office, of [illegible] Acres, 1,620. [illegible] Pop., 5[illegible] Houses, 124. The [illegible] The living is the [illegible] of Holverstone, in the [illegible] the hall of [illegible] The church [illegible] school, and charities, £17.

[illegible] a parish in [illegible] Cumberland. The town [illegible] on the Carlisle and Sil[illegible] 2 miles S of the mouth of the Eden to the [illegible] NW by W of Carlisle; and has a [illegible] of Burgh by Sands [illegible] [illegible] have been here some [illegible] [illegible] Roman wall [illegible] [illegible] in 1174 by William [illegible] in 1293, to the [illegible] but has disappeared. [illegible] Pop., 160. Houses, 106. The [illegible] townships of [illegible] Acres, 7,8[illegible] Pop., [illegible] The [illegible] mills, [illegible] [illegible] [illegible] [illegible] [illegible] [illegible] [illegible] the Sol[illegible] [illegible] Duke of Norf[illegible] [illegible] [illegible] [illegible] Houses, 17.

[illegible] Suffolk, a village and a parish in M[illegible] district, Suffolk. The village stands on the river W[illegible] [illegible] of the [illegible] 1¾ miles WSW of [illegible] and 4 SW by W of Yarmouth. It is ancient [illegible] and has a part of [illegible] Yarmouth. The parish comprises [illegible] [illegible] Real property, £ [illegible] Pop., [illegible] Houses, 7[illegible] The property is divided among a few. The manor belonged to the kings of East Anglia, and [illegible] given, in 630, by King Sigebert to the Irish monk [illegible] for the founding of a monastery. A Roman camp here, occupying fully [illegible] acres, and showing features of strong construction with fine red bricks, and has been identified by many antiquaries with the Roman Gar[illegible] The living is a rectory in the diocese of Norwich. Value, £400.* Patron, the Lord Chancellor. The church is ancient, was recently restored, has in each of the tower fragments of Roman bricks, and is thought to have been built with materials from the Roman [illegible] [illegible] a national school, and charities, £25.

BURGHCLERE, a village and a parish in Kingsclere district, Hants. The village stands on high ground, 4 miles S of Newbury r. station, and 6½ N of Whitchurch, and has a post office under Newbury. A Roman seat or was here, but has not left any traces. The parish includes also the tything of Earlston. Acres, 5,050. Real property, £5,950. Pop., 813. Houses, 16[illegible] The property is divided among a few. Two conspicuous chalk hills are here, Sidon Hill and Beacon hill, [illegible] and 900 feet high, and command extensive views. Sidon Hill is within the park of Highclere, the seat of the Earl of Carnarvon, and is covered with wood. Beacon Hill is close to the park, and has on its summit an ancient camp of irregular outline, with a very deep [illegible] These hills, and others in the vicinity, are supposed to have been the scenes of Border struggles among the early Britons, the Romanized Britons, and the Saxons. The living is a rectory, united with the p. curacy of Newtown, in the diocese of Winchester. Value, £820.* Patron, the Earl of Carnarvon. The church is a modern structure, in the early English style, and has a tower. A school has £20 from endowment, and other charities £25.

BURGHERSH. See BURWASH.

BURGHFIELD, or BURFIELD, a parish in Bradfield district, Berks; on the river Kennet, and on the Reading and Basingstoke railway, [illegible] miles N of [illegible] station, and [illegible] SW of Reading; and has a post office under Reading. Acres, 4,237. Real property, £[illegible]8. Pop., 1,150. Houses, 25[illegible] The property is much sub-divided. Part of the land is common. A bed of sand and coal-like shells, about a inch, under a freestone, is found at Hose hill. The living is a rectory in the diocese of Oxford. Value, £700.* Patron, the Earl of Shrewsbury. The church was rebuilt in 18[illegible] There are two Methodist chapels, a national school, and charities £2[illegible]

BURGHILL, a village, a parish, and a sub-district, in the district and county of Hereford. The village stands near the river Lug, [illegible] miles SW of M[illegible] station, and 3½ NW of Hereford; and has a post office under Hereford. The parish includes also the township of Tillington. Acres, 2,704. Real property, £7,118. Pop., 9[illegible]4. Houses, 1[illegible] The property is divided among a few. Burghill Court is the seat of [illegible] Esq. An ancient square encampment is in the parish, [illegible] to the kestr[illegible] The living is a [illegible] in the diocese of Hereford. Value, £[illegible] Patron, [illegible] [illegible] The church has a Norman [illegible] and [illegible] was recently restored, and contains a screen, a font of [illegible] and a monument of Sir [illegible] Milbourne, [illegible] A school has £[illegible] from endowment, and other charities, £12. The sub-district contains [illegible] parishes, mostly [illegible] and an extra-parochial tract. Acres, 9[illegible] Pop., [illegible]7[illegible]7. Houses, 1[illegible]

BURGH-IN-THE-MARSH, a small town, a parish, and [illegible] Spilsby district, Lincoln. The town [illegible] Burgh [illegible] SW [illegible] and [illegible] S of Spilsby, and [illegible] of [illegible] Burgh on the railway [illegible] [illegible] [illegible] market is held on Thursday, and fairs on the second Thursday of May and Aug., and on 25 Sept. A Roman station was here, and remains of a Roman camp still exist, on high ground, partly natural, partly artificial. Roman coins also have been found, and there are two tumuli, one of them very high, called Cold Hill. There were formerly two churches, but one of them was long ago demolished. The other, now the parish church, is later English, consists of nave, aisles, and chancel, has a fine embattled turretted western tower, the battlements adorned with quatrefoils, and contains a richly carved oaken pulpit and an octagonal font. There are chapels for Baptists and Methodists, a free school, with £60, and other charities, with £71. The parish comprises 4,233 acres. Real property, £10,071. Pop., 1,22[illegible]. Houses, 251. The living is a vicarage, united with the vicarage of Winthorpe, in the diocese of Lincoln. Value, £120.* Patron, the Bishop of Lincoln. The sub-district contains twelve parishes. Acres, 25,252. Pop., [illegible]. Houses, 1,024.

BURGHLEY HOUSE, the seat of the Marquis of Exeter, on the NE border of Northamptonshire, adjacent to the river Welland, and to the Syston and Peterborough railway, in the southern vicinity of Stamford. The mansion was founded in 1575 by Sir William Cecil; is a great hollow Tudor quadrangle; and contains a fine collection of pictures. The park is large, and was laid out by Brown.

BURGH (LITTLE). See BURGH PARVA.

BURGH MATTISHALL, or BURGH MATTISHALL, a parish in Mitford district, Norfolk, on an affluent of the river Wensum, 2¾ miles north of Thuxton r. station, and 5½ E by S of East Dereham. Post town, Mattishall, under Thetford. Acres, 604. Real property, £1,[illegible]28. Pop., 191. Houses, 58. The living is a rectory, annexed to the rectory of Hockering, in the diocese of Norwich. Charities, £19.

BURGH NEXT AYLSHAM, or BURGH ST. MARY, a parish in Aylsham district, Norfolk, on the river Bure, 2 miles SE of Aylsham, near the line of the projected railway from Norwich to Cromer, and 11½ N of Norwich. Post town, Aylsham, under Norwich. Acres, 789. Real property, £1,857. Pop., 227. Houses, 54. The property is divided between three. The living is a rectory in the diocese of Norwich. Value, not reported. Patron, J. H. Holly, Esq. The church is good.

BURGH PARVA, a hamlet in Melton Constable parish, Norfolk, 4½ miles SW of Holt. It was formerly a parish, and it ranks as a rectory, annexed to Melton Constable; but its church is in ruins.

BURGH ST. MARGARET AND ST. MARY, a parish in Flegg district, Norfolk, near the river Bure, 4½ miles NE of Acle, and 7¾ NW of Yarmouth r. station. It has a post office of the name of Burgh, under Norwich, and had formerly a market. Acres, 1,6[illegible]. Real property, £[illegible],110. Pop., 5[illegible]. Houses, 125. The property is much divided. The living is a double [illegible] in the diocese of Norwich. Value, £42. Patron, the Rev. W. Lucas. The church of St. Margaret is good; and that of St. Mary is in ruins. There are a dissenting chapel, a national school, and charities £7[illegible].

BURGH ST. MARY. See BURGH NEXT AYLSHAM.

BURGH ST. PETER, or WHEATACRE BURGH, a parish in Loddon district, Norfolk, on the river Waveney, and on the Lowestoft railway, near Mutford [illegible] miles ENE of Beccles. Post town, Mutford, under Lowestoft. Acres, 2,041. Real property, £[illegible]. Pop., 29[illegible]. Houses, 73. The property is much subdivided. The living is a rectory in the diocese of Norwich. Value, £52[illegible]. Patron, the Rev. W. Boycott. The church is good; and there is a Wesleyan chapel.

BURGH SOUTH, or SOUTHBURGH, a parish in Mitford district, Norfolk, on [illegible] miles NNW of Hingham, and [illegible] WSW of Hardingham r. station. Post town, Hingham, under Attleborough. Acres, 1,210. Real property, £2,[illegible]. Pop., 317. Houses, 62. The property is divided among a few. The living is a rectory in the diocese of Norwich. Value, £21[illegible]. Patron, E. Gurdon, Esq. The church is fair.

BURGH UPON BAIN, or BURGH-ON-BAIN, a parish in Louth district, Lincoln, on the river Bain, near the Wolds, 6¾ miles W of Louth r. station. It includes the hamlet of Girsby, and has a post office under Louth. Acres, 1,500. Real property, £2,[illegible]. Pop., [illegible]3. Houses, 32. The South Wold hounds meet here. The living is a vicarage in the diocese of Lincoln. Value, £1[illegible]. Patron, [illegible], Esq. The church is good.

BURGH UPON THE SANDS. See BURGH BY SANDS.

BURGH WALLIS, a township and a parish in Doncaster district, W. R. Yorkshire. The township lies on the Roman road to York, adjacent to the Dutch river, 1¾ mile SW of Askerne r. station, and 7 NNW of Doncaster; and it includes parts of the hamlets of Robin Hood's Well and Haywood. Pop., 220. Houses, 50. The parish includes also part of the township of Sutton; and its post town is Askerne, under Doncaster. Acres, 1,700. Real property, exclusive of the part of Sutton, £2,[illegible]. Pop., 237. Houses, 42. The property is divided among a few. Burgh Wallis Hall belonged formerly to the Anns, but belongs now to M. Tasburgh, Esq.; and the ancient mansion has given place to a modern one. The living is a rectory in the diocese of York. Value, £275.* Patron, M. Tasburgh, Esq. The church contains some old monuments, and a [illegible].

BURGH WALTER. See BURGH APTON.

BURGODUNUM. See ADEL.

BURHAM, a parish in Malling district, Kent, on the river Medway, adjacent to the Maidstone railway, near Snodland station, 4½ miles NNW of Maidstone. It has a post office under Rochester. Acres, 1,737. Real property, £3,[illegible]08, of which £[illegible]59 are in quarries. Pop., 77[illegible]. Houses, 137. The property is divided among a few. A quarry here, belonging to W. H. Bensted, Esq., forms a fine section of the lower chalk rocks, and is rich in fossils. Lime works here send large supplies to London; and there are extensive pottery and cement works. The living is a vicarage in the diocese of Rochester. Value, £1[illegible]. Patron, Mrs. Anne Cubitt and others. The church is partly early English. There are a Wesleyan chapel, a national school, and charities £2.

BURIAN (ST.). See BURYAN (ST.).

BURINGTON. See BURRINGTON.

BURITON, a tything and a parish in Petersfield district, Hants. The tything lies on the verge of the county, near the Guildford and New Portsmouth railway, 2 miles SSW of Petersfield; and has a post office under Petersfield. The parish includes also the tythings of Nursted and Weston. Acres, 6,305. Real property, £8,03[illegible]. Pop., 1,050. Houses, 1[illegible]. The property is subdivided. Mapledurham here belonged to Gibbon, the historian; was sold by him to Lord Stowell; and belongs now to J. Bonham Carter, Esq. Gray limestone is quarried. The living is a rectory, united with the vicarage of Petersfield, in the diocese of Winchester. Value, £1,1[illegible]. Patron, the Bishop of Winchester. The church is partly Norman, has an ivy-clad square tower, and contains an ancient screen, a modern altar-piece, and [illegible] monuments. There are a Primitive Methodist chapel, three alms-houses, and charities £50.

BURLAND, a township in Acton parish, Cheshire, on the Ellesmere canal, adjacent to the North Western railway, 3½ miles WNW by W of Nantwich. Acres, [illegible]. Real property, £3,122. Pop., 67[illegible]. Houses, 1[illegible].

BURLEIGH ARCHES, a hundred in the rape of Pevensey, Sussex, conterminate with [illegible] parish.

BURLEIGH HOUSE. See BURGHLEY HOUSE.

BURLESCOMBE, a parish in the district of Wellington, on the county of Devon, under [illegible], on the Roman Portway from Somerset to Exeter, and on the Great Western, near the Bristol and Exeter railway, 5 miles SW of Wellington. It has a station on the railway, and it includes the hamlets of Appledore, [illegible], [illegible] of Westleigh, the latter of which has a post office, of the name of Appledore, North Devon. Acres, 3,[illegible]. Real property, £[illegible], of which £700 are in quarries. Pop., [illegible]. Houses, 17[illegible]. The property is subdivided. The manor belongs to [illegible] Sandford, Esq. [illegible]

[illegible] is [illegible] at the time of Henry [illegible], by William de Clareville, conveyed in 1281, to Maud Countess of Gloucester, and changed [illegible] nunnery, passed, after the dissolution, through [illegible] Ireland, and belongs now to the family of [illegible]. Some small remains of it, including [illegible] towers, still [illegible] of superior [illegible], and great quantities of [illegible] sent off by canal [illegible] railway. The living is a vicarage in the diocese of Exeter. Value, £250.* Patron, Rev. T. C. [illegible]. The church chiefly of the time of Henry VII., was restored in 1873, and contains a beautiful [illegible] screen, and [illegible] of the Ashfords. An ancient cross [illegible] on the Ashford estate, and was [illegible] restored.

BURLESTONE, a parish in Dorchester district, Dorset; on the river [illegible], 4 miles NNW of Moreton station, and 7 NE of Dorchester. Post town, [illegible] under Dorchester. Acres, 3[illegible]. Real property, [illegible]. Pop., 4[illegible]. Houses, 7. The living is a rectory, [illegible] to the rectory of [illegible]stone, in the diocese of Salisbury.

BURLEY, a hamlet in [illegible] parish, Gloucester, near Minchinhampton.

BURLEY, a [illegible] and a chapelry in Ringwood district, Hants. The tything is in Ringwood parish, at the [illegible] Forest, 2 miles NW of Holmsley [illegible], and [illegible] S of Ringwood, and [illegible] under [illegible]. Real property, £1,600. Pop., 77. The chapelry includes the tything, and consists mainly [illegible] Burley Walk, and was constituted in 1840. Acres, 2,200. Pop., [illegible]. Houses, [illegible]. Burley House is the seat of [illegible], Esq. The living is a p. curacy in the diocese of Winchester. Value, £100.* Patron, the Bishop of Winchester. An [illegible] church here [illegible] the New Forest. The present church is [illegible] modern. [illegible]

BURLEY, a [illegible] in [illegible] parish, [illegible] 4 miles NNW of [illegible]. Pop., 130.

BURLEY, a township and chapelry in Otley parish, W. R. Yorkshire, on the Leeds and Ilkley railway, [illegible] W by S of Otley. It includes a village, which is built [illegible] about [illegible] of a mile long, and has a post office [illegible] Otley, and a [illegible] station. Acres, 1,6[illegible]. Real property, £5,[illegible]. Pop., 2,1[illegible]. Houses, 417. Burley Hall, Burley New Hall, and Burley Lodge are [illegible] residences, and the latter two were built in the [illegible] part of last century by Mr. [illegible]. Many of the inhabitants are employed in [illegible] mills. The living is a vicarage [illegible] in the diocese of Ripon. Value, £157.* Patron, [illegible] Esq. The church is modern, and has [illegible] chapels.

BURLEY, a village and a chapelry in Leeds parish, W. R. Yorkshire. The village stands near Headingley [illegible] station, 2 miles NNW of Leeds, and has a post office [illegible] Leeds. The chapelry was constituted in 1849. Pop., [illegible]. Houses, 71[illegible]. The living is a vicarage in the diocese of Ripon. Value, £250.* Patrons, Trustees. The church was built in 1837.

BURLEY-ON-THE-HILL, a parish in Oakham district, Rutland, [illegible] 2 miles [illegible] of Oakham [illegible]. Acres, [illegible]. Real property, £4,5[illegible]. Pop., 257. Houses, [illegible]. The manor [illegible] Burley on the Hill [illegible] of the [illegible] [illegible]

true, and [illegible] pictures. The living is a vicarage in the diocese of Peterborough. Value, £[illegible]. Patron, G. Finch, Esq. The church is [illegible] surrounded with trees. There is a free school.

BURLEYDAM, a chapelry in Acton parish, Cheshire, on the verge of the county, [illegible] miles SE of Wrenbury station, and 4½ ENE of Whitchurch. It has a post office under Whitchurch. The statistics are returned with Acton. The living is a p. curacy in the diocese of Chester. Value, £100.* Patron, [illegible].

BURLEY LODGE AND BURLEY LAWN. See BURLEY WALK.

BURLEY WALK WITH EASTERN CLOSES, a [illegible] in Ringwood district, Hants, in the New Forest, within Burley chapelry, contiguous to Ringwood parish. Acres, [illegible] extra-parochial part of Burley Walk, 7,170. Pop., 13. Houses, 1[illegible].

BURLEY WALK, a [illegible] in Ringwood district, Hants, in the New Forest; partly in Ringwood parish, and partly extra-parochial. Acres, 7,740. The extra-parochial part includes Burley Lodge, Burley Lawn, Burley New Lodge, [illegible] Cottage, and Old House. Pop., 62. Houses, 12.

BURLINGHAM ST. ANDREW, a parish in Blofield district, Norfolk, 2½ miles W by S of Acle, and [illegible] by [illegible] of Lingwood r. station. It has a post office, of the name of Burlingham, under Norwich. Acres, 7[illegible]. Real property, £2,01[illegible]. Pop., 1[illegible]. Houses, [illegible]. The property is divided among a few. Burlingham House is the seat of [illegible] Burroughes, Esq. The living is a rectory, united with the rectory of Burlingham St. Edmund, in the diocese of Norwich. Value, £[illegible]. Patron, H. Burroughes, Esq. The church has a painted rood-screen of the 15th century.

BURLINGHAM ST. EDMUND, a parish in Blofield district, Norfolk, contiguous to Burlingham St. Andrew. Post town, Burlingham, under Norwich. Acres, [illegible]. Real property, £[illegible]. Pop., 87. Houses, 1[illegible]. The property is divided among a few. The living is a rectory, annexed to the rectory of Burlingham St. Andrew, in the diocese of Norwich. [illegible] good.

BURLINGHAM ST. PETER, a parish in Blofield district, Norfolk, [illegible] W of Acle, and [illegible] of Lingwood r. station. Post town, Burlingham, under Norwich. Acres, [illegible]. Real property, £1,051. Pop., 80. Houses, 18. The property is [illegible]. The living is a rectory in the diocese of Norwich. Value, £140. Patron, H. N. Burroughes, Esq. The church [illegible] tower [illegible] good [illegible] monuments [illegible].

BURLINSCOMBE. See [illegible].

BURLINGTON. See [illegible].

BURLOW CASTLE. See [illegible], Sussex.

BURLTON, a township in Loppington parish, Salop, [illegible] miles SW by W of Wem. [illegible] Shrewsbury. Pop., 172.

BURMANTOFTS, a chapelry in Leeds parish, W. R. Yorkshire. It was constituted in 1851. [illegible] town is Leeds. Pop., [illegible]. Houses, 1,13[illegible]. [illegible] The living is a p. curacy. [illegible] Trustees. [illegible] £[illegible].

BURMARSH, a parish in Romney Marsh district, Kent, [illegible] SSW of Westenhanger [illegible] station, and [illegible] of Hythe. Post town, [illegible]. Acres, 1,7[illegible]. Real property, £[illegible]. Pop., [illegible]. Houses, [illegible]. The living is a [illegible] in the diocese of [illegible]. Value, £[illegible]. Patron, [illegible] good.

BURMINGTON, a parish in Shipston-on-Stour district, Warwick; on the river Stour [illegible] Shipston-on-Stour [illegible] station, and [illegible] Shipston-on-Stour. [illegible] Real property, £[illegible]. Pop., [illegible]. [illegible] in the diocese of Worcester. The church was recently rebuilt. There is a free school.

BURN, a township in Brayton parish, W. R. Yorkshire, on the Selby canal, adjacent to the river Aire, 3 miles SW of Selby. Acres, 2,672. Real property, £2,923. Pop., 326. Houses, 6[illegible].

BURN (The), a stream of Norfolk, running 6 miles north[ward] to the sea, 3 miles NNE of Burnham Westgate.

BURN or BRUN (The), a stream of Lancashire, running past Burnley to the river Calder.

BURNAGE, a township in Manchester parish, Lancashire, on the river Mersey, adjacent to the Manchester and Sheffield railway, 4 miles S of Manchester. Acres, 658. Real property, £3,7[illegible]. Pop., 621. Houses, 120.

BURNASTON, township in Etwall parish, Derby, adjacent to the Burton-on-Trent and Derby railway, 4½ miles SSW of Derby. Real property, £1,550. Pop., 185. Houses, [illegible].

BURNBY, a parish in Pocklington district, E. R. Yorkshire, on an affluent of the river Derwent, and on the York and Market Weighton railway, 2½ miles ESE of Pocklington. It has a station on the railway, and its post town is Hayton, under York. Acres, 1,667. Real property, £2,515. Pop., 120. Houses, 24. The property is divided among a few. The living is a rectory in the diocese of York. Value, £3[illegible]8.* Patron, Lord Londesborough. The church is fair.

BURNCROSS, a hamlet in Ecclesfield township and parish, W. R. Yorkshire, [illegible] miles N of Sheffield.

BURNESIDE, or BURNESHEAD, a chapelry in Kendal parish, Westmoreland, on the river Kent and the Windermere railway, 2 miles NNW of Kendal. It has a station on the railway, includes the townships of Strickland-Ketel, Strickland-Roger, and part of Skelsmergh, and its post town is Kendal. Rated property, £6,772. Pop., exclusive of the part of Skelsmergh, [illegible]05. Houses, 17[illegible]. The property is much subdivided. The manor belongs to the Earl of Lonsdale. Burneside Hall was formerly the seat of the Braithwaites, one of whom wrote "Drunken Barnaby's Journal," and is now the seat of the [illegible]. Cowmire Hall belonged formerly to the [illegible], and was fortified. There is a "holy well." Paper making is carried on. The living is a p. curacy in the diocese of Carlisle. Value, £120. Patrons, Trustees. The church was rebuilt in 1825.

BURNESS. See BURNESS.

BURNESTON, a township and a parish in Bedale district, N. R. Yorkshire. The township lies near the river Swale, [illegible] miles SE of Bedale, and 3 W of Sinderby station. Acres, [illegible]18[illegible]. Real property, £2,308. Pop., 200. Houses, 70. The parish contains also the townships of Gatenby, Theakston, Carthorpe, and Exelby-Leeming, and Newton, and its post town is Bedale. Acres, 7,411. Real property, £13,2[illegible]. Pop., 1,55[illegible]. Houses, 3[illegible]. The property is much subdivided. The living is a vicarage in the diocese of Ripon. Value, [illegible]. Patron, the Duke of Cleveland. The church was restored in 18[illegible], and has a splendid eastern memorial window to the late Duke of Cleveland. The p. curacy of Leeming is a separate living. There are a Wesleyan chapel and charities £2[illegible].

BURNETT, a parish in Keynsham district, Somerset, on the river Chew, adjacent to the Great Western railway, 2 miles SE of Keynsham. Post-town, Keynsham, under Bristol. Acres, 6[illegible]. Real property, £1,3[illegible]. Pop., [illegible]. Houses, [illegible]. The property is subdivided. The living is a rectory in the diocese of Bath and Wells. Value, £12[illegible]. Patron, the Rev. J. [illegible]. The church [illegible] of 1[illegible]7[illegible], and is good.

BURNGULLOW, a station on the Cornwall railway, in Cornwall, [illegible] miles SW of St. Austell.

BURN HALL, [illegible] county, 2[illegible] miles [illegible] of Dublin, the seat of [illegible], and the site of [illegible] chapel.

BURNHAM, a village, a parish, a sub-district, and a hundred, in [illegible]. The village [illegible] adjacent to the [illegible], near the river Thame, 2½ miles [illegible] of Maidenhead, and has a post office‡ under Maidenhead. It was formerly a market-town, and still has fairs on 25 Feb., 1 May, and 2 Oct. The parish includes the hamlets or liberties of Boveney, Lower, Upper Salt, [illegible], East Burnham, Cippenham, and Wood. Acres, 6,7[illegible]. Real property, £1[illegible],90[illegible]. Pop., 2,2[illegible]. Houses, [illegible]. The property is divided among a few. Burnham Grove is the seat of Sir W. [illegible], but An Augustinian abbey was founded about a mile from the village, in 1265, by Richard, King of the Romans, and given at the dissolution, to William [illegible], and some small remains of it still exist. A fragment of an ancient forest bears the name of Burnham Beeches, [illegible] of venerable beech trees, [illegible] and has been sketched by many artists. The living is a vicarage, united with the p. curacy of Boveney, in the diocese of Oxford. Value, £[illegible]. Patron, [illegible] College. The church is early and decorated English. The p. curacy of Dropmore is a separate benefice. There are an Independent chapel, three schools, and charities [illegible]. Bishop Allen, who died in 157[illegible], was a native, and the learned Jacob Bryant [illegible]. The sub-district contains five parishes, and the greater part of two others, and is in the district of Eton. Acres, 1[illegible],[illegible]0. Pop., [illegible]131. Houses, 1,1[illegible]6. The hundred contains thirteen parishes. Acres, [illegible]8,3[illegible]1. Pop., 2[illegible],[illegible]31. Houses, 4,247.

BURNHAM, a village and a parish in Maldon district, Essex. The village stands on the river Crouch, opposite Wallasea island, 2½ miles NNE of Southminster station, and 10 SE of Maldon. It has a post office‡ under Maldon, dates from old times, includes a good street, is a seaport and a coast guard station, and has two chapels, a custom house, a [illegible], and a fair. Fairs are held at it on 25 April and 24 Sept.; and oyster fishing, boat building, and [illegible] are carried on. The parish includes also the hamlet of [illegible]. Acres, 5,[illegible]. Real property, £11,[illegible], of which £2,072 are in fisheries. Pop., 1,870. Houses, [illegible]. The property is divided among a few. The [illegible] is marshy. The living is a vicarage in the diocese of Rochester. Value, £[illegible]58.* Patron, not reported. The church is good, and is so situated as to serve as a landmark. There is a [illegible] chapel.

BURNHAM, a hamlet in Thornton-Curtis parish, Lincoln, 3½ miles SE of [illegible] upon Humber. [illegible]

BURNHAM, a hamlet in Haxey parish, Lincoln, 2 miles S of Epworth. Pop., 16[illegible]. [illegible] post office under Bawtry.

BURNHAM, a village, a parish, and a sub-district in the district of Axbridge, Somerset. The village stands on the coast, at the mouth of the rivers Brue and Parret, at the terminus of a short branch railway, in connection with the central Somerset and the Bristol and Exeter railways, 2 miles NW of the Highbridge Junction and [illegible] SW by W of [illegible]bridge. It has a post office‡ under Bridgewater, and a [illegible], and is frequented as a watering place. The [illegible] is sand, but is liable, to the breadth of [illegible] miles [illegible]. A project was authorized in [illegible] for constructing a tidal harbour in connection with the [illegible] railway, with the view of [illegible] by steam vessels [illegible] the various ports on the [illegible] of [illegible] and of [illegible]. The [illegible] monthly [illegible]. Two mineral springs [illegible], and two lights for guiding vessels into the [illegible] 2[illegible] feet high, [illegible] the higher one [illegible], the lower [illegible]. The parish includes also the tythings of Highbridge, [illegible], the [illegible] of [illegible] and [illegible], and part of the [illegible]. Acres, [illegible], of which 130 are water. Real property, £1[illegible],57[illegible]. Pop., 2,2[illegible]2. Houses, 4[illegible]. The property is much subdivided. The living is a vicarage in the diocese of Bath and Wells. Value, £[illegible]. Patron, the Dean and Chapter of Wells. The church is [illegible], [illegible] feet in length, with a lofty tower [illegible] of [illegible] by [illegible]. The [illegible] of Highbridge is a separate [illegible]. [illegible] school and charities [illegible].

s e s se n p h A s, Pop. 7,407 Houses 1,21

BURNHAM, a district of Docking, Norfolk, comprises twelve parishes and an extra parochial ... and Burnham Westgate Acres 35,180 ... 1470 See BURNHAM WESTGATE.

BURNHAM OVERY-DALE, a parish in Docking district, Norfolk ... coast 2¼ miles NW by N of Burnham ... station, and ... Wells ... Lynn Acres 1,041 ... Pop., 8 Houses 2 The property ... Much of the surface is naturally ... been partially drained ... and ... The living is a ... Norwich Value, £257 ... The church is Norman ... round tower ... font ... of the Saxon monarchs,

BURNHAM [illegible] ... 4½ miles N of Maidenhead Post ...

BURNHAM FLATS, a series of sands off the NW coast of Norfolk ... Docking ... Holdenby ... Woolpack, the Middle, and ... extends along the coast and ... distance several, flanks the east side of ... and is partly dry at low water, but ...

BURNHAM NORTON, a parish in Docking district, Norfolk ... N of Burnham Westgate station ... W of Wells Post town, Burnham under Lynn ... of which 670 are water Real property ... Pop. 17 Houses 42 A Carmelite priory ... 1241 ... Ralph de Hemenhall ... the house ... Bubb ... the last ... was ... divided ... to ... of Burnham Westgate ... partly to that of ... Norwich

BURNHAM OVERY, a parish in Docking district, Norfolk 1 mile NE of Burnham Westgate station, ... W of Wells Post town, Burnham under Lynn ... of which 210 are water Real property ... Pop., 670 Houses 147 The property is ... The tide ... goes here to ... Burnham harbour ... limestone is worked, and ... of Burnham Sutton in the diocese of Norwich ... and ... small ...

BURNHAM SUTTON CUM BURNHAM ULPH, a parish in Docking district, Norfolk, ... mile S of Burnham Westgate ... 6 W by S of Wells, ... Burnham under Lynn Acres 1,652 Real property, £2,0 ... Pop., 3 ... Houses ... The present parish con... parishes The living of Burnham Sutton is a rectory united with the vicarage of ... of the ... in the diocese of Norwich ... Caius College ... The church ... Burnham Ulph ... of Burnham ...

BURNHAM THORPE, a parish in Docking district, Norfolk ... Burnham Westgate station ... S of Wells ... Its post-town ... under Lynn Acres ... Real property ... Pop. 7 Houses 8 The property is di... The manor ... Cholmondeley ... the diocese of Norwich Value, £47 ... The ... Nelson ... father of Nelson ... Nelson ... Burnham ...

... took from this place the title of ... an Independent chapel and a free school, and ... has £44 from endowment

BURNHAM ULPH. See BURNHAM SUTTON.

BURNHAM WESTGATE, a village and a parish in Docking district ... The village stands ... on the ... and on the ... and Wells railway, 8¼ miles NW of Fakenham ... of the name of Burnham, and ... Lynn, and ... tion was formerly ... to ... and all the ... on ... Acres The parish comprises 3,017 acres Real property £6,21 ... Pop., 1,1 ... Houses, 255 The property is divided among a few Holkham ... is a seat of the Earl of ... There are two iron foundries and an agricultural implement manufactory The living is a rectory united with those of the rectories of Burnham Norton and ... Ulph, in the diocese of Norwich Value, £705 * Patron, Christ's College, Cambridge The church is a neat building of flint and freestone with a square tower There are an Independent chapel, a Primitive Methodist ... National schools and charities £ ...

BURN HILL, a station on the Weardale Extension ... Durham 10 miles NW of Bishop Auckland

BURNHOPE (THE), a head stream of the river Wear on the western border of Durham, joining the main stream 4 miles W of Wolsingham

BURNING CLIFF, a phenomenon on the coast of Dorset ... miles ENE of Weymouth It ... clouds of hot vapour between 182 and 18 7, but its volcanic character was due, not to any deep ... action, but to the ... of ... iron pyrites and bituminous shale

BURNINGHAM. See BRININGHAM

BURNISTON, a township in ... parish ... N R Yorkshire, on the coast 3¾ miles NNW of Scarborough Acres 1,573, of which 123 are ... Real property, £2,5 ... Pop. 30 ... Houses, 80

BURNLEY, a town, a township, four chapelries, a sub-district, a district in Lancashire The town stands on the river Brun ... above its influx ... West Calder 22 miles N ... The Leeds and Liverpool canal ... adjacent ... railways ... directions, toward Skipton ... and Blackburn. A Roman station is supposed to have been here, ... Roman road passed through from Lancaster to Slack ... An adjacent ... called Saxifield, is traditionally believed to have been the scene of a battle in the time of the heptarchy The town itself is almost wholly modern ... undergone vast increase since the latter part of last century and owes its character to the ... manufactures It is ... a fair appearance The town hall ... 1808 The exchange ... St Peter's church is an ancient structure ... altered ... St James' church ... of 1835 in the lancet style St Paul's church ... St Andrew's church ... style, and was ... 1848 ... pointed ... at a cost of ... There are ... Independent chapels ... two ... a Roman Catholic ... cost of £15,000 The grammar school was founded in the time of Edward VI ... free ... Wood ... There are ... national ... Mechanics' institution ... and ... Markets are held ... March ... 10 ... 11 ... Wednesday ... cotton ... The ... coal and ... coarse ... Hall ... Fridays ...

works, rope-walks, tan-yards, and breweries. Much trade is carried on likewise from neighbouring collieries and freestone quarries. Towneley Hall, the seat of the Towneley family, where the late Charles Towneley collected the marbles which were sold to [illegible] the British Museum; also Ormerod Hall, Gawthorpe, [illegible] Shuttleworth Hall, [illegible] in the vicinity. The town was enfranchised by the reform act of 1867, and sends one member to parliament. Pop. in 1851, 20,82[illegible]; in 1861, 28,700. Houses, [illegible].

The township is of less extent than the town, which extends into the township of Habergham Eaves. Acres, 1,8[illegible]. Real property, £71,779, of which £10,13[illegible] are in mines. Pop., 19,9[illegible]. Houses, 3,51[illegible]. The livings are St Peter a rectory, St James and St Paul vicarages, and St Andrew a p. curacy, in the diocese of Manchester; and they are jointly conterminate with the township, or exclusive of Habergham. Value of St Peter, £1,100;* of St James and St Paul each £15[illegible]; of St A, not reported. Patron of St Peter, [illegible] Esq.; of St James and St Paul, alternately the Crown and the Bishop; of St A, the Bishop.—The sub-district contains the townships of Burnley, Habergham Eaves, Ightenhill Park, Dunnockshaw, Cliviger, Worsthorne with Hurstwood, Briercliffe with Extwistle, and [illegible] by Haloves, Filley Close, and New Laund Booth. Acres, 21,148. Pop., 42,702. Houses, 7,[illegible]5.—The district lies entirely within the parish of Whalley, and comprehends, in addition to Burnley sub-district, the sub-district of Padiham, containing the townships of Padiham, Hunscoat, Hapton, Altham, Read, Simonstone, Heyhouses, and Higham with West Close Booth; the sub-district of Colne, containing the townships of Colne, [illegible], Foulridge, [illegible]den, and Little and Great Marsden; and the sub-district of Pendle, containing the townships of Wheatley Carr, Old Laund Booth, [illegible] Booth, Goldshaw Booth, and Barley with Wheatley [illegible]. Acres, 7[illegible],126. Poor rates in 1866, £22,[illegible]. Pop. in 1861, 7[illegible]. Houses, 14,5[illegible]0. Marriages in 186[illegible], 7[illegible]6; births, 2,[illegible]93,—of which 2[illegible] were illegitimate; deaths, 2,1[illegible],—of which 1,037 were at ages under 5 years, and 19 at ages above 85 years. Marriages in the ten years 1851-60, 6,073; births, 25,629; deaths, 16,4[illegible]. The places of worship in 1851 were 23 of the Church of England, with 14,446 sittings; 6 of Independents, with 2,364 s.; 10 of Baptists, with 2,852 s.; 1 of Quakers, with 29[illegible] s.; 1 of [illegible], with 201 s.; 2[illegible] of Wesleyan Methodists, with 7,925 s.; 11 of Primitive Methodists, with 2,09[illegible] s.; 6 of the Wesleyan Association, with 1,17[illegible] s.; 1 of the New Church, with 7[illegible] s.; 3 of [illegible], with 1,080 s.; [illegible] undefined, with 400 s.; and [illegible] of Roman Catholics, with 5[illegible] s. The schools were 42 public day schools, with [illegible]809 scholars; 39 private day schools, with 1,26[illegible] s.; [illegible] Sunday schools, with 16,[illegible] s.; and 20 evening schools for adults, with [illegible] s. The workhouse is in Padiham.

BURNMOOR, a chapelry in Penshaw parish, Durham. Post town, Fence houses. Pop., 1,1[illegible]. Living, a p. curacy. Value, £[illegible]. The church was built in 1[illegible].

BURNMOOR TARN, a mountain lake [illegible] Cumberland, [illegible] 9 miles NE of Ravenglass.

BURNOPFIELD AND BYERMOOR, a township in Lanchester parish, Durham, on the river Derwent, [illegible] miles [illegible] of Durham. Acres, 2,047. Pop., 1[illegible]. Houses, [illegible]. Here is a Wesleyan chapel.

BURNOPFIELD, a hamlet, 7[illegible] miles from Gateshead, in Durham, with a post office under Gateshead.

BURNSALL, a township and a parish in [illegible] district, W. R. Yorkshire. The township bears the name of Burnsall with Thorpe sub Montem, lies on the river Wharfe, 10 miles W by S of Pateley Bridge, and [illegible] NE of Skipton [illegible] and is a [illegible] ton[illegible] [illegible] Skipton [illegible]. Real property, £1,4[illegible]. Pop., [illegible]30. Houses, [illegible]. The parish includes also the townships of Conistone with Kilnsey, Hetton with Bordley, Appletreewick, Thorpe, Rylstone, and Cracoe; the first of which [illegible] has a post office under Skipton. Acres, 31,[illegible]. Real property, £[illegible]. Pop., 1,[illegible]7[illegible]. Houses, 2[illegible]. The property is subdivided. A number of the inhabitants are employed in cotton and woollen manufactures. The living is a rectory of two portions, united with the p. curacies of Rylstone and Coniston, in the diocese of Ripon. Value of the first portion, £1[illegible]; of the second, £270. Patron of the first portion, the [illegible] Graham; of the second, Earl Craven. The church was rebuilt in 18[illegible]. The chapels of Rylstone and Coniston are good; and a chapel at Skyreholme was built in 18[illegible]7. There is an endowed grammar school, with £42 a year.

BURNSIDE. See B[illegible]NSIDE.

BURNT ASH and BURNT ASH GREEN, two localities in the [illegible] of Kent, about 1[illegible] and 2 miles SSE of Lewisham. Burnt Ash Green has a post office under Lewisham, London S.E.

BURNT BRADFIELD. See BRADFIELD COMBUST.

BURNT FEN, an extra-parochial tract, now [illegible], on the mutual border of Cambridge and Suffolk, between the rivers Ouse and Lark, between Mildenhall and Littleport.

BURNT MILL, a station on the Eastern Counties railway, on the western verge of Essex, adjacent to the river Stort, 2[illegible] miles E by N of Roydon.

BURNT MILL, a locality on Icknield street, in Herts, 1 mile NE of Hitchin. It has remains of an ancient station.

BURNT WALLS, the supposed site of the ancient Benaventa, in Northamptonshire, under Borough hill, ½ a mile S of Daventry. It comprises about 6 acres, and has yielded fragments of ancient buildings and other relics.

BURNTWOOD, a hamlet and a township chapelry, in St Michael Lichfield parish, Stafford. The hamlet lies 2 miles NNW of Hammerwich station, and [illegible] W of Lichfield, and has a post office under Lichfield. The chapelry includes also the hamlets of [illegible] and [illegible], and was constituted in 1845. Rated property, £8,7[illegible]. Pop., 1,631. Houses, [illegible]. The property is divided among a few. New coal mines were recently opened. The living is a vicarage in the diocese of Lichfield. Value, £20[illegible]. Patron, the Vicar of St Mary's. The church is good.

BURNTWOOD LANE. See B[illegible].

BURNT YATES, a hamlet in Clint township, Ripley parish, W. R. Yorkshire, 1 mile [illegible] of Ripley.

BURNWOOD, a [illegible] of Walton on Thames parish, Surrey.

BURNWORTHY, a division of Church Stanton parish, Devon.

BURPHAM, a parish in Worthing district, Sussex, on the river Arun, [illegible] miles NE by E of Arundel station, and 4 NNW of Angmering. Post town, Arundel. Acres, 2,722. Real property, £2,[illegible]. Pop., 2[illegible]. Houses, [illegible]2. The property is divided among a few. The living is a vicarage in the diocese of Chichester. Value, £[illegible]. Patrons, the Dean and Chapter of Chichester. The church is [illegible] Norman. There is a national school.

BURPH[illegible], a [illegible] of the Axe, in Devon, [illegible] miles W [illegible]. It has an area of about 10 acres, and is [illegible] at low water [illegible], and [illegible] for the [illegible] fishery.

BURRADON. See [illegible].

BURRALS, a township in Appleby St Lawrence parish, Westmoreland, on a branch of the river Eden, 1[illegible] mile SW of Appleby. Acres, 6[illegible]. Pop., [illegible]. Houses, 1[illegible].

BURRILL WITH COWLING, a township in Bedale parish, N. R. Yorkshire, [illegible] mile SW of Bedale. It has a post office [illegible] of Burrill, under Bedale. Acres, [illegible]. Real property, £1,1[illegible]. Pop., 1[illegible]. Houses, 2[illegible]. [illegible] of Leeds.

BURRINGHAM, a township in Bottesford parish, Lincoln, on the river Trent, [illegible] miles NE of [illegible]. It has a post office under [illegible]. Acres, [illegible],120. Real property, £[illegible]. Pop., [illegible]52. Houses, 1[illegible]. It ranked formerly as a chapelry, and in the vicinity of Bottesford, and it has [illegible] church, and two Methodist chapels. [illegible] is carried on.

BURRINGTON, a parish in South Molton district,

Devon, on the rivers M[illegible] and Taw, [illegible] miles WNW of [illegible] station, and [illegible] NW of Chumleigh. Post town, Chumleigh, North Devon. Acres, 5,3[illegible]0. Real property, £4[illegible]. Pop., [illegible]. Houses, 188. The property is subdivided. [illegible] and belongs now to the Earl of Portsmouth. [illegible] belonged [illegible] to the [illegible] and belongs now to the [illegible]. The surface of the parish is diversified, and shows some romantic scenery. The living is a [illegible] in the diocese of Exeter. Value, £276.* Patron, W. [illegible]. The church is an edifice of different dates, from about 1150 to 1500, consists of nave, [illegible] and south [illegible], with an embattled tower, and has a hand[illegible] screen. There are chapels for Plymouth Brethren and [illegible] Christians.

[illegible]INGTON, a parish in the district of Ludlow and county of Hereford, on the river Teme, 1¾ mile[s] [illegible] of Woofferton [illegible] station, and 5 WSW of Ludlow. Post town, Leintwardine, Herefordshire. Acres, 2,55[illegible]. Real property, with Aston and Downton, £5,7[illegible]. Pop., [illegible]. Houses, 42. The property is divided among a few. The living is a vicarage in the diocese of Hereford. Value, £1[illegible]. [illegible] the Lord Chancellor. The church was [illegible] in 18[illegible] to be very bad.

PUTTINGTON, a village and a parish in Axbridge district, Somerset. The village stands in a romantic [illegible], at the northern [illegible] of the highest part of the Mendip hills, [illegible] miles [illegible] of [illegible], and 5½ SE of [illegible] station, and has a post office, of the name of [illegible], Somerset. The parish comprises 2,009 acres. Real property, £2,4[illegible]. Pop., [illegible]. Houses, 1[illegible]. The property is [illegible] among a few. [illegible] from the village up the Mendips, [illegible] of mountain limestone [illegible] of this about [illegible] discovered in 17[illegible] [illegible] bones, supposed to have been [illegible] and [illegible] bones of horses, sheep, and other animals, supposed to have taken refuge in it, after it [illegible] to be a place of [illegible]. An earthwork, called [illegible], occurs on a hill further up, and is thought to have been a scene of Druidical rites. The living is a vicarage in the diocese of Bath and Wells. Value, £1[illegible].* [illegible]. The church [illegible] in 1800. There are a [illegible] school and charities £1[illegible].

[illegible]. See [illegible].

[illegible]. See [illegible].

[illegible], or [illegible] HILL, a parish in [illegible] district, [illegible], on the [illegible], [illegible] miles S of Melton Mowbray, [illegible], of the name of [illegible]. Acres, 1,0[illegible]. Real property, £2,7[illegible]. Pop., 1[illegible]. Houses, 28. The property is subdivided. [illegible] Hill [illegible] commands a fine view. The living is a [illegible] in the diocese of Peterborough. Value, £[illegible].* [illegible]. The church has [illegible] and the [illegible].

[illegible], a parish in Newport [illegible] [illegible] ESE of [illegible] station [illegible]. Real property, £2,[illegible]. Pop., [illegible]. Houses, [illegible]. The property is [illegible]. The living is a [illegible]. The church is [illegible].

[illegible]

[illegible] ESE of Derby. It has a station on the railway and carries on a [illegible] of hosiery.

BURROW BRIDGE, a chapelry in Stoke St. Gregory, Bridgewater, Lyng, Middlezoy, North Petherton, Othery, and Weston Zoyland parishes, Somerset, on the river Parret, 2 miles NW of South Petherton, and [illegible] of Langport r. station. [illegible] town, South Petherton, under Ilminster. Pop., [illegible]. Houses, 144. The chapelry was constituted in 1840. The living is a p. curacy in the diocese of Bath and Wells. Value, £100.* [illegible] the bishop of Bath and Wells. The church is good.

BURROWDEN. See BORROWDEN.

BURROW WITH BURROW, a township in [illegible] parish, Lancashire, on the river Lune, 2 miles S of Kirkby Lonsdale. Acres, 2,290. Real property, £2,7[illegible]. Pop., 225. Houses, [illegible]. The Roman station [illegible] tonicum is thought to have been here; Roman pavements, altars, [illegible] urns, and coins have been found, and [illegible] is on the road. Burrow Hall is the seat of [illegible] Farrs.

BURROWCATE. See PENRITH.

BURROWS (NORTHAM). See NORTHAM.

BURRY PORT. See PEMBREY.

BURRY RIVER, the estuary of the [illegible] and [illegible] rivers, on the east side of Carmarthen [illegible] [illegible] Carmarthen [illegible] down and [illegible] 1½ miles [illegible] over the [illegible] or spring tides, is 6 [illegible] and the rise of the tide [illegible] is about 1[illegible], and in springs [illegible]. The chief channel [illegible] well buoyed. [illegible], on the north side, [illegible] with [illegible] of 200 tons, is at the [illegible] [illegible].

BURSCOUGH, a township-chapelry in Ormskirk parish, Lancashire, on the Leeds and Liverpool canal, and on the Southport and Ormskirk railway, [illegible] miles NNE of Ormskirk. It includes Burscough Bridge village, and has two stations, of the names of [illegible] and Burscough Bridge, on the railway, and a post office, of the name of Burscough Bridge, under Ormskirk. Acres, 4,959. Real property, £12,1[illegible]. Pop., 2,4[illegible]. Houses, 178. Many of the inhabitants are employed in the cotton manufacture. A priory was founded here, in the time of Richard I., by [illegible] Fitz Henry, lord of Lathom, and was the burial-place of the Stanleys, previous to their adoption of Ormskirk; and some remains of the priory still exist. [illegible] bears the name of Burscough Bridge, and was constituted in 1847. The living is a vicarage in the diocese of Chester. Value, £[illegible].* Patron, the Vicar of Ormskirk. The church was built at a cost of £3,2[illegible]. There are a Wesleyan chapel of 1[illegible], and a national school.

BURSLEDON, a village and a parish in South Stoneham district, Hants. The village stands on the Hamble creek, 4½ miles SSW of Botley, and [illegible] ESE of Southampton, and has a post office, [illegible] [illegible] [illegible] [illegible]. The parish [illegible]. Real property, £[illegible]. Pop., 65[illegible]. Houses, 11[illegible]. The property is [illegible] few. The living is a [illegible] in the diocese of Winchester. Value, £10[illegible].* [illegible] of Winchester. [illegible] at the [illegible].

BURSLEM, a town, a township, a parish, and a [illegible] [illegible] of Wolstanton [illegible] [illegible], Stafford. The town [illegible] [illegible] Stafford, [illegible] NNE [illegible]. It is [illegible] [illegible] town [illegible] and hamlets of England in the pro... nents in pottery. It was the birthplace of Wedgwood and the scene of his many achievements till his removal to Etruria, and it has been called, both on account of its history and on account of its occupying a central spot in the great seat of the fine pottery trade, the "Mother of the Potteries". It is irregularly, though substantially built; it consists of streets and ... so confusedly aligned as to be perplexing to strangers; it has grown into junction with Longport, so as to be practically one place with that town, and it displays everywhere the marks and grotesque features of its staple manufacture. The town hall, built in 1857, is a ... object. The structure is an oblong, of 100 feet by 60, in the Italian style, with pilastered Corinthian arcade, large end portico, and surmounting belfry, consists of three stories, and contains municipal offices, news room, lecture rooms, and a spacious main hall. The Wedgwood Memorial Institute, opened in 1869, near the town hall, and near the place where Wedgwood's manufactory stood, comprehends a school of art, a museum, and a free library, and presents an ornamental façade decorated with terra cotta mouldings, tile mosaics, Della Robbia panels and other products of the ceramic art. St John's church is a brick edifice, with a massive stone Norman tower. St Paul's church, in Longport, is a handsome stone structure of 1828, built with aid of £8,000 from the church commissioners. Christ church, in Cobridge, is an edifice of brick with stone pinnacles, built in 1843. Sneyd church, in Sneyd hamlet, is a fine stone structure of 1852. There are chapels for Independents, Baptists, Wesleyan Methodists, and other dissenters, and there is a school with £27 from endowment. About forty pottery establishments are in the town and its neighbourhood, producing every variety of porcelain and earthenware; and these, together with glass-works, colour mills, smelting furnaces, and various works connected with the potteries and the mines, employ nearly all the inhabitants. The town has a post office under Stoke upon Trent, a railway station with telegraph, two banking offices, and four chief inns, and is a seat of sessions and a polling place. Markets are held on Monday and Saturday; and fairs on the Saturday before Shrove Tuesday, the Saturday on or after 24 June, the Saturday before 11 October... and 26 Dec.

The township includes Longport and Dale Hall. Real property, £51,264, of which £1,380 are in mines. Pop., 17,821. Houses, 3,510.—The parish includes also the hamlet of Sneyd, the rule of Rushton Grange, and the lordship of Abbey Hulton. Acres, 2,940. Real property, £65,240, of which £8,226 are in mines. Pop. in 1841, 16,091; in 1861, 22,327. Houses, 4,390. The property is much subdivided. Potters' clay forms a bed from 2 to 10 feet thick, in clay lies below to considerable depth, and coal lies below the fire clay. The living is a rectory in the diocese of Lichfield. Value, £525.* Patron, J. Morris, Esq. St Paul, Christchurch, and Sneyd are separate charges with p... curacies. Value of St Paul, £300;* of Sneyd, £150;* of Christchurch, £142.* Patron of St P... and Christchurch, the Rector of Burslem; of Sneyd, alternately the Crown and the bishop.—The sub-district is conterminate with the parish.

BURSTALL, a parish in Samford district, Suffolk, on an affluent of the river Orwell, 2¾ miles WSW of Bramford r. station, and 4¾ W of Ipswich. Post town, Bramford, under Ipswich. Acres, 766. Real property, £1,111. Pop., 22... Houses, 49. The living is a p. curacy, annexed to the vicarage of Bramford, in the diocese of Norwich.

BURSTALL, Yorkshire. See BIRSTALL.

BURSTALL GARTH, a hamlet in Skeffling parish, E. R. Yorkshire, 3 miles SE of Patrington. A cell to a Benedictine abbey, near Albemarle in Normandy, was founded here in the 12th century, by Stephen, Earl of Albemarle; passed to the monastery of Kirkstall; and was eventually swept away by the sea.

BURSTEAD (GREAT), a parish and a sub-district, in Billericay district, Essex. The parish lies around, and contains, the town of Billericay, which is near the Eastern Counties railway, and has a head post office. Acres, 3,562. Real property, £8,131. Pop., 2,093. Houses, 4... The property is much subdivided. The living is a vicarage in the diocese of Rochester. Value, £165.* Patron, the ... Francis ... The vicarage of Billericay is a separate ... charge. A school has £60 from endowment, and ... charities £44.—The sub-district ... comprises the greater part of another ... Acres, 20,... 7 Pop., ...803. Houses, 900.

BURSTEAD (LITTLE), a parish in Billericay district, Essex, 2¼ miles SSW of Billericay, and 4½ ... of Brentwood r. station. Post town, Billericay. Acres, 1,823. Real property, £1,697. Pop., 1... Houses, 37. The property is much subdivided. The living is a rectory in the diocese of Rochester. Value, £... Patron, the Bishop of Rochester. The church is good, and there are charities £44.

BURSTOCK, a parish in Beaminster district, Dorset, on the verge of the county, 4¼ miles WNW of Beaminster, and 5 SSW of Crewkerne r. station. Post town, Broadwindsor, under Bridport. Acres, 913. Real property, £1,611. Pop., 220. Houses, 50. The living is a vicarage in the diocese of Salisbury. Value, £150. Patron, Rev. T. Jones. Charities, £14.

BURSTON, a parish in Depwade district, Norfolk, on an affluent of the river Waveney, adjacent to the Eastern Counties railway, 2½ miles NNE of Diss. It has a station on the railway, and its post town is Diss. Acres, 1,449. Real property, £2,731. Pop., 419. Houses, 87. The property is much subdivided. The living is a rectory in the diocese of Norwich. Value, £... Patron, the Lord Chancellor. The church is a diminutive structure in good condition, with round tower and octagonal turret. There is a Wesleyan chapel.

BURSTON, a township in Stone parish, Stafford, on the river Trent, 3 miles SE of Stone. It forms a curacy with Aston.

BURSTON, an old seat in Hunton parish, Kent, 4½ miles SW of Maidstone. It was the seat of the ... but is now a farm house, and it is ... commanding a fine view over the Weald.

BURSTON, Erpingham, Norfolk. See ...

BURSTONE, a hamlet in Zeal Monachorum parish, Devon.

BURSTOW, a parish in Reigate district, Surrey, ... miles SE of Horley r. station, and 7½ S by E of ... It has a post office under Crawley. Acres, 4,717. Real property, £4,265. Pop., 927. Houses, 1... The property is subdivided. Burstow Lodge, formerly called Coultings, and now a farm house, was the seat of the Burstows, and passed to the Bishop... The living is a rectory in the diocese of Winchester. Value, £... Patron, the Lord Chancellor. The church is early English and good. There is a Baptist chapel. Flamsteed, the first astronomer royal, was rector.

BURSTWICK, a township and a parish in Patrington district, E. R. Yorkshire. The township is joined with Skeckling, includes part of Ridgmont, lies on the ... and Holderness railway, near the Humber, 7¼ miles ESE of Hull, and has a station on the railway, and a post office under Hull. Real property, £5,... Pop., 1... Houses, 96. The parish contains also the ... Ryhill and the hamlet of Camerton. Acres, 5,... Real property, £8,872. Pop., 725. Houses, 149. The property is subdivided. The living is a vicarage in the diocese of York. Value, £28... Patron, Sir T. A. C. Constable. The church is later English, and was ... in 185...

BURTERSETT, a hamlet in Hawes township, Aysgarth parish, N. R. Yorkshire, 1 mile E of Hawes.

BURTHOLME, a township in Lanercost parish, Cumberland, on the river Irthing, 3 miles N... of Brampton. Real property, £1,962. Pop., 2... Houses, ...

BURTHOPE. See EASTHOPE ...

BURTLE, a chapelry in Moorlinch parish, Somerset, 3½ miles SSW of Edington Road r. station, and 5½ NE of Bridgewater. Post town, Chilton, under Bridgewater. Pop., 218. Houses, 47. It was constituted in 18... The living is a p. curacy in the diocese of Bath and [illegible] Patron [illegible] The church is [illegible]

BURTON [illegible] in [illegible] West [illegible] parish, Lincoln, 2 [illegible] 278

BURTON, [illegible] a [illegible] burgh town [illegible] where there was [illegible]

BURTON, [illegible] parish in Wirral district, Cheshire. The [illegible] the estuary of the Dee, [illegible] station, and 8 NW by W of Chester, [illegible] formerly a market. Acres 2,1[illegible], of which 20[illegible] water. Real property, £2,178. Pop., [illegible]5. [illegible] The parish includes also the town[ship] of [illegible] post town is Neston, un[der] Chester. Acres, 3,[illegible] Real property, £[illegible]225. Pop., 425. H[ouses], [illegible]7. The property is divided be[tween] [illegible] Burton Hall is the seat of W. W. Con[greve], [illegible] works [illegible] for be[illegible] the Dee. An hospital was founded at [illegible] given to the church of St. John [illegible] The living is a vicarage in the diocese of Chester. Value, £[illegible]4. Patron, W. W. Con[greve], Esq. [illegible] The [illegible] Roman [illegible] and an endowed school, the latter with £[illegible] a year. [illegible] Wilson was a native.

BURTON, a township in Gresford parish, Denbigh, on [illegible] of the county, [illegible] miles NNE of Wrexham. Acres, 2,[illegible] Pop., 579. Houses, 103.

BURTON, a hamlet in Charminster parish, Dorset, 1 [illegible] Dorchester.

BURTON, a [illegible] in [illegible] parish, Dorset, 3[illegible] miles ENE of [illegible]. Marble is quarried.

BURTON, [illegible] Wootton [illegible] parish [illegible]

BURTON, a [illegible] in Christchurch parish, Hants; [illegible] Real property, £2,883. Pop., [illegible]52. [illegible] a curacy [illegible] church.

BURTON, a [illegible] in [illegible] parish, Glamorgan [illegible]

BURTON, a township in [illegible] parish, North [illegible] 5 miles ESE of [illegible] Acres, 1,05[illegible] Pop., 1[illegible]3. Houses, [illegible]

BURTON, a parish in [illegible] district and county of Pem[broke], [illegible] at Pembroke ferry, near [illegible] miles N of Pembroke. It [illegible] Hoaston [illegible] post town is [illegible] Acres, [illegible] of which 400 are water. Real property, £2,241. Pop., [illegible]02[illegible]. Houses, 1[illegible]. The [illegible] Benton Castle is a [illegible] fine view. The living is a rectory in the [illegible] Value, £202.* Patron, the [illegible] Castle. There are chapels for Baptists and Wesleyans, and charities [illegible]

BURTON, a hamlet in Seguries [illegible] parish, Somerset, 3½ miles [illegible] Pop., [illegible]5.

BURTON, a [illegible] in Much Wenlock parish, Salop, [illegible] miles SW [illegible] Much Wenlock station, [illegible] Wellington, Salop. The sta[tion] [illegible] parish. The living is a [illegible] Hereford. Value, £50. Pa[tron] [illegible]

BURTON, [illegible] parish, Westmore[land], [illegible] miles ESE of Appleby. It [illegible] the [illegible] and was the [illegible]

BURTON, [illegible] on [illegible] NW border of Wilts, S [illegible] with a post office under Chippenham.

BURTON, [illegible] See [illegible]

BURTON [illegible] York[shire] [illegible] See BURTON (MONKS).

BURTON, [illegible] York[shire] [illegible] See [illegible]

[illegible]

BURTON [illegible] See BURTON-IN-LONSDALE.

BURTON [illegible] See BURTON-UPON-[illegible], &c.

[illegible] Cheshire [illegible] the county [illegible] miles SSW of [illegible] Acres, 30[illegible] Real property, £[illegible] [illegible] of the [illegible]dulphus. The living is a [illegible] united with the p[er]pe[tual] curacy of Coat[illegible] in the diocese of Chichester. Value, £113. Patron, George W[illegible], Esq.

BURTON AND HO[LME] [illegible] on the Lancaster and Carlisle railway, 10¼ miles N [illegible] Lancaster.

BURTON ABBOTS. See [illegible] BOURTON.

BURTON AGNES, a township and a parish in Bridlington district, E. R. Yorkshire. The township lies on the Hull and Scarborough railway, 5½ miles SW of Bridlington; and has a station on the railway, and a post office under Hull. Acres, 2,4[illegible]. Real property, £4,025. Pop., 344. Houses, [illegible] The parish contains also the townships of Haisthorpe, Thornholme, and Gransmoor. Acres, 6,40[illegible]. Real property, £[illegible],018. Pop., 723. Houses, 11[illegible]. The property is divided between two. Burton Agnes Hall is the seat of Sir H. Boynton, Bart; was built by Inigo Jones; and stands on a fine slope of the Wolds, forming a striking object from the railway. The living is a vicarage, united with the p[erp]etual cur[acy] of Harpham, in the diocese of York. Value, £[illegible]97.* Patron, the Hon. and Rev. A. Duncombe. The church has a nave of three bays, and a good western tower; contains a Norman font, [illegible] tomb of 1[illegible], and a [illegible] with effigies of 1[illegible]; and was restored [illegible] Archdeacon Robert Wilberforce. There are a Wesleyan chapel, an endowed school with £21 a year, and charities £40.

BURTON BISHOP. See BISHOP BURTON.

BURTON (BLACK). See BURTON-IN-LONSDALE.

BURTON-BRADSTOCK, a parish and a sub-district in Bridport district, Dorset. The parish lies on the river Bride, and on the coast, 3 miles SSE of Bridport r. station; includes the tything of [illegible]; and has a post office under Bridport. Acres, 2,6[illegible], of which 155 are water. Real property, with Shipton-George and Stuttphill, £6,436. Pop., 1,010. Houses, 2[illegible]3. Cliffs on the coast consist of fuller's earth. The vale of the Bride here is beautiful. There are flax mill and a twine factory. The living is a rectory, united with the p[erpetual] cur[acy] of Shipton-George, in the diocese of Salisbury. Value, £[illegible]36.* Patron, Lord Rivers. Charities, £4.— The sub-district contains nine parishes and [illegible] parochial chapelry. Acres, 16,30[illegible]. Pop., [illegible],721. Houses, 980.

BURTON-BY-LINCOLN, a parish in the district and county of Lincoln, near the Great Northern railway, [illegible] miles NNW of Lincoln. Post town, Lincoln. Acres, 2,825. Real property, £3,54[illegible]. Pop., 1[illegible]1. Houses, [illegible]6. The manor and Burton House belong to Lord Monson. The living is a rectory in the diocese of Lincoln. Value, £419.* Patron, Lord Monson. The church is modern. Charities, £[illegible]3.

BURTON-BY-TARVIN, a township in Tarvin parish, Cheshire, 3½ miles NW of Tarporley. Acres, [illegible]2[illegible]. Real property, £[illegible]5[illegible]. Pop., 7[illegible]. Houses, 1[illegible].

BURTON CHERRY, a parish in Beverley district, E. R. Yorkshire, near the Hull and Bridlington railway, 3 miles NW by W of Beverley. It has a post office, of the name of Cherry Burton, under Beverley. Acres, 3,061. Real property, £5,[illegible]42. Pop., [illegible]02. Houses, 105. The property is divided among a few. The living is a rectory in the diocese of York. Value, £57[illegible].* Patron, C. Bramwell, Esq. The church is [illegible] in the early decorated English style, and [illegible] of a nave, north aisle, and chancel, with a tower.

BURTON COGGLES, a parish in Grantham district, Lincoln, on an affluent of the river [illegible] near the Great Northern railway, 2 miles NW of Corby. Post town, Corby, under Grantham. Acres, [illegible],[illegible]7[illegible]. Real property, £3,862. Pop., [illegible]3[illegible]. Houses, [illegible]4. The property is divided among a few. The living is a rectory in the diocese of Lincoln. Value, £[illegible]. Patron, the Lord Chancellor. The church is [illegible] A school has £25 from endowment; and other charities £10.

BURTON CONSTABLE, a hamlet in Swine parish, E. R. Yorkshire, with a station on the Hornsea railway, 10[illegible] miles NE of Hull. [illegible] Hall [illegible] formerly the property of the Cliffords, now the seat of Sir T. A. C. Constable, Bart., is a fine [illegible] mansion, with fronts of 1[illegible]8 and 1[illegible] feet, and a tower at each corner, and contains a large collection of [illegible] manuscript history and [illegible], family portraits Races are run in April, over a course of 1½ mile in the park.

BURTON CONSTABLE, a township in Finghall parish, N R Yorkshire, adjacent to the Leyburn railway, 3¼ miles E of Leyburn It includes the hamlet of Stu[illegible]dow Acres, 2,572 Real property, £3,[illegible]38 Pop, 22[illegible] Houses 43

BURTON CUM WALDEN, or West Burton, a township in Aysgarth parish, N R Yorkshire, at the junction of Bishopdale and Wensleydale, 3 miles SW of Aysgarth It has a post office, of the name of West Burton under Bedale, and fairs are held in it on 10 March, 6 May, 30 Aug, 26 Sept, and 3 Nov Acres, 6 790 Real property, £4,038 Pop., 478. Houses 110 There is a Wesleyan chapel

BURTON DASSETT, a village and a parish in Southam district, and a division of Kington hundred, Warwick The village stands 2½ miles W by S of Fenny Compton station and 4 E of Kington, and was once a market town The parish includes also the hamlets of Little Dassett North End, and Knightcote, and its post town is Fenny Compton, under Rugby Acres, 5,400 Real property, £7,4[illegible]1 Pop, 6[illegible]5 Houses, 1[illegible] The manor belonged anciently to the Southleys, and passed to the Belknaps, the Wottons, the Stanhopes and the Temples The surface is hilly and continued long to be a haunt of wild beasts. The living is a vicarage in the diocese of Worcester Value £167 Patrons, Lord Willoughby de Broke and R W Plencowe, Esq Charities, £7[illegible] — The division contains ten parishes and part of another Acres 18,973 Pop. 3,815 Houses 80[illegible]

BURTON EXTRA, a township in Burton upon Trent parish Stafford forming part of the town of Burton upon Trent Real property, £6,941 Pop, 2,849 Houses, [illegible]27 Here is a Baptist chapel

BURTON FLEMING, or NORTH BURTON, a parish in Bridlington district, E R Yorkshire, on the Gypsey race river 3½ miles W by S of Speeton r station, and 7 NW of Bridlington It has a post-office of the name of Burton Fleming under York Acres, 3 790 Real property, £4 [illegible] Pop, 525 Houses 110 The property is subdivided The living is a vicarage in the diocese of York Value, £234 Patron, Admiral Mitford The church has a timber roof of 1576, and a circular Norman font There are two Methodist chapels

BURTON GATE, a parish in Gainsborough district, Lincoln, on the river Trent and on the Lincoln and Gainsborough railway 1½ mile NNW of Marton station, and 5 SSE of Gainsborough Post town Marton under Gainsborough Acres 1,168 Real property, £2,030 Pop, 115 Houses, 24 Burton Hall is the seat of W Hutton, Esq The living is a rectory in the diocese of Lincoln Value, £58 * Patron, W Hutton, Esq

BURTON GRANGE, a village in Monk Bretton township Roystone parish, W R Yorkshire, 1 mile NE of Barnsley

BURTON HASTINGS a parish in the district of Hinckley and county of Warwick, on Watling-street and Ashby de la Zouch canal adjacent to the Trent Valley railway 2 miles N of Bulkington r station and 3½ ESE of Nuneaton Post town, Bulkington, under Rugby Acres 1 [illegible]10 Real property £2,858 Pop 199 Houses, [illegible]8 The manor belonged, in the time of Edward IV to William Lord Hastings and passed by marriage, to the Cotton family The living is a vicarage in the diocese of Worcester Value, £87 Patron W Bucknill, Esq The church is good, and there are charities £28

BURTON (HIGH) a village in Kirk Burton parish, W R Yorkshire 4½ miles SE of Huddersfield

BURTON HILL a tything in Malmsbury St Paul parish Wilts near Malmsbury Pop 2[illegible] Houses, 5[illegible]

BURTON IN BISHOPDALE. See BURTON CUM WALDEN

BURTON IN KENDAL, a small town and a township in Kirkby Lonsdale district, Westmoreland and a parish in the same district but partly in Lancashire The town stands adjacent to the Kendal canal 1½ mile E of Burton and Holme r station, near Farlton Knot, 10 miles NNE of Lancaster It is well built, contains a market place, with handsome stone cross, has a head post office,‡ (designated Burton, Westmoreland Morecambe), a parish church, three other places of worship and a grammar school and is a seat of petty sessions The church is an ancient edifice, with two chapels and a square tower and was recently restored A weekly market is held on Tuesday, and fairs on Easter Monday and 10 Oct The township includes also the hamlet of Clawthorpe Acres, 1,437 Real property, £[illegible],507 Pop., 751 Houses, 172 The parish contains likewise the townships of Holme Preston Patrick, and Dalton, and part of the hamlet of Holmescales Acres, 8,708 Real property, £12,835 Pop 2,118. Houses 3[illegible] The property is much subdivided Preston Patrick Hall, once the seat of the Prestons, is now a farm house Considerable part of the land is reclaimed bog. Sulphate of strontium is found The living is a vicarage in the diocese of Carlisle Value, £19[illegible] * Patrons Simeon's Trustees The chapelries of Holme and Preston Patrick are separate benefices. The grammar school has an endowed income of £27, and other charities have £140 Dr L Dawes, Dr G Langbaine, Dr W Lancaster and several other literary men of the time of Charles I were natives, and William Cockin, the arithmetician and poet, was interred in the churchyard

BURTON IN LONSDALE, or BLACK BURTON, a township chapelry in Thornton in Lonsdale parish, W R Yorkshire on the river Greta, adjacent to the Midland railway, 3 miles WNW of High Bentham r station and 12 NW by W of Settle It has a post office, of the name of Burton in Lonsdale, under Lancaster Acres, 1 380 Real property £3 1[illegible]3 Pop, 5[illegible]7 Houses 134 The living is a vicarage in the diocese of Ripon Value, £[illegible] Patron the Vicar of Thornton The church is old There are a Wesleyan chapel and endowed schools

BURTON JOYCE a village in Basford district, and a parish in Basford and Southwell districts, Notts. The village stands on the river Trent adjacent to the Midland railway, 5 miles NE by E of Nottingham, and has a station on the railway and a post office under Nottingham The parish includes also the chapelry of Bulcote Acres, 1,9[illegible] Real property, £3 [illegible] Pop, 834 Houses, 177 The property is divided among a few The manor belonged to the families of Saccensis Fitz Jose and Stapleton A number of the inhabitants are stocking makers The living is a vicarage united with the p curacy of Bulcote in the diocese of Lincoln Value, £145 Patron, the Earl of Chesterfield The church is ancient but good has a tower and spire and contains a number of monuments There are an Independent chapel of 1869, and a Wesleyan chapel

BURTON KIRK See KIRK BURTON

BURTON LATIMER, a parish in Kettering district Northampton, adjacent to the Leicester and Bedford railway 3½ miles SE of Kettering It has a station jointly with Isham on the railway, and a post-office‡ under Wellingborough Acres, 2 690 Real property, £5,[illegible]3 Pop, 1,1[illegible] Houses, [illegible] The property is subdivided The manor belonged once to the Latimers The living is a rectory in the dio of Peterborough Value, £1,000 * Patron the Rev F L Newman The church was restored in 186[illegible] There are Baptist and Wesleyan chapels a national school and charities £290

BURTON LAZARS a chapelry in Melton Mowbray parish, Leicester, adjacent to the Melton Mowbray and Oakham canal and to the Syston and Peterborough railway 1¾ mile SE by S of Melton Mowbray Post town, Melton Mowbray Acres 2 00[illegible] Real property £4 [illegible]3 Pop, 253 Houses 52 The property is divided among a few A lepers hospital was founded here in the time of Stephen partly by a general collection throughout England, but chiefly by the Mowbrays and was the chief lazar house in England The living is a p curacy, annexed to the vicarage of Melton Mowbray in the diocese of Peterborough The church is good

BURTON LEONARD a parish in Ripon district, W R Yorkshire on the Leeds and Northallerton railway, near Wormald Green station, [illegible] miles SSE of Ripon It has a post-office under Ripon Acres, 1,[illegible]89 Real pro perty, £2,4[illegible] Pop., 507 Houses, 121 The property is much subdivided The living is a vicarage in the diocese of Lincoln Value £110 Patrons, the Dean and Chapter of York The church is tolerable, and there are two Methodist chapels, a national school, and charities £31

BURTON (LONG) See LONG BURTON

BURTON (NORTH) See BURTON FLEMING

BURTON ON THE WOLDS, a township in Prestwold parish, Leicester, 4½ miles ENE of Loughborough Acres 1,690 Real property, £3,812 Pop 441 Houses, 97 Burton Hall here is the seat of the Mundys. There is a Wesleyan chapel

BURTON OVERY, a parish in Billesdon district, Leicestershire, near the Union canal, 6 miles E by S of Wigston r station and 7 SE by E of Leicester It has a post office under Leicester Acres, 1,600 Real property £4,110 Pop, 465 Houses, 110 The property is much subdivided The living is a rectory in the diocese of Peterborough Value, £497 * Patron, Captain W Thorne. The church is decorated and later English, and was recently repaired There are an Independent chapel a national school, and charities £23.

BURTON-PEDWARDINE, a parish in Sleaford district, Lincoln, 2 miles SW of Heckington r station, and 4½ SE of Sleaford. Post-town, Heckington, under Sleaford Acres, 2,380 Real property, £2,427 Pop, 135 Houses, 26 The property is divided among a few The manor was given by the Conqueror to Alan de Craon, and passed to the Pedwardines. The living is a vicarage in the diocese of Lincoln Value £329 * Patron, H Handley, Esq The church is partly ancient, partly of the year 1802 There is a national school of 1869

BURTON PIDSEA, a village and a parish in Patrington district, E R Yorkshire. The village stands on an eminence, with an extensive view, 3½ miles NNE of Marton r station, and 7½ NW by N of Patrington, and has a post office under Hull The parish comprises [illegible] acres Real property, £5,188 Pop., 403 Houses, 84 The property is divided among a few The living is a vicarage in the diocese of York Value £42 * Patrons, the Dean and Chapter of York The church is good

BURTON PYNSENT, a tything in Drayton, Curry Rivel and Fivehead parishes Somerset on the downs 2 miles SW of Langport. Pop, 13 The estate belonged to the Pynsents but was bequeathed to William Pitt afterwards Earl of Chatham and belongs now to Colonel Pinney The Earl of Chatham occasionally resided here, and he erected a column 140 feet high popularly called the Burton steeple, to the memory of Sir William Pynsent This crowns an eminence, with a fine view, and a funeral urn, to his own memory, erected by his Countess, stands in the grounds of the mansion

BURTON ROAD See PONDARY

BURTON SALMON a township in Monk Frystone parish, W R Yorkshire, on the Normanton and York railway 2 miles NE of Pontefract It has a station on the railway Acres, 918 Real property, £1,290 Pop, 2[illegible]7 Houses, 52

BURTON UPON STATHER, a village and a parish in Glanford Brigg district, Lincoln The village stands on a staith or creek of the river Trent, near that river's mouth 3 miles NNE of Kealby r station, and 11½ NW of Glanford Brigg It has a post office under the name of Burton, under Brigg, it figured formerly as a considerable market town it serves now as a depot station for the Hull and Gainsborough steam vessels and it carries on a considerable trade in meal The parish [illegible] also the hamlets of Normanby, Thealby, and [illegible] of Col[illegible] Acres 3,860 Real property, £6,0[illegible]8 Pop 9[illegible]3 Houses, 222 The property is subdivided The living is a vicarage annexed to the rectory of [illegible] in the diocese of Lincoln The church is old and in good condition There are two Methodist chapels and a national school

BURTON UPON TRENT, a township, a town, a parish, a sub-district and a district on the E border of Staffordshire The township is included in the town Real property £[illegible] Pop, 9,[illegible]34 Houses, 1,[illegible]25 The town lies on the river Trent and on the Midland railway, adjacent to the Grand Trunk canal 11 miles SW of Derby A branch canal connects the river with the Grand Trunk and branch railways go off to lines communicating with all parts of the kingdom The town was known to the Saxons as Byrtun or Buryton A religious establishment was founded at it, in the 9th century, by the Irish lady Modwena who had the reputation of a saint and of a great medicine A Benedictine abbey succeeded this establishment in 1004 founded by Wulfric Spot Earl of Mercia, was changed by Henry VIII into a collegiate church, and given, soon afterwards, to Sir William Paget Edward II, in 1322, obtained a decisive victory here, over the Earl of Lancaster, and both parties in the civil war, in the time of Charles I, were here, at several periods, both vanquished and victors The town occupies low level ground, formerly liable to inundation by the Trent, and overlooked by the precipitous thickly wooded hill of Scalpley It does not look well, yet is substantially built, and it consists mainly of two chief streets one of them running parallel with the Trent An edifice, to include a new town hall, municipal offices, assembly rooms library, museum, bath-rooms, and other apartments, was projected in 1865 The bridge across the Trent dates from about the time of the Conquest, is 1,545 feet long and has 36 arches A chapel stood at one end of it, built by Edward II, to commemorate his victory over Lancaster, but has disappeared Some scanty remains of the ancient abbey exist in the churchyard, and opposite the end of New street. The present parish church was built in 1720, stands on the east side of the market place, is a fine large edifice, in the Italian style, with western square tower, and contains a beautiful altar piece of white marble Christ church, near the end of New street, is a neat recent structure in the early English style, with tower and spire 1[illegible]0 feet high Holy Trinity church was built in 1824 at a cost of about £7,000, and is a large and handsome edifice in florid Gothic The Independent chapel, in High street, occupies the site of a previous chapel of 1662, and is an elegant structure in the Gothic style There are chapels also for Baptists, Wesleyan Methodists, Primitive Methodists, and Roman Catholics The grammar school near the parish church was founded in 15[illegible]0 by Abbot Beane and has an endowed income of £401, and other schools and charities have £57[illegible] A building in High street is occupied partly by a museum, established in 18[illegible]2, and partly by the reading room of a literary society, established in 1814 The workhouse, in Horninglow, was erected at a cost of £5,[illegible]00 The town has a head post office ‡ a railway station with telegraph a banking office, and three chief inns, is a seat of sessions and a polling place, and publishes two weekly newspapers A weekly market is held on Thursday and fairs on Candlemas day, 5 April, Holy Thursday, 6 July, 1 Sept, and 29 Oct The chief employment, from remote times, has been the brewing of ale, and this is now carried on to a greater extent than anywhere else in the kingdom Allsopp's brewery cost £40,000, and was designed to be more than twice larger than it is, Bass's occupies fully 20 acres, and there are about eighteen others. Cotton manufacture, tanning and iron working also are carried on The town possesses certain privileges and is sometimes called a borough, but is not governed by the municipal act It comprises the townships of Burton upon Trent, Burton Extra, and part of Horninglow Pop. in 1851, 7,934 in 1861 13,[illegible]71 Houses, 2,[illegible]65. Isaac Hawkins Brown, who died in 1760 was a native

The parish contains all the town all Horninglow township, and the townships of Stretton Branstone, and Winshill,—the last in Derby Acres 7,730 Real property £[illegible]2[illegible] Population of the whole, 16,[illegible]21 Houses [illegible]2[illegible] The property is much subdivided The manor belongs to the Marquis of Anglesey The parochial living and the livings of Christchurch and Holy Trinity, are vicarages in the diocese of Lichfield Value £192, £3[illegible], and £[illegible]207 * Patron of the first [illegible] Vicar of B [illegible] of the others, [illegible] St Paul's church [illegible] and Horninglow and Winshill are separate benefices — The sub district contains also the parish of Tatenhill Acres, 17,138 Pop, 18,715 Houses, 3,633 The district comprehends likewise the sub district of Gresley, containing the parishes of Lullington Coton, Walton upon Trent, Stapenhill, and parts of Church Gresley and Croxall,—all electorally in Derby the sub district of Repton, containing the parishes of Repton, Newton Solney, Foremark, Ladbourne, Dalbury with Lees, Trusley, Twyford, Willington, and parts of Sutton on the hill, Mickleover, and Barrow upon Trent,—all electorally in Derby, and the sub-district of Tutbury, containing the parishes of Tutbury, Rolleston, and part of Hanbury and Scropton, electorally in Stafford, and the parishes of Egginton Church Broughton, Barton Blount, Marston upon-Dove, and parts of Sutton on the Hill and Scropton — electorally in Derby Acres, 90,652 Poor rates in 1863, £13,316 Pop in 1861, 41,065 Houses, 8,217 Marriages in 1866, 401 births, 1,908 —of which 95 were illegitimate, deaths, 1,001,—of which 426 were at ages under 5 years and 21 at ages above 85 Marriages in the ten years 1851–60 2,642, births, 12,462, deaths, 7,501 The places of worship in 1851 were 39 of the Church of England, with 12,403 sittings, 4 of Independents, with 1,357 s, 5 of Baptists, with 1,061 s, 1 of Unitarians, with 74 s, 33 of Wesleyan Methodists, with 4,433 s, 15 of Primitive Methodists, with 1,909 s., 1 of Wesleyan Reformers, with 200 s, 1 of Latter Day Saints, with 80 s., and 1 of Roman Catholics with 180 s The schools were 37 public day schools, with 3,479 scholars, 50 private day schools, with 1,084 s, 51 Sunday schools, with 4,474 s, and 3 evening schools for adults, with 96 s

BURTON UPON URE a township in Masham parish, N R. Yorkshire, 5 miles SW by S of Bedale Acres 2,920 Real property, £3,294 Pop, 120 Houses, 18

BURTON (West), a parish in the district of Gainsborough and county of Nottingham, on the river Trent, 2 miles F of Sturton r station, and 3½ SSW of Gainsborough Post town, Sturton, under Retford. Acres, 710 Real property, £2,080 Pop, 67 Houses, 7 The living is a vicarage in the diocese of Lincoln Value, £65 Patron, John Barrow Esq The church is old.

BURTON (West), a village in Bury parish, Sussex, 4½ miles N of Arundel Pop, 201

BURTON (West) N R Yorkshire. See Burton-cum-Walden

BURTON WOOD, a township chapelry in Warrington parish, Lancashire, adjacent to the Sankey canal and the Liverpool and Manchester railway, 1 mile S of Collins-Green r station, and 4 NW by N of Warrington. Post town, Warrington Acres, 1,144 Real property, £6,5.5 Pop, 900 Houses 188 The property is subdivided The living is a p curacy in the diocese of Chester Value, £96 Patron the Rector of Warrington The church is fair, and there is a school with £12 from endowment

BURWARDSLEY, a township chapelry in Bunbury parish Cheshire, 2 miles SW by S of Beeston r station, and 4½ SSW of Tarporley Post town, Tattenhall, under Chester Acres, 1,039 Real property £1,913 Pop, 500 Houses, 106. The living is a p curacy in the diocese of Chester Value, £50 Patrons, Trustees The church was built in the former part of last century There are a P Methodist chapel, and charities £41

BURWARTON, a parish in Bridgnorth district, Salop, on the river Rea, 9½ miles SW of Bridgnorth r station It has a post-office under Bridgnorth Acres, 1,239 Real property, £3,143. Pop, 156 Houses, 28 Burwarton Hall is the seat of Viscount Boyne The living is a rectory in the diocese of Hereford Value £125 Patron the Rev J. Churton The church is very good, and contains tombs of the Pynes

BURWASH or BURGHERSH a village and a parish in Ticehurst district Sussex. The village stands on an affluent of the river Rother 2½ miles WSW of Etchingham r station, and 8 NW of Battle, and has a post office,‡ of the name of Burwash, under Hurst Green It was formerly a market town and still has fairs on 12 May and 4 Oct, and it is a seat of petty sessions. The parish comprises 7,021 acres Real property, £8,317 Pop 2,143 Houses 422 The property is much subdivided There is a chalybeate spring The living is a rectory and vicarage in the diocese of Chichester Value, £690 * Patron the Rev J Gould The church is early and later English and was restored in 1856 A chapel of ease, in the early English style, was built at Burwash Common in 1867 There are an Independent chapel, a Wesleyan chapel a national school, and charities £ 0 Burwash gives the title of Viscount to the Earl of Westmoreland

BURWELL, a village and a parish in Newmarket district, Cambridge The village stands 1½ miles Fsl of the river Cam, and the same distance NW of Newmarket station, consists chiefly of one irregular street has a post office‡ under Cambridge and was once a market town. Traces of a castle are here built before the Conquest, and besieged in the war between Stephen and the Empress Matilda Seventy eight persons were accidentally burnt to death in a barn here in 1727 The parish includes also part of the hamlet of Reach Acres, 7,332 Real property, £15,227, of which £1 142 are in quarries Pop, 1,957 Houses, 403 About one half of the land is fen The living is a vicarage in the diocese of Ely Value, £335 Patron, the University of Cambridge The church is fine decorated English, was partly restored in 1861 and has a pinnacled tower There are a mission church of 1863, Independent, Baptist, and Wesleyan chapels, an endowed school, two national schools, a British school, and charities £142

BURWELL, a parish in Louth district Lincoln 2¾ miles W by S of Authorpe r station, and 5½ SSE of Louth It has a post office under Louth, and fairs are held on it on 11 May and Old Michaelmas day Acres 2,160 Real property, £2,471 Pop., 159 Houses 25. Burwell Park is the seat of H Lister Esq, and was the birthplace of Sarah Jennings, the famous Duchess of Marlborough A Benedictine priory was founded in the parish, by John de Hay, ancestor of the Lindsey, made a cell to St Mary's abbey Bordeaux, and passed eventually to the Duke of Suffolk The living is a vicarage, united with the p curacy of Walmsgate, in the diocese of Lincoln Value £54 Patron H Lister, Esq The church has a Norman chancel arch

BURWOOD PARK, the seat of Sir Richard Frederick Bart, in Surrey near the Walton station of the South Western railway 2½ miles SE of Chertsey The mansion was built towards the end of last century and contains a fine collection of pictures The orangery is notable

BURY, a name of the same meaning as burgh or burg and applied to a place which had anciently a fort.

BURY, a village 1½ miles SW of Buntingford, in Herts.

BURY, a village 1 mile NE of Stevenage, in Herts

BURY, a seat near Hemel Hempstead, in Herts It belonged once to the Waterhouses and passed to the Wiggines. The house is chiefly modern but includes part of a previous one in which Henry VIII visited J Waterhouse

BURY a hamlet in Brompton Regis parish, Somerset, 2 miles E of Dulverton Bury Castle here was a Roman camp

BURY, a parish in St Ives district Huntingdon on an affluent of the river Nen, ¾ of a mile S of Ramsey r station, and 8 miles N by W of St Ives It has a post office under Huntingdon Acres, 1,615 Real property £3,765 Pop 362 Houses, 75 The property is divided among a few The manor belonged to Ramsey abbey, and passed to successively the Williamses, the Lunbridges, and the Barnards The living is a vicarage in the diocese of Ely Value £167 Patron, the Duke of Manchester The church is partly Norman and early English and is good There is a free school

BURY, a parish and a hundred in Sussex The parish is in Chichester district lies on the river Arun, 1¼ mile NW of Amberley r station, and 5 SSE of Petworth includes the tything of West Burton, and has a post office under Petworth Acres, 3,040 Real property £4,316. Pop, 500 Houses, 105 Bury Hill here is crowned with a large barrow The living is a vicarage in the diocese of Chichester Value, £ 00.* Patrons, the Dean and Chapter of Gloucester The church was recently restored There are national schools and charities £40 --The hundred is in the rape of Arundel, and contains eight parishes and part of another Pop 4 125 Houses 803

BURY a township, a town a parish, two sub districts, and a district in Lancashire The township lies all within the town's assigned boundaries Acres, 2,370 Real property, £26[illegible],[illegible]3 —of which £171,785 are in railways, £1,040 in mines, and £80 in quarries Pop, in 1841, 20,710, in 1861, 30,397 Houses, 5,971 The town lies on the river Irwell 2 miles above its confluence with the Roach, and 8 NNW of Manchester A branch canal goes south westward to the Manchester and Bolton canal, and railways go westward northward, eastward, and southward A Roman station is thought by some to have been on the town's site, a Saxon fort seems certainly to have been here, and a baronial castle, of early date, stood in Castle Croft in the town's vicinity, and was demolished, in 1644 by the troops of Cromwell The manor belonged, in the time of Henry II, to John de Lacy, and passed to successively the Burys the Pilkingtons, and the Stanleys. A muster of 20 000 men, in the royalist cause, was made in 1642, on a heath in the neighbourhood, by Lord Strange, afterwards Earl of Derby

The town was described in 1738 as "a little market town," but it must then have been only a village, and it has risen rapidly to magnitude under manufacturing enterprise It, not long ago, contained old dilapidated buildings, and had a dingy appearance, but it has undergone great improvement, at once by re edification of houses by formation of new streets, and by construction of drainage works, and it now presents a well built and cleanly appearance, and is plentifully supplied with water The new market place was constructed in 1840, is a triangular outline, with open centre, is surrounded by [illegible] and shops, and in 1868, was covered with a roof of wrought iron and glass. A bronze statue of Sir Robert Peel, on a massive pedestal of granite, was erected in the old market place in 1852, at a cost of £2,500 The town hall is a handsome edifice, in the Italian style, contains an assembly room 54 feet by 36 and includes court houses and police office The athenæum adjoins the town hall, was erected in 185[illegible] is a handsome building, and contains a lecture hall 8[illegible] feet by 43, a museum 43 feet by [illegible]0, class rooms and reading rooms The banking offices, the savings bank, the railway station, the [illegible] baths, and the grammar school are good buildings St Mary's church was rebuilt in 1780, and has a tower and spire, rebuilt in 184[illegible] St John's church was built in 1770 St Paul's in 1841 Holy Trinity in 1865, St Thomas', in 18[illegible], and the last is a highly ornate structure in the first pointed style, with tower and spire A Wesleyan chapel and a Roman Catholic chapel are handsome edifices the latter in the pointed style, and built in 1841 There are three Independent chapels two Baptist, 6 Methodist, a Unitarian, a Swedenborgian, and two Roman Catholic, a new cemetery opened in 1869, comprising [illegible] acres, with two ornate chapels, a grammar school, founded in 1726, and with an endowed income of £142, and three exhibitions at the universities, a chorister's school ten national and six denominational schools a dispensary and a variety of other local institutions The town has a head post office,‡ two railway stations with telegraph, two banking offices, several chief inns a weekly market on Saturday, and three annual fairs, is a seat of petty sessions and county courts and a polling place, and publishes four weekly newspapers Woollen manufacture was formerly the main industry and is still carried on in several large factories Cotton manufacture, in various departments is now the staple received a great impulse from inventions by two natives, [illegible] and Robert Kay and from the enterprise of the late Sir Robert Peel's father and maintains at present upwards of twelve factories for spinning and weaving two for printing and bleaching, [illegible] dyeing There are also three large iron foundries several small [illegible] machine making works, hat making houses, and other manufacturing establishments The town was made a parliamentary borough by the act of 1832, and is governed by a body of commissioners under a local act of 1846, and sends one member to parliament. Its boundaries, in addition to all Bury township, include most of the township of Elton Direct taxes, £27,51[illegible] Electors in 1868, 1,366 Pop. in 1851, 31,262, in 1861, 37,563 Houses, 7,257

The parish is chiefly in Bury district, but partly also in the district of Haslingden, and it includes the townships of Bury, Elton, Heap Walmersley-cum Shuttleworth, Tottington Lower End, Tottington Higher End Musbury, and Cowpe Lenches Newhallhey, and Hall Carr Acres, 2[illegible],320 Real property, £421,274, of which £3 544 are in mines and £932 in quarries Pop in 1841, 62 125, in 1861, 80,558 Houses, 15,754 The property is much subdivided The surface is hilly, and the strata yield coal and building stone Chamber Hall, now the seat of Thomas Price, Esq, in the vicinity of the town, was the birthplace of the late Sir Robert Peel St Mary's is a rectory, St John's, St Paul's and Holy Trinity are vicarages, and St. Thomas is a p curacy in the diocese of Manchester Value of St M, £1,[illegible]37, of St. J, £240,* of St P, £300 * of H T not reported, of St. T, £150 Patron of St M the Earl of Derby, of St J, H T, and St. T, the Rector of St P, Trustees The rectories of Holcombe and Heywood the vicarages of Edenfield Elton, Musbury Ramsbottom, Shuttleworth, Tottington, and Waterfoot, and the p curacies of Heap and Walmersley are separate benefices

The two sub districts are North Bury and South Bury Pop of the former, 15,375, of the latter 15,726 The district comprehends the sub district of North Bury, containing part of the township of Bury, the sub district of South Bury containing parts of the townships of Bury, Elton Heap, Pilsworth, and Pilkington and part of the parish of Radcliffe, the sub district of Elton, containing parts of the townships of Elton, Ainsworth, and Walmersley cum Shuttleworth and part of the parish of Radcliffe, the sub district of Pilkington containing part of the township of Pilkington, the sub district of Radcliffe containing parts of the townships of Bury Elton, Ainsworth and Pilkington, and part of the parish of Radcliffe, the sub district of Holcombe, containing parts of the townships of Tottington Lower End and Walmersley cum Shuttleworth, the sub district of Tottington Lower End, containing part of the township of Tottington Lower End, the sub district of Walmersley containing parts of the townships of Elton, Walmersley cum Shuttleworth Tottington Lower end, and Birtle cum Bamford, the sub district of Birtle, containing the township of Ashworth and parts of the townships of Heap and Birtle cum Bamford, and the sub district of Heywood, containing the township of Heywood and parts of the townships of Bury Heap, and Pilsworth The intersections of Radcliffe parish and of the several townships throwing them into different sub districts, are made chiefly by the rivers Irwell and Roach Acres of the district, [illegible] Poor rates in 1866 £34 113 Pop in 1861 101 [illegible] Houses, 19,831 Marriages in 1866, 97[illegible], births, [illegible],579, —of which 222 were illegitimate deaths [illegible] 560,—of which 1,02[illegible] were at ages under 5 years, and 31 at ages above 85 Marriages in the ten years, 1851-60 7 817 births, [illegible]325, deaths, 21,986 The places of worship in 1851 were [illegible]0 of the Church of England with 16,4[illegible] sittings 1 of the Presbyterian Church in England, with 609 s 13 of Independents, with 5,192 s 4 of Baptists, with 1 650 s, [illegible] of Unitarians, with 1 46[illegible] s, 17 of Wesleyan Methodists, with [illegible] 96[illegible] s [illegible] of New Connexion Methodists, with 1 205 s, 6 of Primitive Methodists with 1 27[illegible] s, 3 of the Wesleyan Association with 1,5[illegible] s, 4 of the New Church, with 8[illegible]6 s, 2 of Roman Catholics, with [illegible] s, 2 of Latter Day Saints, with 400 attendants, and 1 of [illegible] with [illegible] The schools were 54 public day schools with 6,528 scholars, 47 private day schools with 3 363 s [illegible] Sunday schools, with [illegible] s and 11 evening schools for adults, with [illegible] s The workhouse is in Bury township

BURY, Suffolk. See BURY ST EDMUNDS.

BURYAN (ST), a parish and a sub district in Penzance district, Cornwall. The parish lies 4½ miles E by N of Lands End, and 4½ SW of Penzance r station, and has a post office under Penzance. Acres, 6,9.. Real property, £8,350. Pop 1,426. Houses 290. The property is divided among a few. The surface consists largely of black granite hills. A small town, of ancient note, was here, but is now represented by only a few cottages. An oratory was founded at it at an early period by St Buriana, a holy woman from Ireland. A secular college also was founded here in 909, by Athelstane, changed afterwards into an exempt deanery and destroyed, in the time of the Commonwealth, by Shrubshall governor of Pendennis Castle. A number of Druidical remains, including the Merry Maidens, the Boscawen Un, and the Rosmodreny circles, occur among the hills. The living is a rectory in the diocese of Exeter, and till 1864 was united with Levan and Sennen. Value, £570.* Patron the Crown. The church stands on a wild open eminence, 415 feet high, has a lofty tower, commanding a view to the Scilly Islands, is an ancient edifice, greatly altered by modern renovations, and contains a fine carved screen, and a curious coffin shaped monument with a Norman French inscription. An ancient chapel called the Sanctuary, stands about a mile to the SE. Attorney general Noy of the time of Charles I, was a native. The sub district contains three parishes. Acres, 11,592. Pop 2,488. Houses 502.

BURY BLUNSDON, a tything in Highworth parish, Wilts, 2 miles W of Highworth. Pop, 17.

BURY DITCHES, an ancient British camp, in Salop, on Tongley Hill, 3½ miles S of Bishops Castle. It commands a fine view.

BURY HILL, the seat of C Barclay, Esq, 1 mile SSE of Dorking, in Surrey. The grounds are ornate and interesting, and are open to the public.

BURY HILL, Hants. See ANDOVER.

BURY LANE, a chapelry with a r station in Newchurch Kenyon parish, Lancashire, on the Liverpool and Manchester railway, 11 miles W by S of Manchester. The living is annexed to Newchurch Kenyon.

BURYMEAD. See ACTON, Middlesex.

BURY (NEW), a chapelry in Deane parish, Lancashire, 4 miles SE of Bolton. Pop about £4 000. Living, a vicarage. The church was built in 1866. See KEARSLEY.

BURY (NORTH). See BURY, Lancashire.

BURY ST EDMUNDS, a town, two parishes, and a district in Suffolk. The town stands on the river Larke, at a meeting of railways from the E, the N, and the W, 14½ miles E of Newmarket. The Larke is navigable to within about a mile of it, and the railway from the N is the Bury and Thetford line, authorised in 1865 but not commenced at the beginning of 1868. The town is thought to have been the Villa Faustina of the Romans. It was made a seat of royalty soon after the settlement of the Saxons, and named Beodericsworth, signifying "the dwelling of Beoderic," after a person who had possessed it. Sigbright the fifth king of East Anglia, on embracing Christianity about 638, founded at it a monastic church. Edmund, who succeeded to the throne of East Anglia in 855, was crowned either here or at Bures, and, upon his being slain by the Danes, and acquiring the reputation of a martyr, his body, after having lain some time elsewhere, was solemnly deposited here, and occasioned the place to be called Bury St. Edmunds. Miracles were alleged to be wrought, and great reputed sanctity was attained. A new church, over the royal remains, was founded in 925, by Athelstane, and a splendid enlargement of this, with the character of a Benedictine abbey, was commenced in 10.. by Canute and consecrated in 1032. A gorgeous shrine for Edmund's body was constructed in it, and Canute came hither in person, and offered his crown. A further enlargement of the edifice was begun soon afterwards and completed in 1095. Edward the Confessor frequently dismounted within a mile of the abbey, and entered it on foot. Henry I did homage in it for his safe return to his dominions. Eustace plundered it in 115.. Henry II was crowned in it, and he carried the banner of St Edmund in front of his troops at the battle of Fornham and ascribed to its influence the victory he obtained. Richard I made a visit to the shrine before going to Palestine. King John was here in 1201 and 1203 and a meeting of barons here shared with that of Runnymede the honour of wresting from him the Magna Charta. The Dauphin Louis plundered the abbey in 1216, and took away Edmund's body. Henry III was several times here, held a parliament here in 1272, and contracted here the disease which terminated in his death. Edward I and his queen visited the shrine five times in the course of his reign and he held a parliament in the town in 1296. Edward II kept his Christmas here in 1326 and his queen Isabella marched hither with the troops from the Prince of Hainault, and made Bury her rallying point. An assault, with great damage, was made on the abbey, in 1327, by the townspeople and suppressed by military force. Edward III and Richard II made visits to the shrine. The insurgents under Jack Straw, in 1381, beheaded Lord Chief Justice Cavendish at Bury, attacked the abbey, and slew the abbot. Henry VI spent his Christmas here in 1433, and held a parliament here in 1446, and Shakspeare lays a scene here in that monarch's reign. Henry VII was here in 1486. The Dukes of Suffolk and Norfolk, in 1525, assembled their troops here to quell the insurrection at Lavenham Sudbury, and the adjacent country. The Duke of Northumberland on proclaiming Lady Jane Grey to be successor of Edward VI made Bury the rendezvous of his troops in support of her cause. Twelve persons were burnt at the stake here on account of religious tenets in the reign of Mary. A visit was made to Bury, in 1578, by Elizabeth. A great fire broke out in 1608 destroyed 160 dwelling houses, and destroyed property to the value of £60,000. The plague made such havoc in 1636 that the grass grew in the streets. Forty persons, in the reign of James I, two of them tried before Sir Matthew Hale, were put to death in Bury for the imaginary crime of witchcraft.

The town occupies a gentle descent, on a sandy soil, amid pleasant environs. It measures about 1½ mile by 1¼, and is well built. The shire hall is a modern erection incorporating part of the ancient church of St Margaret, and contains two convenient courts, for criminal and civil causes. The Guildhall gives name to a street, is a handsome edifice, with an old porch, and contains some interesting old portraits. The county jail cost £30,000, and has capacity for 176 male and .. female prisoners. The bridewell, now used as a police office, outside the prison walls, was once a synagogue, and is a very old Norman building. The corn exchange was built in 1862, has a frontage of 82 feet and a length of 11. feet, consists of nave and aisles and has an elliptical iron roof, glazed for about 20 feet on each side of the arch. The athenæum was built in 1854, is a spacious structure and contains apartments for a public club, a reading room, a museum, a library of about 5,000 volumes, and a large hall. The botanic garden was established in 1820. The theatre was built in 1819. Moyses' hall is a late Norman house, with a vaulted lower story. Mediæval vaults are under the Angel inn. Five gates were in the town walls, but have disappeared. A Franciscan priory, a college, five hospitals, and at least twenty eight churches or chapels, besides the existing parish churches and the abbey chapels, were in the town at the Reformation but most are known now only by their sites or even only by their names. The college was founded by Edward IV, and is now a work house. St Saviour's hospital was founded in 118., appears to have been of great extent, and has all perished except a gateway. St Nicholas hospital was converted into a farm house, the stone chapel became a small inn, and two or three other chapels are represented by fragmentary ruins. The abbey church was cruciform, 505 feet from end to end, 241 feet along the transept, had a nave of thirteen bays, a choir of five bays and an apse containing the shrine several chapels, a central lantern and two octagonal western towers, and was built of flint and boulder cased with barnack stone. The cloisters and other buildings connected with [illegible] were of corresponding magnitude The [illegible] house is now used as a stable, the arches of the west front are incorporated with modern houses the central tower, [illegible] wide and 86 feet high, still stands, was restored in 1847, [illegible] now the grand entrance to the churchyard of the two [illegible] churches, and is a fine specimen of Norman architecture, and the abbey gate house, 50 feet by 40, and 62 feet high, also still stands and is rich decorated English but all the other parts have perished. The revenues were equivalent to about £50,000 of the present day, and passed, at the dissolution, chiefly to the Ayres and the Barons St Mary's church was built in 1005, and rebuilt in 1424–1490, has a west Norman tower is 213 feet long, and contains the tombs of Mary Tudor, Queen of France, and five persons of the 15th century St James church was built in 1200, rebuilt in 1500, and repaired in 1820, and the chancel was rebuilt, very ornately in 1869 St. John's church was built in 1841, at a cost of £5,000 and is a handsome structure St Peter's church is a recent erection at a cost of £3,000 The dissenting chapels are two Independent, two Baptist, one Quaker, one Unitarian, two Methodist, and one Brethren The R Catholic chapel was built in 1837 The grammar-school was founded by Edward VI educates 1[illegible] boys, and has an endowed income of £1,529, with six exhibitions at the universities Three feoffment schools educate 150 boys and 150 girls, and were modified in 18[illegible] to receive orphans There are two national schools The Suffolk general hospital was rebuilt in 1854 at a cost of £13,000 Clopton's asylum and school is an edifice in the Tudor style, built in 18[illegible], and has an endowed income of £[illegible]0 The total endowed charities within the borough amount to £3,923 There are likewise a [illegible] institute, a concert room, and subscription rooms

The town has a head post-office, a railway station with telegraph, four banking offices, and four chief inns, is a seat of assizes and sessions, and a polling place, and publishes two weekly newspapers Weekly markets are held on Wednesday and Saturday and fairs on Easter Tuesday, 2 Oct, and 1 Dec Little manufacture exists, [illegible] large trade arises from the markets and from the demands of numerous wealthy neighbouring families. The town has sent two members to parliament since the time of James I and is governed by a mayor six aldermen, and eighteen councillors Its borough boundaries both parliamentary and municipal are the same as those of the [illegible] [illegible] district. Acres, [illegible]934 Real property, £52 7[illegible] Direct taxes, £10,187 Electors in 1833, 6[illegible]7 Pop in 1841 1[illegible],538, in 1861, 1[illegible] 318 Houses, 2,[illegible]5[illegible] Lord Chancellor Aungervile, Bishop Gardiner Batteley, the antiquary Sir J Cullum Capel Lofft, Bishop Tomline, Bishop Blomfield, and Repton, the landscape gardener, were natives Norwood the antiquarist, Everden the historian, and Lydgate the poet were connected with the abbey, Archbishop Sancroft, Lord Keeper North Anstey Cumberland, the Bunburys, Romilly and a number of other distinguished men were educated at the grammar-school, and Madame de Genlis, [illegible] fox, and Wollaston were residents The town gives the title of Viscount to Earl Albemarle.

The two parishes are St Mary and St James, the latter includes the chapelry of St John and all three are vicarages in the diocese of Ely The value of St Mary's and St James is not reported, of St John £1[illegible]7 * Patrons of St Mary Trustees of St. James H Wilson Esq of St. John the Bishop of Ely The district is [illegible] [illegible] Poor rates in 18[illegible] £6,[illegible]34 Marriages in 18[illegible] 10[illegible] births, [illegible] —of which [illegible]1 were illegitimate, deaths [illegible]17,—of which [illegible]9 were at ages under 5 years and 1[illegible] at ages above [illegible] Marriages in the ten years 1851-60 1,0[illegible]7, births [illegible]0[illegible] deaths [illegible]1[illegible]

BURY (SOUTH) See [illegible]

BURY STREET a ward of Edmonton parish Middlesex, near the New river and the Great Northern [illegible] [illegible] 8 miles N of St Paul's London Pop, 1,172 [illegible] [illegible] [illegible] seat of [illegible] [illegible]

BURYTHORPE, a parish in the district of Malton and E R Yorkshire near the river Derwent, [illegible] miles E by S of Kirkham station and 5 S of New Malton It includes the hamlet of Thornthorpe and its post town is Kirkham, under York Acres, 1,22[illegible] Real property, £1,561 Pop. 2[illegible][illegible] Houses, [illegible]2 The property is divided among few The living is a rectory in the diocese of York Value, £270 Patron, the Lord Chancellor The church was built in 18[illegible]8, is a handsome edifice in the early English style, and contains an ancient Norman font, which belonged to a previous church There is a Wesleyan chapel

BURYTON See BURTON UPON TRENT

BURY WALLS See HAWKSTONE

BURY WOOD a place, with a large and strong Danish camp, near Slaughterford in Wilts

BUSBRIDGE, a chapelry in Godalming parish, Surrey, 1¼ mile S of Godalming Pop, 550 Living, a vicarage Value, £300 * The church was built in 1867

BUSBY (GREAT and LITTLE), two townships in Stokesley parish, N R Yorkshire, 2½ miles S of Stokesley Acres, 1,308 and [illegible]7[illegible]. Real property, £2,423 Pop., 117 and 38. Houses, 21 and 4

BUSCOT, a parish in Faringdon district, Berks on the river Thames, 4¼ miles WNW of Faringdon r station, and 1½ SSE of Lechlade It has a post office under Swindon Acres, 2,846 Real property, £4 556 Pop, 467 Houses 91 The property is subdivided. Buscot Park belonged formerly to the Lovedens and the Stoners and passed to the family of Campbell The parish is a meet for the Old Berks hounds The living is a rectory in the diocese of Oxford. Value, £457 * Patron, [illegible] Campbell, Esq The church is old but good, and contains monuments of the Lovedens Charities, £37

BUSHBURY, a village and a parish in Penkridge district Stafford The village stands adjacent to the Birmingham and Stafford railway, near the Stafford and Worcester canal, 2¾ miles N by E of Wolverhampton, and has a station on the railway The parish includes also the hamlet of Moseley and the township of Essington and its post town is Wolverhampton. Acres, [illegible],377 Real property, £13,101 Pop 2,[illegible]51 Houses, [illegible]93 The property is subdivided Bushbury Hall is a chief residence Coal is worked The living is a vicarage in the diocese of Lichfield Value, £159 * Patrons, [illegible] Horden and others. The church was built in 1[illegible], and is good Charities £35

BUSHBY, a hamlet in Thurnby parish, Leicestershire, [illegible] miles E by S of Leicester Acres, 760 Real property, £1,220 Pop, [illegible]0 Houses, 15

BUSHEY, a village, a parish, and a sub district, in Watford district, Herts The village stands ¾ of a mile E of the North Western railway near the river Colne 1½ mile SE of Watford, has a station on the railway and a post office under Watford, and was once a market-town The parish includes also Bushey Heath, which likewise has a post office under Watford, and is 3 miles from that town Acres, 3,18[illegible] Real property £15 5[illegible] Pop. 3,159 Houses 620 The property is much subdivided The manor was given by William the Conqueror to Geoffrey de Mandeville, and passed afterwards to the Crown Bushey Manor House, Bushey Grove, and Bushey Grange are chief residences The high grounds of Bushey Heath command an extensive and beautiful view The living is a rectory, united with the p curacy of St. Peter in the diocese of Rochester Value £7[illegible] * Patron, Exeter College, Oxford The parish church is tolerable and St Peter's church is modern and very good There are three dissenting chapels and three public schools The sub district contains two parishes. Pop 4,923 Houses, 1,0[illegible]2

BUSHEY HEATH See BUSHEY

BUSHEY PARK See BUSHY PARK

BUSH HILL, a village in the north of Middlesex on the New River, 1½ mile S of Enfield. It has a post office under Edmonton London N Bush Hill Park adjacent to it, belonged to the Mellishes and the [illegible] [illegible], has grounds laid out by Le Notre, and contains some of Gibbons's carvings

BUSHLEY, a parish in Upton on Severn district, Worcester on the river Severn, near the Bristol and

Birmingham railway, 1¾ mile NNW of Tewkesbury Post town Tewkesbury Acres, 1,740 Real property, £3,227 Pop, 282. Houses, 63. Toll Court here is the seat of J E Dowdeswell, Esq The living is a vicarage in the diocese of Worcester Value, £358 Patron J F Dowdeswell Esq The church is good

BUSHMEAD, a seat on the north border of Beds, 5 miles W of St Neots. A priory of Black canons was founded here, in the time of Henry II, by the Beauchamps, came, at the dissolution to Sir W Gascoigne, and passed to the Gerys

BUSHWOOD, a hamlet in Old Stratford parish, Warwick near Stratford on Avon

BUSHY PARK, a royal park in Teddington parish, Middlesex, on the Thames, adjacent to Hampton It comprises 1,110 acres and includes all the enclosures belonging to Hampton Court, except the Home Park Nine avenues are in it, of chestnuts and limes, noted for beauty and magnificence A right of passage through it having been withheld from the public, was recovered by the exertions of an humble resident at Hamptonwick. The house in it is a square brick structure, erected by the Earl of Halifax, and much improved by William IV, and was occupied occasionally by George IV, and much by William IV and his dowager Queen There is a post office of Bushy Park under Hampton, London SW There is also, on the London and Kingston railway, a station of Teddington and Bushy Park.

BUSLINGTHORPE, a parish in Caistor district, Lincoln, adjacent to the Lincoln and Glanford railway, 2 miles NNW of Wickenby station, and 3 SW of Market Rasen. Post town, Market Rasen. Acres, 1,096 Real property, £1,103. Pop, 55 Houses 8 The living is a rectory in the diocese of Lincoln. Value, £241 Patron, the Charter house, London The church is very old and has a brass of 1310

BUSLINGTHORPE, a chapelry in Leeds parish W R. Yorkshire, constituted in 1849 Pop, 4,548 Houses, 998 The property is much subdivided The living is a vicarage in the diocese of Ripon Value, £300 * Patrons Five Trustees

BUSSAGE, a chapelry in Bisley parish Gloucester, adjacent to the Cheltenham and Western Union railway, 3 miles E of Stroud. Post town, Chalford, under Stroud Pop, 312 Houses, 73. The chapelry was constituted in 1848 The living is a vicarage in the diocese of Gloucester and Bristol Value, £30 * Patron, the Bishop of Gloucester and Bristol

BUSSEX, a hamlet in Weston Zoyland parish, Somerset near Sedgemoor 3½ miles SE of Bridgewater

BUSTABECK BOUND, a township in Castle Sowerby parish, Cumberland, 3 miles SE of Hesket Newmarket Pop, 221 Houses, 49

BUSTLEHAM See Bisham

BUSTON (High and Low), two townships in Warkworth parish, Northumberland, on the Northeastern railway, between the Alne and the Coquet rivers, 4½ and 5½ miles SE of Alnwick Acres, 706 and 870 Pop, 120 and 120 Houses, 21 and 20

BUSY GAP, a pass through the hills on the SW border of Northumberland, adjacent to the Roman wall, 3 miles NW of Haltwhistle It used to be infested by moss troopers

BUTCOMBE a parish in Axbridge district, Somerset near the river Yeo, 5 miles SE of Nailsea r station and 8 NE of Axbridge Post town, Chew Stoke, under Bristol Acres, 983 Real property £1 582 Pop, 223 Houses, 52 The property is much subdivided Butcombe Court is a chief residence The living is a rectory in the diocese of Bath and Wells Value, £248 Patron, the Rev W H Cartwright The church is very ancient, and in fair condition

BUTE DOCKS, a harbour in Glamorgan, at the mouth of the river Taff, 1½ mile S of Cardiff It has a post office under Cardiff Docks here were constructed by the Marquis of Bute See Cardiff

BUTELAND See Broomhope

BUTLEIGH, a parish in Wells district Somerset, on the river Brue, 4 miles SSE of Glastonbury r station It includes the hamlet of Butleigh Wootton, and has a post office under Glastonbury Acres, 4 467 Real property £5 130 Pop 1,038 Houses, 212 The property is divided among a few Butleigh Court is the seat of R. Neville Grenville, Esq, was recently rebuilt in part, from designs by Buckler has a saloon 45 feet by 25, and contains some fine portraits Butleigh Hill is prominent, and blue lias is found The living is a vicarage, united with the p curacy of Baltonsborough, in the diocese of Bath and Wells. Value, £380 * Patron R. Neville Grenville, Esq The church is decorated English, and was restored in 1851, and enlarged in 1859 There are an Independent chapel, a national school, and charities £25

BUTLEIGH WOOTTON, a hamlet in Butleigh parish, Somerset, 3 miles NE of Somerton Pop, 212 Wootton House here is the seat of the Hon A Wood.

BUTLER'S COURT, or Gregories, a seat ½ a mile N of Beaconsfield in Bucks. It was the residence and death-place of Burke, was given to him by the Marquis of Rockingham and contains some paintings by Reynolds

BUTLER'S CROSS, a locality 2½ miles SW of Wendover, in Bucks, among the Chiltern hills, 7 miles SW of Tring It has a post office under Tring

BUTLERS MARSTON, a parish in Shipston on Stour district, Warwick, on an affluent of the river Avon 1½ mile SW of Kineton, and 7½ W by S of Fenny Compton r station Post-town Kineton, under Warwick Acres, 1,620 Real property, £2,630 Pop, 271 Houses, 63 The property is subdivided. The living is a vicarage in the diocese of Worcester Value, £169 Patron Christ Church, Oxford The church is Norman There is a Wesleyan chapel

BUTLEY, a township in Prestbury parish, Cheshire, on the Manchester and Birmingham railway, adjacent to Prestbury station, 3 miles N of Macclesfield Acres, 1 500 Real property £3 980 Pop, 674 Houses, 139 Some of the inhabitants are silk weavers. Roman remains have been found There is a Wesleyan chapel Newton the historian of the Saracens, was a native

BUTLEY a parish in Plomesgate district, Suffolk, on a sea creek of its own name, 3 miles W of Orford, and 4½ ESE of Wickham Market Junction r station. Post town, Orford, under Wickham Market Acres 1,941 Real property £1,764 Pop 38_ Houses, 81 The property is divided among a few A priory of Black canons was founded here, in 1171 by Ranulph de Glanville, and given, at the dissolution to the Duke of Norfolk and William Forth Ruins and fragments of the abbey occupy nearly 12 acres, and part of the gateway has been fitted up as a house The living is a vicarage, united with the p curacy of Capel in the diocese of Norwich Value, £130 Patron Lord Rendlesham The church is good There is a national school

BUTSASH, a hamlet in Fawley parish, Hants, 5½ miles W of Fareham

BUTSER HILL, a hill 3 miles SW of Petersfield, in Hants It forms the western termination of the South Downs, has an altitude of 917 feet, and commands a magnificent view

BUTSFIELD, a township in Lanchester parish, Durham, on Watling-street adjacent to the Weardale Extension railway 5½ miles NNE of Wolsingham Acres, 1,423 Real property, £1,324 Pop 310 Houses 6_

BUTTER BUMP, a hamlet in Willoughby parish, Lincoln 3½ miles S of Alford

BUTTERBY a locality on the river Wear, 3 miles S by E of Durham It was formerly called Beautrove, and belonged then to the Lumleys and the Chaytors. It has salt springs

BUTTERCRAMBE a township in Bossall parish, N R Yorkshire, on the river Derwent, under Aldby-Park camp, 3 miles E of Sand Hutton Acres, 1,5_ Real property £3,011 Pop, 120 Houses, 21 It forms a curacy with Bossall

BUTTERHOUSE GREEN, a locality 3 miles from Stockport in Cheshire, with a post office under Stockport

BUTTERLAW, a township in Newburn parish, North

umberland, 5 miles W by N of Newcastle upon Tyne Acres, 250 Pop. 10 Houses, 3

BUTTERLEIGH a parish in Tiverton district Devon, on the river Exe, 2½ miles S by E of Tiverton and 3 W by N of Collumpton r station It has a post office under Collumpton Acres, 479 Real property, £922. Pop 153 Houses 31 The property is much subdivided. The manor belonged to the Courtenays and others, but has been dismembered The living is a rectory in the diocese of Exeter Value, £170 * Patron, the Lord Chancellor The church is small, plain, and ancient, with a small tower

BUTTERLEY, a seat of iron works, 2¼ miles S of Alfreton, in Derbyshire The works were begun in 1792, they lie amid a rich tract of coal and lime, they soon began to employ about 1,500 men, and to make magnificent castings, and they possess ready means of transport by railway and canal

BUTTERLEY, a hamlet in Edwin Ralph parish, Hereford, 3 miles NE by N of Bromyard.

BUTTERLIP-HOWE, a round green hill at the head of Grasmere lake, in Westmoreland It commands a charming view

BUTTERMERE, a village, a township chapelry, and a lake, in Brigham parish, Cumberland The village stands about midway between Buttermere lake and Crummock water, 8½ miles SW of Keswick r station, and 10 S-L of Cockermouth, and consists of only a church two inns, and a few scattered houses The church is new and neat, on the site of a previous one which was said to be the smallest in England, and one of the inns supplies boats for the neighbouring lakes, and is notable for the pathetic story of "Mary of Buttermere" The chapelry includes the village and its post town is Loweswater, under Cockermouth Acres, 4,398 Real property, £1,120 Pop, 101 Houses, 18 The property is divided among a few Hassness, the seat of General Benson is on the NE side of the lake The general surface is a grand vale, engirt with mountains, and much occupied with the lakes A steep mountain pass, called Buttermere Haws, goes from the village, to an elevation of about 1,000 feet, on the road to Keswick Blue slate is quarried The living is a p curacy in the diocese of Carlisle Value, £56 Patron, the Earl of Lonsdale The lake extends from the head of the vale to within a mile of Crummock water, is 1¼ mile long ¾ of a mile broad, and 90 feet deep, and has a surface elevation of 247 feet above the level of the sea Its face looks gloomy, but its skirts are magnificent, being immediately overhung by Honister Crag, with a precipitous front, about 1,500 feet high, and by the Hay Stacks, High-Crag, High Stile, Red Pike, Buttermere Moss, and Great Robinson mountains.

BUTTERMERE, a parish in the district of Hungerford, and county of Wilts, 4½ miles S of Hungerford r station Post-town Shalbourn, under Hungerford. Acres 1,502 Real property, £706 Pop, 128 Houses, 26 The living is a rectory in the diocese of Salisbury Value, £229 Patron, the Bishop of Winchester

BUTTERSHAW, a chapelry in Bradford parish, W R. Yorkshire, near Thornton, constituted in 1842. Post town, Bradford Rated property, £4,334 Pop, 2,247 Houses, 505 The property is subdivided The living is a vicarage in the diocese of Ripon Value £200 * Patron, C Hardy, Esq The church was built in 1838, and a handsome Independent chapel was built in 1868

BUTTERTHWAITE, a hamlet in Ecclesfield township and parish, W R. Yorkshire, 5½ miles N of Sheffield.

BUTTERTON, a township chapelry in Mayfield parish, Stafford, 5½ miles I N E of Leek... station, and 6 ... of Leek Post town, W... under ...bourne Acres, 1,940 Real property £3,8.. Pop 3.. Houses, 8.. The property is divided among a few The living is a p curacy, in the diocese of Lichfield Value, £90 Patron, the Vicar of Mayfield The church has a tower, and is good There are a Wesleyan chapel, and charities ... 7

BUTTERTON, a township in Trentham parish, and a chapelry in Trentham, Swinnerton and Stoke upon-Trent parishes, Stafford The township lies adjacent to the Grand Trunk canal and the Manchester and Birmingham railway, 2 miles S of Newcastle under Lyne, and includes the hamlet of Millstone Green Acres 170 Pop, 57 Houses, 6 Butterton Hall is the seat of the Pilkingtons The chapelry was constituted in 1845 and its post town is Newcastle under Lyne Pop., 679 Houses, 71 The living is a p curacy in the diocese of Lichfield Value, not reported Patrons, Sir ... and Lady Pilkington

BUTTERTON HILL, a hill between South Brent and Ivy Bridge, in Devon Its altitude is 1,203 feet

BUTTERWICK, a township in Sedgefield parish, Durham, near the river Skern 2 miles E by N of Sedgefield. Acres, 1,495. Real property, £924 Pop 48 Houses, 10

BUTTERWICK, a parish in Boston district, Lincoln, on the coast, near Boston Deeps, 4½ miles E of Boston r station It includes an allotment in the East Fen and has a post office under Boston Acres, 4,420, of which 3,050 are water Real property, £4,660 Pop, 605. Houses, 120 A large pond, which medical men declared to be highly pestiferous, was recently filled up and planted with vegetables. The living is a vicarage annexed to the vicarage of Frieston, in the diocese of Lincoln The church has an early English octagonal font, and a rood turret. There are a Wesleyan chapel, an endowed school with £239 a year, and charities £160

BUTTERWICK, a hamlet in Barnpton parish, Westmoreland 7½ miles S of Penrith

BUTTERWICK, a township chapelry in Foxholes parish, E R. Yorkshire, 5½ miles SSE of Sherburn r station, and 10 N of Great Driffield Post town, Weaverthorpe, under York Acres, 1,540 Real property, £1,613 Pop., 109 Houses, 16 The living is a vicarage in the diocese of York. Value, £47 Patron, the Rector of Foxholes. The church has an effigies of a knight

BUTTERWICK, a township in Barton le Street parish N R. Yorkshire, on the river Rye, 4½ miles NW of New Malton Acres, 640 Real property, £976 Pop, 79 Houses, 16 It forms a curacy with Barton le Street

BUTTERWICK (East), a township in Bottesford and Messingham parishes Lincoln on the river Trent 3½ miles S by F of Keadby Real property, £2,397 Pop., 420 There are three dissenting chapels

BUTTERWICK (West), with Kelfield, a township-chapelry in Owston parish, Lincoln on the river Trent, 5½ miles S of Keadby r station It has a post office of the name of West Butterwick, under Bawtry Real property, £4 995 Pop, 937 Houses 203 The property is much subdivided The living is a vicarage in the diocese of Lincoln Value, £300 * Patron, the Vicar of Owston The church was built in 1841 There are three dissenting chapels and a national school

BUTTERWORTH, a township and two sub districts in Rochdale parish, Lancashire The township lies on the verge of the county, near the Manchester and Leeds railway, 3 miles E of Rochdale It includes the hamlets of Clegg, Wildhouse Belfield, Butterworth Hall, Lowhouse Haughs, and Blenked gate cum Roughbank Real property, £26,906 of which £6,305 are in mines. Pop, 6,704 Houses, 1 332 There are cotton and woollen factories, a church of 1795 dissenting chapels, two endowed schools, and charities £32 The sub districts are Freehold side and B Lordship side, and are jointly conterminate with the township

BUTTINGHILL, a hundred in the rape of Lewes, Sussex. It lies round Cuckfield and Hurstpeirpoint, and contains twelve parishes Acres, 60,... Pop in 1851, 15,12.. Houses, 2,547

BUTTINGTON, a parish in the district and county of Montgomery, on Offa's Dyke, the river Severn and the Oswestry and Newtown railway, 2 miles NE of Welshpool It has a station on the railway, and includes the townships of Cletterwood, Hope, and Trewern, and its post town is Welshpool Acres, 6 0.. Real property, £. 100 Pop, 905 Houses, 174 The property is divided among a few A sharp victory was obtained here, in 894, by the Saxons over the Danes, and nearly the last of the sanguinary struggles of the Welsh for national independence was made here Several ancient entrenchments are on the hills, and a vast quantity of human bones was found not many years ago, in digging for a foundation The living is a vicarage in the diocese of St Asaph. Value, £127 * Patron, the Vicar of Welshpool The church is early English, and good

BUTTOLPHS See BOTOLPH

BUTTON HILL, a hamlet in Ecclesall Bierlow township, Sheffield parish, W R Yorkshire, 4½ miles SW of Sheffield

BUTTSBURY, a parish in Chelmsford district, Essex, on the river Wid and on the Eastern Counties railway, 1¼ mile SE of Ingatestone r station, and 6¼ SSW of Chelmsford. Post town, Ingatestone Acres, 2,116 Rated property £2,079 Pop, 531 Houses, 109 The property is divided among a few The living is a vicarage, annexed to the rectory of Ingatestone, in the diocese of Rochester The church is good.

BUXBURY, an eminence projecting from the Downs, 11 miles SW of Salisbury, in Wilts

BUXEY SAND, a shoal at the mouth of the river Crouch, in Essex

BUXHALL, a parish in Stow district, Suffolk, on the rivers Ged and Orwell, near the Eastern Union railway, 3½ miles WSW of Stowmarket. It has a post office under Stowmarket. Acres, 2,120 Real property, £4,374 Pop, 536 Houses, 121 The property is subdivided The living is a rectory in the diocese of Norwich Value, £578 * Patron, the Rev Copinger Hill The church is good

BUXLOW, a hamlet in Knodishall parish, Suffolk, 2½ miles SE of Saxmundham It forms a curacy with Knodishall

BUXTED, a village and a parish in Uckfield district, Sussex The village adjoins the Brighton and Tunbridge-Wells rail, 1½ mile NE of Uckfield, and has a post office under Uckfield, a r station and a fair on 31 July The parish comprises 8,943 acres Real property, £7,324 Pop, 1,624. Houses, 326 The property is much subdivided. Buxted Place is the seat of Colonel Harcourt, and has a picturesque park Hendall is an ancient house, long the seat of the family of Pope Hog House is a structure of 1581 and was the seat of the Hogges. One of this family, Ralph Hogge, in 1543, made the first cast iron cannon ever made in England, and his name, altered into Huggett, is still common among the Sussex blacksmiths A relic of the old iron manufacture, in the form of a hammer post, is at Howbourne An hospital was founded in Buxted, in 1404, by William Hown The living is a rectory in the diocese of Chichester Value £403 * Patron, the Archbishop of Canterbury The church is chiefly early English, in good condition, has a low shingled spire, and contains a brass of 1375 The vicarage of Hadlow Down is a separate benefice Wotton the linguist, and the two Clarkes, grandfather and father of Clarke the traveller, were rectors There are a Calvinist chapel, a national school, and charities £144

BUXTON, a small town, a chapelry, and a sub district in Chapel en le Frith district, Derby The town stands in the bottom of a small valley, at an elevation of nearly 1,000 feet above the level of the sea, almost engirt by lofty hills, near the source of the river Wye, and at the terminus of a branch line from the Manchester and Macclesfield railway, also at the terminus of the Ambergate Junction branch of the Midland railway 10 miles E of Macclesfield and 11 WNW of Bakewell It was formerly called Badestanes, Bawkestanes, and Buckstones It possesses great medicinal springs, and has long been famed for them It is thought by some to have been known to the Druids, and it certainly was known to the Romans Cromlechs and Druidical circles occur on the heights in its neighbourhood, three Roman roads, with branches, went from it, Roman coins and tiles have been found at it, a Roman station, with baths is believed by most antiquaries to have been on its site, Saxon barrows in which interesting relics have been found, are near it, and shrines, with baths images, and offerings made by devotees resorting to it for health, were at it for ages preceding the Reformation The shrines and baths were destroyed by an emissary of Henry VIII, but the baths were speedily restored Mary, Queen of Scots, while in the custody of the Earl of Shrewsbury, came hither four times for health, Lord Burleigh and the Duke of Sussex came in 1577 and 1580, and other personages of note soon followed, giving the place a permanent celebrity The third Earl of Devonshire, in 1670, pulled down a house which had been built for Queen Mary, and replaced it by a larger structure, now known as the Old Hall Hotel Buxton was then a mere hamlet, but it thence grew steadily to be first a village and then a town A pile of buildings, called the crescent, was erected by the Duke of Devonshire, in 1780, at a cost of £120,000 This has a frontage of 316 feet, consisting of two wings 58 feet each, and an intermediate curve of 200 feet, is three stories high and includes two hotels, an assembly room, news room, library, baths, and private residences. The basement story forms an arcade, and is used as a promenade, the upper part is adorned with Doric pilasters, entablature and balustrade, and the ground in front is laid out in beautiful terraces A suit of stables, said to be about the finest in Europe, is behind the crescent, encloses a covered circular ride, 180 feet in diameter used for exercise in bad weather, and includes an upper story, let off as residences The Square, Hall Bank, and Scarsdale Place also consist of good buildings The chief street is wide, but is edificed mainly with small houses The old town stands distinct from the new, is an ordinary village, and has remains of an ancient cross

The waters of Buxton have been much recommended by eminent physicians, and warmly sung by several poets They rise in springs both tepid and cold within 12 inches of each other, and are pellucid and mild An analysis of them, in 1852, by Dr Lyon Playfair, shows, per gallon 0 655 grains of silica, 0 24 of oxide of iron and alumina, 7 773 of carbonate of lime 2 323 of sulphate of lime, 4 543 of carbonate of magnesia, 0 114 of chloride of magnesium, 2 42 of chloride of sodium, 2 5 of chloride of potassium, a trace of fluorine and a trace of phosphoric acid Two elegant recent buildings, covered and lighted with roofs of glass, adjoin the ends of the Crescent, the one for hot baths, the other for natural baths, and a new erection, in room of an old one, called St Anne's well, is over the springs, for the use of drinkers The town can accommodate about 2,000 visitors at a time, and usually has from 12,000 to 14,000 in the course of the season, which lasts from May till October It has a head post office,‡ a railway station with telegraph, a handsome and extensive hotel of 1868, seven other good and spacious hotels, a town hall, a police station, many good shops, and five annual fairs, is a seat of petty sessions and a polling place, and publishes two weekly newspapers A trade is carried on in the manufacture and sale of ornaments in alabaster, spar, and other minerals There are two churches, the one old, the other a structure of 1812, in the Tuscan style with a neat tower, three chapels for Independents, Wesleyans, and Unitarians, a free school, with £91 a year from endowment, and a bath charity, for invalids maintained by subscription Walks, rides, and natural curiosities, of most interesting character, are in the neighbourhood The serpentine walks go along the margin of the Wye, and are variegated with lakelets, mimic cascades, and rustic seats The Duke's drive is a circuit of about four miles, through Ashwood dale, and over Wye-dale A splendid walk goes by Topley Pike, along and across the Wye, and over cliffs to Chee Tor This is a mass of rocks 300 feet high, covered lightly with foliage and commanding a delightful view Poole's Hole, about a mile from the town, is a cavern, with stalactites and stalagmites in grotesque forms, and of fantastic names, one of them traditionally associated with a visit of Mary Queen of Scots. Diamond Hill, not far from Poole's Hole, affords beautiful specimens of quartz crystal, and is crowned by a tower commanding a brilliant view. Other caverns, vales, and mountains of fascinating character in [illegible] all the attractions of the Derby Peak and of some tracts beyond, are within easy distance. Some of the railway works also, on the lines leading to the town and near it—tunnels, viaducts, and cuttings—are very striking.

The chapelry includes the town, is in Bakewell parish, and comprises 1,527 acres. Real property, £10,539. Pop. 1,87[illegible] Houses, 343. The property is not much divided, and the manor belongs to the Duke of Devonshire. The living is a p. curacy in the diocese of Lichfield. Value, £105.* Patron, the Duke of Devonshire.—The sub-district contains parts of three parishes. Acres, 5,741. Pop. 4,142. Houses, 776.

BUXTON, a village, a parish, and a sub-district, in Aylsham district, Norfolk. The village stands on the river Bure, near the line of the projected railway from Norwich to Cromer, 4 miles SSE of Aylsham, and 8 N of Norwich; has a post office under Norwich, and was a seat of petty sessions. A Roman station is supposed to have been here, and Roman urns and other Roman relics have been found. The parish comprises 1,274 acres. Real property, £2,516. Pop., 640. Houses, 134. The property is subdivided. The living is a vicarage, united with the rectories of Oxnead and Skeyton, in the diocese of Norwich. Value, £[illegible].* Patron, Sir H. Stracey, Bart. The church is ancient, has a square tower, and was recently restored. There are a Baptist chapel, a Wesleyan chapel, and charities £168. The sub-district contains twenty-three parishes. Acres, 28,024. Pop., 10,032. Houses, 2,271.

BUXTON, Hereford. See BRCKTON.

BWA[illegible], a very precipitous rock, of remarkable character, near Ystradfellte, on the S border of Brecon. It consists of stratified marble, has the form of the segment of a circle, and is about 50 feet high and 70 feet broad. Its name means "the stone bow," and it is sometimes called also the Chair of the Witch.

BWLCH, a Celtic name signifying a pass, defile, gap, or hollow.

BWLCH, a pass in the F of Breconshire, 9 miles NW of Crickhowell, on the road to Brecon. It commands a fine view.

BWLCH AGRICLA, a pass in Denbigh, near Llanarmon, 3 miles E of Ruthin. It is supposed to have been traversed by Agricola on his way to Anglesey.

BWLCHAN, or BYLCHAN, a chapelry in Henllan and Llansannan parishes, Denbighshire, 6 miles W of Denbigh r station. It was constituted in 1855, and its post town is Denbigh. Pop., 537. Houses, 124. The living is a rectory in the diocese of St Asaph. Value, £[illegible].* Patron, alternately the Crown and the Bishop.

BWLCH COEDEG, a hamlet 1 mile ENE of Dinas Mowddwy, in Merioneth.

BWLCH OFEDDRWS, a grand mountain pass on the road from Dolgelly to Dinas-Mowddy, in Merioneth.

BWLCH PHIWGUP, a pass near Carsygedol, in Merioneth, on the road from Dolgelly to Llanbedr.

BWLCH TRAWYN, a hamlet in Cwmyoy parish, Monmouth, on the river Monnow, 5½ miles N of Abergavenny. It has a post office, of the name of Bwlch, under Crickhowell. Acres, 635. Real property, £654. Pop. 95. Houses, [illegible]

BWLCH TYDDIAD, a pass near Rhinog, in Merioneth, on the road from Harlech to Llanbedr.

BWLCH Y CEFNAN, a hamlet on the NW border of Radnor, 6½ miles NNE of Rhayader.

BWLCH Y CLAWT, a hamlet in Montgomery, under Plinlimmon, 3½ miles NW of Llanidloes.

BWLCH Y CIBAU, a chapelry in Meifod parish, Montgomery. The church was built in 1864, and is in the [illegible] style. See MEIFOD.

BWLCH Y FEDWEN, a mountain pass on the mutual border of Merioneth and Montgomery, 1½ miles E of Dinas Mowddwy, on the road to Llanfair.

BWLCH Y [illegible]RYDD, a hamlet in Montgomery, 3½ miles [illegible] of Newtown.

BWLCH Y GROES, a mountain pass on the mutual border of Merioneth and Montgomery, 8 miles S of Bala, on the road to Dinas Mowddwy. The ascent of it is singular, grand, and stupendous, and used to be reckoned dangerous, and the name, which signifies "the pass of the cross," was given to it on account of a rude crucifix having been placed on its summit to stimulate the faith and courage of travellers.

BWLCH Y GYFYNNG, a hamlet in Merioneth, 6½ miles NE of Towyn.

BYALL FEN, an extra parochial tract 7½ miles NW of Ely, in Cambridge.

BYCHTON, a township in Whitford parish, Flint, 2 miles NW of Holywell. Real property, £2,023, of which £917 are in mines. Pop., 676.

BYERS GREEN, a township and a chapelry in Auckland St Andrew parish, Durham. The township lies on the river Wear, and on the Clarence and Hartlepool railway, 3½ miles NNE of Bishop-Auckland, and has a station on the railway, and a post-office under Ferry Hill. Acres, 997. Real property, £11,030, of which £3,975 are in mines. Pop., 1,634. Houses, 330. The chapelry was constituted in 1845. Pop., 2,691. Houses, 512. The property is subdivided. The living is a rectory in the dio. of Durham. Value, £300. Patron, the Bishop of D. The church is good. There are two Methodist chapels and a national school.

BYFIELD, a parish in Daventry district, Northampton, 6 miles E of Fenny Compton r station, and 7½ SW by S of Daventry. It has a post office‡ under Daventry. Acres, 2,760. Real property, £6,083. Pop., 901. Houses, 224. The property is much subdivided. The living is a rectory in the diocese of Peterborough. Value, £917.* Patron, Caius College, Oxford. The church is ancient. There are Independent and Primitive Methodist chapels, and charities £79.

BYFLEET, a village and a parish in Chertsey district, Surrey. The village stands near the river Wey, the Junction canal, and the Southwestern railway, 2 miles SSW of Weybridge r station, and 2½ WNW of Cobham, and has a post office under Weybridge station. It is a curious picturesque place, and includes several old mansions. The parish comprises 2,068 acres. Real property, £3,991. Pop. 770. Houses, 153. The property is subdivided. The manor belonged anciently to the Crown, was given by Edward II to Piers Gaveston, came again to the Crown, and was settled by James I on Anne of Denmark. Byfleet Park, now a farm house, is said to have been built by the Black Prince, and both it and Dorney House in the village are alleged to have been the nursing place of Henry VIII. A mansion was founded on the manor by Anne of Denmark, and completed by Sir James Fullerton. The living is a rectory in the diocese of Winchester. Value, £295.* Patron, the Lord Chancellor. The church is good, and there are a national school, and charities £23. Stephen Duck, the poetical protege of Queen Caroline, and Joseph Spence, the author of "Polymetis," were rectors.

BYFORD, a parish in Weobly district, Herefordshire, on the river Wey and the Hereford and Brecon railway, near Moorhampton station, 7½ miles WNW of Hereford. Post town, Bishopstone under Hereford. Acres, 903. Real property, £1,787. Pop., 201. Houses, 42. The property is not much divided, and belongs chiefly to Sir H. Cotterell, Bart. The living is a rectory in the diocese of Hereford. Value, £195.* Patron, Sir H. G. Cotterell, Bart. The church is old but very good.

BYGRAVE, a parish in Hitchin district, Herts, on the Hitchin and Royston railway, near Icknield street and Metley Hill, 2½ miles NE of Baldock. Post town, Baldock. Acres, 1,809. Real property, £2,[illegible]92. Pop., 195. Houses, 40. The property is divided among a few. The living is a rectory in the diocese of Rochester. Value, £377. Patron, the Marquis of Salisbury. The church is good.

BYKENOPE. See BICKNOR.

BYKER, a township, two chapelries, and a sub-district, in Newcastle upon Tyne district, Northumberland. The township lies on the river Tyne, near the line of the Roman wall, 1½ mile E of Newcastle upon Tyne, and it has a post office, of the name of Byker Hill, under Newcastle upon Tyne Acres, 687, of which 55 are water Pop, 7,663. Houses, 1,046 The inhabitants are employed variously in potteries, glass works, quarries, collieries, and other manufactories and works The chapelries are B constituted in 1844, and B St Anthony, constituted in 1868, and are in the parish of All Saints. Pop., 10,388 Houses, 1,359 The livings are vicarages in the diocese of Durham Value, £300 and £170 Patron of B, alternately the Crown and the Bishop, of B St. A., Lady James B church was built in 1862, at a cost of £2,500, and is in the decorated English style There is a Wesleyan chapel —The sub district contains three townships and two parishes. Pop, 12,904 Houses, 1,817

BYKLESWADE See BIGGLESWADE

BYLAND ABBEY, a township in Coxwold parish N R Yorkshire, adjacent to the Malton and Driffield railway, at Coxwold station, 8½ miles ESE of Thirsk. Acres 3,130 Real property, £3 392 Pop, 104 Houses, 21 A Cistertian abbey was removed hither, in 1147 from Old Byland, and given, at the dissolution, to Sir William Pickering The west front, one end of the transept, part of the aisles and a fragment of the central tower still stand, and are in transitional Norman. Edward II, while dining here with a small retinue, in 1323, was surprised by a body of Scots, and made a narrow escape

BYLAND (OLD), a parish in Helmsley district, N R Yorkshire, on the river Rye, 4½ miles NW of Helmsley, and 5¼ NNE of Coxwold r station Post town, Helmsley, under York. Acres, 2,733 Real property, £1,942 Pop, 157 Houses, 30 A Cistertian abbey an offshoot from Furness, was founded here, in 1143, by Roger de Mowbray, but was removed, four years afterwards, to Byland Abbey The living is a donative in the diocese of York Value, £55 Patron, G Wombwell, Esq The church is old

BYLAUGH a parish in Mitford district Norfolk, on the river Wensum, 3½ miles ESE of Elmham r station, and 4½ S of Foulsham Post town, Bawdeswell, under Thetford Acres, 1 546 Real property, £1,701 Pop., 82 Houses, 17 The property is divided between two The living is a vicarage in the diocese of Norwich Value, £75 Patron, the Rev H Lombe The church is old but good

BYLCHAN See BWLCHAN

BYLEY, a township in Middlewich parish and a chapelry in Middlewich, Devenham, and Sandbach parishes, Cheshire The township bears the name of Byley-cum Yatehouse, and lies near the Trunk canal, 2 miles N of Middlewich and 3½ NE of Winsford r station Acres, 1 030 Real property, £1 724 Pop., 121 Houses, 21 The chapelry bears the name of Byley with Lees, or St John Byley, and was constituted in 1847 Post town, Middlewich Pop, 460 Houses, 90 The living is a rectory in the diocese of Chester Value £100 Patron, the Vicar of Middlewich

BYNEA, a railway station in Carmarthen, on the Llanelly and Vale of Towy railway, 3¼ miles NE of Llanelly

BYNWESTON a township in Worthen parish, Salop, 7¾ miles NE of Montgomery Pop, 91

BYRAM WITH POOL. See BYROME WITH POOL

BYRTON See BURTON-UPON TRENT

BYRKENHEAD See BIRKENHEAD

BYRLING See BIRLING, Kent

BYRNESHEAD See BURNESIDE

BYRNESS, or BURNESS, a chapelry in Elsdon parish, Northumberland on the river Reed among the Cheviots, 10 miles NW of Otterburn, and 12½ N of Forset station Post town, Elsdon, under Newcastle on Tyne Stats is returned with the parish. The living is a p. curacy in the diocese of Durham Value, £75. Patron, the Rector of Elsdon The church was built in 1793

BYROME WITH POOL a township in Brotherton parish W R Yorkshire, on the river Aire adjacent to the York and Derby railway, 1½ mile NNW of Ferry Bridge Acres 7 5 Real property, £1 C20 Pop, 65 Houses, 9 Byrome Hall is the seat of Sir J W Ramsden, Bart

BYRON, a sub district in the district and borough of Nottingham, consisting of part of the parish of St. Mary Pop 14,673 Houses 3,104.

BYSHAM MONTAGUE See BISHAM

BYSHOTTLES See BRANDON and BYSHOTTLES

BYSICH, a parcel in Llanbedr parish, Brecon, 2 miles NE of Crickhowell. Pop, 150.

BYSTOCK a hamlet in Colyton Rawleigh parish, Devon, 2 miles W of Sidmouth Bystock House is the seat of E Divett, Esq

BYTHAM CASTLE, a village and a parish in Bourn district, Lincoln The village stands on the river Glen, 1¼ mile W by N of Little Bytham r station and 5 S of Corby, and has a post office under Stamford The parish includes also the hamlet of Counthorpe, and the chapelry of Holywell with Aunby Acres, 7,760. Real property, £7,969 Pop, 1 024 Houses, 190 The manor was given by William the Conqueror to his brother in law, Odo, Earl of Albemarle and passed to the Colvilles. An ancient castle stood on it, and was burned by Edward III, and afterwards rebuilt The living is a vicarage in the diocese of Lincoln Value, £450 Patron, the Bishop of Lincoln There is a Wesleyan chapel A school has £40 from endowment

BYTHAM (LITTLE), a parish in Bourn district Lincoln, on the river Glen and the Great Northern railway, 5 miles S by E of Corby It has a station on the railway, and its post town is Castle Bytham, under Stamford Acres, 1,010 Real property, £1,613 Pop, 352. Houses, 64 The living is a rectory in the diocese of Lincoln Value, £329 * Patron, alternately the Bishop of Lincoln and the Dean and Chapter of Lincoln The church is good Charities, £16

BYTHORN, a parish in the district of Thrapston and county of Huntingdon, on the verge of the county, 4 miles ESE of Thrapston r station, and 6½ NW by N of Kimbolton Post town, Thrapston Acres, 1 303 Real property, £2,140 Pop 292 Houses, 59 The living is a p curacy, annexed to the rectory of Brington, in the dio of Ely The church is early English There are a Baptist chapel and charities £16

BYTON, a parish in the district of Presteigne and county of Hereford, on the river Lug near Shobdon hill wood, 4 miles NNW of Pembridge r station, and 4 E of Presteigne Post town, Shobdon, Herefordshire Acres, 946 Real property £1,044 Pop, 214 Houses, 40 The property is divided among a few The living is a rectory in the diocese of Hereford Value, £104 Patron, the Lord Chancellor The church was built in 1860, and is a cruciform structure, in the early English style The previous church was burned Charities, £9

BYWELL, a village and a sub district in Hexham district, Northumberland The village stands in the parishes of Bywell St Andrew and Bywell St Peter, on the river Tyne, adjacent to Stocksfield r station, 7½ miles E of Hexham, and contains the two parish churches, and dissenting chapels. A weir, with a fall of about 10 feet, goes across the river below a bridge, of recent erection, built at the cost of £15,000, spans the river adjacent, and a seat of W B Beaumont, Esq, and the ruins of an ancient castle, are in the vicinity The surrounding manor belonged to the Baliols, passed to the Nevilles and the Fenwicks, and belongs now to W B Beaumont, Esq —The sub-district contains three parishes, large part of another, and an extra parochial tract Acres 47 850 Pop 8 128 Houses 1,522

BYWELL ST ANDREW, a township and a parish in Hexham district, Northumberland The township includes part of Bywell village. Pop, 1? Houses, 7 The parish includes also the townships of Stocksfield Hall, Riding Hard, Styford and Broomhaugh, lies along the river Tyne and the Newcastle and Carlisle railway, and contains the r stations of Stocksfield and Riding Mill and the post offices of Stocksfield, Northumberland and Riding Mill, Northumberland Acres 2,912 Real property, £5 400 Pop 703. Houses, 90 The property is subdivided. The living is a vicarage in the diocese of Durham Value, £159 Patron, W B Beaumont, Esq The church has a lofty steeple, and is very good

BYWELL ST PETER, a township and a parish in Hexham district, Northumberland The township includes part of Bywell village Pop, 94 Houses, 20 The parish includes also the townships of Whittonstall Newlands, Espershields, Healy, High Fortherley, Broomley, Appeiley, Stelling, Newton, and Newton Hall, extends southward to the river Derwent at the boundary with Durham, and is nearly 8 miles long and 5 miles broad. Post town Stocksfield Northumberland. Acres 17 784 Real property, £9,295 Pop, 1,574 Houses, 238. The property is divided among a few Much of the land in the south is high and poor The living is a vicarage in the diocese of Durham Value, £300 Patrons, the Dean and Chapter of Durham The church has a square tower and is good. The p curacy of Whittonstall is a separate charge

BYWORTH, a hamlet in Petworth parish, Sussex, 1¼ mile E of Petworth it has a post office under Petworth

C

CABAS See CABUS.

CABILLO a village in Ystradgunlais parish, Brecon, 9 miles N of Neath

CABOURN, a parish in Caistor district, Lincoln, 2 miles ENE of Caistor, and 4½ ENE of Moortown r station Post town Caistor Acres 2 800 Real property, £3,372 Pop, 171 Houses, 29 The property is divided among a few The living is a vicarage in the diocese of Lincoln. Value, not reported.* Patron, the Earl of Yarborough, The church is tolerable

CABURN-MOUNT, an eminence 2 miles ESE of Lewes, in Sussex, isolated by a pass from the South Downs, overhanging the railway, commanding a fine view and crowned by an ancient round camp

CABUS or CABAS, a township in Garstang parish, Lancashire, on the Lancaster canal adjacent to the Lancaster and Preston railway, 2 miles N of Garstang. Acres, 1 220 Real property, £2,266 Pop, 203 Houses, 39

CACCA DUTTON See DUTTON CACCA

CAD (THE), a stream of Devon, rising in the centre of Dartmoor forest, and running 10 miles south south-westward to the Plym at Shaugh village 8½ miles NNE of Plymouth. It is properly the Plym, being longer than the Leadstream bearing that name Its vale is a wild glen replete with character, overhung by cliffs and rocky hills, and flanked in parts with torrents of fallen masses of granite

CADBURY a parish in Tiverton district, Devon, on the Kennansleigh ridge way 5½ miles W by N of Hele r station, and 6½ ENE of Crediton Post town, Cheriton Fitzpaine, under Crediton Acres, 1,899 Real property £2,399 Pop, 241 Houses 46 The property is divided among three The manor, with Fursdon House, belongs to F Fursdon Esq Cadbury Castle is the remnant of an ancient earthwork, was the rendezvous of Fairfax's army on a day in 1645 and has yielded a quantity of antique ornaments The living is a vicarage in the diocese of Exeter Value £163 * Patron, Rev F J Coleridge The church is a substantial structure of the 15th century

CADBURY (NORTH) a village and a parish in Wincanton district, Somerset The village stands on an eminence, 2 miles NE of Sparkford r station, and 5 WSW of Wincanton and has a post office under Bath The parish includes also the hamlets of Galhampton and Woolston Acres 2,810 Real property £7 229 Pop, 997 Houses 236 The manor belonged to the Newmarshes, the Botreauxes and the Hungerfords and passed to the Hastingses The manor house was built in 1581 by the third Earl of Huntingdon The living is a rectory in the diocese of Bath and Wells Value £700 Patron Emmanuel College, Cambridge The church was built, in the time of Henry VI by the Botreauxes, and contains several ancient monuments There are a Wesleyan chapel and a national school Ralph Cudworth was rector

CADBURY (SOUTH), a parish in Wincanton district, Somerset, adjacent to the Frome and Yeovil railway, 1½ mile E of Sparkford r station, and 6 WSW of Wincanton. Post town, North Cadbury, under Bath Acres, 800 Real property, with Sutton Montis, Weston, and Bampfylde, £4,663 Pop 257 Houses 56 The property is divided among a few Cadbury House is the seat of J Bennett, Esq Cadbury fort, situated on the northern extremity of a ridge of hills, and anciently called Camelet, is thought to have been a Roman station, and probably was the Cathbregion where Arthur routed the Saxons in a great battle, has yielded weapons, articles of camp equipage, a silver horse shoe, and many Roman coins, comprises four concentric deep ditches, and as many massive ramparts, enclosing an area of about 20 acres, and has in the centre a moated mound, called King Arthur's Palace, and in the fourth ditch, a spring called King Arthur's Well The living is a rectory in the diocese of Bath and Wells Value, not reported * Patron, J Bennett, Esq The church is good

CADDINGTON, a parish in the district of Luton and counties of Bedford and Hertford, near the Hertford and Dunstable railway, 2 miles WSW of Luton It includes the Humbershoe portion of Market street village, and its post town is Luton Acres, 4,900 Real property, £6,785 Pop, 1,851 Houses, 359 The living is a vicarage in the diocese of Ely Value, £375 * Patrons, the Dean and Chapter of St Paul's The church is ancient, and has two brasses of the 16th century The vicarage of Market street is a separate charge There are two dissenting chapels, an endowed school with £138 a year, and charities £ 6.

CADLBY, a township and a parish in Market-Bosworth district, Leicester The township lies 1¾ mile SE by S of Market Bosworth, and 5 WSW of Desford r station Acres, 900 Real property £1 692 Pop 104 Houses, 43 The parish contains also the township of Osbaston, and its post town is Market Bosworth, under Hinckley Acres, 2,130 Real property, £4,623 Pop, 422 Houses 85 The property is divided among a few The parish is a meet for the Atherstone hounds The living is a rectory in the diocese of Peterborough Value £223 * Patron, Sir Alex. Dixie Bart The church is very good Charities, £21

CADEBY a hamlet in Wyham parish, Lincoln, 5½ miles NNW of Louth It forms a curacy with Wyham.

CADEBY, a township in Sprotbrough parish, W R Yorkshire, adjacent to the river Don near the South Yorkshire railway 4½ miles SW by S of Doncaster Acres 1,100 Real property £1 536 Pop, 165 Houses, 36 It contains lime and building stone, and forms a curacy with Sprotbrough

CADLEIGH or CADLEIGH, a parish in Tiverton district, Devon, 4½ miles SW of Tiverton r station Post town, Tiverton. Acres, 2,191 Real property, £2,160 Pop 258 Houses, 74 The property is much subdivided The surface rises into bold romantic hills, with brilliant views The living is a rectory in the diocese of Exeter Value, £198 * Patron, Mrs Moore The church is old, consists of nave, chancel, north aisle, and western tower; contains a canopied monument to Sir Simon Leach, and stands on high ground, forming a conspicuous landmark An Independent chapel is at Little Silver, and there are charities £16

CADENHAM, a village 3 miles N of Lyndhurst, in Hants. An oak tree here is remarkable for budding in the depth of winter

CADER, a township in Llanrhaiadr-in Kinmerch parish, Denbighshire, 3½ miles S by W of Denbigh Pop, 183 Cader Gwladus here is an eminence rich in curious minerals, and commanding a fine view

CADER-ARTHUR. See ARTHUR'S CHAIR.

CADER FERWIN See BERWIN MOUNTAINS

CADER GWLADUS. See CADER.

CADER IDRIS, a mountain ridge in the SW of Merioneth, culminating 4½ miles SW by S of Dolgelly, and 6¼ ESE of the sea at Barmouth It extends south west ward from a point about 1½ mile SE of Dolgelly, is 6 miles long as the crow flies, but nearly 10 by the curvatures of its summit line, and varies in breadth from less than ½ a mile to about 3 miles Its highest points are Pen y Gador and Mynydd Moel, 2,914 and 2,817 feet high Its acclivities are generally steep, yet present every variety of gradation, and its breaks, hollows, and other features of contour give it more richness of scenic character than is possessed by almost any other mountain mass in Wales. The views from it are of vast extent, and exhibit striking contrasts Its rocks are eruptive, variously basalt, greenstone, clinkstone, and porphyry

CADGEWITH, a village on the coast of Cornwall, in a romantic valley, 2½ miles NNE of the Lizard It is inhabited chiefly by fishermen, is a coast guard station, and has an inn A pit or amphitheatre is near it, called the Devil's Frying pan nearly 2 acres in area, with sides 200 feet high, and receiving some water of flood tides through an arch which opens to the shore, and here hornblende slate and serpentine occur in junction, and iron pyrites, amianthus, and other minerals are found

CADHAY a seat, 1¼ mile NNW of Ottery St Mary, in Devon It is a Tudor mansion, belonged formerly to the Haydons, and belongs now to Sir Thomas Hare, Bart

CADISHEAD, a hamlet in Barton upon Irwell township, Eccles parish, Lancashire 4½ miles W of Manchester It has a post office under Warrington Pop, 901

CADLANDS, a hamlet in Fawley parish, Hants, on Southampton water, 5½ miles W of Fareham Real property, £2,567 Cadlands Park is the seat of the Drummonds, and has rich grounds, laid out by Brown

CADLEIGH See CADELEIGH

CADLEY See SAVERNAKE (SOUTH)

CADMORE END See ASHAMPSTEAD, Oxford

CADNAM, a tything in Minstead parish, Hants, 6½ miles SW of Romsey Pop, 154

CADNEY CUM HOUSHAM, a parish in Glanford Brigg district Lincoln on the Lincoln and Hull railway, 2½ miles SSE of Glanford Brigg It has a station, of the name of Howsham, on the railway, and its post town is Brigg Acres, with Newstead, 4 860. Real property, £6,383. Pop, 570 Houses, 111 The living is a vicarage in the dio of Lincoln Value £230 * Patron, Lord Yarborough The church is old There are a chapel of ease four dissenting chapels, and a British school

CADOXTON a village, a parish, and a sub district in Neath district, Glamorgan The village stands on the Sarn Helen Roman way and the river Neath, adjacent to the Neath canal and the Vale of Neath railway, ½ a mile N of Neath and is within Neath borough The parish includes the hamlets of Llanhonddan, Dyffryn Clydach, Coedfrank, Ynis y mond, Upper Dylais, Lower Dylais, Lower Neath, Middle Neath and Upper Neath and extends about 15 miles from Briton Ferry to Pont Neath Vaughan Post town, Neath Acres, 32,060, of which 905 are water Real property, £49,268 of which £22,591 are in mines, and £4 800 in iron-works Pop in 1851 5,791, in 1861, 8 203 Houses 1,600 The property is subdivided. The surface is hilly and displays much fine scenery Aberpergwm, the seat of the Williams family, is remarkably picturesque Ynis las, Cadoxton Lodge, and Cadoxton Place also are chief residences Coal and ores abound, and the Neath Abbey iron works, the Crown and Mines Royal copper works, and many other large mineral or manufacturing establishments are within the parish The living is a vicarage, united with the p curacy of Crynant, in the diocese of Llandaff Value, £240 * Patron, R H Miers, Esq The church is good, and contains the pedigree of the Williams family, engraved on sheets of copper. The vicarages of Skewen and Aberpergwm are separate benefices. There is a chapel of ease at Crynant. There are also chapels for Baptists, Wesleyans, and Calvinistic Methodists The parish under a modified form of its name, gives title to Earl Cadogan The sub district contains part of Cadoxton parish and the whole of another Acres, 27,304 Pop, 7,522 Houses, 1,462

CADOXTON JUXTA BARRY, a parish in Cardiff district, Glamorgan, on the coast, 4¾ miles S of St Fagans r station, and 6½ SW of Cardiff Post town, Sully, under Cardiff Acres, 1,028, of which 80 are water Real property, £1,009 Pop, 279 Houses, 64 There are remains of a castle, and lime is worked The living is a rectory in the diocese of Llandaff Value, £100 Patron R F Jenner, Esq, and others

CADWELL, a hamlet in Tathwell parish, Lincoln, 2 miles S of Louth

CADWELL a liberty in Brightwell Baldwin parish, Oxford, 3½ miles WNW of Watlington.

CADWORTH See CAWDEN

CAE COCH a spa on the E border of Carnarvon, in the vale of the Conway, in the vicinity of Trefriw, adjacent to the Conway and Llanrwst railway, 3 miles N of Llanrwst It is called also the Vale of Conway spa. A neat hotel and other houses for visitors have been built, and a great number of invalids have recently come hither

CAE GORLAN, a township in Llangelynin parish, Carnarvon 2 miles S of Conway

CAEGURWAIN See CAERGURWAIN

CAELWYNGRYDD a hamlet in Llanllechid parish, Carnarvon, 3½ miles NE of Bangor

CAENBY, a parish in the district and county of Lincoln, 6½ miles NW of Wickenby r station, and 7 W of Market Rasen Post town, Glentham, under Market Rasen Acres, 1,430 Real property £2,413 Pop, 125 Houses, 25 The manor and property belong to Sir C M L Monck, Bart The living is a rectory in the diocese of Lincoln Value, £301.* Patron, Sir C M L Monck Bart The church is good.

CAEN WOOD, a seat adjacent to the west side of Highgate in Middlesex It belonged formerly to Lord Bute, and belongs now to the Earl of Mansfield The house is in the Ionic style, after a design by Adams and contains valuable paintings and portraits. The Fifth monarchy men in 1661, took refuge in the grounds, and were attacked here by the guards

CAENYNION a township in Oswestry parish Salop, near Oswestry Pop, 142

CAER, CAR, or GAR, a Celtic or old British prefix, signifying a fort or any other artificial military strength.

CAERALLWCH See CAER FALLWCH

CAERARIANRHOD, a submerged town in Carnarvon bay, about 2 miles from the shore, off the mouth of the river Llyfni 7½ miles SW by S of Carnarvon The ruins of it are visible at low water

CAERAU, an old seat of the Lloyds, adjacent to an ancient camp, near Llangammarch, in Brecon

CAERAU Glamorgan See [illegible]

CAER BANNAU, the site of the Roman Bannium in Breconshire, on the Julian way, 3½ miles W of Brecon The Roman works here are still traceable, around an area of 624 feet by 420, and Roman inscriptions and coins have been found A town sprung up in connexion [illegible] the military defences and was the capital of a large circumjacent trade till after the Norman conquest

CAER BRAN, an ancient [illegible] in the south western [illegible] of Cornwall 4½ miles W S W of Penzance It [illegible] and crowns a hill, comprises outer ditch outer [illegible] inner ditch, inner wall, and central circle, and [illegible] traces in [illegible]

CAER CARADOC, or CLADOCK HILL, a hill on the SW border of Salop at the river Clun, near Offa's Dyke, 3 miles [illegible] It was the place of Caractacus' last stand against Ostorius Scapula, and it retains some traces of [illegible] works.

CAER CORI See CIRENCESTER.

CAER CRWYN, an ancient British camp on a hill 5½ miles SW of Corwen, in Merioneth. The hill is crowned [illegible] a pillar erected in honour of Sir W W Wynn, Bart and commands one of the grandest views in Wales

CAER CUSTEINT See CARNARVON

CAER DDEN See GARTHEN

CAERDIFF See CARDIFF

CAER DREWYN, an ancient British fort near Corwen in Merioneth, marked now by only a circle of loose stones, nearly ½ a mile in circumference Owen Gwynedd [illegible] here to repel the invasion of Henry II, and Owen Glendower retreated hither, from the menace of Henry IV

CAER-EGARPY See CAISTOR.

CAEREINION FECHAN, a township in Mallwyd parish Montgomery, on the verge of the county, on the river Dovey [illegible] miles S of Dinas-Mowddwy Acres, 1,894 Real property £707 Pop, 111 Houses, 22.

CAERFAGAN, a locality [illegible] miles ESE of Rhayader, in Radnor It is traversed by a Roman road, and is supposed by many antiquaries to be the site of the Roman station Magos Numerous Roman relics have been found in its neighbourhood

CAER FALLWCH, or CAERFALLWCH, a township in Northop parish, Flintshire, 3½ miles S by E of Flint [illegible] £9,531, of which £6,640 are in mines Pop, 920 Houses, 195 Some of the inhabitants are employed in lead mines. An ancient British camp here, [illegible] Moel Gaer, encloses a circular area of 196 yards [illegible] artificial mound in the centre, commands a very extensive view, is one of the most perfect [illegible] in North Wales and is thought to have been an outpost of the Ordivices for defence against the Romans

CAER FEDWIN a township in Llandyrnog parish, Denbighshire 4½ miles E of Denbigh

CAER FYRDDIN See CARMARTHEN

CAERGAER, an ancient camp on the Julian way, near [illegible] in Glamorgan.

CAERGERIOG a township in Llandderfel parish, Merioneth [illegible] miles E of Bala.

CAERGWRLE, a township in Hope parish Flint on [illegible] the river Alan and the Wrexham and Mold railway [illegible] miles N N W of Wrexham It has a post office under Wrexham, and a r station It was a Roman station [illegible] of Deva Tiles inscribed with the name of the 20th legion, a hypocaust or vapour bath, and other Roman relics have been found at it and traces of Roman [illegible] of two Roman roads are in the neighbourhood A castle stood at it on a lofty hill, [illegible] to the time of Henry II, was visited by Edward I [illegible], was soon afterwards burned down by accident, [illegible] to have been rebuilt in 1307 A [illegible] tower of the castle, and some fragments [illegible] still remain Fairs are held on [illegible] 12 Aug, and 27 Oct Caergwrle is a [illegible] charter from the Black Prince, with [illegible] mayor and two bailiffs and unites with [illegible] in sending a member to [illegible] borough, includes [illegible] or Hope [illegible] Pop, 844 Houses, [illegible]

CAERGWRWAN, or CAERWRWAN, a hamlet in [illegible], on the verge of the county, [illegible] 10 miles N of Neath Real property, [illegible] 2,3[illegible] are in mines. Pop, 84[illegible].

CAERHUN, or CAER RHUN a village and a parish in Conway district, Carnarvon The village stands on the Conway river, near the Conway and Llanrwst railway, 5 miles S of Conway It occupies the site of the Roman Conovium, has yielded many Roman relics, and is a pretty place The parish includes also the townships of Isar-afon, Maen y Bard, Penhe, and Rhwng y Ddwy afon, and its post town is Llanrwst Acres, 13,402 Real property £4,687 Pop, 1,314 Houses, 313. The property is divided among a few The surface comprises mountains glens, and chasms, and is highly picturesque The living is a vicarage, annexed to the rectory of Llanbedr, in the diocese of Bangor The church is good, and there are dissenting chapels

CAERLEON a small town and a sub district in Newport district, Monmouth. The town is in the parish of Llangattock, and stands on the river Usk, 1¾ mile N of the South Wales railway and 2½ NE of Newport It was the Roman Isca Silurum and Isca Colonia, and the capital of Britannia Secunda Akeman street went from it to Caerwent and Bath the maritime Julian way, to Neath and St. Davids, and the mountain Julian way, to Abergavenny, with a branch to Monmouth The Roman city included a great fortress, and is said to have been superbly built, and about 9 miles in circuit A British city succeeded the Roman one, and was the capital of the Welsh princes who styled themselves kings of Gwent and lords of Caerleon The court of King Arthur was held here, and a castle was built at the Conquest, and captured by Edward I Christianity also made a figure here, both in pristine struggles with paganism, and in erecting establishments. Martyrs were slain, a monastery was founded at an early period, and succeeded by an abbey before the time of King John, and a bishop's see was constituted by Dubricius, the opponent of the Arians and removed by his successor David to Menevia, which then took the name of St Davids

The ruins of Caerleon were long very grand Giraldus Cambrensis, writing more than seven centuries after the Romans left it, says —"Many remains of its former magnificence are still visible, splendid palaces which once emulated with their gilded roofs the grandeur of Rome, for it was originally built by the Roman princes, and adorned with stately edifices, a gigantic tower, numerous baths, ruins of temples, and a theatre, the walls of which are partly standing Here we still see, within and without the walls, subterraneous buildings, aqueducts, and vaulted caverns, and what appeared to me most remarkable, stoves so excellently contrived as to diffuse their heat through secret and imperceptible pores " The buildings have now nearly all perished, but very numerous small relics have been preserved, and some great substructions and mounds remain A work published by Mr John F Lee in 1851 figures the antiquities in twenty seven engravings, and a local museum, erected by the Caerleon Antiquarian Association has a rich collection of the relics The chief large remaining works are fragments of the walls of the Roman fortress, 12 feet thick and 1,800 yards in circuit, an oval bank of earth, the vestige of the Roman amphitheatre, 16 feet high and 222 feet by 192 an artificial mound, of doubtful character, 90 feet high and 300 yards round at the base remains of the castle overhanging the Usk, ruins near the bridge, and a round tower near the old fashioned inn the Hanbury Arms An old tradition regards the amphitheatre as the festival scene of King Arthur and his Knights popular nomenclature calls it King Arthur's Round Table, and the Welsh bards have sung—

"How he first ordain'd the circled board,
The knights whose martial deeds far famed that table round
Which trust in their loves which most in arms renowned
The laws which long upheld these Orders, they report,
The Pentecosts prepared at Caerleon in her court,
That table's ancient seat her temples and her groves,
Her palaces, her walls, baths, theatres, and stoves "

The town now consists chiefly of two streets Most of the houses are old, and many of them are partly constructed with Roman bricks The bridge is a handsome modern structure, in room of a curious old wooden one The market house is an ancient weather worn edifice, with four gigantic Tuscan pillars. The church is a handsome Norman edifice, and there are chapels for Independents, Baptists, and Wesleyans, and a free school The town has a post office‡ under Newport, Monmouth, and is a seat of petty sessions Markets are held on Thursdays, and fairs on the third Wednesday of Feb, 1 May, 20 July, and 21 Sept. There are extensive tin-works Pop, 1,268 Houses, 254 The sub district contains sixteen parishes and part of another Acres, 51,398 Pop., 7 615 Houses, 1 548

CAERLEON ULTRA PONTEM a hamlet in Christ-Church parish, Monmouth, on the river Usk, opposite Caerleon, and suburban to that town

CAER LLEON VAWR See CHESTER.

CAERMARTHEN See CARMARTHEN

CAER MERLIN See CARMARTHEN

CAERNARVON See CARNARVON

CAER ODER See BRISTOL

CAER PALLADWR. See SHAFTESBURY

CAERPHILLY, a village, a chapelry a sub-district, and a hundred in Glamorgan. The village is in the hamlet tract of Energlyn, in the parish of Eglwysilan, and stands on a plain, surrounded by barren mountains, adjacent to the Rumney railway, near the Rumney river, 7½ miles by road, and 9½ by railway N by W of Cardiff It most probably was founded by the ancient Britons A monastery early stood at it, dedicated to St Cuydd, and was burnt, in 831, by the Saxons. A fortalice seems to have been built at it soon after the Conquest, was dismantled, in 1219, by Rhys Vychan rebuilt in 1221, by John de Braose, enlarged and strengthened by Ralph Mortimer and Hugh de Spencer, used as a fastness, by the Spencers, for plundering the circumjacent country, made the refuge of Edward II, in his flight from his rebellious barons, sustained then a very vigorous and obstinate siege, was held, in 1400 by Owen Glendower but then was "a fortress great in ruins;" and ceased thereafter to be much noticed in history The ruins of it, now extant, cover an area of 30 acres, display remarkable magnificence, and include outworks, gateways, towers, a grand hall 7 feet by 30, and a ponderous leaning tower, 80 feet high, much shattered, 10 feet out of the perpendicular, and supposed to have sustained its injuries from a steam explosion at the time of the great siege Tennyson resided sometime in the vicinity, lays the scene of his "Idylls of the King" in the immediate neighbourhood, and seems to refer to the castle in the following lines —

> "All was ruinous
> Here stood a shattered archway, plumed with fern,
> And here has fallen a great part of a tower
> Whole like a crag that tumbles from the cliff,
> And, like a crag, was gay with wilding flowers.'

The village is an irregular assemblage of small houses, contiguous to the castle It was formerly a borough, it has a post office‡ under Cardiff, a railway station, and an inn, and it is a seat of petty sessions Markets are held on Thursdays, and fairs on 5 April Trinity Thursday, 19 July, 25 Aug, 9 Oct, 16 Nov, and the Thursday before Christmas. Some blanketing and woollen shawls are made, and numerous collieries and iron works are in the neighbourhood Pop, with Energlyn 1,047 Houses, 237 —The chapelry includes all Energlyn and part of Bedwas, and was constituted in 1850 Pop, 1,193 Houses, 261 The living is a rectory in the diocese of Llandaff Value, £300 Patrons, the Dean and Chapter of Llandaff The church is in the later English style; and there are chapels for Baptists, Calvinistic Methodists, and Wesleyans —The sub district contains six parishes, and part of another, and is in the district of Cardiff Acres, 27,161 Pop 10 013 Houses, 2,089 —The hundred contains four parishes, and parts of three others Acres 62,903 Pop, 67,612 Houses, 13,353

CAERPHA See CAIRN

CAER RHUN See CAERHUN

CAERSEDDFAN, a township in Darowen parish, Montgomery, 6 miles E by N of Machynlleth Real property, £2,057 Pop, 547 Houses, 108

CAER SEGONT See SILCHESTER.

CAER SEIONT See CARNARVON

CAERSWS, a hamlet in Llanwnog parish, Montgomery, on the Sarn Sws Roman way, the Machynlleth railway, and the river Severn, 5¼ miles WNW of New town It has a r station, a post office under Shrewsbury, and three dissenting chapels Pop, 342. A Roman station was here, commanding the neighbouring passes, and a camp still exists, enclosing about 4 acres A farm house is within the enclosure, and many Roman remains have been found.

CAERVORRAN, a locality on the SW border of Northumberland, on the Roman wall, the Maiden way, and the river Tippal near Thirlwall castle and the Newcastle and Carlisle railway, 4¼ miles WNW of Haltwhistle It was the Roman Magna on the Wall,—the place of the second Dalmatian cohort, and altars, inscriptions, and other Roman relics have been found

CAERWENT, a village and a parish in Chepstow district, Monmouth The village stands on Akeman street or the Julian way, 2¼ miles NW of Portskewet r station, and 5 WSW of Chepstow, and has a post office under Chepstow It was the Venta Silurum of the Romans, and it retains considerable fragments of the fortress walls, 505 yards by 390, and in parts from 9 to 12 feet thick and 20 feet high Two tesselated pavements, portions of columns and statues, coins of Severus and Gordian III, and other Roman relics have been found. The parish includes also the hamlet of Crick Acres, 1,952 Real property, £2,907 Pop, 445 Houses, 83 The property is divided among a few The living is a vicarage united with the p curacy of Llanvair Discoed in the diocese of Llandaff Value, £253 * Patrons, the Dean and Chapter of Llandaff The church has a rich porch, and striking early English arcades, was probably built of materials of the Roman city and is in good condition There is a Baptist chapel

CAERWYS, a small town and a parish in Holywell district Flint The town stands 5 miles SW by W of Holywell r station, and 6 E of St Asaph, and has a post office under Holywell It is thought to occupy the site of a Roman station, it was the scene of the court of the last Prince Llewellyn, it witnessed Eisteddfodau, or congresses of bards and minstrels, at various periods till 1798, it was the seat of the county assizes till 1672, and it unites with Flint, and other places, in sending a member to parliament, but, as a borough, includes the townships of Tredre and Tref Edwyn It comprises four streets, crossing each other in the centre, and has a town hall, a church, and three dissenting chapels Markets are held on Tuesdays, and fairs on the 2d Tuesday of Jan, 5 March, the last Tuesday of April, Trinity Thursday, the Tuesday after 7 July, 29 Aug, and 5 Nov Pop, 637 Houses, 150 —The parish includes also the townships of Bryngwyn Issa, and Bryngwyn Ucha Acres, 2,603 Real property £2,952 Pop, 893 Houses, 208 The manor belongs to Lord Mostyn Maes Mynam, the site of the residence of Prince Llewellyn is SW of the town A tumulus is about a mile NE of the town, other tumuli are on the hills to the W, and an ancient camp is on a summit to the N The living is a rectory in the diocese of St Asaph. Value, £125 * Patron, the Bishop of St Asaph Lloyd, the friend of Pennant, was vicar and Bishop Wynne was a native

CAER YN ARFON See CARNARVON

CAERYNWCH, the seat of the Richards family in Merioneth, under Cader Idris, in the south eastern vicinity of Dolgelly The grounds are romantic, and include a series of rapids and cascades about a mile long accompanied by a declivitous path called the Torrent Walk

CÆSAREA See JERSEY

CÆSAR'S CAMP an ancient fortification in Windsor forest, Berks, on an eminence, 3 miles SE of Wokingham It has an irregular outline and a double ditch A Roman road went southward from it across Bagshot heath

CÆSAR'S CAMP, an ancient entrenchment on the confines of Hants and Surrey, on a hill at the western extremity of the North downs, 3 miles W of Aldershot It has an irregular outline and a triple vallum, was probably formed by the ancient Britons, and may have been occupied by Alfred the Great in 893

CAETHYLYD, an old seat of the Morgans in Glamorgan, in Cwm Clydach, near Neath It is now a farm house

CAINHAM, a parish and a sub-district in Ludlow district, Salop The parish lies on an affluent of the river Teme, near the Shrewsbury and Hereford railway, 3¼ miles ESE of Ludlow It includes the township of Bennets End, and its post town is Ludlow Acres, 2,529 Real property, £3,635 Pop, 755 Houses, 161 Cainham Court is the seat of the Calcots The living is a vicarage in the diocese of Hereford. Value, £338 * Patron, C K. Mainwaring, Esq The p. curacy of Knowbury is a separate benefice The sub district contains six parishes Acres, 12,195 Pop, 2,227 Houses, 452

CAINSCROSS, a chapelry in Stonehouse, Stroud and Randwick parishes, Gloucester, on the Western Union railway, 1 mile W of Stroud It has a post office under Stroud It was constituted in 1837 Pop, 1,916 Houses, 425 The living is a p curacy in the diocese of G and Bristol Value, not reported. Patron, Mrs Croome. The church is modern There is a national school

CAIRA, CAIRAU, or **CAERAU**, a parish in Cardiff district, Glamorgan, on the Ithan way and the South Wales railway, near St. Fagans station, 3½ miles W of Cardiff. Post town, St Fagans, under Cardiff Acres, 746 Real property, £901 Pop., 131 Houses 26 The property is divided among a few An ancient camp of about 12 acres is here, and seems to have been British, though often regarded as Roman The living is a vicarage in the diocese of Llandaff Value, £66 Patron, the Bishop of Llandaff The church stands within the camp and is good

CAISTOR, or **CASTOR**, a small town, a parish, a sub district, and a district in Lincoln The town stands on the side of a hill, on the Wolds, 4 miles ENE of Moortown r station, and 7½ SE of Glanford Brigg It was called by the ancient Britons Caer Egarry, and by the Saxons *Thong Ceastre* A Roman station was on its site, and a castle was built at it by the Saxon Hengist Rowena, the daughter of Hengist, was married here to Vortigern, and Egbert in 827, here subdued Wiglof, king of Mercia The town presents a pleasant appearance, is well watered by four springs, called the Cypher well the Pigeon spring, Stot's well, and the Spa, and has a head post office,‡ two banking offices, two chief inns, a church three dissenting chapels, a grammar school, a mechanics institute, and a workhouse The church stands on the site of the ancient castle, is Norman and early English, has a fine tower, contains a brass of 1460, and was repaired in 1863 The grammar school was founded in 1630, and has £185 a year from endowment, with an exhibition at Jesus college, Cambridge A weekly market is held on Saturday, fairs for black cattle and horses on the Saturdays before Palm-Sunday, before Whit sunday before 18 Sept, and after 11 Oct, and fairs for sheep and horses, on the day before each of these fairs Pop, 2,141 Houses, 418 —The parish includes the hamlets of Audleby, Fonaby, and Hundon, and the chapelries of Clixby and Holton le Moor Acres 6,490 Real property £10,388 Pop, 2,318 Houses 460 The property is divided among a few Numerous traces of Roman antiquities exist and remains of a monastery occur a little east of the town The living is a vicarage united with the p curacies of Clixby and Holton le Moor, in the diocese of Lincoln Value £215 * Patron, the Bishop of Lincoln

The sub district contains the parishes of Caistor South Kelsey, North Kelsey, Brocklesby, Keelby, Riby, Limber Magna, Rigby, Somerby Searby with-Owmby Grasby Nettleton Cabourn Swallow, Cuxwold, Rothwell Croxby, Thoresway, Swinhope, Thoresway, Claxby and Normanby on the Wolds and the extra parochial tract of Newsham Acres, 63,511 Pop, 9,005. Houses, 1,817 The district comprehends also the sub district of Great Grimsby, containing the parishes of Great Grimsby, Humberstone, Clee, Scartho, Waltham, Brigsley, Ashby with Fenby, Hawerby with-Beesby, Newton le Wold, East Ravendale, Hatcliffe, Beelsby, Barnoldby le Beck, Irby upon Humber, Aylesby, Laceby, Bradley, Little Coates, Great Coates, Healing, Stallingborough, Immingham, and Habrough, and the sub district of Market Rasen, containing the parishes of Market-Rasen, Middle-Rasen, West Rasen, Usselby, Walesby, Stainton le Vale, Kirmond le Mire, Tealby, North Willingham, Sixhills, East Torrington, Legsby, Lissington Linwood Bushingthorpe, Newton-by Toft, Toft next Newton, Kirkby cum Osgodby, South Owersby, North Owersby, Thornton le Moor, Kingerby, Glentham, Bishop Norton, Snitterby, and Waddingham Acres, 183,164 Poor-rates in 1866 £13,416 Pop in 1861, 37,517 Houses, 7,786 Marriages in 1866, 374, births, 1,474,—of which 71 were illegitimate, deaths, 782,—of which 320 were at ages under 5 years, and 23 at ages above 85 years. Marriages in the ten years 1851-60 2,645 births, 13,349 deaths, 6,746 The places of worship in 1851 were 74 of the Church of England, with 11,963 sittings, 3 of Independents, with 566 s, 2 of Baptists, with 800 s, 47 of Wesleyan Methodists with 8,109 s 31 of Primitive Methodists, with 3,485 s, and 3 of Roman Catholics, with 359 s The schools were 38 public day schools, with 2,260 scholars, 92 private day schools, with 1,955 s, 74 Sunday schools, with 4,407 s, and 1 evening school for adults, with 4 s.

CAISTOR CANAL, a cut, 4 miles long, in Lincoln, eastward from the river Ancholme to Moortown, in South Kelsey parish 3½ miles SW of Caistor

CAISTOR NEXT YARMOUTH, a village and a parish in Flegg district, Norfolk. The village stands on the coast, near the river Bure, 2¼ miles N of Yarmouth, is supposed, by some antiquaries, to occupy the site of the Roman Garianonum, has a post office, of the name of Caistor, under Yarmouth and is a coast guard station The parish comprises 2,832 acres of land and 215 of water Real property, £7,290 Pop, 1 203 Houses, 298 The property is much subdivided A strong moated castle was built, about a mile from the village, in the 15th century, by Sir John Fastolf, a native, the capturer of John II of France, sometimes mistaken for the Falstaff of Shakspeare, and a lofty round tower and part of the north and west walls are still standing An ancient free chapel stood on the manor as early as the time of Edward I, and was erected into a college for seven monks or priests, either by Sir John Fastolf or by one of his successors, and some remains of it exist near the castle ruins The living is a rectory in the diocese of Norwich Value, £942 Patron the Rev G W Steward The church is decorated and later English, and has a lofty square tower There was formerly another church, with parochial jurisdiction, called St Edmunds, but only a part of the tower remains. There are a chapel of ease three Methodist chapels, a reading room, a national school, and charities £97

CAISTOR ST EDMUNDS, a small village and a parish in Henstead district Norfolk. The village stands on the river Tes, near the Eastern Union railway, 3 miles south of Norwich. The Venta Icenorum of the Roman their principal station in the country of the Iceni, was here, and Roman roads went hence to Brancaster Cromer, Burgh Castle, Dunwich Bury Cambridge, Colchester, and London Substructions or traces of Roman buildings occur over an area of 30 acres, and Roman urns bricks numerous coins, and other relics have been found Ancient Norwich is believed to have been built of materials from the Roman structures here, and hence the old rhyme,—

> 'Caistor was a city when Norwich was none,
> And Norwich was built of Caistor stone'

The parish comprises 1,614 acres, and its post town is Norwich Real property £2,754 Pop, 162 Houses, 37 The property is divided among a few Caistor Hall is the seat of Mrs H Dashwood. The living is rectory united with the sinecure rectory of Mukshail, in the diocese of Norwich Value £447 * Patron, Mrs. H Dashwood. The church stands within the old Roman enclosure, and has a few Roman bricks in its masonry Charities, £42

CAISTRON, a township in Rothbury parish, Northumberland, on the river Coquet, 4½ miles W of Rothbury Acres, 400 Pop, 41 Houses, 9

CAIUS COLLEGE. See CAMBRIDGE.

CAKEHAM, a manor in West Wittering parish, Sussex, on the east side of Chichester harbour, 6½ miles SW of Chichester A palace of the Bishops of Chichester formerly stood here, and a lofty brick hexagonal tower connected with it, and built in the early part of the 16th century by Bishop Sherborne, still stands

CAKEMORE, a township in Halesowen parish, Worcester, on the verge of the county, 4 miles E of Stourbridge Pop., 448 Houses, 89

CALBECK. See CALDBECK

CALBOURNE a village, a parish, and a sub district in the Isle of Wight. The village stands 5 miles WSW of Newport, and has a post-office under Newport The parish includes also Newtown borough, and extends from Brixton Down to the Solent Acres, 6,397 of which 265 are water Real property, £[illegible],471 Pop, 728 Houses, 145 The property is divided among a few Westover manor belonged to the Esturs, passed to the Lisles and the Holmeses, and belongs now to the eldest son of Lord Heytesbury, in right of his wife, the daughter of the late Sir Leonard W Holmes The house on it is modern, and the grounds are tasteful Calbourne Bottom 1½ mile SSW of the village, is a depression between Brixton and Moltestone downs The living is a rectory, united with the p curacy of Newtown, in the diocese of Winchester Value, £675 * Patron, the Bishop of Winchester The church is early English, much modernized, and has a brass of 1480 —The sub district contains eight parishes. Acres, 25,050 Pop, 5,117 Houses, 1,071

CALCARIA See TADCASTER

CALCEBY, a parish in Spilsby district, Lincoln, 4½ miles W of Alford r station Post town, Alford Acres, 618 Real property, £938. Pop, 66 Houses, 12 The living is a vicarage, annexed to the rectory of South Ormsby, in the diocese of Lincoln The church is in ruins

CALCETHORPE a parish in Louth district, Lincoln, 6 miles W by N of Louth r station Post town Louth Acres, 1 088 Real property, £1,463 Pop, 81 Houses, 15 The living is a sinecure rectory in the diocese of Lincoln. Value, not reported Patron, the Lord Chancellor The church is in ruins

CALCEWORTH, a hundred or wapentake in the parts of Lindsey, Lincoln, cut into the divisions of marsh and wold The marsh division contains Aby parish and twenty three other parishes Acres, 37,312 The wold division contains Alford parish, and fifteen other parishes. Acres, 26,248 Pop of both, 13 972 Houses, 2 921

CALCOT, a township in Holywell parish, Flint, 2 miles S of Holywell Pop., 170

CALCOTT See BICTON, Salop

CALCOTT PARK, a seat in Berks, on Holybrook, 3 miles WSW of Reading It belonged to John Kendrick, who bequeathed £7,500 to build the Oracle at Reading, was the scene of the romantic marriage of his descendant, "the Berkshire lady," to Benjamin Child, and belongs now to Colonel Plagrave

CALCUTT, a hamlet in Lower Heyford parish, Oxford, 5½ miles WNW of Bicester Pop, 146

CALDBECK a village, three townships, a parish, a sub-district, a range of fells, and a river, in Cumberland The village stands on the river, at the foot of the fells 6½ miles S by W of Curthwaite r station and 7¾ SSE of Wigton and has a post office under Wigton It was founded along with an hospital, soon after the Norman conquest by D Engaine, forester of Inglewood, for the protection of travellers. It has a scattered character, along a rambling vale, yet looks pleasing and even picturesque A number of its inhabitants are employed in different kinds of manufactures.—The three townships are Low Caldbeck, High Caldbeck, and Caldbeck-Haltcliff, and they meet at the village, and are in the district of Wigton Real property of Low C, £2,646, of High C., £2,852, of C Haltcliff £2,602. Pop of Low C, 675, of High C., 213, of C. Haltcliff, 521 Houses, in Low C, 159, in High C, 57, in C Haltcliff, 115 —The parish includes also the township of Mosedale, in the district of Penrith Acres, 24,280 Pop, 1 560 Houses, 342 The property is much subdivided The manor belonged to the Lucys, the Percys, the Dalstons, and the Whartons, and belongs now to the representatives of the late Earl of Egremont. Caldbeck House was the seat of the Backhouse family, and Woodhall was the seat of George Fox, the founder of Quakerism About 13,000 acres are on the fells, and available only for sheep pasture. The living is a rectory in the diocese of Carlisle Value, £600 * Patron, the Bishop of Carlisle The church dates from 1112, but has been modernized, and is good There are a Quaker meeting house, a Wesleyan chapel, and a free school.—The sub-district contains the three Caldbeck townships, and five parishes in Wigton district. Acres, 60,767 Pop., 5 197 Houses, 1,067 —The fells are a north eastern offshoot of the Skiddaw range They culminate on High Pike, at an altitude of 2,101 feet above the level of the sea have a bleak, wild, moorish character, and afford limestone, copper, lead, bismuth, molybdena, and tungsten —The river rises on the fells, and runs 7 miles north eastward to the Caldew, ¾ of a mile north of Hesket Newmarket. Both this stream and the Caldew, at places near the village, make great descents, and are overhung by romantic scenery A deep fall called the Howk, occurs beneath a natural bridge of limestone rock, another fall goes 60 feet over a precipice into a deep rocky hollow, called the Kettle, and a dark, shaggy ravine at one of the falls contains a wild cavern 18 yards long called the Fairy Kirk

CALDBRIDGE, or CALDBERGH a township in Coverham parish, N R Yorkshire 3 miles SW of Middleham It contains the hamlet of East Scrafton Acres, 2,734 Real property, £827 Pop, 97 Houses, 19

CALDECOT, a parish in Swaffham district, Norfolk, 4 miles NE of Stoke Ferry, and 9½ SW of Swaffham r station Post town, Stoke Ferry, under Brandon Acres 930 Real property, £357 Pop, 39 Houses, 6 The living is a sinecure rectory in the diocese of Norwich Value, £6 Patron, Sir H R P Bedingfield, Bart

CALDECOTE, a parish in Caxton district, Cambridge, on an affluent of the river Cem, 3½ miles ESE of Caxton, and 6¾ SW of Histon r station Post town, Caxton, under Royston Acres 833. Real property, £1,02[illegible] Pop, 93 Houses, 22 The property is divided among a few The living is a vicarage, annexed to the rectory of Toft, in the diocese of Ely The church is good.

CALDECOTE, a parish in the district of Peterborough, and county of Huntingdon, 1½ mile WSW of Stilton, and 4 W of Holme r station Post-town, Stilton, under Peterborough Acres, 778. Real property £1,104 Pop, 70 Houses, 14 The property is divided among a few The manor belonged, in the 13th century, to the Hallidays. The living is a rectory in the diocese of Ely Value, £156 Patron, W Wells, Esq The church is good.

CALDECOTE, a hamlet in Towcester parish, Northampton, 2 miles N of Towcester Pop, 98

CALDECOTE, a parish in Nuneaton district, Warwick, on the Coventry canal and the Trent Valley railway, 2¼ miles NNW of Nuneaton Post town, Nuneaton. Acres, 686 Real property, £1,788 Pop, 130 Houses 21 The property is divided among a few Caldecote Hall was defended by the Abbots against Prince Rupert and passed to the Hemmings The living is a rectory in the diocese of Worcester Value, £155 * Patron, K. Fenton, Esq The church is good.

CALDECOTT, a township in Shocklach parish, Cheshire, near the river Dee, 5½ miles NW of Malpas Acres, 430 Real property £1,043. Pop., 66 Houses, 11

CALDECOTT, a parish in Hitchin district, Herts on the verge of the county, near Icknield street, 3¼ miles N by W of Baldock r station Post town Newnham, under-Baldock. Acres, 313 Real property, £484 Pop., 44 Houses, 11 The property is all in one estate Roman urns have been found. The living is a rectory in the diocese of Rochester Value, £75 Patron, C C Hale, Esq The church was reported in 1859 to need repair

CALDECOTT, a hamlet in Chelveston parish, Northampton 2 miles E of Higham Ferrars Pop, 101

CALDECOTT, a parish in Uppingham district, Rutland on the rivers Eye and Welland, and on the Syston and Peterborough railway, adjacent to Rockingham station, 4½ miles S of Uppingham Post-town, Rockingham, under Leicester Acres, 1,440 Real property, £2,510 Pop., 3-3 Houses, 73 The living is a vicarage annexed to the rectory of Liddington, in the diocese of Peterborough The church is good.

CALDECOTT, Monmouth and Beds See CALDICOTT

CALDER (THE), a stream of Cumberland. It rises in Copland forest, near Ennerdale water and runs 9 miles south south westward, between Cold fell and Ponsonby fell, and past Calder Abbey and Calder Bridge, to the sea near Sellafield r station.

CALDER (THE), a stream of Lancashire It rises on the eastern border of the county, E of Burnley, and runs 13 miles west north westward, through the north eastern part of Blackburn district, to the river Ribble, a little below Whalley

CALDER (THE), a stream of Lancashire It rises on Calder fell, on the east border of the county, and runs 6 miles south westward to the Wyre, near Garstang

CALDER (THE), a river of Lancashire and W R Yorkshire. It rises at Cliviger dean, among the back-bone mountains, not far from Burnley, and runs about 45 miles eastward, exclusive of numerous windings, past Todmorden, Sowerby, Rastrick, and Wakefield, to the Aire at Castleford. It first traverses a moorish region, and then flows through picturesque and populous tracts, all increasing ornature and industry It is followed, down much of its descent, by the Manchester and Leeds railway and is connected with various canals, which give water communication between the eastern and the western seas, from Liverpool to Hull

CALDER BRIDGE, a village and a chapelry in Ponsonby parish, Cumberland The village stands on the Calder river 1½ mile NNE of Sellafield r station, and 4 SE by S of Egremont, and has a post office under Whitehaven, and two inns. The chapelry includes the village, and is a p curacy, annexed to Beckermet St Bridget, in the diocese of Carlisle The church was built in 1842, and is a cruciform structure, in the early English style, with a pinnacled tower Ponsonby Hall, the seat of J E Stanley Esq, is in the southern vicinity of the village, and Calder Abbey, the seat of Captain Irwin, adjoins abbey ruins, on the left bank of the river, about a mile above The abbey was founded, in 113-, by Ranulph, second Earl of Chester for Cistertian monks, became a dependency of the abbey of Furness, and was given at the dissolution, to Thomas Leigh A large portion of its remains, in mingled Norman and early English, with the central tower, and richly robed in parasitic plants, still stands Vestiges of a Roman camp are on the opposite side of the river

CALDERBROOK See PLATCHINWORTH

CALDERVALE, a chapelry in Churchtown or Garstang parish, Lancashire near the Lancaster and Preston railway, 4 miles NW of Garstang It has a post office under Garstang Statistics returned with the parish The living is a vicarage in the diocese of Manchester Value not reported Patrons, the Vicar of Churchtown and H Garnet Esq The church was built in 1863

CALDEW (THE), a river of Cumberland It rises on the east brow of Skiddaw receives headstreams from ... and the Caldbeck fells, and runs about 25 miles north eastward past Hesket Newmarket, Sebergham, Highhead, Rose Castle, Dalston, and ... to the Eden at Carlisle It receives the Caldbeck river near Hesket Newmarket, making the ... in the vicinity of the influx of that stream and runs under ground, about 4 miles, from Holt Close Bridge to Spout's Dub See CALDBECK

CALDEWGATE, a township in St. Mary-Carlisle parish, Cumberland, on the Caldew river, within Carlisle city Acres, 1,564 Pop, 9,732 Houses, 1,563. See CARLISLE.

CALDEY See CALDY

CALDICOTT, a village, a parish, a stream, a level, and a hundred in Monmouth. The village stands on the stream, near the South Wales railway and the estuary of the Severn, 1½ mile W of Portskewet r station, and 5 SW of Chepstow, and has a post office under Chepstow The parish is in Chepstow district, and comprises 1,938 acres of land, and 1,220 of water Real property, £3,171 Pop, 579 Houses 136 The property is subdivided The land is part of the low flat tract of Caldicott level. A stately castle ruin, with round towers, remarkable for the excellence of its masonry, partly Norman, but mostly late decorated English, stands adjacent to the village The castle belonged to the Bohuns, passed to the Duke of Gloucester, and was annexed, by Henry VIII, to the duchy of Lancaster The living is a vicarage in the diocese of Llandaff Value, £240 Patron, M H Noel, Esq The church is ancient and good, consists of nave, chancel, and aisles, with a bold tower, and has decorated cinquefoils in the chancel. There are a Wesleyan chapel, and charities £17 The stream bears the name of Caldicott Pill, rises in Wentwood chase, within 2½ miles of the Usk, and runs 7 miles south south eastward to the estuary of the Severn at Portskewet. The level lies along the Severn estuary and the Bristol channel, extends about 11 miles to the mouth of the Usk, was at one time subject to continual inundation, was drained and brought into cultivation, by the monks of Goldcliff, and is now a rich grazing tract The hundred is cut into two divisions, Higher and Lower The Higher div contains Caldicott parish, twelve other parishes, and part of another Acres, 27 930 The Lower div contains Goldcliff parish, and sixteen other parishes Acres, 53,000 Pop of both, 13,624 Houses, 2,741

CALDICOTT, Huntingdon, &c See CALDECOTT

CALDICOTT (LOWER and UPPER) two hamlets in Northill parish, Beds, 1½ mile NW of Biggleswade Pop, 591 Houses 127

CALDON CANAL, a canal in the NW of Stafford shire. It commences near Apedall Hall, goes south south eastward, past Newcastle under Lyne, to Handford, and deflects thence to the Grand Trunk canal, at Stoke upon Trent

CALDRON SNOUT, a remarkable waterfall on the river Tees, a few miles below its source, near the meeting point of Westmoreland, Durham, and Yorkshire

CALDWELL, a township in St John Stanwick parish, N R Yorkshire, on an affluent of the river Tees, 8 miles N of Richmond. Acres, 2,000 Real property, £2,102 Pop, 162 Houses 34.

CALDWELL, Leicester See CHADWELL.

CALDWELL, Derby See CAULDWELL

CALDY, a township in West Kirby parish Cheshire, on the estuary of the Dee 6½ miles NW of Great Neston Acres, 2,102, of which 1,355 are water Real property, £1 160 Pop., 147 Houses, 22

CALDY ISLAND, or YNYS PYR, an extra parochial island in the district and county of Pembroke near Giltar head on the SW side of Carmarthen bay, 2½ miles S of Tenby Its length is about a mile and its area, 162 acres Pop, with St Margaret's Island, 73 Houses 16 Upwards of one third is in good cultivation, and limestone is found A priory was founded here, in the time of Henry I by Robert de Tours and made a cell to Dogmaels abbey and some remains of it including the church tower, still exist The residence of C. Kynaston, Esq, the proprietor of the island, adjoins the ruins Several islets and shoals are adjacent to the coast A lighthouse, built in 1829, showing a fixed light, partly bright and partly red at a height of 210 feet, is on the south side, and there is good anchorage on the north.

CALE (THE), a stream of Somerset and Dorset. It rises near Wincanton, and runs about 12 miles south ward, along the vale of Blackmoor, to the river Stour, near Sturminster

CALEDONIAN RAILWAY, a railway in Cumberland, commencing in a junction with the Carlisle and Lancaster, the Carlisle and Newcastle, the Carlisle and Maryport, and the Carlisle and Silloth railways at Carlisle, and going north north westward to the boundary with Scotland at Gretna It proceeds, in Scotland, to a central point, at Carstairs junction, sends off thence main lines to Edinburgh and Glasgow, and ramifies to Biggar, Lanark towards Stirling and in other directions

CALEDONIAN ROAD, a street in the NW of London, leading out from King's Cross and Pentonville to the model prison and the new cattle market, and crossed by the North London railway It has a station on the railway

CALEHILL, a seat, a sub district and a hundred in Kent. The seat is in Little Chart parish, 5 miles WNW of Ashford, and has belonged to the Darell family since the time of Henry IV The sub district is in West Ashford district, and contains Little Chart parish, and five other parishes Acres, 22 535 Pop, 5,311 Houses, 1,007 The hundred is in the lathe of Shepway, and conterminate with the sub-district

CALF-FELL, a mountain on the confines of Yorkshire and Westmoreland, in the neighbourhood of Sedbergh A fine waterfall, called Cantley Spout, occurs on its skirt See CAUTLEY

CALF OF MAN, an island in Rushen parish, Isle of Man, near the south western extremity of the main island, 6 miles SW by W of Castletown It is about 4 miles in circuit, has cliffs upwards of 400 feet high, swarms with sea fowls and rabbits, is partly under good culture, and belongs to the Careys Pop, 25 Two lighthouses are on it, erected in 1818 560 feet apart, with revolving lights 305 and 395 feet high

CALGARTH, a seat on the east side of Windermere, 3¼ miles SSE of Ambleside, in Westmoreland It was built and occupied by Bishop Watson of Llandaff

CALIFORNIA a station on the Epsom Downs railway, in Surrey, between Sutton and Banstead

CALKE, or CAUK, a parish in the district of Ashby de la Zouch and county of Derby, on the SE verge of the county, 4 miles N of Ashby de la Zouch r station Post town, Ticknall, under Derby Acres, 880 Real property £987 Pop 78. Houses, 14 An Augustinian priory was founded here, in 1160, by the Countess of Chester, a mansion on the site of the priory, and called Calke Abbey, was erected, in the early part of last century by Sir John Harpur, and this is now the seat of Sir J H Crewe, Bart. The living is a donative in the diocese of Lichfield Value, £84 Patron, Sir J H Crewe, Bart. The church was built in 1826, is a handsome Gothic edifice, with a square tower, and contains a fine monument to the Harpurs

CALKERTON a tything in Rodmarton parish, Gloucester, 3½ miles NE of Tetbury Pop, 145

CALLALLY AND YETLINGTON, a township in Whittingham parish, Northumberland, 5 miles N by W of Rothbury Acres, 3 970 Pop, 261 Houses, 51 Callaley Hall is the seat of the Claverings, and includes some portions of an old castle Callaley crag is crowned with remains of a Roman entrenchment

CALLAUGHTON, a township in Much Wenlock parish, Salop, 2 miles S of Much Wenlock Pop, 149

CALLERTON (BLACK) See BLACK CALLERTON

CALLERTON (HIGH), a township in Ponteland and Newburn parishes Northumberland 7 miles NW by N of Newcastle upon Tyne. Acres, 795 Pop, 97 Houses, 23

CALLERTON (LITTLE), a township in Ponteland parish Northumberland, near High Callerton Acres, 673 Pop 20 Houses 5

CALLESTICK, a locality 5 miles from Truro, in Cornwall, with a post office under Truro.

CALLEVA See SILCHESTER

CALLINGTON, formerly KELLINGTON, a small town, a parish, and a sub district in Liskeard district Cornwall The town stands on a gentle acclivity near the river Lynher, 6 miles N of St Germans r station, and 11 S of Launceston It consists chiefly of one broad street, irregularly built, is a seat of petty sessions, and a polling place, and has a head post office,‡ (designated Callington, Cornwall,) two banking offices, a hotel, a church two dissenting chapels, a literary institution, and a free school The church was built, on the site of a previous one, in 1460, is perpendicular English, was restored in 1859 and contains a very curious old Norman font, and an elaborate monument to Lord Willoughby de Broke A fine gabled sculptured cross is in the church yard. Many of the inhabitants are miners A weekly market is held on Wednesday, and fairs on the second Thursday of March and Nov, and on the first Thursday of May and after 19 Sept The town was made a borough in the time of Elizabeth, and sent two members to parliament, till disfranchised by the act of 1832.—The parish comprises 2,492 acres Real property £6,962, of which £700 are in mines. Pop 2 202 Houses, 347 The manor belonged to successively the Champernounes, the Ferrers, the Dennises, the Brokes and others. Kit Hill, about 2 miles N of the town, consists of granite, is 1 067 feet high, and commands an extensive view Stream tin and copper ore are worked The living is a rectory, annexed to the rectory of Southill, in the diocese of Exeter —The sub district contains six parishes Acres, 28,984 Pop 8 899 Houses, 1,595

CALLIS COURT and CALLIS GRANGE a hamlet and a tything in St Peter parish, Thanet, Kent, 2 miles N of Ramsgate

CALLIVEL, BERRACH, AND BRYNGWYNE, a conjoint hamlet in Llanfihangel Aberbythych parish, Carmarthen near Llandeilofawr Pop, 267

CALLOES See KELLAWAYS

CALLOW, a township in Wirksworth parish, Derby, 2 miles SW of Wirksworth Real property, £1,801 Pop, 91 Houses, 16

CALLOW, a parish in the district and county of Hereford, 2 miles E of Tram Inn r station, and 4 S by W of Hereford Post town, Hereford Acres, 621 Real property, £486 Pop, 137 Houses, 30 The property is much subdivided The living is a vicarage, annexed to the vicarage of Dewsall, in the diocese of Hereford The church is tolerable

CALLOW DOWN, an eminence 2 miles SW of Princes Risborough, in Bucks

CALLOW HILL, an eminence, 5 miles SE of Bromsgrove, in Worcester

CALLWEN, or GLYNTAWE, a chapelry in Devynnock parish, Brecon Pop, 49 Living, a p curacy Value, £80

CALMSDEN, a tything in North Cerney parish, Gloucester, 4½ miles NNE of Cirencester Pop, 65

CALNE, a town a parish, a sub district, a district, and a hundred in Wilts The town stands on the rivulet Marlan, at the end of a branch railway from the Great Western, and of a branch canal from the Wilts and Berks, 5½ miles E by S of Chippenham Its environs are a fine mixture of dale and hill, and adjoin, on the SW, the Marquis of Lansdowne's seat of Bowood It rose originally from the ruins of a Roman station, dates from the Saxon times, and was the scene of the synod in 977, at which St Dunstan presided for settling the disputes respecting the celibacy of the clergy when all present, except the president, went down by the falling in of the floor It is a quaint old place with small stone houses, either weather worn or white washed, and consists of one long chief street and a few minor ones, all narrow, and paved with pebbles It had an hospital so early as the time of Henry III, and has now a post office‡ under Chippenham, two banking offices three chief inns, a town-hall, a parish church, a chapel of ease five dissenting chapels, a free school, and a workhouse The church is early English, with traces of Norman has a pinnacled tower 93 feet high, and was recently restored The chapel of the Free Christians was erected in 1848, and is a structure of some elegance The free school was founded in 1660 by John Bentley and has an endowed income of £51 with two scholarships at Queen's college, Oxford The workhouse is at Northfield, and cost about £5,000 A large cloth trade was formerly carried on but has become nearly extinct There are now flour mills, flax mills, and paper mills A weekly market is held on Wednesday and fairs on 6 May and 29 Sept. The town is a borough by prescription, is governed by a mayor, four aldermen, and twelve councillors, sent two members to parliament, from the time of Richard II till the act of 1832 and now sends one Its municipal limits comprise only 800 acres, while its parliamentary limits comprise all Calne parish and parts of Blackland and Calstone Welington parishes Direct taxes, £3,038 Electors in 1868, 175 Pop of the m borough, 2,494 of the p borough, 5,179 Houses in the m borough, 501, in the p borough, 1,105

The parish comprises, in addition to the m borough, the tythings of Blackland Calstone, Eastmead street, Quemerford, Stock, Stockley, Studley, Whetham, Whitley, and part of Beversbrook. Acres, 8,079 Real property, exclusive of the part of Beversbrook, £25,974 Pop, 5,098. Houses 1,087 The manor was given by Edward I. to the Cantilupes, and passed to the Zouches The living is a vicarage united with the chapelry of Trinity, in the diocese of Salisbury Value, £769 * Patron the Bishop of Salisbury The vicarage of Christchurch at Derryhill, is a separate benefice —The sub district and the district are co-extensive, and contain the parishes of Calne, Blackland, Calstone Wellington, Bremhill, Heddington, Cherhill, Compton-Basset, Hilmarton, Highway, and Yatesbury, and the liberty of Bowood Acres, 28,610 Poor rates in 1866, £8,028 Pop in 1861, 8,885. Houses, 1,939 Marriages in 1866, 72, births, 278,—of which 9 were illegitimate, deaths, 142,—of which 36 were at ages under 5 years, and 5 at ages above 85 Marriages in the ten years 1851–60, 642, births, 2,651, deaths, 1,788 The places of worship in 1851 were 11 of the Church of England, with 2,186 sittings 1 of Independents, with 150 s, 5 of Baptists, with 925 s, 1 of Quakers, with 160 s, 5 of Wesleyan Methodists, with 633 s, 3 of Primitive Methodists, with 419 s, 1 of Moravians, with 200 s., and 1 of Brethren, with 100 s The schools were 14 public day schools, with 1,270 scholars, 12 private day schools, with 251 s, 13 Sunday schools, with 1,232 s, and 1 evening school for adults, with 40 s —The hundred contains eight parishes and a liberty Acres, 19,083 Pop, 1,297 Houses, 972

CALNE RAILWAY, a railway in Wilts, 5¼ miles long, eastward from the Great Western at Chippenham, to Calne It was authorized in May 1860, and opened in November 1863

CALOW, a township in Chesterfield parish, Derby, 2¼ miles E of Chesterfield Real property £1 844 Pop, 375 Coal is worked There are a chapel of ease of 1867, an Independent chapel and a national school

CALSHOT CASTLE an extra parochial tract in New Forest district, Hants, at the W side of the mouth of Southampton water 7 miles SSE of Southampton Pop, 23 Houses, 6 A castle here was one of the numerous small forts built by Henry VIII for protecting the south coast, and is now a dwelling house A lighthouse is here with a fixed light, bright and red, and a light vessel, called the Calshot Spit Light, is in the neighbourhood, with a minute revolving light Calshot Castle is also a coast guard station

CALSTOCK, a village and a parish in Liskeard district, Cornwall The village stands on the river Tamar, near the Tavistock canal, 5½ miles WNW of Horrabridge r station, and 6 SW of Tavistock, is a sub port to Plymouth and has a post office, under Tavistock, and an inn The parish comprises 6,1[illegible] acres Real property, £14 2[illegible], of which £4,173 are in mines, £30 in quarries, and [illegible] in fisheries Pop, 7,0[illegible] Houses 1,[illegible]77 The property is much subdivided The manor belonged to the duchy of Cornwall Cothele House is an old mansion, the seat of the Earl of Mount Edgcumbe, and Harewood House is the seat of Sir W Trelawny, Bart Porphyritic elvan, called Hobborough stone, is quarried, granite abounds and tin copper, manganese, and lead ore, have been mined The living is a rectory in the diocese of Exeter Value, £710 * Patron, the Prince of Wales The church is a granite structure, with a lofty pinnacled tower, and contains the vault of the Edgcumbes, and monuments to Pearse Edgcumbe and the Countess of Sandwich. There is a Baptist chapel Blackburn, Archbishop of York, was rector

CALSTONE, a tything in Calne parish, Wilts, near Calne Pop, 219

CALSTONE-WELLINGTON, or CALSTONE WILLINGTON, a parish in Calne district, Wilts on the Roman road from Bath, near Wans Dyke, 2½ miles SE of Calne r station It has a post office under Chippenham Acres, 308 Real property, £1,945 Pop, 36 Houses, 9 The property is divided among a few The manor belonged to the Cantilupes and the Zouches, and passed to the Lords Willington. The living is a rectory in the diocese of Salisbury Value, £192 * Patron, the Marquis of Lansdowne The church was repaired in 1859 to need repair

CALTEGFA, a township in Llanfwrog parish, Denbigh, near Ruthin.

CALTHORPE, a parish in Aylsham district, Norfolk, on an affluent of the river Bure, 2½ miles W of the line of the projected railway to Cromer 3½ N of Aylsham, and 15 NNE of Elmham r station Post-town, Aylsham, under Norwich Acres, 1,048 Real property, £2,328 Pop, 187 Houses, 44 The property is all in one estate The living is a vicarage in the diocese of Norwich Value, £143 * Patron, Sir W Foster, Bart. The church is good, and there are charities £13

CALTHORPE a hamlet in Neithrop township, Banbury parish, Oxford in the north western vicinity of Banbury

CALTHORPE, Leicester See CATTHORPE

CALTHWAITE a township in Hesket in the Forest parish, Cumberland, on the river Petterill, and the Lancaster and Carlisle railway, 7½ miles NNW of Penrith It has a station on the railway Acres, 1,876 Real property £1,790 Pop, 269 Houses, 48

CALTON, three townships, a chapelry, and a sub-district in the district of Ashborne and county of Stafford. The townships are Calton in Mayfield, Calton in Blore and Calton in Waterfall, they lie in three several parishes, designated in their respective names, and they are contiguous to one another, at a point 2½ miles W of the river Dove, 4½ ENE of Froghall r station, and 6½ NW by W of Ashborne Acres of the three, 2,480 Real property, £1 911 Pop of C in M, 70, of C in B, 72, of C in W, 65 Houses of C in M, 17 of C in B, 17, of C in W 13 The chapelry includes also a detached part of Croxden parish, and its post town is Ashborne The living is a donative in the diocese of Lichfield. Value, £33 * Patron the Vicar of Mayfield Fairs are held on 15 Aug and 20 Sept —The sub district contains eight parishes, parts of three other parishes, and an extra parochial tract Acres, 17,689 Pop, 3,0[illegible] Houses, 618

CALTON a township in Kirkby in Malham Dale parish, W R Yorkshire on an affluent of the river Aire, near the Midland railway 7 miles SE by E of Settle Acres 1 730 Real property, £1,286 Pop, 56 Houses, 12 General Lambert, one of the parliamentarian leaders in the civil wars, was a native

CALVELEY a township in Bunbury parish, Cheshire, on the Chester canal, adjacent to the Chester and Crewe railway 8 miles W by N of Crewe It has a station on the railway and it forms a curacy with Bunbury Acres, 1,517 Real property £2,502 Pop, 285 Houses, 48 The manor belonged to Sir Hugh Calveley, the "glory of Cheshire," and belongs now to the Davenports

CALVER, a township in Bakewell parish, Derby, on the river Derwent [illegible] miles N by E of Bakewell It has a post office under Sheffield Real property £1 5[illegible]0 Pop 617 Houses, 129 The inhabitants are chiefly lime burners and cotton spinners, and there are extensive cotton mills

CALVERHALL, or CORRA, a chapelry in Prees parish Salop [illegible] miles NE of Prees r station, and 4½ SE of Whitchurch Its post town Prees, under Shrewsbury Rated property, £2 518 Pop, 270 Houses, 51 The property is divided among a few The chapelry was constituted in 1558 The living is a vicarage in the diocese of Lichfield Value, £83 * Patron, John W Dod Esq The church is recent and Gothic

CALVERLEIGH, a parish in Tiverton district, Devon, in the vicinity of the Western canal, 2¼ miles NW of Tiverton r station Post town Tiverton Acres, 591 Real property, £874 Pop, 86 Houses, 17 The property is divided among a few The manor belonged, from the time of King John till that of Henry VIII, to the Calwoodleys, and belongs now to J C Nagle, Esq The living is a rectory in the diocese of Exeter Value, £101 Patron, G W Owen, Esq The church is old and good, with a low turreted tower

CALVERLEY, a village, a township, a sub district, and a parish, in Bradford district, W R Yorkshire The village stands adjacent to the river Aire and to the Leeds and Bradford railway, 4½ miles NE of Bradford, and has a station on the railway, and a post office under Leeds The township includes also the hamlets of Woodhall Hill, Womersley Row, and Bagley, and parts of the villages of Apperley Bridge, Podley, and Stanningley, and bears the name of Calverley with Farsley Acres, 3,500 Real property, £15,857, of which £300 are in mines, and £330 in quarries Pop, 5,559 Houses, 1,231 The sub district is conterminate with the township The parish includes also the townships of Pudsey, Bolton, and Idle Acres, 8,918 Rated property, £52,195 Pop in 1841, 21,039, in 1861, 28,503 Houses, 6 354 The property is much subdivided Calverley Hall was the seat of the ancient family of Calverley, and the scene in 1604 of the subject of the 'Yorkshire Tragedy,' erroneously ascribed to Shakspeare, and was converted, early in the present century, into separate tenements for manufacturers Many of the inhabitants are employed in woollen and worsted mills. The living is a vicarage, united with the p curacy of Bolton, in the diocese of Ripon Value, £230 * Patron, the Bishop of Ripon The church is good The chapelries of Farsley Pudsey, St Paul's and Idle are separate benefices There are four dissenting chapels, a mechanics' institute, four public schools, and charities £54

CALVERLEY, Sussex. See TONBRIDGE WELLS.

CALVERT FENTON See FENTON CULVERT

CALVERT HOUSE, a hamlet in Muker chapelry, Grinton parish, N R Yorkshire, near Muker

CALVERTON, a parish in the district of Potterspury and county of Buckingham on Watling street and the river Ouse, adjacent to the Buckingham canal, 1 mile S of Stony Stratford, and 2¼ WSW of Wolverton r station Post-town, Stony-Stratford Acres, 1,930 Real property, £3,372. Pop, 595 Houses, 112 The property is divided among a few A Roman camp lay around the site of the church and Roman relics have been found there The living is a rectory in the diocese of Oxford. Value £346 * Patron, the Earl of Egmont. The church was built in 1818 Charities, £30

CALVERTON, a village and a parish in Basford district, Notts. The village stands near an affluent of the river Trent 4½ miles NNW of Burton-Joyce r station, and 6½ NNE of Nottingham and has a post office under Nottingham The parish includes Satterford manor Acres, 3,320 Real property, £4,724 Pop, 1,372 Houses, 288 The property is much subdivided Roofing stone is quarried Many of the inhabitants are lace and stocking makers The living is a vicarage in the diocese of Lincoln Value, £127 * Patron, alternately the Bishop of Manchester and the Prebendary of Oxton The church is good, and there are chapels for Baptists, Wesleyans and Primitive Methodists A school has £12 from endowment, and other charities £12 Lee, the inventor of the stocking frame, was a native

CALVERTON (LOWER) See CALVERTON, Bucks

CALWICH a township in Ellastone parish, Stafford, on the river Dove 3½ miles SW of Ashborne Pop, 87 Houses, 22 A black priory was founded here, in the 12th century, by Fitz Nigel and given at the dissolution to John Fleetwood Calwich Hall is the seat of the Granvilles, and has a fine collection of pictures.

CAM (THE), a stream of Gloucester It rises on the Cotswolds, 4 miles W of Nailsworth, and runs 7 miles north westward to the Severn near Frampton

CAM (THE) a river of Cambridge It rises at Ashwell, near the boundary with Beds, runs 14 miles north-eastward, past Barrington, to Granchester, receives there the Granta coming 12 miles from the west, and becomes navigable, proceeds thence 2¾ miles north by eastward to Cambridge, and goes thence 13 miles north north eastward, past Chesterton, Waterbeach, and Upware, to a confluence with the Ouse, 3½ miles above Ely It was widened and otherwise improved, in its course past Cambridge, in 1869, at a cost of about £6,000

CAM, a parish in Dursley district, Gloucester; on the Cam rivulet and the Dursley railway, under the Cotswolds, 1 mile N of Dursley It has a station on the railway and its post town is Dursley Acres, 2,946 Real property, £9,079 Pop, 1,500 Houses, 373 The property is divided among a few Excellent cheese is produced. Cloth manufacture is carried on in a large establishment A battle was fought here, in the time of Edward the Elder, between the Danes and the Saxons The living is a vicarage, united with the p curacy of Low Cam, in the diocese of Gloucester and Bristol Value, £150 * Patron, the Bishop of Gloucester and Bristol The church is early English There are endowed and national schools and large charities

CAMALLT See CADBURY (SOUTH)

CAMALODUNUM See COLCHESTER.

CAMARON (THE), an affluent of the river Ithon, in Radnor

CAMBECK FORT See CASTLESTEADS

CAMBECK (THE), an affluent of the river Irthing, in Cumberland

CAMBER CASTLE, a ruined fortalice on the coast of Sussex, nearly midway between Winchelsea and Rye It was one of the strengths built by Henry VIII, for defence of the coast, was dismantled in 1642, and has a central tower, surmounted by smaller ones, with connecting curtains The sea once washed its walls, but has considerably receded.

CAMBERFORD - See COMBERFORD

CAMBERWELL, a district in the NE corner of Surrey It lies within the borough of Lambeth, is partly a suburb of London, partly rural, with considerable extent of open field, and includes the suburbs of Dulwich and Peckham The suburban part of it is 1½ mile SSW of the terminus of the Bricklayers Arms Extension railway, has two railway stations, called Camberwell Gate and Camberwell New Road, is 1½ mile ESE of the Vauxhall station of the Southwestern railway, and 2¾ miles S of St. Paul's, lies across the terminal part of the Grand Surrey canal, and consists chiefly of streets, places, and outskirts with modern houses Ermine street, coming up from Lambeth ferry, passed through south eastward, going into Kent at Oak of Honour Hill, and traces of it were found at the cutting of the canal Oak of Honour Hill is said to have acquired its name from Queen Elizabeth's dining on it under an oak St. Thomas Watering, near this, was a resting place of the Canterbury pilgrims, and a marble head of Janus was found there Camberwell Grove, in the suburb, now occupied by a handsome range of modern houses, was the place where George Barnwell murdered his uncle Camberwell manor house, near Denmark Hill, was a curious ancient mansion, converted latterly into a school Camberwell Green is notorious as the scene of a crowded pleasure fair on three days in August, but was recently surrounded by iron railings, and laid out in gravel walks, flower plots and shrubbery The district is a polling place, and has a post office‡ under London S with seven receiving houses and five pillar boxes Acres, 4 342 Real property, £127,523 Poor rates in 1866, £32,584 Pop in 1861, 71,488 Houses, 12 093 Marriages in 1866, 856, births, 3,343 —of which 138 were illegitimate, deaths, 2,056, —of which 888 were at ages under 5 years and 31 at ages above 85. Marriages in the ten years 1851-60, 4 410 births, 19,973, deaths 13,631 There are four sub-districts,—Camberwell, Dulwich, Peckham, and St. George. Acres of C., 1,339; of D., 1,423; of P., [illegible]; of St. G., 434. Pop. of C., 21,297; of D., 1,723; of P., 2[illegible],165; of St. G., 20,333. Houses of C., 3,[illegible]; of D., 2[illegible]; of P., 4,943; of St. G., 3,421.

The district is conterminate with one ancient parish, which is still a single parish for civil purposes, but is now divided ecclesiastically into thirteen parishes and two separate chapelries, and also includes two annexed chapelries, all in the diocese of Winchester. Six of the divisions, Christchurch, St. Mary Magdalene, Camden, St. Andrew, St. Michael and St. Chrysostom, are noticed in our article on Peckham; four, Dulwich College, East Dulwich, St. Stephen, and St. Peter, are noticed in that on Dulwich, and one, partly in Lambeth, is noticed in that on Herne-Hill. The others are St. Giles, around the mother church, St. George, constituted in 1524, Emmanuel, constituted in 18[illegible], and St. Philip, constituted in 1866. The living of St. Giles is a vicarage united with the chapelry of Forest-Hill; the livings of St. George and Emmanuel are vicarages, and that of St. Philip is a p. curacy. Value of St. Giles, with Forest Hill, £1,600;* of St. George, £400; of Emmanuel, £450;* of St. Philip, £200. Patron of St. Giles, F. F. Kelly, Esq.; of St. George, Sir W. B. Smith, Bart.; of Emmanuel, the Rev. W. Harker; of St. Philip, the Bishop of Winchester. St. Giles' church was built in 1[illegible]2-4, on the site of an old one burnt in 1841; and is a large, elegant, cruciform edifice, in the later English style, with a lofty spire. St. George's church was built in 1[illegible]24, and is a Doric edifice, with hexastyle portico. The total places of worship in 1851 were 13 of the Church of England, with 11,212 sittings; 6 of Independents, with 3,536 s.; 1 of Baptists, with 350 s.; 1 of Quakers, with 231 s.; 2 of Wesleyan Methodists, with 680 s.; 1 of Primitive Methodists, with 30 s.; 1 of Latter Day Saints, with 250 s.; and 1 undefined, with 150 s. The schools were 27 public day schools, with 3,730 scholars; 151 private day schools, with 3,091 s.; 20 Sunday schools, with 3,317 s.; and 4 evening schools for adults, with [illegible]3 s. One of the public schools is Dulwich college; another is a grammar school; six others are endowed; and six are National. Tyrrell, the historian, was educated in the grammar school; and Parr, the biographer and chaplain of Archbishop Usher, was thirty eight years vicar. The charities amount to nearly £300.

CAMBLESFORTH, a township in Drax parish, W. R. Yorkshire; between the rivers Ouse and Aire, 2¼ miles N of Snaith. It has a post-office under Selby. Acres, [illegible]49[illegible]. Real property, £2,017. Pop., 3[illegible]2. Houses, 72. Camblesforth Hall belongs to Sir C. Blois, Bart.

CAMBO, a township and a chapelry in Hartburn parish, Northumberland. The township lies near an affluent of the river Wansbeck, and near the Wansbeck Valley railway, in the vicinity of Scot's Gap station, 11 miles SE by S of Otterburn; and has a post office‡ under Newcastle upon Tyne. Acres, 630. Pop., 111. Houses, 2[illegible]. The chapelry is much more extensive than the township, and was constituted in 1844. Rated property, £7,[illegible]7. Pop., 7[illegible]0. Houses, 151. The property is divided between two. The living is a vicarage in the diocese of Durham. Value, £113. Patron, the Vicar of Hartburn. The church is good.

CAMBOIS, or CHAMBOIS, a township and a chapelry in Bedlington parish, Northumberland. The township lies on the coast, at the mouth of the river Wansbeck, near North-Seaton r. station, 2¾ miles N by W of Blythe. The chapelry was constituted in 1863. Post town, Bedlington, Northumberland. Pop., about 3,000. The living is a vicarage in the diocese of Durham. Value, £3[illegible].* Patrons, the Dean and Chapter of Durham. Brown, the landscape gardener, was a native.

CAMBORICUM. See CAMBRIDGE.

CAMBORNE, a town, a parish, and a sub district, in Redruth district, Cornwall. The town stands adjacent to the West Cornwall railway, in the centre of a rich mining tract, 14½ miles WSW of Truro. It is a thriving place, a scene of considerable trade, and a seat of petty sessions; and has a head post-office,‡ a r. station with telegraph, a banking office, a hotel, a market house of 1866, a church, four dissenting chapels, and charities £70. The church is perpendicular English, in granite, large, but very low; was restored in 1862; contains a carved wooden pulpit, a new granite font, and monuments of the family of Pendarves; and has, on the outside, an ancient inscribed stone, placed in its present position by the late Lord de Dunstanville, and believed to have been originally an altar cover. A weekly market is held on Saturday, and fairs on 7 March, Whit Tuesday, 29 June, and 11 Nov. Pop., 7,208. Houses, 1,415.—The parish includes also the villages of Tucking mill, Penponds, Beripp[illegible], Trewithan, and others. Acres, 6,744. Real property, £39,102; of which £26,315 are in mines. Pop., 14,0[illegible]6. Houses, 2,737. Pendarves, about a mile S of the town, the seat of the late E. W. W. Pendarves, Esq., is a modern granite edifice, contains some good pictures and a rich mineral cabinet, and stands in a fine park, formed entirely out of a moor. Tehidy, the seat of J. F. Basset, Esq., has a good collection of pictures, and stands in a park of upwards of 700 acres. Carnbrea, a rocky eminence 740 feet high, is regarded by Borlase as having been the chief seat of the Druids in the west of England; and Carwinnen, a wild moorish hill confronting Pendarves, has at its foot a cromlech, called the Pendarves Quoit. Extensive mines are worked, and employ most of the inhabitants. Dolcoath mine, about 3 miles W of Carnbrea, has been sunk to the depth of 1,080 feet, and extends under ground fully a mile. The living is a rectory in the diocese of Exeter. Value, £600.* Patron, J. F. Basset, Esq. The vicarages of Tucking mill, Penponds, and Treslothan are separate charges. A modern chapel, in the Norman style, is at Tucking mill; and a handsome one, built in 1842, is on an eminence in Pendarves park. An ancient chapel stood on the latter's site; another stood at Trewin, adjacent to a medicinal well; and four or five more stood in other places. The sub district is conterminate with the parish.

CAMBRIA. See WALES.

CAMBRIDGE, a university town, the capital of Cambridgeshire. It stands on the Via Devana, the river Cam, and the Eastern Counties railway, 51 miles by road, and 57½ by railway, N by E of London. The Cam is navigable to it; and railways go from it in six directions, toward London, Hitchin, Bedford, Huntingdon, Ely, and Ipswich, ramifying toward all parts of the kingdom.

History.—Cambridge is the Granta, perhaps also the Camboricum of the Romans, and most probably the Grantaceaster of the Saxons. It was burnt by the Danes in 870 and 1010. A military station seems to have been at it in the times of the Saxons, certainly in those of the Romans; and a castle was built at it, probably on the site of the previous station, by William the Conqueror, to overawe the Isle of Ely. In the castle was received Sir Osborn, whose legendary conflict with a demon knight on Gogmagog hill was used by Sir Walter Scott for an episode in "Marmion." The town was injured by both parties in the wars of the Barons and the Roses, especially in 1216 and 1267; suffered from insurrections of the townsmen against the University, in 1249, 1322, and 1381; was occupied on behalf of Queen Mary, after the attempt to place Lady Jane Grey on the throne; and was seized and occupied under Cromwell, for the parliamentarians. Royal visits were made to it by Stephen, in 1139; by John, in 1200 and 1216; by Henry III., in 1265 and 1270; by Edward I., in 1293; by Edward II., in 1325; by Edward III., in 1328; by Richard II., in 1390; by Edward IV., in 1463; by Richard III., in 1483 and 1485; by Henry VII., in 1486, 1487, 1491, 149[illegible], and 1506; by Queen Catherine, in 1520; by Henry VIII., in 1522; by Elizabeth, in 1564; by James I., in 1614, 1615, 1623, and 1624; by Charles I., in 1628, 1632, and 1641; by Charles II., in 1671 and 1681; by William III., in 1689; by Anne, in 1705; by George I., in 1717; by George II., in 1728; and by Victoria, in 1847.

Site and Streets.—The town stands amid a great flat tract; is not clearly seen on any approach to it, till near; and appears relieved, even then, by only the tower of St. Mary, the spire of Trinity, and the four turrets of King's, over a line of trees. Tradition alleges it to have anciently extended 3 miles along the Cam, from Gra[illegible] chester to Chesterton, but this is not to be believed The present borough limits indeed include a space about 3½ miles long with a mean breadth of 1½ mile, comprising 3,470 acres, but the town itself, exclusive of the suburb of Chesterton, which is not in the borough, covers only about one fifth of the space Regent street is a fine street, Trumpington and St Andrew's streets also are broad, airy, and pleasant, and many new streets of small houses have recently been formed, but the other streets, generally, are narrow, winding, and irregularly edificed. The town has, of late years, been much improved by extension or renovation of public buildings, by removal of old private houses, and by erection of new ones, and, as the seat of a great university, it necessarily possesses great wealth of structure and ornament, yet it fails to impress a stranger with a fair idea of either beauty or dignity It suffers severely from dearth of stone, and has betaken itself largely to brick and stucco, and, owing to the recent rebuilding of some of its colleges, and to the Grecian or Italian character of large portions of others, its university looks almost modern

Antiquities —Dr Stukeley notes that the site of the Roman Granta is very traceable on the side of Cambridge towards the castle, that the Roman agger is identical with a fine terrace walk in the garden of Magdalene college, that the gateway of the castle, and the churches of St Giles and St Peter are marked antiquities that many Roman bricks have been found in the latter church s walls, and many small Roman relics in the adjoining fields, and that remains exist of three bastions raised by Cromwell Other antiquities will be noticed in connexion with the churches and the colleges

Public Buildings —An elegant suite of buildings to comprise guild hall, public rooms, and municipal offices, was commenced in 1860, on an immediate scale to cost about £6,000, but on a plan to be ultimately extended, at a cost of nearly £40,000 The new county courts occupy the site of the castle, contiguous to the ancient gateway and are commodious. The county jail has capacity for 72 male prisoners, but has no cells for females. The borough jail was built subsequent to 1827, at a cost of £15,738, has capacity for 62 males and 26 females, and, by arrangement of the authorities, serves also for county female prisoners. The spinning house was founded in 1628, and is used as a place of confinement for lewd and disorderly females The market place was originally spacious was recently enlarged and improved, and has a handsome restored conduit, originally erected in 1614, and a statue of Jonas Webb, erected in 1866 The corn exchange is a recent and ugly structure The theatre is small but neat The Union Buildings were erected in 1867, at a cost of £10,000, are in the pointed style of the 13th century, and include a debating room 60 feet by 43

Parishes —Downing college is in the parish of St Benedict, the new buildings of St John s, and the grove of Catherine s also are within parishes, but all the other colleges are extra parochial The parishes are All Saints, St Andrew the Great, St Andrew the Less or Barnwell, St Benedict, St Botolph, St Clement, St Edward, St. Giles, St Peter, St Mary the Great, St. Mary the Less, St Michael, St Sepulchre, and Holy Trinity Only St Andrew the Less and St Giles extend much beyond the limits of the town St. Paul s cn pelrs also is ecclesiastically a parish The living of St Botolph is a rectory that of St Edward is a donative the others are vicarages, that of St Peter is annexed to that of St Giles, and all are in the diocese of Ely Value of All Saints, £130, of St. Andrew the Great £120, of St Paul, £120,* of St Andrew the Less, £18,* of St Benedict, £151, of St Botolph, £122, of St. Clement, £56, of St Edward £58, of St Giles, with St Peter £170 of St Mary the Great, £104, of St Mary the Less and St Michael, each £55, of St Sepulchre, £123 of Holy Trinity, £96 Patron of All Saints and St Clement, Jesus College, of St Andrew the Great, the Dean and Chapter of Ely of St Andrew the Less and St Paul, Trustees, of St Benedict Corpus Christi College, of St. Botolph, Queen s College, of St Edward, Trinity Hall of Holy Trinity not reported, of St. Giles, the Bishop of Ely, of St. Mary the Great and St Michael, Trinity College, of St. Mary the Less, St Peter's College, of St. Sepulchre, the parishioners

Ancient Monasteries —An Augustinian priory was founded, on the left bank of the river, in 1092, by Picot, a Norman lord of Bourne, removed to Barnwell, in 1112 by Payne Peverell, standard bearer in Palestine to the Duke of Normandy and given, after the dissolution, to Lord Clinton Some portions of the building still exist. A Gilbertine priory was founded at the old chapel of St Edmund, in 1291, by Bishop Fitzwalter, and given, at the dissolution, to Edward Elrington and Humphrey Metcalf A Benedictine priory was founded on the site of Trinity hall, at the beginning of the reign of Edward III, by John de Craulen but was granted, in a few years, to the Bishop of Norwich, and gave place to Trinity hall A Benedictine nunnery was founded on the site of Jesus' college, in 1130, and part of it is included in the college chapel. A Bethlehemite friary, the only one in England, was founded at Trumpington street in 1257 A friary de Sacco was founded in 1258, a friary of St Mary, in 1273, a grey friary, on the site of Sidney Sussex college, in 1225, an Augustinian friary, by Pitchford, in 1259, a white friary, at King's college garden in 1316, and a black friary, on the site of Emmanuel college, in 1275

Churches.—The church of All Saints was reconstructed on a new site in 1864, is an ornamental edifice and contains a monument by Chantrey, to Henry Kirke White The church of St Andrew the Great was rebuilt in 1643, and again in 1845 and contains a cenotaph to Cook, the navigator The church of St Andrew the Less, or Barnwell was partly built out of Barnwell priory, and was recently restored The church of St Benedict has a Saxon tower was recently repaired and enlarged, contains some interesting monuments, and was some time served by Thomas Fuller The church of St Botolph was recently restored, and has many monuments The church of St Clement has an early English door, and a fine tower and spire of 1821, was restored in 1856, and contains an octagonal font, and a monument of 1329 The church of St Edward is early English, was recently restored, has a good font and was served by Latimer The church of St Giles is partly as old as 1100, and was recently restored The church of St Peter, now disused, includes Roman bricks, and has a Norman door The church of St Mary the Great is the University church, was built in 1478-1519, has a conspicuous tower of 1593-1608, surmounted by octagonal turrets, shows the architectural features of the age in which it was erected, measures, within walls, 120 feet by 68, was recently restored and beautified at large expense and contains the grave of Martin Bucer The church of St Mary the Less is later English, was recently restored has a rich east window, and contains a Norman font The church of St. Michael was built in 1337, and restored in 1849, is pure decorated English, possesses the old stalls of Trinity college chapel, and had the grave of Fagius The church of St Sepulchre was built by the Templars in 1101 and restored by the Camden Society in 1843, is a round Norman edifice, with short massive piers, and includes restored windows south aisle, domical ribbed vault, and campanile The church of Holy Trinity was built in the 15th century, and recently repaired has a good tower and spire, contains an altar tomb to Sir Robert Tabor, the physician and a monument to Henry Martyn, the missionary and was served by Charles Simeon The church of St Paul and another called Christ church, are recent erections and the church of St Barnabas was founded in 1861 The total places of worship within the borough, in 1851, were 16 of the Church of England, with 9 334 sittings 1 of Independents, with 630 s, 3 of Baptists, with 2,170 s, 1 of Wesleyan Methodists with 1 000 s., 1 of Primitive Methodists with 250 s, 1 of Latter Day Saints with 150 s, and 1 of Roman Catholics, with 230 s The new cemetery was laid out by London, and contains a chapel by G G Scott

Schools, &c.—A grammar school was founded in 1615 by bequest of Dr Perse, was recently rebuilt, and gives its pupils, of 3 years standing a preference to the Perse fellowships and scholarships at Caius college Whiston's charity schools for boys and girls were instituted in 1703 and have an endowed income of £64, but have long been united with the National schools The total schools within the borough in 1851, were 18 public day schools, with 2,734 scholars, 54 private day schools, with 1,121 s , and 22 Sunday schools, with 3,477 s Eleven of the public schools were National, and one was a ragged school There are a Union Society, a Philo Union Society, a Philosophical Society, several students' clubs and associations a free library, founded in 1855, a lending library, founded in 1858, and largely aided by the late Prince Consort and a working men's college and reading room Addenbrooke's hospital or infirmary was founded in 1766, by bequest of Dr John Addenbrooke, and enlarged in 1813, by bequest of John Bowtell, has upwards of £1,500 from endowment, and a large income from subscription, and was undergoing enlargement and improvement in 1864, at a cost of about £10,000 Storey's alms houses, for clergymen's widows, have £813 Wray's have £215, Knight's, £94, and the Spital, £25 The Victoria and Royal Albert asylums are modern institutions, munificently maintained by donation and subscription The total endowed charities of the borough amount to £5,000

Trade, &c.—The town is maintained chiefly by supplying the wants of the university, yet conducts a large trade in land produce, and carries on some manufactures in leather, ropes, baskets, pattens, mustard, vinegar, iron ware, brass ware, and other articles. Markets are held daily, chief markets, on Wednesdays and Saturdays and fairs on 24 June and 25 Sept The town has a head post office,‡ a railway station with telegraph, two other telegraph stations, four banking offices, and six chief inns, is a seat of assizes and sessions, a place of election, and the head of an excise district, and publishes two weekly newspapers Races are run on Midsummer Common and boat races, among the University men, from the vicinity of Ditton church A fine public park, called Parker's Piece, contains about 20 acres, and is almost square

The Borough—Cambridge is a borough by prescription, was incorporated by Henry I , has sent two members to parliament since the time of Edward I , and is governed by a mayor, ten aldermen, and thirty councillors Real property of the town, £117,307, of the corporation £2,400, of the university, £33,758 Corporation revenue, £17,258 Direct taxes £24,559 Electors, in 1868, 1,926 Pop in 1841, 24,453, in 1861, 26,361 Houses, 5,383. The borough forms a registration district —Poor rates, in 1866, £1? 938 Marriages, 1?7, births, 829,—of which 41 were illegitimate, deaths, 635,—of which 227 were at ages under 5 years, and 15 at ages above 85 Marriages in the ten years 1851-60, 1,868, births, 7,709, deaths 5,504 The town gives the title of Duke to a prince of the blood royal Sir J Cheke tutor of Edward VI Gibbons, the organist Bishops Thirlby Goldsborough, Rust, Townson and Musgrave, Bernet the martyr, Dean Duport, Jeremy Taylor, Lady D Masham, Essex the antiquary, Drake, the translator of Herodotus and Cumberland the dramatist, were natives

The University—Cambridge university is an incorporated society of students in all the liberal arts and sciences It originated with or was restored by Sigebert, king of East Anglia and was revived by Edward the Elder but first acquired consequence about 1209, under the abbot of Croyland The students lived, for some time in inns and hostels, built for their reception, but were afterwards provided with seventeen colleges The colleges possess equal privileges form an aggregate body under one supreme authority, and at the same time are ruled separately each by its own statutes The supreme authority comprises legislative and executive The legislative is a senate, composed of all the masters of arts, and doctors in divinity, civil law, and physic, whose names are on the boards,—divided till recently into two houses, of regents and non regents, or white hoods and black hoods, but now voting as one body,—and controlled by a council consisting of the chancellor, the vice-chancellor, four heads of colleges, four professors, and eight other members of senate chosen annually from the roll, who must approve all business before it can be offered to the senate The executive includes a chancellor, generally a person of rank and non resident, a vice chancellor or acting governor, a high steward, or judge in cases of felony, a commissary or assessor, a public orator, who acts also as official secretary and several other officials The members of the university are variously heads of colleges, professors, fellows, noblemen, graduates, doctors in the several faculties, bachelors in divinity, graduates, bachelors in civil law and in physic, bachelors of arts, fellow commoners, pensioners, scholars, and sizers, and all, in their several ranks and also in their several colleges, are distinguished by differences of costume There are 27 professorships, 410 fellowships, about 900 scholarships or exhibitions, and about 1,800 residents Two-thirds, or nearly so, of the residents, live in the colleges, and the rest live in lodgings. The doctors and regent masters of arts in convocation send two members to parliament, and amounted, in 1868, to 5,184 The income of all the colleges is £184,994

University Buildings—The senate house stands on the north side of a spacious square, near the centre of the town, was built in 1722-30, after a design by Burrough, at a cost of £20,000, is exteriorly Corinthian, and interiorly Doric, measures 101 feet by 42, with a height of 32 feet, has galleries of Norway oak, and contains statues of George I and the Duke of Somerset by Rysbrack George II by Wilton, and W Pitt by Nollekens The public schools stand on the west side of the same square, were first founded in 1443, form three sides of a small court, and contain apartments for the philosophy, divinity, law, and physic schools, and for disputations, exercises, and lectures The old library is over the schools, was rebuilt in 1775, and contains a colossal Ceres from Eleusis, 100,000 volumes and 2,000 manuscripts The new library was built in 1837, after designs by Cockerell is an elegant edifice, 167 feet by 45 with a new wing begun in 1864, and contains on the base, Dr Woodward's geological specimens The Fitzwilliam museum, in Trumpington street, originated in 1816, in a bequest of £100,000, a library and a collection of works of art from Viscount Fitzwilliam, was built in 1837 and following years, after a design of Basevi, covers an area of 160 feet by 162, has a noble octastyle Corinthian portico, 76 feet high, and contains 144 paintings of the Italian, Dutch, and Flemish schools, statuary, books, and a valuable manuscript collection of music New museums and lecture rooms, in the Gothic style, estimated to cost about £30,000, on the site of the old botanic garden were built in 1862-4 The observatory, on a rising ground, on the Madingley road, about a mile from the college walks was built in 1822-5, by Mead at a cost of £19,000 is 120 feet long, and has a domed house for a 20 feet telescope, presented by the Duke of Northumberland The university printing office, in Trumpington street, was built in 1831-3 by Blore is in the perpendicular English style, with a lofty central tower, and looks like a church The botanical gardens formerly lay around the site of the ancient Augustinian priory, and occupied upwards of three acres, but were recently removed to a new site between Trumpington road and Hills road and they occupy there an area of about twenty one acres, and are both rich in specimens and ornamentally laid out The college walks have avenues of limes elms and horse chestnuts and are overlooked by the backs of most of the larger colleges

St Peter's College, or *Peterhouse*—This is the oldest of the colleges, and was founded, in 1284, by Hugh de Balsham, bishop of Ely It stands in Trumpington street, on ground previously occupied by two hostels, and comprises two old courts the larger 144 feet by 84, and a new court built in 1826 Its chapel was erected

1632, has a fine east window, with painted glass representing the crucifixion, and got all its side windows filled, in 1858–64, with painted glass from Munich The college has 14 fellowships, 59 scholarships 2 exhibitions, 11 livings, and an income of £7,341 Eminent men educated at it were Cardinal Beaufort, Archbishop Whitgift, Bishops Cosin, Law, and Walton Dean Sherlock, the poets Crashaw, Gray and Garth, Jer Markland, Col Hutchinson, the Duke of Grafton, and Lord Ellenborough

Clare College.—This was founded in 1326 by Dr Richard Badew, under the name of University Hall, was burned to the ground about 1342 was rebuilt by the sister and co-heiress of Gilbert Earl of Clare, and took then the name of Clare Hall, and was begun to be rebuilt again in 1638. It stands on the east bank of the Cam, has, over the river a fine old stone bridge, and comprises a noble quadrangle, 150 feet by 111 Its chapel was rebuilt in 1769, at a cost of £7 000, and has a picture of the Salutation, by Cipriani The college has 17 fellowships, 24 scholarships, and 18 livings. Eminent men educated at it were Archbishops Heath and Tillotson, Bishop Gunning, Chaucer, Cudworth, Whiston, W Whitehead, Parkhurst, Nicholas Ferrar, Hervey, Dr Dodd, and the Duke of Newcastle

Pembroke College.—This was founded, in 1347, by the Countess of Pembroke It stands in Trumpington street, nearly opposite St Peters, and consists of two courts, 95 feet by 55, with intermediate hall Its chapel was built by Bishop Wren, after a design by his nephew, Sir Christopher Wren, and has a picture of the entombment by Baroccio A large and curious orrery, made by Dr Long in 1730, is in the inner court, and water works are in the gardens The college has 14 fellowships, 2 bye fellowships, 20 scholarships, 10 livings, and an income of £14,013 Eminent men educated at it were Archbishops Grindall and Whitgift, Bishops Lyndwood, Ridley, Andrews, Wren, Tomlin, and Middleton, the martyrs Bradford and Rogers, the poets Spencer, Gray, and Mason, E Calamy, W Pitt, and Dr Long

Gonville and Caius College.—This was founded in 1348, by Sir Nicholas Gonville, and enlarged in 1557, by Dr John Caius. It stands at the corner of Trumpington and Trinity streets, comprises three courts, with a picturesque new one in progress in 1869, and includes three gates by John of Padua. Its chapel is small but beautiful, and contains a brass of 1500, a monument of Dr Caius, and a picture of the Annunciation by Retz The college has 30 fellowships, 36 scholarships and 22 livings Eminent men educated at it were Dr Harvey and many other distinguished physicians, Jeremy Taylor Sir T Gresham, Shadwell, Henry Wharton, Lord Thurlow, Dr Shuckford, Jeremy Collier, Dr S Clarke, and the antiquaries Grater, Chauncey, and Blomefield

Trinity Hall.—This was founded, in 1350, by Bateman, bishop of Norwich It stands near Clare College on ground previously occupied by a hostel for the monks of Ely, and comprises two courts, one of which is modern Its library is rich in law-works, and its chapel contains three brasses, and a painting of the Presentation by Stella A range of students' residences, in strictly collegiate style, but of earlier character than the rest of the college buildings, with a plain oriel over the entrance doorway, and an octagonal oriel turret at the angle crowned with a short spire, was built in 1861 at a cost of about £10,000, and replaced previous buildings burnt down in 1851 Trinity Hall has 13 fellowships, 19 scholarships 3 livings, and an income of £3 917 Eminent men educated at it were Bishops Gardiner and Horsley, the martyr Bilney, Corbet, Tusser Dr Andrews, Sir R. Naunton, Lord Chesterfield Earl Fitzwilliam, Sir Bulwer Lytton, and Lord Chief Justice Cockburn

Corpus Christi, or *Bene't College.*—This was founded, in 1359, by the two Guilds of Corpus Christi and the Saint Mary It stands in Trumpington street, and comprises an old court of the 14th century, and a new one built in 1823 The new court measures 158 feet by [illegible], and has a frontage of 222 feet, with grand gateway and four massive towers The library measures 87 feet by 22, and contains many valuable manuscripts, bequeathed by Archbishop Parker The chapel was built in 1827, is in the Gothic style, and has windows filled with stained glass from a previous chapel of 1570, built by Lord Keeper Bacon. The college has 12 fellowships, 6 scholarships, and 11 livings Eminent men educated at it were Archbishops Parker and Tenison the martyr Wishart, Bishop Latimer, the poet Fletcher, Sir Nicholas Bacon, Lord Keeper Bacon, and the antiquaries Gough, Salmon, and Stukeley

King's College.—This was founded, in 1441, by Henry VI It occupies a central situation, consists of two courts, partly Italian, partly later English, and forms the finest group of buildings in the town The hall measures 102 feet by 36, the library, 93 feet by 27, the chapel, 316 feet by 45½ The last is esteemed the best specimen of later English in the kingdom, was mainly built in 1441–1530, partly built in last century, and partly restored by Wilkins in 1826, has eleven pinnacles on each side, and four octagonal towers at the corners, and commands, from the leads, an extensive panoramic view, reaching on one side to Ely cathedral The pinnacles are 101 feet high, and rise from buttresses including a range of chantries between their projections, the towers are 146½ feet high, and capped with cupolas, the side windows, twenty four in number, are nearly 50 feet high, and filled with scripture subjects in stained glass of the time of Henry VIII, the doors are very fine, the roof is stone, groined, with fan tracery, in twelve compartments, without the support of a single pillar, the largest and richest of its kind in England the stalls and screen are of the 17th century, and the altar-piece is the Descent from the Cross by Volterra. The college enjoys special privileges and has 46 fellowships 48 scholarships from Eton, 39 livings, and an income of £26,857 Eminent men educated at it were Archbishop Rotherham, Bishops Aldrich, Close and Pearson, the martyr Frith, the chronicler Hall, the poets Waller, P Fletcher and Anstey, the mathematician Oughtred the historian Coxe, the antiquary Cole, Jacob Bryant A. Collins, Sir John Cheke, Sir F Walsingham, Sir W Temple, Sir R Walpole, Sir W Draper, Horace Walpole and Lord Camden

Queen's College.—This was founded, in 1446, by Margaret of Anjou, and enlarged, in 1465 by the queen of Edward IV Its grounds lie on both sides of the Cam, and are connected by a rustic bridge, rebuilt in 1746 Its buildings comprise three ancient looking courts, with gateway tower and cloisters, and were reconstructed about 1833 The gateway is of noble design, perpendicular, with a lierne vault. The inner court has three alleys, each 80 feet long, and contains the room of Erasmus The hall has a fine open roof, the library, about 30,000 volumes, and the chapel four brasses. The college has 14 fellowships, 14 scholarships, 10 livings, and an income of £5,347 Eminent men educated at it were Erasmus Bishops Fisher and Patrick the antiquary Wallis, the poets Beaumont and Pomfret, T Fuller, S Ockley, Milner, Weever Rymer, Shaw, and Manning

Catherine's College.—This was founded, in 1473, by Chancellor Woodlark It stands in Trumpington street, and forms a court, 180 feet by 120, rebuilt in 1700, of plain appearance, but undergoing ornamental change in 1869 The hall measures 42 feet by 24 the chapel, 75 by 30 The college has 9 fellowships, 23 scholarships, and 4 livings. Eminent men educated at it were Archbishops Sands and Dawes Bishops Headley, Sherlock, Blackall and Overall Dr Lightfoot, Strype, and Sparrow

Jesus College.—This was founded, in 1496, by Bishop Alcock. It stands in Jesus' lane, on the site of the Benedictine nunnery, and comprises three courts, one of them 140 feet by 120 The frontage extends 180 feet, the gateway is fine perpendicular, the second court has an ancient cloister, the hall has a peculiarly elegant oriel, and a fine wooden roof and the chapel was the church of the nunnery is cruciform belonged to the 12th century includes recent restorations, and has an altar piece of the Presentation by Jouvenet The college has 16 fellowships, 1 honorary fellowship, 34 scholarships, and

16 livings. Eminent men educated at it were Archbishops Cranmer, Bancroft and Sterne Bishops Goodrich, Beadon, Bale, and Pearson, the poets Fenton, Fanshaw and Coleridge, the metaphysician Hartley, the traveller Clarke, Flamstead, Venn, Sterne, Jortin, Wakefield, and R North

Christ's College.—This was founded, in 1456, under the name of God s house, by Henry VI, and refounded, in 1505 under its present name, by the mother of Henry VII It stands in St Andrew's street, and forms two courts partly built by Inigo Jones, one of them 140 feet by 120 The chapel is 84 feet long, and has paintings of Henry VII and others, and the gravestone of Cudworth, and the gardens contain a mulberry tree planted by Milton The college has 15 fellowships, 29 scholarships, 18 livings, and an income of £9,179 Eminent men educated at it were Archbishops Sharp and Cornwallis, Bishops Latimer, Law, and Porteous, the poets Milton, Cleland, and Quarles, the platonist More, the blind professor Saunderson Leland, Mede, Cudworth T Burnet, L Echard, Harrington, and Paley

St John s College.—This was founded, in 1511, by the will of the mother of Henry VII It stands in St John s-street, on ground previously occupied by a canons' hospital, and comprises three old courts and a new one The entrance gate is of brick, with four large turrets, the first court is the oldest, built in 1510-14, and measuring 228 feet by 216, the second court is of the same century, and measures 270 feet by 240, the third court is smaller than either of the former and the fourth court was built in 1830 by Rickman and Hutchinson, measures 430 feet by 130, is in the perpendicular English and the Tudor styles, and has a tower 120 feet high The hall is 60 feet by 39, the library is spacious, and contains a very extensive and valuable collection of books, and the chapel measures 120 feet by 27, and has excellent stall work and a painting of St John by Sir R, K Porter A covered bridge of three arches crosses the Cam within the grounds, and is nicknamed "the Bridge of Sighs" A spacious new court, a new Master's lodge, and a magnificent new chapel, after designs by G G Scott, was founded in 1864 These buildings cost an immense sum, they occupy the site of a large number of houses, which were removed to make way for them, the new chapel abuts upon St John street, was opened in May 1869, alone cost about £57,000, and is a chief ornament of the town, and the other new buildings stand between the previously existing body of the college and the river on the Bridge-street side The college has 60 fellowships, about 60 scholarships, 9 sizarships, 54 livings, and an income of £26,167 Eminent men educated at it were Bishops Fisher, Stillingfleet, Watson Beveridge, and Morgan, the poets Sackville, Wyatt, Ben Jonson, Herrick, Hammond, Prior, Brome, Otway, A Phillips, Browne, Kirke White, and Wordsworth, the historian Carte, the antiquary Baker, Sir J Cheke R Ascham, Sir J Wyatt, Sir K Digby Lord Burleigh, Lord Chancellor Egerton, Lord Falkland, the Earl of Strafford, Lord Keeper Guildford, Fairfax, Cartwright, Stackhouse, Whittaker, Dr Bentley, Bowyer, Pegge, S Jenyns, Briggs, Horne Tooke, the Marquis of Rockingham, and Wilberforce

Magdalene College.—This was begun, in 1509, by the Duke of Buckingham, and completed in 1542, by Lord Chancellor Audley It stands in Bridge street, on the site of the original Augustinian priory, and comprises two courts, one of them 110 feet by 78 The library contains the collection of Secretary Pepys The college has 13 fellowships 25 scholarships and exhibitions, 7 livings, and an income of £4 130 Eminent men educated at it were Archbishop Grindall Bishops Cumberland and Walton, Lord-Keeper Bridgman, the mathematician Waring Pepys, Duport, and Waterland

Trinity College.—This was founded, in 1546, by Henry VIII It stands in Trinity street, on ground previously occupied by seven hostels and two colleges One of the colleges bore the name of Michael house, and was founded, in 1324, by Hervey de Stanton, the other bore the name of King's hall, and was founded, in 1337, by Edward III, and both were suppressed by Henry VIII The present college comprises three courts, called the great court, Nevile s court, and King's court The great court is entered by a fine old gateway, measures 1,202 feet in circuit, and has an octagonal conduit in the centre Nevile s court was built in 1609, by D Nevile, and measures 229 feet by 148 King s court was built in 1823-6, after designs by Wilkins at a cost of £40,000 displays much elegance, and was named in honour of George IV, who headed the subscription for it with a donation of £1,000 The hall in the great court, is 100 feet long, 40 feet wide, and 50 feet high, and is in the Tudor style The master s lodge, in the same court, is large and lofty, and has, since the time of Elizabeth, been the residence of the sovereigns visiting the university The library in Nevile s court, was designed by Wren, is 190 feet long, 40 feet wide, and 38 feet high, and contains the manuscript of Paradise Lost, a statue of Lord Byron by Thorwaldsen, and busts of eminent members of the college by Roubiliac The chapel, in the great court, is late perpendicular, 204 feet long, 34 feet wide and 44 feet high, and has an altar piece by West, and the ante chapel contains Roubiliac's statue of Newton The college has 60 fellowships, 72 scholarships, 16 sizarships, 3 professorships, 74 livings, and an income of £34,522 Eminent men educated at it were Bishops Tunstal and Watson, the poets Cowley, Dryden, Donne, Herbert, G Fletcher, Marvel V Bourne Lee, Hayley, Byron, and Crabbe, the astrologer Dee, Robert Earl of Essex Whitgift, Sir Edward Coke, Lord Bacon, Fulke Lord Brooke, Sir R Cotton, Sir H Spelman, P Holland, Hacket, Wilkins, Pearson, Barrow, Willoughby, Bentley, Gale, Ray, Cotes, Robert Nelson, C Middleton, Le Neve, Maskelyne, Sir Isaac Newton, Villiers, Governor Pownall, Sir R. Filmer, Sp Perceval, Lord Lansdowne, Lord Macaulay, Dr Whewell and Professor Sedgwick A statue of Macaulay was prepared in 1866

Emmanuel College.—This was founded, in 1584, by Sir W Mildmay It stands in St Andrew's street, on the site of the Dominican priory, and comprises two courts, one of them 128 feet by 107 The chapel was finished, in 1677, by Archbishop Sancroft after designs by Wren, and has an altar piece of the Prodigal Son by Amiconi The college has 13 fellowships, about 22 scholarships, 25 livings, and an income of £6 517 Eminent men educated at it were Archbishops Sancroft and Manners-Sutton, Bishops Hall, Bedell, Hurd, and Percy, the commentator Poole, the bible translator Chaderton the mathematician Wallis, the orientalist Castell the antiquaries Twysden and Morton Sir W Temple, Joshua Barnes, Blackwall, Farmer, Martyn, Parr, Temple, and Akenside

Sidney-Sussex College.—This was founded, in 1596, by the will of Frances Sidney, Countess of Sussex It stands in Sidney street, on the site of the Greyfriars' monastery, and comprises two courts, restored by Wyatville The hall measures 60 feet by 27, and the chapel has an altar piece of the Repose of the Holy Family by Pittoni The college has 10 fellowships 20 scholarships, 8 livings, and an income of £5,393 Eminent men educated at it were Archbishop Bramhall, Bishops Reynolds, Seth Ward, and Wilson of Sodor O Cromwell, Chief Baron Atkyns, the historian May, Fuller, Comber, L'Estrange and Twining

Downing College.—This was chartered in 1800 and founded in 1807, by will of Sir George Downing Bart The buildings stand between Trumpington street and Regent street were erected after designs by Wilkins, at a cost of £60,000, and form a quadrangle in the Grecian style The college has 8 fellowships, 10 scholarships, 2 professorships, 2 livings, and an income of £7 240

CAMBRIDGE a hamlet in Slimbridge parish, Gloucester, on the river Cam 4 miles NNW of Dursley It has a post office under Stonehouse It was known to the Saxons as Cwatbrige and was the scene of a battle, in the time of Edward the Elder, between the Saxons and the Danes.

CAMBRIDGE HEATH, a locality in the north eastern outskirts of London, on the Regent's canal, near Hack ney It has a post office‡ under Hackney, London, N E

CAMBRIDGESHIRE an inland county, bounded, on the NW, by Northampton, on the N by Lincoln, on the E, by Norfolk and Suffolk, on the S, by Essex and Herts, and on the W, by Beds and Huntingdon Its greatest length from north to south is about 50 miles, its greatest breadth, about 30 miles, its circumference, about 138 miles and its area, 523,861 acres. The surface throughout the N, is mostly low, level, fen land, intersected by canals and ditches, and even elsewhere consists mainly of low flat tracts, diversified only by hillocks, Orwell hill about 300 feet high, and the bleak bare range of the Gogmagog hills The chief rivers are the Ouse, the Cam, the Lark, and the Nen Alluvial and diluvial deposits form the fen tracts throughout the N, chalk rocks form the tracts throughout the S, and middle oolite, lower greensand, and upper greensand rocks form small tracts along the Cam Clunch appears about Burwell, and is the material of Ely cathedral, blue clay or gault abounds about Ely, and is used there for white bricks and earthenware, and Portland oolite appears in parts farther N

The soil is very diversified, and generally fertile That of much of the fens is a very rich vegetable mould, that of the fens about Wisbeach is a good loam that of other parts of the fens is a strong black earth, incumbent on gravel, that of the chalk tracts is variously clay, loam, chalk, and gravel, and that of the highest and poorest parts of these tracts is so thin and incohesive as to be unsuitable for tillage About one third of the entire area is fenny, and the rest is variously arable, meadow, and pasture The farms, for the most part, are small The fens, in their several parts and different conditions, yield variously turf fuel, hay, green crops hemp, flax, and rich crops of corn Other arable tracts yield excellent wheat, beans turnips, and sainfoin Dairy lands, about the centre, are famous for butter, and about Cottenham and Soham for cream cheese The heath lands are depastured by short wooled sheep, the fen pastures, by long wooled sheep, and the tracts of different kinds maintain great numbers of cattle, draught horses, pigeons, and wild fowl Much produce, of various kinds, is sent to London The only manufactures, of any note, are white bricks, coarse pottery, baskets, and reed matting Numerous canals intersect the fen-tracts, all cut originally for the purpose of drainage but a number of them serving also for navigation, and a canal, called the London and Cambridge Junction, connects the Cam with the Stort, and through that with the Lea and the Thames Railways belonging to the Eastern Counties, the East Anglian, and the Great Northern systems, intersect all parts of the county One comes in near Linton, and goes north north eastward, past Brinkley and Newmarket, toward Bury St Edmund, another deflecting from the former at Great Chesterford on the north border of Essex, goes northward to Cambridge, and thence north north eastward, past Ely, toward Lynn another comes in at Royston, and goes north north eastward to Cambridge, another comes in from Bedford and goes north eastward to Cambridge, another goes from Cambridge, eastward, to the first at Brinkley another goes from Cambridge, north westward, toward St Ives and Huntingdon, another, connecting with the last at St Ives, goes east north eastward past Ely toward Brandon, another, also connecting at St Ives, and going north north-eastward, passes March and proceeds to Wisbeach, and another goes from Ely north westward to March, and thence westward toward Peterborough

The county contains 153 parishes, part of another parish, and 3 extra parochial tracts, besides the parishes and extra parochial colleges of Cambridge It is divided into the hundreds of Armingford, Chesterton, Cheveley, Chilford, Flendish Longstow Northstow Papworth, Radfield, Staine, Staploe, Triplow, Wetherley, Whittlesford, Ely, Wisbeach North Witchford, and South Witchford, the liberty of Whittlesey and Thorney, and the boroughs of Cambridge and Wisbeach The northern section of it forms the Isle of Ely and contains the hundreds of Ely, Wisbeach and Witchford, the liberty of Whittlesey and Thorney, and the borough of Wisbeach The registration county is more extensive than the electoral county, includes 114,735 acres from adjoining counties, excludes 17 590 acres, contains 571,7?8 acres, and is divided into the districts of Caxton, Chesterton, Cambridge, Linton, Newmarket, Ely, North Witchford, Whittlesey, and Wisbeach The market towns are Cambridge, Ely, Linton, March, Thorney, Wisbeach, and parts of Newmarket and Royston, and the towns next in note are Caxton, Chesterton Whittlesey, and Soham The chief seats are Cheveley Park, Wimpole Hall, Bourne House, Waresley Park, Madingley Park, Gogmagog Hill, Abington Hall, Wratting Park, Branches Park, Croxton Park, Chippenham Park, Babraham, Papworth, Fordham Abbey, Hadley Park Fulbourne House, Horseheath Lodge, Stetchworth House, Shudy Camps Park, Sawston Hall, Milton, and Swaffham Real property in 1815, £705,372 in 1843 £1,102,415 in 1851, £1,138,314, in 1860, £1,234,465.

The county is governed by a lord lieutenant, a deputy a high sheriff, and about 48 magistrates. It is in the Home military district, and in the Norfolk judicial circuit The assizes are held at Cambridge, and quarter sessions at Cambridge Ely, and Wisbeach The police force, in 1864, comprised 11 men in the borough of Wisbeach, 52 in the rest of the Isle of Ely, 34 in the borough of Cambridge, and 70 in the rest of the county, the crimes committed were 14 in the borough of Wisbeach, 49 in the rest of the Isle of Ely, 41 in the borough of Cambridge, and 56 in the rest of the county, the known depredators and suspected persons at large were 137 in the borough of Wisbeach, 499 in the rest of the Isle of Ely, 303 in the borough of Cambridge, and 305 in the rest of the county, and the houses of bad character were 51 in the borough of Wisbeach, 50 in the rest of the Isle of Ely, 54 in the borough of Cambridge, and 26 in the rest of the county The prisons are houses of correction in Wisbeach and Ely, and borough jail and county jail at Cambridge Two members of parliament are returned by the borough of Cambridge, two by the university, and three by the county The county electors in 1868 were 7,060 The county is in the diocese of Ely, and constitutes the archdeaconry of Ely, and the deanery of Fordham in the archdeaconry of Sudbury The poor rates, for the registration county in 1863, were £119,809 Marriages in 1866, 1,228,—of which 122 were not according to the rites of the Established church, births, 6,067 —of which 460 were illegitimate, deaths, 3,582,—of which 1,260 were at ages under 5 years, and 126 at ages above 85 Marriages in the ten years 1851-60, 13,898, births, 62,065, deaths 38,447 The places of worship, in 1851, in the county proper, were 176 of the Church of England, with 52 917 sittings, 38 of Independents, with 12,195 s 72 of Baptists, with 17,897 s, 3 of Quakers, with 440 s, 2 of Unitarians, with 330 s., 57 of Wesleyan Methodists, with 11,764 s, 39 of Primitive Methodists with 5,105 s, 5 of Wesleyan Reformers, with 1,430 s., 1 of Lady Huntingdon's Connexion, with 650 s, 5 of isolated congregations, with 1,293 s, 2 of Latter Day Saints, with 270 s, 3 of Roman Catholics, with 350 s, and 1 of Jews The schools were 188 public day schools, with 16,559 scholars, 398 private day schools, with 7,770 s, 23? Sunday schools, with 24,006 s, and 11 evening schools for adults, with 156 s Pop in 1801, 89,346, in 1821, 122,387, in 1841, 161,459, in 1861 176,016 Inhabited houses, 37,634, uninhabited, 1,838 building, 74

The territory now forming Cambridgeshire belonged first to the Iberians, and afterwards to the Iceni It became part of the Roman province of Flavia Cæsariensis, and subsequently was included mainly in East Anglia, and partly in Mercia The Danes overran it in 870 held it in subjection during 50 years, were driven from it in 921, by Edward the Elder, and again overran it in 1010 The Isle of Ely was a separate jurisdiction, under the name of South Girwa, and the rest of the county took the name of Grentebrigscire or Grantbridgeshire. The Isle of Ely made resistance to William the Conqueror, and held out against him till 1074 The county in general, and the Isle of Ely in particular suffered severely during the civil wars in the times of Stephen, John, and Henry III, and they stood strongly for the parliament in the wars of Charles I—Icknield street went along the southern border, past Royston and Hixton, toward Newmarket Ermine street went across the south west, north north westward, from Royston, toward Godmanchester The Via Devana went across the south centre, north westward from the vicinity of Linton, past Cambridge toward Godmanchester The Devil's Ditch goes across the south east, a little west of Burwell Traces of British earthworks occur at the Devil's Ditch and at Fleam Dyke Roman coins, urns, and other remains, have been found at Cambridge, Ely, March, Soham, Chatteris, Wilney, the Gogmagog hills, and other places. Remains of abbeys and priories occur at Thorney, Denny, Cambridge, Isleham, and Barham. Saxon or Norman bits of architecture occur in Ely cathedral and in Duxford, Stuntney, Ickleton, and other churches. Nine castles of note stood at different places but all, except the gateway of one at Cambridge, have disappeared

CAMDDWR (THE), a stream of Cardigan, rising under Tregaron mountain, and running 7 miles south-east ward to the Towy, 3 miles above Capel Ystrad-fin

CAMDEN PLACE, a seat of the Marquis of Camden in the north west of Kent, 2 miles ENE of Bromley It was the residence and death place of Camden the antiquary, and, passing to Lord Chancellor Pratt, who was raised to the peerage in 1765, gave to him his title of Baron Camden of Camden Place

CAMDEN TOWN, a suburb of London, a sub district, and three chapelries in St Pancras parish and district, Middlesex. The suburb adjoins the north east side of Regent's Park, 3½ miles NW of St Paul's; is intersected by the Regent's canal and by the North London and Northwestern railways, and has a railway station of Camden with telegraph, a railway station of Camden Road, and three post-offices Camden Town High street, Camden Town Park street, and Camden Road,‡ all under London N W It was founded in 1791, it took its name from the first Marquis of Camden, the lessee of the manor and it contains good streets, crescents, and places Here are a veterinary college, St. Martin's alms house, St Pancras workhouse, a cemetery, with the graves of C Dibdin and Sir J Barrow, and the depôt of the Northwestern railway, with the stationary engines for drawing the trains up an inclined plan — The sub district is bounded by lines along High street, the Regent's canal, Gloucester-place, Pancras-road, Brewer street, Skinner street and New-road Acres, 171 Pop, 23,260 Houses, 2,550 The chapelries are Camden Town St Paul Camden New Town, and St Thomas Camden New Town Pop., 15,822 5,145, and 5,000 The livings are vicarages in the diocese of London Value of C. T, £300, of St P, £350, of St T, £120 * Patron of C T, the Vicar of St Pancras, of St P, the Dean and Chapter of St Paul's, of St T, alternately the Crown and the Bishop. C. T church stands in Camden-street, was built in 1828, and has an lonic portico. St Paul's church stands in Camden square, and is recent and elegant St Thomas church stands in Wrotham road, was built in 1863, has a well-proportioned tower, with a spire roof and presents a picturesque but foreign appearance There are several dissenting chapels Extensive public baths were erected in 1867, and a memorial statue of Richard Cobden, in 1868

CAMEL (THE) See ALAN (THE)

CAMELEY, a parish in Clutton district, Somerset 5½ miles WNW of Radstock r station It contains Temple Cloud village with post office under Bristol Acres 1 135 Real property, £2 805 Pop, 526 Houses 102 Bath stone is quarried The living is a rectory in the diocese of Bath and Wells Value, £256 * Patron J Hippisley Esq The church is ancient There are a national school and charities £21

CAMELFORD, a small town a parish a sub district, and a district in Cornwall The town stands on the river Camel, on the skirt of a moorish upland tract, 12 miles N by E of Bodmin, and 14 N of Bodmin road r station It is an ancient place, was incorporated by one of the Cornish Earls, sent two members to parliament, till disfranchised by the act of 1832, and has still a corporation Two battles were fought near it, the one in 543, between King Arthur and his nephew Mordred, fatal to both, the other in 823, between Egbert and the Cornishmen "Ossian Macpherson represented the borough in parliament, and Captain Wallis, the discoverer of Tahiti, was born in its vicinity The town has recently undergone considerable improvement, and it contains a town hall, with market house, a free school, used as an evening chapel of ease, and places of worship for Wesleyans, Un Free Methodists, and Bible Christians It has a head post office,‡ two banking offices, and two chief inns, and is a seat of petty sessions, and a polling-place A weekly market is held on Friday, and fairs on the Friday after 10 March, and on 26 May 17 and 18 July, 6 Sept, and the second Wednesday of Nov The town gave the title of Baron to the Pitts of Boconnoc, and the Smiths.—The parish bears also the name of Lanteglos, or is called properly Lanteglos by Camelford Acres, 3 951 Real property, £5,359 Pop, 1,620 Houses, 323 The property is much subdivided. The manor belongs to the Duchy of Cornwall A deer park, attached to the manor, was disparked by Henry VIII Slate and stone are worked. Traces of an ancient camp are seen on St Syths Beacon The living is a rectory, united with the rectory of Advent, in the diocese of Exeter Value, £700 * Patron, the Prince of Wales. The church stands 1½ mile west of the town was restored in 1866 and contains a fine font, and monuments of several old Cornish families A chantry chapel of the 14th century stood in the town, but was shut up at the Reformation, and has disappeared

The sub district contains the parishes of Camelford Advent, Davidstow, St Clether, Michaelstow, St Teath, and St Breward Acres, 34,479 Pop., 5,355 Houses 1,083 The district comprehends also the sub district of Boscastle, containing the parishes of Minster, Forrabury, Trevalga, Tintagel, Otterham Lesnewth, and St Juliot Acres, 51,647 Poor-rates in 1866, £5,149 Pop in 1861, 7,774 Houses, 1 613 Marriages in 1866, 61, births, 273 —of which 21 were illegitimate, deaths, 140,—of which 47 were at ages under 5 years, and 13 at ages above 85 Marriages in the ten years 1851-60, 560, births, 2,781, deaths, 1 532 The places of worship in 1851 were 14 of the Church of England with 3,880 sittings, 9 of Wesleyan Methodists with 798 s, 15 of the Wesleyan Association, with 2,130 s, and 16 of Bible Christians, with 1 778 s The schools were 7 public day schools with 275 scholars, 18 private day schools, with 413 s 25 Sunday schools, with 1,253 s, and 3 evening schools for adults, with 48 s

CAMEL (QUEEN), a village and a parish in Wincanton district, Somerset The village stands near the river Yeo, on an affluent of that river 1 mile SW of Sparkford r station and 6 ENE of Ilchester, and has a post office‡ under Taunton Fairs are held at it on 11 June and 25 Oct, and a sulphureous spring of some note, is a mile to the west. The parish comprises 2 498 acres Real property, £4,977 Pop 734 Houses 152 The property is divided among a few The living is a vicarage in the diocese of Bath and Wells Value £222 * Patron, P S J Mildmay, Esq The church is very good, and there are a Wesleyan chapel and charities £11

CAMEL (WEST) a parish in Yeovil district, Somerset, on the river Yeo, 2 miles NW of Marston r station and 4 ENE of Ilchester It includes the hamlets of Downhead, Sterthill and Urgashay, and its post town is Queen Camel under Taunton Acres 1 953 Real property, £3 4-3 Pop 338 Houses, 72 The property is subdivided The living is a rectory in the diocese of Bath and Wells Value £275 * Patron, the Bishop of Bath and Wells The church is good

CAMELEY See CAMELEY

CAMERINGHAM See CAMMERINGHAM

CAMERTON, a parish in Clutton district, Somerset on the Fosse way and the Radford canal, 5½ miles SSW of Twerton station and 6½ SW of Bath An act was passed in 1863 to construct a railway from the Great Western at Bristol to Radstock, with a branch to Camerton The parish includes part of Carlingcott hamlet, and its post town is Timsbury, under Bath Acres, 1,748. Real property, £6 532. Pop, 1,368 Houses, 279 The property is divided among a few Camerton Park is the seat of John Jarrett Esq Coal is worked. Roman pottery, glass, and other relics, and remains of Roman villas, have been found. The Living is a rectory in the diocese of Bath and Wells Value, £481 * Patron, John Jarrett, Esq The church is good, and contains several very fine tombs of the Carews There are chapels for Baptists and Wesleyans

CAMERTON, a hamlet in Burstwick parish E R Yorkshire, 3¼ miles SE of Hedon Pop, 29 Houses, 4

CAMERTON, Cumberland See CAMMERTON

CAMES ASH a tything in Bishops Lydeard parish, Somerset, 4½ miles NE of Milverton

CAM FELL, a mountain 4 miles SSW of Hawes, N R Yorkshire Its height is 1,926 feet

CAM HOUSES, a hamlet in High Abbotside township Aysgarth parish, N R Yorkshire, under Cam Fell, 5 miles NW of Hawes

CAMLAN a township in Mallwyd parish, Merioneth on the river Dovey, 2 miles S of Dinas-Mowddwy Real property, £573 Pop, 180

CAMLAS (THE), an affluent of the river Usk, in Brecon

CAMLET (THE), an affluent of the river Severn, in Salop

CAM (LOW). See CAM

CAMLYN, a bay on the N coast of Anglesey, 7 miles W of Amlwch

CAMMERINGHAM a parish in the district and county of Lincoln, on the wolds, 5¾ miles E of Marton station, and 7 NNW of Lincoln Post town, Stow, under Gainsborough Acres, 1 806 Real property 2,162 Pop, 137 Houses, 27 The property is divided among three Limestone occurs. The living is a vicarage in the diocese of Lincoln Value, £152 Patron, Lord Monson. The church is modern

CAMMERTON, a township and a parish in Cockermouth district, Cumberland. The township lies on the river Derwent, and on the Workington and Cockermouth railway, 3 miles E by N of Workington and has a station on the railway Acres, 788 Real property, £1,022 Pop., 224 Houses 41 The parish includes also the township of Seaton, and extends down the Derwent to the sea Post town, Workington Acres, 3,727, of which 347 are water Real property, £8,344, of which £3,000 are in mines, and £350 in iron works Pop 1,326 Houses, 277 The property is subdivided. Cammerton Hall is a chief residence Coal is largely worked, brick making is carried on, and there are tin plate and iron works The living is a vicarage in the diocese of Carlisle Value, £300 Patrons, the Dean and Chapter of Carlisle The church is very good, and contains the tomb of Black Tom of the north

CAMMON, a township in Llanfyllin parish Montgomery near Llanfyllin Pop, 44

CAMP, a hamlet in Miserden parish, Gloucester, 5½ miles NE of Stroud

CAMPDEN a sub district in the district of Shipston on Stour, and county of Gloucester It lies around Chipping Campden, and contains four parishes in Gloucester, and one partly in Gloucester and partly in Warwick Acres, 20,186 Pop, 4,845 Houses 1,114

CAMPDEN (BROAD), a hamlet in Chipping Campden parish, Gloucester, 1 mile SE of Chipping Campden Real property £2 744

CAMPDEN (CHIPPING), a small town and a parish in the district of Shipston on Stour, and county of Gloucester The town stands in a fertile valley, surrounded by cultivated hills and hanging woods, adjacent to the West Midland railway, 6 miles NNW of Morton in the Marsh It consists chiefly of one street nearly a mile long, and has about the centre, a court-house and a market house, the former a structure of the beginning of the 15th century or earlier, the latter erected, in 1624, by Sir Baptist Hickes It was the meeting place of the Saxon kings, in 687, for consulting on the war against the Britons, and it became, in the 14th century a principal mart for wool, and the residence of many opulent merchants but it has lost nearly all of its manufacturing consequence A large extant mansion, of nearly the same age as the court house, is believed to have been the dwelling of one of the wool merchants The town has a post office‡ under Moreton in the Marsh, a station, with telegraph, on the railway, a grammar school with endowed income of £170, and an exhibition at Pembroke college, Oxford, two endowed schools, with £130 and £26, suites of alms houses, founded by Sir Baptist Hickes, with income of £140 and a chief inn called the Noel Arms A weekly market is held on Wednesday, and fairs on Ash Wednesday, 23 April, 5 Aug and 11 Dec The Cotswold games, instituted in the time of James I, and sung by Ben Jonson, Drayton, and other poets, were held on Dovers hill, about ½ a mile from the town Dr Harris, the famous preacher, born in 1628, and George Ballard, author of "Memoirs of British Ladies," were natives

The parish includes also the hamlets of Berrington, Broad Campden, and Westington with Combe Acres, 4,660 Real property, £10,725 Pop, 1 975 Houses, 474 The property is not much divided The manor belonged at Domesday to Hugh Lupus, Earl of Chester was purchased, in the time of James I by Sir Baptist Hickes, who was created Viscount Campden, passed to the family of Noel, Earls of Gainsborough, and was bequeathed, in 1798, by the sixth Earl, to his nephew G Noel Edwards, Esq, who assumed the name of Noel A magnificent mansion was built on the manor by Sir Baptist Hickes, at a cost of £29,000, and was destroyed by Lord Noel, grandson of Sir Baptist, but has left some remains Campden House, now the seat of Viscount Campden, is a large modern mansion A great battle was fought between the Mercians and the West Saxons at Berrington, and the "barrows over the bodies of the slain are supposed to have given rise to its name The living is a vicarage in the diocese of Gloucester and Bristol Value, £640 * Patron the Earl of Gainsborough The church is fine decorated English A memorial chapel, in the early English style, was built in 1868 A chapel of ease is at Westington There are three dissenting chapels and charities £489

CAMPDEN HILL a chapelry in Kensington parish, Middlesex, constituted in 1864 Pop., 6,500 Living, a vicarage Patron, J Bennett, Esq

CAMPHILL, a station on the Bristol and Birmingham railway 3 miles SSW of Birmingham.

CAMP (NORTH), a station on the Reading branch of the Southeastern railway, at Aldershot, in Hants It has a post-office under Farnborough station See ALDERSHOT

CAMPODUNUM See ALMONDBURY

CAMPS See CASTLE CAMPS

CAMPSALL a township a parish and a sub-district in Doncaster district, W R Yorkshire. The township adjoins the Doncaster and Wakefield railway, 1½ mile W of Askern station, and 7½ N by W of Doncaster and includes the hamlet of Barnsdale Acres, 1,470 Real property, £2,480 Pop, 349 Houses 64 The parish contains also the townships of Askern, Norton, Fenwick, Moss, and part of Sutton, and its post town is Askern under Doncaster Acres, 9,390 Real property, with the rest of Sutton, £14,816 Pop, 1 948 Houses, 427 The property is not much divided. Campsall Hall is the seat of F B Frank Esq The living is a vicarage in the diocese of York Value, £140 * Patron G C Yarborough, Esq The church is ancient The vicarage of Askern is a separate benefice There are three Methodist chapels an endowed school for girls, a national school and some charities The sub districts contain six parishes, and parts of two others. Acres, 25,671 Pop, 4,549 Houses, 1 003

CAMPSEY ASH, a parish in Plomesgate district Suffolk on the river Deben and the East Suffolk railway, near Wickham Market-Junction station, 2½ miles E by

N of Wickham Market It has a post-office under Wickham-Market. Acres, 1,873 Real property, £2 982 Pop., 27[illegible] Houses, [illegible] The property is divided among a few Ash House is the seat of the Sheppards A nunnery of St. Clare was founded here, in the time of King John, by Theobald de Valoines, and some remains of it exist. The living is a rectory in the diocese of Norwich Value, £250.* Patron, Lord Pendlesham. The church has an ancient tower, contains a brass of a priest, and is [illegible]

CAMPTON a village and a parish in Biggleswade district, Beds. The village stands on the river Ivel, 1¼ mile W of Shefford r station, and 6 SW of Biggleswade, and has a post-office under Biggleswade The parish includes also the township of Shefford. Acres, 1,120 Real property £4,4[illegible]6 Pop, 1,544 Houses, 327 The property is much subdivided. The living is a rectory, united with the p curacy of Shefford, in the diocese of Ely Value, £374 * Patron, Sir G R Osborn, Bart Both churches are good, and the mother one has a brass of 14[illegible] R. Bloomfield, the poet, was buried here in 1823 There are a national school and charities £11.

CAMPOSE, or CAMROS, a village and a parish in Haverfordwest district, Pembroke. The village stands on an affluent of the river Cleddy, 3½ miles NNW of Haverfordwest r station and has a post office under Haverfordwest, and fairs on 13 Feb and 12 Nov The parish includes also the villages of Keston, Wolfsdale, and Pelcomo Acres, 8 129 Real property, £6,348 Pop, 1 126. Houses, 2[illegible] The property is much subdivided Camrose House is the seat of H W Bowen, Esq The living is a vicarage in the diocese of St Davids Value, £[illegible]* Patron, H W Bowen, Esq The church is not good. There are two dissenting chapels

CAMSCOTT, a hamlet in Ilfracombe parish, Somerset

CAMS HILL an eminence near Malmesbury, in Wilts It was the scene of a battle between Stephen and the Empress Matilda and it has three ancient camps, two of them British, the other supposed to be Saxon

CAMVELIN a village in Llangan parish, Carmarthen, [illegible] miles NE of [illegible]arberth

CAN (THE), an affluent of the river Chelmer, at a point near Chelmsford, in Essex

CANBURY, a manor adjacent to Kingston, in Surrey It belonged to Merton priory, and has remains of a curious monastic barn, about 90 feet square

CANCANI PROMONTORIUM. See BRAICH Y PWLL

CANDA (THE), a stream of Cumberland, running 9 miles south westward to the Eden, in the vicinity of Carlisle.

CANDLESBY, a parish in Spilsby district, Lincoln, 2 miles WNW of Burgh r station and 3½ ENE of Spilsby It has a post-office under Spilsby Acres, 850 Real property £ 8[illegible]2 Pop, 240 Houses, 56 The property is much subdivided Candlesby Hall is a chief residence. Several pieces of old armour and weapons have been found. The living is a rectory in the diocese of Lincoln. Value £200 * Patron, Magdalene College, Oxford. The church is good.

CANDLESHOE, a wapentake in the parts of Lindsey, Lincoln, cut into two divisions, Marsh and Wold. The Marsh div contains Addlethorpe, Burgh, and nine other parishes. Acres, 43,8[illegible] The Wold div contains [illegible], Candlesby, and twelve other parishes. Acres, 17,2[illegible] Pop of both div 10,[illegible]02 Houses, 2,237

CANDOVER BROWN See BROWN CANDOVER.

CANDOVER-CHILTON a parish in Alresford district, Hants, on the river Itchen 5 miles N of New Alresford r station and [illegible] NE of Winchester Post town Brown Candover, under Mitcheldever station Acres 1 472 Real property £[illegible] Pop 142 Houses, 21 The property all belongs to Lord Ashburton The living is a rectory annexed to the rectory of Brown Candover, in the diocese of Winchester The church is a [illegible] small and good

CANDOVER PRESTON, a parish in Basingstoke district, Hants, on the river Itchen [illegible] miles N by E of New Alresford r station, and 10½ NE of Winchester It has a post-office under Mitcheldever station. Acres, 3,413 Real property, £2,793 Pop., 476 Houses, 95 The property is divided among a few Preston House is the seat of E C Rumbolt, Esq The living is a vicarage, united with the p curacy of Nutley, in the diocese of Winchester Value, £228 Patrons, the Dean and Chapter of Winchester The church is ancient and very good, and contains a handsome monument, surmounted by a brass

CANEWDON, a village and a parish in Rochford district, Essex. The village stands on the river Crouch 3½ miles NNE of Rochford, and 6½ N of Southend r station, and has a post office under Chelmsford, and a fair on 24 June Canute, the Dane, held his court here, and the name Canewdon is a corruption of Canute s Town A Roman station also was here, and several Roman urns and a torso have been found The parish includes part of Wallasea island Acres, 4 071, of which 100 are water Real property, £7,8[illegible]8 Pop, 664 Houses, 140 The property is much subdivided. The living is a vicarage in the diocese of Rochester Value, £49[illegible] * Patron, the Bishop of Peterborough The church is later English, has a massive tower, and is very good There are an Independent chapel, and charities £132

CANFIELD (GREAT) a parish in Dunmow district, Essex, on the river Roding 2 miles S of the Bishop Stortford, Dunmow and Braintree railway, and 3½ SW of Dunmow It has a post office under Chelmsford Acres, 2,472. Real property, £3,575 Pop, 468 Houses, 115 The property is subdivided Canfield House is the seat of the Barnards. There are remains of a moated castle, built by the De Veres. The living is a vicarage in the diocese of Rochester Value, £140 * Patron J M Wilson, Esq The church is tolerable and has two brasses of the 16th century

CANFIELD (LITTLE), a parish in Dunmow district, Essex, on the river Roding, and on the Bishop Stortford Dunmow, and Braintree railway, 3 miles W by S of Dunmow It has a post office under Chelmsford Acres 1,479 Real property, £2,315 Pop, 314 Houses, 74 The property is much subdivided The living is a rectory in the diocese of Rochester Value, £32[illegible] * Patron, Christ's College Cambridge The church is partly ancient, partly a renovation of 1817, partly a reconstruction of 1859, shows Norman, perpendicular, and decorated characters in fine blending, has a tower and spire of 1817, and contains a richly sculptured monument, erected by the present rector to the memory of his mother

CANFORD, a sub district in Poole district, Dorset It comprises part of Great Canford parish, excluding Longfleet and Parkstone tythings. Acres, 12,768 Pop., 2,326 Houses, 468

CANFORD (GREAT), a village and a parish in Poole district, Dorset. The village stands on the river Stour, near the South western railway, 2 miles E of Wimborne Minster, and has a post office under Wimborne, and an iron foundry The parish contains also the village of Little Canford and the tythings of Kinson, Longfleet and Parkstone, extends southward to Poole harbour and includes part of Poole borough Acres, 17,750 of which 1,740 are water Rated property, exclusive of the parts within Poole borough, £6,401 Pop 4,877 Houses, 976 The property is much subdivided. The manor belonged once to John of Gaunt belongs now to Sir J L Guest, Bart, and is of great extent The mansion on it, Canford Hall, occupies the site of an Ursuline convent, is an edifice in the Tudor style, built, in 1826, for Lord de Mauley includes remains of the convent kitchen, with two huge fireplaces, and has a very fine hall A gallery, connected by a cloister with the mansion, contains Assyrian sculptures from Nineveh, and drives go through fir woods to the vicinity of Poole Merly House, to the west, the seat of Willett I Adye Esq, contains paintings by Hogarth, and the sketches of his "Marriage a la Mode The living is a vicarage in the dio of Salisbury, and till 1865 included Kinson chapelry Value, £450 * Patron, Sir J B Guest, Bart. The church has Norman features, particularly in the tower, and contains monuments, by Bacon, to the Willetts of Merly The chapelries of Kinson, Longfleet, and Parkstone are separate benefices Charities, £22

CANFORD (LITTLE), a village in Great Canford parish, Dorset, 2 miles N E of Great Canford. It has a post office under Wimborne

CANKLOW, a hamlet in Whiston parish, W R York shire, 2 miles SSE of Rotherham.

CANLEY, a hamlet in Stoneleigh parish, Warwick, 2 miles SW of Coventry

CANN, or SHASTON ST RUMBOLD, a parish in Shaftesbury district, Dorset on the verge of the county, 1¼ mile SE of Shaftesbury, and 1¼ SSE of Semley r station Post-town, Shaftesbury under Salisbury Acres, 930 Pop, 547 Houses, 126 The area is all included in the borough of Shaftesbury The living is a rectory in the diocese of Salisbury Value, £196 * Patron, the Earl of Shaftesbury

CANNA MILL, a hamlet in West Newton township Kirknewton parish, Northumberland, 6½ miles WNW of Wooler

CANN HALL, a locality adjacent to Epping forest, Essex, ½ a mile N by W of Forest Gate r station, and 5¼ NE of St. Paul s, London. It has a post office under Leytonstone, London N F

CANNINGS (ALL) See ALL CANNINGS

CANNINGS BISHOPS See BISHOPS CANNINGS.

CANNINGTON a village, a parish, and a hundred, in Somerset The village stands 2 miles SSW of a bend of the river Parret, and 3½ NW by W of Bridgewater r station, and has a post office‡ under Bridgewater It dates from ancient times, was known to the Saxons as Cuningannmersys, had a Benedictine nunnery founded in the time of King Stephen, by Robert de Courcy, and is supposed to have been the birth place of the Fair Rosamond, of ballad notoriety The parish includes also the hamlets of Edstock and Beer, impinges some distance on the Parret, and is in the district of Bridgewater Acres, 5,015 of which 350 are water Real property, £4,850 Pop, 1,419 Houses, 320 The manor belongs to Lord Clifford Cannington Park the seat of Lord Clifford's ancestors, is now occupied as a grazing farm Brymore House is the seat of the Hon P Pleydell Bouverie Kithill, in the vicinity has an altitude of 1,067 feet The living is a vicarage in the diocese of Bath and Wells. Value, £371 * Patron Lord Clifford The church was part of the Benedictine nunnery, is later English, and fine, and contains tombs of the Cliffords There are a Wesleyan chapel, a Roman Catholic chapel, a national school, a charity for alms houses and for the poor amounting to £330 a year, and other charities £34 —The hundred contains ten parishes Acres, 23,411 Pop., 5,700 Houses, 1,252

CANNING-TOWN, a chapelry in West Ham parish, Essex, adjacent to the Victoria docks and North Woolwich railway, 5½ miles E of London Bridge It was constituted in 1866, and it has a post office‡ under London E Living a p curacy

CANNOCK, a village a parish a sub district, an ancient forest, and two railways in Staffordshire The village stands adjacent to the Walsall and Stafford railway, near Watling street, 7¾ miles NNW of Walsall, and has a station on the railway, a post office‡ under Stafford public rooms, a banking office and fairs on 8 May, 24 Aug and 18 Oct The public rooms were erected in 1862, and include a large hall for lectures or concerts, a room for magistrates meetings and a reading room The making of edge tools is carried on The parish includes also the townships of Cannock Wood Hednesford, Leacroft, Huntington, and Great Wyrley Acres, 10 775 Real property £12 153 Pop, 3,964 Houses, 749 The property is much subdivided Much of the surface is part of the ancient forest and partakes its character of moor and mineral The living is a vicarage in the diocese of Lichfield Value £185 * Patrons, the Dean and Chapter of Lichfield The church was repaired in 1859 Dr Sacheverell was for some time incumbent The vicarage of Great Wyrley is a separate benefice There are an Independent chapel a Wesleyan chapel, and charities £30 —The sub district contains also two other parishes, parts of two more, and an extra parochial tract, and is in the district of Penkridge Acres, 22,583 Pop, 8,773. Houses, 1,674 —The ancient forest bears the name of Cannock Chase, extends to the vicinity of Bednal, Lichfield, and the Trent, with an area of about 25 000 acres, and was anciently a hunting ground of the Mercian and the Norman kings. It long was covered with wood, but is now bleak, moorish, and wild, yet is so rich in coal and ironstone as to have been much encroached upon both for mining and for cultivation Large portions of it present the attractions of a hill country, and some spots have ancient standing-stones, supposed to be Druidical Castle Hill in it is crowned by an ancient, British, double trenched camp of 8 or 10 acres, and commands a good view A place called the Old Nunnery, at Radmore, near Castle Hill, was the site of a Cistercian abbey, founded in the time of Stephen, and soon transferred to Stoneleigh in Warwickshire —The two railways are called the Cannock Mineral and the Cannock Chase railways. The former was opened in 1859, and goes from the Walsall and Stafford at Cannock to the Trent Valley at Rugeley The latter is in four parts authorised in 1860, 1862, 1864, and 1866, is aggregately 21½ miles long, and goes to Wolverhampton and Hednesford.

CANNOCK CHASE See CANNOCK

CANNOCK WOOD, a township in Cannock parish, Stafford near Cannock Pop, 275

CANN-OFFICE, a village in Llangadfan parish, Montgomery, 6½ miles WNW of Llanfair It occupies the site of a camp, has a post office under Welshpool, and a good inn, and is a resort of anglers A shooting box of Lord Powis is near it

CANNONBY (CROSS) See CANONBY (CROSS)

CANNON FEE, a tithing in Crediton parish, Devon Pop, 1 411

CANNONHOLD, a tything in Melksham parish, Wilts, near Melksham Pop., 321

CANN QUARRY, an excavation in dark blue slate, 4½ miles NNE of Plymouth, in Devon It is finely overhung by foliage, and has workings of the slate by water machinery

CANN ST RUMBOLD See CANN

CANOLE a village in Trefeirig township, Llanbadarn fawr parish, Cardigan near Aberystwith

CANONBURY an ancient manor in Islington, 2 miles N of St Paul s, London. It belonged, at the Conquest, to Ralph de Berners, was given by him to the priory of St Bartholomew, went, at the dissolution, to Lord Cromwell afterwards Earl of Essex, and passed to successively the Earl of Warwick, Sir John Spencer, and Lord Compton, ancestor of the Marquis of Northampton Canonbury House on it was built about 1362, as a mansion of the priors of St Bartholomew, and Canonbury Tower, 17 feet square and 58 feet high, was added to the house either by Bolton the last prior or by Sir John Spencer Newberry, the bookseller, C Smart, the poet, Chambers, the cyclopedist, and Oliver Goldsmith had apartments in the tower, and the last is said to have written here his "Vicar of Wakefield" Much of the manor is now built upon and two suites of buildings on it are called Canonbury square and Canonbury grove

CANONBY (CROSS), a township and a parish in Cockermouth district, Cumberland The township lies on the river Ellen the Maryport and Carlisle railway, and the Solway frith, 2 miles NE of Maryport Acres, 1,093 of which 426 are water Real property, £4,571, of which £630 are in mines Pop, 87 Houses 17 The parish includes also the townships of Crosby and Birkby, and the chapelry of Maryport, and its post town is Maryport Acres, 3,911 of which 993 are water Rated property £11 111 Pop, 6 900 Houses, 1 192 The property is much subdivided Coal and stone are worked The living is a vicarage in the diocese of Carlisle Value, £200 * Patrons, the Dean and Chapter of Carlisle The church is partly Norman, and very good The p curacy of Maryport is a separate benefice

CANON FROME, a parish in Ledbury district, Hereford, on the river Frome 2 miles N of Ashperton r sta tion, and 6 NW by N of Ledbury Post town Bosbury, under Ledbury Acres, 1,023 Real property, £1,278. Pop., 115 Houses, 18 The property is divided among a few Canon-Frome Court is the seat of the Rev John Hopton The living is a vicarage in the diocese of Hereford. Value, £200 Patron, the Rev John Hopton. The church was built in 1861, is in the early English style, with ornate chancel and alabaster reredos, and retains the tower of a previous church.

CANONGATE, a township in Alnwick parish, Northumberland near Alnwick Pop, 336 Houses, 76

CANON-PYON, a parish in Weobly district, Hereford, 4 miles SE of Weobly, and 4½ WNW of Moreton r station It has a post office under Hereford. Acres, 3,706 Real property £5,630 Pop, 768 Houses, 172 The property is much subdivided. Canon Pyon House is a chief residence The living is a vicarage in the diocese of Hereford. Value, not reported. Patrons, the Dean and Chapter of Hereford. The church is early English, in tolerable condition, and has a large old font and a screen

CANONS a property in Little Stanmore parish, Middlesex, 1½ mile NW of Edgeware It belonged to the priory of St. Bartholomew, went, at the dissolution, to the Losses, and passed to the Lakes, and to the first Duke of Chandos, the "Timon" of Pope. A palace was built on it by the Duke of Chandos, and pulled down in 1747 Canons Park here was the residence of the sportsman, O Kelly, and figured in connexion with his famous horse "Eclipse"

CANONS ASHBY See ASHBY CANONS

CANONSLEIGH See BURLESCOMBE

CANONTEIGN, the seat of Viscount Exmouth, in Devon, on the river Teign, 8 miles SW of Exeter The mansion is an elegant edifice, erected by the late Viscount The previous mansion was built in the time of Elizabeth was garrisoned for Charles I, and taken by Fairfax, and is now used as a farm house. The remains of the hero of Algiers were interred in the neighbouring church of Christow

CANSFIELD See CANTFIELD

CANTELOFF, an ancient parish, now incorporated with Hethersett parish, in Norfolk, but still ranking as a distinct rectory, annexed to the rectory of Hethersett.

CANTERBURY, a city in Kent and a diocese in Kent and Surrey The city partly forms a district of itself and is partly in the districts of Bridge and Blean It stands on Watling street, the river Stour and the London and Dover railway 6 miles S by E of Whitstable and 53 by road, but 65 by railway, E by S of London Railways go from it in five directions, toward Whitstable, London, Ashford, Dover, and Ramsgate, and give it communication with all the principal towns in the kingdom Its site is a valley, surrounded by hills, its appearance, as seen from any point, is highly picturesque, and its environs are diversified and very pleasant

History.—Canterbury rose prior to the era of authentic history and comes into view as a British town under the name of Durwhern The Romans made it one of their principal stations, rebuilt and strengthened it over nearly the whole area occupied by the modern town and called it Durovernum The Saxons made it the capital of the kingdom of Kent and called it Cant-wara-byrig, the stronghold of the men of Kent. The arrival of Augustine in 597, followed by the conversion of Ethelbert, gave it consequence as the source of Christianity to England and as the cradle of the metropolitical see The Danes took it in 843 852 918 and 1011 but were expelled by successive Eldreds and Canute It had a castle before the Conquest, and was called Civitas Cantuariae at Domesday It had begun at the end of the Heptarchy, to be eclipsed by Winchester and London and it continued, for ages, to decrease in comparative importance but, at the murder of Thomas à Becket in its cathedral in 1170, it burst into celebrity as one of the most notable towns in Europe Pilgrims of all ranks from all parts of Christendom, crowded to its gates and the romancers placed it side by side with Cologne and Compostella Henry II visited it in 1172, 1179, and 1184, Richard I in 1194, Richard II, in 1389, and Henry VIII, the emperor Charles V, and the Queen of France, in 1519 Elizabeth also visited in 1573, Charles I, in 1625, and Charles II, in 1660 Other historical notices will occur in our accounts of the ancient buildings

Walls and Streets.—Walls most probably were built around the town by the Romans, walls certainly stood around it in the time of the Saxons, new walls and a ditch were formed in the time of Richard I, and these were renovated, in 1374–81, by Archbishop Simon of Sudbury The area within them has been found to contain many Roman bricks, pavements, vases, lachrymatories, and personal ornaments, at about 6 or 9 feet beneath the surface, and therefore was occupied by Roman houses. The walls were 6 feet thick, composed of large masses of chalk, cemented with a strong mortar, and lined and faced with flint, were surmounted by twenty-one turrets, at equal distances, and had six gates Portions of the walls, with two or three of the turrets, still stand in Broad-street. The west gate also still stands, contiguous to the river, and is a noble embattled structure, flanked by two lofty round towers The ditch around the walls was originally 150 feet wide, but most of it is now built upon, or converted into gardens. Part of the present town is without the walls, and much is modern, handsome, and substantial, but most of it within the walls is ancient. The High street presents gabled ends and projecting fronts Alleys and lanes toward the cathedral and its precincts look antiquely picturesque Mercery lane, leading off the High-street, was named from the mercery stalls at which pilgrims bought memorials of their visit, and contains some window arches of the "Chequers of the Hope," noted by the lively and laughter loving Chaucer, and the first opening west of this lane shows part of the court into which the pilgrims rode An inn still standing, called the Red Lion, entertained the ambassadors of Charles V in 1520, and another ancient but modernized inn, called the Star, in the suburb of St Dunstan on the way from the railway station to the centre of the city, was a hostel for pilgrims who arrived after the shutting of the gates at night fall The city within the walls extends about ¾ a mile from east to west, and somewhat more from north to south, and has an oval outline "No city," remarks Mr Walcott, "can shew a greater number of churches, monuments, and sites of interest, and no city has done less to preserve them Till within a hundred years, town walls, gates, towers, and old buildings stood as in centuries since, but happily, a better feeling is now prevalent, and the good work of restoration and repair has been begun"

Public Buildings.—The guild hall, at the corner of High street and Guild hall street was built in 1439, and rebuilt in 1697, has been exteriorly modernized, and contains pieces of ancient armour and some curious portraits. The court or sessions house is a modern structure in the suburb of St Augustine The city jail is partly the upper portion of the west gate, partly a contiguous erection of 1820, and has capacity for 21 male and 4 female prisoners, but is fit only to be used as a lock up, and for debtors The county jail adjoins the court house, in the suburb of St Augustine, is an erection of 1808 on the radiating plan, with the keeper's house and chapel in the centre, and has capacity for 76 male and 30 female prisoners. The music hall is in St Margaret street The theatre is in Guild hall street, and was built in 1861 The royal cavalry barracks were built in 1794, form three sides of a square, and present a striking appearance The old infantry barracks were built in 1798, with accommodation for 2,000 men, formed, for some time a station for the horse and foot artillery, and are now to be used for depots of cavalry The new infantry barracks were built in 1811 The keep of the ancient castle stands in Castle street, adjacent to the site of one of the city gates, measures 88 feet by 80, and is now used as a gas work The castle was taken, without resistance, in the time of King John by Louis of France became afterwards a prison and was remarkable for the incarceration of Jews The mound on which the donjon stood, now called the Dane John, has, along with part of the city walls, been converted into a city mall, 1,130 feet long, laid out in spiral walks and shrubberies, and commanding a grand view of the cathedral. An adjacent field, outside the walls, was the scene of the martyrdoms in the reign of Mary and bears the name of the Martyrs field. The Archbishop's palace, founded in the time of the Saxons, rebuilt by Lanfranc and extended by Hubert Walter and Stephen Langton, stood in Palace street, but is now represented by little else than an arched doorway. This was the scene of the death of the Black Prince, of the prelude of the murder of Thomas à Becket, of the bridal feast of Edward I., and of banquets to Henry VIII., Charles V., and Elizabeth. Other public buildings will be noticed in subsequent paragraphs.

The Cathedral.—A church was built, by St. Augustine, on the site of the cathedral, greatly injured by the Danes in 938, restored by Archbishop Odo, in 940–60, damaged again by the Danes in 1011, and almost destroyed by fire in 1067, and contained the bodies of St. Blaize, St. Wilfred, St. Dunstan, St. Alphege, and St. Andoen, the heads of St. Swithin and St. Furseus, and the arm of St. Bartholomew. The present edifice was commenced in 1070–86 by Archbishop Lanfranc, extended, altered, and restored by successive prelates till 1495, and has undergone great, costly, recent renovations. It exhibits, in its various parts, all the styles of architecture, from early Norman to perpendicular, makes grand displays of them both in their respective features, and in their junctions with one another; and is especially rich and large in transition-Norman and perpendicular English. It has a crypt, with vaulted roof 14 feet high, supported on massive pillars, and it stands aloft on a height of base and with a force of character unsurpassed in any other cathedral, dominating over the city around it like an abrupt, isolated, spiry hill over some miles of plain. It consists of a south porch, a nave of nine bays, with aisles, a central transept, with two chapels, a choir of six bays, with aisles, a choir transept, with two apsidal chapels in each wing, a presbytery of two bays, with aisles, and with northern and southern apsidal chapels, an eastern ambulatory, with aisles, a main apsidal chapel of four bays, with magnificent procession path and aisles, and a circular structure to the east of this, called A' Becket's Crown, and it has a central tower and two western towers. The nave is 178 feet long, 71 feet wide, and 80 feet high, the choir, 180 feet long, 40 feet wide, and 71 feet high, the central transept, 124 feet long, the choir transept, 154 feet long, the central tower, 35 feet square and 235 feet high, and the western towers, 130 feet high. The nave has no triforium, the main transept has no aisles, the choir is approached by noble flights of stairs, and offers the earliest instance of the pointed arch in England, the screen is of the 15th century, with niched imagery of founders and saints, and was recently restored, the throne was carved by Flemish workmen, and cost £1,200, the pulpit is of stone, by Butterfield of London, and was put up in 1846, the main apsidal chapel is approached by broad flights of stairs, contained the gorgeous shrine of St. Thomas à Becket, and has a curious mosaic pavement, with the signs of the zodiac, the central tower is of two stages, with octagonal turrets at the angles, and has been called "the glory of all towers," and the western towers are each of six stages and much beauty, one of them rebuilt in 1840, at a cost of £25,000. Effigies, altar tombs, and other monuments, in great variety, are dispersed through the various parts of the pile to the memory of the archbishops and other notable persons, including Henry IV., Queen Joan of Navarre, Edward the Black Prince, a Lady Mohun, a Countess of Athole, Admiral Sir G. Rooke, Sir John Boys, Hadrian Saravia, Orlando Gibbons, W. Shuckford, Odo Coligny, a Marquis of Dorset, and a Duke of Clarence.

The edifice served, throughout the Romish times, both as a cathedral and as a conventual church. A Benedictine priory stood connected with it, and was known as the convent of Christ's Church. A massive wall surrounded the precincts, and served at once for defence and for seclusion. The passage from the priory led to the choir transept through a circular chamber, now used as a baptistery. The library is to the north of this, and occupies the site of the prior's chapel. The chapter-house stands parallel with the north side of the north-west transept, and is 87 feet long, 35 feet wide, and 52 feet high. The cloisters are on the north side of the nave, measure 144 feet by 144, and have eight bays on every side. "The space southward of the choir formed the cemetery, or God's acre, sown with the seed of the resurrection. 'The Oaks' was the convent garden, the Norman doorway is in the precinct gate eastward of the choir. The ancient stone house on the left side turning round the Becket's Crown formed the Honours, the guest hall (a nave and aisles 150 feet by 40 feet), for the reception of visitors. Considerable remains of the infirmary are observable, the chapel and common hall, of flint, with three tall pointed windows, built in 1342. Near it was St. Thomas' well. At this point occurs 'the Dark entry,' a Norman cloister built by Prior Wibert about 1167, with a curious bell-shaped tower, which served as the monks' conduit, above it is now the baptistery. On one side is the gate of the great cloisters. The arch and ruins towards the Green Court are those of La Gloriette, the prior's rooms built by Prior Hathbrand, 1379. Passing the chapter, once the prior's chapel library, the Prior's or Court Gate, leads into the Green Court. On the east side is the deanery, built by Dean Godwin, 1570, after a fire on the site of the Prior's lodgings. In it Hooper welcomed Queen Mary. At the north-east corner a large gateway opens into the follings or forings, the space beyond the conventual jurisdiction. On the north side, were the ancient dean's great hall, water house, granary, refectory, frater house, brew-house, bake house, and domestic buildings, among which great part of the dormitory remains, with a gateway and steps. At the north-west angle is the Norman precinct gate of the priory, which stood on the south side of the court, the back entrance to it, or Larder Gate, still remains. At the south-west angle is the arched door which led to the palace. The strangers' hall was on the west side. In the north-west angle is likewise the Norman staircase, with an open arcade which led into the north hall, 150 feet by 40 feet, allotted to the stewards of the prior court, the arches on which it was supported alone remain, above them the King's school has been built by Mr. Austen, 1855. They form a passage into the Mint yard. It is the only staircase of the period known to be in existence. In the King's school were educated Harvey, the physician, Lord Thurlow, and Lord Tenterden. Within the ancient almonry on the north-west of the Green Court, stood the chantry of St. Thomas à Becket, which Henry VIII. converted into a mint, and Cardinal Pole made the King's school. In the high wall, probably a portion of Lanfranc's building, leading to the north-west entrance of the cathedral, are the remains of the covered way to the cloisters, by which the primates entered, but their ordinary approach was through a large gateway with a square tower of flint and ashlar.

Ancient Monasteries.—An abbey was founded by St. Augustine, outside the walls, in the eastern suburb of Longport. It was designed by him mainly as a mausoleum for bishops and kings, it became the burial place of himself and his successors, and of Ethelbert and his successors, it possessed much grandeur as an edifice and great wealth and consequence as a monastery, it was always regarded as more sacred and important than the cathedral, till the latter outshone it by means of the glory of A' Becket's shrine, and it competed to the last with the convent of Christ Church in the splendours and fetes of its guest hall. The buildings of it were greatly injured at the Reformation, were, some time after, partly converted into a royal palace, were subsequently given to Lord Wotton, were several times damaged by fire and by flood, were eventually degraded to the uses of a brewery, and were purchased, in 1844, by A. J. Beresford Hope, Esq., to give place to a Missionary college. Richard II. and his queen were guests in them, in their original condition, and Elizabeth, Charles I, Henrietta, and Charles II were in them when a palace. Their guest hall seems to be preserved in the refectory of the Missionary college, but the only other portions of them which remain are some wall fragments of late Norman character, the cemetery gate built in the time of Richard II, and a superb great gateway built in 1287 flanked by two turrets and embattled. A ruined chapel 31 feet by 21, at the north east angle of the cemetery, was originally Ethelbert's heathen place of worship, was changed, at his conversion, into a Christian church, dedicated to St Pancras, and was rebuilt in 1387. A Dominican friary, in St. Peter's street, was founded in the time of Henry III and has left considerable remains. Part of it was formed into private dwellings and a wool house, part became a Baptist meeting house, and the refectory, with windows high in the wall, is now a Unitarian chapel, and was noted for the preaching of Defoe. A Franciscan friary, in the same vicinity, was founded in 1220, but has disappeared. Lord Badlesmere, steward of the household to Edward II, and many other men were buried in it. A priory of St Gregory for Augustinian black canons in Northgate street, was founded by Lanfranc but also has disappeared. A house of the Knights-Templars stood near the Dominican friary and, after the suppression of the Templars, was used by the priests of the Black Prince's chantry. A Benedictine nunnery, in the eastern suburb, contiguous to Watling street, about ¼ of a mile from the city walls, was founded by Archbishop Anselm, had for one of its nuns, Elizabeth Barton, the "Maid of Kent," after her removal from Aldington, and has left some small remains.

Churches.—The livings within the city are the rectory of All Saints, with the rectories of St Mary in the Castle and St Mildred, the rectory of St Alphage with the vicarage of St. Mary Northgate, the rectory of St Andrew with the rectory of St. Mary Bredman, the vicarage of St. Dunstan, the rectory of St George the Martyr, with the rectory of St Mary-Magdalene, the vicarage of St Gregory the Great, the rectory of St Margaret, the rectory of St Martin, with the vicarage of St. Paul, the vicarage of St Mary Bredin, and the rectory of St Peter, with the vicarage of Holy Cross, and all are in the diocese of Canterbury. Value of All Saints, £150, of St Alphage, £150,* of St Andrew, £203,* of St Dunstan £120, of St Peter, £120,* of St George-the Martyr, £140,* of St Gregory the Great, not reported, of St. Margaret, £120,* of St Martin £300, of St Mary Bredin £149.* Patron of All Saints the Lord Chancellor, of St. Alphege, St Dunstan, and St. Gregory-the Great, the Archbishop of Canterbury, of St Andrew, the Archbishop for two turns, and the Dean and Chapter for one, of St George the Martyr, the Dean and Chapter, of St Margaret, the Archdeacon, of St. Martin and St. Peter, the Archbishop and the Dean and Chapter alternately, of St Mary Bredin, the Rev H Lee Warner.

St Mildred's church occupies the site of a previous church, is partly later English, consists of three aisles and three chancels with a square tower, includes Roman bricks in its walls, and contains monuments of the Attwoods, the Cranmers, and others. St Alphage's church, in Palace street, is of considerable antiquity, consists of two aisles and two chancels with a square tower, and has some curious epitaphs. St Andrew's church superseded a previous one about 1763, is a brick structure, and consists of two aisles and a chancel with a steeple. St Mary Bredman's church shows Norman features, and has a monument of Herne, the historian of Peculver. St Dunstan's church, without the walls, is a modernized ancient structure with Norman features, consists of two aisles, a small western chancel, and two large eastern ones, with western tower and contiguous half circular tower, and contains a piscina, a font, an ancient chantry, and the burial vault of the Ropers with the head of Sir Thomas More. A brick gateway nearly opposite, now part of a brewery, is a remnant of the Ropers' manor house, where Margaret, the learned daughter of Sir Thomas More, spent her married life. St George's church is a modernized, ancient Norman structure, consists of two chancels and two aisles, with a square tower and a narrow turret, and contains an ancient octagonal font and a brass of 1531. St Mary Magdalene's church, in Burgate-street, shows Norman features of the earliest Norman time, has a tower, added in 1503, and contains a fine old, octangular, Norman font. St Gregory's church without the walls, beyond Broad street, is a modern edifice in the early English style, by Scott. St Margaret's church, in St Margaret's street, has suffered much from mutilation, was partially restored in 1831, consists of three chancels and three aisles, with a square tower, and contains a monument of Somner, the city historian. St. Martin's church, without the walls, on a hill, with a fine view, about ½ a mile from the cathedral, was originally the oratory of Queen Bertha, became the first church or cathedral of St Augustine, and afterwards the church of a resident suffragan bishop, is a small rough cast edifice, rebuilt at a remote date on the site of the original church, and including portions of that church's walls, with Roman bricks and fragments of Roman mortar, was recently well restored, at the expense of the Hon Daniel Finch, auditor of the cathedral, has modern stained glass windows, with subjects of its early history, and contains a large Norman font, traditionally alleged to have been that in which Ethelbert was baptized. Byzantine and Merovingian looped coins have been found in the church yard. St Paul's church is early English, comprises two chancels and two aisles, with a rudely formed square tower, and contains a very curious pillared font, and a tomb of Admiral Rooke. St Mary Bredin's church was originally Norman, was rebuilt in 1867, at a cost of £4 000, and is in the early English style, of flint with dressings of Bath stone. St Peter's church, at the corner of St Peter's lane, has very thick walls, curious square columns, and an old square font. Holy Cross church, close to Westgate, was rebuilt about 1381, and consists of three aisles, and a chancel, with a square tower. A suite of Carmelite conventual buildings, comprising church, convent, and farm offices, after designs by Pugin, on a site of thirty acres, within a high brick wall enclosure, to cost £34 354 for the buildings alone, was contracted for in 1868 by Miss Hales, proprietress of Hales Place estate, (on which the Royal Agricultural Society of England held their show in 1860,) to be erected on her own grounds and at her own expense.

Schools, &c—The King's school, already incidentally mentioned, was founded by Henry VIII, for the education of 50 scholars from all parts of the kingdom, and has about 24 scholarships or exhibitions in Cambridge university. A portion of its old buildings which still stood was taken down in 1863, to give place to new erections. The Blue-coat school was founded by the city corporation out of a gift by Queen Elizabeth of an hospital and its lands, clothes, maintains, and educates 16 boys, and has an income of £475. The grey coat school educates 30 boys and 30 girls, and is supported chiefly by the dean and chapter. St Augustine's missionary college, at St. Augustine's abbey, was incorporated in 1849, consists of warden, sub warden, and six fellows, trains young men for the service of the Church of England in the distant dependencies of the empire, possesses endowments and exhibitions from a number of different benefactors, and forms a quadrangle, including hall, chapel, library, cloisters, and corridor in the monastic style, by Butterfield. The philosophical institution, in Guild hall street, was built by subscription in 1826, is an ornamental edifice, with Ionic portico, and contains a museum with some interesting collections.

Eastbridge hospital was founded either by Lanfranc or by A' Becket, originally to receive "wayfaring and hurt men," maintains inmates, and gives out door relief, is connected with a school for 20 children founded by Whitgift, and has an income of £512. St John's hospital was founded by Lanfranc, was recently restored, includes an ancient arched wooden gateway, and has an income of £155. Harbledown hospital also was founded by Lanfranc, possesses still its original chapel, and has an income of £250. Jesus' hospital was founded in 1595, by Sir John Boys, for persons above 55 years of age, and has an income of £618 Maynard's hospital was founded in the time of Henry II, and has an income of £244 Cogan's hospital, for clergymen's widows, was founded in 1657, and has an income of £248 Hackington hospital has £26, Smith's alms houses, £260, Harris's, £68 The Kent and Canterbury infirmary contains accommodation for about 200 patients, and is liberally supported by annual subscriptions The total amount of endowed charities is £4 899

Trade, &c.—Pelic making and the supplying of the wants of pilgrims were the only trade in the Romish times. Silk weaving was introduced by refugee Walloons and French protestants after the Reformation. This flourished for a period, but gave place to the manufacture of cotton and silk, and that also has ceased Some trade in wool is now carried on, but the chief source of industry is the export of agricultural produce especially hops Markets are held on Wednesday and Saturday, and a fair on 11 Oct The city has a head post-office,‡ two railway stations with telegraph, two banking offices, and several good inns, and publishes seven weekly newspapers Races are run in April and August, over an uneven course of two miles on Barnham downs.

The District—The registration district contains the parishes of All Saints, St. Mildred, St. Alphage, St Mary Northgate St Andrew, and St. Mary Bredman, St. George the Martyr, St Mary Magdalene, St Margaret, St. Martin St Paul, St Mary Bredin and St Peter, part of the parish of Holy Cross, and the extra parochial places of St John's Hospital precincts, Old Castle precincts, Eastbridge Hospital precincts, Black Prince's Chantry precincts and Whitefriars House The return for St Paul's parish includes Longport which is a borough under the old common law division of the county, and St Augustine's abbey precinct, the precise limits of which are not known Acres of the district, 3,121 Poor rates in 1866, £6,936 Pop in 1861, 16,643 Houses 2 919 Marriages in 1866, 164, births, 487,—of which 25 were illegitimate deaths, 309,—of which 118 were at ages under 5 years, and 11 at ages above 85 Marriages in the ten years 1851–60, 1,548, births, 3,980 deaths, 3,517 The places of worship in 1851 were 13 of the Church of England, with 4 886 sittings, 1 of Independents, with 650 s., 3 of Baptists, with 670 s, 1 of Quakers, with 125 s 1 of Wesleyan Methodists, with 1 100 s, 1 of Primitive Methodists, with 500 s, 1 of Lady Huntingdon's Connexion, with 275 s, and 1 of Jews, with 73 s The schools were 8 public day schools, with 1,292 scholars, 44 private day schools, with 867 s., and 10 Sunday schools, with 1,044 s

The Borough.—The city includes all the registration district, also parts of Holy Cross, Nackington Thanington, Patrixbourne. Littlebourne and Fordwich parishes in the district of Bridge also Archbishop's Palace and Christchurch precincts, Staplegate and St. Gregory villes and parts of St Dunstan and Hackington parishes in the district of Blean It is a seat of sessions, a place of elections, the head of an excise collection and a head quarters of militia. It received municipal privileges from Henry II, and an incorporation charter from Henry VI, is governed by a mayor, a sheriff, six aldermen, and eighteen councillors, and sends two members to parliament Real property £51,390 Direct taxes, £11 498 Electors in 1861, 1,837 Pop., in 1841, 15 435 in 1861, 21,324 Houses, 3 908 The city gives the title of Viscount to the Manners Suttons Gostling and Somner, the antiquaries Dean Nevile, Dr Linacre Aphra Behn, Marlowe Richard the great Earl of Cork, and Lord Tenterden were natives

The Diocese—Canterbury, at once as a bishopric as an archbishopric and is the metropolitan see of England, dates from St Augustine Among its prelates were Dunstan, Theodore Lanfranc, Anselm Pascal II A'Becket Langton Bradwardine, Langham Chichele, Warham Cranmer, Pole Parker, Whitgift, Laud, Sancroft Wake Tillotson Tenison Secker Sutton and Howley The archbishop ranks as first peer of the realm, next to the royal family and places the crown on the sovereign's head, at a coronation His seats are Lambeth palace and Addington park, and his income is £15,000 His archiepiscopal jurisdiction extends over twenty suffragan bishops, and includes all Wales, and all England except the six northern counties

The diocese includes all Kent, except the parishes of Charlton, Lee, Lewisham, Greenwich, Woolwich, Eltham, Plumstead, Deptford St. Nicholas part of Deptford St Paul, and the city and deanery of Rochester It includes likewise the part of Surrey comprising the parishes of Addington and Croydon, and the district of Lambeth Palace Its pop, in 1861, was 474,603, inhabiting 88,073 houses It is divided into the archdeaconries of Canterbury and Maidstone The chapter includes a dean with £2,000 a year, two archdeacons, six canons, and six minor canons Eight deaneries are comprised in each of the two archdeaconries, and from eleven to thirty one livings are in each deanery Some of the livings have recently been raised in status chiefly p curacies raised to be vicarages, and are named as they now rank in the separate articles on them in our work, but all will be named here as they ranked in 1861

The deanery of Canterbury includes the livings within Canterbury city, the rectories of Fordwich, Harbledown, Lower Hardres, and Milton next Canterbury, the vicarages of Hackington, and Sturry, and the p curacies of Nackington and Thanington The deanery of Bridge includes the rectories of Adisham, Bishopsbourne, Brook, Chartham, Chillenden, Crundall Elmstone, Kingstone, Stourmouth, Upper Hardres, Ickham, and Wickhambreux, the vicarages of Ash, Boughton Aluph, Chilham, Godmersham, Weld, Littlebourne, Patrixbourne, Bridge, Preston next Wingham, Waltham, and Petham, the p curacies of Staple, Trinity-Ash, Barham Molash, Challock, Goodnestone next Wingham, Stelling Nunnington, Wingham, Womenswold, and Wye, and the donative of Stodmarsh The deanery of Dover includes the rectories of St James Dover, Charlton near Dover, Cheriton, Ewell Temple, and Hawkinge, the vicarages of Alkham, Newington Folkstone Hougham Lydden, St. Margarets at Cliffe, River, and Westcliffe, and the p curacies of Capel le Fern Beauxfield, Buckland near Dover, St Mary Dover, Trinity Dover, Christ church Folkstone, Christ church Hougham, Guston, Sandgate, and Swingfield The deanery of Elham includes the rectories of Acrise, Monks Horton, Denton, Hastingleigh, Lyminge, Saltwood, St Mary Stowting, and Woolton, the vicarages of Elham Brabourne, Elmsted and Postling, and the p curacies of Horton, Standford Paddlesworth, and Hythe The deaneries of North and South Lympne include the rectories of Aldington, Bonnington, Burmarsh, Dymchurch, Hinxhill, Ivy-Church Ken Ardington, Kingsnorth, Mersham, Orlestone Old Romney, St. Mary-Romney Marsh Newchurch Romney Marsh, Pluckley, Sevington, Shadoxhurst, Snargate, Snave, Warehorne, Willesborough, and Woodchurch, the vicarages of Appledore, Brenzett Brookland Lydd, Lympne St Mary Sellinge, Stone, and Willesborough and the p curacies of Smeeth, Bilsington, Ebony, and Fairfield The deanery of Ospringe includes the rectories of Luddenham Leaveland, Eastling, Hever, Luddenham Newnton, and Otterden the vicarages of Boughton under Blean, Doddington, Faversham Goodnestone Graveney Hernhill Linstead, Newnham Ospringe, Preston by Faversham, Selling, Sheldwich Stalisfield, Teynham, and Throwley, the p curacies of Isle of Harty, and Oare, and the donative of Davington The deanery of Sandwich includes the rectories of Barfrestone, Betshanger, Deal, Eythorne, Ham, Knowlton, East Langdon Great Mongeham Little Mongeham Ringwould, Ripple, and St Peter Sandwich the vicarages of Eastry, Northbourne St Clement Sandwich, St. Mary Sandwich Sibbertswold, Coldred Tilmanstone, Waldershare and Woodnesborough, and the p. curacies of St Andrew Deal, St George Deal West Langdon, Shoulden, Kingsdown, Sutton next Dover Walmer, and Worth The deanery of Westbere includes the rectories of Westbere and Swalecliffe the vicarages of Chislet, Herne St Laurence in Thanet St John Margate Minster Thanet, Monkton St Nicholas at Wade, St Peter-in Thanet, Ramsgate Reculver, and St Walter, and the p curacies of Herne Bay, Trinity in Thanet, Trinity-in Margate, Birchington Acol, Broadstairs, Christchurch Ramsgate, Heath and Whitstable

The deanery of Dartford includes the rectories of Beckenham, Chelsfield Chiselhurst, Crayford Footscray, North Cray St Paul's Cray and Keston, the vicarages of Addington, Bexley Croydon, Cudham, Dartford, Erith, Hayes Horton-Kirby Orpington Sutton at Home, West Wickham, and Wilmington, and the p curacies of Bexley Heath, Bromley, Trinity Bromley, Sidcup, St. Mary Cray, Crocken Hill, Southend-Croyden, Broad green Croyden Croyden Common, Norwood Croyden, South Norwood Croyden, Shirley Croyden Downe, Farnborough, and Lamorbey The deanery of North Malling includes the rectories of Addington, Allington, Barming, Ditton, Hunton, Leybourne, Mereworth, Nettlestead, West Barming, Offham, West Peckham, and Trotters cliffe, the vicarages of Birling, East Farleigh, West Farleigh Hadlow, East Malling, West Malling, East Peckham, Frarsh Teston Wateringbury, and Yalding, the p curacies of New Hythe, Trinity Peckham, and St Margaret Yalding and the donative of Shipbourne The deanery of South Malling includes the rectories of Ashurst, Bidborough, Chiddingstone, Cowden, Hever, Horsemonden, Penshurst, and Speldhurst, the vicarages of Brenchley, Lamberhurst, Leigh, Pembury, Tudeley, and Tunbridge, and the p curacies of Mark Beech, Fordcomb, Groombridge, Rusthall, Capel, St. Stephen Tunbridge, Hildenborough Southborough, Tunbridge Wells Trinity-Tunbridge Wells, and Christchurch Tunbridge Wells. The deanery of East Charing includes the rectories of Boughton Malherbe, Great Chart, Little Chart Eastwell, Pluckley and Pevington, the vicarages of Ashford Charing, Hothfield, Kennington and Westwell, and the p curacy of Egerton The deanery of West Charing includes the rectories of Biddenden, Frittenden, Newenden, Sandhurst, and Smarden, the vicarages of Benenden, Bethersden, Cranbrook, Headcorn, Rolvenden, and Tenterden, the p curacies of Trinity-Cranbrook and Hawkhurst and the donative of Small hythe The deanery of Shoreham includes the rectories of Brasted, Chevening, Halstead, Ightham, Lullingstone, Sevenoaks, Stanstead, Sundridge, and Wrotham the vicarages of Eynesford, Farningham, Kemsing, Shoreham and Westerham, and the p curacies of Edenbridge, Seal Knockholt, Otford, Riverhead, Weald, Ide Hill, Grockham-Hill, Woodlands, Platt, and Plaxtol The deanery of Sittingbourne includes the rectories of Hartchurch, Bicknor, Elmly, Kingsdown, Milkstead, Murston, Tunstall, Warden, and Wichling, the vicarages of Bapchild Bobbing, Borden, Bredgar, Lower Halstow, Hartlip Leysdown Milton next Sittingbourne, Newington next Sittingbourne, Rainham, Rodmersham, Sittingbourne, Stockbury Tong, and Upchurch, and the p curacies of Iwade, Minster in Sheppey Queenborough, and Sheerness in Minster The deanery of Sutton includes the rectories of Frinstead, Harrietsham Langley Otham, Staplehurst, Allington Ulcombe, and Wormshill the vicarages of Bearsted, Boughton Monchelsea, Boxley, Chart by Sutton, Detling Goudhurst Hollingborne, Lenham, Linton, Marden, Sutton Valence, and Thornham, and the p curacies of Bredhurst, Linlown, Hucking Leeds Bromfield, Loose All Saints-Maidstone, Trinity Maidstone St Peter Maidstone, Tovil, and East Sutton

CANTERTON, a tything in Minstead parish Hants 8½ miles SW of Romsey Real property, with Fritham, £1 316 Pop 38.

CANTIUM, the North Foreland promontory at the NE extremity of Kent The Cantii of the Romans were the ancient Britons of Kent.

CANTLEY a parish in Blofield district, Norfolk on the river Yare and the Yarmouth railway, 10 miles ESE of Norwich It has a station on the railway and a post office under Norwich Acres 1,570 Real property, £2,5[illegible]2 Pop, 2[illegible] Houses 1[illegible] Cantley House is a chief residence The living is a rectory in the diocese of Norwich Value £203 * Patron, W A Gilbert, Esq

CANTLEY, a parish in Doncaster district, W R Yorkshire near the river Idle, 3 miles N by W of Rossington r station, and 3½ ESE of Doncaster It includes the hamlets of Bessacar, Branton, Gatewood, and High and Low Ellers, and has a post office under Doncaster Acres 5,100 Real property, £5,373 Pop., 665. Houses, 127 The property is divided between two Cantley House is the seat of J W Childers, Esq The living is a vicarage in the diocese of York. Value, £233 * Patron J W Childers, Esq The church is good, and there is a national school

CANTON, a chapelry, with a village, in Llandaff parish, Glamorgan, adjacent to the Taff Valley and the Pymney railways, 1 mile NW of Cardiff It has a post office‡ under Cardiff. Rated property, £5,539 Pop, 3 920 Houses, 709 The property is much subdivided The chapelry was constituted in 1858 The living is a rectory in the diocese of Llandaff Value, £300 Patron the Bishop of Llandaff A Baptist chapel, in the Lombardic style, was built in 1858.

CANTREFF, or CYNNFDD, a parish in the district and county of Brecon, near the river Usk and the Brecon and Hereford railway 2½ miles SSE of Brecon It includes the chapelry of Nantddu, and its post-town is Brecon Acres, about 20,000 Real property, £1,807 Pop, 221 Houses 39 The property is divided among a few The surface includes the BRECKNOCK BEACONS which see. The living is a rectory in the diocese of St. David's. Value, not reported. Patron, the P[illegible] I Powell The church is good. The p curacy of Nantddu is a separate benefice The learned T Powell was rector

CANTREF GWAELOD, a submerged tract, 12 miles by 5, off Gwallog and Aberystwith, in Cardigan, now forming the Sarn Gwalod shoal It was a low flat tract, defended by dykes and dams, and said to contain sixteen towns and was submerged in 520

CANTSFIELD, a township in Tunstall parish Lancashire, near the river Greta, 4½ miles SE of Kirkby Lonsdale It has a post office under Burton in Kendal. Acres 1 221 Real property £1 786 Pop., 116 Houses, 20 Cantsfield Hall is the seat of the Lushains.

CANTWARABYRIG See CANTERBURY

CANVEY ISLAND, a chapelry in Billericay and Rochford districts Essex encircled by the Thames, opposite the Hope, adjacent to Benfleet r station, 4½ miles SW of Rayleigh It comprises parts of Vange, Pitsea Bowers Gifford, North Benfleet, South Benfleet, Hadleigh, Prittlewell and Southchurch parishes and its post town is South Benfleet, under Chelmsford Acres about 3,500 Pop 111 The property is much subdivided The surface is marshland sheep pasture, and it is protected all round by embankments, and connected with the mainland by a causeway Fairs are held on 25 June and 25 Sept The living is a p curacy in the diocese of Rochester Value, £58 Patron, the Bishop of Rochester The church is good

CANWELL, an extra parochial tract in Tamworth district Stafford on the verge of the county, 5 miles SW of Tamworth Acres, 2[illegible]0 Real property, £[illegible] Pop 43 Houses 7 Canwell Hall is the seat of Sir F Lawley, Bart A Benedictine priory was founded here in 1142, by Geva daughter of Hugh Lupus, and given, at the dissolution to Cardinal Wolsey

CANWICK, a parish in the district and county of Lincoln on the Gainsborough and Boston railway, within the borough, and 1½ mile SE of the town of Lincoln Post town, Lincoln Acres, returned with Lincoln city Real property, £3,223 Pop 22[illegible] Houses 42 The property is not much divided Canwick House is the seat of the Sibthorpes. The living is a vicarage in the diocese of Lincoln Value £231 * Patrons, the Mercers Company The church is Norman Charities £1[illegible]

CAPAS HEIGHT, a hamlet in Pudsey township and parish W R Yorkshire, 5½ miles NW of Wakefield

CAPE CORNWALL, a headland in the SW of Cornwall 1 mile WNW of St Just, and 4[illegible] N by E of Land's End It is 2[illegible] feet high contains quartz jasper, tin copper ore, and iron, and [illegible] minerals, and has, on the face of its cliffs, the engine of a mine which is worked to depths below the sea

CAPEL, an ancient British name signifying an oratory or a chapel.

CAPEL, a village in Llanfihangel Ystrad parish, Cardigan 6½ miles NW of Lampeter

CAPEL, Suffolk See CAPEL ST ANDREW and CAPEL-ST MARY

CAPEL, a parish and a sub-district in Dorking district, Surrey The parish lies 5 miles NW by N of Faygate r station, and 6 S of Dorking, and has a post office under Dorking Acres, 5,522 Real property, £4,566 Pop, 1,074 Houses, 201 The property is divided among a few Part of the surface is moorish The living is a vicarage in the diocese of Winchester Value, £84 * Patron Charles Webb, Esq The church is good. The vicarage of Cold Harbour is a separate benefice There are a Quakers meeting house, a national school, and charities £15 —The sub district contains five parishes Pop., 4 094

CAPEL, or CAPLE, a parish in Tunbridge district, Kent, near the Southeastern railway, 3 miles SE of Tunbridge Post town, Tunbridge. Acres, 1,568 Real property, £3 261 Pop, 611 Houses, 115 The property is much subdivided The living is a vicarage, annexed to Tudeley, in the dio. of Canterbury The church is small, but has a steeple There is a national school

CAPEL ARTHOG, a hamlet in Llangelynin parish, Merioneth, on the river Maw, under Cader Idris, 6½ miles WSW of Dolgelly It has a post office under Corwen, and a chapel of ease

CAPEL BANGOR. See BANGOR, N Cardigan

CAPEL-BETTWS See BETTWS CLYRO and PENPONT

CAPEL CADWALADR, a ruined church in Llanddaniel parish, Anglesey, 2 miles NNW of Llanidan It is very ancient, and makes a claim but against good evidence, to have been the first church ever erected in the county

CAPEL CALLWEN See GLYNTAWE

CAPEL COELBREN, a chapelry in Ystradgynlas parish, Brecon, on the river Llech, 5 miles NNW of Glyn Neath r station, and 12 NNE of Neath. Post town, Ystradgynlas, under Swansea Statistics, with the parish The scenery is picturesque, and borrows grandeur from the Cribarth mountain The Llech makes a noble fall of 100 feet. Some erect coal trees, of the sigillaria class, have been found in the bed of the stream There are remains of a Roman road The living is a p curacy in the diocese of St David's. Value, £100 Patron, the Rector of Ystradgynlas. The church is a small primitive structure, and contains a curious old tombstone

CAPEL COLMAN See CHAPEL COLMAN

CAPEL CURIG, a hamlet and a chapelry in Llandegai parish, Carnarvon The hamlet lies on the river Llugwy at the foot of Moel Siabod and Snowdon, 5½ miles WSW of Llanrwst r station It has a post office under Conway, and a hotel, and is a polling place, and a resort for tourists and anglers Public coaches daily pass through it The surrounding scenery is most romantic, and the route hither to the top of Snowdon, though the most toilsome, is the best The chapelry includes the hamlet, and is a vicarage in the diocese of Bangor Value, £89 Patron, the Bishop of Bangor The church is very old but good.

CAPEL CYNON, a chapelry in Llandisilio Gogo parish, Cardigan, 8 miles NNE of Newcastle Emlyn r station Post town, Newcastle Emlyn under Carmarthen Pop, 413. Houses, 90 Henry VII encamped here on his march to Bosworth Fairs are held on Holy Thursday and on the second Thursday after 10 Oct. The chapelry was constituted in 1859 The living is a rectory in the diocese of St David's. Value, £100 Patron, the Bishop of St David s

CAPEL-DDEWI, a hamlet in Llandyssil parish, Cardigan, 6½ miles E of Newcastle Emlyn Pop, 394 It forms a curacy with Llandyssil

CAPEL EVAN, a village in Kilrhedin parish, Carmarthen, 2½ miles S of Newcastle Emlyn

CAPEL GARMON, or CARTH GARMON, a chapelry in Llanrwst parish, Denbigh, on the river Conway, 4½ miles S by E of Llanrwst r station Post town, Llanrwst Statistics returned with the parish The property is much subdivided The living is a p curacy in the diocese of St Asaph Value, not reported Patron, the Rector of Llanrwst The church is not good. There is an Independent chapel

CAPEL KINGS See KINGS CAPLE

CAPELLANTE, a mountain in the south of Brecon, 7 miles W by S of the Brecknock Beacons Its altitude is 2,394 feet

CAPEL LE FERNE, a parish in Dover district, Kent, on the coast, and on the Dover and Folkestone railway, 3 miles NE of Folkestone Post town, Folkestone Acres, 1,736, of which 100 are water Real property, £1,450 Pop, 193 Houses, 37 The property is much subdivided The living is a vicarage, annexed to the vicarage of Alkham, in the diocese of Canterbury The church consists of nave and chancel, with a western tower, shows interesting internal features of early English, and contains a piscina, a sedilia, and a brass of 1526

CAPEL LLANDURY, a hamlet in Pembrey parish, Carmarthen, 2 miles SE of Kidwelly It has a chapel, and forms a curacy with Pembrey

CAPEL-NANT DDU, a place, with a church of 1864, in the S of Brecon, 6 miles NNW of Merthyr Tydvil

CAPEL NEWYDD, a chapelry in the NW of Monmouth, 4½ miles N by W of Pontypool See BLAENAVON

CAPEL ST ANDREW, a parish in Woodbridge district, Suffolk, near the coast, 6 miles ESE of Melton r station, and 7 E of Woodbridge Post town, Orford, under Wickham Market. Acres, 2,272 Real property, £851 Pop, 231 Houses, 48 The living is a p. curacy, annexed to the p curacy of Butley, in the diocese of Norwich There is no church.

CAPEL ST MARY, a parish and a sub district in Samford district, Suffolk The parish lies on the Hadleigh railway, 5 miles SE of Hadleigh, and has a station on the railway and a post office under Ipswich, both of the name of Capel Acres, 1,910 Real property, £3,723 Pop, 669 Houses, 145. The property is subdivided The living is a rectory, united with the rectory of Little Wenham, in the diocese of Norwich Value, £632 * Patron, the Rev J Tweed The church is good —The sub district contains fifteen parishes Acres, 23,565 Pop, 6,592 Houses, 1 486

CAPEL VOELAS See PENTRE VOELAS

CAPEL Y-LLOCHWY See HOLYHEAD.

CAPENHURST, a township in Shotwick parish, and a chapelry in Shotwick and Neston parishes, Cheshire The township lies on the Birkenhead railway, 2 miles NNW of Mollington station, and 5½ NNW of Chester Acres, 1 173 Real property, £1,315 Pop 131 Houses, 25 The chapelry was constituted in 1859, and its post town is Sutton, under Chester Pop 224 Houses, 40 Capenhurst Hall is the seat of the Rev R Richardson The living is a rectory in the diocese of Chester Value, £120 Patron, the Rev R Richardson The church is recent.

CAPERNWRAY, a hamlet in Over-Kellet township, Bolton parish, Lancashire, 3½ miles S of Burton in Kendal Pop, 113. Capernwray Hall is the seat of the Mortons

CAPESTHORNE, a township-chapelry in Prestbury parish Cheshire 2½ miles ESE of Chelford r station, and 5 W by S of Macclesfield. Post town, Chelford, under Congleton Acres, 748 Real property, £1,294 Pop 111 Houses, 20 Capesthorne Hall is the seat of the Davenports, and was burnt in 1861 The living is a p curacy in the diocese of Chester Value, £70 * Patron E D Davenport, Esq The church is good

CAPHEATON, a township in Kirkwhelpington parish, Northumberland, near the Wansbeck Valley railway, 7½ miles N of the Roman wall, and 11 WSW of Morpeth It has a post office under Newcastle upon Tyne Acres, 2,213 Pop, 195 Houses, 44 Capheaton Castle dates from 1267, is the seat of Sir J E.

Swinburne, Bart, and belonged to his ancestors from the time of Henry VIII Roman coins and silver vessels have been found.

CAPLAND, a tything in Broadway parish, Somerset, 2 miles NW of Ilminster Acres, 410 Real property, £346 Pop, 113

CAPLE. See CAPEL, Kent.

CAPLE-CROSS, a hamlet in Horsemonden parish, Kent 7½ miles E by S of Tunbridge Wells

CAPLE-KINGS See KINGS-CAPLE.

CAPPENHURST See CAPENHURST

CAPTON, a hamlet in Dittisham parish, Devon, near the river Dart, 3½ miles N of Dartmouth. Pop 104 It has a Wesleyan chapel.

CAPTON, a hamlet in Stogumber parish, Somerset, 4½ miles SSE of Watchet.

CAR. See CARR.

CAR, or CHAR (THE), a stream of Dorset running 5 miles south westward to the English Channel at Charmouth.

CARADOC See CAER CARADOC.

CARADON, a hill and copper mines in Cornwall, 4 miles N of Liskeard. The hill is 1,208 feet high, and commands a fine view The mines are at the south foot of the hill, excavated in granite A mineral railway, called the Liskeard and Caradon railway, 8¾ miles long, opened in 1846, connects them with Liskeard.

CARAN (THE) a stream of Gloucester, falling into the Avon, near its influx to the Severn, in the vicinity of Tewkesbury

CARBECK, a hamlet in Lunedale township Romald Kirk parish, N R. Yorkshire; 10 miles NW of Barnard Castle.

CARBROOK, a hamlet in Attercliffe chapelry, W R. Yorkshire, 2 miles NE of Sheffield

CARBROOKE, a parish in Wayland district, Norfolk, near the river Wissey, 2 miles NE of Watton, and 8 SSW of Dereham r station Post town, Watton, under Thetford. Acres, 3,033 Real property, £5,296 Pop., 751 Houses, 172. The property is divided among a few Carbrooke Hall is the seat of J Wing, Esq A commandery of the Knights Templars was founded, near the church, in 1173, by Roger, Earl of Clare. The living is a vicarage in the diocese of Norwich. Value, £170 Patron, R. Dewing Esq The church is later English and good consists of nave, two aisles, a chancel and two porches, with a lofty square tower, and is seated with open benches. There are a national school, and charities £70

CARBURTON, a chapelry and a sub district in Worksop district, Notts The chapelry is in Edwinstowe parish, and lies contiguous to Clumber Park, 4 miles SSE of Worksop r station. Post town, Worksop Real property, £1,216 Pop, 177 Houses, 31 Carburton Lodge was the seat of Dr Aldrich The living is a p. curacy, annexed to the vicarage of Edwinstowe in the diocese of Lincoln. The sub district contains also five other parishes and an extra parochial tract Acres 13,140 Pop 5 523 Houses, 1,096

CARCAFRICK TOR, an eminence 6½ miles WNW of Callington, in Cornwall.

CARCLAZE, a range of moorish downs, 2 miles N of St Austell, in Cornwall It has an altitude of 665 feet, and commands an extensive view Its substance, some way down from the surface, is disintegrated schorlaceous granite and deeper down comparatively compact granite. A tin mine open to the day, has been worked in it from time immemorial, is now about a mile in circumference and fully 130 feet deep, and exhibits a striking contrast in the whiteness of its cliffs to the sombreness of the surrounding moor

CARCLEW a seat 3½ miles N of Penryn in Cornwall It belonged formerly to the De Angerses, the Bonythons, and others, and belongs now to Sir C Lemon, Bart The gardens are rich in rare plants, and the park is of great extent and grandly timbered

CARCLIFF TOR, an eminence on Stanton moor, in Derby 2 miles N of Winster Some rock basins are on it, and a hermitage is below

CAR COLSTON, a parish in Bingham district Notts, near the Car Dyke and the river Trent, 3 miles NNE of Bingham r station Post town, Bingham, under Nottingham Acres, 1,200 Real property, £3,166 Pop, 299 Houses, 49 The property is much subdivided The living is a vicarage in the diocese of Lincoln Value, £203 * Patron, the Rev J C. Girardot The church is good, and there are a Wesleyan chapel, and charities £18

CARCROFT, a hamlet in Owston township and parish, W R Yorkshire, 5½ miles N of Doncaster

CARDEN, a township in Tilston parish, Cheshire, under Broxton hills, 4½ miles N by W of Malpas Acres, 802 Real property, £1,269 Pop, 208 Houses, 40 Carden Hall is a fine old seat, and figured in the public events of 1643

CARDESTON, or CARDISTON, a parish in Atcham district, Salop, near the river Severn, 5 miles S by W of Baschurch r station, and 6¾ W of Shrewsbury It includes part of Wattlesborough township, and its post town is Alberbury, under Shrewsbury Acres, 2,400 Real property, £3,478 Pop, 294 Houses, 65 The property is divided among a few The living is a rectory in the diocese of Hereford Value, £274 Patron, Sir B Leighton, Bart The church is very good

CARDIFF, a town, two parishes, a sub district, and a district in Glamorgan The town is a seaport, a borough, a head quarters of militia, and a polling place, and shares with Swansea the dignity of being the capital of the county It stands on the Julian way, the river Taff, the Glamorgan canal, and the South Wales railway 1½ mile N of the Bristol Channel, 11¾ miles SW of Newport, Monmouth, and 45¼ by railway ESE of Swansea. The tract around it is rich low land, artificially protected from inundation by spring tides, and overlooked on the north by well wooded hills. Great works, variously railway, canal, and docks, connect it with the Bristol Channel, the Taff Vale and the Rhymney railways connect it with the rich mineral fields of Glamorgan and Monmouth, and the South Wales railway, with its ramifications and connexions, gives it communication with all parts of the kingdom

Caerdydd is the Welsh name of the place, and is supposed to be a corruption either of Caer Taf, "the port of the Taff," or Caer Didi, "the port of Didius" Didius was a Roman general, who succeeded Ostorius, in the command of the legions, and is thought to have had a camp here, on the Julian way Jestyn ap Gwrgan, lord of Glamorgan, removed hither from Caerleon, raised some fortifications on the spot, probably around a previous stronghold, and gave assistance to the overthrow, in 1091, of Rhys, Prince of Wales The Norman Fitzhamon, with twelve knights, had been taken into alliance with him, but turned against him, fought and defeated him on a battle ground in the neighbourhood took possession of his fortifications and estates, and built a new strong castle at Cardiff The manor descended from Fitzhamon to the De Clares, the De Spensers, the Beauchamps, and the Nevilles, passed, at Bosworth, to the Crown, was given to Herbert, first Earl of Pembroke, and went, by marriage, first to the Windsors, and next to the Marquis of Bute Robert, Duke of Normandy, eldest son of the Conqueror, was kept a prisoner twenty six years in the castle, and died here in 1144 The town afterwards was strongly fortified, and had an encompassing wall, of five gates Owen Glendower took the castle and destroyed the town The royalists held the place in the civil wars of the 17th century, and are said to have made such stout resistance here to Cromwell as to have been eventually overcome and expelled only by the aid of a traitor, who disclosed a subterraneous passage Rawlins White, a poor but zealous protestant, in the terrible year 1555, was first imprisoned in the castle, and then burnt at the stake in the market place

The ancient gates have disappeared, but portions of the walls on the east side with a watch tower, are preserved. The castle adjoins the Taff, is partly ancient, partly modernized, and includes inhabited buildings, forming a seat of the Marquis of Bute. It consists of a spacious quadrangular court, defended toward the river by a lofty wall, and enclosed on the other side by a lofty earthwork. The gateway and the gate house tower are on the south side, and the latter is alleged to have been the prison of the Duke of Normandy, but shows clear marks of much later date An artificial mound, 75 feet high, is on the north side, was evidently the site of an ancient edifice, and is now crowned by a polygonal shell and perpendicular English tower The inhabited buildings are on the west side, toward the river, were partly renovated, partly built, about the beginning of the present century, include a fine central multangular tower, and some early English turrets, and contain pictures of the Herberts and the Windsors. Four monastic establishments were founded in the town and its vicinity, in the 12th and 13th centuries, some traces of one of them and considerable ruins of another, still exist, and the buildings of the latter were long a seat of the Herberts.

The town was, not long ago, an ill built, dirty village, but is now large, well built, and agreeable It possesses tolerably regular streets, is, in great measure, new, has been much improved in every part, and includes modern suburbs towards Roath and Mundy, at Penarth, Canton, and along the road to Llandaff It displays great public spirit, and, owing to the docks being at some distance from the bulk of the population, it shows less of the unpleasant accompaniments of commerce than almost any other considerable seaport of the kingdom The town-hall is a good modern edifice, and was the scene of an "eisteddfod in 1850 The county jail is on Mr Howard's plan was built in 1832 at a cost of £12,000, and has capacity for 164 male and 61 female prisoners. A handsome bridge, of five arches, built by Parry in 1796, spans the river St John's church is a plain Norman structure of the 13th century, has a lofty, conspicuous, and very beautiful tower, of perpendicular date and character, with open battlements and pinnacles, and contains two curious altar tombs of Sir William and Sir John Herbert St Mary's church is a structure in strange taste, erected in 1842 St Andrew's-church was built in 1863, at a cost of £4,800, and is in the geometric decorated style A chapel of ease in Roath was reconstructed from a secular building in 1859 Two Baptist chapels are recent structures in the Lombardic style A Roman Catholic church was built in 1861, at a cost of upwards of £4 000 A building, for free library and museum, was projected in 1869, to cost £12,900 Other public buildings are several dissenting chapels, a new neat hall of the Young Men's Christian Association, a market-house, a custom house, a theatre, barracks, an infirmary, a free school, alms houses, and a workhouse

The Glamorgan canal, opened in 1794, and 25 miles long, commences in the Taff, near its mouth, with gates 27 feet wide, and has an area of 12½ acres adapted to loading and discharging with from 9 to 13 feet of water The Taff-Vale railway, which is also the Rhymney railway to a deflecting point at Walnut tree Bridge commences at the harbour, and has a station there, called the Cardiff Docks station. The docks comprise the East and West Bute docks, with communication canal, a tidal dock, and three graving docks, and were constructed by the late Marquis of Bute, and by his trustees, at a cost of probably not less than a million of pounds The West Bute dock was opened in 1839 Its length is 4 000 feet, its width 200 feet height of water in springs 28 feet 8½ inches, at neaps 18 feet 7½ inches width of sea gates, 45 feet The East Bute dock was constructed in three successive portions, and completed in 1860 Its length is 4,300 feet, its greatest width, 500 feet, height of water in springs 31 feet 8½ inches, at neaps, 21 feet 7½ inches, width of sea gates, 55 feet The tidal dock was opened in 1857 Its length is ¼ of a mile, its width, 150 feet, average depth of water at springs 26 feet 8½ inches, at neaps, 16 feet 7½ inches All the docks are provided with steam cranes and staiths, the former capable of discharging 40 tons per hour, the latter capable of shipping 150 tons of coal per hour The steam packet harbour has been undergoing an extension and improvement, at an estimated cost of about £10,000 An import warehouse was erected in 1860-1 at the north end of the East Bute dock, at a cost of about £9,000, and a large new basin and a low water pier at the mouth of the Taff, with other works, were in progress in 1869 The harbour of Penarth, at the mouth of the river Ely, opened in 1859, is also practically a harbour of Cardiff See PENARTH The anchorage off the mouth of the Taff protected by Penarth head about 200 feet high, is very good.

The general trade of the port and the town arises from their being the outlet of the agricultural produce of a considerable tract of country, and specially of the mineral produce, coal and iron, of the Taff and its tributary valleys, brought hither by the canal and the railways, and attracted by the magnificent docks The export of coal rose, in the twenty years following 1826, from 40,718 to 626,443 tons, and that of iron, from 64 303 to 222,491 tons The vessels registered at the port, in the beginning of 1868, were 30 small sailing vessels, of aggregately 807 tons, 55 larger sailing vessels, of aggregately 17,960 tons, 33 small steam vessels of aggregately 606 tons, and 5 larger steam vessels, of jointly 733 tons The vessels which entered in 1867, from the British colonies and foreign countries were 441 British sailing-vessels, of aggregately 141,221 tons, 1,356 foreign sailing vessels, of aggregately 325 875 tons, 419 British steam vessels, of aggregately 222,022 tons, and 28 foreign steam vessels, of aggregately 11,667 tons, and coastwise, 2,015 sailing-vessels, of aggregately 165,961 tons, and 831 steam vessels, of aggregately 81,965 tons The vessels which cleared in 1867 were, for abroad, 3,829 sailing vessels of 1,120,972 tons, and 644 steam vessels of 347,390 tons, and coastwise, 7,397 vessels of 630,438 tons The customs amounted in 1858 to £16,647, in 1867, to £14,297 Steamers sail regularly to Burnham, Bristol, Ilfracombe, and Cork. The town has a head post-office‡ a railway station with telegraph, three banking offices, and four chief inns, and publishes two weekly newspapers Markets are held on Wednesdays and Saturdays and fairs on the second Wednesday of March, April, and May, and on 29 June 19 Sept, and 30 Nov Quarter sessions are held on 1 Jan and 2 July, and assizes at the summer circuit. An area, exclusive of suburbs, but conterminate with the two parishes, forms the borough, is governed by a mayor, six aldermen, and eighteen councillors, and unites with Cowbridge and Llantrisaint in sending a member to parliament Electors of all the boroughs in 1868 2,123 Direct taxes, £19 744 Pop of Cardiff borough in 1841, 10,077, in 1861, 32,954 Houses, 4,606 The town gives the title of Baron to the Marquis of Bute The famous King Arthur and Wilson the painter were natives

The two parishes are St. John and St Mary, and there are also chapelries of St Andrew and All Saints, constituted in 1863 and in 1857 Acres, 2,321 Real property, £237,036, of which £91,831 are in railways and £2,686 in gas works Pop the same as the borough The livings of St John, St Mary, and All Saints are vicarages, and that of St. Andrew is a p curacy, in the diocese of Llandaff Value of St John, £260,* of St Mary and All Saints, each £200, of St Andrew, not reported Patron of St John, the Dean and Chapter of Gloucester, of St Mary, the Marquis of Bute, of All Saints, the Bishop of Llandaff, of St Andrew not reported Charities, £137.—The sub district contains also the parishes of Roath, Llandaff, Radyr, St Fagan, Cairau, Leckwith, Penarth, Cogan Lavernock, Michael-stone le Pit Llandough juxta Penarth, St Mellons, and Rumney—the two last electorally in Monmouth Acres, 26,543 Pop, 46 954 Houses, 7,030—The district comprehends also the sub district of Caerphilly, containing the parishes of Eglwysilan, Rudrry, Lisvane Llanedarn Llanishen, Whitchurch, and part of Bedwas, the sub-district of Llantrisaint containing the parishes of Llantrisaint, Llantwit vardre, Pentyrch, Pendoylan, St Bride-super Ely, Peterstone super Ely, and the parochial chapelry of Llanilltern, and the sub district of St Nicholas, containing the parishes of St. Nicholas, St Lythans, St Andrew, St George, Wenvoe, Bonvilston, Michaelstone super Ely, Sully, Coldoxton juxta Barry, Merthyr Dovan, Barry, Porthkerry Penmarl Llancarvan

Llantrithyd, and Welsh St Donats, and the extra parochial tracts of Highlight and Llanvithin Acres, 117 797 Poor rates in 1866, £36 074 Pop in 1861, 74 575 Houses, 12 710 Marriages in 1866 677, births, 2,417,—of which 71 were illegitimate deaths, 1,426,—of which 570 were at ages under 5 years, and 26 at ages above 85 Marriages in the ten years 1851-60 6 238 births, 22,636, deaths, 14,096 The places of worship in 1851 were 50 of the Church of England, with 9,188 sittings, 19 of Independents, with 5,038 s, 24 of Baptists with 6 184 s, 1 of Quakers, with 200 s, 18 of Wesleyan Methodists, with 2 601 s, 25 of Calvinistic Methodists, with 5,731 s, 1 undefined, with 60 s, 1 of Roman Catholics, with 9̣3 s, and 1 of Latter Day Saints, with 250 attendants. The schools were 33 public day schools, with 2,832 scholars, 40 private day schools, with 1,335 s, and 75 Sunday schools, with 5 795 s.

CARDIGAN, a town, a parish, a sub district, and a district in Cardiganshire. The town is a seaport, a borough, and the capital of the county It stands on the river Teifi, 3½ miles from its mouth, 10 miles WNW of Newcastle Emlyn, at the terminus of a railway to it from Carmarthen, originally authorised in 1854, re authorised from Newcastle Emlyn in 1863, opened to Llandyssil in 1864, and near completion to Cardigan in July 1869 The Welsh call it Aberteifi A castle was built at it, in 1160, by Gilbert de Clare, sustained many assaults by alternately the Welsh and the English, changed owners at least half a score of times before 1240, when it was rebuilt by Gilbert Marshall, and was garrisoned by the royalists in the wars of Charles I, sustained then a regular siege, and surrendered to the parliamentarian forces under General Langhorne Remains of it stand on a low cliff, at the foot of the ancient bridge, consist of little more than two bastions and part of a curtain-wall, and are hidden within the enclosure of a modern mansion erected by Mr Bowen A Benedictine priory, a cell to Chertsey, stood in the vicinity of the church, and a modern mansion the seat of the Miles family, occupies its site, and was inhabited by Mrs Philips, who wrote "Letters of Orinda

The town stands on a gentle eminence, comprises two principal streets, contains several good houses, has a suburb on the Pembroke side of the river, called Bridg end, looks well in the distance, and presents a good subject for the pencil, as seen from the bridge It once was walled, but the walls have disappeared A suite of buildings, of picturesque appearance, comprising town hall news room, library grammar school, corn exchange, and public markets, was erected in 1860 at a cost of about £5 000 The previous town hall, used as the county court house was built in 1764 The county jail was erected, in 1793, by Nash and has capacity for 19 male and 4 female prisoners The barracks were constructed in 1847 A handsome seven arched bridge spans the Teifi The church is chiefly perpendicular English, recently restored, consists of spacious nave and elegant chancel, with western square tower, and contains a good canopied piscina There are chapels for Independents, Baptists, Wesleyans, and Calvinistic Methodists. The town has a head post office ‡ a banking office, and three chief inns A weekly market is held on Saturday and fairs on 13 Feb, 5 April, 8 Sept., 10 Nov, and 19 Dec

A good herring fishery and a very productive salmon fishery, are carried on Commerce is much cramped by a dangerous bar in the river where the depth of water at low tides is sometimes so little as 6 feet, and in the average of neaps, 11 feet Vessels of 400 tons occasionally come up to the bridge, but vessels of from 20 to 100 tons are chiefly employed The port s jurisdiction extends from Aberaypon to a point 4 miles below Fishguard The vessels registered at the beginning of 1868 were 89 of 50 tons and under, aggregately 2,587 and 61 of upwards of 50 tons, aggregately 6 944 tons Those which entered in 1867 from the colonies and foreign ports were 2 of jointly 557 tons, and coastwise 574 of aggregately 17 437 tons Those which cleared in 1867 were none for abroad, and 2 sailing of 903 tons, and 8 steam of 600 tons coastwise The chief exports are grain, slates, and bark The customs, in 1867, amounted to nothing The borough includes both the town and the Bridgend suburb, was incorporated by Edward I, is governed by a mayor, four aldermen, and twelve councillors, and unites with Aberystwith, Adpar, and Lampeter, in sending a member to parliament Electors of all the boroughs in 1868, 692 Direct taxes, £4,476 Pop of Cardigan borough in 1841 3,800, in 1861 3,543 Houses, 900 The town gives the title of Earl to the family of Brudenell

The parish comprises 2 412 acres of land and 105 of water Real property, £7,132 Pop., 2,706 Houses, 680 The property is much subdivided. The living is a vicarage in the diocese of St Davids. Value, £173 Patron, the Lord Chancellor —The sub-district contains also the parishes of Llangoedmore, Verwick, Mount, Llantood Bridell, Kilgerran, Monington, Moylgrove, and St Dogmells,—the last six electorally in Pembroke Acres, 27,982 Pop, 8 886 Houses, 2,171 —The district comprehends also the sub district of Llandygwydd, containing the parochial chapelry of Llechryd, and the parishes of Llandygwydd, Aberporth, Blaenporth, Tremain, Mounteddwy, and Llanfihangel Penbedw,—the last two electorally in Pembroke, and the sub district of Newport, containing the parishes of Newport, Dinas, Llanychllwydog, Nevern, Bayvil, Meline, Eglwyswrw, Whitchurch, and Llanfair Nant Gwyn —all electorally in Pembroke Acres 85,481 Poor rates in 1866, £9,713 Pop in 1861, 19,535 Houses, 4,533 Marriages in 1866, 125, births, 436,—of which 21 were illegitimate, deaths, 345 —of which 61 were at ages under 5 years, and 27 at ages above 85 Marriages in the ten years 1851-60, 1,149, births, 4,845, deaths, 3,770 The places of worship in 1851 were 27 of the Church of England, with 4,373 sittings, 17 of Independents, with 4 901 s, 20 of Baptists with 6 092 s 13 of Calvinistic Methodists, with 3,356 s, and 1 of Wesleyan Methodists, with 196 s The schools were 11 public day schools, with 1,079 scholars 17 private day schools with 532 s, 49 Sunday schools, with 6,257 s, and 2 evening schools for adults with 31 s The workhouse is in St Dogmells

CARDIGAN BAY, a gulf on the west coast of Wales, along the counties of Cardigan, Merioneth, and Carnarvon, from Cardigan Head to Braich y Pwll Its length, across the entrance north and south, is 48 miles, its length, from Cardigan Head to the top of a projection between Merioneth and Carnarvon, north north eastward is 64 miles, and its greatest breadth, from the line of entrance to the mouth of the river Dyfi, eastward, is 30 miles Part of its bottom is the submerged tract of Cantref Gwaelod, and is there beset by the reefs of Sarn y Gynfelyn, Sarn y Bwch, and Badrig but the rest is free from obstacles to navigation, and has a depth of from 3 to 30 fathoms Bardsey Island studs it in the vicinity of Braich y Pwll, and is washed by a strong current setting from the south The chief harbours are those of Cardigan Aberaeron Aberystwith, Aberdovey, Barmouth Mochres, Pwllheli, Portmadoc, and Aberdaron See CANTREF GWAELOD and BARDSEY ISLAND

CARDIGAN HEAD, a headland at the northern extremity of Pembrokeshire, on the left side of the mouth of the river Teifi 3½ miles NW of Cardigan

CARDIGAN ISLE, an island in Cardiganshire on the right side of the mouth of the river Teifi, 3½ miles NNW of Cardigan It measures about 40 acres, and is pastured by sheep

CARDIGAN RAILWAY See CARMARTHEN and CARDIGAN RAILWAY

CARDIGANSHIRE a maritime county of South Wales, bounded on the west by Cardigan Bay, on the north by Merioneth on the north east by Montgomery on the east by Radnor and Brecon, on the south by Carmarthen and Pembroke Its length north eastward is 45 miles, its greatest breadth is 35 miles, its circumference is about 150 miles, and its area is 443,387 acres It is the most primitive and the wildest county of South Wales The coast, for the most part, is low and rather tame The interior, except in three valleys, has little level land, includes vast sweeping ranges of hills, and is largely mountainous. The south western portion may comparatively speaking, be called low country, while the north eastern is high, and culminates in Plinlimmon Some parts contain grand scenery, in varieties of the picturesque, but the upland parts generally, exhibit a dreary sameness. The river Dyfi goes to the sea on the northern boundary, the river Teifi goes to the sea on the southern boundary, and the Rheidol, the Ystwith, the Mynach, the Ayron, the Dothie, the Pyscottwr, the Claerwen, the Elan, the Belwyn, the Gwyrai, the Lery, and other streams water the interior Lakes are numerous, but none of them are large Rocks of the lower silurian series occupy the entire area. Metal mines, of high celebrity, yielding great wealth, were worked in the 16th century, were, for a long time, almost wholly abandoned, and have, of late years, been partially resumed Lead, zinc, and silver ores are the chief, and copper ore also is found Slate, for roofs and floors, is worked

The soil, in much of the valleys, is peat or vegetable mould, in the vales among the uplands, chiefly stiff clay, with mixture of light loam, on the higher grounds of the lowland tracts, generally a light sandy loam, from four to twelve inches deep, and on the uplands for the most part a coarse, shallow, barren detritus About one half of the entire area is waste Tolerably good farming is practised in the valleys of the Teifi and the Ayron, and in some other parts, but the husbandry elsewhere is rude and unimproved Lime is brought from Pembroke, and much used as a manure, but sea weed and peat ashes also are much used. Barley and oats are the chief crops while wheat, rye, pease, beans, potatoes, and turnips also are raised. The arable farms may average about 150 acres. Farm buildings have begun to be improved, but the cottages are miserable Butter and pork are produced for the market. The cattle are a small hardy black breed, the sheep also are small, but have begun to be improved by crosses with the Southdowns, the Leicesters, and the Dorsets, and the horses seldom exceed fourteen hands in height, but are strong and hardy Ancient woods were extensive, but have been nearly all swept away Oak, ash, and alder are native trees, and some large plantations of larch have been made The only manufactures of any note are woollens and gloves for local use The Llanelly railway and the Carmarthen and Cardigan railway give facilities to the southeastern and the southern borders, the Aberystwith and Welsh Coast railway gives facilities to the northern districts, and a railway partly in progress in 1869, partly then in operation, in connection with the Central Wales system from Llanidloes to the neighbourhood of Newcastle Emlyn, is of value to the central districts Good roads connect the towns, and traverse much of the interior

The county contains sixty five parishes and is divided into the boroughs of Cardigan and Aberystwith, and the hundreds of Geneur, Ilar, Moyddyn, Penarth, and Troedyraur The registration county excludes 11,264 acres to Montgomery, includes 162,760 acres of Carmarthen and Pembroke, measures 594,883 acres, and is divided into the districts of Cardigan, Newcastle Emlyn, Lampeter, Aberayron, Aberystwith, and Tregaron The market towns are Cardigan, Aberystwith, Lampeter, Tregaron, and part of Newcastle Emlyn The chief seats are Gogerthan, Nanteos, Peterwell Crosswood Blaenhant, Coedmore, Hafod, Mabus, Allt yr Odyn, Llanina, Tyglyn, and Llanerchayron Real property in 1815, £145,933 in 1843, £205,328, in 1851, £216,835, in 1860, £226,552 The county is governed by a lord lieutenant, a high sheriff, and about forty five magistrates It is in the South Wales judicial circuit, and the Home military district The assizes are held at Cardigan, and quarter sessions at Aberayron The police force, in 1864, consisted of 3? men, at a cost of £2 553, the crimes committed were 40 the depredators and suspected persons at large were 113, and the houses of bad character, 47 One member is sent to parliament for the county, and one for the boroughs of Cardigan, Aberystwith Lampeter, and Adpar The electors for the county in 1868 were 3,520 The county is in the diocese of St David's and, with parts of adjoining counties, forms an archdeaconry Pop in 1801, 42,956, in 1821, 57,784, in 1841, 68,766, in 1861, 72,245 Inhabited houses, 15,754, uninhabited 529, building, 105

The territory now forming Cardiganshire was anciently part of Dimetia. It had an important station of the Romans, called Loventium, at Llanio isan, and was nominally included in their Britannia Secunda. The Danes harassed it in 987 and 1071 The Normans came into it in 1093, but were driven out in 1097 Henry I granted it to the Strongbows, Henry II restored it to Prince Rhys, and Edward I, in 1284, on the overthrow of the last Llewelyn, united it to England Druidical monuments occur at Yspytty Cynwyn, Alltgoch near Lampeter, Carrog near Llanllwchairn and in other places The Roman road, called Sarn Helen, went through Loventium toward Penalt and Carnarvon British fortifications stood at Cardigan, Aberystwith, Ystradmeiric, Lampeter Llanrhysted, Kilcennin, Dinerth, Abercenion, Castell Gwalter, Castell Flemish, Moyddyn, Penweddic, Aberayron, and a number of other places. A famous abbey stood at Strata Florida, now Ystrad flur, on the Roman way, and monastic houses stood at Cardigan, Llanrhysted, Lampeter, and Llandewi Brefi

CARDINAL'S CAP See WHITE HILL.

CARDINGTON, a village and a parish in the district and county of Bedford The village stands on an affluent of the river Ouse, adjacent to the Midland railway, 2½ miles SE of Bedford, and has a station on the railway The parish includes also the township of East Cotts Post town, Bedford Acres, 5 170 Real property, £9,079 Pop, 1,419 Houses, 275 Cardington House is the seat of the Whitbreads, and was, for some years, the residence of the philanthropist Howard The living is a vicarage in the diocese of Ely Value, £245.* Patron, Trinity College Cambridge The church is later English There are an Independent chapel, a handsome industrial school, a British school, alms houses with £50 a year, and other charities £28.

CARDINGTON, a village and a parish in Church Stretton district, Salop The village stands on a pleasant spot, under Cardington hill, 2½ miles E of the Shrewsbury and Hereford railway, and 4 ENE of Church Stretton, and has a post office under Church Stretton The parish includes also the townships of Broom, Chatwall, Comley, Enchmarsh, Holt Preen, Lydley Hayes, Plaish Willstone, and part of Gretton Acres, 6,713 Real property, £4,723 Pop, 769 Houses, 141 The property is much subdivided Fine clay and quartz for the potteries are found The living is a vicarage in the diocese of Hereford Value, £287 * Patron, R Hunt, Esq The church is good A school has £25 from endowment, and other charities, £53

CARDINHAM, a parish in Bodmin district, Cornwall, on the river Fowey, 3 miles NNE of Bodmin Road r station, and 4 E by N of Bodmin It has a post office under Bodmin Acres, 9,534 Real property £3,881 Pop, 717 Houses 129 The property is subdivided The manor belonged to Robert de Cardinnam, ancestor of the Lords Dinham, and has traces of an ancient castle Glynn, a beautiful place on the Fowey, is the seat of Lord Vivian, and contains an early portrait by Reynolds, which opened the way to his career as an artist Cardinham Bury is an ancient circular entrenchment. The living is a rectory in the diocese of Exeter Value, £524 * Patron, Mrs Vivian The church is good, and has a brass of a priest

CARDISTON See CARDESTON

CAR DYKE a cut in the fens of Lincoln, from Thurlby, northward to Sleaford canal It is 20 miles long and 60 feet wide, extended formerly to the rivers Welland and Witham, and is thought to have been a work of the Romans

CAREBY, a parish in Bourn district, Lincoln on a branch of the river Glen 1½ mile SW of little Bytham r station, and 5½ WSW of Bourn Post town, Castle-Bytham, under Stamford Acres, 1 451 Real property, £1,878 Pop, 107 Houses, 23 The property is divided among a few The manor belonged formerly to the Hatchers, and belongs now to G B Reynardson, Esq The living is a rectory, united with the p curacy of Holywell and Aunby, in the diocese of Lincoln Value, £400 * Patron, G B Reynardson, Esq The church is very good.

CARESWELL. See CAVERSWALL.

CAREW, or CAREY, a village and a parish in the district and county of Pembroke. The village stands on a creek of Milford haven, near the Pembroke and Tenby railway, 4 miles ENE of Pembroke. Here is a very ancient and beautiful cross, probably Saxon or Danish, of a single shaft, 14 feet high, covered with Runic carvings. The parish comprises 5,256 acres of land, and 380 of water, and its post town is Pembroke Real property, £5,953, of which £458 are in quarries. Pop. 993. Houses, 216 The property is much subdivided The manor belonged to the princes of South Wales, was given as a dowry with Nesta, daughter of Rhys ap Tewdwr, to Gerald de Windsor, passed to Sir Rhys ap Thomas, gave entertainment to the Earl of Richmond, on his way to Bosworth field, was, soon afterwards, the scene of a great tournament, the first show of its kind in Wales, and belongs now to the Carews of Crocomb. A fortress stood here in the times of the Welsh princes, and a magnificent mansion was added to this in the time of Henry VII Some part of the ancient fortress seems still to exist in a shattered, ivy-clad barbican, and the shell of the added mansion still stands, and is one of the finest ruins in Wales. The architecture is rich late perpendicular, the windows are large, square, and lantern-like, and the great hall has a lofty porch and measures 102 feet by 20 Milton House, Freestone Hall, and Wilsdon are fine mansions and the last occupies ground on which Cromwell had his quarters when besieging Pembroke castle Extensive limestone quarries were worked, but have been stopped The living is a vicarage in the diocese of St David's Value, £182 * Patron, the Bishop of St David's. The church is early English, with good perpendicular tower and contains monuments of the Carews and others. The vicarage of Redberth is a separate benefice

CAREY, a locality 6½ miles from Ross, in Hereford with a post office under Ross

CAREY, Northumberland See CARY COATS.

CARFAN See PRISK and CARFAN

CARGO, or CRAGHOW, a township in Stanwix parish Cumberland on the river Eden, adjacent to the Silloth railway, 3 miles NW of Carlisle Acres, 1,196 Real property, £2,553 Pop, 262 Houses, 63

CARGO FLEET See CLEVELAND PORT

CARHAM, a village and a parish in Glendale district, Northumberland The village stands adjacent to the river Tweed, to the Tweedmouth and Kelso railway, and to the boundary with Scotland, 5½ miles WSW of Cornhill, and has a station on the railway The parish includes also the townships of Shidlaw, Downham, Hagg, New Learmouth, West Learmouth, East and West Mindrim Moneylaws, Preston, Tythehill, Wark, and Wark Common, and its post town is Coldstream Acres 10,382, of which 127 are water Real property, £17,411 Pop, 1,274 Houses, 236 The property is divided among a few Carham Hall belongs to the heirs of A Compton, Esq Shidlaw hill and other offsets of the Cheviots are in the south, and command charming views A house of black monks, a cell to Kirkham priory in Yorkshire, anciently stood here, and was burned by the Scots under Wallace, whose place of encampment is still called Campfield Three sanguinary battles were fought in the parish, one at an early period, between the Saxons and the Danes, the other two, in 1018 and 1370, between the English and the Scots. The living is a vicarage in the diocese of Durham Value, £233 * Patrons, the heirs of A Compton Esq The church is good

CARHAMPTON, a village, a parish, and a hundred in Somerset The village stands near the coast, 1¼ mile SE of Dunster, and 4 W of Watchet r station It dates from ancient times, under the name of Carumtune, and is a seat of petty sessions The parish includes also the hamlet of Rodhuish, and is in the district of Williton Post town, Dunster, under Taunton Acres, 5,724, of which 525 are water Real property, £6,076 Pop, 706 Houses, 141 The property is divided among a few The surface is diversified with glen and hill The living is a vicarage united with the p curacy of Rodhuish, in the diocese of Bath and Wells Value, £182 Patron, J F Luttrell, Esq The church is ancient, interesting, and good and contains a screen Charities, £9 —The hundred contains sixteen parishes. Acres, 60 350 Pop, 8,502 Houses, 1,674

CARHARRACK, a locality 2 miles from Scorrier Gate r station, in Cornwall, with a post office under Scorrier

CARHAYES BARTON, a hamlet in St. Michael Carhayes parish, Cornwall, 3 miles SE of Tregony

CARHAYES ST MICHAEL. See MICHAEL-CARHAYES, (ST)

CARINGTON See CARRINGTON

CARISBROOKE, a village and a parish in the Isle of Wight The village stands on an affluent of the river Medina, 1 mile SW of Newport, was formerly the capital of the island and a market town, and has a post office under Newport A Roman station seems to have been here, and previously, perhaps, a British city The presence of the Romans here, or even anywhere in the island, has been doubted, but was fully proved in 1859 by the discovery of a Roman villa of about 120 feet by 50, with two large halls, tesselated pavements, a semicircular bath, a hypocaust, some coins, and a few small articles. An early fortress crowned an adjacent hill, 239 feet high, and was taken, in 530, by Cerdic, the Saxon A castle, on the site of this, was built by William Fitz Osborne the first Norman lord of Wight, rebuilt, in the time of Henry I, by Richard de Redvers, Earl of Devon, enlarged, in 1262-93, by Isabella de Fortibus, repaired and outwardly strengthened by Elizabeth, used as a state prison by Cromwell, and made then the prison of Charles I and his children, used as a state prison also by Charles II, long occupied by the governor and the garrison of the Isle of Wight, allowed eventually to go greatly to decay and subjected recently to considerable restoration The site is very fine, the appearance of the castle is picturesque, and a walk of about a mile goes round it, commanding delightful views The encompassing bastions, faced with stone, are of the time of Elizabeth, the entrance, by archway stone bridge, and machicolated gatehouse, with flanking circular towers, is partly of the time of Edward IV, partly of the time of Elizabeth, the range of building containing Charles I's prison rooms, on the left past the gatehouse, belongs to the later years of the 15th century, the polygonal keep, on a moated mound, in the north east corner of the inner court, was probably the work of Richard de Redvers, the great hall, now divided into two stories, and otherwise modernized, is early English, and was probably the work of Isabella de Fortibus, and the chapel, at right angles with the hall, seems to have been constructed along with it, and was long desecrated, and afterwards restored The castle well is a regular excavation through solid rock, and famous for its depth, reputed to be 300 feet, though really no more than 145, and is covered by a structure of the 15th century, recently restored Sir William Davenant, the poet, was confined in the castle

The parish includes also the hamlets of Bowcombe, Billingham and part of Chillerton, Parkhurst forest with part of Parkhurst prison, Albany barracks, and the Isle of Wight house of industry Acres, 7,409 Real property, £24,7?4 Pop, 7,502 Houses, 1,1?6 The property is much subdivided A priory was founded near the church by Fitz Osborne attached to the Benedictine abbey of Lire, and given by Henry V to his new establishment at Sheen The living is a vicarage, united with the p curacy of Northwood, in the diocese of Winchester Value £?00 * Patron, Queen's College Oxford The church was built by Fitz Osborne, deprived of its chancel and north aisle in the time of

Elizabeth, has a fine tower, with pinnacles and an octagonal turret, and contains two interesting monuments of Lady Wadham and William Keeling The p curacy of St John and that of St Nicholas in the Castle are separate charges Value of St John, not reported,* of St Nicholas, £24 There are an Independent chapel and charities £30 A Dominican priory for eighteen nuns was built in 1867, at a cost of £12,000, defrayed by the Countess of Clare

CARK, a village on the west coast of Morecambe bay in Lancashire, 2 miles SW by S of Cartmel It has a post office under Newton-in Cartmel, and a station, jointly with Cartmel, on the Ulverstone and Lancaster railway, and a public coach runs daily from it to Newby Bridge

CARKIN, a township in Forcett parish, N R Yorkshire, 8 miles NNE of Richmond Acres, 650 Pop, 55 Houses, 13

CARLATION, an extra parochial tract in Brampton district, Cumberland, 10 miles ESE of Carlisle. Acres, 1,810 Pop, 71 Houses, 10

CARLBURY, a hamlet in Coniscliffe parish, Durham, on the river Tees, 5½ miles WNW of Darlington. Pop, 44 Limestone is worked

CARLBY, a parish in Bourn district Lincoln, on the river Glen and the Great Northern railway, near Essendine r station, and 5 miles NNE of Stamford Post town, Stamford. Acres, 1 020 Real property, £1,535 Pop, 183 Houses, 40 The property is divided among a few The living is a rectory in the diocese of Lincoln Value, £195 * Patrons, the Marquis of Exeter and Sir E Smith, Bart The church is good. Charities, £7

CARLCOATES, a hamlet in Thurlestone township, Penistone parish W R Yorkshire, 1 mile W of Penistone Pop, 332.

CARLEOL See CARLISLE

CARLESFORD See CARLFORD

CARLES WORK, a stone embankment on the moors, between Castleton and Hathersage, in Derby It is, in some parts, 8 feet high Its origin is unknown

CARLETON a township in St Cuthbert parish, Cumberland, adjacent to the Newcastle railway, 2 miles SE of Carlisle Pop, 181 Houses 33

CARLETON, a township in Drigg parish, Cumberland, on the river Mite, near the coast, 2 miles NNE of Ravenglass Pop, 143 Carleton Hall is the seat of the Burroughs

CARLETON, a hamlet in Penrith parish, Cumberland, on the river Eamont, 1 mile SSE of Penrith Pop, 81 Carleton Hall was formerly the seat of the Carletons, and belongs now to the Cowpers.

CARLETON, a township in Pontefract parish, W R Yorkshire, 1 mile S of Pontefract Acres, 620 Real property, £2,012 Pop, 191 Houses, 44

CARLETON, Durham, Notts, Leicester, Suffolk, and Yorkshire See CARLTON

CARLETON, or CARLTON, a township chapelry in Snaith parish, W R Yorkshire, near the river Aire and the Goole railway, 2 miles N of Snaith It has a post office under Selby Acres, 3,070 Real property, £7,479 Pop, 752 Houses, 183 The property is much subdivided. The living is a p curacy in the diocese of York Value, £168 * Patron, the Rev W W Ware The church was built in 1863 There are a Roman Catholic chapel, a national school and charities £25

CARLETON FOREHOE, a parish in Forehoe district, Norfolk, on the river Yare, 2 miles NE of Kimberley r station, and 3½ N by W of Wymondham Post town, Wymondham Acres 772 Real property, £1,732 Pop, 121 Houses, 25 The property is divided among a few The living is a rectory in the diocese of Norwich Value, £150 * Patron, Lord Wodehouse The church is later English with a square tower, and was repaired in 1839 Charities £26

CARLETON (GREAT AND LITTLE), a township in Poulton le Fylde parish, Lancashire, adjacent to the Blackpool railway, 1 mile SW of Poulton Acres, 1,979 Real property, £3 905 Pop 363 Houses 76

CARLETON ST PETER, a parish in Loddon district, Norfolk near the river Yare, 3 miles NNW of Loddon, and 3½ SW by S of Buckenham r station Post town, Loddon, under Norwich Acres, 772 Real property, £1,159 Pop, 79 Houses, 18 The property is divided among a few The living is a rectory, united with the rectory of Ashby, in the diocese of Norwich Value, £294 Patrons, Sir W B Proctor and Sir C H Rich, Barts The church is good

CARLFORD, a sub district and a hundred in Suffolk The sub district is in Woodbridge district, lies between Woodbridge and Ipswich and contains thirteen parishes Acres, 19,834 Pop., 5,359 Houses, 1,201 The hundred contains the same parishes as the sub district, and two more, but is joined to Colneis.

CARLINGCOTT, a hamlet in Camerton and Dunkerton parishes, Somerset, 4½ miles SE of Bath

CARLINGHOW a hamlet in Guisbrough township and parish, N R Yorkshire, near Guisbrough.

CARLINGHOW, a hamlet in Batley township and parish, W R Yorkshire, 6½ miles NW of Wakefield

CARLISLE, a city and a district in Cumberland, and a diocese in Cumberland, Westmoreland, and Lancashire The city stands on the river Eden, at the influx of the Petterill and the Caldew, on the great western line of communication from England to Scotland, within a mile of the Roman wall, 9½ miles SSE of Gretna, and 301 NNW of London Railways go from it in six directions, toward Hawick, Annandale, Silloth, Maryport, Lancaster, and Newcastle upon Tyne, and give it communication with all parts of Great Britain, and all of them meet in one central station

History —A Roman station stood on the city's site, and bore the name of Lugavallum, signifying the "tower by the wall" This was shortened by the Britons into Luel, and prefixed with Caer, their word for a fort, and the name Caer Luel passed, in course of time, into Carleol and Carlisle Roman altars, inscriptions, vases, coins, and other relics have been found within the city, and Roman roads went from it to Longtown, Ellenborough, and Lancaster A native fortress succeeded the Roman station, was maintained by both the Saxons and the Normans, and made resistance to the Picts and the Scots A city wall was constructed at an early period, perhaps in the 7th century, was reconstructed at subsequent periods, enclosed a triangular space of 2,000, 650, and 460 yards, and had three gates The Cumbrian king Arthur figures in two famous ancient ballads —the one on the marriage of his knight Sir Gawaine, the other entitled the "Boy and the Mantle"—as having held his court at Carlisle The Northumbrian king Egfred founded here a religious house, and placed it under his establishment at Lindesfarne The Danes took and wasted the town in 875 William Rufus revived it, and gave it a new fortress Stephen resided some time in it, and greatly improved its defences. The Scots besieged it under their kings David I, Malcolm IV, William the Lion, and Alexander II, and held possession of it during an aggregate of eighteen years. Edward I retreated to it from Falkirk in 1298, convoked his barons and knights at it in 1300, and held his last parliament in it in 1307 It suffered much and often in the subsequent wars, resisted a siege, in 1315, by Bruce, and both then and afterwards endured great disaster It also figured in the raid, in 1388, which led to the battle of Otterburn, and served for ages as the main bulwark, in the west against the Scottish forays Mary queen of Scots, was here taken into custody, Kinmont Willie, the notable Border trooper, celebrated in song and story was rescued from durance here by a bold exploit of Scott of Buccleuch, and "Hughie the Graeme, Hobbie Noble, and other famous Scottish reivers, were here put to death The city shared much in the troubles which followed the Reformation, sustained a siege of six months, in 1645, from General Leslie's army, and was held by Prince Charles Edward, in 1745, from the time of his advance into England till after the retreat of his main force to Scotland Executions in it, during about two centuries were more numerous than in any other provincial town in the kingdom, and those which fol lowed the affair of Prince Charles Edward were rendered memorable and ghastly by the fixing of the heads of the victims on the city gates Hence says a poetical fragment preserved in Scott's Border Antiquities—

' When I first cam by merry Carlisle,
Was ne'er a town sae sweetly seeming;
The white rose flaunted o'er the wall
The thistled banners far were streaming!
When I cam next by merry Carlisle
O sad sad seem'd the town an eerie!
The auld auld men cam out and wept—
O maiden come ye to seek yere dearie!
* * *
His lang lang hair in yellow hanks
Waved o'er his cheeks sae sweet and ruddie,
But now they wave o'er Carlisle yetts
In dripping ringlets clotting bloodie!

Site and Streets —The city occupies a swell or gentle eminence in the midst of an extensive, fertile, well wooded plain. The environs are all rich low country, profusely adorned with water, culture, parks, and mansions. The higher points both within the city and around it command a brilliant panorama, away to the Northumberland hills, the Scottish mountains, Criffel beyond the Solway, and the group of Skiddaw The exterior of the city, as seen from various approaches, presents a striking appearance, and looks as if combining modern elegance with remains of antiquity The interior, as entered from the railway station, seems entirely, neatly, and briskly modern The castle, which most prominently links it with the past, does not come immediately into view, and the cathedral which also speaks largely of the past, has been so outwardly renovated as to appear almost new The three principal streets, English street, Scotch street, and Castle street, diverge from the market place, adjacent to the central railway station, and are wide and handsome Other streets are straight, airy, and well built, and the city as a whole, seems little different from a well planned, lively, thriving, modern town

Public Buildings.—The court houses and the county jail form a grand suite of buildings, and were erected, after designs by Smirke, at a cost of about £100,000 The court houses stand partly on the site of what was called the citadel, comprising two very strong circular towers for defending the city gates, and they themselves form two circular Gothic towers, on opposite sides of the upper end of English street. The county jail stands on the site of a black friary, was partly remodelled, and principally rebuilt in 1869, and now has capacity for 112 male and 55 female prisoners An elegant bridge, of five elliptical arches spans the Eden on the great road to the north was erected by Smirke, at a cost of upwards of £70 000 and is connected with the city by an arched causeway, nearly ¼ of a mile long Two small bridges span the Petteril and the Caldew The central railway station stands partly on the site of the citadel, presents a neat front to the head of English street is a long, spacious, well-contrived arcade, and contains handsome refreshment and waiting rooms The news room, reading and coffee rooms, are a beautiful recent structure, erected by subscription from a design by Rickman An octagonal chimney stalk, 305 feet high, connected with a large cotton factory, is a conspicuous object Other noticeable things are a market cross of 1682, an old town hall where the mayor's court and the city sessions are held, a new town hall, where the city council and other corporate bodies meet a statue of the late Earl of Lonsdale on a pedestal in Court square a statue of Mr Steel in Market square a theatre, assembly rooms the water works formed in 1848, and the great public buildings to be noticed in subsequent paragraphs

The Castle —The fortress built by William Rufus probably occupied the site of the previous Saxon fortress and Roman station Buildings were added to it, or erected around by several kings, forming fortifications, prisons and palace, and all were called the castle but they have, in recent times, been greatly altered The site is a bold but not high eminence, overlooking the Eden, and commands one of the best prospects which the city or the environs afford, over the great rich surrounding country The chief existing structures are a very thick enclosing wall, and buildings used as barracks The entrance is an embattled gateway, with the ancient portcullis, and a defaced sculpture, believed to represent the arms of Henry II A half moon battery formerly defended the inner court, but is now dismantled The great keep still stands, and is a lofty massive tower, but has been converted into an armoury The hall of the palace was destroyed in 1827, the chapel of it was turned into barracks in 1835, and a small staircase is the only other part of it that remains Sir William Wallace rested a night under the castle gate, and Waverley, in Sir Walter Scott's novel, watched from the gatehouse Fergus MacIvor going out to execution

The Cathedral —This was originally the church of an Augustinian priory, built, in 1101, by Walter the Norman and endowed by Henry I, but it has undergone sweeping changes, and great recent restorations "The cloisters of the priory have disappeared, but the entrance-gateway and the fratry or refectory remains The gateway has a circular arch with an inscription recording it to have been built by the prior, Christopher Slee. The fratry is lighted on the south side by a row of well proportioned Tudor windows, and adorned on the opposite wall with three niches, surmounted by elegant crocketted canopies, and it contains a curious stone chair, with impanelled foliated ceiling called the confessional This is the place in which Edward I. held his parliament and it is now used as the chapter room The cathedral is cruciform and has a square embattled tower, 127 feet high, rising over the intersection of the cross The nave and the transepts are Norman, narrow and without aisles Their columns are very massive, each 17½ feet in circumference, and 14 feet 2 inches high The nave was deprived of about 90 feet of its length in the time of Cromwell to yield material for the erection of guard houses and batteries, and the rest of it was afterwards closed with a wall, and fitted up as a parish church The transepts measure 124 feet in length and 28 feet in width and the north one is now used as the consistory court The choir was built at great expense, with vast effort, by aid of money obtained through sale of indulgences and remissions, in the reign of Edward III Most of it is early English, but the east end is the decorated Its length is 137 feet, its width, 71 feet, its height, 75 feet The north side makes a fine appearance to the street, and is divided from the thoroughfare by a new enclosure wall and elegant iron railing and by a belt of ground with a row of trees The east end shows rich grandeur of design, with a most magnificent central window, with other windows to correspond, and with bold buttresses, crocketted pinnacles, and gable crosses The interior is arranged in side aisles and central aisle, with triforium and clerestory The columns are clustered, and the capitals are adorned with carved figures and flowers The clerestory has a rich parapet pierced with foliated circles The great east window, as seen in the interior has been pronounced by many competent judges the finest decorated window in the kingdom It measures 60 feet by 30, contains nine lights, and is filled in the head with surpassingly rich flowing tracery The windows of the side aisles have a corresponding character A row of beautiful niches appears below them, and is continued all round the walls A very fine organ, erected in 1856, stands above the entrance to the choir The stalls are embellished with tabernacle work, in carved oak, black with age The bishop's throne and the pulpit are modern and not so rich in design, yet elegant and stately The screens in the aisles show some curious legendary paintings from the histories of St Augustine, St Anthony, and St Cuthbert A fine mural monument to Dr Paley simply recording his name and age, appears in the north aisle, and monuments to Bishops Bell Law, Smith, Robinson Barrow, and other distinguished men are in other parts A small chapel, dedicated to St. Catherine, founded and endowed by John de Capella, a citizen of Carlisle, stands in the south aisle, adjoining the transept. The deanery stands within the precincts of the cathedral. It was built by Prior Senhouse, in 1507, and contains a fine apartment used as a drawing-room, with a remarkably ornate ceiling in carved emblazoned oak."

Churches.—St. Mary's church is part of the cathedral nave. St. Cuthbert's church is a plain structure of 1778, on the site of a previous very old one; and has a monument of Dean Carlyle. Trinity church, in Caldewgate, and Christ church, in Botchergate, are handsome structures of 1830, the former in the Tudor style, the latter in the early English, each with a tower and spire. St. Stephen's and St. John's are beautiful edifices of 1865, the former in early and decorated English, the latter in pure early English. The first five are vicarages, and the last a p. curacy, in the dio. of C. Value of each, £300. Patrons of the first four, the Dean and Chapter; of St. Stephen's, the Bishop; of St. John, Five Trustees. The places of worship, in 1851, were 5 of the Ch. of England, with 4,039 sittings; 1 of the Ch. of Scotland, with 750 s.; 1 of U. Presbyterians, with 470 s.; 3 of Independents, with 1,370 s.; 1 of Baptists, with 1,000 s.; 1 of Quakers, with 360 s.; 2 of Wesleyan Methodists, with 1,000 s.; 1 of the Wesleyan Association, with 1,000 s.; 1 of Latter Day Saints, with 89 s.; and one of Roman Catholics, with 1,000 s. Four other churches are in the rural parts of the parish; a new church of St. Mary-Without, to cost £4,000, was projected in 1869; a new Presbyterian church, in plain Gothic, was built in 1863; and an Evangelical Union chapel also is recent.

Schools, &c.—The grammar-school was founded in 1546, by Henry VIII.; has two exhibitions to Queen's college, Oxford; and numbers among its pupils Bishop Thomas and Dean Carlyle. A girls' school has an endowed income of £37. There are an academy of arts, and a literary, philosophical, and mechanical institution. The infirmary is a recent edifice, built by subscription; and has a tetrastyle Doric portico. The dispensary is notable for a child born in 1788 without a brain, who lived six days. Alms-houses and other charities have an endowed income of £85.

Trade, &c.—Manufactures of cotton thread, ginghams, checks, hats, whips, hooks, and other articles are carried on. The large factory, with the lofty chimney stalk, employs about 550 hands. There are also iron-foundries, tan-yards, and breweries. Vast stir and much business arise from the traffic on the railways. Markets are held on Wednesdays and Saturdays; and fairs on 26 Aug., 19 Sept., and the first and second Saturday after 10 Oct. The city was formerly connected with the Solway by a ship canal, now superseded by the Silloth railway; and it ranks as a seaport, with Allonby and Port-Carlisle as sub-ports. The vessels registered at it in 1868 were 8 sailing-vessels, of aggregately 288 tons, 14 sailing-vessels, of aggregately 1,883 tons, and 6 steam-vessels, of aggregately 1,202 tons; and the vessels which entered in that year were 8 from British colonies, of aggregately 3,705 tons, 7 from foreign countries, of aggregately 1,812 tons, 36 sailing-vessels coastwise, of aggregately 2,757 tons, and 343 steam-vessels coastwise, of aggregately 53,013 tons. The vessels registered at the end of 1862 were 23 sailing-vessels of aggregately 2,370 tons, and 5 steam-vessels of aggregately 806 tons; and the commerce in that year, with foreign and colonial ports, comprised 13 vessels inwards of aggregately 3,301 tons, and 8 vessels outwards of aggregately 2,695 tons. The customs amounted, in 1858, to £25,535; in 1867, to £21,967. The city has a head post-office,‡ a telegraph-office, three banking-offices, and seven chief inns; and publishes several newspapers. Races are run, in the immediate neighbourhood, on a fine course of 1 mile 90 yards, in July.

The Borough.—The city is a borough by prescription; was chartered by Henry II.; is governed by a mayor, 10 aldermen, and thirty councillors; and sends two members to parliament. Its borough limits, both for government and for representation, comprise the townships of Botchergate and English-street in St. Cuthbert parish; the townships of Scotch-street, Fisher-street, Castle-street, Abbey-street, and part of Caldewgate, in St. Mary parish; and the extra-parochial place of Eaglesfield-abbey. Assizes are held at both circuits of the judges; and quarter sessions on 1 Jan., 9 April, 2 July, and 15 Oct. Real property, £86,723; of which £7,119 are in railways, and £2,734 in gas-works. *Direct taxes,* £14,348. Electors in 1868, 1,606. Pop. in 1841, 20,815; in 1861, 29,417. Houses, 5,140. The city gives the title of Earl to a branch of the Howard family.

The District.—The registration district comprehends the sub-district of St. Mary, containing all the borough parts of St. Mary parish, with the rest of Caldewgate township; the sub-district of St. Cuthbert, containing all the townships of St. Cuthbert parish, and Wreay chapelry in St. Mary; the sub-district of Stanwix, containing the parishes of Stanwix and Rockliffe, and the extra-parochial tract of King-Moor; the sub-district of Burgh, containing the parishes of Burgh-by-Sands, Kirkandrews-upon-Eden, Beaumont, and Grinsdale; the sub-district of Dalston, containing the parishes of Dalston and Orton, and the Cummersdale township of St. Mary; and the sub-district of Wetheral, containing the parishes of Crosby-upon-Eden, Warwick, and five townships of Wetheral. Acres, 70,810. Poor-rates in 1866, £17,364. Pop. in 1861, 41,820. *Houses,* 8,299. *Marriages in* 1866, 421; births, 1,412,—of which 153 were illegitimate; deaths, 977,—of which 321 were at ages under 5 years, and 20 at ages above 85. Marriages in the ten years 1851-60, 2,644; births, 14,681; deaths, 9,983. The places of worship in 1851 were 21 of the Church of England, with 8,464 sittings; 1 of the Church of Scotland, with 750 s.; 1 of the United Presbyterian church, with 470 s.; 3 of Independents, with 1,370 s.; 1 of Baptists, with 1,000 s.; 3 of Quakers, with 710 s.; 5 of Wesleyan Methodists, with 1,260 s.; 12 of the Wesleyan Methodist Association, with 1,430 s.; 2 of Primitive Methodists with 100 s.; 1 undefined, with 100 s.; 2 of Latter Day Saints, with 141 s.; and 2 of Roman Catholics, with 1,130 s. The schools were 35 public day schools, with 3,640 scholars; 64 private day schools, with 1,830 s.; 35 Sunday schools, with 3,913 s.; and 6 evening schools for adults, with 251 s. There are two workhouses, both in the city.

The Diocese.—The see was founded, in 1132, by Henry I. The first bishop was Athelwold, the king's confessor; and among his successors have been De Everdon, De Kirkby, Merks, Oglethorpe, Usher, Nicholson, and Sterne. The bishop's income is £4,500; and his residence is Rose Castle. The chapter comprises a dean, two archdeacons, four canons, four honorary canons, and a chancellor. The diocese comprehends all Cumberland, except Alston parish, all Westmoreland, and the Lancashire deaneries of Cartmel and Ulverstone; and is divided into the archdeaconries of Carlisle and Westmoreland. Pop. in 1861, 266,591. Some livings have recently been raised in status, as named in our articles on them; but all will be named here as they stood in 1861.

The archdeaconry of Carlisle comprises the rural deaneries of Appleby, Brampton, Carlisle, Greystoke, Keswick, Kirkby-Stephen, Lowther, Penrith, and Wigton. The deanery of Appleby includes the rectories of Asby, Dufton, Kirkby-Thore, Long Marton, Newbiggin, and Ormside; the vicarages of Appleby-St. Lawrence and Appleby-St. Michael; and the p. curacies of Milburn and Temple-Sowerby. The deanery of Brampton includes the rectories of Bewcastle, Castlecarrock, Nether Denton, and Stapleton; the vicarages of Brampton and Irthington; and the p. curacies of Cumrew, Cumwhitton, Over Denton, Farlam, Hayton, Lanercost, Gilsland, Nichol-Forest, and Walton. The deanery of Carlisle includes the rectories of Arthuret, Kirkandrews-upon-Eden, Beaumont, Kirkandrews-upon-Esk, Kirkbampton, Kirklinton, Orton, and Scaleby; the vicarages of Burgh-by-Sands, Crosby-upon-Eden, and Stanwix; and the p. curacies of Carlisle-St. Mary, Carlisle-St. Cuthbert, Carlisle-Trinity, Carlisle-Christchurch, Upperby, Wreay, Grinsdale, Hesket-in-the-Forest, Armathwaite, Rockliffe, Houghton, Wetheral, Warwick, Holm-Eden, and Scotby. The deanery of Greystoke includes the rectories of Greystoke, Skelton, and Hutton-in-the-Forest; the vicarages of Castle-Sowerby and Dacre; and the p. curacies of

Naughton Head, Matterdale, Mungrisedale, Watermillock, Patterdale, and Sebergham. The deanery of Keswick includes the vicarage of Crosthwaite, and the p. curacies of Keswick St John, Borrowdale, Grange, Newlands, St John in the-Vale, Thornthwaite, Wythburn, Bassenthwaite, Buttermere, Lorton, Threlkeld, and Wythop. The deanery of Kirkby Stephen includes the rectories of Crosby Garret and Great Musgrave, the vicarages of Brough under Stainmore, Kirkby Stephen, and Warcop, and the p. curacies of Stainmore, Mallerstang, Soulby, and Ravenstonedale. The deanery of Lowther includes the rectories of Cliburn, Clifton, and Lowther, the vicarages of Askham, Bampton, Crosby Ravensworth, Morland, Orton, and Shap, and the p. curacies of Martindale, Bolton, Thrimby, Mardale, and Swindale. The deanery of Penrith includes the rectories of Brougham, Melmerby, Ousby, and Great Salkeld, the vicarages of Addingham, Ainstable, Barton, Edenhall, Kirkland, Kirkoswald, Lazonby, and Penrith, and the p. curacies of Langwathby, Culgaith, Skirwith, Plumpton, Newton Regny, Renwick, and Christchurch Penrith. The deanery of Wigton includes the rectories of Aikton, Bolton, Bowness, Caldbeck, Kirkbride, and Uldale, the vicarages of Bromfield, Dalston, Thursby, and Wigton, and the p. curacies of Allonby, West Newton, Highet, Holme Cultram, St. Cuthbert, St Paul, Newton Arlosh, Ireby, and Westward.

The archdeaconry of Westmoreland comprises the rural deaneries of Aldingham, Ambleside, Cartmel, Cockermouth, Gosforth, Kendal, Kirkby Lonsdale, Ulverstone, and Whitehaven. The deanery of Aldingham includes the rectory of Aldingham, the vicarages of Dalton in Furness, Pennington, and Urswick, and the p. curacies of Dendron, Lindale, Staveley, Kirkby Ireleth, Rampside, Walney, and Bardsea. The deanery of Ambleside includes the rectories of Grasmere and Windermere, the vicarage of Hawkshead, and the p. curacies of Ambleside, Langdale, Rydal, Brathay, Low Wray, Satterthwaite, Applethwaite, and Troutbeck. The deanery of Cartmel includes the p. curacies of Cartmel, Cartmel-Fell, Field Broughton, Flookburgh, Grange, Lindale, Staveley, Colton, Finsthwaite, Haverthwaite, and Rusland. The deanery of Cockermouth includes the rectory of Plumbland, the vicarages of Aspatria, Bridekirk, Brigham, Dearham, Gilcrux, Isell, and Torpenhow, and the p. curacies of Allhallows, Great Broughton, Cockermouth, Embleton, Mosser, Setmurthy, Camerton, Clifton, Crosscanonby, Maryport, and Flimby. The deanery of Gosforth includes the rectories of Bootle, Corney, Gosforth, Waberthwaite, and Whicham, the vicarage of Millom, and the p. curacies of Drigg, Eskdale, Irton, Thwaites, Muncaster, Ponsonby, Wastdale Head, Nether Wastdale, and Whitbeck. The deanery of Kendal includes the vicarage of Kendal, and the p. curacies of Kendal St George, Kendal St Thomas, Burneyside, Crook, Grayrigg, Helsington, Hugil, New Hutton, Old Hutton, Kentmere, Long Sleddale, Natland, Selside, Staveley, Underbarrow, and Winster. The deanery of Kirkby Lonsdale includes the vicarages of Beetham, Burton in Kendal, Heversham, and Kirkby Lonsdale, and the p. curacies of Witherslack, Holme, Preston Patrick, Crosthwaite, Crosscrake, Levens, Milnthorpe, Barbon, Casterton, Firbank, Hutton Roof, Killington, Mansergh, and Middleton. The deanery of Ulverstone includes the vicarage of Kirkby Ireleth, and the p. curacies of Broughton in-Furness, Seathwaite, Woodland, Ulpha, Ulverstone, Ulverstone Trinity, Blawith, Coniston, Egton cum Newland, Lowick, and Torver. The deanery of Whitehaven includes the rectories of Dean, Distington, Egremont, Harrington, Lamplugh, Moresby, and Workington, and the p. curacies of Arlecdon, Beckermet St Bridget, Beckermet St John, St Bees, Ennerdale, Hensingham, Loweswater, Whitehaven St James, Whitehaven St Nicholas, Whitehaven Trinity, Whitehaven Christchurch, Workington St John, Cleator, and Hayle.

CARLISLE AND SILLOTH RAILWAY, a railway in Cumberland, from Carlisle westward to Silloth bay. The first reach of it, 8½ miles long, from Carlisle to Drumburgh, goes west-north-westward, along the course of the old ship canal, a branch 2¾ miles long goes thence, in the same direction, to Port Carlisle, and the remaining reach, 12¾ miles long, from Drumburgh to Silloth, goes south westward to Abbey, and west north westward thence to Silloth. This last part was authorized, in 1855, in connection with the scheme for Silloth dock, and the railway was opened in 1856,—the dock in 1859. See PORT CARLISLE and SILLOTH.

CARLISLE (OLD), a locality 2 miles S of Wigton, in Cumberland, the site of the Roman station Olenacum, on the Roman road from Carlisle to Ellenborough. Materials were taken from ancient buildings on it toward the erection of Wigton, and numbers of Roman relics have been found.

CARLISLE (PORT). See PORT CARLISLE.

CARLISLES QUARTER. See BILCES QUARTER.

CARL LOFTS, a remarkable antiquity, either Druidical or Scandinavian, in Westmoreland, on the Lancaster and Carlisle railway, 2 miles S of Shap. It was originally an enclosure about ½ a mile long, and from 30 to 60 feet wide, by lines of unhewn granite blocks of great size, with a terminating circle, about 40 feet in diameter, of similar character, but it has been extensively demolished by blastings for building material, and by the forming of the railway.

CARLTON, a parish in the district and county of Bedford, on the verge of the county, near the river Ouse, 4½ miles NE of Olney, and 5¼ SW by W of Sharnbrook r. station. It has a post office under Bedford. Acres, 1,530. Real property, £2,174. Pop., 470. Houses, 109. Carlton Hall is a chief residence. The living is a rectory united with the rectory of Chellington, in the diocese of Ely. Value £370. Patron, Lord Dynevor. There is a Baptist chapel.

CARLTON, a township in Redmarshall parish, Durham, on the Clarence railway, 4 miles NW of Stockton upon Tees. It has a station on the railway. Acres, 1,453. Real property, £1,324. Pop., 176. Houses, 37.

CARLTON, a chapelry in Market Bosworth parish, Leicester, on the Ashby de la-Zouch canal, 1¼ mile NW by N of Market Bosworth, and 5 WSW of Bagworth r. station. Post town, Market Bosworth, under Hinckley. Acres, 680. Real property, £1,755. Pop., 277. Houses, 63. The property is divided among a few. The chapelry was constituted in 1863. The living is a vicarage in the diocese of Peterborough. Value, £173.

CARLTON, a township and a sub district in Basford district, Notts. The township is in Gedling parish, lies on the Nottingham and Lincoln railway, adjacent to the river Trent, 3 miles ENE of Nottingham, and has a station on the railway, and a post office under Nottingham. Real property, £5,733. Pop., 2,559. Houses, 564. Many of the inhabitants are lace and stocking makers. There are a chapel of ease, and chapels for Baptists, Wesleyans, and Free Methodists.—The sub district contains three parishes, and great part of another. Acres, 8,435. Pop., 4,328. Houses, 939.

CARLTON, a village, two townships, a parish, and a sub district in Worksop district, Notts. The village stands 4 miles N of the Manchester and Sheffield railway at Worksop, was a place of some consequence in the Saxon times, and has a post office under Worksop. The townships comprise all the parish, are for highway purposes only, and bear the names of North and South. The parish is called Carlton in Lindrick, and contains 3,980 acres. Real property, £6,354. Pop., 1,035. Houses, 227. The property is much subdivided. The manor was given at the conquest to Roger de Busli. Carlton Hall belonged formerly to the Cliftons and others, and passed to the Ramsdens. The living is a rectory in the diocese of Lincoln. Value, £576.* Patron, the Archbishop of York. The church is partly Norman, has a lofty square tower, and is pretty good. There are a Wesleyan chapel and a free school.—The sub d. contains four parishes, part of another, and an extra parochial tract. Acres, 25,200. Pop., 3,556. Houses, 787.

CARLTON, a parish in Blything district, Suffolk, on the East Suffolk railway, ¾ of a mile NW of Saxmundham. Post town, Saxmundham. Acres, 5[illegible]3. Real property £1 132 Pop, 116 Houses, 26 A chantry was founded here, in 1330, by John Framlingham, and given to the Homings. Carlton Hall belongs to Lady Stradbroke The living is a rectory, annexed to the rectory of Kelsale, in the diocese of Norwich The church is Norman Charities, £56

CARLTON, a township in Coverham parish, N R Yorkshire in Highdale 5 miles SSW by W of Middleham It has a post office under Bedale Acres, 2,716 Real property, £1,931 Pop, 276 Houses, 69 The surface is the lower part of an upland vale, traversed by a tributary of the river Ure See CARLTON HIGHDALE

CARLTON, a parish in Stokesley district, N R York shire, on an affluent of the river Tees, adjacent to the Northallerton and Stokesley railway, 3½ miles SW of Stokesley It has a post office under Northallerton Acres, 830 Real property, £1,803 Pop, 243 Houses, 66 The property is divided among a few There formerly were extensive alum works The living is a vicarage in the diocese of York. Value, £56 * Patron, G Reeve, Esq The church is good, and there are a Wesleyan chapel and charities £24

CARLTON, a hamlet in Helmsley township and parish, N R Yorkshire, 2 miles N of Helmsley

CARLTON, a township in Husthwaite parish, N R Yorkshire, 5 miles NNW of Easingwold Acres, 810 Real property, £1,367 Pop, 170 Houses, 34

CARLTON, a village and a parish in Skipton district, W R Yorkshire The village stands on the river Aire, near the Leeds and Liverpool canal and the North Midland railway, 2 miles SW of Skipton, and has a post office under Skipton The parish includes also the hamlet of Lothersdale Acres, 5,117 Real property, £5,919 Pop 1,506 Houses, 311 The property is subdivided The living is a vicarage in the diocese of Ripon Value, £400 * Patron, Christ Church, Oxford The church was rebuilt in 18,9 The vicarage of Lothersdale is a separate benefice Almshouses founded in 1700 by Mr Spence, have £231 a year and a school, founded in 1709, by Elizabeth Wilkinson, has £120

CARLTON, a township in Guiseley parish, W R Yorkshire on the river Warp, 24 miles SE of Otley Acres 1,270 Real property, £1,272 Pop, 192 Houses, 20

CARLTON, a township in Royston parish, W R Yorkshire, adjacent to the Barnesley canal, and the York and Derby railway, 3 miles NNE of Barnesley Acres, 1,953 Real property, £4,049, of which £1,500 are in mines Pop, 351 Houses, 84

CARLTON, Rothwell, W R Yorkshire See LOFT HOUSE WITH CARLTON

CARLTON, Cumberland See CARLETON

CARLTON, Pontefract and Snaith, W R. Yorkshire See CARLETON

CARLTON CASTLE, a parish in Louth district, Lincoln, adjacent to the East Lincoln railway, near Authorpe station, 5 miles SE of Louth Post town, Carlton, under Louth Acres, 700 Rated property, £427 Pop 45 Houses, 9 The property is divided among a few A populous market town was formerly here, enjoying many privileges Sir Hugh Bardolph held the manor in the time of Henry I, and had a castle on one of three artificial mounds called the Castle hills The living is a rectory in the diocese of Lincoln Value, £69 Patron John Forster Esq The church is good

CARLTON COLVILLE a parish in Mutford district, Suffolk, on the East Suffolk railway, between the rivers Lothing and Waveney, 3½ miles SW by W of Lowestoft It has a station on the railway, and its post town is Lowestoft. Acres, 2,894 Real property £5,256 Pop, 946 Houses 202 The property is subdivided The living is a rectory in the diocese of Norwich. Value £34? * Patron, V Andrews, Esq The church is old but good There are a Wesleyan chapel, a national school, and a private lunatic asylum

CARLTON CUM WILLINGHAM, a parish in Linton district, Cambridge, on the verge of the county 4½ miles ESE of Six Mile Bottom r station, and 7½ S of Newmarket It has a post office, of the name of Carlton, under Newmarket Acres 2 200 Real property, £3,102 Pop, 402 Houses, 87 The property is divided among a few Part of the land is common The living is a rectory in the diocese of Ely Value, £287 * Patrons, the Trustees of the Rev W S P Wilder The church is old but good, and has a monument of Sir T Elliot, author of a Latin Dictionary and other works There is a Primitive Methodist chapel

CARLTON CURLIEW, a village and a parish in Billesdon district, Leicester The village stands on an affluent of the river Welland, 2 miles NE of Kibworth r station, and 7½ NNW of Market Harborough The parish includes also the township of Ilston on the Hill, and its post town is Great Glen, under Leicester Acres, 2,970 Real property, £4,838 Pop., 308 Houses, 61 The property is divided among a few Carlton-Curlieu Hall, a Tudor edifice, is the seat of Capt E Sutton The living is a rectory in the diocese of Peterborough Value, £242 Patron, Sir J H Palmer, Bart The church is good, and has some old monuments

CARLTON (EAST), a parish in Henstead district, Norfolk, on the Norfolk railway, near Hethersett station, 4½ miles E of Wymondham Post town, Hethersett, under Wymondham Acres, 1,213 Real property, £2,400 Pop, 244 Houses, 56 The property is divided among a few There were formerly two parishes, St. Mary and St Peter The living is a rectory in the diocese of Norwich Value, £176 Patron, Mr Peter Day The church is very good

CARLTON (EAST), a parish in Kettering district, Northampton, near the river Welland, 3½ miles SW of Rockingham r station, and 7 E by N of Market Harborough Post town, Rockingham, under Leicester Acres 1,598 Real property, £3,293 Pop, 70 Houses, 17 The property is divided among a few Carlton House is a seat of Sir J H Palmer, Bart The living is a rectory in the diocese of Peterborough Value, £108 * Patron, Sir J H Palmer, Bart The church is modern, and has a tower

CARLTON (GREAT) a parish in Louth district, Lincoln, 2½ miles E of Legbourne r station, and 6 ESE of Louth It has a post office, of the name of Carlton, under Louth Acres 2,190 Real property £4,231 Pop, 338 Houses, 64 The property is divided among a few The living is a vicarage in the diocese of Lincoln Value, £500 * Patrons, the Dean and Chapter of Lincoln The church is good, and there are a Wesleyan chapel and an endowed school, the latter with £26 a year

CARLTON (GREAT), Lancashire See CARLETON (GREAT and LITTLE)

CARLTON HIGHDALE, a township in Coverham parish, N R Yorkshire, in Highdale, 9 miles SW of Middleham It includes the hamlets of Gammersgill, Horsehouse Swineside, Arkleside, Blackrake, Bradley, Woodale, Hindlethwaite, Pickill West Close, Flersop and Coverhead Acres, 12 480 Real property £2,863 Pop, 363 Houses, 69 The surface is the upper part of a mountain vale, traversed by a tributary of the river Ure, and ascends in high bleak tracts, called Carlton-Moors, at the boundary with the west riding

CARLTON HUSTHWAITE See CARLTON, Husthwaite N R. Yorkshire

CARLTON IN LINDRICK See CARLTON, Worksop Notts

CARLTON ISLEBECK See CARLTON MINIOTT

CARLTON LE MOORLAND, a parish in the district of Newark and county of Lincoln, between the rivers Witham and Brant 2½ miles SSE of Swinderby r station, and 7 ENE of Newark Post town, Bassingham, under Newark Acres, 2,610 Real property, £3,931 Pop, 394 Houses 80 The property is divided among a few The living is a vicarage united with the vicarage of Stapleford in the diocese of Lincoln Value, £158 Patron, Lord Middleton The church is good, and there are a Baptist chapel, and charities £10

CARLTON (LITTLE), a parish in Louth district Lincoln 2 miles E of Legbourne r station, and 4½ ESE of Louth Post town Carlton under Louth Acres 1,006

Real property, £1,735 Pop, 181 Houses, 33 The property is much subdivided The living is a rectory in the diocese of Lincoln Value, £159 * Patron, John Foster Esq The church is good

CARLTON (LITTLE), Lancashire See CARLTON (GREAT and LITTLE)

CARLTON (LITTLE or SOUTH), a hamlet in South Muskham parish, Notts, 3¼ miles NW of Newark Pop 79

CARLTON MAGNA See CARLTON (GREAT)

CARLTON MINIOTT or CARLTON ISLEBECK, a township-chapelry in Thirsk parish, N R Yorkshire, adjacent to the Great Northern railway, 2 miles W of Thirsk. Post town, Thirsk. Acres, 1,555 Real property, £3,?07 Pop, 314 Houses, 70 The property is subdivided. The living is a p curacy in the diocese of York Value £125 Patron, the Archbishop of York. The church is very old.

CARLTON-MOORS See CARLTON HIGHDALE

CARLTON (NORTH), a parish in the district and county of Lincoln. 3½ miles E by N of Saxelby r station, and 5 NNW of Lincoln. Post town, Saxelby, under Lincoln Acres, 1,795 Real property, £2,500 Pop, 1?3. Houses, 27 The property is divided between two. The living is a vicarage in the diocese of Lincoln. Value, £35 Patron, the Bishop of Lincoln

CARLTON (NORTH and SOUTH) See CARLTON, Worksop, Notts

CARLTON ON TRENT See CARLTON-UPON TRENT

CARLTON-PARVA. See CARLTON (LITTLE)

CARLTON RODE, a parish in Depwade district, Norfolk, 2 miles NE of New Buckenham, and 4 ESE of Attleborough r station. Post town, New Buckenham, under Attleborough Acres, 2,631 Real property, £5,823 Pop, 90? Houses, 203 The property is much subdivided. An ancient rood or cross gave rise to the suffix Rode The living is a rectory in the diocese of Norwich Value, £850 * Patron, Sir R. J Buxton, Bart The church is good, and there are a Baptist chapel a national school, and charities £65

CARLTON SCROOP, a parish in Grantham district, Lincoln, on a branch of the river Witham, 2¾ miles W of Ancaster r station, and 6 NNE of Grantham It has a post-office under Grantham Acres, 1,342 Real property, £2,937 Pop., 266 Houses, 53 The property is subdivided The living is a rectory in the diocese of Lincoln Value, £356 * Patron, alt Earl Brownlow and two others The church is good There are a Wesleyan chapel, a national school, and charities £13

CARLTON (SOUTH), a parish in the district and county of Lincoln, 3¼ miles E of Saxelby r station, and 4 NNW of Lincoln Post town, Lincoln Acres, 1,910. Real property, £2,282 Pop, 181 Houses, 32 The property is divided between two The living is a vicarage in the diocese of Lincoln Value, £200 Patron, the Bishop of Lincoln. The church is tolerable Admirable Sir W Monson, of the time of Elizabeth, was a native

CARLTON (SOUTH) Notts See CARLTON, Worksop, and CARLTON (LITTLE or SOUTH)

CARLTON UPON TRENT a chapelry in Norwell parish, Notts, on the river Trent, at a ferry, and on the Great Northern railway, 6½ miles N of Newark It has a station on the railway and a post office under Newark Acres, 1,1?? Real property, £2,151 Pop, 290 Houses, 61 The Living is a p curacy, annexed to the vicarage of Norwell, in the diocese of Lincoln The church is modern, in the early English style, and has a tall spire There is a parochial school

CARLTON-WITH ASHBY See CARLTON-SCROOP

CARLTON WITH FOSHAM a hamlet in Aldborough township and parish, E. R Yorkshire, 6½ miles S of Hornsea Real property, £1,530

CARLYON a locality 2 miles S of Truro, in Cornwall, the reputed birthplace of Sir Tristram the companion of King Arthur

CARMARTHEN a town, a parish a sub district and a district in Carmarthenshire. The town stands on the Julian ways the river Towy, and the South Wales railway, 9 miles NNE of the Towy's mouth, and 19¾, by railway NNW of Llanelly The two lines of the Julian way met at it the river Towy is navigable to it for sea borne vessels, and makes it a sub port to Llanelly, railways strike from it in four directions, the South Wales one southward and westward, the Carmarthen and Cardigan north-westward, and the Carmarthen and Llandilo eastward into connexion at Llandilo with the Central Wales system It was known to the Romans as Maridunum, and, for a long time to the Welsh, as Caer Fyrddyn and Caer Merlin It figured as the capital of Wales till the removal of the princes to Dynevor in 877, and it retained the chancery and the exchequer of South Wales, from the annexation of the principality till the abolition of the Welsh jurisdiction A Roman station stood at it, remains of a Roman camp are still visible in a field adjacent to it, called the Bulrach, traces of a Roman causeway, from this camp nearly parallel with Priory street, have been discovered, and Roman bricks, coins, and other relics have been found A castle of the Welsh princes succeeded the Roman station, occupied the brow of a hill, rising abruptly from the river, was extended and strengthened into a fortress almost impregnable, included a citadel, interior buildings, exterior towers and bastions, and a strong encompassing rampart on a ground plan nearly square, was taken in 1113 by Gruffydd ab Rhys, in 1140 by Owen Gwynedd, in 1215 by Llewelyn ap Jorwerth, in 1223 by the Normans under the Earl of Pembroke, in 1405 by Owen Glendower, and in the civil wars of the 17th century by the parliamentarians under Laughorne, was dismantled in 1648, and converted into a prison, and continued to be used as prison till 1787, when a portion of it, left standing, was incorporated with the new county jail The famous reputed magician Merlin was a native and gave rise to the alternative name Caer Merlin, and a spot 3 miles distant is alleged to have been the place of his entombment by the Lady of the Lake, and bears the name of Merlin's cave Lewis Bayly, chaplain to James I, afterwards Bishop of Bangor Sir Thomas Picton, the hero of Waterloo, and Sir William Nott, the recent hero of the East, also were natives Sir Richard Steele spent his later years partly in a house of the town which was converted into the Ivy Bush hotel, and partly in a house in the vicinity called Ty Gwyn, and composed here his "Conscious Lovers and other pieces Spenser speaks of Carmarthen, in allusion to its old history, in the lines,—

"To Maridunum that is now by change
Of name Cayr Marrddin call'd, they took their way

The town occupies irregular ground, sloping to the river, and commands extensive and beautiful views It is about a mile long and half a mile broad Several of the streets are very narrow, some have been partially widened, and the best contain many good houses A lovely public walk, called the Parade, is at the upper end, overlooking a fine reach of the river A grand view of the town itself, the picturesque vale of the Towy, and the ruins of Dynevor castle, is got from Grongar hill celebrated in the descriptive poem of Dyer The guildhall, in the middle of the town, is a large, handsome, pillared, modern building, with market place below, and a grand front staircase The county jail is a substantial structure, on the plan of Howard, with a recent addition, and has capacity for 30 male and 16 female prisoners A bridge of six spacious arches, with four auxiliaries spans the river A bronze statue of Sir William Nott, on a granite pedestal, is in front of the guild hall, and an obelisk to the memory of Sir Thomas Picton, in room of a monument by Nash, pulled down in 1846, is at the west end of the town Barracks for about 1 500 men, erected since 1847, are 2 miles to the west The lunatic asylum, for the counties of Carmarthen, Cardigan, and Pembroke, erected in 1863–4, after designs by D Brandon, with accommodation for 260 patients, is also in the neighbourhood The parish church is a large plain edifice, ancient and originally cruciform, but renovated and altered, has a lofty square tower, and contains a fine altar tomb to Sir Rhys ap Thomas, who died in 1527, a monument to Bishop Farr, who was burnt in the market place for his religion, and a monument to Sir William Nott St. David's church is a recent Gothic structure, raised at a cost of £1,450. There are chapels for Independents, Baptists, Unitarians, Wesleyan Methodists, and Calvinistic Methodists Vestiges exist, behind the guild hall, of an ancient church or chapel. A priory of black canons, founded before 1148, stood at some distance NE of the parish church, and part of an arched gateway of it, with some other remains, are still standing A house of greyfriars, a cell to St Augustine's monastery at Bristol, stood at the other end of the town, but has disappeared The grammar school, founded in the 17th century, by Bishop Owen has £20 from endowment, with three exhibitions The collegiate institution, for training young men for the dissenting ministry, is supported by a fund in London. The training school for South Wales, founded in 1847, stands ½ a mile west of the town, and is a very handsome edifice, raised at a cost of £8,000 There are a literary and scientific institution, a theatre, an infirmary, alms houses, and a workhouse. The yearly aggregate of endowed charities is £180

The town has a head post office,‡ a railway station with telegraph, two banking-offices, and three chief inns publishes two weekly newspapers, and is the capital of the county, the seat of assizes at both circuits, and of quarter sessions in April and Oct Markets are held on Wednesday and Saturday, and fairs on 15 and 16 April, 3 and 4 June, 10 July, 12 Aug., 9 Sept, 9 Oct, and 14 and 15 Nov Some manufacture is carried on in flannel, malt, ropes, and leather, much business is done in connexion with numerous copper and tin works, and coal and lead mines, in the neighbourhood, and considerable traffic exists in the export of agricultural produce, and import of miscellaneous goods Upwards of 50 vessels belong to the town, and vessels of about 300 tons come up to the quay. Steam communication is maintained with Tenby, Bristol, and Wexford The town was chartered by Henry VIII, is governed by a mayor, six aldermen, and eighteen councillors, and unites with Llanelly in sending a member to parliament. The borough limits include all the parish, together with the extra parochial tract of Castle Green Electors of Carmarthen and Llanelly in 1868, 889 Direct taxes, £10,253 Pop of Carmarthen in 1841, 9,526, in 1861, 9 993 Houses, 1,763 The town gives the title of Marquis to the Duke of Leeds

The parish encircles the extra parochial tract of Castle Green, which is in the town, around the jail Acres, including this, 5,155 Real property, £31,298 Pop, exclusive of Castle Green, 9,798 Houses, 1,746 The living is a vicarage in the diocese of St David's Value, £176* Patron, St. David's College, Lampeter The vicarages of St David's and Llanllwch are separate charges, and the former has an income of £190,* and is in the patronage of the vicar The sub district includes also the parishes of Llangain and Abergwilly Acres 18,563 Pop, 12,583. Houses, 2,303 The district comprehends likewise the sub district of Llangendeirne, containing the parishes of Llangendeirne, Llanddarog, Llanarthney, Llangunnor Llandeilo, and St Ishmaels, the sub district of St Clears, containing the parishes of St Clears, Llanstephan Laugharne Llansadurnen Llandawke Llandowror, Llanginning, Llangunnock, Llanfihangel abercowin, and Llandilo abercowin, and the sub district of Conwil, containing the parishes of Llanllawddog, Llanpumpsaint, Newchurch Merthyr, Abernant, Treleach a Bettws, Mydrim, and Llanwinio and the parochial chapelry of Conwil-in Elvet Acres, 172,546 Poor rates in 1866 £18,013 Pop. in 1861, 33,675 Houses 7,451 Marriages in 1866, 292, births, 1,097,—of which 100 were illegitimate, deaths, 895,—of which 211 were at ages under 5 years, and 53 at ages above 85 Marriages in the ten years 1851-60, 2,879, births, 11 793, deaths, 7,933 The places of worship in 1851 were 35 of the Church of England, with 8 611 sittings, 32 of Independents with 7,389 s, 17 of Baptists, with 3,511 s, 2 of Unitarians, with 316 s, 6 of Wesleyan Methodists, with 1 459 s., 29 of Calvinistic Methodists, with 5 828 s., 1 of Latter Day Saints, with 100 s., and 1 of Roman Catholics, with 120 s The schools were 37 public day schools, with 2,523 scholars, 46 private day schools, with 1,136 s, and 113 Sunday schools with 11,973 s.

CARMARTHEN AND CARDIGAN RAILWAY, a railway in South Wales. It commences in a junction with the South Wales railway at Carmarthen, and goes north north westward to Newcastle Emlyn, and thence west north westward to Cardigan It was authorized in 1854, was opened to Llandyssil in 1864, and was empowered in 1864-5 to have branch connexion to Kidwelly

CARMARTHEN BAY, a large bay of South Wales, on the coast of Pembroke, Carmarthen and Glamorgan It opens from the Bristol Channel, between Giltar Point and Worms Head, measures 17 miles, east south eastward, across the entrance, makes a somewhat semicircular sweep, with offsets at the Towy and the Burry rivers, and penetrates about 9 miles from the line of entrance to the Towy's mouth Caldy Island lies at the west side of the entrance, the Cefn Sidan sandbank spreads over the north eastern portion, and the ports of Tenby, Saundersfoot, Carmarthen, and Llanelly are on the minor baylets or rivers Caldy island forms a natural breakwater, and lights are there and elsewhere to guide the navigation A very productive fishery might be carried on, but has been strangely neglected

CARMARTHENSHIRE a maritime county of South Wales, bounded, on the W by Pembroke, on the N, by Cardigan, on the E, by Brecon, on the SE, by Glamorgan, on the S, by Carmarthen bay Its length, north-eastward, is 50 miles, its greatest breadth, 35 miles, its circuit, about 155 miles, its area, 606 331 acres. A low tract, reclaimed from the sea, lies round Laugharne another low tract lies along the Towy, a great congeries of hills and uplands fills most of the interior, a range of mountains, striking away to Plinlimmon in Cardigan is in the north and a loftier range, forming the main part of the Black mountains, culminating at an altitude of 2,596 feet, is in the east The chief rivers are the Towy, with the Gwili, the Cothi, the Bran, the Sawddy, and the Cennen, the Tave, with the Gwynin, the Cowin, and the Morlais, the Teifi on the boundary with Cardigan, the Llonghor on the eastern boundary to the sea the two Gwendraeths, and the Amman Several lakes occur, of no great size, yet full of interest either to the angler or to the tourist. Numerous medicinal springs exist, and one, at Middleton-park, is chalybeate of greater strength than the Tunbridge waters. Lower silurian rocks form the northern and the central districts, upper silurian rocks form narrow belts in the SE, old red sandstone rocks form a considerable belt on the coast, from the western boundary to the east of the Towy, and thence east north eastward, and rocks of the carboniferous series, rich in the coal measures, constituting part of the great coal field of South Wales, form all the tracts on the SE, both sea board and inland. Lead ore, copper ore, ironstone, slate, building stone fire stone, and dark blue marble are worked, and there are 87 collieries

The soils on the higher tracts over all the different kinds of rocks, are, for the most part, rather poor, while those in the valleys, especially in the lower parts of those of the Towy and the Tave are, in general, very fertile About one third of all the land is waste, and a large aggregate of the rest is so miserably cultivated as to yield a niggard produce Agriculture, generally, is in a primitive or backward condition yet has begun to be incited, and much improved, by the influence of Agricultural Societies Lime, not only on the tracts where limestone abounds but on others to which it has to be brought from a considerable distance, is profusely used, and the system of augmenting farm yard manure by the best appliances of cropping and house feeding has been much on the increase The enclosing and the cultivating of wastes also have been going on Peat is the only fuel throughout much of the uplands, and crushed coal, mixed with clay, and formed into balls, is the chief fuel in the other tracts The enclosures are chiefly of stone, the farm buildings, generally, are inferior, and the cottages for the most part, are of mud and thatched Oats are the chief grain crop, both for home use and for exportation Butter and bacon are sent, from dairy tracts, to market. The cattle are chiefly a small or middle sized native breed, but in some of the best parts of the valleys, are large kinds from other counties The sheep also are small, native, and degenerate, but have begun to be much improved by crosses with the Southdowns The draught horses are mostly compact, bony, middle-sized animals, and saddle horses, of a fine breed, have begun to be reared Woods formerly were abundant, but have, of late years, been greatly demolished A large export trade is carried on in coal, stone, and iron, and some manufactures exist in woollens and leather Several tram railways, one of them 15 miles long, serve for the mining produce, the South Wales railway goes along the whole seaboard, the Llanelly and the Vale of Towy railways traverse the centre northward, the Carmarthenshire railway, authorised in 1864, comprises three lines in conjunction with the Llanelly, and the Cardigan railway traverses the northwest

The county contains 72 parishes parts of four others, and an extra parochial place, and is divided into the boroughs of Carmarthen and Llandovery, and the hundreds of Carnwallon, Cartainog, Cayo, Derllys Elvet, Iskennen, Kidwelly, and Perfedd The registration county gives off 12 parishes to Pembroke and 10 to Cardigan, takes in a parish from Glamorgan and two from Brecon, comprises 497,776 acres, and is divided into the districts of Carmarthen, Llandilofawr, Llandovery, and Llanelly The market towns are Carmarthen, Llanelly, Llandilofawr, Llandovery, Newcastle Emlyn, Kidwelly, Laugharne, and Llangadock, and the other chief towns are Llandybie and St Clears The chief seats are Golden Grove, Abergwili, Newton, Lacced, Edwinsford, Dolcolhy, Middleton, Henllys, Llwyn y-Wermod, Llanstephan, Ystrad, Maesgwynne, Kilgwyn, and Aberglasney Real property in 1815 £282,030 in 1843, £396,917, in 1851, £385,600, in 1860, £430,056 The county is governed by a lord lieutenant, a high sheriff, and about thirty five magistrates and is in the Home military district, and the South Wales judicial circuit. The assizes are held at Carmarthen, and quarter sessions, at Carmarthen and Llandilo The police force, in 1864, comprised 62 men, at a cost of £4,426, the crimes committed were 95, the depredators and suspected persons at large, 330, the houses of bad character, 89 Two members are sent to parliament by the county and one by the boroughs County electors, in 1865, 4,633 Pop, in 1801, 67,317, in 1821, 90,239, in 1841, 106,326, in 1861, 111,796 Inhabited houses, 23,070, uninhabited, 925, building, 129

The territory now forming Carmarthenshire belonged to the Demetæ or Dyfed, was included in the Roman Britannia Secunda, afterwards formed part of Ceredigion or Dynevor, made very stout resistance to the Normans, gave way to the forces of Edward I, and was not entirely subdued by England till the commencement of the 16th century Druidical antiquities have been discovered in the parishes of Llanboidy, Conwil in Elvet, Eglwys Newydd, and Penboyr The maritime Julian way ran through the county nearly in the route of the South Wales railway, the mountain Julian way went up the vale of the Towy from Carmarthen, and the Western way or Sarn Helen is distinctly traceable in several parts of the parish of Llanfairarybryn Ruins or remains of castles exist at Dynevor Dryslwyn, Llandovery, Carreg Cennen, Carmarthen Llanstephan, Laugharne, Kidwelly, and Newcastle Emlyn and remains of monasteries are at Talley Whitland Llanllwny, and Carmarthen

CARMEARS, a valley in Cornwall, descending from the hills of Hensbarrow, south eastward, past Luxulian, to the vicinity of St Blazey It is traversed by a romantic stream and by a railway from the china clay works of Hensbarrow to the harbour of Par is flanked by granite cliffs and tors, in picturesque arrangement has in one part, a grand cascade through a wood, and presents finer groups of scenery, with water, wood, and rock than any other valley of Cornwall

CARMEL HEAD a headland at the NE side of the entrance of Holyhead bay, 7 miles NNE of Holyhead, in Anglesey

CARN, a Celtic name, signifying "a heap or a prominence," and used as a prefix.

CARNABY, a parish in Bridlington district, E R Yorkshire, on the Hull and Scarborough railway, 2½ miles SW of Bridlington It has a station on the railway, and its post-town is Bridlington under Hull Acres, 2 000 Real property, £2,616 Pop, 152 Houses, 25. The property is divided among a few The living is a vicarage, united with the vicarage of Fraisthorpe, in the diocese of York. Value, £82 Patron, Sir G Strickland, Bart. The church shows some early English features, has a good later English tower, and contains a circular Norman font

CARNANTON, a seat 2½ miles WNW of St Columb, in Cornwall It belonged, in the time of Charles I, to Attorney General Noy, and belongs now to H Willyams, Esq

CARNARVON, a town, a sub district, and a district, in Carnarvonshire. The town stands adjacent to the Carnarvon railways, on the Sarn Helen way, at the mouth of the river Seiont, on the SE side of the Menai strait, in the parish of Llanbeblig, 8¾ miles SW by S of Bangor The Roman station Segontium was at Llanbeblig, within ½ a mile, on the road to Beddgelert It occupied a quadrangular area of about 7 acres, on the summit of an eminence gradually sloping on every side, and was defended with strong walls of masonry Extensive portions of these walls, on the south side, still exist, and traces of a Roman villa and baths were discovered in 1835 Roman coins and other relics also have been found, and one of the coins is that of Vespasian struck at the capture of Judea. A strong fort, some remains of which are still standing, was near the Seiont, to secure a landing place at high water, other outposts, which can still be traced were on the opposite side of the Seiont a well in the vicinity still bears the name of Helena, the mother of Constantine the Great, and a very strong, conspicuous, circular, artificial mound, on the sea shore, where Roman coins have been found, and which is now called Dinas Dinlle, was the chief outpost Constantine the Great and other Roman emperors visited Segontium, and Helena, Constantine's mother, was born at it The Welsh appear to have called it Caer-Seiont and Caer-Custeint,—"the fort of the Seiont" and "the fort of Constantine," and, on building a strength of their own in its vicinity, within a district then named Arfon, called this Caer-yn Arfon, now changed into Carnarvon The Welsh princes had their seat here till 873, when they went back to Aberffraw Edward I took possession of it in 1282, and came to it in person and founded a castle at it in 1284, and his son, the Prince of Wales, afterwards Edward II, was born here in the same year Walls were built round the town in 1286 the castle continued to be in progress in 1291, both the walls and the castle were much demolished at Madoc's insurrection in 1295, and were afterwards refounded, and the grandest part of the castle, called the Eagle tower was built by Edward II, and finished in 1320 Owen Glendower besieged the place in 1402, but failed to take it. Both parties in the civil wars of Charles I repeatedly took and retook it, till the parliamentarians eventually got the mastery, A warrant was issued by Charles II in 1660 for destroying the fortifications, but did not take effect. The castle still stands, on strong ground, at the west end of the town, was recently repaired, under the direction of the Board of Woods and Forests, at a cost of upwards of £3,000, and is exceedingly grand and imposing 'It covers about 2½ acres, and forms an oblong irregular square The external walls are very high, and have within them a lofty series of galleries with numerous eillets or arrow slips There are 13 great towers, of pentagonal, hexagonal and octagonal designs The very massive pentagonal Eagle tower, guarding the mouth of the Seiont, is so called from a now shapeless figure of that bird brought, it is alleged, from the ruins of Segontium, but an eagle was one of Edward's crests. This majestic tower has three turrets and its battlements display a mutilated series of armed heads of the time of Edward I In front of the august Gothic main entrance is a mutilated statue of Edward I sheathing a sword with a defaced shield under his feet The grooves of four portcullises remain On the east side of the castle is the Queen's gate, so called according to tradition, because Queen Eleanor entered this way, it is now much above the level of the ground, but a very high bank existed opposite to it from which a drawbridge was let down The interior, which is greatly dilapidated is divided into an outer and inner ward, and the state rooms were fitted with spacious windows and elegant tracery, of which little is left. The only staircase that remains perfect is that to the Eagle tower —155 steps" The town was visited by the Prince and Princess of Wales in 1868

The environs are strikingly picturesque, comprise great views of the Menai strait and the Snowdon and Eifl mountains, and contain charming drives and walks The Twr hill, immediately adjacent, resembles the Calton hill of Edinburgh, and commands a brilliant panoramic prospect The town walls, defended by many round towers, remain nearly complete round all the circuit, but have mainly become private property, and are much blocked up by houses, and only a small part of their summit, adjoining the town church, is available for the public, but a broad pleasant terrace runs on the outside of them, from the north end to the quay, and forms a fashionable promenade The town consists of ten streets inside the walls, and twice that number outside, with many handsome villas The suburbs are very pleasant, and have undergone recent extensions, as a sea bathing resort The baths unite elegance and utility, comprise suites of hot and cold sea water baths, with large swimming bath and dressing rooms, and were erected by the Marquis of Anglesey, at a cost of upwards of £10,000 The county hall, opposite the main entrance to the castle is a poor looking structure The guild hall, over the east town gate is occasionally used for balls and concerts The county gaol is part of the castle and has capacity for 49 male and 6 female prisoners The market house is a recent erection. The museum adjoining the baths, contains a good collection in natural history, and many Roman and British antiquities. The custom house stands at the south end of the terrace a pier and landing slip are at the north end and the harbour extends under the walls of the castle New harbour works, on the north side of the town, estimated to cost £50,000, were commenced in 1869 The town church is a chapel of ease to the parish church and was formerly the garrison chapel The services here are always in English, while those in the parish church are in Welsh There are nine chapels for dissenters, a national school erected in 1844, a training college, said to be the cheapest for pupils in the kingdom, a mechanics institute, a commodious news room, and two excellent libraries

The town has a head post office,‡ a railway station with telegraph, two banking offices and three chief inns, is the capital of the county, with assizes, sessions, elections, and militia head quarters, and publishes two weekly newspapers A weekly market is held on Saturday, and fairs on the second Thursday of Feb, March, and April, the first Thursday of May, the third Thursday of June, Sept, and Oct, the fourth Thursday of Aug, 9 Nov, and the first Friday and Saturday of Dec A steam ferry boat runs to the opposite shore of Anglesey a steamer plies twice a day to Menai Bridge, and they can load and discharge at all states of the tide The port includes Barmouth, Port Madoc, and Porthdynllaen as sub ports. The vessels belonging to it, at the beginning of 1868, were 170 small sailing vessels, of aggregately 6 619 tons, 351 larger sailing vessels, of aggregately 35,259 tons, and 5 steam vessels, of aggregately 280 tons The vessels which entered, in 1867, from abroad were 37, of aggregately 8,916 tons, and coastwise 1,337 sailing vessels, of aggregately 70 264 tons, and 104 steam vessels, of aggregately 16,626 tons The vessels which cleared, in 1867 for the colonies were 103 of 18,978 tons, and coastwise 74 of 5,258 tons The customs amounted, in 1858, to £7,759, in 1867, to £9,527 The chief exports are slates and copper ore, and the chief imports, timber, coal and foreign produce The annual average export of slates is 91,000 tons The town was chartered by Edward I, is governed by a mayor six aldermen and eight councillors, and unites with Bangor and four other boroughs in sending a member to parliament Its borough limits include about three fourths of the parish, and extend, in some directions, two miles from the town Electors of the six boroughs in 1868 1 023 Direct taxes, £6 903 Real property of Carnarvon town, £23,846, of which £2 000 are in railways Pop of Carnarvon borough in 1851, 8,001, in 1861, 8 512 Houses, 1,820 The town gives the title of Earl to the family of Herbert

The sub district contains the parishes of Llanbeblig and Llanfaglan Acres, 8,676 Pop, 10,190 Houses, 2,149 —The district comprehends also the sub district of Llandwrog, containing the parishes of Llandwrog, Llanwnda, Llanllyfni, and Clynnog, the sub district of Llanrug, containing the parishes of Llanrug, Llanberis, Llanddeiniolen, Llanfair is Gaer, and Bettws Garmon, and the sub district of Llanidan, in Anglesey, containing the parishes of Llanidan, Llangaffo, Llangeinwen, and St. Peter Newborough, and the parochial chapelry of Llanfairynycwmmwd. Acres, 97,635 Poor rates in 1866 £14,329 Pop in 1861, 32,425 Houses 7 023 Marriages in 1866, 300, births, 1,195,—of which 84 were illegitimate deaths 1,022, —of which 379 were at ages under 5 years, and 24 at ages above 85 Marriages in the ten years 1851-60, 2,265, births, 9 909, deaths, 6,941 The places of worship in 1851 were 21 of the Church of England, with 5,464 sittings, 23 of Independents, with 4,453 s. 8 of Baptists, with 1,250 s, 9 of Wesleyan Methodists, with 2,159 s, 35 of Calvinistic Methodists, with 11,678 s. and 1 of Latter Day Saints, with 58 attendants The schools were 25 public day schools, with 2,423 scholars, 16 private day schools, with 400 s, 55 Sunday schools, with 11,973 s, and 1 evening school for adults, with 58 s. The workhouse is in Carnarvon

CARNARVON BAY, an offset of the Irish sea on the west coast of Anglesey and Carnarvonshire It commences between Holyhead on the north and Pwllheli on the south, measures 36 miles across the entrance, has a somewhat triangular outline, and penetrates 18¼ miles eastward to the SW mouth of the Menai strait.

CARNARVON RAILWAYS, four railways in Carnarvonshire One the Bangor and C, goes from Bangor station to C Another, the C. and Nantlle, goes 9 miles from C to Llandwrog, and was authorised in 1867 to go 8½ miles further Another, the Carnarvonshire goes 17 miles from C to Avon Wen became united with the preceding, and was opened in Sept. 1867 Another, the C and Llanberis, was authorised in 1864 to go 9 miles from C to L, and in 1865, to have an extension to the Bangor and C, and a branch into the Bettws Garmon Valley

CARNARVONSHIRE, a maritime county of North Wales, bounded, on the north, by Beaumaris bay and the Irish sea, on the north east, by Denbigh, on the south east and the south, by Merioneth and by Cardigan bay, on the south west by Carnarvon bay, and on the north west, by the Menai strait, dividing it from Anglesey Its length, south westward, is 50 miles, its greatest breadth, 23½ miles, its circuit, about 150 miles, its area, 370,273 acres The part between Cardigan bay and Carnarvon bay 28 miles long and diminishing in breadth from 13 miles to a point, is the peninsula of Lleyn, and the other parts are mainly filled with the vales and mountains of Snowdonia Much of the Lleyn peninsula is low country, parts of the other seaboards also are low yet these tracts abound in bold picturesque diversities while the mountains of Snowdonia regarded either in the group or in detail, are the richest for grandeur, force, and beauty, in the British Isles. The Conway river goes along the north eastern boundary to the sea, the Machno the Lleder, and the Llugwy go into the Conway, the Glas Llyn, a romantic stream, goes to Cardigan bay, and the Seiont and the Gwrfai descend from Snowdon to the

Menai strait. Numerous lakes lie among the mountains, and innumerable rivulets run around their bases. Cambrian and silurian rocks, with vast and manifold protrusions of eruptive rocks, fill nearly all the area. The cambrian form considerable belts in the north west and the south west; the lower silurian spread from the middle west, through all the centre, to the south and the east; and the upper silurian form a small tract in the north-east. The erupted rocks range from granite, through all the traps, to the simply volcanic, and include great uplifted masses of clay slate and other schists. Old red sandstone appears on the coast from Conway to Bangor,—also in Beach -Pwll, and carboniferous limestone appears in Orme's Head, and in a strip along part of the Menai strait. Copper, lead and zinc, are worked, roofing slates, in vast quantities, are quarried, and mill stone and ochre are found.

Not more than 8 000 acres are in tillage, rather more than half the entire area is enclosed pasture, and the rest is either waste or can be depastured only in the summer months. Wheat is grown in a few fertile spots on the sea-boards but oats, barley, and potatoes are the chief crops and sometimes very precarious. Husbandry, in general, is rude, yet has been much improved. The black cattle are smaller than those of Anglesey, the sheep are a very lean native breed, with long legs and slender bodies, and the hogs are unshapely creatures, tall and meagre, like those of Ireland. Butter, wool, and lambs are sent to the market, and stockings, flannel, and coarse woollen cloth are manufactured. The Chester and Holyhead railway goes along the northern seaboard; the Llanrwst railway serves for the tracts on the Conway, and the Carnarvon railways go along the Menai strait and traverse the interior. Tram railways also connect the great quarries with the ports, and good roads traverse the most populous tracts.

The county contains 68 parishes, parts of 5 other parishes, and 2 extra parochial places, and is divided into the boroughs of Carnarvon and Pwllheli, and the hundreds of Cwmwd maen, Creyddyn, Dinllaen, Fifionydd, Gaffligion, Isaf, Isgorfai, Nant Conway, Uchaf, and Uwchgorfai. The registration county includes 68,317 acres of Denbigh and Anglesey, excludes 78,527 acres to Denbigh and Merioneth, and is divided into the districts of Carnarvon, Bangor, Conway and Pwllheli. The towns are Carnarvon, Bangor, Pwllheli, Conway, Criccieth, Nevin and Tremadoc. The chief seats are Glynllifon Park, Glynllifon Hall, Gloddaeth, Nant Hall, Penrhyn Castle, Nanthoran, Llanvair, Madryn, Cefn-Amwlch, Tanyrallt, Vaenol, and Coed Helen. Real property in 1815, £131 213; in 1843, £251 044; in 1851, £258,893; in 1860, £379 623, of which £119 002 are in quarries, £1 127 in mines and £2 000 in canals. The county is governed by a lord lieutenant, a high sheriff, and about thirty magistrates. It is in the Home Military district, and in the North Wales judicial circuit. The assizes and the quarter sessions are held at Carnarvon. The police force, in 1864, comprised 51 men at a cost of £5 525; the crimes committed were 114, the depredators and suspected persons at large were 269, the houses of bad character 70. One member is sent to parliament by the county at large, and one by the boroughs. County electors in 1868, 2 190. Pop in 1801, 41 521; in 1821, 58 099; in 1841, 81,093; in 1861, 95 694. Inhabited houses, 20,256; uninhabited 593; building 171. The county is in the diocese of Bangor.

The territory now forming Carnarvonshire belonged anciently to the Cangi and the Ordovices; was included by the Romans in their Britannia Secunda, and formed part of Venedotia or Gwynedd. It was the chief theatre of the successive and protracted struggles of Romans, Saxons, Normans, and English for the subjugation of Wales; and it possessed the stoutest means for offering resistance. Its natural defences, themselves of the highest order, were so strengthened by artificial strongholds as to make the parts of it around Snowdon one vast mountain fortress. The passage of the Conway was guarded by Castell Diganwy, the pass of Bwlch y ddeufaen, by a fort at Caerhun, the northern seaboard by the great hill camp of Penmaen Mawr, and by forts at Aber and in Nant-Francon, the pass of Llanberis, by Dolbadarn Castle, the pass under Mynydd-Mawr, by a fort overlooking it, and the passage over the Traeth Mawr or great sands, by the castle of Harlech in Merioneth on the one side, and by that of Criccieth on the other, with a watch tower at Castell Gwyvarch, and a fort at Dolbenmaen. Snowdonia thus could not be entered without a siege, or penetrated without encountering the double resistance of artificial defences and stupendous natural fastnesses, and it, in consequence, was the scene of continued and desperate warfare, because the last retreat of unconquered freedom,—

> "The Briton's last resource—his mountains hoar—
> Where weeping Freedom from the contest fled,
> And Cambria saw her dearest heroes dead."

Cromlechs occur at Bacheren, Cefn Amlwch, Ystym Cegid, Ymeinauhirion, and Penmorfa, and other Celtic antiquities exist, while many more have been destroyed since the latter part of last century. Several large ancient British camps or forts especially at Diganwy, Dolbenmaen, Dinas Dinorwig, Dinas Dinlle, Braich y Dinas, and Tre'r Caeri, still exist. Roman stations stood at Caerhun and Carnarvon, a branch of the northern Watling street joined the main Roman road at Caerhun, the Sarn Helen way went from Carnarvon to Heriri Mons in Merioneth, and many Roman antiquities have been found. The castles of Carnarvon and Conway are two of the finest extant specimens of their class in the kingdom, and those of Dolbadarn and Criccieth still present features of interest. Vestiges of monastic houses are at Bangor, Beddgelert, Clynnog Vawr, Maenan and Bardsey, and a large ancient church is at Clynnog.

CARN-BODUAN, a hill, with traces of ancient buildings, near Nevin, in Carnarvon.

CARNBREA. See CAMBORNE.

CARNCOED, a village in Llangurig parish, Montgomery, 3½ miles S of Llanidloes.

CARNED, a township in Llandinam parish, Montgomery, 5½ miles NNE of Llanidloes.

CARNEDD DAVYD and CARNEDD LLEWELYN, two peaks of Snowdonia, in Carnarvon, 5 miles NW and NNW of Capel Curig. They have altitudes of 3 426 and 3,469 feet, and are joined by a narrow ridge, 2 miles long. Carnedd Llewelyn commands a very magnificent prospect, and has traces of an ancient camp.

CARNEDDI, a hamlet in Llanllechid parish, Carnarvon, near Bangor.

CARNEDDI HENGWM, a defile 5½ miles N of Barmouth, in Merioneth. Several cairns are here, one of them 60 yards long, and containing a cistvaen.

CARNEDD LLEWELYN. See CARNEDD DAVYD.

CARNELIAN BAY, a pretty little bay 3 miles S of Scarborough, N R Yorkshire. Carnelians, jaspers, moss agates, and other pebbles are found on its shore.

CARNFORTH, a township in Warton parish, Lancashire, on the Lancaster and Carlisle railway, 6 miles NNE of Lancaster. It has a r station with telegraph, a post office‡ under Lancaster, six blast furnaces erected in 1865, and an endowed school used as a church. Acres, 1 492. Real property, £2 269. Pop, 393. Houses, 82. A subterranean brook bursts up here, after having run 2 miles under ground from a limestone cavern at Dunald mill hole. The Furness and Ulverston railway makes its junction with the Lancaster and Carlisle at Carnforth, and the Furness and Midland, connecting the former with the Little Northwestern, and opened in 1867, goes hence to Wennington.

CARN GALVA, a hill on the coast of Cornwall, 7 miles NNW of Penzance. It is beautifully crested with granite, and commands a good view.

CARNGIWCH, a parish in Pwllheli district, Carnarvon, on the river Erch, 3¾ miles NW of Nevin, and 5½ WNW of Avon Wen r station. Post town, Nevin, under Pwllheli. Acres, 1 344. Real property, £412. Pop, 130. Houses, 28. The property is divided among a few. The living is a vicarage, annexed to the rectory of Elern, in the diocese of Bangor The church is tolerable.

CARN LLECHART, a Druidical circle in Llangyfelach parish, Glamorgan, near the top of Mynydd Maen Coch, in the neighbourhood of Swansea It is in a state of almost perfect preservation

CARN MADRYN, a hill 7 miles W by S of Pwllheli, in Carnarvon It is 1,205 feet high, and has some ancient ruins

CARN MARTH, a hill in the south eastern vicinity of Redruth, in Cornwall Its height is 757 feet An excavation in the side of it, called Gwennap pit, was the scene of Wesley's famous preaching to the miners, and is still used, by the Wesleyans, for an anniversary celebration, generally attended by upwards of 20,000 persons.

CARNMENELLIS, or CARN MENELEZ a chapelry in Wendron parish, Cornwall, on the river Kennal, near the Cornwall railway, 3 miles S of Redruth It was constituted in 1846 Post town, Redruth Pop, 3,094 Houses, 559 Carn Menelez hill here is 822 feet high The living is a vicarage in the diocese of Exeter Value, £134 * Patron, Mrs Broadley

CARN MINNIS, a hill 3 miles W by S of St Ives in Cornwall Its height is 805 feet, and it commands an extensive view

CARNO, a river, a village, and a parish in Montgomeryshire The river rises near the watershed with the Dyfi, and runs 9 miles south eastward to the Severn, 2½ miles N of Llandinam The village stands on the river, adjacent to the Newtown and Machynlleth railway, 10 miles W by N of Newtown and has a station on the railway, and a post office under Shrewsbury The parish comprises the townships of Derlwyn, Llysyn, and Trowscoed and is in the district of Newtown Acres, 10,982 Real property £3 168, Pop 909 Houses, 160 The property is much subdivided Great part of the surface is mountainous Remains of a Roman fortress, called Caer Noddfa, are contiguous to the village, and vestiges of two castles are on a hill above Avon Cerniog and on a spur of Allt Mawr, both within a mile of the village A battle, decisive of the sovereignty of North Wales, was fought, in 946 at the village, and another, of fierce character, with similar result, was fought, in 1077, on Mynydd Carn The living is vicarage in the diocese of Bangor Value, £95 Patron, Sir W W Wynn Bart The church occupies the site of an old one of the Knights of St John, and was built in 1807 There are chapels for Independents, Baptists, Calvinistic Methodists and Wesleyans

CARNO, a locality in the southern vicinity of Crickhowell, in Brecon Ethelbald, king of Mercia, on his invasion of Wales in 728, was met and defeated here by the Britons

CARNON, a stream and a village in Cornwall The stream runs 4 miles south eastward, down a valley, to the head of a creek of Falmouth harbour 4 miles N of Falmouth Great tin stream works were carried on at its mouth, over a space 300 yards wide upwards of a mile long, some distance into the bed of the estuary, and banked round to keep off the water but have been abandoned The village stands a short way up the stream, and has extensive works for preparing arsenic from arsenical pyrites

CARNSMERRY, a locality 5 miles from St Austell, in Cornwall It has a post office under St Austell, and fairs on 13 July and 20 Oct

CARNWALLON, a hundred in Carmarthen, 9 miles along the Loughor river to the coast It contains five parishes Acres 61,282 Pop, 20 944 Houses, 4,045

CAROGE, a township in Llanbister parish, Radnor 11 miles W of Knighton Real property, £533. Pop, 144

CARON See CARON YS CLAWDD

CARON UWCH CLAWDD or STRATA FLORIDA, a township chapelry in Caron ys Clawdd parish Cardigan, on the Sarn Helen way and the river Teifi, 4 miles NNE of Tregaron r station, and 22½ N by W of Llandovery It includes the village of Rhydfendigaed and its post-town is Tregaron, under Carmarthen Rated property, £363 Pop, 868 Houses 181 The property is divided among a few The surface consists of mountains, intersected by narrow vales A Cistertian abbey, often called Ystrad Flwr abbey, was founded here, in 1164, by Rhys ap Gryfydd, prince of South Wales, burnt down in the wars of Edward I, restored afterwards to more than its original splendour, and given, at the dissolution, to the Stedmans It was the repository of the national records from 1156 till 1270, and the scene of a grand assembly of lords and barons in 1238, and was the burial-place of many of the Cambrian princes It stood on the Teifi overshadowed by mountains, and was alike secluded and magnificent, but almost the only part of it now remaining is a very beautiful Norman arch, which formed the west entrance to its church An older but small monastic house stood two miles to the south, at a spot still showing ancient foundations, and called Llan Monachlog, "the old monastery" The living is a vicarage in the diocese of St Davids Value, £80 Patron, W E Powell, Esq The church is a small mean structure within the precincts of the abbey There is a Calvinistic Methodist chapel

CARON YS CLAWDD a parish in Tregaron district, Cardigan, on the Sarn Helen way and the rivers Berwyn and Teifi at Tregaron r station, and 18½ miles NNW of Llandovery It is called also Caron, Tregaron, and Trefgaron, and it contains the townships of Caron Uwch Clawdd, Braen Aeron, Tre Cefel, Bron Caron, Tref Lynn, Croes and Berwyn, and Aigoed and Ystrad, the last of which includes the town of Tregaron, with a post office under Carmarthen Acres, 39 138 Real property, £4,056 Pop., 2,608 Houses, 567 Much of the surface is bog and mountain The living is a vicarage in the diocese of St Davids Value £176 * Patron, the Bishop of St Davids The church has a good tower, and the churchyard contains some ancient monumental stones There is a Calvinistic Methodist chapel Twm Shon Catti, the famous robber of the 17th century, who afterwards became high sheriff of the county was a native

CARPERBY CUM-THORESBY, a township in Aysgarth parish N R Yorkshire 3½ miles E of Askrigg Acres, 4 950 Real property, £3,245 Pop, 315 Houses 74

CARR, a hamlet in Laughten en le Morthen parish, W R Yorkshire 5½ miles SW of Tickhill Pop, 66

CARRATON HILL, a hill 4 miles NNE of Liskeard, in Cornwall Its height is 1,208 feet Prince Rupert's army encamped on it in 1644

CARR BANK, a shoal in Milford haven, Pembroke, off Milford A floating light is on it

CARRE (THE), a tributary of the river Parret, in Somerset.

CARRLDFYNYDD, a township in Llannefydd parish Denbighshire, 5½ miles NW of Denbigh Real property, £3,009

CARREG CENNEN CASTLE, an ancient ruin 2½ miles SE of Llandeilofawr, in Carmarthen It crowns a precipitous, isolated, limestone rock, nearly 300 feet high, overhanging the river Cennen, almost surrounded by bare sandstone hills, and commanding extensive vista views along valleys and to the sea It covers a platform of fully an acre, is inaccessible on all sides except one, and must, in old times, have been almost impregnable Its history is not known, and its origin has been ascribed variously to the ancient Britons and the Romans Its remains comprise two square towers, defending the entrance, a large round tower, and an octagonal tower, and do not appear to be older than the time of Henry III or Edward I

CARREG GWASTAD POINT, a headland in Llanwnda parish, Pembroke, 4½ miles WNW of Fishguard A French force of 1 400 men landed here in 1797 and were beaten and captured by a body of yeomanry under Lord Cawdor

CARREGHOVA a township in Llanymynech parish Montgomery, on the river Vyrnwy, near Offa's Dyke and the Montgomery canal, 5½ miles SSW of Oswestry Acres, 1,223 Real property, £3,111, of which £1,432 are in quarries, and £30 in mines Pop, 400 Houses, 92 Limestone is extensively quarried

CARR END, a hamlet in Bainbridge township, Aysgarth parish N R. Yorkshire, 1 mile SW of Askrigg

CARR GREEN, a hamlet in Dirton township and parish W R Yorkshire, 3¼ miles NW of Barnesley

CARRHOUSE, a hamlet in Belton parish, Lincoln, 2 miles N of Epworth Pop, 148

CARRINGTON, a township chapelry in Bowden parish, Cheshire, on the Mersey, 3¼ miles NW of Broadheath r station Post-town Ashton on Mersey Acres, 2 333 Real property, £4 480 Pop., 521 Houses, 102 The living is a vicarage in the dio. of Chester Value, £375 Patron, the Earl of Stamford The church is good There are two Methodist chapels and a n school

CARRINGTON, a parochial chapelry in Boston district, Lincoln, in the fens, 4 miles NE of Langrick r station, and 7½ N of Boston. Post town New Bolingbroke, under Boston. Acres, 2,660 Real property, £5,056 Pop, 197 Houses, 28 It was formerly a township of Helpringham, but was made parochial on the draining of Wildman fen in 1812, and named after Lord Carrington, the principal proprietor The living is a vicarage in the diocese of Lincoln Value, £[illegible]5 Patrons, certain Trustees

CARRINGTON, a hamlet and a chapelry in Basford parish, Notts The hamlet stands 1¼ mile N of Nottingham, and has a post office under Nottingham Pop 353 The chapelry was constituted in 1843 Pop., 2,426 Houses, 519 The living is a p curacy in the diocese of Lincoln Value, £150 Patron the Bishop of L. There are Baptist and Wesleyan chapels, and a national school

CARR LANE, a hamlet in North Bierley township, Bradford parish, W R Yorkshire, near Bradford

CARROCK FELL, a mountain of the Skiddaw group, in Cumberland 3½ miles S of Hesket Newmarket Much of it is rocky and broken, many parts are interesting to the mineralogist, and the summit has an altitude of 2,1[illegible]0 feet, is biforked, and appears to have once been surrounded by a wall.

CARROG a township, with a r station, in Corwen parish Merioneth, 3 miles E of Corwen Pop, 199

CARROW, a hamlet in Trowse parish, Norfolk, within the city boundaries of Norwich

CARROW, a hamlet in Warden parish, Northumberland, on the Roman wall, 4¾ miles N of Haydon Bridge Carrowburgh here was the Procolitia on the Wall, where the Batavian cohort was stationed, and two Roman altars have been found

CARSHALTON—pronounced CASHORTON or CARSHORTON—a village, a parish, and a sub district in Epsom district, Surrey The village stands near the river Wandle and the Epsom railway, 3 miles W by S of Croydon, and has a station on the railway, and a post office under London, S It was known at Domesday as Aulton, and was once a market town The parish comprises 2,904 acres Real property £14 178 Pop 2 538 Houses, 492 The property is subdivided Carshalton Park was formerly the seat of Sir N Throckmorton, Dr Radcliffe and the Scawens, and is now occupied by James Aitken, Esq The parish is watered by the Wandle and its head streams, and has flour, paper, oil, and snuff mills. A spring, overarched with stone close to the churchyard, is traditionally associated with Queen Anne Boleyn, and bears her name The living is a rectory in the diocese of Winchester Value, £575 * Patron Albert Cator, Esq The church is early English, much altered but in good condition, and contains a remarkable brass of Sheriff Gaynesford, who died in 1490, and three elaborate monuments of last century There are gas works a police station a British school, a national school an infant school, and charities £78 The sub district contains four parishes. Acres 12,119 Pop, 8,[illegible]11 Houses, 1,451

CARSICK HILL, a hamlet in Upper Hallam township, Sheffield parish, W R Yorkshire 2 miles W of Sheffield

CARSINGTON, a parish in Ashborne district, Derby on the Peak railway, 2 miles W of Wirksworth r station, and 5 W of Whatstandwell Bridge Post town, Wirksworth Acres, 1,118 Real property £1 965 Pop, 259 Houses, 54 The property is divided among a few Limestone abounds, and lead ore occurs The living is a rectory in the diocese of Lichfield Value, £176 Patron, the Bishop of Lichfield The church is good An endowed school has £50 Oldfield, the non conformist, and Farneworth, the translator of Machiavel, were rectors.

CARSWELL See BUCKLAND, Berks.

CARTER FELL, one of the Cheviots, on the boundary of Northumberland with Scotland, 16 miles NW of Otterburn Its height is 1,602 feet A depression on its NE shoulder, called Carter-Bar is traversed by Watling-street, a principal inland route to Scotland, and was always a noted pass in the times of the Border forays A smart skirmish took place, in the vicinity of the pass, on the Red Swire, in 1575, at a judicial meeting for redressing Border wrongs, and nearly kindled national hostilities between the Scottish king and Elizabeth The skirmish is commemorated in a fine old ballad, given in the "Border Minstrelsy"

CARTER KNOWL, a hamlet in Ecclesall Bierlow township, Sheffield parish, W R Yorkshire, 4¼ miles SW of Sheffield.

CARTERMOOR, a hamlet in Kirkley township, Ponteland parish, Northumberland, 6¼ miles SSW of Morpeth

CARTHAMARTHA ROCKS, a group of picturesque limestone cliffs 6 miles S of Launceston in Cornwall

CARTHKENNY (THE), a tributary of the river Cynin at St. Clear in Carmarthen

CARTHORPE, a township in Burneston parish, N R. Yorkshire, near the river Swale 4½ miles SE of Bedale Acres 2,035 Real property, £2,401 Pop, 3[illegible]7 Houses, 81 There is a Wesleyan chapel

CARTINGTON, a township in Rothbury parish, Northumberland, on an affluent of the river Coquet, 3 miles NW by N of Rothbury It includes the township of Bankhead and the hamlet of Sandylands. Acres, 1,912 Pop 84 Houses, 15 Cartington Castle was a seat of the Ratcliffes and the Widdringtons

CARTLETT, a hamlet in Lower Guyting parish, Gloucester, 4¼ miles EbE of Winchcomb.

CARTLETT a suburb of Haverfordwest in Pembroke

CARTMEL, a small town, a parish, and a sub district in Ulverstone district, Lancashire The town stands in a fine valley, overhung by the Coniston fells, within 2½ miles of the Leven sands, 2 NE of Cark and Cartmel r station, and 6½ E of Ulverstone Egfrid King of Northumbria, gave the surrounding lands to St. Cuthbert, Ethelred a successor of Egfrid, put to death here two rivals to his throne, and William Mareschal Earl of Pembroke founded here in 1188, a grand Augustinian priory The priory enjoyed the privilege of providing guides for the Leven and Morecambe sands, and was given at the dissolution to Thomas Holcroft The church of it still stands, measures 157 feet along the nave and choir, 100 along the transepts, and is now the parish church The nave was rebuilt in the 15th century, the rest is early English, the choir has an eight light, transomed, east window, the central steeple exhibits the curious feature of a diagonal belfry on a square basement, and the church contains carved stalls, two ancient monuments of Prior Walton and Sir J Harrington, and monuments of the Prestons, the Lowthers, and others The town consists of good stone houses in narrow irregular streets, and has a post office‡ under Newton in Cartmel. It once had a weekly market, and it still has fairs on the Wednesday before Easter, Whit Monday, the Tuesday after 23 Oct, and 5 Nov A grammar school has £116 from endowment, and other charities £49 Bishop Law was a native, and was educated in the grammar school The parish includes also the village of Newton in Cartmel and contains the townships of Cartmel Fell Staveley, East Broughton, Upper Allithwaite Lower Allithwaite, Upper Holker and Lower Holker Acres, 28 7[illegible]7 Real property, £29,658 Pop 5,103 Houses, 1 033 The property in many parts, is much subdivided Some of the inhabitants are employed in cotton mills A medicinal spring called the Holy Well, occurs about 3 miles south of the town and draws numerous visitors. The living is a vicarage in the diocese of Carlisle Value, £200 * Patron, the Duke of Devonshire The p. curacies of Cartmel Fell, Grange, Field Broughton, Flookburgh, Lindale, Allithwaite, and Staveley are separate benefices The sub district is conterminate with the parish

CARTMEL FELL, a township chapelry in Cartmel parish, Lancashire, on the river Winster, 4¾ miles N of Grange r station, and 6½ NNE of Cartmel Post town Newton in Cartmel Acres, 2,900 Real property, £3,114 Pop, 308 Houses, 61 The property is subdivided The living is a p curacy in the diocese of Carlisle Value, £130 Patron, the Duke of Devonshire. The church is good, and there is a Quakers' chapel

CARTWORTH, a township in Kirkburton parish, W R Yorkshire, on a branch of the river Colne, 6 miles S of Huddersfield It includes part of the village of Holmfirth, and part of the hamlet of Scholes Acres, 2,820 Real property, £7,930, of which £122 are in quarries Pop, 2,503 Houses, 503 Many of the inhabitants are employed in the woollen manufacture

CARUMTUNE See CARHAMPTON

CARVARCHELL, a village in St David's parish, Pembroke, 3½ miles ENE of St David's

CARWINNEN See CAMBORNE

CARWOOD a township in Hopesev parish, Salop, 6½ miles SE of Bishops Castle

CARY CASTLE See CASTLE CARY

CARY COATS, a township in Thockrington parish, Northumberland, 6½ miles ESE of Bellingham Acres, 1,799 Pop, 41 Houses, 9

CARY FITZPAINE, a hamlet in Charlton Mackrell parish, Somerset, 3½ miles NW of Ilchester Real property, £825

CARY LYTES, a picturesque old seat in Somerset, 2 miles N of Ilchester A wing of it, forming a chapel, is of the time of Edward III, and the rest is of the time of Henry VIII

CARY'S SCONCE See ALUM BAY

CASCOB, a township and a parish in Presteigne district, Radnor The township lies in Radnor forest, near the river Lug, partly within the borough boundaries of New Radnor 5½ miles W by N of Presteigne, and 5¾ SW by S of Knighton r station Pop, 117 Houses, 22 The parish includes also part of the township of Litton and Cascob, and its post town is Presteigne, Radnorshire Acres, 2 548 Real property, with the rest of Litton and Cascob £1,941 Pop, 153 Houses, 29 The property is subdivided The living is a rectory in the diocese of St David's Value, £190 * Patron, the Bishop of St David's The church is not good

CASEHORTON See CARSHALTON

CASEWICK, a hamlet in Uffington parish, Lincoln, 3½ miles ENE of Stamford

CASEY GREEN, a hamlet in New Forest township, Kirkby Ravensworth parish, N R Yorkshire, 4½ miles N of Richmond

CASHIO, a hamlet and a hundred in Herts The hamlet is in Watford parish, and lies adjacent to Watford town, the river Gade, and the Northwestern railway It bears also the name of Cashiobury, and it occupies the site of an ancient town of the Cassii, and was given by King Offa to St Alban's abbey Cashiobury Park immediately N of it, belonged once to the Morrisons and the Capels, and is now the seat of the Earl of Essex The mansion is a Tudor edifice, containing many fine family portraits, and the park is spacious, and was laid out by Le Notre The hundred extends from Bucks and Middlesex, north north eastward past the hamlet and past St. Alban's, to within 2½ miles of Stevenage, and contains nineteen parishes. Acres, 82 090 Pop in 1851, 31,009, in 1861, 33,038 Houses, 6,522

CASKETS, or CASQUETS (THE), a group of rocks in the English channel, 8 miles W of Alderney They are about a mile in circuit, granitic, fantastically shaped, barren, and so abrupt that a line of battle ship can pass within an oar's length of them They were long a terror to mariners, but have now three lighthouses, put up in 1723, placed triangularly, connected by strong walls, and showing revolving lights, visible all round, at the distance of 15 miles Admiral Balchen was wrecked on them in 1744

CASLLWCHWR. See LOUGHOR

CASQUETS (THE) See CASKETS (THE)

CASSIBELAN See ALBANS (ST)

CASSINGTON, a village and a parish in Woodstock district Oxford The village stands near the river Isis, and near Handborough Junction r station, 5 miles NW of Oxford The parish includes also the hamlet of Worton, and its post town is Oxford. Acres, 2,990 Real property, £2,899 Pop., 433 Houses, 92 The manor belonged anciently to the Montacutes, and had a castle. The paper mill of Oxford university is here The living is a vicarage in the diocese of Oxford Value, £166 Patron, Christ Church, Oxford The church was built by Geoffrey de Clinton, chamberlain to Henry II

CASSINO (GREAT and LITTLE), two seats in Aldborough parish, Suffolk.

CASSOP, a township and a chapelry in Kelloe parish, Durham The township lies on the Hartlepool railway 4½ miles SE by E of Durham and has a post-office, of the name of Cassop Colliery, under Ferryhill Acres, 1,622 Real property, £5,248, of which £2,839 are in mines. Pop, 1,661 Houses, 321 The chapelry includes Quarrington Pop., 3,130 Living a p. curacy Value, £300 The church was built in 1868

CASTELDWYRAN See CASTLE DYRRAN

CASTELL, a township in Llanuwchllyn parish, Merioneth, 6½ miles SW of Bala. Real property, £429 Pop, 78

CASTELL ABER LLEINIOG a small ruined fort on the E coast of Anglesey, 2 miles NNE of Beaumaris. It was built, in 1098, by Hugh Lupus, has turrets at the corners, and was taken, in 1645, by the royalists

CASTELLAN, a chapelry in Penrith parish, Pembroke, under Vrenin vawr, 6 miles SSE of Cardigan Acres, 890 Pop., 165 Houses, 43 The church is in ruins

CASTELL BYTHE. See CASTLE-BYTHE

CASTELL CADWGAN See ABERAYRON

CASTELL CAERLINION See CASTLE CAERENION

CASTELL CAERSEION, a ruined ancient British town on the coast of Carnarvon, on the summit of a serrated ridge, 1¾ mile W of Conway It comprises very distinct circular houses, a citadel, and outworks, and commands an exquisite view

CASTELL CIDWM, an ancient British fort in Snowdonia, Carnarvonshire, on a rugged steep of Mynydd-Mawr, 6½ miles SE of Carnarvon Its name signifies "the Wolf's Castle

CASTELL COCH, an ancient fort in a pass of its own name, in Glamorgan, on the river Taf 3 miles SW by S of Caerphilly Its site is a precipitous escarpment, overhanging the pass, its plan was triangular, with a round tower at each corner, and its remains show features of the time of Henry III Its name signifies "the Red Castle, and alludes to the tint of the sandstone of which it is built

CASTELL CARNDOCHAN an ancient British fort in Merioneth, 6½ miles SW of Bala.

CASTELL-CYMARON, an old baronial fortalice in Llandewy Ystradenny parish, Radnor, 10 miles E of Rhayader It was built by the Normans, and became a seat of the Mortimers

CASTELL DINAS BRAN, an ancient fortress at the Valle Crucis, in Denbigh, on a conical eminence 910 feet high, rising from the Dee in the north eastern vicinity of Llangollen It dates from very early times, was the chief seat of the lords of Yale and Bromfield, gave refuge to Gryffydd ap Madoc, at his alliance with Henry III, and sustained a siege in the conflict between Owen Glendower and Lord Grey De Ruthin Little more than substructions of it exist, but they show it to have been an oblong, 290 feet by 110, and very strong Traces of entrenchments also are seen on the shoulders of the hill The site commands extensive and very interesting views.

CASTELL DOLBADARN See DOLBADARN CASTLE.

CASTELL DOLWYDDELAN See DOLWYDDELAN

CASTELL DWYRAN See CASTLE DYRRAN

CASTELL EDWIN, an ancient British fort in Flint, 3½ miles E of Rhuddlan

CASTELL EINION SAIS, an old baronial fortalice in Brecon, in the valley of the Usk, near Capel Bettws. It was built by Einion, who fought under Edward III

CASTELL FLEMING, an ancient British fort in Cardigan, near the Sarn Helen way, 3 miles NW of Tregaron

CASTELL GLAS, a ruined fort in Cardigan, on the river Ebwy, 2 miles NW of Tregaron. It was built during the baronial wars, and a tower and traces of the walls remain

CASTELL GLYN ITHON See CEFNLLYS

CASTELL GWALTER, an ancient hill fort on the coast of Cardigan, 8 miles NE of Aberystwith. A castle is said to have been built on it by Walter L Espec, the ancestor of the Duke of Rutland, and destroyed, in 1135, by Owen Gwynedd, but no vestige of this exists.

CASTELL LLEINIOG See CASTELL-ABER LLEINIOG

CASTELLMAI, a village in Llanbeblig parish, Carnarvonshire near Carnarvon

CASTELLMOCH, a township in Llanrhaiadr-yn Mochnant parish, Montgomery, 3¼ miles N of Llanfyllin Pop., 98

CASTELL-NADOLIG See PENBRYN

CASTELL-PRYSOR, an old fort in a defile of Merioneth, between Moel Uchaf and the lofty heights of the Garn 4 miles S by E of Festiniog It is now a mere fragment, and it has been ascribed variously to the Britons and the Romans Roman coins and urns have been found at it

CASTELL RHYFELL, an ancient camp in Cardigan, near a remarkable ancient British road 4½ miles E by N of Tregaron

CASTELL Y BERE, an ancient castle, 7½ miles NE of Towyn, in Merioneth It was visited by Edward I, and was in a defensible state during the wars of the Roses.

CASTELNAU See BARNES

CASTER, CESTER, or CHESTER, a word varied from the Saxon "ceaster" or the Latin "castrum," signifying a camp, a fort, a castle, a fortified town, or a city, and used often, in conjunction with other words to designate places which had ancient military strengths.

CASTERLEY CAMP, an entrenched area of 64 acres in Salisbury plain, Wilts, 8½ miles SE of Devizes It is surrounded by a single vallum, 28 feet high, and has a sacred circle in the centre Sir R C Hoare pronounces it "one of the most original and unaltered works of the British era in the county"

CASTERN, a hamlet in Ilam parish, Stafford, 10 miles ESE of Leek Pop, 45

CASTERTON, a township chapelry in Kirkby Lonsdale parish Westmorland, on the river Lune, adjacent to the Ingleton branch of the Northwestern railway, 1½ mile NE of Kirkby Lonsdale It has a post office under Burton in Kendal Acres, 1,230 Real property, £3 444 Pop, 587 Houses, 61 The property is divided among a few Casterton Hall is the seat of the Wilsons The scenery is so fine as to have been called "the pride of Lonsdale Coal and limestone are found The living is a p curacy in the diocese of Carlisle Value, not reported * Patrons, Trustees The church was built in 1833, and has a tower Schools established by the late Rev W Carus Wilson, are widely known to fame

CASTERTON (GREAT), or BRIDGE CASTERTON, a parish in the district of Stamford and county of Rutland, on Ermine street and the river Gwash near the Leicester and Peterborough railway, 2½ miles NW of Stamford It has a post office, of the name of Great Casterton, under Stamford Acres, 1 590 Real property, £2,021 Pop 323 Houses 76. The property is divided among a few The manor belonged formerly to the Husseys, the Scroops the Delawarrs, and others, and belongs now to the Marquis of Exeter A Roman station, burnt by the Picts, is thought by some to have been here. The living is a rectory, united with the rectory of Pickworth, in the diocese of Peterborough Value, £450 * Patron, the Marquis of Exeter The church was later English but has been rebuilt. National schools were erected in 1861

CASTERTON (LITTLE), a parish in the district of Stamford and county of Rutland, on the river Gwash, near the Leicester and Peterborough railway, 2½ miles N by W of Stamford It includes the hamlet of Tolethorpe, and its post town is Stamford Acres, 1,450 Real property, £2,117 Pop, 118 Houses, 24 The manor belongs to Lord Chesham The living is a rectory, united with the p curacy of Tolethorpe, in the diocese of Peterborough Value, £254 * Patron, Lord Chesham The church is partly Norman and later English, but has been modernized There is a free school

CASTHORPE, a hamlet in Barrowby parish, Lincoln, 2 miles W of Grantham Pop, 51

CASTLE, a hamlet adjacent to the river Brue, and to the Mid Somerset railway, 8½ miles NNE of Glastonbury, in Somerset It has an ancient cross, and an eminence adjoining it, called Castle Hill was the site of an ancient stronghold

CASTLE, a hamlet in Pentyrch parish, Glamorgan, 3½ miles NW of Llandaff Real property, £1,195 Pop, 195

CASTLE, a township in Castle Caereinion parish, Montgomery, 4½ miles WSW of Welshpool Pop, 197

CASTLE, Llanwnog, Montgomery See ESGOB AND CASTLE

CASTLE, Notts See NOTTINGHAM.

CASTLE, Northumberland See CASTLE-WARD.

CASTLE ACRE, a village and a parish in Freebridge-Lynn district, Norfolk The village stands on the Peddar way and the river Nar 3½ miles NW of Dunham r station, and 4 N of Swaffham, and has a post office under Brandon, and fairs on 1 May and 5 Aug Here are extensive remains of a castle and a priory founded in 1085, by the Earl of Warrenne The castle occupies the site of previous works, covered an area of about 18 acres, and had an encircling embattled wall, 7 feet thick The priory was a cell to Lewes included an area of 29 acres, had a cruciform church 218 feet long, a chapter house 40 feet by 20, and a refectory 110 feet by 26, and was given, at the dissolution, to the Duke of Norfolk Part of the south west tower, some pillars of the nave, the walls of the transepts, the chapter house, the refectory the prior s lodge, and the gatehouse are still standing, exhibit features from Norman to perpendicular and look very picturesque —The parish comprises 3,249 acres. Real property, £5,427 Pop, 1,403 Houses, 334 The property is much subdivided The living is a vicarage in the diocese of Norwich Value, not reported Patron, the Earl of Leicester The church is ancient, large, and good, has a lofty square tower, and contains an ancient font and some curious monuments There are chapels for Baptists, Wesleyans, and Primitive Methodists, and a national school

CASTLE AN DINAS a hill 2½ miles ESE of St Columb in Cornwall Its summit has a height of 735 feet, commands a superb panoramic view, was occupied, as a military strength by Britons, Romans, and Danes, and is crowned by an earthwork and a ruined tower

CASTLE ASHBY See ASHBY CASTLE

CASTLE BARNARD See BARNARD (CASTLE)

CASTLEBEAR HILL a locality between the river Brent and the Great Western railway, 2¼ miles N of Brentford in Middlesex It has a post office under Ealing, London W A mansion here was the seat of the Duke of Kent

CASTLEBERG, a limestone cliff contiguous to Settle W R Yorkshire It is about 300 feet high, and commands a fine prospect

CASTLE BIGH See CASTLE BYTHE

CASTLE BOLTON See BOLTON CASTLE

CASTLE BROMWICH See BROMWICH (CASTLE)

CASTLE BYTHAM See BYTHAM CASTLE.

CASTLE BYTHE or CASTLE BIGH a parish in Haverfordwest district, Pembroke 5 miles N of Clar heston Road r station, and 10 NE of Haverfordwest Post town Haverfordwest Acres, 2,537 Real property, £1,056 Pop, 227 Houses 48 Part of the surface is upland on the skirt of the Percelly mountains An ancient military strength was here, supposed to be the Roman Ad Vigesimum, on the maritime Julian way The living is a rectory in the diocese of St Davids Value, not reported Patron, the Lord Chancellor

CASTLE CAEREINION, a parish in the district and county of Montgomery 4 miles WNW of Forden r station, and 4 WSW of Welshpool It includes the townships of Castle Gaer, Moydog, Sylfaen, Trefnant, Cwmgoron, Hydan Uchaf, Hydan Dol, Nantforch, and Trehelig, and has a post office under Welshpool Acres, 6,540 Rated property, £4 619 Pop, 682 Houses, 134 The property is divided among a few A castle of the princes of Powys was here The living is a rectory in the diocese of St Asaph Value, £575 * Patron, the Lord Chancellor The church was recently in a dilapidated state A school has £17 from endowment, and other charities £15

CASTLE CAMPS, a parish in Linton district, Cambridge, on the verge of the county, 3½ miles SW by W of Haverhill r station It has a post office under Cambridge Acres, 2 703 Real property, £3,885. Pop, 901 Houses, 199 The property is divided among a few The manor was given, at the Conquest, to Aubrey de Vere, conveyed, in 1580, by his successor, one of the Earls of Oxford, to Sutton, and given, by the latter, to the Charter House, London A castle of the De Veres stood on it, and appears to have been magnificent, but is now represented by only a deep moat round a farm house on its site Large entrenchments of the East Angles and the Danes were in the parish, and these, with the castle, gave rise to the name of Castle Camps. The living is a rectory in the diocese of Ely Value £570 * Patron the Charter House of London The church is good, and there are an Independent chapel and a charity school

CASTLE CARY See CASTLE CARY

CASTLE CARLTON See CARLTON CASTLE

CASTLE CARROCK, a parish in Brampton district, Cumberland, on the river Gelt under Cumrew fell, 3 miles SE of How Mill r station, and 4 S of Brampton It has a post office under Carlisle Acres 3,640 Real property, £2,026 Pop, 337 Houses, 65 The property is much subdivided Limestone and freestone abound and there are two mineral springs Traces exist of two ancient military strengths The living is a rectory in the diocese of Carlisle. Value, £159 * Patrons, the Dean and Chapter of Carlisle The church was rebuilt in 1828 There are an Independent chapel and an endowed school—the latter with £14

CASTLE CARY, a small town, a parish, and a sub district in Wincanton district, Somerset. The town stands on valley and on slopes, amid charming environs, adjacent to the East Somerset railway, 12 miles NNE of Yeovil A castle at it was built by the Lovells, and made a figure in the civil wars of the time of Stephen, but has disappeared A manor house adjacent, gave shelter to Charles II after the battle of Worcester but has been almost demolished A beautifully broken hill side, called Castle Cary Park was probably the chase of the lords of the manor, and commands a very splendid and extensive view The principal street of the town runs up a hollow between two hills The market house is an elegant edifice, built in 1855, at a cost of £2 300, and contains an assembly room upwards of 50 feet long The parish church surmounts a hillock, has a tower and spire, erected in 1855, is itself partly decorated English of the time of Henry I, partly recent reconstruction, and contains an old font and a richly carved pulpit There are Independent and Wesleyan chapels, a national school, a post office‡ under Bath a railway station, a banking office, and three chief inns Markets are held on Mondays, and fairs on the Tuesday before Palm Sunday, 1 May, Whit Tuesday, and the Tuesday after 19 Sept. Some trade is carried on in flax spinning and hair cloth weaving.—The parish includes also the hamlets of Clanville, Dimmer, and Cockhill, and the manor of Foxcombe Acres 2,625 Real property, with Almsford, £11,977 Pop., 2 060 Houses, 433 The living is a vicarage in the diocese of Bath and Wells Value, £312 * Patron, the Bishop of Bath and Wells —The sub district contains fifteen parishes Acres, 16,906 Pop, 6,129 Houses, 1,303

CASTLE CHURCH, a parish and a sub-district in the district and county of Stafford The parish adjoins the south western suburbs of Stafford, and includes the townships of Forebridge and Rickerscote Post town, Stafford. Acres, 3,774 Rated property, £15,772 Pop 3,362 Houses, 669 The property is much subdivided The living is a vicarage in the diocese of Lichfield Value, £120 * Patron, the Lord Chancellor The church is old but good A district church, forming a separate charge, is in Forebridge, and there is a neat Roman Catholic chapel —The sub district contains three parishes and part of another Acres, 13,071 Pop, 5,413 Houses, 1,089

CASTLE COMBE, a village, a parish, and a sub district, in Chippenham district Wilts The village stands on the Box rivulet, near Akeman-street, 5 miles NNW of Corsham r station and 5½ WNW of Chippenham, and has a post office under Chippenham, and an inn It was once a place of some note, and had a weekly market, and it still has a fair, for cattle, sheep, and horses, on 4 May An ancient market cross is in it, a number of gable fronted old houses line its streets, and an old dowry house and an old manor house stand, the one at the end of its principal street, the other in the near neighbourhood. A Saxon fort, or even a Roman camp, is supposed to have crowned an adjacent hill and a great castle of the Dunstanvilles was built there about the year 1200, and dismantled before the close of the 14th century Both the earlier fort and the later castle, perhaps the former quite as much as the latter are now represented only by remains of a fosse and rampart The manor passed from the Dunstanvilles to the Badlesmeres and others but has belonged, for about 500 years, to the Scropes The present mansion occupies a romantic site on the Box, deeply embosomed among steep and wooded slopes Two notable occupants of the manor were Lord Chancellor Scrope, of the time of Richard II, and William Scrope, author of "Days of Deer Stalking" The parish comprises 1,494 acres Real property, £3,21[illegible] Pop 534 Houses, 122 The property is not much divided The living is a rectory in the diocese of Gloucester and Bristol. Value not reported Patron, G P Scrope, Esq The church is early English, consists of nave, chancel, and two aisles, with a square tower, was restored in 1851, at a cost of £3,000, and contains an octagonal font and a cenotaph of the Scropes. There are chapels for Independents and Baptists. The sub district contains eight parishes. Acres, 14,011 Pop, 3,286 Houses 701

CASTLE COYTY See COYTY

CASTLE CRAG See BORROWDALE, Cumberland

CASTLE DITCH an ancient camp on Little Haldon Hill, 2½ miles W of Dawlish, in Devon It is circular and 124 yards in diameter

CASTLE DITCH, an ancient camp, 4 miles SE of Hindon, in Wilts It is triangular includes 24 acres and has a treble ditch and ramparts 40 feet high

CASTLE DONINGTON, a town, a parish, and a sub district in the district of Shardlow, and county of Leicester The town stands near the river Trent, 3½ miles W of Kegworth r station, and 7½ NW by N of Loughborough It was known at Domesday as Dunitone, it takes the first part of its present name from an old castle, now a fragment, said to have belonged to John of Gaunt, and it contains vestiges of a monastery, founded in the time of Henry II It has a church four dissenting chapels, a large handsome parochial school a post office‡ under Derby, and two chief inns The church is very old, has a large chancel, with fine east window, and a handsome spire, 160 feet high, and contains a double canopied brass of 1458 and some old effigies. A weekly market is held on Saturday, and fairs on 18th March and 29

Sep. Several departments of manufacture are carried on. Pop., 2,291 Houses 561 The parish comprises 4,250 acres Real property, £12,856 Pop, 2 445 Houses, 617 The property is subdivided The manor belonged formerly to the Plantagenets and the Huntingdons and belongs now to the Marquis of Hastings. Donington Park the seat of the Marquis, a mile west of the town, is a grand edifice, in a mixed style of pointed and Tudor, by Wilkins, has picturesque grounds of 350 acres and contains an extensive library and a large collection of valuable paintings. The living is a vicarage in the diocese of Peterborough Value, £223 * Patron, the Marquis of Hastings. The sub district contains six parishes and an extra parochial tract Acres 13,355 Pop, 5 775 Houses, 1,385

CASTLEDOOR or CASTLE DOR, a locality 2½ miles N of Fowey, in Cornwall It takes name from a small ancient camp, probably Danish, and has a post office under Par Station

CASTLE DURRAN See CASTLE DYRRAN

CASTLE DYKE, an ancient camp on high mounds, in Ugbrooke Park, 1½ mile SSE of Chudleigh, in Devon It is circular, and thought to be Danish, but has outworks of a much later time than that of the Danes.

CASTLE DYKES, a Roman camp at Farthingo in Northampton It includes 13 acres, and is double ditched. It is thought to have been occupied by Ethelfleda and burnt in 1013, by the Danes

CASTLE DYKINGS, an extra parochial tract in the district and county of Lincoln, within the city boundaries of Lincoln Pop, 188 Houses 33

CASTLE-DYRRAN, a hamlet in Cilymaenllwyd parish Carmarthen, 3½ miles NE of Narbeth Pop, 61 It forms a curacy with Cilymaenllwyd

CASTLE EATON, a small village and a parish in Highworth district Wilts. The village stands on the river Thames adjacent to the Thames and Severn canal 3½ miles ENE of Cricklade, and 6¼ NE of Purton r station. The parish includes also the tything of Lushill, and its post town is Kempsford under Swindon Acres, 1,936 Real property, with Lushill and Marston Maisey, £6,171 Pop, 286 Houses, 64 The property is divided among a few Lushill House is the seat of the Archers. A place called the Butts seems to have been notable, in old times, for the practice of archery The parish is famous for cheese. The living is a rectory in the diocese of Gloucester and Bristol Value, £633 * Patron the Rev C E Bowlby The church dates from about 1400 has a singular cupola, and is very good

CASTLE EDEN, a rivulet, two villages, and a parish in Easington district Durham The rivulet traverses a romantic dell, called Castle Eden dean and goes eastward to the sea The villages are Castle Eden and Castle Eden Colliery, they stand near the Hartlepool and Ferryhill railway, 7½ and 6¾ miles NW by W of Hartlepool, and they have stations on the railway, and post offices under Ferryhill There is also a post office‡ of Castle-Eden Station under Ferryhill The parish comprises 1,035 acres Real property £1,942 of which, £1,500 are in mines. Pop 535 Houses, 110 The property is divided among a few The manor belonged anciently to Guisborne priory and the see of Durham Castle Eden Hall the seat of R. Burdon, Esq is a handsome modern castellated edifice surmounting a wooded precipice contiguous to Castle Eden dean, and commanding brilliant views Coal is extensively worked, and there are brick works and a brewery The living is a rectory in the diocese of Durham. Value, £212.* Patron, R Burdon, Esq The church was built in 1764, and has a [illegible] The vicarage of Wingate Grange is a separate benefice There are Wesleyan and P. Methodist chapels

CASTLE FLEMISH See AMBLESTON

CASTLEFORD, a township and a parish in Pontefract district [illegible] Yorkshire The township lies on Watling street, the river Aire and the York and Leeds railway 7½ miles NNE of Wakefield, and has a station on the railway and a post office‡ under Normanton The Roman station Legeolium is supposed to have been here, and Roman coins, urns, pavements, and substructions have been found Coal mining, glass making and earthenware manufacture are largely carried on, and have occasioned much recent increase of population A railway hence to Ardsley was opened in May, 1869 Acres, 540 Real property, £9,023 Pop, 3 870 Houses, 813 The parish includes also the township of Glass Houghton Acres, 2,040 Real property, £11,295 Pop, 4,365 Houses, 926 The property is much subdivided The living is a rectory in the diocese of York Value, £335 * Patron, the Duchy of Lancaster The church is ancient and cruciform There are a school church, an Independent chapel of 1862, four Methodist chapels, and two public schools.

CASTLEFORD, a hamlet in Ipplepen parish, Devon

CASTLE FROME a parish in Ledbury district, Hereford, on the river Frome, 3 miles NNE of Ashperton r station, and 6 NNW of Ledbury Post town Bishops-Frome under Worcester Acres, 1,511 Real property £2,012 Pop, 115 Houses, 18 The property is divided among a few The living is a rectory in the diocese of Hereford Value £300 * Patron, F T Freeman, Esq The church is good

CASTLEGATE See YORK

CASTLE GREEN See CARMARTHEN

CASTLE GRESLEY, a township in Church Gresley parish, Derby, 4½ miles SE by E of Burton upon Trent. Pop, 236 Houses, 52

CASTLE HALL a chapelry in Dukinfield township Stockport parish, Cheshire, on the verge of the county adjacent to the river Tame, the Manchester and Sheffield railway, and Stalybridge It was constituted in 1846 Post town Stalybridge, Lancashire Pop, 7,612 Houses, 1,479 The Living is a vicarage in the diocese of Chester Value, £300 Patrons Trustees

CASTLE HEAD See DERWENT WATER

CASTLE HEDINGHAM, a village and a parish in Halstead district, Essex The village stands on the river Colne, and on the Colne Valley railway, 4½ miles NW of Halstead, is a seat of petty sessions and a polling place, and has a post-office under Halstead a railway station, and an inn Fairs are held on 14 May and 25 July A grand castle was built on an adjacent eminence in the early part of the 12th century by Aubrey de Vere, Earl of Oxford, was the death place of Queen Maud, made a great figure in the wars in the time of King John, was the scene of a sumptuous entertainment to Henry VII, suffered much demolition in 1592 by Edward de Vere and was reduced to ruin, in 1666, in the first Dutch war Only the keep of it now stands, and this is pure Anglo Norman, 62 feet wide, 55 feet broad and about 100 feet high —the walls, from 10 to 13 feet thick —the height disposed in five storeys, pierced with loop holes and narrow windows A Benedictine nunnery and an hospital also were founded here by the De Veres, —the former in 1198, the latter in 1250,—part of the nunnery is now a farm house The parish comprises 2 429 acres Real property, £6 027 Pop 1,203 Houses, 300 The property is divided among a few The manor passed from the De Veres to the Ashursts and the Houghtons, and belongs now to A Majendie, Esq The parish is notable for its produce of Essex hops The living is a p. curacy in the diocese of Rochester Value, £100 Patron, A Majendie Esq The church dates from the time of King John, shows Norman traces, has a tower of 1616 and contains monuments of the De Veres and the Ashursts There are a large Independent chapel and several alms houses

CASTLE HEWIN an extinct ancient stronghold, at Tarn Wadling Cumberland under the north side of Blaze fell, in the eastern vicinity of High Hesket It is mentioned in the old ballad of the 'Marriage of Sir Gawaine'

CASTLE HILL, any one of numerous eminences in all parts of England, either now or formerly crowned with military works Most of them possess little interest, except the name, a few have vestiges of ruins of ancient camps, forts, or castles and some give name to contiguous localities

CASTLE HILL [illegible] the seat of Earl Fortescue in D[illegible]

on the river Bray 3 miles NW by W of South Molton An adjacent place of the same name has a post office under South Molton

CASTLE HILL SIDE, a hamlet in Almondbury township and parish, W R Yorkshire, 1 mile SE of Huddersfield

CASTLE HORNECK, a seat in the western vicinity of Penzance, in Cornwall It belongs to S Borlase, Esq, and takes name from an ancient entrenchment, encircling an adjoining eminence

CASTLE HOW See ENNERDALE WATER.

CASTLE HOWARD, a railway station and a noble mansion in N R Yorkshire. The station is on the York and Scarborough railway, adjacent to the river Derwent, 3¾ miles SW of New Malton There is also a post office of the name under York. The mansion is the seat of the Earl of Carlisle, and stands 3 miles NNW of the station It occupies the site of the old castle of Hinderskelf,—destroyed by accidental fire, and was built, in 1702, after designs by Sir John Vanbrugh The south front is 323 feet long, consists of a centre and two wings, and is adorned at the centre, with an attached Corinthian portico The north front also has a Corinthian centre, and is surmounted there by a cupola. The great hall, situated beneath the cupola, is 35 feet square, the dining room, 27 feet by 23 the saloon, 34 feet by 24, the drawing room, 27 feet by 23, the state bed room, 26 feet by 22, the museum, 24 feet square and the antique gallery 160 feet by 20 The decorations, paintings, and curiosities are exceedingly rich The gardens occupy 12 acres, and the pleasure grounds contain statues, temples, an obelisk, a pyramid, and a grand mausoleum Queen Victoria visited Castle Howard in 1850, and planted a tree in the grounds

CASTLE INN See BRECKNOCK

CASTLE LEAVINGTON, a township in Kirk Leavington parish, N R Yorkshire, on a branch of the river Tees, 3½ miles SE of Yarm Acres, 1,828 Real property £1,327 Pop 53 Houses, 6

CASTLE MAELGWN, the seat of the Gower family, in Pembroke, on the river Teifi, 3¼ miles SE by E of Cardigan

CASTLE MALWOOD, a walk in the New Forest, Hants, 8¼ miles NW of Lyndhurst It takes name from an old fort in it the keep of which is still standing

CASTLE MARTIN, a village a parish, and a hundred in Pembrokeshire The village stands on the coast, 5¼ miles WSW of Pembroke, and 7¼ SW of New Milford r station and has a post office under Pembroke An ancient castle, of uncertain origin, or perhaps an ancient British fort, stood here, and has left some vestiges The parish extends a considerable way, along a rugged coast and is in the district of Pembroke Acres, 4,867, of which 365 are water Real property £4,024, of which £143 are in quarries Pop, 422 Houses, 65 The property is divided among a few Brownslade House is a chief residence Several ancient British and Danish remains are on the coast The living is a vicarage in the diocese of St David's Value, £315 * Patron, Earl Cawdor The church is old but excellent —The hundred contains fifteen parishes, and parts of two others, and is famous for its breed of black cattle Acres, 48 122 Pop., 5,856 Houses, 1,035

CASTLE MONA, the quondam residence of the Dukes of Athole, in the Isle of Man, adjacent to Douglas It was a magnificent place, and is still surrounded by fine plantations

CASTLE MORTON or MORTON FOLIOT, a parish in Upton on Severn district Worcester, under the Malvern hills, 4½ miles SW by W of Upton on Severn, and 3½ S by E of Malvern r station Post town Longdon, under Tewkesbury Acres, 3 656 Real property, £5 569 Pop, 818 Houses, 195 The property is much subdivided A castle of the De Moutes stood here The living is a vicarage, annexed to the vicarage of Longdon, in the diocese of Worcester The church is ancient but good, and a chapel for the outlying portions of Castle Morton and Berrow was built in 1869 There are a national school, and charities £28

CASTLL NADOLIG See CASTELL NADOLIG

CASTLE-NORTHWICH, a township in Great Budworth parish, Cheshire on the river Weaver, in the south western vicinity of Northwich Acres, 100 Real property, £18,218, of which £15,484 are in canals Pop, 1,395. Houses, 308 See NORTHWICH

CASTLE (OLD) See OLD CASTLE

CASTLE PRECINCTS, extra parochial places in the city of Durham, the city of Bristol, and the borough of Lewes

CASTLE RIGG, an eminence 1½ mile SE of Keswick in Cumberland It commands an extensive and most gorgeous view, much admired by all lakers, and specially noted by the poets Gray and Wordsworth

CASTLE RING See CANNOCK

CASTLE RINGS, an ancient entrenchment on the SW border of Wilts, on Tittlepath hill, 2½ miles NE of Shaftesbury It consists of ditch and lofty rampart, encloses 15½ acres, encircles the hill, and gives it a singular shape

CASTLE RINGS or WEATHERBURY CASTLE, an ancient British camp in Dorset 3 miles WNW of Bere Regis It is rectangular, and has two ramparts and ditches A fir plantation and a modern obelisk are within it

CASTLE RISING, a decayed town, a parish, and a sub district in Freebridge Lynn district, Norfolk. The town stands 2¾ miles NE of Wootton r station, and 4¾ NE by N of Lynn, and has a post office under Lynn A Roman station and a Saxon fort probably were here, and a great castle was erected on their site some time before 1176 by William de Albini, first Earl of Sussex. Remains of the castle still exist, and show it to have been a place of much importance. The interior is greatly dilapidated but is least so in the room where the court leet was held The walls of the keep are 9 feet thick, the encompassing ditch is deep, and the rampart bold, a strong wall, with three towers, formerly surmounted the rampart, and the entire place was on a similar plan to Norwich castle, and nearly as large Several kings made visits to it, and Isabel, the queen of Edward III was confined in it from 1330, after the murder of her husband, till her death in 1358 The town is now a paltry village, but was formerly a seat of great markets, a centre of political influence, a borough by prescription, and probably a seaport, and it sent two members to parliament, till disfranchised by the act of 1832. Tradition assumes that the sea came up to it in the same manner that it now does to Lynn and an old rhyme says,—

"Rising was a seaport town,
When Lynn was but a marsh,
Now Lynn it is a seaport town
And Rising fares the worse!"

The parish comprises 2,090 acres Real property, £2 298. Pop, 377 Houses, 79 The property all belongs to the Howard family The living is a rectory, united with the rectory of Roydon in the diocese of Norwich Value, £419 * Patrons the Heirs of the late Hon Col Howard The church is partly Norman, partly early English, and was restored in 1844 and 1857 There are a national school and an alms house hospital, and the latter was founded, in the time of James II, by Henry Howard, Earl of Northampton and has £100 a year —The sub district contains seven parishes. Acres 19 006 Pop 2 420 Houses, 529

CASTLE ROCK a picturesque crag at the head of the Vale of St John, in Cumberland, 3 miles ESE of Keswick It looks as if castellated and might be mistaken by a stranger in some states of the atmosphere for an actual, great, lofty fortress Sir Walter Scott, describing it in his "Bridal of Triermain," as it appeared to the charmed eye of King Arthur, says—

"A mound
Arose with airy turrets crowned,
Buttress and rampart circling bound,
And mighty keep and tower

Seem'd some primeval giant's hand
The castle's massive walls had plann'd,
A ponderous bulwark, to withstand
Ambitious Nimrod's power '

CASTLE ROUGH, an ancient camp on the N coast of Kent, in Kemsley marsh, 2 miles N by E of Sittingbourne It is an earthwork about 100 feet square, with broad ditch and single rampart, and was formed by Hasten the Dane, at his landing in 892

CASTLE RUSHEN See CASTLETOWN, Isle of Man

CASTLESIDE, a chapelry in Lanchester parish Durham, 3 miles SSW of Shotley-Bridge It was constituted in 1864, and it has a post office under Gateshead Pop 1,178 The living is a vicarage in the diocese of Durham Value, £300

CASTLE-SOWERBY, a parish in Penrith district, Cumberland in Inglewood forest, under Carrock fell, 3 miles SE by E of Hesket Newmarket, and 7 W of Plumpton r station It contains the townships of Bustabeck Bound, How Bound, Row-Bound, Southernby Bound, and Stockdalewath Bound, and its post town is Hesket Newmarket, under Wigton Acres, 7,940 Real property £5,112 Pop, 906 Houses, 194 The property is much subdivided The manor belongs to the Duke of Devonshire An ancient fortress stood near the church, and an old circular fort is at How hill The living is a vicarage in the diocese of Carlisle Value, £90 * Patrons the Dean and Chapter of Carlisle The church is tolerable The p curacy of Raughton Head is a separate benefice

CASTLESTEADS, or CAMBECK FORT the Roman station Petriani, on the Wall, near Brampton, in Cumberland It measures 450 feet by 300, has yielded altars, inscriptions, coins, and other relics, and gives name to an adjacent mansion formerly the seat of the Dacres

CASTLE STREET, a locality on the confines of Lancashire and Yorkshire, 1 mile from Todmorden, with a post office under Todmorden

CASTLE STREET, a township in St. Mary Carlisle parish, Cumberland, within the city of Carlisle

CASTLE THORPE, a parish in Newport Pagnell district, Bucks, on the verge of the county, the river Ouse, and the Northwestern railway, 2¼ miles NNW of Wolverton r station, and 3½ NNE of Stony Stratford It has a post office under Stony Stratford Acres, 1,380 Real property, £2,844 Pop, 338 Houses, 69 The property is divided among a few, but belongs chiefly to Lord Carrington The ancient castle of the barony of Hanslope stood here, but is represented now by only a deep ditch and an artificial mound The living is a vicarage, annexed to the rectory of Hanslope, in the diocese of Oxford The church is an old edifice, with low square tower and has a monument of Judge Tyrrell, of the time of Charles II

CASTLE THORPE, a township in Broughton parish, Lincoln, on the river Ancholme, 1 mile N of Glanford Brigg Pop, 346

CASTLE TOLL See NEWENDEN

CASTLETON, a village, a township, and a parish in Chapel en le Frith district, Derby The village stands in a deep hollow at the foot of Mam Tor mountain, 6 miles N of Millers Dale r station, and 10 NE of Buxton A steep and commanding eminence at it, upwards of 200 feet high, is crowned by the ruined castle of ' Peveril of the Peak This is supposed by some to have been preceded by a Saxon fort, by others, to have been built originally by William Peveril, a son of the Conqueror It passed from the Peverils in the time of Henry II, was held by the Earl of Montaigne, afterwards King John was given in the time of Edward II to the Earl of Warren, passed afterwards to John of Gaunt, and has belonged, since his time, to the duchy of Lancaster The keep and portions of the walls still stand they consist of massive masonry, 9 feet thick, and they present a most interesting specimen of the features of Norman architecture The Peak cavern is adjacent while all the other grand attractions of the High Peak [illegible] on or near and they draw hither great numbers of summer visitors and tourists The village has a post office‡ under Sheffield, three chief inns a church, a Wesleyan chapel a Primitive Methodist chapel, an endowed school and an excellent library The church is partly early English, neat and in good repair, and has three interesting monuments to the mineralogist Mawe the Rev E Bagshaw, and Micha Hall Fairs are held on the third Wednesday of March 21 April, the first Wednesday of Oct, and the third Wednesday of Nov —The township includes the village, and extends over neighbouring mountains. Real property, £5,006 Pop, 771 Houses, 167 The property is much subdivided Lead ore, fluor spar, mountain limestone, and other useful minerals abound. The working of lead mines long employed a large portion of the inhabitants, but, of late years, has been unproductive.—The parish includes also the township of Edale Acres, 10,205 Real property, £8,156 Pop., 1,157 Houses, 213 The manor belongs to the duchy of Lancaster, and is leased by the Duke of Devonshire The living is a vicarage in the diocese of Lichfield Value, £186 Patron, the Bishop of Lichfield. The vicarage of Edale is a separate benefice

CASTLETON, a parish in Sherborne district, Dorset, on the Yeovil and Salisbury railway, ¾ of a mile ENE of Sherborne Post town, Sherborne Acres, 69 Real property, £581 Pop, 59 Houses, 13. The living is a vicarage in the diocese of Salisbury Value, £81 Patron, G D W Digby, Esq A fair is held on the Wednesday before Holy Thursday

CASTLETON, a township and two sub districts in Rochdale parish and district, Lancashire The township stands on the Rochdale canal and the Manchester and Leeds railway, partly within the borough of Rochdale, partly in the south eastern suburbs and environs Real property, £102,077 of which £24,424 are in the canal Pop in 1841 14 279, in 1861, 23,771 Houses, 4,884 The part without the borough includes the villages and hamlets of Buersill Lowerplace, Newbold, Marland, Lower Lane, Broad Lane, Backlanes, Roeacre, Captain fold, Castleton Moor, and Bluepits There are traces of a castle, supposed to have been built before the Conquest —The sub districts are C Within and C Without and are jointly conterminate with the township Pop of C Within, 13 071 Houses, 2,692

CASTLETON, a village in Marshfield parish Monmouth, 5 miles SW of Newport It has a post-office under Cardiff, two dissenting chapels, remains of a Norman castle and three annual fairs.

CASTLETON, a village in Danby parish N R Yorkshire, on the North Yorkshire and Cleveland railway 7½ miles SE of Guisbrough It has a r station with telegraph, a post office under Yarm, and a weekly market

CASTLETON, Glamorgan See ATHANS (St)

CASTLETON MOOR, a chapelry in Castleton township, Lancashire, 2¼ miles SSW of Rochdale Pop, about 3 000 Living, a vicarage Value, £300 The church was built in 1862, and is a fine edifice with a spire

CASTLETOWN, a seaport village in Portland isle Dorset, 4½ miles S by E of Weymouth It has a post office under Weymouth, a hotel, and a stone wharf and pier

CASTLETOWN, a town in Kirk Malew parish Isle of Man, on a bay of its own name, near the southern extremity of the island, 10 miles SW of Douglas The bay is separated, on the NE, by only the narrow isthmus of Longness peninsula, from Derby haven, measures about 2½ miles by 2, and has an occasional light, seen at the distance of 8 miles, but is unsheltered from southerly winds, beset with sunken rocks and comparatively shallow Some vessels frequent it, in a good corn and coasting trade, but most prefer Derby haven The town is thought to be the oldest in the island, was the residence of its kings and is still the seat of its government, yet consists chiefly of modern houses, in regular streets. A rivulet runs through it to the bay, and is crossed by two bridges, for carriages and pedestrians. A market place, a large square, is near the centre Castle Rushen, once the abode of royalty, now variously court house, prison, and barracks, stands on a rock between the market square and the rivulet, and overlooks the country for many miles This was originally built, about 945, by Guthred, the Dane, is said to resemble Elsinore Castle, the scene of Hamlet, was the theatre of the events which form the plot of Sir Walter Scott's "Peveril of the Peak," retains the formidable gloomy grandeur of the mediæval architecture, with massive walls and square towers, one of them 80 feet high, and was partially restored in 1815 A memorial to Governor Smelt, a Doric pillar, is on the parade St Mary's church, facing the parade, is an ornamental structure, built on the site of a previous church, in 1828 Three Roman coins were got at the founding of the church, and a Roman altar is at the governor's house King William's college, founded in 1830, stands at Hango-hill, and is an imposing edifice, in the pointed style, 210 feet by 135, with a tower and lantern 115 feet high The training here is liberal, preparatory for the church, and several of the masters, as also many of the pupils, have been distinguished There are also chapels for Wesleyans Primitive Methodists, and Roman Catholics a free school, and a literary institution, and the town has a post office‡ under Douglas, a banking office, and a weekly market Pop, 2,373 Houses, 442

CASTLETOWN QUARTER, a township in Rockliff parish, Cumberland, on the river Eden and the Caledonian railway, 5 miles NNW of Carlisle Acres, 5,225, of which 1 134 are water Pop, 509 Houses 106

CASTLE VIEW, a liberty within the borough of Leicester Pop, 139 Houses, 29

CASTLE WARD, a district and two divisions in Northumberland extending northward from the borough boundaries of Newcastle The district comprehends the sub district of Ponteland, containing the parishes of Ponteland, Dinnington Stannington, Gosforth, Whalton, Bolan, and part of Morpeth, and the sub district of Stamfordham, containing the parishes of Stamfordham, Newburn, Heddon on the Wall, parts of Hartburn, Kirkwhelpington, and Ovingham, and the chapelry of Kirkheaton Acres, 88,537 Poor rates in 1866, £8 991 Pop in 1861, 14,943 Houses, 3,018 Marriages in 1866, 39, births, 517,—of which 41 were illegitimate, deaths, 264,—of which 94 were at ages under 3 years, and 10 at ages above 85 Marriages in the ten years 1851-60, 433, births, 4,514 deaths, 2,747 The places of worship in 1851 were 17 of the Church of England, with 3 521 sittings 3 of the United Presbyterian Church, with 223 s, 14 of Wesleyan Methodists, with 2,070 s, 3 of Primitive Methodists, with 468 s, 5 of Wesleyan Reformers, with 448 s, and 1 of Roman Catholics, with 170 s The schools were 23 public day schools, with 1,377 scholars, 13 private day schools, with 418 s 27 Sunday schools, with 1,432 s, and 1 evening school for adults, with 20 s. The workhouse is in Ponteland township The two divisions are East and West, and they include most of the district, but extend beyond it, and are jointly larger The E div contains six parishes and parts of four others Acres, 39,163. The W div contains five parishes and parts of eight others Acres, 56,571 Pop of both, 58,132 Houses 11,063

CASTLEWRIGHT, a township in Mainstone parish, Montgomeryshire, 5¼ miles S of Montgomery Acres, 1,332 Pop, 145. Houses, 32

CASTLEY, a township in Leathley parish, W R Yorkshire, on the river Wharfe, 4½ miles E of Otley Acres 527 Real property, £927 Pop., 73 Houses, 14

CASTLE YARD, an extra parochial place in the city of Exeter Pop, 4 House, 1

CASTON, a parish in Wayland district, Norfolk, 3½ miles SE of Watton, and 6 WNW of Attleborough r station It has a post office under Attleborough Acres, 1,557 Real property, £3 122 Pop, 510 Houses, 116 The property is subdivided The living is a rectory in the diocese of Norwich Value, £495 * Patron, Henry Dover, Esq The church is good, and there are a Wesleyan chapel, a n school, and charities £10

CASTOR a village and a parish in Peterborough district, Northampton The village stands on Ermine street adjacent to the river Nen and to the Peterborough and Northampton railway, 5 miles W of Peterborough and has a station on the railway and a post office under Peterborough It occupies part of the site of the Roman station Durobrivæ and was known to the Saxons as Castra or Kyneburgecastre Numerous Roman relics, including a Jupiter Terminalis, pavements, urns, and coins from Trajan to Valens, have been found around it A nunnery was founded at it in the 7th century, by a daughter of King Penda, and destroyed in 1010, by the Danes —The parish contains also the hamlet of Ailesworth, and the chapelries of Sutton and Upton Acres, 7 020 Rated property, £8 519 Pop, 1,323 Houses, 272 The property is divided among a few The living is a rectory in the diocese of Peterborough Value, £528 Patron, the Bishop of Peterborough. The church is Norman, with early English tower and spire, exhibits curiously the features and decorations of the Norman period, and underwent recently a thorough renovation The vicarages of Sutton and Upton are separate charges Bishop Madan was rector There are an Independent chapel and a national school

CASTOR, Lincoln See CAISTOR.

CASWELL, a tything in Portbury parish Somerset, 5½ miles W of Bristol Pop, 74

CASWELL BAY, a small bay in Glamorgan, 4½ miles SW of Swansea Its shores are picturesque, and have a hotel and boarding house

CATARACTONUM See CATTERICK

CAT BELLS, a mountain on the SW of Derwent water in Cumberland. Its height is 1,448 feet

CATCHBURN a village in Morpeth Castle township, Morpeth parish, Northumberland, 1½ mile S of Morpeth

CATCHEDECAM See HELVELLYN

CATCHEMS END, a hamlet in Pattishall parish, Northampton, 4½ miles NNW of Towcester

CATCHERSIDE, a township in Kirkwhelpington parish, Northumberland, 7½ miles SE of Otterburn Acres, 593 Pop 19 Houses, 2

CATCLIFFE, a township in Rotherham parish W R Yorkshire on the York and Derby railway, 3 miles S of Rotherham Acres 648. Pop, 279 Houses 61

CATCOMB, a tything in Hillmarton parish, Wilts 3½ miles NNE of Calne Pop, 68

CATCOTT, a chapelry in Moorlinch parish, Somerset, 3 miles SSW of Shapwick r station, and 7 ENE of Bridgewater It includes part of Burtle hamlet Post town Bridgewater Acres, 2,256 Real property, £3,701 Pop, 740 Houses, 159 The property is much subdivided The living is a donative in the diocese of Bath and Wells Value, £100 * Patron, A Henniker, Esq The church is Norman There are two Methodist chapels, a free school, a national school, and charities £60

CATEBY See CADEBY, Yorkshire

CATEL or ST MARY DE CASTRO, a parish in Guernsey, 1½ mile WNW of St Peter Port It contains the village of King's Mills, and has a post office under Guernsey Pop, 2,071 Houses, 366 The castle of a sea king, named Le Grand Jeffroi, stood here on an eminence, commanding an extensive view of the sea, and was destroyed in 1061 by William Duke of Normandy A church, dedicated to the Virgin, was built on the castle's site out of its materials, and hence the name St. Mary de Castro. The living is a rectory in the diocese of Winchester Value, £150 Patron, the Governor The church appears still to retain portions of the original one of the castle, has a Norman transept and a tower, and was recently repaired Cattle fairs are held at Easter, Midsummer, and Michaelmas

CATERHAM, a village and a parish in Godstone district Surrey The village stands at the terminus of a branch of the South eastern railway, 7 miles S by E of Croydon and has a r station with telegraph and a post office under Red Hill The branch railway deflects from the Brighton line at Caterham Junction station, 2½ miles S of Croydon, is 4½ miles long was opened in 1856, and has stations at Kenley and Warlingham An omnibus runs from Caterham station to Westerham The parish comprises 2,400 acres Real property, £2,997 Pop,

81. Houses, 140 The property is much subdivided The Roman vicinal way, called Stane-street, went through the parish, and ancient works indicative of warlike operations, are in it, near a place called War Coppice. The living is a rectory in the diocese of Winchester Value, £235 Patron, the Rev J L Hesse The church is mainly early English The p curacy of Caterham Valley is a separate charge, and was constituted in 1866 The Warehousemen and Clerks Orphan asylum, reported to be in Caterham, but really in Beddington, was built in 1866 at a cost of about £20,000, is in the Venetian Gothic style, and has accommodation for 150 boys and girls.

CATESBY, or CATESBY ABBEY, a parish in Daventry district Northampton, on the verge of the county near the Oxford canal 5 miles SW of Daventry, and 6 ESE of Southam Road r station It includes the hamlet of Newbold grounds, and its post town is Daventry Acres, 1,940 Real property, £3,583, Pop., 107 Houses 2 A Benedictine nunnery was founded here, as early as at least as the time of Richard I, by Robert de Esseby, and given, at the dissolution, to John Onley Catesby House occupies the nunnery's site, belonged to the Parkhursts was the birth place of Parkhurst, the Greek and Hebrew lexicographer, and passed to James Attenborough Esq, of Brampton Ash The parish is a resort of sportsmen The living is a vicarage in the diocese of Peterborough. Value, not reported Patrons, T and M Scrafton, Esqs The church was long in ruins, and a new one, instead of it, incorporating some fine materials of the old, was recently erected by Mr Attenborough

CATFIELD, a parish in Tunstead district, Norfolk, adjacent to Barton and Hickling meres, 5½ miles SE of Worstead, and 10 NNE of Brundall r station It has a post office under Norwich Acres, 2,393 Real property £4 413 Pop, 630 Houses 162 The property is much subdivided Catfield House is the seat of the Rev B. L. Cubitt The living is a rectory and vicarage in the diocese of Norwich Value, £606 Patron, alt. the Bishop of N and the Rev B L Cubitt The church is very late English There is a P Methodist chapel

CATFORD BRIDGE a railway station in the west of Kent on the Beckenham railway, adjacent to Ravensbourne river 6 miles SE of London Bridge

CATFOSS, a township in Sigglesthorne parish, E R Yorkshire, 4½ miles W of Hornsea Acres, 1,050 Real property £1,200 Pop., 63 Houses, 8

CATHANGER CUM STOWEY, a tything in Fivehead parish Somerset, 4½ miles SW of Langport Pop, 20

CATHARGOED CATHILAS, AND GLYNN, a conjoint hamlet in Llanfihangel Aberbythych parish, Carmarthen 3½ miles S of Llandeilofawr Pop, 466

CATHBREGION See CADBURY (SOUTH)

CATHEDINE, a parish in the district and county of Brecon on an affluent of the river Wye, near the Hereford and Brecon railway, 6 miles SSW of Talgarth It contains the nominal ancient borough of Blaenllynfi, and its post town is Llangorse under Hereford Acres, 1,757 Real property £1,403 Pop., 191 Houses, 41 Cathedine House is the seat of the Ven R W P Davies The living is a rectory in the diocese of St. Davids. Value £141 Patron the Ven R W P Davies

CATHEDRAL CHURCH, an extra parochial place in Brecon eccl. dist., contiguous to St Nicholas parish Pop, 26 Houses, 3

CATHEDRAL CHURCH, an extra parochial place in Chester city, Cheshire contiguous to St John Baptist parish. Pop, 376 Houses, 65

CATHEDRAL CLOSE, an extra parochial place in Chichester city Sussex Pop, 156 Houses 21

CATHEDRAL YARD, an extra parochial place in Winchester city Hants

CATHERINE HALL. See CAMBRIDGE

CATHERINE (ST), a village and a parish in the district and county of Gloucester The village is suburban to Gloucester city within the borough, on its north side Pop 1 270 Houses, 233 The parish includes also the hamlets of Kingsholm and Longford, the former within the borough, the latter not Acres, 200 Pop., 2 478 Houses, 480 The living is a p curacy in the diocese of Gloucester and Bristol Value, £34 Patrons, the Dean and Chapter of Bristol

CATHERINE (ST), a parish in Bath district, Somerset, on the verge of the county, 3½ miles WNW of Box r station and 3¾ NE by N of Bath Post town, Batheaston, under Bath Acres, 1 040 Real property, with Easton Amoril, £11,100 Pop, 34 Houses, 22 The manor belonged to the abbots of St. Peters, Bath, and their residence, an edifice of 1499 with a porch added in the time of Charles I, is still standing The living is a p. curacy, annexed to the vicarage of Batheaston, in the diocese of Bath and Wells The church was built about the same time as the abbots residence and contains a carved pulpit, a Norman font, and an altar tomb of 1631

CATHERINE (ST), one of the tower hamlets in London, on the Thames immediately below the Tower Most of it was destroyed in 1828, to give place to the St Catherine docks A church and an hospital were founded at it, in 1148, by Queen Maud, refounded by Queen Eleanor, and enlarged by Queen Philippa The church was rebuilt by Henry VI, claimed at the Reformation, as Queen's property, by Anne Boleyn, and used by the inhabitants till 1825 A new church and hospital, in lieu of the demolished ones, were erected by the Dock company in the Regent's park The docks occupy a space of 24 acres and were formed at a cost of £195,640 per acre Upwards of 1,200 houses were demolished to clear the site Pop of the hamlet in 1801, 2,652, in 1831, 72.

CATHERINE (ST) a western suburb of Guildford, in Surrey It has a post office under Guildford, and a fair on 2 Oct A small hill at it is surmounted by a ruined chapel, of the time of Edward II, commanding a fine view

CATHERINE'S BAY (ST), a bay on the east side of Jersey, 3½ miles E by N of the south eastern extremity of the island It measures nearly 2 miles across the entrance, but does not penetrate more than ¾ of a mile Vast works, by government, are far advanced to convert it all, with some area out ward, into an artificial harbour 3 miles in circumference, to serve as a harbour of refuge, and as a war naval station

CATHERINE'S CHAPEL (ST), a ruined chapel, serving as a sea mark, on the coast of Dorset, 8¾ miles NW of Weymouth

CATHERINE'S DOWN (ST), a hill on the south coast of the Isle of Wight, 4½ miles W of Ventnor It is 769 feet high, and about a mile long, and commands a full view of most part of the island, and of a great tract of the mainland A hermitage was built on it at an early period a chapel succeeded the hermitage in 1323, and the belfry of this an octagonal structure, 35 feet high, with a pyramidal roof still stands, and serves as a sea mark A lighthouse was commenced adjacent about 1780 but never finished, and stands as a mere shell A column, 72 feet high is on the north end of the hill, erected by Michael Hay, a Russian merchant, to commemorate the Emperor Alexander's visit to England in 1814

CATHERINE'S HILL (ST), an eminence adjacent to the river Itchen, 1½ mile SSE of Winchester, in Hants Its summit has foundations of an ancient chapel is engirt by a deep fosse, which probably belonged to a Roman camp, and commands a fine view of Winchester and the circumjacent country

CATHERINE'S HILL (ST), an eminence on the southwest border of Hants adjacent to the river Avon, 2 miles NW of Christchurch It has barrows, ancient earthworks, and remains of a small, square, double ditched camp and commands a fine view

CATHERINE SLACK, a village in Northowram township, Halifax parish, W R Yorkshire, 2 miles NE of Halifax

CATHERINE'S POINT (ST) a headland in the Isle of Wight, the southernmost land of the island, under St Catherine's Down, 4¾ miles WNW of Ventnor A coast guard station and a lighthouse are here, the latter a handsome structure of 1840, with a fixed light visible at the distance of 18 miles.

CATHERINE'S TOR (St.), a conical hill on the north coast of Devon; in the western vicinity of Hartland. The foundations of a Roman building have been discovered on its summit.

CATHERINGTON, a village, a parish, and a district in Hants. The village stands about a mile NNW of Horndean, under Catherington down, near Bere forest, 3¼ miles NW by W of Rowlands-Castle r. station, and 5¼ NNW of Havant. The parish comprises 5,139 acres. Post-town, Horndean. Real property, £7,265. Pop., 1,151. Houses, 231. The property is subdivided. Catherington House is the seat of the Rev. N. Pearse. The living is a vicarage in the diocese of Winchester. Value, £280.* Patron, C. Pritchard, Esq. The church is early Norman; has a massive tower; and contains a fine old monument of Chief-Justice Hyde. Charities, £16.—The district includes only the sub-district of Horndean, containing the parishes of Catherington, Blendworth, Chalton, and Clanfield, and the ville of Waterloo. Acres, 10,561. Poor-rates in 1866, £1,802. Pop. in 1861, 2,497. Houses, 502. Marriages in 1866, 22; births, 95,—of which 2 were illegitimate; deaths, 47,—of which 11 were at ages under 3 years, and 3 at ages above 85 years. Marriages in the ten years 1851-60, 163; births, 776; deaths, 478. The places of worship in 1851 were 6 of the Church of England, with 1,340 sittings; and 5 of Independents, with 510 s. The schools were 5 public day schools, with 200 scholars; 4 private day schools, with 83 s.; and 9 Sunday schools, with 457 s. The workhouse is in Catherington.

CATHERSTON-LEWSTON, a parish in Bridport district, Dorset; on the river Char, 4 miles NE of Lyme-Regis, and 6¼ WNW of Bridport r. station. Post-town, Whitchurch-Canonicorum, under Bridport. Acres, 248. Real property, with Marshwood, Griddleshay, Sarum-Wells, Wild, Wootton-Abbas, and Wootton-Fitzpaine, £12,618. Pop., 34. Houses, 9. Catherston was the seat of Judge Jeffreys; and his judge's cap is preserved in the church. The living is a rectory in the diocese of Salisbury. Value, £67. Patron, Mrs. Hildyard. The church was built in 1859, and is in the decorated English style.

CATHILAS, a hamlet in Llanfynydd parish, Carmarthen; 5½ miles SE of Llandeilofawr. Pop., 79. See also CATHARGOED.

CATHINOG, a hundred in Carmarthen. It marches with Cardigan, in the vicinity of Lampeter; extends 16½ miles southward; and contains nine parishes and parts of two others. Acres, 85,064. Pop., 10,161. Houses, 2,262.

CATHORPE. See CATTHORPE.

CATISFIELD, a hamlet in Fareham parish, Hants; near Fareham.

CATLEY. See BOSBURY.

CATLEY-LANE, a hamlet in Spotland township, Rochdale parish, Lancashire; near Rochdale.

CATMORE, a parish in Wantage district, Berks; near the Ridge way, 2¾ miles WSW of East Ilsley, and 8 N by W of Newbury r. station. It includes Lilley tything; and once had a market. Post-town, East Ilsley, under Newbury. Acres, 696. Pop., 121. Houses, 22. The manor has been held, for upwards of five centuries, by the Eystons. The living is a rectory in the diocese of Oxford. Value, £200. Patron, C. Eyre, Esq. The church is Norman, without porch or tower; and was recently restored.

CATON, a township, a chapelry, and a sub-district in Lancaster district, Lancashire. The township lies on the river Lune and the Midland railway, 4¼ miles NE of Lancaster; is in Lancaster parish; includes Littledale hamlet; and has a station on the railway, and a post-office under Lancaster. Acres, 8,278. Real property, £6,652. Pop., 1,150. Houses, 223. The property is much subdivided. A rising ground commands a noble view, much praised by the poet Gray, of the valley of the Lune, backed by Ingleborough mountain. Coal and slate are found; and the cotton manufacture is carried on.—The chapelry comprises all the township, except Littledale hamlet. The living is a vicarage in the diocese of Manchester. Value, £100.* Patron, the Vicar of Lancaster. The church was rebuilt in 1864. There are Independent and Wesleyan chapels, a national school, and charities £20.—The sub-district contains also Quernmoor township and Claughton parish. Pop., 1,817. Houses, 316.

CATON, a hamlet on Erme river, near Ivy-Bridge, in Devon.

CATOR, a hamlet in Widecombe-in-the-Moor parish, Devon; 6 miles NW by N of Ashburton.

CATSASH, a hundred in Somerset. It contains Alford parish and eighteen other parishes. Acres, 24,093. Pop., 7,912. Houses, 1,683.

CATS-DEANS, a hamlet in Monks-Risborough parish, Bucks; near Princes-Risborough.

CATSFIELD, a parish in Battle district, Sussex; near the Tunbridge-Wells and Hastings railway, 2¼ miles SW of Battle. It has a post-office under Battle. Acres, 2,944. Real property, £2,819. Pop., 584. Houses, 109. The property is much subdivided. Catsfield Place is a chief residence. The living is a rectory in the diocese of Chichester. Value, £311.* Patron, the Earl of Ashburnham. The church is decorated English. There are a national school and a charity for the blind, the latter £60 a-year.

CATSGORE, a hamlet in Somerton parish, Somerset; near Somerton.

CATSGORE, formerly KEATS-GORE, a locality 2 miles N of East Ilsley, in Berks. Here were the great stables erected by the Duke of Cumberland for his race-horses.

CATSHALL, a tything in Godalming parish, Surrey; near Godalming. Real property, £796.

CATSHILL, a chapelry in Bromsgrove parish, Worcester; 2¼ miles from Bromsgrove r. station. It was constituted in 1844; and has a post-office under Bromsgrove. Pop., 2,393. Houses, 509. The living is a vicarage in the diocese of Worcester. Value, £120. Patron, the Vicar of Bromsgrove. The church was built in 1838. There are four dissenting chapels.

CATSHILL, a hamlet in Shenstone parish, Stafford.

CATSTREE, a township in Worfield parish, Salop.

CATTAL, a township in Hunsingore parish, W. R. Yorkshire; on the river Nidd, and on the York and High Harrogate railway, 6½ miles ESE of Knaresborough. It has a station on the railway. Acres, 950. Real property, £1,891. Pop., 189. Houses, 40.

CATTERALL, a township in Garstang parish, Lancashire; on the river Wyre, adjacent to the Lancaster canal, and to the Lancaster and Preston railway, 1¼ mile S by W of Garstang. It has a post-office under Garstang. Acres, 1,738. Real property, £6,851. Pop., 867. Houses, 168. Catterall House is the seat of A. Simpson, Esq. There are two large cotton mills, Caldervale church, and a Wesleyan chapel.

CATTERHAM. See CATERHAM.

CATTERICK, a village, a township, and a sub-district, in Richmond district, and a parish in Richmond, Northallerton, and Bedale districts, N. R. Yorkshire. The village stands on the river Swale, near Ermine-street, 1½ mile S of Catterick-Bridge r. station, and 5½ SE of Richmond; and has a head post-office,‡ and an inn. An ancient camp was here, probably around the area now occupied by the churchyard; and an hospital was founded in the time of Henry III.—The township comprises 1,561 acres. Real property, £4,206. Pop., 623. Houses, 146.—The sub-district includes three townships in three other parishes; and contains the townships of Catterick, Colburn, Scotton, East and West Appleton, Brough, Tunstall, Scorton, Uckerby, Ellerton-upon-Swale, and Bolton-upon-Swale, in Catterick parish. Acres, 29,179. Pop., 3,164. Houses, 681.—The parish includes also the townships of Hudswell, Hipswell, Killerby, Whitwell, and Kiplin. Acres, 22,699. Real property, £35,475. Pop., 2,914. Houses, 608. The property is much subdivided. Brough Hall is the seat of Sir W. Lawson, Bart. Ermine-street crossed the Swale at Catterick-Bridge, about a mile north of the village The Roman station Cataractonium was on the site of Thornbrough, ¼ of a mile from Catterick-bridge, enclosed an area of about 9 acres, and was walled along the sides, respectively 240 and 175 yards. Substructions, pavements, an altar, a bronze vessel, coins, fragments of pottery and other Roman relics have been found at it An ancient camp is on a hill about a mile SE of the village, and several tumuli are near Races are run in April on a fine oval course of 1 mile 60 yards, in the vicinity of Catterick-bridge The living is a vicarage united with the p curacy of Tunstall, in the diocese of Ripon Value, £678 * Patron, the Bishop of Ripon The church is early and perpendicular English, in good condition The p curacies of Bolton on Swale, Hipswell, and Hudswell are separate benefices. Tunstall's hospital has £45 a year, and other charities ...

CATTERICK BRIDGE, a station on the Richmond and Darlington railway, 3½ miles E of Richmond, N R Yorkshire See CATTERICK.

CATTERICK-FORCE, a romantic waterfall, 2½ miles N W of Settle W R Yorkshire

CATTERLEN, a township in Newton Regny parish, Cumberland, 3½ miles NW by N of Penrith. Real property £1 092 Pop, 112 Houses, 21

CATTERTON, a township in Tadcaster parish, W R Yorkshire, 2½ miles NE of Tadcaster Acres, 712 Real property, £536 Pop 43. Houses, 9

CATTHORPE, or CALTHORPE, a parish in Lutterworth district, Leicester, on the verge of the county Warwick, and the river Avon, near the Midland railway 4 miles ENE of Rugby It has a post-office under Rugby Acres, 625 Real property, £1,493 Pop, 1..5 Houses, .. The property is divided among a few The parish is a meet for the Pytchley hounds The living is a rectory in the diocese of Peterborough Value £290 * Patron the Rev L Harper The church is good and has a very old font Charities £17

CATTISTOCK a parish in Dorchester district Dorset, on the river Frome and on the Dorchester and Yeovil railway near Maiden-Newton station, 4½ miles WSW of Cerne Abbas. It has a post office under Dorchester Acres, 3,030 Real property, £1,912 Pop, 510 Houses 133 The property is subdivided Cattistock House is the seat of the Farquharsons The living is a rectory in the diocese of Salisbury Value, £500 * Patron ... Still The church is good

CATTO See LANDMOTH WITH CATTO

CATTON a township in Croxall parish, Derby, on the river Trent adjacent to the Birmingham and Derby railway, 5½ miles SSW of Burton upon Trent Acres, 1,... Real property, £2,329 Pop, 76 Houses, 13

CATTON a village and a parish in St Faith district Norfolk The village stands on high ground, amid pleasant environs, 2 miles N of Norwich, contains several large and elegant houses, and has a post office under Norwich. The parish comprises 805 acres Real property, £4,305 Pop 649 Houses 133. The property is divided among a few The manor belonged, at the Conquest, to Archbishop Stigand, and was given, afterwards, to Norwich cathedral. The living is a vicarage in the diocese of Norwich Value £1.2 Patrons the Dean and Chapter of Norwich The church is early and perpendicular English, has a round tower surmounted by an octagon, and contains a rich monument to T C ... Esq There are a free school and charities £10

CATTON, a grieve ship in Allendale parish, Northumberland near Catton road station, and 1½ mile NW of Allendale It has a post office under Carlisle Pop, 535

CATTON two townships in Pocklington district, and a parish in Pocklington and York districts, E R York shire The townships are High and Low Catton, they lie contiguous to each other and the latter is on the river Derwent, 1 mile S of Stamford Bridge r station and 7 E by N of York Acres, 1,640 and 2,110 Real property £1,5.9 and £1 651 Pop 215 and 179 Houses, 42 and 33 The parish contains also the townships of East Stamford bridge, Kexby, and Stamford bridge with Scoreby, and has post offices at Stamford bridge and Kexby, both under York Acres, 8,102. Real property, £9,623, of which £151 are in quarries Pop, 1,180 Houses, 223 The property is much subdivided The living is a rectory in the diocese of York Value £410 Patron, Lord Leconfield The church is tolerable The vicarage of Kexby is a separate benefice There are a Wesleyan chapel an endowed school with £2.. and other charities with £11

CATTON, a township in Topcliffe parish, N R Yorkshire, on the river Swale, 5 miles SW of Thirsk Acres, 804 Real property £1 306 Pop, 104 Houses, 26

CATWATER, or PLYM (THE), a river of Devon It rises in Dartmoor, near Sheep's Tor, and runs 16 miles south south westward to Plymouth sound, at Plymouth It there forms inside of Mount Batten, a good estuarial harbour, and is crossed by a five arched iron bridge, 500 feet long, erected in 1827

CATWICK, a parish in Skirlaugh district, E R Yorkshire 4 miles WNW of Hatfield r station, and 5½ WSW of Hornsea Post town Leven, under Beverley Acres, 1 650 Real property £2,723 Pop, 218 Houses, 51 The property is divided among a few The living is a rectory in the diocese of York Value £119 * Patron, the Lord Chancellor The church was rebuilt in 1864 and is in the decorated English style Charities, £7

CATWORTH (GREAT), a parish in St Neots district Huntingdon, 3¾ miles N by W of Kimbolton r station, and 7 ESE of Thrapston It has a post office, of the name of Catworth, under Thrapston Acres, £2,090 Real property, £2,816 Pop, 640 Houses, 143 The property is subdivided The living is a rectory in the diocese of Ely Value, £337 * Patron, Brasenose College Oxford The church is early and later English There are Baptist and Wesleyan chapels, a national school, and charities £32 Lord Mayor Dixie was a native.

CATWORTH (LITTLE), a chapelry in Stow parish Huntingdon, 3¾ miles N of Kimbolton, and 8 ESE of Thrapston r station Post town, Catworth, under Thrapston Pop, 52 Houses, 12. The church is in ruins

CAUCA ARIXA See CHARMOUTH

CAUDLE GREEN, a hamlet in Brimpsfield parish, Gloucestershire, 8¾ miles SE of Gloucester

CAUGHALL, a township in Backford parish, Cheshire 3¼ miles NNE of Chester Acres, 328 Pop, 19 Houses, 2

CAULCUTT, a hamlet in Grandborough parish, Warwick, 5½ miles NE of Southam

CAULDON, a parish in Cheadle district, Stafford, on the river Hamps, 3¼ miles ENE of Froghall r station, and 7 WNW of Ashborne Post town, Ashborne Acres, 1,458 Real property, £2,985, of which £1,011 are in quarries. Pop, 400 Houses, 77 The property is divided among a few Much of the surface is barren moor Excellent limestone is extensively quarried on the lofty hill of Cauldon Lowe, and sent, on a railway of three inclined planes, to Froghall Good fossil marble also is found, and limestone is burnt The river Hamps runs a long distance, in the neighbourhood, under ground Urns and flint headed arrows have been found at Big Lowe The living is a vicarage in the diocese of Lichfield Value, £80 Patron, A Heumber, Esq The church has a square tower, and contains monuments to the Croppers Wilmots, Marshalls, and Sheldons

CAULDWELL, a hamlet in Stapenhill parish Derby, 4 miles NNE of Burton upon Trent It has a post office under Burton upon Trent, and a Baptist chapel Real property, £2,092 Pop, 132 Houses, 26

CAULEDGE PARK a hamlet in Alnwick parish, Northumberland, 2 miles S of Alnwick Pop 33

CAULK See CALKE

CAUNANT MAWR or CEUNANT MAWR, a fine waterfall of 60 feet, in Carnarvon, under Snowdon, 2 miles WNW of Llanberis

CAUNDLE BISHOP, or BISHOPS CAUNDLE a parish in Sherborne district, Dorset, 4 miles S by E of Milborne Port r station, and 5 SE of Sherborne It includes Caundle Wake, Wything and Bishopstown hamlet, and has a post office, of the name of Bishops Caundle, under

Sherborne. Acres, 1,297. Real property, of Caundle-Bishop only, £677. Pop., 371. Houses, 92. The living is a rectory in the diocese of Salisbury. Value, £226.* Patron, G. D. W. Digby, Esq. The church is old, and has a tower. Charities, £12.

CAUNDLE-MARSH, a parish in Sherborne district, Dorset; 2¾ miles S by W of Milborne-Port r. station, and 4 SE of Sherborne. Post-town, Bishops-Caundle, under Sherborne. Acres, 792. Real property, 1,128. Pop., 84. Houses, 16. The living is a rectory in the diocese of Salisbury. Value, £143. Patron, Sir H. A. Hoare, Bart.

CAUNDLE-PURSE, a parish in Sherborne district, Dorset; on the verge of the county, 1¼ mile SE of Milborne-Port r. station, and 4¾ E of Sherborne. Post-town, Milborne-Port, under Sherborne. Acres, 1,470. Real property, £1,498. Pop., 185. Houses, 36. The living is a rectory in the diocese of Salisbury. Value, £160. Patron, Sir H. A. Hoare, Bart.

CAUNDLE-STOURTON, a parish in Sturminster district, Dorset; 3¼ miles SE of Milborne-Port r. station, and 4¼ WNW of Sturminster. Post-town, Stalbridge, under Blandford. Acres, 1,975. Real property, with Lydlinch, Wake, and Stock-Gaylard, £8,445. Pop., 395. Houses, 94. The living is a vicarage in the diocese of Salisbury. Value, £48. Patron, Sir H. A. Hoare, Bart. The church is ancient, and has a tower. Bishop Mew was a native.

CAUNDLE-WAKE, a tything in Caundle-Bishop parish, Dorset. It belonged to Archbishop Wake.

CAUNSALL, a hamlet in Wolverley parish, Worcester; near Kidderminster.

CAUNTON, a parish in Southwell district, Notts; on an affluent of the river Trent, 5 miles SW of Carlton r. station, and 6 NW by N of Newark. It includes the hamlets of Knapthorpe, Beesthorpe, and Deanhall; and has a post-office under Newark. Acres, 3,130. Real property, £3,845. Pop., 596. Houses, 133. The property is divided among a few. Beesthorpe Hall belongs to S. E. Bristowe, Esq. The living is a vicarage in the diocese of Lincoln. Value, £171. Patron, the Bishop of Ripon. The church is old and has a tower. There are chapels for Wesleyans and Primitive Methodists, and a parochial school.

CAUSE, a township in Westbury parish, Salop; 9¾ miles WSW of Shrewsbury. Traces exist of an ancient castle of the Corbets, on a spot commanding an extensive view.

CAUSENNÆ. See ANCASTER.

CAUSEY-PARK, a township in Hebburn parish, Northumberland; 5¼ miles NNW of Morpeth. Acres, 1,117. Pop., 101. Houses, 19. Causey-Park House is the seat of the Ogles; and was built in 1582.

CAUSEY-PIKE, a mountain on the north flank of Keskadale, in Cumberland; 5 miles SW of Keswick. It has a height of 2,030 feet; and figures conspicuously in the grand surrounding scenery.

CAUSTON, a township in Chobury parish, Salop; 6¼ miles SE of Bishops-Castle. Pop., 21.

CAUTLEY, a hamlet and a chapelry in Sedbergh parish, W. R. Yorkshire. The hamlet lies among grand mountain scenery, adjacent to Westmoreland, in the vicinity of Sedbergh. A waterfall here, called Cautley Spout, makes three descents, of aggregately about 860 feet, between such screens, precipices, and cliffs, that those on one side can be scaled only by much care and effort, and those on the other not at all.—The chapelry includes also the hamlet of Dowbiggin; was constituted in 1853; and bears the name of Cautley and Dowbiggin. Post-town, Sedbergh, under Kendal. Pop., 276. Houses, 55. The living is a p. curacy in the diocese of Ripon. Value, £55. Patron, the Vicar of Sedbergh.

CAVE. See CAVE (NORTH) and CAVE (SOUTH).

CAVE HILL. See ABERGELE.

CAVE HOLE, a cavernous hollow, near Portland light, on the coast of Dorset. It is swept by sea-billows during storms.

CAVENDISH, a parish, with a village, in Sudbury district, Suffolk; on the Haverhill and Melford railway, 2½ miles E of Clare. It has a post-office under Sudbury, a r. station, and a fair on 11 June. Acres, 3,354. Real property, £5,510. Pop., 1,301. Houses, 298. The property is subdivided. The manor belonged anciently to the Cavendish family, ancestors of the Dukes of Devonshire. The living is a rectory in the diocese of Ely. Value, £733.* Patron, Jesus' College, Cambridge. The church is later English. An endowed school has £115 a-year, and a lecture-hall was built in 1869.

CAVENHAM, a parish in Mildenhall district, Suffolk; on the river Lark, 2¼ miles N of Higham r. station, and 4½ SE of Mildenhall. Post-town, Tuddenham, under Soham. Acres, 2,630. Real property, £1,270. Pop., 229. Houses, 48. The property is divided among a few. Cavenham-Hall is the seat of the Waddingtons. The living is a vicarage in the diocese of Ely. Value, £113. Patron, the Lord Chancellor. The church is a neat small edifice, with a tower. Charities, £48.

CAVE (NORTH), a township in Howden district, and a parish in Howden and Pocklington districts, E. R. Yorkshire. The township lies 4½ miles NE of Staddlethorpe r. station, and 6¾ S by E of Market-Weighton; and has a post-office‡ under Brough, Yorkshire. Acres, 3,270. Real property, £5,489. Pop., 976. Houses, 219. The parish contains also the townships of South Cliff and Drewton-with-Everthorpe. Acres, 6,913. Real property, £9,358. Pop., 1,281. Houses, 269. The property is much subdivided. The living is a vicarage in the diocese of York. Value, £247.* Patrons, H. and S. Burton. The church is good; and there are three dissenting chapels and an endowed school.

CAVERSFIELD, a parish in Bicester district, Oxford; near the Oxford and Bletchley railway, 1¾ mile N of Bicester. Post-town, Bicester. Acres, 1,200. Real property, £2,142. Pop., 183. Houses, 30. The property is divided among a few. Caversfield House is the seat of the Marsham family. Roman coins have been found. The living is a vicarage in the diocese of Oxford. Value, £69. Patron, R. B. Marsham, Esq. The church is old, of various dates, but good; and has a Norman porch and a very ancient font.

CAVERSHAM, a village and a parish in Henley district, Oxford. The village stands on the river Thames, in the vicinity of the Great Western railway, 1 mile N of Reading; and has a post-office under Reading. It is a long straggling place, partly mean, partly well-built, partly winged with neat new villas. A bridge connects it with Reading; was the scene of a sharp skirmish in 1643; was rebuilt in 1869; and in the clear, is 290 feet long. An island below the bridge was the place where Robert de Montfort and Henry de Essex fought in the presence of Henry II. A priory of black canons, a cell to Nutley abbey, stood at the village; and was famous, in the old Romish times, for some boasted relics. The martial Earl of Pembroke, protector of Henry III., died at Caversham; South, the celebrated preacher, prepared his sermons at it for the press; and Earl Cadogan takes from it the title of Viscount.—The parish comprises 4,772 acres. Real property, £11,167. Pop., 1,783. Houses, 335. The manor belonged, at the Conquest, to the Giffords; passed to the Marsaes and the Cadogans; and belongs now to W. Crawshay, Esq. The mansion, called Caversham Park, occupies a commanding site, amid fine grounds laid out by Brown; and was destroyed by fire in the time of George I., and again in 1850, and each time immediately rebuilt. Queen Anne of Denmark was splendidly entertained in the original edifice; and Charles I. was for some time kept prisoner in it, and allowed to have interviews with his children. The living is a vicarage in the diocese of Oxford. Value, £116.* Patron, Christ Church, Oxford. The church is partly Norman, partly later styles; lost its north side and its tower in the civil wars; and was partly restored in 1857. The vicarage of Kidmore is a separate charge. There are a Baptist chapel of 1866, another dissenting chapel, a national school, a British school, and charities £13.

CAVERSWALL, or CARESWELL, a township and a parish in Cheadle district, Stafford. The township lies on the river Blythe, 1 mile NE of Blythe-Bridge r. sta-

…n, and 4 W of Cheadle and has a post office, of the name of Caverswall, under Stafford. Real property, £7,941, of which £1,200 are in mines The parish contains also the township of Weston Coyney with Hulme Acres, 5,000 Real property, £16,937, of which £4,460 are in mines Pop, 3,046 Houses, 609 The property is much subdivided. Caverswall Hall is a chief residence Caverswall castle is a large edifice with lofty keep and four corner towers was built originally, in the time of Edward II, by Sir William de Caverswall, rebuilt, in the time of James I, by Sir William Cravdock, and converted, in 1810, into a Benedictine nunnery The living is a vicarage in the diocese of Lichfield. Value, £217 * Patron the Hon E. S Jervis The church is ancient and contains monuments of Sir William de Caverswall and Earl St Vincent There are a Wesleyan chapel and charities £31

CAVE (SOUTH), a small town, a township and a sub-district in Beverley district, and a parish in Beverley and Howden districts, E R. Yorkshire. The town stands in a hollow, on the Roman road from Brough to York, 3 miles NNW of Brough r station, and 12 W by N of Hull, is a seat of petty sessions, and has a post-office‡ under Brough, a banking office, 3 inns, a weekly market on Monday, and a cattle fair on Trinity Monday The township extends to the Humber, and comprises 4,520 acres of land, and 194 of water Real property, £8,652 Pop, 894 Houses, 211 The parish contains also the townships of Faxfleet and Broomfleet. Acres 8,6[illegible] Real property £13,388 Pop, 1,37[illegible] Houses, 31[illegible] The property is much subdivided The manor belonged formerly to the Bolleros, and belongs now to Mrs. Barnard of Cave Castle John Washington grandfather of George Washington, the liberator of America, held landed property here, and emigrated hence in 1657 The living is a vicarage in the diocese of York Value £258 * Patron, Mrs Barnard The church was built in 1601, and is in excellent condition The vicarage of Broomfleet is a separate charge There are three dissenting chapels, and an endowed school

CAVIL. See PORTINGTON AND CAVIL

CAWDEN AND CADWORTH, a hundred in Wilts It contains fourteen parishes, and parts of two others, and includes part of Salisbury Plain Acres, 22,769 Pop, 4,621 Houses, 976

CAWDRY a detached portion of Bradnop township, Leek parish, Stafford, near Leek

CAWKWELL a parish in Horncastle district, Lincoln, 6½ miles SW of Legbourne r station, and 7 N of Horncastle Post town, Scamblesby, under Horncastle Acres 540 Real property, £870 Pop, 35 Houses, 7 The property is divided among a few The living is a vicarage in the diocese of Lincoln Value £46 Patron, Lord Yarborough The church is good

CAWOOD, a village and a parish in Selby district, W R Yorkshire The village stands on the river Ouse, 3 miles ENE of Ulleskelf r station, and 4½ WNW of Selby It was formerly a market town is a seat of petty sessions and has a post-office‡ under Selby, and fairs on 12 May and 23 Sept A castle was built at it, about 930 by King Athelstane, given to the see of York, rebuilt in splendid style in the time of Henry VI, by Archbishops Bowett and Kempe, held, for two years, by the royalists, in the wars of Charles I and taken and dismantled by the parliamentarians Many of the archbishops lived in the castle as their chief residence, Archbishop Mathew, famed for extemporaneous preaching, and Archbishop Montaigne a native of Cawood died in it and Cardinal Wolsey retired to it after his fall, and was arrested in it by the Earl of Northumberland The only remains of it are the gateway tower, square and but tressed, and a brick building, which seems to have been a chapel The parish comprises 2 840 acres Real property, £5,500 Pop, 1,213 Houses, 301 The property is much subdivided The living is a vicarage in the diocese of York Value, £300 * Patron, the Archbishop of York The church is early English and good, and there are Wesleyan and Primitive Methodist chapels An hospital has £76 from endowment, a school, £10[illegible], and other charities £252

CAWOOD, Lancashire See ARKHOLME

CAWRSE, a hundred in Montgomery It contains Forden parish, and parts of five other parishes Acres 16,808 Pop, 2,548 Houses, 453

CAWSAND, a village on the coast of Cornwall, on a small bay of its own name, on the west side of Plymouth sound, opposite the Breakwater, 4 miles SW of Plymouth It has a post office under Devonport, and is a coast guard and pilot station The bay has an anchorage for the largest ships, is well sheltered, and was used as the chief anchorage of the sound prior to the construction of the Breakwater

CAWSAND BEACON, or COSDON a mountain in the north of Dartmoor, Devon, 4 miles SE by E of Okehampton Its height is 1,792 feet It was a station of the Ordnance survey, and it commands a very extensive and most striking view

CAWSTON, a village and a parish in Aylsham district, Norfolk. The village stands on a pleasant spot, near an affluent of the river Wensum, 4 miles WSW of Aylsham, and 9½ E of Elmham r station, and has a post office under Norwich, and fairs on 1 Feb and the last Wednesday of April and Aug The parish comprises 4 2[illegible]6 acres Real property, £5,374 Pop, 1,019 Houses, 245. The property is divided among a few The living is a rectory in the diocese of Norwich Value, £1,015 * Patron, Pembroke Hall, Cambridge The church is decorated perpendicular, and was partly restored in 18[illegible] There are a Wesleyan chapel, and charities £11

CAWSTON a hamlet in Dunchurch parish Warwick 2 miles SW of Rugby It is a meet for the North Warwick hounds Cawston House is the seat of Lady John Scott

CAWTHORN, a township in Middleton parish, N R. Yorkshire, 3½ miles NNW of Pickering Acres 1,5[illegible] Pop, 33 Houses, 3 Here are four Roman camps, in good preservation, one of them square and double ditched, another, nearly oval, 850 feet long and 320 broad Some British tumuli are near

CAWTHORNE, a village, a parish, and a sub district in Wortley district W R Yorkshire The village stands 2 miles NNW of Silkstone r station, and 4 WNW of Barnesley, and has a post office under Barnesley The parish includes also Barnby Basin hamlet, at the end of Barnesley canal, and the hamlets of Barnby Furnace, Deacon Brook, and Norcroft Acres, 3,4[illegible] Real property, £5 684 Pop, 1,283 Houses, 271 The property is divided among six Coal, limestone, and ironstone are worked The living is a p curacy, under the vicarage of Silkstone in the diocese of Ripon Value £119 Patron, J S Stanhope Esq The church is old but fair, and there are Wesleyan and Primitive Methodist chapels and a slightly endowed school —The sub-district contains also parts of two other parishes. Acres, 8 396 Pop, 4,825 Houses 973

CAWTHORPE, a hamlet in Bourn parish, Lincoln near Bourn. Pop, 94 Houses, 19 There is a Baptist chapel

CAWTHORPE (LITTLE), a parish in Louth district, Lincoln, 1½ mile WSW of Legbourne r station, and 3½ SSE of Louth Post town, Louth Acres 460 Real property, £942 Pop, 223 Houses, 46 The property is much subdivided. The living is a rectory in the diocese of Lincoln Value £69 Patron, not reported The church was built in 1860, and is a structure of light coloured bricks, striped with lines of black There are Wesleyan and Free Methodist chapels.

CAWTON, a township in Gilling parish N R Yorkshire, 5 miles S of Helmsley Acres, 1,038 Real property £1 255 Pop, 79 Houses, 18.

CAXTON a decayed town, a parish a sub district and a district in Cambridgeshire The town stands on Ermine street, 3½ miles NNW of North Road r station, and 9½ W of Cambridge and has a post office‡ under Royston and two inns It had a market from the 13th century till the middle of the 18th, and it still has a fair on the 12th of Oct —The parish comprises 2,00[illegible] acres.

Real property, £2,278. Pop., 515. Houses, 97. The property is divided among a few. The manor belonged to the D'Eschallerses, the Freviles, the Burgoynes, and others. The living is a vicarage in the diocese of Ely. Value, £80.* Patrons, the Dean and Canons of Windsor. The church contains some old tombs; and was recently restored. There are a national school and a workhouse. M. Paris, the historian, was a native.—The sub-district and the district are co-extensive; and contain the parishes of Caxton, Bourn, Knapwell, Elsworth, Longstow, Hatley-St. George, East Hatley, Tadlow, Croydon-cum-Clapton, Arrington, Wimpole, Orwell, Little Eversden, Great Eversden, Kingston, Caldecote, Toft, Hardwicke, Gamlingay, Eltisley, Croxton, Papworth-St. Everard, Little Gransden, Great Gransden, Yelling, and Papworth-St. Agnes,—the last partly and the two previous wholly in Huntingdon-proper. Acres, 49,885. Poor-rates in 1866, £5,414. Pop. in 1861, 10,966. Houses, 2,200. Marriages in 1866, 56; births, 416,—of which 30 were illegitimate; deaths, 236,—of which 113 were at ages under 5 years, and 12 at ages above 85. Marriages in the ten years 1851-60, 733; births, 3,907; deaths, 2,046. The places of worship in 1851 were 26 of the Church of England, with 4,951 sittings; 2 of Independents, with 740 s.; 7 of Baptists, with 1,757 s.; 5 of Wesleyan Methodists, with 685 s.; and 1 of Primitive Methodists, with 70 s. The schools were 17 public day schools, with 1,282 scholars; 8 private day schools, with 196 s.; and 27 Sunday schools, with 1,718 s. The workhouse has capacity for 215 inmates.

CAYNE (THE), a stream of Merioneth; running 7 miles south-south-westward to the Maw, 4 miles N of Dolgelly. A fall of nearly 200 feet occurs on it, called the Pistyll-y-Cayne, over a mural precipice.

CAYNHAM. See CAINHAM.

CAYNTON, a township in Edgmond parish, Salop; 3½ miles NW of Newport. Pop., 61.

CAYO, a village and a hundred in Carmarthen. The village is in Conwil-Cayo parish, 6½ miles NW of Llandovery; and has fairs on 21 Aug. and 6 Oct. The hundred lies around the village; extends from the boundary with Cardigan to the vicinity of Llandeilofawr; and contains six parishes, and parts of three others. Acres, 107,889. Pop., 12,339. Houses, 2,593.

CAYTHORPE, a village and a parish in the district of Newark and county of Lincoln. The village stands near the Grantham and Lincoln railway, 9 miles N by E of Grantham; and has a post-office‡ under Grantham, a r. station, and a fair on the second Friday after Good Friday. The parish includes also Friston hamlet. Acres, 4,210. Real property, £8,038. Pop., 822. Houses, 178. The property is much subdivided. Caythorpe Hall is the seat of G. H. Packe, Esq. The living is a rectory in the diocese of Lincoln. Value, £976.* Patron, G. H. Packe, Esq. The church is cruciform and decorated English; suffered extensive injury, with destruction of a beautiful spire, by a storm in 1859; and has been subsequently restored. There are a Wesleyan chapel, and charities £7.

CAYTHORPE, a township in Lowdham parish, Notts; on the river Trent, 5½ miles S of Southwell. Real property, £1,413. Pop., 315.

CAYTHORPE, a hamlet in Rudstone parish, E. R. Yorkshire; 3½ miles NE of Great Driffield.

CAYTON, a township and a parish in Scarborough district, N. R. Yorkshire. The township lies on the coast, and on the Scarborough and Hull railway, 4 miles SSE of Scarborough; includes the hamlets of Deepdale and Killerby; and has a station on the railway. Acres, 1,298; of which 63 are water. Pop., 457. Houses, 131. The parish contains also the township of Osgodby; and its post-town is Seamer under Scarborough. Acres, 2,553,—of which 153 are water. Real property, £6,295. Pop., 534. Houses, 111. The property is much subdivided. The living is a p. curacy, annexed to the vicarage of Seamer, in the diocese of York. The church is good; and has an embattled tower. There is a Wesleyan chapel.

CAYTON, a hamlet in South Stainley parish, W. R. Yorkshire; 3½ miles NE of Ripley.

CEALSCYTHE. See CHELSEA.

CEDRIS, a township in Talyllyn and Llanfihangel-y-Pennant parishes, Merioneth; 6½ miles SSW of Dolgelly. Real property, £752. Pop., 166.

CEFEN-COCH, a township in Llanrhaiadr-yn-Mochnant parish, Montgomery; on the verge of the county, 5½ miles N of Llanfyllin. Pop., 301.

CEFFENPAWL. See CEFNPAWL.

CEFN, a Welsh or ancient British word, signifying the ridge or upper part of a mountain, and used much as a prefix of local names.

CEFN, a hamlet in Gelligaer parish, Glamorgan; 6½ miles N of Caerphilly. Real property, £9,719; of which £7,191 are in mines. Pop., 659. Houses, 120.

CEFN, a chapelry in St. Asaph parish, Denbigh; 3 miles SW of St. Asaph. It has a post-office under Rhyl. Pop., 620. The living is a rectory. Value, £292. The church was built in 1864, and is handsome.

CEFN, a railway station in the east of Denbigh; on the Shrewsbury railway, 6½ miles SSW of Wrexham.

CEFN, a railway station in Glamorgan; on the Porthcawl railway, 4½ miles SW of Bridgend.

CEFN, or CEFYN, a township in Cilcen parish, Flint; 5½ miles NW of Mold. Pop., 220. Houses, 44.

CEFN-AMWLCH, the seat of the Finch family, in the vicinity of Nevin, Carnarvon.

CEFNBLAIDD, a hamlet in Talley parish, Carmarthen; 7½ miles N of Llandeilofawr. Pop., 376.

CEFN-BRYN, a hill ridge across the western peninsula of Glamorgan; in the vicinity of Reynoldstone. Its height is 581 feet. A famous cromlech, called Arthur's Stone, and numerous cairns and Druidical circles are on it.

•CEFN-COED, a village on the north-east border of Glamorgan; 2½ miles NNW of Merthyr-Tydvil. It has a post-office under Merthyr-Tydvil, and a r. station.

CEFN-CYMER, a township in Llangwyfan parish, Denbigh; 14 miles SW of Ruthin. Pop., 119.

CEFNDEISIOG, a township in Llanfihangel parish, Montgomery; 4½ miles SW of Llanfyllin.

CEFNDU, a township in Rhuddlan parish, Flint; near Rhuddlan.

CEFNHAFODAN, a township in Llangurig parish, Montgomery; 5½ miles S of Llanidloes. Pop., 326.

CEFNI (THE), a river of Anglesey. It rises near the centre of the county; runs 5 miles south-eastward to Llangefni; and goes thence 7 miles southward and south-westward to Malldraeth bay. The Chester and Holyhead railway crosses it, about 1½ mile above its mouth, on a nineteen-arched viaduct.

CEFNLENYD, an extra-parochial tract in Llanfyllin district, Montgomery; 7½ miles E of Llanfyllin. Pop., 15.

CEFNLLYFNOG, a township in Meifod parish, Montgomery; 3½ miles S of Llanfyllin. Pop., 52.

CEFNLLYS, or KEVENLLECE, a village, a parish, and a hundred, in Radnor. The village stands on the river Ithon, 2½ miles SSW of Penybont r. station, and 16 W by N of Kington; and is a contributary borough to New Radnor, and a polling-place. The parish includes also the townships of Cwmbreath, Trefonnon, and Trelegoed. Post-town, Penybont, Radnorshire. Acres, 4,135. Real property, £1,590. Pop., 395. Houses, 62. The vale of the Ithon here is strikingly picturesque. A fortress, called Castell-Glyn-Ithon, crowned a steep hill adjacent to the village; was erected, in 1242, by Ralph Mortimer; and passed, in the time of Edward IV., into the possession of the Crown. The living is a rectory in the diocese of St. Davids. Value, £135. Patron, the Bishop of St. Davids. Charities, £22.—The hundred contains also five other parishes, and parts of four others. Acres, 37,291. Pop., 3,579. Houses, 696.

CEFNLLYS-ISAF and CEFNLLYS-UCHAF, two townships in Llanerfyl parish, Montgomery; 4½ miles WNW of Llanfair. Pop., 192 and 223.

CEFN-MABLEY, the seat of the Kemes family, in Glamorgan; on the Rhymney river, 6½ miles NNE of Cardiff. The house is old and curious.

CEFN-OGO. See ABERGELE.

CEFNPAWL, a township in Abbey-cwm-Hir parish, Radnor; at the influx of the Clywedog river to the Ithon,

6½ miles ENE of Rhayader Real property, £525 Pop., 161 Houses, 27

CEFNPENNAR a hamlet in Aberdare parish, Glamorgan on the river Cynon, the Merthyr Tydvil canal, and the Taf Valley railway, under Twynmawr, 4½ miles SW of Merthyr Tydvil Real property, £32,667, of which £15 096 are in mines, £8,000 in iron works, £2,185 in canals and £60 in quarries. Pop, 834

CEFNPOST a township in Llanfihangel Glyn Myfyr parish, Merioneth, 6½ miles NW of Corwen Acres, 3,?35. Pop, 70 Houses, 16

CEFNRHOS-ISAF and CEFNRHOS UCHAF, or ISAF CEFNRHOS and UCHAF CEFNRHOS, two townships in Towyn parish, Merioneth, near Towyn Real property, £1,479 and £533 Pop, 633 and 93.

CEFN SIDAN SANDS, a shoal in Carmarthen bay, extending about 6 miles south south eastward, from the north of the Towy river It has been fatal to many ships

CEFNTREFFRAW, a tything in Aberffraw parish, Anglesey, near Aberffraw

CEFN Y BEDD, a locality on the east border of Denbigh, 3¾ miles NNW of Wrexham It has a post-office under Wrexham, and r station

CEFN Y BEREN a township in Kerry parish, Montgomery, 2 miles ESE of Newtown Pop, 83

CEFN Y COED, a township in Eglwysfach parish, Denbigh 4½ miles SSE of Conway

CEFN Y GWRDY, a township in Llangwyfan parish, Denbigh, 5½ miles N of Ruthin Pop, 114

CEFN YR OGO See ABERGELE

CEFN YR OWEN, a township in Dolgelly parish, Merioneth, near Dolgelly Real property, £116 Pop, 66

CEFYN See CEFN, Flint

CEGID (THE), a river of Carnarvon It rises on the east side of Snowdon, and runs 12 miles, north northwestward, to the head of Beaumaris bay, in the vicinity of Bangor The Chester and Holyhead railway crosses it on a viaduct 600 feet long

CEGIDOG See GEORGE (ST) Denbigh

CEIDIO a parish in Pwllheli district Carnarvon, 2¾ miles SW by W of Nevin, and 7 SW of Pwllheli Post town, Nevin, under Pwllheli. Acres, 1,081 Real property, £1,044 Pop, 154 Houses, 25 The living is a vicarage in the diocese of Bangor Value, £85 Patron 1 P J Parry, Esq

CEIDIO, Anglesey See RHODOGEIDIO

CEIRCHIOG a parochial chapelry in the district and county of Anglesey, 2 miles NNE of Ty Croes r station, and 4½ N by W of Aberffraw Post town, Bryngwran, under Holyhead Acres, 613 Real property, £6?7 Pop, 174. Houses, 37 The living is a p curacy annexed to the rectory of Llanbeulan, in the diocese of Bangor

CEIRIOG (THE) a river of Denbigh and Salop It rises under Cader Berwyn, in Denbigh, and runs 18 miles in great curves prevailingly eastward, past Glynn and Chirk to the river Dee, 3 miles NE of Chirk

CELLIAN, or KELLIAN, a parish in Lampeter district, Cardigan on the river Teifi 3 miles NE of Lampeter r station, and 11 NW of Llandovery Post town, Lampeter, under Carmarthen Acres, 3 645 Real property £1,184 Pop, 532 Houses, 128 An ancient road, British and Roman, passed through, and numerous antiquities exist, including cairns, camps, standing stones, the Bedd y Cowryn or Virgin's Grave, and the Llech-Cynon, an enormous stone on an artificial circular tumulus. The living is a rectory in the diocese of St Davids Value £83 * Patron the Bishop of St Davids The church has an ancient font The Rev M Williams, the antiquary, was a native

CELLAR HEAD a hamlet in Cheddleton parish, Stafford, 4½ miles NW of Cheadle

CELLIWS, a township in Llanbadarn fawr parish, Radnor, 7½ miles SE of Rhayader Pop 101

CEMAS COED, a village in Trewalchmai parochial chapelry Anglesey, 5½ miles NNE of Aberffraw

CEMMAES, a township in Llanbadrig parish, Anglesey, on Kemlyn bay 4½ miles W of Amlwch It has a post office under Bangor Real property, £2 ?66 of which £100 are in quarries Pop 909 A creek is here, with a small pier A small church was built in 1865

CEMMAES or CEMMES, a village and a parish in Machynlleth district, Montgomery The village stands in Gwernybwlch township, on the river Dyfi and the Mawddwy railway, 8 miles NE of Machynlleth, and has a post office‡ under Shrewsbury, and a r station The parish consists of the townships of Gwernybwlch and Brynuchel Tafolog Acres, 9,247 Rated property, £2 805 Pop, 872 Houses, 187 The property is divided among a few Some remains exist of an ancient circle for games The living is a rectory in the diocese of Bangor Value £288 * Patron, the Bishop of Bangor The church is good, and there is an Independent chapel

CEMMAES ROAD, a railway station in North Wales on the Newtown and Machynlleth railway, 5 miles E of Machynlleth

CENARTH, or KENARTH, a township in St Harmon parish, Radnor, 4½ miles N of Rhayader Real property, £1 575 Pop, 300 Houses, 60

CENARTH, or KENARTH, a hamlet, a parish, and a sub district in the district of Newcastle in Emlyn, and county of Carmarthen The hamlet lies on the river Teifi adjacent to the Cardigan railway, 3 miles W by N of Newcastle Emlyn and has a post office under Carmarthen The parish includes also the town of Newcastle Emlyn, and the hamlets of Dolbryn, Emlyn and Gellygally Acres, 6 429 Real property, £4 110 Pop, 1,744 Houses, 404 The Teifi is crossed, at Cenarth hamlet by a picturesque bridge, falls, immediately above the bridge over a bold ledge of rocks, and has there a famous salmon leap, at which 100 fish have been taken in a single morning Gelli-Dewyll is the seat of the Brigstokes The living is a vicarage in the diocese of St Davids Value, £159 Patron, the Bishop of St. Davids. There is a Calvinistic Methodist chapel The sub-district contains eight parishes Acres, 47,459 Pop, 6,072 Houses, 1,544

CENIN, a village in Llanfihangel-y Pennant parish, Carnarvon, 5½ miles N of Criccieth Pop., 215

CENNANT MAWR. See CANNANT MAWR

CENNEN (THE) A stream of Carmarthen running 7 miles to the Loughor, 3 miles S of Llandeilo fawr

CENOL, a parcel in Llanfihangel cwmdu parish, Brecon, 5½ miles NW of Crickhowell Pop, 204

CENTRAL CORNWALL RAILWAY, a railway in Cornwall, first of 21 miles, authorised in 1864, from Launceston to the Bodmin and Wadebridge, next of 2? miles authorised in 1865, from Ruthern to Truro

CENTRAL WALES RAILWAY, a railway in South Wales. It commences at Knighton, on the verge of Wales adjacent to Salop, and goes south westward, through the counties of Radnor and Brecon to Llandovery in Carmarthenshire The part of it to Llandrindod, 20 miles long, was authorized in 1859, under the name of the Central Wales, and the part thence to Llandovery, 26¼ miles long, was authorized in 1860, under the name of the Central Wales Extension It has such junctions and connexions with other railways, and such extensions of its own, as to give a continuous and direct route from Manchester and Central England through Shrewsbury, to Swansea, Llanelly, and Milford Haven It was opened to Llanwrtyd in May 1867, and further in 1868, and it is worked by the Northwestern

CEORTESEGE See CHERTSEY

CERCHEDE. See CHELSEA

CERDICESFORD See CHARFORD (NORTH)

CERDICESLEAGH See CHARDSLEY

CERDRE See CHARD

CERDYN (THE), a stream of Cardigan running 5 miles south eastward to the Teifi, near Llandyssil

CERIST, a township in Mallwyd parish, Merioneth 2 miles S of Dinas Mowddwy Real property, £ ?68 Pop 137

CERNE, a river a sub district a hundred, and a division in Dorset The river rises near Minterne, and runs 10 miles southward past Cerne Abbas Nether Cerne, and Forston, through a tract of chalk hills to the Frome in the vicinity of Dorchester The sub district lies round Cerne Abbas, is in the district of Dorchester, and contains nineteen parishes and a parochial chapelry Acres, 45,363 Pop, 7,318 Houses, 1,543 The hundred also lies round Cerne Abbas, is partly in Bridport and Dorchester divisions, but chiefly in Cerne division, bears the name of Cerne, Totcombe and Modbury and contains five parishes of the sub district, together with one parish and part of another not in the sub district Acres, 10 501 —The division is more extensive than the sub district, and contains the hundreds or liberties of Alton Pancras, Buckland Newton, Piddletrenthide, and Sydling St. Nicholas, and parts of Fordington, Bindon, Sherborne, Tollerford, Whiteway, Yetminster, and Cerne, Totcombe, and Modbury Acres, 47,653 Pop, 7,318. Houses, 1,543.

CERNE ABBAS, a small town and a parish in Dorchester district, Dorset The town stands on the river Cerne, 4¾ miles ESE of Evershot r station, and 7½ N by W of Dorchester It includes four or five streets is a seat of petty sessions, and has a post-office,‡ of the name of Cerne, under Dorchester, three inns and a workhouse, a church, two dissenting chapels, and some remains of a Benedictine abbey The church is perpendicular English, and has a tower The abbey was founded, in 987, by Aylmer, Earl of Cornwall, plundered, in 1015, by Canute, and occupied, in 1471, by Queen Margaret, on her way to Tewkesbury St Augustine is said by some to have founded it, Edwald, the brother of St Edmund the martyr, is said by others to have founded it, and to have been buried in it, and Cardinal Morton, born at Bere Regis, was one of its monks The remains of it are a gatehouse, bearing escutcheons, a long buttressed barn, still used as a granary, and some traces of the gardens and park An ancient earthwork, unknown to record is north of the churchyard A lofty eminence, called Trendle hill or the Giant's hill, rises adjacent to the town, has the figure of a man, 180 feet high cut on its chalky surface, and is crowned by an ancient camp Markets are held on Wednesdays fairs are held on Mid lent Monday, 28 April, and 2 Oct, and some trade is carried on in malting, brewing and leather dressing —The parish comprises 3,063 acres Real property, with Upper Cerne, £6,389 Pop, 1,185 Houses, 254 The property is not much divided, and the manor belongs to Lord Rivers The living is a vicarage in the diocese of Salisbury Value, £81 * Patron, Lord Rivers.

CERNE NETHER, a parish in Dorchester district, Dorset, on the river Cerne, 4¼ miles E of Maiden Newton r station, and 5½ N by W of Dorchester Post town, Cerne, under Dorchester Acres, 845 Real property, with Godmanstone, £2,204 Pop, 95 Houses 16 The property is all in one estate The living is a vicarage in the diocese of Salisbury Value, £60 Patron, R B Sheridan, Esq The church is small but neat, and has an ivy clad tower

CERNE (UPPER), a parish in Dorchester district, Dorset, on the river Cerne 1¾ mile N by W of Cerne Abbas, and 4 E by S of Evershot r station Post town Cerne, under Dorchester Acres, 1,103 Real property, with Cerne Abbas, £6,389 Pop, 75 Houses, 13 The property is all in one estate The living is a rectory in the diocese of Salisbury Value, £132 * Patron, J White Esq The church was reported in 1859 as very bad

CERNEY (NORTH), a parish in Cirencester district, Gloucester, near Ermine street, 4 miles N of Cirencester r station It includes the tythings of Calmsden and Woodmancote, and has a post office under Cirencester Acres, 4,153. Real property, £5,19[illegible] Pop, 692 Houses, 153 The property is divided among a few Cerney House is the seat of the Croomes The living is a rectory in the diocese of Gloucester and Bristol Value, £654 * Patron, University College, Oxford The church is very good, and there is a national school.

CERNEY (SOUTH), a parish in Cirencester district, Gloucester, adjacent to the Thames and Severn canal and near the Cheltenham and Western Union railway, 4 miles SSE of Cirencester It has a post office under Cirencester Acres, 3 100 Real property, £6,364 Pop, 1,006 Houses, 247 The property is much subdivided The living is a vicarage united with the p curacy of Cerney-Wick in the diocese of Gloucester and Bristol Value £221 Patron, the Bishop of Gloucester and Bristol The church ranges from transition Norman to decorated English, and was partly rebuilt in 1862. There are a chapel of ease, an Independent chapel, a national school, an asylum college on a bequest of £11,000 in 1834 for widows and orphans of poor clergymen and other charities £70

CERNEY WICK. See CERNEY (SOUTH)

CERNIOGE, a locality 10 miles SE of Llanrwst, in Denbigh A famous inn stood here, on the road from London to Holyhead, and is now a farm house The ground is high, adjacent to the watershed between the Dee and the Conway and a spot in the vicinity commands a very grand view of Snowdonia.

CERRIG CEINWEN, a parish in the district and county of Anglesey, 3 miles N of Bodorgan r station, and 5½ NE of Aberffraw Post town, Llangefni, under Bangor Acres, 1,582 Real property, £1,621 Pop, 465 Houses, 108 The property is much subdivided The living is a vicarage, annexed to the rectory of Llangristiolus, in the diocese of Bangor The church was built in 1861, is in the early English style, and consists of nave and chancel, with bell turret and vestry

CERRIG DEWI, a hill near Ystrad Ffin, in Cardigan It is about 600 feet high, and it commands a fine view of the upper part of the Towy The cave of Thomas ap Catherine, the Robin Hood of Wales, is in it

CERRIG Y DRUIDION, a village and a parish in the district of Corwen and county of Denbigh The village stands on a headstream of the river Dee, on the quondam mail road from London to Holyhead, 10 miles WNW of Corwen r station, and 13 SSW of Denbigh, and has a post office under Corwen, and fairs on 14 March, 27 April, 27 Aug, 20 Oct, and 7 Dec The parish includes also the townships of Clust y blaidd Cwmpenanner Gwernheurn, Hafod y Maidd, Llaethwryd, Tyak, and Voel Acres, 11,556 Assessed property, in 1815, £4,016. Pop, 1,243 Houses, 256 The property is much subdivided The land lies high, and is chiefly moor and upland pasture A collection of large stones, including cistvaens, was formerly at the village, but has disappeared An ancient British fort with a circular rampart was on Pen y Gaer, about a mile to the east and is said to have been the place where Caractacus was taken prisoner, but is now reduced to slight vestiges The living is a rectory in the diocese of St. Asaph Value, £500 * Patron, the Bishop of St. Asaph The church is tolerable, and there is a Calvinistic Methodist chapel An almshouse has £95, and other charities £104

CERTHAM See CHARTHAM

CESTOR. See CASTOR.

CETEHAM See CHATHAM

CEULAN Y MAES MAWR, a township in Llanfihangel Geneur Glynn parish Cardigan, on an affluent of the river Lery, 5¾ miles ENE of Aberystwith It contains the village of Penrhyncoch Acres, 7,439 Pop, 840 Houses, 172

CEUSWYN, a township in Talyllyn parish, Merioneth 5½ miles S of Dolgelly Pop, 362.

CHACELEY See CHASELEY

CHACEWATER. See CHASEWATER.

CHACKMORE, a hamlet in Radclive parish, Bucks, 1 mile NNW of Buckingham Pop, 238

CHACOMBE See CHALCOMBE.

CHAD See CHAD (ST)

CHADBURY, a tything in Norton parish, Worcester, 2 miles N of Evesham Pop, 23

CHADD See CHAD (ST)

CHADDENWICK, a tything in Mere parish, Wilts, 2 miles from Mere Real property, with West Knoyle, £2,591 Pop, 21 Houses 6

CHADDERTON, a township two chapelries, and a sub district in Oldham district, Lancashire The township lies on the Oldham railways, the river Irk and the Rochdale canal, within Oldham borough, and 1 mile

ESE of Middleton, and has a post office under Manchester Acres, 2,978. Real property, £29 797, of which 6,907 are in mines Pop 7,486 Houses 1 503 The property is much subdivided Chadderton Hall was formerly the seat of the Hortons. Many of the inhabitants are employed in collieries, and in cotton and silk factories —The chapelries are Chadderton St John and Chadderton St Matthew, were constituted in 1844, and jointly are a little more extensive than the township The livings are vicarages in the diocese of Manchester Value, £300 and £300 Patron, alternately the Crown and the Bishop St M s church was built, at a cost of £1,900, in 1857 There are chapels for Baptists and Wesleyans The Oldham cemetery also is here —The sub district consists of Chadderton and Tonge townships Acres, 3 345. Pop, 12 092 Houses, 2,456

CHADDESDEN, a parish in Shardlow district Derbyshire, adjacent to the Derby canal and the Midland railway 2 miles E of Derby It has a post office under Derby Acres, 2,080 Real property £4 551 Pop, 465 Houses, 99 The property is divided among a few Chaddesden Hall is the seat of Sir H Wilmot, Bart The living is a vicarage in the diocese of Lichfield Value, £89 Patron, Sir H Wilmot, Bart The church was restored in 1859, at a cost of £2,000 There are a Wesleyan chapel a national school, six alms houses, and the Derby new cemetery, comprising 32 acres, and containing two mortuary chapels

CHADDESLEY CORBETT, a village, a parish, and a sub district, in Kidderminster district, Worcester The village stands on an affluent of the river Severn 3¼ miles NE of Hartlebury r station, and 4½ SE of Kidderminster, and has a post-office under Kidderminster, and fairs on the last Monday of April and the Monday before 18 Oct. The parish comprises 5 914 acres Real property £13,509 Pop, 1,457 Houses 311 The property is not much divided. There are coal pits, some forges, and a yarn factory The living is a vicarage in the diocese of Worcester Value, £341 * Patron, the Lord Chancellor The church is partly Norman, partly later There are P Methodist and R Catholic chapels, two endowed schools, five alms houses, and other charities £320 —The sub district contains three parishes Acres, 9,782 Pop 2 091 Houses, 418

CHADDLEHANGLE, a hamlet in Lamerton parish, Devon

CHADDLEWORTH, a parish in Wantage district Berks, 6 miles WSW of East Ilsley and 7 NNE of Hungerford r station It includes Woolley tything, and has a post office under Wantage Acres 3,319 Real property, £4 099 Pop, 539 Houses, 99 The property is divided among a few The manor was given by the Conqueror to Robert D'Oyley, and belonged afterwards to the mother of Edward I Chaddleworth House, the seat of the Pipons, was rebuilt in 1810 and Woolley Park the seat of the Wroughtons, was built in 1690, and much altered in 1799 An Augustinian priory was founded at Ellensfordsmere, in 1161 by Ralph of Chaddleworth, and destroyed in 1532 The living is a vicarage in the diocese of Oxford. Value, £272 * Patrons the Dean and Chapter of Westminster The church has a Norman doorway and is good An endowed school has £100 and other charities £22

CHADKIRK See ROMELEY

CHADLINGTON, a village, a chapelry a tything, and a hundred in Oxford The village stands near the river Evenlode and the Oxford and Worcester railway 2½ miles NW by N of Charlbury r station, and 3½ SSE of Chipping Norton, and has a post office under Enstone The chapelry includes the village, and bears the name of East Chadlington The tything lies a mile to the NW and bears the name of West Chadlington and both are in Charlbury parish Acres of both 4,800 Real property of E Chadlington £1 355, of W Chadlington, £2,520 Pop of both 733 Houses, 157 The chapelry living is annexed to the vicarage of Charlbury The church is ancient There are a Baptist chapel and a national school —The hundred extends to the boundary with Warwick and Gloucester, and contains twenty three parishes, and part of another Acres, 67,695 Pop in 1851 13 804, in 1861 13,837 Houses, 2,986

CHAD (ST), a parish and a sub district in Shrewsbury district Salop The parish lies on the river Severn, the Ellesmere canal, and the Shrewsbury and Oswestry railway, partly within Shrewsbury borough, and extending thence to the NW, and it comprises the townships of Longney, Crow-Meole, Onslow Frankwell, Betton and Almere, Bicton and Calcott, Shelton and Oxon, Whitley and Welbatch, and Woodcote and Horton Post-town, Shrewsbury Rated property, £36,014 Pop 8 318 Houses, 1,690 The property is much subdivided The living is a vicarage in the diocese of Lichfield Value £350 Patron, the Lord Chancellor The original church was built by the Mercian kings was long collegiate and a royal free chapel, was burned in 1393 afterwards restored and finally ruined by the fall of the tower in 1788 but an aisle of it, of Norman character, was refitted for funeral services, and afterwards appropriated to a charity school The present church was built in 1792 at a cost of £20,000, is a circular Grecian edifice, 100 feet in diameter, with dome and handsome tower, 150 feet high and has the "Resurrection" by Egginton after West brought from Lichfield cathedral The vicarages of Bicton, Betton Strange, Frankwell and Oxon and Shelton are separate benefices. Job Orton the biographer of Doddridge, was a native.—The sub district contains also the parish of Meole Brace. Pop 9 533 Houses 1,950

CHAD (ST), Stafford See LICHFIELD

CHAD, or CHADD (ST), a chapelry in Malpas parish, Cheshire, on the verge of the county, 3½ miles NNW of Whitchurch r station. Post town, Whitchurch Statistics, with the parish The living is a p curacy in the diocese of Chester Value, £140 * Patrons, the Rectors of Malpas The church was built in 1863

CHADSHUNT a parish in Southam district, Warwick, 1½ mile NE of Kineton and 5 W of Fenny Compton r station Post-town, Kineton under Warwick Acres 1,306 Real property, £1,770 Pop, 37 Houses, 5 The manor belonged early to the monks of Coventry, and passed to the see of Lichfield The living is a p curacy, annexed to the vicarage of Bishops Itchington, in the diocese of Worcester An image of St Chad in the Romish times, stood in the churchyard, and attracted many pilgrims

CHADSTONE, a hamlet in Castle Ashby parish, Northamptonshire, 7½ miles E of Northampton Pop, 52

CHADWELL, or CHADWELL HEATH, a ward in Barking parish, Essex on the Eastern Counties railway, 2½ miles E by N of Great Ilford It has a station on the railway and a post office under London E Real property, £3 615 Pop 882 Houses, 131 There is a Baptist chapel

CHADWELL, or CALDWELL, a chapelry in Rothley parish, Leicester, near the Salt way 5 miles NNW of Saxby r station and 5 NE of Melton Mowbray Post town, Scalford under Melton Mowbray Acres, 1,730 Pop 139 Houses, 27 The living is a p curacy annexed to the vicarage of Rothley in the diocese of Peterborough The church is good and has a tower

CHADWELL ST MARY, a parish in Orsett district, Essex, on the Thames, and on the Tilbury and Southend railway, 2 miles E of Grays r station, and 2½ S of Orsett Post town, Grays, under Romford Acres, 1 977, of which 180 are water Real property £2,946 Pop, 457 Houses, 85 The property is divided among a few Chalk caves occur here, called Daneholds and Cunobelin s gold mines Tilbury fort is partly within the border The living is a rectory in the diocese of Rochester Value, £427 * Patron the Rev J P Herringham The church is old but good Charities, £12

CHADWELL SPRINGS, one of the sources of the New River near Ware Park in Herts

CHADWICK a hamlet in Spotland township Rochdale parish Lancashire 2 miles W of Rochdale

CHADWICK a hamlet in Bromsgrove parish, Worcester 3½ miles N of Bromsgrove

CHALCOMBE a parish in Chard district Somer

st, on the Chard canal, 2 miles NE of Chard r station, and 3½ S by W of Ilminster Post town, Ilminster Acres 999 Real property, with Knowle St. Giles, £2,896 Pop., 246. Houses 50 The property is divided among a few The living is a rectory in the diocese of Bath and Wells Value, £140 Patron, Earl Poulett The church is early English, and was restored in 1859

CHAFFORD, a hundred in Essex. It touches the Thames for 7 miles above and below Purfleet, extends 12½ miles northward and contains fourteen parishes. Acres, 35,712 Pop, 16,001 Houses 3 769

CHAGFORD a small town, a parish and a sub district in Okehampton district, Devon The town stands on elevated ground, near the river Teign, on the skirts of Dartmoor, 4 miles WNW of Moreton Hampstead r. station, and 12 SW of Crediton, and has a post-office‡ under Exeter, and two inns It is a picturesque old place, amid romantic environs, in a bracing climate, repulsive during winter, but attractive to tourists and to invalids in summer It was made a stannary town in 1328, and it sustained an attack by the royalists in the wars of Charles I The Three Crowns inn at it was built as a mansion, by Judge Whyddon, in the time of James I, and served afterwards as the dower house of Whyddon Park. Markets are held on Saturdays, and fairs on the first Thursday of May and the last Thursday of March, Sept., and Oct. The parish comprises 7,492 acres Real property, £7,014 Pop, 1,379 Houses, 283 The property is much subdivided. The manor belonged to Dodo the Saxon, was given by the Conqueror to the Bishop of Coutances, and passed, in the time of Henry III, to Sir Hugh de Chagford and afterwards to Judge Whyddon Several ancient British antiquities occur among the hills. The living is a rectory in the diocese of Exeter Value, £539 * Patron, the Rev H G Hames. The church is a good ancient structure, with a square embattled tower, and contains a grand monument of Judge Whyddon There are chapels for Wesleyan Methodists and Bible Christians Charities, £14 The sub district contains four parishes. Acres, 19,821 Pop, 2,907 Houses, 608

CHAIGLEY, a hamlet in Mitton parish, Lancashire, 5½ miles W of Clitheroe Pop, 266

CHAILEY, a village, a parish, and a sub district in Lewes district, Sussex The village stands 3 miles E of Cook s Bridge r station, and 5½ N by W of Lewes, and has a post office under Lewes and a fair on 29 July The parish comprises 5,839 acres. Real property, £5,610 Pop, 1,344 Houses, 247 The property is divided among a few The living is a rectory in the diocese of Chichester Value, £505 * Patrons, Mrs Hepburne and Mrs Blencowe The church is early English, and good There are a national school a workhouse and charities £9 The sub district contains four parishes Acres, 18,464 Pop., 4,947 Houses, 931

CHAIR LEDDER, a remarkable group of columnar rocks on the coast of Cornwall, a little SE of Lands End.

CHAIR OF THE WITCH See LWA MAEN

CHALENDEN See CHECKENDON

CHALBURY, a parish in Wimborne district Dorset near the Roman road from Dorchester 3 miles NNE of Bailey Gate r station and 5 N by E of Wimborne Minster It includes Didlington tything, and its post town is Horton, under Wimborne Acres, 1,344 Real property, £1,409 Pop, 194. Houses, 41 The property is divided among a few Part of the land is high, has an ancient entrenchment, and commands a fine view, to the sea. The living is a rectory in the diocese of Salisbury Value, £165 * Patron, the Earl of Pembroke The church is tolerable

CHALCOMBE, or CHACOMBE, a parish in the district of Banbury and county of Northampton adjacent to the river Cherwell, near the Oxford and Rugby and the Buckinghamshire railways, 3¾ miles NE of Banbury It has a post office under Banbury Acres, 1,691 Real property, £4,213 Pop 464 Houses 111 The property is much subdivided A number of the inhabitants are stocking makers. A priory was founded here, in the time of Henry II by Hugh de Chacombe, and given at the dissolution, to the Foxes The living is a vicarage in the diocese of Peterborough Value £250 * Patron, C W Martin, Esq The church is chiefly decorated English, has a porch and a tower, and contains a fine Norman font and a brass of 1609 There are Wesleyan and Primitive Methodist chapels.

CHALDON, a parish in Reigate district Surrey near the Brighton and the Caterham r lways, 2 miles NE by N of Merstham r station, and 5 NE of Reigate Post town, Merstham, under Red Hill Acres, 1,622 Real property, £1,253. Pop 169 Houses, 32 The property is divided among a few The living is a rectory in the diocese of Winchester Value, £255 * Patron, the Rev H Shepherd. The church is partly early English and has a spire.

CHALDON-BOYS, or WEST CHALDON, a quondam parish in Wareham district, Dorset, near the coast, 10½ miles WSW of Wareham. It was incorporated, in 1446, with Chaldon-Herring

CHALDON HERRING, or EAST CHALDON, a parish in Wareham district Dorset, near the coast, 3¾ miles S of Moreton r station, and 9½ WSW of Wareham Post town, Winfrith, under Dorchester Acres, 2,981 Real property with Chaldon Boys and Holworth £3,285 Pop, 341 Houses, 63 The property is all in one estate The living is a vicarage in the diocese of Salisbury Value, £62 Patron, Joseph Weld, Esq The church is good

CHALE, a parish in the Isle of Wight, on the south coast, 6½ miles W of Ventnor It has a post office under Southampton Acres, 2,375, of which 80 are water Real property, £3,940 Pop, 584 Houses, 130 The property is divided among a few The manor belonged to Carisbrooke priory, and passed to the Pelhams. Chale Farm house is an interesting architectural relic, with features of decorated English The coast includes black gang chine, and the interior includes St. Catherine s hill. A slight indentation of the coast, 3 miles long, bears the name of Chale bay, is overhung by terrific cliffs, and was the scene of the shipwreck of the "Clarendon" in 1836 The living is a rectory in the diocese of Winchester Value £334 * Patron, James Theobald, Esq The church is partly transition Norman has a perpendicular English tower, and contains a piscina, and a handsome monument to Major General Sir Henry Worsley The graves of many of the passengers and crew of the Clarendon, with a monument to the Shutes, are in the churchyard An endowed school has £22

CHALFIELD (GREAT), a parish in Bradford district, Wilts, on an affluent of the river Avon 1½ mile N of Holt Junction r station, and 3 W of Melksham Post town, Holt, under Trowbridge Acres, 700 Real property, with Little Chalfield and Cottles, £2,432 Pop, 12 Houses, 3 The property is divided among three The manor belonged to the Tropenells, and passed to the Eyres and the manor house, built by the former, still stands, is surrounded by a moat, and forms a beautiful specimen of a mansion of the time of Edward IV The living is a rectory in the diocese of Salisbury Value, £162 Patron, Lady Neale The church is fair

CHALFIELD (LITTLE), AND COTTLES, an extra parochial tract in Bradford district Wilts contiguous to Great Chalfield, 3½ miles W of Melksham Acres, 560 Pop., 43 Houses, 7 The manor belonged to the Eyres, and the manor house is Tudor

CHALFONT a sub district in Amersham district Bucks. It consists of the two Chalfont parishes and Chenies Acres 10,192 Pop 3 029 Houses, 670

CHALFONT ST GILES, a village and a parish in Amersham district, Bucks. The village stands on the Misbourn rivulet, 3 miles SE by S of Amersham, and 6 E by N of Loudwater r station, and has a post office‡ under Slough The poet Milton resided here during the plague of London in 1665 and finished here his "Paradise Lost," and the house which he occupied, a half timbered cottage, still exists, and has his name on its front The parish comprises 3,641 acres. Real property, £6 117 Pop, 1,217 Houses, 255 The property is

. I ailed. The manor belongs to T N Allen Esq. The House or the Vache, is a modernized ancient edifice, was long held by the Hare family, belonged previously to the Alstons, and is said to have been built originally on a dairy farm of King John. The living is a rectory in the diocese of Oxford. Value, £615.* Patron the Bishop of Oxford. The church is ancient, has a Norman tower, was restored in 1863, and contains brasses and monuments of the Gardiners, the Fleetwoods, the Claytons, and Bishop Hare. There are chapels for Independents, Primitive Methodists, Free Methodists and Quakers, and the remains of William Penn, the founder of Pennsylvania, and Thomas Elwood, the friend of Milton, are in the Quakers' burying-ground. A school has £58 from endowment, and other charities £100.

CHALFONT ST PETER, a village and a parish in Amersham district, Bucks. The village stands on the Misbourn rivulet 5 miles SSE of Amersham and 6½ miles N of Woburn Green r station, is a seat of petty sessions and has a post-office under Slough. The parish comprises 4,717 acres. Real property, £7,335. Pop, 1,3?4. Houses, 303. The property is divided among a few. Chalfont House was built by General Churchill, the brother in law of Horace Walpole, owed much of its original character to Walpole's taste, but has been much altered and improved, and is now the seat of J Hibbert, Esq. A house called the Grange was for some time the residence of Judge Jeffreys. The living is a vicarage in the diocese of Oxford. Value, £731.* Patron, St John's College, Oxford. The church is a brick edifice of 1725, highly improved by Street in 1854, and contains three good brasses. The p. curacy of Gerrard's Cross is a separate benefice. There are a Baptist chapel, a national school, and charities £25.

CHALFORD, a chapelry in Bisley parish, Gloucester, on the Stroudwater canal and the Cheltenham and Western Union railway, adjacent to Brimscomb r station, and 3½ miles ESE of Stroud. It has a post office‡ under Stroud. It was constituted in 1842. Pop, 2,008. Houses, 504. Much of the surface is a picturesque reach of valley, called Chalford Bottom, and many of the inhabitants are employed in various manufactures. The living is a vicarage in the diocese of Gloucester and Bristol. Value, £150.* Patron, the Archdeacon of Gloucester. The church was built in 1724. There are chapels for Independents, Baptists, Wesleyans, and Primitive Methodists, and two public schools.

CHALFORD, a liberty in Aston Rowant parish, Oxford, 3½ miles S of Thame. Real property, £692.

CHALGRAVE, a parish in Woburn district, Beds, 3½ miles N by W of Dunstable r station, and 5½ ENE of Leighton Buzzard. It includes the hamlets of Tebworth and Wingfield, and its post town is Hockliffe, under Leighton Buzzard. Acres, 2,130. Real property, £4,055. Pop, 761. Houses, 207. The property is subdivided. The living is a vicarage in the diocese of Ely. Value, £250. Patron, the Rev J M Hamilton. The church is ancient. There are a Wesleyan chapel and a n school.

CHALGROVE, a village and a parish in Thame district, Oxford. The village stands on an affluent of the Thame, 5 miles SW of Tetsworth, and 3½ NNE of Wallingford r station, and has a post office under Tetsworth. The parish includes also the liberty of Rufford. Acres, 2,394. Real property, £3,747. Pop, 5?9. Houses, 1?4. A skirmish was fought on Chalgrove Field, in 1643, between the royalists under Prince Rupert and the parliamentarians. John Hampden at first mustered the parliamentarians on the same ground, and he led them in the skirmish, and received then his death wound. A monument to his memory, bearing a medallion portrait and an inscription, was erected on the spot in 1843. The living is a vicarage, united with the p. curacy of Berwick Salome, in the diocese of Oxford. Value, £600.* Patron, Christ Church, Oxford. The church is Norman, consists of nave, two aisles and chancel, with a tower, and contains an octagonal font, and several fine monuments. There are a Wesleyan chapel, and charities £97.

CHALK, a parish in North Aylesford district, Kent, on the river Thames and the North Kent railway, 2½ miles SE by E of Gravesend. It has a post office under Gravesend, and a fair on Whit Monday. Acres, 2,246, of which 305 are water. Real property, with Denton, £5,177. Pop, 382. Houses, 74. The property is divided among a few. The surface is variously marshy and chalky. Gun flints of prime quality were formerly manufactured, and much fruit is sent to the London market. The living is a vicarage in the diocese of Rochester. Value £200. Patron the Lord Chancellor. The church is of flint, very ancient and good, has two grotesque figures on the porch, and contains curious monuments and sedilia.

CHALK, a hundred in Wilts. It lies around Broad Chalk, and contains seven parishes and part of another. Acres, 24,832. Pop., 3,493. Houses, 733.

CHALK (BROAD). See BROAD CHALK.

CHALK FARM, a place of 32 acres in the north western suburbs of London, now partly occupied by the Northwestern railway and its depot, adjacent to the Zoological Gardens and Primrose Hill, 3½ miles NW of St Paul's. It was notorious for duels fought on it, specially for one between Col Montgomery and Capt. Macnamara in 1803.

CHALKTON. See CHALTON, Hants.

CHALLACOMBE, a parish in Barnstaple district, Devon, on the river Bray, near its sources, on the verge of the county at Exmoor forest, 10 miles NE of Barnstaple r station. Post town, Paracombe, under Barnstaple. Acres, 5,343. Real property, £1,471. Pop, 282. Houses, 57. The manor and most of the property belong to Earl Fortescue. The surface is hilly, and, to a large extent, high wild moorland. The living is a rectory in the diocese of Exeter. Value, £200.* Patron, Earl Fortescue. The church is a recent erection, in the Gothic style, with a tower.

CHALLOCK, a parish in East Ashford district, Kent, adjacent to the river Stour and to the Ashford and Canterbury railway, 2½ miles NW by W of Wye r station and 5 N by E of Ashford. It has a post office under Ashford, and a fair on 8 Oct. Acres, 2,837. Real property, £2,643. Pop, 373. Houses, 78. The property is subdivided. Eastwell Park, the seat of the Earl of Winchelsea, is on the south. The living is a p. curacy, annexed to the vicarage of Godmersham, in the diocese of Canterbury. The church is ancient. Charities, £5.

CHALLOW. See FARINGDON ROAD.

CHALLOW (EAST), a chapelry in Letcombe Regis parish, Berks, on the Berks and Wilts canal, 1 mile WNW of Wantage, and 2 SE by S of Faringdon Road r station. Post town, Wantage. Real property, £3,136. Pop, 391. Houses, 84. The property is much subdivided. There are extensive agricultural implement works. The living is a p. curacy, united with West Challow, in the dio of Oxford. Value, £100.* Patron, C Eyrard, Esq. The church was restored in 1858.

CHALLOW (WEST), a chapelry in Letcombe Regis parish, Berks, on the Berks and Wilts canal, 2 miles W by N of Wantage, and 1½ S of Faringdon Road r station. Post town, Wantage. Real property, £1,455. Pop, 192. Houses, 43. The property is divided among a few. The living is a p. curacy annexed to East Challow, in the diocese of Oxford. The church is good.

CHALTON, a hamlet in Toddington parish, Beds, 3½ miles N of Dunstable. Real property, £1,714. Pop., 224.

CHALTON, or CHALKTON, a parish in Catherington district, Hants, on the verge of the county, 2½ miles NNW of Rowland's Castle r station, and 5½ S by W of Petersfield. It includes the chapelry of Idsworth, and its post town is Horndean. Acres, 1,723. Real property, £1,261. Pop, 619. Houses, 125. The property is all in one estate. Part of the surface is high, and bears the name of Chalton Down. The living is a rectory, united with the p. curacy of Idsworth and the rectory of Clanfield, in the diocese of Winchester. Value, £600.* Patron, King's College, Cambridge. The church is ancient, and was repaired in 1859.

CHALVEY, a chapelry in Upton parish, Bucks, adjacent to the Great Western railway, 1 mile W of Slough

Post town, Slough Pop., 574 The living is a p cu racy, annexed to the vicarage of Upton, in the diocese of Oxford The church was built in 1861, and is in the early decorated English style, with some peculiarities of design

CHALVINGTON, a parish in Hailes district Sussex, adjacent to the river Cuckmere, 2½ miles NNW of Berwick r station and 5 W of Hailsham Post town, Ripe, under Hurst Green Acres, 729 Real property, £1,037 Pop, 119 Houses, 26 The property is much sub divided. The living is a rectory in the diocese of Chichester Value, £200 * Patron, O Fuller Meyrick, Esq The church is decorated English

CHAMBER HALL See BURY, Lancashire.

CHAMBOIS See CAMBOIS

CHAMPION HILL, a suburb of London, in Camberwell parish, 4 miles S of St Pauls It has a post office‡ under Camberwell, London S, and a r station

CHANCTONBURY, an ancient camp in Wiston parish, Sussex, on one of the Downs, 814 feet high, 3½ miles W by N of Steyning It has a dark clump of trees, and figures in the landscape views of half the county It is circular, and may have been originally British, but it lies near a Roman road running east and west, and has yielded Roman coins The prospect from it is extensive, panoramic, and grand.

CHANDLER'S FORD, a railway station in Hants, on the Salisbury railway, 3½ miles ESE of Romsey

CHANDLINGS, an extra-parochial tract in Abingdon district, Berks, near Abingdon Pop, 5 House 1

CHANNEL (BRISTOL). See BRISTOL CHANNEL

CHANNEL (BRITISH or ENGLISH) See ENGLISH CHANNEL.

CHANNEL ISLANDS, a group of islands in the English Channel, near the coasts of Normandy and Brittany in France The chief are Jersey, Guernsey, Alderney, and Sark, and others are Herm, Jethou, Le Marchant, and the Caskets They were known to the Romans, were early occupied by the Gauls, were an asylum of refugee Britons, fleeing from the Roman power in England received Christianity, early in the 6th century, from Wales, were ceded by France, in 912, to Rollo first Duke of Normandy, continued to be held by William, the seventh duke, at his conquest of England and though frequently attacked by France, and sometimes severely shaken by political changes in England, have, with slight interruption, remained ever since annexed to the English crown The several islands will be separately described, in separate articles, in their alphabetical place

CHANTRY, a chapelry in Whatley, Great Elm, and Mells parishes Somerset, near the East Somerset railway, 2 miles W of Frome. Post town, Frome The chapelry was constituted in 1846 Pop, 264 Houses, 49 The living is a vicarage in the diocese of Bath and Wells Value, £90 * Patron, the Rev J Russell The church was built in 1846 There are a Wesleyan chapel and a girls' industrial and boarding school.

CHAPEL CHAPEL, or PONTISBRIGHT, a parish in Lexden district, Essex, on the Colne river and the Colne Valley railway, 7 miles WNW of Colchester It has a station, of the name of Chapel, on the railway, and its post town is Marks Tey, under Colchester Acres, 1,146 Real property, £2,021 Pop, 370 Houses, 86 The property is much subdivided The living is a p curacy, under the vicarage of Great Tey in the diocese of Rochester Value, £70 Patrons the Parishioners The church is old but good, and has a spire

CHAPEL ALLERTON See ALLERTON CHAPEL

CHAPEL AMBLE, a locality 3 miles from Wadebridge, in Cornwall with a post-office und r Wadebridge

CHAPEL ASCOTE See ASCOTE (CHAPEL)

CHAPEL BILLINGE See BILLINGE

CHAPEL BRAMPTON See BRAMPTON CHAPEL

CHAPEL BRIDGE, a railway station in Monmouth, on the Western Valleys railway, 9½ miles NW of Newport

CHAPEL BROKE See ASTERLEY

CHAPEL CARNBREA a rocky hill at the south western extremity of Cornwall, 2 miles SE of Lands End. It is 640 feet high, and it commands a grand view

CHAPEL CHORLTON See CHORLTON Stafford

CHAPEL CLEEVE, a hamlet in Old Cleeve parish Somerset, on the coast, 2 miles W of Watchet A chapel here, dedicated to the Virgin, was much frequented in the Romish times, by pilgrims, and the remnant of a cross, for guiding them h ther stands midway between Washford and Old Cleeve church

CHAPEL COLMAN, or CAPEL COLMAN, a parish in the district of Newcastle in Emlyn, and county of Pembroke, near the Cardigan railway, 6 miles SE of Cardigan Post town, Cardigan Acres, 770 Rated property, £510 Pop, 157 Houses, 30. The property is divided among a few The living is a vicarage in the diocese of St Davids. Value £72 Patron, Miss Jones The church was reported in 1859 to need repair

CHAPEL DALE See CHAPEL LE DALE.

CHAPEL END, a locality on the NE border of Warwickshire, 3 miles from Nuneaton and 4 from Atherstone It has a post office under Atherstone

CHAPEL EN LE FRITH, a small town, a parish, a sub district, and a district in Derby The town stands on the slope of a high hill, near the High Peak, adjacent to the Buxton and Whaley Bridge railway, and 5 miles N of Buxton It sprang from an ancient church or chapel within the Peak "frith or forest, and is now a neat centre of local trade, a seat of petty sessions, and a polling place It has a post office‡ under Stockport, a railway station, two chief inns, a town hall a church, two dissenting chapels, and a suite of schools The town hall is a neat edifice of 1851 The church is an ancient structure with a square tower, renovated in 1837 The schools were built in 1840, at a cost of fully £1,100 Manufacture is carried on in cotton and paper mills, and considerable traffic exists in the transfer of lead, coal, and limes one from neighbouring works to distant places Markets are held on Thursdays, and fairs on the Thursday before 14 Feb, 3 March, 29 March, Easter, 30 April 24 Aug, and 11 Nov, Holy Thursday, the third Thursday after Holy Thursday and the Thursday after 29 Sept —The parish includes also the townships of Coombs Edge, Bradshaw Edge and Bowden Edge Acres, 13,220 Real property, £14,389 Pop 4,264 Houses, 780 The property is subdivided Much of the surface is hill and moor The canal reservoir is a fine sheet of water, and the Larm re Clough well is an ebbing and flowing spring The living is a vicarage in the diocese of Lichfield Value, £300 * Patrons, Resident Freeholders

The sub district contains the parishes of Chapel en le Frith and Castleton, parts of the parishes of Hope Hathersage, Glossop, and Tideswell, and the liberty of Peak Forest Acres, 57,507 Pop, 9,878 Houses, 1,923 The district includes also the sub district of Buxton, containing parts of the parishes of Bakewell, Hope and Hartington Acres, 63,248 Poor rates in 1866, £3,725 Pop. in 1861 14,020 Houses, 2,690 Marriages in 1866, 110, births, 586 —of which 23 were illegitimate, deaths 300,—of which 127 were at ages under 3 years, and 11 at ages above 85 years Marriages in the ten years 1851–60 815, births 3 826, deaths, 2,513 The places of worship in 1851 were 10 of the church of England, with 3 483 sittings 2 of Independents, with 475 s, 1 of Baptists, with 150 s, 17 of Wesleyan Methodists with 2,795 s., and 6 of Primitive Methodists, with 590 s The schools were 11 public day schools, with 1,009 scholars, 15 private day schools with 336 s., 25 Sunday schools, with 2,035 s., and 3 evening schools for adults with 46 s.

CHAPEL FOLD, a hamlet in Batley parish, W R Yorkshire 6½ miles NW of Wakefield

CHAPELGATE See BILSDALE-MIDCABLE and RYEFORD (EAST)

CHAPEL HADDLESEY a township chapelry in Birkin parish, W R Yorkshire, on the river Aire 4½ miles SSW of Selby r station Acres, 1 000 Real property £1,833 Pop., 210 Houses 47 A three arched iron bridge here spans the Aire The living is a p curacy, annexed to the rectory of Birkin, in the diocese of York. There is a Wesleyan chapel

CHAPEL HILL, a chapelry in Swineshead parish, Lincoln, near the Lincoln and Boston railway, 3 miles from Coningsby It has a post office under Boston Statistics, with the parish The living is a p curacy in the diocese of Lincoln Value, £47 Patron the Vicar of Swineshead

CHAPEL HILL a seat in Mardale, Westmoreland, near the head of Hawes water, 6½ miles WSW of Shap. It belongs to the Holmes, descendants of a follower of William the Conqueror, and took its name from a place of worship built by one of them after enduring political disaster in the time of King John

CHAPEL HILL, a parish in Chepstow district, Monmouth, on the river Wye, 4½ miles N of Chepstow r station It contains Tintern Abbey, which has a post office under Chepstow Acres, 820 Real property £1,503 Pop, 497 Houses, 101 The property is divided among a few The living is a vicarage in the diocese of Llandaff Value, £60 Patron, the Duke of Beaufort The church was reported in 1859 as dilapidated. Charities, £63 See TINTERN ABBEY

CHAPEL HOUSE, a quondam famous inn, 1 mile NE of Chipping Norton, in Oxford. A chapel of Cold Norton priory once occupied its site, and stone coffins have been found near it.

CHAPEL LE DALE, or INGLETON FELLS a chapelry in Bentham parish, W R Yorkshire, 5 miles NNE of Bentham r station, and 10½ NW of Settle Post town, Bentham, under Lancaster Pop, 190 The surface is mountainous The living is a vicarage in the diocese of Ripon. Value, £122 * Patron, the Rector of Bentham

CHAPEL (LOWER), a locality 5 miles from Brecon, in Breconshire, with a post office under Brecon

CHAPEL MUMBY, a hamlet in Mumby parish, Lincoln, on the coast, 5½ miles ESE of Alford Pop, 316

CHAPEL (NORTH) See NORTH CHAPEL

CHAPEL PLASTER, a place 3 miles SW of Corsham, in Wilts. It was, in the Romish times, a resting place of pilgrims on the way to Glastonbury abbey, and, in last century, the retreat of the notorious highwayman, John Baxter

CHAPEL POINT, a headland in Gorran parish Cornwall 8 miles S of S Austell. A ruined chapel is on it

CHAPEL ROW, a locality 3½ miles SE of Bishop Auckland, in Durham It has a post office under Darlington

CHAPEL SUCKEN, a township in Millom parish, Cumberland, on the river Duddon, 12 miles SE by S of Ravenglass Acres, 2,054 Real property, £1,893. Pop. 291 Houses, 59

CHAPELTHORPE, a chapelry in Great Sandall parish, W R Yorkshire adjacent to the North Midland railway, 3½ miles S of Wakefield It was constituted in 1843, and it has a post office under Wakefield Pop, 2 021 Houses, 431 Many of the inhabitants are coal miners The living is a vicarage in the diocese of Ripon Value, £159 * Patron, the Vicar of Great Sandall

CHAPELTOWN, a railway station and a village in Lancashire on the Bolton and Blackburn railway, 7½ miles N by E of Bolton

CHAPELTOWN, a sub district in Hunslet district, W R Yorkshire It contains Chapel Allerton and Potter Newton townships in Leeds parish Shadwell township in Thorner parish and Roundhay township in Barwick in Elmet parish Acres, 7,271 Pop, 5,930 Houses, 1 252.

CHAPELTOWN a chapelry in Ecclesfield parish, W R Yorkshire, adjacent to the Sheffield and Barnsley railway, 7 miles N of Sheffield It has a post office under Sheffield, and a station, jointly with Thorncliffe on the railway It was constituted in 1844 Pop. 1 063 Houses, 797 Many of the inhabitants are colliers The living is a vicarage in the diocese of York Value, £300 Patron, alternately the Crown and the Bishop The church was built in 1860 There are three dissenting chapels two public schools, and endowed alms houses with £160 a year

CHAPELTOWN a hamlet in Tawstock parish, Devon

CHAPELWICK, a hamlet in Ashbury parish, Berks.

CHAPELYATE See BIRSDALE MIDGARTH

CHAPMAN BARROWS, a mountain in the western part of Exmoor, on the confines of Somerset and Devon Its altitude is 1,540 feet

CHAPMAN SAND, a shoal in the Thames, off the south side of Canvey island A beacon is on it

CHAPMANSLADE, a village in Westbury, Upton Scudamore, and Corsley parishes, Wilts, 3½ miles SW of Westbury It has a post office under Westbury, a church built in 1867, and an Independent chapel

CHAPMAN'S POOL, a small bay on the coast of Dorset immediately west of St. Alban's head, and 3½ miles S of Corfe Castle A lofty eminence of Kimmeridge clay rising from cliffs, overhangs it, and contains beds of bituminous shale which have long been in slow combustion

CHAPPEL See CHAPEL Essex

CHAR (THE) See CAR (THE)

CHARBOROUGH, a hamlet in Morden parish, Dorset, on an affluent of the river Stour, 6 miles W of Wimborne Minster It was formerly a separate parish and it still ranks as a rectory, in the diocese of Salisbury Value, not reported Patron, Mrs Drax. Charborough House, formerly the seat of the Erles, now the seat of the Draxes, has on the ceiling of the staircase a painting of the Judgment of Paris by Thornhill, and the park contains a small building in which the revolution of 1688 was concerted, and a conspicuous obelisk

CHARD, a town, a parish, a sub district, and a district in Somerset The town stands on high ground at a watershed between the Bristol and the English channels, within a mile of the boundary with Dorset 3½ miles E of the boundary with Devon, and 13 SSE of Taunton, and is connected by a branch railway of 3 miles with the trunk line of the South western, at Chard Junction. It was known to the Saxons as Cerdre, was visited, in 1644, by Charles I, on his return from Cornwall, was the scene of a defeat of the royalists, under the conduct of Col Penruddock and witnessed a sanguinary execution, in 1685, in connexion with the affair of the Duke of Monmouth It comprises three chief thoroughfares, presents an irregular appearance, with very much recent improvement, and has a head post office,‡ a railway station, two banking offices, a town-hall an assembly room, a parish church, four dissenting chapels, a grammar school, a national school an alms house, with £844 a year, a workhouse, two large iron foundries, and two large lace factories The town hall is a recent erection in the Tuscan style, with market hall, and superseded an ancient Gothic one The church is later English, long, low, and cruciform, was restored in 1828, has a window representing Christ in the garden, put up in 1829 and contains an elaborate monument of 1614 An Independent chapel, at a cost of £3 000 was built in 1869 Well attended markets are held on Mondays, and fairs on the first Wednesday of May, Aug, and Nov A good trade exists in agricultural produce and was much aided by a canal northward to the Bridgewater and Taunton canal, 3 miles E of Taunton The town was made a borough in the time of Edward I sent members to parliament till the time of Edward III, and is now governed by a mayor, four aldermen, and twelve councillors The borough formerly comprised only 52 acres, but now comprises about 180 Real property £6,102 Pop, 2,276 Houses, 446. Sandford, the divine of the 16th century and Sir Simon Every who figured as a royalist in the civil war, were natives The branch railway of 3 miles to the town was authorized in 1860, and opened in the spring of 1863 Another railway, called the Chard and Taunton 15½ miles long to connect the Chard line with the Bristol and Exeter, was authorized in 1861, to be completed within four years, but the scheme for it broke down in 1863, was then transferred to the Bristol and Exeter, and was in operation in 1863

The parish includes also the tythings of Old Chard, South Chard, Crim Chard and Forton and Tatworth

Acres, 5,449 Real property, £20,144 Pop, 5,316 Houses 1,037 The property is much subdivided Snowdon, a high hill, connected with the Black Downs, rises immediately above the town, and commands a magnificent prospect over Somerset and Devon Several barrows called Robin Hood's butts and traditionally associated with the exploits of Robin Hood and Little John, are on Brown Down The living is a vicarage in the diocese of Bath and Wells Value £510 * Patron, the Bishop of Bath and Wells The vicarage of Tatworth is a separate charge The sub district contains also the parishes of Chaffcombe, Winsham, and Cricket St Thomas Acres, 10,276 Pop, 6,661 Houses, 1,307 The district comprehends likewise the sub district of Crewkerne, containing the parishes of Crewkerne, Wayford, Cudworth, Chillington, Dinnington, Hinton St George, Lopen, and Merriott, the sub district of Ilminster, containing the parishes of Ilminster, Shepton Beauchamp, Stocklinch Magdalen, Stocklinch Ottersey, Seavington St Michael, Seavington St Mary, White Lackington, Kingstone, Dowlish Wake, West Dowlish, Cricket Malherbie, Donyatt, Ilton, Ashill, and Broadway, and the sub district of Combe St Nicholas, containing the parishes of Combe-St Nicholas Buckland St. Mary, White Staunton, Knowle St Giles, Yarcombe, and Wambrook,—the last electorally in Dorset, the next last electorally in Devon Acres 60,312 Poor rates in 1866, £12,752 Pop in 1861, 25,591 Houses 5,224 Marriages in 1866, 179, births, 840,—of which 51 were illegitimate, deaths, 41,—of which 153 were at ages under 5 years, and 13 at ages above 85 Marriages in the ten years 1851-60, 1 860 births, 8,183 deaths, 5 264 The places of worship in 1851 were 33 of the Church of England, with 11 097 sittings, 6 of Independents, with 2,173 s., 8 of Baptists, with 2,100 s , 2 of Unitarians, with 276 s., 10 of Wesleyan Methodists with 1,408 s , 2 of Bible Christians, with 160 s , 2 of Latter Day Saints, with 90 s., and 2 undefined with 190 s. The schools were 26 public day schools, with 1,880 scholars, 39 private day schools, with 750 s , 46 Sunday schools, with 4,523 s., and 1 evening school for adults, with 10 s

CHARD AND TAUNTON RAILWAY See CHARD

CHARD (CRIM), a tything in Chard parish, Somerset, ½ a mile N of Chard Pop , 517

CHARD (OLD), a tything in Chard parish, Somerset Pop 1,331

CHARD-JUNCTION, formerly CHARD ROAD, a railway station near the confines of Somerset and Dorset, on the South western railway, 7 miles WSW of Crewkerne

CHARD (SOUTH), a tything in Chard parish, Somerset, 2 miles S by E of Chard It includes the hamlet of Chilson, and part of the hamlet of Perry street, and has a post office under Chard Pop 471

CHARDSTOCK, a village, a parish, and a sub district in the district of Axminster, and county of Dorset The village stands on the river Kitbridge, near the Yeovil and Exeter railway between the Chard Road and Axminster stations, 3½ miles SSW of Chard, and has a post office under Chard, and a fair on Old Michaelmas day The parish comprises 5,800 acres. Real property, with Wambrook £9,543 Pop., 1,161 Houses 233. The property is much subdivided A number of the inhabitants are employed in woollen mills The living is a vicarage in the diocese of Salisbury Value, £450 * Patron the Bishop of Salisbury The church was rebuilt in 1840 Charities, £82 The sub district contains three parishes. Acres, 17 417 Pop , 3,827 Houses, 714

CHARDSTOCK ALL SAINTS, a chapelry in Chardstock and Axminster parishes, Dorset and Devon adjacent to the Yeovil and Exeter railway, 2 miles NNE of Axminster Post town, Axminster The chapelry was constituted in 1840 Pop , 453 Houses, 93 The living is a rectory in the diocese of Salisbury Value £300 * Patron the vicar of Chardstock

CHARFIELD, a parish in Thornbury district, Gloucester, on an affluent of the Severn, and on the Gloucester and Bristol railway, under the Cotswolds, 2 miles N of Wickwar It has a station on the railway, and a post office under Wotton under Edge Acres, 1,369 Real property, £3,977 Pop., 629 Houses, 137 The property is divided among a few The living is a rectory in the diocese of G and Bristol. Value, £351 * Patron Sir J Neeld, Bart The church is ancient and good There are an Independent chapel and an endowed school

CHARFORD, a hamlet in South Brent parish, Devon

CHARFORD (NORTH), a parish in Fordingbridge district, Hants, on the river Avon, at the verge of the county 6½ miles SSE of Salisbury r station Post town, Downton, under Salisbury Acres, 570 Real property, £1,045 Pop , 70 Houses, 15. It was known to the Saxons as Cerdicesford, and is said to have taken that name from Cerdic having formed his court at or near it, on the founding of Wessex. It has no ecclesiastical status and its church is in ruins.

CHARFORD (SOUTH), a parish in Fordingbridge district, Hants, formerly reckoned a tything of North Charford, and lying contiguous to it, 7 miles SSE of Salisbury Acres 833 Real property £1,068 Pop , 70 Houses, 13 It has no ecclesiastical status

CHARING, a village and a parish in West Ashford district, Kent The village stands on the ancient road called the Pilgrims' way, near the source of the Len 5 miles N by E of Pluckley r station, and 5½ NW of Ashford It is an ancient place, known at Domesday as Cheringes, and it has a post office‡ under Ashford, an inn, and fairs on 29 April, and 29 Oct The parish comprises 4,551 acres Real property, £7,610 Pop., 1,285 Houses, 265 The property is divided among a few The manor belonged early to the see of Canterbury, was held some time by the Saxon kings, reverted to the Archbishops, was given up by Cranmer to Henry VIII , and passed to the Whelers of Otterden A palace of the Archbishops stood here, was rebuilt in the 14th century, and gave entertainment to Henry VII and Henry VIII The edifice was in the early decorated style, and badly executed, and considerable ruins of it still exist The living is a vicarage in the diocese of Canterbury Value, £475 * Patrons, the Dean and Chapter of St Paul's The church was chiefly rebuilt after a destruction of it by fire in 1590, but retains portions in early English and perpendicular, and it contains monuments of the Brents, the Sayers, the Honeywoods, and Mrs Ludwell A school founded by Mrs. Ludwell who died in 1765 has £88 a year from endowment, and two exhibitions at Oriel college

CHARING CROSS, a sub district and a railway in London The sub district is part of the parish and district of St Martin in the Fields, includes St James Palace and Whitehall, and comprises 241 acres of land and 22 of the Thames Pop 11,071 Houses, 1,248 The railway was authorised in 1859-61, to go from Charing Cross to the South Eastern at London bridge, and thence, across the Thames to Cannon street, and was opened to London bridge in 1864 to Cannon street in 1866

CHARINGWORTH, a hamlet in Ebrington parish, Gloucester, 2 miles E of Chipping Campden

CHARLBURY, a small town, a parish and a sub district in Chipping Norton district, Oxford The town stands on an eminence adjacent to the river Evenlode, and to the Oxford and Worcester railway, near Cornbury Park and Wychwood Forest 6 miles SE of Chipping Norton and has a station on the railway, a post-office‡ under Enstone, a banking office an inn, a church, several dissenting chapels, and a grammar-school The church is variously Norman early English, and decorated, has a tower of the 13th century, and contains monuments of the Somersets and the Jenkinsons The grammar school has £40 a year from endowment, with two exhibitions at Brasenose college, and other charities have £70 A weekly market is held on Friday, fairs are held on 1 Jan the second Friday in Lent, the second Friday after 13 May and 11 Oct , and some trade is done in glove making and leather dressing —The parish contains also the hamlets of Finstock, Fawler, and Walcott, the tything of West Chadlington, and the chapelries of Shorthampton and East Chadlington Acres, 11,320 Real property, £17,117 Pop , 1,388 Houses, 331 The property is much subdivided The manor belonged to the Mercian kings, was given by them to the Bishops of Lincoln, passed to the Abbey of Evesham, and went, at the dissolution, to St John's College, Oxford. The living is a vicarage, united to the p. curacies of Shorthampton and Chadlington, in the diocese of Oxford. Value, £290.* Patron, St John's College, Oxford. The vicarage of Finstock is a separate benefice. The sub-district contains eight parishes, part of another parish, and two extra-parochial tracts. Acres, 40,268. Pop., 6,915. Houses, 1,563.

CHARLCOMBE, a parish in Bath district, Somerset, near the Great Western railway, 1½ mile N of Bath. Post-town, Bath. Acres, 571. Real property, £3,604. Pop., 378. Houses, 37. The property is divided among a few. Water works are here for supplying the city of Bath. The living is a rectory in the diocese of Bath and Wells. Value, £20[illegible].* Patrons, the Mayor and Corporation of Bath. The church is ancient and curious, but good, and the churchyard contains a very old yew tree.

CHARLCOTE, a village and a parish in Stratford-on-Avon district, Warwick. The village stands on the river Avon, 3¾ miles W of the Fosse way, and 4½ ENE of Stratford-on-Avon r. station. The parish includes also the hamlets of Thelsford and Hunscote, and its post-town is Hampton Lucy, under Warwick. Acres, 2,190. Real property, £4,025. Pop., 245. Houses, 54. The manor, with all the property, belongs to Henry Lucy, Esq. The Lucys have been in possession since the time of Richard I. The manor house, Charlcote House, was built in 1558, by Sir Thomas Lucy, believed to be the Justice Shallow of Shakspeare. It forms three sides of a quadrangle, shows all the characteristics of the Tudor architecture, has been altered and renovated in strict keeping with its original character, has a gatehouse with an oriel window, flanked by octagon towers, and stands in an extensive well wooded park. The great hall is believed to have been the scene of Shakspeare's examination consequent on his deer-stealing exploit, and retains many of the features which it originally possessed. The living is a vicarage in the diocese of Worcester. Value, £153. Patron, Henry Lucy, Esq. The church was rebuilt in 1853, in the decorated style of the 14th century, and the Lucy chapel, separated from the chancel by a richly carved oaken screen, contains the monument of Sir Thomas Lucy and his lady by Bernini, and two other interesting monuments. Charities, £10.

CHARLCOTT, a tything in Whitchurch parish, Hants, near Whitchurch. Pop., 2[illegible].

CHARLCOTT, a tything in Bremhill parish, Wilts, 2½ miles N of Calne.

CHARLES, a village and a parish in South Molton district, Devon. The village stands on the river Bray, 5 miles NNW of South Molton, and 9 E of Barnstaple r. station. The parish includes also the hamlet of Brayford. Post-town, South Molton, North Devon. Acres, 2,429. Real property, £2,527. Pop., 306. Houses, [illegible]7. The property is subdivided. The manor belongs to Sir T. D. Acland, Bart. The living is a rectory in the diocese of Exeter. Value, £[illegible]90.* Patron, the Rev. R. [illegible]ckmore. The church is perpendicular English, with a tower.

CHARLES THE MARTYR, a sub-district in the district of Plymouth, and a parish in the districts of Plymouth and Plympton, on St Mary, Devon. The sub-district is part of the borough of Plymouth. Acres, 870 of land, and 2[illegible]0 of water. Pop., 2[illegible],300. Houses, 2,121. —The parish includes also the tything of Compton Gifford. Acres, 1,[illegible]17 of land, and 240 of water. Pop., 2[illegible],270. Houses, 2,[illegible]. The living is a vicarage, with the p. curacy of Compton Gifford, in the diocese of Exeter. Value, £575. Patrons, the Executors of the late Sir C. Lemon, Bart. See PLYMOUTH.

CHARLESTON. See ASHTON-UNDER-LYNE.

CHARLESTOWN, a small seaport town and a chapelry in St Austell parish, Cornwall. The town stands on the coast, 2 miles SE of St Austell, is a sub-port to Fowey, and has a post-office under St Austell. It was founded, towards the close of last century, by Charles Rashleigh, Esq., has harbour and docks, capable of receiving large ships, has also building yards and pilchard fisheries, carries on a large export trade in lime, china clay, and other mineral produce, and is connected, by tram railway, with St Austell, and with extensive tin mines of its own name, employing about 430 hands.—The chapelry includes the town, and was constituted in 1846. Pop., 3,[illegible]7. Houses, 675. The living is a vicarage in the diocese of Exeter. Value, £100. Patron, alternately the Crown and the Bishop. The church is good.

CHARLESTOWN, a village and a chapelry in Northowram township, Halifax parish, W. R. Yorkshire, 2 miles NE of Halifax. The chapelry was constituted in 1861, and its post town is Halifax. The living is a vicarage in the diocese of York. Value, £[illegible]00. Patron, the Vicar of Halifax. The church was built in 1860.

CHARLESTOWN, a chapelry in Eccles parish, Lancashire, adjacent to the Manchester and Preston railway, near the river Irwell, in the northern part of Salford, suburban to Manchester. Post town, Manchester. Pop., about 5,000. The living is a vicarage in the diocese of Manchester. Value, £300. Patron, the Bishop of Manchester.

CHARLESWORTH, a township and a chapelry in Glossop parish, Derby. The township lies on the river Etherow, near the High Peak, 1¼ mile SSW of Glossop r. station, and 8½ N of Chapel en le Frith, and has a post-office under Manchester. Pop., 1,565. Houses, 306. The chapelry is more extensive than the township, and was constituted in 1845. Pop., 2,564. Houses, 508. The property is all in one estate. The inhabitants are chiefly cotton spinners and colliers. The living is a vicarage in the diocese of Lichfield. Value, £150.* Patron, alternately the Crown and the Bishop. The church is modern; and there are chapels for Independents, Baptists, Wesleyans, and Primitive Methodists.

CHARLETON, a village and a parish in Kingsbridge district, Devon. The village stands on a sea creek, 2 miles SSE of Kingsbridge, and 11 S by E of Kingsbridge Road r. station, and is a straggling place, in two parts, called East and West. The parish includes also the hamlets of Goveton, Lidstone, and part of Frogmore. Post town, Kingsbridge. Acres, 2,779, of which 400 are water. Real property, with Sherford, £7,131. Pop., 568. Houses, 127. The living is a rectory in the diocese of Exeter. Value, £[illegible]2.* Patron, Mrs. J. Twysden. The church is ancient, consists of nave, chancel, and aisles, with a tower, and has an ancient carved screen.

CHARLETON, Berks, &c. See CHARLTON.

CHARLETON (QUEEN), a parish in Keynsham district, Somerset, near Wans Dyke, 2 miles SW of Keynsham r. station, and 5 SE of Bristol. Post town, Keynsham, under Bristol. Acres, 935. Real property, £1,956. Pop., 141. Houses, 31. The property is all in one estate. The manor belonged to Keynsham abbey, and was given by Henry VIII. to Queen Catherine. The gateway of the Abbey grange, a Norman structure, still stands. The living is a vicarage in the diocese of Bath and Wells. Value, £65. Patron, Mrs Dickinson. The church was recently restored.

CHARLEY, or CHARNWOOD, an extra parochial tract in Loughborough district, Leicester, on the Wolds, near Charnwood forest, 5½ miles SW of Loughborough. Acres, 600. Real property, £6[illegible]. Pop., 34. Houses, [illegible]. An Augustinian priory was founded here, in the time of Henry II., by the Blanchmains, and some remains of it exist.

CHARLEY MOUNT, a locality 2 miles from Wednesbury, in Stafford, with a post office under Wednesbury.

CHARLINCH, or CHARLINCH, a parish in Bridgewater district, Somerset, on an affluent of the river Parret, near the Quantock hills, 4 miles W by N of Bridgewater r. station. Post town, Bridgewater. Acres, 1,132. Assessed property, £1,916. Pop., 241. Houses, 41. The property is divided among a few. The Agapemone or Love's Abode here is an establishment of Communists, founded by Henry James Prince, originally a curate, and called after him Princeites. The living is a rectory in the diocese of Bath and Wells. Value, £180. Patron, Lord Taunton. The church is old but good. There are a national school and charities £9.

CHARLTON, a hamlet in Wantage parish, Berks; adjacent to the Berks and Wilts canal, near the Great Western railway, 1 mile NE of Wantage. Real property, £2,708. Pop., 255. Houses, 53. The hamlet forms a curacy with Wantage, in the diocese of Oxford; and is a meet for the Vale of White Horse hounds. Charlton House belonged once to the Wilmots; was visited in their time, by Charles I.; and passed to the Freemans.

CHARLTON, a hundred in Berks. It marches with Hants, at the Blackwater river; is 7 miles long; and contains Barkham and Finchampstead parishes, and parts of three others. Acres, 18,840. Pop., 3,292. Houses, 660.

CHARLTON, a tything in Henbury parish, Gloucester; 5 miles N of Bristol. Acres, 1,329. Real property, £2,548. Pop., 425. Houses, 83.

CHARLTON, a tything in Tetbury parish, Gloucester; near Tetbury. Real property, £1,890.

CHARLTON, a hamlet in Andover parish, Hants; within Andover borough. Pop., 323.

CHARLTON, a hamlet in Sunbury parish, Middlesex; 3¼ miles SE of Staines. Pop., 106.

CHARLTON, a hamlet in Newbottle and Kings-Sutton parishes, Northampton; 4 miles W by S of Brackley. Pop., 446. There is an Independent chapel.

CHARLTON, a township in Wrockwardine parish, Salop; 3¼ miles W of Wellington. Pop., 101.

CHARLTON, a hamlet in Kilmersdon parish, Somerset; 6½ miles WNW of Frome. Pop., 241.

CHARLTON, a hamlet, partly extra-parochial, partly in Shepton-Mallet parish, Somerset; 1½ mile E of Shepton-Mallet.

CHARLTON, a hamlet in Cropthorne parish, Worcester; near the river Avon, 2 miles NW of Evesham. Pop., 274. There is a Baptist chapel.

CHARLTON, a hamlet in Singleton parish, Sussex; 5¼ miles S of Midhurst.

CHARLTON, a tything in Donhead-St. Mary parish, Wilts; 7¼ miles S of Hindon. It forms a curacy with Donhead-St. Mary, in the diocese of Salisbury; but its church is in ruins.

CHARLTON, a chapelry in Downton and Standlinch parishes, Wilts; on the river Avon, 4 miles SSE of Salisbury. It was constituted in 1851; and it has a post-office under Salisbury. Pop., 393. Houses, 74. The living is a vicarage in the diocese of Salisbury. Value, not reported. Patron, the Vicar of Downton.

CHARLTON, a parish in Malmsbury district, Wilts; 2½ miles NE of Malmsbury, and 4 WSW of Minety r. station. It has a post-office under Chippenham. Acres, 4,750. Real property, £4,926. Pop., 621. Houses, 129. The property is not much divided. The manor belonged to Malmsbury abbey; passed to the Knevits; and belongs now to the Earl of Suffolk. The mansion on it, Charlton House, is a stately edifice, of Jacobean architecture, with west front by Inigo Jones; contains a large collection of valuable paintings; and was frequently visited by the poet Dryden. The living is a vicarage, annexed to the vicarage of Westport, in the diocese of Gloucester and Bristol. The church is early English; and contains the burial-vault of the Earls of Suffolk. Charities, £10.

CHARLTON, a parish in Fewsey district, Wilts; on the river Avon, near Salisbury plain, 8¼ miles S of Woodborough r. station, and 8¼ SE by E of Devizes. Post-town, Pewsey, under Marlborough. Acres, 1,706. Real property, £1,835. Pop., 222. Houses, 44. The property is divided among three. An alien priory was founded here, in 1187, by Reginald de Paveley; given, at the suppression of alien monasteries, to St. Catherine's hospital; and transferred, in the time of Edward VI., to the Sheringtons. A Roman camp is at Casterley. The living is a vicarage in the diocese of Salisbury. Value, £143.* Patron, Christ Church, Oxford. The church is old but excellent; with a tower; and has a mural brass of 1524. Stephen Duck, the author of the "Thrasher's Labour," was a native.

CHARLTON, a station on the Border Counties railway in Northumberland; at Charlton-East-Quarter and Charlton-West-Quarter townships, 2¼ miles NW of Bellingham.

CHARLTON, Devon. See CHARLTON.

CHARLTON, Dorset. See CHARLTON-MARSHALL.

CHARLTON, Kent. See CHARLTON-NEAR-DOVER and CHARLTON-NEXT-WOOLWICH.

CHARLTON-ABBOTS, a parish in Winchcomb district, Gloucester; under the Cotswolds, 2¼ miles S by E of Winchcomb, and 6 E by N of Cheltenham r. station. Post-town, Winchcomb, under Cheltenham. Acres, 2,160. Real property, £1,247. Pop., 109. Houses, 18. The living is a vicarage in the diocese of Gloucester and Bristol. Value, £38. Patron, C. J. Chamberlayne, Esq. The church is old.

CHARLTON-ADAM, a parish in Langport district, Somerset; on the Fosse way, 2¾ miles NNE of Martock r. station, and 7 ENE of Langport. Post-town, Charlton-Mackrell, under Taunton. Acres, with Charlton-Mackrell, 3,910. Real property of C.-A. only, £2,011. Pop., 530. Houses, 119. The property is divided among a few. The living is a vicarage in the diocese of Bath and Wells. Value, £127. Patron, the Rev. Guy Bryan. The church is later English. There is a Wesleyan chapel.

CHARLTON-BY-DOVER. See CHARLTON-NEAR-DOVER.

CHARLTON CROSS, an extra-parochial tract in Somerset; 5¼ miles N of Frome.

CHARLTON-EAST-QUARTER, a township in Bellingham parish, Northumberland; on the North Tyne river, and the Border Counties railway, 2 miles NW of Bellingham. Pop., 119. Houses, 25. See CHARLTON.

CHARLTON-HORETHORNE, a parish in Wincanton district, Somerset; 3 miles N of Milborne-Port r. station, and 5¼ SW of Wincanton. It has a post-office under Sherborne. Acres, 2,368. Real property, £4,331. Pop., 506. Houses, 122. The property is divided among a few. The living is a vicarage in the diocese of Bath and Wells. Value, £384.* Patron, the Marquis of Anglesey. The church was restored in 1846. There are a Wesleyan chapel, a national school, and charities £11.

CHARLTON-KINGS, a parish and a sub-district in Cheltenham district, Gloucester. The parish lies in the south-eastern environs of Cheltenham, nominally 1¾ mile distant; and has a post-office under Cheltenham. Acres, 3,170. Real property, £17,974. Pop., 3,443. Houses, 741. The property is much subdivided. Charlton Park is a chief residence. There are mineral springs. The living is a vicarage in the diocese of Gloucester and Bristol. Value, £177. Patron, Jesus College, Oxford. The church is later English, with enlargement in 1842; and has a tower. The churchyard contains a stone cross. There are a Wesleyan chapel, national schools, and charities £69.—The sub-district comprises all Cheltenham district, except Cheltenham parish. Acres, 21,136. Pop., 10,099. Houses, 2,032.

CHARLTON-MACKRELL, a parish in Langport district, Somerset; on the river Cary and the Fosse way, 3¼ miles N of Martock r. station, and 5¼ ENE of Langport. It includes the hamlets of Cary-Fitzpaine and Lyte's-cary; and has a post-office under Taunton. Acres, with Charlton-Adam, 3,910. Real property of C.-M. only, £2,637. Pop., 387. Houses, 77. The property is divided among a few. The living is a rectory in the diocese of Bath and Wells. Value, £499.* Patron, John Brymer, Esq. The church was recently restored. There are endowed schools with £45 a-year, and charities £3.

CHARLTON-MARSHALL, a parish in Blandford district, Dorset; on the river Stour, near the Blandford railway, 2 miles S of Blandford-Forum. It has a post-office, of the name of Charlton, under Blandford. Acres, 2,100. Real property, £2,782. Pop., 553. Houses, 114. The property is divided among a few. Roman coins have been found. The parish is a meet for the Blackmoor harriers. The living is a p. curacy, annexed to the rectory of Spetisbury, in the diocese of Salisbury. The church was built in 1727; and contains a monument of Wake, the founder of the corporation for the sons of the clergy. There is an Independent chapel.

CHARLTON-MUSGROVE, a parish in Wincanton

district Somerset, on the river Cale near the Somerset and Dorset railway, 1 mile NNW of Wincanton r station Post town Wincanton, under Bath Acres, 2,153 Real property, £3,762 Pop, 418 Houses, 102 Part of the land is recently enclosed common The living is a rectory in the diocese of Bath and Wells Value, £493 Patron, the Rev Paul Leir The church is decorated English and has a fine tower There are a Baptist chapel and a national school

CHARLTON NEAR DOVER, a parish in Dover district, Kent, on the river Dour and the Southeastern railway, contiguous to the north side of Dover and mostly within Dover borough It has a post-office,‡ of the name of Charlton, under Dover Acres, 387 Rated property, £7,254 Pop, 4,093 Houses, 761 The property is much subdivided The surface is hilly and picturesque, and there are paper oil, and corn mills The living is a rectory in the diocese of Canterbury Value £93 * Patron, the Rev J Monins The church was rebuilt in 1820 There is a national school

CHARLTON (NEW), a locality in Charlton next Woolwich parish, Kent, between *Charlton next Woolwich* village and the Thames It has a post office under Charlton See next article

CHARLTON NEXT WOOLWICH, a village and a parish in Lewisham district, Kent The village lies among the low hills between Blackheath and Woolwich adjacent to the North Kent railway near the river Thames, 8 miles E by S of London Bridge, and has a station on the railway, and a post office under London S E both of the name of Charlton It formerly was a market town, and it still has a famous fair on 18 Oct, known as Horn Fair The parish comprises 1 251 acres of land and 191 of water Real property, £36,162 Pop, 8,472 Houses, 1,117 The manor was given by William Rufus to Bermondsey abbey, went, at the dissolution, to the Newtons passed to the Langhornes, the Dacres, and the Maryons, and belongs now to Sir T M Wilson, Bart Charlton House was built, about 1612, by Sir Adam Newton, forms a fine specimen of the architecture of its age, contains a good portrait of Henry, Prince of Wales, to whom Sir Adam Newton acted as tutor, was the death place, in 1679, of Lord Downe, and is now the seat of Sir T M Wilson The grounds connected with it have some very old cypresses, the "Hanging Wood adjoining it affords a charming walk, and some sand pits in the vicinity present great attractions to geologists A farm house in the parish, called Cherry Garden, is said to have been erected by Inigo Jones for his own residence Several handsome villas have recently been built The living is a rectory in the diocese of London Value, £350 * Patron, Sir T M Wilson, Bart The church is a plain brick edifice of 1640 The rectories of St Thomas and St Paul and the chapelries of Blackheath Park and St Germans Blackheath are separate charges Value of St Thomas £400,* of St Paul, £286 Patron of both Sir T M Wilson Bart St Thomas church stands at New Charlton is a handsome structure, and was built in 1850, at a cost of £7 000 St Pauls church was built in 1867, is in the second pointed style cruciform and highly ornate, and has a SW tower and spire There are a Wesleyan chapel, the cottages on Woolwich Common Morden college for decayed merchants, national schools, Langhorne s school and alms houses and other charities £80

CHARLTON (NORTH), a township in Ellingham parish, Northumberland 6½ miles N by W of Alnwick Acres 2,731 Pop, 184 Houses, 13

CHARLTON (SOUTH), a township chapelry in Ellingham parish, Northumberland, 3¾ miles SW of Christon Bank station and 5 NNW of Alnwick Post town, Lock under Alnwick Acres, 1,806 Pop, 167 Houses, 23 The living is a p. curacy in the diocese of Durham Value, £200 Patron the Duke of Northumberland The church was built in 1862

CHARLTON UPON OTMOOR, a village and a parish in Bicester district, Oxford The village stands adjacent to the river Ray near the Roman road over Otmoor and near the Oxford and Bletchley railway, 2½ miles NE of Islip r station and 5 SSW of Bicester The parish includes also the hamlets of Fencott and Murcott Post town Islip under Oxford Acres, 1 864 Real property, £1,811 Pop, 657 Houses, 152 The property is much subdivided Part of the land is marshy The living is a rectory in the diocese of Oxford Value, not reported * Patron, Queens College, Oxford The church is cruciform early English, and good, and contains a richly carved oaken rood screen, stone stalls and an ancient brass There are chapels for Baptists, Wesleyans, and Primitive Methodists

CHARLTON WEST QUARTER a township in Bellingham parish, Northumberland, on the North Tyne river and the Border Counties railway, 2½ miles NW of Bellingham Pop, 134 Houses, 39 See CHARLTON

CHARLWOOD, a parish in Reigate district Surrey, on an affluent of the river Mole, 3½ miles SW by W of Horley r station, and 6½ S by W of Reigate It has a post office under Crawley Acres, 7,000 Real property, £6 668 Pop 1 342 Houses, 263 The property is subdivided Charlwood Park and Charlwood Place are chief residences The living is a rectory in the diocese of Winchester Value, £650 * Patron, H C Wise Esq The church is partly Norman, and was repaired in 1859 There are an Independent chapel, an endowed school, and charities £25

CHARMINSTER, a village and a parish in Dorchester district, Dorset The village stands on a branch of the river Froom, adjacent to the Dorchester and Yeovil railway, 2 miles NNW of Dorchester, and has a post office under Dorchester The parish contains also the hamlets of Burton and Forston, and the county lunatic asylum Acres, 4,095 Real property, £2 608 Pop, 1 020 Houses, 148 The property is divided among a few The living is a vicarage, united with the vicarage of Stratton, in the diocese of Salisbury Value, £137 Patron, Henry Pickard Esq The church is very good.

CHARMOUTH, a village and a parish in the district of Axminster and county of Dorset The village stands on the coast, at the mouth of the river Char, under Charmouth hill, adjacent to the line of a Roman road 2 miles NE by E of Lyme Regis, and 6½ W of Bridport r station It occupies the site of the Cauca Arixa of the Romans is itself an ancient place, and consists now of one long street, or edificed road with a sprinkling of villas on a declivity. It was the scene of two battles, in 8_0 and 840, between the Saxons and the Danes, and the scene of a narrow escape of Charles II from capture, on the eve of his embarkation for France after the battle of Worcester It has a post office ‡ under Bridport, and two chief inns is a watering place and a coast guard station, was once a market town, and contains an old cottage, originally part of an inn in which Charles II spent the night of his peril The parish comprises _33 acres of land and 83 of water Real property £3,314 Pop 678 Houses, 151 Charmouth Hill is about 1 000 feet high, and was called by Hutchins the Pinlimmon of Dorset The ground rises from the sea in cliffs and dark slopes, and presents features of great interest to geologists A part of the cliffs, rich in pyrites, ignited in 1751, and another part underwent a great landslip with a shock like an earthquake in 1839 The living is a rectory in the diocese of Salisbury Value £150 * Patron, J Hunt Esq The church was rebuilt about 1503, and contains a screen and some curious old oaken carvings There are chapels for Independents and Wesleyans, and charities £48

CHARNDON, a hamlet in Twyford parish, Bucks, 6½ miles SSW of Buckingham Acres, 1 880 Real property £2,070 Pop, 170 Houses, 41

CHARNES a township in Eccleshall parish Stafford near the river Sow, 4½ miles NW of Eccleshall Acres, 570 Pop 107 Houses, 13

CHARNEY, a chapelry in Longworth parish, Berks, on the river Ock, 3 miles NE by N of Faringdon Road r station and 4½ NNW of Wantage Post town Longworth under Faringdon Acres, 1,220 Real property, £1 915 Pop 241 Houses, 53 The property is divided among a few The living is a vicarage united to the rectory of Longworth, in the diocese of Oxford The church has a Norman doorway, and is good.

CHARNHAM STREET, a tything in Hungerford parish, Wilts, about a mile from Hungerford Acres, 2 490 Pop, 450 Houses, 95

CHARNOCK HEATH, a township in Standish parish, Lancashire, on the Bolton and Preston railway, at Adlington station, 2½ miles SE by S of Chorley Acres, 1,596 Real property, £4,207, of which £450 are in mines, and £250 in quarries. Pop, 772 Houses, 150 There are brick works and a cotton mill

CHARNOCK RICHARD a township chapelry in Standish parish, Lancashire, adjacent to the Wigan and Preston railway, near Coppull station, 3 miles SW by W of Chorley Post town, Coppull, under Chorley Acres, 1,948 Real property, £6,253 of which £2,700 are in mines Pop, 899 Houses 161. The living is a vicarage in the diocese of Manchester Value, £141 * Patron, James Darlington, Esq The church was built in 1861, is in the perpendicular English style, and consists of nave and chancel, with tower and vestry

CHARNWOOD FOREST, a bare hilly tract, about 20 miles in circuit in the NE of Leicester, near Charley, 5 miles SW of Loughborough It was disforested after the Conquest It consists chiefly of trap rocks, but includes slate, freestone, and coal Its highest ground is Bardon hill, which has an altitude of 853 feet, and commands a very extensive view Charley hermitage and Ulvescroft priory were within it, and a monastery of St Bernard was built in it, near Bardon hill, in 18-5, and has a chapel, a chapter house, and cloisters in the early English style The three vicarages of Oaks, Copt Oaks, and Woodhouse Eaves are in it and will be separately noticed The property of it is in six manors, belonging to different owners

CHARSFIELD a parish in Woodbridge district, Suffolk, 3½ miles WNW of Wickham Market r station, and 5½ N of Woodbridge Post town, Wickham Market Acres, 1,299 Real property, £2,397 Pop, 484 Houses, 108 The living is a vicarage in the diocese of Norwich Value, £100 * Patron, Earl Howe The church is a neat brick structure There are a Baptist chapel, a national school, and charities £8

CHART, or CHIRT, or CHURT, a chapelry in Frensham parish, Surrey, 5 miles SSE of Farnham r station It was constituted in 1865, and it has a post office under Farnham Pop 425 The living is a p curacy Value £100 Patron, the Archdeacon of Surrey

CHART AND LONGBRIDGE, a hundred in the lathe of Shepway, Kent, containing Great Chart parish and ten other parishes Acres, 21,655 Pop 5 303

CHART CORNER, a locality in Chart next Sutton Valence parish Kent, 5 miles N by E of Staplehurst It has a post office under Staplehurst

CHARTER HOUSE, an extra parochial place in Holborn district, London, near Aldersgate Street and Smithfield, ¾ of a mile N of St Paul's It includes a square and gardens, comprises 10 acres, and extends slightly into the extra parochial liberty of Glasshouse yard It was purchased, in 1349 by Bishop Stratford to be a burial place for victims of the plague became the site, in 1371, of a Carthusian priory, founded by Sir Walter Manny, passed, in 1537, to the Crown and was purchased, in 1611, for £81,217, by Thomas Sutton, to be made the place of a public school The buildings are partly ancient partly modern, form seven courts, of collegiate appearance, and include an ancient pointed gateway and a great Tudor hall the latter erected by the Duke of Norfolk and the Earl of Suffolk The school has an income of about £28 000, is governed by the Queen, the Prince of Wales, the two Archbishops, the bishop of London, and twelve elected noblemen and gentlemen, consists of 44 scholars on the foundation, and usually from 120 to 180 "extras," and numbers among its famous pupils bishops Monk and Thirlwall Judge Blackstone, Lord Chief-Justice Ellenborough, Dr Barrow, Addison, Steele John Wesley, Grote, the Earl of Liverpool, Sir Charles Eastlake, Thackeray, and General Havelock.

CHARTER HOUSE an extra parochial place in Sculcoates parish, E R Yorkshire, 1 mile N of Hull

CHARTER HOUSE HINTON, a parish in Bath district Somerset, on the verge of the county, near the Ridge way, 1 mile S of Freshford r station, and 4½ SSE of Bath It has a post office under Bath Acres 2 890 Real property £4,527 Pop, 615 Houses, 135 A Carthusian priory was founded here, in 1232, by Ela, Countess of Salisbury and some remains of it, supposed to have been the chapter house, the refectory and the dormitory, still exist Hinton Great Abbey House belonged formerly to the Hungerfords, is now the seat of Lieut Col Gotgrave, and contains some fine paintings Some Roman relics, including coins, pottery, and traces of an amphitheatre, have been found The living is a vicarage in the diocese of Bath and Wells. Value, £100 * Patron the Vicar of Norton St Philip The church is ancient There is a national school

CHARTER HOUSE ON MENDIP, an extra parochial ville in Axbridge district, Somerset, adjacent to Blagdon parish 5 miles E by N of Axbridge. Acres 2,410 Pop., 82 Houses, 16 It had anciently a cell to Witham Carthusian priory and it is still ecclesiastically connected with Witham Friary parish

CHARTERIDGE, a hamlet in Chesham parish, Bucks, near Chesham Real property £1,960 Pop, 404

CHART (GREAT) a village and a parish in West Ashford district Kent The village stands adjacent to the Ashford and Tunbridge railway, near the river Stour, 2 miles W by S of Ashford, and has a post office under Ashford It was formerly a market town, and it still has a fair on 5 April The parish comprises 3,281 acres Real property, £4,989 Pop, 806 Houses, 152 The property is divided among a few The manor belonged anciently to Christ Church Canterbury, and belongs now to the Chapter there An earthquake was felt here in 1580 The living is a rectory in the diocese of Canterbury Value, £600 * Patron, the Archbishop of Canterbury The church is chiefly perpendicular English, was much repaired in the 15th century, by the Goldwell family, and contains monuments of the Goldwells, the Tokes and others There are a Wesleyan chapel, a national school, and two alms-houses

CHARTHAM a village, a parish, and a sub district in Bridge district, Kent The village stands on the river Stour and the South eastern railway, 3½ miles SW of Canterbury, and has a r station, and a post office under Canterbury It was known at Domesday as Certeham it occupies a low site, round a green, and it contains a house built by Dr Delangle, a French refugee who became rector here, and marked by a bust of Charles II The parish includes also Horton, consisting of 399 acres, and the hamlets of Chartham Hatch and Shalmsford Street Acres, 4 530 Real property, £6,672 Pop, 1,094 Houses, 2-2 The property is much subdivided The manor was given in 871, to Christ Church, Canterbury belongs now to the Chapter there, and is still called the Deanery Chartham downs, above the village, have remains of a number of tumuli, called Danes' Banks, and are marked by lines of ancient entrenchments One of the earliest discoveries of great fossil bones giving rise to the modern science of palæontology, was made, in 1668, at Chartham, in the sinking of a well A large paper mill is at the back of the village The living is a rectory in the diocese of Canterbury Value £800 * Patron, the Archbishop of Canterbury The church is cruciform variously early and decorated English, has rare and very beautiful tracery in the windows, and an embattled tower at the west end, and contains brasses monumental slabs, a monument of Dr Delangle, and an elaborate monument, by Rysbrach, of Sir William Young There is a Wesleyan chapel —The sub district contains nine parishes, part of another, and an extra parochial tract. Acres, 18,523 Pop, 5,020 Houses, 1 071

CHARTHAM HATCH, a hamlet in Chartham parish, Kent 1 mile N of Chartham village

CHARTINGTON See CALLINGTON

CHARTLEY HOLME, or CHARTLEY LODGE, an extra